P9-EJT-913

LIFE-SPAN DEVELOPMENT

FIFTH CANADIAN EDITION

John W. Santrock
University of Texas at Dallas

Anne MacKenzie-Rivers
George Brown College

Thomas Malcomson
George Brown College

Kwan Ho Leung
George Brown College

Verna Pangman
University of Manitoba

McGraw-Hill Ryerson

McGraw-Hill
Ryerson

Copyright © 2014, 2011, 2008, 2005, 2002 by McGraw-Hill Ryerson Limited. Copyright © 2013, 2011, 2009, 2008, 2006, 2004, 2002, 1999 by McGraw-Hill Education LLC. All rights reserved. No part of this publication may be reproduced or transmitted in any form or by any means, or stored in a data base or retrieval system, without the prior written permission of McGraw-Hill Ryerson Limited, or in the case of photocopying or other reprographic copying, a licence from The Canadian Copyright Licensing Agency (Access Copyright). For an Access Copyright licence, visit www.accesscopyright.ca or call toll-free to 1-800-893-5777.

Statistics Canada information is used with the permission of Statistics Canada. Users are forbidden to copy this material and/or redisseminate the data, in an original or modified form, for commercial purposes, without the expressed permission of Statistics Canada. Information on the availability of the wide range of data from Statistics Canada can be obtained from Statistics Canada's Regional Offices, its Web site at www.statcan.gc.ca and its toll-free access number 1-800-263-1136.

The Internet addresses listed in the text were accurate at the time of publication. The inclusion of a Web site does not indicate an endorsement by the authors or McGraw-Hill Ryerson, and McGraw-Hill Ryerson does not guarantee the accuracy of information presented at these sites.

ISBN-13: 978-0-07-087819-8
ISBN-10: 0-07-087819-6

1 2 3 4 5 6 7 8 9 0 TCP 1 9 8 7 6 5 4

Printed and bound in Canada

Care has been taken to trace ownership of copyright material contained in this text; however, the publisher will welcome any information that enables it to rectify any reference or credit for subsequent editions.

Director of Product Management: *Rhondda McNabb*
Group Product Manager: *Leanna MacLean*
Senior Product Manager: *Marcia Siekowski*
Marketing Manager: *Margaret Janzen*
Senior Product Developer: *Katherine Goodes*
Supervising Editor: *Cathy Biribauer*
Senior Product Team Associate: *Marina Seguin*
Photo/Permissions Researcher: *Robyn Craig*
Copy Editor: *Kelli Howey*
Proofreader: *Ashley Rayner*
Plant Production Coordinator: *Michelle Saddler*
Manufacturing Production Coordinator: *Emily Hickey*
Cover and Inside Design: *David Montle/Pixel Hive Studio*
Composition: *Laserwords Private Limited*
Cover Photo: © *Paul Tomlins/http://www.flowerphotos.com/Eye Ubiquitous/Corbis*
Printer: *Transcontinental Printing Group*

Library and Archives Canada Cataloguing in Publication Data

Santrock, John W., author
Life-span development/John W. Santrock, Anne MacKenzie-Rivers, Thomas Malcomson, Kwan Ho Leung, Verna Pangman.—Fifth Canadian edition.

Revision of: Life-span development/John W. Santrock.—4th Canadian ed.—[Toronto] : McGraw-Hill Ryerson, c2011.

Includes bibliographical references and index.
ISBN 978-0-07-087819-8 (pbk.)

1. Developmental psychology—Textbooks.
2. Life cycle, Human—Textbooks.   I. MacKenzie-Rivers, Anne, author   II. Title.

BF713.L53 2014   155   C2013-904544-9

*With special appreciation to my mother, Ruth Santrock,
and the memory of my father, John Santrock.*
—John W. Santrock

*To my family and friends for their love and support.
To the editorial staff at McGraw-Hill Ryerson for their
collegiality, patience, and diligence.*
—Anne MacKenzie-Rivers

For Peggy, with love.
—Tom Malcomson

*For God's blessings, especially my parents, sister
and brother-in-law, and dear relatives,
friends, and teachers.*
—Kwan Ho Leung

*To students, who have inspired me.
To my husband, Clare, who has lovingly supported me.
To my colleagues and friends for their assistance and patience.*
—Verna Pangman

About the Authors

John W. Santrock received his Ph.D. from the University of Minnesota in 1973. He taught at the University of Charleston and the University of Georgia before joining the Program in Psychology and Human Development at the University of Texas at Dallas, where he currently teaches a number of undergraduate courses and was given the University's Effective Teaching Award in 2006. In 2010, he created the UT-Dallas Santrock undergraduate scholarship, an annual award that is given to outstanding undergraduate students majoring in developmental psychology to enable them to attend research conventions.

John has been a member of the editorial boards of *Child Development* and *Developmental Psychology*. His research on father custody is widely cited and is used in expert witness testimony to promote flexibility and alternative considerations in custody disputes. John also has authored these exceptional McGraw-Hill texts: *Children* (12th edition), *Adolescence* (14th edition), *A Topical Approach to Life-Span Development* (6th edition), and *Educational Psychology* (5th edition).

For many years, John was involved in tennis as a player, teaching professional, and coach of professional tennis players. At the University of Miami (FL), the tennis team on which he played still holds the NCAA Division I record for most consecutive wins (137) in any sport. His wife, Mary Jo, has a Master's degree in special education and has worked as a teacher and a realtor. He has two daughters—Tracy, who also is a realtor, and Jennifer, who is a medical sales specialist. He has one granddaughter, Jordan, age 21, currently an undergraduate student at Southern Methodist University, and two grandsons, Alex, age 8, and Luke, age 6. In the last two decades, John has also spent time painting expressionist art.

Anne MacKenzie-Rivers retired from a rewarding career as teacher and administrator at George Brown College. Her interest in psychology focuses on social psychology, positive psychology, and contemporary research on the brain. Throughout her career, she has enjoyed the design and delivery of a diverse range of courses such as the Politics of Language, Cross-cultural Communication, and modules geared to incorporating writing across the curriculum. As an administrator, she worked closely with faculty to support the development and delivery of general education, science, math, and English courses, as well as innovative programs with the College's School of Labour and Aboriginal Centre.

Her degrees are in English and educational psychology. As well as spending time with her children and grandchildren, Anne enjoys volunteering.

Thomas Malcomson has taught at George Brown College for the past 25 years. He has a Master's Degree in Experimental Psychology and a Ph.D. in History. His areas of interest in psychology centre on social psychology, gerontology, and the experience of bereavement and grief. Dr. Malcomson has taught courses in introductory, social, and developmental psychology, death, dying, and bereavement, and the history of eugenics. Thomas lives in Toronto with his wife, Peggy, and their son, Nathan.

Kwan Ho Leung enjoys teaching psychology and English—especially infancy, childhood, and grammar—at George Brown College. He has graduate degrees in psychology and economics and certificates in teaching ESL and adults. In his leisure time, Kwan Ho does paid copywriting and also volunteers for worthwhile causes. He enjoys reading, eating, and travelling—he has maintained a streak of annual visits to Europe since 2001!

Verna Pangman holds the rank of a Senior Instructor in the Faculty of Nursing, University of Manitoba. She has taught Human Growth and Development for a number of years at the undergraduate level. Verna is the primary author of the leadership textbook *Nursing Leadership from a Canadian Perspective*. In addition, she has been invited to insert Canadian data in several textbooks and chapters. She is the recipient of the Excellence in Professional Nursing Award from the College of Registered Nurses of Manitoba. She serves as a Research Affiliate at both Riverview Health Centre Winnipeg and Centre on Aging, University of Manitoba. Verna and her husband reside in a small harbour town on the shores of Lake Winnipeg. They both enjoy outdoor activities and rural community life.

brief contents

contents

SECTION 1   The Life-Span Developmental Perspective

SECTION 2 Beginnings

SECTION 3 Infancy

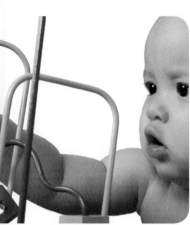

SECTION 4   Early Childhood

SECTION 6 Adolescence

SECTION 7 Early Adulthood

SECTION 8 Middle Adulthood

SECTION 9 Late Adulthood

SECTION 10 Endings

Preface

The fifth Canadian edition builds on the tradition of consistently current research, intellectually engaging materials, student-friendly writing style and pedagogy, and enticing illustrations to include even more Canadian research and content, expanded research citations, and an increased emphasis on discussions relevant to the Canadian context more fully integrate the Canadian experience.

This edition introduces a new Connections theme to provide a systematic, integrative approach to the course material. This theme was developed by John Santrock based on feedback from his students, who said that highlighting connections among the different aspects of life-span development would help them to better understand the concepts. Here's how the new theme is presented:

— **Connecting with Today's Students.** To help students learn about life-span development more effectively.

— **Connecting through Research.** To provide students with the best and most recent theory and research in the world today about each of the periods of human life span.

— **Connecting Developmental Processes.** To guide students in making developmental connections across different points in the human life span.

— **Connecting Development to Life.** To help students understand ways to apply content about the human life span to the real world and improve people's lives; and to motivate them to think deeply about their own personal journey through life and better understand who they were, are, and will be.

Connecting with Today's Students

In *Life-Span Development*, we recognize that today's students are as different in some ways from the learners of the last generation as today's discipline of the life-span development is different from the field 30 years ago. Students now learn in multiple modalities; rather than sitting down and reading traditional printed chapters in linear fashion from beginning to end, their work preferences tend to be more visual and more interactive, and their reading and study often occur in short bursts. For many students, a traditionally formatted printed textbook is no longer enough when they have instant, 24/7 access to news and information from around the globe. Two features that specifically support today's students are the adaptive diagnostic tool (discussed in more detail under Supplements) and the learning objectives system.

The Learning Objectives System

Students often report the life-span development course to be challenging because of the amount of material covered. To help today's students focus on the key ideas, the Learning Objectives System developed for *Life-Span Development* provides extensive learning connections throughout the chapters. The learning system connects the chapter opening outline, learning objectives for the chapter, mini-chapter maps that open each main section of the chapter, and Reach Your Learning Objectives and Review, Connect, Reflect at the end of each chapter. Key terms are defined in the margins as they appear in the text.

CHAPTER OUTLINE

Physical Changes and Health
LO1 Describe physical changes and health in middle and late childhood.
Body Growth and Change
The Brain
Motor Development
Exercise
Health, Illness, and Disease

Cognitive Development
LO2 Explain cognitive changes in middle and late childhood.
Piaget's Concrete Operational Stage
Information Processing
Intelligence

Language Development
LO3 Discuss language development in middle and late childhood.
Vocabulary, Grammar, and Metalinguistic Awareness
Reading
Bilingualism

Educational Approaches and Issues
LO4 Discuss approaches and issues related to education.
Approaches to Student Learning
Educational Issues
International Comparisons
Private Schools and Home Education

Children with Disabilities
LO5 Identify different types of disabilities and discuss issues relating to their education.
Learning Disabilities
Attention Deficit Hyperactivity Disorder (ADHD)
Autism Spectrum Disorders
Physical Disabilities
Children's Disabilities and the Family
Educational Issues

connecting through research ←----------

The Magic Brain—Neuroplasticity

At the beginning of the twentieth century, Freud was certain that repressed trauma impacted the individual whether or not the individual remembered it. As a neurologist and a psychoanalyst, Freud was certain of the connection, but was unable to prove it. Today, brain imaging and case studies support Freud's hunch that an interactive synergy exists between the conscious and unconscious processes of the mind (Doidge, 2007; Wexler, 2006). The focus of much of today's research is aimed at better understanding the interaction between the internal structure of the mind and the external environment.

The brain is an incredible organ, with physiological properties that lend themselves to the development of complex, dynamic, and flexible human minds. It can produce new neurons or nerves ("neuro"), resulting in a brain that is malleable or adaptable ("plastic"), hence the word neuroplasticity (Doidge, 2007; Wexler, 2006). When one part of the brain is damaged—by stroke, accident, or trauma, for example—it is able to recruit

capacity from another area of the brain to increase processing power (Doidge, 2007; Wexler, 2006). With intensive therapeutic treatment, patients have regained eyesight, recovered functioning after strokes, and ameliorated learning disorders (Doidge, 2007).

Psychiatrist and psychoanalyst Dr. Norman Doidge, who holds appointments at both the University of Toronto and Columbia University in New York, believes that as the body of knowledge grows, we will come to understand how the brain is changed by such things as emotional experiences, addictions, and learning experiences, as well as cultural factors such as technology.

As neuroscience progresses, the potential for understanding and healing traumatic experiences (conscious or not) and degenerative diseases such as Alzheimer's disease becomes more plausible (Doidge, 2007). As brain imaging becomes more refined and sophisticated, therapists will be able to more effectively help individuals who have been diagnosed with mental illnesses or are facing difficult emotional circumstances (Pugh, 2004).

Connecting through Research

This boxed feature looks closely at specific areas of research, involving experts in related fields and current research throughout. Connecting through Research describes a study or program to illustrate how research in life-span development is conducted and how it influences our understanding of the discipline.

Connecting through Social Policy

Connecting development to social policy helps students connect to the social policies that mould our development throughout life. These Connecting through Social Policy boxes highlight life-span development research activities and their influence on social policy and students' lives.

connecting development to life ←----------

Culture and Child Rearing

Child-rearing practices often reflect a culture's values, values that often are reflected in what is called locus of control (Bornstein, 2006; Cole, 2006; Shiraev & Levy, 2007). Locus of control refers to an individual's ability to affect events: those with an internal locus of control believe they can affect outcomes; on the other hand, those with an external locus of control believe that events are more likely controlled by forces outside the individual's control. Chances are that if you were born and raised in a Western culture such as one in North America or Europe you would endorse an internal locus of control, and raise children to behave and think independently. However, if you were born and raised in an Eastern culture such as one in Asia or the Middle East you are more likely to endorse an external locus of control, and raise children to consider what is best for the group first. Indeed, researchers have found that parents' child-rearing goals depend less on their personal characteristics and more on the values of the culture in which the parents live (Chao & Tseng, 2002; Trommsdorff, 2002).

Children raised on the premise of an external locus of control are more likely to show a concern for social harmony (Keller, 2002). They grow up with a stronger sense of "family self" than children in most Western cultures, believing that what they do reflects upon not just one's self but also one's family. In communal cultures, do something wrong or deviant and you shame your family; do something right or approved of and you honour your family. Conversely, individuals from Western cultures are

more apt to believe that when a person thinks independently, he or she will be more likely to contribute to the overall well-being of family and society. An interesting example of how this plays out is lying. Children learn about "appropriate lies" within a social context. In the Chinese culture, for example, where harmony and modesty are valued over individualism, children will preserve their modesty by denying having done something that is for the good of the group. In cultures such as Canada, where individuality is championed, children will seek credit for doing something that makes a positive contribution to the group (Sweet, Heyman, Fu, & Lee, 2010).

People who immigrate to Canada bring child-rearing views and practices with them from their native country, and these may conflict with the views of their new culture (Fuligni & Witkow, 2004; Parke & Buriel, 2006). For example, spanking, even beatings, are disciplinary measures applied to children and even to wives in many countries of the world but may be problematic in Canada, where such practices are highly criticized and, if done to excess, may result in legal interventions. Further, children and adolescents from immigrant families may want as much independence as their North American peers and friends have; they may want to work part time, or date someone from outside their cultural background. Such behaviour may conflict with the wishes of their parents and grandparents who want to preserve the traditions of their native culture.

Connecting Development to Life

In addition to helping students make research and developmental connections, *Life-Span Development* shows the important connections between the concepts discussed and the real world. Students in life-span development have increasingly said that they want more of this type of information. In this edition, real-life connections are explicitly made through the chapter opening vignette, the Connecting Development to Life boxes, and the new Milestones program that helps students watch life as it unfolds.

Each chapter begins with a **vignette** designed to increase students' interest and motivation to read the chapter. Each vignette establishes the Canadian or international context and uses personal stories to set the tone for the content that follows. The **Connecting Development to Life** feature can be found within the chapter and describes the influence of development in a real-world context with special attention to culture, ethnicity, and gender.

The **Milestones** program shows students what developmental concepts look like by watching actual humans develop. Starting from infancy, students track several individuals, seeing them achieve major developmental milestones, both physically and cognitively. Clips continue through adolescence and adulthood, capturing attitudes toward issues such as family, sexuality, and death and dying. Part of applying development to the real world is understanding its impact on oneself.

Critical thinking questions are also seen throughout the chapter to encourage students to critically consider what they have just read and challenge students to discuss and debate contemporary issues of concern to Canadians. To further encourage students to make personal connections to content in the text, **Reflect: Your Own Personal Journey of Life** appears in the end-of-chapter review in each chapter. This feature involves a question that asks students to reflect on some aspect of the discussion in the section they have just read and connect it to their own life.

connect

McGraw-Hill Connect provides you with a powerful tool for improving academic performance and truly mastering course material. You can diagnose your knowledge with pre and posttests, identify the areas where you need help, search the entire learning package, including the eBook, for content specific to the topic you're studying, and add these resources to your personalized study plan. CONNECT for Life-Span Development, fifth Canadian edition, offers the following:

- chapter-specific online quizzes
- groupwork
- presentations
- writing assignments
- case studies
- and much more!

Visit CONNECT today!

review → *connect* → reflect

review

Characterize the changes that occur in the brain's development during middle and late childhood. **LO1**

How does Piaget's stage of concrete operational thought differ from the earlier preoperational stage? **LO2**

What are some of the different types of intelligence? **LO3**

What is metalinguistic awareness? **LO3**

What are some of the major issues in education that affect academic performance? **LO4**

connect

In this chapter, you read about the role of exercise and nutrition on children's health. With this information in mind, design a child's day that would optimize his or her health and development. What would the child have for meals and snacks? In addition to school, in what activities would you engage the child?

reflect *Your Own Personal Journey of Life*

Consider Gardner's Eight Frames of Mind. Create a list that puts in order your strengths and weaknesses, putting your major strength on top, and your major weakness on the bottom. What activities do you enjoy the most? How do these activities compare with your list of strengths and weaknesses?

What's New in the Fifth Canadian Edition?

The fifth Canadian edition has been thoroughly revised and updated throughout to continue meeting the needs of Canadian instructors and students.

Chapter 1

- New data and updates added in the sections covering centenarians, homelessness, social age, the interactionist view, life expectancy, generations in Canada, and the *Tri-Council Policy Statement*
- Research challenges discussion revised

Chapter 2

- Added contemporary approaches to psychology section that includes brief introductions to dynamic systems, evolutionary psychology, neuroscience, and positive psychology
- Added well-known scientist and animal activist Jane Goodall to the ethological approach section
- Content condensed and made more concise throughout

Chapter 3

- Genetic foundations section revised to include information on the Human Genome Project and Genome Canada's role in the research
- Connecting Research and Social Policy feature "Ethical Considerations of Stem Cell Research and Genetic Screening: An Overview" revised to include new information highlighting the debate over stem cell research in Canada and elsewhere
- Connecting through Social Policy feature "Eugenics and Social Policy" added
- Epigenetics discussion revised and updated to include investigation between suicide and childhood abuse

Chapter 4

- New sections added on "Healthy Beginnings" and on ecstasy
- Prescription and non-prescription drugs section reworked and new content added

Chapter 5

- Updated discussion of physical growth, neurons, shaken baby syndrome, breastfeeding, sudden infant death syndrome, and conditioning
- New and updated data added on Baringa work on songbirds, the new research on cross-cultural sleep, research on vitamin D, colour vision, hearing music, and critique of Piaget
- New Canadian information added to the discussion of failure to thrive

- New research inserted on culture and developmental consequences of early parenting and on visual perception; section on the other senses condensed

Chapter 6

- New research added on crying, temperament, intentions, and social referencing
- Area of evolutionary psychology added
- Canadian references added to family section
- Inserted mention of Woodgate, the Canadian Research Chair in Child Care
- Added Lamb to paternal caregiving
- Child care section reorganized and Canadian Child Care Federation added
- New section added on infants with special needs

Chapter 7

- Discussion of Vygotsky and language development revised
- Updated section on nutrition and exercise to include information about obesity in Canadian children as well as the role of nutrition in brain development
- Added Canadian research on children and lying (Talwar & Lee)
- Discussion of the impact of poverty on development threaded throughout the chapter

Chapter 8

- Parenting styles expanded to include research findings on immigrant and refugee families and co-parenting
- Added information on the changing nature of families; includes challenges to stepfamilies and blended families
- Information added on child maltreatment

Chapter 9

- Social media information expanded
- Intelligence section revised and EI added
- Giftedness section updated

Chapter 10

- Information on families revised and updated to include data related to the role of parents in blended or stepfamilies

- Child maltreatment section revised and updated to include the impact of alcohol, social media, and parental role modelling, and long-term consequences such as leaving home to live on the streets, difficulty in establishing and maintaining relationships, substance abuse, and anxiety and depression
- Bullying section revised and updated to include four roles people play—bully, bullied, bystander, and upstander—cyberbullying, and the impact of bullying not only to the victim but to the bully and others
- The impact of poverty threaded throughout, including data on the use of food banks and the dropout rate among First Nations children

Chapter 11
- Added updated research on the brain
- New content on the timing of adolescent sexual behaviours
- Updated information on eating disorders and substance abuse

Chapter 12
- New data inserted on suicide, both urban and rural
- New data added in areas of the brain, adolescent sexuality, the timing of adolescent behaviours, adolescent sexual identity, dating violence, STI, HPV, rates of adolescent pregnancy in Canada and globally, eating disorders, risk and vulnerability, ecstasy and the adolescent brain, gambling, combating substance use, second language learners, and effective schools
- Substance use and addiction and prescription and non-prescription drugs sections revised and new data added
- Revised sections on physical changes in puberty, sexual maturation in height and weight, teen perspective on maturity, and depression

Chapter 13
- New data added on moral development, self-esteem, balancing freedom and control, parent–adolescent conflict, racial, ethnic, and cultural identity, social exclusion as a health determinant, traditions and changes in adolescence, bullying, sexting, and peer pressure
- Revised discussion of identity development, autonomy, and attachment
- Family influence added and sexual orientation given a new definition

Chapter 14
- New data added on addiction, sexual assault, and work during university
- Physical development health and wellness section revised

Chapter 15
- New opening vignette highlighting the paradigm shift defining middle adulthood, family diversity, economic realities, and healthier lifestyles
- Career and work revised to include economic impacts and the impact of leaves on women for caregiving and birth
- Added the impact of mental health on individuals and their families
- Section on religion and meaning in life revised to Meaning in Life: Meditation, Religion, and Spirituality

Chapter 16
- New opening vignette indicating how very complicated life is for people in middle adulthood as they balance home, work, community, and relationships
- Challenges on the empty nest and its refilling updated
- Intergenerational relationships section revised and updated

Chapter 17
- New opening vignette illustrates the life of Leonard Cohen as an example of healthy aging
- Updated information about changing demographics, including life expectancy and the number of centenarians
- Addition of Ursula Franklin as an example of healthy cognition in late adulthood
- Addition of new research broadening the field of neuroscience and findings supporting the robust impact on the brain of meditation, prayer, and practices in spirituality

Chapter 18
- Research added related to the impact of social determinants on health (education income, social inclusion, housing)
- New research on loneliness added to the section on the aging couple
- Economic realities threaded throughout
- New Connecting through Social Policy box describes end of life decisions

Chapter 19
- Living wills and palliative care updated and further Canadianized
- Research study added on euthanasia
- Better care for dying patients updated and further Canadianized
- Changing historical times and death in different cultures added
- Updated discussion of causes of death; life-span perspectives in adulthood, childhood, adolescence, and young adulthood; communicating with a dying person; and losing a life partner

Supplements

McGraw-Hill Connect™ is a Web-based assignment and assessment platform that gives students the means to better connect with their coursework, with their instructors, and with the important concepts that they will need to know for success now and in the future.

With Connect, instructors can deliver assignments, quizzes, and tests online. Instructors can edit existing questions and author entirely new problems. Track individual student performance—by question, assignment, or in relation to the class overall—with detailed grade reports. Integrate grade reports easily with Learning Management Systems (LMS).

By choosing Connect, instructors are providing their students with a powerful tool for improving academic performance and truly mastering course material. Connect allows students to practise important skills at their own pace and on their own schedule. Importantly, students' assessment results and instructors' feedback are all saved online—so students can continually review their progress and plot their course to success.

Connect also provides 24/7 online access to an eBook—an online edition of the text—to aid them in successfully completing their work, wherever and whenever they choose.

Key Features

Simple Assignment Management

With Connect, creating assignments is easier than ever, so you can spend more time teaching and less time managing.

- Create and deliver assignments easily with selectable questions and testbank material to assign online.
- Streamline lesson planning, student progress reporting, and assignment grading to make classroom management more efficient than ever.
- Go paperless with the eBook and online submission and grading of student assignments.

Smart Grading

When it comes to studying, time is precious. Connect helps students learn more efficiently by providing feedback and practice material when they need it, where they need it.

- Automatically score assignments, giving students immediate feedback on their work and side-by-side comparisons with correct answers.
- Access and review each response; manually change grades or leave comments for students to review.
- Reinforce classroom concepts with practice tests and instant quizzes.

Instructor Library

The Connect Instructor Library is your course creation hub. It provides all the critical resources you'll need to build your course, just how you want to teach it.

- Assign eBook readings and draw from a rich collection of textbook-specific assignments.
- Access instructor resources, including ready-made PowerPoint presentations and media to use in your lectures.
- View assignments and resources created for past sections.
- Post your own resources for students to use.

eBook

Connect reinvents the textbook learning experience for the modern student. Every Connect subject area is seamlessly integrated with Connect eBooks, which are designed to keep students focused on the concepts key to their success.

- Provide students with a Connect eBook, allowing for anytime, anywhere access to the textbook.
- Merge media, animation, and assessments with the text's narrative to engage students and improve learning and retention.
- Pinpoint and connect key concepts in a snap using the powerful eBook search engine.
- Manage notes, highlights, and bookmarks in one place for simple, comprehensive review.

LEARNSMART®

No two students are alike. McGraw-Hill LearnSmart™ is an intelligent learning system that uses a series of adaptive questions to pinpoint each student's knowledge gaps. LearnSmart then provides an optimal learning path for each student, so that they spend less time in areas they already know and more time in areas they don't. The result is that LearnSmart's adaptive learning path helps students retain more knowledge, learn faster, and study more efficiently.

SMARTBOOK™

As the first and only adaptive reading experience, SmartBook is changing the way students read and learn. SmartBook creates a personalized reading experience by highlighting the most important concepts a student needs to learn at that moment in time. As a student engages with SmartBook, the reading experience continuously adapts by highlighting content based on what each student knows and doesn't know. This ensures that he or she is focused on the content needed to close specific knowledge gaps, while it simultaneously promotes long-term learning.

Milestones

McGraw-Hill's Milestones is a powerful tool that allows students to experience life as it unfolds, from infancy to late adulthood. Milestones consists of two essential components that work together to capture key changes throughout the lifespan—Milestones of Child Development and Milestones: Transitions.

In Milestones of Child Development, students track the early stages of physical, social, and emotional development. By watching one child over time or comparing various children, Milestones provides a unique, experiential learning environment that can only be achieved by watching real human development as it happens—all in pre-, transitional, and post-milestone segments.

In Milestones: Transitions, students meet a series of people—from teenagers to individuals in late adulthood—to hear individual perspectives on changes that occur throughout the life span. Through a series of interviews, students are given the opportunity to think critically while exploring the differences in attitudes on everything from body image to changes in emotion, sexuality, cognitive processes, and death and dying.

Instructor Resources

Connect is a one-stop shop for instructor resources, including:

Instructor's Manual   Revised by the text authors, Verna Pangman, University of Winnipeg, and Anne MacKenzie-Rivers, this comprehensive guide includes an overview of each chapter, learning objectives, suggestions and resources for lecture topics, classroom activities, projects, and suggestions for video and multimedia lecture enhancements.

Test Bank   The *Test Bank* provides a wide variety of book-specific test questions. Revised and updated by the text author, Verna Pangman, University of Winnipeg, accuracy-checked to ensure it meets our highest standards of excellence, and available as Word files, the questions in the *Test Bank* are also provided in an easy-to-use electronic testing program. It accommodates a wide range of question types and allows instructors to add their own questions. The program is available for Windows and Macintosh environments.

Microsoft® PowerPoint® Presentations   These presentations cover the key points of the chapter and include graphics. Revised by Lucia New, Saskatchewan Institute of Applied Science and Technology (SIAST), the presentation slides can be used as-is or modified to meet the instructor's needs.

Visual Assets Database   The Visual Assets Database (VAD) provides hundreds of easily accessible media resources for use with life-span and developmental psychology courses. These resources include video demonstrations and interviews, photographs, audio clips, Web links, figures and graphs, and suggested in-class activities. For more information, visit vad.mhhe.com.

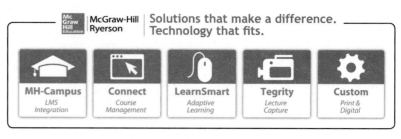

Superior Learning Solutions and Support

The McGraw-Hill Ryerson team is ready to help you assess and integrate any of our products, technology, and services into your course for optimal teaching and learning performance. Whether it's helping your students improve their grades, or putting your entire course online, the McGraw-Hill Ryerson team is here to help you do it. Contact your *Learning Solutions Consultant* today to learn how to maximize all of McGraw-Hill Ryerson's resources!

For more information on the latest technology and Learning Solutions offered by McGraw-Hill Ryerson and its partners, please visit us online: www.mcgrawhill.ca/he/solutions.

Acknowledgements

The Canadian authors would like to thank Marcia Siekowski, Senior Product Manager; Katherine Goodes, Product Developer; Cathy Biribauer, Supervising Editor; Kelli Howey, Copy Editor; Ashley Rayner, Proofreader; Robyn Craig, Permissions Editor; and the helpful, thoughtful team of people at McGraw-Hill Ryerson whose professionalism, insights, suggestions, and cheerfulness made working on this text a pleasure.

Last, but not least, we extend our thanks to those instructors whose thoughtful reviews informed the text:

Cathy Mondloch, Brock University

Carol Prechotko, Cambrian College of Applied Arts and Technology

Susan Hartwell, Durham College

Theresa Steger, Humber College Institute of Technology and Advanced Learning

Nancy Ogden, Mount Royal University

Thomas Keenan, Niagara College

Susan Chuang, University of Guelph

Catherine Hedlin, MacEwan University

Gregory Bird, Lethbridge College

Dana Murphy, Nipissing University

Lucia New, Saskatchewan Institute of Applied Science and Technology

Andrew Starzomski, Saint Mary's University

Wendy Bourque, St. Thomas University

Anne MacKenzie-Rivers and *Verna Pangman*

CHAPTER 1 # The Life-Span Perspective

CHAPTER OUTLINE

"We reach backward to our parents and forward to our children, and through our children to a future we will never see, but about which we need to care."

—CARL JUNG, TWENTIETH-CENTURY SWISS PSYCHIATRIST

1

Our Amazing Brain Over the Life Span

Undoubtedly you have observed changes in yourself over the years. How different are you now from your baby pictures? How does your behaviour today differ from when you were ten years old? Fifteen? How do you account for these changes? Not as obvious as some of the physical and behavioural changes, but equally important, is the growth and development of our brain over the course of our lives. From the moment of conception and throughout our life span, changes in the brain enable us to understand and respond to the world around us. Neuroscientists are just beginning to understand the magnitude of these changes.

Fetus Development

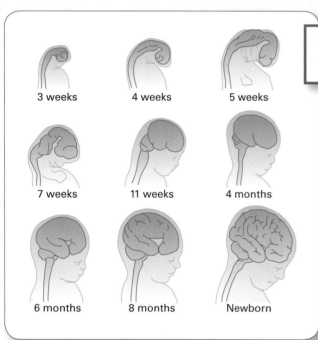

3 weeks   4 weeks   5 weeks

7 weeks   11 weeks   4 months

6 months   8 months   Newborn

Warning!
Take special care: cell explosions!

- Approximately 250,000 new nerve cells are created every minute. One billion are created by the time of birth.
- At the end of four weeks, the zygote's brain emerges.
- At the end of four weeks, the neurons begin to take on specialized tasks.
- Before birth, genes mainly direct the brain's development.

From Birth to Approximately 8–10 Years of Age:

Caution!
Work in progress—will begin to interact with the world!

- After birth, environmental experiences associated with the five senses direct the brain's development.
- At birth, the infant's brain weighs 25 percent of its adult weight. By two years of age, the brain weighs 75 percent of its adult weight; by six years, 90 percent.
- The younger the brain, the more plastic it is; therefore, learning new things, such as language, is easier and more natural.
- The prefrontal cortex, which plays an important role in higher-order cognitive functioning such as decision making, attention, and memory, develops extensively between three and six years.

From Approximately 8–10 Years of Age Through Ages 20–25:

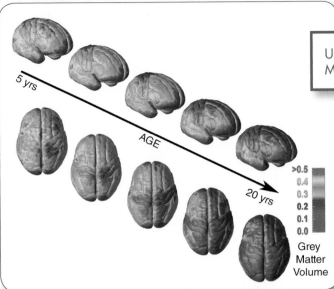

Under Renovation:
Much growth and exuberance! Please excuse our dust!

- As the brain adds the last 10 percent of its weight, its ability to regulate emotions increases.
- The amygdala, which processes emotion, matures earlier than the prefrontal cortex.
- Magnetic resonance imaging (MRI) shows that activity level in the amygdala of teens is considerably more active than in adults.
- Researchers call the rapid growth and pruning of synapses that occurs during adolescence *exuberance*.

From Approximately 20–25 Years of Age Through Ages 60–65:

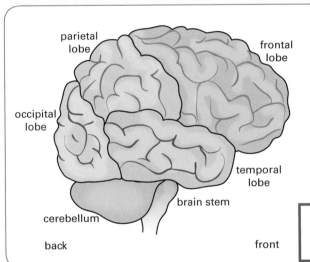

- The exuberance of the adolescent brain is not completed until somewhere between the ages of 20 and 25.
- The myelin sheath, the layer of fat cells that insulates nerve cells and enables nerve impulses to travel rapidly, plays an important role in inhibiting behaviour. Myelination of the prefrontal cortex is not completed until our early twenties.
- Athleticism and physical strength peak in early adulthood.
- Creativity, which requires patience and practice and considerable self-regulation, peaks in middle adulthood.
- Unless compromised by disease, the adult brain remains plastic and grows more efficient.

Welcome!
Newly renovated and fully functioning!

From Approximately 60–65 Years of Age Through Age 120

Welcome!
Please be mindful of possible loose connections!

- Physical, mental, and social activity, as well as a sense of purpose, are associated with healthy brain activity in late adulthood. A subject of contemporary research is to determine whether the brain remains healthy because of these activities or whether disengagement is an early sign of dementia.
- The first system of the brain to show age is memory. The prefrontal cortex loses its ability to hold information.
- Active brains maintain their capacity for abstract and analytical thinking.

With conception, when one heroic sperm among millions—one with its own genetic makeup and cultural legacy—manages to penetrate an ovum, with its own unique genetic makeup and cultural legacy, the story of prenatal development begins to unfold. The details of the story depend, however, on the individual situation. Many individuals who are unable to conceive through sexual intercourse turn to alternative methods of reproductive technologies to fulfill their parental desires. A few questions may arise, such as: Was the pregnancy planned? Is this the first pregnancy? Has the couple been taking fertility treatments? Is the mother a teenager? How is the father reacting to the pregnancy? Equally important are the responses from the prospective grandparents, brothers and sisters, relatives, and friends. Whatever the situation, everyone involved will be bubbling over with myriad thoughts and emotions. Everyone's brain will also be highly engaged, working night and day, celebrating, planning, worrying, and anticipating. At the same time, the brain of the unborn fetus continues to explode as the actual brain starts to become a fully fledged organ with specialized parts and hemispheres. Our brain continues to change throughout the life span.

The sketches and *fast facts* above highlight some of the significant changes in the brain at various points in the life span.

Throughout the text, you will learn about the growth and development of the brain. You will read more about the lightning-speed rate of growth during the prenatal and infancy stages, the consolidation in childhood, the restructuring in adolescence, the further consolidation in adulthood, and the changes in connectivity in late adulthood. You will also read about how the brain is affected by chemical substances, injury, and disease. Our brain's ability to respond consciously and unconsciously to myriad stimuli, to accommodate injury, heal, and much more, is truly inspiring.

> *But here's the most inspiring of insights about the brain: We can enhance our brain's performance by our own efforts. Thus, learning about the brain provides a wonderful mix of instruction, amazement, and self-improvement. As you gain knowledge, you're in a better position to improve its functioning and thereby increase the quality of your life.*
>
> —Dr. Richard Restak, neurologist, psychologist, and author of many books about the brain
> (Sweeney, 2009, p. 152).

Family photographs of your grandmother or grandfather's wedding, like those of yourself as a baby, illustrate some of the changes that take place over a lifetime. The changes we see in photographs show the more obvious physical or biological changes. We are also well aware of accompanying emotional changes; certainly, a baby does not have the same emotional response to a loved one as newlyweds have to each other, and we have more strategies to help us cope with disappointment than we did when we were four years old. As the opening vignette illustrates, the physiology of our brain, and thus our capacity for thinking, understanding, and creating meaning, changes throughout our lives. The neuroplasticity of the brain enables us to heal, accommodate injury, make decisions, and sustain ourselves.

The Life-Span Perspective

LO1 Define life-span development and describe the characteristics of the life-span perspective.

Life-Span Development

Each life is a unique and fascinating biography. Understanding the rhythms and patterns of growth and development allows us to better understand and weave together the portrait of our present, our past, and, to some extent, our future.

Life-Span Development

The Importance of Studying Life-Span Development

How might we benefit from examining life-span development? Perhaps you are, or will be, a parent, social worker, law-enforcement officer, nurse, or teacher. If so, understanding others is, or will be, a part of your everyday life. The more you learn about them, the more rewarding your relationships will be. Most development involves growth, but it also includes decline (as in dying). In exploring development, we will examine the life span from the point of conception until the time when life (at least, life as we know it) ends. You will see yourself as an infant, as a child, and as an adolescent, and be stimulated to think about how those years influenced the kind of individual you are today. Not only will you gain greater insights about yourself and those with whom you interact professionally and socially, you may better understand the challenges facing the loved ones in your life as well.

Although growth and development are dramatic during the first two decades of life, they continue throughout the life span. The life-span approach emphasizes developmental change throughout adulthood as well as childhood (Baltes, 2009; Birren, 2007; Park & Schwarz, 2009; Schaie, 2007). **Life-span development** *is the pattern of movement or change that begins at conception and continues through the human life span.*

life-span development The pattern of change that begins at conception and continues through the life cycle.

The Importance of Studying Life-Span Development
Characteristics of the Life-Span Perspective
The belief that development occurs throughout life is central to the life-span perspective on human development, but this perspective has other characteristics as well. According to life-span development expert Paul Baltes (1939–2006), the **life-span perspective** *views development as lifelong, multidimensional, multidirectional, plastic, multidisciplinary, and contextual, and as a process that involves growth, maintenance, and regulation of loss* (Baltes, 2003, 2009; Baltes, Lindenberger, & Staudinger, 2006). In Baltes's view, it is important to understand that development is constructed through biological, socio-cultural, and individual factors working together (Baltes, Reuter-Lorenz, & Rösler, 2006). Let's look at each of these characteristics.

life-span perspective The view that development is lifelong, multidimensional, multidirectional, plastic, contextual, and multidisciplinary and involves growth, maintenance, and regulation.

DEVELOPMENT IS LIFELONG   Is early adulthood the endpoint of development? According to the life-span perspective, it is not. In addition, no age period dominates development. Researchers are increasingly studying the experiences and psychological orientations of adults at different points in their development. Later in this chapter, we will describe the age periods of development and their characteristics.

DEVELOPMENT IS MULTIDIMENSIONAL   Development consists of biological, cognitive, and socio-emotional processes (later in the chapter, we will explore these key processes of life-span development). Even within a process such as cognition, various components such as opportunity, internalization, and support play a vital role.

DEVELOPMENT IS MULTIDIRECTIONAL   During early adulthood, as individuals establish romantic relationships, the time spent with their friends may decrease. During late adulthood, older adults might become wiser by being able to call on experience to guide their intellectual decision making, but they perform more poorly on tasks that require speed in processing information (Baltes, 2009; Baltes & Kunzmann, 2007; Salthouse, 2009b).

Paul Baltes (1939–2006) was a leading architect of the life-span perspective of development. Here he is seen conversing with one of the long-time research participants in the Berlin Aging Study that he directed. She joined the study in the early 1990s and participated six times in extensive physical, medical, psychological, and social assessments. In her professional life, she was a medical doctor. At the time of this picture, she was 96 years of age.

plasticity Refers to the capacity for change.

context The settings, influenced by historical, political, economic, social, and cultural factors, in which development occurs.

How might growth versus maintenance and regulation be reflected in the development of this grandmother and her granddaughter?

DEVELOPMENT IS PLASTIC   A key developmental research agenda item is the search for plasticity and its constraints (Baltes, Lindenberger, & Staudinger, 2006). **Plasticity** *means the capacity for change.* For example, can intellectual skills still be improved through education for individuals in their seventies or eighties? Is there a possibility that these intellectual abilities are cast in stone by the time people are in their thirties so that further improvement is impossible? In one research study, the reasoning abilities of older adults were improved through retraining (Boron, Willis, & Schaie, 2007; Kramer & Morrow, 2009). However, it is possible we possess less capacity for change when we become older (Baltes, Reuter-Lorenz, & Rösler, 2006). The search for plasticity and its constraints is a key element on the contemporary agenda for developmental research; in fact, the contemporary studies of neuroplasticity and neuropsychology have developed around this concept (Kramer & Morrow, 2009).

DEVELOPMENT IS MULTIDISCIPLINARY   Psychologists, sociologists, anthropologists, neuroscientists, and medical researchers all study human development and share an interest in unlocking the mysteries of development through the life span. What constraints on intelligence are set by the individual's heredity and health status? How universal are cognitive and socio-emotional changes? How do environmental contexts influence intellectual development?

DEVELOPMENT INVOLVES GROWTH, MAINTENANCE, AND REGULATION   Baltes and his colleagues (Baltes, Staudinger, & Lindenberger, 2006) believe that the mastery of life often involves conflict and competition among three goals of human development: growth, maintenance, and regulation. As individuals enter middle and late adulthood, the maintenance and regulation of their capacities take centre stage away from growth. Thus, a 70-year-old woman may aim not to improve her tennis shot, but to maintain her independence and continue to play. As we age, the goal to seek growth in intellectual capacities (such as memory) or physical capacities may yield to maintenance of skills or minimizing deterioration. In Section 9, "Late Adulthood," we will discuss these ideas in greater depth.

DEVELOPMENT IS A CO-CONSTRUCTION OF BIOLOGY, CULTURE, AND THE INDIVIDUAL Development is a co-construction of biological, cultural, and individual factors working together (Baltes, 2009; Baltes, Reuter-Lorenz, & Rösler, 2006). For example, our brain shapes and interprets culture, but it is also shaped by culture and the experiences that we have or pursue. We can author a unique developmental path by actively choosing from the environment the things that optimize our lives (Rathunde & Csikszentmihalyi, 2006).

DEVELOPMENT IS CONTEXTUAL   All development occurs within a **context**, or a setting. Contexts include families, socio-economic statuses, schools, peer groups, churches, cities, neighbourhoods, university laboratories, countries, and so on. Each of these settings is influenced by historical, economic, geological, social, and cultural factors (Matsumoto & Juang, 2008; Mehrotra & Wagner, 2009).

To this point, we have discussed the life-span perspective. For a review, see the Reach Your Learning Objectives section at the end of this chapter.

The Role of Context

LO2 Define the term *context* and examine the role it plays in understanding growth and development.

Context

As we just noted, all development occurs within a context; however, like individuals, contexts also can change. Thus, individuals are changing beings in a changing world. As a result of these changes, contexts exert three types of influences (Baltes, 2003): (1) normative age-graded influences, (2) normative history-graded influences, and (3) non-normative or highly individualized life events. Each of these types can have a biological or environmental impact on development.

NORMATIVE AGE-GRADED INFLUENCES are similar for individuals in a particular age group. These influences include biological processes such as puberty and menopause. They also include socio-cultural, environmental processes such as beginning formal education (usually at about age five in Canada), and retirement (which often occurs in the fifties or sixties). Forty or fifty years ago, Canadians married in their late teens or early twenties and rarely lived together prior to marriage. Now, couples typically cohabitate, postponing marriage until closer to age 30.

NORMATIVE HISTORY-GRADED INFLUENCES are common to people of a particular generation because of historical circumstances. For example, in their youth, North American baby boomers shared the experience of the Separatist Movement in Quebec, Trudeau-mania, and the British invasion. Other examples of normative history-graded influences include economic, political, and social upheavals such as the war in Afghanistan, the LGBTQ rights movements of the 1990s, the terrorist attacks of 9/11/2001, as well as the integration of computers and cell phones into everyday life (Elder & Shanahan, 2006; Schaie, 2007). In Canada in 2013, tropical storm Leslie could be considered a non-normative history-graded influence, as the storm affected thousands of lives on the eastern coastline. The Canadian Hurricane Centre warned the people of Newfoundland and Labrador to expect 12 hours of intense weather over the land; people had to cope with power outages and road hazards, which influenced their lives.

NON-NORMATIVE LIFE EVENTS are occurrences that are not anticipated but have a major impact on an individual's life. For example, most of us anticipate that we will outlive our parents; however, a parent who dies unexpectedly when a child is young illustrates a non-normative life event. Non-normative life events can also be positive events, such as winning the lottery or getting an unexpected career opportunity with special privileges. An important aspect of understanding the role of non-normative life events is to focus on how people adapt to them.

Life Expectancy

Life expectancy *refers to the number of years an individual is expected to live starting from birth.* Life expectancy is based on specific mortality statistics for a given observation period, typically three years. In 2007–2009, life expectancy for Canadians averaged 81.1 years. Males and females averaged 78.8 and 83.3 years, respectively. During that same period (2007–2009), males continued to have a lower life expectancy than females. The life expectancy difference in years between males and females has become smaller, from a difference of 4.7 years in 2005–2007 to 4.5 years in 2007–2009 (Health Canada, 2010; Statistics Canada, 2012g).

For both men and women, life expectancy has been significantly higher in urban areas compared to rural areas (CIHR, 2006). Higher overall mortality rates seem to be driven by higher death rates from causes such as circulatory disease, injury, and suicide rates. On the other hand, more rural residents than urban residents reported a strong sense of community belonging, a measure of social capital (DesMeules et al., 2012).

Perhaps more than any other single factor, context plays a vital role in life expectancy because context determines access to water, hygiene, health care, and social services. The country and community in which we live plays a determining factor in personal safety. Here again, context is critical, as life expectancy represents one of the planet's greatest disparities. In some parts of the world, many children do not live long enough to even go to school, and many young women die during childbirth.

The 2010 Human Development Report indicates that substantial progress has been made in many aspects of human development. For example, the recent pro-democracy protests across Arab States began in Tunisia and Egypt, and most significantly have been driven by educated

What are some of the personal, historical, and cultural factors that are changed by a normative history-graded influence, such as the natural disaster in Haiti pictured here?

life expectancy The average age a child born in a given year can expect to live to, based on specific mortality rates calculated for a given year

urban youth. This democratization movement can be considered a direct consequence of human development progress. Another instance is that, in 1970, Tunisia had a lower life expectancy than that of the Democratic Republic of the Congo; Tunisia had fewer children in school than Malawi. However, by 2010 Tunisia was in the high category on the Human Development Index, with an average life expectancy of 74 years and the greatest number of children enrolled in secondary school (United Nations, 2011).

The Human Development Index (HDI) combines data related to life expectancy, educational levels, and per capita income to measure the overall well-being of individuals. Additional, related factors such as the availability of fresh water, a healthy childhood, nutritious foods, hygiene, sanitation, and access to health care further contribute to overall health (United Nations, 2011). In examining the HDI trend (1980–2011), Canada ranks 6th among 187 countries; the country that ranks first is Norway, and the lowest ranking country is the Democratic Republic of the Congo. However, there have been large improvements in life expectancy, school enrolment, literacy, and income in all countries (United Nations, 2011). See Figure 1.1 for an illustration of life expectancy in different parts of the world.

Today, most people live longer, are more educated, and have more access to goods and services than ever before. Even in economically impoverished countries, the health and education of their people have improved greatly. Progress has been credited, at least in part, to individuals who now exercise their voices to select leaders, influence public decisions, and share knowledge to improve their quality of life. However, not all countries have seen rapid progress, and the variations are striking. People in the former Soviet Union and in Southern Africa have endured times of regress, especially in health matters (United Nations, 2011).

Figure 1.1

World Variations in Life Expectancy

This map illustrates the disparities in life expectancy around the world. Notice the many areas where the average of life expectancy is undisclosed. **What factors might contribute to this? What factors contribute to those areas of the world where life expectancy is less than 50 years?**

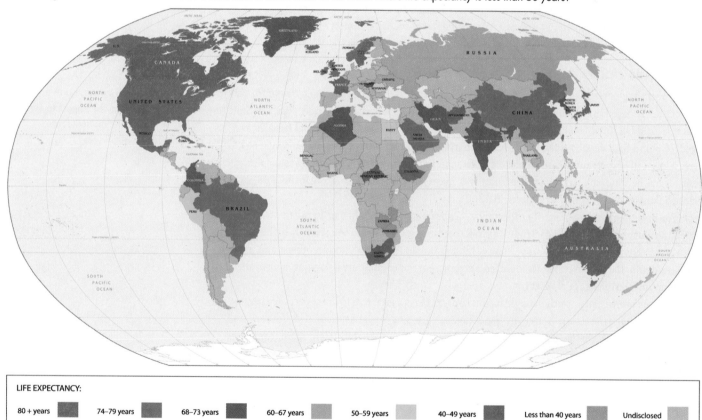

LIFE EXPECTANCY:

80 + years   74–79 years   68–73 years   60–67 years   50–59 years   40–49 years   Less than 40 years   Undisclosed

Although consistently ranked among the healthiest countries of the world, disparities occur in our peaceful nation, particularly in the northern areas inhabited by Aboriginal Canadians. The life expectancy for Aboriginal Canadians, although improving, remains lower than that of the rest of the Canadian population. For example, the prevalence of obesity is significantly higher among Aboriginal compared to non-Aboriginal populations, particularly in Alberta, Manitoba, Ontario, and Quebec; however, this is not the case in Nunavut (CIHI, 2011).

Median Age and Centenarians

Between the 2006 and 2011 censuses, Canada's population increased 5.9 percent compared with the 5.4 percent increase during the previous five-year period (Statistics Canada, 2012h). In fact, between 2006 and 2011, Canada's population increased at a faster rate than the population of any other member of the G8 group of industrialized nations. During the past ten years, net international migration (the difference between the number of immigrants and emigrants) accounted for two-thirds of Canada's population growth. Meanwhile, natural increase (the difference between births and deaths) was accountable for only about one-third (Statistics Canada, 2012h).

In July 2011 the median age of Canada's population was estimated at 39.9 years, up 0.2 years from the same date a year earlier. Two major factors believed to have contributed to the increase in median age were decreased fertility rates and increased life expectancy (Statistics Canada, 2011a). Interestingly, as a result of gains in life expectancy, an increasing number of Canadians, called centenarians, are reaching the age of 100 (Statistics Canada, 2013b). The 2011 census counted 4,870 women and 955 men aged 100 and over. More women than men reach the age of 100 because, compared to men, women experience a lower probability of dying at all ages (Statistics Canada, 2013b). In the United States, the rate of centenarians was slightly lower than it was in Canada. Japan had the highest rate at nearly at 37 centenarians per 100,000 persons. Meanwhile, Russia had only 4 centenarians per 100,000 persons (Statistics in Canada, 2013b). These demographic estimates are interesting because they portray the life-span development of individuals from birth to death. See Figure 1.2 for an illustration of the aging population in Canada.

Generations in Canada

In 2011, many generations comprised the Canadian population. The best-known generation is the baby boomers. The largest annual increase in the number of births since 1921 occurred between 1945 and 1946. This particular period of time showed an increase of about 15 percent in the population,

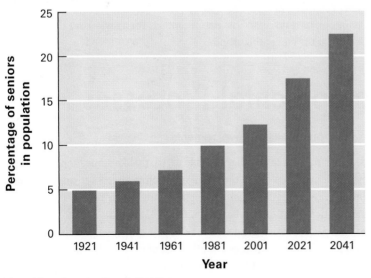

Figure 1.2

The Aging Senior Population in Canada

The percentage of seniors in the general population has been increasing.

Adapted from Statistics Canada (2002).

critical thinking

A natural implication of an increasing median age is that the population of those under 25 is decreasing. **1.** What do you think are the personal, social, economic, and political implications of our aging population? **2.** Compare and contrast relevant characteristics (housing, communication, and possible others) between the young population (under 25) and the aging population in Canada. **3.** Draw a representation of the centenarian's perception about his/her quality of life today. **4.** Specify the social environment of your centenarian.

and it marked the beginning of the baby boom period (Statistics Canada, 2011a). In the near future, many baby boomers will reach the age of 65; the result will be an acceleration of the aging population in Canada. By 2031 all baby boomers will have reached the age of 65, and the proportion of seniors is expected to reach 23 percent compared to 15 percent in 2011 (Statistics Canada, 2011c).

The second significant generation is that of the parents of the baby boomers. This generation can be defined as all individuals born during the 22-year inter-war period (1919–1940). In 2011, these people were between 71 and 92 years of age (Statistics Canada, 2011c).

According to Statistics Canada (2011a), 27 percent of the total population belongs to the children of the baby boomers, best known as Generation X. This generation may also be called Generation Y or "echo of the baby boom." Generation X is smaller than the baby boom generation because the baby boomers had fewer children than their parents did. Generation X individuals grew up in a world of mind-blowing technological invention. That is, not only did Generation X experience the impact of personal computers and other advanced technology throughout their developmental years, but in addition many experienced a tense environment of separation and divorce, two-parent working families, and institutional daycare, as well as more permissive parenting (Morton, 2003; Sudheimer, 2009). It is interesting to note whether the stresses experienced by current university students might be rooted in the events that have occurred in their lives. Results of a 2011 survey of 1,600 students at the University of Alberta indicate that 51 percent of students reported that within the past 12 months they "felt things were hopeless." A shocking 7 percent admitted that they had "seriously considered suicide," and about 1 percent had attempted it (Lunau, 2012). A discussion paper delivered in June 2011 at Queen's University in Ontario offered a range of explanations. One such explanation claimed that students are grappling with mental health problems while being surrounded by heavy academic demands. Another explanation had to do with their parents' expectations regarding their grades. A frequently stated reason for the student stress seems to be the looming recognition of a tough job market, aggravated by the student debt facing them at graduation (Lunau, 2012). It can be argued that these are factors the baby boomers were not forced to face during their developmental years.

Finally, individuals born since 1993 have sometimes been designated as the new Generation Z, or the Internet Generation. In the 2011 census of Canada, 22 percent of the total population was born between 1993 and 2011. In 2011, these people were 18 years old or under, and a few were just starting to enter the labour market (Statistics Canada, 2011c).

Socio-Economic Status (SES)

Another major contextual influence is our socio-economic status. Poverty is a great inhibitor to growth and development because access to health services and recreational and educational programs is limited. You will read more about the impact of poverty throughout the text.

To this point, we have discussed the role of context. For a review, see the **Reach Your Learning Objectives** section at the end of this chapter.

Developmental Processes

LO3 Review the processes of development.

Biological, Cognitive, and Socio-Emotional Processes

Each of us develops partly like all other individuals, partly like some other individuals, and partly like no other individual. Most of the time, our attention is directed to an individual's uniqueness. But psychologists who study life-span development are drawn to our shared, as well as to our unique, characteristics. Most of us—Leonardo da Vinci, Sir John A. Macdonald, Stephen Harper, Clara Hughes, Terry Fox, you—walked at about one year of age, engaged in fantasy play as a young child, and became more independent as a youth. Each of us, if we live long enough, will experience the aging process and the deaths of family members and friends.

At the beginning of this chapter, we defined life-span development as the pattern of change that begins at conception and continues through the life span. The opening vignette illustrates how the brain changes throughout the course of life; however, the patterns are incredibly complex because our growth and development reflect the integrative and fluid product of biological, cognitive, and socio-emotional processes (see Figure 1.3). The following discussion provides brief definitions of these processes around which this text is organized. As you read, you will learn how these processes develop at different stages of the life span.

Biological, Cognitive, and Socio-Emotional Processes

Biological processes *produce changes in an individual's physical nature.* Genes inherited from parents, the development of the brain, height and weight gains, changes in motor skills, the hormonal changes of puberty, and cardiovascular decline all reflect the role of biological processes in development.

Cognitive processes *refer to changes in the individual's thought, intelligence, and language.* Watching a colourful mobile swinging above the crib, putting together a two-word sentence, memorizing a poem, imagining what it would be like to be a movie star, and solving a crossword puzzle all involve cognitive processes.

Socio-emotional processes *involve changes in the individual's relationships with other people, changes in emotions, and changes in personality.* An infant's smile in response to her mother's touch, a young boy's aggressive attack on a playmate, a girl's development of assertiveness, an older sibling's concern for a younger sibling, an adolescent's joy at the senior prom, and the affection of an elderly couple all reflect the role of the socio-emotional processes in development.

In many instances, biological, cognitive, and socio-emotional processes are bidirectional. For example, biological processes can influence cognitive processes and vice versa. Thus, although usually we will study the different processes of development (biological, cognitive, and socio-emotional) in separate locations, keep in mind that we are talking about the development of an integrated individual with a mind and body that are interdependent.

biological processes Changes in an individual's physical nature.

cognitive processes Changes in an individual's thought, intelligence, and language.

socio-emotional processes Changes in an individual's relationships with other people, emotions, and personality.

Figure 1.3

Processes and Periods of Development

The unfolding of life's periods of development is influenced by the interaction of biological, cognitive, and socio-emotional processes.

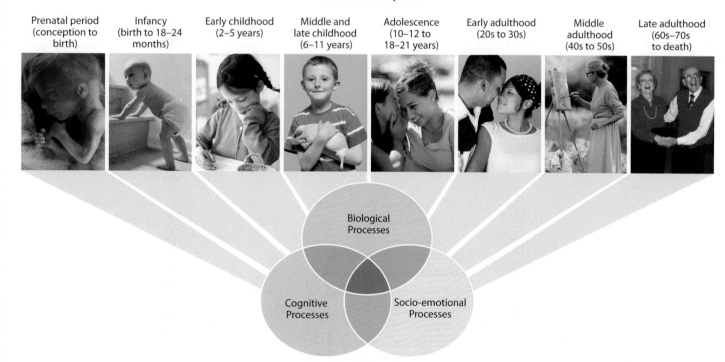

Periods of Development

Prenatal period (conception to birth) · Infancy (birth to 18–24 months) · Early childhood (2–5 years) · Middle and late childhood (6–11 years) · Adolescence (10–12 to 18–21 years) · Early adulthood (20s to 30s) · Middle adulthood (40s to 50s) · Late adulthood (60s–70s to death)

Biological Processes

Cognitive Processes

Socio-emotional Processes

Processes of Development

To this point, we have discussed developmental processes. For a review, see the Reach Your Learning Objectives section at the end of this chapter.

Periods of Development

LO4 Describe the periods of development and concept of age.

The Periods of Development

The interplay of biological, cognitive, and socio-emotional processes produces the periods of the human life span. A developmental period refers to a time frame in a person's life that is characterized by certain features. For example, in the opening vignette you read about changes that occur to our brains at different periods in our lives. For the purposes of organization and understanding, we commonly describe development in terms of these periods. The most widely used classification of developmental periods involves the eight-period sequence shown in Figure 1.3. Approximate age ranges are listed for the periods to provide a general idea of when a period begins and ends.

The *prenatal period* is the time from conception to birth. It involves tremendous growth—from a single cell to an organism complete with brain and behavioural capabilities, produced in approximately a nine-month period.

Infancy is the developmental period extending from birth to 18 or 24 months. Infancy is a time of extreme dependence upon adults. Many psychological activities are just beginning—language, symbolic thought, sensorimotor coordination, and social learning, for example.

Early childhood is the developmental period extending from the end of infancy to about five or six years. This period is sometimes called the "preschool years." During this time, young children learn to become more self-sufficient and to care for themselves, develop school readiness skills (following instructions, identifying letters), and spend many hours in play with peers. Grade 1 typically marks the end of early childhood.

Middle and late childhood is the developmental period extending from about 6 to 11 years of age. This period is sometimes called the "elementary school years." The fundamental skills of reading, writing, and arithmetic are mastered. The child is formally exposed to the larger world and its culture. Achievement becomes a more central theme of the child's world, and self-control increases.

Adolescence is the developmental period of transition from childhood to early adulthood, entered at approximately 10 to 12 years of age and ending at 18 to 21 years of age. Adolescence begins with rapid physical changes—dramatic gains in height and weight, changes in body contour, and the development of sexual characteristics, such as enlargement of the breasts, development of pubic and facial hair, and deepening of the voice. At this point in development, the pursuit of independence and an identity is prominent. Thought is more logical, abstract, and idealistic. More time is spent outside of the family with a peer group.

Early adulthood is the developmental period beginning in the late teens or early twenties and lasting through the thirties. It is a time of establishing personal and economic independence, career development, and, for many, selecting a mate, learning to live with someone in an intimate way, starting a family, and rearing children.

Middle adulthood is the developmental period beginning at approximately 40 years of age and extending to about age 60. It is a time of expanding personal and social involvement and responsibility; of assisting the next generation in becoming competent, mature individuals; and of reaching and maintaining satisfaction in a career.

Late adulthood has the longest span of any period of development, and as noted earlier, the number of people in this age group has been increasing dramatically. As a result, life-span developmentalists have been paying more attention to differences within late adulthood (Scheibe, Freund, & Baltes, 2007). Paul Baltes and Jacqui Smith (2003) argue that a major change takes place in older adults' lives as they become the "oldest-old," on average at about 85 years of age. For example, the "young-old" (classified as 65 through 84 in this analysis) have substantial potential for physical and cognitive fitness, retain much of their cognitive capacity, and can develop strategies to cope with the gains and losses of aging. In contrast, the oldest-old (85 and older) show considerable loss in cognitive skills, experience an increase in chronic stress, and are more frail (Baltes & Smith, 2003).

Thus, Baltes and Smith concluded that considerable plasticity and adaptability characterize adults from their sixties until their mid-eighties, but that the oldest-old have reached the limits of their functional capacity, which makes interventions to improve their lives difficult. Nonetheless, as will be described in later chapters, considerable variation exists in how much the oldest-old retain their capabilities (Perls, 2007).

Life-span developmentalists who focus on adult development and aging increasingly describe life-span development in terms of four "ages" (Baltes, 2006; Willis & Schaie, 2006):

- *First age:* Childhood and adolescence
- *Second age:* Prime adulthood, twenties through fifties
- *Third age:* Approximately 60 to 79 years of age
- *Fourth age:* Approximately 80 years and older

The major emphasis in this conceptualization is on the third and fourth ages, especially the increasing evidence that individuals in the third age are healthier and can lead more active, productive lives than their predecessors in earlier generations. However, when older adults reach their eighties, especially 85 and over (fourth age), health and well-being decline.

The Concept of Age

In our description of the periods of the life span, we linked approximate age ranges with the periods. But we also have noted that there are variations in the capabilities of individuals of the same age, and we have seen how changes with age can be exaggerated. How important is age when we try to understand an individual? Are age and happiness related?

Age and Happiness

Consider a recent large-scale, U.S. study of approximately 28,000 individuals from 18 to 88 that revealed happiness increased with age (Yang, 2008). For example, about 33 percent were very happy at 88 years of age, compared with only about 24 percent in their late teens and early twenties. Why might older people report as much or more happiness and life satisfaction as younger people? Despite the increase in physical problems and losses older adults experience, they are more content with what they have in their lives, have better relationships with the people who matter to them, are less pressured to achieve, have more time for leisurely pursuits, and have many years of experience that may help them adapt to their circumstances with wisdom better than younger adults do (Cornwell, Laumann, & Schumm, 2008; Ram, Morelli, Lindberg, & Carstensen, 2008).

The study also stated that baby boomers (those born from 1944 to 1964) reported being less happy than individuals born earlier, possibly because they are not lowering their aspirations and idealistic hopes as they age as earlier generations did. Because growing older is a certain outcome of living, it is good to know that we are likely to be just as happy or happier as older adults as when we were younger.

A prime example of a Canadian older adult who has been successful is Jean Chrétien. His public life spanned a course of 40 years. During that time he served as Prime Minister of Canada for a decade and led his party to three successive majority governments. He was the fourth Canadian to be honoured with the Order of Merit, considered to be a personal gift from Queen Elizabeth. Jean Chrétien married Aline Chaîné on September 10, 1957, and together they recently celebrated 44 years of married life. Aline Chrétien's most important role was that of confidante and closest adviser to her husband. Together, their love for one another weathered many political storms and family issues. As Jean Chrétien once stated, "I am what I am . . . and I survived" (CBC Newsworld, 2003).

Conceptions of Age

Like happiness, age can be defined in different ways. The clichés "You're only as old as you feel" or "She is wise beyond her years" illustrate, to some degree, the different connotations of age. The five ways psychologists define age are *chronological, biological, mental, psychological,* and *social.*

--- **critical** thinking ------------

1. What different responses might a person have to a major disappointment if the person were 4 years old? 10 years? 16 years? 22 years? 35 years? 50 years? 70 years? **2.** Would the reactions differ if the individual were male or female? **3.** In what ways would you respond to a major celebration in your life today? Would the response be different in another 10 years?

Jean Chrétien and his wife, leading active and successful lives.

chronological age The number of years that has elapsed since a person's birth; what is usually meant by "age."

biological age A person's age in terms of biological health.

mental age An individual's ability to solve problems on a diagnostic instrument relative to others of the same chronological age.

psychological age An individual's adaptive capacities compared with those of other individuals of the same chronological age.

social age Social roles and expectations related to a person's age.

CHRONOLOGICAL AGE **Chronological age** *is the number of years that have elapsed since a person's birth. Many people consider chronological age synonymous with the concept of age.* However, some developmentalists argue that chronological age is not relevant to understanding a person's psychological development. A person's age does not cause an individual's development. Rather, events and experiences that accumulate over the years contribute to shaping us. Time is a crude index of many events and experiences and is not in itself a causal factor.

BIOLOGICAL AGE **Biological age** *is a person's age in terms of biological health.* Determining biological age involves knowing the functional capacities of a person's vital organ system. One person's vital capacities may be better or worse than those of others of comparable age. The younger the person's biological age, the longer the person is expected to live, regardless of chronological age.

MENTAL AGE **Mental age** *is an individual's ability to solve problems on a standardized instrument compared with others of the same chronological age.* A child's mental age is used to understand the child's intelligence quotient (IQ). Binet first developed testing instruments in response to educators who wished to provide appropriate guidance to families about children's academic progress.

PSYCHOLOGICAL AGE **Psychological age** *is an individual's adaptive capacities relative to those of other individuals of the same chronological age.* Thus, older adults who continue to learn may be more flexible and motivated. These and other attributes, such as emotional control and lucid thinking, mean that the individual has more strategies available with which to effectively adapt to change. The adaptability of these older adults contrasts sharply with that of chronological age mates who are not motivated, do not continue to learn, are rigid, and do not control their emotions or think clearly.

SOCIAL AGE According to Marsh, Keating, Punch, and Harden (2009), **social age** *refers to the social understandings and significance that are attached to a person's age.* In fact, age-relevant behaviours are probably more influenced by social rules/norms than by biological ones. In predicting the behaviour of an adult woman, it is probably more relevant to know that she is the mother of a 3-year-old child than to know whether she is 20 or 30 years of age.

Life-span expert Bernice Neugarten (1988) believes we are rapidly becoming an age-irrelevant society. She says we are already familiar with the 28-year-old mayor, the 35-year-old grandmother, the 65-year-old father of a preschooler, the 55-year-old widow who starts a business, and the 70-year-old student. Neugarten's ideas raise questions about how age should be conceptualized. Some of the ways age has been conceptualized are as chronological age, biological age, mental age, psychological age, and social age (Hoyer, Rybash, & Roodin, 1999). These definitions of age are tools that offer a more complex means of understanding human behaviour than chronological age alone.

To this point, we have discussed the periods of development. For a review, see the **Reach Your Learning Objectives** section at the end of this chapter.

Issues in Life-Span Development

LO5 Outline three prominent issues in life-span development.

Are we born with specific intellectual capacities, or do life experiences sculpt our talents? When you consider your family members, is one more mathematical than another? More musical? More athletic? Is one more extraverted? More conscientious? If so, why do you suppose that is? Did early experiences determine our later lives? Are our journeys through life marked out ahead of time, or can our experiences change our paths? Are the experiences we have early in our journeys more important than later ones? These questions point to three issues about the nature of development: the roles played by nature and nurture, stability and change, and continuity and discontinuity.

Interactional Model

Continuity and Discontinuity

Stability and Change

Evaluating Developmental Issues

(Left) Pam McSwain, 60, competing in the Senior Olympics in Memphis, Tennessee in 2009. *(Right)* A sedentary, overweight middle-aged man. **Even if Pam McSwain's chronological age is older, might her biological age be younger than the middle-aged man's?**

Interactional Model

Developmentalists have, for some time now, debated the question of whether developmental change is due to nature (hereditary factors) or to nurture (environmental factors). This historical debate is called the nature–nurture controversy (Berger, 2011). In essence, nature always affects nurture and nurture affects nature. This tendency prompted developmentalists to shift toward an understanding that development could not be understood as a result of separate personal and situational factors. Rather, they claimed, development is a product of a reciprocal interaction between biological and situational factors (Mischel, Shoda, & Ayduk, 2008).

Many theorists have adopted the interactionist view that considers development to be the result of an ongoing dynamic interaction of individual differences and particular conditions and not caused entirely by the individual or the context (Berger, 2011). The interactionist's models proposed are a vast improvement over the either–or theories of depression. Wade, Tavris, Saucier, and Elias (2007) argue that by understanding the causes of depression as an interaction among a person's biology, ways of thinking, and experiences, one is then able to comprehend why the same precipitating event, such as a minor setback or even the loss of a loved one, might emit feelings of sadness in one person and extreme depression in another.

Continuity and Discontinuity

Think about your development for a moment. Did you become the person you are gradually, like the slow, cumulative way a seedling grows into a giant oak? Or did you experience sudden, distinct changes in your growth, like the way a caterpillar changes into a butterfly? (See Figure 1.4.)

The **continuity–discontinuity issue** *focuses on the extent to which development involves gradual, cumulative change (continuity) or distinct stages (discontinuity).* In terms of continuity, a child's first word, though seemingly an abrupt, discontinuous event, is actually the result of weeks and months of growth and practice. Puberty, though also seemingly an abrupt, discontinuous occurrence, is actually a gradual process occurring over several years.

---- **critical** thinking -----------

Siblings differ considerably; one may be extraverted, seeking the limelight, while another may be introverted, preferring books to people. The oldest may excel in math, a middle child in sports, and the youngest in art. One may be intellectually brilliant, another socially intuitive and skilled. Each family member is unique, and the family of former Prime Minister Jean Chrétien is no different. As we know, Jean Chrétien decided to enter public life, whereas his brother Michael chose biochemistry and is known for his dedication to research. Jean Chrétien's adopted son was born with fetal alcohol syndrome.
1. In what ways does the dynamic interplay that results from the interaction of environment and biological processes shape human development over time?
2. What makes the various aspects that you have identified in your development stand out for you?

continuity–discontinuity issue Regards whether development involves gradual, cumulative change (continuity) or distinct stages (discontinuity).

Discontinuity

Continuity

In terms of discontinuity, each person is described as passing through a sequence of stages in which change occurs qualitatively, rather than quantitatively. As the oak moves from seedling to giant oak, it becomes *more* oak—its development is continuous. As the caterpillar changes to a butterfly, it is not just more caterpillar; it is a *different kind of organism*—its development is discontinuous. For example, at some point a child moves from the limits of concrete thinking to being able to think abstractly about the world. This is a qualitative, discontinuous change in development, not a quantitative, continuous change.

----------------------------------- **Figure 1.4**

Continuity and Discontinuity in Development Is our development like that of a seedling gradually growing into a giant oak? Or is it more like that of a caterpillar suddenly becoming a butterfly?

stability–change issue Regards whether development is best described as involving stability or as involving change; involves the degree to which we become older renditions of our early experience or, instead, develop into someone different from who we were at an earlier point in development.

Stability and Change

Another important developmental topic is the **stability–change issue**, *which addresses whether development is best described by stability or by change. The stability–change issue involves the degree to which we become older renditions of our early experience or, instead, develop into someone different from who we were at an earlier point in development.* Will the shy child who hides behind the sofa when visitors arrive be a wallflower at college dances, or will this child become a sociable, talkative individual?

Many developmentalists who emphasize stability in development argue that stability is the result of heredity and possibly early experiences in life. For example, many argue that if an individual is shy throughout life, this stability is due to heredity and possibly early experiences in which the infant or young child encountered considerable stress when interacting with people.

Developmentalists who emphasize change take the more optimistic view that later experiences can produce change. Recall that in the life-span perspective, plasticity—the potential for change—exists throughout the life span. Experts such as Paul Baltes (2003) argue that with increasing age, and on average, older adults often show less capacity for change in the sense of learning new things than younger adults. However, many older adults continue to be good at practising what they have learned in earlier times.

The roles of early and later experience are an aspect of the stability–change issue that has long been hotly debated (Caspi & Shiner, 2006). Some argue that unless infants experience warm, nurturant caregiving in the first year or so of life, their development will never be optimal (Sroufe, 2007). The later-experience advocates see children as malleable throughout development and later sensitive caregiving as equally important to earlier sensitive caregiving.

What is the nature of the early/later experience issue in development?

Evaluating Developmental Issues

Most life-span developmentalists acknowledge that development is a reciprocal dynamic interaction among an individual's genetic heritage and social experiences and not caused entirely by nature or nurture separately (Berger, 2011; Mischel, Shoda, & Ayduk, 2008).

How can we answer questions about the roles of interactional model, stability and change, and continuity and discontinuity in development? How can we determine, for example, whether memory declines in older adults can be prevented or whether special care can repair the harm inflicted by child neglect? Research using the scientific method is the best tool we have to answer such questions.

To this point, we have discussed issues in life-span development. For a review, see the **Reach Your Learning Objectives** section at the end of this chapter.

connecting through social policy ‹----------

Dr. J. Douglas Willms

Dr. J. Douglas Willms is the Director of the Canadian Research Institute for Social Policy (CRISP) at the University of New Brunswick (UNB). He holds the Canada Research Chair in Human Development at UNB and is a Fellow of the Royal Society of Canada, the International Academy of Education, and the Canadian Institute for Advanced Research. In 2002, Willms received the Canadian Policy Research Award for his role on the expert advisory group for planning, implementation, and data analysis of the National Longitudinal Survey of Children and Youth (NLSCY). Through his research, Willms has demonstrated that the learning potential of youth is linked to family environment, classroom disciplinary climates, parental involvement, and teacher expectations.

In 2000 and 2003, the Program for Student International Assessment (PISA) surveyed 15-year-olds from 42 participating nations, including 30,000 Canadian youths. Although Canadian youth performed very well overall, coming second in reading, fifth in science, and sixth in math, performance levels within Canada varied considerably when analyzed in terms of gender and social class. Educators and policymakers expressed concern that social and economic factors have the effect of segregating children from differing racial, ethnic, and class backgrounds within the school system (Statistics Canada, 2004a). Willms's research on this problem demonstrates that when children are segregated along lines of social class, those from less privileged families tend to have substantially worse academic and social outcomes while those from privileged families do only marginally better (Statistics Canada, 2004a).

In 2005, Willms and his colleagues designed *Tell Them From Me* (2005), an evaluation system for the continuous monitoring of school climate that provides information for school administrators and faculty. Using Barbara Haynes's (U.S.) study, which illustrates the relationship of summer learning to social economic status, Willms pointed out that children whose families can afford camps, vacations, educational outings, and so forth gain skills and enhanced self-esteem. Children whose families do not have the financial resources for these activities are disadvantaged and fall back. Willms suggested that this could be offset in part by camps that would run in June and be organized by skill development rather than by grade and age. Although impressive in themselves, Willms's studies illustrate how research can be applied to benefit educational curriculum and social policy. You will read more applications of Willms's studies, particularly NLSCY, throughout the text.

Some Contemporary Concerns

LO6 Appraise several major contemporary concerns.

Using the Internet, you might read a blog about a political figure, skype with a family member who is out of the country, play a game with someone from another part of the world, or text a friend. You can also read the news either in your local or national newspaper or online. You might read about how to improve your memory, about a test to predict Alzheimer's disease, or about Native land claims. These are some of the areas of contemporary concern. Further, research on these areas and others, including health and well-being, parenting, education, and socio-cultural contexts, influences social policy. One example of research influencing social policy is that the research on the adolescent brain is being used to help determine whether or not a youth should be tried in an adult or juvenile court.

Health and Well-Being

Health and well-being have been important goals for just about everyone for most of human history. Just as Asian physicians in 2600 B.C. and Greek physicians in 500 B.C. recognized that good habits are essential for good health, professionals today recognize the power of lifestyles and psychological states in health and well-being (Fahey, Insel, & Roth, 2009; Hahn, Payne, & Lucas, 2009). In every chapter of this book, issues of health and well-being—such as genetic counselling, school health programs, breast versus bottle-feeding, and geriatric concerns, including dementia and Alzheimer's disease—are integrated into our discussion.

Education

A sound education is an important ingredient of a democratic society. Research in education includes curriculum development to ensure currency and to provide an appropriate knowledge base for children who are gifted, as well as for those who are intellectually challenged. Research also supports programs aimed at addressing social needs such as dropout rates, the influence of computers on the brain, and bullying. Approaches to education such as school hours, the age to start kindergarten, the ethnic or racial composition of a school, or the constructivist approach to learning, which you will read about in later chapters, are some of the issues rooted in research.

The use of social media has revolutionized education and communication. The Internet and online communication tools including Facebook and instant messaging (IM) have become common ways for young people to communicate with peers, friends, and family. Social media has shifted the modes and speed of communication dramatically, allowing information "data" to be collected, analyzed, and used differently than was possible a decade ago. To meaningfully engage with the current generation of students in any faculty, teaching needs to be presented in a context that is relevant to the social media generation. The explosion of available information needs to be communicated in a way that will assist students to learn and to think critically about issues (Ratzan, 2011).

The results of a study conducted with Canadian and Israeli undergraduate participants concluded that instant messaging (IM) was used primarily, but not exclusively, to maintain existing ties with close friends rather than to develop new ties (Mesch, Talmud, & Quan-Haase, 2012). These researchers argue that as this study is limited to university students, future studies need to examine the development of instant messaging (IM) relational patterns over the life span.

Socio-Cultural Contexts

The tapestry of Canadian culture has changed dramatically in recent years. Nowhere is the change more dramatic than in the increasing ethnic diversity of Canada's citizens. This changing demographic landscape promises not only the richness that diversity produces, but also difficult challenges in extending support and equal opportunity to all individuals.

Socio-cultural contexts include five important concepts: context, culture, ethnicity, gender, and race. Recall that a *context* is the setting in which development occurs. This setting is influenced by historical, political, economic, geographic, social, and cultural factors. Every person's development occurs against the backdrop of cultural contexts. These contexts or settings include homes, schools, peer groups, churches, workplaces, shelters, cities, neighbourhoods, university laboratories, as well as the larger society. Each of these settings has meaningful historical, economic, social, and cultural legacies (Brislin, 2000; Rogoff, 2001).

Culture *is the behaviour patterns, beliefs, and all other products of a particular group of people that are passed on from generation to generation.* Culture results from the interaction of people over many years. A cultural group can be as large as a country, such as Canada, or as small as an isolated town, such as Rankin Inlet. Regardless of its size, a group's culture influences the behaviour of its members (Taylor & Whittaker, 2009). Since culture influences behaviour, it also impacts our understanding of human development.

Cross-cultural studies *involve a comparison of a culture with one or more other cultures. The comparison provides information about the degree to which development is similar, or universal, across cultures or is instead culture-specific.* For example, a study by University of Toronto researchers Duane Rudy and Joan Grusec (2006) found authoritarian parenting strategies effective for their Egyptian-Canadian subjects, but not for their European-Canadian participants. The findings of Rudy and Grusec show that one culture may benefit from a parenting style that is not effective in other cultural groups. Rudy and Grusec's work highlights the need for further cross-cultural research to develop a better understanding of the impact of culture on human development.

Children learn to love when they are loved.

culture The behaviour patterns, beliefs, and all other products of a group that are passed on from generation to generation.

cross-cultural studies Comparisons of one culture with one or more other cultures; provide information about the degree to which children's development is similar, or universal, across cultures, and the degree to which it is culture-specific.

Ethnicity *is based on cultural heritage, nationality characteristics, race, religion, and language* (the word "ethnic" comes from the Greek word for nation). Not only is there diversity within a country such as Canada, or a racial group such as Caucasian, there also is diversity within each ethnic group. Not all Aboriginal peoples live in low-income circumstances. Not all Italian-Canadians are Catholic. It is easy to fall into the trap of stereotyping an ethnic group by thinking that all its members are alike, whereas in reality each grouping represents a diverse group of people. Diversity exists within each ethnic group (Banks, 2008; Kim, Su, Yancurra, & Yee, 2009; Gollnick & Chinn, 2009).

Race is sometimes used interchangeably with ethnicity. This can lead to misunderstanding, because *race is a controversial classification of people according to real or imagined biological characteristics, such as skin colour and blood group* (Corsini, 1999). An individual's ethnicity can include his or her race, but also many other characteristics. Thus, an individual might be white (a racial category) and a first-generation Quebecois who is Jewish, speaks English, French, Hebrew, and Polish, and is of Polish descent.

Gender *is the socio-cultural dimension of being female or male.* Sex refers to the biological dimension of being female or male. Few aspects of our development are more central to our identity and social relationships than gender (Blakemore, Berenbaum, & Liben, 2009; Matlin, 2008; Zosuls, Lurye, & Ruble, 2008). Society's gender attitudes are changing. But how much?

The twentieth century has witnessed a growing equality between women and men in many countries, including Canada. One indicator of the worldwide progress of women is the annual computation of the Gender Inequality Index (GII) provided by the United Nations. This index is a composite measure reflecting inequality in achievements between men and women along three dimensions: reproductive health, empowerment, and the labour market (United Nations, 2011). According to the United Nations Human Development Report 2011, Canada ranked twentieth among 187 nations included in the Gender Inequality Index. Meanwhile, the greatest gender egalitarian countries, and those that ranked well above Canada, were situated in northern Europe (e.g., Sweden ranked first). Canadian women, it seems, still have a considerable way to go before they achieve top-level equality with men. For example, although the gender gap in earnings is shrinking, the gap is expected to disappear only in 2085, provided the Canadian difference continues to diminish at a consistent rate (Brym, Roberts, Lie, & Rytina, 2013). Canadians can take some encouragement in two significant developments in recent decades: the number of Canadian women in politics has increased significantly, and birth control technology has enabled women to experience greater control over reproductive issues (Macionis, Jansson, & Benoit, 2013).

Social Policy

Social policy *is a national government's course of action designed to influence the welfare of its citizens.* A current trend is to conduct developmental research that will lead to effective social policy. Given that 1 child in 10 is living in poverty (Campaign 2000, 2009), low income is related to children's poor health and academic performance (Campaign 2000, 2012), children and young adolescents are giving birth, the use and abuse of drugs is widespread, the spectre of AIDS is present, and the provision of health care for the elderly is inadequate, our nation needs responsible and progressive social policies. Research conducted by the Canadian Research Institute for Social Policy is an example of how research shapes social policy in Canada. (See the Connecting through Research box "Longitudinal Studies" later in this chapter for more information.)

Social policy is responsive to demographics such as median age, life expectancy, immigration rates, fertility rates, gender, and sexual orientation. Many data are gathered from hospital admission charts or census forms. You may have noted that typically these forms ask participants to identify as either male or female. After the last census, an Internet campaign circulated requesting that the gender identifier be changed to include more inclusive identifiers, such as transsexual, or intersexed. Without more inclusive identifiers, all findings can be classified only as belonging to either male or female groups, which is not helpful when tracking social trends and health conditions of the LBGQTI communities.

ethnicity A characteristic based on cultural heritage, nationality characteristics, race, religion, and language.

race A classification of people according to real or imagined biological characteristics, such as skin colour and blood group.

gender The social and psychological dimensions of being male or female.

Classrooms today have become more diverse, especially those in urban centres.

social policy A national government's course of action designed to influence the welfare of its citizens.

An example of how social policy impacts individuals is evidenced in the Canadian government's relationship with the Aboriginal peoples of Canada. In an effort to address some of the concerns, the Royal Commission on Aboriginal Peoples was established in 1991. The Commission held 178 days of public hearings, visited 96 communities, consulted dozens of experts, commissioned scores of research studies, and reviewed numerous past inquiries and reports. The Commission's summary of its central conclusion was that "The main policy direction, pursued for more than 150 years, first by colonial then by Canadian governments, has been wrong" (Department of Indian and Northern Affairs Canada, 1996).

Assimilation policies of the past have almost obliterated Aboriginal cultures and identities, "leaving a legacy of brokenness affecting Aboriginal individuals, families and communities. The damage has been equally serious to the spirit of Canada—the spirit of generosity and mutual accommodation in which Canadians take pride" (Department of Indian and Northern Affairs Canada, 1996). In short, these policies have failed.

Aboriginal people continue to face injustice and oppression; however, the future holds hope for a people deeply proud of their culture and heritage. To fulfill the promise of hope for all citizens, the underlying assumptions of policy must be informed by Aboriginal traditions of self-governance in partnership with Canada. The Commission reminds policymakers that "*Aboriginal peoples are nations.* That is, they are political and cultural groups with values and lifeways distinct from those of other Canadians" (Canadian Institute of Health Research, 2006).

The shape and scope of social policy is strongly tied to our political system. Our country's policy agenda and the welfare of the nation's citizens are influenced by demographics, the values held by individual lawmakers, the nation's economic strengths and weaknesses, and partisan politics.

Health care, more than any other major social institution, exemplifies the impact of politics, demographics, and competing values. Saskatchewan Premier Tommy Douglas (1904–1986) fought for universal health care, the forerunner of the healthcare system that Canadians enjoy today. The Romanow Commission, headed by Roy Romanow and established in 2001 to engage Canadians in a national dialogue about health care, released its findings in 2002 (Romanow, 2002). Recommendations for change were made that would ensure the sustainability of a publicly funded universal healthcare system in spite of rising costs, an aging population, and privatization arguments modelled by the practices and policies of the United States. The Commission continues to fuel the debate about whether Canada should have a privatized and multi-tiered healthcare system.

Who should get the bulk of government dollars for improved well-being? Children? Their parents? Their grandparents or their great-grandparents? **Generational inequity**, *a social policy concern, is the possible condition in which an aging society is being unfair to its younger members.* This occurs because older adults pile up advantages by receiving inequitably large allocations of resources; for example, seniors are more likely to require assisted living facilities or medications. Generational inequity raises questions about whether the young should have to pay for the old and whether an "advantaged" older population is using up resources that should go to disadvantaged children.

If Canada were like many countries of the world where no social insurance systems exist, many adults would have to bear the financial burden of supporting their elderly parents, leaving fewer of their resources for educating their children. Our aging demographic spawns a host of social concerns ranging from health care, retirement age, and pension plans to elder abuse.

A somewhat uncomfortable ambiguity has persisted in Canadian society regarding home care for the elderly (Firbank, 2011). This prime contentious issue has been the debate of governments for quite some time. The controversy in social policy formation has been evident in regard to informal caregivers and home support services. The possibility of designing a national "standard model" of home care is the logical first step for seeking federal/provincial consensus (Firbank, 2011). Developing and applying such a model may prove to be considerably more difficult than is sometimes acknowledged.

A shift in ethnicity—another demographic determinant—affects all levels of society, especially when it is propelled by spikes in immigration. The desire to sustain the growth spurt is Canada's open-arms approach to immigration. This phenomenon, which has become twice as important as that of natural population increase (the difference between births and deaths), is driving the country's population upward. The 2011 census of Canada indicates clearly that Saskatchewan has

critical thinking

Healthcare expenses continue to skyrocket at the same time that the population is aging and more are in need of care. **1.** How do you think taxpayers can meet the increasing demands of universal health care? **2.** Select one or two disparities and design a plan based upon one or two relevant factors (location, cost, need, resources, etc.). **3.** Compare and contrast universal health care and privatization in Canada.

generational inequity An aging society's unfairness to its younger members due to older adults piling up advantages by receiving inequitably large allocations of resources.

emerged as a full partner with Alberta in the oil and gas–fuelled economic boom that is attracting immigrants from abroad and migrants from other parts of Canada. The same magnetic attraction that oil wealth appears to be having in Western Canada seems to be boosting the number of people—and keeping them—in petroleum-rich Newfoundland and Labrador (Statistics Canada, 2012h). More than one-third of all Canadians, 35 percent of the population, now live in one of Canada's largest cities: Toronto, Montreal, or Vancouver. Each of these centres has grown substantially over the past five years. The gains are driven by the arrival of tens of thousands of immigrants (Statistics Canada, 2012h).

These urban areas struggle to provide adequate supports to newcomers; however, language training and social assistance are not always enough. Our notions of common sense are deeply rooted in the culture of our birth. No matter what the policy or service, the needs are greater and therefore gaps and surprises will continue to exist (Statistics Canada, 2001).

Available estimates suggest that, in Canada, 150,000 to 3000,000 people will experience homelessness during the course of a year (Aubry, Klodawsky, & Coulombe, 2012). Despite these high numbers, the population of homeless people indicates greater diversity. No longer is homelessness characterized simply as a problem among single men. In particular, the number of people experiencing homelessness includes a significant number of women, families, and youth (Klodawsky, 2006).

Given this growing diversity, developing effective social policies will facilitate meaningful advances in housing and shelter to help combat the different aspects of problems (Aubry, Klodawsky, & Coulombe, 2012). The promotion of health equity requires the promotion of social policy to strengthen the quality of social determinants of health (Raphael, 2010). Calling for housing security, as well as affordable child care, universal health care, living wages, and improved food and income, are all essential means of promoting health equity. Canadian action on improving health equity by addressing the social determinants of health has been profoundly lacking. The housing crisis in Canada has seen explosive increases in homelessness. Researchers have noted that it is well within the reach of Canadian governments to end the homelessness crisis by increasing their allocation for housing by 1 percent. However, few Canadian governments seem willing to make such a commitment.

To this point, we have discussed some contemporary concerns. For a review, see the **Reach Your Learning Objectives** section at the end of this chapter.

Research Methods and Challenges

LO7 Compare and contrast research methodology and challenges.

As you can see from the prominent issues and contemporary concerns, as well as in this chapter's opening vignette, research is vital to the field of psychology. In fact, the study of life-span development is a science based on theories and systematic investigative strategies to explain human development and behaviour. Historically, many have argued that the social sciences, such as psychology and sociology, were not sciences, because they did not test empirical data in the same way that chemistry, physics, or biology did. However, today most agree that studies aimed at understanding human behaviour are scientific because a rigorous analytical approach is applied. Studies about whether watching TV for many hours is linked to obesity, or about the characteristics of lasting relationships, are conducted in a rigorous manner and contribute to our understanding of human behaviour. In other words, *how* we investigate, rather than *what* we investigate, defines whether or not research is scientific. Life-span development is a provocative, intriguing interdisciplinary field filled with information about who we are, how we have come to be this way, and where our futures may take us.

Generally, research in life-span development is designed to test hypotheses that, in some cases, are derived from the theories you will read about in Chapter 2. Through research, theories are modified to reflect new data, and occasionally new theories arise. What types of research are conducted in life-span development? If researchers want to study people of different ages, what research designs can they use? These are questions we will examine next.

Methods of Collecting Data

Research Designs

Research Challenges

All scientific knowledge stems from a rigorous, systematic method of investigation (Pittenger, 2003; Salkind, 2003). Research has both quantitative and qualitative components. *Quantitative* research involves the collection of data in numerical form and provides statistical analysis. "How many?" and "How strong is the association of variables?" are quantitative questions. Data collected through interviews and observations, for example, are qualitative and provide descriptive and inferential information. "What?" and "Why?" are *qualitative* questions. Strict adherence to scientific method is essential in both components to maximize the objectivity of information and minimize bias. The *scientific method* is essentially a four-step process:

1. Conceptualize a process or problem to be studied.
2. Collect research information (data).
3. Analyze data.
4. Draw conclusions.

In step 1, when researchers are formulating a problem to study, they often draw on theories and develop hypotheses (Loiselle, Profetto-McGrath, Polit, & Beck, 2011). A **theory** *is an interrelated, coherent set of ideas that help explain and make predictions.* **Hypotheses** *are specific assumptions and predictions that can be tested to determine their accuracy.* For example, a theory on mentoring might attempt to explain and predict why sustained support, guidance, and concrete experience make a difference in the lives of children from impoverished backgrounds. The theory might focus on children's opportunities to model the behaviour and strategies of mentors, or it might focus on the effects of individualized attention.

Methods of Collecting Data

Whether we are interested in studying attachment in infants, the cognitive skills of children, or social relationships in older adults, we can choose from several ways of collecting data. Here we outline the measures most often used, beginning with observation.

Observation

Scientific **observation** requires an important set of skills (Rosnow & Rosenthal, 2008; Wiersma & Jurs, 2009). For observations to be effective, they have to be systematic. We have to have some idea of what we are looking for. We have to know whom we are observing, when and where we will observe, how the observations will be made, and how they will be recorded. Where should we make our observations? We have two choices: the laboratory and the everyday world.

When we observe scientifically, we often need to control certain factors that determine behaviour but are not the focus of our inquiry (McMillan, 2008). For this reason, some research in life-span development is conducted in a **laboratory**, *a controlled setting where many of the complex factors of the "real world" are absent.* For example, suppose you want to observe how children react when they see other people act aggressively. If you observe children in their homes or schools, you have no control over how much aggression the children observe, what kind of aggression they see, which people they see acting aggressively, or how other people treat the children. In contrast, if you observe the children in a laboratory, you can control these and other factors and therefore have more confidence about how to interpret your observations.

Laboratory research does have some drawbacks, however, including the following:

- It is almost impossible to conduct research without the participants knowing they are being studied.
- The laboratory setting is unnatural and therefore can cause the participants to behave unnaturally.
- People who are willing to come to a university laboratory may not fairly represent groups from diverse cultural backgrounds.
- People who are unfamiliar with university settings, and with the idea of "helping science," may be intimidated by the laboratory setting.

theory An interrelated, coherent set of ideas that help explain and make predictions.

hypotheses Specific assumptions and predictions that can be tested to determine their accuracy.

observation A systematic and scientific inquiry into behaviour that may be conducted in a natural environment or a laboratory setting.

laboratory A controlled setting where many of the complex factors of the "real world" are absent.

Naturalistic observation provides insights that we sometimes cannot achieve in the laboratory (Jackson, 2008). **Naturalistic observation** *means observing behaviour in real-world settings, making no effort to manipulate or control the situation.* Life-span researchers conduct naturalistic observations at sporting events, child care centres, work settings, malls, and other places people live in and frequent.

Naturalistic observation was used in one study that focused on conversations in a children's science museum (Crowley, Callahan, Tenenbaum, & Allen, 2001). When visiting exhibits at the science museum, parents were far more likely to engage boys than girls in explanatory talk. This finding suggests a gender bias that encourages boys more than girls to be interested in science (see Figure 1.5). A team of researchers from Canadian universities in Ontario have been observing mother–infant interactions in the more convenient and natural home settings rather than in a laboratory (Bailey, Moran, Pederson, & Bento, 2007). In what ways would the home interaction be more realistic than a laboratory observation?

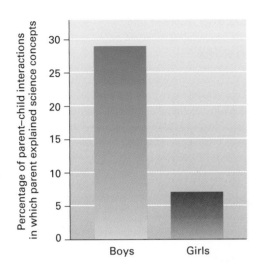

Figure 1.5 -

Parents' Explanations of Science to Sons and Daughters at a Science Museum

In a naturalistic observation study at a children's science museum, parents were three times more likely to explain science to boys than to girls (Crowley et al., 2001). The gender difference occurred regardless of whether the father, the mother, or both parents were with the child, although the gender difference was greatest for fathers' science explanations to sons and daughters.

naturalistic observation Observing behaviour in real-world settings, making no effort to manipulate or control the situation.

Survey and Interview

Sometimes the best and quickest way to get information about people is to ask them for it. One technique is to interview them directly. A related method is the survey (sometimes referred to as a questionnaire), which is especially useful when information from many people is needed. A standard set of questions is used to obtain people's self-reported attitudes or beliefs about a particular topic. In a good survey the questions are clear and unbiased, allowing respondents to answer unambiguously.

Surveys and interviews can be used to study a wide range of topics, from religious beliefs to sexual habits to attitudes about gun control to beliefs about how to improve schools. Surveys and interviews may be conducted in person, over the telephone, and over the Internet.

One problem with surveys and interviews is the tendency of participants to answer questions in a way that they think is socially acceptable or desirable, rather than to say what they truly think or feel (Creswell, 2008). For example, on a survey or in an interview, some individuals might say that they do not take drugs even though they do.

Standardized Test

A **standardized test** *has uniform procedures for administration and scoring.* Many standardized tests compare a person's performance with that of other individuals; thus, they provide information about individual differences among people (Kingston, 2008). One example is the Stanford-Binet intelligence test, which is described in Chapter 9. Your score on the Stanford-Binet test tells you how your performance compares with that of thousands of other people who have taken the test (Bart & Peterson, 2008).

One criticism of standardized tests is that they assume a person's behaviour is consistent and stable, yet personality and intelligence—two primary targets of standardized testing—can vary

standardized test Has uniform procedures for administration and scoring.

with the situation. For example, a person may perform poorly on a standardized intelligence test in an office setting but score much higher at home, where he or she is less anxious.

Case Study

case study An in-depth look at a single individual.

A **case study** is *an in-depth look at a single individual.* Case studies are performed mainly by mental health professionals when, for either practical or ethical reasons, the unique aspects of an individual's life cannot be duplicated and tested in other individuals. A case study provides information about one person's experiences; it may focus on nearly any aspect of the subject's life that helps the researcher understand the person's mind, behaviour, or other attributes. A researcher may gather information for a case study from interviews and medical records.

A case study can provide a dramatic, in-depth portrayal of an individual's life, but we must be cautious when generalizing from this information. The subject of a case study is unique, with a genetic makeup and personal history that no one else shares. In addition, case studies involve judgments of unknown reliability. Researchers who conduct case studies rarely check to see if other professionals agree with their observations or findings.

Physiological Measures

Researchers increasingly are using physiological measures when they study development at different points in the life span. For example, as puberty unfolds, the blood levels of certain hormones increase. To determine the nature of these hormonal changes, researchers analyze blood samples from adolescent volunteers (Dorn, Dahl, Woodward, & Biro, 2006).

Another physiological measure that is increasingly being used is neuroimaging, especially functional magnetic resonance imaging (fMRI), in which electromagnetic waves are used to construct images of a person's brain tissue and biochemical activity (Hofheimer & Lester, 2008; Moulson & Nelson, 2008). We will have much more to say about neuroimaging and other physiological measures in later chapters.

Research Designs

In addition to methods of collecting data, researchers also need a research design. The three basic types of research design are descriptive, correlational, and experimental. Each has strengths and weaknesses.

Descriptive Research

descriptive research Has the purpose of observing and recording behaviour.

Some important theories have grown out of **descriptive research**, *which has the purpose of observing and recording behaviour.* For example, a psychologist might observe the extent to which people are altruistic or aggressive toward each other. By itself, descriptive research cannot prove what causes some phenomenon, but it can reveal important information about people's behaviour and attitudes. Descriptive research methods include observation, surveys and interviews, standardized tests, case studies, and life-history records.

Correlational Research

correlational research The goal is to describe the strength of the relationship between two or more events or characteristics.

In contrast to descriptive research, correlational research goes beyond describing phenomena; it provides information that will help us to predict how people will behave. In correlational research, the goal is to describe the strength of the relationship between two or more events or characteristics. The more strongly the two events are correlated (or related or associated), the more effectively we can predict one event from the other (Jackson, 2008; Kraska, 2008). In **correlational research**, *the goal is to describe the strength of the relationship between two or more events or characteristics.* The more strongly the two events are correlated (or related or associated), the more effectively we can predict one event from the other (Whitley, 2002).

For example, to study whether children of permissive parents have less self-control than other children, you would need to carefully record observations of parents' permissiveness and their children's self-control. You might observe that the higher a parent was in permissiveness, the lower the child was in self-control. You would then analyze these data statistically to yield a numerical measure, called a correlation coefficient, a number based on a statistical analysis that is used to describe the degree of association between two variables. The correlation coefficient ranges from +1.00 to −1.00. A negative number means an inverse relation. In this example, you might find an inverse correlation between permissive parenting and children's self-control with a coefficient of, say, −.30. By contrast, you might find a positive correlation of +.30 between parental monitoring of children and children's self-control.

The higher the correlation coefficient (whether positive or negative), the stronger the association between the two variables. A correlation of 0 means there is no association between the variables. A correlation of −.40 is stronger than a correlation of +.20 because we disregard whether the correlation is positive or negative in determining the strength of the correlation.

A caution is in order, however: correlation does not equal causation (Aron, Aron, & Coupos, 2008). Figure 1.6 illustrates these possible interpretations of correlational data.

Experimental Research

An **experiment** *is a carefully regulated procedure in which one or more factors believed to influence the behaviour being studied are manipulated, while all other factors are held constant.* If the behaviour under study changes when a factor is manipulated, we say that the manipulated factor has caused the behaviour to change (Kirk, 2003). In other words, the experiment has demonstrated cause and effect. The cause is the factor that was manipulated. The effect is the behaviour that changed because of the manipulation (see Figure 1.7). Non-experimental research methods (descriptive and correlational research) cannot establish cause and effect because they do not involve manipulating factors in a controlled way. Other chapters will cite studies that have been conducted using empirical methodology.

INDEPENDENT AND DEPENDENT VARIABLES
Experiments include two types of changeable factors, or variables: independent and dependent. An *independent variable* is a manipulated, influential, experimental factor. It is a potential cause. The label "independent" is used because this variable can be manipulated independently of other factors to determine its effect. Researchers have a vast array of options open to them in selecting independent variables, and one experiment may include several independent variables.

A *dependent variable* is a factor that can change in an experiment, in response to changes in the independent variable. As researchers manipulate the independent variable, they measure the dependent variable for any resulting effect.

EXPERIMENTAL AND CONTROL GROUPS
Experiments can involve one or more experimental groups and one or more control groups.

experiment A carefully regulated procedure in which one or more of the factors believed to influence the behaviour being studied are manipulated, while all other factors are held constant.

Figure 1.6

Possible Explanations for Correlational Data

An observed correlation between two events cannot be used to conclude that one event caused the other. Some possibilities are that the second event caused the first event, or that a third, unknown event caused the correlation between the first two events.

Observed Correlation: As permissive parenting increases, children's self-control decreases.

Permissive parenting	causes →	Children's lack of self-control
Children's lack of self-control	causes →	Permissive parenting
A third factor such as genetic tendencies or poverty	causes both →	Permissive parenting and children's lack of self-control

Figure 1.7

Principles of Experimental Research

Imagine that you decide to conduct an experimental study of the effects of aerobic exercise by pregnant women on their newborns' breathing and sleeping patterns. You would randomly assign pregnant women to experimental and control groups. The experimental group women would engage in aerobic exercise over a specified number of sessions and weeks. The control group would not. Then, when the infants are born, you would assess their breathing and sleeping patterns. If the breathing and sleeping patterns of the newborns whose mothers were in the experimental group are more positive than those of the control group, you would conclude that aerobic exercise caused the positive effects.

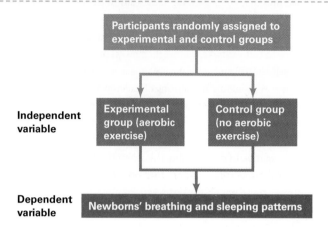

An *experimental group* is a group whose experience is manipulated. A *control group* is a comparison group that is as much like the experimental group as possible and that is treated in every way like the experimental group except for the manipulated factor (independent variable). The control group serves as a baseline against which the effects of the manipulated condition can be compared.

Random assignment is an important principle for deciding whether each participant will be placed in the experimental group or in the control group (Shaughnessy, Zechmeister, & Zechmeister, 2003). *Random assignment* means that researchers assign participants to experimental and control groups by chance. It reduces the likelihood that the experiment's results will be due to any pre-existing differences between groups. Figure 1.7 illustrates the nature of experimental research.

Time Span of Research

A special concern of developmentalists is the time span of a research investigation. Studies that focus on the relation of age to some other variable are common in life-span development. We have several options: researchers can study different individuals of different ages and compare them; they can study the same individuals as they age over time; or they can use some combination of these two approaches.

cross-sectional approach A research strategy in which individuals of different ages are compared at one time.

CROSS-SECTIONAL APPROACH   The **cross-sectional approach** *is a research strategy in which individuals of different ages are compared at one time.* A typical cross-sectional study might include a group of 5-year-olds, 8-year-olds, and 11-year-olds. Another might include a group of 15-year-olds, 25-year-olds, and 45-year-olds. The different groups can be compared with respect to a variety of dependent variables: IQ, memory, peer relations, attachment to parents, hormonal changes, and so on. All of this can be accomplished in a short time. In some studies, data are collected in a single day. Even in large-scale cross-sectional studies with hundreds of subjects, data collection does not usually take longer than several months to complete.

The main advantage of the cross-sectional study is that the researcher does not have to wait for the individuals to grow up or become older. Despite its time efficiency, the cross-sectional approach has its drawbacks. It gives no information about how individuals change or about the stability of their characteristics. The increases and decreases of development—the hills and valleys of growth and development—can become obscured in the cross-sectional approach. For example, in a cross-sectional approach to perceptions of life satisfaction, average increases and decreases might be revealed. But the study would not show how the life satisfaction of individual adults waxed and waned over the years. It also would not tell us whether adults who had positive or negative perceptions of life satisfaction as young adults maintained their relative degree of life satisfaction as middle-aged or older adults.

longitudinal approach A research strategy in which the same individuals are studied over a period of time, usually several years or more.

LONGITUDINAL APPROACH   The **longitudinal approach** *is a research strategy in which the same individuals are studied over a period of time, usually several years or more.* For example, if a study of life satisfaction were conducted longitudinally, the same adults might be assessed periodically over a 70-year time span—at the ages of 20, 35, 45, 65, and 90, for example. Figure 1.8 compares the cross-sectional and longitudinal approaches.

Although longitudinal studies provide a wealth of information about such important issues as stability and change in development and the importance of early experience for later development, they are not without their problems (Raudenbush, 2001). They are expensive and time consuming. The longer the study lasts, the more participants drop out—they move, get sick, lose interest, and so forth. Participants can bias the outcome of a study because those who remain may be dissimilar to those who drop out. Those individuals who remain in a longitudinal study over a number of years may be more compulsive and conformity-oriented, for example, or they might have more stable lives.

SEQUENTIAL APPROACH   Sometimes, developmentalists also combine the cross-sectional and longitudinal approaches to learn about life-span development (Schaie, 1993). The **sequential approach** *is the combined cross-sectional, longitudinal design.* In most instances, this approach starts with a cross-sectional study that includes individuals of different ages. A number of months after the initial assessment, the same individuals are tested again—this is the longitudinal aspect of the design. At this later time, a new group of participants is assessed at each age level. The new groups at each level are added at the later time to control for changes that might have taken place in the original group—some might have dropped out of the study, or retesting might have improved their performance, for example. The sequential approach is complex, expensive, and time consuming, but it does provide information that is impossible to obtain from cross-sectional or longitudinal approaches alone. The sequential approach has been especially helpful in examining cohort effects in life-span development, which we will discuss next.

COHORT EFFECTS   A *cohort* is a group of people who were born at a similar point in history and share similar experiences as a result, such as growing up in the same city around the same time. For example, cohorts can differ in years of education, child-rearing practices, health, attitudes toward sex, religious values, and economic status. In life-span development research, **cohort effects** *are due to a person's time of birth or generation but not to actual age.* Cohort effects are important because they can powerfully affect the dependent measures in a study ostensibly concerned with age. Researchers have shown it is especially important to be aware of cohort effects in the assessment of adult intelligence (Schaie, 1996). Individuals born in different decades, for example, may have had varying opportunities for education.

Cross-sectional studies can show how different cohorts respond, but they can confuse age changes and cohort effects. Longitudinal studies are effective in studying age changes, but only within one cohort. With sequential studies, age changes in one cohort can be examined and compared with age changes in another cohort.

An important point to make is that theories often are linked with a particular research method or methods. Thus, the method(s) researchers use are associated with their particular theoretical approach. Figure 1.9 illustrates the connections between research methods and theories.

sequential approach A combined cross-sectional, longitudinal design.

cohort effects Occur due to a person's time of birth or generation but not to actual age.

critical thinking

Life-span researchers are especially concerned about cohort effects because they shape an individual's understanding of the world, including what might be taken as common sense. For example, a woman born in Canada in 1998 might assume she would make an economic contribution to her family by having a career outside the home, whereas her grandmother may have shaped her identity around being a mother and homemaker. The individual born in the mid-70s may find some of the newer technologies more challenging than an individual born in 1990. The child born in Canada in 2015 will have a very different view of the world than a child born in Zimbabwe in 2015. **1.** What changes can you foresee that may shape the development of your children and grandchildren? **2.** In what ways do you believe that you can contribute to the development of your children and grandchildren? **3.** Write a detailed narrative, providing specifics, of your developmental plans and activities for when you are older as you might describe them to a friend.

Figure 1.8

A Comparison of Cross-Sectional and Longitudinal Approaches

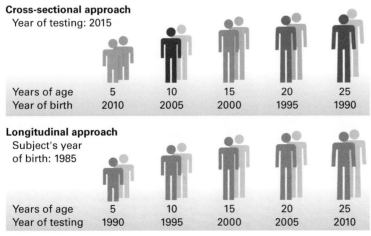

Cross-sectional approach
Year of testing: 2015

| Years of age | 5 | 10 | 15 | 20 | 25 |
| Year of birth | 2010 | 2005 | 2000 | 1995 | 1990 |

Longitudinal approach
Subject's year of birth: 1985

| Years of age | 5 | 10 | 15 | 20 | 25 |
| Year of testing | 1990 | 1995 | 2000 | 2005 | 2010 |

connecting through research ◄-------------------

Longitudinal Studies

The National Longitudinal Survey of Children and Youth (NLSCY) is a comprehensive survey of Canadians from birth to adulthood (Statistics Canada, 2004a). Fifteen thousand children are already participating in the study; an additional 5,000 will be added, making the study cohort approximately 20,000 people. A database of information about such characteristics as behaviour and academic performance, as well as life experiences such as family structure, health, language, and cognitive, social, emotional, and behavioural outcomes, is being built by this research. This national database, supporting research on each stage of development, informs the development of policies and strategies to help children and youth.

Another longitudinal study, the Youth in Transition Survey (YITS), focuses on the transition from school to work by young adults in more than 50 countries. This study, a project of the Organisation for Economic Co-operation and Development (OECD), is designed to provide policy-oriented international indicators of the skills and knowledge base of 15-year-old students in the domains of reading, math, and science (OECD, 2010).

This research not only is designed to discover and understand the challenges facing children growing up in Canada and the dynamics between social context and individual action in determining positive or negative outcomes, but also aims to shape social policy. In Canada, social policy has attempted to create a nation in which people have equal opportunity to achieve positive life experiences. Where differences or difficulties exist, social policy sets up programs, agencies, and institutions to attempt to facilitate solutions to the problem or direct assistance to meet the basics for equal outcome. Information from the NLSCY will help shape social policy to assist children and their families to avoid, or rise out of, the conditions and choices that lead to vulnerability. Whereas in the past the belief that the elimination of poverty would be the direct route to significantly decreasing childhood vulnerability, Dr. Doug Willms, Director of the Canadian Research Institute for Social Policy at the University of New Brunswick and editor of the study, notes that the root of vulnerability is most likely a complex interaction of variables, which may be more clearly addressed by social policies focusing on "building an infrastructure for a family-enabling society" (Willms, 2002, p. 361).

In the end, a picture of the participants' life path from their mothers' pregnancies to their own entry into young adulthood will exist and serve to shape social policy and intervention. You will find references to this study throughout the text.

Figure 1.9 -------------------

Connections between Research Methods and Theories

Research Method	Theory
Observation	• All theories emphasize some form of observation. • Behavioural and social cognitive theories place the strongest emphasis on laboratory observation. • Ethological theory places the strongest emphasis on naturalistic observation.
Survey/interview	• Psychoanalytic and cognitive studies (Piaget, Vygotsky) often used interviews. • Behavioural, social cognitive, and ethological theories are the least likely to use surveys or interviews.
Case study	• Psychoanalytic theories (Freud, Erikson) were the most likely to use this method.
Correlational	• All of the theories use this research method, although psychoanalytic theories are the least likely to use it.
Experimental research	• The behavioural and social cognitive theories and the information-processing theories are the most likely to use the experimental method. • Psychoanalytic theories are the least likely to use it.
Cross-sectional/ longitudinal/sequential methods	• National Longitudinal Survey of Children and Youth (NLSCY) is an example of this method. • The sequential method is the least likely to be used by any theory.

Research Challenges

Conducting ethical research and minimizing bias are vital to protecting the rights of participants and representing information accurately.

Conducting Ethical Research

Ethics in research may affect you personally if you ever serve as a participant in a study. In that event, you need to know your rights as a participant and the responsibilities of researchers to ensure that these rights are safeguarded.

If you ever become a researcher in life-span development yourself, you will need an even deeper understanding of ethics. Even if you only carry out experimental projects in psychology courses, you must consider the rights of the participants in those projects. A student might think, "I volunteer in a home for people with intellectual disabilities several hours per week. I can use the residents of the home in my study to see if a particular treatment helps improve their memory for everyday tasks." But without proper permissions, the most well-meaning, kind, and considerate studies still violate the rights of the participants.

In Canada, for the protection of human participants in research, the collaboration of the three major funding agencies—the Canadian Institutes of Health Research (CIHR), the Natural Sciences and Engineering Research Council of Canada (NSERC), and the Social Sciences and Humanities Research Council (SSHRC)—has led to a joint development of the document *Tri-Council Policy Statement: Ethical Conduct for Research Involving Humans* (Canadian Institutes of Health Research et al., 2010). The second edition of the *Tri-Council Policy Statement: Ethical Conduct for Research Involving Humans* (TCPS 2) was developed to keep pace with changes in research and society at large. The document continues to be based on respect for human dignity, and includes a consolidated set of three core principles identified as follows (Canadian Institutes of Health Research et al., 2010):

- RESPECT FOR PERSONS: Both the intrinsic value of human beings and the respect and consideration to which they are entitled are recognized. Respect for persons is critical because it incorporates the dual moral obligations to respect autonomy and to protect those with developing, impaired, or diminished autonomy. One highly important research mechanism that strives to respect participants' autonomy is the requirement to obtain their free, informed, and ongoing consent. For those participants who lack full capacity to make their own decisions to participate, additional measures are needed to protect their interests and to ensure that their wishes (to the extent that their desires are known) are respected.

- CONCERN FOR WELFARE: Welfare in research refers to the impact of factors such as a participant's physical, mental, and spiritual health or their well-being. Additional factors that must be considered are the participant's physical, economic, and social circumstances. For example, relevant determinants of welfare could be housing, community membership, and the extent of social participation in various aspects of life. The welfare of a person, or of a group, is affected in turn by the welfare of those who are important to them. Harm to a person or group includes any negative effect on welfare. Therefore, researchers must plan to protect the welfare of participants regarding any foreseeable risks associated with that research.

- JUSTICE: Justice refers to the obligation of the researcher to treat participants fairly and equitably. Fairness entails treating all people with equal respect and concern. Equity requires distributing the burdens and benefits of research participation in such a way that no segment of the population is unduly burdened by any harm that might arise during the research project. In addition, participants must not be denied any benefits of knowledge generated from the investigation. Individuals or groups whose circumstances cause them to be vulnerable or marginalized must be afforded special attention in order that they are treated justly in research. Vulnerability is often created by one's limited capacity, or a limited access to social goods such as rights, opportunities, and power (Canadian Institutes of Health Research et al., 2010).

One of the most valuable assets realized for developing the second edition is the feature included in chapter 9 with Aboriginal partners. This feature discusses the latest thinking about ethical research involving Canada's Aboriginal peoples. The chapter emphasizes the need for equitable

Look at these two photographs, one of all white males, the other of a diverse group of females and males from different ethnic groups, including some white individuals. Consider a topic in psychology, such as parenting, love, or cultural values. **If you were conducting research on this topic, might the results of the study be different depending on whether the participants in your study were the individuals in the left photograph or the right one?**

partnerships, and it explains safeguards specific to First Nations, Inuit, and Métis people (Macionis, Jansson, & Benoit, 2013).

Minimizing Bias

Studies of life-span development are most useful when they are conducted without bias or prejudice toward any particular group of people. Of special concern are bias based on gender and bias based on culture or ethnicity.

GENDER BIAS   Sociological research frowns upon the process of using data from one gender to draw conclusions about populations. Consequently, approaching research problems from an exclusively male perspective is less common today (Brym, Roberts, Lie, & Rytina, 2013). Pohlhaus, Jiang, Wagner, Schaffer, and Wood (2011) conducted an analysis of sex differences in National Institutes of Health (NIH) award programs. The findings of this cross-sectional analysis indicated that women and men were equally successful at all career stages. Meanwhile, the results of the longitudinal analysis revealed that men with previous experiences as NIH grantees had higher application and funding rates than women at similar career points. The researchers conclude that while greater participation of women in NIH programs is underway, further action will be required to eradicate remaining sex differences. In the recent report *Women in Canada: A Gender-Based Statistical Report* (2010–2011), a deeper understanding of the roles of women in Canadian society is presented with indications of ways in which these roles have changed over time. One example from the report dwells upon women in the labour markets. Regardless of educational attainment, women remain less likely than men to be employed, although the gaps are most narrow among women with higher levels of education. Among women with university degrees, 75 percent of women versus 77 percent of men were employed in 2009. However, these patterns are reversed among younger women aged 15–24 years. Young women with higher levels of education found greater rates of employment than did men. For example, 77 percent of women under age 25 with a non-university, post-secondary certificate or diploma were employed in 2009, compared with 73 percent of men (Statistics Canada, 2010d). A significant question is generated by such a finding: "What accounts for the differences in the age group under 25?"

Fortunately, studies pioneered by Karen Horney, Erich Fromm, and, more recently, Carol Gilligan, Betty Jean Miller, and Harriet Lerner have opened the doors to wide examination of gender differences. See the Connecting Development to Life box "Gender Makes a Difference" for more information.

ETHNIC AND CULTURAL BIAS   Essentially, from a historical point of view, research on ethnic groups has been ignored. At best they have been viewed simply as variations from the norm. The

connecting development to life ←-------

Gender Makes a Difference

Four prominent clinical psychoanalysts have significantly influenced the field of psychology. Arguing that the primary framework in the field, put forward by Freud, Jung, Erikson, Kohlberg, and others, is a framework designed by and for men, Karen Horney, Jean Baker Miller, Carol Gilligan, and Harriet Lerner have made an enormous contribution.

Karen Horney (1885–1952) was the first woman to challenge prevalent thinking by proposing that cultural and experiential factors are primary determinants of personality for both men and women. While Horney agreed with much of Freud's work, she firmly disagreed with what she thought to be a preoccupation with male genitalia. Arguing "anatomy is not destiny," Horney proposed that men should experience womb-envy rather than women experiencing penis envy because women are the bearers of future generations—something men cannot do. Horney founded the American Institute for Psychoanalysis so that research and training would not be constrained by prevalent thought. Her major contribution to the field was her theory of neurosis, the struggle between our real self and our idealized self. She also argued that neglect, not abuse, is the single most damaging factor in a child's development, because the child has no way to rail against neglect.

Jean Baker Miller (1927–2006) was the founding director of the Jean Baker Miller Training Institute at Wellesley College. In her groundbreaking book *Toward a New Psychology of Women,* first published in 1970, she argues that "all life has been underdeveloped and distorted because our past explanations have been created by only one half of the human species." Miller believed that the dominant–subordinate grouping is inadequate because it defines and distorts members of both groups in different ways. Dominant groups define oppressed groups falsely, just as oppressed groups define dominant groups falsely. This distortion undermines the development of both groups and can be applied to all political contexts, including gender.

Carol Gilligan (1936–), psychoanalyst, ethicist, and feminist, was a colleague of Erikson and Kohlberg. She disagreed with Kohlberg, who believed that men had superior moral reasoning capacities. Gilligan asserted that men and women have different but equal moral and psychological tendencies. In her text *In a Different Voice: Psychological Theory and Women's Development* (1982), Gilligan observed that because of socialization, women not only define themselves in the context of relationships, but also judge themselves in terms of their ability to provide care and nurturance (p. 17). In addition, women alter their feelings and judgments in deference to others (pp. 95–101).

Harriet Lerner (1944–) is best known for her work on the psychology of women and the process of change in families. Lerner proposes that the rigidity of corporate culture disadvantages both male and female ability to manage and sustain relationships, thereby undermining the family unit. Lerner advocates that the corporate world demonstrate its valuing of family life by offering parental leaves, leaves to care for elderly parents or sick children, flexible hours, convenient daycare settings, and flexible work settings. These ideas are either very new to us or somewhere on the horizon (Lerner, 1998).

In different ways, Gilligan, Horney, Lerner, and Miller suggest that societal conventions and norms surrounding female identity, work, social, familial, and intimate relationships are strengthened when women and men both have healthy self-esteem and an equal voice.

developmental and educational problems experienced by ethnic groups have been viewed as "confounds" or "noise" in the data. It now appears obvious that more individuals and groups from different ethnic backgrounds need to be included in cultural research (Graham, 2006; Mehrotra & Wagner, 2009). In 2008, the Multiculturalism and Human Rights Branch of the Department of Canadian Heritage commissioned six academic investigators to conduct a socio-economic scan of the regions of Canada and to identify and specify significant research themes related to Canadian multiculturalism. Consequently, two of the ten research themes for 2008–2010 were patterns of ethnic community formation, and racism and discrimination (Minister of Public Works and Government Services Canada, 2010).

Researchers also have tended to practise what is called "ethnic gloss" when they select and describe ethnic minority samples (Banks, 2008; Markides, Rudkin, & Wallace, 2007). Ethnic gloss is using a superficial label that makes an ethnic group look more homogeneous than it really is. Ethnic gloss can cause researchers to obtain samples of ethnic groups that either are not representative or conceal the group's diversity, which can lead to overgeneralization and stereotyping.

Also, historically, when researchers have studied ethnic groups they have mainly focused on their problems. It is important to study the difficulties, such as poverty, that groups face, but it is equally important to examine methods by which these difficulties are negotiated, such as taking pride in one's community, self-esteem, problem-solving skills, and extended family support systems. In the context of a more pluralistic view of our society, researchers are increasingly studying the positive dimensions of behaviour (Swanson, 1997).

The World Health Organization (WHO) notes the lack of research in underdeveloped nations, where people are suffering the traumas of war, famine, acquired immune deficiency syndrome (AIDS), and diseases related to the lack of fresh water and immunization. Today's concerns differ widely from the concerns of the researchers and analysts who lay the formative foundations of psychology. Currrent researchers, building on the theories of the past, are equally excited about new discoveries. Unlike their historical predecessors, however, they concern themselves with sensitive ethical dilemmas, rigorous scientific procedures, and critical issues that influence social policy.

THE CANADIAN PSYCHOLOGICAL ASSOCIATION (CPA)   The Canadian Psychological Association (CPA) publishes and periodically updates ethical guidelines for both clinical and research psychologists in this country. Now in its third edition, the *Canadian Code of Ethics for Psychologists* (CPA, 2000) states that the primary professional goal for psychologists is "to respect the dignity of all persons with whom they come in contact in their role as psychologists."

For research, investigators must obtain informed consent from potential subjects before a study begins. To secure consent, investigators should describe in clear terms the purpose of the study, the procedure and materials used, the risks—both physical and psychological—to the subjects, and the issue of confidentiality. Potential subjects then can decide if they would like to participate in the study. Even after subjects have given their informed consent, they have a right to refuse to participate in certain parts of the study and to discontinue their participation completely during the course of the research.

To ensure that truthful responses from subjects can be obtained, researchers sometimes have to conceal information from potential subjects or distort certain information in their description of a study. On these occasions, the CPA (2000) suggests that researchers debrief subjects—that is, describe the actual intentions and answer subjects' inquiries—after the procedure has been completed. Canadian universities normally require students to submit a research proposal to their ethics committee.

To this point, we have discussed research methods and challenges. For a review, see the **Reach Your Learning Objectives** section at the end of this chapter.

reach your **learning objectives**

The Life-Span Perspective

LO1 Define life-span development and describe the characteristics of the life-span perspective.

Life-Span Development	Life-span development is the pattern of movement or change that begins at conception and continues throughout the human life span.
The Importance of Studying Life-Span Development	Studying life-span development provides insights that will enrich both personal and professional understanding of self and others.
	According to Paul Baltes, life-span development is:
	■ multidimensional
	■ multidirectional
	■ multidisciplinary
	■ plastic
	■ contextual
	■ concerned with growth, maintenance, and regulation
	■ a co-construct of biology, culture, and the individual

The Role of Context

LO2 Define the term *context* and examine the role it plays in understanding growth and development.

Context influences major aspects of growth and development including life expectancy, median age, and the demographics related to baby boomers. Major contextual influences include:

- normative age-graded influences
- normative history-graded influences
- non-normative life events

Socio-economic status (SES) is a major aspect of context.

Developmental Processes

LO3 Review the processes of development.

Biological, Cognitive, and Socio-Emotional Processes

Three intricate and complex processes of development are:

- biological/physical
- cognitive
- socio-emotional

These processes interact in a fluid manner, each shaping the growth and development of the other.

Periods of Development

LO4 Describe the periods of development and the concept of age.

The Periods of Development

Periods of development refer to the time frames in life that are characterized by certain features.

The periods of development include:

- prenatal
- infancy
- early childhood
- middle and late childhood
- adolescence
- early adulthood
- middle adulthood
- late adulthood

The Concept of Age

There are five conceptions of age:

- chronological
- biological
- mental
- psychological
- social

Issues in Life-Span Development

LO5 Outline three prominent issues in life-span development.

Interactional Model	■ Are we primarily influenced by the reciprocal interaction of both our biological inheritance or by our environment?
Continuity and Discontinuity	■ Do we change gradually or in distinct stages?
Stability and Change	■ Do we become older renditions of our childhood selves?
Evaluating Developmental Issues	■ Life-span development lists do not take extreme positions on the three developmental issues.

Some Contemporary Concerns

LO6 Appraise several major contemporary concerns.

Health and Well-Being	■ Research is a major focus of health and well-being, encompassing many areas of concern from genetics to geriatrics. ■ Fitness, nutrition, mental health, stress, and dementia are some of the research areas.
Education	■ Research in the area of education focuses on a wide range of topics from curriculum development, dropout rates, approaches to education, and neuroplasticity of the brain. Social media is drawing much attention to enhance critical thinking as well as enhancing relatedness.
Socio-Cultural Contexts	■ Culture refers to patterns of behaviour and beliefs, as well as other products of a group that are passed on from generation to generation. ■ Research in this area focuses primarily on cross-cultural studies, ethnicity, race, and gender.
Social Policy	■ Social policy refers to a national government's course of action designed to influence the welfare of its citizens (e.g., Canada's approach to First Nations or Aboriginal peoples; generational inequity—the economic fairness to younger people who may shoulder the tax burden of facilities to care for older people; homecare support for the elderly; the infrastructure needed to provide support to immigrants; housing security for the homeless).

Research Methods and Challenges

LO7 Compare and contrast research methodology and challenges.

Methods of Collecting Data	■ Theory is an interrelated, coherent set of ideas that help explain and make predictions. ■ Hypotheses are specific assumptions and predictions that can be tested to determine their accuracy. ■ Data are collected by observation, both naturalistic and observational, survey and interview, standardized tests, case studies, and physiological measures, including functional magnetic resonance imaging (fMRI).

Research Designs	■ Descriptive research includes observation, both in laboratory and natural settings, survey (questionnaire) or interview, standardized tests, case study, and life history record.
	■ Correlational research has as its goal the explanation or description of the strength of the relationship between two or more events or characteristics.
	■ Experimental research uses both independent and dependent variables to conduct an experiment to determine cause and effect. The independent variable is the manipulated, influential, experimental factor. The dependent variable responds to changes in the independent variable.
	■ Cross-sectional approach is a research strategy in which individuals of different ages are compared at one time.
	■ Longitudinal approach is a research strategy in which individuals are studied over a period of time, usually several years or more.
	■ Sequential approach combines the methods of both cross-sectional and longitudinal approaches.
	■ Cohort effects are the effects related to the historical time or generational time of an individual's birth, but not to actual age.
Research Challenges	■ Conduct ethical research. According to the Canadian Psychological Association (CPA), the primary goal for psychologists is "to respect the dignity of all persons with whom they come in contact. . . ." Guidelines to ensure that research complies with this goal are established and reviewed periodically.
	■ Minimize bias. Researchers make every effort to guard against gender, cultural, and ethnic biases in research. In particular, researchers must avoid ethnic gloss. Ethnic gloss is using a superficial label, such as "immigrant" or "visible minority," in such a way that it portrays a group as being more homogeneous than it really is.

review ---> *connect* ---> reflect

review

What is meant by the concept of development? **LO1**

List several characteristics of development. **LO1**

Why is the study of life-span development important? **LO1**

How is context related to growth and development? Provide an example. **LO2**

What are the three key developmental processes of development? **LO3**

How is age related to development? **LO4**

What are three main developmental issues? **LO5**

What are some contemporary concerns in life-span development? **LO6**

What research designs are used to study development? **LO7**

What are the researchers' ethical responsibilities to the individuals they study? **LO7**

connect

Reflect upon your own experience. How do you think biology and culture interact to affect development?

reflect *Your Own Personal Journey of Life*

You and your parents grew up at different points in time. Consider some of the ways you are different from your parents. What are several differences that may be caused by cohort effects?

McGraw-Hill Connect provides you with a powerful tool for improving academic performance and truly mastering course material. You can diagnose your knowledge with pre- and post-tests, identify the areas where you need help, search the entire learning package, including the eBook, for content specific to the topic you're studying, and add these resources to your personalized study plan. CONNECT for *Life-Span Development*, fifth Canadian edition, offers the following:

■ chapter-specific online quizzes

■ groupwork

■ presentations

■ writing assignments

■ case studies

■ and much more!

Visit CONNECT today!

CHAPTER 2

Prominent Approaches in Life-Span Development

CHAPTER OUTLINE

"A man is but the product of his thoughts—what he thinks, he becomes."

MAHATMA GANDHI,
FATHER OF INDIAN
INDEPENDENCE MOVEMENT

The Legacy of Sigmund Freud (1856–1939)

Many people consider Sigmund Freud, the "Father of Psychology," to be one of the most influential minds of the twentieth century because he revolutionized our understanding of human behaviour by suggesting we are motivated by both conscious and unconscious drives. He also theorized that the mind has structure (id, ego, superego), that human development passes through five psychosexual stages, and that defence mechanisms operate to protect the ego.

Born in 1856, Freud was the eldest son of a Jewish wool merchant who moved from the Czech Republic to Vienna. There, Freud studied in a variety of literary and philosophical areas until he settled on medicine and became a neuroscientist. Believing dreams to be the "royal road to the unconscious," Freud published his masterpiece, *The Interpretation of Dreams*, in 1900. In this work, Freud argued that meaning exists in everything we do, from our wildest nightmares to our most casual slips of the tongue. Humorous "Freudian slips" are verbal errors believed to reflect unconscious thoughts, desires, or emotions. "Saying one thing but meaning your mother" is an example of a Freudian slip. Such plays on words have provided writers, comedians, and others with a lively source of comedy; however, Freud's theory of the unconscious has broadened their meanings.

A man of broad intellectual interests, Freud formed the Vienna Psychoanalytic Society in 1908. This was a group of well-known thinkers of the time, including Carl Jung and Alfred Adler, who met weekly to debate ideas and examine case studies. Freud's contribution to psychology and German literary culture earned him the Goethe Prize in 1930.

Unfortunately, the Nazis burned his books when they took control of Germany in 1933. The Gestapo arrested his daughter Anna; in addition, his two sisters were arrested and murdered. Freud was able to emigrate to England with his wife and Anna so that he might "die in freedom." He died in London on September 23, 1939, three weeks after the beginning of World War II.

His pioneering work legitimized the field of psychology as a science and his theories continue to be the subject of interest, speculation, and debate. Freud believed that the mind changed in relationship to conscious or repressed entities. This idea anticipated prevalent theories in neurology today (Doidge, 2006). Contemporary neuroscientists find that Freudian theories provide a model integrating the interactions of the brain and the mind. Eric Kandel, one of Freud's contemporary proponents, won the Nobel Prize in 2000 for proving that the process of thinking changes brain structure. Further support for Freud's theories is illustrated by brain scans of infants who have endured trauma. These scans show structural changes that become encoded in an individual's implicit memory systems even though the individual does not consciously recall the incident in later years (Doidge, 2006). Freud's continuing relevance in a field that is being massively transformed by technological advances is a solid indication of his importance as a theorist.

Freud's work is not without its critics, who point to three main concerns: the originality of his ideas; his privileged white European male perspective; and his lack of consideration of cultural variables such as gender. Nevertheless, important theorists, including those who disagreed with him such as Adler, Jung, and Karen Horney, as well as Erikson and Bowlby, all acknowledge Freud's influence.

Sigmund Freud, the pioneering architect of psychoanalytic theory. **How did Freud believe each individual's personality is organized?**

The Psychoanalytic Approach

LO1 Describe the psychoanalytic approach and the contributions of major theorists.

Characteristics of the Psychoanalytic Approach

The **psychoanalytic approach** *describes development as primarily unconscious—that is, beyond awareness—and as heavily coloured by emotion.* Psychoanalytic theorists believe that behaviour is merely a surface characteristic and that to truly understand development we have to analyze the symbolic meanings of behaviour and the deep inner workings of the mind. Sigmund Freud was the revolutionary founder of psychoanalytic theory. As noted in the opening vignette, his theories are rooted in the scientific method and have formed the basis for much study and debate (Carveth, 2006).

Sigmund Freud

Freud's (1856–1939) major contributions include the exploration of the unconscious, from which his personality theory emerged; dream analysis; defence mechanisms; and the five psychosexual stages of development. Though famed for his work in psychoanalysis, few realize that Freud was a trained neurologist and spent as many hours in a laboratory studying neurons as he did in an office practising psychoanalysis (Doidge, 2006).

In 1917, Freud proposed that personality has three structures: the *id*, the *ego*, and the *superego*. The **id** *consists of instincts, which are an individual's reservoir of psychic energy.* In Freud's view, the id is totally unconscious and not concerned with reality. As children experience the demands and constraints of their worlds, a new structure of personality emerges—the ego, which deals with the demands of reality. The **ego** *is called the "executive branch" of the psyche because it uses reasoning to make decisions.* The id and the ego are not moral entities. The moral branch of the personality is the **superego**, *which takes into account whether something is right or wrong.* The superego is what we often refer to as our "conscience."

In Freud's view, the rational ego must resolve conflicts between the demands of reality, the wishes and dreams of the id, and the constraints of the superego. Such conflicts cause anxiety that alerts the ego to use protective measures to resolve the conflict. These protective measures are called defence mechanisms, and they reduce anxiety and conflict by unconsciously distorting reality. As Freud listened to, probed, and analyzed his patients, he became convinced that their problems were the result of traumatic experiences early in life that they had repressed. Freud believed that *repression* is the most powerful and pervasive defence mechanism, because it pushes unacceptable id impulses (such as intense sexual and aggressive desires) into the unconscious mind. He further believed that dreams provide insights into repressed experiences.

Freud's five psychosexual stages illustrate discontinuity as development is accomplished in stages. *The theory is that as children grow up their focus of pleasure and sexual impulses shifts from the oral stage to the anal stage, followed by the phallic stage, the latency period, and finally the genital stage* (see Figure 2.1). Each stage provides a **critical period** during which an individual resolves conflicts between sources of pleasure and the demands of reality. The adult personality is determined by how these conflicts are resolved. Freud believed that the individual is capable of developing a mature love relationship and functioning independently as an adult only when unresolved conflicts from childhood and adolescence are resolved.

Freud's theory has been significantly revised by a number of psychoanalytic theorists. Many of today's psychoanalytic theorists maintain that Freud overemphasized sexual instincts. Theorists such as Adler, Horney, Maslow, and Erikson placed more emphasis on cultural experiences as

psychoanalytic approach Development is primarily unconscious and heavily coloured by emotion. Behaviour is merely a surface characteristic. It is important to analyze the symbolic meanings of behaviour. Early experience is important to development.

id According to Freud, the element of personality consisting of instincts, which are an individual's reservoir of psychic energy.

ego According to Freud, the "executive branch" of the psyche, used for reasoning and decision making.

superego According to Freud, the moral branch of the personality, which takes into account whether something is right or wrong.

Freud's five psychosexual stages Freud postulated that as children grow up, their focus of pleasure and sexual impulses shifts from the oral stage to the anal stage, followed by the phallic stage, the latency period, and finally the genital stage.

critical period A period of time in each of Freud's psychosexual stages during which an individual resolves conflicts between sources of pleasure and the demands of reality.

Figure 2.1

Comparison of Freud's Five Psychosexual Stages and Erikson's Eight Psychosocial Stages

Age of Freud's Stages	Freud's Psychosexual Stages of Development	Age of Erikson's Stages	Erikson's Psychosocial Stages of Development
Birth–18 months	**Oral stage:** Pleasure centres around the mouth: chewing, sucking, and biting.	Birth–12 months	**Trust vs. mistrust:** Trust emerges when baby feels comfortable and safe. Needs are responded to lovingly. **Resolution:** Hope
15 months–3 years	**Anal:** Pleasure centres around the anus muscles and from elimination. Conflict occurs when child is punished too harshly or neglected.	1–3 years	**Autonomy vs. shame and doubt:** Toddler exercises will and independence. Shame and doubt result when toddler is restrained too much or punished too harshly. **Resolution:** Will
3–6 years	**Phallic:** Children discover that manipulation of their own genitals brings pleasure. During this stage, the Oedipus complex for boys and the Electra complex for girls occurs. This is when children first come face to face with the realities of their family life and a conscience emerges as they learn some things are taboo.	Preschool–4 or 5 years	**Initiative vs. guilt:** As children enter a wider social world, they learn to take responsibility for their toys, their behaviour, their bodies, etc. Their behaviour becomes more purposeful and a sense of accomplishment becomes more important. Guilt is quickly overcome when the child is able to accomplish something. **Resolution:** Purpose
6 years–puberty	**Latency:** The child represses interests in sexuality and develops social and intellectual skills.	Grades K–6	**Industry vs. inferiority:** Children enthusiastically pursue mastery of skills: spelling, multiplication tables, sports, etc. Children enjoy using their creativity and imagination. A sense of inferiority emerges when the child is unproductive or made to feel incompetent. **Resolution:** Competence
Puberty–late adulthood	**Genital:** Reawakening of sexual pleasure. The source of sexual pleasure becomes someone outside the family.	Adolescence	**Identity vs. identity confusion:** Self-discovery occurs at this stage. **Resolution:** Fidelity
		Early Adulthood	**Intimacy vs. isolation:** With a sense of self, the individual is able to commit to a relationship and to responsibilities such as managing one's own resources: health, time, money, relationships. **Resolution:** Love
		Middle Adulthood	**Generativity vs. stagnation:** Concern for the next generation. Stagnation occurs when the adult believes they can't contribute to the next generation. **Resolution:** Care
		Late Adulthood	**Integrity vs. despair:** In their senior years, individuals reflect on their lives and conclude that their life has or has not been well spent. **Resolution:** Wisdom

Erik Erikson generated one of the most important developmental theories of the twentieth century. **Which stage of Erikson's theory are you in? Does Erikson's description of this stage characterize you?**

---- **critical** thinking ----

A number of psychoanalysts and psychologists have taken exception to the stages proposed by both Freud and Erikson, arguing that the progression from stage to stage differs for men and women or that development does not occur in stages. Do you believe your personal growth has progressed from one stage to the next, or have you developed more continuously? Do you think the cultural variables in your life including your gender have influenced your growth and development? If so, how?

Erikson's theory Eight stages of psychosocial development unfold throughout the human life span. Each stage consists of a unique developmental task that confronts individuals with a crisis that must be faced.

determinants of an individual's development. Many argue that unconscious thought remains a central theme, but conscious thought plays a greater role than Freud envisioned. Next, we will outline the ideas of an important revisionist of Freud's ideas—Erik Erikson.

Erik Erikson

Unlike Freud, who believed that motivation was sexual in nature, Erik Erikson (1902–1994) believed that motivation was highly social by nature and reflects a desire to affiliate with others. Both theorists believed development occurs in stages (discontinuity); however, Erikson believed that development occurs over the life span, whereas Freud believed our basic personalities are formed by five years of age. Additionally, in contrast to Freud's five *psychosexual stages*, **Erikson's theory** identified eight stages and called them *psychosocial stages* (see Figure 2.1).

Each stage consists of a unique developmental task that confronts individuals with a crisis that must be faced. According to Erikson, the crisis is more of a turning point and is indicative of both increased vulnerability and enhanced potential. Like Freud, Erikson believed that the more successfully individuals resolve the crises or turning points, the healthier development will be (Hopkins, 2000).

Erikson believed that the proper resolution of a stage is not always completely positive. Some of the negative aspects to conflict are inevitable—you cannot trust all people under all circumstances and survive, for example. Nonetheless, in the healthy resolution to a stage crisis balance is achieved and virtues, or emotional strengths, emerge.

As you know, historical time provides a context that influences thinking and behaviour. More than just music and fashion undergo change; attitudes and beliefs about a variety of concepts such as gender and human rights undergo major paradigm shifts as well. For example, although Canadians hold dear their right to vote, it wasn't until 1960 that First Nations peoples were given that right. Same-sex marriage illustrates another major paradigm shift. Although some provinces had granted the right to marry earlier, 2005 marks the year that Canada as a nation extended the right for couples of the same sex to marry; in 2013, nation-wide rights to same-sex marriage were passed in England, Wales, Uruguay, and France. In 2014, when these laws go into effect, the total number of countries sanctioning same-sex marriage will rise to 17 (Encyclopedia Britannica, 2013; ILGA Europe, 2013). Our thinking, laws, and norms change with time. Scholars such as Freud and Erikson developed their theories within a historical and social milieu as well. For example, Freud's argument that wars were the result of pent-up aggression may have been influenced by the historic World Wars I and II that took place in Europe and affected his life directly. Erikson's belief that the key elements of women's identity were that of mother and wife were developed in the 1950s, a time when women did not enter the workforce as they do today and one income was sufficient to support a family.

Other Psychoanalytic Theories

The term *neo-Freudians* refers to psychologists who have contributed further to the psychoanalytic approach initiated by Freud. Some psychoanalysts thought that Freud's view of human nature was too negative and overly concerned with sex and aggression. Others believed that environmental, social, and biological factors as well as both conscious and unconscious forces influence personality development. A myriad of divergent ideas sprung forth from this group, which included Alfred Adler, Carl Jung, Karen Horney, and Freud's daughter Anna Freud. None of these prominent theorists proposed a stage theory; instead, they looked at personality development more holistically. Figure 2.2 provides a synopsis of the contributions of the neo-Freudians.

Evaluating the Psychoanalytic Approach

Contributions of psychoanalytic theories include an emphasis on a developmental framework, family relationships, and the unconscious aspects of the mind. Criticisms include a lack of scientific rigour, too much emphasis on sexual underpinnings, and a relatively negative view of human nature.

To this point, we have discussed the various theories of the psychoanalytic approach. For a review, see the **Reach Your Learning Objectives** section at the end of this chapter.

Figure 2.2

Major Contributions of the Neo-Freudian Psychoanalytic Theorists

Neo-Freudian	Theory
Alfred Adler 1870–1937	Alfred Adler developed *individual psychology* because he believed each person is unique and is striving toward emotional health and well-being. He identified the inferiority complex to describe our feelings of lack of self-worth; we struggle to overcome our inferiority (Fisher, 2001).
Carl Jung 1875–1961	Carl Jung believed the psyche includes three parts: the *ego*, or the conscious mind; the *personal unconscious*, which includes everything not presently conscious, and the *collective unconscious*, or "psychic inheritance." *Déjà vu*, love at first sight, and immediate responses to various symbols are examples of the collective unconscious (Boeree, 2006). Jung developed a personality typology that distinguished between introversion and extraversion and identified preferred ways of dealing with the world. This typology is the groundwork for the Myers-Briggs Personality Inventory.
Karen Horney 1885–1952	Horney, a student of Freud's, criticized his work on the grounds of gender and cultural differences. Well-known for her work on neurosis, Horney identified ten neurotic trends that she believed resulted from parental indifference and which she called the "basic evil." The child's reaction to parental indifference, basic hostility, and basic anxiety leads the child to develop coping strategies; as the individual matures, neuroses may develop.
Anna Freud 1895–1982	Sigmund Freud's daughter Anna Freud made significant contributions to the fields of child psychoanalysis and child development psychology from her work in the analysis of children and adolescents. She was concerned with the ego, its conflicts with reality, and the defence mechanisms.
Eric Fromm 1900–1980	Fromm believed human nature is influenced by dysfunctional social patterns, such as poverty, war, power, and capitalistic greed, as well as biological factors. He endorsed the concepts of feminism and supported Horney's assertions of gender differences by arguing that men had to prove themselves in the world and thus were driven to acquire wealth and power at the expense of people and environment. Women, on the other hand, feared being abandoned and submitted to male power. Fromm, who studied the theories of Karl Marx, believed that capitalistic societies damaged the psychological well-being of those who were marginalized or impoverished. Thus, he, along with Horney, was one of the first to consider the influence of racism, sexism, and economic inequities on personality growth.

The Cognitive Approach

LO2 Compare and contrast the theories within the cognitive approach.

Whereas psychoanalytic theories stress the importance of unconscious thoughts, **cognitive theories** *emphasize conscious thoughts*. Three important cognitive theories are Piaget's cognitive development theory, Vygotsky's socio-cultural cognitive theory, and the information-processing approach.

Piaget's Cognitive Developmental Theory

Swiss psychologist Jean Piaget (1896–1980) proposed an important theory of cognitive development that illustrates discontinuity. **Piaget's theory** *states that children actively construct their understanding of the world and go through four stages of cognitive development.* Two processes underlie this cognitive construction of the world: organization and adaptation. To make sense of our world, we organize our experiences (Carpendale, Muller, & Bibok, 2008). For example, we separate important ideas from less important ideas. We connect one idea to another. But not only do we organize our observations and experiences, we also adapt our thinking to include new ideas because additional information furthers understanding (Byrnes, 2008). Piaget (1954) believed that we adapt in two ways: assimilation and accommodation.

Assimilation *occurs when individuals incorporate new information into their existing knowledge.* **Accommodation** *occurs when individuals adjust to new information,* for example when an infant who drops a rattle over the side of the crib learns gravity (Elkind, 1997–2012). Consider the circumstance in which a 9-year-old girl is given a hammer and nails to hang a picture on the wall. She has never used a hammer, but from observation she realizes that a hammer is an object to be held, that it is swung by the handle to hit the nail, and that it is usually swung a number of times. Recognizing each of these things, she fits her behaviour to the information she already has (assimilation). However, the hammer is heavy, and so she holds it near the top. She swings too hard and the nail bends, and so she adjusts the pressure of her strikes. These adjustments reveal her ability to alter slightly her conception of the world (accommodation). Learning progresses from one stage to the next, including from reflex to determined behaviour, as information is first assimilated and then accommodated.

Piaget thought that assimilation and accommodation operate in the very young infant's life. Newborns reflexively suck everything that touches their lips (assimilation), but after several months of experience they construct their understanding of the world differently. Some objects, such as fingers and the mother's breast, can be sucked, but others, such as fuzzy blankets, should not be sucked (accommodation).

Each of the four stages we go through as we seek an understanding of the world around us is age-related and consists of distinct ways of thinking (see Figure 2.3). According to Piaget, it is the different way of understanding the world that makes one stage more advanced than another; knowing more information does not make the child's thinking more advanced. This is what Piaget meant when he said the child's cognition is qualitatively different in one stage than in another (Vidal, 2000).

The *sensorimotor stage*, from birth to about two years of age, is the first Piagetian stage. In this stage, infants construct an understanding of the world by coordinating sensory experiences (such as seeing and hearing) with physical, motoric actions—hence the term sensorimotor. At the beginning of this stage, newborns have little more than reflexive patterns with which to work. At the end of the stage, 2-year-olds have complex sensorimotor patterns and are beginning to operate with primitive symbols.

The *preoperational stage*, from approximately two to seven years of age, is the second Piagetian stage. In this stage, children begin to represent the world with words, images, and drawings. However, although preschool children can symbolically represent the world, according to Piaget they still lack the ability to perform operations, the Piagetian term for internalized mental actions that allow children to do mentally what they previously did physically.

cognitive theories Emphasize conscious thoughts.

Piaget's theory Children actively construct their understanding of the world and go through four stages of cognitive development.

assimilation In Piaget's theory, individuals incorporate new information into their existing knowledge.

accommodation In Piaget's theory, individuals adjust to new information.

Jean Piaget, the famous Swiss developmental psychologist, changed the way we think about the development of children's minds.
What are some key ideas in Piaget's theory?

connecting development to life

Culture and Child Rearing

Child-rearing practices often reflect a culture's values, values that often are reflected in what is called locus of control (Bornstein, 2006; Cole, 2006; Shiraev & Levy, 2007). Locus of control refers to an individual's ability to affect events: those with an internal locus of control believe they can affect outcomes; on the other hand, those with an external locus of control believe that events are more likely controlled by forces outside the individual's control. Chances are that if you were born and raised in a Western culture such as one in North America or Europe you would endorse an internal locus of control, and raise children to behave and think independently. However, if you were born and raised in an Eastern culture such as one in Asia or the Middle East you are more likely to endorse an external locus of control, and raise children to consider what is best for the group first. Indeed, researchers have found that parents' child-rearing goals depend less on their personal characteristics and more on the values of the culture in which the parents live (Chao & Tseng, 2002; Trommsdorff, 2002).

Children raised on the premise of an external locus of control are more likely to show a concern for social harmony (Keller, 2002). They grow up with a stronger sense of "family self" than children in most Western cultures, believing that what they do reflects upon not just one's self but also one's family. In communal cultures, do something wrong or deviant and you shame your family; do something right or approved of and you honour your family. Conversely, individuals from Western cultures are more apt to believe that when a person thinks independently, he or she will be more likely to contribute to the overall well-being of family and society. An interesting example of how this plays out is lying. Children learn about "appropriate lies" within a social context. In the Chinese culture, for example, where harmony and modesty are valued over individualism, children will preserve their modesty by denying having done something that is for the good of the group. In cultures such as Canada, where individuality is championed, children will seek credit for doing something that makes a positive contribution to the group (Sweet, Heyman, Fu, & Lee, 2010).

People who immigrate to Canada bring child-rearing views and practices with them from their native country, and these may conflict with the views of their new culture (Fuligni & Witkow, 2004; Parke & Buriel, 2006). For example, spanking, even beatings, are disciplinary measures applied to children and even to wives in many countries of the world but may be problematic in Canada, where such practices are highly criticized and, if done to excess, may result in legal interventions. Further, children and adolescents from immigrant families may want as much independence as their North American peers and friends have; they may want to work part time, or date someone from outside their cultural background. Such behaviour may conflict with the wishes of their parents and grandparents who want to preserve the traditions of their native culture.

The *concrete operational stage*, from approximately 7 to 11 years of age, is the third Piagetian stage. In this stage, children can perform operations and logical reasoning replaces intuitive thought, as long as reasoning can be applied to specific or concrete examples. For instance, concrete operational thinkers cannot imagine the steps necessary to complete an algebraic equation because manipulating unknowns is too abstract at this stage of development.

Figure 2.3

Piaget's Four Stages of Cognitive Development

SENSORIMOTOR STAGE	PREOPERATIONAL STAGE	CONCRETE OPERATIONAL STAGE	FORMAL OPERATIONAL STAGE
The infant constructs an understanding of the world by coordinating sensory experiences with physical actions. An infant progresses from reflexive, instinctual action at birth to the beginning of symbolic thought toward the end of the stage.	The child begins to represent the world with words and images. These words and images reflect increased symbolic thinking and go beyond the connection of sensory information and physical action.	The child can now reason logically about concrete events and classify objects into different sets.	The adolescent reasons in more abstract, idealistic, and logical ways.
Birth to 2 years of age	2–7 years of age	7–11 years of age	11 years of age through adulthood

connecting through research

The Magic Brain—Neuroplasticity

At the beginning of the twentieth century, Freud was certain that repressed trauma impacted the individual whether or not the individual remembered it. As a neurologist and a psychoanalyst, Freud was certain of the connection, but was unable to prove it. Today, brain imaging and case studies support Freud's hunch that an interactive synergy exists between the conscious and unconscious processes of the mind (Doidge, 2007; Wexler, 2006). The focus of much of today's research is aimed at better understanding the interaction between the internal structure of the mind and the external environment.

The brain is an incredible organ, with physiological properties that lend themselves to the development of complex, dynamic, and flexible human minds. It can produce new neurons or nerves ("neuro"), resulting in a brain that is malleable or adaptable ("plastic"), hence the word *neuroplasticity* (Doidge, 2007; Wexler, 2006). When one part of the brain is damaged—by stroke, accident, or trauma, for example—it is able to recruit capacity from another area of the brain to increase processing power (Doidge, 2007; Wexler, 2006). With intensive therapeutic treatment, patients have regained eyesight, recovered functioning after strokes, and ameliorated learning disorders (Doidge, 2007).

Psychiatrist and psychoanalyst Dr. Norman Doidge, who holds appointments at both the University of Toronto and Columbia University in New York, believes that as the body of knowledge grows, we will come to understand how the brain is changed by such things as emotional experiences, addictions, and learning experiences, as well as cultural factors such as technology.

As neuroscience progresses, the potential for understanding and healing traumatic experiences (conscious or not) and degenerative diseases such as Alzheimer's disease becomes more plausible (Doidge, 2007). As brain imaging becomes more refined and sophisticated, therapists will be able to more effectively help individuals who have been diagnosed with mental illnesses or are facing difficult emotional circumstances (Pugh, 2004).

There is considerable interest today in Lev Vygotsky's socio-cultural cognitive theory of child development. **What were Vygotsky's three basic claims about children's development?**

Vygotsky's theory A socio-cultural cognitive theory that emphasizes developmental analysis, the role of language, and social relations.

The formal operational stage, which appears between the ages of 11 and 15, is the fourth and final Piagetian stage. In this stage, individuals move beyond concrete experiences and think in abstract and more logical terms. As part of thinking more abstractly, adolescents develop images of ideal circumstances. They might think about what an ideal parent is like and compare their parents to this ideal standard. They begin to entertain possibilities for the future and are fascinated with what they can be. In solving problems, they become more systematic, developing hypotheses about why something is happening the way it is and then testing these hypotheses.

Since Piaget's time, researchers have broadened Piaget's theories to include ideas from other traditions. Robbie Case (1994–2000), Director of the University of Toronto's Institute of Child Study prior to his death, is considered the quintessential neo-Piagetian. Case broadened Piaget's stages by incorporating Vygotsky's social-constructivist theory, information processing, linguistics, and current findings in neuroscience (Jackson, 2003).

Vygotsky's Socio-Cultural Cognitive Theory

Like Piaget, the Russian psychologist Lev Vygotsky (1896–1934) also believed that children actively construct their knowledge. However, Vygotsky gave social interaction and culture far more important roles than did Piaget. **Vygotsky's theory** *is a socio-cultural cognitive theory that emphasizes how culture and social interaction guide cognitive development.* Vygotsky was born the same year as Piaget, but he died much earlier, from tuberculosis at the age of 37. Again, the social-political context emerged, this time in Russia. Unfortunately, the Russian government repudiated Vygotsky's theories; fortunately, they were recovered in 1957 and are widely considered by psychologists, educators, and parents today.

Vygotsky portrayed child development as inseparable from social and cultural activities (Cole & Gajdamaschko, 2007; Gredler, 2008). He believed that the development of *memory, attention, and reasoning* involves learning to use the inventions of society, such as language, mathematical systems, and memory strategies. In one culture, this might consist of learning to count with the help of a calculator. In another, it might consist of counting on one's fingers or using beads.

Vygotsky's theory has stimulated considerable interest in the view that knowledge is *situated and collaborative* (Tudge, 2004). In this view, knowledge is not generated from within the individual, but instead is constructed through interaction with other people and objects in the culture, such as books. This suggests that knowing can best be advanced through interaction with others in cooperative activities. According to Vygotsky, children's social interaction with more-skilled adults and peers is indispensable to their cognitive development (Holzman, 2009). Through this interaction, they learn to use the tools that will help them adapt and be successful in their culture.

The Information-Processing Approach

The **information-processing approach** *emphasizes that individuals manipulate information, monitor it, and strategize about it.* Central to this approach are the processes of memory and thinking. According to the information-processing approach, individuals develop a gradually increasing capacity for processing information, which allows them to acquire increasingly complex knowledge and skills (Halford, 2008; Vallotton & Fischer, 2008). Unlike Piaget's cognitive developmental theory, but like Vygotsky's theory, the information-processing approach does not describe development as being stage-like.

Robert Siegler (2006, 2007), a leading expert on children's information processing, believes that thinking is information processing. He says that when individuals perceive, encode, represent, store, and retrieve information, they are thinking. Siegler believes that an important aspect of development is learning good strategies for processing information. For example, becoming a better reader might involve learning to monitor the key themes of the material being read.

Dr. Kang Lee (2010) notes that telling lies involves processing and manipulating information while at the same time keeping the truth in mind. Although most conscious lying starts at about age three, some very intelligent, perhaps gifted, children start telling lies at as young as two years old. As children mature they get better at lying, and their skills peak at age 12. About age 16, the tendency to tell lies falls off. Lee's studies have indicated that telling lies illustrates brain activity and does not mean the child is to become deceptive or will cheat; rather, because it is developmental and involves so much brain activity, lying serves as a predictor of future success (Alleyene, 2010).

information-processing approach Emphasizes that individuals manipulate information, monitor it, and strategize about it. Central to information processing are the processes of memory and thinking.

Evaluating the Cognitive Approach

Contributions of the cognitive theories include a positive view of development and an emphasis on the active construction of understanding. Criticisms include skepticism about the pureness of Piaget's stages and the insufficient attention to individual variations.

To this point, we have studied a number of ideas about the cognitive approach. For a review, see the **Reach Your Learning Objectives** section at the end of this chapter.

The Behavioural and Social Cognitive Approach

LO3 Discuss and examine the behavioural and social cognitive approach, including the contributions of Pavlov, Skinner, and Bandura.

At about the same time that Freud was interpreting patients' unconscious minds through their early childhood experiences, Ivan Pavlov and John B. Watson were conducting detailed observations of behaviour in controlled laboratory settings. Their work provided the foundations of *behaviourism*, which essentially holds that only what can be directly observed and measured can be studied in a scientific way. Out of the behavioural tradition grew the belief that development is observable behaviour that can be learned through experience with the environment (Watson & Tharp, 2007). In terms of the continuity–discontinuity issue discussed in Chapter 1, the behavioural and social cognitive theories emphasize continuity in development and argue that development does not occur in stage-like fashion. The three versions of the behavioural approach that we will explore are Pavlov's classical conditioning, Skinner's operant conditioning, and Bandura's social cognitive theory.

Pavlov's Classical Conditioning

Skinner's Operant Conditioning

Bandura's Social Cognitive Theory

Evaluating the Behavioural and Social Cognitive Approach

Pavlov's Classical Conditioning

In the early 1900s, Russian physiologist Ivan Pavlov (1927) knew that dogs innately salivate when they taste food. He became curious when he observed that dogs salivate in reaction to various sights and sounds even before eating their food. For example, when an individual paired the ringing of a bell with the food, the bell ringing subsequently developed the ability to elicit the salivation of the dogs, even when the bell ringing was presented by itself. Pavlov discovered the principle of *classical conditioning*, in which a neutral stimulus (in this case, ringing a bell) acquires the ability to produce a response originally produced by another stimulus (in this example, food).

Many of our fears—fear of the dentist following a painful experience, fear of driving after being in an automobile accident, fear of heights—may have been learned through classical conditioning. As well, much of our stereotypical assumptions or fears may have been learned. For example, does the pairing of a word such as "terrorist" to a particular group stir up negative stereotypical images and create fear?

Skinner's Operant Conditioning

Classical conditioning may explain how we develop many involuntary responses such as fear, but B. F. Skinner (1904–1990) argued that a second type of conditioning accounts for the development of types of behaviour. According to Skinner's theory of *operant conditioning* (1938), the consequences of a behaviour produce changes in the probability of the behaviour's future occurrence. If a behaviour is followed by a rewarding stimulus, it is more likely to recur, but if a behaviour is followed by a punishing stimulus, it is less likely to recur. For example, when a person smiles at a child after the child has done something, the child is more likely to engage in the activity than if the person gives the child a disapproving look.

In Skinner's view (1936), such rewards and punishments shape individuals' development. For example, Skinner's approach argues that shy people learned to be shy because of the environmental experiences they had while growing up. It follows that modifications to an environment can help a shy person become more socially oriented. Skinner emphasized that behavioural changes are brought about by rewards and punishments, not by thoughts and feelings.

Bandura's Social Cognitive Theory

Some psychologists believe that the behaviourists are basically right when they say development is learned and is influenced strongly by environmental experiences. However, they also see cognition as important in understanding development (Mischel, 2004). The **behavioural and social cognitive approach** *is the view of psychologists who emphasize behaviour, environment, and cognition as the key factors in development.*

Canadian-born psychologist Albert Bandura (1925–) and Austrian-born Walter Mischel (1930–) are the leading architects of social cognitive theory. Bandura (1986, 2001, 2004, 2006, 2008, 2009a) and Mischel both believe that cognitive processes are important mediators of environment–behaviour connections. Bandura's early research focused heavily on observational learning, learning that occurs through observing what others do. Observational learning is also referred to as imitation or modelling. For example, a toddler may observe his older brother playing hockey and imitate his movements. Social cognitive theorists stress that people acquire a wide range of behaviours, thoughts, and feelings through observing the behaviour of others, and that these observations form an important part of life-span development.

Bandura believes that people cognitively represent the behaviour of others and then sometimes adopt this behaviour themselves. For example, a parent who often tells her child that he has three options, a, b, or c, may hear her child resolve a conflict with a friend by saying, "Tristan, we have three options. . . ." These observations form an important part of life-span development.

Bandura's (2001, 2004, 2006) most recent model of learning and development involves three elements: behaviour, the person, and the environment. An individual's confidence that he or she can control his or her success is an example of a person factor; strategies to do so are an example of a cognitive factor. As shown in Figure 2.4, behaviour, personal (and cognitive), and environmental

---

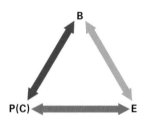

Albert Bandura has been one of the leading architects of social cognitive theory. **How does Bandura's theory differ from Skinner's?**

behavioural and social cognitive approach The theory that behaviour, environment, and person/cognitive factors are important in understanding development.

Figure 2.4

Bandura's Social Cognitive Model

B

P(C)   E

P(C) stands for personal and cognitive factors, *B* for behaviour, and *E* for environment. The arrows reflect how relations among these factors are reciprocal, rather than unidirectional.

factors operate interactively. Behaviour can influence personal factors and vice versa. The person's cognitive activities can influence the environment, the environment can change the person's cognition, and so on.

Consider how Bandura's model might work in the case of a university student's achievement behaviour. As the student diligently studies and gets good grades, her behaviour produces positive thoughts about her abilities. As part of her effort to make good grades, she plans and develops a number of strategies to make her studying more efficient. In these ways, her behaviour has influenced her thought, and her thought has influenced her behaviour. At the beginning of the term, her school made a special effort to involve students in a study skills program, and she decided to join it. Her success, along with that of other students who attended the program, has led the university to expand the program next semester. In these ways, environment influenced behaviour, and behaviour changed the environment. The administrators' expectations that the study skills program would work made it possible in the first place. The program's success has spurred expectations that this type of program could work in other universities. In these ways, cognition changed the environment, and the environment changed cognition.

Evaluating the Behavioural and Social Cognitive Approach

Contributions of the behavioural and social cognitive theories include an emphasis on scientific research and environmental determinants of behaviour. Criticisms include too little emphasis on cognition and too much attention on environmental determinants.

To this point, we have discussed the behavioural and social cognitive approach. For a review, see the **Reach Your Learning Objectives** section at the end of this chapter.

The Ethological Approach

LO4 Describe the ethological approach and distinguish among the major contributions of Darwin, Lorenz, Bowlby, and Goodall.

Ethology *is the study of animals to discover their responses to the environment, their physiological makeup, their communication abilities, and their evolutionary aspects.* For example, ethologists would study a trait such as dominance, mating, or aggression in many different types of animals to understand whether the behaviour is innate or learned. Ethologists believe behaviour is influenced by biology and that a critical or sensitive period was essential for healthy development. The presence or absence of certain experiences has a long-lasting influence on individuals.

Ethologists use three methods of study to understand the origins of non-verbal behaviours, social grooming, and other innate behaviours. They compare the behaviour of closely related species, for example humans and apes. They also study the responses of healthy children with those who have physical or intellectual challenges, such as deafness or blindness. Additionally, ethologists consider whether behaviours occur in more than one culture, as the more universally a behaviour is observed, the stronger the possibility that it is innate. Research shows that many non-verbal behaviours, such as smiles, raised eyebrows, and even flirting, are similar among cultures, and are therefore thought to be innate. Let's look at the contribution of four ethological theorists.

Charles Darwin

Charles Darwin (1809–1882), a British naturalist, was one of the first to theorize about the connection between humans and the rest of the animal kingdom. His theories of evolution and natural selection and survival of the fittest were based on years of scientific study and observation.

critical thinking

The Children's Aid Society placed two teenaged brothers, 17 and 18 years old, in a group home. Their aunt and uncle had adopted them when they were 3 and 4 years of age because their mother, who has since died, was unable to care for them due to her drug and alcohol dependency. The boys were caged for 13 years and deprived of food, sanitation, and nurturing. In January 2004, their adoptive parents pleaded guilty to forcible confinement, assault with a weapon, and failure to provide the necessities of life.

Based on your readings, observations, and experiences, how do you think the boys' physical, mental, and emotional growth would be affected? Imagine that you may interact with one or both of the brothers either professionally or as a neighbour. How might you understand them? Which of the theories we've discussed would be most useful to you? Which do you think would not be helpful?

Charles Darwin

Konrad Lorenz

John Bowlby

Jane Goodall

Evaluating the Ethological Approach

ethology The study of animals to discover their responses to the environment, their physiological makeup, their communication abilities, and their evolutionary aspects.

Konrad Lorenz

The European zoologist Konrad Lorenz (1903–1989) is often called the "father of ethology" because of his studies of the innate behaviour of animals, especially imprinting in young birds. Through an elaborate set of experiments, mostly with greylag geese, Lorenz (1965) determined that newly hatched goslings attach themselves to the first "mother" figure they see. In fact, the goslings that were hatched in an incubator followed Lorenz everywhere because he was the first "mother" figure they saw, whereas those hatched in their natural habitat by their mother immediately bonded with her. He called this process *imprinting*, the rapid, innate learning within a limited critical period of time that involves attachment to the first moving object seen.

Konrad Lorenz, a pioneering student of animal behaviour, is followed through the water by three imprinted greylag geese. Describe Lorenz's experiment with the geese. **Do you think his experiment would have the same results with human babies? Explain.**

John Bowlby

John Bowlby (1907–1990), the "father of attachment theory," contributed one of the most important applications of the ethological approach to human development. Bowlby stressed that all infants form enduring emotional bonds with their caregivers beyond the need for physical nourishment. The caregiver's role to protect the infant from harm ensures the survival of the species. Smiling, crying, and cooing are all part of the infant's innate repertoire of behaviours that elicit caregiver responses. The infant's senses—touch, smell, taste, sight, and hearing—all become intimately bound with the nurturer. In this manner, an infant elicits loving, protective responses from the caregiver, which in turn strengthen attachment. If the attachment is negative and insecure, life-span development will likely not be optimal.

As the infant grows and develops, he or she seeks the proximity of the caregiver, usually the mother. The child may wander off, but frequently checks back with or returns to the mother or primary caregiver, thus ensuring availability and attentiveness. The young child does not seek out any caregiver, but only the one with whom a strong bond has been established. In a sense, this has been imprinted, thereby reducing the number of people the child will seek out.

A secure attachment during the critical period of the first two years of life contributes to the child's ability to develop a sense of self. According to Bowlby, there is no such thing as responding too much in the first 18 months. Responding reinforces attachment, and this strong bond enables the child to develop healthy relationships later in life. Secure attachments are associated with lower levels of depression, closer friendships, and more stable romantic relationships.

Jane Goodall

Jane Goodall (1934–), a well-known animal activist and scientist, has been dedicated to learning about animals since childhood. She studied chimpanzees in Tanzania and, gaining their trust, was able to document the complex social system of the chimps, including their ability to communicate, to make tools, to comfort each other, their social status signs, and their gender roles. Through her programs and writings, she challenged scientists to redefine their long-held ideas on differences between humans and other primates. In recognition of her work she has received many awards, and was appointed a United Nations Messenger of Peace in 2002.

Jane Goodall is a well-known ethologist and animal activist whose studies of chimpanzees challenged previous ideas of how humans differed from other species.

Evaluating the Ethological Approach

Contributions of the ethological approach include a focus on biological and evolutionary bases of development, the role of sensitive or critical periods, and the use of careful observations in naturalistic settings. Criticisms include too much emphasis on biological foundations and the rigid timeframe for the sensitive or critical periods.

To this point, we have discussed the ethological approach. For a review, see the **Reach Your Learning Objectives** section at the end of this chapter.

The Humanist Approach

LO5 Describe and evaluate the humanist approach, including the contributions of Rogers and Maslow.

In the various schools of thought that you have read about so far, behaviour is rooted in either unconscious drives or biological processes. That there are other schools of thought comes as no surprise, because neither biology nor empirical behaviour fully satisfied many prominent psychologists. As such, Abraham Maslow and Carl Rogers, believing they were onto a new frontier of understanding, founded the humanist school of thought.

The **humanists** *believe that people work hard to become the best they can possibly become.* Abraham Maslow called this striving self-actualization, whereas Rogers called it an actualizing tendency. These terms differ in that Maslow believed very few of us (two percent or fewer) self-actualize, while Rogers believed all of us tend to self-actualize. Putting this difference aside, they agreed that all human behaviour is intrinsically motivated toward self-improvement and that values, intentions, and meaning play an important role in growth and development.

Carl Rogers

Carl Rogers (1902–1987) believed that in order for growth individuals need an environment that provides openness, acceptance, and empathy. Given those three components, individuals can flourish and become fully functioning. He defined **congruence** *as a state when our self-worth, "self-image, and ideal self ideal" are consistent with each other.* Another core concept is that our actualizing tendency refers to our efforts to reduce incongruity, the gap between the *real self* (the "I am") and the *ideal self* (the "I should be"). Rogers referred to this gap as **incongruity**.

Rogers believed that human nature strives to be healthy and that mental illness, criminality, and other human problems are distortions of the motivation toward health. According to Rogers (1961), a healthy, fully functioning person has the following characteristics: openness; existential living or engagement in the present; reliance on gut instincts when making decisions; freedom to experiment and assume responsibility; creativity; reliability and constructiveness for maintaining balance; and living a rich, full life (McLeod, 2012; Rogers, 1961).

Abraham Maslow

Abraham Maslow's (1908–1970) *hierarchy of needs* (1943) is familiar to many as it has been widely used to understand and explain human motivation. Believing that human nature was either neutral or inherently good, Maslow broke with prevailing thinking and is credited with being the creative founder of the humanist approach to psychology. His argument that some needs take precedence over others was based on observation and critical analysis. He noted things such as the fact that when we are critically ill, our need for sleep overtakes our need for self-esteem; once we are rested and healthy, we can resume fulfilling our esteem needs and return to work. In Canada, the hierarchy of needs is realized in accordance with Canadian norms and standards of living, which are quite different from those in many parts of the world. For example, people in many countries do not have universal health care, nor is water so readily available.

Maslow applied the principle of *homeostasis*—the body's desire to maintain balance—to explain his theory. Homeostasis functions as an internal monitor, alerting us when we need to put on a sweater or quench our thirst. Similarly, the first four needs in the hierarchy (physiological, safety and security, love and belonging, esteem needs) are primarily physical in nature and go relatively unnoticed in Canadian life unless they are not met.

According to Maslow, the esteem needs have a "lower" and "higher" order. The lower-order esteem needs are satisfied when we experience respect and recognition from others. Because recognition from others is often temporary and elusive, it can be lost just as easily as it was gained. The higher-order self-esteem needs, however, are not so easily lost as they are based on the respect we have for ourselves. Feelings of self-confidence, competence, autonomy, and freedom characterize

Carl Rogers

Abraham Maslow

Evaluating the Humanist Approach

humanists Psychologists who believe people work hard to become the best they can possibly become.

congruence The relationship between a person's ideal self and real self as determined by self-selected descriptors.

incongruity The gap between the real self (the "I am") and the ideal self (the "I should be").

this higher order. If our esteem needs are not met, we may suffer from inferiority complexes. Maslow called these needs *D-needs*, or *deficit needs*. When one is not met, an individual experiences anxiety and is motivated to find a way to fulfill this need.

Maslow believed that the primarily physical needs become dormant once they are met, leaving us free to pursue more psychological needs. Being intelligent and restless by nature, we strive to use our capacities and develop to our fullest potential. Thus, Maslow expanded his original hierarchy to include cognitive and aesthetic needs as well as self-actualizing needs. These growth needs he called *being needs*, or *B-needs*. He believed that failure to develop and use our capacities results in atrophy, anxiety, and neuroses.

Believing that we turn from ugliness and that we feel calmer and healthier in beautiful surroundings, Maslow further postulated that we strive for what he termed aesthetic needs. When the earlier needs are met, we wish to create and surround ourselves with beauty. The creation of music, art, architecture, and museums, as well as our appreciation of nature, illustrate this need (Maslow, 1970).

Self-actualization *is the individualized expression of self in terms of reaching one's fullest potential without concern for praise or rewards.* He regarded self-actualization as peak moments during which we are able to transcend physical and social conventions. The more completely the earlier needs are satisfied, the more peak moments we can experience. If forced to live without the freedom to be one's authentic self, the self-actualizer is vulnerable to depression, despair, disgust, alienation, and a degree of cynicism. Maslow believed that only two percent of the population and few, if any, young people could attain self-actualization because social and economic pressures keep our internal monitors directed at filling deficits (Maslow, 1954, 1968, 1970).

Maslow postulated that "a desire to understand, to systematize, to organize, to analyze, to look for relations and meanings" is an innate cognitive need (Maslow, 1970, p. 385). He attempted to distinguish between, yet also rank in order of importance, the desire for information and the desire for understanding, and wrote, "insight is usually a bright, happy, emotional spot in any person's life, perhaps even a high spot in the life span" (Maslow, 1970, p. 158).

Evaluating the Humanist Approach

The contributions of the humanist approach are the positive regard for human nature and the consideration of the environment on development. Criticisms include that the interpretation is too subjective and the approach lacks scientific rigour.

To this point, we have discussed the humanist approach. For a review, see the **Reach Your Learning Objectives** section at the end of this chapter.

The Bio-Ecological Approach

LO6 Describe Bronfenbrenner's bio-ecological approach and illustrate how each system affects human growth and development.

Urie Bronfenbrenner

Urie Bronfenbrenner's (1917–2005) **bio-ecological approach** (1986, 2000, 2004) holds that development reflects the influence of five environmental systems (see Figure 2.5). The five environmental systems are:

- *Microsystem*—the setting in which the individual lives. These contexts include the person's family, peers, school, and neighbourhood. It is in the microsystem that the most direct interactions with social agents take place—with parents, peers, and teachers, for example. The individual is viewed not as a passive recipient of experiences in these settings, but as someone who helps construct them.
- *Mesosystem*—involves relations between microsystems or connections between contexts. Examples are the relation of family experiences to school experiences, school experiences to

self-actualization The individualized expression of self in terms of reaching one's fullest potential without concern for praise or rewards.

------ **critical** thinking ------

To what degree do you act in accordance with Maslow's hierarchy of needs? Can you think of times when you acted in a way that was consistent with this theory, and others when you did not? Do you think the theory holds true for most people in most situations? If you were living in a war-torn country such as Syria, how might Maslow's hierarchy of needs apply?

Urie Bronfenbrenner

Evaluating the Bio-Ecological Approach

bio-ecological approach Focuses on five environmental systems: microsystem, mesosystem, exosystem, macrosystem, and chronosystem.

church experiences, and family experiences to peer experiences. For example, children whose parents have rejected them may have difficulty developing positive relations with teachers.

- *Exosystem*—is involved when experiences in another social setting in which the individual does not have an active role influence what the individual experiences in an immediate context. For example, work experiences can affect a woman's relationship with her husband and their child. The mother might receive a promotion that requires more travel, which might increase marital conflict and change patterns of parent–child interaction.
- *Macrosystem*—the culture in which individuals live. Remember from Chapter 1 that culture refers to the behaviour patterns, beliefs, and all other products of a group of people that are passed on from generation to generation. Remember also that cross-cultural studies—the comparison of one culture with one or more other cultures—provide information about the generality of development. For example, Canadians believe paying taxes is vital to support education and health care.
- *Chronosystem*—the patterning of environmental events and transitions over the life course, as well as socio-historical circumstances. For example, the socio-historical aspects of social media differ remarkably depending on determinants such as age, education, socio-economic status, and geography. Babies born today in societies where Internet access is readily available will never experience the technological revolution in the same way as their parents or grandparents or those born in regions or countries without such access. Every year, technologies are redefining each of the systems, including personal space, individual behaviour, family life, education, health, community relationships, and work life, as well as legal boundaries and political systems.

Although Bronfenbrenner added biological influences to his theory, environmental contexts dominate (Bronfenbrenner & Morris, 1998, 2006; Ceci, 2000).

Evaluating the Bio-Ecological Approach

Contributions of the bio-ecological approach include a systematic examination of the macro- and micro-dimensions of environmental systems and attention to connections between environmental settings and historical influences. A further contribution of Bronfenbrenner's theory is an emphasis

Urie Bronfenbrenner developed the bio-ecological approach, a perspective that is receiving increased attention. His theory emphasizes the importance of both the micro- and macro-dimensions of the environment in which an individual lives.

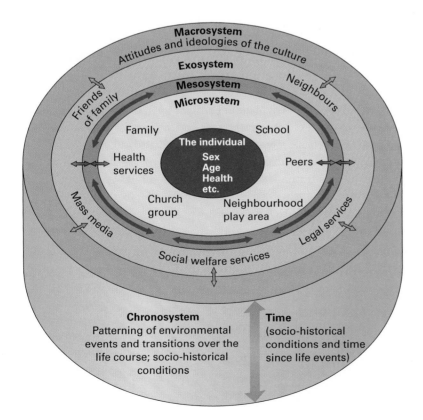

Figure 2.5

Bio-Ecological Theory of Development

Bronfenbrenner's bio-ecological theory consists of five environmental systems: microsystem, mesosystem, exosystem, macrosystem, and chronosystem.

critical thinking

Urie Bronfenbrenner argued that every child should have a champion, someone who would defend him or her no matter what. How would having such a champion enable the individual to cope with the various systems as an adult?

on a range of social contexts beyond the family, such as neighbourhood, religion, school, and workplace, as influential in children's development (Gauvain & Parke, 2010a, 2010b). Criticism includes giving inadequate attention to biological and cognitive factors.

To this point, we have discussed the bio-ecological approach. For a review, see the **Reach Your Learning Objectives** section at the end of this chapter.

Contemporary Approaches to Psychology

LO7 Compare and contrast four contemporary approaches to human growth and development.

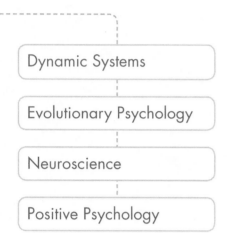

The historical approaches we have discussed thus far are quite divergent; nevertheless, they have provided an important springboard for contemporary research. Traditionally, the processes of our biological, cognitive, and socio-emotional development (see Chapter 1) have been considered separately; however, contemporary researchers are seeking frameworks that integrate these processes and explain our development in a more coherent way. Four relatively new approaches are dynamic systems, evolutionary psychology, neuroscience, and positive psychology.

Dynamic Systems

The dynamic systems (DS) approach attempts to encompass all that explains human growth and development. Esther Thelen of the University of Indiana (1941–) brought an entirely new approach to Piaget's learning theory by conducting a number of experiments investigating how babies learn to manage movement. Her experiments showed that instead of isolated brain development, learning is connected firmly to physical experience.

Based on her experiments, Thelen concluded that skill development, such as walking and later abstract thinking and formal operations, results from "perceiving the world and activity in it throughout life." In her presidential address to the Society for Research in Child Development, Thelen described how we might acquire skills via an embedded system—the nervous system—interacting with the rest of the body, which interacts with the world outside the body (Fausto-Sterling, 2011). This interaction among the nervous system, the rest of the body, and the surrounding environment helps us to make sense of the world and is called self-organization (Lewis, 2000).

According to Marc Lewis, formerly of the University of Toronto and now of Radboud University in the Netherlands, self-organization has four dominant characteristics: (1) it allows developmental spontaneity and novelty, (2) it becomes more complex and sophisticated with experience, (3) phase transition, or points of instability and turbulence, lead to new levels of complexity, and (4) self-organizing systems are both intrinsic and extrinsic due to the coupling of feedback with other systems, for example a toddler shifting from crawling to walking in response to the texture of the ground (Lewis, 2000).

The dynamic systems approach is being applied to a diverse range of activities, from coaching athletes to parenting.

Evolutionary Psychology

Natural selection and survival of the fittest—Darwin's signature theories, put forward in his book *On the Origin of Species* well over a century ago, in 1869—remain vital to today's discourse, forming the basis of the *nature versus nurture* debate that you read about in Chapter 1. Have we evolved from earlier and more primitive species? If so, how? Are we the product of our genetic makeup, our environment, or both? If both, which influence dominates? What adaptations have we made? How closely linked are these adaptations to our mate selection? How closely is mate selection linked to our survival? Evolutionary psychology synthesizes modern evolutionary biology and psychology in the search for meaning to life's penetrating mysteries—Why is sex so important? Why is the world riddled with so much conflict? (Buss, 2009). You will read more about genetic influence in Chapter 3.

Neuroscience

Fascinating discoveries about our brain, its development, and its ability to accommodate and heal have opened doorways to a relatively new area of study: neuroscience, the study of the brain, the nervous system, and the spinal column. The Chapter 1 opening vignette features the development and *neuroplasticity* of the brain. Thanks to modern imaging technology, contemporary neuroscientists can now observe how events trigger the formation of patterns in the brain in a self-organizing manner. Scientists are learning more and more about how the brain maps our personal narratives by connecting our experiences with neurotransmitters such as serotonin and dopamine (Lewis, 2000).

Research in the field is mushrooming, and for good reason. According to Brain Canada, "1 in 3 Canadians will be affected by a disease, disorder or injury of the brain, spinal cord or nervous system at some point in their lives" (Brain Canada, 2012, n.p.). Motivated by his own experience, Dr. Marc D. Lewis uses neuroscience to understand the brain's link to addictions. He proposes that the brain is attentive to all experience and our emotional responses to them (Lewis, 2012).

Other areas of investigation include causes and treatments of Parkinson's disease, Alzheimer's disease, autism, multiple sclerosis, and eating or sleep disorders (Canadian Association for Neuroscience, 2012).

Positive Psychology

Traditionally, psychology has concerned itself with illness—identifying, understanding, and treating conditions such as anxiety, stress, sadness, depression, delusions, neurosis, psychosis, and so forth. In doing so, the prominent approaches you just read about have contributed a wealth of information enabling us to better understand our motivations and cope with a host of disorders. Contemporary psychologists agree that all of this is important and helpful; however, in the words of "father of positive psychology" Martin Seligman, as a science "psychology can do better" (Seligman, 2004). He and Hungarian-born Mihaly Csikszentmihalyi, who is highly regarded for his work on creativity and flow, championed research in this area (APA, 2012). The result is an explosion of work on happiness, optimism, emotions, and healthy character traits.

So far, the findings indicate that we are most happy when what we're doing captivates our attention fully. Csikszentmihalyi defined this heightened state as "flow." Athletes, musicians, artists, and others sometimes refer to this state of total concentration as being "in the zone," or "in the moment." Time becomes inconsequential because purpose and the pleasure of the activity engage us completely. This heightened state usually, but not always, has three ingredients: pleasure, meaningfulness, and engagement. Frequently, pleasure comes last.

To this point, we have discussed contemporary approaches to psychology. For a review, see the **Reach Your Learning Objectives** section at the end of this chapter.

An Eclectic Theoretical Orientation

LO8 Discuss the eclectic approach.

Eclectic Approach

The Eclectic Approach

No single theory described in this chapter can explain entirely the rich complexity of life-span development, but each has contributed to our understanding of development. Psychoanalytic theory best explains the unconscious mind. Erikson's theory best describes the changes that occur in adult development. The views of Piaget, Vygotsky, and the information-processing approach provide the most complete description of cognitive development. The behavioural and social cognitive approaches of

Pavlov, Skinner, and Bandura give an adept examination of environmental determinants of development. On the other hand, the ethological approach of Darwin, Lorenz, and Bowlby has heightened today's awareness of biology's role and the importance of sensitive periods in development. The humanist approach of Rogers and Maslow contributes a more optimistic framework by theorizing that individuals strive to be the best they can possibly be. Bronfenbrenner's bio-ecological approach is adept at examining the role society plays in our development. The more contemporary approaches, such as neuroscience, dynamic systems, and positive psychology, further complement our understanding of learning, motivation, and development.

In short, although theories are helpful guides, relying on a single theory to explain development is probably a mistake. This book instead takes an **eclectic theoretical orientation**, *which does not follow any one theoretical approach but rather selects from each theory whatever is considered its best features.* In this way, you can view the study of development as it actually exists—with different theorists making different assumptions, stressing different empirical problems, and using different strategies to discover information.

The theories that we have discussed were developed at different points in history. Figure 2.6 shows when these theories were proposed.

These theoretical perspectives, along with the research methods and challenges discussed in Chapter 1, provide a sense of the scientific nature in the field of psychology. Context plays a major role in the formation of theories. For example, each generation is influenced by the building blocks provided by the generation before and contributes to the generations that follow. In 1935, Freud stated that he had reached the very climax of his psychoanalytic work in 1912, a year before Karen Horney received her medical degree (Horney, 1967). By the time Horney began publishing her findings, social and cultural paradigms, especially those related to women and culture, had shifted considerably.

The theorist chart available on Connect (www.mcgrawhillconnect.ca) is a chronological listing of the prominent theorists and their primary publications. Imagine the kind of debates Freud and Erikson may have had about whether personality is shaped more by psychosexual drives and repression or by social experiences. Perhaps Maslow and Rogers argued into the wee hours of the morning about whether all creatures strive for fulfillment, or whether only a few whose more basic needs had been met could realize their potential. Today, researchers such as Czikszentmihalyi, Elkind, Gilligan, Seligman, Thelen, and many others continue the study of human growth and development, building on the insights of past generations and opening up new avenues of debate, inquiry, and thought for today and for generations to come.

To this point, we have discussed an eclectic theoretical orientation. For a review, see the **Reach Your Learning Objectives** section at the end of this chapter.

eclectic theoretical orientation An orientation that does not follow any one theoretical approach, but rather selects the best features from each theory.

Figure 2.6

Timeline for Major Developmental Theories

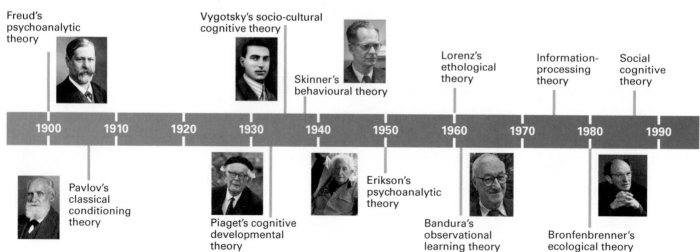

reach your learning objectives

The Psychoanalytic Approach

LO1 Describe the psychoanalytic approach and the contributions of major theorists.

Characteristics of the Psychoanalytic Approach	■ Development is primarily unconscious and influenced largely by emotion and biological factors. ■ Theorists attempt to analyze the symbolic meanings of behaviour to understand the inner workings of the mind. ■ Early experiences with caregivers shape development.
Sigmund Freud (1856–1939)	Freud's theory: ■ Personality is made up of the id, the ego, and the superego. ■ Conflicting demands of these structures produce anxiety and trigger defence mechanisms. ■ Freud was convinced that problems develop because of early experiences. ■ Freud believed individuals go through five psychosexual stages: oral, anal, phallic, latent, and genital.
Erik Erikson (1902–1994)	Erikson emphasized eight psychosocial stages of development: ■ trust versus mistrust ■ autonomy versus shame and doubt ■ initiative versus guilt ■ industry versus inferiority ■ identity versus identity confusion ■ intimacy versus isolation ■ generativity versus stagnation ■ integrity versus despair No stage is completely resolved; however, when balance is achieved virtues, or emotional strengths, emerge in the healthy personality.
Other Psychoanalytic Theories (the Neo-Freudians)	Alfred Adler (1870–1937) ■ Developed individual psychology and believed that striving for perfection to fulfill one's potential is the single motivating drive behind all behaviour. Carl Jung (1875–1961) ■ Believed the psyche had three parts: the ego or the conscious mind, the personal unconscious, and the collective unconscious. Karen Horney (1885–1952) ■ Criticized Freud's argument on the grounds of gender and cultural differences. Anna Freud (1895–1982) ■ Opened the field of psychoanalysis to include children and adolescents. Eric Fromm (1900–1980) ■ Believed human nature to be influenced by dysfunctional social patterns.
Evaluating the Psychoanalytic Approach	■ The contribution of psychoanalytic thought is its emphasis on a developmental framework, the role of parents or caregivers, and the role of the unconscious in personality growth and development. ■ Criticisms are that the theories lack scientific rigour, portray human nature negatively, and do not adequately factor in culture and gender differences.

The Cognitive Approach

LO2 Compare and contrast the theories within the cognitive approach.

Piaget's Cognitive Developmental Theory	■ Children play an active role in their cognitive development. ■ Children use the processes of assimilation and accommodation to understand their world. ■ Children go through four cognitive stages: sensorimotor, preoperational, concrete operational, and formal operational. ■ Neo-Piagetian Robbie Case extended Piaget's theory to include aspects of culture, information processing, linguistics, and neuroscience.
Vygotsky's Socio-Cultural Cognitive Theory	■ Social and cultural contexts are primary factors in a child's development. ■ Knowledge is situated and collaborative. ■ Interaction with skillful adults or peers is essential for cognitive development.
The Information-Processing Approach	■ Emphasizes that individuals manipulate information, monitor it, and strategize about it. ■ Thinking is a form of information processing.
Evaluating the Cognitive Approach	■ Contributions include an emphasis on the active construction of understanding. ■ One criticism is that the approach gives too little attention to individual variation.

The Behavioural and Social Cognitive Approach

LO3 Discuss and examine the behavioural and social cognitive approach, including the contributions of Pavlov, Skinner, and Bandura.

Pavlov's Classical Conditioning (1849–1936)	■ Demonstrated that a neutral stimulus acquires the ability to produce a response originally produced by another stimulus.
Skinner's Operant Conditioning (1904–1990)	■ Demonstrated that the consequences of a behaviour produce changes in the probability of the behaviour's future occurrence.
Bandura's Social Cognitive Theory (1925–)	■ Emphasized that cognitive processes are important mediators of environment–behaviour connections. Observational learning, or imitation and modelling, is cognitive in that individuals sometimes adopt the behaviours of others.
Evaluating the Behavioural and Social Cognitive Approach	■ Emphasized scientific research and the role of environmental determinants of behaviour. ■ Too little emphasis on cognition and inadequate attention to developmental changes.

The Ethological Approach

LO4 Describe the ethological approach and distinguish among the major contributions of Darwin, Lorenz, Bowlby, and Goodall.

Charles Darwin (1809–1882)	■ One of the first theorists to note the connection between animal behaviour and human behaviour. ■ Developed the theory of evolution and natural selection.
Konrad Lorenz (1903–1989)	■ Won the Nobel Prize in 1973 for his study establishing the key concepts of imprinting and critical periods.
John Bowlby (1907–1990)	■ Often called the "father of attachment theory" for his work on the innate bond between infant and caregiver.
Jane Goodall (1934–)	■ Ethologist and animal activist who has documented in chimpanzees behaviours previously believed to be specific to humans.
Evaluating the Ethological Approach	■ Contributions include a focus on the biological and evolutionary bases of development. ■ Criticisms include a belief that the critical and sensitive period concepts are too rigid.

The Humanist Approach

LO5 Describe and evaluate the humanist approach, including the contributions of Rogers and Maslow.

Carl Rogers (1902–1987)	■ Reshaped the interaction between client and therapist. ■ Believed all living creatures worked hard to realize their fullest potential.
Abraham Maslow (1908–1970)	■ Defined a hierarchy of needs: physiological, safety and security, love and belonging, esteem, and self-actualization.
Evaluating the Humanist Approach	■ Contributed to establishing a positive regard for human nature. ■ Criticisms include unscientific methods of study.

The Bio-Ecological Approach

LO6 Describe Bronfenbrenner's bio-ecological approach and illustrate how each system affects human growth and development.

Urie Bronfenbrenner (1917–2005)	■ Identified five environmental systems that impact individual growth and development: microsystem, mesosystem, exosystem, macrosystem, and chronosystem.
Evaluating the Bio-Ecological Approach	■ Contributions include a systematic explanation of environmental systems and the connections between these systems. ■ One criticism is that inadequate attention is given to biological and cognitive factors.

Contemporary Approaches to Psychology

LO7 Compare and contrast four contemporary approaches to human growth and development.

Dynamic Systems	■ This approach posits that human growth and development is linked to physical experience, which becomes embedded in the nervous system.
Evolutionary Psychology	■ Scientific study in this approach synthesizes modern evolutionary biology and psychology in a search for meaning to life's penetrating mysteries, such as why sex is so important and why the world is riddled with so much conflict.
Neuroscience	■ Scientific study of the brain, the nervous system, and the spinal cord in an effort to understand how these organs and systems work, as well as how to respond when they malfunction.
Positive Psychology	■ This approach contends that understanding happiness can facilitate human growth and development.

An Eclectic Theoretical Orientation

LO8 Discuss the eclectic approach.

The Eclectic Approach	■ Because of the diversity theories, many psychologists (and this text) will select one or a combination of approaches depending what fits best with a particular context.

review ---→ *connect* ---→ reflect

McGraw-Hill Connect provides you with a powerful tool for improving academic performance and truly mastering course material. You can diagnose your knowledge with pre- and post-tests, identify the areas where you need help, search the entire learning package, including the eBook, for content specific to the topic you're studying, and add these resources to your personalized study plan. CONNECT for *Life-Span Development*, fifth Canadian edition, offers the following:

- chapter-specific online quizzes
- groupwork
- presentations
- writing assignments
- case studies
- and much more!

Visit CONNECT today!

review

What are the main psychoanalytic theories? **LO1**

What are some contributions and criticisms of psychoanalytic theories? **LO1**

What are three main cognitive theories? **LO2**

What are some contributions and criticisms of cognitive theories? **LO2**

What are two main behavioural and social cognitive theories? **LO3**

What are some contributions and criticisms of behavioural and social cognitive theories? **LO3**

What is the nature of ethological theory? **LO4**

Which psychologists contributed to the humanistic theory? **LO5**

What are some contributions and criticisms of Bronfenbrenner's bio-ecological theory? **LO6**

What differentiates the approach of the neuroscience theory and the dynamic systems approach? **LO7**

What is an eclectic theoretical orientation? **LO8**

connect

Karen Horney considers child neglect the most damaging type of child maltreatment because the child can not fight back. Imagine that you believe a child you know, perhaps one in your neighbourhood, is being neglected. On what evidence do you base your suspicion? What might be the long-term implications of this neglect? What theories outlined in this chapter might be useful in helping this child?

reflect *Your Own Personal Journey of Life*

Imagine what your development would have been like in a culture that offered fewer or distinctly different choices. How might your development have been different if your family had been significantly richer or poorer?

CHAPTER 3

Biological Beginnings

CHAPTER OUTLINE

The Evolutionary Perspective

LO1   Discuss the evolutionary perspective on life-span development.

Natural Selection and Adaptive Behaviour

Evolutionary Psychology

Genetic Foundations

LO2   Describe what genes are and how they influence human development.

The Collaborative Gene

Genes and Chromosomes

Genetic Principles

Chromosome and Gene-Linked Variations

The Human Genome Project

Reproduction Challenges and Choices

LO3   Identify some important reproductive challenges and choices.

Prenatal Diagnostic Tests

Infertility and Reproductive Technology

Adoption

Heredity–Environment Interaction: The Nature–Nurture Debate

LO4   Explain some of the ways that heredity and environment interact to produce individual differences in development.

Behaviour Genetics

Heredity–Environment Correlations

Shared and Nonshared Environmental Experiences

The Epigenetic View

Conclusions about Heredity–Environment Interaction

> " *There are one hundred and ninety-three living species of monkeys and apes. One hundred and ninety-two of them are covered with hair. The exception is the naked ape, self-named Homo sapiens.* "
>
> —DESMOND MORRIS, CONTEMPORARY BRITISH ZOOLOGIST

Three Dilemmas

After three years of marriage, Usha and Henri think they would like to have a baby. Henri's younger brother is autistic and Henri isn't sure if he carries the gene for this condition. Usha's cousin has the mental age of three months although she is 10 years old. These troubling thoughts are a barrier to their having children. However, recently Usha and Henri have learned that some prenatal procedures can diagnose brain conditions in the fetus. They decide they will undergo genetic screening before becoming pregnant to see if they carry the genes involved in autism and brain conditions.

Stephanie and her partner, Ray, have learned through maternal serum screening that their unborn child could be born with Down syndrome. Stephanie, who has worked as a volunteer with physically challenged children, knows that many resources are available, including support groups for parents and families. They realize that one of them will likely have to forgo a successful career in order to provide adequate home care and support for their child, because most of the resources they will need are not government subsidized. They worry about their financial strength and have sought genetic counselling. The thought that "Every child brings his or her own special love" echoes in Stephanie's mind.

Moira and her partner Joanne are considering in vitro fertilization so they can have a child. Moira's parents are thrilled at the prospect of becoming grandparents, but Joanne's parents are anxious because they will have to acknowledge their daughter's homosexual relationship publicly, plus they harbour concerns about a child raised by homosexual parents. Everyone involved worries about the safety and expenses of the procedure.

Are we, as Urie Bronfenbrenner suggests, intensified by our environment? Or are we very much a product of our inherited genetic makeup? Does the presence of grandparents influence decisions and choices, or are our decisions and choices more influenced by information gathered on the Internet? Environmental experiences and biological foundations work together to make us who we are. Our coverage of life's biological beginnings in this chapter focuses on theories and research about evolution, genetic foundations, reproduction challenges and choices, and the interaction of heredity and environment.

What if parents could choose the genetic makeup of their child? Would they choose the child's gender, physical attractiveness, intelligence, and strength? What are some of the factors you would consider if you were in a situation like one of these?

The Evolutionary Perspective

LO1 Discuss the evolutionary perspective on life-span development.

In evolutionary time humans are relative newcomers to Earth, yet we have established ourselves as the most successful and dominant species. As our earliest ancestors left the forest to feed on the savannah, and finally to form hunting societies on the open plains, their minds and behaviours changed. How did this evolution come about?

Natural Selection and Adaptive Behaviour

Evolutionary Psychology

Natural Selection and Adaptive Behaviour

Natural selection is the evolutionary process that favours individuals of a species that are best adapted to survive and reproduce. Recall that in Chapter 2 you read about Charles Darwin, who, after extensive travel observing many different species of animals in their natural surroundings, published his observations and thoughts in *On the Origin of Species* over a century ago in 1859. Darwin noted that most organisms reproduce at rates that would cause enormous increases in the population of many species, and yet populations remain nearly constant. He reasoned that an intense, constant struggle for food, water, and resources must occur among the young because many do not survive. Those that do survive pass on their genes to the next generation. Darwin believed that the survivors are better adapted and more able to reproduce than the non-survivors to their world (Brooker, 2011). Over the course of many generations, this could produce a gradual modification of the whole population. Dramatic environmental changes such as non-normative events occur, other characteristics emerge or become favoured, and the process of natural selection could move the species in a different direction (Mader, 2011).

All organisms must adapt to particular places, climates, food sources, and ways of life (Audesirk, Audesirk, & Byers, 2011). Adaptive behaviour is behaviour that promotes an organism's survival in the natural habitat (Johnson & Losos, 2010). For example, attachment between a caregiver and a baby ensures the infant's closeness to a caregiver for feeding and protection from danger, thus increasing the infant's chances of survival. For an illustration of the brain sizes of various primates and humans in relation to the length of the childhood period, see Figure 3.1.

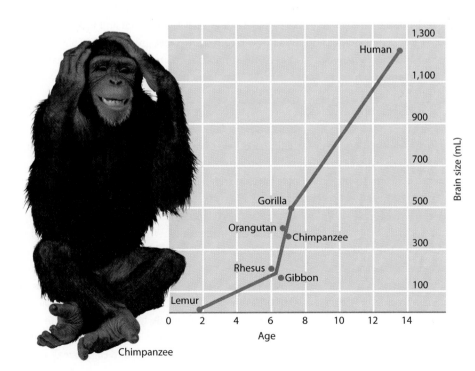

Chimpanzee

Figure 3.1

The Brain Sizes of Various Primates and Humans in Relation to the Length of the Childhood Period

Compared with other primates, humans have both a larger brain and a longer childhood period. **What conclusions can you draw from the relationship indicated by this graph?**

Evolutionary Psychology

evolutionary psychology A contemporary approach that emphasizes that behaviour is a function of mechanisms, requires input for activation, and is ultimately related to survival and reproduction.

Darwin's theory of evolution by natural selection, introduced in 1859, has recently become popular as a framework for explaining behaviour (Silverman, 2003). One of psychology's contemporary approaches, introduced in Chapter 2, **evolutionary psychology**, *emphasizes the importance of adaptation, reproduction, and "survival of the fittest" in explaining behaviour.* "Fit" in this sense refers to the ability to bear offspring that survive long enough to bear offspring of their own. The evolutionary process of natural selection favours behaviours that increase organisms' reproductive success and their ability to pass their genes to the next generation (Bjorklund, 2006; Geary, 2006).

David Buss (1999, 2000, 2008) has been especially influential in stimulating new interest in how evolution can explain human behaviour. He reasons that just as evolution shapes our physical features, such as body shape and height, it also pervasively influences how we make decisions, how aggressive we are, our fears, and our mating patterns. For example, assume that our ancestors were hunters and gatherers on the plains and that men did most of the hunting and women stayed close to home gathering seeds and plants for food. If you have to travel some distance from your home in an effort to find and slay a fleeing animal, you need not only certain physical traits but also the ability for certain types of spatial thinking. Men born with these traits would be more likely than men without them to survive, to bring home lots of food, and to be considered attractive mates—and thus to reproduce and pass on these characteristics to their children. In other words, these traits would provide a reproductive advantage for males; consequently, over many generations, men with good spatial thinking skills might become more numerous in the population. Critics point out that this scenario might or might not have actually happened.

Evolution and Development

Recently, interest has grown in using the concepts of evolutionary psychology to understand human development (Bjorklund, 2006, 2007; Geary, 2006). A few ideas proposed by evolutionary developmental psychologists (Bjorklund & Pellegrini, 2002, pp. 336–340) include the following:

- *An extended juvenile period evolved because humans require time to develop a large brain and learn the complexity of human social communities.* Humans take longer to become reproductively mature than any other mammal.
- *"Many aspects of childhood function as preparations for adulthood and were selected over the course of evolution."* Play is one possible example. Beginning in the preschool years, boys in all cultures engage in more rough-and-tumble play than girls. Perhaps rough-and-tumble play prepares boys for fighting and hunting as adults. In contrast to boys, girls engage in play that involves more imitation of parents, such as caring for dolls. This, according to evolutionary psychologists, is an evolved tendency that prepares females for becoming the primary caregivers for their offspring.
- *Some characteristics of childhood were selected because they are adaptive at specific points in development, not because they prepare children for adulthood.* For example, some aspects of play may function not to prepare us for adulthood, but to help children adapt to their immediate circumstances, perhaps to learn about their current environment. Sports activities illustrate this concept. Although very few people become professional athletes, many children enjoy participating in a variety of sports activities.
- *Many evolved psychological mechanisms are domain-specific.* That is, the mechanisms apply to only a specific aspect of a person's makeup (Atkinson & Wheeler, 2004; Rubenstein, 2004). According to evolutionary psychology, information processing is one example. In this view, the mind is not a general-purpose device that can be applied equally to a vast array of problems. Instead, as our ancestors dealt with certain recurring problems, specialized modules evolved that process information related to those problems. This includes a module for physical knowledge, a module for mathematical knowledge, and a module for language. Also in this view, "infants enter the world 'prepared' to process and learn some information more readily than others, and these preparations serve as the foundation for social and cognitive development"

(p. 338). For example, much as goslings in Lorenz's experiment (described in Chapter 2) were "prepared" to follow their mother, human infants are biologically prepared to learn the sounds that are part of human language.

■ *Evolved mechanisms are not always adaptive in contemporary society.* Some behaviours that were adaptive for our prehistoric ancestors may not serve us well today. For example, the food-scarce environment of our ancestors likely led to humans' gorging and craving high-caloric foods. This trait, as adaptive as it may seem, might be partially responsible for the growing number of obese children in the world.

Humans, more than any other animal, adapt to and control most types of environments. Because of longer parental care, humans learn more complex behaviour patterns, which contribute to adaptation. **What are some other adaptive aspects of human behaviour that might be tied to evolution?**

Connecting Evolution and Life-Span Development

In evolutionary theory, what matters is that individuals live long enough to reproduce and pass on their genetic characteristics (Johnson, 2006; Mader, 2006, 2007; Promislow, Fedorka, & Burger, 2006; Raven, 2011). Why, then, do humans live so long after viable reproduction? Perhaps evolution favoured longevity because the work and presence of social elders improves the survival rates of babies. For example, the ability of grandparents to care for the young while parents were out hunting and gathering food created an evolutionary advantage. In contemporary terms, grandparents are caring for children whose parents have died from the AIDS pandemic or whose lives are severely affected by poverty.

According to life-span developmentalist Paul Baltes (2003), the benefits of evolutionary selection decrease with age. Natural selection has not weeded out many conditions and nonadaptive characteristics that mostly affect older adults such as dementia and arthritis. Why? Natural selection operates primarily on characteristics that are tied to reproductive fitness, which extends through the earlier part of adulthood. Thus, says Baltes, selection primarily operates during the first half of life.

Unaided by evolutionary pressures against nonadaptive conditions, we suffer the aches, pains, and infirmities of aging. And as the benefits of evolutionary selection decrease with age, argues Baltes, the need for culture increases (see Figure 3.2). That is, as older adults weaken biologically, they need culture-based resources such as cognitive skills, literacy, medical technology, and social support. For example, older adults may need help and training from other people to maintain their cognitive skills (Knight & Sayegh, 2010).

A concrete example of a decrease in evolutionary-selection benefits in older adults involves Alzheimer's disease, a progressive, irreversible brain disorder characterized by gradual deterioration. This disease does not typically appear before age 70. If the disease struck 20-year-olds, perhaps natural selection would have eliminated it eons before the birth of Dr. Alois Alzheimer, the German physician who first discovered the anatomical changes in the brain associated with it (Alzheimer Society, 2009a). Possibly, diseases such as Alzheimer's emerge in later life because evolutionary pressures based on reproductive fitness do not select against individuals prone to them.

Evaluating Evolutionary Psychology

Evolutionary psychology is one theoretical approach, and like other approaches, it has limitations, weaknesses, and critics. Albert Bandura (1998), whose social cognitive theory was described in Chapter 2, acknowledges the important influence of evolution on human adaptation and change. However, he rejects what he calls "one-sided evolutionism," which sees social behaviour as the product of evolved biology. An alternative is the *bi-directional view*, in which environment and biological conditions influence each other. Evolutionary pressures created changes in biological structures for the use of tools, which enabled organisms to manipulate, alter, and construct new environmental conditions. Increasingly complex environmental innovations in turn produced new selection pressures for the evolution of specialized biological systems for consciousness, thought, and language.

Human evolution gave us bodily structures and biological potentialities, but does not dictate behaviour. Having evolved, advanced biological capacities can be used to produce diverse cultures—aggressive, pacific, egalitarian, or autocratic. The "big picture" idea of natural selection leading to the development of human traits and behaviours is difficult to refute or test because it is on a time

Figure 3.2

Baltes's View of Evolution and Culture across the Life Span

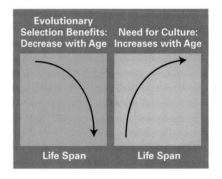

developmental **connection**

Bandura's Social Cognitive Theory

scale that does not lend itself to empirical study. Thus, studying specific genes in humans and other species—and their links to traits and behaviours—may be a more effective approach for testing ideas emanating from evolutionary psychology.

To this point, we have discussed the evolutionary perspective. For a review, see the **Reach Your Learning Objectives** section at the end of this chapter.

Genetic Foundations

LO2 Describe what genes are and how they influence human development.

Every species must have a mechanism for transmitting characteristics from one generation to the next. This mechanism is explained by the principles of genetics. Each of us carries a genetic code that we inherited from our parents. This code is located within every cell in our bodies. Our genetic codes are alike in one important way—they all contain the human genetic code. Because of the human genetic code, a fertilized human egg cannot grow into an egret, eagle, or elephant.

Genetics is a fascinating, complex field and researchers are discovering new intricacies almost daily. Darwin's cousin, Francis Galton, engaged in twin studies and their relationship to heredity in 1876 (Minnesota Centre, 2012). About a century later, in 1979, the Minnesota Study of Twins Reared Apart, undertaken by Thomas Bouchard and his colleagues, brought identical twins (identical genetically because they come from the same fertilized egg) and fraternal twins (dissimilar genetically because they come from different fertilized eggs) who had been separated at birth or shortly thereafter to Minneapolis from all over the world in order to investigate their lives (Bouchard et al., 1990). They found genetically identical twins who had been separated as infants showed striking similarities in their tastes and habits and choices, including the names they chose for their children, the types of jobs they held, the names of their spouses, or unique behaviours they exhibited. Can we conclude that their genes must have caused the development of those similar tastes and habits and choices? Other possible causes need to be considered.

The twins shared not only the same genes but also many common experiences. Some of the separated twins lived together for several months prior to their adoption; some of the twins had been reunited prior to testing (in some cases, many years earlier); adoption agencies often place twins in similar homes; and even strangers who spend several hours together and start comparing their lives are likely to come up with some coincidental similarities (Joseph, 2006). The Minnesota study of identical twins points to both the importance of the genetic basis of human development and the need for further research on genetic and environmental factors (Lykken, 2001).

And, of course, further research is ongoing. For example, a team of researchers from the University of Western Ontario have also been investigating the genetic makeup of twins. One might believe that identical twins would be totally identical; for example, if one twin had schizophrenia, wouldn't the other suffer from the same disease? However, their studies revealed that growth and development (mitosis and meiosis, discussed later in this chapter) create additional changes in our genetic makeup, even adding new DNA. These studies continue to further our understanding of evolution and genetic individuality, showing that each of us is unique (Maiti et al., 2011).

The Collaborative Gene

Each of us began life as a single cell weighing about one-fifty-millionth of a gram. Imagine! This tiny piece of matter housed our genetic code—instructions that orchestrated growth from that single cell to a person made of trillions of cells, each containing information that replicates the original genetic code.

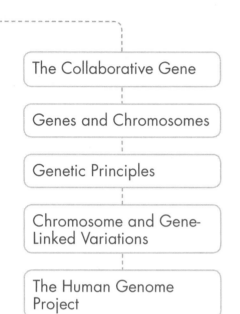

The Collaborative Gene

Genes and Chromosomes

Genetic Principles

Chromosome and Gene-Linked Variations

The Human Genome Project

Figure 3.3

Cells, Chromosomes, Genes, and DNA

(Left) The body contains trillions of cells, which are the basic structural units of life. Each cell contains a central structure, the nucleus. *(Middle)* Chromosomes and genes are located in the nucleus of the cell. Chromosomes are made up of threadlike structures composed of DNA molecules. *(Right)* A gene, a segment of DNA that contains the hereditary code. The structure of DNA is a spiralled double chain.

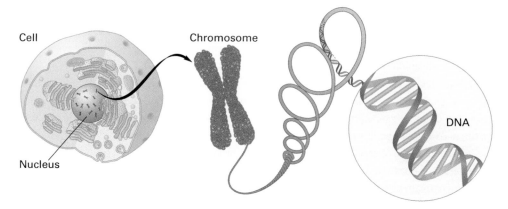

Cell Chromosome DNA Nucleus

The nucleus of each human cell contains **chromosomes,** *which are threadlike structures that are made up of deoxyribonucleic acid, or DNA.* **DNA** *is a complex molecule that has a double helix shape (like a spiral staircase), and contains genetic information.* **Genes,** *the units of hereditary information, are short segments composed of DNA.* Genes act as a blueprint for cells to reproduce themselves and manufacture the proteins that maintain life. Proteins are the building blocks of cells as well as the regulators that direct the body's processes (Freeman, 2011). As noted earlier, chromosomes, DNA, and genes change during meiosis and mitosis (Maiti et al., 2011). Figure 3.3 will help you turn mystery to understanding.

Genes and Chromosomes

Genes are not only collaborative; they are enduring. How do the genes manage to get passed from generation to generation and end up in all of the trillion cells in the body? Three processes explain the heart of the story: mitosis, meiosis, and fertilization.

Mitosis, Meiosis, and Fertilization

All cells in your body, except the sperm and egg, have 46 chromosomes arranged in 23 pairs. These cells reproduce by a process called mitosis. During **mitosis,** *the cell's nucleus—including the chromosomes—duplicates itself and the cell divides.* Two new cells are formed, each containing the same DNA as the original cell, arranged in the same 23 pairs of chromosomes.

However, a different type of cell division—meiosis—forms eggs and sperm (or gametes). During **meiosis,** *a cell of the testes (in men) or ovaries (in women) duplicates its chromosomes but then divides twice, thus forming four cells, each of which has only half of the genetic material of the parent cell* (Klug et al., 2010). By the end of meiosis, each egg or sperm has 23 unpaired chromosomes.

During **fertilization,** *an egg and a sperm fuse to create a single cell, called a zygote* (see Figure 3.4). In the **zygote,** *the 23 unpaired chromosomes from the egg and the 23 unpaired chromosomes from the sperm combine to form one set of 23 paired chromosomes*—one chromosome of each pair from the mother's egg and the other from the father's sperm. In this manner, each parent contributes half of the offspring's genetic material.

chromosomes Threadlike structures that are made up of deoxyribonucleic acid, or DNA.

DNA (deoxyribonucleic acid) A molecule in the shape of a double helix; contains genetic information.

genes Units of hereditary information composed of DNA; act as a blueprint for cells to reproduce themselves and manufacture the proteins that maintain life.

mitosis The process of cellular division during which cellular material is duplicated and two daughter cells are formed.

meiosis The process of cellular division that divides sex cells and produces four daughter cells, each with 23 single chromosomes.

fertilization The process that, in humans, begins when a female gamete (ovum) fuses with a male gamete (sperm) to create a zygote.

zygote A single cell formed when an ovum is fertilized by a sperm.

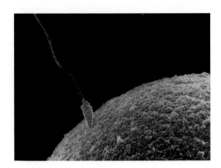

-------------------------------- **Figure 3.4**

Union of Sperm and Egg

-------- **critical** thinking --------

Although Genome Canada (2012) is funding a host of exciting research initiatives, some have warned that many of these initiatives raise a host of complex ethical issues including the nature of life. What are the arguments for and against developments such as cloning, genetic screening, and genetically modified foods? Should our genetic information be stored? If so, who should have access? Should we patent our genes? Or, should we weed out undesirable genetic traits? If so, who decides which traits are desirable and which are not?

genotype A person's genetic heritage; the actual genetic material.

phenotype The way an individual's genotype is expressed in observed and measurable characteristics.

Sources of Variability

Combining the genes of two parents in offspring increases genetic variability in the population, which is valuable for a species because it provides more characteristics for natural selection. In fact, the human genetic process creates several important sources of variability.

First, the chromosomes in the zygote are not exact copies of those in the mother's ovaries and the father's testes. During the formation of the sperm and egg in meiosis, the members of each pair of chromosomes are separated, but which chromosome in the pair goes to the gamete is a matter of chance. In addition, before the pairs separate, pieces of the two chromosomes in each pair are exchanged, creating a new combination of genes on each chromosome (Mader, 2011). Thus, when chromosomes from the mother's egg and the father's sperm are brought together in the zygote, the result is a truly unique combination of genes (Starr, Evers, & Starr, 2010).

If each zygote is unique, how do identical twins exist? *Identical twins* (also called monozygotic twins) develop from a single zygote that splits into two genetically identical replicas, each of which becomes a person. *Fraternal twins* (called dizygotic twins) develop from separate eggs and separate sperm, making them genetically no more similar than ordinary siblings.

A second source of variability comes from DNA (Brooker, 2011). Chance, a mistake by cellular machinery, or damage from an environmental agent such as radiation may produce a *mutated gene*, which is a permanently altered segment of DNA (Lewis, 2010).

There is increasing interest in studying susceptibility genes, those that make the individual more vulnerable to specific diseases or acceleration of aging, and longevity genes, those that make the individual less vulnerable to certain diseases and be more likely to live to an older age (Marques, Markus, & Morris, 2010; Tacutu, Budovsky, & Fraifeld, 2010). Even when their genes are identical, however, people vary. The difference between genotypes and phenotypes helps us to understand this source of variability. *All of a person's genetic material makes up his or her* **genotype**. However, not all of the genetic material is apparent in our observed and measurable characteristics. A **phenotype** *consists of observable characteristics*. Phenotypes include physical characteristics (such as height, weight, and hair colour) and psychological characteristics (such as personality and intelligence).

For each genotype, a range of phenotypes can be expressed, providing another source of variability (Gottlieb, 2007; Meaney, 2010). An individual can inherit the genetic potential to grow very large, for example, but good nutrition, among other things, will be essential to achieving that potential.

Calvin and Hobbes © 1991 Watterson. Reprinted with permission of Universal Press Syndicate. All rights reserved.

Genetic Principles

Genetic determination is a complex affair, and much is unknown about the way genes work (Starr, 2011). Three genetic principles such as dominant–recessive genes, sex-linked genes, and polygenically inherited characteristics are outlined here.

Dominant–Recessive Genes Principle

A recessive gene exerts its influence only if both genes of a pair are recessive. If you inherit a recessive gene for a trait from both your parents, you will show the trait. If you inherit a recessive gene from only one parent, you may never know you carry the gene. Brown eyes, farsightedness, and dimples rule over blue eyes, nearsightedness, and freckles in the world of dominant recessive genes.

Can two brown-eyed parents have a blue-eyed child? Yes, they can. Since dominant genes override recessive genes, the parents have brown eyes, but both are carriers of blueness and pass on their recessive genes for blue eyes. With no dominant gene to override them, the recessive genes can make the child's eyes blue.

Figure 3.5 shows 23 paired chromosomes of a male and female. The members of each pair of chromosomes are both similar and different: each chromosome in the pair contains varying forms of the same genes, at the same location on the chromosome. A gene for hair colour, for example, is located in the same place on both members of the same pairing. However, one of those chromosomes might carry the gene for blond hair and the other for brown hair.

Do you notice any obvious differences between the chromosomes of the male and the chromosomes of the female in Figure 3.5? The difference lies in the 23rd pair. Ordinarily, in females this pair consists of two chromosomes called X chromosomes; in males, the 23rd pair consists of an X and a Y chromosome. The presence of a Y chromosome is what makes an individual male.

Sex-Linked Genes

Most mutated genes are recessive. When a mutated gene is carried on the X chromosome, the result is called *X-linked inheritance* (Turner, 2006). The implications for males may be very different from those of females (Agrelo & Wutz, 2010). Remember that males have only one X chromosome. Thus, if there is an altered, disease-creating gene on the X chromosome, males have no "backup" copy to counter the harmful gene and therefore may carry an X-linked disease. However, females have a second X chromosome, which is likely to be unchanged. As a result, they are not likely to have the X-linked disease. Thus, most individuals who have X-linked diseases are males. Females who have one changed copy of the X gene are known as "carriers," and they usually do not show any signs of the X-linked disease. Thus, they may not realize they are carriers until they have male children.

Figure 3.5 --

The Genetic Difference between Males and Females

Set (a) shows the chromosome structure of a male, and set (b) shows the chromosome structure of a female. The last pair of 23 pairs of chromosomes is in the bottom right box of each set. Note that the Y chromosome of the male is smaller than the X chromosome of the female. To obtain this kind of chromosomal picture, a cell is removed from a person's body, usually from the inside of the mouth. The chromosomes are stained by chemical treatment, magnified, and then photographed.

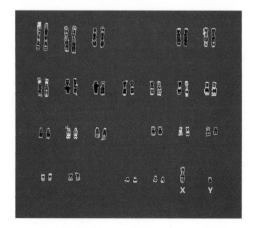
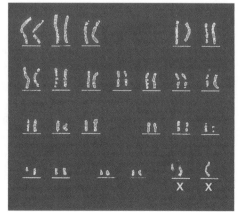

Hemophilia and fragile X syndrome are examples of X-linked inheritance (Gonzalez-del Angel et al., 2000; Rogaev et al., 2009).

Genetic Imprinting

Genetic imprinting occurs when genes have differing effects depending on whether they are inherited from the mother or the father (Zaitoun et al., 2010). A chemical process "silences" one member of the gene pair. For example, as a result of imprinting, only the maternally derived copy of a gene might be active, while the paternally derived copy of the same gene is silenced—or vice versa. Only a small percentage of human genes appear to undergo imprinting, but it is a normal and important aspect of development (Koerner & Barlow, 2010). When imprinting goes awry, development is disturbed, as in the case of Beckwith-Wiedemann syndrome, a growth variation, and Wilms' tumour, a type of cancer (Hartwig et al., 2010).

POLYGENIC INHERITANCE   Genetic transmission is usually more complex than the simple examples we have examined thus far (Brooker, 2011). Few characteristics reflect the influence of only a single gene or pair of genes. Most are determined by the interaction of many different genes; they are said to be polygenically determined (Meaney, 2010). Even a simple characteristic such as height, for example, reflects the interaction of many genes, as well as the influence of the environment. Most diseases, such as cancer and diabetes, develop as a consequence of complex gene interactions and environmental factors (Ekeblad, 2010; Vimaleswaran & Loos, 2010).

The term *gene–gene interaction* is increasingly used to describe studies that focus on the interdependence of two or more genes in influencing characteristics, behaviours, diseases, and development (Costanzo & et al., 2010). For example, recent studies have documented gene–gene interaction in cancer (Chen et al., 2009) and cardiovascular disease (Jylhava et al., 2009).

Chromosome and Gene-Linked Variations

Variations can be produced by an uneven number of chromosomes; they can also result from harmful genes.

Chromosome Variations

When gametes are formed, the 46 chromosomes do not always divide evenly. In this case, the resulting sperm and ovum do not have their normal 23 chromosomes. The most notable instances when this occurs involve Down syndrome and gene-linked variations (see Figure 3.6).

Other diseases that result from genetic variations include cystic fibrosis, diabetes, hemophilia, Huntington's disease, spina bifida, and Tay-Sachs disease. Someday, scientists may identify why these and other genetic variations occur and discover cures. The Human Genome Project has already linked specific DNA variations with increased risk of a number of diseases and conditions, including Huntington's disease (in which the central nervous system deteriorates), some forms of cancer, asthma, diabetes, hypertension, and Alzheimer's disease.

Gene-Linked Variations

Variations not only can be produced by an uneven number of chromosomes, but also can result from harmful genes (Croyle, 2000). Apart from the single pair of sex chromosomes, the 22 other pairs of chromosomes are referred to as autosomes and account for most of the genetic disorders. The inheritance of the disorders follows one of two paths, either *autosomal-dominant* or *autosomal-recessive*. In the autosomal-dominant pattern, one parent will usually be affected with the disorder. If only one parent has the dominant gene, then half the children will exhibit the disorder. If both parents have the gene, then all the children will have the disorder. Examples of disorders generated by the autosomal-dominant gene include achondroplasia, a bone growth disorder; hereditary colon cancer; and neurofibromatosis I, which causes light brown birthmarks and soft skin lumps over peripheral nerves. In the autosomal-recessive pattern, if both parents are carriers, but not

These athletes, many of whom have Down syndrome, are participating in a Special Olympics competition. Notice the distinctive facial features of the individuals with Down syndrome, such as a round face and a flattened skull. **What causes Down syndrome?**

Figure 3.6

Some Chromosome Variations

Name	Description	Treatment	Incidence
Down syndrome	Extra or altered 21st chromosome causes mild to severe retardation and physical variations.	Surgery, early intervention, infant stimulation, and special learning programs.	1 in 1,900 births at maternal age 20; 1 in 300 births at maternal age 35; 1 in 30 births at maternal age 45
Klinefelter syndrome	An extra X chromosome causes physical variations	Hormone therapy can be effective	1 in 800 males
Fragile X syndrome	A variation in the X chromosome can cause mental retardation, intellectual disabilities, or short attention span	Special education, speech and language therapy	1 in 1,500 males; 1 in 2,500 females
Turner syndrome	A missing X chromosome in females can cause intellectual disabilities and sexual underdevelopment	Hormone therapy in childhood and puberty	1 in 3,000 female births
XYY syndrome	An extra Y chromosome can cause above-average height	No special treatment required	1 in 1,000 male births

affected by the disorder, each offspring will have a one-in-four chance of being affected. If both parents are affected, then all their children will be as well. If one is affected and the other not at all (not a carrier), then their children will be unaffected but carriers. If one parent is affected and the other is a carrier, then half their offspring will be affected. Phenylketonuria, sickle-cell anemia, Tay-Sachs disease, and cystic fibrosis are autosomal-recessive disorders. In both patterns, male and female babies are equally affected. More than 7,000 such genetic disorders have been identified, although most of them are rare. Other genetic variations include diabetes, hemophilia, Huntington's disease, and spina bifida. Figure 3.7 provides further information about the genetic variations we have discussed.

Every individual carries DNA variations that might predispose the person to serious physical disease or mental disorder. But not all individuals who carry a genetic disorder display the disorder. Other genes or developmental events sometimes compensate for genetic variations (Gottlieb, 2004; Gottlieb, Wahlsten, & Lickliter, 2006).

Thus, genes are not destiny, but genes that are missing, nonfunctional, or mutated can be associated with disorders (Zaghloul & Katsanis, 2010). Identifying such genetic variations could enable doctors to predict an individual's risks, recommend healthy practices, and prescribe the safest and most effective drugs (Wider, Foroud, & Wszolek, 2010). A decade or two from now, parents of a newborn baby may be able to leave the hospital with a full genome analysis of their offspring that reveals disease risks.

However, this knowledge might bring important costs as well as benefits. Who would have access to a person's genetic profile? An individual's ability to land and hold jobs or obtain insurance might be threatened if it is known that a person is considered at risk for some disease. For example, should an airline pilot or a neurosurgeon who is predisposed to develop a disorder that makes one's hands shake be required to leave that job early? Might this affect their ability to attain the education that would allow them to enter those professions in the first place?

Genetic counsellors, usually physicians or biologists who are well versed in the field of medical genetics, understand the kinds of situations just described, the odds of encountering them, and helpful strategies for offsetting some of their effects (Berkowitz, Roberts, & Minkoff, 2005; Finn & Smoller, 2006; Mayeux, 2005; Watson et al., 2005).

Figure 3.7

Some Gene-Linked Variations

Name	Description	Treatment	Incidence
Cystic fibrosis	Glandular dysfunction that interferes with mucus production; breathing and digestion are hampered, resulting in a shortened life span	Physical and oxygen therapy, synthetic enzymes, and antibiotics; most individuals live to middle age	1 in 2,000 births
Diabetes	Body does not produce enough insulin, which causes abnormal metabolism of sugar	Early onset can be fatal unless treated with insulin	1 in 2,500 births
Hemophilia	Delayed blood clotting causes internal and external bleeding	Blood transfusions/injections can reduce or prevent damage due to internal bleeding	1 in 10,000 males
Huntington's disease	Central nervous system deteriorates, producing problems in muscle coordination and mental deterioration	Does not usually appear until age 35 or older; death likely 10 to 20 years after symptoms appear	1 in 20,000 births
Phenylketonuria (PKU)	Metabolic disorder that, left untreated, causes mental retardation	Special diet can result in average intelligence and normal life span	1 in 14,000 births
Sickle-cell anemia	Blood disorder that limits the body's oxygen supply; it can cause joint swelling, sickle-cell crises; heart and kidney failure	Penicillin, medication for pain, antibiotics, and blood transfusions	1 in 400 North American children of African descent (lower among other groups)
Spina bifida	Neural tube disorder that causes brain and spine variations	Corrective surgery at birth, orthopedic devices, and physical/medical therapy	2 in 1,000 births
Tay-Sachs disease	Deceleration of mental and physical development caused by an accumulation of lipids in the nervous system	Medication and special diet are used, but death is likely by five years of age	1 in 30 North American Jews is a carrier

The Human Genome Project

Each gene has its own location, its own designated place on a particular chromosome. Today, there is a great deal of enthusiasm about efforts to discover the specific locations of genes that are linked to certain functions (Lewis, 2010). An important step in this direction is the Human Genome Project. The term "genome" is a combination of the words gene and chromosome, and the project is as enormous as it is complex. According to Dr. Hsein-Hsein Lei, if the genome were a book, it would be as large as 800 dictionaries. Further, it would take a person typing 60 words a minute, 8 hours a day, about 50 years to type it (Genome Canada, 2012). Human Genome Projects are international efforts to map the human genome—the complete set of developmental instructions for creating proteins that initiate the making of a human organism (Willey, Sherwood, & Woolverton, 2011).

One of the big surprises of the Human Genome Project was an early report indicating that humans have only about 30,000 genes (Human Genome Project Information, 2001). More recently, the number of human genes has been revised further downward to approximately 20,500 (Ensembl Human, 2010; *Science Daily*, 2008). Scientists had thought that humans had as many as 100,000 or more genes. They had also maintained that each gene programmed just one protein. In fact, humans have far more proteins than they have genes, so there cannot be a one-to-one correspondence between genes and proteins (Commoner, 2002).

Rather than being a group of independent genes, the human genome consists of many genes that collaborate both with each other and with nongenetic factors inside and outside the body. The collaboration operates at many points. For example, the cellular machinery mixes, matches, and links small pieces of DNA to reproduce the genes—and that machinery is influenced by what is going on around it.

Whether a gene is "turned on"—working to assemble proteins—is also a matter of collaboration. The activity of genes (*genetic expression*) is affected by their environment (Gottlieb, 2007; Meaney, 2010). For example, hormones that circulate in the blood make their way into the cell where they can turn genes "on" and "off." And the flow of hormones can be affected by environmental conditions, such as light, day length, nutrition, and behaviour. Numerous studies have shown that external events outside of the original cell and the person, as well as events inside the cell, can excite or inhibit gene expression (Gottlieb, Wahlsten, & Lickliter, 2006). For example, one recent study revealed that an increase in the concentration of stress hormones such as cortisol produced a fivefold increase in DNA damage (Flint et al., 2007). Other research has shown that experiences early in development can alter gene expression and this expression is related to later behaviour (Francis et al., 2003). In short, a single gene is rarely the source of a protein's genetic information, much less of an inherited trait (Gottlieb, 2007).

With funding from Genome Canada, physicians are finding ways to diagnose and treat diseases. For example, one team under the leadership of Dr. Tony Pawson of the Simon Lunenfeld Research Institute at Mount Sinai Hospital in Toronto is discovering drugs that may halt the division of cancerous cells and lead to recovery. Dr. Stephen Scherer of Sick Kids Hospital in Toronto is the lead researcher of the Autism Genome Project, an unprecedented international initiative involving 10 countries (Genome Canada, 2012). Both health care and social policy will be greatly influenced by these developments.

To this point, we have explored a number of ideas about genetic foundations. For a review, see the **Reach Your Learning Objectives** section at the end of this chapter.

Reproduction Challenges and Choices

LO3 Identify some important reproductive challenges and choices.

The facts and principles we have discussed regarding mitosis, meiosis, fertilization, and genetics are a small part of the current explosion of knowledge and research about human biology. This research not only will help us understand human development, but also will open up many new choices for prospective parents, choices that can also raise ethical questions.

Prenatal Diagnostic Tests

Infertility and Reproductive Technology

Adoption

Prenatal Diagnostic Tests

Scientists have developed a number of tests to determine whether a fetus is developing normally, among them amniocentesis, ultrasonography, chorionic villus sampling, and maternal serum screening. These developments have opened up a host of choices for prospective mothers.

Amniocentesis is a prenatal medical procedure in which a sample of amniotic fluid is withdrawn by syringe and tested to discover if the fetus is suffering from any chromosomal or metabolic disorders (Ramsay et al., 2004). Amniocentesis is performed between the 15th and 18th weeks of pregnancy. The later amniocentesis is performed, the better is its diagnostic potential (Pinette, Wax, & Wilson, 2004). It may take two weeks for enough cells to grow and amniocentesis test results to be obtained.

connecting through social policy

Eugenics and Social Policy

What we learn about ourselves, and the world around us, is often shaped by advances in scientific knowledge; such advances influence social policy, for better and for worse. For example, when Darwin's cousin, Francis Galton, proposed the idea of eugenics in the late 1880s, he perceived it as a science that would promote improvement of the human race. His ideas caught on like wildfire, resulting in many countries promoting laws to either sterilize, incarcerate, or otherwise prevent those deemed defective from reproducing (Black, 2003; Dowbiggin, 1997; Kevles, 1985; McLaren, 1990; Lombardo, 2008). Who were those deemed defective? They were the poor, the criminal, those viewed as immoral (the alcoholic, the prostitute), the mentally ill, the disabled, the chronically ill, the feeble elderly, and members of minority racialized groups. Further, those deemed defective were blamed for all kinds of social ills (from poverty and crime to high taxes). One of the most extreme and blatant expressions of eugenics was Nazi Germany, where nearly 300,000 physically, mentally, or emotionally disabled people were killed between 1939 and 1945 (Evans, 2004).

Consequently, after the genocide perpetrated in the Second World War, the field of eugenics lost much support. Critics further cited methodological problems and an inherent bias undermined the evidence offered in support of conclusions. How is it, then, that the field has regained momentum?

Health and wellness may be a primary motivating trigger. With the Human Genome mapped, the next step is to decipher and read the map. Such an accomplishment is expected to identify the genes involved in nearly every aspect of human behaviour. Genetic research is increasingly finding genes that appear connected to one or more of a long list of common conditions such as asthma, heart problems, arthritis, diabetes, Alzheimer's disease, and cancer, as well as skin pigmentation, temperament, and development of hair follicles (Braithwaite et al., 2004; Sabeti et al., 2007; Rifkin, 2005). The early eugenicists could not make such scientific predictions.

In 2007, the Society of Obstetricians and Gynaecologists of Canada recommended that all pregnant women be screened for Down syndrome and be given the alternative choices to keep or abort the baby (Summers et al., 2007). If, through genetic screening, we can learn that a child has the potential for particular diseases or conditions, what would we do with that information? Religious beliefs, economic conditions, the family size and its unique context all influence the response to information obtained in genetic counselling sessions. Dixon (2008) found medical professionals who gave genetic counselling were rarely neutral and tended to favour the abortion of babies with potential disabilities.

The counsellors are not alone in their bias. Many women who have had children with Down syndrome experience social rejection, often in the form of direct statements questioning the decision to give birth to a child with a disability (Shriver, 2007). A socially responsive country such as Canada will likely never employ practices described above; however, many troubling questions persist. For example, would genetic counselling assist a variation of the eugenic idea that some people are better than others and should be allowed to live, while the less capable or undesirable should not? If so, who would decide? On what criteria? Would employment opportunities be affected? Additionally, is the reliability of genetic information from screening 100 percent accurate?

Dr. Calliopi Havele and Dr. Peter Bretscher, of the Department of Microbiology and Immunology at the University of Saskatchewan, sound cautionary notes. Dr. Havele says, "Our genetic composition is incredibly complex," to which Dr. Bretscher adds, "A genetic tendency towards one trait may easily be offset by something else which counteracts the tendency" (interview, May 2007). A single gene is rarely the source of a protein's genetic information, much less of an inherited trait (Gottlieb, Wahlsten, & Lickliter, 2006; Rusk & Rusk, 2007). Therefore, rather than individualized and unwavering self-replicators, genes can be considered to be both interdependent and highly influenced by external factors. Perhaps even more critical is that our view of how a gene(s) might shape a portion of a person's life is dependent on our personal values and society's values, and our experience with people who might be different from ourselves. How will our social policies grapple with scientific advances?

Chorionic villi sampling is a prenatal medical procedure in which a small sample of the placenta is removed at some point between the 10th and 12th weeks of pregnancy to detect genetic variations (Health Canada, 2002). Diagnosis takes approximately 10 days. Chorionic villi sampling has a slightly higher risk of miscarriage than amniocentesis and is linked to a slight risk of limb deformities (Figure 3.8).

Ultrasonography or *ultrasound test*, often conducted seven weeks into a pregnancy and again at various times later, is a risk-free prenatal medical procedure in which high-frequency sound waves are directed into the pregnant woman's uterus. The echo from the sounds is transformed into a visual representation of the fetus's inner structures. This technique has been able to detect such disorders as microencephaly, a form of mental retardation involving an unusually small brain. Ultrasonography is often used in conjunction with amniocentesis to determine the precise location of the fetus and the number of fetuses in the mother's uterus. It can also give clues to the baby's sex (Gerards et al., 2008).

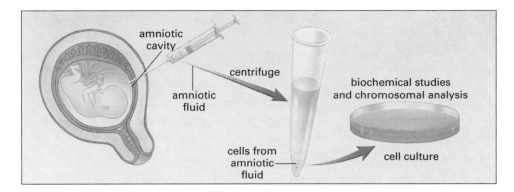

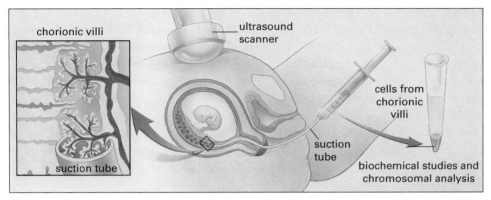

Figure 3.8

Amniocentesis
and Chorionic Villi
Sampling

Fetal MRI is a brain-imaging technique used to diagnose fetal malformations (Daltro et al., 2010; Duczkowska et al., 2010) (see Figure 3.9). MRI stands for magnetic resonance imaging and uses a powerful magnet and radio images to generate detailed images of the body's organs and structures. Currently, ultrasound is still the first choice in fetal screening, but fetal MRI can provide more detailed images than ultrasound. In many instances, ultrasound will indicate a possible abnormality and then fetal MRI will be used to obtain a clearer, more detailed image (Obenauer & Maestre, 2008). Among the fetal malformations that fetal MRI may be able to detect better than ultrasound sonography are certain central nervous system, chest, gastrointestinal, genital/urinary, and placental abnormalities (Baysinger, 2010; Panigrahy, Borzage, & Blümi, 2010; Weston, 2010).

Maternal blood screening may be performed during the 16th to 18th weeks of pregnancy. This process identifies pregnancies that have an elevated risk for birth defects such as spina bifida (a defect in the spinal cord) and Down syndrome (Bustamante-Aragonés et al., 2010). The current blood test is called the triple screen because it measures three substances in the mother's blood. After an abnormal triple screen result, the next step is usually an ultrasound examination. If an ultrasound does not explain the abnormal triple screen results, amniocentesis is typically used.

Noninvasive prenatal diagnosis (NIPD) is increasingly being explored as an alternative to such procedures as chorionic villus sampling and amniocentesis (Susman et al., 2010). At this point, NIPD has mainly focused on the isolation and examination of fetal cells circulating in the mother's blood and analysis of cell-free fetal DNA in maternal plasma (Prakash, Powell, & Geva, 2010). Researchers already have used NIPD to successfully test for genes inherited from a father that cause cystic fibrosis and Huntington's disease. They also are exploring the potential for using NIPD to diagnose a baby's sex, as early as five weeks after conception, and Down syndrome (Avent et al., 2008). Being able to detect an offspring's sex and various diseases and defects so early raises ethical concerns about couples' motivation to terminate a pregnancy (Benn & Chapman, 2010).

Maternal serum screening (alpha-fetoprotein—AFP) is a prenatal diagnostic technique that is used to identify pregnancies that have an elevated risk for spina bifida, Down syndrome, and other conditions (Echevarria & Avellón, 2006; Nicolaides, 2005). The blood test is the first level of screening for possible fetal variations and may be administered in the first trimester. If it is, there is a 1-in-10 to 1-in-20 chance of a false-positive reading, depending on maternal age

Figure 3.9

A fetal MRI, which is
increasingly being used
in prenatal diagnosis of
fetal malformations.

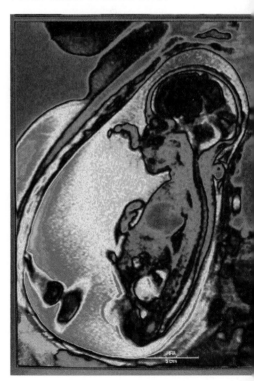

(Health Canada, 2002). This test is administered to women 14 to 20 weeks into pregnancy only when they are at risk of bearing a child with defects in the formation of the brain and spinal cord.

These techniques provide valuable information about the presence of disabilities, but they also raise issues pertaining to whether an abortion should be obtained if disabilities are present. The International Clearinghouse for Birth Defects Monitoring Systems (2001) surveyed a number of countries and reported that due to prenatal tests diagnosing Down syndrome, 53.2 percent of pregnancies were terminated. The lowest percentage of aborted pregnancies due to the possible presence of Down syndrome was 26.7, in Alberta, while the highest (84 percent) was found in Paris, France.

Infertility and Reproductive Technology

In 2012, Canada's fertility rate was reported to be 1.59 births per woman. This represents a drop from 1.65 in 2007 (CIA World Factbook, 2012). The "replacement rate"—that is, the number of births that sustain a population—is 2.1 children per woman, so birthrates below that trigger a number of social and economic concerns. Women are waiting longer to have a baby; for example, the fertility rate of women between ages 30 and 34 is now higher than that of women between 25 and 29. Both nationally and internationally, more women over 40 are having children. The rate in Canada is up slightly from 2.6 percent in 2002 to 2.9 percent in 2006; the numbers coming out of studies in northern and western Europe are considerably higher, ranging from 10 percent to 12 percent in Sweden (Wheeler, 2008). In terms of population growth, Quebec and Alberta are leading the way with increases of 7.3 percent and 7.4 percent, respectively.

Infertility is defined as the inability to conceive a child after 12 months of regular intercourse without contraception. The cause of infertility can rest with the woman or the man (Verhaak et al., 2010; Walsh, Pera, & Turek, 2009). The woman may not be ovulating, she may be producing abnormal ova, her fallopian tubes may be blocked, or she may have a disease that prevents implantation of the ova. The man may have a seminal problem, either too few sperm (a condition called *oligospermia*), or no sperm (a condition called *azoospermia*), the sperm may lack motility (the ability to move adequately), or the man may have a blocked passageway (Kini et al., 2010). (See Figure 3.10.) William Buckett of McGill University suggests that without treatment, women who ovulate infrequently might take up to a decade or more to become pregnant (Buckett, 2004). In the past, this timeline was not a major issue in a marriage that could begin at age 18 or 20. But with women today waiting longer to get married and start a family (possibly into their early thirties), this period of time would place them in the age range where fertility normally declines, thus not giving them enough time to successfully conceive. Other causes for fertility problems noted by Buckett include tubal disease (related to sexually transmitted diseases) and obesity-related infertility.

In some cases of infertility, surgery may correct the cause. The Royal Commission on New Reproductive Technologies examined three forms of infertility treatment: fertility drugs, assisted insemination (AI), and in vitro fertilization (IVF). The most common form of fertility treatment in Canada is the use of fertility drugs. The Commission found that many of the drugs in use do not have research that clearly supports their effectiveness.

The oldest form of assisting a woman to become pregnant when she or her partner are subfertile, or her partner is infertile, or she wishes to have a baby without a male partner, is assisted insemination, or AI. In this procedure, the sperm of either the woman's partner or of a donor is placed in the vagina, near the cervix, or in the uterus. AI is the most common fertility procedure available in Canada. The Commission found AI to have "the potential to be a safe, inexpensive, and relatively low-tech" method to treat infertility. Yet, they raised concerns for the storage and handling of sperm, the definition of success, and the variations in procedural technique employed across the country.

The third form of infertility treatment studied by the Commission, the use of high-tech IVF procedures, has received the most media coverage. The basic idea of IVF is that the egg and sperm are removed from the couple, and one or both of them are subjected to procedures intended to enhance the likelihood of fertilization. The Canadian Fertility and Andrology Society (CFAS, 2012) reported that 9,904 live births were reported from in vitro treatment cycles at Canada's 28 IVF centres. Quebec is the only province that covers IVF treatment in its provincial health plan (CFAS, 2012).

Figure 3.10

Fertility Problems, Possible Causes, and Treatments

MEN		
Problem	**Possible Causes**	**Treatment**
Low sperm count	Hormone imbalance, varicose vein in scrotum, possibly environmental pollutants Drugs (cocaine, marijuana, lead, arsenic, some steroids and antibiotics) Y chromosome gene deletions	Hormone therapy, surgery, avoiding excessive heat
Immobile sperm	Abnormal sperm shape Infection Malfunctioning prostate	None Antibiotics Hormones
Antibodies against sperm	Problem in immune system	Drugs

WOMEN		
Problem	**Possible Causes**	**Treatment**
Ovulation problems	Pituitary or ovarian tumour Underactive thyroid	Surgery Drugs
Antisperm secretions	Unknown	Acid or alkaline douche, estrogen therapy
Blocked fallopian tubes	Infection caused by IUD or abortion or by sexually transmitted disease	Surgical incision, cells removed from ovary and placed in uterus
Endometriosis (tissue buildup in uterus)	Delayed parenthood until the thirties	Hormones, surgical incision

One consequence of fertility treatments is an increase in multiple births. Twenty-five to 30 percent of pregnancies achieved by fertility treatments—including in vitro fertilization—now result in multiple births. A recent meta-analysis (a statistical technique that combines the results of multiple studies to determine the strength of the effect) revealed that in vitro fertilization twins have a slightly increased risk of low birth weight (McDonald et al., 2010) and another meta-analysis found that in vitro fertilization singletons have a significant risk of low birth weight (McDonald et al., 2009).

Adoption

Although surgery and fertility drugs may solve an infertility problem, another choice is adoption, the social and legal process by which a parent–child relationship is established between persons unrelated by birth. Citizenship and Immigration Canada reports that in 2010, there were 1,968 international adoptions, down from 2,130 in 2009, and 2,180 in 2003. By contrast, international adoption in the U.S. has dropped from 22,991 in 2004 to 9,320 in 2011 Changes in laws and costs involved have impacted adoption rates (Pearce, 2012). China has been the most popular country for adopting children, particularly girls. On the other hand, although international adoptions are declining, Ontario's Ministry of Children and Youth Services reports that Ontario increased domestic adoptions by 21% since 2008, and is making efforts to make adoption a smoother process (Pearce, T., 2012).

critical thinking

According to Dr. Robert Glossop, former Executive Director of Programs and Research at the Vanier Institute of the Family, "what is personal is political and what is political is personal." Private decisions are very much linked with public policies. With that in mind, how affordable is in vitro fertilization (IVF)? Should all provinces follow Quebec's example and cover health care costs? Suppose that you learn you are infertile; what steps would you take? What considerations would affect your decision?

Wanting to be a parent and choosing to adopt, or conversely, deciding to place an infant up for adoption are both riddled with emotion. According to Origins Canada (2010), mothers who have given their baby up for adoption have a higher than average likelihood of suffering from a variety of mental disorders including complex post-traumatic stress disorder, postpartum depression following the birth of a subsequent child, anxiety disorders, grief lasting a lifetime, depression, stress related ailments including fibromyalgia, migraines, etc., plus difficulty developing and maintaining intimate relationships.

Adopted children fare considerably better than their biological mothers. A recent study (2012) of internationally adopted Chinese girls, reported the children to be relatively well-adjusted and to demonstrate resilience and characteristics of love, creativity, humour, curiosity, and kindness. As they entered their teens, traits such as teamwork and gratitude are added (Loker, T., et. al. 2012). At the same time, persons who have been adopted identified issues related to problems with attachment, identity, abandonment, and parenting of their own children (Origins Canada, 2012).

The amount of time a child spends in an orphanage is linked to adjustment; hence the earlier the adoption the better the outcomes. At age six, children adopted from an orphanage in the first six months of their lives showed no lasting negative effects of their early experience. However, children from the orphanage who were adopted after they were six months of age had abnormally high levels of cortisol, indicating that their stress regulation had not developed adequately (Ambert, 2003). York University professor Anne-Marie Ambert (2003) reports that adoptive parents are usually equally attached to their adopted children and their biological children, if they have them.

To this point, we have discussed a number of ideas about reproduction challenges and choices. For a review, see the **Reach Your Learning Objectives** section at the end of this chapter.

Heredity–Environment Interaction: The Nature–Nurture Debate

LO4 Explain some of the ways that heredity and environment interact to produce individual differences in development.

Heredity and environment interact to produce development (McGuire, 2001). To explore this interaction, we will focus on an important area of development—intelligence —and then explore many other aspects of heredity–environment interaction.

Behaviour Genetics

Behaviour genetics is the field that seeks to discover the influence of heredity and environment on individual differences in human traits and development. Note that behaviour genetics does not determine the extent to which genetics or the environment affects an individual's traits. Instead, what behaviour geneticists try to do is to figure out what is responsible for the differences among people—that is, to what extent do people differ because of differences in genes, environment, or a combination of these (Silberg, Maes, & Eaves, 2010). To study the influence of heredity on behaviour, behaviour geneticists often use either twins or adoption situations (Goldsmith, 2011).

In the most common twin study, the behavioural similarity of identical twins (who are genetically identical) is compared with the behavioural similarity of fraternal twins. Recall that although fraternal twins share the same womb, they are no more genetically alike than brothers or sisters. Thus by comparing groups of identical and fraternal twins, behaviour geneticists capitalize on the basic knowledge that identical twins are more similar genetically than are fraternal twins (Loehlin, 2010). For example, one study found that conduct problems were more prevalent in identical twins than fraternal twins; the researchers concluded that the study demonstrated an important role for heredity in conduct problems (Scourfield et al., 2004).

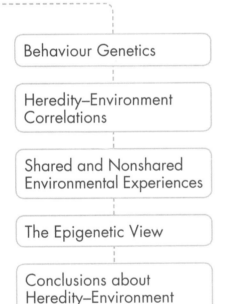

Behaviour Genetics

Heredity–Environment Correlations

Shared and Nonshared Environmental Experiences

The Epigenetic View

Conclusions about Heredity–Environment Interaction

connecting through research ←----------

Ethical Considerations of Stem Cell Research and Genetic Screening: An Overview

When scientific inquiry collides with chance, the future may be irrevocably transformed. Such is the story behind stem cell research. Over half a century ago, in 1961, two men, who some now refer to as the founding fathers of stem cell research, physicist James Till and biologist Ernest McCulloch, were experimenting with bone marrow and mice when, much to their surprise, they observed a startling phenomenon: cells were renewing themselves! From these beginnings in a modest Toronto lab to today's activity in multi-million-dollar facilities around the world, stem cell research has created quite a furor of activity and spawned heated debate.

Till and McCulloch's discovery paved the way for life-saving bone marrow transplants that have not only prolonged the lives of leukemia patients, but also sparked a plethora of research for more effective treatments of life-threatening conditions such as cancer, heart disease, and spinal cord and neurological disorders (Smith, 2005; UHN, 2006).

The tension between research possibilities and ethical concerns ignited passionate debates about when and how life begins; who, if anyone, can create life; and how evolution will be determined. So heated was the controversy that in 2006, after lengthy debate, the US House of Representatives and the Senate passed a bill to allow government funding of stem cell research. However, President Bush categorized the stem cell research as a form of abortion, and vetoed the bill (Nature, 2006). Private labs, however, may operate lawfully but without government funding. Only a few days after Bush's veto, the United Kingdom and the European Union both announced funding for stem cell research. Recall that in 1997, the first mammal, Dolly the sheep, was cloned by Scottish scientists at the Roslin Institute of the University of Edinburgh (Human Genome Project Information, 2009). This event triggered speculation about human cloning and little more than a decade later, Dr. Zavos, often referred to as the father of andrology, working out of a secret lab in the Middle East, where

Drs. McCulloch and Till's incisive findings won them the prestigious Gairdner Foundation International Award in 1969 and the 2005 Albert Lasker Award for Basic Medical Research. They were inducted into the Canadian Medical Hall of Fame in 2004 (NET, 2006).

no laws prohibiting human cloning exist, became the first to inseminate women with cloned embryos (Connor, 2009; Human Cloning Foundation, 2012).

In 2007, Dr. Andras Nagy and his research team at the Samuel Lunenfeld Research Institute of Mount Sinai Hospital in Toronto, building on research conducted in Japan and the United States, made another major breakthrough. They were able to use skin cells to grow embryonic stem cells without the use of unpredictable virus cells. This discovery may lay to rest many of the contentions that stem cell research is immoral and dangerous. Because cloned organs could be used not only for transplants but also to test new medical therapies, research continues worldwide. In fact, as recently as 2012, British researcher Sir John Gurdon and Shinya Yamanaka of Japan won the Nobel Prize in medicine for their innovative work on stem cell reprogramming.

Recognizing that Canadian researchers have been pioneers in the area of stem cell research and the tension generated between the potential to provide treatment for many debilitating diseases and the ethical, social, and legal issues, the Canadian Institutes of Health Research worked to establish guiding principles guidelines. To receive federal or provincial funding research must adhere to these guidelines, which, according to Alan Bernstein, chair of the board of directors of the Canadian Stem Cell Foundation, have become the gold standard for other countries (Bernstein, 2012; CIHR, 2012b).

As the controversy and debate continue to capture worldwide media attention, public expectation and speculation escalates. On the one hand, some embrace the possibility of cures and treatments that will ease the lives of many, while on the other hand, some are horrified by the notion of growing human organs in a laboratory and infuriated by the possibility of human cloning. Even countries such as Canada, where stem cell research is publicly funded and lawful, are proceeding cautiously because of ethical concerns.

However, several issues complicate interpretation of twin studies. For example, perhaps the environments of identical twins are more similar than the environments of fraternal twins. Adults might stress the similarities of identical twins more than those of fraternal twins, and identical twins might perceive themselves as a "set" and play together more than fraternal twins do. If so, the influence of the environment on the observed similarities between identical and fraternal twins might be very significant.

In an adoption study, investigators seek to discover whether the behaviour and psychological characteristics of adopted children are more like those of their adoptive parents, who have provided

Twin studies compare identical twins with fraternal twins. Identical twins develop from a single fertilized egg that splits into two genetically identical organisms. Fraternal twins develop from separate eggs, making them genetically no more similar than non-twin siblings. **What is the nature of the twin study method?**

passive genotype–environment correlations Exist when the natural parents, who are genetically related to the child, provide a rearing environment for the child.

evocative genotype–environment correlations Exist when the child's genotype elicits certain types of physical and social environments.

active (niche-picking) genotype–environment correlations Exist when children seek out environments they find compatible and stimulating.

According to Sandra Scarr, what are three ways that parents can contribute to genotype–environment correlations?

a home environment, or more like those of their biological parents, who have contributed their heredity (Loehlin, Horn, & Ernst, 2007). Another form of the adoption study compares adoptive and biological siblings.

As noted earlier, scholarly research can occasionally be quite biased, sparking sometimes contentious and hostile controversy. Assigning aptitudes and abilities to one gender or the other is also controversial. You may have heard or read that some researchers have suggested that male brains are better at math and female brains are better in languages, or that people from one part of the world excel in math over those from another part of the world. No definitive research supports these findings; however, on January 14, 2006, Harvard University President L.H. Summers proposed that innate genetic differences between men and women may be one explanation for why fewer women succeed in science careers. Like many, The National Organization for Women (NOW), finding these remarks sexist and offensive, demanded his resignation. Within a month Summers resigned (February 2006), but his remarks fuelled the debate once again (Eltis, 2007).

Most experts today agree that the environment plays an important role in intelligence. This means that improving children's environments can raise their intelligence.

Heredity–Environment Correlations

Heredity–environment correlations involve the interpretation of the complexities of heredity–environment interactions. An individual's genes may influence the types of environments to which they are exposed. In a sense, individuals inherit environments that may be related or linked to genetic tendencies (Plomin et al., 2003). Behaviour geneticist Sandra Scarr (1993) described three ways that heredity and environment are correlated: passively, evocatively, and actively.

Passive genotype–environment correlations *occur when biological parents, who are genetically related to the child, provide a rearing environment for the child.* For example, the parents might have a genetic predisposition to be intelligent and read skillfully. Because they read well and enjoy reading, they provide their children with books to read. The likely outcome is that their children, given their own inherited predispositions, will become skilled readers.

Evocative genotype–environment correlations *occur because a child's genotype elicits certain types of physical and social environments.* For example, active, smiling children receive more social stimulation than passive, quiet children do. Athletically inclined youth tend to elicit encouragement to engage in school sports. As a consequence, these adolescents tend to be the ones who try out for sport teams and go on to participate in athletically oriented environments.

Active (niche-picking) genotype–environment correlations *occur when children and adolescents seek out environments they find compatible and stimulating.* Niche-picking refers to finding a niche or setting that is suited to one's abilities. Adolescents select from their surrounding environment some aspect that they respond to, learn about, or ignore. Their active selections of environments are related to their particular genotype. Adolescents who are musically inclined are likely to select musical environments in which they can successfully employ their skills.

Scarr believes that the relative importance of the three genotype–environment correlations changes as children develop from infancy through adolescence. In infancy, much of the environment that children experience is provided by adults. Thus, passive genotype–environment correlations are more common in the lives of infants and young children than they are for older children and adolescents, who can extend their experiences beyond the family's influence and create their environments to a greater degree. The neuro structures in children are moulded and transformed by environment; however, in adolescence, we stop changing our minds to fit the world and instead try to change the world to fit our minds (Wexler, 2006).

Shared and Nonshared Environmental Experiences

Shared environmental experiences *are children's common experiences, such as their parents' personalities and intellectual orientation, the family's social class, and the neighbourhood in which they live.* By contrast, **nonshared environmental experiences** *are a child's unique experiences, both within*

Hockey legends Ken and Dave Dryden. After hockey, Ken became a lawyer, author, and politician. Dave became a teacher and principal and manages the charity Sleeping Children Around the World, which their father founded. **What shared and nonshared environmental experiences contributed to their lives?**

the family and outside the family, that are not shared with another sibling. Thus, experiences occurring within the family can also be part of the "nonshared environment."

Behaviour geneticist Robert Plomin (2004) has found that common rearing, or shared environment, accounts for little of the variation in children's personality or interests. In other words, even though two children live under the same roof with the same parents, their personalities often are very different. Heredity influences the nonshared environments of siblings through the heredity–environment correlations described earlier. For example, a child who has inherited a genetic tendency to be athletic is likely to spend more time in environments related to sports, while the child who has inherited a tendency to be musically inclined may spend more time in environments related to music.

Canadian psychologist Gordon Neufeld and physician Gabor Maté (2004) support the nurture argument. In their book *Hold On to Your Kids: Why Parents Matter*, they find that some parents distance themselves from their children during the early years, allowing the children to spend most of their time with other children. Neufeld and Maté say this results in a stronger attachment with peers than with parents for these children. The results are often a complete rejection of parental authority, influence, and connection during adolescence, a time when parental attachment might prevent or at least soften some of the problems teenagers can encounter. Thus, Neufeld and Maté believe a strong and nurturing attachment with their parents is critical for adolescents' positive experience of life. Perhaps it is in our nature to be nurtured.

Jean Chrétien was the 18th child of 19 born into a working class family in Shawinigan; nine of the 18 births survived. After receiving his law degree, Chrétien became active in politics and was prime minister for a decade, from 1993–2003. **How might Chrétien's environment have shaped his political life?**

shared environmental experiences Children's common environmental experiences that are shared with their siblings, such as their parents' personalities and intellectual orientation, the family's social class, and the neighbourhood in which they live.

nonshared environmental experiences The child's own unique experiences, both within the family and outside the family, that are not shared by another sibling. Thus, experiences occurring within the family can be part of the "nonshared environment."

epigenetics The study of ongoing, bidirectional interchange of biological and environmental factors that result in heritable modifications, but which do not alter DNA, our genetic code.

The Epigenetic View

Darwin believed that genetic changes evolved over generations as a result of natural selection; in other words, choices that parents make would not influence the genetic makeup of their children. More recently, however, scientific investigation suggests that environmental factors, including choices such as whether or not to smoke, may in fact trigger changes in inherited characteristics for generations to come. How and why this occurs is the focus of **epigenetics**, *the study of ongoing, bidirectional interchange of biological and environmental factors that result in heritable modifications, but which do not alter DNA, our genetic code.* A baby inherits genes from both parents at conception. During prenatal development, toxins, nutrition, and stress can influence some genes to stop functioning while others become stronger or weaker. In the epigenetic view, environmental factors, both imposed (such as famine, poverty, or war) or chosen (such as nutrition or smoking), can change ways that genes interact and collaborate. In other words, heredity and environment operate together—or collaborate—to produce a person's intelligence, temperament, height, weight, ability to pitch a baseball, ability to read, and so on (Gottlieb, 2007; Meaney, 2010). During infancy, environmental experiences such as toxins, nutrition, stress, learning, and encouragement continue to modify genetic activity and the activity of the nervous system that directly underlies behaviour. This also helps to explain why identical twins can be quite different.

Dr. Michael Meaney and Dr. Moshe Szyf, working with rat models at the Michael Meaney Lab at McGill University (2004), reported that the gene expression in rat pups could be affected by maternal care in infancy. Excited by this finding, Patrick McGowan, who had once studied with Meaney, wanted to expand this research to humans; he wondered if there is a link between

critical thinking

Review the scenarios in the opening vignette. Do any of them resonate with you? If you were a family counsellor, or if you were in any one of the three situations, what might you do? What are the factors you would include in your decision-making process?

critical thinking

Being a primary contact with the world, families often contribute to an individual's understanding of the world in many ways. For example, what is considered common sense in one family may be completely different in another family. Typically family members share similar political and religious views and often share common body gestures, facial expressions, and even sense of humour. Compare and contrast your life and choices so far with those of your siblings. If you do not have siblings, consider siblings you know fairly well—perhaps good friends or relatives—and compare and contrast their lives and choices. How are the choices made by siblings similar? How are they distinctly different? How has the environmental contributed to the similarities and differences? What contribution do you think genetics has made? Of all the domains of family life considered here, what do you think would be easiest to change? What might be the most difficult?

child abuse and adult suicide. McGowan analyzed brain tissue from the Quebec Suicide Brain Bank, where brain tissue from dozens of people who committed suicide is stored in Pyrex containers, and conducted validating interviews with family members of those whose brain tissue was stored. Having both the brains and the histories, McGowan, in collaboration with scientists at the newly formed Sackler Program for Epigenetics and Psychobiology at McGill University, discovered a biological link to some male suicides. Although the connection between childhood abuse and suicide was known, this study demonstrated, at least to some extent, the biological factors, representing another step forward for the field of epigentics. Dr. Gustavo Turecki, director of the McGill Group for Suicide Studies, notes that his study represents another step forward for the field of epigenetics but cautions that conclusions are tentative. Further, he notes that "Abuse and its severity is subjective; however impact is important" (Reynolds, 2012). According to Dr. E. Whitelaw and Dr. N.C. Whitelaw of the Queensland Institute of Medical Research in Brisbane, Australia, "Over the next decade, many of these processes will be better understood, heralding a greater capacity for us to correlate measurable molecular marks with phenotype and providing the opportunity for improved diagnosis and presymptomatic health-care" (p. 131). Cancers, mental illnesses, and suicides may one day be detected and treated earlier (Whitelaw & Whitelaw, 2006).

Conclusions about Heredity–Environment Interaction

In sum, both genes and environment are necessary for a person even to exist. Because the environment's influence depends on genetically endowed characteristics, we say the two factors interact. Humans are driven to match their internal neurological structures to the external environment (Wexler, 2006).

The relative contributions of heredity and environment are not formulaic, one part genes, one part environment; nor does full genetic expression occur at any one time such as at conception or birth. Genes produce proteins throughout the life span, in many different environments. Or they don't produce these proteins, depending in part on how harsh or nourishing those environments are.

The emerging view is that complex behaviours have some genetic loading that gives people a propensity for a particular developmental trajectory (Goldsmith, 2011). Environment is as complex as the mixture of genes we inherit (Bronfenbrenner & Morris, 2006; Parke & Buriel, 2006; Scheidt & Windley, 2006; Spencer, 2006). Environmental influences range from the things we lump together under "nurture" (such as parenting, family dynamics, schooling, and neighbourhood quality) to biological encounters (such as viruses, birth complications, and even biological events in cells).

Growing up with many of the "advantages" does not guarantee success any more than growing up with many disadvantages guarantees failure. People who grew up in privileged families might take opportunities for granted and fail to develop the motivation to succeed. By the same token, people who grow up in impoverished conditions may make the best of the opportunities available to them and learn to seek out advantages that can help them improve their lives.

If heredity and environment interact to determine the course of development, is that all there is to answering the question of what causes development? Are humans completely at the mercy of their genes and environment as they develop through the life span? Our genetic heritage and environmental experiences are pervasive influences on development (Sameroff, 2010; Wermter et al., 2010). But in thinking about what causes development, recall from Chapter 1 our discussion of development as the co-construction of biology, culture, and the individual. We not only are the outcomes of our heredity and the environment we experience, but we also can author a unique developmental path by changing the environment.

To this point, we have discussed heredity–environment interaction and the nature–nurture debate. For a review, see the **Reach Your Learning Objectives** section at the end of this chapter.

reach your **learning objectives**

The Evolutionary Perspective

LO1 Discuss the evolutionary perspective on life-span development.

Natural Selection and Adaptive Behaviour	▪ Natural selection, originally proposed by Charles Darwin in 1859, is the process that favours individuals of a species that are best adapted to survive and reproduce. ▪ In evolutionary theory, adaptive behaviour is behaviour that promotes the organism's survival in a natural habitat. ▪ Biological evolution shaped human beings into a culture-making species. ▪ In this view, adaptation, reproduction, and "survival of the fittest" are important in explaining behaviour.
Evolutionary Psychology	▪ A contemporary approach that emphasizes that behaviour is a function of mechanisms, requires input for activation, and is ultimately related to survival and reproduction. ▪ Developmentalists propose that behaviour may evolve. ▪ According to Baltes, the benefits of evolutionary selection decrease with age mainly because of a decline in reproductive fitness. ▪ While evolutionary selection benefits decrease with age, cultural and social support need increase. ▪ Social cognitive theorist Albert Bandura acknowledges evolution's important role in human adaptation and change, but argues for a bi-directional view that enables organisms to alter and construct new environmental conditions. ▪ Biology allows for a broad range of cultural possibilities.

Genetic Foundations

LO2 Describe what genes are and how they influence human development.

The Collaborative Gene	▪ Genes are short segments of DNA. ▪ Hereditary information that directs cells to reproduce and manufacture proteins is contained in genes. ▪ The nucleus of each human cell contains 46 chromosomes, which are composed of DNA. ▪ Genes act collaboratively, not independently.
Genes and Chromosomes	▪ Reproduction takes place when a female gamete (ovum) is fertilized by male gamete (sperm) to create a zygote. ▪ Mitosis is the process of cell division.
Genetic Principles	▪ Genes are transmitted from parents to offspring by gametes, or sex cells. ▪ Gametes are formed by the splitting of cells, a process called meiosis. ▪ Genetic principles include those involving dominant-recessive genes, sex-linked genes, and polygenically inherited characteristics.

Chromosome and Gene-Linked Variations	■ Occasionally chromosomes are harmful or they do not divide evenly, causing variations.
	■ Sex-linked chromosomal abnormalities include Klinefelter syndrome, fragile X syndrome, Turner syndrome, and XYY syndrome.
	■ Gene-linked disorders include phenylketonuria (PKU) and sickle-cell anemia.
The Human Genome Project	■ The Human Genome Project has made stunning progress in mapping the human genome.
	■ Current research is aimed at finding ways to diagnose and treat diseases, as well as to shape health care policies.

Reproduction Challenges and Choices

LO3 Identify some important reproductive challenges and choices.

Prenatal Diagnostic Tests	■ Amniocentesis, ultrasonography, chorionic villi sampling, and the maternal blood test are used to determine the presence of defects once pregnancy has begun.
Infertility and Reproductive Technology	■ Genetic counselling has increased in popularity because couples desire information about their risk of having a child with defective characteristics.
	■ Some infertility problems can be corrected through surgery or fertility drugs.
	■ Methods include in vitro fertilization and other more recently developed techniques.
Adoption	■ Adopted children and adolescents are relatively well-adjusted, but report difficulties with issues related to attachment, identity, abandonment, and parenting their own children.
	■ When adoption occurs very early in development, the outcomes for the child are improved.

Heredity–Environment Interaction: The Nature–Nurture Debate

LO4 Explain some of the ways that heredity and environment interact to produce individual differences in development.

Behaviour Genetics	■ The nature–nurture debate: Heredity and environment interact to produce individual differences in development.
	■ Behaviour genetics is the field concerned with the influence of heredity and environment on individual differences in human traits and development. Methods used by behavioural geneticists include twin studies and adoption studies.
Heredity–Environment Correlations	■ Sandra Scarr argues that the environments parents select for their children depend on the parents' genotypes.
	■ Passive genotype–environment, evocative genotype–environment, and active (niche-picking) genotype–environment are three correlations.
	■ Scarr believes the relative importance of these three genotype–environment correlations changes as children develop.
Shared and Nonshared Environmental Experiences	■ Shared environmental experiences refer to siblings' common experiences such as parents' personalities, the family's socio-economic status, and the neighbourhood in which they live.
	■ Non-shared environmental experiences refer to the child's unique experiences, such as those both within and outside of the family environment.

The Epigenetic View	■ Development is the result of ongoing, bi-directional interaction between environment and heredity.
	■ Epigentic research is heralding the potential to use information about gene activity to diagnose and treat both mental and physical health prior to the disease becoming symptomatic.
Conclusions about Heredity–Environment Interaction	■ Many complex behaviours have some genetic loading that gives people a propensity for a particular developmental trajectory.
	■ Actual development also requires an environment, and that environment is complex.
	■ The interaction of heredity and environment is extensive.

review ---→ *connect* ---→ reflect

review

How would you describe the evolutionary perspective? **LO1**

What are genes and why are they considered collaborative? **LO2**

How do mitosis and meiosis differ? **LO2**

What is the Human Genome Project about? **LO2**

What happens when chromosomes do not divide evenly? **LO2**

What strategies are people using to address reproductive challenges? **LO3**

What are some of the ethical considerations of stem cell research and genetic screening? **LO3**

What is the epigenetic view? **LO4**

connect

When you consider all the members of your family, including those you may not have met but of whom you have heard, what are the commonalities? With one of your family members in mind, describe how you think the interaction of genetics and heredity may have affected personality and development.

reflect *Your Own Personal Journey of Life*

How much of your behavior and personality development reflect your home environment, and how much might be genetic? Consider the possibility that you or a friend you know fairly well were adopted. What questions might you have about your genetic make-up? How may environmental factors have played a role in your personality development?

McGraw Hill Education **connect**

McGraw-Hill Connect provides you with a powerful tool for improving academic performance and truly mastering course material. You can diagnose your knowledge with pre- and post-tests, identify the areas where you need help, search the entire learning package, including the eBook, for content specific to the topic you're studying, and add these resources to your personalized study plan. CONNECT for *Life-Span Development*, fifth Canadian edition, offers the following:

■ chapter-specific online quizzes

■ groupwork

■ presentations

■ writing assignments

■ case studies

■ and much more!

Visit CONNECT today!

CHAPTER 4

Prenatal Development and Birth

CHAPTER OUTLINE

"Each time you look at your child you see something mysterious and contradictory— bits and pieces of other people—grandparents, your mate, yourself, all captured in a certain stance, a shape of the head, a look in the eye, combined with something very precious—a new human soul rich in individuality and possibility. That's immortality."

—JOAN SUTTON, CANADIAN AUTHOR

Birth: Yesterday, Today, and Tomorrow

Anticipating or witnessing the birth of another species or our own inspires a sense of awe at the wonders of nature. From the first news of conception, the biological beginnings (discussed in Chapter 3), through prenatal development, to birth, we are reminded of the vast complexities of life. Seeing a newborn's tiny features, hearing her first cry, or touching his silken skin moves us deeply. Such is the wonder of birth. To appreciate fully the successive stages of pregnancy, an essential guide called "Healthy Beginnings" has been developed by the Society of Obstetricians and Gynaecologists of Canada (SOGC). This valuable guideline assists mothers-to-be and caregivers to understand more completely not only how a body prepares itself for birth, but also what the growing baby requires during pregnancy (Schuurmans, Senikas, & Lalonde, 2009).

When a child is born in the developed world, whether in the hospital under the care of a physician or at home under the care of a midwife, the child and mother have all the resources of the medical world. This includes neonatal intensive care units, ready or on standby to assist them. To understand the differences, compare the births of today with the birth of the Dionne quintuplets in 1934. The "quints" were born to Oliva and Elzire Dionne, a French-Canadian couple from a small town in Northern Ontario. Assisted into the world by two midwives and one physician, they were the first medically recorded quintuplets. Their combined weight at birth was less than 6,500 grams. Against all odds, they survived.

Although today multiple births are not uncommon, the rarity of such an event in 1934 created quite a media stir. The news of the Dionne quintuplets' birth spread like wildfire. Media and public response afforded the family virtually no privacy.

Two months after their births, the five babies—Yvonne, Émilie, Annette, Cécile, and Marie—were made wards of the state. The Ontario government appointed a board of guardians to protect the health and interests of the girls, thereby effectively stripping control from the parents. The parents, Oliva and Elzire, along with the quints' seven sisters and brothers, were allowed to visit the quints, but the parents were completely excluded from any decisions about how their daughters were to be raised.

The miracle of their births was a magnet for human-interest news stories; the quints immediately became celebrities and a major tourist attraction. People travelled for hundreds of kilometres to view them in their sheltered environment. Stories of their birthdays, Christmases, vacations, hobbies, education, and even family arguments were popular news items.

"Quintland" became an instant money-maker for the provincial government. The five identical sisters' lives were displayed in glass bubbles, for all the world to see. In 1998, the three surviving quints, Cécile, Yvonne, and Annette, received a $4 million settlement from the government in response to their request for an inquiry into the management of the funds and for compensation. They are still seeking a detailed examination of their guardianship.

Major advances have occurred in the sciences of fertility and neonatal medicine. Where medical resources are in place, delivery is now much safer for both mother and infant. The use of hormone-based fertility treatments or in vitro fertilization has given rise to more multiple and premature births. Parents today have the opportunity to make choices and decisions that were not available to parents 20 years ago. Some decisions may be influenced by spiritual beliefs. Contemporary scientists investigate the possibilities of DNA manipulation and cloning. Possibilities unimagined in 1934 are reality today, just as possibilities unimagined today will be tomorrow's reality. These advances raise a number of interesting and ethical questions about how life is defined and sustained.

Let us now explore the development of a fetus from the time of conception through the moment of birth.

The birth and lives of the Dionne quints became an international event that captured the hearts and interests of the world. Their story contrasts remarkably with the births and lives of multiples today. **What are some of the major changes in hospital care available today that were unavailable in 1934? In media and public response? How would the Canadian federal or provincial governmental responses be different? What are some of the ethical questions posed by the treatment of the Dionne quintuplets? What are some of the ethical questions posed by fertility treatments?**

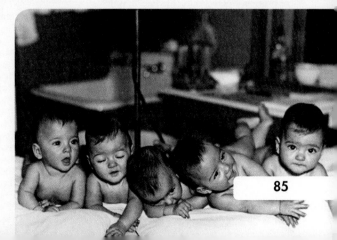

Prenatal Development

LO1 Explain prenatal development.

Imagine how a baby comes to be. Out of thousands of eggs and millions of sperm, one egg and one sperm unite to produce a baby. If the union of sperm and egg come a day or even an hour earlier or later, the results may be very different. Remember from Chapter 3 that conception occurs when a single sperm cell from the male unites with an ovum (egg) in the female's fallopian tube in a process called fertilization, and that the fertilized egg is called a zygote. By the time the zygote ends its three-to-four-day journey through the fallopian tube and reaches the uterus, it has divided into approximately 12 to 16 cells. Two hundred and sixty-six to 280 days (38 to 40 weeks) after fertilization, a fully formed baby makes its way from the womb to the outside world, prepared to breathe, take nourishment, and interact with the new environment. Prenatal development concerns the incredible story of the journey from fertilization through transition to the outside world.

The Course of Prenatal Development

Prenatal development is divided into three periods: germinal, embryonic, and fetal.

The Germinal Period

The **germinal period** *is the period of prenatal development that takes place in the first two weeks after conception. It includes the creation of the zygote, continued cell division, and the attachment of the zygote to the uterine wall.* By approximately one week after conception, the zygote is composed of 100 to 150 cells. The differentiation of cells has already commenced, as inner and outer layers of the organism are formed. The **blastocyst** *is the inner mass of cells that develops during the germinal period. These cells later develop into the embryo.* The **trophoblast** *is the outer layer of cells that develops during the germinal period. It later provides nutrition and support for the embryo.* Implantation, the attachment of the zygote to the uterine wall, takes place 11 to 15 days after conception. Figure 4.1 illustrates some of the most significant developments during the germinal period.

The Embryonic Period

The **embryonic period** *is the period of prenatal development that occurs from two to eight weeks after conception. During the embryonic period, the rate of cell differentiation intensifies, support systems for the cells form, and organs appear.* As the zygote attaches to the uterine wall, its cells form two layers. At this time, the name of the mass of cells changes from zygote to embryo. The embryo's endoderm is the inner mass of cells, which will develop into the digestive and respiratory systems. The outer layer of cells is divided into two parts. The ectoderm is the outermost layer, which will become the nervous system, sensory receptors (ears, nose, and eyes, for example), and skin parts (hair and nails, for example). The mesoderm is the middle layer, which will become the circulatory system, bones, muscles, excretory system, and reproductive system. Every body part eventually develops from these three layers. The endoderm primarily produces internal body parts, the mesoderm primarily produces parts that surround the internal areas, and the ectoderm primarily produces surface parts.

As the embryo's three layers form, life-support systems for the embryo mature and develop rapidly. These life-support systems include the amnion, the placenta, and the umbilical cord. The **amnion** *is like a bag or an envelope that contains a clear fluid in which the developing embryo floats.* The amniotic fluid provides an environment that is temperature- and humidity-controlled, as well as shockproof. The **placenta** *consists of a disc-shaped group of tissues in which small blood vessels from the mother and the offspring intertwine but do not join.* The **umbilical cord** *contains two arteries and one vein, and connects the fetus to the placenta.*

---

germinal period Prenatal development in the first two weeks after conception; includes the creation of the zygote, continued cell division, and the attachment of the zygote to the uterine wall.

blastocyst The inner mass of cells that develops during the germinal period. These cells later develop into the embryo.

trophoblast The outer layer of cells that develops in the germinal period to provide nutrition and support for the embryo.

embryonic period Prenatal development that occurs two to eight weeks after conception, during which the rate of cell differentiation intensifies, support systems for the cells form, and organs appear.

amnion A life-support system that is like a bag or envelope containing a clear fluid in which the developing embryo floats.

placenta A life-support system that consists of a disc-shaped group of tissues in which small blood vessels from the mother and offspring intertwine but do not join.

umbilical cord A life-support system containing two arteries and one vein that connects the baby to the placenta.

Figure 4.1

Significant Developments in the Germinal Period

Just one week after conception, cells of the blastocyst have already begun specializing. The germination period ends when the blastocyst attaches to the uterine wall. **Which of the steps shown in the drawing occur in the laboratory when IVF (described in Chapter 3) is used?**

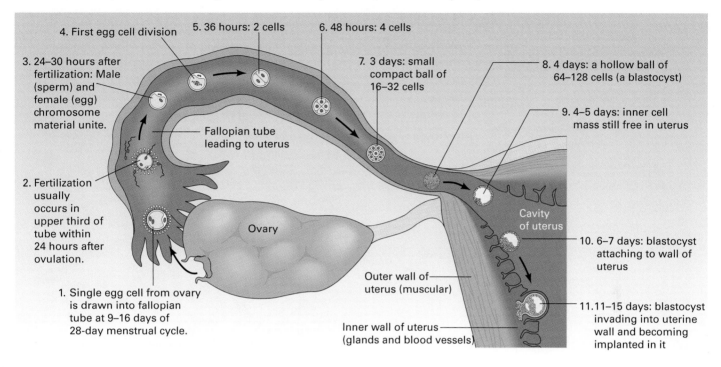

Figure 4.2 provides an illustration of the placenta, the umbilical cord, and the blood flow in the expectant mother and developing fetus in the uterus. Very small molecules—oxygen, water, salt, food from the mother's blood, as well as carbon dioxide and digestive wastes from the embryo's blood—pass back and forth between mother and fetus.

Large molecules cannot pass through the placental wall; these include red blood cells and harmful substances, such as most bacteria, maternal wastes, and hormones. The mechanisms that govern the transfer of substances across the placental barrier are complex and still not entirely understood (Klieger, Pollex, & Koren, 2008; Nanovskaya et al., 2008). At approximately 16 weeks, the kidneys of the fetus begin to produce urine. This fetal urine remains the main source of the amniotic fluid until the third trimester, when some of the fluid is excreted from the lungs of the growing fetus. Although the amniotic fluid increases in volume tenfold from the 12th to the 40th week of pregnancy, it is also removed in various ways. Some of it is swallowed by the fetus and some is absorbed through the umbilical cord and the membranes covering the placenta.

Organogenesis *is the process of organ formation that takes place during the first two months of prenatal development.* While organs are being formed, they are especially vulnerable to environmental changes (Mullis & Tonella, 2008). In the third week, the neural tube that eventually becomes the spinal cord forms. At about 21 days, eyes begin to appear, and at 24 days, the cells for the heart begin to differentiate. During the fourth week, the first appearance of the urogenital system is apparent, and arm and leg buds emerge. The four chambers of the heart take shape, as do blood vessels. From the fifth to the eighth week, arms and legs differentiate further; at this time, the face starts to form but still is not very recognizable. The intestinal tract develops, and the facial structures fuse. At eight weeks, the developing organism weighs about one gram and is just over 1.27 cm long.

organogenesis Organ formation that takes place during the first two months of prenatal development.

Figure 4.2

The Placenta and the Umbilical Cord

Maternal blood flows through the uterine arteries to the spaces housing the placenta, and it returns through the uterine veins to the maternal circulation. Fetal blood flows through the umbilical arteries into the capillaries of the placenta and returns through the umbilical veins to the fetal circulation. The exchange of materials takes place across the layer separating the maternal and fetal blood supplies, and so the bloods never come into contact. *Note:* The area bound by the square is enlarged in the right half of the illustration. Arrows indicate the direction of blood flow.

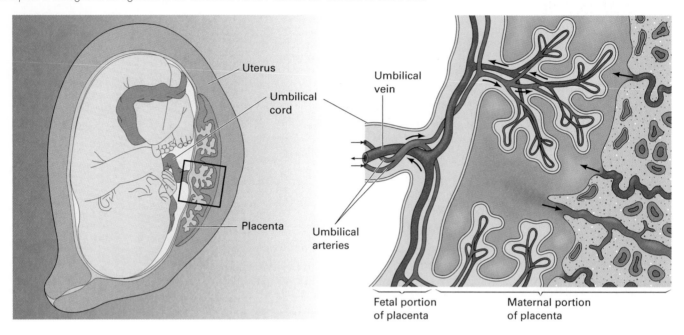

fetal period Prenatal development that begins two months after conception and lasts for seven months, on average.

The Fetal Period

The **fetal period** *is the prenatal period of development that begins two months after conception and lasts for seven months, on average.* Growth and development continue their dramatic course during this time. Three months after conception, the fetus is about 7.62 cm long and weighs about 28 grams. It has become active, moving its arms and legs, opening and closing its mouth, and moving its head. The face, forehead, eyelids, nose, and chin are distinguishable, as are the upper arms, lower arms, hands, and lower limbs. In most cases, the genitals can be identified as male or female. By the end of the fourth month, the fetus has grown to 15.2 cm in length and weighs 112 to 196 grams. At this time, a growth spurt occurs in the body's lower parts. Prenatal reflexes are stronger; arm and leg movements can be felt for the first time by the mother.

By the end of the fifth month, the fetus is about 30 cm long and weighs close to 454 grams. Structures of the skin have formed—toenails and fingernails, for example. The fetus is more active, showing a preference for a particular position in the womb. By the end of the sixth month, the fetus is about 35.6 cm long and already has gained another 225 to 450 grams. The eyes and eyelids are completely formed, and a fine layer of hair covers the head. A grasping reflex is present, and irregular breathing movements occur.

By the sixth month of pregnancy (about 24 to 25 weeks after conception), the fetus for the first time has a chance of surviving outside of the womb—that is, it is viable (Hernandez-Reif, 2007). Infants born early, or between 24 and 37 weeks of pregnancy, usually need help breathing because their lungs are not yet fully mature. By the end of the seventh month, the fetus is about 40 cm long and has gained another 450 grams; it now weighs about 1.4 kg.

During the eighth and ninth months, the fetus grows longer and gains substantial weight—about another 1.8 kg. At birth, the average North American baby weighs 3.2 kg and is about 50.8 cm long. In these last two months, fatty tissues develop, and the functioning of various organ systems—heart and kidneys, for example—steps up.

Figure 4.3

The Three Trimesters of Prenatal Development

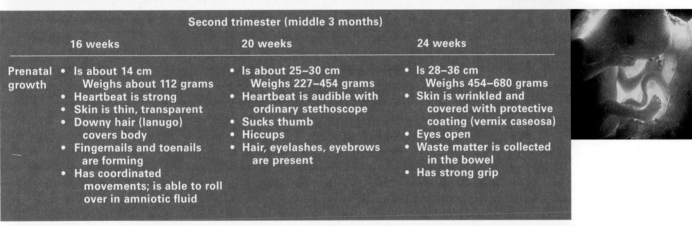

First trimester (first 3 months)		
Conception to 4 weeks	8 weeks	12 weeks
Prenatal growth • Is less than 0.25 cm • Beginning development of spinal cord, nervous system, gastrointestinal system, heart, and lungs • Amniotic sac envelops the preliminary tissues of entire body • Is called a "zygote"	• Is less than 2.54 cm • Face is forming with rudimentary eyes, ears, mouth, and tooth buds • Arms and legs are moving • Brain is forming • Fetal heartbeat is detectable with ultrasound • Is called an "embryo"	• Is about 7.6 cm Weighs about 28 grams • Can move arms, legs, fingers, and toes • Fingerprints are present • Can smile, frown, suck, and swallow • Sex is distinguishable • Can urinate • Is called a "fetus"

Second trimester (middle 3 months)		
16 weeks	20 weeks	24 weeks

Prenatal growth • Is about 14 cm
   Weighs about 112 grams
• Heartbeat is strong
• Skin is thin, transparent
• Downy hair (lanugo) covers body
• Fingernails and toenails are forming
• Has coordinated movements; is able to roll over in amniotic fluid
	• Is about 25–30 cm
	   Weighs 227–454 grams
	• Heartbeat is audible with ordinary stethoscope
	• Sucks thumb
	• Hiccups
	• Hair, eyelashes, eyebrows are present
		• Is 28–36 cm
		   Weighs 454–680 grams
		• Skin is wrinkled and covered with protective coating (vernix caseosa)
		• Eyes open
		• Waste matter is collected in the bowel
		• Has strong grip

Third trimester (last 3 months)		
28 weeks	32 weeks	36 to 40 weeks

Prenatal growth • Is 36–43 cm
   Weighs 1,100–1,400 grams
• Is adding body fat
• Is very active
• Rudimentary breathing movements are present
	• Is 42–46 cm
	   Weighs 1,800–2,300 grams
	• Has periods of sleep and wakefulness
	• Responds to sounds
	• May assume birth position
	• Bones of head are soft and flexible
	• Iron is being stored in liver
		• Is 50 cm
		   Weighs 3,200 grams
		• Skin is less wrinkled
		• Vernix caseosa is thick
		• Lanugo is mostly gone
		• Is less active
		• Is gaining immunities from mother

An overview of some of the main developments we have discussed and some more specific changes in prenatal development is presented in Figure 4.3. Note that we have divided these changes into trimesters, or three equal time periods. The three trimesters are not the same as the three prenatal periods we have discussed—germinal, embryonic, and fetal. An important point is that the first time a fetus has a chance of surviving outside of the womb is the beginning of the third trimester (at about seven months). Even when infants are born in the seventh month, they usually need assistance in breathing.

THE BRAIN One of the most remarkable aspects of the prenatal period is the development of the brain (Fair & Schlaggar, 2008; Nelson, 2009). By the time babies are born, they have approximately 100 billion *neurons*, or nerve cells, which handle information processing at the cellular level in the

Figure 4.4

Development of the Nervous System

This photograph shows the primitive, tubular appearance of the nervous system at six weeks in the human embryo.

brain. During prenatal development, neurons spend time moving to the right locations and start to become connected. The basic architecture of the human brain is assembled during the first two trimesters of prenatal development. In typical development, the third trimester of prenatal development and the first two years of postnatal life are characterized by connectivity and functioning of neurons (Moulson & Nelson, 2008).

As the human embryo develops inside its mother's womb, the nervous system begins forming as a long, hollow tube located on the embryo's back. This pear-shaped *neural tube*, which forms at about 18 to 24 days after conception, develops out of the ectoderm. The tube closes at the top and bottom ends at about 24 days after conception. Figure 4.4 shows that the nervous system still has a tubular appearance six weeks after conception.

Two birth defects related to a failure of the neural tube to close are anencephaly and spina bifida. The highest regions of the brain fail to develop when fetuses have anencephaly or when the head end of the neural tube fails to close, and they die in the womb, during childbirth, or shortly after birth (Koukoura et al., 2006). Spina bifida results in varying degrees of paralysis of the lower limbs. Individuals with spina bifida usually need assistive devices such as crutches, braces, or wheelchairs. A strategy that can help to prevent neural tube defects is for women to take adequate amounts of the B vitamin folic acid, a topic we will further discuss later in the chapter (Johnston, 2008; Ryan-Harshman & Aldoori, 2008).

In a normal pregnancy, once the neural tube has closed a massive proliferation of new immature neurons begins to take place at about the fifth prenatal week, and continues throughout the remainder of the prenatal period. The generation of new neurons is called *neurogenesis*. Up to half a million brain cells per minute are created at peak growth mid-pregnancy (Dowling, 2004).

At approximately 6 to 24 weeks after conception, *neuronal migration* occurs (Nelson, 2009). This involves cells moving outward from their point of origin to their appropriate locations and creating the different levels, structures, and regions of the brain (Hepper, 2007). Once a cell has migrated to its target destination, it must mature and develop a more complex structure.

At about the 23rd prenatal week, connections between neurons begin to occur, a process that continues postnatally (Moulson & Nelson, 2008). We will have much more to say about the structure of neurons, their connectivity, and the development of the infant brain in Chapter 5.

Teratology and Hazards to Prenatal Development

Some expectant mothers carefully tiptoe about in the belief that everything they do and feel has a direct effect on their unborn child. Others behave casually, assuming that their experiences will have little effect. The truth lies somewhere between these two extremes. A mother's womb can provide a protective environment or affect the fetus adversely in many well-documented ways.

General Principles

teratogen Any agent that causes a birth defect or negatively alters cognitive and behavioural outcomes. The field of study that investigates the causes of birth variations is called *teratology*. From the Greek word *tera*, meaning "monster."

A **teratogen** *is any agent that can potentially cause a birth defect or negatively alter cognitive and behavioural outcomes* (the word comes from the Greek word *tera*, meaning "monster"). The field of study that investigates the causes of birth variations is called *teratology*. Teratogens include drugs, incompatible blood types, infectious diseases, nutritional deficiencies, maternal stress, advanced maternal and paternal age, and environmental pollutants. In fact, fetuses can sometimes be affected by events that occurred in the mother's life as early as one or two months before conception. Additionally, some factors related to the health of the sperm can influence prenatal development.

So many teratogens exist that practically every fetus is exposed to some degree. For this reason, it can be difficult to determine which teratogen causes which problem. In addition, it may take a long time for the effects of a teratogen to show up. Only about half of all potential effects appear at birth.

The dose, genetic susceptibility, and the time of exposure to a particular teratogen influence both the type and severity of effect.

DOSE–REPONSE RELATIONSHIP   The dose effect is rather obvious—the greater the dose of an agent, such as a drug, the greater the effect. That is, there should be a relationship between the "dose" or the amount of exposure and the outcome (Holmes, 2011).

GENETIC SUSCEPTIBILITY   The use of genetic information to determine an individual's susceptibility to disease is part of the growing practice of personalized medicine (Nussbaum, McInnes, & Willard, 2007). The steadily increasing body of evidence supports the important genetic contribution to the pathogenesis of sepsis (Winning, Claus, Huse, & Bauer, 2006). Further, certain genetic markers have been identified, which indicate an increased risk of susceptibility for a given disorder such as Type I diabetes (Viken et al., 2007). Prenatal screening is offered routinely to pregnant women at any age; in higher risk pregnancies more invasive and risky procedures are being used. Mackoff et al. (2010) explain that future research is expected to focus on better understanding the concerns of genetic counsellors surrounding genetic susceptibility testing in children.

TIME OF EXPOSURE   Teratogens have greater effect when they occur at some points in development rather than at others (Nava-Ocampo & Koren, 2007; Rifas-Shiman et al., 2006). During the germinal period they may even prevent implantation. In general, the embryonic period is most vulnerable (Wong, Hockenberry, Wilson, Perry, & Lowdermilk, 2006).

Figure 4.5 summarizes additional information about the effects of time of exposure to a teratogen. The probability of a structural defect is greatest early in the embryonic period, when organs are being formed (Hill, 2007). Each body structure has its own critical period of formation. Recall from Chapter 2 that a *critical period* is a fixed time period very early in development during which certain experiences or events can have a long-lasting effect on development. The critical period for the nervous system (week 3) is earlier than for arms and legs (weeks 4 and 5). After organogenesis is complete, teratogens are less likely to cause anatomical defects. Instead, exposure during the fetal period is more likely to stunt growth or to create problems in the way organs function. To examine some key terotogens and their effects, let's begin with drugs.

Prescription and Non-Prescription Drugs

The Society of Obstetricians and Gynaecologists of Canada (SOGC, 2011b) has advised women that, before and during pregnancy, consultation with a health care professional is highly warranted prior taking any prescription or non-prescription medication, herbal remedy, or drug.

It should be stressed that prescription as well as over-the counter-medications, herbal products, topical creams, inhalers, and mega doses of vitamins can all cross the placenta into the fetal bloodstream. Prescription drugs that can function as teratogens include certain antidepressants and some hormones, such as progestin and synthetic estrogen (Garcia-Bournissen et al., 2008). Interestingly, an antimicrobial, such as tetracycline, can cause tooth enamel discoloration of deciduous teeth in the second and third trimesters (Wilson, 2007). During the period from 1957 to 1962, thalidomide was prescribed to women to offset morning sickness during the early stages of pregnancy. The drug was withdrawn from the Canadian market in 1962 after over 100 children were born with limb defects and other organ anomalies (Benegbi, 2007; Greener, 2011). According to SOGC, the only prescription medication approved by Health Canada for the treatment of nausea and vomiting in pregnancy is Diclectin (SOGC, 2011b).

Although clinical studies have indicated that a small number of medications are safe for use during pregnancy, the effects of many other drugs are not known. The safe use of all medication is essential to optimize the health of both a pregnant woman and her unborn child. The Motherrisk Program at the Hospital for Sick Children in Toronto is a recognized leader in providing valuable information about medications during pregnancy as well as breastfeeding. The toll-free number is 1-877-439-2744, or visit www.motherrisk.org.

Non-prescription drugs that can be harmful include diet pills and Aspirin (Nørgård et al., 2006). A recent research review indicated that low doses of Aspirin pose no harm for the fetus, but high doses can contribute to maternal and fetal bleeding (James, Brancazio, & Price, 2008).

Figure 4.5

Teratogens and the Timing of Their Effects on Prenatal Development

The danger of structural defects caused by teratogens is greatest early in embryonic development. This period of organogenesis (red colour) lasts for about six weeks. Later assaults by teratogens (blue colour) typically occur in the fetal period and, instead of structural damage, are more likely to inhibit growth or cause problems of organ function.

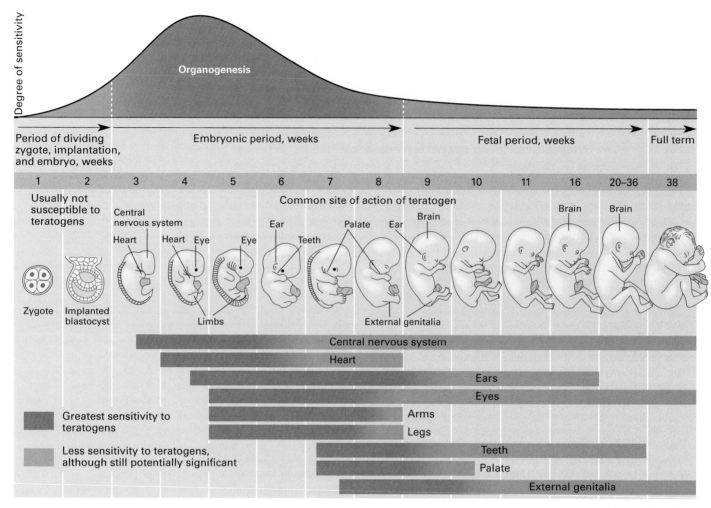

PSYCHOACTIVE DRUGS *Psychoactive drugs* act on the nervous system to alter states of consciousness, modify perceptions, and change moods. Examples include caffeine, alcohol, and nicotine, as well as illicit drugs such as cocaine, methamphetamine, marijuana, heroin, and ecstasy.

CAFFEINE People often consume caffeine by drinking coffee, tea, or colas, or by eating chocolate. A recent study revealed that pregnant women who consumed 200 or more milligrams of caffeine a day had an increased risk of miscarriage (Weng, Odouli, & Li, 2008). Taking these results into account, the Public Health Agency of Canada (PHAC, 2009a) recommends that pregnant women either not consume caffeine, or consume less than 300 mg of caffeine per day.

ALCOHOL Heavy drinking can be devastating to the fetus. No one knows with certainty the extent to which drinking causes fetal alcohol spectrum disorders. In essence, there is no safe amount of alcohol that pregnant mothers can consume (PHAC, 2011g). One study revealed that the intake of alcohol by both men and women during the week of conception increased the risk of early pregnancy loss (Henriksen et al. 2004).

Fetal alcohol spectrum disorders (FASD) are a cluster of abnormalities and problems that appear in the offspring of mothers who drink alcohol heavily during pregnancy (Olson, King, & Jirikowic, 2008). The abnormalities include facial deformities and defective limbs, face, and heart (see Figure 4.6). Most children with FASD have learning problems and many are below average in intelligence, while some are intellectually disabled (Casey et al., 2008; Cuzon et al., 2008). Although many mothers of FASD infants are heavy drinkers, heavy drinking does not always result in a child being born with FASD.

Drinking alcohol during pregnancy can have serious effects on offspring even when they are not afflicted with FASD (Pollard, 2007; Sayal et al., 2007). For example, birth defects related to pre-natal alcohol consumption and exposure, known as alcohol-related birth defects (ARBD), include abnormalities in the heart, kidneys, bones, and/or hearing (Gallicano, 2010; Khalil & O'Brien, 2010).

Although FASD is often viewed as an issue that does not affect all populations in Canada, it is commonly seen as affecting families primarily from low socio-economic status, Aboriginal commu-nities, and among mothers who seem not to care about their children. However, such views tend to cre-ate harmful assumptions and stigmatization associated with this disability (Healthy Child Manitoba, 2012). FASD is a nation-wide health concern. It does not discriminate on the basis of race, socio-economic status or sex (Health Canada, 2012). In fact, national prevalence data demonstrate that women from all financial and ethnic backgrounds tend to consume some alcohol during pregnancy. The Public Health Agency of Canada has provided a grant (2011–2012) to the province of Manitoba to lead the development of a national prevalence plan (Healthy Child Manitoba, 2012). The focus of this plan is to collect, analyze, and distribute information in a timely fashion to direct policy, create evidence-based programs, implement prevention and intervention strategies, and inform public awareness.

What are some guidelines for alcohol use during pregnancy? Even drinking just one or two servings of beer or wine or one serving of hard liquor a few days a week can have negative effects on the fetus, although it is generally agreed that this level of alcohol use will not cause fetal alcohol syndrome. Health Canada recommends that if a women is pregnant or is trying to become pregnant, she should not drink any alcohol.

NICOTINE The Public Health Agency of Canada (PHAC, 2009e) conducted the Canadian Mater-nity Experiences Survey (MES) in order to facilitate understanding, and to promote and improve the health of new mothers across Canada. The sample of women to whom the survey was administered comprised mothers 15 years of age or older who had given birth to a single child in Canada during a three-month period prior to the 2006 Canadian Census of the Population. The MES included women who had smoked before, during, and following their pregnancy. The sample excluded First Nations women living on the reserve and institutionalized women.

Overall, the proportions of women who smoked during pregnancy showed variations between provinces and territories, from 9 percent in British Columbia and Ontario to 25 percent in the Northwest Territories and 64 percent in Nunavut. The proportion of women who smoked during pregnancy was highest in the younger age group (15–24 years). During the last trimester of their pregnancy 90 percent of women did not smoke at all. Interesting to note is that those women who did not smoke during the third trimester of pregnancy had resumed smoking either daily or occa-sionally by the time of the interview. This rate indicates a high proportion of postpartum relapse among those who quit smoking during pregnancy.

These smoking rates are based solely on self-reports made by the survey participants. Actually, this finding is somewhat problematic because, as research studies have demonstrated, self-reports of smoking tend to underestimate smoking prevalence. Other studies have concluded that the non-disclosure of smoking ranges from 23 to 28 percent (Dietz et al., 2010). According to Al-Sahab, Saqib, Hauser, and Tamim (2010), conclusive data on the prevalence and predictors of smoking among Canadian women during pregnancy are limited.

Cigarette smoking by pregnant women can adversely influence prenatal development, birth, and postnatal development (Cooper & Moley, 2008). Preterm births and low birth weights (see Figure 4.7), fetal and neonatal deaths, respiratory problems, and sudden infant death syndrome

Figure 4.6

Fetal Alcohol Spectrum Disorder

Fetal alcohol spectrum disorders (FASD) are characterized by a number of physical abnormalities and learning problems. Notice the wide-set eyes, flat cheekbones, and thin upper lip in this child with FASD.

Figure 4.7

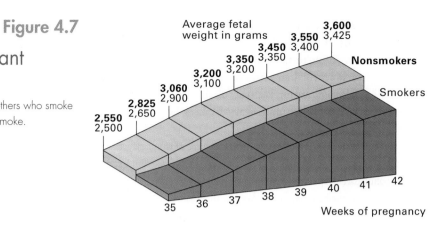

The Effects of Smoking by Expectant Mothers on Fetal Weight

Throughout prenatal development, the fetuses of expectant mothers who smoke weigh less than the fetuses of expectant mothers who do not smoke.

(SIDS; also known as crib death) are all more common among the offspring of mothers who smoked during pregnancy (Henderson, 2008; Landau, 2008). One study linked heavy smoking during pregnancy to nicotine withdrawal symptoms in newborns (Godding et al., 2004). Prenatal exposure to cigarette smoking during pregnancy is also related to increased incidence of attention deficit hyperactivity disorder at 5 to 16 years of age (Thapar et al., 2003). A recent study revealed that environmental tobacco smoke or second-hand smoke was linked to increased risk of low birth weight in offspring (Leonardi-Bee et al., 2008).

Intervention programs designed to help pregnant women stop smoking can reduce some of smoking's negative effects, especially by raising birth weights (Barron et al., 2007). A recent study revealed that women who quit smoking during pregnancy had offspring with higher birth weights than their counterparts who continued smoking (Jaddoe et al., 2008). Another intervention is nicotine replacement therapy (NRT), which has been widely developed as a pharmacotherapy of smoking cessation. It is considered to be a safer alternative for women to smoking during pregnancy (Bruin, Gerstein, & Holloway, 2010).

COCAINE   Prenatal cocaine exposure has been linked to impaired motor development at two years of age; to a slower rate of growth through 10 years of age (Richardson, Goldschmidt, & Willford, 2008); and to impaired language development and information processing (Beeghly et al., 2006), including attention deficits in preschool and elementary school children (Accornero et al., 2007; Noland et al., 2005). In addition, lower birth weight, length, and head circumference (dose dependent) as well as congenital anomalies and genitourinary malformations were found (Wong, Ordean, & Kahan, 2011).

Some researchers argue that these findings should be interpreted cautiously (Accornero et al., 2007). Why? Because other factors in the lives of pregnant women who use cocaine (such as poverty, malnutrition, and other substance abuse) often cannot be ruled out as possible contributors to the problems found in their children (Hurt et al., 2005). For example, cocaine users are more likely than non-users to smoke cigarettes, use marijuana, drink alcohol, and take amphetamines. Interestingly, Singer et al. (2004) compared the cognitive outcomes of preschool children with prenatal exposure to cocaine to those children who were not exposed to prenatal cocaine. The results indicated that when a better home environment was provided to the cocaine-exposed children their IQ scores were similar to IQ scores of children who were not exposed to prenatal cocaine.

Despite these cautions, the weight of research evidence indicates that children born to mothers who use cocaine are likely to have neurological and cognitive deficits (Field, 2007; Richardson, Goldschmidt, & Larkby, 2008). Cocaine use by pregnant women is never recommended.

METHAMPHETAMINE   Methamphetamine, like cocaine, is a stimulant, speeding up an individual's nervous system. Babies born to mothers who use methamphetamine, or "meth," during pregnancy are at risk for a number of problems, including high infant mortality, low birth weight, and developmental and behavioural problems (Forester & Merz, 2007). Meth use during pregnancy is increasing, and some experts conclude that its use during pregnancy has become a greater problem in the United States than cocaine use (Elliott, 2004). A recent study revealed that meth exposure during prenatal development was linked to decreased arousal, increased stress, and poor movement quality in newborns (Smith et al., 2008).

MARIJUANA   An increasing number of studies have found that marijuana use by pregnant women also has negative outcomes for offspring (Huizink & Mulder, 2006; Williams & Ross, 2007). A recent study found that prenatal marijuana exposure was related to lower intelligence in children (Goldschmidt et al., 2008). Another study revealed that prenatal marijuana exposure was linked with depressive symptoms at 10 years of age (Gray et al., 2005). Further, a recent study indicated that prenatal exposure to marijuana was linked to marijuana use at 14 years of age (Day, Goldschmidt, & Thomas, 2006). In sum, marijuana use is not recommended for pregnant women.

HEROIN   It is well-documented that infants whose mothers are addicted to heroin show several behavioural difficulties at birth (Steinhausen, Blattmann, & Pfund, 2007). The difficulties include withdrawal symptoms, such as tremors, irritability, abnormal crying, disturbed sleep, and impaired motor control. The most common treatment for heroin addiction, methadone, is associated with very severe withdrawal symptoms in newborns (Binder & Vavrinkova, 2008). Even though methadone has definite treatment advantages for the mother, there is mounting evidence of adverse effects upon developing cortical function in the unborn child (Mactier, 2011).

A recent study revealed that, when compared to pregnant women who entered methadone treatment late (less than six months prior to birth), continuous methadone treatment during pregnancy was linked to improved neonatal outcomes (Burns et al., 2007).

ECSTASY   Ecstasy, referred to as MDMA, is, among young adults, one of most widely used illicit recreational drugs. Singer and colleagues (2012) conducted a study to examine the neurobehavioural outcomes of infants (one to four months) exposed to ecstasy and other recreational drugs taken by mothers during pregnancy. The results indicated a difference in sex ratio; that is, a greater number of male births was associated with ecstasy use. The mechanisms by which such alterations in sex ratio occur are not known. However, a speculative explanation poses several possibilities: an increase in XY embryos, an enhanced loss of XX embryos, and the survival of Y sperm over X sperm (Tildo et al., 2005). Another finding indicated that the ecstasy-associated infants also had lower quality of motor functioning and, at four months, lower milestone attainment, such as the ability to sit up without support, or to roll from their back to their side. These findings suggest risk to the developing infant following MDMA exposure, and that continued research studies are warranted to determine whether early motor delays persist or become resolved (Singer et al., 2012).

Incompatible Blood Types

Incompatibility between the mother's and father's blood types poses another risk to prenatal development. Blood types are created by differences in the surface structure of red blood cells. The most common blood type in Canada is O Rh positive (Canadian Blood Services, 2012).

One type of difference in the surface of red blood cells creates the familiar blood groups—A, B, O, and AB. A second difference creates what is called Rh-positive and Rh-negative blood. If a surface marker, called the *Rh factor*, is present in an individual's red blood cells, the person is said to be Rh-positive; if the Rh-marker is not present, the person is said to be Rh-negative. If a pregnant woman is Rh-negative and her partner is Rh-positive, the fetus may be Rh-positive. If the fetus's blood is Rh-positive and the mother's is Rh-negative, the mother's immune system may produce antibodies that will attack the fetus. This can result in any number of problems, including miscarriage or stillbirth, anemia, jaundice, heart defects, brain damage, or death soon after birth (Moise, 2005).

Generally, the first Rh-positive baby of an Rh-negative mother is not at risk, but with each subsequent pregnancy the risk increases. A vaccine (RhoGAM) may be given to the mother within three days of the first child's birth to prevent her body from making antibodies that will attack any future Rh-positive fetuses in subsequent pregnancies. Also, babies affected by Rh incompatibility can be given blood transfusions before or right after birth (Flegal, 2007).

---

critical thinking

As noted above, thalidomide was used as a treatment for morning sickness in Canada and resulted in over 100 children being born with shortened arms, cleft lip or palate, missing limbs and/or heart, and kidney and genital abnormalities (Pannikar, 2003). Worldwide, over 10,000 people were born with defects due to exposure to the drug. Banned in most countries by 1962, it is still being used in some countries, such as Brazil, and still causing birth defects. Since the late 1990s, thalidomide has been used to treat leprosy, myeloma, and HIV. With special permission from Health Canada and their provincial Ministry of Health, some Canadians have been able to gain access to the banned drug (its current name is Thalomid) to treat either myeloma or HIV. Reflect on the genetic abnormalities that occurred in babies caused by the ingestion of thalidomide by pregnant women. In what ways should Thalomid be made accessible for treatment to individuals with myeloma or HIV? Examine your ideas with a classmate, and together create a list of reasons to support your position.

Environmental Hazards

Many aspects of our industrial world can endanger the embryo or fetus (O'Connor & Roy, 2008). An embryo or fetus may be harmed if the mother's diet includes toxins such as mercury, or if the father's exposure to certain chemicals caused changes in his sperm. Some specific hazards to the embryo or fetus that are worth a closer look include radiation, toxic wastes, and other chemical pollutants (Orecchia, Lucignani, & Tosi, 2008; Raabe & Muller, 2008).

Prior to the time when a woman is aware of her pregnancy, a pregnant women is at risk to exposure to nonionizing and ionizing radiation. Such risks can arise from necessary medical procedures, workplace exposure, and therapeutic or diagnostic interventions during pregnancy (Williams & Fletcher, 2010). In utero exposure to nonionizing radiation, such as microwaves or electromagnetic waves, is not associated with significant risks. However, in utero exposure to ionizing radiation, such as gamma rays and x-rays, can have a negative impact on the fetus (Groen, Bae, & Lim, 2012). In fact, the effects of such exposures are directly related not only to the level of exposure but also to the stage of fetal development. The fetus is most susceptible to radiation during organogenesis, two to seven weeks after conception, and in the early fetal period (8 to 15 weeks after conception). It is important for pregnant women and their physician to weigh the risk of exposure to radiation from an x-ray when an actual, or potential, pregnancy is involved (Menias et al., 2007).

Environmental pollutants and toxic wastes are also sources of danger to the fetus. A recent extensive review of the literature by University of Ottawa's Donald T. Wigle and colleagues (2008) noted that the timing of the exposure in the life of either parent and/or during prenatal development influenced the impact of the environmental chemical contaminant. Among the dangerous pollutants and wastes are carbon monoxide, mercury, and lead. During pregnancy, lead can cross the placenta and affect the unborn child; no "safe" level of exposure to lead has been identified (Health Canada, 2011b). Several epidemiological studies have reported an association between early-life lead exposure and adverse developmental effects (Health Canada, 2011a). One study, by Hu et al. (2006), revealed that a moderately high maternal lead level during the first trimester of pregnancy showed links to lower scores on an index of mental development in infancy. Wigle et al. (2008) found evidence that any exposure was dangerous and impacted the cognitive functioning of the infant. They urged that health policies should strive to eliminate all lead exposure in "housing (paint, plumbing), ambient air, consumer products, such as artist's supplies, and drinking water" (p. 486).

In Canada, lead was eliminated from all paints in 1991; however, homes built and painted between 1960 and 1990 frequently revealed small amounts of lead in some of the painted indoor surfaces. Highest amounts of lead were used in exterior paints (Health Canada, 2011b). In the United States the risk of lead exposure is higher among poor, urban, and immigrant populations than among other groups (Cleveland, Minter, Cobb, Scott, & German, 2008).

Maternal Factors

Maternal diseases and infections can produce defects in offspring by crossing the placental barrier, or they can cause damage during birth. Rubella (German measles) is one disease that can cause prenatal defects. Women who plan to have children should have a blood test before they become pregnant to determine if they are immune to the disease (Dontigny et al., 2008).

Syphilis (a sexually transmitted infection) is more damaging later in prenatal development—four months or more after conception. Rather than affecting organogenesis, as rubella does, syphilis damages organs after they have formed. Damage includes eye lesions, which can cause blindness, and skin lesions. When syphilis is present at birth, problems can develop in the central nervous system and gastrointestinal tract (Johnson, Erbelding, & Ghanem, 2007).

Another infection that has received widespread attention recently is genital herpes. Newborns contract this virus when they are delivered through the birth canal of a mother with genital herpes (Hollier & Wendel, 2008). About one-third of babies delivered through an infected birth canal die; another one-quarter become brain damaged. If an active case of genital herpes is detected in a pregnant woman close to her delivery date, a caesarean section can be performed (in which the infant is delivered through an incision in the mother's abdomen) to keep the virus from infecting the newborn (Baker, 2007).

Human papillomavirus (HPV) is very common among reproductive-age women. HPV is known as anogenital warts, and is one of the most frequently diagnosed sexually transmitted infections (Porterfield, 2011). A critical clinical consequence of HPV infection is cervical cancer (Garolla, Pizzol, & Foresta, 2011). Generally, the acquisition of HPV is attributed to sexual transmission, or by skin-to-skin contact (Porterfield, 2011). HPV occurrence during pregnancy has not been well studied. Although indications are that the infection has been linked with spontaneous abortion, this finding yet has to be confirmed (Narducci, Einarson, & Bozzo, 2012). On the other hand, the fact that this infection can be transmitted from mother to infant has been demonstrated (LaCour & Trimble, 2012). Given the prevalence of HPV in the population, it is now essential to research the manner in which this virus is actually transmitted to the newborn and to substantiate such findings with clinical relevance (LaCour & Trimble, 2012).

AIDS is a sexually transmitted infection that is caused by the human immunodeficiency virus (HIV). The demographic profile of HIV-infected women varies widely across Canada and may reflect the distribution of different racial groups as well as immigrant populations (Forbes et al., 2011). As a result of HIV infection among women of childbearing age, fetal exposure to HIV during pregnancy has been on the rise in Canada (PHAC, 2011d). Mother-to-child transmission can occur in three ways: (1) during gestation (in utero transmission), (2) during delivery as the newborn comes into contact with maternal blood and cervical–vaginal secretions, and (3) postpartum (after birth) through breastfeeding (PHAC, 2011d). Antiretroviral therapy is effective in reducing mother-to-child transmission of HIV, and yet several infants prenatally exposed to HIV are confirmed infected each year in Canada (PHAC, 2011d). In addition, prenatal HIV testing is offered to all pregnant women in Canada; however, the approach to testing varies by province and territory (PHAC, 2011d). A significant knowledge gap remains regarding issues related to HIV and its implications for the pregnant woman and her infant (Dorval, Ritchie, & Gruslin, 2007). Whenever possible, it is essential for health care professionals to provide HIV-infected women with information required to make an informed choice about pregnancy, contraception, and reduction of vertical transmission. In this manner, the health of women and their partners as well as the protection of future children is maximized (Loutfy et al., 2012; McCall & Vicol, 2011).

Diabetes is a disorder of the metabolism that most often is caused by the inability of the body to properly absorb sugar and starch from the blood. A woman may be diabetic before she becomes pregnant, or may develop a form of diabetes called gestational diabetes during her pregnancy, usually during the 24th week. The presence of diabetes poses considerable risk to both the mother and the fetus; however, good medical care and rigorous self-management increase the likelihood of a successful pregnancy and a healthy baby for women with diabetes (Barnes, 2003).

A recent research review concluded that the offspring of diabetic mothers are at risk for metabolic disease (Doblado & Moley, 2007). And one study revealed that both chronic (long-standing) and gestational (onset or first recognition during pregnancy) diabetes were significant risks for caesarean delivery and preterm birth (Rosenberg et al., 2005). Women who have gestational diabetes also may deliver very large infants (weighing 4 kg or more), and the infants may be at risk for diabetes themselves. Figure 4.8 details some other maternal diseases that can affect the fetus.

MATERNAL AGE   When the mother's age is considered in terms of possible harmful effects on the fetus and infant, two maternal ages are of special interest: adolescence and women 35 or older (Chen et al., 2007; Maconochie et al., 2007). One recent study revealed that the rate of stillbirth was elevated for adolescent girls and women 35 years and older (Bateman & Simpson, 2006). The mortality rate of infants born to adolescent mothers is double that of infants born to mothers in their twenties. Although this high rate probably reflects the immaturity of the mother's reproductive system, poor nutrition, lack of prenatal care, and low socio-economic status may also play a role (Smith Battle, 2007). Adequate prenatal care decreases the probability that a child born to an

Figure 4.8

Maternal Diseases Impacting Perinatal Development

Diseases	Effects
Rubella (German measles)	▪ Rubella contracted in the third or fourth week of pregnancy as well as in the second month may cause intellectual disability, blindness, deafness, and heart problems. Preventive vaccines are routinely administered.

Sexually transmitted infections
▪ Syphilis
▪ Genital herpes can be contracted through the birth canal
▪ HPV common among reproductive-age women
▪ AIDS—caused by the human immunodeficiency virus (HIV), which damages the body's immune system in three ways:
  – through the placenta
  – through fluid exchange between baby and mother
  – through breastfeeding
	▪ Syphilis damages organs in the fourth month after conception. Eye lesions which may cause blindness, skin lesions, and damage to the central nervous system and the gastrointestinal tract are also linked to syphilis.
	▪ About one-third of babies delivered through a birth canal infected with genital herpes die; another one-quarter become brain damaged. A caesarean section can prevent the virus from infecting the newborn.
	▪ AIDS—transmission of HIV has been reduced due to counselling, voluntary testing, and the use of Atripla. Prenatal screening can lead to antiretroviral therapy, use of formula feeding, and elective caesarean section births (Burdge et al., 2003a, b; Loutfy et al., 2012).

What are some of the risks for infants born to adolescent mothers?

adolescent girl will have physical problems. However, adolescents are the least likely of women in all age groups to obtain prenatal assistance from clinics, pediatricians, and health services.

The birth rate among teenage mothers has decreased constantly over the last three decades, from about 30 births per 1,000 in 1974, to 12 births per 1,000 in 2009 (HRSDC, 2012b). Despite the evidence of a birth rate decrease, teenage motherhood is still an important public health issue due to various adverse maternal and health outcomes (PHAC, 2008). Health problems during teenage pregnancies include poor maternal weight gain and anemia. Many factors contribute to the poor outcomes associated with teenage childbearing. Included among them are disadvantaged social environment, biological immaturity, inadequate antenatal care, physical and sexual abuse, smoking, and drug use (PHAC, 2008). It is likely, however, that the declining trends in teen pregnancy rates could reflect several of the following: increasing levels of effective contraceptive use, exposure to higher quality sexual health education and/or shifting social norms in a direction that provides greater support for the capacity of young women to exercise reproductive choice (SIECCAN, 2012).

In 2009, Nunavut had an average age of mothers at birth that was significantly younger (25.1 years) compared to the national average, which was 29.4 years (HRSDC, 2012b). The rate of births to teens in Nunavut was almost eight times the Canadian average. In contrast, Ontario and British Columbia had the highest numbers of mothers, as well as the highest percentage of births to mothers, 30 and over (HRSDC, 2012b).

It should be noted that the decline in teen pregnancy rate in Canada during 1996–2006 was greater than in other countries including the United States and England, where teen pregnancy rates did decline but to a lesser extent than in Canada (McKay, 2006).

The chances of having a baby with Down syndrome, a form of developmental disability, increases relative to the mother's age (Soergel et al., 2006). A baby with Down syndrome is rarely born to a mother under the age of 35, but the risk increases after the mother reaches 30. By age 40, the probability is slightly over 1 in 100, and by age 50 it is almost 1 in 10. The risk also is higher before age 18.

One of the most important changes in reproductive behaviour during recent decades has been the rising proportions of births among mothers at advanced ages (Billari et al., 2011). The Canadian average age of childbearing mothers is increasing, and older mothers tend to be married, highly educated, and affluent (Joseph et al., 2005). However, many Canadian women stay in school longer and seek to establish their careers before beginning a family (Vézina & Turcotte, 2009). Policy decision makers must be cognizant of the need for additional high-risk obstetric and neonatal health services when societal norms especially encourage women to delay childbearing in favour of education and career objectives (Benzies et al., 2006).

When mothers are 35 years and older, risks also increase for low birth weight, preterm delivery, and fetal death (Fretts, Zera, & Heffner, 2008). In one study fetal death was low for women 30 to 34 years of age, but increased progressively for women 35 to 39 and 40 to 44 years of age (Canterino et al., 2004). Carolan and Nelson (2007) found that concern over the expected risk of a pregnancy after age 35 created stress for pregnant women in this age group. However, if women remain active, exercise regularly, and are careful about their nutrition, their reproductive systems may remain healthier at older ages than was thought possible in the past.

Crompton and Keown (2009) found Canadian women might be forestalling having children until they have access to maternal benefits. In combination with the existing maternity leave benefit of 15 weeks, an amendment to Canada's *Employment Insurance Act* in 2000 increased prenatal leave benefits from 10 to 35 weeks. The total employment-protected (not necessarily paid) maternity and parental leave period increased from six months to one year (PHAC, 2009e).

DIET, NUTRITION, AND EXERCISE   A developing embryo or fetus depends completely on the mother for nutrition, which comes from the mother's blood (Derbyshire, 2007a, b). The nutritional status of the embryo or fetus is determined by the mother's total caloric intake and her intake of proteins, vitamins, and minerals. Children born to malnourished mothers are more likely than other children to have physical disabilities.

Being overweight before and during pregnancy can also put the embryo or fetus at risk (Reece, 2008). Researchers have found that obese women had a significant risk of fetal death (Nohr et al., 2005). Recent studies indicate that maternal obesity doubles the risk of stillbirth and neonatal death, and is linked with problems in the central nervous system, including spina bifida (Frederick et al., 2008; Guelinckx, Devlieger, & Vansant, 2008; Kriebs, 2009). Further, a recent analysis proposed that overeating by pregnant women results in a series of neuroendocrine changes in the fetus that in turn program the development of fat cells and appetite regulation system (McMillen et al., 2008). In this analysis, it was predicted that such early fetal programming is likely linked to being overweight in childhood and adolescence. Health Canada's recommended weight gain for pregnant women, based on pre-pregnancy body mass index (BMI), is given in Figure 4.9.

Figure 4.9

Health Canada Suggested Weight Gain during Pregnancy based on Pre-Pregnancy BMI (weight in kg divided by height in metres squared)

Pre-Pregnancy BMI Category	Recommended Range of Total Weight Gain
BMI < 18.5 underweight	12.5 to 18 kg
BMI 18.5 to 24.9 normal weight	11.5 to 16 kg
BMI 25.0 to 29.9 overweight	7.0 to 11.5 kg
BMI ≥ 30 obese	5.0 to 9.0 kg

Reprinted with permission from Table S-1, Weight Gain During Pregnancy: Re-examining the Guidelines, 2009 by the National Academy of Sciences. Courtesy of the National Academies Press, Washington, D.C.

Inuit infants in Nunavik have higher levels of PCBs in their umbilical cord blood than other children due to the large amounts of fish and marine animals eaten by their mothers (Muckle, Dewailly, & Ayotte, 1998).

One aspect of maternal nutrition that is important for normal prenatal development is folic acid, a B-complex vitamin (Goh & Koren, 2008). As noted earlier in the chapter, a lack of folic acid is linked with neural tube defects in offspring, such as spina bifida, a typically fatal defect in the spinal cord (Ryan-Harshman & Aldoori, 2008). Health officials recommend that pregnant women consume a minimum of .4 mg of folic acid per day (about twice the amount the average woman gets in one day). Orange juice and spinach and broccoli are examples of foods rich in folic acid (Health Canada, 2007a).

Fish is often recommended as part of a healthy diet, but increased pollution has made many fish a risky choice for pregnant women. Some fish contain high levels of mercury, which is released into the air both naturally and by industrial pollution (Fitzgerald et al., 2004). When mercury falls into the water, it can become toxic and accumulate in large fish, such as shark, swordfish, king mackerel, and some species of large tuna. Mercury is easily transferred across the placenta, and the embryo's developing brain and nervous system are highly sensitive to the metal (Gliori et al., 2006; Sato, Li, & Shaha, 2006). In Eating Well with Canada's Food Guide, Health Canada (2007a) recommends eating cooked fish and shellfish.

PCBs (polychlorinated biphenyls) are chemicals that were used in manufacturing until they were banned in the 1970s, but they are still present in landfills, sediments, and wildlife. One concern focuses on pregnant women eating PCB-polluted fish (Hertz-Picciotto et al., 2008). A recent research review concluded that PCB-polluted fish pose a potential risk to prenatal neurodevelopment (Korrick & Sagiv, 2008). Inuit infants in Nunavut currently have much higher levels of PCBs in their umbilical cord blood than other children, presumably due to the large amounts of fish and marine animals eaten by their mothers.

Proper exercise during pregnancy is an important activity to ensure appropriate weight gain, to promote better sleep, to relax and reduce stress, and to offset the risk of gestational diabetes. Health Canada recommends that drinking water during exercise is important to avoid overheating and dehydration. Before undertaking a new exercise program, the pregnant woman should consult with her doctor or nurse (PHAC, 2011g).

EMOTIONAL STATES AND STRESS   When a pregnant woman experiences intense fears, anxieties, and other emotions or negative mood states, physiological changes occur that may affect her fetus (Taige et al., 2007). Maternal stress may increase the level of corticotropin-releasing hormone (CRH), a precursor of the stress hormone cortisol, early in pregnancy (Nakamura, Sheps, & Arck, 2008). Elevated levels of CRH and cortisol in the fetus have been linked to premature delivery in infants (Field, 2007). A recent study also revealed that a decline in stress during pregnancy was linked to a lower incidence of preterm birth (Glynn et al., 2008). A mother's stress may also influence the fetus indirectly by increasing the likelihood that the mother will engage in unhealthy behaviours, such as taking drugs and engaging in poor prenatal care.

The mother's emotional state during pregnancy can influence the birth process, too. An emotionally distraught mother might have irregular contractions and a more difficult labour, which can cause irregularities in the supply of oxygen to the fetus or other problems after birth. Babies born after extended labour also may adjust more slowly to their world and be more irritable.

High maternal anxiety and stress during pregnancy can have long-term consequences for the offspring (Bowen & Muhajarine, 2006; Bowen, Bowen, Maslany, & Muhajarine, 2008; Davis et al., 2007). A recent research review indicated that pregnant women with high levels of stress are at increased risk for having a child with emotional or cognitive problems, attention deficit hyperactivity disorder (ADHD), and language delay (Taige et al., 2007).

Paternal Factors

Some paternal factors such as age and exposure to environmental hazards, including exposing the mother and fetus to secondhand smoke, may also influence prenatal and child development. Men's exposure to lead, radiation, certain pesticides, and petrochemicals may cause abnormalities in sperm that lead to miscarriage or diseases such as childhood cancer (Cordier, 2008;

critical thinking

You are aware that the spraying of pesticides to control mosquitoes is occurring in some cities. Compare and contrast the responsibilities of the individual relative to those of the provincial and federal government toward environmental teratogens. In what ways do social determinants, such as family income and education, play a role in people's lives regarding their health and safety in the environment? What policies could be developed to promote health in society? What would be required to enact these policies? Analyze and make comparisons regarding the severity of environmental teratogens on the health of individuals, first in rural and then in urban communities.

Monge et al., 2007). In one study, heavy paternal smoking was associated with the risk of early pregnancy loss (Venners et al., 2004).

The father's age also makes a difference (Maconochie et al., 2007; Yang et al., 2007). About 5 percent of children with Down syndrome have older fathers. The offspring of older fathers also face increased risk for other birth defects, including dwarfism and Marfan syndrome, which involves head and limb deformities.

Prenatal Care

Prenatal care varies enormously, but usually involves a package of medical care services in a defined schedule of visits. In addition to medical care, prenatal care programs often include comprehensive educational, social, and nutritional services (Moos, 2006).

Prenatal care usually includes screening that can reveal manageable conditions and/or treatable diseases that can affect the baby or the mother (Lu & Lu, 2008). The education an expectant woman receives about pregnancy, labour and delivery, and caring for the newborn can be extremely valuable, especially for first-time mothers. Prenatal programs include comprehensive educational, social, and nutritional services (Massey, Rising, & Ickovics, 2006; Moos, 2006).

Inadequate prenatal care can occur for a variety of reasons. These include the health care system, provider practices, and individual and social characteristics (Conway & Kutinova, 2006). According to the College of Family Physicians of Canada, approximately one-third of Canadian women who live in rural areas (80 or more kilometres from an urban centre) find accessing advanced maternity care difficult. Lack of transportation and child care, as well as financial difficulties, were commonly cited as barriers to getting prenatal care. Women who have unplanned or unwanted pregnancies, or who have negative attitudes about being pregnant, are more likely to delay prenatal care or to miss appointments.

Because, a healthy pregnancy and infancy are key to optimal child development, the Canadian Perinatal Surveillance System (CPSS) of Health Canada (PHAC, 2012b) monitors care provided and outcomes. Chalmers and Wen (2003) suggest that given the expensive nature of perinatal care, more exploration of unnecessary, excessive, and non-evidence-based methods of care be made to eliminate useless and costly procedures.

Positive Prenatal Development

For the vast majority of pregnancies, prenatal development does not go awry, and development occurs along the positive path described at the beginning of the chapter (Lester, 2000). That said, it is still important for prospective parents to avoid the risks to fetal development to the greatest degree possible.

To this point, we have discussed a number of ideas about prenatal development. For a review, see the **Reach Your Learning Objectives** section at the end of this chapter.

Birth

LO2 Outline the birth process.

As we saw in the opening vignette, many changes have taken place in giving birth to a baby since 1934, when the Dionne quintuplets were born. Today, there are more multiple births, fewer home births, and more extensive medical care.

The Birth Process

To learn more about the birth process, we will examine the stages of birth, the transition from fetus to newborn, childbirth strategies, special neonatal (newborn) considerations, and measures of neonatal health and responsiveness.

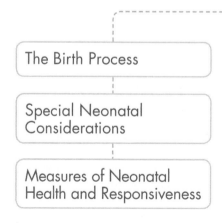

The Birth Process

Special Neonatal Considerations

Measures of Neonatal Health and Responsiveness

Stages of Birth

The birth process occurs in three stages. For a woman having her first child, the first stage lasts an average of 12 to 24 hours; it is the longest of the three stages. In the first stage, uterine contractions are 15 to 20 minutes apart at the beginning and last up to a minute. These contractions cause the woman's cervix to stretch and open. As the first stage progresses, the contractions come closer together, appearing every two to five minutes. Their intensity increases, too. By the end of the first birth stage, contractions dilate the cervix to an opening of about 10 cm so that the baby can move from the uterus to the birth canal.

The second birth stage begins when the baby's head starts to move through the cervix and the birth canal. It terminates when the baby completely emerges from the mother's body. This stage lasts approximately 1.5 hours. With each contraction, the mother bears down hard to push the baby out of her body. By the time the baby's head is out of the mother's body, the contractions come almost every minute and last for about a minute. **Afterbirth** *is the third stage, when the placenta, umbilical cord, and other membranes get detached and expelled.* This final stage is the shortest of the three birth stages, lasting only minutes.

The Transition from Fetus to Newborn

Being born involves considerable stress for the baby. During each contraction, when the placenta and umbilical cord are compressed as the uterine muscles draw together, the supply of oxygen to the fetus is decreased. If the delivery takes too long, the baby can develop *anoxia*, a condition in which the fetus or newborn has an insufficient supply of oxygen. Anoxia can cause brain damage (Smith, 2008).

The baby has considerable capacity to withstand the stress of birth. Large quantities of adrenaline and noradrenalin, hormones that help protect the fetus in the event of oxygen deficiency, are secreted in stressful circumstances. These hormones increase the heart's pumping activity, speed up heart rate, channel blood flow to the brain, and raise blood-sugar levels. This circumstance underscores how stressful it is to be born, but also how prepared and adapted the fetus is for birth (Von Beveren, 2008).

At the time of birth, the baby is covered with what is called *vernix caseosa*, a protective skin grease. This vernix consists of fatty secretions and dead cells, thought to protect the baby's skin against heat loss before and during birth.

The umbilical cord is cut immediately after birth, and the baby is on its own; 25 million little air sacs in the lungs must be filled with air. Until now, oxygen came from the mother via the umbilical cord, but now the baby has to be self-sufficient and breathe on its own. The newborn's bloodstream is redirected through the lungs and to all parts of the body. These first breaths may be the hardest ones at any point in the life span (Wong et al., 2006).

CHILDBIRTH SETTING AND ATTENDANTS   Although an increasing number of home births occur, as evidenced by the increased number of midwifery programs to train midwives, most births take place in hospitals and are attended by physicians. Many hospitals now have birthing centres, where fathers or birth coaches may be with the mother during labour and delivery. Some people believe this so-called alternative birthing centre offers a good compromise between a technological, depersonalized hospital birth (which cannot offer the emotional experience of a home birth) and a birth at home (which cannot offer the immediate medical backup of a hospital). The birthing room allows for a full range of birth experiences, from a totally unmedicated, natural birth to the most complex, medically intensive care.

Midwifery in Canada is an autonomous self-regulating profession that has undergone tremendous growth since 2010. Some form of regulated midwifery care is available in 8 of 10 Canadian provinces, and 2 of 3 territories (O'Brien et al., 2011). In all regulated provinces and territories, midwives must be registered with the regulatory authority in order to legally call themselves a midwife and to practise their profession. As such, the **midwife** is recognized as *a responsible and accountable professional who works in partnership with women to give the necessary support, care, and advice during*

afterbirth The third stage of birth when the placenta, umbilical cord, and other membranes are detached and expelled.

After the long journey of prenatal development, birth takes place. During birth, the baby is on a threshold between two worlds. **What is the fetus-to-newborn transition like?**

midwife A responsible and accountable professional who works in partnership with women to give the necessary support, care, and advice during pregnancy, labour, and the postpartum period.

Home or Hospital: Where Would You Like to Give Birth?

"There's no place like home!" "Home is where the heart is!" We have all heard these refrains; but is home the best place to give birth? In preparing for the birth of a baby, parents consider the health and well-being of both mother and newborn, as well as the role of a midwife. Should a woman choose to give birth in a hospital, she will have immediate care and reassurance from health care providers intent on making her comfortable. Full health care services are ready should they be required. Should she choose to give birth at home, she will be surrounded by her family and have all the comforts of home, including food to her liking, available to her (Johnson & Daviss, 2005).

Canadian research indicates that home births and hospital births are equally safe for both mothers and infants (Janssen et al., 2009). To qualify for a home birth, the woman must be in good health and be assessed in the low-risk category. A low-risk pregnancy is one without complications for the mother or the infant. Generally, the mother is in good health, seeks prenatal care as soon as she believes she is pregnant, and continues seeing her health care provider. Women with low-risk pregnancies require minimum medical attention.

Although midwifery is relatively new to many parts of Canada, education and training for midwifery is now offered at many universities. Knowing that reliable studies have attested to the safety of home births and that midwives are highly trained to deliver the newborn and assist the mother, a woman can make the decision with her family with considerable confidence. What decision would you make regarding the birth of your child?

pregnancy, labour, and the postpartum period. Midwives conduct births on their own responsibility and provide care for the newborn and the infant (ICM, 2011). Midwifery education in Canada is offered at a university baccalaureate level (Canadian Midwifery Regulators Consortium, 2012). The Society of Obstetricians and Gynaecologists of Canada (SOGC) continues its support of ongoing evaluation and accreditation of midwifery education and supports the integration of midwifery into the obstetrical interprofessional health care team to foster excellence in maternity care for women living in Canada. Where midwifery is provided within an obstetrical health care team, women then have a familiar caregiver with them during labour and birth, and for their postpartum care (SOGC, 2009). Registered midwives remain current on maternity-related research. The evidence, available in journals and research studies, allows them to provide comprehensive information so that women and their families can make informed choices about all aspects of their care (Canadian Midwifery Regulators Consortium, 2012). On May 5, 2011, the National Aboriginal Health Organization (NAHO) joined midwives and their supporters from across Canada to mark the International Day of the Midwife (NAHO, 2012).

In many countries, a doula attends a childbearing woman. Doula is a Greek word that means "a woman who helps." A **doula** *is a caregiver who provides continuous physical, emotional, and educational support for the mother before, during, and after childbirth.* Doulas remain with the mother throughout labour, assessing and responding to her needs. Researchers have found positive effects when a doula is present at the birth of a child (Campbell et al., 2007; Stein, Kennell, & Fulcher, 2004). In a recent study, low-income pregnant women who were given doula support spent a shorter time in labour and their newborn had a higher health rating at one and five minutes after birth than their low-income counterparts who did not receive doula support (Campbell et al., 2006). Gilliland (2010) states that doula support during labour is considered one of the more positive interventions in childbirth.

doula A caregiver who provides continuous physical, emotional, and educational support to the mother before, during, and after childbirth.

BIRTH PLANS   Canadian women deserve quality maternity care whether they live in an urban, rural, or remote community (Miller et al., 2012). Childbirth is a very natural event and, coupled with the advent of family-centred care, childbearing families and health care providers now realize the advantage of a birth plan. A birth plan informs the health care provider about the following: the type of delivery the mother-to-be wants, the choice of birth companion (usually the father), the choice of medication management to be implemented or not during labour, and finally the care of the baby postpartum (SOGC, 2011a).

In *hospital settings* that provide obstetrical care and birthing units, a specialized interprofessional health care team is on hand. Analgesics can be used to reduce the discomfort of labour. An *epidural block* is regional anaesthesia that numbs the woman's body from the waist down. Even this drug, thought to be relatively safe, has come under recent criticism because it is associated with fever, extended labour, and increased risk of caesarean delivery (Glantz, 2005). *Oxytocics* are synthetic hormones that are used to stimulate contractions; pitocin is the most commonly used oxytocic. The benefits and risks of oxytocin as a part of childbirth continue to be debated (Vasdev, 2008).

Predicting how a particular drug will affect an individual pregnant woman and the fetus is difficult (Funai, Evans, & Lockwood, 2008). It is important for the mother to assess her level of pain and be an important voice in the decision of whether she should receive medication.

Martell (2003) conducted a study to explore the perceptions of postpartum women on the hospital environment and how it affects their postpartum experience. The results of her study indicated that the physical and socio-cultural environments of the hospital do, in fact, affect the mother's experience. For example, concern about privacy and safety caused anxiety for several participants. Bothersome sensory stimuli such as light and noise interfered with their sleep. The lack of clarity in the care setting possibly accounts for the high incidence of negative perceptions held by the mothers of newborns in the special care nursery.

The emphasis today is on broadly educating the pregnant woman so that she can be reassured and confident in her birthing experience. This objective is most relevant in light of the Canadian Maternity Experiences Survey (PHAC, 2009e). Chalmers, Kaczorowski, O' Brien, and Royle (2012), in examining the results of the survey, found that women need to be better informed about the advantages and disadvantages of different birthing procedures and technologies to make informed decisions. Though the trend at one time was toward natural childbirth without any medication, today the emphasis is on using some medication, but keeping it to a minimum when possible.

Debate regarding the safety implications of *home births* is still prevalent in the literature. The Society of Obstetricians and Gynaecologists of Canada does not take a specific stand on home births (SOGC, 2003). The results of one study conducted by Janssen and her colleagues (2009) revealed that planned home births attended by a registered midwife were associated not only with very low rates of perinatal death, but also with reduced rates of obstetric interventions and adverse maternal outcomes, compared to planned hospital birth attended by a midwife or physician.

Natural childbirth *was developed in 1914 by an English obstetrician, Grantley Dick-Read. It attempts to reduce the mother's pain by decreasing her fear through education about childbirth and by teaching her to use breathing methods and relaxation techniques during delivery.* Dick-Read also believed that the doctor's relationship with the mother is an important factor in reducing her pain. He said the doctor should be present during her active labour prior to delivery and should provide reassurance.

Prepared childbirth *was developed by French obstetrician Fernand Lamaze. This childbirth strategy is similar to natural childbirth but includes a special breathing technique to control pushing in the final stages of labour and a more detailed anatomy and physiology course.* The Lamaze method has become very popular in the United States. The pregnant woman's partner or a friend usually serves as a coach, and attends childbirth classes with her and helps with her breathing and relaxation during delivery.

Many other prepared childbirth techniques also have been developed (Davidson, London, & Ladewig, 2008). They usually include elements of Dick-Read's natural childbirth or Lamaze's method, plus one or more new components. French obstetrician Frederick Leboyer opposed the standard techniques of childbirth and advocated "birth without violence." In the *Leboyer method*, soft lights are used in the delivery room, and the newborn is placed on the mother's abdomen immediately after birth to foster bonding and then immersed in lukewarm water to relax. The umbilical cord is not cut until the newborn is able to breathe on his or her own. Virtually all of the prepared childbirth methods emphasize some degree of education, relaxation, and breathing exercises and

natural childbirth Developed in 1914 by Dick-Read, this method attempts to reduce the mother's pain by decreasing her fear through education about childbirth and relaxation techniques during delivery.

prepared childbirth A childbirth strategy similar to natural childbirth but that includes a special breathing technique to control pushing in the final stages of labour and a more detailed anatomy and physiology course; developed by Fernand Lamaze.

support. In recent years, new ways of teaching relaxation have been offered, including guided mental imagery, massage, and meditation. In sum, the current belief in prepared childbirth is that when information and support are provided, women *know* how to give birth.

In a **caesarean delivery**, *the baby is removed from the mother's uterus through an incision made in her abdomen.* This is sometimes called a caesarean section, or c-section. A caesarean section is usually performed if the baby is in a **breech position**, *which causes the baby's buttocks to be the first part to emerge from the vagina.*

The benefits and risks of caesarean section continue to be debated (Declercq et al., 2008; Vendittelli et al., 2008). Caesarean deliveries are safer than breech deliveries, but they involve a higher infection rate, a longer hospital stay, and the greater expense and stress that accompany any surgery. Liston, Allen, O'Connell, and Jangaard (2008) conducted a study to determine the impact of caesarean delivery on the incidence of neonatal outcome. They found that caesarean delivery in labour, compared with vaginal delivery, is more likely to be associated with an increased risk for respiratory conditions and depression at birth than is the case with caesarean delivery without labour. It is interesting to note that caesarean delivery appears to be somewhat protective against neonatal birth trauma, especially when performed without labour. Further, client-initiated elective caesarean delivery is emerging as an urgent issue for practitioners, hospitals, and policy makers and for pregnant women. For many childbearing mothers the persuasive influence of positive caesarean stories and negative vaginal stories must be considered by health care professionals. Care providers need to become familiar with the social influences impacting women's decisions for mode of delivery so that realistic informed discussions can be pursued with the childbearing woman (Munro, Kornelson, & Hutton, 2009).

Currently, women who rarely have witnessed a live birth are using technological interventions, such as caesarean section, because they believe it will reduce the pain, stress, and uncertainty of labour (Romano & Lothian, 2008). Some obstetricians, wanting to be safe rather than sorry, opt for caesarean births. Some health care providers argue that women should have the right to choose either vaginal delivery or caesarean section; others who oppose this choice note that caesarean section should not be used unless absolutely necessary. Opponents argue that postpartum depression, risk of infection, and hospital costs all increase with caesarean section (Simpson, 2010).

Canada's obstetricians have extended warnings recently that the percentage of babies being born by caesarean section is at an all-time high and continues to rise. According to SOGC (2008), from 2003 to 2006 the rate of c-sections in Canada increased from 17.6 to 26.3 percent. This increase is exposing mothers and infants to more risks that would be less pronounced during natural birth. Liu et al. (2007) state that even though the absolute difference is small, the risks of severe maternal morbidity associated with planned caesarean delivery are higher than those associated with planned vaginal delivery.

Special Neonatal Considerations

Some newborns present special situations that require additional consideration. For example, how can we distinguish between a preterm infant and a low-birth-weight infant? How do children with special needs gain access to all aspects of life available to the able-bodied child?

Preterm and Low-Birth-Weight Infants

Three related conditions pose threats to many newborns: low birth weight, being preterm, and being small for date. **Low-birth-weight infants** weigh less than 2.5 kilograms at birth. *Very-low-birth-weight* newborns weigh under 1.6 kilograms, and *extremely-low-birth-weight* newborns weigh under .9 kilograms. **Preterm infants** are those born three weeks or more before the pregnancy has reached its full term—in other words, prior to 38 weeks after conception. **Small-for-date infants** (also called *small-for-gestational-age infants*) *are those whose birth weight is below normal when the length of the pregnancy is considered.* They weigh less than 90 percent of all babies of the same gestational age. Small-for-date infants may be preterm or full-term. One study found that small-for-date infants had more than a fourfold risk of death (Regev et al., 2003). An infant is full-term when it has grown in the womb for a full 38 to 42 weeks between conception and delivery. Between 1991 and 2004, preterm births

caesarean delivery The baby is removed from the mother's uterus through an incision made in her abdomen.

breech position The baby's position in the uterus that causes the buttocks to be the first part to emerge from the vagina.

--- **critical** thinking ------------

From 1993 to 2006, Canada's c-section rate increased from 18 to 26 percent. For Canada, one of the safest places in the world to give birth, this increasing rate presents a concerning trend for the future. Design a plan for women to facilitate the decision-making process between a vaginal birth or a caesarean birth. Compare and contrast complications between vaginal and caesarean births.

low-birth-weight infant Born after a regular period of gestation (the length of time between conception and birth) of 38 to 42 weeks but who weighs less than 2.5 kg.

preterm infant Born prior to 38 weeks after conception.

small-for-date infants Born with birth weight below normal when length of the pregnancy is considered; may be preterm or full-term; also called *small-for-gestational-age infants*.

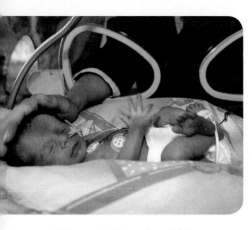

A "kilogram kid," weighing 1 kilogram or less at birth. **What are some long-term potential consequences from weighing so little at birth?**

increased from 6.6 per 100 to 8.2 per 100 live births (PHAC, 2008). The increase in preterm birth is likely due to such factors as the increasing number of births to women 35 years and older, increasing rates of multiple births, increased management of maternal and fetal conditions (for example, inducing labour preterm if medical technology indicates it will increase the likelihood of survival), increased substance abuse (tobacco, alcohol), and increased stress (Goldenberg & Culhane, 2007).

Recently, considerable interest has been generated in the role that progestin might play in reducing preterm births (Basaran, 2007; Thornton, 2007). Several studies provide further support for the use of progestin in the second trimester of pregnancy in reducing the risk of preterm delivery (da Fonseca et al., 2007; Lamont & Jaggat, 2007). However, one study did not find a reduction in preterm labour when progestin was given to women who were pregnant with twins (Rouse et al., 2007). Another survey indicated that the use of progestin to prevent preterm birth increased from 38 percent of maternal–fetal medicine specialists in 2003 to 67 percent in 2005 (Ness et al., 2006).

The incidence of low birth weight varies considerably from country to country. The U.S. low-birth-weight rate of 8 percent in 2004 is quite high for a developed country (Hoyert et al., 2006). In Canada, 6 percent of newborns were considered of low birth weight in 2005 (Statistics Canada, 2008). The causes of low birth weight also vary. In the developing world, low birth weight stems mainly from the mother's poor health and nutrition (Lasker et al., 2005). For example, diarrhea and malaria, which are common in developing countries, can impair fetal growth if the mother becomes affected while she is pregnant. In developed countries, cigarette smoking during pregnancy is the leading cause of low birth weight (Nabet et al., 2007). In both developed and developing countries, adolescents who give birth when their bodies have not fully matured are at risk for having low-birth-weight babies (Malamitsi-Puchner & Boutsikou, 2006).

Long-Term Outcomes for Low-Birth-Weight Infants

Although most preterm and low-birth-weight infants are healthy, as a group they have more health and developmental problems than normal-birth-weight infants (Minde & Zelkowitz, 2008; van de Weijer-Bergsma, Wijnroks, & Jongmans, 2008). For preterm birth, the terms *extremely preterm* and *very preterm* are increasingly used (Smith, 2008). Extremely preterm infants are those born less than 28 weeks preterm, and very preterm infants are those born less than 33 weeks of gestational age. Figure 4.10 shows the results of a recent Norwegian study indicating that the earlier preterm infants are born, the more likely they will drop out of school (Swamy, Ostbye, & Skjaerven, 2008). Another recent study found that extremely preterm infants were more likely to show pervasive delays in early language development (such as vocabulary size and quality of word use) than very preterm infants, who in turn showed more early language delays than full-term infants (Foster-Cohen et al., 2007). A research review also revealed that very preterm infants had lower IQ scores, less effective information-processing skills, and were more at risk for behavioural problems than were full-term infants (Johnson, 2007).

The number and severity of these problems increase as birth weight decreases (Marlow et al., 2007). Survival rates for infants who are born very early and very small have risen, but with this improved survival rate has come increases in rates of severe brain damage (Allen, 2008; Casey, 2008). A recent MRI study revealed that adolescents who had experienced very preterm birth were more likely to show reduced prefrontal lobe and corpus callosum functioning than full-term adolescents (Narberhaus et al., 2007).

At school age, children who were born low in birth weight are more likely than their normal-birth-weight counterparts to have a learning disability, attention deficit disorder, or breathing problems such as asthma (Greenough, 2007; Joshi & Kotecha, 2007). Children born very low in birth weight have more learning problems and lower levels of achievement in reading and math than moderately low-birth-weight children (Breslau, Paneth, & Lucia, 2004). Approximately 50 percent of all low-birth-weight children are enrolled in special education programs.

Not all of these adverse consequences can be attributed solely to being born low in birth weight. Some of the less severe but more common developmental and physical delays occur because many low-birth-weight children come from disadvantaged environments (Malamitsi-Puchner & Boutsikou, 2006).

-------------- **Figure 4.10**

Percentage of Preterm and Full-term Birth Infants Who Dropped Out of School

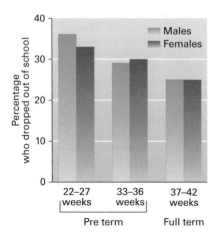

Some of the devastating effects of being born low in birth weight can be reversed. Intensive enrichment programs that provide medical and educational services for both the parents and the child have been shown to improve short-term developmental outcomes for low-birth-weight children.

Kangaroo Care and Massage Therapy

Beginning life as a preterm or low-birth-weight baby in a neonatal intensive-care unit (NICU) is to live in an incubator attached to monitoring equipment and trying to sleep in an often very noisy environment. Kangaroo care is a way of holding a preterm infant so that there is skin-to-skin contact. One survey has indicated that kangaroo care is used by 82 to 97 percent of nurses in NCIUs in the United States (Engler et al., 2002; Field et al. 2006). The baby, wearing only a diaper, is held upright against the parent's bare chest, much as a baby kangaroo is carried by its mother. Kangaroo care is typically practised for two to three hours per day, skin-to-skin, over an extended time in early infancy (Feldman & Eidelman, 2003).

Why use kangaroo care with preterm infants? Preterm infants often have difficulty coordinating their breathing and heart rate, and the close physical contact with the parent provided by kangaroo care can help to stabilize the preterm infant's heartbeat, temperature, and breathing (Walters et al., 2007). Further, preterm infants who experience kangaroo care have longer periods of sleep, gain more weight, decrease their crying, have longer periods of alertness, and have earlier hospital discharge (Ludington-Hoe et al., 2006). A review of the literature on kangaroo care found it increased infants' weight gain and duration and intake of breastfeeding, facilitated mother–infant bonding, and had a positive effect on temperament (Charpak et al., 2005). Canadian researchers found kangaroo care helped to diminish pain responses in infants undergoing procedures involving a heel lance (Johnston et al., 2008). Increasingly, kangaroo care is being recommended for full-term infants as well (Ferber & Makhoul, 2008; Walters et al., 2007).

Many preterm infants experience less touch than full-term infants because they are isolated in temperature-controlled incubators (Chia, Sellick, & Gan, 2006). Tiffany Field's (2007) research has led to a surge of interest in the role that massage might play in improving the developmental outcomes of low-birth-weight infants. In a recent study, preterm infants in a NICU were randomly assigned to a massage therapy group or a control group. Behaviour indicators of stress such as crying, grimacing, leg movements, and startles were recorded. The therapy group then received three 15-minute massage sessions per day for five days, while the control did not. At the end of the five days, the preterm infants in the massage therapy group showed a significantly lower stress response rating than the control group (Hernandez-Reif & Field, 2007).

Measures of Neonatal Health and Responsiveness

The **Apgar scale** *is widely used to assess the health of newborns at one and five minutes after birth by evaluating infants' heart rate, respiratory effort, muscle tone, body colour, and reflex irritability.* An obstetrician or a nurse does the evaluation and gives the newborn a score, or reading, of 0, 1, or 2 on each of these five health signs (see Figure 4.11). A total score of 7 to 10 indicates that the newborn's condition is good. A score of 5 indicates there may be developmental difficulties. A score of 3 or below signals an emergency and indicates that the baby might not survive. The Apgar scale also identifies high-risk infants who need resuscitation.

To evaluate the newborn more thoroughly, the **Brazelton Neonatal Behavioral Assessment Scale (NBAS)** *is performed within 24 to 36 hours after birth to evaluate the newborn's neurological development, reflexes, and reactions to people and objects.* It is also used as a sensitive index of neurological competence up to one month after birth for typical infants, and as a measure in many studies of infant development (Mamtani, Patel, & Kulkarni, 2008).

An "offspring" of the NBAS, the **Neonatal Intensive Care Unit Network Neurobehavioral Scale (NNNS)**, *provides a more comprehensive analysis of the newborn's behaviour, neurological and stress responses, and regulatory capacities* (Brazelton, 2004; Lester, Tronick, & Brazelton, 2004). Whereas the NBAS was developed to assess normal, healthy term infants, T. Berry Brazelton, along with Barry Lester and Edward Tronick, developed the NNNS to assess the "at-risk" infant. It is especially useful

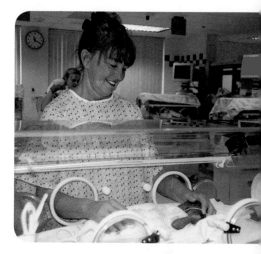

Shown here is Tiffany Field massaging a newborn infant. **What types of infants has massage therapy been shown to help?**

Apgar scale A widely used method to assess the health of newborns at one and five minutes after birth; evaluates infants' heart rate, respiratory effort, muscle tone, body colour, and reflex irritability.

Brazelton Neonatal Behavioral Assessment Scale (NBAS) A test given 24 to 36 hours after birth to assess newborns' neurological development, reflexes, and reactions to people and objects.

Neonatal Intensive Care Unit Network Neurobehavioral Scale (NNNS) Provides a more comprehensive analysis of the newborn's behaviour, neurological and stress responses, and regulatory capacities; an offspring of the NBAS.

Figure 4.11

The Apgar Scale

SCORE	0	1	2
Respiratory effort	No breathing for more than one minute	Irregular and slow	Good breathing with normal crying
Body colour	Blue and pale	Body pink, but extremities blue	Entire body pink
Heart rate	Absent	Slow—less than 100 beats per minute	Fast—100–140 beats per minute
Muscle tone	Limp and flaccid	Weak, inactive, but some flexion of extremities	Strong, active motion
Reflex irritability	No response	Grimace	Coughing, sneezing, and crying

for evaluating preterm infants (although it may not be appropriate for those less than 30 weeks' gestational age) and substance-exposed infants (Boukydis & Lester, 2008; Smith et al., 2008).

A very low Brazelton score can indicate brain damage or can reflect stress to the brain that may heal in time. However, if an infant merely seems sluggish in responding to social circumstances, parents are encouraged to give the infant attention and become more sensitive to its needs. Parents are shown how the newborn can respond to people and how to stimulate such responses. Researchers have found that the social interaction skills of both high-risk infants and healthy, responsive infants can be improved through such communication with parents (Girling, 2006).

To this point, we have studied a number of ideas about birth. For a review, see the **Reach Your Learning Objectives** section at the end of this chapter.

The Postpartum Period

LO3 Understand the changes that take place in the postpartum period.

What Is the Postpartum Period?

The **postpartum period** *is the period after childbirth or delivery. It is a time when the woman's body adjusts, both physically and psychologically, to the process of childbirth. It lasts for about six weeks or until the body has completed its adjustment and has returned to a near pre-pregnant state.* Some health professionals refer to the postpartum period as the "fourth trimester." Though the time span of the postpartum period does not necessarily cover three months, the terminology of fourth trimester demonstrates the idea of continuity and the importance of the first several months after birth for the mother.

Parenting during the early postpartum period is a time of maternal learning and adaptation. Mothers are called upon to learn new behaviours to be able to care effectively for their infants and to achieve maximum satisfaction with parenting (Leahy-Warren & McCarthy, 2011). During this period families may receive home visits from a public health nurse. Postpartum care by the nurse in the home usually includes monitoring the physical and emotional well-being of all family members; identifying potential or developing complications for the mother and newborn; and acting as an advocate between mother and other health care providers such as a lactation consultant. While providing effective care, it is essential to understand the postpartum health needs of the new mother and to teach her to care for her infant, her family, and herself. Doing so will help the mother respond to physical and emotional postpartum changes, and to the transition to parenthood (PHAC, 2009e).

What Is the Postpartum Period?

Physical Adjustments

Emotional and Psychological Adjustments

postpartum period Occurs after childbirth when the mother adjusts, both physically and psychologically, to the process of child-birth; lasts for about six weeks or until her body has completed its adjustment and returned to a near pre-pregnant state.

Physical Adjustments

The woman's body makes numerous physical adjustments in the first days and weeks after childbirth (London et al., 2007). A concern is the loss of sleep that the primary caregiver experiences in the postpartum period (Gunderson et al., 2008; Signal et al., 2007). A recent analysis indicated that the primary caregiver loses as much as 700 hours of sleep in the first year following the baby's birth (Maas, 2008). The loss of sleep can contribute to stress, marital conflict, and impaired decision making (Meerlo, Sgoifo, & Suchecki, 2008). Even after their newborn begins to sleep better through the night by the middle of the baby's first year, many mothers report waking up several times a night even when their baby is asleep. Sleep experts say it takes several weeks to several months for parents' internal sleep clocks to adjust.

Some women and men want to resume sexual intercourse as soon as possible after the birth. Others feel constrained or afraid. A sore perineum (the area between the female's anus and vagina), a demanding baby, lack of help, and extreme fatigue can affect a woman's ability to relax and enjoy making love. Many couples resume sexual activity before the postpartum check-up six weeks after childbirth (Wong et al., 2006). If the woman regularly engaged in conditioning exercises during pregnancy, exercise will help her recover her former body contour and strength during the postpartum period. With a caregiver's approval, the woman can begin some exercises as soon as one hour after delivery. A recent study found that women who maintained or increased their exercise from pre-pregnancy to postpartum had better maternal well-being than women who engaged in no exercise or decreased their exercise from pre-pregnancy to postpartum (Blum, Beaudoin, & Caton-Lemos, 2005). Queen's University researcher Gregory Davies and colleagues (2003) found postpartum pelvic floor exercises reduced the incidence of later urinary incontinence.

Relaxation techniques are also helpful during the postpartum period. Five minutes of slow breathing on a stressful day in the postpartum period can relax and refresh the new mother, as well as the new baby.

The weeks following childbirth are likely to present many challenges to new parents and their offspring. Many health professionals believe that the best postpartum care is family centred, using the family's resources to support an early and smooth adjustment to the newborn by all family members.

Emotional and Psychological Adjustments

Emotional fluctuations are common for mothers in the postpartum period. These emotional fluctuations, called the baby blues, may be due to any of a number of factors: hormonal changes, fatigue, inexperience or lack of confidence with newborn babies, or the extensive time and demands involved in caring for a newborn. For some women, the emotional fluctuations decrease within several weeks after the delivery and are a minor aspect of their motherhood. For others, they are more long-lasting and can produce feelings of anxiety, depression, and difficulty in coping with stress (Morrissey, 2007; Tam & Chung, 2007). Mothers whose feelings of depression last more than a few weeks, even when they are getting adequate rest, may benefit from professional help in dealing with their problems. Some signs that can indicate a need for professional counselling about postpartum adaptation include excessive worrying, depression, extreme changes in appetite, crying spells, and inability to sleep.

Postpartum depression *involves a major depressive episode that typically occurs about four weeks after delivery. In other words, women with postpartum depression have such strong feelings of sadness, anxiety, or despair that for at least a two-week period they have trouble coping with their daily tasks.* Without treatment, postpartum depression may become worse and last for many months (Gjerdingen, Katon, & Rich, 2008). Canadian researchers noted that anxiety during pregnancy was correlated with postpartum depression (Bowen et al., 2008). Thus, identifying pregnant women experiencing clinical levels of anxiety and treating the anxiety would be one possible method of preventing or reducing their experience of postpartum depression. These researchers noted that younger pregnant women tended to be more anxious than older women.

Maternal postpartum depression in rural areas is a particularly critical issue. One of the main factors in decreasing the likelihood that a rural mother will seek treatment is the lack of the availability of resources (Brannen, Dyck, Hardy, & Mushquash, 2012). One research project, by Brannen and her colleagues (2006), provided accessible appropriate treatment for mothers with postpartum depression. Mothers were provided with a manual and DVDs to provide information

A mother bonds with her infant moments after it is born. **How critical is bonding for the development of social competence later in childhood?**

postpartum depression A major depressive episode that typically occurs about four weeks after delivery. Women with postpartum depression have such strong feelings of sadness, anxiety, or despair, that for at least a two-week period they have trouble coping with daily tasks.

about postpartum depression (PPD), along with cognitive-behavioural techniques used for managing symptoms. Weekly evaluations of PPD were undertaken and a baseline maintained during a 12-month follow-up by a trained assessment assistant. Results from the pilot study indicated that all participants reported significant improvements in their symptoms, and all but one of the 27 participants had resolved her clinical depression.

Hormonal changes occurring after childbirth are believed to play a role in postpartum depression (Groer & Morgan, 2007; Jolley et al., 2007). Estrogen helps some women with postpartum depression, but estrogen also has some possible problematic side effects (Grigoriadis & Kennedy, 2002). Several antidepressant drugs are effective in treating postpartum depression and appear to be safe for breast-feeding women (Horowitz & Cousins, 2006). Psychotherapy, especially cognitive therapy, also is an effective treatment of postpartum depression for many women (Beck, 2006). Also, engaging in regular exercise may help in treating postpartum depression (Daley, Macarthur, & Winter, 2007).

One concern about postpartum depression is that breastfeeding is less common among postpartum-depressed women. They may not breastfeed because of their concern about potentially negative effects of antidepressants that can be transmitted to their young infant through breast milk (Einarson & Ito, 2007). Currently, little research has been conducted on whether the positive effects of breastfeeding might outweigh the positive effects of antidepressants for both the mother and the infant (Field, 2008).

Can a mother's postpartum depression affect her child? Researchers have found that depressed mothers interact less with their infants and are less likely to respond to their infant's efforts to get attention (Teti & Towe-Goodman, 2008). A recent national survey indicated that mothers who are depressed were 1.5 times more likely to provide less healthy feeding and sleeping practices for their newborns (Paulson, Dauber, & Leiferman, 2006). Another recent study revealed that postpartum depression was more common in mothers who had preterm than full-term infants (Feldman & Eidelman, 2007). In this study, with both preterm and full-term infants, mothers with postpartum depression showed a low level of maternal–infant synchrony.

A Father's Adjustment

Fathers also undergo considerable adjustment in the postpartum period, even when they work away from home all day (Cox, 2006; Pinheiro et al., 2006). Many fathers feel that the baby comes first and gets all of the mother's attention; some feel that they have been replaced by the baby. Becoming a father is a major milestone for men (Bartlett, 2004).

A study conducted by Yu and colleagues (2012) assessed expectant fathers' support network, marital intimacy, and health status during the third trimester of their partner's pregnancy. The results indicated that fathers who perceived more marital intimacy and support from their partners were actually more attached to their infants. The researchers concluded that marital intimacy and partner support are important predictors for father–infant attachment. It is interesting to note that a longitudinal study examined perceptions of fatherhood over the first 18 months after the birth of a first child. The results suggested that when couples become parents, the reciprocal interaction of new mothers and fathers influences their perspective perceptions relative to fatherhood (Tremblay & Pierce, 2011).

With the support of the Public Health Agency of Canada, the Father Involvement Initiative–Ontario Network (FII-ON) has produced a new Web site that will serve as an online booklet for new and expecting fathers. The Web site provides detailed information using a combination of articles and videos to provide answers to the most common new-dad questions using a father-friendly approach (FIRA, 2012).

To help the father adjust, parents should set aside some special time to be together with each other. The father's postpartum reaction also likely will be improved if he has taken childbirth classes with the mother and is an active participant in caring for the baby.

In recognition of the belief that bonding may have a positive effect on getting the parent–infant relationship off to a good start, many hospitals now offer a *rooming-in* arrangement, in which

critical thinking

Postpartum depression is a very serious and potentially dangerous state for a new mother to experience. Based on information in this chapter, construct a set of "helpful tips" that you could provide to an expectant mother and father to decrease the likelihood of postpartum depression developing. The list ought to include both information and activities in which the parents-to-be could engage. How would you interact with a mother who is experiencing postpartum depression? What support would you give to the mother and father, as well as the baby?

connecting development to life ⟵--------

Global Responses to Pregnancy and Attachment after Birth

All cultures have beliefs and rituals that surround life's major events, including pregnancy and birth.

Pregnancy: Some cultures view pregnancy and infancy as a natural occurrence; others see it as a medical condition (Mathole et al., 2004; Paredes et al., 2005; Walsh, 2006). How expectant mothers behave during pregnancy may depend in part on the prevalence of traditional homecare remedies and folk beliefs, the importance of indigenous healers, and the influence of health care professionals in their culture (Walsh, 2006). In various cultures, pregnant women may turn to herbalists, faith healers, root doctors, or spiritualists for help (Mbonye, Neema, & Magnussen, 2006).

Chinese expectant mothers commonly listen to classical music during pregnancy because they believe it will help the offspring develop patience, wisdom, and artistic sensitivity. Many Chinese people also think that a child's moral disposition is at least partially developed in the womb. As a consequence, expectant Chinese mothers may avoid contact with people they perceive to be dishonest, may engage in charitable deeds, and try to avoid having negative thoughts or feelings. In some Asian countries, such as the Philippines, many expectant mothers will not take any medication during pregnancy. Also, some immigrant Asian women return to their parents' home in their native country to deliver their baby, especially if it is their firstborn child (American Public Health, 2006).

Infancy: A special component of the parent–infant relationship is **bonding**, *the occurrence of close contact, especially physical, between parents and newborn in the period shortly after birth.* During the period immediately following birth, the parents "fall in love" with the child they have and that newborn elicits protection and loving responses from caregivers. Whether humans have a critical period for bonding is inconclusive and debatable, but varying levels of attachment emerge as a result of caregiver and child interaction during the first months of the child's life (Kennell, 2006; Rode et al., 1981).

The degree of security of attachment is related to the level of sensitivity caregivers provide newborns, as evidenced by responsive behaviours to distress, vocalization, gazing, as well as proximity, holding, and carrying behaviours (Whaley et al., 2002, Tulviste & Ahtonen, 2007). Infant security is not related to gender, economic status, or who the primary caregiver is (Tulviste & Ahtonen, 2007).

Secure attachment is linked to desirable childhood and adulthood behaviours, whether the cultural values favour individualism or collectivism. Considerable variation exists in the extent to which behaviours, particularly self-directed behaviours, are valued and

how behaviours associated with security are defined and interpreted (Rothbaum et al., 2007; Tulviste & Ahtonen, 2007; Whaley et al., 2002). Cultural contexts shape caregiver responses (Rothbaum et al., 2007; True, Pisani, & Oumar, 2001; Whaley et al., 2002). To North Americans (economically secure mothers who spent most of their lives in Canada or the United States), secure attachment is the balance between closeness and exploration and leads to the development of autonomy, self-esteem, and self-reliance (Rothbaum et al., 2007). In contrast, Puerto Ricans view secure attachment as the balance between emotional connectedness and proper demeanour and leads to respect, obedience, and calmness (Rothbaum et al., 2007). In Japan, secure attachment leads to the development of empathy, accommodation, and interdependence. Whereas North American parents associate insecure attachment with anger and aggression in adulthood, Japanese mothers attribute inappropriate behaviours as security-seeking behaviours (Rothbaum et al., 2007).

How women behave toward their newly born children is also related to cultural norms and interpretation. In North America, mutual gazing and vocal maternal behaviours are thought to be predictors of optimal development. In Kenya, however, maternal vocalization and gazing are comparatively absent. Patterns of shared caregiving by multiple family and community members exist in several countries, such as Botswana, India, Kenya, and Zaire. In these countries, older siblings frequently care for infants and younger siblings, a practice for which a North American parent would be deemed irresponsible. At all ages, Kenyan caregivers hold or carry infants more than North American mothers, who decrease the amount of carrying and holding time as infants age. Kenyan mothers spend less time engaged in vocalization and gazing than their North American counterparts, but when multiple caregiver responses were factored in, the amount of such behaviours doubled in Kenya while increasing by only 2 percent in North America (Whaley et al., 2002).

Findings such as these are based on naturalistic observation by trained experts, which was discussed in Chapter 1. You can conduct your own mini–field research by observing and questioning practices in your own family. For example, are multiple caregivers from family and/or community involved in responding to a newborn in your family? How much gazing and vocalization does the mother engage in compared to other family members? What are the benefits or drawbacks to having greater or less involvement of extended family in child rearing? How might this change in different social contexts?

---

the baby remains in the mother's room most of the time during the hospital stay. However, the weight of the research evidence suggests it will not harm the infant emotionally if parents choose not to use this rooming-in arrangement (Lamb, 1994).

To this point, we have discussed the postpartum period. For a review, see the **Reach Your Learning Objectives** section at the end of this chapter.

bonding Close contact, especially physical, between parents and their newborn in the period shortly after birth.

reach your **learning objectives**

Prenatal Development

LO1 Explain prenatal development.

The Course of Prenatal Development

Germinal Period
- From conception until 10 to 14 days later.
- A fertilized egg is called a zygote.
- This period ends when the zygote attaches to the uterine wall.

Embryonic Period
- Approximately two to eight weeks after conception.
- The embryo differentiates into three layers, life-support systems develop, and organ systems form (organogenesis).

Fetal Period
- Lasts from about two months after conception until nine months, or when the baby is born.
- Growth and development continue their dramatic course, and organ systems mature to the point at which life can be sustained outside of the womb.

The Brain
- The nervous system begins as a hollow tube in the embryo's neck, closing at both ends about day 24.
- The nearly 100 billion neurons are formed over the remainder of the prenatal period.
- The neurons migrate to their appropriate location in the brain and begin to build interconnections and form the various brain structures.
- Brain growth and development continues after delivery.

Teratology and Hazards to Prenatal Development
- Teratology investigates the causes of congenital (birth) disabilities.
- Any agent that causes disability in the offspring by the time of birth is called a teratogen.
- The dose, genetic susceptibility, and the time of exposure will influence the type and severity of the effect.

Prenatal Care
- Prenatal care varies considerably, but usually involves medical care services with a defined schedule of visits.

Positive Prenatal Development
- Most pregnancies and prenatal development go well, although it is important to avoid the vulnerabilities that teratogens produce.

Birth

LO2 Outline the birth process.

The Birth Process
- The first stage of labour lasts about 12 to 24 hours for a woman having her first child. The cervix dilates to about 10 cm.
- The second stage begins when the baby's head moves through the cervix and ends with the baby's complete emergence.
- The third stage is the delivery of the placenta and membranes, commonly called the afterbirth.

Special Neonatal Considerations	▪ Preterm infants are those born after an abnormally short time in the womb.
	▪ Infants who are born after a regular gestation period of 38 to 42 weeks but who weigh less than 2,500 grams are called low-birth-weight infants.
	▪ Although most low-birth-weight infants are normal and healthy, as a group, they have more health and developmental problems than normal-birth-weight infants.
Measures of Neonatal Health and Responsiveness	▪ For many years, the Apgar scale has been used to assess the newborn's health.
	▪ The Brazelton Neonatal Behavioral Assessment Scale, a more recently developed scale, is used for long-term neurological assessment and social responsiveness.
	▪ The Neonatal Intensive Care Unit Neurobehavioral Scale provides a more comprehensive analysis of the newborn's behaviour, neurological and stress responses, and regulatory capacities.

The Postpartum Period

LO3 Understand the changes that take place in the postpartum period.

What Is the Postpartum Period?	▪ This is the period after childbirth or delivery.
	▪ The woman's body adjusts physically and psychologically to the process of childbearing.
	▪ It lasts for about six weeks or until the body has completed its adjustment.
Physical Adjustments	▪ These include fatigue, involution (the process by which the uterus returns to its pre-pregnant size five or six weeks after birth), hormonal changes, when to resume sexual intercourse, and exercises to recover body contour and strength.
Emotional and Psychological Adjustments	▪ Emotional fluctuations on the part of the mother are common in this period, and they can vary a great deal from one mother to the next.
	▪ The father also goes through a postpartum adjustment.

review ----> *connect* ----> reflect

review

Why is it important to take a positive approach to prenatal development? **LO1**

What is meant by the term *teratology*? What are the significant hazards to prenatal development? **LO1**

What is the course of the birth process? **LO2**

What are a few measures of neonatal health and assessment? **LO2**

What physical and emotional adjustments characterize the postpartum period? **LO3**

What role does the father play during pregnancy? **LO3**

connect

You are asked to design a health teaching program for pregnant mothers who smoke. What will you include in this plan?

reflect *Your Own Personal Journey of Life*

If you are a female, which birthing process would you prefer? Explain. If you are a male, how involved would you want to be in helping your partner through the birth of your baby? Explain.

Mc Graw Hill Education **connect**®

McGraw-Hill Connect provides you with a powerful tool for improving academic performance and truly mastering course material. You can diagnose your knowledge with pre- and post-tests, identify the areas where you need help, search the entire learning package, including the eBook, for content specific to the topic you're studying, and add these resources to your personalized study plan. CONNECT for *Life-Span Development*, fifth Canadian edition, offers the following:

▪ chapter-specific online quizzes
▪ groupwork
▪ presentations
▪ writing assignments
▪ case studies
▪ and much more!

Visit CONNECT today!

CHAPTER 5 | Physical and Cognitive Development in Infancy

CHAPTER OUTLINE

Physical Development and Health

LO1 Outline steps involved in physical growth and development in infancy.

Physical Growth

Brain

Sleep

Health

Motor, Sensory, and Perceptual Development

LO2 Examine infant motor development and summarize the course of sensory and perceptual development in infancy.

Motor Development

Sensory and Perceptual Development

Cognitive Development

LO3 Determine how infants learn, remember, and conceptualize.

Piaget's Sensorimotor Stage

Information Processing

Infant Intelligence

Language Development

LO4 Explain the nature of language and how it develops in infancy.

Language Acquisition

Biological Foundations of Language

Behavioural and Environmental Influences

"*A baby is an angel whose wings decrease as his legs increase.*"

—FRENCH PROVERB

Bottle- and Breastfeeding in Africa and Canada

Latonya is a newborn baby in the African country of Ghana. The culture of the area in which she was born discourages breastfeeding. She has been kept apart from her mother and bottle-fed in her first days of infancy. Manufacturers of infant formula provide the hospital where she was born with free or subsidized milk powder. Her mother has been persuaded to bottle-feed her, rather than breastfeed.

When her mother bottle-feeds Latonya, she overdilutes the milk formula with unclean water. Latonya's feeding bottles also have not been sterilized. She starts to get sick—very sick. She dies before her first birthday.

By contrast, Ramona lives in nearby Nigeria. Her mother is breastfeeding her. Ramona was born at a Nigerian hospital where a "baby-friendly" program has been initiated. In this program, babies are not separated from their mothers when they are born, and the mothers are encouraged to breastfeed. The mothers are told of the perils that bottle-feeding can bring because of unsafe water and unsterilized bottles. They also are informed about the advantages of breast milk, such as its nutritious and hygienic qualities, its ability to immunize babies against common illnesses, and its role in reducing the mother's risk of breast and ovarian cancers. At one year of age, Ramona is very healthy.

The World Health Organization and UNICEF have been trying to reverse the trend toward bottle-feeding of infants in many impoverished countries. They have instituted the baby-friendly initiative program in many of them. In fact, the Baby-Friendly Hospital Initiative was launched by the World Health Organization and UNICEF in 1989 to promote, protect, and support breastfeeding worldwide (Chalmers et al., 2009).

The advantages of breastfeeding in impoverished countries are substantial. However, these advantages must be balanced against the risk of passing the human immunodeficiency virus (HIV) to the babies through breast milk if the mothers have the virus; the majority of mothers don't know that they are infected (Doherty et al., 2006; Dube et al., 2008). In some areas of Africa, more than 30 percent of mothers have HIV.

According to Canadian researchers Levitt and colleagues (2011), the Baby-Friendly Hospital Initiative (BFHI) promotes both the World Health Organization International Code of Marketing of Breast-Milk Substitutes (WHO Code) and the WHO/UNICEF's Ten Steps to Successful Breastfeeding (Ten Steps). Between 1993 and 2007, Levitt and her team of researchers surveyed all Canadian maternity hospitals on routine maternity practices and policies including infant feeding. They concluded that in the 14 years separating the two surveys, Canadian maternity hospitals substantially improved their implementation of the WHO Code and their adherence to the WHO/UNICEF Ten Steps (Levitt et al., 2011). Clear and robust evidence is available to support breastfeeding's essential benefits to the health of infants and children (Phillipp & Merewood, 2004). Breastfeeding has been shown to be related to a lower risk of obesity (Cope and Allison, 2008).

(Left) A Canadian mother breastfeeding her baby. (Right) A Rwandan mother bottle-feeding her baby. **What are some concerns about bottle- versus breastfeeding in impoverished African countries?**

Physical Development and Health

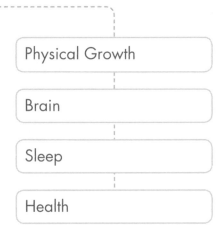

LO1 Outline steps involved in physical growth and development in infancy.

Infants' physical development in the first two years after birth is extensive (Caulfield, 2001). Their bodies and brains experience rapid growth. Two important elements that promote this growth are sleep and health.

Physical Growth

Typically, the full-term newborn is 48 to 53 cm, and weighs 2,500 to 4,000 grams. In the first several days the newborn typically loses approximately 10 percent of its initial birth weight secondary to the loss of meconium and extracellular fluid as well as limited food intake (Chow, Ateah, Scott, Ricci, & Kyle, 2013). It is expected that this newborn weight loss will be regained within 10 to 14 days. Weight loss of more than 10 percent requires close monitoring (Burns, Dunn, Brady, Starr, & Blosser, 2013).

Once an infant has adjusted to sucking, swallowing, and digesting it grows rapidly, gaining 150 to 210 grams weekly until 5 to 6 months, when typically the birth weight has doubled. By one year of age, the infant's birth weight has tripled. Infants who are breastfed beyond four to six months of age typically gain less weight than those who are bottle-fed. Infants grow about 2.5 cm per month during the first six months of life; growth slows during the second six months (Hockenberry & Wilson, 2013).

The growth rate of infants is considerably slower in the second year of life. By two years of age, infants weigh approximately 12 kg. The birth weight is quadrupled by 2.5 years of age. At two years of age, the average height is 86.6 cm, which is nearly one-half of their adult height (Hockenberry & Wilson, 2013).

Physical development tends to follow two patterns. The **cephalocaudal pattern** *is the sequence in which the greatest growth in size, weight, and feature differentiation gradually works down from top to bottom*. This same pattern occurs in the head area: the top parts of the head—the eyes and brain—grow faster than the lower parts, such as the jaw. A large proportion of the total body is occupied by the head during prenatal development and early infancy (see Figure 5.1).

Later in the chapter, you will see that sensory development and motor development also proceed according to the cephalocaudal principle. For example, infants can use their hands long before they can crawl or walk.

The **proximodistal pattern** *is the sequence in which growth starts at the centre of the body and moves toward the extremities*. An example of this is the early maturation of muscular control of the trunk and arms, as compared with that of the hands and fingers. Furthermore, infants use their whole hand as a unit before they can control several fingers.

Brain

By the time it is born, the infant that began as a single cell is estimated to have a brain that contains approximately 100 billion nerve cells, or neurons. Extensive brain development continues after birth, through infancy and later (de Haan & Martinos, 2008; Nelson, 2011). Because the brain is still developing so rapidly in infancy, the infant's head should be protected from falls or other injuries and the baby should never be shaken. *Shaken baby syndrome*, which includes brain swelling and hemorrhaging, affects hundreds of babies in North America each year (Altimer, 2008; King et al., 2003; Squire, 2008).

Goulet and colleagues (2009) conducted a study in Canada to evaluate the opinions of parents and nurses regarding the benefit program on shaken baby syndrome: the Perinatal Shaken Baby Syndrome Prevention Program (PSBSPP). These researchers found that the program achieved two important goals. First, it increased parents' knowledge about infant crying, anger, and shaken baby

cephalocaudal pattern The sequence in which the greatest growth in size, weight, and feature differentiation gradually works down from top to bottom.

proximodistal pattern The sequence in which growth starts at the centre of the body and moves toward the extremities.

Physical Growth

Brain

Sleep

Health

Figure 5.1

Changes in Proportions of the Human Body during Growth

As individuals develop from infancy through adulthood, one of the most noticeable physical changes is that the head becomes smaller in relation to the rest of the body. The fractions listed refer to head size as a proportion of total body length at different ages.

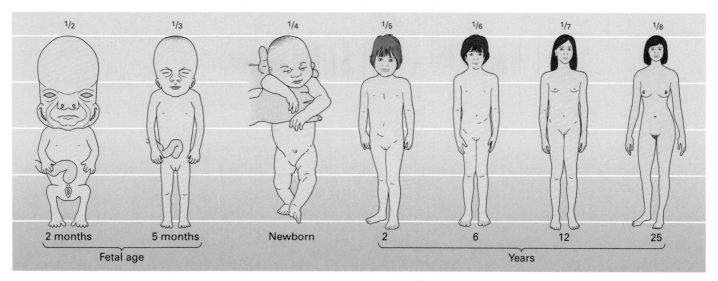

| 1/2 | 1/3 | 1/4 | 1/5 | 1/6 | 1/7 | 1/8 |

| 2 months | 5 months | Newborn | 2 | 6 | 12 | 25 |

Fetal age   Years

syndrome. Secondly, the program helped parents to identify coping strategies. The study concluded that introducing the PSBSPP in all birthing institutions is highly relevant.

Health Canada, together with a diverse group of professionals and advocacy associations, has developed the Joint Statement on Shaken Baby Syndrome (SBS) as an essential step to stimulate action across Canada to address this problem. The statement was developed to create a common understanding of the definition, causes, outcomes, and consequences of SBS and to encourage effective strategies to prevent SBS (PHAC, 2011b).

Brain Development

At birth, the newborn's brain is about 25 percent of its adult weight. By the second birthday, the brain is about 75 percent of its adult weight. However, the brain's areas do not mature uniformly. Some areas, such as the primary motor areas, develop earlier than others, such as the primary sensory areas.

It is amazing that the infant began life as a single cell and nine months later is born with a brain and nervous system that contain approximately 100 billion nerve cells, or neurons. A **neuron** *is a nerve cell that handles information processing at the cellular level.* Among the most dramatic changes in the brain in the first two years of life are the spreading connections of dendrites. Figure 5.2 illustrates these changes.

A neuron is made of several parts: the cell body, many dendrites, and an axon. The dendrites are short fibres that extend from the cell body and receive information from other neurons and carry it into the cell body. The neuron's axon carries the message (an electrical signal) from the cell body to the point where it is passed to the next neuron. This point is at the end of the axon, which splits into multiple finger-like filaments that end with a structure called the terminal button. Here the electrical signal triggers the release of one or more of the many neurotransmitters (chemical substances, such as serotonin) that cross a very small gap (called the synaptic gap) between the terminal button on the axon to a dendrite of another neuron. When the neurotransmitter bonds with the next dendrite, it serves to trigger that neuron. A myelin sheath, which is a layer of fat cells, encases most axons. Not only does the myelin sheath insulate nerve cells, it also helps nerve impulses travel faster (Zalc, 2006). Myelination, the process of encasing axons with fat cells, begins

neuron Nerve cell that handles information processing at the cellular level.

Figure 5.2

The Development of Dendritic Spreading

Note the increase in connectedness between neurons over the course of the first two years of life. Reprinted by permission of the publisher from *The Postnatal Development of the Human Cerebral Cortex, Vols I-VIII* by Jesse LeRoy Conel, Cambridge, Mass.: Harvard University Press, Copyright © 1939, 1975, by the President and Fellows of Harvard College.

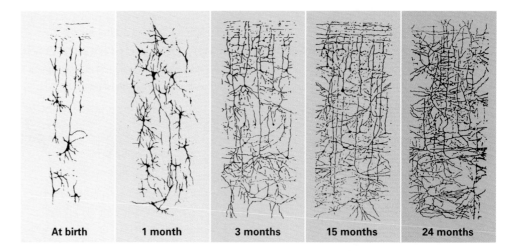

| At birth | 1 month | 3 months | 15 months | 24 months |

Figure 5.3

The Human Brain's Hemispheres

The two hemispheres of the human brain are clearly seen in this photograph. It is a myth that the left hemisphere is the exclusive location of language and logical thinking or that the right hemisphere is the exclusive location of emotion and creative thinking.

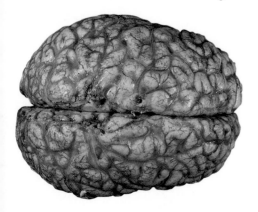

prenatally and continues after birth. Myelination for visual pathways occurs rapidly after birth and is completed in the first six months. Auditory myelination is not completed until four or five years of age. Some aspects of myelination continue even into adolescence (Dubois et al., 2007; Fair & Schlaggar, 2008).

The connections that are used become strengthened and survive, while the unused ones are replaced by other pathways or disappear. In the language of neuroscience, these connections will be "pruned" (Giedd, 2008). For example, the more babies engage in physical activity or use language, the more those pathways will be strengthened.

The notion of the development of new neurons in the brains of mammals has received considerable research attention, and related investigations are ongoing. Baringa (2003) claims that certain brain regions are at least replenished with the development of new neurons. Researchers are not certain, however, what exactly is the contribution of these "newcomer" neurons and what they contribute to the behaviours controlled by certain brain regions, such as singing, smelling, and learning. Some of the most persuasive research has been conducted on songbirds. It has been posited that newly generated neurons have been found in the high vocal centre (HVC) of canaries, a brain area that helps produce their characteristic song. For example, during breeding season, male canaries seem to learn new song elements believed to be due to the HVC enlargement caused by the addition of new neurons (Baringa, 2003). Based on this rather interesting evidence regarding songbirds, what assumptions can you hypothesize regarding these findings to the behaviour of infants that just might be caused by the development of new neurons in the infant's brain?

MAPPING THE BRAIN   Scientists analyze and categorize areas of the brain in numerous ways (Fischer & Immordino-Yang, 2008; Nelson, 2011). We are most concerned with the portion farthest from the spinal cord, known as the *forebrain*, which includes the cerebral cortex and several structures beneath it. The *cerebral cortex* covers the forebrain like a wrinkled cap. It has two halves, or hemispheres (see Figure 5.3). Based on ridges and valleys in the cortex, scientists distinguish four main areas, called lobes, in each hemisphere. Although the lobes usually work together, each has a somewhat different primary function (see Figure 5.4):

- Frontal lobes are involved in voluntary movement, thinking, personality, and intentionality or purpose.
- Occipital lobes function in vision.
- Temporal lobes have an active role in hearing, language processing, and memory.
- Parietal lobes play important roles in registering spatial location, attention, and motor control.

To some extent, the type of information handled by neurons depends on whether they are in the left or right hemisphere of the cortex (Bianco et al., 2008; Spironelli & Angrilli, 2008). Speech and grammar, for example, depend on activity in the left hemisphere in most people; humour and the use of metaphors depend on activity in the right hemisphere (Imada et al., 2007). *This specialization of function in one hemisphere of the cerebral cortex or the other is called* **lateralization**. However, most neuroscientists agree that complex functions such as reading or performing music involve both hemispheres. Labelling people as "left-brained" because they are logical thinkers and "right-brained" because they are creative thinkers does not correspond to the way the brain's hemispheres work. Complex thinking in normal people is the outcome of communication between both hemispheres of the brain (Liégeois et al., 2008).

At birth, the hemispheres of the cerebral cortex already have started to specialize: newborns show greater electrical brain activity in the left hemisphere than the right hemisphere when they are listening to speech sounds (Hahn, 1987). How are the areas of the brain different in the newborn and the infant from those in an adult, and why do the differences matter? Important differences have been documented at both the cellular and the structural level.

Early Experience and the Brain

Children who grow up in a deprived environment may have depressed brain activity (Nelson, Zeanah, & Fox, 2007; Reeb et al., 2008). As shown in Figure 5.5, a child who grew up in the unresponsive and unstimulating environment of a Romanian orphanage showed considerably depressed brain activity compared with a normal child.

Are the effects of deprived environments irreversible? There is reason to think the answer is no. The brain demonstrates both flexibility and resilience. Consider 14-year-old Michael Rehbein. At age seven, he began to experience uncontrollable seizures—as many as 400 a day. Doctors said the only solution was to remove the left hemisphere of his brain where the seizures were occurring. Recovery was slow, but his right hemisphere began to reorganize and take over functions that normally occur in the brain's left hemisphere, including speech.

Neuroscientists believe that what wires the brain—or rewires it, in the case of Michael Rehbein—is repeated experience. Each time a baby tries to touch an attractive object or gazes intently at a face, tiny bursts of electricity shoot through the brain, knitting together neurons into circuits. The results are some of the behavioural milestones we discuss in this chapter.

In sum, the infant's brain depends on experiences to determine how connections are made (Dalton & Bergenn, 2007). Before birth, it appears that genes mainly direct basic wiring patterns. Neurons grow and travel to distant places awaiting further instructions (Sheridan & Nelson, 2008). After birth, the inflowing stream of sights, sounds, smells, touches, language, and eye contact help shape the brain's neural connections (Nelson, 2011).

lateralization Specialization of function in one hemisphere of the cerebral cortex or the other.

Figure 5.4 ----------

The Brain's Four Lobes

Shown here are the locations of the brain's four lobes: frontal, occipital, temporal, and parietal.

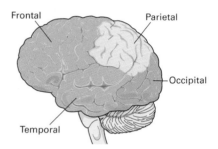

developmental **connection** ----------

Stability vs. Change

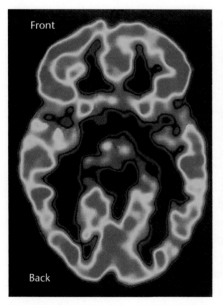

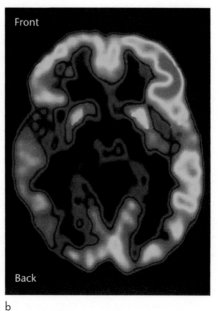

a   b

Figure 5.5 ----------

Early Deprivation and Brain Activity

These two photographs are PET (positron emission tomography) scans (which use radioactive tracers to image and analyze blood flow and metabolic activity in the body's organs) of the brains of (a) a normal child, and (b) an institutionalized Romanian orphan who experienced substantial deprivation since birth. In PET scans, the highest to lowest brain activity is reflected in the colours red, yellow, green, blue, and black, respectively. As can be seen, red and yellow show up to a much greater degree in the PET scan of the normal child than that of the deprived Romanian orphan.

Sleep

Sleep Patterns and Arrangements

When we were infants, sleep consumed more of our time than it does now (Sadeh, 2008; Taveras et al., 2008). Newborns sleep 16 to 17 hours a day, although some sleep more and others less. The range is from a low of about 10 hours to a high of about 21 hours. Infants' sleep during the day does not always follow a rhythmic pattern. An infant might change from sleeping several long bouts of seven or eight hours to three or four shorter sessions only a few hours in duration. By about one month of age, most infants have begun to sleep longer at night, and by about four months of age, they usually have moved closer to adult-like sleep patterns, having their longest span of sleep at night (Daws, 2000).

Cultural variations exist in infant sleeping patterns. Mindell and colleagues (2010) examined cross-cultural sleep patterns and sleep problems in a large sample of children from birth to 36 months of age in countries with predominantly Asian and Caucasian cultures. This study concluded that, overall, children from predominantly Asian countries had significantly shorter total sleep times, later bedtimes, and high parentally perceived sleep problems. Asian children were more likely to room-share than were children from predominantly Caucasian countries/regions. These researchers report substantial differences in sleep patterns among young children across culturally diverse countries/regions. Further research will seek to understand the bases for, and impact of, these interesting differences.

Researchers are intrigued by the various forms of infant sleep. They are especially interested in **REM (rapid eye movement) sleep**, *a recurring sleep stage during which vivid dreams commonly occur*. Most adults spend about one-fifth of their night in REM sleep, and REM sleep usually appears about one hour after non-REM sleep. However, about one-half of an infant's sleep is REM sleep, and infants often begin their sleep cycle with REM sleep, rather than non-REM sleep. By the time infants reach three months of age, the percentage of time they spend in REM sleep falls to about 40 percent, and no longer does REM sleep begin their sleep cycle. The large amount of REM sleep may provide infants with added self-stimulation since they spend less time awake than do older children (Zuk & Zuk, 2002) and might promote the brain's development (McNamara, Lijowska, & Thach, 2002). Figure 5.6 illustrates the amount of time spent in REM sleep across the human life span.

Some child experts believe there are benefits to shared sleeping, such as promoting breastfeeding, responding more quickly to the baby's cries, and detecting breathing pauses in the baby that might be dangerous (Pelayo et al., 2006). In a review prepared for the Public Health Agency of Canada, Wendy Trifunov (2009) noted that no studies of bed sharing in Canada had appeared in the academic literature. In Canada and the United States, there is great concern over the relationship between bed sharing and the incidence of sudden infant death syndrome (SIDS) (Ruys et al., 2007). Trifunov (2009) notes that it is very difficult to separate the practice of bed sharing from the bed environment and other factors that might contribute to SIDS (discussed below). In her review of the literature, Trifunov found that the percentage of infant deaths due to SIDS while sleeping "with a parent rose from 12 percent in the 1980s to 50 percent in 1999–2003" (p. 7). In addition, the rate of SIDS while in a crib has been cut by one-sixth, as opposed to SIDS deaths while sharing a bed with a parent which has only been halved.

SIDS

SIDS is one serious condition that is frequently associated with sleep. **Sudden infant death syndrome (SIDS)** *is a condition that occurs when an infant stops breathing, usually during the night, and suddenly dies without apparent cause.* SIDS is the leading cause of postneonatal death in Canada (Rusen et al., 2004). SIDS is the leading cause of death in infants between birth and 12 months of age, but is most likely to occur between two and six months of age (Maindonald, 2005). Boys are more likely to die from SIDS than girls. The incidence of SIDS among First Nations and Inuit populations is significantly higher than among non-Aboriginal Canadian groups, as much as five to seven times as high (Allard, Wilkins, & Berthelot, 2004; Hunt & Hauck, 2006; Luo et al., 2004; McShane, Smylie, & Adomako, 2009).

REM (rapid eye movement) sleep A recurring sleep stage during which vivid dreams commonly occur.

sudden infant death syndrome (SIDS) A condition that occurs when an infant stops breathing, usually during the night, and suddenly dies without apparent cause.

Figure 5.6

Sleep across the Human Life Span

Considerable variation exists across cultures in newborns' sleeping arrangements. For example, sharing a bed with a mother is a common practice in many cultures, such as Guatemala and China, whereas in others, such as the United States and Great Britain, newborns sleep in a crib, either in the same room as the parents or in a separate room. In some cultures, infants sleep with the mother until they are weaned, after which they sleep with siblings until middle and late childhood (Walker, 2006).

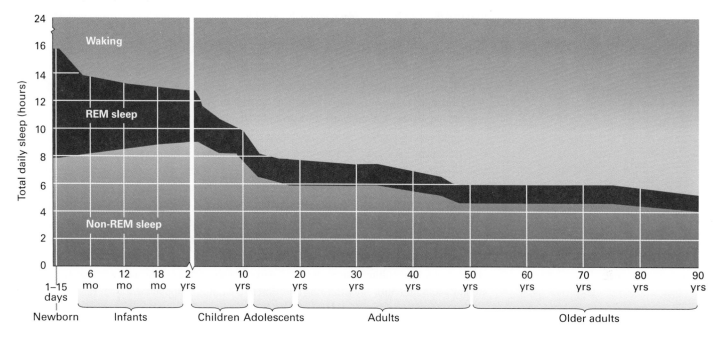

There is no definitive way to predict which infants will become victims of SIDS. However, researchers have found the following:

- Low-birth-weight infants are five to ten times more likely to die of SIDS than are their normal-weight counterparts (Horne et al., 2002).
- Subsequent siblings of an infant who has died of SIDS have a higher risk of also dying from SIDS (Hunt & Hauck, 2006).
- SIDS is more common in infants who are passively exposed to cigarette smoke (Shea & Steiner, 2008).
- Six percent of infants with sleep apnea, a temporary cessation of breathing in which the airway is completely blocked for usually ten seconds or longer, die of SIDS (McNamara & Sullivan, 2000).
- SIDS is more common in lower socio-economic groups (Mitchell et al., 2000; Rusen et al., 2004).

The Public Health Agency of Canada recognizes SIDS, and other infant deaths, as a major public health concern that occurs during sleep. The *Joint Statement on Safe Sleep: Preventing Sudden Infant Deaths in Canada* (PHAC, 2011a) is part of the Canadian government's commitment to raise awareness of sudden infant deaths and sleeping environments. Several recommendations are for infants be placed to sleep on their backs, the environment be smoke-free, and infants not to be placed on soft chairs, sofas, waterbeds, or cushions whether sleeping with another person or not (Hunt & Hauck, 2006; Trifunov, 2009). Health Canada (2005) suggests that firm flat bedding is best for normal healthy infants, with sheets and light blankets as required, and recommends the avoidance of products to maintain the sleeping position.

Since the onset of risk-reduction education the incidence of SIDS has declined, although it remains the leading cause of infant mortality from one month to one year (Ostfeld, Esposito, Perl, & Hegyi, 2010).

Health

Infants' physical growth depends on appropriate intake of nutrients. Here we examine their nutritional needs, breastfeeding, and malnutrition.

Nutritional Needs

The importance of adequate energy and nutrient intake consumed in a loving and supportive environment during the infant years cannot be overstated. From birth to one year of age, infants' weight triples and their length increases by 50 percent. Individual differences among infants in terms of their nutrient reserves, body composition, growth rates, and activity patterns make defining actual nutrient needs difficult. However, nutritionists recommend that infants consume approximately 242 joules per day for each kilogram they weigh—more than twice an adult's requirement per kilogram. In addition, parents should know that fat is also very important to an infant's health. It is recommended that children under the age of two should not consume skim milk.

Children in Canada are at risk of vitamin D deficiency. Sunlight stimulates vitamin D production in the skin. Because of the long winters in Canada, there can be little exposure of the skin to the sun. Therefore, vitamin D supplements, either in the form of fortified infant formula milk or other sources, are recommended by the Public Health Agency of Canada (2009a).

Crocker and her Canadian researchers (2011) conducted a survey of breastfeeding mothers of healthy infants to determine whether or not parents and caregivers follow the advice of Health Canada, which urges that all breastfed infants receive a daily supplement of 400 IU of vitamin D. It was found that although 90 percent of infants received breast milk at two months of age, the vitamin supplementation rate was only 80 percent. One of the conclusions was that subsequent studies should monitor breastfeeding duration and vitamin D supplementation rates as children get older.

Another health concern is iron deficiency. Among other functions, iron is involved in the production of energy, the function of the brain, and transportation of oxygen and carbon dioxide. When the iron level is low, a condition called anemia can occur. Anemia is the reduction of the blood's ability to carry oxygen—an important process for the rapid growth in infancy—and is more prevalent among Aboriginal Canadians than the general population in Canada (Christofides, Schauer, & Zlotkin, 2005). A study of 4-to-18-month-old Cree infants in Northern Ontario and Inuit infants in Nunavut found a 36 percent prevalence rate of anemia, much higher than the 4 to 5 percent among infants in urban Canada (Christofides et al., 2005). To reduce the risk of anemia and iron deficiency, foods containing iron, such as iron-fortified cereals and formula milk, should be given to the babies, and cow's or evaporated milk should be avoided. Breast-fed children should also have iron-rich supplements in their diets.

A mother's weight gain during pregnancy and a mother's own high weight before pregnancy may result in the newborn being overweight and staying overweight through infancy (Hockenberry & Wilson, 2013; Wardlaw & Smith, 2009). One likely important factor is whether an infant is breastfed or bottle-fed. Breast-fed infants have lower rates of weight gain than bottle-fed infants by school age, and it is estimated that breastfeeding reduces the risk of obesity by approximately 20 percent (Li et al., 2006).

Twells and Newhook (2010) conducted a study to examine the prevalence of overweight and obesity in a Canadian preschool population located in eastern Canada and to examine the relationship between exclusive breastfeeding and preschool obesity. Their results indicated that exclusive breastfeeding appeared to be a protective factor for obesity in preschoolers.

Crucial to the proper intake of nutrients is oral health. One issue is how soon children should be seen by a dentist. While many parents are told age three is the ideal earliest age, University of Toronto's Dr. Lynn Poranganel and her colleagues' answer is "within six months of the eruption of the first teeth and no later than one year of age" (Poranganel, Titley, & Kulkarni, 2006, p. 11). These researchers have developed a video to help parents and expectant parents anticipate and handle their babies' oral health. You can find out more on Connect at www.mcgrawhillconnect.ca.

---- **critical** thinking ----

What three pieces of advice about the infant's physical development and health would you want to give a friend who has just had a baby? Why those three? Compare and contrast breastfeeding and bottle-feeding as each applies to the infant's health. How would you explain to a group of mothers how cultural forces and geographic locations, such as rural areas, influence breastfeeding?

Breastfeeding

For years, debate has focused on the benefits of breastfeeding versus those of bottle-feeding. The growing consensus is that breastfeeding is better for the baby's health (Gartner et al., 2005; Wong, 2006) and the mother's health. Health Canada (2012b) recommends that women breastfeed their babies for the first six months of life as breast milk is the best food for optimal growth of the infant. Breastfeeding has been associated with improved health outcomes for mother and infant. If possible, breastfeeding (along with the introduction of solid foods) is recommended to continue through age two and beyond.

Breastfeeding results in benefits in many areas during the first two years of life and later:

- *Gastrointestinal infections.* Breast-fed infants have fewer gastrointestinal infections (Newburg & Walker, 2007).
- *Lower respiratory tract infections.* Breast-fed infants have fewer lower respiratory tract infections (Ip et al., 2007).
- *Allergies.* A recent research review by the American Academy of Pediatrics indicated that there is no evidence that breastfeeding reduces the risk of allergies in children (Greer et al., 2008). The research review also concluded that modest evidence exists for feeding hypoallergenic formulas to susceptible babies if they are not solely breastfed.
- *Asthma.* The recent research review by the American Academy of Pediatrics concluded that exclusive breastfeeding for three months protects against wheezing in babies, but whether it prevents asthma in older children is unclear (Greer et al., 2008).
- *Otitis media.* Breast-fed infants are less likely to develop this middle ear infection (Rovers, de Kok, & Schilder, 2006).
- *Atopic dermatitis.* Breast-fed babies are less likely to have this chronic inflammation of the skin (Snijders et al., 2007). The recent research review by the American Academy of Pediatrics also concluded that for infants with a family history of allergies, breastfeeding exclusively for at least four months is linked to a lower risk of skin rashes (Greer et al., 2008).
- *Overweight and obesity.* Consistent evidence indicates that breast-fed infants are less likely to become overweight or obese in childhood, adolescence, and adulthood (Moschonis, Grammatikaki, & Manios, 2008).
- *Diabetes.* Breast-fed infants are less likely to develop Type 1 diabetes in childhood (Ping & Hagopian, 2006) and Type 2 diabetes in adulthood (Villegas et al., 2008).
- *SIDS.* Breast-fed infants are less likely to experience SIDS (Alm, Lagercrantz, & Wennergren, 2006).

In Canada, while over 75 percent of women breastfeed their infants, 22 percent stop the practice within three months (Palda et al., 2004). One of the reasons for the cessation is the absence of support and information (Palda et al., 2004).

Effective ways to promote breastfeeding include pre-partum breastfeeding education, in conjunction with postpartum telephone and in-person contacts with nursing professionals and peer counsellors (Palda et al., 2004). Mothers who are encouraged to breastfeed within minutes of giving birth and those who receive information and guidance about breastfeeding maintain breastfeeding longer than mothers who wait several hours to breastfeed or who receive little or no support (Kramer et al. 2008). As for mothers who return to work in the infant's first year of life, they can extract breast milk by using a breast pump, and store the milk for later use.

Benefits of breastfeeding for the mother are observed in the following areas:

- *Breast cancer.* Consistent evidence indicates a lower incidence of breast cancer in women who breastfeed their infants (Shema et al., 2007).
- *Ovarian cancer.* Evidence also reveals a reduction in ovarian cancer in women who breastfeed their infants (Jordan et al., 2008).
- *Type 2 diabetes.* Some evidence suggests a small reduction in Type 2 diabetes in women who breastfeed their infants (Ip et al., 2007).

Are there circumstances when mothers should not breastfeed? A mother should not breastfeed (1) if she is infected with HIV or some other infectious disease that can be transmitted through her milk, (2) if she has active tuberculosis, or (3) if she is taking any drug that may not be safe for the infant (Chatzimichael et al., 2007; Dube et al., 2008).

Some women cannot breastfeed their infants because of physical difficulties; others feel guilty if they terminate breastfeeding early. Mothers may also worry that they are depriving their infants of important emotional and psychological benefits if they bottle-feed rather than breastfeed. Some researchers have found, however, that there are no psychological differences between breast-fed and bottle-fed infants (Ferguson, Harwood, & Shannon, 1987; Young, 1990).

For women who cannot or choose not to breastfeed, Health Canada (2012b) recommends using powdered infant formula (PIF). They caution that proper preparation, handling, and storage is necessary to avoid contamination with harmful bacteria (such as *Enterobacter sakazakii* and *Salmonella enterica*). For pre-term, low-birth-weight, or infants with compromised immune systems, they advise consultation with a physician, who will likely recommend using commercially produced liquid infant formulas.

In either breastfeeding or infant formula use, the Public Health Agency of Canada (2012) suggests starting to introduce solid foods at six months of age. Foods should be introduced one at a time for a week or so to test the infant's response, looking for any allergenic response. Foods rich in iron should be introduced first (single grains or iron-fortified infant cereal), followed by meats and well-cooked legumes. Salt, sugar, and spices should be avoided. By one year of age, the infant should have a variety of foods based on Eating Well with Canada's Food Guide (Health Canada, 2007a).

Malnutrition in Infancy

Malnutrition can result in serious health problems among infants. Two of these problems are marasmus and kwashiorkor. **Marasmus** *is a wasting away of body tissues in the infant's first year, caused by severe protein-calorie deficiency.* The infant becomes grossly underweight, and the muscles atrophy. **Kwashiorkor** *is a condition caused by a deficiency in protein, in which the child's abdomen and feet swell with water.* This disease usually appears between one and three years of age. Kwashiorkor sometimes makes children appear well-fed, even though they are not. It causes a child's vital organs to collect the nutrients that are present and deprive other parts of the body of them. The child's hair becomes thin, brittle, and colourless, and the child's behaviour often becomes listless. The main cause of marasmus and kwashiorkor is early weaning from breast milk to inadequate nutrients, such as unsuitable and unsanitary cow's milk formula.

Growth failure, or *failure to thrive* (FTT), is a sign of inadequate growth resulting from the inability to obtain or use the calories required for proper growth. FTT has no universal definition. One criterion that has been used, however, considers weight and sometimes height that falls below the fifth percentile for the child's age (Hockenberry & Wilson, 2013). At the Hospital for Sick Children (Sick Kids) in Toronto, several special-interest clinics form part of the Paediatric Consultation Clinic (PCC). One such clinic is the Infant and Toddler Growth and Feeding Program (for children under three years showing failure to thrive). Dr. Emma Cory is a director of the PCC. One of Dr. Cory's clinical interests includes failure to thrive in infants and toddlers (Sick Kids, 2012).

As a final note for this section, nutrition is not the only factor for infants' growth: other environmental factors such as a safe environment and immunization are also important. To learn more about what the Canadian Paediatric Society and Health Canada say about these issues, visit Connect at www.mcgrawhillconnect.ca and follow the links.

To this point, we have studied a number of ideas about infants' physical development and health. For a review, see the **Reach Your Learning Objectives** section at the end of this chapter.

marasmus A wasting away of body tissues in the infant's first year, caused by severe protein-calorie deficiency.

kwashiorkor A condition caused by a deficiency in protein, in which the child's abdomen and feet swell with water.

This Honduran child has kwashiorkor. Note the tell-tale sign—a greatly expanded abdomen. **What are some other characteristics of kwashiorkor?**

Motor, Sensory, and Perceptual Development

LO2 Examine infant motor development and summarize the course of sensory and perceptual development in infancy.

Along with the development of the brain, infants also experience rapid progress in their motor, sensory, and perceptual skills. In this section, we explore these advances.

Motor Development

As a newborn, Ramona could suck, fling her arms, and tightly grip a finger placed in her tiny hand. Within just two years, she is toddling around on her own, opening doors and jars as she explores her little world. Are her accomplishments inevitable? How do infants develop their motor skills, and which skills do they develop when?

Dynamic Systems Theory

According to dynamic systems theory, infants assemble motor skills for perceiving and acting (Smith & Breazeal, 2007; Thelen & Smith, 2006). In this theory, "assembly" means the coordination or convergence of a number of factors, such as the development of the nervous system, the body's physical properties and movement possibilities, the goal the infant is motivated to reach, and the environmental support for the skill. This theory also emphasizes that perception and action work together in the infant's mastery of a skill.

The dynamic systems view contrasts with the traditional maturational view by proposing that even the universal milestones, such as crawling, reaching, and walking, are learned through a process of adaptation (Adolph & Joh, 2008). It emphasizes exploration and selection in finding solutions to new task demands. In other words, infants modify their movement patterns to fit a new task by exploring and selecting various configurations. The assumption is that the infant is motivated by the new challenge—desire to get a new toy in one's mouth or to cross the room to join other family members. It is the new task—the challenge of the context, not a genetic program—that represents the driving force for change.

Reflexes

The newborn is not completely helpless. Among other things, it has some basic reflexes, which are genetically carried survival mechanisms. For example, the newborn has no fear of water, naturally holding its breath and contracting its throat to keep water out. Reflexes can serve as important building blocks for subsequent purposeful motor activity.

Reflexes *are built-in reactions to stimuli; they govern the newborn's movements, which are automatic and beyond the newborn's control.* The **sucking reflex** *occurs when the newborn automatically sucks an object placed in its mouth.* The sucking reflex enables the newborn to get nourishment before it has associated a nipple with food. The **rooting reflex** *occurs when the infant's cheek is stroked or the side of the mouth is touched. In response, the infant turns its head toward the side that was touched in an apparent effort to find something to suck.* The sucking and rooting reflexes disappear when the infant is three to four months old. They are replaced by the infant's voluntary eating. The sucking and rooting reflexes have survival value for newborn mammals, which must find the mother's breast to obtain nourishment. The **Moro reflex** *is a neonatal startle response that occurs in response to a sudden, intense noise or movement. When startled, the newborn arches its back, throws back its head, and flings out its arms and legs. Then, the newborn rapidly draws its arms and legs close to the centre of its body.*

Some reflexes present in the newborn—coughing, blinking, and yawning, for example—persist throughout life. Other reflexes disappear or eventually become incorporated into complex, voluntary

---

Motor Development

Sensory and Perceptual Development

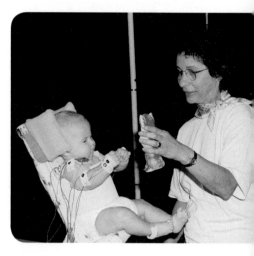

Esther Thelen is shown conducting an experiment to discover how infants learn to control their arms to reach and grasp for objects. A computer device monitors the infant's arm movements and tracks muscle patterns. Thelen's research is conducted from a dynamic systems perspective. **What is the nature of this perspective?**

dynamic systems theory The perspective on motor development that seeks to explain how motor behaviours are assembled for perceiving and acting.

- - developmental **connection** - - - - - -

Ethological Approach

reflexes Built-in reactions to stimuli; they govern the newborn's movements, which are automatic and beyond the newborn's control.

sucking reflex A newborn automatically sucks an object placed in its mouth.

rooting reflex When the infant's cheek is stroked or the side of the mouth is touched, the infant turns its head toward the side that was touched in an apparent effort to find something to suck.

Moro reflex A neonatal startle response that occurs in reaction to a sudden, intense noise or movement. When startled, the newborn arches its back, throws its head back, and flings out its arms and legs. Then the newborn rapidly draws its arms and legs close to the centre of the body.

grasping reflex A neonatal reflex that occurs when something touches the infant's palm; the infant responds by grasping tightly.

gross motor skills Involve large muscle activities, such as moving one's arms and walking.

actions. One example is the **grasping reflex**, *which occurs when something touches the infant's palm; the infant responds by grasping tightly.* By the end of the third month, the grasping reflex diminishes, and the infant shows a voluntary grasp, which is often produced by visual stimuli (Hockenberry & Wilson, 2013).

An overview of some of the main reflexes is given in Figure 5.7.

Gross Motor Skills

Gross motor skills *involve large muscle activities, such as moving one's arms and walking.* New motor skills are the most dramatic and observable changes in the infant's first year. These motor progressions transform babies from being unable even to lift their heads, to being able to grab things off the grocery store shelf, to chase the cat, and to participate actively in the family's social life. How do gross motor skills develop? As a foundation, these skills require postural control. Posture is more than just holding still and straight. Posture is a dynamic process that is linked with sensory information in the skin, joints, and muscles, which tell us where we are in space; in vestibular organs in the inner ear that regulate balance and equilibrium; and in vision and hearing (Thelen & Smith, 2006).

Figure 5.7

Infant Reflexes

Reflex	Stimulation	Infant's Response	Developmental Pattern
Babinski	Sole of foot stroked	Fans out toes, twists foot in	Disappears after nine months to one year
Blinking	Flash of light, puff of air	Closes both eyes	Permanent
Grasping	Palms touched	Grasps tightly	Weakens after three months, disappears after one year
Moro (startle)	Sudden stimulation, such as hearing loud noise or being dropped	Startles, arches back, throws head back, flings out arms and legs and then rapidly closes them to centre of body	Disappears after three to four months
Rooting	Cheek stroked or side of mouth touched	Turns head, opens mouth, begins sucking	Disappears after three to four months
Stepping	Infant held above surface and feet lowered to touch surface	Moves feet as if to walk	Disappears after three to four months
Sucking	Object touching mouth	Sucks automatically	Disappears after three to four months
Swimming	Infant put face down in water	Makes coordinated swimming movements	Disappears after six to seven months
Tonic neck	Infant placed on back	Forms fists with both hands and usually turns head to the right (sometimes called the "fencer's pose" because the infant looks like it is assuming a fencer's position)	Disappears after two months

A summary of the accomplishments in gross motor skills is shown in Figure 5.8. The actual month at which the milestones occur varies, especially among older infants. What remains fairly uniform, however, is the sequence of accomplishments. An important implication of these motor accomplishments is the increasing degree of independence they bring.

If infants can produce forward-stepping movements so early in their first year of life, why does it take them so long to learn to walk? The key skills in learning to walk appear to be stabilizing balance on one leg long enough to swing the other forward and shifting the weight without falling. This is a difficult biomechanical problem to solve, and it takes infants about a year to do it.

After their first birthday, toddlers become more motorically skilled and mobile. By 13 to 18 months, toddlers can pull a toy attached to a string, use their hands and legs to climb up a number of steps, and ride four-wheel wagons. By 18 to 24 months, toddlers can walk quickly or run stiffly for a short distance, walk backward without losing their balance, stand and throw a ball, and jump in place.

With the increased interest in fitness today, some parents have tried to give their infants a head start on becoming physically fit and physically talented. However, it may not be good to give structured exercise classes for babies. When an adult is stretching and moving an infant's limbs, it is easy to go beyond the infant's physical limits without realizing it.

Fine Motor Skills

Fine motor skills *involve more finely tuned movements, such as finger dexterity.* Infants have hardly any control over fine motor skills at birth, although they have many components of what later become finely coordinated arm, hand, and finger movements (Rosenblith, 1992). The onset of reaching and

- - critical thinking - - - - - - - - - - -

Many parents worry that their infants are behind other babies when it comes to motor performance. On the basis of what you have learned in the milestone charts in this section, how would you respond to their concern? A mother informs you that she would like to take her infant, Robbie, to exercise class with her. She wants to involve Robbie in some stretches and movement to accelerate his physical growth. How would you respond to the mother? Differentiate between the palmer grasp and the pincer grasp.

fine motor skills Motor skills that involve more finely tuned movements, such as finger dexterity.

Figure 5.8 -

Milestones in Gross Motor Development

Although infants usually learn to walk around the time of their first birthday, the neural pathways that control the leg alteration component of walking are in place from a very early age, possibly even at birth or before. The clue for this belief is that when one-to-two-month-olds are given support with their feet in contact with a motorized treadmill, they show well-coordinated, alternating steps.

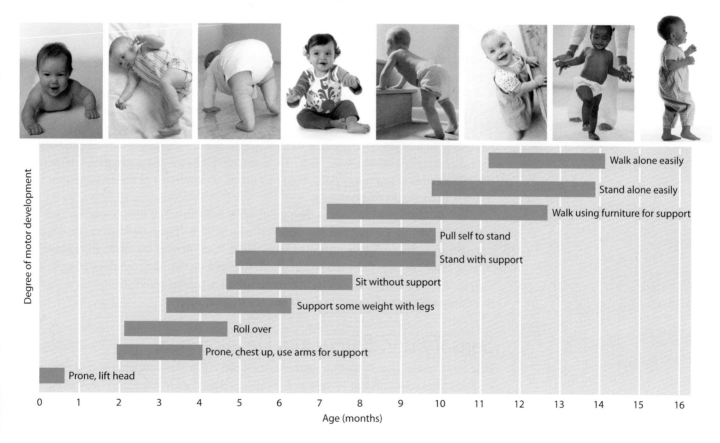

connecting development to life ←--------------

Culture and Developmental Consequences of Early Parenting Experiences on Self-Recognition and Self-Regulation of Infants

A growing awareness is emerging that universal developmental tasks may be solved differently in various socio-cultural environments (Greenfield, Keller, Fuligni, & Maynard, 2003). Keller and colleagues (2004a) conducted a study in three different cultural communities to relate parenting styles (proximal and distal) of three-month-old children to children's self-recognition and self-regulation at 18 and 20 months. The proximal parenting style emphasizes body contact and supports the development of a more independent self. This style is related to the development of the acceptance of norms and values of the family, compliance, and obedience. Meanwhile, the distal style emphasizes face-to-face contact. This style supports the development of an independent self; it is related to the development of autonomy and separateness (Keller et al., 2004b). The combination of both proximal and distal parenting strategies supports the development of an autonomous self whereby eye contact and object play support

autonomy and body contact, with body stimulation supporting relatedness. The data collected revealed observable differences in the socio-cultural orientations, not only in the parenting styles of the three socio-cultural samples, but in the development of self-recognition and self-regulation among toddlers. As specific examples, children of the Cameroonian Nso farmers, who experience a proximal parenting style, develop self-regulation early. Meanwhile, children of Greek urban middle-class families, who experience distal parenting style, develop self-recognition earlier. Finally, children of Costa Rican middle-class families, who experience both aspects of proximal and distal parenting style, fall between the other two groups on both self-regulation and self-recognition. One of the recommendations put forward by the researchers is that it is important to assess parenting styles beyond infancy to understand continuities and discontinuities in parenting across cultural environments.

grasping marks a significant achievement in infants' functional interaction with their surroundings (van Hof, van der Kamp, & Savelsbergh, 2008).

The development of reaching and grasping becomes more and more refined during the first two years. Initially, infants show only crude shoulder and elbow movements; later, they show wrist movements, hand rotation, and coordination of the thumb and forefinger. Four-month-old infants rely greatly on touch to determine how they will grip an object; eight-month-olds are more likely to use vision as a guide (Newell et al., 1989). The maturation of hand–eye coordination is reflected in the improvement of fine motor skills. Figure 5.9 provides an overview of the development of fine motor skills during the first two years.

Just as infants need to exercise their gross motor skills, they also need to exercise their fine motor skills (Barrett, Davis, & Needham, 2007; Needham, 2008). Especially when they can manage a pincer grip, infants delight in picking up small objects. Many develop the pincer grip and begin to crawl at about the same time, and infants at this time pick up virtually everything in sight, especially on the floor, and put the objects in their mouth. Thus, parents need to be vigilant in regularly monitoring what objects are within the infant's reach (Keen, 2005).

Sensory and Perceptual Development

How does a newborn know that her mother's skin is soft rather than rough? How does a five-year-old know what colour his hair is? Infants and children "know" these things as a result of information that comes through the senses. Without vision, hearing, touch, taste, and smell, we would be isolated from the world; we would live in dark silence, a tasteless, colourless, feelingless void.

Figure 5.9

The Development of Fine Motor Skills in Infancy

Birth to 6 Months	Fine Motor Skill
2 mo.	Holds rattle briefly
2½ mo.	Glances from one object to another
3–4 mo.	Plays in simple way with rattle; inspects fingers; reaches for dangling ring; visually follows ball across table
4 mo.	Carries object to mouth
4–5 mo.	Recovers rattle from chest; holds two objects
5 mo.	Transfers object from hand to hand
5–6 mo.	Bangs in play; looks for object while sitting
6–12 Months	
6 mo.	Secures cube on sight; follows adult's movements across room; immediately fixates on small objects and stretches out to grasp them; retains rattle
6½ mo.	Manipulates and examines an object; reaches for, grabs, and retains rattle
7 mo.	Pulls string to obtain an object
7½–8½ mo.	Grasps with thumb and finger
8–9 mo.	Persists in reaching for toy out of reach on table; shows hand preference; bangs spoon; searches in correct place for toys dropped within reach of hands; may find toy hidden under cup
10 mo.	Hits cup with spoon; crude release of object
10½–11 mo.	Picks up raisin with thumb and forefinger; pincer grasp; pushes car along
11–12 mo.	Puts three or more objects in a container
12–18 Months	
	Places one 5-cm block on top of another 5-cm block (in imitation) Scribbles with a large crayon on large piece of paper
	Turns two to three pages in a large book with cardboard pages while sitting in an adult's lap
	Places three 2.5-cm cube blocks in a 15-cm diameter cup (in imitation)
	Holds a pencil and makes a mark on a sheet of paper
	Builds a four-block tower with 5-cm cube blocks (in imitation)
18–24 Months	
	Draws an arc on piece of unlined paper with a pencil after being shown how
	Turns a doorknob that is within reach, using both hands
	Unscrews a lid put loosely on a small jar after being shown how
	Places large pegs in a pegboard
	Connects and takes apart a pop bead string of five beads
	Zips and unzips a large zipper after being shown how

Figure 5.10

Visual Acuity during the First Months of Life

The four photographs represent a computer estimation of what a picture of a face looks like to a one-month-old, two-month-old, three-month-old, and one-year-old (which approximates that of an adult).

sensation Occurs when a stimulus reaches sensory receptors—the eyes, ears, tongue, nostrils, and skin.

perception The interpretation of what is sensed.

Figure 5.11

Fantz's Experiment on Infants' Visual Perception

(a) Infants two to three weeks old preferred to look at some stimuli more than others. In Fantz's experiment, infants preferred to look at patterns, rather than at colour or brightness. (b) Fantz used a "looking chamber" to study infants' perception of stimuli.

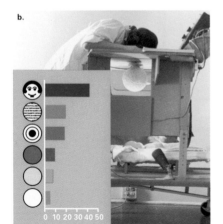

Sensation and Perception

All information comes to the infant through the senses. **Sensation** *occurs when a stimulus reaches sensory receptors—the eyes, ears, tongue, nostrils, and skin.* The sensation of hearing occurs when waves of pulsating air are collected by the outer ear and transmitted through the bones of the inner ear to the auditory nerve. The sensation of vision occurs as rays of light contact the eyes and become focused on the retina. **Perception** *is the interpretation of what is sensed.* The information about physical events that contacts the ears may be interpreted as musical sounds, for example. The physical energy transmitted to the retina may be interpreted as a particular colour, pattern, or shape.

Visual Perception

Can newborns see? How does visual perception develop in infancy?

ACUITY AND COLOUR   Just how well can infants see? At birth, the nerves and muscles and lens of the eye are still developing. As a result, newborns cannot see small things that are far away. The newborn's vision is estimated to be 20/240 on the well-known Snellen chart used for eye examinations, which means that a newborn can see at 20 feet what a normal adult can see at 240 feet (Aslin & Lathrop, 2008). In other words, an object 20 feet away is only as clear to the newborn as it would be if it were 240 feet away from an adult with normal vision (20/20). By six months of age, though, on average vision is 20/40 (Aslin & Lathrop, 2008). Figure 5.10 shows a computer estimation of what a picture of a face looks like to an infant at different points in development from a distance of about 15 cm.

Young infants can perceive certain patterns. With the help of his "looking chamber" (see Figure 5.11), Robert Fantz (1963) revealed that even two- to three-week-old infants prefer to look at patterned displays rather than non-patterned displays. For example, they prefer to look at a normal human face rather than one with scrambled features, and prefer to look at a bull's-eye target or black-and-white stripes rather than a plain circle.

According to Lewis and Maurer (2009), visual capabilities continue to improve after early infancy but the age at which the vision of children is as good as that of adults varies widely with the particular aspect of vision under study. For example, by six to seven years of age children are as accurate as adults on the measures of acuity, and holistic and featural face processing, but at age six children are not as accurate as adults on sensitivity to global form (the ability to integrate individual dots forming a swirl among randomly positioned dots). In addition, Mondloch, Geldart, Maurer, and Le Grand (2003) found that the slow development of sensitivity to second-order relations (processing the spacing among internal features of the face) caused the children, as compared to adults, to be especially poor at recognizing the identity of a face when seen in a new orientation.

Lewis and Maurer (2009) studied children treated for dense cataracts in one or both eyes. The cataracts were so dense that they prevented patterned vision from reaching the retina until the cataracts were removed surgically, replacing the natural lens with a contact lens of a suitable refractive power. It was found in studying the visual outcomes of such children that visual deprivation has different effects on various aspects of vision, and at different times, during development. The infant's colour vision also improves (Kellman & Arterberry, 2006).

One study found that for normal vision to develop satisfactorily, experience is necessary (Sugita, 2004). In a classic study, Bornstein (1975) found that by four months of age infants sometimes show colour preferences that mirror those of adults. That is, they prefer saturated colours, such as royal blue over pale blues. Meanwhile, other researchers claim that the "hue" preference of infants possibly arises from the preferred stimuli hues that adults see as blue, purple, and red. These hues appear to be more visually compelling to the infant than do greens and yellows (Zemach, Chang, & Teller, 2007).

In part, these changes in vision reflect maturation. Experience, however, is also necessary for vision to develop normally. For example, one study found that experience is necessary for normal colour vision to develop (Sugita, 2004).

DEPTH PERCEPTION   How early can infants perceive depth? To investigate this question, infant perception researchers Eleanor Gibson and Richard Walk (1960) conducted a classic experiment. They constructed a miniature cliff with a drop-off covered by glass. Then, they placed infants on the edge of a visual cliff and had their mothers coax them to crawl onto the glass (see Figure 5.12). Most infants would not crawl out on the glass, choosing instead to remain on the shallow side, indicating that they could perceive depth. However, because the 6- to 14-month-old infants had extensive visual experience, this research did not answer the question of whether depth perception is innate.

What about younger infants? Research with two- to four-month-old infants shows differences in heart rate when they are placed directly on the deep side of the visual cliff instead of on the shallow side (Campos, Langer, & Krowitz, 1970). However, an alternative interpretation is that young infants respond to differences in some visual characteristics of the deep and shallow cliffs with no actual knowledge of depth.

VISUAL EXPECTATIONS   Amazingly, infants develop expectations about future events in their world by the time they are three months of age. Marshall Haith and his colleagues (Canfield & Haith, 1991; Haith, Hazen, & Goodman, 1988) presented infants with pictures in either a regularly alternating sequence—such as left, right, left, right—or an unpredictable sequence. When the sequence was predictable, three-month-old infants began to anticipate the location of the picture, looking to the side on which it was expected to appear. The young infants formed this visual expectation in less than one minute. However, younger infants did not develop expectations about where a picture would be presented.

Hearing

During the last two months of pregnancy, as the fetus nestles in the mother's womb, it can hear sounds such as the mother's voice, music, and so on (Kisilevsky et al., 2004; Saffran, Werker, & Werner, 2006). Two psychologists wanted to find out if a fetus that heard Dr. Seuss's classic story *The Cat in the Hat* while still in the mother's womb would prefer hearing the story after birth (DeCasper & Spence, 1986) (Figure 5.13). During the last months of pregnancy, 16 women read the story to their fetuses. Then shortly after they were born, the mothers read either *The Cat in the Hat* or a story with a different rhyme and pace, *The King, the Mice and the Cheese*. The infants sucked on a nipple in a different way when the mothers read the two stories, suggesting that the infants recognized the pattern and tone of *The Cat in the Hat*. This study illustrates not only that fetuses can hear, but also that we have a remarkable ability to learn even in the mother's womb.

The fetus can also recognize the mother's voice. In one study (Kisilevsky et al., 2003), 60 fetuses (mean gestational age, 38.4 weeks) were exposed to a tape recording either of their mother or of a female stranger reading a passage. The sounds of the tape were delivered through a loudspeaker

Figure 5.12

Examining Infants' Depth Perception on the Visual Cliff

Eleanor Gibson and Richard Walk (1960) found that most infants would not crawl out on the glass, which indicated that they had depth perception.

Figure 5.13

Mom Reading to Fetus

A pregnant mom reading to her fetus.

Figure 5.14

Newborns' Facial Responses to Basic Tastes

Facial expressions elicited by (a) a sweet solution, (b) a sour solution, and (c) a bitter solution.

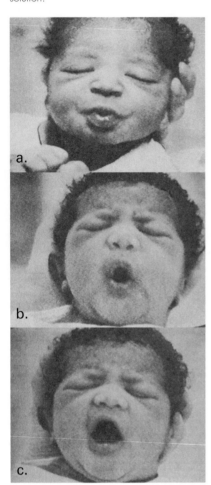

a.

b.

c.

intermodal perception The ability to relate and integrate information from two or more sensory modalities, such as vision and hearing.

held just above the mother's abdomen. Fetal heart rate increased in response to the mother's voice but decreased in response to the stranger's voice.

What kinds of changes in hearing take place from infancy on? It seems that these changes involve perceptual changes in the loudness, pitch, and localization of the sound (Saffran, Werker, & Werner, 2006). Newborns can determine the general direction of the source of the sound. By the age of six months, however, they are significantly more proficient at localizing sounds, and detecting their origins. The ability to localize sounds continues to improve during the second year (Saffran, Werker, & Werner, 2006).

It is likely that melodic aspects of the mother's speech, perhaps involving signature tunes that are individually distinctive pitch patterns, contribute to the preference of the mother's voice. Bergeson and Trehub (2007) state that signature tunes, and other recurring maternal vocalizations, may together facilitate the infant's ability to process speech. The purpose of a study conducted by Hannon and Trehub (2005) was to demonstrate that 12-month-old infants show an adult-like culture-specific pattern of responding to musical rhythms. This is in contrast to the culture-general responding that is evident at six months of age. Hannon and Trehub (2005) found that brief exposures to foreign music enables 12-month-olds, but not adults, to perceive rhythmic distinctions in foreign music contexts. These results may possibly indicate a sensitive period early in life for the acquisition of rhythm.

Other Senses

In addition to vision and hearing, the senses of touch and pain, smell, and taste also experience changes in infancy.

Newborns respond readily to touch. This might suggest that touch is the most well-developed sense at that age. A touch to the cheek produces a turning of the head, whereas a touch to the lips produces sucking movements. Increasing documentation suggests that touch and motion are essential to normal growth and development (Hockenberry & Wilson, 2013). Newborns, it seems, can also feel pain (Field & Hernandez-Reif, 2008; Gunnar & Quevedo, 2007). Newborns cry in protest when pricked by the needle by a technician drawing blood for a laboratory test. Similar adaptation to the social world occurs for the sense of smell and taste, even though these senses have been studied less extensively.

Newborns are able to differentiate odours (Doty & Shah, 2008). As babies learn to recognize the smell and handling procedure of each adult, they relax when cradled by that familiar caregiver, and they even close their eyes (Berger, 2011). The newborn has the ability to distinguish among tastes. A tasteless solution elicits no facial expression. On the other hand, a sweet solution elicits an eager suck, a sour solution causes the usual puckering of the lips, and a bitter solution produces an angry expression (Hockenberry & Wilson, 2013). See Figure 5.14.

Intermodal Perception

When mature observers look and listen to an event, they experience a unitary episode. But can very young infants, with little practice at perceiving, put vision and sound together as precisely as adults do?

Intermodal perception *is the ability to relate and integrate information from two or more sensory modalities, such as vision and hearing.* Early, exploratory forms of intermodal perception exist even in newborns (Bahrick & Hollich, 2008; Sann & Streri, 2007). Early forms of intermodal perception become sharpened with experience in the first year of life (Hollich, Newman, & Jusczyk, 2005). That is, Bahrick (2006) suggests that the senses are united in early infancy, fostering the rapid development of intermodal perception. Sai (2005) conducted four experiments that investigated the role of the mother's voice in facilitating recognition of the mother's face at birth. The conclusion drawn is that a prior experience with the mother's voice and face is necessary for the development of face recognition. As a result, intermodal perception is evident at birth.

Similarly, in a study by Michelle Patterson and Janet Werker (2003) at the University of British Columbia, the length of infants' gaze at one of two faces presented side-by-side was used as an indicator of their having put the language sound and visual information together. The sound they heard was a vowel; the photo of the face was of the person making the sound. Infants as early as two months of age gazed longer at the faces that matched the vowel sounds produced. The findings suggest that the capacity to connect visual information and sounds in the human language may be inborn. Trehub, Plantinga, and Brcic (2009) from the University of Toronto demonstrated that six- to eight-month-old infants will watch the silent video of a stranger speaking whose voice sound track they had previously been exposed to, rather than a stranger whose voice sound track they had not heard. Infants' intermodal skills develop quickly from combining single sounds with the features of a familiar face that accompany the sound to matching spoken statements with the numerous facial features that a stranger's face makes during the production of the sentence.

Just as they can coordinate perceptions from various modalities, infants also can manage perceptual and motor skills as a unit. In a study on visual expectations and motor reactions (Claxton, Keen, & McCarty, 2003), ten-month-olds were given two tasks: placing a ball into a narrow tube and throwing a ball into a plastic tub. Previous research had shown that adults reach for a target object more slowly before performing a precise action than before engaging in a non-precise action, as if they needed more time to plan their reaching before the task. In this study, infants showed similar differences—it took them longer to reach for a ball before the fitting task than before the throwing task, suggesting that young infants coordinate their actions and their perceptual expectations (Claxton et al., 2003).

Perceptual-Motor Coupling

As we come to the end of this section, we return to the important theme of perceptual-motor coupling. Babies continually coordinate their movements with perceptual information to learn how to maintain balance, reach for objects in space, and move across various surfaces and terrains (Adolph & Joh, 2007, 2008; Thelen & Smith, 2006). They are motivated to move by what they perceive. Consider the sight of an attractive toy across the room. In this situation, infants must perceive the current state of their bodies and learn how to use their limbs to reach the toy. Although their movements at first are awkward and uncoordinated, babies soon learn to select patterns that are appropriate for reaching their goals.

Equally important is the other part of the perception-action coupling. That is, action educates perception (Adolph & Joh, 2007, 2008; Smith & Breazeal, 2007; Thelen & Smith, 2006). For example, watching an object while exploring it manually helps infants to discriminate its texture, size, and hardness. Locomoting in the environment teaches babies about how objects and people look from different perspectives, or whether surfaces will support their weight. Individuals perceive in order to move and move in order to perceive. Perceptual and motor development do not occur in isolation from each other, but instead are coupled.

To this point, we have discussed a number of ideas about infants' motor, sensory, and perceptual development. For a review, see the **Reach Your Learning Objectives** section at the end of this chapter.

Cognitive Development

LO3 Determine how infants learn, remember, and conceptualize.

Piaget's Sensorimotor Stage

Recall from Chapter 2 that Piaget proposed a theory that emphasized the qualitative changes in cognitive development from infancy to adolescence. Because thinking is qualitatively different in each stage, progression can be seen in stages, with each later one being more advanced in terms of the way people understand the world. For example, an infant may understand an object only by seeing and touching it, while an adolescent can think about the same object in terms of its possible uses in various situations without the object being present.

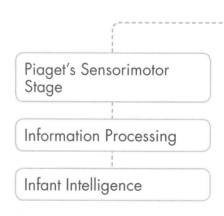

Piaget's Sensorimotor Stage

Information Processing

Infant Intelligence

scheme In Piaget's theory, a cognitive structure that helps individuals organize and understand their experiences.

organization Piaget's concept of grouping isolated behaviours and thoughts into a higher-order system.

equilibration A mechanism that Piaget proposed to explain how children shift from one stage of thought to the next.

simple reflexes Piaget's first sensorimotor substage, which corresponds to the first month after birth. In this substage, sensation and action are coordinated primarily through reflexive behaviours.

first habits and primary circular reactions Piaget's second sensorimotor substage, which develops between one and four months of age. In this substage, the infant coordinates sensation and two types of schemes: habits and primary circular reactions.

secondary circular reactions Piaget's third sensorimotor substage, which develops between four and eight months of age. In this substage, the infant becomes more object-oriented, moving beyond preoccupation with the self.

coordination of secondary circular reactions Piaget's fourth sensorimotor substage, which develops between 8 and 12 months of age. Actions become more outwardly directed, and infants coordinate schemes and act with intentionality.

tertiary circular reactions, novelty, and curiosity Piaget's fifth sensorimotor substage, which develops between 12 and 18 months of age. In this substage, infants become intrigued by the many properties of objects and by the many things that they can make happen to objects.

internalization of schemes Piaget's sixth and final sensorimotor substage, which develops between 18 and 24 months of age. In this substage, the infant develops the ability to use primitive symbols.

object permanence The Piagetian term for one of an infant's most important accomplishments: understanding that objects and events continue to exist even when they cannot directly be seen, heard, or touched.

Piaget introduced the concept of **scheme**, *a cognitive structure that helps individuals organize and understand their experiences.* Schemes change over time, and the changes involve two processes you learned in Chapter 2: assimilation (incorporating new information into existing knowledge) and accommodation (changing the existing knowledge to fit the new information). Infants assimilate all sorts of objects into their sucking scheme. Over a short time, they learn that some items such as fingers and mother's breast can be sucked, but others such as fuzzy blankets should not be; thus, they accommodate their sucking scheme.

To make sense out of their world, said Piaget, children cognitively organize their experiences. **Organization** *in Piaget's theory is the grouping of isolated behaviours and thoughts into a higher-order system.* Continual refinement of this organization is an inherent part of development. A boy who has only a vague idea about how to use a hammer may also have a vague idea about how to use other tools. After learning how to use each one, he relates these uses, organizing his knowledge.

Assimilation and accommodation always take the child to a higher ground, according to Piaget. In trying to understand the world, the child inevitably experiences cognitive conflict, or disequilibrium. That is, the child is constantly faced with counterexamples to his or her existing schemes and with inconsistencies. For example, if a child believes that pouring water from a short and wide container into a tall and narrow container changes the amount of water, then the child might be puzzled by where the "extra" water came from and whether there is actually more water to drink. The puzzle creates disequilibrium; for Piaget, an internal search for equilibrium creates motivation for change. The child assimilates and accommodates, adjusting old schemes, developing new schemes, and organizing and reorganizing the old and new schemes. Eventually, the organization is fundamentally different from the old organization; it is a new way of thinking. **Equilibration** *is the name Piaget gave to this mechanism by which children shift from one stage of thought to the next.*

According to Piaget, mental development in this early age is characterized by the infant's ability to organize and coordinate sensations with physical movements and actions, and he termed this period in cognitive development the sensorimotor stage. Piaget divided the sensorimotor stage into six substages: (1) **simple reflexes**; (2) **first habits and primary circular reactions**; (3) **secondary circular reactions**; (4) **coordination of secondary circular reactions**; (5) **tertiary circular reactions, novelty, and curiosity**; and (6) **internalization of schemes** (see Figure 5.15).

Object Permanence

Object permanence *is the Piagetian term for one of an infant's most important accomplishments: understanding that objects and events continue to exist even when they cannot directly be seen, heard, or touched.* The principal way that object permanence is studied is by watching an infant's reaction when an interesting object or event disappears (see Figure 5.16). If infants show no reaction, it is assumed they believe the object no longer exists. By contrast, if infants are surprised at the disappearance and search for the object, it is assumed they believe it continues to exist.

Causality

Piaget was very interested in infants' knowledge of cause and effect. His conclusions about infants' understanding of causality were based mainly on his observations of the extent to which infants acted to produce a desired outcome, such as pushing aside an obstacle to reach a goal.

One study on infants' understanding of causality found that even young infants comprehend that the size of a moving object determines how far it will move a stationary object if it collides with it (Kotovsky & Baillargeon, 1994). In this research, a cylinder rolled down a ramp and hit a toy bug that was located at the bottom of the ramp. By 5½ to 6½ months of age, infants understand that the bug would roll farther if it is hit by a large cylinder than if it is hit by a small cylinder, after they had observed how far it would be pushed by a medium-sized cylinder. Thus, by the middle of the

Figure 5.15

Piaget's Six Substages of Sensorimotor Development

Substage	Name	Age Range	Description and Examples
1	Simple Reflexes	1st month	Reflexive behaviour determines the coordination of sensation and action; e.g., a newborn will suck a nipple or bottle when it is placed directly in the baby's mouth or touched to the lips
2	First Habits and Primary Circular Reactions	1 to 4 months	Reflexes evolve into more refined and coordinated adaptive schemes. The infant develops schemes to reproduce an interesting or pleasurable event that initially occurred by chance; e.g., infant might suck on anything he/she brings to mouth
3	Secondary Circular Reactions	4 to 8 months	The infant becomes more object-oriented, or focused on the world, moving beyond a preoccupation with the self in sensorimotor interactions; e.g., by chance infant might shake a rattle, and will repeat the action for the sake of fascination
4	Coordination of Secondary Circular Reactions	8 to 12 months	Several significant changes take place that involve the coordination of schemes and intentionality; e.g., infants might look at an object and grasp it simultaneously, or they might visually inspect a toy and finger it simultaneously, exploring it tactilely
5	Tertiary Circular Reactions, Novelty, and Curiosity	12 to 18 months	The infant becomes intrigued by the variety of properties that objects possess and the multiplicity of things it can make happen to objects; e.g., infant explores new possibilities with new objects, doing new things to them and exploring the results, a trial-and-error exploration
6	Internalization of Schemes	18 to 24 months	The infant's mental functioning shifts from a purely sensorimotor plane to a symbolic plane, and the infant develops the ability to use primitive symbols; e.g., infant develops the use of symbols to represent objects or events. Symbols allow the infant to manipulate and transform the represented events in simple ways.

first year, these infants understood that the size of the cylinder was a causal factor in determining how far the bug would move when it was hit by the cylinder. Figure 5.17 outlines this main characteristic of sensorimotor thought.

Critiques

Piaget opened up a whole new way of looking at the development of infants' understanding of the world. However, he constructed his view of infancy mainly by observing the development of his own three children. Few laboratory techniques were available at the time, and much of the new research suggests that Piaget's view of sensorimotor development needs to be modified (Carlson & Zelazo, 2008; Meltzoff, 2007).

An ongoing debate is occurring in developmental psychology regarding whether or not the stage models are valid. Stages are problematic and discontinuous over different domains of development. Alternative conceptions of development contend that development is quantitative, continuous, modular, and gradual, implying that development can be understood without recourse to stage models. For example, neo-Piagetian models have been constructed to allow for the construct of individual differences in cognitive development (Young, 2011).

Figure 5.16

Object Permanence

Piaget thought that object permanence is one of infancy's landmark cognitive accomplishments. For this five-month-old boy, "out-of-sight" is literally out of mind. The infant looks at the toy monkey (*left*), but when his view of the toy is blocked (*right*), he does not search for it. Several months later, he will search for the hidden toy monkey, reflecting the presence of object permanence.

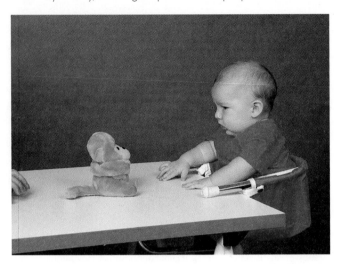

Theorists such as Eleanor Gibson (2001) and Elizabeth Spelke (1991; Spelke & Kinzler, 2007a, b) believe that infants' perceptual abilities are highly developed very early in development, challenging the slow progress toward object permanence understood by Piaget.

The violation-of-expectation (VOE) method has been used to investigate the fact that young infants can represent and reason about hidden objects. The apparent success of young infants in the VOE method reflects novelty and familiarity preferences brought about by habituation or familiarization trials in the tasks. To challenge some of the controversy regarding the VOE method, Wang, Baillargeon, and Brueckner (2004) concluded from their study that young infants can succeed at VOE tasks involving hidden objects even when given no habituation or familiarization. Several studies have examined ways in which infants respond to a moving object that temporarily disappears beyond a screen, but are delighted when it reappears (Aguiar & Baillargeon, 2002; Rosander & von Hofsten, 2004). These findings indicate that infants are capable of maintaining in mind a representation of the hidden object when it is behind the screen: the essence of object permanence. Xu and Baker (2005) investigated object individuation in infants. Object individuation is the process

Figure 5.17

Infants' Understanding of Causality

After young infants saw how far the medium-sized cylinder (a) pushed a toy bug, they showed more surprise at the event in (c) that showed a very small cylinder pushing the toy bug as far as the large cylinder (b). Their surprise, indicated by looking at (c) longer than (b), indicated that they understood the size of a cylinder was a causal factor in determining how far the toy bug would be pushed when it was hit by the cylinder.

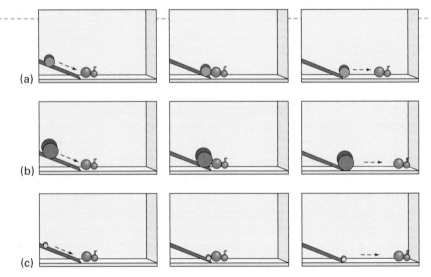

of establishing the number of objects that are involved in an event. They hypothesized that infants younger than 12 months rely heavily on spatiotemporal information—that is, information about location and motion. Spatiotemporal information overrides any conflicting property information, which refers to the perceptual features of objects such as colour, texture, and size. They concluded that when spatiotemporal evidence specifying a single object that changes properties is weak, 10-month-old infants succeed in using property information for object individuation.

It is further believed that the cognitive abilities of young infants may be richer and more continuous than previously believed by Piaget. Unfortunately, Piaget did not have access to the sophisticated new methods available to researchers today. Consequently, his conclusions tended to underestimate the physical knowledge and reasoning abilities of infants (Baillargeon, 2004).

Many researchers have concluded that Piaget wasn't specific enough about how infants learn about their world, and that infants are more competent than Piaget thought (Bremner, 2007; Spelke & Kinzler, 2007a, b). As they have examined the specific ways that infants learn, the field of infant cognition has become very specialized. If there is a unifying theme, it is that investigators in infant development seek to understand more precisely how developmental changes in cognition take place, and the big issue of nature and nurture (Spelke & Kinzler, 2007b).

Information Processing

In this section, we will explore aspects of how infants learn, remember, and sort information. The approaches we look at here do not describe infant development in terms of stages, but adopt a continuous view of development.

Conditioning

In Chapter 2, we described Pavlov's classical conditioning (in which, as a result of pairing, a new stimulus comes to elicit a response previously given to another stimulus) and Skinner's operant conditioning (in which the consequences of behaviour produce changes in the probability of the behaviour's occurrence). Infants can learn through both types of conditioning. For example, if an infant's behaviour is followed by a rewarding stimulus, the behaviour is likely to recur.

Carolyn Rovee-Collier (1987) has demonstrated that infants can retain information from the experience of being conditioned. In one study, she placed a 2½-month-old baby in a crib under an elaborate mobile (see Figure 5.18). She then tied one end of a ribbon to the baby's ankle and the other end to the mobile. Subsequently, she observed that the baby kicked and made the mobile move. The movement of the mobile was the reinforcing stimulus (which increased the baby's kicking behaviour). Weeks later, the baby was returned to the crib, but its foot was not tied to the mobile. The baby kicked, indicating retention of the information that kicking moved the mobile.

In addition, Campanella & Rovee-Collier (2005) have found that three-month-old infants can make associations between objects and their physical surroundings. The concept of association is fundamental and is invoked to explain a variety of both simple and complex cognitive phenomena. It was concluded that latent learning by very young infants is both extensive and enduring, and that their knowledge base begins to form early in life. In fact, such learning can occur long before infants are able to express what they know. Giles and Rovee-Collier (2011) conducted an experiment with six- and nine-month-old infants to discover first how long an association between events remains latent before being forgotten, and second what exposure conditions affect their persistence. The two groups were pre-exposed to two puppets for one hour per day for two days, one hour on one day or one hour on one day in two sessions: 1–27 days later, target actions were modelled on one puppet, and infants were tested with the other puppet one day later. The data revealed that the pre-exposure regimen determined retention. Regardless of exposure time, both ages remembered the association longer after two sessions, and younger infants remembered longer than older infants.

Cuevas, Rovee-Collier, and Learmonth (2006) found that infants as young as six months cannot only form new associations between objects, but also can form new associations with memories of objects. These results provide evidence that what infants merely see "brings to mind" what they saw before, and

developmental **connection**

Pavlov's Classical Conditioning and Skinner's Operant Conditioning

Figure 5.18

The Technique Used in Rovee-Collier's Investigation of Infant Memory

In Rovee-Collier's experiment, operant conditioning was used to demonstrate that infants as young as 2½ months of age can retain information from the experience of being conditioned.

that events and memories can combine in new ways. These results go far to highlight the important role that early experiences combined with enriching environments have upon cognitive development.

Attention

attention The focusing of mental resources on select information.

Attention, *the focusing of mental resources on select information,* improves cognitive processing on many tasks. Even newborns can detect a contour and fix their attention on it. Older infants scan patterns more thoroughly. By four months, infants can selectively attend to an object. Attention in the first year of life is dominated by an *orienting/investigative process* (Posner & Rothbart, 2007). This process involves directing attention to potentially important locations in the environment (that is, *where*) and recognizing objects and their features, such as colour and form (that is, *what*) (Courage & Richards, 2008). From three to nine months of age, infants can deploy their attention more flexibly and quickly. Another important type of attention is *sustained attention*, also referred to as *focused attention* (Courage & Richards, 2008).

New stimuli typically elicit an orienting response followed by sustained attention. This sustained attention allows infants to learn about and remember characteristics of a stimulus as it becomes familiar. Researchers have found that infants as young as three months of age engage in five to ten seconds of sustained attention. From this age through the second year, the length of sustained attention increases (Courage & Richards, 2008). Memorial University's Mary Courage and associates (2006) found infants nearing one year of age held sustained attention for longer time periods when attending to more complex rather than simple stimuli (faces and *Sesame Street* material versus achromatic patterns, respectively) than did younger infants, who showed no preference.

Habituation and Dishabituation

habituation Decreased responsiveness to a stimulus after repeated presentations of the stimulus.

dishabituation The increase in responsiveness after a change in stimulation.

If a stimulus—a sight or sound—is presented to infants several times in a row, they usually pay less attention to it each time. This is the process of **habituation**—*decreased responsiveness to a stimulus after repeated presentations of the stimulus.* **Dishabituation** *is the increase in responsiveness after a change in stimulation.* Among the measures researchers use to study whether habituation is occurring are sucking behaviour (sucking behaviour stops when the young infant attends to a novel object), heart and respiration rates, and the length of time the infant looks at an object. Habituation can be used to indicate infants' perception, such as the extent to which they can see, hear, smell, taste, and experience touch (Cohen & Cashon, 2003; Slater, 2002).

Infants' attention is strongly governed by novelty and habituation (Courage & Richards, 2008; Snyder & Torrence, 2008). When an object becomes familiar, attention becomes shorter, making infants more vulnerable to distraction (Oakes, Kannass, & Shaddy, 2002). One study found that 10-month-olds were more distractible than 26-month-olds (Ruff & Capozzoli, 2003). Knowing about habituation and dishabituation can help parents interact effectively with infants. Infants respond to changes in stimulation. Wise parents sense when an infant shows an interest and realize that they may have to repeat something many times for the infant to process information. But if the stimulation is repeated often, the infant stops responding to the parent. In parent–infant interaction, it is important for parents to do novel things and to repeat them often until the infant stops responding.

Imitation and Memory

developmental **connection**

Ethological Approach

Can infants imitate someone else's facial expressions? If an adult opens his mouth, widens his eyes, and raises his eyebrows, will the baby follow suit?

Infant development researcher Andrew Meltzoff (2004, 2005, 2007; Meltzoff & Moore, 1999; Meltzoff & Williamson, 2008) believes infants' imitative abilities are biologically based because infants can imitate a facial expression within the first few days after birth. Meltzoff also emphasizes that the infant's imitative abilities are not like what ethologists conceptualize as a hardwired, reflexive, innate releasing mechanism, but rather involve flexibility, adaptability, and intermodal perception. In Meltzoff's observations of infants in the first 72 hours after birth, the infants gradually displayed a full imitative response of an adult's facial expression, such as protruding the tongue or opening the mouth wide.

Meltzoff (2005) also has studied **deferred imitation**, *which occurs after a time delay of hours or days.* In one study, Meltzoff (1988) demonstrated that nine-month-old infants could imitate actions that they had seen performed 24 hours earlier. Each action consisted of an unusual gesture—such as pushing a recessed button in a box (which produced a beeping sound). Piaget believed that deferred imitation does not occur until about 18 months of age. Meltzoff's research suggested that it occurs much earlier.

deferred imitation Imitation that occurs after a time delay of hours or days.

Can young infants remember? Some infant researchers, such as Carolyn Rovee-Collier, argue that infants as young as two to six months of age can remember some experiences through 1½ to 2 years of age (Rovee-Collier, 2008). However, critics such as Jean Mandler (2004), a leading expert on infant cognition, argue that Rovee-Collier fails to distinguish between retention of a perceptual motor activity that is involved in conditioning tasks (such as that involved in kicking a mobile), often referred to as *implicit memory*, and the ability to consciously recall the past, often referred to as *explicit memory*.

When people talk about memory, they are usually referring to explicit memory. Most researchers find that babies do not show explicit memory until the second half of the first year (Bauer, 2007, 2008; Bauer et al., 2003). Then, explicit memory improves substantially during the second year of life (Bauer, 2007, 2008; Carver & Bauer, 2001). In one longitudinal study, one-year-old infants were assessed several times (Bauer et al., 2000). These infants showed more accurate memory and required fewer prompts to demonstrate their memory than infants under the age of one.

What changes in the brain are linked to infants' memory development? From about 6 to 12 months of age, the maturation of the hippocampus and the surrounding cerebral cortex, especially the frontal lobes, make the emergence of explicit memory possible (Nelson, Thomas, & de Haan, 2006). Explicit memory continues to improve in the second year, as these brain structures further mature and connections between them increase. Less is known about the areas of the brain involved in implicit memory in infancy.

Most adults cannot remember anything from the first three years of their life: this is referred to as *infantile amnesia*. The few reported adult memories of life at age two or three are at best very sketchy (Newcombe, 2008). Elementary school children also do not remember much of their early childhood years (Lie & Newcombe, 1999). One reason older children and adults have difficulty recalling events from their infant and early child years is that during these early years the prefrontal lobes of the brain are immature; this area of the brain is believed to play an important role in storing memories for events (Boyer & Diamond, 1992). After reviewing recent research, Canadian researchers Mark Howe and Mary Courage (2004) concluded that "memory . . . begins well after our entrance into this world." An alternative description is that memory formed in infancy cannot be expressed by the representational tools—like words—we learn later (Richardson & Hayne, 2007).

Concept Formation and Categorization

Along with attention, memory, and imitation, concepts are key aspects of infants' cognitive development (Oakes, 2008; Quinn, Bhatt, & Hayden, 2008). To understand what concepts are, we first have to define *categories*: they group objects, events, and characteristics on the basis of common properties. Concepts are members of a category. *Concepts* and categories help people to simplify and summarize information. Without concepts, each object and event would appear unique, memory would be overloaded easily, and no generalization could be made.

Do infants have concepts? They do, but we do not know just how early concept formation begins (Mandler, 2004). It is not until about seven to nine months of age that infants form *conceptual* categories that are characterized by perceptual variability. Further advances in categorization occur in the second year of life (Booth, 2006). Many infants' "first concepts are broad and global in nature, such as *animal* or *indoor thing*. Gradually, over the first two years, these broad concepts become more differentiated into concepts such as *land animal*, then *dog*, or to *furniture*, then *chair*" (Mandler, 2006, p. 1). In sum, the infant's skills in processing information—through attention, memory, imitation, and concept formation—are rich. As Jean Mandler (2004) concluded, "The human infant shows a remarkable degree of learning power and complexity in what is being learned and in the way it is represented" (p. 304).

critical thinking

If a one-year-old infant does well on a developmental scale, how confident should the parents be that this baby is going to be a genius later in life? Determine the value of implicit and explicit memory in infants. Justify the conclusion arrived by Canadian researchers (Howe & Courage, 2004), that "memory. . .begins well after our entrance into this world."

Infant Intelligence

So far, we have stressed general statements about how the cognitive development of infants progresses. We have emphasized what is typical of the largest number of infants or the average infant, but the results obtained for most infants do not apply to all infants. Individual differences in infant cognitive development have been studied primarily through the use of developmental scales, or infant intelligence tests.

The **Bayley Scales of Infant Development**, *developed by Nancy Bayley (1969) to assess infant behaviour and predict later development, is widely used in the assessment of infant development.* The current version, Bayley-III, has five scales: cognitive, language, motor, socio-emotional, and adaptive (Bayley, 2005). The first three scales are administered directly to the infant, while the latter two are questionnaires given to the caregiver. The Bayley-III also is more appropriate for use in clinical settings than the two previous editions (Lennon et al., 2008).

How well should a six-month-old perform on the Bayley mental scale? The six-month-old infant should be able to vocalize pleasure and displeasure, persistently search for objects that are just out of immediate reach, and approach a mirror that is placed in front of the infant by the examiner. By 12 months of age, an infant should be able to inhibit behaviour when commanded to do so, imitate words the examiner says (such as "Mama"), and respond to simple requests (such as "Take a drink").

Another assessment tool, the Fagan Test of Infant Intelligence (Fagan, 1992), focuses on the infant's ability to process information, including encoding the attributes of objects, detecting similarities and differences between objects, forming mental representations, and retrieving these representations. The Fagan test estimates babies' intelligence by comparing the amount of time they look at a new object with the amount of time they spend looking at a familiar object. This test elicits similar results from infants in different cultures and is correlated with measures of intelligence in older children. In fact, evidence is accumulating that measures of habituation and dishabituation are linked to intelligence in childhood and adolescence (Kavsek, 2004; Sigman, Cohen, & Beckwith, 2000). A recent longitudinal study found that the Fagan test when administered to 6- and 12-month-old infants was moderately predictable of the infants' IQ and academic achievement at 21 years of age (Fagan, Holland, & Wheeler, 2007).

It is important, however, not to go too far and think that the connections between early infant cognitive development and later childhood cognitive development are so strong that no discontinuity takes place. Rather, we should be examining the ways cognitive development is both continuous and discontinuous. We will describe these changes in cognitive development in subsequent chapters.

To this point, we have studied a number of ideas about infants' cognitive development. For a review, see the **Reach Your Learning Objectives** section at the end of this chapter.

Language Development

LO4 Explain the nature of language and how it develops in infancy.

What is language? **Language** *is a form of communication, whether spoken, written, or signed, that is based on a system of symbols.* All human languages have some common characteristics. These include infinite generativity and organizational rules. **Infinite generativity** *is the ability to produce a seemingly endless number of meaningful sentences using a finite set of words and rules.* This quality makes language a highly creative enterprise.

Language Acquisition

As infants develop, they reach a number of language milestones. At birth they communicate by crying, but by about two years of age, most can say approximately 200 words in the language their parents use. How does this remarkable ability develop?

Bayley Scales of Infant Development Scales developed by Nancy Bayley and widely used in the assessment of infant development. The current version has five scales: cognitive, language, motor, socio-emotional, and adaptive.

Language Acquisition

Biological Foundations of Language

Behavioural and Environmental Influences

Babbling and Other Vocalizations

Babies actively produce sounds and try to communicate with the outside world from birth onward. In the first year, the infant's effort to communicate is characterized by the following:

- *Crying.* This is present at birth, and, as you will discover in Chapter 6, different types of crying can signal different things.
- *Cooing.* This first occurs at about one to two months. These are /oo/ sounds such as /coo/ or /goo/ that usually occur during interaction with the caregiver.
- *Babbling.* This first occurs in the middle of the first year and includes strings of consonant–vowel combinations.
- *Gestures.* Infants use gestures, such as showing and pointing, at about 8 to 12 months of age. Some examples are waving bye-bye, nodding one's head to mean "yes," and pointing to a pet to draw attention to it.

Deaf infants born to deaf parents who use sign language babble with their hands and fingers at about the same age as hearing children babble vocally (Bloom, 1998). Such similarities in timing and structure between manual and vocal babbling indicate the presence of a unified language capacity that underlies signed and spoken language (Petitto & Marentette, 1991).

Recognizing Language Sounds

Long before infants learn words, they can make fine distinctions among the sounds of the language (Sebastian-Galles, 2007). Not only do they notice human speech sounds, infants as young as 2½ months old actually prefer human speech sounds to similar non-speech sounds, as a team at the University of British Columbia has discovered (Vouloumanos & Werker, 2004).

Kuhl (2007) argues that from birth up to about six months of age, infants are "universal linguists": they recognize when sounds change most of the time, no matter what language the syllables come from. But over the next six months, infants get even better at perceiving the changes in sounds from their "own" language, the one their parents speak, and gradually lose the ability to recognize differences that are not important in their own language.

Infants also appear to prefer certain categories of words to others. In English, lexical words such as nouns and verbs tend to carry more meaning and have different acoustic characteristics (e.g., longer vowel durations) than grammatical words such as prepositions. A pair of Canadian researchers found that six-month-olds from both English-speaking and Chinese-speaking families paid more attention when hearing lexical words such as "hide" and "chair" than they did when hearing grammatical words such as "the" and "you" (Shi & Werker, 2001, 2003). These findings suggest that infants noticed the different acoustic features of these two categories of words and preferred those of lexical words. This preference may help them to understand and produce these words first.

First Words

Spoken vocabulary begins when the infant utters its first word. As early as five months of age, infants recognize their name when someone says it. Thus, in infancy *receptive vocabulary* (words the child understands) considerably exceeds *spoken vocabulary* (words the child uses).

A child's first words include those that name important people (*dada*), familiar animals (*kitty*), vehicles (*car*), toys (*ball*), food (*milk*), body parts (*eye*), clothes (*hat*), household items (*clock*), and greeting terms (*bye*). These were the first words of babies 50 years ago. They are the first words of babies today.

The infant's spoken vocabulary rapidly increases once the first word is spoken (Pan & Uccelli, 2009). The average 18-month-old can speak about 50 words, but by the age of two years can speak about 200 words. This rapid increase in vocabulary that begins at approximately 18 months is called the *vocabulary spurt* (Bloom, Lifter, & Broughton, 1985). Like the timing of a child's first word, the timing of the vocabulary spurt varies (Lieven, 2008). Children sometimes overextend or underextend the meanings of the words they use (Woodward & Markman, 1998). *Overextension* is the

language A form of communication, whether spoken, written, or signed, that is based on a system of symbols.

infinite generativity The ability to produce a seemingly endless number of meaningful sentences using a finite set of words and rules.

Young children learn to speak in two-word utterances, in most cases, at about 18 to 24 months of age. **What are some examples of these two-word utterances?**

Figure 5.19

Some Language Milestones in Infancy

Despite great variations in the language input received by infants, around the world they follow a similar path in learning to speak.

Typical Age	Language Milestones
Birth	Crying
2 to 4 months	Cooing begins
5 months	Understands first word
6 months	Babbling begins
7 to 11 months	Change from universal linguist to language-specific listener
8 to 12 months	Use gestures, such as showing and pointing Comprehension of words appears
13 months	First word spoken
18 months	Vocabulary spurt starts
18 to 24 months	Uses two-word utterances Rapid expansion of understanding of words

telegraphic speech The use of short and precise words to communicate.

-------- developmental **connection** --

Brain Development and Evolutionary Psychology

⟵ -

Broca's area An area in the brain's left frontal lobe involved in producing words.

Wernicke's area A region of the brain's left hemisphere involved in language comprehension

language acquisition device (LAD) A biological endowment that enables the child to detect certain language categories, such as phonology, syntax, and semantics.

tendency to apply a word to objects that are inappropriate for the word's meaning. For example, children at first may say "*dada*" not only for "father" but also for other men, strangers, or boys. With time, overextensions decrease and eventually disappear. *Underextension* is the tendency to apply a word too narrowly; it occurs when children fail to use a word to name a relevant event or object. For example, a child might use the word *boy* to describe a five-year-old neighbour, but not apply the word to a male infant or to a nine-year-old male. Figure 5.19 shows some of the language milestones in infancy.

Two-Word Utterances

By the time children are 18 to 24 months of age, they usually can utter two-word statements. During this two-word stage, they quickly grasp the importance of expressing concepts and of the role that language plays in communicating with others. To convey meaning with two-word utterances, the child relies heavily on gesture, tone, and context.

Although two-word sentences omit many parts of speech, they are remarkably succinct in conveying many messages. In fact, in every language, a child's first combinations of words have this economical quality: **telegraphic speech**, *the use of short and precise words to communicate*. In a telegram, articles, auxiliary verbs, and other connectives usually are omitted, and young children's two- and three-word utterances are characteristically telegraphic.

Biological Foundations of Language

The strongest evidence for the biological basis of language is that children all over the world reach language milestones at about the same time developmentally and in about the same order. This occurs despite the vast variation in the language input they receive. For example, in some cultures, adults do not talk to children under one year of age, yet these infants still acquire language. There is no other convincing way to explain how quickly children learn language than through biological foundations.

A number of experts believe that biological evolution has undeniably shaped humans into linguistic creatures (Jackendoff & Pinker, 2005). The brain, nervous system, and vocal apparatus of our predecessors changed over hundreds of thousands of years. Physically equipped to do so, *Homo sapiens* went beyond grunting and shrieking to develop abstract speech. Language clearly gave humans an enormous edge over other animals and increased their chances of survival (Lachlan & Feldman, 2003; Pinker, 1994).

There is evidence that particular regions of the brain are predisposed to be used for language (Opitz & Friederici, 2007; Skipper et al., 2007). Two regions involved in language were first discovered in studies of brain-damaged individuals: **Broca's area**, *an area in the left frontal lobe of the brain involved in producing words,* and **Wernicke's area**, *a region of the brain's left hemisphere involved in language comprehension* (see Figure 5.20). Individuals with damage to Broca's area have difficulty producing words correctly; individuals with damage to Wernicke's area have poor comprehension and often produce fluent but incomprehensible speech.

McMaster University researchers have established that four-month-old infants have developed an automated skill, located in their auditory cortex, to monitor repeating sound input for any change (He, Hotson, & Trainor, 2009). This automated function is absent in two-month-old infants. The four-month-old infant's skill mirrors the stimulus change detection ability noted in adults. This ability is an essential element in infants' early language development, and appears to be located in the right frontal hemisphere. This type of research helps to understand the areas of the brain where language acquisition begins.

Linguist Noam Chomsky (1957) believes humans are biologically prewired to learn language at a certain time and in a certain way. He believes children are born into the world with a **language acquisition device (LAD)**, *a biological endowment that enables the child to detect certain language*

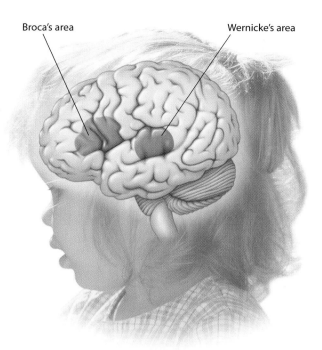

Broca's area

Wernicke's area

Figure 5.20

Broca's Area and Wernicke's Area

Broca's area is located in the frontal lobe of the brain's left hemisphere, and it is involved in the control of speech. Wernicke's area is a portion of the left hemisphere's temporal lobe that is involved in understanding language. **How does the role of these areas of the brain relate to lateralization?**

categories, such as phonology, syntax, and semantics. Phenomena such as the uniformity of language milestones across languages and cultures, biological substrates for language, and evidence that children create language even in the absence of well-formed input suggest the existence of an LAD. Moreover, research by McGill University's Fred Genesee (2001) demonstrates that, starting when they can produce the first words, infants can use two languages at the same time. He further states that studies show that children learn to be bilingual with the same relative ease as they learn to be monolingual. Hence, the language acquisition device appears to be capable of developing more than one language at a time.

Behavioural and Environmental Influences

Behaviourists view language as just another behaviour. They argue that language represents chains of responses (Skinner, 1957) or imitation (Bandura, 1977). However, many of the sentences we produce are novel; we have not heard them or spoken them before. For example, a child hears the sentence "The plate fell on the floor," and then says, "My mirror fell on the blanket," after dropping the mirror on the blanket. The behavioural mechanisms of reinforcement and imitation cannot completely explain this.

However, as we will see shortly, many parents do expand on their young children's grammatically incorrect utterances and recast many of those that have grammatical errors (Bonvillian, 2005).

Another criticism of the behavioural view is that it fails to explain the extensive orderliness of language. The behavioural view predicts that vast individual differences should appear in children's speech development because of each child's unique learning history. However, as we have seen, all infants coo before they babble; all toddlers produce one-word utterances before two-word utterances; and all state sentences in the active form before they state them in the passive form.

Nevertheless, people do not learn language in a social vacuum. Most children are bathed in language from a very early age (Tomasello, 2006). The Wild Boy of Aveyron, who never learned to communicate effectively, had lived in social isolation for years. The support and involvement of caregivers and teachers greatly facilitate a child's language learning (Snow & Yang, 2006).

> developmental **connection**
>
> **Skinner's Operant Conditioning and Bandura's Social Cognitive Theory**

It is a good idea for parents to begin talking to their babies from the start. The best language teaching occurs when the talking is begun before the infant becomes capable of intelligible speech. **What are some other guidelines for parents to follow in helping their infants and toddlers develop their language? What are some characteristics of infant-directed speech?**

child-directed speech This type of speech has a higher-than-normal pitch and involves the use of simple words and sentences.

- - - - - - - **critical** thinking - - - - - - - -

Should infants be exposed to numerous languages because they could easily acquire languages at an early age? Would this kind of language learning be harmful to a baby? Develop a research question to determine the effects on an infant's visual fixation caused by the mothers' singing and talking to them. In what ways can you assist adolescent mothers from a low socio-economic class in increase language development over the first two years of the child's life?

For example, one study found that when mothers immediately smiled and touched their eight-month-old infants after they babbled, the infants subsequently made more complex speech-like sounds than when mothers responded to their infants in a random manner (Goldstein, King, & West, 2003).

Researchers have found that the child's vocabulary development is linked to the family's socio-economic status and the type of talk that parents direct to their children. LaCroix and colleagues (2001) conducted a study in Montreal, examining language development over the first two years of life. They found that children of adolescent mothers and of mothers of low socio-economic status lagged behind the children of mothers ranked as higher in socio-economic status in language development. LaCroix and colleagues established that maternal vocalization to the children at 6 and 18 months of age is correlated to language development at 18 and 24 months, respectively.

An intriguing aspect of the environment in the young child's acquisition of language is called **child-directed speech**. *This type of speech has a higher-than-normal pitch and involves the use of simple words and sentences.* Parents and even other children make use of this speech pattern, often without conscious awareness. Infant-directed speech has the important functions of capturing the infant's attention and maintaining communication.

It appears that mothers have a "signature tune" in their speech patterns for their infants. In a series of audio recorded interactions between mother and infant, identifiable tunes with unique pitch contours were detected for each mother when speaking to their baby (Bergeson & Trehub, 2007). Nakata and Trehub (2004) found mothers singing to their infants created a stronger visual fixation along with movement reduction (indicating greater attention) than when mothers spoke to their infants. While we all might use child-directed speech, mothers' speech and singing are unique to their infants. Whether father's voice arouses the same attention and has the same unique character remains to be discovered.

While infant-directed speech helps maintain infants' interest in oral interactions, adults sometimes use specific strategies to enhance children's acquisition of language. Four such techniques are recasting, echoing, expanding, and labelling. *Recasting* is rephrasing something the child has said in a different way, perhaps turning it into a question. For example, if the child says, "The dog was barking," the adult can respond by asking, "When was the dog barking?" Recasting fits with the idea that letting a child initially indicate an interest and then proceeding to elaborate that interest—commenting, demonstrating, and explaining—improves communication and helps language acquisition. *Echoing* is repeating what a child says, especially if it is an incomplete phrase or sentence. *Expanding* is restating, in a linguistically sophisticated form, what a child has said. *Labelling* is identifying the names of objects. When adults ask young children to identify the names of objects, the youngsters acquire vocabulary.

Each of the techniques mentioned above and child-directed speech indicate that we should make special effort to speak to and teach language to children. Melanie Soderstrom (2007) reminds us, however, that children also learn about language as adults engage in conversation with other adults in the presence of the child. What we say and how we say it can be easily observed and learned by the child to whom we are not directly speaking.

An interactionist view emphasizes that both biology and experience contribute to language development. How much of the language is biologically determined, and how much depends on interaction with others, is a subject of debate among linguists and psychologists. However, all agree that both biological capacity and relevant experience are necessary (Gathercole & Hoff, 2007; Tomasello, Carpenter, & Liszkowski, 2007).

To this point, we have discussed a number of ideas about infants' language development. For a review, see the **Reach Your Learning Objectives** section at the end of this chapter.

reach your **learning objectives**

Physical Development and Health

LO1 Outline steps involved in physical growth and development in infancy.

Physical Growth	■ The average full-term newborn is 48–53 centimetres long and weighs 2,500 to 4,000 grams.
	■ Infants grow about 2.5 centimetres per month in the first 6 months of life, but growth slows during the second 6 months.
	■ The cephalocaudal pattern refers to growth that occurs from top down.
	■ The proximodistal pattern refers to growth that occurs from centre out.
Brain	■ Dendritic spreading is dramatic in the first two years.
	■ Myelination continues to develop in infancy and childhood.
	■ Connections between neurons increase.
	■ Lateralization refers to specialization of function in one hemisphere or the other.
	■ Early experience is important for the development of the brain.
Sleep	■ Newborns usually sleep 16 to 17 hours a day. By four months of age, many Canadian infants' sleeping patterns approach adult patterns.
	■ REM sleep, which might promote brain development, is present more in early infancy than in childhood or adulthood.
	■ There is no foolproof method to predict the occurrence of sudden infant death syndrome. Some risk factors include low birth weight and exposure to cigarette smoke.
Health	■ High-calorie, high-energy foods are part of a balanced diet for infants.
	■ Deficiencies in vitamin D and iron are two health concerns in infancy.
	■ Infants should be taken to the dentist for the first time within six months of the eruption of the first teeth.
	■ Breastfeeding is superior to bottle-feeding.
	■ One cause of malnutrition in infancy is early weaning from breast milk to inadequate nutrients.

Motor, Sensory, and Perceptual Development

LO2 Examine infant motor development and summarize the course of sensory and perceptual development in infancy

Motor Development	■ Reflexes are automatic movements that govern the newborn's behaviour.
	■ Gross motor skills involve large muscle activities, such as moving one's arms and walking.
	■ Fine motor skills involve movements that are fine tuned, such as using fingers to grasp an object.
	■ A number of milestones in these motor skills are achieved in infancy.

| Sensory and Perceptual Development | <ul><li>Sensation occurs when a stimulus reaches sensory receptors, such as the eyes and skin.</li><li>Perception is the interpretation of what is sensed.</li><li>By age one, the infant's visual acuity nears that of an adult.</li><li>Gibson and Walk's visual cliff study showed that babies as young as six months have depth perception.</li><li>Visual expectation has been found among three-month-old babies.</li><li>The fetus can hear sounds such as the mother's voice and music in the last two months of pregnancy. Both fetuses and newborns prefer the mother's voice.</li><li>Newborns can feel touch and pain and prefer certain odours and tastes.</li><li>Intermodal perception of matches between vowels and the face that produced them occurs as early as two months of age.</li><li>Babies are constantly coordinating their motor movements with concurrent perceptual information.</li></ul> |

Cognitive Development

LO3 Determine how infants learn, remember, and conceptualize.

Piaget's Sensorimotor Stage	<ul><li>A scheme is a cognitive structure that helps a person organize experience and changes with age.</li><li>This stage lasts from birth to about two years of age.</li><li>The infant is able to organize and coordinate sensations with physical movements.</li><li>The infant's understanding of the physical world is shown by the attainment of object permanence and a sense of causality.</li><li>Object permanence refers to the ability to understand that objects continue to exist, even though the infant is no longer observing them.</li><li>Research suggests that children acquire perceptual and conceptual skills earlier than Piaget thought.</li></ul>
Information Processing	<ul><li>Habituation is the repeated presentation of the same stimulus, causing reduced attention to the stimulus. It has been used to demonstrate infants' perception.</li><li>Explicit memory—that is, the ability to recall the past consciously—does not emerge until the second half of the first year after birth.</li><li>Concepts and categories help simplify and summarize information. Research has shown that infants can form concepts.</li></ul>
Infant Intelligence	<ul><li>The infant testing movement grew out of the tradition of IQ testing of older children.</li><li>The Bayley-III has five scales: cognitive, language, motor, socio-emotional, and adaptive. The first three scales are administered directly to the infant, while the latter two are questionnaires given to the caregiver.</li><li>The Fagan test of infant intelligence focuses on the infant's ability to process information.</li><li>Development of cognitive skills from infancy to childhood shows both continuity and discontinuity.</li></ul>

Language Development

LO4 Explain the nature of language and how it develops in infancy.

Language Acquisition	■ In the first year, infants use crying, cooing, then babbling as well as gestures to communicate.
	■ Infants utter their first word at about 10 to 15 months of age. Their vocabulary spurt begins at around 18 months, when infants can speak about 50 words; six months later, they have a vocabulary of about 200 words.
	■ In the so-called two-word stage, infant speech is "telegraphic."
	■ In infancy, receptive vocabulary exceeds spoken vocabulary.
Biological Foundations of Language	■ Broca's area is involved in producing words. Wernicke's area is involved in language comprehension.
	■ Chomsky's notion of a language acquisition device is one example to show how a biological endowment allows children to detect language categories.
Behavioural and Environmental Influences	■ Environmental influences on language acquisition can be seen in research contrasting middle-income and low-income children's language performance.
	■ Among the ways that adults teach language to children are infant-directed speech, recasting, echoing, expanding, and labelling.

review ---> *connect* ---> reflect

review

What are some key features of the brain and its development in infancy? **LO1**

What are the infant's nutritional needs? **LO1**

How do gross motor skills develop in infancy? **LO2**

How do fine motor skills develop in infancy? **LO2**

How is imitation involved in infant learning? **LO3**

What is intermodal perception? **LO3**

What are some biological and environmental influences on language? **LO4**

connect

What are the main differences between the grasping reflex present at birth and the fine motor grasping skills an infant develops between 4 and 12 months of age?

reflect *Your Own Personal Journey of Life*

What types of sensory stimulation would you provide to your own baby on a daily basis? Is it possible for you to overstimulate your baby? Explain.

McGraw Hill Education **connect**

McGraw-Hill Connect provides you with a powerful tool for improving academic performance and truly mastering course material. You can diagnose your knowledge with pre- and post-tests, identify the areas where you need help, search the entire learning package, including the eBook, for content specific to the topic you're studying, and add these resources to your personalized study plan. CONNECT for *Life-Span Development*, fifth Canadian edition, offers the following:

■ chapter-specific online quizzes

■ groupwork

■ presentations

■ writing assignments

■ case studies

■ and much more!

Visit CONNECT today!

CHAPTER 6

Socio-Emotional Development in Infancy

CHAPTER OUTLINE

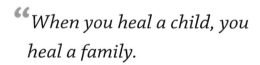

> "*When you heal a child, you heal a family.*
>
> *When you heal a family, you heal a community.*
>
> *When you heal a community, you heal a nation.*"
>
> —SHAWN ATLEO, NATIONAL CHIEF OF THE ASSEMBLY OF THE FIRST NATIONS

Tom and His Father

Tom is a one-year-old infant who is being reared by his father during the day. His mother works full-time at her job away from home, and his father is a writer who works at home; they prefer this arrangement over putting Tom in daycare. Tom's father is doing a great job of caring for him. Tom's father keeps Tom nearby while he is writing and spends lots of time talking to him and playing with him. From their interaction, it is clear that they genuinely enjoy each other.

Tom's father looks to the future and imagines the hockey and soccer games Tom will play in and the many other activities he can enjoy with Tom. Remembering how little time his own father spent with him, he is dedicated to making sure that Tom has an involved, nurturing experience with his father.

When Tom's mother comes home in the evening, she spends considerable time with him. Tom shows a positive attachment to both his mother and his father. His parents have cooperated and successfully juggled their careers and work schedules to provide one-year-old Tom with excellent child care.

Tom's experience highlights some developmental issues related to a child's future outcomes: child care arrangements, parenting style, paternal caregiving, and attachment. These issues concern many researchers and families and will be discussed in this chapter.

Many fathers are spending more time with their infants today than in the past.

Emotional Development

LO1 Outline the development of emotions in infancy.

Infants can express a number of emotions. We will explore what these are and how they develop, but first we need to define *emotion*.

Defining Emotion

Defining emotion is difficult because it is not easy to tell when a child or an adult is in an emotional state. Is a child in an emotional state when his/her heart beats fast, palms sweat, and stomach churns? Or is a child in an emotional state when he/she smiles or grimaces? For our purposes, we will define **emotion** *as feeling, or affect, that occurs when a person is in a state or an interaction that is important to him or her, especially to his or her well-being* (Campos, 2005). Psychologists classify the broad range of emotions in many ways, but almost all classifications designate an emotion as either positive or negative (Barrett et al., 2007). Positive emotions include enthusiasm, joy, and love. Negative emotions include anxiety, anger, guilt, and sadness.

Biological and Environmental Influences

Emotions are influenced both by biological foundations and by a person's experience. Biology's importance to emotion is also apparent in the changes in a baby's emotional capacities (Bell & Wolfe, 2007). Certain regions of the brain that develop early in life (such as the brain stem, hippocampus, and amygdala) play a role in distress, excitement, and rage, and even infants display these emotions (Buss & Goldsmith, 2007). But, as we discuss later in the chapter, infants develop the ability to regulate their emotions only gradually, and this ability seems tied to the gradual maturation of the frontal regions of the cerebral cortex (discussed in Chapter 4) that can exert control over other areas of the brain (Thompson & Goodvin, 2007).

These biological factors, however, are only part of the story of emotion. Emotions serve important functions in our relationships (Perez & Gauvain, 2007). As we discuss later in this section, emotions are the first language with which parents and infants communicate. Emotion-linked interchanges, as when Tom cries and his father sensitively responds, provide the foundation for the infant's developing attachment to the parent.

Social relationships, in turn, provide the setting for the development of a rich variety of emotions (Brownell & Kopp, 2007; Thompson, 2009a). When toddlers hear their parents quarrelling, they often react with distress and inhibit their play. Well-functioning families make each other laugh and may develop a light mood to defuse conflicts. Biological evolution has allowed human beings to be *emotional*, but embeddedness in relationships and culture with others provides diversity in emotional experiences (Perez & Gauvain, 2007; Thompson & Virmani, 2009). For example, Japanese parents try to prevent their children from experiencing negative emotions, whereas non-Latino White mothers are more likely to respond after their children become distressed and then help them cope (Rothbaum & Trommsdorff, 2007).

Early Emotions

The leading expert on infant emotional development, Michael Lewis (2007), distinguishes between primary emotions and self-conscious emotions. **Primary emotions** are *emotions that are present in humans and other animals;* these emotions appear in the first six months of the human infant's development. Primary emotions include surprise, interest, joy, anger, sadness, fear, and disgust (see Figure 6.1 for infants' facial expressions of some of these early emotions). In Lewis's classification, **self-conscious emotions** *require self-awareness that involves consciousness and a sense of "me."* Self-conscious emotions include jealousy, empathy, embarrassment, pride, shame, and guilt, most of which occur for the first time at some point in the second half of the first year through the second

emotion Feeling, or affect, that occurs when a person is in a state or an interaction that is important to him or her, especially to his or her well-being.

developmental **connection**

Bandura's Social Cognitive Theory and Evolutionary Psychology

primary emotions Present in humans and other animals and emerge early in life; examples are joy, anger, sadness, fear, and disgust.

self-conscious emotions Require self-awareness, especially consciousness and a sense of "me"; examples include jealousy, empathy, and embarrassment.

Figure 6.1

Expression of Different Emotions in Infants

| Joy | Sadness | Fear | Surprise |

year. Some experts on emotion call self-conscious emotions such as embarrassment, shame, guilt, and pride *other-conscious emotions* because they involve the emotional reactions of others when they are generated (Saarni et al., 2006). For example, approval from parents is linked to toddlers beginning to show pride when they successfully complete a task.

Researchers such as Joseph Campos (2005) and Michael Lewis (2007) debate how early in the infant and toddler years these emotions first appear and their sequence. As an indication of the controversy regarding when certain emotions first are displayed by infants, consider jealousy. Some researchers argue that jealousy does not emerge until approximately 18 months of age (Lewis, 2007), whereas others emphasize that it is displayed much earlier (Draghi-Lorenz, 2007; Draghi-Lorenz, Reddy, & Costall, 2001). Consider a research study in which six-month-old infants observed their mothers either giving attention to a lifelike baby doll (hugging or gently rocking it, for example) or to a book (Hart & Carrington, 2002). When mothers directed their attention to the doll, the infants were more likely to display negative emotions, such as anger and sadness, which may have indicated their jealousy (see Figure 6.2). On the other hand, their expressions of anger and sadness may have reflected frustration in not being able to have the novel doll to play with. Debate about the onset of an emotion such as jealousy illustrates the complexity and difficulty in indexing early emotions.

Emotion Expression and Social Relationships

Emotional expressions are involved in infants' first relationships. The ability of infants to communicate emotions permits coordinated interactions with their caregivers and the beginning of an emotional bond between them (Thomann & Carter, 2008; Thompson, 2009b). Not only do parents change their emotional expressions in response to infants' emotional expressions, but infants also modify their emotional expressions in response to their parents' emotional expressions. In other words, these interactions are mutually regulated. Because of this coordination, the interactions are described as *reciprocal*, or *synchronous*, when all is going well. Sensitive, responsive parents help their infants grow emotionally, whether the infants respond in distressed or happy ways (Thompson & Newton, 2009).

Cries and smiles are two emotional expressions that infants display when interacting with parents. These are babies' first forms of emotional communication.

Crying

Crying is the most important mechanism newborns have for communicating with others. This is true for the first cry, which tells the mother and doctor the baby's lungs have filled with air. Cries also may tell physicians and researchers something about the central nervous system. Newborns even tend to respond with cries and negative facial expressions when they hear other newborns cry (Dondi, Simion, & Caltran, 1999).

Figure 6.2

Research Setting for Sybil Hart's Attempt to Assess the Early Development of Jealousy

An infant becomes distressed when his mother gives attention to a lifelike baby doll. **What are some possible interpretations of the infant's distress?**

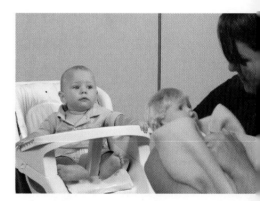

What are some developmental changes in emotion during infancy? What are some different types of crying that infants display?

basic cry A rhythmic pattern usually consisting of a cry, a briefer silence, a shorter inspiratory whistle that is higher pitched than the main cry, and then a brief rest before the next cry.

anger cry Similar to the basic cry, with more excess air forced through the vocal chords.

pain cry A sudden appearance of loud crying without preliminary moaning and a long initial cry followed by an extended period of breath holding.

Babies do not have just one type of cry; they have at least three. The **basic cry** is a *rhythmic pattern that usually consists of a cry, followed by a briefer silence, then a shorter inspiratory whistle that is somewhat higher in pitch than the main cry, then another brief rest before the next cry*. Some infancy experts believe that hunger is one of the conditions that incite the basic cry. The **anger cry** is a *variation of the basic cry*. However, in the anger cry, more excess air is forced through the vocal cords. The **pain cry**, which *is stimulated by high-intensity stimuli, differs from other types of cries. A sudden appearance of loud crying without preliminary moaning and a long initial cry followed by an extended period of breath holding characterize the pain cry*.

Most adults can determine whether an infant's cries signify anger or pain (Zeskind, 2009; Zeskind, Klein, & Marshall, 1992). Parents also can distinguish the cries of their own baby better than those of another baby. There is little consistent evidence to support the idea that mothers and other females, but not fathers and other males, are innately programmed to respond in a comforting way to an infant's crying.

To soothe or not to soothe—should a crying baby be given attention and soothed, or does this spoil the infant? Many years ago, famous behaviourist John Watson (1928) argued that parents spent too much time responding to infant crying. As a consequence, he said, parents were actually rewarding infant crying and increasing its incidence. More recently, infancy experts Mary Ainsworth (1979) and John Bowlby (1989) considered the caregiver's quick, comforting response to the infant's cries an important ingredient in the development of secure attachment. Overall, developmentalists increasingly argue that an infant cannot be spoiled in the first year of life, which suggests that parents should soothe a crying infant, rather than be unresponsive; in this manner, infants likely will develop a sense of trust and secure attachment to the caregiver in the first year of life. Feldman and Eidelman (2003) and Feldman, Weller, Sirota, and Eidelman (2003) found that a tactile stimulus could be useful for terminating an infant's crying behaviour.

Evolutionary psychologists look to nature—that is, the inborn biological forces that have evolved to promote survival—to explain why individuals act in certain ways. According to them, such individuals cannot be changed by modifying the reinforcers. These reactions are based on the human genetic code which we all share. However, evolutionary psychologists alert us to the fact that we do need to pay close attention to basic human needs (Belsky, 2010).

Nakayama (2010) examined the development of infant crying behaviour after six months of age. Two female infants were observed twice a month for six months when the infants were between 7 and 14 months of age. It appeared that the crying behaviour of the infants became more sophisticated and communicative with increasing age. This behaviour suggested a proactive stance by the infant in interacting with the mother. The findings seemed to indicate that at 11–12 months of age, "fake crying" was observed during naturalistic interaction with the mother. Fake crying is the behaviour used by an infant to convey attention to the mother so that the mother would come nearer and provide attention to the infant. This study indicated that normal infants might be capable of deceptive behaviour such as "fake crying" by the end of the first year. The results also provided strong evidence that infants communicate proactively with the mother by using crying behaviour. Fake crying has come to be regarded as a favourable sign of a normal infant's social development.

In summary, primary health care professionals have a responsibility to provide parents with information and strategies to help them understand and manage both the infant's crying as well as their own frustration with crying (Evanoo, 2007).

------- developmental **connection** -------

Bowlby's Attachment Theory

←-------------------------------

Smiling

Smiling is another important communicative affective behaviour of the infant. Two types of smiling can be distinguished in infants—one reflexive, the other social. A **reflexive smile** *does not occur in response to external stimuli*. It appears during the first month after birth, usually during irregular patterns of sleep. By contrast, a **social smile** *occurs in response to an external stimulus, which, early in development, typically is a face*. The power of the infant's smiles was appropriately captured by British attachment theorist John Bowlby (1969): "Can we doubt that the more and better an infant smiles, the better he is loved and cared for? It is fortunate for their survival that babies are so designed by nature that they beguile and enslave mothers."

reflexive smile Does not occur in response to external stimuli. It happens during the month after birth, usually during irregular patterns of sleep.

social smile Occurs in response to an external stimulus, which, early in development, typically is a face.

Daniel Messinger (2008) recently described the developmental course of infant smiling. From two to six months after birth, infants' social smiling increases considerably, both in self-initiated smiles and smiles in response to others' smiles. At 6 to 12 months, smiles that couple what is called the Duchenne marker (eye constriction) and mouth opening occur in the midst of highly enjoyable interactions and play with parents. In the second year, smiling continues to occur in such positive circumstances with parents, and in many cases an increase in smiling occurs when interacting with peers. Also in the second year, toddlers become increasingly aware of the social meaning of smiles, especially in their relationship with parents.

Fear

One of a baby's earliest emotions is fear, which typically first appears at about six months of age and peaks at about 18 months. However, abused and neglected infants can show fear as early as three months (Campos, 2005). Researchers have found that infant fear is linked to guilt, empathy, and low aggression at six to seven years of age (Rothbart, 2007).

The most frequent expression of an infant's fear involves **stranger anxiety**, *in which an infant shows fear and wariness of strangers*. This reaction starts to appear in the second half of the first year. There are individual variations in stranger anxiety, and not all infants show distress when they encounter a stranger. Stranger anxiety usually emerges gradually, first appearing at about six months of age in the form of wary reactions. By age nine months, the fear of strangers is often more intense, reaching a peak toward the end of the first year of life, then decreasing thereafter (Scher & Harel, 2008).

In addition to stranger anxiety, infants experience fear of being separated from their caregivers. The result is **separation protest**—*crying when the caregiver leaves*. Separation protest is initially displayed by infants at approximately 7 to 8 months and peaks at about 15 months (Kagan, 2008).

Emotion Regulation and Coping

Emotion regulation *consists of effectively managing arousal to adapt to and reach a goal* (Eisenberg et al., 2002). Arousal involves a state of alertness or activation, which can reach levels that are too high for effective functioning.

During the first year after birth, the infant gradually develops an ability to inhibit or minimize the intensity and duration of emotional reactions (Calkins, 2007; Kopp, 2008). From early in infancy, many babies put their thumbs in their mouths to soothe themselves. They also depend on caregivers to help them soothe their emotions by rocking them to sleep, singing lullabies to them, gently stroking them, and so on. The caregivers' actions influence the infant's neurobiological regulation of emotions (Thompson, Meyer, & Jochem, 2008). By soothing the infant, caregivers help infants to modulate their emotion and reduce the level of stress hormones (Gunnar & Quevedo, 2007). Many developmentalists stress that it is a good strategy for a caregiver to soothe an infant before the infant gets into an intense, agitated, uncontrolled state (McElwain & Booth-LaForce, 2006). Contexts can influence emotional regulation (Thompson & Goodvin, 2007). Infants are often affected by such factors as fatigue, hunger, time of day, and the people around them. Infants must learn to adapt to different contexts that require emotional regulation. Further, new context demands appear as the infant becomes older and parents modify their expectations. For example, a parent may not expect a 1½-year-old to scream loudly in a restaurant, but may not have been as bothered by this when the child was six months old.

By two years of age, toddlers can use language to define their feeling states and the context that is upsetting them (Kopp, 2008). A toddler might say, "Feel bad. Dog scare." The communication of this type of information about feeling states and context may help caregivers to assist the child in regulating emotion. Toddlers can also be very good at using physically aggressive behaviour to express feeling states, such as anxiety, fear, and jealousy, instead of using their language abilities. In a study following a group of children in Quebec from ages four months through seven years, Barker and colleagues (2008) found that children who showed a higher level of aggressive behaviour

stranger anxiety An infant's fear and wariness of strangers; it tends to appear in the second half of the first year of life.

separation protest An infant's crying when the caregiver leaves.

emotion regulation Effectively managing arousal to adapt to and reach a goal.

"Oh, he's cute, all right, but he's got the temperament of a car alarm." © The New Yorker Collection 1999 Barbara Smaller from cartoonbank.com. All Rights Reserved.

developmental **connection**

Language Development

(biting, kicking, hitting, etc.) by age 17 months were more likely to be subject to peer victimization by the time they entered Grade 2. Their inappropriate interpersonal skills made them liable to bullying. This finding underlines the importance of teaching toddlers to verbally express and resolve negative emotional states.

To this point, we have studied a number of ideas about emotional development in infancy. For a review, see the **Reach Your Learning Objectives** section at the end of this chapter.

Temperament and Personality Development

Temperament

Personality Development

LO2 Summarize the development of temperament and personality during infancy.

Infants show different emotional responses. One infant might be cheerful and happy much of the time; another baby might cry constantly. These behaviours reflect differences in temperament (Halpern & Brand, 1999).

Temperament

temperament An individual's behavioural style and characteristic way of emotionally responding.

Temperament *is an individual's behavioural style and characteristic way of emotionally responding.* Developmentalists are especially interested in the temperament of infants.

Defining and Classifying Temperaments

Given the uniqueness of infants' temperamental responses, many developmentalists have attempted to classify temperament into different styles.

CHESS AND THOMAS'S CLASSIFICATION   Psychiatrists Alexander Chess and Stella Thomas (Chess & Thomas, 1977; Thomas & Chess, 1991) believe there are three basic types, or clusters, of temperament—easy, difficult, and slow to warm up.

easy child Generally is in a positive mood, quickly establishes regular routines in infancy, and adapts easily to new experiences.

difficult child Tends to react negatively and cry frequently, engages in irregular daily routines, and is slow to accept new experiences.

slow-to-warm-up child Has a low activity level, is somewhat negative, shows low adaptability, and displays a low intensity of mood.

1. An **easy child** *is generally in a positive mood, quickly establishes regular routines in infancy, and adapts easily to new experiences.*
2. A **difficult child** *tends to react negatively and cry frequently, engages in irregular daily routines, and is slow to accept new experiences.*
3. A **slow-to-warm-up** child *has a low activity level, is somewhat negative, shows low adaptability, and displays a low intensity of mood.*

Various dimensions make up these three basic clusters of temperament. Chess and Thomas found that 40 percent of the children they studied could be classified as easy, 10 percent as difficult, and 15 percent as slow-to-warm-up (35 percent did not fit any of the three patterns). These three basic clusters of temperament are moderately stable across the childhood years.

KAGAN'S BEHAVIOURAL INHIBITION   Another way of classifying temperament focuses on the differences between a shy, subdued, timid child and a sociable, extraverted, bold child (Asendorph, 2008). Jerome Kagan (2002; Kagan et al., 2007) regards shyness with strangers (peers or adults) as one feature of a broad temperament category called *inhibition to the unfamiliar*. Inhibited children react to many aspects of unfamiliarity with initial avoidance, distress, or subdued affect, beginning at about seven to nine months of age.

Kagan has found that inhibition shows considerable stability from infancy through early childhood. One study classified toddlers into extremely inhibited, extremely uninhibited, and intermediate groups (Pfeifer et al., 2002). Follow-up assessments occurred at four and seven years of age. Continuity was demonstrated for both inhibition and lack of inhibition, although a substantial number of the inhibited children moved into the intermediate groups at seven years of age. In a

developmental **connection**

Stability and Change

recent meta-analysis to determine the magnitude of gender differences in temperament, the findings were revealed that girls have greater inhibitory control and higher perceptual sensitivity, while boys have higher levels of activity and higher intensity levels of pleasure (Else-Quest, Hyde, Goldsmith, & Van Hulle, 2006).

ROTHBART AND BATES'S CLASSIFICATION   Mary Rothbart and John Bates (2006) argue that three broad dimensions best represent what researchers have found to characterize the structure of temperament: extraversion/surgency, negative affectivity, and effortful control (self-regulation):

- *Extraversion/surgency* includes "positive anticipation, impulsivity, activity level, and sensation seeking" (Rothbart, 2004, p. 495). Kagan's uninhibited children fit into this category.
- *Negative affectivity* includes "fear, frustration, sadness, and discomfort" (Rothbart, 2004, p. 495). These children are easily distressed; they may fret and cry often. Kagan's inhibited children fit this category.
- *Effortful control (self-regulation)* includes "attentional focusing and shifting, inhibitory control, perceptual sensitivity, and low-intensity pleasure" (Rothbart, 2004, p. 495). Infants who are high on effortful control show an ability to keep their arousal from getting too high and have strategies for soothing themselves. By contrast, children low on effortful control often are unable to control their arousal; they become easily agitated and intensely emotional.

In Rothbart's (2004, p. 497) view, "early theoretical models of temperament stressed the way we are moved by our positive and negative emotions or level of arousal, with our actions driven by these tendencies." The more recent emphasis on effortful control, however, advocates that individuals can engage in a more cognitive, flexible approach to stressful circumstances.

Rothbart and Maria Gartstein (2008) recently described the following developmental changes in temperament during infancy. During early infancy, smiling and laughter emerge as part of the positive affectivity dimension of temperament. Also, by two months of age, infants show anger and frustration when their actions don't produce an interesting outcome. During this time, infants often are susceptible to distress and overstimulation. From 4 to 12 months of age, fear and irritability become more differentiated with inhibition (fear) increasingly linked to new and unpredictable experiences. Not all temperament characteristics are in place by the first birthday. Positive emotionality becomes more stable later in infancy, and the characteristics of extraversion/surgency can be determined in the toddler period. Improved attention skills in the toddler and preschool years are related to an increase in effortful control, which serves as a foundation for improved self-regulation.

Biological Foundations and Experience

How does a child acquire a certain temperament? Kagan (2002) argues that children inherit a physiology that biases them to have a particular type of temperament. However, through experience they may learn to modify their temperament to some degree. For example, children may inherit a physiology that biases them to be fearful and inhibited, but they learn to reduce their fear and inhibition to some degree.

BIOLOGICAL INFLUENCES   Physiological characteristics have been linked with different temperaments (Rothbart & Bates, 2006). In particular, an inhibited temperament is associated with a unique physiological pattern that includes high and stable heart rate, high level of the hormone cortisol, and high activity in the right frontal lobe of the brain (Kagan, 2008). This pattern may be tied to the excitability of the amygdala, a structure of the brain that plays an important role in fear and inhibition. Canadian researchers Louis Schmidt and his colleagues (2009) reported evidence for a gene–endoenvironment (i.e., resting frontal brain electroencephalogram, EEG, asymmetry) interaction in predicting child temperament. The dopamine D4 receptor (DRD4) gene (long allele vs. short allele) moderated the relation between resting frontal EEG asymmetry (left vs. right) at 9 months, and temperament at 48 months. Children who exhibited left frontal EEG asymmetry at 9 months and who possessed the DRD4 long allele were significantly more soothable at 48 months than other children

> **critical** thinking
>
> How would you describe your temperament now and in childhood? Are they the same? Is your present temperament similar to what your parents remember about your temperament in your early years? What is temperament in an infant? Compare and contrast infant gender differences of temperament.

-------- developmental **connection** --

Brain Development

who exhibited right EEG asymmetry and possessed the DRD4 long allele. The researchers conclude that evidence was found that a gene involved in the regulation of dopamine moderated the relation between frontal brain activity and two basic components of early temperament, one cognitive and the other affective. Furthermore, their data serve as a starting point for considering the impact of endogenous factors and other exogenous environmental factors on gene expression to explain the complexities of temperament and other complex traits.

What is heredity's role in the biological foundations of temperament? Twin and adoption studies suggest that heredity has a moderate influence on differences in temperament within a group of people (Buss & Goldsmith, 2007). The contemporary view is that temperament is a biologically based but evolving aspect of behaviour; it evolves as the child's experiences are incorporated into a network of self-perceptions and behavioural preferences that characterize the child's personality (Thompson & Goodvin, 2005). The fact that temperament interacts with environmental influences is not surprising, because development is complex and is rarely guided by one or a few primary influences.

GENDER, CULTURE, AND TEMPERAMENT   Gender may be an important factor in shaping the context that influences the fate of temperament. Parents might react differently to an infant's temperament depending on whether the baby is a boy or a girl.

Similarly, the reaction to an infant's temperament may depend in part on culture (Perez & Gauvain, 2007). For example, an active temperament might be valued in some cultures (such as Canada), but not in other cultures (such as China). Indeed, children's temperament can vary across cultures (Putnam, Sanson, & Rothbart, 2002). Behavioural inhibition is more highly valued in China than in North America, and researchers have found that Chinese children are more inhibited than Canadian infants (Chen et al., 1998). The cultural differences in temperament were linked to parent attitude and behaviours. Canadian mothers of inhibited two-year-olds were less accepting of their infants' inhibited temperament, whereas Chinese mothers were more accepting.

In short, many aspects of a child's environment can encourage or discourage the persistence of temperament characteristics (Bates & Pettit, 2007; Rothbart & Sheese, 2007). One useful way of thinking about these relationships applies the concept of goodness of fit, which we examine next.

What are some ways that developmentalists have classified infants' temperaments? Which classification makes the most sense to you, on the basis of your observations of infants?

Goodness of Fit and Parenting

Goodness of fit refers to the match between a child's temperament and the environmental demands the child must cope with (Schoppe-Sullivan et al., 2007; Thompson, Meyer, & Jochem, 2008). Goodness of fit can be important to the child's adjustment. For example, consider an active child who is made to sit still for long periods of time or lives in a small apartment. Consider also a slow-to-warm-up child who is abruptly pushed into new situations on a regular basis. Such a lack of fit between the child's temperament and environmental demands can produce adjustment problems for the child.

Therefore, adults, especially parents, should be aware of children's temperament. Interestingly, many parents do not realize temperament's importance until the birth of their second child and view the first child's behaviour as being solely a result of how they socialized the child. However, management strategies that worked with the first child might not be as effective with the second child. Problems experienced with the first child (such as those involved in feeding, sleeping, and coping with strangers) might not exist with the second child, but new problems might arise. Such experiences strongly suggest that nature as well as nurture influences child development, that children differ from each other very early on in life, and that these differences have important implications for parent–child interaction (Rothbart & Putnam, 2002).

What are the implications of temperamental variations for parenting? Some experts have reached the following conclusions:

- *Attention to and respect for individuality.* An important implication of taking children's individuality seriously is that it becomes difficult to generate prescriptions for "good parenting," other

than possibly specifying that parents need to be sensitive and flexible. Parents need to be sensitive to the infant's signals and needs. A goal of parenting might be accomplished in one way with one child and in another way with another child, depending on the child's temperament (Putnam, Sanson, & Rothbart, 2002; Sanson & Rothbart, 1995).
- *Structuring the child's environment.* Crowded, noisy environments can pose greater problems for a "difficult" child than an "easygoing" child. Similarly, a fearful, withdrawing child could benefit from slower entry into new contexts.
- *The "difficult child" and packaged parenting programs.* Some books and programs for parents focus on temperament (Cameron, Hansen, & Rosen, 1989; Turecki & Tonner, 1989), usually *difficult* temperaments. Acknowledgment that some children are harder to parent is often helpful, and advice on how to handle particular difficult temperament characteristics can also be useful. However, the label *difficult* should be used with care because whether a particular characteristic of a child is difficult, by and large, depends on its fit with the environment.

What are some good strategies for parents to adopt when responding to their infant's temperament?

These implications all point to the need for parents to take into account children's temperament in everyday caregiving situations. Many parents apparently have heeded this advice. For example, George M. Tarabulsy at the Université Laval (Tarabulsy et al., 2003) showed that maternal sensitivity in everyday life was related to infants' self-soothing behaviour under stress. Importantly, this relationship is weaker among fussy infants than among easy babies. These results suggest that sensitive mothers interact differently with infants with different temperaments. Continuing in the matter of temperament, Costa and Figueiredo (2011) conducted a study to analyze, first, differences in infant temperament at 3 and 12 months according to infants psychophysiological profiles: "withdrawn," "extroverted," and "underaroused," and second, changes in infant temperament from 3 to 12 months according to the infant psychophysiological profile and the quality of mother–infant interaction. These researchers concluded that significant differences in mothers' perception of infant temperament were found at both 3 and 12 months in infants with distinct psychophysiological profiles. For example, mothers of withdrawn infants perceived them as more difficult. These difficulties then predispose to difficulties in the relational level between mother and infant, which may be indicative of an increased probability of developmental problems in the infant. However, it becomes apparent that when a good mother–infant interaction is established an increased positive emotionality is possible to develop, which may act as a protective factor in infant development.

As a final note on sensitive caregiving, the importance of parental responsiveness cannot be overemphasized. Another study in Quebec (Pomerleau, Scuccimarri, & Malcuit, 2003) showed that maternal responsiveness at one month had a moderate positive correlation with infants' mental performance on the Bayley Scales of Infant Development (Bayley, 1993) at six months. Although correlational, the findings indicate that parental behaviour may have implications for infants' cognitive development—in addition to their social adjustment. A U.S. study examined the contributions of infant temperament, marital functioning, and the division of parenting on the quality of the co-parenting relationship for couples parenting six-month-old infants. The researchers found that mothers who perceived their infants as more reactive reported more negative co-parenting only if their infants were also not easily soothed, or if mothers were dissatisfied with how parenting tasks were divided and performed given their prior expectations. Meanwhile, fathers reported more negative co-parenting when faced with a more reactive infant and when they reported a low-quality marital relationship (Burney and Leerkes, 2010).

Personality Development

We have explored some important aspects of emotional development and temperament. What about personality development?

Trust

According to Erik Erikson (1968), the trust-versus-mistrust stage of development characterizes the first year after birth. Following a life of regularity, warmth, and protection in the mother's womb, the infant faces a world that is less secure. Erikson believes that infants learn trust when they are cared for in a consistent, warm manner. If the infant is not well-fed and kept warm on a consistent basis, a sense of mistrust is likely to develop.

Trust versus mistrust is not resolved once and for all in the first year of life. It arises again at each successive stage of development. There is hope as well as danger in this. Children who enter school with a sense of mistrust may regain a sense of trust because of a responsive teacher. By contrast, children who leave infancy with a sense of trust can still have their sense of mistrust activated at a later stage, perhaps if their parents separate or divorce under acrimonious circumstances.

Self

Individuals carry with them a sense of who they are and what makes them different from everyone else. Real or imagined, this sense of self is a strong motivating force in life. When does the individual begin to sense a separate existence from others? Infants are not "given" a self by their parents or the culture. Rather, they find and construct selves. Studying the self in infancy is difficult, mainly because infants are unable to describe with language their experiences of themselves (Thompson, 2007).

To determine whether infants can recognize themselves, psychologists have used mirrors. First, the mother puts a dot of rouge on her infant's nose. The observer watches to see how often the infant touches its nose. Next, the infant is placed in front of a mirror, and observers detect whether nose touching increases. In two independent investigations, it was discovered that not until the second half of the second year of life did infants recognize their own image and coordinate the image they saw with the actions of touching their own body (Amsterdam, 1968; Lewis & Brooks-Gunn, 1979). Signs of self-recognition began to appear among some infants when they were 15 to 18 months old. By the time they were two years old, most children recognized themselves in the mirror. In sum, infants begin to develop a self-understanding called self-recognition at approximately 18 months of age (Lewis, 2005). Figure 6.3 shows the findings of these studies. Late in the second year and early in the third year, toddlers show other emerging forms of self-awareness that reflect a sense of "me" (Laible & Thompson, 2007).

What about blind infants? How do we know if they have developed a sense of self? The answer may lie in research on joint attention—people's realization of each other's involvement in an object. Joint attention observed in infants signals their awareness of their role as an agent in the environment. In a recent study, Ann Bigelow (2003) of St. Francis Xavier University noticed joint attention in blind infants. In one situation, an infant and his mother responded to the other's actions on a toy: The child jiggled the toy and then put it down, and the mother moved it to another position; then another sequence of these actions followed. This infant clearly was aware of his impact on the environment. Overall, blind children do have a sense of self at a young age, though, as Bigelow's data suggest, this sense may develop more slowly than is the case with other infants.

Independence

Independence is an important theme in the infant's life. The theories of Margaret Mahler and Erik Erikson have important implications for both self-development and independence. Mahler (1979) believed that the child goes through a separation and then an individuation process. Separation involves the infant's movement away from the mother. Individuation involves the development of self.

Erikson (1968), like Mahler, believed that independence is an important issue in the second year of life. Erikson described the second stage of development as the stage of autonomy versus shame and doubt. Autonomy builds on the infant's developing mental and motor abilities. At this point in development, infants can not only walk, but also climb, open and close, drop, push and pull, and hold and let go. Infants feel pride in these new accomplishments and want to do everything themselves, whether it is flushing a toilet, pulling the wrapping off a package, or deciding what to eat. It is important for parents to recognize the motivation of toddlers to do what they are capable of doing at their own pace. Then the infants can learn to control their muscles and their impulses themselves. But when caregivers are impatient and do for toddlers what they are capable of doing themselves, shame and doubt develop. Every parent has rushed a child from time to time. It is only when parents consistently overprotect toddlers or criticize accidents (wetting, soiling, or breaking, for example) that children develop an excessive sense of shame and doubt about their ability to control themselves and their world.

Erikson also believed that the stage of autonomy versus shame and doubt has important implications for the development of independence and identity during adolescence. The development of autonomy during the toddler years gives adolescents the courage to be independent individuals who can choose and guide their own future.

To this point, we have studied a number of ideas about the infant's temperament and personality development. For a review, see the **Reach Your Learning Objectives** section at the end of this chapter.

Figure 6.3

The Development of Self-Recognition in Infancy

The graph shows the findings of the two studies in which infants less than one year of age did not recognize themselves in the mirror. A slight increase in the percentage of infant self-recognition occurred around 15 to 18 months of age. By two years of age, a majority of children recognized themselves. **Why do researchers study whether infants recognize themselves in a mirror?**

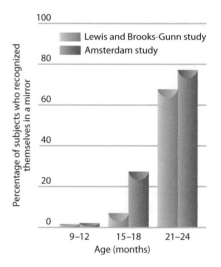

Social Orientation/Understanding and Attachment

LO3 Analyze social orientation/understanding and the development of attachment in infancy.

So far, we have discussed how emotions and emotional competence change as children develop. We have also examined the role of emotional style; in effect, we have seen how emotions set the tone of our experiences in life. But emotions also write the lyrics, because they are at the core of our relationships with others.

Social Orientation/Understanding

As socio-emotional beings, infants show a strong interest in the social world and are motivated to orient to it and understand it. In earlier chapters, we described many of the biological and cognitive foundations that contribute to the infant's development of social orientation and understanding. We will call attention to relevant biological and cognitive factors as we explore social orientation; locomotion; intention, goal-directed behaviour, and cooperation; and social referencing. Discussing biological, cognitive, and social processes together reminds us of an important aspect of development that was pointed out in Chapter 1: these processes are intricately intertwined (Diamond, 2007).

Social Orientation

From early in their development, infants are captivated by the social world. As we discussed in our coverage of infant perception in Chapter 4, young infants stare intently at faces and are attuned to the sounds of human voices, especially their caregiver's (Ramsey-Rennels & Langlois, 2007). Later, they become adept at interpreting the meaning of facial expressions.

Face-to-face play often begins to characterize caregiver–infant interactions when the infant is about two to three months of age. The focused social interaction of face-to-face play may include vocalizations, touch, and gestures (Leppanen et al., 2007). Such play is part of many mothers' motivation to create a positive emotional state in their infants (Laible & Thompson, 2007; Thompson, 2009a).

Infants also learn about the social world through contexts other than face-to-face play with a caregiver (Thompson, 2009b; Thompson & Newton, 2009). Even though infants as young as six months of age show an interest in each other, their interaction with peers increases considerably in the last half of the second year. One recent study involved presenting one- and two-year-olds with a simple cooperative task that consisted of pulling a lever to get an attractive toy (Brownell, Ramani, & Zerwas, 2006) (see Figure 6.4). Any coordinated actions of the one-year-olds appeared to be more coincidental than cooperative, whereas the two-year-olds' behaviour was characterized as more active cooperation to reach a goal. As increasing numbers of North American infants experience child care outside the home, they are spending more time in social play with other peers (Field, 2007). Later in the chapter, we will further discuss child care.

Locomotion

Recall from earlier in the chapter how important independence is for infants, especially in the second year of life. As infants develop the ability to crawl, walk, and run, they are able to explore and expand their social world. These newly developed self-produced locomotor skills allow the infant to independently initiate social interchanges on a more frequent basis (Laible & Thompson, 2007; Thompson, 2006). Remember from Chapter 4 that the development of these gross motor skills is the result of a number of factors, including the development of the nervous system, the goal the infant is motivated to reach, and environmental support for the skill (Adolph, 2008; Adolph & Joh, 2008).

Locomotion is also important for its motivational implications (Thompson, 2008). Once infants have the ability to move in goal-directed pursuits, the reward from these pursuits leads to further efforts to explore and develop skills.

developmental **connection**

Bandura's Social Cognitive Approach

Intention, Goal-Directed Behaviour, and Cooperation

Perceiving people as engaging in intentional and goal-directed behaviour is an important social cognitive accomplishment, and this initially occurs toward the end of the first year (Laible & Thompson, 2007; Thompson, 2006). Joint attention and gaze following help the infant to understand that other people have intentions (Meltzoff, 2007; Tomasello & Carpenter, 2007). Joint attention is defined as a state during which both social partners are actively focused on a particular object, event, or topic, and both are aware of each other's active participation and focus (Nowakowski, 2009). That is, the capability to pay attention to both another person's intentions and an object at the same time is related later to social competence, such as language and behavioural skills (D'Entremont & Hartung, 2003).

Emerging aspects of joint attention occur at about seven to eight months, but at about 10 to 11 months of age joint attention intensifies and infants begin to follow the caregiver's gaze. By their first birthday, infants have begun to direct the caregiver's attention to objects that capture their interest (Heimann et al., 2006). In fact, some Canadian theorists, including Racine and Carpendale (2007), propose that during joint attention pointing is often thought to be the clearest indicator of early social understanding.

In the study on cooperating to reach a goal that was discussed earlier, one- and two-year-olds also were assessed with two social understanding tasks: observation of children's behaviour in a joint attention task, and the parents' perceptions of the language the children use about the self and others (Brownell, Ramani, & Zerwas, 2006). Those with more advanced social understanding were more likely to cooperate. To cooperate, the children had to connect their own intentions with the peer's intentions and put this understanding to use in interacting with the peer to reach a goal. Carpendale and Lewis (2004) argue that knowledge is gradually constructed within social interaction. That is, children's social knowledge is based on action and the mind is defined in and through action (Racine & Carpendale, 2007). At first the interaction between infant and other is dyadic and not yet referential, but by the latter part of the first year this interaction becomes triadic among the infant, caregiver, and objects. A child's understanding of mind develops gradually in the context of social interaction (Carpendale & Lewis, 2004).

Further, a recent study revealed that initiating and responding to joint attention at 12 months of age were linked to being socially competent (for example, not aggressive or defiant, showing empathy, and engaging in sustained attention) at 30 months of age (Vaughan et al., 2007).

Social Referencing

Social referencing *involves "reading" emotional cues in others to help determine how to act in a particular situation.* The development of social referencing helps infants to interpret ambiguous situations more accurately, as when they encounter a stranger and need to know whether to fear the person (de Rosnay et al., 2006; Thompson, 2006). Infants become better at social referencing in the second year after birth. In one interesting study, Muir and Lee (2003) used a face inversion procedure to investigate the development of infant processing of dynamic emotional facial expression between three and six months of age. A three-period ABA design was used. In A, an adult (mother or female stranger) engaged infants in a face-to-face interaction, without touch; in B, the adult's face was inverted. Infants engaged in interactions with adults that were presented either "in person" over closed circuit TV, or as a TV virtual adult that was driven by experimenters using computer software to simulate the contingent social behaviour adults used during face-to-face interactions. The findings indicated that the visual attention between three and six months was similar during A and B periods. The usual U-shaped function (e.g., Muir & Hains, 1999) did not occur. By contrast, infant smiling dropped substantially during all inverted face periods (B) relative to the upright face in A periods. The researchers concluded that while infants were interested in faces irrespective of their orientation, the loss of smiling at the inverted face suggests that they, similar to adults, may find it difficult to process emotional expressions in inverted faces irrespective of age. A consideration of the U-shaped function of social referencing of infants continues.

Figure 6.4 ----------------------------

The Cooperation Task

The cooperation task consisted of two handles on a box, atop of which was an animal musical toy, surreptitiously activated by remote control when both handles were pulled. The handles were placed far enough apart that one child could not pull both handles. The experimenter demonstrated the task, saying, "Watch! If you pull the handles, the doggie will sing" (Brownell, Ramani, & Zerwas, 2006).

social referencing Involves "reading" emotional cues in others to help determine how to act in a particular situation.

developmental **connection**

Bowlby's Attachment Theory
←

Infants' Social Sophistication and Insight

In sum, researchers are discovering that infants are more socially sophisticated and insightful at younger ages than previously envisioned (Hamlin, Hallinan, & Woodward, 2008; Thompson, 2008, 2009a, b). This sophistication and insight is reflected in infants' perceptions of others' actions as intentionally motivated and goal-directed (Brune & Woodward, 2007), and their motivation by their first birthday to share and participate in that intentionality (Tomasello & Carpenter, 2007). The more advanced social cognitive skills of infants could be expected to influence their understanding and awareness of attachment to a caregiver.

Attachment and Its Development

In everyday language, attachment is a relationship between two individuals who feel strongly about each other and do a number of things to continue the relationship. In the language of developmental psychology, though, **attachment** is *a close emotional bond between two people*. During infancy, the infant's attachment is usually with one or more adult caregivers, and the phenomenon is a close emotional bond (Bowlby, 1969, 1989).

attachment A close emotional bond between two people.

There is no shortage of theories about infant attachment. Freud believed that infants become attached to the person or object that provides oral satisfaction. For most infants this is the mother, because she is most likely to feed the infant.

Is feeding as important as Freud thought? A classic study by Harry Harlow (1958) reveals that the answer is no (see Figure 6.5). Harlow evaluated whether feeding or contact comfort was more important to infant attachment. Infant monkeys were removed from their mothers at birth and reared for six months by surrogate "mothers." One of the mothers was made of wire, the other of cloth. Half the infant monkeys were fed by the wire mother, half by the cloth mother. Periodically, the amount of time the infant monkeys spent with either the wire or the cloth mother was computed. Regardless of whether they were fed by the wire or the cloth mother, the infant monkeys spent far more time with the cloth mother. This study clearly demonstrated that feeding is not the crucial element in the attachment process, and that contact comfort is important.

developmental **connection**

Freud's Psychoanalytic Theory
←

Erik Erikson (1968) believed that the trust versus mistrust stage in the first year of infancy is the key time frame for the development of attachment. A sense of trust requires a feeling of physical comfort and a minimal amount of fear and apprehension about the future. Trust in infancy sets the stage for a lifelong expectation that the world will be a good and pleasant place.

The ethological perspective of British psychiatrist John Bowlby (1969, 1989) also stresses the importance of attachment and the responsiveness of the caregiver early in life. Bowlby believes that an infant and the primary caregiver form an attachment. The baby cries, clings, coos, and smiles. Later, the infant crawls, walks, and follows the mother. The immediate result is to keep the primary caregiver nearby; the long-term effect is to increase the infant's chances of survival (Thompson, 2006).

Attachment does not emerge suddenly but rather develops in a series of phases, moving from a baby's general preference for human beings to a partnership with primary caregivers. The following are four such phases based on Bowlby's (1969) conceptualization of attachment:

Figure 6.5

Harlow's Classic "Contact Comfort" Study

Regardless of whether they were fed by a wire mother or by a cloth mother, the infant monkeys overwhelmingly preferred to be in contact with the cloth mother, demonstrating the importance of contact comfort in attachment.

Phase 1:	Birth to 2 months	Infants instinctively direct their attachment to human figures. Strangers, siblings, and parents are equally likely to elicit smiling or crying from the infant.
Phase 2:	2 to 7 months	Attachment becomes focused on one figure, usually the primary caregiver, as the baby gradually learns to distinguish familiar people from unfamiliar ones.
Phase 3:	7 to 24 months	Specific attachments develop. With increased locomotor skills, babies actively seek contact with regular caregivers, such as the mother or father.
Phase 4:	24 months on	A goal-directed partnership is formed in which children become aware of others' feelings, goals, and plans and begin to take these into account in forming their own actions.

As the phases above indicate, attachment focuses on specific individuals and is reflected by infants' behaviour in the second half of the first year after birth. You may recall in an earlier discussion that stranger anxiety also emerges at around the same time. This suggests that stressful situations may provoke attempts to seek comfort from a trusted individual. The occurrence of these phenomena at approximately the same time also indicates that the infant visually recognizes the differences between the caregiver and the stranger, has some knowledge of causality of his or her own action (e.g., crawling toward the caregiver in the hope of getting comforted), and uses locomotor skills to achieve goals. Together, these phenomena serve to remind us that physical, cognitive, and social developments are interrelated.

developmental **connection**

Erikson's Theory of Psychosocial Development

Individual Differences in Attachment

Although attachment to a caregiver intensifies midway through the first year, isn't it likely that some babies have a more positive attachment experience than others? Mary Ainsworth (1979) thought so. Ainsworth created the **Strange Situation**, *an observational measure of infant attachment that requires the infant to move through a series of introductions, separations, and reunions with the caregiver and an adult stranger in a prescribed order* (see Figure 6.6). In using the Strange Situation, researchers hope that their observations will provide information about the infant's motivation to be near the caregiver and the degree to which the caregiver's presence provides the infant with security and confidence. Based on how babies respond in the Strange Situation, they are described as being securely attached or insecurely attached (in one of three ways) to the caregiver.

Securely attached babies *use the caregiver as a secure base from which to explore the environment.* When in the presence of their caregiver, securely attached infants explore the room and examine

Strange Situation An observational measure of infant attachment that requires the infant to move through a series of introductions, separations, and reunions with the caregiver and an adult stranger in a prescribed order.

securely attached babies Use the caregiver as a secure base from which to explore the environment.

Figure 6.6

The Ainsworth Strange Situation

Mary Ainsworth developed the Strange Situation to assess whether infants are securely or insecurely attached to their caregiver. The episodes involved in the Ainsworth Strange Situation are described here.

Episode	Participants	Duration of Episode	Description of Setting
1	Caregiver, baby, and observer	30 seconds	Observer introduces caregiver and baby to experimental room, then leaves. (Room contains many appealing toys scattered about.)
2	Caregiver and baby	3 minutes	Caregiver is non-participant while baby explores; if necessary, play is stimulated after two minutes.
3	Stranger, caregiver, and baby	3 minutes	Stranger enters. First minute: stranger is silent. Second minute: stranger converses with caregiver. Third minute: stranger approaches baby. After three minutes caregiver leaves unobtrusively.
4	Stranger and baby	3 minutes or less	First separation episode. Stranger's behaviour is geared to that of baby.
5	Caregiver and baby	3 minutes or more	First reunion episode. Caregiver greets and/or comforts baby, then tries to settle the baby again in play. Caregiver then leaves, saying "bye-bye."
6	Baby alone	3 minutes or less	Second separation episode.
7	Stranger and baby	3 minutes or less	Continuation of second separation. Stranger enters and gears behaviour to that of baby.
8	Caregiver and baby	3 minutes	Second reunion episode. Caregiver enters, greets baby, then picks baby up. Meanwhile stranger leaves unobtrusively.

toys that have been placed in it. When the caregiver departs, securely attached infants might mildly protest, and when the caregiver returns these infants re-establish positive interaction with her, perhaps by smiling or climbing on her lap. Subsequently, they often resume playing with the toys in the room.

insecure avoidant babies Show insecurity by avoiding the caregiver.

Insecure avoidant babies *show insecurity by avoiding the caregiver.* In the Strange Situation, these babies engage in little interaction with the caregiver, often display distress by crying when the adult leaves the room, usually do not re-establish contact upon reunion, and may even turn their back on the caregiver at this point. If contact is established, the infants usually lean away or look away.

insecure resistant babies Often cling to the caregiver, then resist by fighting against the closeness, perhaps by kicking or pushing away.

Insecure resistant babies *often cling to the caregivers and then resist them by fighting against the closeness, perhaps by kicking or pushing away.* In the Strange Situation, these babies often cling anxiously to the caregivers and do not explore the playroom. When the caregivers leave, they often cry loudly and push away if they try to comfort them on their return.

insecure disorganized babies Show insecurity by being disorganized and disoriented.

Insecure disorganized babies *show insecurity by being disorganized and disoriented.* In the Strange Situation, these babies might appear dazed, confused, and fearful. To be classified as disorganized, strong patterns of avoidance and resistance must be shown or certain select behaviours, such as extreme fearfulness around the caregiver, must be present.

Although the Strange Situation has been used in a large number of studies of infant attachment, some critics believe that the isolated, controlled events of the setting might not necessarily reflect what would happen if infants were observed with their caregiver in a natural environment. Moreover, Bowlby's attachment theory does not indicate that attachment behaviour must fall into specific patterns, even as attachment categories do provide one way of understanding how infants organize their behaviour (Waters & Beauchaine, 2003).

Whipple, Bernier, and Mageau (2009) of the University of Montreal suggest that self-determination theory could add to our understanding of how attachment occurs. Self-determination theory holds that children are active agents, naturally inclined to explore their world through interaction with its various elements. This inclination does not assure exploration, however, as the social forces (for example parents) influence the child's exploration activity. Since secure attachment strikes a balance between attachment and exploration, examination of how mothers (and fathers) promote or limit self-determined exploratory behaviour could add much to our understanding of attachment.

Caregiving Styles and Attachment Classifications

Is the parent's caregiving style linked to this close emotional bond called attachment? Securely attached babies have caregivers who are sensitive to their signals and are consistently available to respond to their infants' needs (Juffer et al., 2007). These caregivers often let their babies have an active part in determining the onset and pacing of interaction in the first year of life. Researchers have found infants whose parents are married are more likely to be securely attached than infants whose parents are either cohabitating or single (Aronson & Huston, 2004).

How do the caregivers of insecurely attached babies interact with them? Caregivers of avoidant babies tend to be unavailable or rejecting (Bakermans-Kranenburg et al., 2007). They often do not respond to their babies' signals and have little physical contact with them. When they do interact with their babies, they may behave in an angry and irritable way toward them. Caregivers of insecure-resistant babies tend to be inconsistently available to their babies (Cassidy & Berlin, 1994). That is, sometimes they respond to their babies' needs, and sometimes they do not. In general, they tend not to be very affectionate with their babies and show little synchrony when interacting with them. Caregivers of disorganized babies often neglect or physically abuse their babies (Benoit, 2009; Toth, 2009). In some cases, these caregivers also have depression (Thompson, 2008). The mother's behaviours are reflective of her state of mind with regards to her attachment with her baby.

Research by Leslie Atkinson and associates (2005) has put into question the above conceptualization that the mother's state of mind mediates directly the infant's level of attachment. Their research using samples of new mothers in London, Ontario, and Toronto found that not only did state of mind have an influence, but so did the mother's sensitivity to her infant's needs. The

What is the nature of secure and insecure attachments?

researchers proposed that an interaction between these two qualities of the mothers helped to shape the infant's attachment.

Changes in the caregiving relationship over time may affect the stability of attachment patterns. While 44 percent to 72 percent of the various attachment patterns remained stable over a two-year period, Ellen Moss of the Université du Québec à Montréal and her colleagues (Moss, Cyr, Bureau, Tarabulsy, & Dubois-Comtois, 2005) found that intense changes in the quality of mother–child interaction, low marital satisfaction, and significant family events (death of parent or grandparent, hospitalization of a parent) were related to a shift from secure to insecure attachment patterns.

critical thinking

What character strengths of fathers would promote secure attachments? What other factors, besides the child's environment and family history, should be taken into account in assessing attachment behaviours?

Attachment, Temperament, and the Wider Social World

If early attachment to a caregiver is important, it should relate to a child's social behaviour later in development. For some children, early attachments seem to foreshadow later functioning (Cassidy, 2009; Egeland, 2009). In the extensive longitudinal study conducted by Alan Sroufe and his colleagues (2005), early secure attachment (assessed by the Strange Situation at 12 and 18 months) was linked with positive emotional health, high self-esteem, self-confidence, and socially competent interaction with peers, teachers, camp counsellors, and romantic partners through adolescence. Another study revealed that being classified as insecure resistant in infancy was a negative predictor of cognitive development in elementary school (O'Connor & McCartney, 2007).

For some children, though, there is less continuity (Thompson & Goodvin, 2007). Not all research reveals the power of infant attachment to predict subsequent development. In one longitudinal study, attachment classification in infancy did not predict attachment classification at 18 years of age (Lewis, Feiring, & Rosenthal, 2000). In this study, the best predictor of an insecure attachment classification at 18 was the occurrence of parental divorce in the intervening years. Consistently positive caregiving over a number of years is likely an important factor in connecting early attachment and the child's functioning later in development. Indeed, researchers have found that early secure attachment *and* subsequent experiences, especially maternal care and life stresses, are linked with children's later behaviour and adjustment (Belsky & Pasco Fearon, 2002a; Thompson, 2006).

Some developmentalists conclude that too much emphasis has been placed on the attachment bond in infancy (Newcombe, 2007). Jerome Kagan (1987, 2002), for example, points out that infants are highly resilient and adaptive; he argues that they are evolutionarily equipped to stay on a positive developmental course, even in the face of wide variations in parenting. Kagan and colleagues stress that genetic characteristics and temperament play more important roles in a child's social competence than the attachment theorists, such as Bowlby and Ainsworth, are willing to acknowledge (Bakermans-Kranenburg et al., 2007). For example, if some infants inherit a low tolerance for stress, this, rather than an insecure attachment bond, may be responsible for an inability to get along with peers.

Another criticism of attachment theory is that it ignores the diversity of socializing agents and contexts that exist in an infant's world. A culture's value system can influence the nature of attachment (Grossman & Grossman, 2009; van Ijzendoorn & Sagi-Schwartz, 2009). For example, Aboriginal concepts of the family range from the extended family concept, where lineage and bloodlines are important, to the wider view where totems, clans, and kin can include elders, leaders, and communities (Okpik, 2005). A collective responsibility for the caring and nurturing of the child is shared by all these members (McShane & Hastings, 2004). The bond between the parent and the child as well as other caregivers in the Aboriginal culture is multi-layered rather than dyadic. Attachment theory, in contrast, concentrates on the linear relationship between the mother and the infant and does not include in the theory wider social relationships except to suggest that the mother–infant relationship becomes a template for all future relationships (Lewis, 2005). Therefore, attachment theory does not fully reflect the reality of an Aboriginal infant's life and socialization experiences. Figure 6.7 shows a cross-cultural comparison of attachment among the United States, Germany, and Japan.

developmental **connection**

Stability and Change

developmental **connection**

Evolutionary Psychology

Figure 6.7 -
Cross-Cultural Comparison of Attachment

In one study, infant attachment in three countries—the United States, Germany, and Japan—was measured in the Ainsworth Strange Situation (van Ijzendoorn & Kroonenberg, 1988). The dominant attachment pattern in all three countries was secure attachment. However, German infants were more avoidant and Japanese infants were less avoidant and more resistant than American infants.

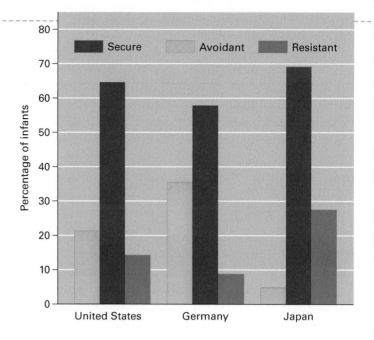

Infants in agricultural societies tend to form attachments to older siblings who are assigned a major responsibility for younger siblings' care. Researchers recognize the importance of competent, nurturing caregivers in an infant's development (Parke & Buriel, 2006). At issue, though, is whether or not secure attachment, especially to a single caregiver, is critical (Lamb, 2005; Thompson, 2006).

Despite such criticisms, there is ample evidence that security of attachment is important to development (Posada, 2008; Thompson, 2009b). Secure attachment in infancy is important because it reflects a positive parent–infant relationship and provides the foundation that supports healthy socio-emotional development in the years that follow. Secure attachment's importance has led to the suggestion that attachment theory–based interventions be developed for dealing with abusive family situations (Tarabulsy et al., 2008). In this approach, the parents' attachment to the child, their sensitivity to the child's needs, and the child's own level of attachment are all assessed. A treatment plan to move everyone in the family to a more secure attachment pattern is established and implemented.

To this point, we have discussed a number of ideas about the infant's social orientation/understanding and attachment. For a review, see the **Reach Your Learning Objectives** section at the end of this chapter.

Social Contexts

LO4 Determine how social contexts influence the infant's development.

The Family

The family can be thought of as a constellation of subsystems—a complex whole made up of interrelated, interacting parts—defined in terms of generation, gender, and role. Each family member participates in several subsystems (Fiese & Winter, 2008; Parke et al., 2008). The father and child represent one subsystem, the mother and father another, the mother-father-child yet another, and so on. At the same time, the family is but one unit nested in larger suprasystems, such as neighbourhoods, organizations, and church communities. The hierarchy of systems and the boundaries that create systems are useful concepts to apply when working with, and attempting to conceptualize, the uniqueness of each particular family (Wright & Leahey, 2013).

These subsystems have reciprocal influences on each other (Belsky, 2009), as Figure 6.8 highlights. For example, Jay Belsky (1981) emphasizes that marital relations, parenting, and infant behaviour and development can have both direct and indirect effects on each other. An example of a direct effect is the influence of the parents' behaviour on the child. An indirect effect is how the relationship between the spouses mediates the way a parent acts toward the child (Hsu, 2004). For example, marital conflict might reduce the efficiency of parenting, in which case marital conflict would indirectly affect the child's behaviour. The simple fact that two people are becoming parents may have profound effects on their relationship.

The Transition to Parenthood

When people become parents through pregnancy, adoption, or step-parenting, they face disequilibrium and must adapt. Parents want to develop a strong attachment to their infant, but they still want to maintain strong attachments to each other and to friends, and possibly continue their careers. Parents ask themselves how this new being will change their lives. A baby places new restrictions on parents; no longer will they be able to rush out to a movie on a moment's notice, and money may not be as readily available for vacations and other luxuries. Dual-career parents ask, "Will it harm the baby to place her in daycare? Will we be able to find responsible babysitters?"

In a longitudinal investigation of couples from late pregnancy until three years after the baby was born, some couples said that they had enjoyed more positive marital relations before the baby was born than after (Cowan & Cowan, 2000; Cowan et al., 2005). Still, almost one-third showed an increase in marital satisfaction. Some couples said that the baby had both brought them closer together and moved them farther apart. They commented that being parents enhanced their sense of themselves and gave them a new, more stable identity as a couple. Babies opened men up to a concern with intimate relationships, and the demands of juggling work and family roles stimulated women to manage family tasks more efficiently and pay attention to their personal growth.

At some point during the early years of the child's life, parents face the difficult task of juggling their roles as parents and as self-actualizing adults. Until recently, nurturing children and having a career were thought to be incompatible. In fact, as a recent study with female health care workers in Ontario—a group highly vulnerable to sleep difficulty—showed that positive family relationships actually helped the subjects deal with work-related stress and improved the sleep quality of this sample of women, most of whom were parents (Williams, Franche, Ibrahim, Mustard, & Layton, 2006).

Reciprocal Socialization

For many years, socialization between parents and children was viewed as a one-way process: children were considered to be the products of their parents' socialization techniques. However, parent–child interaction is reciprocal (Fiese & Winter, 2008; Thompson & Newton, 2009). **Reciprocal socialization** *is socialization that is bi-directional. That is, children socialize parents just as parents socialize children.*

When reciprocal socialization has been studied in infancy, mutual gaze, or eye contact, has been found to play an important role in early social interaction. A recent study revealed that *parent–infant synchrony*—the temporal coordination of social behaviour—played an important role in children's development (Feldman, 2007). In this study, parent–infant synchrony at three and nine months of age were positively linked to children's self-regulation from two to six years of age. In sum, the behaviours of mothers and infants involve substantial interconnection, mutual regulation, and synchronization (Moreno, Posada, & Goldyn, 2006).

An important form of reciprocal socialization is **scaffolding**, *in which parents time interactions in such a way that the infant experiences turn-taking with the parents.* Scaffolding involves parental behaviour that supports children's efforts, allowing them to be more skillful than they would be if they were to rely only on their own abilities (Field, 2007). In using scaffolding, caregivers provide a positive, reciprocal framework in which they and their children interact. For example, in the game peek-a-boo, the mother initially covers the baby. Then she removes the cover and registers

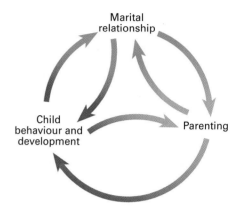

developmental **connection**

Research Methods: Longitudinal Research

reciprocal socialization The idea that children socialize parents, just as parents socialize children.

scaffolding Parents time interactions in such a way that the infant experiences turn-taking with the parents.

connecting through research ←

Canadians have contributed greatly to the understanding of caregiver–infant interaction. Mary Ainsworth, the creator of the Strange Situation, began her academic career at the University of Toronto. From the same school comes Sandra Trehub, who has conducted much research on maternal singing—which, like motherese, helps regulate a child's attention and emotion.

In one study (Milligan, Atkinson, Trehub, Benoit, & Poulton, 2003), maternal singing when infants were in distress was examined. When their infants showed signs of discomfort, many mothers sang with less intense emotion than when the infants were calm. However, some mothers sang with the same intensity, regardless of their infants' psychological state. These mothers tended to have an adult attachment style characterized by a dislike to deal with negative emotions. This style is typical of mothers of infants with avoidant attachments. These results highlight the role of caregiver adjustment to infant behaviour in adult–infant interactions.

- - - - developmental **connection** - -

Vygotsky

←- - - - - - - - - - - - - - - -

"surprise" at the infant's reappearance. As infants become more skilled at peek-a-boo, pat-a-cake, and so on, other caregiver games exemplify scaffolding and turn-taking sequences.

Caregivers can provide a positive, reciprocal framework in which they and their children interact. The stress and anxiety associated with poverty, though, may make this difficult to achieve in poor families. For example, a study with low-income Aboriginal and non-Aboriginal families in Alberta showed that the parent–infant interaction quality in these families was lower than the norm. Interestingly, despite less vocalization by Aboriginal parents, the interaction quality for both ethnic groups was the same. These findings suggest that attempts to improve parent–child interaction in poor families should respect these families' cultural practices (Letourneau, Hungler, & Fisher, 2005).

Maternal and Paternal Caregiving

Today, 51 percent of Canadian two-parent families with children are in a position where one parent works full-time while the other works less than full-time hours to be at home with the children, for at least part of the day (LaRochelle-Côté & Dionne, 2009). A recent study revealed that stay-at-home fathers were as satisfied with their marriage as traditional parents, although they indicated that they missed their daily life in the workplace (Rochlen et al., 2008). In this study, stay-at-home fathers reported that they tended to be ostracized when they took their children to playgrounds and often were excluded from parent groups.

Can fathers take care of infants as competently as mothers can? Observations of fathers and their infants suggest that fathers have the ability to act as sensitively and responsively as mothers with their infants (Parke, 2004; Parke & Buriel, 2006). Maternal interactions usually centre on child care activities—feeding, changing diapers, bathing. Paternal interactions are more likely to include play (Parke, 2004; Parke & Buriel, 2006). When men actively care for their children, they adapt behaviourally and physiologically (Gettler, McDade, Feranil & Kuzawa, 2011). The extent of paternal involvement may also differ depending on the personality of the father as well as on the amount of encouragement and support the fathers receive (Lamb & Lewis, 2010). Harmony between the parents seems to be an especially important key predictor of father–child relationships.

An analysis of 23 parenting books found that only about 4 percent of the paragraphs mentioned the father's role (Fleming & Tobin, 2005). Of this small amount, many focused on negative aspects about fathering such as being inaccessible, and less than 10 percent mentioned the challenges and adjustments of fathering, information that is important to most fathers (Fleming & Tobin, 2005).

At the same time, many social service organizations have developed programs for current and prospective fathers. For example, in Ontario, Catholic Community Services of York Region's Focus on Fathers teaches fathering skills and, to accommodate immigrant communities, the program has instructional materials in nine languages (Gordon, 2007).

In summary, according to Lamb (2010), it is a well-established fact that both men and women have the capacity to be good parents. The quality of parent–child relationships is determined by the degree to which parents offer love, affection, emotional commitment, reliability, and consistency (Lamb, 2012). Another relevant factor is the extent to which parents can effectively "read" their children or adolescents and provide the appropriate guidance, stimulation, and limit setting that is important (Lamb & Lewis, 2011).

Parental Leaves

Regardless of differing parental styles, taking care of children, especially newborns, requires a substantial amount of time. In Canada, both the federal and provincial/territorial governments have parental leave policies. Federal programs, such as Employment Insurance, also help parents during their leave. Some employers in Canada add to the government benefits when their employees take a maternity or parental leave. Under the current *Employment Insurance Act*, a couple can split 35 weeks of partially paid parental leave, in addition to 15 weeks of maternity leave after the birth or adoption of a child (Marshall, 2008). These provisions, however, do not apply to self-employed individuals or those who have not worked for 600 hours in the past 52 weeks. The Quebec provincial government introduced its own Parental Insurance Plan in 2006, with 18 weeks of maternity leave, up to 70 percent of wages, no waiting period, and inclusion of self-employed people. They offer 32 weeks of parental leave to birth parents and 37 weeks to adoptive parents. Because parental benefits cover only 55 percent of weekly earnings (outside of Quebec), lower-income mothers tend to return to work earlier than do higher-income mothers (Marshall, 2003). Moreover, as shown in the graph in the Connecting Development to Life box, Canadian fathers outside of Quebec are very unlikely to take advantage of the parental leave benefits. Still, the number of men taking parental leave rose over the first six years of the twenty-first century to the point where one in five dads elected to take some or all of the parental leave available to them (Marshall, 2008). Decisions to claim are very complex, involving the incomes of both parents, job type, and values toward parental leave both in their work environment and the larger community.

critical thinking

In addition to parental leaves, what other arrangements in the workplace can allow parents to spend more time with their children? Can you come up with some suggestions for employers? What are some advantages and disadvantages of parental leave? In your province or territory, what are the policies for parental leave? Discuss them with your peers.

Child Care

The type and nature of the child care into which infants are placed have major impact on their development. Mustard (2009) draws our attention to the fact that "brain development is highly sensitive to external influences" (p. 689). Most children gain certain amounts of cognitive and language benefits when they are in high-quality daycare (Belsky, 2007). Geoffroy, Côté, Parent, and Séguin (2006) found stress levels (as measured by increases in cortisol levels) went up for children in low quality daycare and for those children with difficult temperaments. Children are more likely to experience poor quality child care if they come from families with few resources (psychological, social, and economic) (Cabrera, Hutchens, & Peters, 2006; McCartney, 2009). Many researchers have examined the role of poverty in the quality of child care (Giannarelli, Sonenstein, & Stagner, 2006). One study found that extensive child care was harmful to low-income children only when the care was of low quality (Votruba-Drzal, Coley, & Chase-Lansdale, 2004). Even if the child was in child care more than 45 hours a week, high-quality care was linked with fewer internalizing problems (anxiety, for example) and externalizing problems (aggressive and destructive behaviours, for example). A recent study revealed that children from low-income families benefited in terms of school readiness and language development when their parents selected higher-quality child care (McCartney et al., 2007). Côté and associates (2007) found that children whose mother had not finished high school were more likely to be among the 17 percent of their sample with high levels of physical aggression. Those children in their sample whose mothers had not finished high school, and who had a non-maternal caregiver prior to nine months of age, were not in the aggressive group.

Different options for non-parental care exist: care can be provided in a regulated facility where provincial standards are maintained and checked; care can also be given by a relative or non-relative at or outside the child's home. Approximately 80 percent of children under the age of four years

connecting development to life

Child Care Policy around the World

Sheila Kamerman (1989, 2000a, b) has conducted extensive examinations of parental leave policies around the world. Parental leaves were first enacted as maternity policies more than a century ago to protect the physical health of working women at the time of childbirth. More recently, childrearing, parental, and paternity leaves were created not only in response to the needs of working women (and parents), but also because of concern for the child's well-being.

Sweden has one of the most extensive leave policies. One year of parental leave is allowed (including maternity leave),

paid for by the government at 80 percent of wages. Maternity leave may begin 60 days prior to the expected birth of the baby and ends 6 weeks after birth. Another six months of parental leave can be used until the child's eighth birthday (Kamerman, 2000a). Many Swedish parents take advantage of these leave policies. As shown in Figure 6.9 (Marshall, 2008), Swedish fathers are much more likely than Canadian fathers to take time off from work to care for their young children.

Figure 6.9

Percentage of Fathers Who Used or Planned to Use Parental Leave Benefits

Source: Marshall, 2008, International comparison, p 7.
Note: Percentage of usage does not indicate whether those studied took all the time available or only a portion of the time.

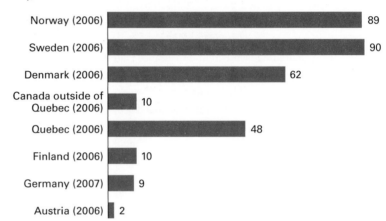

Norway (2006)	89
Sweden (2006)	90
Denmark (2006)	62
Canada outside of Quebec (2006)	10
Quebec (2006)	48
Finland (2006)	10
Germany (2007)	9
Austria (2006)	2

whose mothers are working or studying are involved in some form of child care (Beach et al., 2009). Just over 600,000 children under the age of two years had a mother in the labour force in 2007. In 2007, there were 837,923 regulated child care spaces in Canada for the more than 3 million children under the age of 12 years whose mothers worked. Beach and colleagues report that nearly 70 percent of children with both parents working or a working single parent were cared for by a relative, an in-home caregiver, or an unregulated child care provider.

What constitutes a high-quality child care program for infants? In high-quality child care (Clarke-Stewart & Miner, 2008, p. 273):

> Caregivers encourage the children to be actively engaged in a variety of activities, have frequent, positive interactions that include smiling, touching, holding, and speaking at the child's eye level, respond properly to the child's questions or requests, and encourage children to talk about their experiences, feelings, and ideas.

The Canadian Child Care Confederation values children. In order to promote the child's safety and their healthy pattern of evolving growth and development, the organization is committed to providing Canadians with the very best in early learning and child care knowledge and best practices (Canadian Child Care Confederation, 2013).

critical thinking

What are the characteristics of competent caregivers? Would you have different criteria for caregivers in a family (e.g., parents and grandparents) and for caregivers in an institution (e.g., nurses and daycare workers)? What criteria are essential for the safety of children in a regulated child care facility? You are thinking of becoming an unregulated child care provider; what steps would you take to get started?

Not surprisingly, a high adult-to-child ratio and small group sizes are important elements of quality daycare. Across Canada, provincial and territorial requirements regarding caregiver-to-child ratios are similar to the ones proposed in Figure 6.10. Nevertheless, there remain large differences in the maximum group size allowed in different provinces and territories (Beach et al., 2009).

What is the quality of daycare in Canada? Keon (2009) noted that Canada placed 21st out of 29 countries for "over-all child well-being" in the Organisation for Economic Co-operation

Figure 6.10

What Is High-Quality Daycare?

The following recommendations are based on criteria proposed by Canadian researchers and a review of research literature (Friendly, Doherty, & Beach, 2006). Quality refers to elements that protect "children's health and safety," nurture their "emotional and prosocial development," and provide "intellectual stimulation through play and hands-on activities" (as paraphrased in Friendly et al., 2006 from Harms, 2005).

Adult Caregivers

- Have formal training in child development and curriculum planning
- Show consistent expectations of children's behaviours
- Receive training in cultural diversity

Organization

- Encourages staff in decision-making process
- Offers decent salaries to reduce likelihood of staff turnover
- Maintains a high staff–child ratio and small group size

Age of Children	Adult–Child Ratio	Maximum Group Size
0–1 year	1:3	6
1–2 years	1:4	8
2–3 years	1:6	12
3–4 years	1:7	14
4–5 years	1:9	18
5–6 years	1:9	18

Program

- Has daily routines for children
- Promotes positive child–adult and child–child interactions
- Gives children ample opportunity to talk with adults

and Development's (OECD) 2007 assessment. The United Nations Children's Fund found Canada only reached one of ten benchmarks on early learning and care, placing us 26 out of 26 (Hertzman, 2009). To overcome this poor showing, Canada has initiated efforts to revitalize its commitment to early childhood development. Keon (2009) reports the Canadian Senate is exploring what other jurisdictions are doing and making recommendations to Parliament to study and advance the provision of universal child development services in Canada. Compared to Sweden, where the national child care system begins with prenatal care and extends through the early years of school, Canada has a ways to go (Hertzman, 2009). Sweden met all ten of the OECD's benchmarks.

The shift to a new paradigm is occurring across Canada. Quebec is ahead of the rest of Canada in establishing the universality of child care, although creating a high standard of quality care is still a concern (Hertzman, 2009). Prince Edward Island has shifted responsibility for child care programs to the Department of Education, as has Saskatchewan (Beach & Bertrand, 2009). Most provinces are moving to initiate education programs that link early childhood development with the schooling that begins at age four. Ontario, as we will see in the following chapter, initiated an extensive pilot project in full-day kindergarten (for four- and five-year-olds) in 2011. While these initiatives may cost taxpayers more money, Daniel Trefler (2009) suggests the benefits arising from a better-educated and healthier population will offset the initial investment in a "high-quality, universal early child development program" (p. 684).

Infants with Special Needs

The organization of health and other community services in ways that enhance their access and coordination can substantially benefit children and families with special needs (Perrin et al. 2007). Historically, hospital-based institution care has been the only option for most children with complex medical conditions, technology dependence, and significant emotional and behavioural needs (Murphy, Carbone, & Council on Children with Disabilities, 2011). In fact, social policy has promoted community-based programs that provide care for children with disabilities in their homes and communities (McPherson et al., 2004).

Patient and family-centred care is an innovative approach that is grounded in a mutually beneficial partnership with participation among patients, families, and health care providers. According to the Committee on Hospital Care and the Institute for Patient and Family-Centred Care (2012), patient and family-centred care can significantly improve patient and family outcomes. In one important study, conducted by Woodgate, Edwards, and Ripat (2012), parents' conceptualizations of participation were examined, including their perspectives of participation involving themselves, their children, and their family unit. The findings revealed that the parents in this study described participation as a dynamic and reciprocal social process of involvement in being with others. For participation in everyday life to be meaningful, according to parents, the attributes of choice, safety, acceptance, accessibility, and accommodation had to be present. In fact, participation was valued highly by parents because it resulted in positive outcomes. To summate, meaningful participation contributed not only to them, but to their children striving to have a life.

To this point, we have studied how social contexts influence the infant's development. For a review, see the **Reach Your Learning Objectives** section at the end of this chapter.

reach your **learning objectives**

Emotional Development

LO1 Outline the development of emotions in infancy.

Defining Emotion	▪ Emotion can involve physiological arousal, conscious experience, and behavioural expression.
Biological and Environmental Influences	▪ Brain areas such as the brain stem, hippocampus, and amygdala are involved in emotions. ▪ Social relationships provide the setting for the development of a rich variety of emotions.
Early Emotions	▪ Primary emotions are present in humans and other animals and emerge early in life; examples are joy, anger, sadness, fear, and disgust. ▪ Self-conscious emotions require self-awareness, especially consciousness and a sense of "me"; examples include jealousy, empathy, and embarrassment.
Emotion Expression and Social Relationships	▪ The basic cry, the anger cry, and the pain cry are observed in babies. ▪ The reflexive smile occurs at birth and the social smile comes around two to three months of age. ▪ The most frequent expression of an infant's fear is stranger anxiety. ▪ Stranger anxiety emerges gradually, starting at about age six months and escalating through the first birthday.

Emotion Regulation and Coping	■ Emotion regulation consists of managing arousal to adapt to and reach a goal.
	■ One example of emotion regulation is when infants suck their thumbs to soothe themselves.
	■ In early infancy, babies mainly depend on caregivers for soothing.
	■ Factors such as parental expectation can influence an infant's emotion regulation.
	■ The use of language helps toddlers to communicate their feelings.

Temperament and Personality Development

LO2 Summarize the development of temperament and personality during infancy.

Temperament	■ Temperament is an individual's behavioural style and characteristic way of emotional responding. Developmentalists are especially interested in the temperament of infants.
	■ Chess and Thomas classified infants as (1) easy, (2) difficult, or (3) slow to warm up.
	■ Kagan proposed the temperament category of inhibition to the unfamiliar.
	■ According to Rothbart and Bates, the structure of temperament consists of (1) extraversion/surgency, (2) negative affectivity, and (3) effortful control.
	■ Goodness of fit refers to the match between a child's temperament and the environmental demands the child must cope with.
	■ Although research evidence is sketchy at this point in time, some general recommendations are that caregivers should (1) be sensitive to the individual characteristics of the child, (2) be flexible in responding to these characteristics, and (3) avoid negative labelling of the child.
Personality Development	■ Erikson argued that the first year is characterized by the crisis of trust versus mistrust.
	■ At some point in the second half of the second year of life, the infant develops a sense of self.
	■ Blind babies also develop a sense of self in infancy, even though this may come at a later time than is the case with other infants.
	■ Independence becomes a central theme in the second year of life. Mahler argued that the infant separates itself from the mother and then develops individuation. Erikson stressed that the second year of life is characterized by the stage of autonomy versus shame and doubt.

Social Orientation/Understanding and Attachment

LO3 Analyze social orientation/understanding and the development of attachment in infancy.

Social Orientation/ Understanding	■ Social orientation is infants' captivation with the social world around them made up of parents and other children.
	■ Locomotion allows infants to initiate social interaction on their own through exploration.
	■ Development of intention, goal-directed behaviour, and cooperation facilitate social interactions.
	■ Social referencing involves "reading" emotional cues in others, such as the mother, to learn how to act in a situation.
	■ Infants' perceptions of others' actions reveals an earlier development of social sophistication and insight than previously imagined.

Attachment and Its Development	■ Attachment is a close emotional bond between the infant and caregiver.
	■ Feeding is not an important aspect of attachment, although contact comfort and trust are.
	■ Bowlby's ethological theory stresses that the caregiver and the infant instinctively trigger attachment.
	■ Attachment develops in four phases.
Individual Differences in Attachment	■ Securely attached babies use the caregiver, usually the mother, as a secure base from which to explore the environment.
	■ Three types of insecure attachment are avoidant, resistant, and disorganized.
	■ Mary Ainsworth created the Strange Situation, an observational measure of attachment.
Caregiving Styles and Attachment Classifications	■ Caregivers of secure babies are sensitive to the babies' signals and are consistently available to meet their needs.
	■ Caregivers of avoidant babies tend to be unavailable or rejecting.
	■ Caregivers of resistant babies tend to be inconsistently available to their babies and are usually not very affectionate.
	■ Caregivers of disorganized babies often neglect or physically abuse their babies.
	■ Changes in the caregiving relationship over time may affect the stability of attachment patterns.
Attachment, Temperament, and the Wider Social World	■ Early attachment relationships and subsequent experiences with the caregiver are linked with later behaviour and adjustment.
	■ Some critics argue that attachment theorists have not given adequate attention to genetics and temperament.
	■ Other critics stress that they have not adequately taken into account the diversity of social agents and contexts.
	■ Cultural variations in attachment have been found, but in all cultures studied to date, secure attachment is the most common classification.

Social Contexts

LO4 Determine how social contexts influence the infant's development.

The Family	■ The transition to parenthood requires considerable adaptation and adjustment on the part of parents.
	■ Children socialize parents just as parents socialize children.
	■ Belsky's model describes direct and indirect effects.
	■ Mothers tend to be the primary caregiver to children, and children prefer their mothers to fathers during stressful times.
	■ Many fathers perform both instrumental and expressive functions in their children's lives, but parenting publications tend to ignore their role.
Child Care	■ Daycare has become a basic need of the Canadian family.
	■ Early daycare experiences are related to later social adjustment.
	■ The Canadian Child Care Federation values children and is an excellent resource.
Infants with Special Needs	■ Patient and family-centred health care is important.

review ---> *connect* ---> reflect

review

What is the nature of an infant's emotions? In what ways do they change? **LO1**

What is temperament? How does it develop in infancy? **LO2**

How is secure attachment developed in infancy? **LO3**

What are some individual variations in attachment? **LO3**

What are some important family processes in infant development? **LO4**

connect

According to Bowlby, attachment is important to the infant. Explain the importance of an internal working model of attachment as the infant grows and develops.

reflect *Your Own Personal Journey of Life*

If you had an opportunity to design a child care facility for infants, what type of play activity would you suggest for infants as they progress from one month to one year?

McGraw Hill Education **connect**

McGraw-Hill Connect provides you with a powerful tool for improving academic performance and truly mastering course material. You can diagnose your knowledge with pre- and post-tests, identify the areas where you need help, search the entire learning package, including the eBook, for content specific to the topic you're studying, and add these resources to your personalized study plan. CONNECT for *Life-Span Development*, fifth Canadian edition, offers the following:

- chapter-specific online quizzes
- groupwork
- presentations
- writing assignments
- case studies
- and much more!

Visit CONNECT today!

CHAPTER 7

Physical and Cognitive Development in Early Childhood

CHAPTER OUTLINE

Physical Development

LO1 Identify physical changes in early childhood.

Body Growth

The Brain

Motor Development

Health and Wellness

LO2 Identify the factors involved in determining the health and wellness of children in Canada and in other countries.

Nutrition and Exercise

Wellness in Canada

Wellness in Other Countries

Cognitive Development

LO3 Describe three views of the cognitive changes that occur in early childhood.

Piaget's Preoperational Stage

Vygotsky's Theory

Information Processing

Language Development

LO4 Summarize how language develops in early childhood.

Early Childhood Education

LO5 Identify different approaches to early childhood education.

The Child-Centred Kindergarten

Developmentally Appropriate and Inappropriate Practices

Young Children's Literacy and Numeracy

Education for Children Who Are Disadvantaged

> "*You are troubled at seeing him spend his early years doing nothing. What! Is it nothing to be happy? Is it nothing to skip, to play, to run about all day long? Never in his life will he be so busy as now.*"
>
> —JEAN-JACQUES ROUSSEAU, SWISS-BORN FRENCH PHILOSOPHER, EIGHTEENTH CENTURY

> "*You have to colour outside the lines once in a while if you want to make your life a masterpiece.*"
>
> —HALLMARK CARD

Oh, Brother!

In early childhood, our greatest untold poem was being only four years old. We skipped and ran and played all the sunlight long, never in our lives so busy, busy being something we had not quite grasped yet. Who knew our thoughts, which we worked up into small mythologies all our own? Our thoughts and images and drawings took wings. The blossoms of our heart, no wind could touch. Our small world widened as we discovered new refuges and new people. When we said, "I," we meant something totally unique, not to be confused with any other. Section 4 consists of two chapters: "Physical and Cognitive Development in Early Childhood" (Chapter 7) and "Socio-Emotional Development in Early Childhood" (Chapter 8).

One day four-year-old Alex and his two-year-old brother, Chris, were left with a babysitter named Nathan. Nathan took them to a nearby park where they could play on a swing set, slides, and climbers. Alex engaged in a noisy game of tag with a couple of children his age. They also played hide and seek, and had discussions about who would be the "baddies" for imaginary play. Chris played on the swings, wandered around with Nathan, then sat on Nathan's knee. At lunch time, Nathan brought them home and made them lunch of macaroni and cheese and juice. Then to much merriment and laughter, Nathan arranged the apple slices with some raisins to make funny faces and Chris named his apple-raisin face A-Ray and invented a dialogue about how A-Ray would capture the baddies in outer space in his "thing-a-ma-jig."

After lunch, Alex got out his horse collection, lined them up in a circle, and started to make up a story while Chris watched. Chris wanted to play with the horses, but Alex wouldn't let him so Chris started to cry and kicked them over. Alex pushed him away. Nathan intervened and said, "Let's go watch a movie." Alex said, "Yea!" and Chris smiled. During the movie, Chris fell asleep but Alex was glued to the events on the television screen.

After the movie, Chris woke up and Alex took the storybooks off a bookshelf and started "reading." Alex tried to read to Chris, but within a matter of minutes they threw down the books and ran to the basement, where Alex rode his scooter and Chris played with a car. Next, Alex took the lead and started making noises like a siren and Chris began running around and falling down. Nathan suggested they go for a walk and said that Alex could take his scooter.

After their walk, Alex asked for a cookie, one that his mom had said he could have after supper. Nathan said no, but that he could have more apple slices. Alex argued, stamped his feet, pouted, and said things like, "You never let me have anything!" With a laugh in his voice, Nathan said to Alex, "Now Alex, don't you dare smile! Don't even grin, and don't come over here when I read this story to Chris." Nathan started reading the story to Chris and Alex became quiet. Nathan looked up and asked Alex if he'd like to read the story to Chris but Alex turned away and continued to pout. When Nathan repeated, "Be careful, Alex, don't smile now," Alex laughed and joined Nathan and Chris. Nathan began reading the story, but Alex started making faces which made Chris laugh. Then Chris started to cry, saying that he wanted his mommy and Alex tried to soothe him. Chris and Alex lay down on the couch with their sippy-cups and watched television for half an hour.

After their show Nathan took the boys for a walk, and then he engaged the boys in an art activity with chalk and coloured paper—a present for their parents when they got home.

When the parents returned, the boys proudly gave them their artwork-presents, and Nathan reported how energetic and intelligent they were. Alex ran fast, played creatively with toys, spoke clearly, made jokes, argued, comforted his brother, described the storyline of the movie to his babysitter and made a wonderfully artistic drawing for his parents. Chris ran more slowly than Alex and imitated his older brother's behaviour throughout the day. He loved the swings, the trucks, and the walk. His speech was somewhat jumbled, but he exhibited reasoning skills and knew who Swiper was.

In this chapter, we will discuss the physical and cognitive development of children in the same age group as these two brothers, examining such questions as: How does the body grow and develop? What are young children's motor skills like? What are the theories and findings pertaining to children's cognitive abilities? We will also talk about early childhood education in Canada. As you are reading, you might be able to envision Alex and Chris running, playing, thinking, and talking.

Remember from Chapter 5 that an infant's growth in the first year is rapid and follows cephalocaudal and proximodistal patterns. Improvement in fine motor skills—such as being able to turn the pages of a book one at a time—also contributes to the infant's sense of mastery in the second year. The growth rate continues to slow down in early childhood. (Otherwise, we would be a species of giants!)

Physical Development

LO1 Identify physical changes in early childhood.

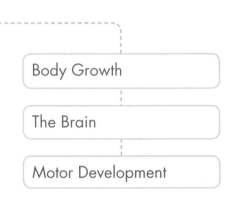

Body Growth

The Brain

Motor Development

Body Growth

Growth in height and weight is the obvious physical change that characterizes early childhood. Unseen changes in the brain and nervous system are no less significant, however, in preparing children for advances in cognition and language.

Height and Weight

The average child grows about 6.4 cm in height and gains between 2.2 and 3.2 kg a year during early childhood. As the preschool child grows older, the percentage of increase in height and weight decreases with each additional year (Darrah, Senthilselvan, & Magill-Evans, 2009). Girls are slightly smaller and lighter than boys during these years, a difference that continues until puberty. During the preschool years, both boys and girls slim down as the trunks of their bodies lengthen. Although their heads are still somewhat large for their bodies, by the end of the preschool years most children have lost their top-heavy look. Body fat also shows a slow, steady decline during the preschool years. Growth patterns vary individually (Hockenberry, 2010). Much of the variation is due to heredity, but environmental experiences are involved to some extent. Urban, middle-socio-economic status, and firstborn children were taller than rural, lower-socio-economic status, and later-born children. Both height and weight of children whose mothers smoked during pregnancy are adversely affected (Clayson, 2007).

The Brain

One of the most important physical developments during early childhood is the continuing development of the brain and nervous system (Edin et al., 2007; Nelson, 2011). The changes that occur during this period enable children to plan their actions, to react to stimuli more effectively, and to make considerable strides in language development.

Brain Size and Growth

Brain growth continues, but at a slower pace. By the time children reach three years of age, the brain is three-quarters of its adult size. By age six, the brain has reached about 95 percent of its adult volume (Lenroot & Giedd, 2006). Thus, the brain of a five-year-old is nearly the size it will be when the child reaches adulthood, but as we will see in later chapters, the development that occurs inside the brain continues through the remaining childhood and adolescent years (Blakemore, 2010; Romer et al., 2010). Figure 7.1 reveals how the growth curve for the head and brain advances more rapidly than the growth curve for height and weight.

Some of the brain's interior changes involve increases in dendritic connections as well as **myelination**, *in which nerve cells are covered and insulated with a layer of fat cells*. This has the effect of increasing the speed of information travelling through the nervous system (Fair & Schlaggar, 2008). Myelination is important in the maturation of a number of children's abilities (Diamond, Casey, & Munakata, 2011). For example, myelination in the areas of the brain related to hand–eye coordination is not complete until about four years of age. Myelination in the areas of the brain related to focusing attention is not complete until the end of middle or late childhood.

myelination The process in which nerve cells are covered and insulated with a layer of fat cells, increasing the speed at which information travels through the nervous system.

Figure 7.1

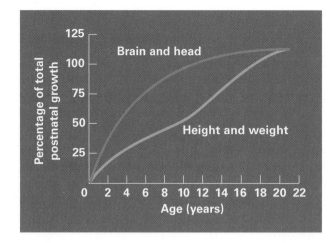

The more rapid growth of the brain and head can easily be seen. Height and weight advance more gradually over the first two decades of life.

The Brain and Cognitive Development

The increasing maturation of the brain, combined with opportunities to experience a widening world, contribute to children's emerging cognitive abilities. Consider a child who is learning to read aloud. Input from the child's eyes is transmitted to the child's brain, then passed through many brain systems that translate (process) the patterns of black and white into codes for letters, words, and associations. The output occurs in the form of messages to the child's lips and tongue. The child's own gift of speech is possible because brain systems are organized in ways that permit language processing.

The brain is organized in many neural circuits, which consist of neurons with certain functions. One neural circuit has an important function in attention and working memory (a type of memory similar to short-term memory that is like a mental workbench in performing many cognitive tasks) (Krimer & Goldman-Rakic, 2001). This neural circuit involves the *prefrontal cortex* and the neurotransmitter dopamine (Diamond, 2001) (see Figure 7.2).

Researchers also have discovered that children's brains undergo dramatic anatomical changes between the ages of 3 and 15 (Gogtay & Thompson, 2010; Thompson et al., 2000). By repeatedly obtaining brain scans of the same children for up to four years, they have found that children's brains experience rapid, distinct spurts of growth. The amount of brain material in some areas can nearly double within a year, followed by a drastic loss of tissue as unneeded cells are purged and the brain continues to reorganize itself. Local patterns within the brain change dramatically between 3 and 15 years of age. Researchers have found that in children from 3 to 6 years of age the most rapid growth takes place in the frontal lobe areas involved in planning and organizing new actions, and in maintaining attention to tasks (Diamond, Casey, & Munakata, 2011; Gogtay & Thompson, 2010).

Parents and educators know intuitively that reading books to and with children is vital to cognitive development. Is there scientific evidence to support this intuitive knowledge? Martha Farer of the University of Pennsylvania tracked children from lower socio-economic homes, many of them single-parent homes, for a 20-year period. Basically, she and her colleagues walked around the homes noting the number of books and educational toys available to the children. When the children were 18 or 19 years of age, brain scans revealed a high correlation between the amount of stimulation children had at age 4 and the development of the brain dedicated to language and cognition. In other words, stimulation, particularly at age 4, is critical to cortex development (Jha, 2012). Referring to the tremendous difficulty people of lower socio-economic means have in trying to break the cycle of poverty, Farer says, "It is a tragic irony that they so often face this challenge with diminished capabilities as a result of the hardships experienced early in life" (Farer, 2011).

As advances in technology allow scientists to "look inside" the brain and observe its activity, we will likely understand more precisely how the brain functions in cognitive development.

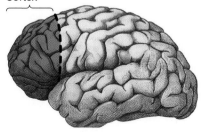

The bodies of five-year-olds and two-year-olds are different. Note how the five-year-old not only is taller and weighs more, but also has a longer trunk and longer legs than the two-year-old. **What might be some other physical differences between two- and five-year-olds?**

Figure 7.2

The Prefrontal Cortex

This evolutionarily advanced portion (shaded in purple) of the brain shows extensive development from three to six years of age and is believed to play important roles in attention and working memory.

Prefrontal Cortex

------ developmental **connection**

Chomsky's Language Acquisition Device

←-------------------------

Motor Development

Running as fast as they can, falling down, getting right back up and running just as fast as they can some more . . . building towers with blocks . . . scribbling, scribbling, scribbling . . . cutting paper with scissors. Most preschool children are as active as they will ever be—running as fast as they can, falling down, getting up, running again. Let's explore what this activity involves in young children's lives.

Gross Motor Skills

The preschool child no longer has to make an effort simply to stay upright and to move around. As children move their legs with more confidence and carry themselves more purposefully, moving around in the environment becomes more automatic.

At three years of age, children enjoy simple movements, such as hopping, jumping, and running back and forth, just for the sheer delight of performing these activities. They take considerable pride in showing how they can run across a room and jump all of 15 cm. The run-and-jump will win no Olympic gold medals, but for the three-year-old, the activity is a source of considerable pride and accomplishment.

At four years of age, children are still enjoying the same kind of activities, but they have become more adventurous. They scramble over low jungle gyms as they display their athletic prowess.

At five years of age, children are even more adventuresome. It is not unusual for self-assured five-year-olds to perform hair-raising stunts on practically any climbing object. A summary of development in gross motor skills during early childhood is shown in Figure 7.3.

You probably have arrived at one important conclusion about preschool children: They are very, very active. Indeed, three-year-old children have the highest activity level of any age in the entire human life span. They fidget when they watch television. They fidget when they sit at the dinner table. Even when they sleep, they move around quite a bit. Because of their activity level and the development of large muscles, especially in the arms and legs, preschool children need daily exercise.

Figure 7.3 --

The Development of Gross Motor Skills in Early Childhood

37–48 Months	49–60 Months	61–72 Months
Throws ball underhand (1.2 m)	Bounces and catches ball	Throws ball (13.4 m boys; 7.6 m girls)
Pedals tricycle 3 m	Runs 3 m and stops	Carries a 7-kg object
Catches large ball	Pushes/pulls a wagon/doll buggy	Kicks rolling ball
Completes forward somersault (aided)	Kicks 0.25 m ball toward target	Skips alternating feet
Jumps to floor from 0.3 m	Carries 5.4 kg object	Roller skates
Hops three hops with both feet	Catches ball	Skips rope
Steps on footprint pattern	Bounces ball under control	Rolls ball to hit object
Catches bounced ball	Hops on one foot four hops	Rides two-wheel bike with training wheels

Fine Motor Skills

At three years of age, children are still emerging from the infant ability to place and handle things. Although they have had the ability to pick up the tiniest objects between their thumb and forefinger for some time, they are still somewhat clumsy at it. Three-year-olds can build surprisingly high block towers, each block placed with intense concentration but often not in a completely straight line. When they play with a form board or a simple jigsaw puzzle, they are rather rough in placing the pieces. Even when they recognize the hole a piece fits into, they are not very precise at positioning the piece. They often try to force the piece in the hole or pat it vigorously.

By four years of age, children's fine motor coordination has become much more precise. Sometimes, four-year-old children have trouble building high towers with blocks because in their desire to place each of the blocks perfectly, they may upset those already stacked. By age five, children's fine motor coordination has improved further. Hand, arm, and body all move together under better command of the eye. Mere towers no longer interest the five-year-old, who now wants to build a house or a church, complete with steeple, though adults might still need to be told what each finished project is meant to be. A summary of the development of fine motor skills in early childhood is shown in Figure 7.4.

Figure 7.4

The Development of Fine Motor Skills in Early Childhood

37–48 Months	49–60 Months	61–72 Months
Approximates circle	Strings and laces shoelace	Folds paper into halves and quarters
Cuts paper	Cuts following line	Traces around hand
Pastes using pointer finger	Strings 10 beads	Draws rectangle, circle, square, and triangle
Builds three-block bridge	Copies figure X	Cuts interior piece from paper
Builds eight-block tower	Opens and places clothespins (one-handed)	Uses crayons appropriately
Draws 0 and 1	Builds a five-block bridge	Makes clay object with two small parts
Dresses and undresses doll	Pours from various containers	Reproduces letters
Pours from pitcher without spilling	Prints first name	Copies two short words

Note: The skills are listed in the approximate order of difficulty within each age period.

To this point, we have studied many ideas about physical development in early childhood. For a review, see the **Reach Your Learning Objectives** section at the end of this chapter.

Health and Wellness

LO2 Identify the factors involved in determining the health and wellness of children in Canada and in other countries.

What are a preschool child's energy needs? What is a preschooler's eating behaviour like? How do habits formed in early childhood affect growth and development?

Nutrition and Exercise

Eating habits are an important aspect of development during early childhood (Schiff, 2011; Wardlaw & Smith, 2011). What children eat affects their skeletal growth, body shape, and susceptibility to disease. Exercise and physical activity also are very important aspects of young children's lives (Lumpkin, 2011).

The average preschool child requires 1,700 calories per day and appears to be getting this amount . . . and more. According to the 2004 Canadian Community Health Survey *Nutrition*, the

Nutrition and Exercise

Wellness in Canada

Wellness in Other Countries

body mass index (BMI) A measure of weight in relation to height.

average daily energy intake by children aged four to eight in the 10 provinces was 1,895 calories; more than one-quarter of this amount came from "between-meal consumption," meaning that Canadian children consume a lot of snacks (Garriguet, 2007). **Body Mass Index (BMI)**, *a measure of weight in relation to height*, is used to indicate if a person has the expected weight or is overweight or obese. Figure 7.5 shows the Body Mass Index score indicating that a child is overweight or obese for ages two through five.

Figure 7.5

Body Mass Index (BMI) Cut-Off Points for Overweight and Obese Children Ages Two to Five Years*

| | Overweight | | Obese | |
| | BMI** greater than or equal to: | | BMI greater than or equal to: | |
Age (years)	Boys	Girls	Boys	Girls
2	18.41	18.02	20.09	19.81
3	17.89	17.56	19.57	19.36
4	17.55	17.28	19.29	19.15
5	17.42	17.15	19.30	19.17

* Figure adapted from Table E.1 in Chief Public Health Officer (2009) p. 95.
** BMI is calculated by dividing the person's body weight (in kilograms) by their height (in metres) squared.
Source: The Chief Public Health Officer's Report on the State of Public Health in Canada "Growing Up Well: Priorities for a Healthy Future" 2009, 138 pages, http://www. phac-aspc.gc.ca/cphorsphc-respcacsp/2009/fr-rc/pdf/cphorsphc-respcacsp-eng.pdf, Health Canada, 2009. Reproduced with the permission of the Minister of Public Works and Government Services Canada, 2013.

basal metabolism rate (BMR) The minimum amount of energy a person uses in a resting state.

Energy requirements for individual children are determined by the **basal metabolism rate (BMR)**, which is the *minimum amount of energy a person uses in a resting state*. Energy needs of individual children of the same age, sex, and size vary. Reasons for these differences remain unexplained. Differences in physical activity, basal metabolism, and the efficiency with which children use energy are possible explanations.

Childhood obesity contributes to a number of problems, including psychological adjustment. For example, as early as five years of age, being overweight is linked with lower self-esteem, negative self-image, a pervading sense of sadness, loneliness, and an increase in high-risk behaviours (Chief Public Health Officer, 2009). Being overweight or obese in early childhood is a significant predictor of later-life health care issues, including continued weight issues.

Young children's eating behaviour is strongly influenced by their caregivers' behaviour (Black & Hurley, 2007; Ventura, Gromis, & Lohse, 2010). Young children's eating behaviour improves when caregivers eat with children on a predictable schedule, model eating healthy food, make mealtimes pleasant occasions, and engage in certain feeding styles. Distractions from television, family arguments, and competing activities should be minimized so that children can focus on eating. A sensitive/responsive caregiver feeding style, in which the caregiver is nurturant, provides clear information about what is expected, and appropriately responds to children's cues, is recommended (Black & Lozoff, 2008).

Studies indicate that overweight young children will continue to be overweight when they become older. In one study, 80 percent of the children who were at risk for being overweight at 3 years of age were also at risk for being overweight or were overweight at 12 years of age (Nader et al., 2006). Another study found that children's weight at 5 years of age was significantly linked to their weight at 9 years of age (Gardner et al., 2009). Yet another study revealed that the prevalence

182   CHAPTER 7 | Physical and Cognitive Development in Early Childhood of being overweight remained stable from 4 to 11 years of age for children with lean parents but more than doubled across this time frame for children with obese parents (17 percent to 45 percent) (Semmler et al., 2009).

In Canada, 15.2 percent of children between ages two and five are overweight and another 6.3 percent are obese (Wilkinson & McCarger, 2008). Childhood obesity contributes to a number of health problems in young children (Oliver et al., 2010; Raghuveer, 2010). For example, physicians are now seeing type 2 (adult-onset) diabetes (a condition directly linked with obesity and a low level of fitness) in children as young as five years of age (Amed et al., 2010; Danne & Becker, 2007). Except for extreme cases of obesity, overweight preschool children are usually not encouraged to lose a great deal of weight. Consulting a physician and/or nutritionist is recommended before engaging in any effort to help a child lose weight.

The food children eat affects brain development as well. A study of 7,000 children who were tracked at ages 15 months, 2 years old, and 8 years old reported that IQ could be affected by as much as two points depending on the children's diets. Dr. Lisa Smithers of the University of Adelaide in South Australia led the study and found that children who were breastfed at six months and who had a healthy diet regularly including foods such as legumes, cheese, fruit, and vegetables at 15 and 24 months had an IQ up to 2 points higher by age 8. While the difference is small, it does reinforce the importance of nutrition on young children (Smithers, 2012).

Most children gain weight prior to a growth spurt, then thin out as they grow taller. Also, routine physical activity should be a daily occurrence. Apart from fat, a healthy diet includes various nutrients as well. To help Canadians achieve healthy eating habits, Health Canada published the first food guide in 1942 and has revised it periodically (Garriguet, 2007). The first food guide for First Nations, Inuit, and Métis, which takes into account the content of their traditional meals, was published in 2007. Similarly, the latest edition of Canada's Food Guide includes guidelines based on the dietary practices of various cultures.

We will have much more to consider about children's eating behaviour and weight status in Chapter 9.

As mentioned above, the daily needs of energy for Canadian four- to eight-year-olds are satisfied by their food intake. However, more than 70 percent of these young children do not eat enough vegetables and fruit and more than 2 percent do not eat enough grain products daily. In addition, the daily minimum amount of milk products was missed by over 35 percent of 4- to 9-year-olds in 2004 (Garriguet, 2007).

Wellness in Canada

In recent decades, vaccines have nearly eradicated disabling bacterial meningitis and have become available to prevent measles, rubella, mumps, and chicken pox. The disorders still most likely to be fatal during early childhood today are birth defects, cancer, and diseases of the nervous system. Although the dangers of many diseases for children have been greatly diminished, it still is important for parents to keep young children on an immunization schedule.

More than any disease, unintentional injuries (most notably automobile accidents) are the leading cause of death among children between ages 1 and 11, totalling 33 percent of all deaths in this age group (Chief Public Health Officer, 2009). After motor vehicle accidents, drowning, threats to breathing, and fire are the most common causes of death in this group. Although these injuries are lethal, they are also preventable—if safety precautions are taken.

Another concern about children's health is exposure to parental smoking. A number of studies have concluded that children are at risk for health problems when they live in homes in which a parent smokes (Arshad, 2005; Lloyd & Wise, 2004; Sheahan & Free, 2005). Children exposed to tobacco smoke in the home are more likely to have weakened immune systems, pneumonia, or pulmonary bronchitis, and to develop wheezing symptoms and asthma than children in non-smoking homes (Arshad, 2005; Clayson, 2007; Murray et al., 2004). They may also have significantly lower levels of vitamin C in their blood than their counterparts in non-smoking homes. In one study, the more parents smoked, the less vitamin C the children and adolescents had in their blood (Strauss, 2001).

Children exposed to environmental smoke should be encouraged to eat foods rich in vitamin C or be given this vitamin as a supplement (Preston, Rodriguez, Rivera, & Sahai, 2003).

Canada has no official definition of poverty as several different approaches are applied to studies (Pohl, 2002); however, almost 900,000 people, 38 percent of them children, access food banks (Food Banks Canada, 2012). No matter which criteria to define poverty are used, certain trends can be noted: poverty rates are higher among lone-parent and immigrant families, visible minorities, and people with disabilities (Pohl, 2002). Of special concern is the poor health status of many young children from low-income families. According to the Conference Board of Canada (2010), 15.1 percent of children (under 18 years of age) in Canada live in poverty, putting Canada 13th out 17 countries assessed. In Inuit and First Nations communities, one of every four children are living in poverty (Make Poverty History, 2010).

Living in poverty has a negative impact on physical and emotional health (Raphael, 2002; Phipps, 2003; Canadian Nurses Association, 2009; Gupta, de Wit, & McKeown, 2007). In a review of Canadian research, Gupta and associates (2007) found that children under five years of age living in a low-income family had higher rates of asthma and injuries (both lethal and non-lethal), were more likely to be overweight or obese, had poorer mental health ratings, and had a lower level of readiness for school and functional health than children in middle- or high-income families.

As noted above, poverty rates for Inuit and First Nations children are considerably higher than average; it follows that their health is poorer than that of many other children. The number of Aboriginal children who are obese or overweight has become a major concern in Aboriginal communities (Ferris, 2010). In 2004, 58 percent of Aboriginal children living on reserve, between 2 and 11 years of age, were overweight or obese (Chief Public Health Officer, 2009). Type 2 diabetes is on the increase among obese and overweight children, bringing with it significant health issues. Another concern for Aboriginal people is a tuberculosis rate 4.8 times higher than the rate for the general population in 2004 (Public Health Agency of Canada, 2008). The rate is actually 26.4 times higher for Aboriginal people compared with Canadian-born non-Aboriginals. The larger rate results from removing foreign-born Canadians, for whom the tuberculosis rate is 18.4 times higher than for Canadian-born non-Aboriginals. Tuberculosis among Aboriginals may be due, in part, to the higher housing densities in which many live (Clark, Riben, & Nowgesic, 2002). Health issues for many Aboriginal Canadians are further complicated by the fact that they live in isolated communities beyond the easy reach of health care providers, which impacts diagnosis and timely treatment.

Wellness in Other Countries

The link between poverty and children's health is an issue not only in Canada, but also in the rest of the world. The poor of the world often experience lives of hunger, malnutrition, unsafe water, and inadequate access to health care (UNICEF, 2006). Compared with Canada, poor countries tend to have worse records on child health. For example, in 2009, the mortality rate among children under age 5 was 6 per 1,000 in Canada, but the rate was 262 per 1,000 in Sierra Leone, 181 per 1,000 in Rwanda, 59 per 1,000 in South Africa, and three per 1,000 in Sweden (World Health Organization, 2009). The rate of low-birth-weight infants was 1.6 percent in Bulgaria, 14.9 percent in Tajikistan, and 38.4 percent in the Sudan (WHO, 2009).

In 15 countries studied, pneumonia and dehydration from diarrhea are the two leading causes of death of the world's children (WHO, 2008a). Giving the child plenty of water and liquids usually prevents dehydration, but the source of the water must be uncontaminated. Measles, tetanus, and whooping cough also cause deaths among children around the world, although increased immunization programs in the last several decades have led to a decrease in deaths due to these diseases (Foege, 2000).

Another leading cause of death among children under five is "preventable injuries" resulting from accidents. Road accidents kill an estimated 260,000 children per year, followed by drowning, burns, falls, and poisonings (WHO, 2008b). These are all possibly preventable deaths.

critical thinking

What are the implications of the link between poverty and malnutrition inside and outside Canada's borders? For example, would it be more cost-effective to deal with childhood poverty now than to pay for the lost productivity and medical treatment of malnourished people in the future? Is a hungry child able free, creative, and active? How do you think it feels to access a food bank? What would you do if you lived in a rural area and there was no food bank?

In the last decade, there has been a dramatic increase in the number of young children who have died because of HIV/AIDS transmitted to them by their parents (UNICEF, 2008). Deaths in young children due to HIV/AIDS occur especially in countries with high rates of poverty and low levels of education (Boeving & Forsyth, 2008). For example, the uneducated are four times more likely to believe that there is no way to avoid AIDS and three times more likely to be unaware that the virus can be transmitted from mother to child (UNICEF, 2006). Another complication is that over 50 percent of the world's population now live in cities, where they hope to gain employment, access to health care, and support. Unfortunately, cities around the world are unable to keep up with the rapid change and this has led to scarcity and deprivation in urban areas (UNICEF, 2012). In one report, UNICEF (2006) concluded that the under-five mortality rate is the result of a wide range of factors, including the nutritional health and health knowledge of mothers, the level of immunization, dehydration, availability of maternal and child health services, income and food availability in the family, availability of clean water and safe sanitation, and the overall safety of the child's environment. Many of the deaths of young children around the world can be prevented by a reduction in poverty and improvements in nutrition, sanitation, education, and health services (UNICEF 2006, 2012).

To this point, we have studied a number of ideas about health and wellness in early childhood. For a review, see the **Reach Your Learning Objectives** section at the end of this chapter.

Cognitive Development

LO3 Describe three views of the cognitive changes that occur in early childhood.

The cognitive world of the preschool child is creative, free, and fanciful. Preschool children's imaginations work overtime, and their mental grasp of the world improves. Our coverage of cognitive development in early childhood focuses on three theories: Piaget's, Vygotsky's, and information processing.

Piaget's Preoperational Stage

Recall from Chapter 5 that during Piaget's sensorimotor stage of development, the infant progresses in the ability to organize and coordinate sensations and perceptions with physical movements and actions. The second stage, Piaget's **preoperational stage**, *lasts from approximately two to seven years of age.* Piaget used the label preoperational to emphasize that children at this stage do not yet think in an operational way; in other words, children can add and subtract when they are able to move objects physically, but they are unable to perform these functions mentally. Piaget believed that the ability to perform functions such as these mentally comes in the third stage, which he labelled the concrete operational stage. **Operations** *are internalized and reversible sets of actions that allow children to do mentally what before they could do physically.*

Preoperational thought is the beginning of the ability to reconstruct in thought what has been established in behaviour. Language is a hallmark of this stage; as well, children form stable concepts and begin to reason and to represent the world with words, images, drawings, and imaginary play. For example, the child may develop an imaginary friend, build a fort from blankets and pillows, or pretend that a broom is a horse. At the same time, the young child's cognitive world is dominated by egocentrism and magical beliefs.

The preoperational stage can be divided into two substages: the symbolic function substage and the intuitive thought substage.

Symbolic Function Substage

In the **symbolic function substage**, *roughly between the ages of two and four, the young child gains the ability to mentally represent an object that is not present.* The ability to engage in such symbolic thought is called symbolic function, and it vastly expands the child's mental world (Carlson &

Piaget's Preoperational Stage

Vygotsky's Theory

Information Processing

preoperational stage Piaget's second stage, lasting from two to seven years of age, during which children begin to represent the world with words, images, and drawings. They form stable concepts and begin to reason.

operations In Piaget's theory, an internalized set of actions that allow a child to do mentally what before he or she did physically.

symbolic function substage Piaget's first substage of preoperational thought, in which the child gains the ability to mentally represent an object that is not present (occurs between two and four years of age).

Zelazo, 2008). Young children use scribbled designs to represent people, houses, cars, clouds, and so on. Other examples of symbolism in early childhood are language and the prevalence of pretend play. However, although young children make distinct progress during this substage, their thinking still has several important limitations, two of which are egocentrism and animism.

egocentrism The inability to distinguish between one's own perspective and someone else's perspective.

Egocentrism *is the inability to distinguish between one's own perspective and that of someone else.* Piaget and Barbel Inhelder (1969) initially studied young children's egocentrism by devising the three mountains task (see Figure 7.6). The child walks around the model of the mountains and becomes familiar with what the mountains look like from different perspectives. The child is then seated on one side of the table. The experimenter moves a doll to different locations around the table, at each location asking the child to select, from a series of photos, the one photo that most accurately reflects the view the doll is seeing. Children in the preoperational stage often pick the view from where they are sitting, rather than the doll's view. **Animism**, another limitation within preoperational thought, *is the belief that inanimate objects have "lifelike" qualities and are capable of action.* A young child might show animism by saying, "The sidewalk made me mad; it made me fall down" (Gelman & Opfer, 2002).

animism The belief that inanimate objects have "lifelike" qualities and are capable of action.

Possibly because young children are not very concerned about reality, their drawings are fanciful and inventive. One 3½-year-old looked at a scribble he had just drawn and described it as a pelican kissing a seal (see Figure 7.7a). In the elementary school years, a child's drawings become more realistic, neat, and precise (see Figure 7.7b).

Intuitive Thought Substage

intuitive thought substage Occurs between approximately four and seven years of age, when children begin to use primitive reasoning and want to know the answers to all sorts of questions.

The **intuitive thought substage** *occurs between approximately four and seven years of age. In this substage, children begin to use primitive reasoning and want to know the answers to all sorts of questions.* Piaget called this time period intuitive because young children seem quite sure about their knowledge and understanding, yet are unaware of how they know what they know. That is, they say they know something but know it without the use of rational thinking.

In this substage, children begin to use primitive reasoning and want to know the answers to all sorts of questions. Consider four-year-old Ryan, who is at the beginning of the intuitive thought substage. Although he is starting to develop his own ideas about the world he lives in, his ideas are still simple, and he is not very good at thinking things out. He has difficulty understanding events that he knows are taking place but that he cannot see. His fantasized thoughts bear little resemblance to reality. He cannot yet answer the question "What if?" in any reliable way. For example, he has only a vague idea of what would happen if a car were to hit him. He also has difficulty negotiating traffic because he cannot do the mental calculations necessary to estimate whether an approaching car will hit him when he crosses the road.

Figure 7.6

The Three Mountains Task

View 1 shows the child's perspective from where he or she is sitting. View 2 is an example of one of the photographs the child would be shown, along with other photographs taken from different perspectives. It shows what the mountains look like to a person sitting at spot B. When asked what a view of the mountains looks like from position B, the preoperational child selects a photograph taken from location A, the child's view at the time. A child who thinks in a preoperational way cannot take the perspective of a person sitting at another spot.

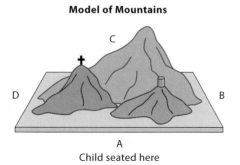

Model of Mountains

C

D

B

A

Child seated here

Photo 1
(View from A)

Photo 2
(View from B)

Photo 3
(View from C)

Photo 4
(View from D)

Figure 7.7

The Symbolic Drawings of Young Children

(a) A 3½-year-old's symbolic drawing. Halfway into this drawing, the 3½-year-old artist said it was "a pelican kissing a seal." *(b)* This 11-year-old's drawing is neater and more realistic, but also less inventive.

By the age of five, children have just about exhausted the adults around them with "why" questions. The child's questions signal the emergence of interest in reasoning and in figuring out why things are the way they are. Following are some samples of the questions children ask during the questioning period of four to six years of age (Elkind, 1976): "What makes you grow up?" "Who was the mother when everybody was a baby?" "Why do leaves fall?" "Why does the sun shine?"

Centration and the Limits of Preoperational Thought

One characteristic of preoperational thought is **centration**—*the focusing, or centring, of attention on one characteristic to the exclusion of all others.* Centration is most clearly evidenced in young children's lack of **conservation**—*awareness that altering an object's or a substance's appearance does not change its basic properties.* In the conservation task, a child is presented with two identical beakers, each filled to the same level with liquid (see Figure 7.8). The child is asked if these beakers have the same amount of liquid, and the child usually replies yes. Then, the liquid from one beaker is poured into a third beaker, which is taller and thinner than the first two. The child is then asked if the amount of liquid in the tall, thin beaker is equal to that which remains in one of the original beakers. Children younger than seven or eight years old usually say no and justify their answers in terms of the differing height or width of the beakers. This kind of justification shows centration in that children are focusing on just one aspect of the event. In contrast, older children usually answer yes and justify their answers appropriately ("If you poured the milk back, the amount would still be the same").

centration The focusing, or centring, of attention on one characteristic to the exclusion of all others.

conservation Awareness that altering an object's or a substance's appearance does not change its basic properties.

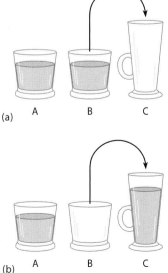

Figure 7.8

Piaget's Conservation Task

The beaker test is a well-known Piagetian test to determine whether a child can think operationally.

Figure 7.9

Some Dimensions of Conservation: Number, Matter, and Length

Type of Conservation	Initial Presentation	Manipulation	Preoperational Child's Answer
Number	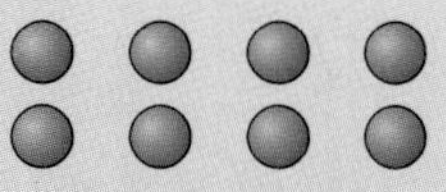 Two identical rows of objects are shown to the child, who agrees they have the same number.	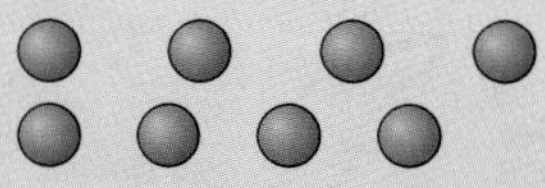 One row is lengthened and the child is asked whether one row now has more objects.	Yes, the longer row.
Matter	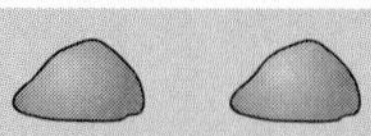 Two identical balls of clay are shown to the child. The child agrees that they are equal.	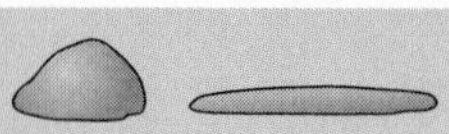 The experimenter changes the shape of one of the balls and asks the child whether they still contain equal amounts of clay.	No, the longer one has more.
Length	 Two sticks are aligned in front of the child. The child agrees that they are the same length.	 The experimenter moves one stick to the right, then asks the child if they are equal in length.	No, the one on the top is longer.

In addition to the conservation of liquid, Piaget also studied other conservation tasks: number, matter, length, volume, and area (Figure 7.9 portrays several of these). Children often vary in their performance on different conservation tasks. Thus, a child might be able to conserve volume but not number.

The child's inability to reverse actions mentally is an important characteristic of preoperational thought. For example, in the conservation of matter, preoperational children say that the longer shape has more clay because they assume that "longer is more." They cannot mentally reverse the clay-rolling process to see that the amount of clay is the same in both the shorter ball shape and the longer stick shape.

Some developmentalists believe Piaget was not entirely correct in his estimate of when children's conservation skills emerge. For example, Rochel Gelman (1969) showed that when the child's attention to relevant aspects of the conservation task is improved, the child is more likely to conserve. Gelman also believes that conservation appears earlier than Piaget thought, and that attention is especially important in explaining conservation.

Some other aspects of the preoperational stage have also been called into question. For example, due to egocentrism, children should not realize that they need to provide an audience with information concerning the time and location, not just the action, of their past experiences if the audience were not present at the same events. A child may recall, "The dog barked and I was scared," without mentioning when and where this experience occurred. However, Carole Peterson of Memorial University of Newfoundland (e.g., Peterson & McCabe, 1994) showed that children as young as 26 to 31 months could actually provide the when and where information in their description of past experiences, suggesting children may not be as egocentric as Piaget suggested. Further, recent research finds that preschool-aged children are able to make up stories and tell falsehoods indicates some awareness of differing perspectives (Talwar & Lee, 2006).

As for the notion of animism, Quebec researchers Diane Poulin-Dubois and Gisèle Héroux (1994) found that both adults and children (five- to nine-year-olds) considered an object that can move as "more alive" than one that cannot, indicating that children's cognitive structure regarding the "aliveness" of objects may not be different from that of adults. The animism that preoperational children sometimes show may reflect a lack of knowledge of certain objects, rather than the presence of a qualitatively different cognitive structure. Figure 7.10 summarizes the characteristics of preoperational thought.

Figure 7.10

Characteristics of Preoperational Thought

| More symbolic than sensorimotor thought | Inability to engage in operations; cannot mentally reverse actions; lacks conservation skills | Egocentric (inability to distinguish between own perspective and someone else's) | Intuitive, rather than logical |

Vygotsky's Theory

In Chapter 2, we described the basic principles of Vygotsky's theory: (1) the child's cognitive skills can be understood only when they are developmentally analyzed and interpreted; (2) cognitive skills are mediated by words, language, and forms of discourse, which serve as psychological tools for facilitating and transforming mental activity; and (3) cognitive skills have their origins in social relations and are embedded in a socio-cultural background.

The Zone of Proximal Development

The **zone of proximal development (ZPD)** *is Vygotsky's term for the range of tasks too difficult for a child to master alone but that can be learned with the guidance and assistance of adults or more-skilled children.* ZPD reflects Vygotsky's belief in the importance of social influences, especially instruction on children's cognitive development. As shown in Figure 7.11, the lower limit of the ZPD is the level of problem solving reached by the child working independently. The upper limit is the level of additional responsibility the child can accept with the assistance of an able instructor. An example of the ZPD is an adult helping a child put together a jigsaw puzzle.

The ZPD captures the child's cognitive skills that are in the process of maturing and can be accomplished only with the assistance of a more-skilled person (Alvarez & del Rio, 2007; Gauvain & Perez, 2007). Vygotsky (1962) called these the "buds" or "flowers" of development, to distinguish them from the "fruits" of development, which the child already can accomplish independently.

Scaffolding

Closely linked to the idea of zone of proximal development is the concept of scaffolding. **Scaffolding** *means changing the level of support.* Over the course of a teaching session, a more-skilled person (perhaps a teacher or a more advanced peer) adjusts the amount of guidance to fit the child's current performance (Daniels, 2007). When the student is learning a new skill, the more-skilled person may use direct instruction. As the student's competence increases, less guidance is given.

Language and Thought

The use of dialogue as a tool for scaffolding is only one example of the important role of language in a child's development. According to Vygotsky, children use speech not only to communicate socially but also to help them solve tasks. Vygotsky (1962) further believed that young children use language to plan, guide, and monitor their behaviour. This use of language for self-regulation is called private speech. For Piaget, private speech is egocentric and immature, but for Vygotsky it is an important tool of thought during the early childhood years (John-Steiner, 2007).

Dialogue is an important tool of scaffolding in the zone of proximal development (Tappan, 1998). Vygotsky viewed children as having rich but unsystematic, disorganized, and spontaneous concepts. In a dialogue, these concepts meet with the skilled helper's more systematic, logical, and rational concepts. As a result, the child's concepts become more systematic, logical, and rational. For example, a dialogue might take place between a teacher and a child when the teacher uses scaffolding to help a child understand a concept like "transportation."

"I still don't have all the answers, but I'm beginning to ask the right questions." The New Yorker Collection, 1989, Lee Lorenz from the cartoonbank.com. All rights reserved.

zone of proximal development Vygotsky's term for the range of tasks too difficult for a child to master alone but that can be learned with the guidance and assistance of adults or more-skilled children.

scaffolding In cognitive development, Vygotsky used this term to describe the changing support over the course of a teaching session, with the more-skilled person adjusting the amount of guidance to fit the child's current performance level.

In Vygotsky's theory, an important point is that children need to learn the skills that will help them do well in their culture. Vygotsky believed that this should be accomplished through interaction with more-skilled members of the culture, such as this boy learning to read with the guidance of his father. **What are some other ways that skilled members of a society can interact with young children?**

Figure 7.11

Vygotsky's Zone of Proximal Development

Vygotsky's zone of proximal development has a lower limit and an upper limit. Tasks in the ZPD are too difficult for the child to perform alone. They require assistance from an adult or a skilled child. As children experience the verbal instruction or demonstration, they organize the information in their existing mental structures so that they can eventually perform the skill or task alone.

Upper limit
Level of additional responsibility child can accept with assistance of an able instructor

Zone of proximal development (ZPD)

Lower limit
Level of problem solving reached on these tasks by child working alone

Vygotsky believed that language and thought initially develop independently of each other and then merge. He said that all mental functions have external, or social, origins. Children must use language to communicate with others before they can focus inward on their own thoughts. Children also must communicate externally and use language for a long period of time before the transition from external to internal speech takes place. This transition period occurs between the ages of three and seven years of age and involves talking to oneself. After a while, the self-talk becomes second nature to children, and they can act without verbalizing. When this occurs, children have internalized their egocentric speech in the form of inner speech, which becomes their thoughts.

Vygotsky reasoned that children who use a lot of private speech are more socially competent than those who do not. He argued that private speech represents an early transition to becoming more socially communicative. Piaget maintained that self-talk is egocentric and reflects immaturity. However, researchers have found support for Vygotsky's view that private speech plays a positive role in children's development (Winsler, Carlton, & Barry, 2000). Researchers have found that children use private speech more when tasks are difficult, following errors, and when they are not sure how to proceed. They also have revealed that children who use private speech are more attentive and improve their performance more than children who do not use private speech (Berk & Spuhl, 1995).

Teaching Strategies

Vygotsky's theory has been embraced by many teachers and has been successfully applied to education (Daniels, 2007; Holzman, 2009). Here are some ways Vygotsky's theory can be incorporated in classrooms:

1. *Assess the child's ZPD.* Like Piaget, Vygotsky did not recommend formal, standardized tests as the best way to assess children's learning. Rather, Vygotsky argued that assessment should focus on determining the child's zone of proximal development. The skilled helper presents the child with tasks of varying difficulty to determine the best level at which to begin instruction.

2. *Use the child's ZPD in teaching.* Teaching should begin toward the zone's upper limit, so that the child can reach the goal with help and move to a higher level of skill and knowledge. Offer just enough assistance. You might ask, "What can I do to help you?" Or simply observe the child's intentions and attempts and provide support when it is needed. When the child hesitates, offer encouragement. And encourage the child to practise the skill. You may watch and appreciate the child's practice or offer support when the child forgets what to do.

3. *Use more-skilled peers as teachers.* Remember that it is not just adults who are important in helping children learn. Children also benefit from the support and guidance of more-skilled children.

4. *Place instruction in a meaningful context.* Educators today are moving away from abstract presentations of material; instead, they provide students with opportunities to experience learning in real-world settings. For example, rather than just memorizing math formulas, students work on math problems with real-world implications.

5. *Transform the classroom with Vygotskian ideas.* What does a Vygotskian classroom look like? The Kamehameha Elementary Education Program (KEEP) in Hawaii is based on Vygotsky's theory (Tharp, 1994). The ZPD is the key element of instruction in this program. Children might read a story and then interpret its meaning. Many of the learning activities take place in small groups. All children spend at least 20 minutes each morning in a setting called "Center One." In this context, scaffolding is used to improve children's literary skills. The instructor asks questions, responds to students' queries, and builds on the ideas that students generate.

Unlike Piaget, for Vygotsky the conceptual shift is one from the individual to collaboration, social interaction, and sociocultural activity (Halford, 2008). The endpoint of cognitive development for Piaget is formal operational thought. For Vygotsky, the endpoint can differ depending on which skills are considered to be the most important in a particular culture. For Piaget, children construct knowledge by transforming, organizing, and reorganizing previous knowledge. The implication of Piaget's theory for teaching is that children need support to explore their world and discover knowledge. The main implication of Vygotsky's theory for teaching is that students need many opportunities to learn with the teacher and more-skilled peers. In both Piaget's and Vygotsky's theories, teachers serve as facilitators and guides, rather than as directors of learning. Figure 7.12 compares Vygotsky's and Piaget's theories.

Evaluating Vygotsky's Theory

Even though Vygotsky's work was not translated into English until the 1960s, and thus has not been evaluated as thoroughly as Piaget's ideas, both theorists were actually contemporaries. Moreover, their theories are both constructivist and state that children actively construct knowledge and understanding, rather than being passive receptacles. However, Vygotsky's **social constructivist approach** *emphasizes that both learning and the construction of knowledge occur in social contexts.* On the other hand, Piaget's theory does not have this social emphasis. Moving from Piaget to Vygotsky, the conceptual shift is from the individual to collaboration, social interaction, and socio-cultural activity (Holzman, 2009).

Some critics point out that Vygotsky was not specific enough about age-related changes (Gauvain, 2008; Gauvain & Parke, 2010). Another criticism suggests that Vygotsky did not adequately describe how changes in socio-emotional capabilities contribute to cognitive development. Yet another criticism is that he overemphasized the role of language in thinking. Additionally, his emphasis on collaboration and guidance has potential pitfalls. Might facilitators be too helpful in

social constructivist approach An approach that emphasizes that both learning and the construction of knowledge occur in social contexts.

Figure 7.12

Comparison of Vygotsky's and Piaget's Theories

Vygotsky		Piaget
Constructivism	**Social Constructivist**	**Cognitive Constructivist**
Stages	No general stages of development proposed	Strong emphasis on stages (sensorimotor, preoperational, concrete operational, and formal operational)
Key processes	Zone of proximal development, language, dialogue, tools of the culture	Schema, assimilation, accommodation, operations, conservation, classification, hypothetical-deductive reasoning
Role of language	A major role; language plays a powerful role in shaping thought	Language has a minimal role; cognition primarily directs language
View on education	Education plays a central role, helping children learn the tools of the culture	Education merely refines the child's cognitive skills that already have emerged
Teaching implications	Teacher is a facilitator and guide, not a director; establish many opportunities for children to learn with the teacher and more-skilled peers	Also views teacher as a facilitator and guide, not a director; provide support for children to explore their world and discover knowledge

some cases, as when a parent becomes too overbearing and controlling? Further, some children might become lazy and expect help when they might have done something on their own.

Information Processing

Piaget's and Vygotsky's theories provided important ideas about how young children think and how their thinking changes. More recently, the information-processing approach has generated research that illuminates how children process information during the preschool years (Galotti, 2010). What are the limitations and advances in the young child's ability to pay attention to the environment, to remember, to develop strategies and solve problems, and to understand their own mental processes and those of others?

Attention

In Chapter 5, we defined attention as the focusing of mental resources on select information. The child's ability to pay attention improves significantly during the preschool years (Posner & Rothbart, 2007). The toddler wanders around, shifts attention from one activity to another, and seems to spend little time focused on any one object or event. By comparison, the preschool child might be observed building a fort for half an hour.

Young children especially make advances in two aspects of attention—executive attention and sustained attention (Rothbart & Gartstein, 2008). **Executive attention** *involves action planning, allocating attention to goals, error detection and compensation, monitoring progress on tasks, and dealing with novel or difficult circumstances.* **Sustained attention** *is focused and extended engagement with an object, task, event, or other aspect of the environment.*

Mary Rothbart and Maria Gartstein (2008) recently described why advances in executive and sustained attention are so important in early childhood:

> The development of the . . . executive attention system supports the rapid increases in effortful control in the toddler and preschool years. Increases in attention are due, in part, to advances in comprehension and language development. As children are better able to understand their environment, this increased appreciation of their surroundings helps them to sustain attention for longer periods of time. (p. 332)

In at least two ways, however, the preschool child's control of attention is still deficient:

- *Salient versus relevant dimensions.* Preschool children are likely to pay attention to stimuli that stand out, or are salient, even when those stimuli are not relevant to solving a problem or performing a task. For example, if a flashy, attractive clown presents the directions for solving a problem, preschool children are likely to pay more attention to the clown than to the directions. After the age of six or seven, children attend more efficiently to the dimensions of the task that are relevant, such as the directions for solving a problem. This change reflects a shift to cognitive control of attention, so that children act less impulsively and reflect more.
- *Planfulness.* When experimenters ask children to judge whether two complex pictures are the same, preschool children tend to use a haphazard comparison strategy, not examining all of the details before making a judgment. By comparison, elementary school age children are more likely to systematically compare the details across the pictures, one detail at a time (Vurpillot, 1968) (see Figure 7.13).

In Central European countries such as Hungary, kindergarten children participate in exercises designed to improve their attention (Mills & Mills, 2000; Posner & Rothbart, 2007). For example, in one eye-contact exercise the teacher sits in the centre of a circle of children and each child is required to catch the teacher's eye before being permitted to leave the group. In other exercises created to improve attention, teachers have children participate in stop-go activities during which they have to listen for a specific signal, such as a drumbeat or an exact number of rhythmic beats, before stopping the activity.

executive attention Action planning, allocating attention to goals, error detection and compensation, monitoring progress on tasks, and dealing with novel or difficult circumstances.

sustained attention Focused and extended engagement with an object, task, event, or other aspect of the environment.

Computer exercises recently have been developed to improve children's attention (Jaeggi, Berman, & Jonides, 2009; Tang & Posner, 2009). For example, one study revealed that five days of computer exercises that involved learning how to use a joystick, working memory, and the resolution of conflict improved the attention of four- to six-year-old children (Rueda et al., 2005).

Preschool children's ability to control and sustain their attention is related to their school readiness (Posner & Rothbart, 2007). For example, one recent study of more than 1,000 children found that the ability to sustain attention at 54 months of age is linked to school readiness, which includes achievement and language skills (NICHD Early Child Care Research Network, 2005). Also, young children who have difficulty regulating their attention are more likely than other children to experience peer rejection and to engage in aggressive behaviour (Eisenberg, Spinrad, & Smith, 2004).

Memory

Memory is a central process in children's cognitive development that involves the retention of information over time. Conscious memory comes into play as early as seven months of age, although children and adults have little or no memory of events experienced before the age of three. Recall that in Chapter 5 we saw that to understand the infant's capacity to remember we need to distinguish implicit memory, the ability to repeat certain tasks without conscious awareness, from explicit memory, the ability to consciously recall events. Explicit memory itself, however, comes in many forms. One distinction occurs between relatively permanent or long-term memory and short-term memory.

Among the interesting questions about memory in the preschool years are those involving short-term memory.

SHORT-TERM MEMORY   In **short-term memory**, *individuals retain information for up to 15 to 30 seconds, assuming there is no rehearsal.* Using rehearsal (repeating information after it has been presented), people can keep information in short-term memory for a much longer period. One method of assessing short-term memory is the memory-span task. Children hear a short list of stimuli—usually digits—presented at a rapid pace (one per second, for example). Then, they are asked to repeat the digits. Research with the memory-span task suggests that short-term memory increases during early childhood. For example, in one investigation, memory span increased from about two digits in two- to three-year-old children to about five digits in seven-year-old children; yet, between 7 and 13 years of age, memory span increased only by 1½ digits (Dempster, 1981). Keep in mind, though, that there are individual differences in memory span.

Why does memory span change with age? Rehearsal of information is important: Older children rehearse the digits more than younger children do. Speed and efficiency of processing information are also important, especially the speed with which memory items can be identified (Schneider, 2004). The speed with which a child processes information is an important aspect of the child's cognitive abilities, and abundant evidence exists that the speed with which many cognitive tasks are completed improves dramatically across the childhood years (Kail, 2007).

LONG-TERM MEMORY   In Chapter 5, we saw that infants' memories are, for the most part, short-lived—except for their memory of perceptual-motor actions, which can be substantial (Mandler, 2000). Fortunately, memory becomes more accurate as children grow older. Further, young children can remember a great deal of information if they are given appropriate cues and prompts.

Because of the importance of cues, research has been conducted to look at how cues may affect children's eyewitness testimony. The findings show that under certain circumstances young children can be led to incorporate false suggestions into their accounts, and even into legal testimony (Hyman & Loftus, 2001). An outrageous case of injustice against innocent people because of children's false memories occurred in Martensville, Saskatchewan, in the early 1990s. Nine adults were accused of performing Satanic rituals against children. After over a decade of living with pain and others' angry suspicions, eight of the nine were cleared of any wrongdoing and some were compensated. It is now known that investigators used leading questions to obtain the children's false

Figure 7.13

The Planfulness of Attention

In one study, children were given pairs of houses to examine, like the ones shown here (Vurpillot, 1968). For three pairs of houses, what was in the windows was identical (a). For the other three pairs, the windows had different items in them (b). By filming the reflection in the children's eyes, it could be determined what they were looking at, how long they looked, and the sequence of their eye movements. Children under six years of age examined only a fragmentary portion of each display and made their judgments on the basis of insufficient information. By contrast, older children scanned the windows in more detailed ways and were more accurate in their judgments of which windows were identical.

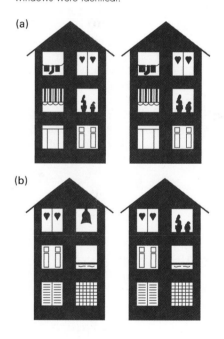

(a)

(b)

short-term memory The memory component in which individuals retain information for 15 to 30 seconds, assuming there is no rehearsal.

testimonies (Cook, 2004). Children are suggestible not just about peripheral details but also about the central aspects of an event and can be highly influenced by interviewing techniques (Bruck, Ceci, & Principe, 2006).

Several factors can influence the accuracy of a young child's memory:

- *Age differences exist in children's susceptibility to suggestion.* Preschoolers are the most suggestible age group in comparison with older children and adults (Lehman et al., 2010; Pipe, 2008). For example, preschool children are more susceptible to believing misleading or incorrect information given after an event (Ghetti & Alexander, 2004). Despite these age differences, there is still concern about the reaction of older children when they are subjected to suggestive interviews (Ceci et al., 2007).
- *Individual differences exist in susceptibility.* Some preschoolers are highly resistant to interviewers' suggestions, whereas others immediately succumb to the slightest suggestion. A recent study revealed that preschool children's ability to produce a high-quality narrative was linked to their resistance to suggestion (Kulkofsky & Klemfuss, 2008).

critical thinking

Would you, as a juror, believe a child's testimony of past abuses? What evidence would you need to make a decision beyond reasonable doubt—the criminal record of the accused? The testimonies of a teacher or neighbour? Have you ever been surprised by a young child's memory? If so, how accurate was the memory? How might your interactions with young children affect your ability as a juror to believe a child's testimony? What other factors might influence you?

Strategies and Problem Solving

Strategies consist of using deliberate mental activities to improve the processing of information (Bjorklund, 2008; Pressley, 2007). For example, rehearsing information and organizing it are two typical strategies for remembering information. What strategies do young children use? The relatively stimulus-driven toddler may become transformed into a child capable of flexible, goal-directed problem solving (Zelazo & Müller, 2004). Consider a problem in which children must sort stimuli using the rule of colour. In the course of the colour sorting, a child may describe a red rabbit as "a red one" to solve the problem. However, in a subsequent task, the child may need to discover a rule that describes the rabbit as just "a rabbit" to solve the problem. If three- to four-year-olds fail to understand that it is possible to provide multiple descriptions of the same stimulus, they persist in describing the stimulus as "a red rabbit." Researchers have found that at about four years of age children acquire the concept of perspectives, which allows them to appreciate that a single stimulus can be described in two different ways (Frye, 1999).

Zhe Chen and Robert Siegler (2000) placed young children at a table at which an attractive toy was placed too far away for the child to reach it. On the table, between the child and the toy, were six potential tools (see Figure 7.14). Only one of them was likely to be useful in obtaining the toy. After initially assessing the young children's attempts to obtain the toy on their own, the experimenters either modelled how to obtain the toy (using the appropriate tool) or gave the child a hint (telling the child to use the particular tool). These two-year-olds learned the strategy and subsequently mapped it onto new problems. This study shows that children as young as two years of age can learn a strategy.

Figure 7.14

The Toy-Retrieval Task in the Study of Young Children's Problem-Solving Strategies

The child needed to choose the target tool (in this illustration, the toy rake) to pull in the toy (in this case, the turtle).

Theory of Mind

Theory of mind *refers to the awareness of one's own mental processes and the mental processes of others.* Even young children are curious about the nature of the human mind, and developmentalists have shown a flurry of interest in children's thoughts about what the human mind is like (Wellman et al., 2008). Studies of theory of mind view the child as "a thinker who is trying to explain, predict, and understand people's thoughts, feelings, and utterances" (Harris, 2006, p. 847).

Children's theory of mind changes as they develop through childhood (Flavell, Miller, & Miller, 2002). From 18 months through age 3, children begin to understand three mental states:

- *Perceptions.* Children realize that other people see what is in front of their eyes and not necessarily what is in front of the child's eyes.
- *Desires.* Children understand that if people want something, they will try to get it.
- *Emotions.* Children can distinguish between positive (for example, happy) and negative (sad, for example) emotions.

Between three and five years of age, children come to understand that the mind can represent objects and events accurately or inaccurately. This realization can be seen in two phenomena: false beliefs and preference of information source. The knowledge that people can have false beliefs—beliefs that are not true—develops in a majority of children by the time they are five years old (Wellman, Cross, & Watson, 2001). This point is often described as a pivotal one in understanding the mind—recognizing that beliefs are not just mapped directly into the mind from the surrounding world, but that different people can also have different, and sometimes incorrect, beliefs (Gelman, 2009).

While age-related memory and conceptual deficits may explain young children's problems with false beliefs, as Susan Birch (2005) from the University of British Columbia points out, the "curse" of knowledge—people who are knowledgeable about an issue assume others to have the same information—may be the reason here. The younger we are, the less we are able to resist making this assumption.

In addition to an understanding of false beliefs, four-year-olds can use the past accuracy of someone's knowledge to evaluate the new information provided by this person. In one study (Jaswal & Neely, 2006), children were shown four *familiar* objects (e.g., shoe) and heard a child or an adult label the items. When the adult was inaccurate and the child was accurate, children preferred the child's labels for *unfamiliar* items (e.g., dish scrubber) in a subsequent task.

Victoria Talwar and Kang Lee of Queen's University and the University of Toronto conducted many studies on children's lying. In one, children between ages three and seven were left alone in a room with a music-playing toy placed behind their back. The children were told not to peek at the toy; however, most, unable to resist the temptation, peeked. When asked whether or not they had peeked, about half of the three-year-olds said yes, whereas most of the older children denied peeking.

Can adults tell when children are telling a lie? According to Lee and Talwar, no. Even police officers, social workers, parents, and lawyers are unable to tell whether or not a three-year-old is lying by looking at their facial expressions. Children under the age of seven or eight years have difficulty crafting a lie. After age seven or eight, children are much more capable liars and adults have difficulty detecting whether the child is telling the truth (Talwar et al., 2006).

INDIVIDUAL DIFFERENCES   As in other developmental research, individual differences exist in when children reach certain milestones in their theory of mind (Pellicano, 2010). For example, preschoolers who have more siblings, especially older siblings, perform better on theory of mind tasks than preschoolers with fewer siblings (McAlister & Peterson, 2007). Two-year-olds who talk with their parents about feelings frequently show better performance on theory of mind tasks (Ruffman, Slade, & Crowe, 2002), as do children who frequently engage in pretend play (Harris, 2000). Children who are deaf but have hearing parents perform more poorly on theory of mind tasks than deaf children raised by deaf parents, presumably because they have fewer opportunities to engage in communication with their parents about mental states (Courtin, 2000).

Executive function, which describes several functions (such as inhibition and planning) that are important for flexible, future-oriented behaviour, also may be connected to theory of mind development

theory of mind The awareness of one's own mental processes and the mental processes of others.

---

developmental **connection**

Research Methods: Experimental Research

Carole Peterson, Narrative Researcher

Although some people might not find children's storytelling interesting, Carole Peterson sees it differently. "I really enjoy children's views of their adventures and experiences," she says. A professor at Memorial University of Newfoundland, Dr. Peterson has studied issues around children's narrative (storytelling) skills, including parents' input and socio-economic factors.

In a recent study (Peterson & Roberts, 2003), Dr. Peterson wondered whether there would be any correspondence between children's recall of a recent event and their same-sex parents' recall of the same situation. Her question was based on theories about the development of children's gender identification and research on differences in language exposure between boys and girls. She examined preschool and school-age children's

recall of their recent medical treatments for severe injuries and their parents' recall of the same events, and found positive correlations in the number of words, descriptors, and connecting words (e.g., then, and, and so on) between the narratives of school-age girls and those of their mothers. Other dyads (e.g., mother–younger daughter, father–older daughter, mother–older son, and so on) showed few or none of these correlations. These findings—leading to the title of the paper, "Like Mother, Like Daughter: Similarities in Narrative Style"—may reflect both the long time mothers typically spend with their daughters and the mutual influence of narrative styles that occur during their interactions.

Source: From author's personal correspondence with Dr. Carole Peterson.

(Doherty, 2008). Cultural and genetic factors may also influence a child's awareness of his or her own state of mind as well as that of others, an aspect of executive functioning. For example, parental expectations, largely a product of cultural norms, may be a factor. Impulse control is more highly valued and expected in children from China than children from Western cultures. A gene (DRD4) related to hyperactivity is prevalent in Western cultures whereas it is very rare in Asian cultures, thereby linking the interaction of environment and genetics to impulse control (Sabbagh et al., 2006).

Another individual difference in understanding the mind involves autism (Doherty, 2008). To learn how theory of mind differs in children with autism, see Connecting through Research.

THEORY OF MIND AND AUTISM   Another individual difference in understanding the mind involves autism (Doherty, 2008; Tager-Flusberg, 2007). Autism Canada defines autism spectrum disorder (ASD) as a complex neurobiological condition that can not only affect normal body function of the gastrointestinal, immune, hepatic, endocrine, and nervous systems, but also impacts normal brain development (Autism Canada, 2011). Approximately one in 200 Canadian children is estimated to have some sort of autism spectrum disorder (Autism Society of Canada, 2004). Autism can usually be diagnosed by the age of three years, and sometimes earlier. Children with autism show a number of behaviours different from children their age, including deficits in social interaction and communication as well as repetitive behaviours or interests. They often show indifference toward others, in many instances preferring to be alone and showing more interest in objects than people. It now is accepted that autism is linked to genetic and brain abnormalities (Iacoboni & Dapretto, 2006).

Children and adults with autism have difficulty in social interactions, often ascribed to huge deficits in theory of mind. Researchers have found that autistic children have difficulty in developing a theory of mind, especially in understanding others' beliefs and emotions (Harris, 2006). Although children with autism tend to demonstrate poor reasoning in false-belief tasks (Peterson, 2005), they can perform much better on reasoning tasks requiring an understanding of physical causality.

However, it is important to keep in mind that autism is a spectrum of disorders, and so autistic children are not a homogeneous group. Some have less severe social and communication problems than others. For example, higher-functioning autistic children show reasonable progress in understanding others' desires (Harris, 2006).

A further important consideration in thinking about autism and theory of mind is that autistic children's difficulty in understanding others' beliefs and emotions might not be due solely to theory of mind deficits, but also to other aspects of cognition such as problems in focusing attention or some general intellectual impairment (Renner, Grofer Klinger, & Klinger, 2006). Some recent theories of autism suggest that weaknesses in executive functioning may relate to the problems that some people with autism have on theory of mind tasks. Other theories have pointed out that typically developing individuals process information by extracting the big picture, whereas those with autism process information in a very detailed, almost obsessive way. It may be that in autism, a number of different but related deficits lead to the social cognitive deficits (Rajendran & Mitchell, 2007).

To this point, we have studied many ideas about cognitive development in early childhood. For a review, see the **Reach Your Learning Objectives** section at the end of this chapter.

Language Development

LO4 Summarize how language develops in early childhood.

As you learned in Chapter 5, most infants go from crying to using words orally. As young children learn the special features of their own language, there are extensive regularities in how they acquire that particular language (Berko Gleason, 2009). These rule systems include morphology (the meaningfulness of parts of words), syntax (how words should be ordered in a sentence), semantics (the meaning of words, phrases, and sentences), and pragmatics (rules of conversation).

developmental **connection**

Research Methods: Experimental Research

Understanding Phonology and Morphology

During the preschool years, most children gradually become more sensitive to the sounds of spoken words and become increasingly capable of producing all the sounds of their language. By the time children are three years of age, they can produce all the vowel sounds and most of the consonant sounds (Menn & Stoel-Gammon, 2009). In fact, children have fun rhyming words. This demonstrates an increasing understanding of **phonology**, *the study of how sounds are organized and used.*

By the time children move beyond two-word utterances they demonstrate a knowledge of **rules of morphology**, *the study of the structure and form of words, including inflection, derivation, and compound words* (Tager-Flusberg & Zukowski, 2009). Children begin using the plural and possessive forms of nouns (such as *dogs* and *dog's*). They put appropriate endings on verbs (such as *-s* when the subject is third-person singular and *-ed* for the past tense). They use prepositions (such as *in* and *on*), articles (such as *a* and *the*), and various forms of the verb *to be* (such as "I am going to the store"). Some of the best evidence for changes in children's use of morphological rules occurs in their overgeneralization of the rules, as when a preschool child says "foots" instead of "feet," or "goed" instead of "went."

In a classic experiment that was designed to study children's knowledge of morphological rules, such as how to make a plural, Jean Berko (1958) presented preschool children and first-grade children with cards such as the one shown in Figure 7.15. Children were asked to look at the card while the experimenter read aloud the words on the card. Then the children were asked to supply the missing word. This might sound easy, but Berko was interested in the children's ability to apply the appropriate morphological rule, in this case to say "wugs" with the *z* sound that indicates the plural.

Although the children's answers were not perfect, they were much better than chance. What makes Berko's study impressive is that most of the words were made up for the experiment. Thus, the children could not base their responses on remembering past instances of hearing the words. That they could make the plurals or past tenses of words they had never heard before was proof that they knew the morphological rules.

Changes in Syntax and Semantics

Preschool children also learn and apply rules of **syntax**, *the formation of gramatically correct sentences* (Lieven, 2008; Tager-Flusberg & Zukowski, 2009). They show a growing mastery of complex rules for how words should be ordered. Consider *wh-* questions, such as "Where is Daddy going?" or "What is that boy doing?" To ask these questions properly, the child must know two important differences between *wh-* questions and affirmative statements (for instance, "Daddy is going to work" and "That boy is

phonology The study of how sounds are organized and used.

rules of morphology The study of the structure and form of words, including inflection, derivation, and compound words.

syntax The formation of gramatically correct sentences.

Figure 7.15

Stimuli in Berko's Study of Young Children's Understanding of Morphological Rules

In Jean Berko's (1958) study, young children were presented with cards, such as this one with a "wug" on it. Then the children were asked to supply the missing word; in supplying the missing word, they had to say it correctly too. "Wugs" is the correct response here.

This is a wug.

Now there is another one.
There are two of them.
There are two _____.

semantics The meaning of words

- - - - - developmental **connection** - -

Stability and Change

←- - - - - - - - - - - - - - - - - - -

waiting for the school bus"). First, a *wh*- word must be added at the beginning of the sentence. Second, the auxiliary verb must be inverted—that is, exchanged with the subject of the sentence. Young children learn quite early where to put the *wh*- word, but they take much longer to learn the auxiliary-inversion rule. Thus, preschool children might ask, "Where Daddy is going?" and "What that boy is doing?"

Gains in **semantics**, *the meaning of words*, also characterize early childhood. Vocabulary development is dramatic (Pan & Uccelli, 2009). Some experts have concluded that between 18 months and 6 years of age, young children learn about one new word every waking hour (Gelman & Kalish, 2006)! By the time they enter first grade, it is estimated that children know about 14,000 words (Clark, 1993).

Advances in Pragmatics

Changes in pragmatics also characterize young children's language development (Bryant, 2009). A six-year-old is simply a much better conversationalist than a two-year-old is. What are some of the improvements in pragmatics during the preschool years?

Young children begin to engage in extended discourse (Akhtar & Herold, 2008, p. 581). For example, they learn culturally specific rules of conversation and politeness and become sensitive to the need to adapt their speech in different settings. They even learn to tell white lies (Lee, 2010). Their developing linguistic skills and increasing ability to take the perspective of others contribute to their generation of more competent narratives.

As children get older, they become increasingly able to talk about things that are not here (grandma's house, for example) and not now (what happened to them yesterday or might happen tomorrow, for example). A preschool child can tell you what she wants for lunch tomorrow, something that would not have been possible at the two-word stage of language development.

University of Waterloo researchers Daniela O'Neill, Rebecca Main, and Renata Ziemski (2009) examined peer-to-peer conversations of preschoolers. They found the children overwhelmingly initiated conversation to express a particular personal desire or need, or to direct the listener to do something. The subject matter of the conversations led the researchers to surmise that children may have used their developing sense of theory of mind to establish mutual understanding with their listener. Further, around four to five years of age, children develop a sense of audience. For example, even four-year-old children speak differently to a two-year-old than to a same-aged peer; they use shorter sentences with the two-year-old. They also speak differently to an adult than to a same-aged peer, using more polite and formal language with the adult.

Young Children's Literacy

Early precursors of literacy and academic success include language skills, phonological and syntactic knowledge, letter identification, and conceptual knowledge about print and its conventions and functions (Morrow, 2009; Otto, 2010). Children should be active participants and be immersed in a wide range of interesting listening, talking, writing, and reading experiences (Beaty & Pratt, 2011). A recent study revealed that children whose mothers had more education had more advanced emergent literacy levels than children whose mothers had less education (Korat, 2009). Another recent study found that literacy experiences (such as how often the child was read to), the quality of the mother's engagement with her child (such as attempts to cognitively stimulate the child), and provision of learning materials (such as age-appropriate learning materials and books) were important home literacy experiences in low-income families that were linked to the children's language development in positive ways (Rodriguez et al., 2009). Instruction should be built on what children already know about oral language, reading, and writing. The following three longitudinal studies indicate the importance of early language skills and children's school readiness:

- Phonological awareness, letter name and sound knowledge, and naming speed in kindergarten were linked to reading success in the first and second grade (Schattschneider et al., 2004).
- Children's early home environment influenced their early language skills, which in turn predicted their readiness for school (Forget-Dubois et al., 2009).
- The number of letters children knew in kindergarten was highly correlated (.52) with their reading achievement in high school (Stevenson & Newman, 1986).

Children's speech in the preschool years shows another characteristic: questions. Children's earliest questions appear around the age of three, and by the age of five they have just about exhausted the adults around them with "why" questions. Children's questions yield clues about their mental development and reflect intellectual curiosity, signalling the emergence of an interest in verbal reasoning and figuring out why things are the way they are.

To this point, we have discussed language development in early childhood. For a review, see the **Reach Your Learning Objectives** section at the end of this chapter.

Early Childhood Education

LO5 Identify different approaches to early childhood education.

In the 1840s, Friedrich Froebel's concern for quality education for young children led to the founding of the kindergarten—literally, "a garden for children." The founder of the kindergarten understood that like growing plants, raising children required careful nurturing.

The Child-Centred Kindergarten

As noted earlier in the chapter, both parents work in almost 70 percent of Canadian homes; consequently, for many all-day kindergarten seemed to be a panacea. However, because the all-day program hours usually end at 2:30 or 3:00, and most parents work beyond that, after-school programs also are part of the scene. Quite often children go to daycare, then to kindergarten, then back to daycare. In each scenario, curriculum is set to assist the child's social, emotional, and academic development.

In the **child-centred kindergarten**, *education involves the whole child and includes concern for the child's physical, cognitive, and social development* (Follari, 2007). Instruction is organized around the child's needs, interests, and learning styles. Emphasis is on the process of learning, rather than on what is learned (Morrison, 2008). Each child follows a unique developmental pattern, and young children learn through first-hand experience with people and materials. Moreover, play is considered extremely important in the child's total development. These programs emphasize experimenting, exploring, discovering, trying out, restructuring, speaking, and listening.

The kindergarten experience varies across Canada (Friendly & Prabhu, 2010). Only New Brunswick has a compulsory kindergarten program; all other provinces and territories offer voluntary programs. The Northwest Territories and Yukon offer either half- or full-day kindergarten. Most provinces and Nunavut offer half-day programs (the exceptions being Ontario and Quebec, which offer full-day kindergarten). As noted in Chapter 6, Ontario began moving toward full-day kindergarten at both the junior and senior level, beginning in selected schools in 2010–2011 (Ontario Government, 2010). The expectation is that the full-day program will lay the foundation for the skills, concepts, and positive orientation to learning necessary for successful learning in subsequent grades.

Yukon, Ontario, and Quebec offer kindergarten programs for both four- and five-year-olds (sometimes referred to as junior and senior kindergarten, respectively). All other jurisdictions provide only five-year-olds with kindergarten. The curriculum for kindergarten is different for each province and territory except in Yukon, which adopts the British Columbia curriculum. Most kindergarten programs have targeted achievement goals in such areas as language arts, social sciences, art, physical education, and math. Manitoba uses an "activity-based approach," Saskatchewan uses "learning through play," while New Brunswick employs a "student-centred" focus. In Nunavut, the Elders Advisory Committee works with teachers to develop an Inuit perspective to the curriculum, focusing on knowledge, skills, and values.

The Montessori Approach

Montessori schools are patterned after the educational philosophy of Maria Montessori (1870–1952), an Italian physician-turned-educator who crafted a revolutionary approach to young children's education at the beginning of the twentieth century. Her work began in Rome with a group

The Child-Centred Kindergarten

Developmentally Appropriate and Inappropriate Practices

Young Children's Literacy and Numeracy

Education for Children Who Are Disadvantaged

child-centred kindergarten Education that involves the whole child and includes concern for the child's physical, cognitive, and social development.

of children who were intellectually disabled. She was successful in teaching them to read, write, and pass examinations designed for normal children. Some time later, she turned her attention to poor children from the slums of Rome and had similar success in teaching them. Her approach has since been adopted by many nursery schools.

The **Montessori approach** *is a philosophy of education in which children are given considerable freedom and spontaneity in choosing activities.* They are allowed to move from one activity to another as they desire. The teacher acts as a facilitator, rather than a director of learning. The teacher shows the child how to perform intellectual activities, demonstrates interesting ways to explore curriculum materials, and offers help when the child requests it. "By encouraging children to make decisions from an early age, Montessori programs seek to develop self-regulated problem solvers who can make choices and manage their time effectively" (Hyson, Copple, & Jones, 2006, p. 14).

Some developmentalists favour the Montessori approach, but others believe that it neglects children's social development. For example, although Montessori fosters independence and the development of cognitive skills, it de-emphasizes verbal interaction between the teacher and child and peer interaction. Montessori's critics also argue that it restricts imaginative play.

Developmentally Appropriate and Inappropriate Practices

A number of educators and psychologists believe that preschool and young elementary school children learn best through active, hands-on teaching methods such as games and dramatic play. They recognize that children develop at varying rates and that schools need to allow for these individual differences (Miranda, 2004). They also believe that schools should focus on improving children's social development, as well as their cognitive development (Bredekamp, 2011; Kostelnik, Soderman, & Whiren, 2011). Educators refer to this type of schooling as **developmentally appropriate practice**, *which is based on knowledge of the typical development of children within an age span (age appropriateness) and the uniqueness of the child (individual appropriateness).* Developmentally appropriate practice emphasizes the importance of creating settings that encourage children to be active learners and reflect children's interests and capabilities (Bredekamp, 2011; Kostelnik, Soderman, & Whiren, 2011). Desired outcomes for developmentally appropriate practice include thinking critically, working cooperatively, solving problems, developing self-regulatory skills, and enjoying learning. The emphasis in DAP is on the process of learning rather than its content (Barbarin & Miller, 2009; Ritchie, Maxwell, & Bredekamp, 2009).

Young Children's Literacy and Numeracy

Literacy is important for school achievement. Phonological awareness, letter name and sound knowledge, and naming speed in kindergarten have been linked to reading success in Grades 1 and 2 (Schattschneider et al., 2004). What should an early literacy program have? First, instruction should be built on what children already know about oral language, reading, and writing. Also, reading should be integrated into the broad communication process, which includes speaking, listening, and writing, as well as other communication systems, such as art, math, and music (Christie, Vukelich, & Enz, 2007; Combs, 2006; May, 2006). Moreover, parents and teachers should take time to read to children from a wide variety of poetry, fiction, and non-fiction (Temple et al., 2005). During the shared reading session, parents and teachers need to engage the child in working together at vocabulary, word recognition, and actually looking at the text, which most children do not do, as adults read to them (Phillips, Norris, & Anderson, 2008). Adults also should present models for young children to emulate by using language appropriately, listening and responding to children's talk, and engaging in their own reading and writing. Johnston, Barnes, and Desrochers (2008) suggest that individualized attention should address the different areas of developmental challenge that preschoolers encounter in developing literacy skills. Ability to infer and follow a story line, the richness of a child's vocabulary, and issues around dealing with text material need to be addressed early to promote later literacy development.

Montessori approach An educational philosophy in which children are given considerable freedom and spontaneity in choosing activities.

critical thinking

Put yourself in the shoes of a single parent with a kindergarten-aged child. Your job demands that you be onsite from 9 to 5:30; your child may attend an all-day kindergarten from 9 to 2:30. Because you live in an urban setting, you are able to manage this by enrolling your child in a daycare. The daycare provides lunch, walks the children to school, and meets them after school to walk them back to the daycare facility. How do you think you would manage this if you lived in a rural setting without such daycare accommodations? What criteria would you use in choosing a daycare for your child? What adjustments would both you and the child have to make? How much energy at the end of the day would you and your child have? What additional stresses may you encounter?

developmentally appropriate practice Education based on knowledge of the typical development of children within an age span (age appropriateness) and the uniqueness of the child (individual appropriateness).

developmental **connection**

Piaget; Vygotsky; Information Processing Theory

Finally, children should be encouraged to be active participants in the learning process, rather than passive recipients of knowledge. This can be accomplished by using activities that stimulate experimentation with talking, listening, writing, and reading (Barone, Hardman, & Taylor, 2006). Where reading problems are suspected, Vellutino and colleagues (2006) suggest that one-on-one reading remedial assistance be offered throughout kindergarten and into Grade 1.

Numeracy is just as important as literacy in early childhood. Most children at age two begin to learn a few number words, and by age five will be able to count backwards from ten and work at counting up from pre-designated numbers (e.g., "start counting from seven") (Canadian Child Care Federation, 2009). They can use the concept of ordinal place to order such things as the sequence of events, winners of a race, or their top five favourite toys. In the next year they will expand their counting range to one hundred, the use of units of ten, and simple multiplication and fractions. Like literacy, numeracy skills need to be addressed and fostered through interactive activity with adults.

Education for Children Who Are Disadvantaged

A risk factor for children's readiness for formal education is the education approach of another culture. In one longitudinal study in Montreal (Pagani, Jalbert, Lapointe, & Hébert, 2006), children with foreign-born parents who did not speak French at home lagged behind children with Canadian-born French-speaking parents in number and receptive vocabulary skills at the beginning of kindergarten. The deficit in number skills was due to the children's difficulty with French. Hence, language knowledge appears to be the key for the academic success of children in a linguistic minority. This result is corroborated by another Quebec study's finding that preschoolers' storytelling skills were related to their school readiness (Fiorentino & Howe, 2004). Teachers certainly can help children in this situation: as the study by Pagani and colleagues showed, linguistic-minority children who achieved better progress in verbal skills over time tended to have teachers who were willing to switch away from child-driven methods popular in Canadian schools to adult-driven techniques that many immigrant families feel comfortable with.

For deaf children, school readiness appears to involve learning sign language at home as their native language, along with a familiarity with oral language (Meristo et al., 2007). Children with a background in both forms of language (with sign language as their native language) developed a better ability to express a theory of mind promoting the understanding of the emotional states of others when compared to deaf children who did not develop sign language within the home from infancy. Bailes and associates (2009) stress the importance of parents (especially hearing parents) of deaf children using American Sign Language as early as possible in interactions with their infant. The evidence suggests that later literacy and academic success depends on learning a language as the child experiences the first few years of life to develop a medium in which they can interact with and learn from their environment.

Another risk factor for school readiness is low income. Children from poor families tend to fare worse in their readiness to learn. In one study, Canadian children from lower-income families were more likely to have delays in cognitive and language development in the preschool years and were more likely to repeat a grade in elementary schools than their peers. Similarly, in a recent analysis of five-year-olds (Thomas, 2006), household income, children's activities (the likelihood of being read to daily and participation in organized sports and other physical activities), and school readiness variables (vocabulary and number skills) were found to be interrelated. These results suggest that children in low-income families may be disadvantaged in the area of school preparedness because of adults' lack of time and resources for activities that may promote such readiness.

What can be done to solve this problem? A comprehensive child care approach may be an answer. In Canada, one of the programs that follows this approach is Aboriginal Head Start. Launched in 1995 and funded by Health Canada, this program mirrors Project Head Start in the United States, which was started in the 1960s. The U.S. program was based on a belief that compensatory intervention to help low-income children to succeed in school should involve both academic and non-academic aspects of their lives, such as health and the local community.

Aboriginal Head Start is offered in 168 sites across the country, serving almost 7,000 children up to age 6 and their families. The program recognizes not only the need to provide comprehensive care to preschool children, but also the importance of Aboriginal cultures on the children. As a result, the program consists of six components, including culture and language training for children, preschool education, promotion of caregivers' health, parental input in management and activities, and community resources for families. Elders and parents in each locale also participate in developing projects appropriate for the community (Public Health Agency of Canada, 2013). In a pilot study to assess the success of Head Start programs in urban and northern communities in Alberta, researchers found graduates of the program scored as well in verbal abilities and language development as age-matched non-Aboriginal peers, as assessed by standardized tests (dela Cruz & McCarthy, 2010).

Jessica Ball (2009) notes that community-based program staff, teachers, and speech pathologists have described language problems among Aboriginal preschoolers that will interfere with "their later learning and overall development" (p. 20). Fewer Aboriginal children are learning their indigenous language, a significant threat to Aboriginal culture. One possible approach is being explored by researchers from the University of Calgary, who suggest the use of oral storytelling coupled with reading to develop literacy skills in preschoolers (McKeough et al., 2008). The study is not yet completed, but the idea is that storytelling is a forerunner to reading and is a significant part of Aboriginal tradition. As such, it motivates and prepares preschoolers to develop language skills necessary for literacy.

To this point, we have studied a number of ideas about early childhood education. For a review, see the **Reach Your Learning Objectives** section at the end of this chapter.

reach your learning Objectives

Physical Development

LO1 Identify physical changes in early childhood.

Body Growth	■ The average child grows in height and gains between 2.2 and 3.2 kg a year during early childhood. Growth patterns vary individually.
	■ Some children are unusually short because of congenital problems, a physical or emotional problem that develops in childhood, or growth hormone deficiency.
The Brain	■ Some of the brain's increase in size is due to increases in the number and size of nerve endings, while some is due to myelination.
	■ From ages 3 to 15, local patterns of the brain experience major changes. The frontal lobe areas involving planning and organizing functions show rapid growth between ages 3 and 6, while temporal and parietal lobe areas responsible for language and spatial functions develop quickly from age 6 to puberty.
	■ Increasing brain maturation contributes to improved cognitive abilities.
Motor Development	■ Gross motor skills increase dramatically during early childhood.
	■ Children become increasingly adventuresome as their gross motor skills improve.
	■ Fine motor skills also improve substantially during early childhood.

Health and Wellness

LO2 Identify the factors involved in determining the health and wellness of children in Canada and in other countries.

Nutrition and Exercise	■ Energy requirements vary according to basal metabolism, rate of growth, and level of activity.
	■ A special concern is that too many young children are being raised on diets that are too high in fat. Eating habits formed in early childhood are critical to healthy eating habits and good health as the child matures.
Wellness in Canada	■ Congenital anomalies, cancer, diseases of the nervous system, unintentional injuries, and exposure to parental smoking are major health concerns for children in early childhood.
Wellness in Other Countries	■ Poor countries around the world have higher mortality rates for children under age five than do Western industrialized nations.
	■ Pneumonia, dehydration from diarrheal diseases, and preventable injuries are the main causes of death among the world's children.
	■ Child deaths due to the transmission of HIV/AIDS from parents have increased in poor countries.
	■ Many childhood diseases and deaths can be prevented by a reduction in poverty and improvements in nutrition, sanitation, education, and health services.

Cognitive Development

LO3 Describe three views of the cognitive changes that occur in early childhood.

Piaget's Preoperational Stage	■ This stage marks the beginning of the ability to reconstruct at the level of thought what has been established in behaviour.
	■ The two substages are the symbolic function substage and the intuitive thought substage.
	■ Preoperational thinking is characterized by egocentrism, animism, and centration, the last of which can be shown in the lack of conservation.
Vygotsky's Theory	■ The zone of proximal development refers to a range of tasks too difficult for children to master alone, but that can be learned with the guidance and assistance of people with greater expertise.
	■ Scaffolding involves changing support over the course of a teaching session to fit a learner's current performance level.
	■ Language plays a key role in guiding cognition.
	■ Teaching strategies may be based on Vygotsky's theory.
Information Processing	■ Preschool children's attention is strongly influenced by the salient features of a task.
	■ Short-term memory increases during early childhood.
	■ Appropriate cues can improve young children's long-term memory. At the same time, children can be led into developing false memories.
	■ Preschool children are capable of learning simple problem-solving strategies.
	■ Theory of mind refers to thoughts about how mental processes work. Children's theory of mind changes during the early childhood years. By age five, children have some understanding of false beliefs and use past accuracy to judge sources of information.

Language Development

LO4 Summarize how language develops in early childhood

- Children's grasp of the morphological rules improves during early childhood, as Jean Berko's (1958) study and overregularization errors show.
- At age 6, the size of a child's speaking vocabulary is about 14,000 words.
- Children have some understanding of the parts of speech.
- Early childhood also witnesses improved performance in pragmatics.
- Children's questions indicate not only language skills, but also intellectual curiosity at this age.

Phonology and Morphology

- Children's understanding of phonology and morphology improves as children age; in other words, they demonstrate a better understanding of how sounds are organized and used as well as the structure and form of words, including inflection, suffixes and prefixes, and compound words.

Syntax and Semantics

- Children's grasp of syntax and semantics improves as evidenced by their mastery of grammatically correct sentence structure.

Pragmatics

- Children become increasingly more adept in pragmatics as they are increasingly able to understand the social context, have a sense of audience, and become more capable of conversation.

Young Children's Literacy

- Studies indicate that exposure to reading materials is important to the child's development of language skills.
- Studies also indicated that early development of language skills is highly linked to the child's readiness for school.

Early Childhood Education

LO5 Identify different approaches to early childhood education.

The Child-Centred Kindergarten

- The child-centred kindergarten emphasizes the whole child's physical, cognitive, and social development.
- There is a very wide range of kindergarten programs across Canada.
- In a Montessori school, children are given considerable freedom and spontaneity in choosing activities.

Developmentally Appropriate and Inappropriate Practices

- Developmentally appropriate practice focuses on the typical patterns of children and the uniqueness of each child.
- Literacy skills in early childhood are related to reading performance in elementary and secondary schools.
- Development of numeracy skills between the ages of two and five are critical to later number learning.

Young Children's Literacy and Numeracy	■ Literacy is important for school achievement.
	■ Early literacy programs should include instruction built on what children already know; reading integrated into the communication process; a wide variety of reading materials; adults as models for using language appropriately; individualized attention; children as active participants in the learning process.
	■ Numeracy is just as important as literacy in early childhood.
	■ Numeracy skills should be addressed and fostered through interactive activity with adults.
Education for Children Who Are Disadvantaged	■ Child-driven teaching may not help linguistic-minority children achieve progress in verbal skills.
	■ Comprehensive preschool programs that provide academic and non-academic support, such as Head Start, may have positive effects on children from disadvantaged economic backgrounds.

review ---> *connect* ---> reflect

review

Describe the development of gross and fine motor skills in early childhood. **LO1**

What role do nutrition and exercise play in early childhood? **LO2**

Compare and contrast Piaget's and Vygotsky's theories of cognitive development. **LO3**

What is theory of mind and how does this change in the early childhood years? **LO3**

Describe the primary changes in language development in early childhood. **LO4**

What is meant by a child-centred kindergarten? **LO5**

connect

In this chapter you read about children and lying. In your interaction with young children, have you been able to tell when they are telling the truth and when they might be lying? What are some of the signals that might be tell-tale? How does language development play a role in a child's ability to tell a lie successfully?

reflect *Your Own Personal Journey of Life*

What were your eating habits like as a young child? In what ways are they similar to or different from your current eating habits? Were your early eating habits a forerunner of whether or not you have weight problems today? If you are a parent, have your eating habits changed? If you are not a parent, do you think your eating habits may change when and if you decide to become a parent? Why or why not?

Mc Graw Hill Education **connect**

McGraw-Hill Connect provides you with a powerful tool for improving academic performance and truly mastering course material. You can diagnose your knowledge with pre- and post-tests, identify the areas where you need help, search the entire learning package, including the eBook, for content specific to the topic you're studying, and add these resources to your personalized study plan. CONNECT for *Life-Span Development*, fifth Canadian edition, offers the following:

■ chapter-specific online quizzes

■ groupwork

■ presentations

■ writing assignments

■ case studies

■ and much more!

Visit CONNECT today!

CHAPTER 8

Socio-Emotional Development in Early Childhood

CHAPTER OUTLINE

The Self and Emotional Development

LO1 Discuss the emergence of the self and emotional development in early childhood.

The Self

Emotional Development

Moral Development and Gender

LO2 Summarize moral development and gender in early childhood.

Moral Development

Gender

Families

LO3 Explain how families can influence young children's development.

Parenting

Divorce

Sibling Relationships and Birth Order

Peer Relations, Play, and Social Media

LO4 Describe the roles of peers, play, and social media in young children's development.

Peer Relations

Play

Social Media

"What are little boys made of? Frogs and snails and puppy dogs' tails. What are little girls made of? Sugar and spice and all that's nice."

—J.O. HALLIWELL, NINETEENTH-CENTURY ENGLISH AUTHOR

Is the Sky the Limit for a Parent's Love?

How often does a mother write a song for her children? And how often does such a song draw tears from strangers outside the family? For Canadian songwriter and singer Amy Sky's children, the answers would have been "one for each child" and "all the time."

Although autobiographical—talking about the milestones of her own life—the song for her first child, "I Will Take Care of You," showed an unconditional commitment to raising her daughter. She promised that:

I will take care of you

The very best that I can

With all of the love here in my heart

And all of the strength in my hands

Your every joy I'll share

For every tear I'll be there

My whole life through

I will take care of you

Her immense motherly love did not subside with the arrival of her second-born. To her, seeing him grow was like witnessing "Ordinary Miracles" every day, something that she would cherish even when her boy became a grown-up.

Amy Sky's lyrics and decision to write the songs demonstrate a parent's love for her children. At the same time, as a successful song writer and performer, she may experience the same challenges that many parents face today, like coordinating with spouses in their caregiving approach and maintaining a family–work balance, especially when one or both parents have to work unusual schedules. This chapter will examine these parenting issues and how they may affect the child.

In addition, significant developmental tasks for children in early childhood—like an emergent understanding of the self, an awareness of one's own biological sex, moral reasoning and action, and relationships with siblings and peers—will also be discussed. To students, researchers, and policy-makers, these make interesting research topics and policy issues. To parents, however, each of these pieces in the child's early childhood—like every one before this time and every one after—is truly an "ordinary miracle."

The Self

Emotional Development

The Self and Emotional Development

LO1 Discuss the emergence of the self and emotional development in early childhood.

Amy Sky's songs on motherhood reflect on the love and importance of parents. At the same time, as young children's social worlds are expanding and they start to take initiatives on their own, they learn more and more about people other than their parents, like their peers . . . and themselves. We will begin our discussion of socio-emotional development with a look at the child's understanding of the self and emotions.

The Self

We learned in Chapter 6 that toward the end of the second year of life, children develop a sense of self. During early childhood, some important developments in the self take place.

Initiative versus Guilt

According to Erik Erikson (1968), the psychosocial stage that characterizes early childhood is initiative versus guilt. By now, children have become convinced that they are their own persons. During early childhood, children use their perceptual, motor, cognitive, and language skills to make things happen. They have a surplus of energy that permits them to approach new areas that seem desirable—even if they seem dangerous—with undiminished zest and some increased sense of direction. On their own initiative, then, children at this stage move out exuberantly into a wider social world.

The great governor of initiative is *conscience*. Children now not only feel afraid of being found out, but also begin to hear the inner voice of self-observation, self-guidance, and self-punishment. Their initiative and enthusiasm may bring them not only rewards, but also punishments. Widespread disappointment at this stage may lead to an unleashing of guilt that lowers the child's self-esteem.

Self-Understanding

self-understanding The child's cognitive representation of self, the substance and content of self-conceptions.

In Erikson's portrait of early childhood, the young child clearly has begun to develop **self-understanding**, *which is the representation of self, the substance and content of self-conceptions* (Harter, 2006). Though not the whole of personal identity, self-understanding provides its rational underpinnings. Mainly through interviews, researchers have probed many aspects of children's self-understanding. Recent studies show that young children are more psychologically aware—of themselves and others—than was once thought (Carpendale & Lewis, 2011; Hughes & Ensor, 2010; Thompson & Virmani, 2010). This increased psychological awareness reflects young children's expanding psychological sophistication.

developmental **connection**

Infant Sensory Development

Early self-understanding involves self-recognition. Recall that recognizing one's body parts in a mirror takes place by approximately 18 months of age (see Chapter 6). A sense of "me" emerges later in the second year and early in the third year. In early childhood, young children distinguish themselves from others through many physical and material attributes. Says four-year-old Sandra, "I'm different from Jennifer because I have brown hair and she has blond hair." Says four-year-old Ralph, "I am different from Solomon because I am taller and I am different from my sister because I have a bicycle." Preschool children often describe themselves in terms of activities such as play. Although young children mainly describe themselves in terms of concrete, observable features and action tendencies, at about four to five years of age, as they hear others use psychological trait and emotion terms, they begin to include these in their own self-descriptions (Marsh, Ellis, & Craven, 2002). Thus, in a self-description, a four-year-old might say, "I'm not scared. I'm always happy."

Young children's self-descriptions are typically unrealistically positive, as reflected in the comment of the four-year-old who says he is always happy, which he is not (Harter, 2006). They express this optimism because they don't yet distinguish between their desired competence and their actual competence, tend to confuse ability and effort (thinking that differences in ability can be changed as easily as can differences in effort), don't engage in spontaneous social comparison of their abilities with those of others, and tend to compare their present abilities with what they could do at an earlier age (by which they usually look quite good). Perhaps as adults we should all be so optimistic about our abilities (Thompson, 2008).

Understanding Others

--developmental **connection** ---------

Theory of Mind

Children also make advances in their understanding of others in early childhood (Carpendale & Lewis, 2011). As we saw in Chapter 7, "Physical and Cognitive Development in Early Childhood," young children's theory of mind includes understanding that other people have emotions and desires. And at about four to five years, children not only start describing themselves in terms of psychological traits, but also begin to perceive others in terms of psychological traits. Thus, a four year-old might say, "My teacher is nice."

Individual differences characterize young children's social understanding (Laible & Thompson, 2007). Some young children are better than others at understanding what people are feeling and what they desire, for example. To some degree, these individual differences are linked to conversations caregivers have with young children about other people's feelings and desires, and children's opportunities to observe others talking about people's feelings and desires. For example, a mother might say to her three-year-old, "You should think about Raphael's feelings next time before you hit him."

Both the extensive theory of mind research and the recent research on young children's social understanding underscore that young children are not as egocentric as Piaget envisioned (Sokol, Snjezana, & Muller, 2010). Leading expert on children's socio-emotional development Ross Thompson (2009b) recently commented about how amazed he is that Piaget's concept of egocentrism has become so ingrained in people's thinking about young children given the fact that the current research on social awareness in infancy and early childhood is so dissonant with Piaget's egocentrism concept.

Emotional Development

Children develop a better and better understanding of emotions in early childhood because of greater cognitive skills, knowledge of the self, and social interactions in this age than in infancy.

Self-Conscious Emotions

As noted in Chapter 6, even young infants experience emotions such as joy and fear. But to experience *self-conscious emotions*, children must be able to refer to themselves and be aware of themselves as distinct from others (Lewis, 2007). Pride, shame, embarrassment, and guilt are examples of self-conscious emotions. Self-conscious emotions do not appear to develop until self-awareness appears in the last half of the second year of life.

During the early childhood years, emotions such as pride and guilt become more common. They are especially influenced by parents' responses to children's behaviour. For example, a young child may experience shame when a parent says, "You should feel bad about biting your sister."

Emotion Language and Understanding of Emotion

Among the most important changes in emotional development in early childhood are the gradually increased use of emotion language and the understanding of emotion. Preschoolers are also learning about the causes and consequences of feelings (Denham, Bassett, & Wyatt, 2007). Young children increasingly understand that certain situations are likely to evoke particular emotions, facial expressions indicate specific emotions, emotions affect behaviour, and emotions can be used to influence others' emotions (Cole et al., 2009). A recent meta-analysis revealed that emotion knowledge (such as understanding emotional cues; for example, when a young child understands that a peer feels sad about being left out of a game) was positively related to three- to five-year-olds' social competence (such as offering an empathic response to the child left out of a game) and negatively related to their internalizing (high level of anxiety, for example) and externalizing problems (high level of aggressive behaviour, for example) (Trentacosta & Fine, 2009). A recent study also found that young children's emotion understanding was linked to their prosocial behaviour (Ensor, Spencer, & Hughes, 2010).

At four to five years of age, children show an increased ability to reflect on emotions. They also begin to understand that the same event can elicit different feelings in different people. Moreover, they show a growing awareness of the need to control and manage emotions to meet social standards (Cole et al., 2009).

Shyness

What exactly is shyness? Carleton University researcher Robert Coplan has studied children's emotions extensively. In one study, Coplan identified two conditions when preschoolers tended to withdraw from peer interactions, conflicted shyness and social disinterest. "Conflicted shyness" refers to high anxiety toward social interactions, whereas "social disinterest" refers to children's preference to be on their own (Coplan, Prakash, O'Neil, & Armer, 2004). Conflicted shyness is negatively correlated to the perceived competence of children. Interestingly, the mother's overprotective tendency is related to the son's, not the daughter's, conflicted shyness. Neither perceived competence nor maternal overprotectiveness is related to social disinterest. In another study (Coplan & Armer, 2005), parental ratings of children's shyness were more strongly related to boys' withdrawn behaviour in school than they were to girls. This result suggests that shyness can lead to a higher risk of maladjustment for shy boys than for shy girls (Coplan & Armer, 2005).

Regulating Emotions

As we saw in Chapter 6, emotion regulation is an important aspect of development (Kopp, 2011). Emotion regulation plays a key role in children's ability to manage the demands and conflicts they face in interacting with others (Cole et al., 2009; Lewis, Todd, & Xu, 2011).

Emotion-Coaching and Emotion-Dismissing Parents

Parents can play an important role in helping young children regulate their emotions (Klimes-Dougan & Zeman, 2007; Stocker et al., 2007). Depending on how they talk with their children about emotion, parents can be described as taking an emotion-coaching or an emotion-dismissing approach (Gottman, 2008). *Emotion-coaching parents* monitor their children's emotions, view their children's negative emotions as opportunities for teaching, assist them in labelling emotions, and coach them in how to deal effectively with emotions. In contrast, *emotion-dismissing parents* deny, ignore, or change negative emotions.

Researchers have found that when interacting with their children, emotion-coaching parents are less rejecting, use more scaffolding and praise, and are more nurturing than emotion-dismissing parents. The children of emotion-coaching parents were better at soothing themselves when they got upset, more effective in regulating their negative affect, focused their attention better, and had fewer behaviour problems than the children of emotion-dismissing parents.

To this point, we have discussed a number of ideas about the self and emotional development. For a review, see the **Reach Your Learning Objectives** section at the end of this chapter.

Moral Development and Gender

LO2 Summarize moral development and gender in early childhood.

Moral Development

Moral development *involves the development of thoughts and feelings regarding standards of right and wrong and behaviours regarding rules and conventions about what people should do in their interactions*

critical thinking

Based on your experience and observations, are boys more shy than girls? What role do parents play in children's shyness? Is there a greater risk of maladjustment for shy boys than shy girls? Why or why not? How might a parent or older sibling help a shy child?

A young child expressing the emotion of shame, which occurs when a child evaluates his or her actions as not living up to standards. A child experiencing shame wishes to hide or disappear. **Why is shame called a self-conscious emotion?**

Moral Development

Gender

with others. Major developmental theories have focused on different aspects of moral development. Knowledge of morality and one's own sex is important for self-understanding and interaction with others. This knowledge develops rather rapidly in early childhood. In this section, we will look at how and what children know about the moral standard and sex differences in society.

Moral Feelings

Feelings of anxiety and guilt are central to the account of moral development provided by Freud's psychoanalytic theory (introduced in Chapter 1). According to Freud, to reduce anxiety, avoid punishment, and maintain parental affection, children identify with parents, internalize their standards of right and wrong, and thus form the *superego*, the moral element of personality.

Freud's ideas are not backed by research, but guilt certainly can motivate moral behaviour. Other emotions, however, also contribute to the child's moral development, including positive feelings. One important example is *empathy*, which is responding to another person's feelings with an emotion that echoes the other's feelings (Eisenberg, Fabes, & Spinrad, 2006).

Infants have the capacity for some purely empathic responses, but empathy often requires the ability to discern another's inner psychological states, or what is called *perspective taking*. Learning how to identify a wide range of emotional states in others and to anticipate what kinds of action will improve another person's emotional state help to advance children's moral development (Johansson, 2006).

Moral Reasoning

Interest in how the child thinks about moral issues was stimulated by Jean Piaget (1932). He extensively observed and interviewed children from ages 4 to 12. He watched them play marbles, seeking to learn how they used and thought about the game's rules. He also asked children questions about ethical rules—theft, lies, punishment, and justice, for example. Piaget concluded that children think in two distinctly different ways about morality:

- **Heteronomous morality** *occurs from approximately four to seven years of age. Justice and rules are conceived of as unchangeable properties of the world, removed from the control of people.*
- **Autonomous morality** *is displayed by older children (about 10 years of age and older). The child becomes aware that rules and laws are created by people and that in judging an action, one should consider the actor's intentions as well as the consequences.*

Children 7 to 10 years of age are in a transition between the two stages, showing some features of both.

Because preschool-age children are heteronomous moralists, they judge the rightness or goodness of behaviour by considering the consequences of the behaviour, not the intentions of the actor. For example, accidentally breaking 12 cups is considered worse than breaking 1 cup intentionally. For the moral autonomist, the reverse is true. The actor's intentions assume paramount importance.

The heteronomous thinker also believes that rules are unchangeable and are handed down by all-powerful authorities. When Piaget suggested that new rules be introduced into the game of marbles, the young children resisted. They insisted that the rules had always been the same and could not be altered. By contrast, older children—who were moral autonomists—recognized that rules are merely convenient, socially agreed-upon conventions, subject to change by consensus.

In addition, the heteronomous thinker believes in **imminent justice**, *the concept that if a rule is broken, punishment will be meted out immediately.* The young child believes that a violation is connected automatically to its punishment. Thus, young children often look around worriedly after doing something wrong, expecting inevitable punishment.

How do these changes in moral reasoning occur? According to Piaget, as children develop they become more sophisticated in thinking about social matters, especially about the possibilities and conditions of cooperation. This understanding comes about through the mutual give-and-take of peer relations. In the peer group, all members have similar power and status, plans are negotiated and coordinated, and disagreements are reasoned about and eventually settled. Parent–child relations, in which parents have the power and the child does not, are less likely to advance moral reasoning because rules are often handed down in an authoritarian way.

moral development Thoughts and feelings regarding standards of right and wrong and behaviours regarding rules and conventions about what people should do in their interactions with others.

- - developmental **connection** - - - - - - -

Freud's Psychoanalytical Theory

- - developmental **connection** - - - - - - -

Piaget's Cognitive Development Theory

heteronomous morality The first stage of moral development in Piaget's theory, occurring from approximately four to seven years of age. Justice and rules are conceived of as unchangeable properties of the world, removed from the control of people.

autonomous morality The second stage of moral development, displayed by older children (about 10 years of age and older). The child becomes aware that rules and laws are created by people and that in judging an action one should consider the actor's intentions as well as the consequences.

imminent justice The concept that if a rule is broken, punishment will be meted out immediately.

Lying to Make Others Happy

Children, like adults, lie to cover up their mistakes. Nevertheless, in some way, the occurrence of lying is good news because it signifies advanced cognitive skills: Awareness of another person's possible ignorance of the wrongdoing and an appreciation of one's skills to continue such ignorance. Lying is also considered appropriate when it is used to make others happy, as in the case of telling white lies.

Telling white lies serves a socialization purpose—being polite—which is much different from telling lies to hide one's transgression to avoid punishment. In a recent paper (Talwar, Murphy, & Lee, 2007), a team of Canadian researchers created a situation involving an undesirable gift—a bar of soap—to examine white lying among children ages 3 to 11. Children were given the soap and were left alone for a few minutes. Then the experimenter returned and asked for the child's opinion about the gift.

Sixty-eight percent of the children lied, saying that they liked the soap. Not only did they lie, they did it well by deliberately coordinating verbal and non-verbal performance. These children showed a reduction in negative emotion and an increase in smiling between the time they received the gift and the time they answered how they liked the gift. In contrast, in a control condition where children received a desirable gift, the intensity of smiling dropped between the two time points, maybe because it

was natural for the initial excitement of receiving the gift to taper off quickly.

In another condition, parents were asked to teach their children to tell white lies. There was an interesting link between parents' instruction and children's lies: children were likely to use reasons to support their lies (e.g., the family needed soap) when their parents suggested to the children what to say. This supports the idea that pragmatics can be taught explicitly. Moreover, the children who told white lies showed more positive emotion when the parents told them in detail what to say, suggesting that parents' efforts may have prompted children to mobilize the whole arsenal of verbal and non-verbal behaviours appropriate for lying.

Overall, older children lied more and elaborated more when lying than younger children. This suggests that cognitive skills and socialization experience with others are crucial for being successful tellers of white lies, at least in this early age.

This study showcases a few things: the early occurrence of white-lie telling, young children's awareness of politeness and their skills in deceiving others, the power of adult input in white lying, and the creative way researchers develop to examine touchy issues such as lying.

By the way, children who got the soap were given an opportunity to exchange it for a better gift at the end of the research session.

Building on Piaget's ideas, Lawrence Kohlberg developed a theory of moral development that also emphasized moral reasoning and the influence of the give-and-take of peer relations. Like Piaget, Kohlberg concluded from his research that children begin as heteronomous moralists. Later, in Chapter 10, we will examine Kohlberg's theory and stages of moral development, the evidence his theory is based on, and its critics.

Moral Behaviour

Behaviour is as important as thinking when it comes to moral development. The processes of reinforcement, punishment, and imitation can explain the development of moral behaviour (Bugental & Grusec, 2006). When children are rewarded for behaviour that is consistent with laws and social conventions, they are likely to repeat that behaviour in the same situation. Likewise, after punishment, the target behaviour is likely to be reduced in the same situation. Also, when models who behave morally are provided, children are likely to adopt their actions. And, when children are punished for immoral behaviour, those behaviours are likely to be reduced or eliminated. However, because punishment may have adverse side effects, as discussed later in this chapter, it needs to be used judiciously and cautiously.

The phrase "in the same situation" was mentioned twice in the previous paragraph because the situation influences behaviour. More than half a century ago, a study of thousands of children in many situations—at home, at school, and at church, for example—found that the totally honest child was virtually non-existent; so was the child who cheated in all environments (Hartshorne & May, 1928–1930). Behavioural and social cognitive researchers emphasize that what children do in one situation is often only weakly related to what they do in other situations. A child might cheat in class but not in a game; a child might steal a piece of candy when alone but not steal it when others are present. This situational approach to moral development is consistent with the theory developed by Urie Bronfenbrenner, which is discussed in Chapter 14.

Social cognitive theorists also believe that the ability to resist temptation is closely tied to the development of self-control. To achieve this self-control, children must learn to delay gratification. According to the theorists, cognitive factors are important in the child's development of self-control (Bandura, 2007a, b).

Conscience

Conscience refers to an internal regulation of standards of right and wrong that involves an integration of all three components of moral development we have described so far—moral thought, feeling, and behaviour (Kochanska & Aksan, 2007). Researchers have found that young children are aware of right and wrong, have the capacity to show empathy toward others, experience guilt, indicate discomfort following a transgression, and are sensitive to violating rules (Kochanska & Aksan, 2007; Kochanska et al., 2009).

A major interest in young children's conscience focuses on the children's relationship with their caregivers (Thompson, 2009d). Especially important in this regard is the emergence of the young children's willingness to embrace the values of their parents that flows from a positive, close relationship (Kochanska & Aksan, 2007). For example, children who are securely attached are more likely to internalize their parents' values and rules (Thompson, 2009d).

Parenting and Young Children's Moral Development

Both Piaget and Lawrence Kohlberg held that parents are responsible for providing role-taking opportunities and cognitive conflict, but peers play the primary role in moral development. Research reveals that both parents and peers contribute to children's moral maturity (Hastings, Utendale, & Sullivan, 2007).

In Ross Thompson's (2006; Laible & Thompson, 2007) view, young children are moral apprentices, striving to understand what is moral. They can be assisted in this quest by the "sensitive guidance of adult mentors in the home who provide lessons about morality in everyday experiences" (Thompson, Meyer, & McGinley, 2006, p. 290). Among the most important aspects of the relationship between parents and children that contribute to children's moral development are relational quality, parental discipline, proactive strategies (such as diversion), and conversational dialogue.

Secure attachment may play an important role in children's moral development. A secure attachment can place the child on a positive path for internalizing parents' socializing goals and family values (Kochanska et al., 2008). And a recent study revealed that an early mutually responsive orientation between parents and their infant and a decrease in parents' use of power assertion in disciplining a young child were linked to an increase in the child's internalization and self-regulation (Kochanska et al., 2008). With younger children, being proactive means using diversion, such as distracting their attention or moving them to alternative activities. With older children, being proactive may involve talking with them about values that the parents deem important. Transmitting these values can help older children and adolescents resist the temptations that inevitably emerge in contexts as outside the scope of direct parental monitoring such as peer relations and social media.

Conversations related to moral development can benefit children whether they occur as part of a discipline encounter or outside the encounter in the everyday stream of parent–child interaction (Thompson, 2012; Thompson, Meyer, & McGinley, 2006). The conversations can be planned or spontaneous and can focus on topics such as past events (for example, a child's prior misbehaviour or positive moral conduct), shared future events (for example, going somewhere that may involve a temptation and requires positive moral behaviour), and immediate events (for example, talking with the child about a sibling's tantrums).

developmental **connection**

Bandura's Social Cognitive Theory

developmental **connection**

Attachment Theory

Gender

So far in this chapter, we have studied the self, emotional development, and moral development. Another important dimension of young children's socio-emotional development is gender.

What Is Gender?

gender The social and psychological dimensions of being male or female.

gender identity The sense of being male or female, which most children acquire by the time they are three years old.

gender role A set of expectations that prescribe how females or males should think, act, and feel.

Sex refers to the biological dimension of being male or female, and **gender** *refers to the social and psychological dimensions of being male or female.* **Gender identity** *is the sense of being male or female, which most children acquire by the time they are three years old.* **Gender role** *is a set of expectations that prescribe how females or males should think, act, and feel.* One aspect of gender identity involves knowing whether you are a girl or boy, which most children do by about 2½ years of age (Blakemore, Berenbaum, & Liben, 2009). During the preschool years, most children increasingly act in ways that match their culture's gender roles. Gender typing refers to acquisition of a traditional masculine or feminine role. For example, fighting is more characteristic of a traditional masculine role and crying is more characteristic of a traditional feminine role. A recent study revealed that sex-typed behaviour (boys playing with cars and girls with jewellery, for example) increased during the preschool years and that children engaging in the most sex-typed behaviour during the preschool years still did so at eight years of age (Golombok et al., 2008).

Biological Influences

Biology clearly plays a role in sex development. Among the possible biological influences are chromosomes, hormones, and evolution.

CHROMOSOMES AND HORMONES   Recall that humans normally have 46 chromosomes arranged in pairs (see Chapter 3). The 23rd pair consists of a combination of X and Y chromosomes, usually two X chromosomes in a female and an X and a Y in a male. In the first few weeks of gestation, however, female and male embryos look alike.

Males start to differ from females when genes on the Y chromosome in the male embryo trigger the development of testes rather than ovaries; the testes secrete copious amounts of the class of hormones known as androgens, which leads to the development of male sex organs. Low levels of androgens in the female embryo allow the normal development of female sex organs.

Thus, hormones play a critical role in the development of sex differences (Lippa, 2005). The two main classes of sex hormones are estrogens and androgens, which are secreted by the *gonads* (ovaries in females, testes in males). *Estrogens*, such as estradiol, influence the development of female physical sex characteristics. *Androgens*, such as testosterone, promote the development of male physical sex characteristics. A recent study revealed that a higher fetal testosterone level measured from amniotic fluid was linked to increased male-typical play in 6- to 10-year-old boys and girls (Auyeung et al., 2009).

THE EVOLUTIONARY PSYCHOLOGY VIEW   How might physical differences between the sexes give rise to psychological differences between males and females? Evolutionary psychology offers one answer. According to evolutionary psychology, adaptation during human evolution has produced psychological differences between males and females (Buss, 2008; Cosmides, 2011). Because of their differing roles in reproduction, males and females faced differing pressures when the human species was evolving. In particular, because having multiple sexual liaisons improves the likelihood that males will pass on their genes, natural selection favours males who adopt short-term mating strategies. These are strategies that allow a male to win the competition with other males for sexual access to females. Therefore, say evolutionary psychologists, males have evolved dispositions that favour violence, competition, and risk taking.

In contrast, females' contributions to the gene pool are improved when they secure resources that ensure the survival of their offspring; this outcome is promoted by obtaining long-term mates who can support a family (Geher & Miller, 2007). As a consequence, natural selection favours females who devote effort to parenting and choose successful, ambitious mates who can provide their offspring with resources and protection.

Critics of evolutionary psychology argue that its hypotheses are backed by speculations about prehistory, not evidence, and that in any event people are not locked into behaviour that was adaptive in the evolutionary past. Critics also claim that the evolutionary view pays little attention to cultural and individual variations in gender differences (Best, 2010; Matlin, 2008).

Social Influences

Many social scientists argue that gender differences are due to social experiences (Denmark, Rabinowitz, & Sechzer, 2005).

SOCIAL THEORIES OF GENDER   Three main social theories of gender have been proposed—social role theory, psychoanalytic theory, and social cognitive theory. Alice Eagly (2001, 2009; Eagly & Fischer, 2009; Eagly & Sczesny, 2009) proposed the **social role theory**, *which states that gender differences result from the contrasting roles of women and men.* In most cultures, women have less power and status and control fewer resources than men do (UNICEF, 2010). In this view, as women adapted to roles with less power and less status in society, they showed more cooperative, less dominant profiles than men. Thus, the social hierarchy and division of labour may be important causes of gender differences in power, assertiveness, and nurture.

The **psychoanalytic theory of gender** *stems from Freud's view that the preschool child develops a sexual attraction to the opposite-sex parent.* At five or six years of age, the child renounces this attraction because of anxious feelings. Subsequently, the child identifies with the same-sex parent, unconsciously adopting the same-sex parent's characteristics. However, some developmentalists argue that children become gender-typed much earlier than five or six years of age, and they become masculine or feminine even when the same-sex parent is not present in the family.

The **social cognitive theory of gender** *explains that children's gender development occurs through observing and imitating what other people say and do, and through being rewarded and punished for gender-appropriate and gender-inappropriate behaviour* (Bussey & Bandura, 1999). From birth onward, males and females are treated differently. When infants and toddlers show gender differences, parents tend to reward them. In addition to parents, environmental factors such as culture, schools, peers, the media, and other family members also provide gender role models (Smith, B., 2007). Let's take a closer look at the influence of parents and peers.

PARENTAL INFLUENCES   Parents, by action and by example, influence their children's gender development (Gore, 2009). Cultures around the world, however, tend to give mothers and fathers different roles (Kagitcibasi, 2007). A recent research review provided these conclusions (Bronstein, 2006):

- *Mothers' socialization strategies.* In many cultures, mothers socialize their daughters to be more obedient and responsible than their sons. They also place more restrictions on daughters' autonomy.
- *Fathers' socialization strategies.* Fathers show more attention to sons than daughters, engage in more activities with sons, and put forth more effort to promote sons' intellectual development.

Thus, according to Bronstein (2006, pp. 269–270), "Despite an increased awareness in the United States and other Western cultures of the detrimental effects of gender stereotyping, many parents continue to foster behaviors and perceptions that are consonant with traditional gender role norms."

PEER INFLUENCES   Parents provide the earliest influence on gender roles, but before long peers join the process of responding to and modelling masculine and feminine behaviour (Blakemore, Berenbaum, & Liben, 2009). Peers extensively reward and punish gender-appropriate behaviour and often reject children who act in a manner that is considered more characteristic of the other sex

social role theory A theory that gender differences result from the contrasting roles of men and women.

psychoanalytic theory of gender Derived from Freud's view that the preschool child develops a sexual attraction to the opposite-sex parent, renounces this attraction by approximately five or six years of age because of anxious feelings, and subsequently identifies with the same-sex parent, unconsciously adopting the same-sex parent's characteristics.

social cognitive theory of gender Explains that children's gender development occurs through observing and imitating what other people say and do, and through being rewarded and punished for gender-appropriate and gender-inappropriate behaviour.

developmental **connection**

Freud's Psychoanalytic Theory

developmental **connection**

Bandura's Social Cognitive Theory

Nurturing

critical thinking

Do you recall how old you were when you realized what sex you are? Do you remember when you learned that not everyone was the same sex as yourself? What are some of the factors that have influenced your gender identity? Which theory of gender development do you like the best? What might an eclectic theoretical view of gender development be like? (You might want to review the discussion of an eclectic theoretical orientation in Chapter 2.)

developmental connection

Piaget

gender schema theory The idea that gender-typing emerges as children gradually develop gender schemas of what is gender-appropriate and gender-inappropriate in their culture.

As reflected in this tug-of-war battle between boys and girls, the playground in elementary school is like going to "gender school." Elementary school children show a clear preference for being with and liking same-sex peers. Think back to when you were in elementary school. **Did you prefer being with peers of the same sex?**

(Leaper & Friedman, 2007; Matlin, 2008). A little girl who brings a doll to the park may find herself surrounded by new friends; a little boy might be jeered.

However, there is greater pressure for boys to conform to a traditional male role than for girls to conform to a traditional female role (Fagot, Rogers, & Leinbach, 2000). For example, a preschool girl who wants to wear boys' clothing receives considerably more approval than a boy who wants to wear a dress. The very term "tomboy" implies broad social acceptance of girls' adopting traditional male behaviours.

Gender moulds important aspects of peer relations (Best, 2010). It influences the composition of children's groups, the size of groups, and interactions within a group (Maccoby, 1998, 2002):

- *Gender composition of children's groups.* Around the age of three, children already show a preference to spend time with same-sex playmates. From 4 to 12 years of age, this preference for playing in same-sex groups increases, and during the elementary school years children spend a large majority of their free time with children of their own sex.
- *Group size.* Research by Joyce Benenson at McGill University shows that, from about five years of age onward, boys are more likely to associate together in larger clusters than girls (Benenson & Heath, 2006). Moreover, girls are more likely than boys to play in dyads or triads, while boys are more likely to interact in larger groups and seek to attain a group goal (Benenson, Apostoleris, & Parnass, 1997).
- *Interaction in same-sex groups.* Boys are more likely than girls to engage in rough-and-tumble play, competition, conflict, ego displays, risk taking, and seeking dominance. By contrast, girls are more likely to engage in "collaborative discourse," in which they talk and act in a more reciprocal manner.

Cognitive Influences

Observation, imitation, rewards, and punishment—these are the mechanisms by which gender develops according to social cognitive theory. Interactions between the child and the social environment are the main keys to gender development in this view. Some critics who adopt a cognitive approach argue that this explanation pays too little attention to the child's own mind and understanding, and portrays the child as passively acquiring gender roles (Martin & Ruble, 2004).

One influential cognitive theory is **gender schema theory**, *which states that gender-typing emerges as children gradually develop gender schemas of what is gender-appropriate and gender-inappropriate in their culture* (Blakemore, Berenbaum, & Liben, 2009; Zosuls, Lurye, & Ruble, 2008). A *schema* is a cognitive structure, a network of associations that guide an individual's perceptions. A *gender schema* organizes the world in terms of female and male. Children are internally motivated to perceive the world and to act in accordance with their developing schemas. Bit by bit, children pick up what is gender-appropriate and gender-inappropriate in their culture, and develop gender schemas that shape how they perceive the world and what they remember (Blakemore, Berenbaum, & Liben, 2009). Children are motivated to act in ways that conform with these gender schemas. Thus, gender schemas fuel gender-typing.

To this point, we have studied a number of ideas about moral development and gender. For a review, see the **Reach Your Learning Objectives** section at the end of this chapter.

Families

LO3 Explain how families can influence young children's development.

Families everywhere reflect the wider social and cultural environment; for example, families living in urban areas such as Vancouver, Montreal, Ottawa, and Toronto are accustomed to city density, pavement, and relatively easy access to facilities. By contrast, families living in rural settings such as Nunavut, Bonnyville, or Notre-Dame-de-Ham experience life very differently—quieter, more farmland, and much less access to facilities such as health care and education. Urie Bronfenbrenner, whose bio-ecological systems you read about in Chapter 2, believed that we are intensified by our environment and that parents are the champions guiding children through all the elements within the ecological systems. This section will explore parenting styles, sibling relationships, and family cohesion as they interact reciprocally within the environment and reflect the wider national cultural and economic shifts.

> Parenting
>
> Divorce
>
> Sibling Relationships and Birth Order

Parenting

Shifting Parental Roles

Given the economic burdens facing families, more women are working outside the home, and their incomes are essential to the financial security of most households. Eighty-two percent of women between ages 25 and 54 are active participants in the workforce. While the number of women has increased, the same is not true for men, whose participation has declined slightly (Vanier Institute, 2010).

Work can produce positive and negative effects on parenting (Han, 2009). Recent research indicates that what matters for children's development is the nature of the parents' work rather than whether one or both parents works outside the home (Goldberg & Lucas-Thompson, 2008). In her research, Ann Crouter (2006) concluded that parents who have poor working conditions, such as long hours and overtime, stressful jobs, and a lack of autonomy at work are likely to be more irritable at home and engage in less effective parenting than their counterparts who have better work conditions in their jobs. A consistent finding is the children (especially girls) of working mothers engage in less gender stereotyping and have more egalitarian views of gender (Goldberg & Lucas-Thompson, 2008).

The Vanier Institute (2012) reports that more fathers today, 75 percent, claim to be actively engaged with their children, spending an average of 3.1 hours daily caring for them. Not only are more fathers taking parental leave—an increase from 3 percent to 27 percent between 2001 and 2007—but also 10 percent of all stay-at-home parents in 2008 were men. A greater proportion of working men in dual-income families were doing housework daily and were spending more time on it in 2005 than their counterparts were in 1992, while the reverse was true for employed women. Nevertheless, the wives still assumed 62 percent of household work in 2005. In addition, working mothers were more likely to feel stressed about time and less likely to be happy with their work–life balance than working fathers (Marshall, 2006).

It's not just the quantity of time parents spend with children that is important for children's development—the quality of the parenting is also clearly important (Bornstein & Zlotnik, 2008; Grusec, 2009; Landry, 2009). To understand variations in parenting, let's consider the styles parents use when they interact with their children, how they discipline their children, and co-parenting.

Baumrind's Parenting Styles

Diana Baumrind (1971) argues parents should be neither punitive nor aloof. Rather, they should develop rules for their children and be affectionate with them. She has described four types of parenting styles: authoritarian, authoritative, neglectful, and indulgent.

Authoritarian parenting *is a restrictive, punitive style in which parents exhort the child to follow their directions and to respect work and effort.* The authoritarian parent places firm limits and

authoritarian parenting A restrictive, punitive style in which parents exhort the child to follow their directions and to respect work and effort. The authoritarian parent places firm limits and controls on the child and allows little verbal exchange.

controls on the child and allows little verbal exchange. For example, a parent might say, "You do it my way or else."

Authoritarian parents also might enforce rules rigidly but not explain them, and show rage toward the child. Children of authoritarian parents are often unhappy, fearful, and anxious about comparing themselves with others, fail to initiate activity, and have weak communication skills.

Authoritative parenting *encourages children to be independent but still places limits and controls on their actions.* Extensive verbal give-and-take is allowed, and parents are warm and nurturing toward the child. An authoritative parent might put his arm around the child in a comforting way and say, "You know you should not have done that. Let's talk about how you can handle the situation better next time." Authoritative parents show pleasure and support of children's constructive behaviour. They also expect mature, independent, and age-appropriate behaviour of children. Children whose parents are authoritative are often cheerful, self-controlled and self-reliant, and achievement-oriented. They also maintain friendly relations with peers, cooperate with adults, and cope well with stress.

Neglectful parenting *is a style in which the parent is very uninvolved in the child's life.* Recall from Chapter 1 that well-known psychoanalyst Karen Horney argued that neglect is the single most damaging factor in a child's development because the child has no way to rail against neglect. Children whose parents are neglectful develop the sense that other aspects of the parents' lives are more important than they are. These children tend to be socially incompetent. Many have poor self-control and do not handle independence well. They frequently have low self-esteem, are immature, and may be alienated from the family. In adolescence, they may show patterns of truancy and delinquency.

authoritative parenting A style in which parents encourage their children to be independent but still place limits and controls on their actions. Extensive verbal give-and-take is allowed, and parents are warm and nurturing toward the child.

neglectful parenting A style in which the parent is very uninvolved in the child's life.

indulgent parenting A style in which parents are highly involved with their children but place few demands or controls on them.

Calvin and Hobbes

WHAT ASSURANCE DO I HAVE THAT YOUR PARENTING ISN'T SCREWING ME UP?

Calvin and Hobbes, Copyright © 1993 Watterson. Reprinted with permission of Universal Press Syndicate. All rights reserved.

Indulgent parenting *is a style of parenting in which parents are highly involved with their children but place few demands or controls on them.* Such parents let their children do what they want. The result is that the children never learn to control their own behaviour and always expect to get their way. Some parents deliberately rear their children in this way because they believe the combination of warm involvement and few restraints will produce a creative, confident child. However, children whose parents are indulgent rarely learn respect for others and have difficulty controlling their behaviour. They might be aggressive, domineering, and non-compliant.

These four classifications of parenting involve combinations of acceptance and responsiveness on the one hand, and demand and control on the other (Maccoby & Martin, 1983). How these dimensions combine to produce authoritarian, authoritative, neglectful, and indulgent parenting is shown in Figure 8.1.

Keep in mind that research on parenting styles and children's development is correlational, not causal, in nature. Thus, if a study reveals that authoritarian parenting is linked to higher levels of children's aggression, it may be that aggressive children elicited authoritarian parenting just as much as authoritarian parenting produced aggressive children. Also recall from Chapter 1 that, in correlational studies, a third factor may influence the correlation between two factors. Thus, in the example of the correlation between authoritarian parenting and children's aggression, possibly authoritarian parents (first factor) and aggressive children (second factor) share genes (third factor) that predispose them to behave in ways that produced the correlation.

Figure 8.1

Classification of Parenting Styles

	Accepting, responsive	Rejecting, unresponsive
Demanding, controlling	Authoritative	Authoritarian
Undemanding, uncontrolling	Indulgent	Neglectful

The four types of parenting styles (authoritative, authoritarian, neglectful, and indulgent) involve the dimensions of acceptance and responsiveness on the one hand, and demand and control on the other. For example, authoritative parenting involves being both accepting/responsive and demanding/controlling.

Parenting Styles in Context

Parenting is influenced by culture, ethnicity, and socio-economic status (Tamis-LeMonda & McFadden, 2010). Recall from Bronfenbrenner's ecological theory (see Chapter 2) that a number of social contexts influence the child's development. In Bronfenbrenner's theory, culture, ethnicity, and socio-economic status are classified as part of the macrosystem because they represent broader societal contexts that influence the individual. Although occasional exceptions have been found, evidence linking authoritative parenting with competence on the part of the child occurs in research across a wide range of ethnic groups, social strata, cultures, and family structures (Steinberg & Silk, 2002).

Researchers have found that in some ethnic groups, aspects of the authoritarian style may be associated with more positive child outcomes than Baumrind predicts (Parke & Buriel, 2006). Elements of the authoritarian style may take on different meanings and have different effects depending on the context. In a study examining the use of authoritative or authoritarian styles by Chinese parents in Canada and China, Chuang and Su (2009) found that parents in China were more apt to be authoritarian, while Chinese Canadian parents were more authoritative. They suggested that cultural socialization accounted for the difference in parenting style.

Diversity

Canada prides itself on its diversity and supports a host of programs to assist immigrants with resettlement; nevertheless, challenges faced by immigrant families are multifaceted and complex. Limited language knowledge is one major challenge that has an enormous ripple effect. Many immigrants (46 percent in 2001) report limited ability to speak in either English or French, and the consequences range from poor diagnosis of health and learning problems to confusion, anxiety, withdrawal, and depression (Chuang, 2010). For many immigrant families, parenting can also be affected by how individual family members adjust to the mainstream culture. Less assimilated and more assimilated family members may have different views on discipline and the child's freedom, resulting in conflicts and confusion. Not only can this type of situation influence parenting behaviour, it can also affect parent–child interactions in general.

Frequently, immigrant and refugee families are separated, with one or both parents immigrating to or seeking refuge in Canada, working and sending support to the family in the home country. In such cases the children may live with their grandparents, occasionally connecting with the parent or parents perhaps through social media. Once the adult is able, he or she may initiate the long process of family reunification. In the case of refugee claimants, such reunion of parents and children may take several years (Canadian Council for Refugees, 2012).

Some differences may be partially explained by environment. Living in dangerous neighbourhoods may encourage parents to enforce rules and be strict to prevent their children from engaging in antisocial behaviour, such as imitating or joining street gangs, and from being victimized by others.

What are some characteristics of families within different ethnic groups?

Parents in different socio-economic groups also tend to think differently about education (Hoff et al., 2002; Magnuson & Duncan, 2002). Middle- and upper-income parents more often think of education as something that should be mutually encouraged by parents and teachers. By contrast, low-income parents are more likely to view education as the teacher's job.

Although there are a lot of parenting differences among various cultures and economic situations, as well as between individuals within the same group, authoritative parenting has been linked to competence on the part of the child in research across a wide range of ethnic groups, social strata, cultures, and family structures (Steinberg, Blatt-Eisengart, & Cauffman, 2006; Steinberg & Silk, 2002), suggesting the "safest" way of parenting may be the balance of control and warmth.

Working Parents

In 2005, more than 70 percent of two-parent families with children under age 16 were dual-income families; this number almost doubled the 36 percent in 1976 (Marshall, 2006). Just over 30 percent of dual-income families have one parent working full-time while the other has part-time employment. In approximately 15 percent of dual-income families, both parents work part-time. Corresponding to these numbers is a steady increase in working mothers with one child under age six (Bushnik, 2006). In fact, in 2005, 67.2 percent of women with a young child were employed (Statistics Canada, 2006e). LaRochelle-Côté, Gougeon, and Pinard (2009) report that 51 percent of single mothers work full-time, while 65 percent of single fathers have full-time employment. As noted in Chapter 6, this change has exposed more and more children to non-parental care in their early years.

A special challenge for many dual-income families is having either or both parents work non-standard schedules—weekends, nights, and evenings. Non-standard schedules can ensure that at least one parent is at home with the children. A pioneering study of dual-income families with children aged 2 to 11 in the National Longitudinal Survey of Children and Youth found that working non-standard hours was related to ineffective parenting, parental depression, and weakened family functioning in areas such as showing support and communicating feelings. This, in turn, was linked to children's behavioural and emotional difficulties (Strazdins, Clements, Korda, Broom, & D'Souza, 2006).

Co-Parenting

Co-parenting refers to the support that parents provide each other in jointly raising a child. Poor coordination between parents, active undermining of the other parent, lack of cooperation and warmth, and disconnection by one parent—either alone or in combination with overinvolvement by the other—are conditions that place children at developmental risk (Doherty & Beaton, 2004; McHale, Kuersten-Hogan, & Rao, 2004; McHale et al., 2002; Van Egeren & Hawkins, 2004). An analysis of the National Longitudinal Survey of Children and Youth showed that witnessing violence at home was related to children's explicit aggression, such as fighting and threatening, four years later (Moss, 2003). Therefore, parents should avoid fighting or other kinds of aggression in the home. In fact, they should keep in mind that parental cooperation and warmth have clear ties to children's prosocial behaviour and competence in peer relations.

Parenting is not just an activity that the parents do together toward their child. Canadian researchers Burton, Phipps, and Curtis (2005) argue that it is an interactive process, an engagement between people acting in various ways. The parent's and child's behaviour each influence the responses given by the other. In this view, we might see co-parenting as involving both the parents and the children.

Punishment

Early in 2004, the Supreme Court of Canada upheld the provision in the *Criminal Code* allowing spanking with non-excessive force as a form of punishment. The Court, however, added that spanking could be used only on children between the ages of 2 and 12. As for public opinion, a cross-cultural comparison found that Canadians were among those most favourable toward corporal punishment and most remembered it being used by their parents (Curran et al., 2001) (see Figure 8.2).

critical thinking

In thinking about parenting styles, consider the style or styles your parents used in rearing you. Were they both authoritative; one authoritarian, the other indulgent; and so on? Or, was there a mix of styles? What do you understand about your parents' upbringing that may have contributed to their parenting practices? What effects do you think their parenting styles had on your development? What parenting practices might you keep? What might you change? Why?

Figure 8.2

Corporal Punishment in Different Countries

A 5-point scale was used to assess attitudes toward corporal punishment. Scores closer to 1 indicated an attitude against its use, and scores closer to 5 suggested an attitude for its use (Curran et al., 2001).

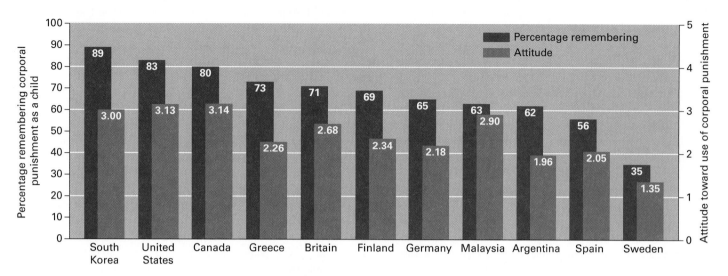

In contrast, Swedes, whose country outlawed physical punishment in 1979, had a very unfavourable view toward this form of punishment.

A research review concluded that corporal punishment by parents is associated with higher levels of immediate compliance and aggression by the children (Gershoff, 2002). The review also found that corporal punishment is associated with lower levels of moral internalization and mental health (Gershoff, 2002). One study revealed that children whose parents hit or slapped them in the prior two weeks showed more emotional and adjustment problems than children who had not been hit or slapped by parents in the same time frame (Aucoin, Frick, & Bodin, 2006). A recent study also found a link between the use of physical punishment by parents and children's negative behavioural adjustment at 36 months and in Grade 1 (Mulvaney & Mebert, 2007). Another recent study also discovered that a history of harsh physical discipline was linked to adolescent depression and externalized problems, such as juvenile delinquency (Bender et al., 2007).

Canada's National Longitudinal Survey of Children and Youth (2006) found punitive parenting was related to increased aggressive behaviour, more anxiety, and lower prosocial behaviour in children under five years of age. If the parenting style had not changed, these results were found again when measured at age 10 to 13 years, compared with children whose parents practised a non-punitive style. However, the results were different if parents had moved from punitive to non-punitive parenting style in the intervening years. At the later measure (ages 10 to 13), the children's aggression, anxiety, and prosocial behaviour had changed and were the same as those children whose parents were non-punitive at both assessments. Unfortunately, when parents adopted a punitive style in the intervening years, their children had higher aggression, more anxiety, and lower prosocial behaviour than the non-punitive parents at one or both of the two assessments. The research suggests that changing from a punitive to a non-punitive parenting style can have positive results in children's behaviour and their sense of self.

Some experts recommend reasoning with the child, especially explaining the consequences of the child's actions as the best way to handle children's transgressions (Straus, 2003). Time-out, in which the child is removed from a setting where the child experiences positive reinforcement, can also be effective. Susan O'Leary cautions parents to be careful enforcing the time-out. Because the child may resist staying in the "isolated spot" and leave or talk with the parent from the spot, parents may give up or hold the child in the time-out spot, both of which undermine the lesson that

Parental Attitudes of the Sami

When Canadians think of Norway, they may see an ethnically homogeneous country with beautiful mountains and fjords. However, just like Canada, Norway has a sizeable minority group living in the circumpolar area. These are the Sami, a traditionally nomadic people. Despite their assimilation with the mainstream Norwegian culture, researchers wonder if the childrearing values among the Sami remain different from the Western values dominant in the country.

In a recent study of both Norwegian and Sami parents of preschoolers, researchers asked the parents about their attitudes toward child behaviour in everyday situations, such as mealtime and bedtime, and found some interesting differences—and similarities—between the two groups (Javo, Rønning, & Heyerdahl, 2004).

Overall, there is greater emphasis on child autonomy among the Sami (Javo et al., 2004). In contrast to Norwegian mothers, Sami mothers are less comfortable with their children's clingy behaviour, but are more flexible with mealtime and bedtime rules. For example, Sami mothers did not find children's talking while eating and their desire to stay up late as annoying as Norwegian mothers did. At the same time, Sami mothers are less tolerant of children's temper tantrums and expressions of jealousy, and are more willing to slap or threaten their misbehaving children than are Norwegian mothers. This highlights the importance of self-control and communal harmony in the pursuit of independence.

Despite these differences, both groups have similar parental attitudes in several areas, one of which is the expectations parents have for their daughters (Javo et al., 2004). Girls are expected to take care of simple everyday tasks, such as dressing and undressing, earlier than boys are. Such similarities may be the result of assimilation, or simply that of longstanding beliefs independently held by each group.

In sum, the Sami parents are more likely to expect and encourage child autonomy than Norwegian parents are. Interestingly, the Sami's attitudes are similar to those of the Inuit in Canada (Javo et al., 2004). Maybe the unforgiving conditions of the north have developed in both Sami and the Inuit parents this strong desire to foster their children's independence.

critical thinking

Some argue that the line between corporal punishment and child maltreatment is a very fine one that can easily be crossed. What do you think? Is corporal punishment a valid parenting strategy? If so, when? What other strategies might be used? At what age, if any, should corporal punishment be used? Were you spanked as a child? Was there any relationship between the punishment and your parent's temper? What impact did the spanking(s) have? What punishments did your parents administer? What did you learn from these punishments? Given what you have learned about moral development, parenting style, and punishment, what would be the most appropriate way for a parent to teach his/her child the values the parent feel are most important?

undesirable behaviour needs to change. Another example of consequences might be the removal of privileges such as social media, TV, bicycles, and so forth. Of course, children need to be told, before and/or after, what behaviour is appropriate.

Divorce

According to the Vanier Institute of the Family, 4 in 10 marriages end in divorce (2010). Consequently, many children have to adjust to the changes that follow their parents' divorce. Most common-law relationships that fail do so before the couple are 30 years of age, and in 70 percent of these no children are involved (Beaupré & Cloutier, 2006). Where there are children, the children are usually under the age of six. Divorces in a marriage relationship usually occur a bit later and the children are usually older.

Should parents stay together in an unhappy or conflicted marriage for the sake of the children? If the stresses and disruptions in family relationships associated with an unhappy, conflictual marriage that erode the well-being of children are reduced by the move to a divorced, single-parent family, divorce can be advantageous. However, if the diminished resources and increased risks associated with divorce are accompanied by inept parenting and sustained or increased conflict, the best choice for the children would be that an unhappy marriage is retained (Hetherington & Stanley-Hagan, 2002). It is difficult to determine how these "ifs" will play out when parents either remain together in an acrimonious marriage or become divorced.

Children in Divorced Families

Most researchers agree that children from divorced families show poorer adjustment than their counterparts in non-divorced families (Hetherington, 2006; Wallerstein, 2008). Those who have experienced multiple divorces are at greater risk. One recent study linked individuals' experiences with the divorce of their parents in childhood and adolescence to having unstable romantic or marital relationships as well as low levels of education in adulthood (Amato, 2006). Note that marital conflict may have negative consequences for children in the context of marriage or divorce (Cox et al., 2008). And many of the problems that children from divorced homes experience begin during the pre-divorce period, a time when parents are often in active conflict with each other. Thus, when children from divorced homes show problems, the problems may not be due only to the divorce, but also to the marital conflict that led to it (Thompson, 2008). However, the majority of children in divorced families do not have significant adjustment problems (Ahrons, 2007). One study found that 20 years after their parents had divorced when they were children, approximately 80 percent of adults concluded that their parents' decision to divorce was a wise one (Ahrons, 2004).

When couples separate, issues of child custody and support are of primary concern. Arrangements are made in the best interest of the child, and while most agreements are made by the parents, some parents may turn to the courts to settle disputes. When this is the case, joint custody is awarded in 47 percent of the cases, up from 21 percent in 1995 (Vanier Institute, 2010). Research on whether different types of custodial arrangements are better for children in divorced families has been inconsistent (Spruijt & Duindam, 2010). An analysis of studies found that children in joint-custody families were better adjusted than children in sole-custody families (Bauserman, 2002). Some studies have shown that boys adjust better in father-custody families, girls in mother-custody families, whereas other studies have not (Ziol-Guest, 2009). A relatively harmonious relationship between the divorcing parents coupled with the constructive use of authoritative parenting assists the child or children's adjustment (Hetherington, 2006). In sum, many factors are involved in determining how divorce influences a child's development (Amato & Dorius, 2010; Hetherington, 2006).

Marital break-up is also associated with an increase in the likelihood for depressive symptoms, with the odds being three times higher for divorced men and two-and-a-half times higher among divorced women than their married peers. For most, though, the depression appears to subside after two years (Rotermann, 2007).

Among the factors involved in the child's risk and vulnerability are the child's adjustment prior to the divorce, as well as the child's personality and temperament, gender, and custody situation (Hetherington, 2006). Children whose parents later divorce show poorer adjustment before the break-up. Children who are socially mature and responsible, who show few behavioural problems, and who have an easy temperament are better able to cope with their parents' divorce. Children with a difficult temperament often have problems in coping with their parents' divorce (Hetherington, 2000).

Programs to help divorced parents are available across Canada. For example, the six-hour For the Sake of the Children program in Manitoba is designed to help parents learn about children's adjustment, financial issues, legal options, and so on, after a divorce or separation (Government of Manitoba, n.d.). A study of 10 such programs across the country indicates participants have a high level of satisfaction with the programs immediately following participation. Three months later, most reported the programs helped them, especially in the areas of dealing with children and the ex-spouse. The authors of the study did caution that the lack of a control group and many parents' concurrent uses of counselling and other help did not allow for a simple cause-and-effect conclusion for the effectiveness of the programs (McKenzie & Bacon, 2002).

Socio-Economic Status

What role does socio-economic status play in the lives of children in divorced families? Lone-parent families account for 15.9 percent of families and, although more men are lone parents, most—80 percent—are headed by single moms (Vanier Institute, 2010). Custodial mothers experience the loss of about one-fourth to one-half of their pre-divorce income, in comparison with a loss of only one-tenth by custodial fathers. This income loss for divorced mothers is accompanied by increased workloads, high rates of job instability, and residential moves to less desirable neighbourhoods with inferior schools (Sayer, 2006). Poverty is a significant factor in growth and development. According to a UNICEF report released in 2012, 14 percent of Canadian children live in poverty; this high rate puts Canada in the bottom third of the countries measured. Poverty poses additional major challenges for racialized minority and immigrant families.

In Japan, only 6 percent of children live in lone-parent families, compared with 15.9 percent in Canada and 27 percent in the United States (Martin & Kats, 2003; Vanier Institute, 2010). **What might explain this difference?**

developmental **connection**

Temperament

Stepfamilies

Nearly half a million Canadian families in 2001 were stepfamilies (Judy, 2003–2004). Most involved a man forming a relationship with a woman who had children from a previous relationship. Only one in six stepfamilies involved a father and his children being joined by a woman without children, but even rarer were situations in which both adults brought children to the new family formation. Facing the issues of family loyalty, distinct past experiences, and the need to be loved, as well as various daily habits, both children and adults in blended families have to adjust to a new reality (Preece, 2003–2004). Early adolescence seems to be an especially difficult time in which to have a remarriage occur, possibly because it exacerbates normal concerns about autonomy, identity, and sexuality during this period. Re-stabilization may take longer in stepfamilies—up to five years or more—than in divorced families, in which it often occurs in one to two years.

Remarried parents need to adjust, too. Stepfathers often attempt to engage the children of their new mate, and if successful this can result in very positive relationships within the family (Preece, 2003–2004). If rejected, the stepfather often responds by withdrawing emotionally and physically from the children, which leads to more problems. Stepfathers sometimes try to win over the children by being lax on rules and non-punitive, another situation that can cause problems. The most common attitude to be assumed by stepfathers is a more disengaged one. Stepmothers have a more difficult time integrating themselves into stepfamilies than do stepfathers. Overall, children's relationships with custodial parents tend to be better than with stepparents.

Gay and Lesbian Parents

Most children of gay and lesbian parents were born in a heterosexual relationship that ended in a divorce. In most cases, the divorce was brought about because one or both parents only later identified themselves as gay or lesbian. In other cases, lesbians and gays became parents as a result of donor insemination and surrogates, or through adoption. Obtaining artificial insemination or adopting may be difficult and prospective parents may face numerous barriers (Foster, 2005). Researchers have found few differences in the emotional development between children growing up with lesbian mothers or gay fathers and children growing up with heterosexual parents (Golombok & Tasker, 2010; Patterson, 2009a, b). For example, children growing up in gay or lesbian families are just as popular with their peers, and no differences are found in the adjustment and mental health of children living in these families when they are compared with children in heterosexual families (Hyde, 2007). Contrary to the once-popular expectation that being raised by a gay or lesbian parent would result in the child growing up to be gay or lesbian, in fact the overwhelming majority of children from gay or lesbian families have a heterosexual orientation (Golombok & Tasker, 2010).

Sibling Relationships and Birth Order

Today's children are more likely to live in smaller households than those in older cohorts. According to an estimate, the average family size is three, a decrease of 0.7 from 1971 (Canadian Council on Social Development, 2002). Still, many children have siblings. In this section, we will examine what it is like to have siblings and what it is like to be an only child.

Sibling Relationships

For many, sibling relationships are the longest relationships they have with any individual in life. Curiously, siblings' impact on development was largely overlooked by researchers until recently (Dunn, 2005; Kramer & Bank, 2005). Siblings very likely have rich memories of aggressive, hostile interchanges. Such disputes can be resolved through various means, from ignoring to arguing to fighting. In home observations of two- and four-year-old siblings, University of Toronto's Michal Perlman and University of Waterloo's Hildy Ross found that verbal and physical aggression to resolve a dispute tended to lead to disruptive reactions like unwillingness to comply in the older sibling and crying in the younger sibling. In contrast, there was some indication of both parties' willingness to reason if the other one used reasoning first (Perlman & Ross, 2005).

How does living in a stepfamily influence a child's development?

critical thinking

Considering the challenges that both divorce and entry into a step or blended family can have for a child, what are some of the factors that could help to ease the difficulties for each situation? What are some of the possible positive outcomes of divorce? How might joint-custody arrangements be helpful? What are some of the complications that would arise in a blended family? How might parents facilitate adjustment?

Judy Dunn (2007), a leading expert on sibling relationships, has described three important characteristics of sibling relationships:

- *Emotional quality of the relationship.* Both intensive positive and negative emotions are often expressed by siblings toward each other. Many children and adolescents have mixed feelings toward their siblings.
- *Familiarity and intimacy of the relationship.* Siblings typically know each other very well, and this intimacy suggests that they can either provide support or tease and undermine each other, depending on the situation.
- *Variation in sibling relationships.* Some siblings describe their relationships more positively than others. Thus, there is considerable variation in sibling relationships. While many siblings have mixed feelings about each other, some children and adolescents mainly describe their sibling in warm, affectionate ways, whereas others primarily talk about how irritating and mean a sibling is.

Birth Order

Whether a child has older or younger siblings has been linked to development of certain personality characteristics. For example, a recent review concluded that "firstborns are the most intelligent, achieving, and conscientious, while later-borns are the most rebellious, liberal, and agreeable" (Paulhus, 2008, p. 210). Compared with later-born children, firstborn children have also been described as more adult-oriented, helpful, conforming, and self-controlled. However, when such birth-order differences are reported, they often are small.

Proposed explanations for these differences usually point to variations in interactions with parents and siblings associated with being in a particular position in the family. This is especially true in the case of the firstborn child (Teti, 2001). The oldest child is the only one who does not have to share parental love and affection with other siblings—until another sibling comes along. An infant requires more attention than an older child; this means that the firstborn sibling receives less attention after the newborn arrives.

What is the only child like? While some people have the stereotype that the only child is a "spoiled brat," researchers present a more positive portrayal. Only children are often achievement-oriented and display a desirable personality, especially in comparison with later-borns and children from large families (Falbo & Poston, 1993; Jiao, Ji, & Jing, 1996).

So far, our discussion suggests that birth order might be a strong predictor of behaviour. However, an increasing number of family researchers stress that when all of the factors that influence behaviour are considered, birth order itself shows limited ability to predict behaviour. Think about some of the other important factors in children's lives that influence their behaviour beyond birth order. They include heredity, family size, models of competency or incompetency that parents present to children on a daily basis, peer influences, school influences, socio-economic factors, socio-historical factors, and cultural variations. Families are very complex micro-environments and the experience of each member is related to age, gender, power, or status within the family as well as influences from outside the family. So-called "shared events" have a unique impact on each member.

To this point, we have studied many aspects of families. For a review, see the **Reach Your Learning Objectives** section at the end of this chapter.

Peer Relations, Play, and Social Media

LO4 Describe the roles of peers, play, and social media in young children's development.

The family is an important social context for children's development. However, children's development is also strongly influenced by what goes on in other social contexts, such as peer relations and play.

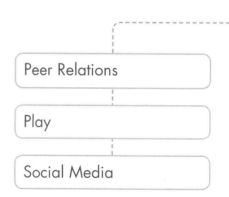

Peer Relations

Play

Social Media

Peer Relations

As children grow older, peer relations consume an increasing amount of their time. What is the function of a child's peer group?

Peers are children of about the same age or maturity level. One of the most important functions of the peer group is to provide a source of information and comparison about the world outside the family. Children receive feedback about their abilities from their peer group. Children evaluate what they do in terms of whether it is better than, as good as, or worse than what other children do. It is hard to do this at home because siblings are usually older or younger.

Good peer relations can be necessary for normal socio-emotional development (Howes, 2008; Prinstein & Dodge, 2008). Special concerns focus on children who are withdrawn and aggressive (Bukowski, Brendgen, & Vitaro, 2007). Withdrawn children who are rejected by peers or are victimized and feel lonely are at risk for depression. Children who are aggressive with their peers are at risk for developing a number of problems, including delinquency and dropping out of school (Dishion, Piehler, & Myers, 2008; Dodge, Coie, & Lynam, 2006; Tremblay, Gervais, & Petitclerc, 2008).

Just like parenting, peer relations can be influenced by cultural values. In Canada, reticent, quiet behaviour signals lack of social competence in children, while in Mainland China the same type of behaviour shows maturity. A recent study with four-year-olds in both countries found that Canadian children who displayed this behaviour were more likely to be rejected and less likely to receive positive affect and compliance from peers when they did initiate peer interaction than Chinese children in the same situation. These young children reacted to one another according to their culture's views of reticent behaviour (Chen, DeSouza, Chen, & Wang, 2006).

Play

An extensive amount of peer interaction during childhood involves play. Play is a pleasurable activity that is engaged in for its own sake. It ranges from an infant's simple exercise of a new-found sensorimotor talent, to a preschool child's riding a tricycle, to an older child's participation in organized games.

Play's Functions

Play is essential to the young child's development. Play increases affiliation with peers, releases tension, advances cognitive development, increases exploration, and provides a safe haven in which to engage in potentially dangerous behaviour.

According to Freud and Erikson, play is a useful form of human adjustment, helping the child master anxieties and conflicts. Because tensions are relieved in play, the child can cope with life's problems. Play permits the child to work off excess physical energy and to release pent-up tensions. Through *play therapy*, the therapist can analyze the child's conflicts and ways of coping with them. Children may feel less threatened and be more likely to express their true feelings in the context of play.

Piaget (1962) believed that play advances children's cognitive development. At the same time, he said that children's cognitive development constrains the way they play. Piaget thought that cognitive structures need to be exercised, and play provides the perfect setting for this exercise. For example, children who have just learned to add or multiply begin to play with numbers in different ways as they perfect these operations, laughing as they do so.

Vygotsky (1962), whose developmental theory was discussed in Chapter 7, also believed that play is an excellent setting for cognitive development. He was especially interested in the symbolic and make-believe aspects of play, such as when a child substitutes a stick for a horse and rides the stick as if it were a horse. For young children, the imaginary situation is real. Parents should encourage such imaginary play because it advances the child's cognitive development, especially creative thought.

Mildred Parten classified play into six categories. Study this photograph. **Which of Parten's categories are reflected in the behaviour of the children?**

developmental **connection**

Piaget and Vygotsky

Figure 8.3

Parten's and Bergen's Classifications of Play

Parten's (1932) Classification of Play

- **Unoccupied play** is not play as it is commonly understood. The child may stand in one spot, look around the room, or perform random movements that do not seem to have a goal.
- **Solitary play** occurs when the child plays alone and independently of others. The child seems engrossed in the activity and does not care much about anything else that is happening.
- **Parallel play** occurs when the child plays separately from others, but with toys like those the others are using or in a manner that mimics their play.
- **Onlooker play** occurs when the child watches other children play and maintains an active interest in their action. The child may talk with other children but does not enter into their play behaviour.
- **Associative play** involves social interaction with little or no organization. Children seem to be more interested in each other than in the tasks they are performing. Borrowing toys and following or leading one another in line are examples of this.
- **Cooperative play** involves social interaction in a group with a sense of group identity and organized activity.

Bergen's (1988) Classification of Play

- **Sensorimotor play** is behaviour engaged in by infants to derive pleasure from exercising their existing sensorimotor schemas, like shaking a rattle to make noise. The development of this type of play follows Piaget's description of sensorimotor thought (discussed in Chapter 5).
- **Practice play** involves the repetition of behaviour when new skills are being learned or when physical or mental mastery and coordination of skills are required for games or sports.
- **Pretence/symbolic play** occurs when children transform the physical environment into a symbol. They act toward objects as if these were other items.
- **Social play** involves social interaction with peers. It increases in the preschool years. One example is rough-and-tumble play. Although behaviours such as chasing and hitting are similar to those in hostile actions, laughter and exaggerated movement indicate this is play.
- **Constructive play** occurs when children engage in self-regulated creation or construction of a product or a problem solution.
- **Games** are activities engaged in for pleasure. They include rules and often competition with one or more individuals.

Types of Play

Depending on the behaviour children show, the amount of social interaction they engage in, and the functions an activity serves, play can be classified in many ways. Figure 8.3 shows both a classic and a contemporary classification of play.

Social Media

Few developments in society in the second half of the twentieth century have had a greater impact on children than television and technology (Brooks-Gunn & Donahue, 2008; Murray & Murray, 2008). Although television is only one of the many types of mass media that affect children's behaviour, it remains the most influential. The persuasive capabilities of television are staggering (Comstock & Scharrer, 2006).

Some children spend more time in front of the television set than they do with their parents. Statistics Canada (2006d) reports that in 2004, children aged 2 to 11 watched on average 14 hours of television a week. Television can have a negative influence on children by making them passive learners, distracting them from doing homework, teaching them stereotypes, providing them with violent models of aggression, and presenting them with unrealistic views of the world (Murray, 2007). However, television can have a positive influence on children's development by presenting motivating educational programs, increasing their information about the world beyond their immediate environment, and providing models of prosocial behaviour (Bryant, 2007; Wilson, 2008).

developmental **connection**

Bandura's Social Cognitive Theory

Effects of Social Media on Children's Aggression

The extent to which children are exposed to violence and aggression on television and in computer games raises special concern (Murray & Murray, 2008; Wilson, 2008). Research has found links between watching television violence as a child and acting aggressively years later. For example, in one study, exposure to media violence at 6 to 10 years of age was linked with young adult aggressive behaviour (Huesmann et al., 2003). In addition to television violence, there is increased concern about children who play violent video games, especially those that are highly realistic (Escobar-Chaves & Anderson, 2008). Children can become so deeply immersed in some electronic games that they experience an altered state of consciousness in which rational thought is suspended and arousing aggressive scripts are learned (Roberts, Henrikson, & Foehr, 2004). The direct rewards that players receive ("winning points") for their actions may also enhance the influence of video games.

These studies are correlational, so we can conclude from them that television violence is associated with aggressive behaviour. Experiments have not yet been conducted to demonstrate increased aggression subsequent to playing violent video games, although a recent analysis of research studies concluded that playing violent video games is linked to aggression in both males and females (Carnagey, Anderson, & Bushman, 2007).

developmental **connection**

Research Methods: Correlational Study

Effects of Social Media on Children's Prosocial Behaviour

Social media also can teach children that it is better to behave in positive, prosocial ways than in negative, antisocial ways as well as facilitate learning. LeapFrog offers a range of learning activities for children to enhance numeracy and literacy competence. Many of the cartoons on TVO or Treehouse, for example, illustrate creative exploration of nature, constructive conflict resolution, and problem solving-skills.

To this point, we have discussed a number of ideas about peer relations, play, and social media. For a review, see the **Reach Your Learning Objectives** section at the end of this chapter.

reach your **learning objectives**

The Self and Emotional Development

LO1 Discuss the emergence of the self and emotional development in early childhood.

The Self	■ Erikson believed that early childhood is a period when development involves resolving the conflict of initiative versus guilt.
	■ In early childhood, the self is understood in terms of physical or material attributes.
Emotional Development	■ Self-conscious emotions like pride and shame develop later than basic emotions like joy and fear.
	■ Preschoolers become more and more adept at talking about their own and others' emotions.
	■ Two- and three-year-olds can use a large number of terms to describe emotion.
	■ At four to five years of age, children show an increased ability to reflect on emotions. They also show a growing awareness of the need to control and manage emotions to meet social standards.
	■ Shyness can be classified into "conflicted shyness" and "social disinterest." Shy boys may be at more risk for maladjustment than shy girls.
	■ Emotion-coaching and emotion-dismissing parents act differently toward their children's expressions of emotions.
	■ Ability to control one's emotions is related to children's peer relationships.

Moral Development and Gender

LO2 Summarize moral development and gender in early childhood.

Moral Development	■ Moral development refers to the development of thoughts, feelings, and behaviours regarding standards of right and wrong.
	■ Piaget distinguished between the heteronomous morality of younger children and the autonomous morality of older children.
	■ There is considerable situational variability in moral behaviour.
	■ According to Freud's psychoanalytic theory, the superego, the moral branch of personality, develops through the Oedipus conflict and identification with the same-gender parent. In Freud's view, children conform to societal standards to avoid guilt.
Gender	■ Gender is the social dimension of being male or female.
	■ For most children, gender identity is acquired by three years of age.
	■ A gender role is a set of expectations that prescribes how females or males should think, act, and feel.
	■ The 23rd pair of chromosomes may have two X chromosomes to produce a female or one X and one Y chromosome to produce a male.
	■ The two main classes of sex hormones are estrogens, which are dominant in females, and androgens, which are dominant in males.
	■ Evolutionary psychology explains behavioural differences in males and females in terms of adapting to their different roles in reproduction.
	■ The social role theory, the psychoanalytic theory, and the social cognitive approach explain how people acquire gender-appropriate behaviour through interaction with the environment.
	■ Gender schema theory emphasizes the role of cognition in gender development.

Families

LO3 Explain how families can influence young children's development.

Parenting	■ Parental roles have shifted; economic pressures require dual incomes and fathers are more engaged with child raising.
	■ Baumrind's four parenting styles are authoritarian, authoritative, neglectful, and indulgent.
	■ Parenting styles in context: cultural and economic factors shape parenting styles.
	■ Diversity: Immigrant and refugee families face challenges of language and separation in addition to cultural adjustment.
	■ Culture and ethnicity are influential factors and include multifaceted challenges facing immigrant and refugee families such as language, poverty, and family reunification.
	■ Co-parenting refers to the support that parents provide each other in jointly raising a child.
	■ Punishment: In 2004, the Supreme Court ruled that spanking is legal so long as excessive force is not used. Research links harsh punitive punishment to aggressive behaviour.
Divorce	■ Divorce: 4 in 10 marriages end in divorce. Children adjust more readily when parents maintain a relatively harmonious relationship and engage in authoritative parenting styles.
	■ Gay and lesbian marriages were legalized in 2005 and most gay and lesbian families include children from a previous marriage.
	■ Step or blended families pose many challenges for both children and parents.

Sibling Relationships and Birth Order	■ Families are smaller and more diverse.
	■ Siblings interact with each other in positive and negative ways.
	■ Birth order is related in certain ways to children's characteristics, but some critics argue that birth order is not a good predictor of behaviour.

Peer Relations, Play, and Social Media

LO4 Describe the roles of peers, play, and social media in young children's development.

Peer Relations	■ Peers are children who are of about the same age or maturity level.
	■ Peers are powerful socialization agents.
	■ Peers provide a source of information and comparison about the world outside the family.
Play	■ Play's functions include affiliation with peers, tension release, advances in cognitive development, exploration, and provision of a safe haven.
	■ Freud and Erikson saw play as a way to help children deal with anxiety.
	■ Piaget and Vygotsky suggested that play was important for cognitive development.
Social Media	■ Viewing television and playing some computer games can negatively influence later learning ability and encourage the expression of violence.
	■ Social media can also increase prosocial behaviour and assist children with early literacy milestones.

McGraw-Hill Connect

McGraw-Hill Connect provides you with a powerful tool for improving academic performance and truly mastering course material. You can diagnose your knowledge with pre- and post-tests, identify the areas where you need help, search the entire learning package, including the eBook, for content specific to the topic you're studying, and add these resources to your personalized study plan. CONNECT for *Life-Span Development*, fifth Canadian edition, offers the following:

■ chapter-specific online quizzes
■ groupwork
■ presentations
■ writing assignments
■ case studies
■ and much more!

Visit CONNECT today!

review ---> *connect* ---> reflect

review

How might Erikson's fourth stage, initiative versus guilt, be resolved? **LO1**

How do self-esteem and self-concept differ? Give an example of each. **LO1**

How do heteronomous and autonomous morality differ? **LO2**

What is meant by the term *gender*? **LO2**

How do the definition and assumptions of family today differ from the definition and assumptions about family a generation ago? **LO3**

What are the long-term effects of child maltreatment? **LO3**

What are some of the positive and negative impacts of social media? **LO4**

connect

You read in this chapter that research has linked harsh punishment to aggressive behaviour. You also read that the Supreme Court of Canada has determined that spanking is legal as long as it does not include excessive force. How might you define the terms *harsh punishment, spanking,* and *excessive force*?

reflect *Your Own Personal Journey of Life*

Did your parents monitor your use of television and the Internet? If so, what strategies did they use? If not, why? What might be some of the challenges facing parents? What guidelines might you develop or recommend to monitor children's use of television and other forms of social media? What safety net could be offered to a child who is the victim of cyberspace bullying?

CHAPTER 9 Physical and Cognitive Development in Middle and Late Childhood

CHAPTER OUTLINE

Physical Changes and Health

LO1 Describe physical changes and health in middle and late childhood.

Body Growth and Change

The Brain

Motor Development

Exercise

Health, Illness, and Disease

Cognitive Development

LO2 Explain cognitive changes in middle and late childhood.

Piaget's Concrete Operational Stage

Information Processing

Intelligence

Language Development

LO3 Discuss language development in middle and late childhood.

Vocabulary, Grammar, and Metalinguistic Awareness

Reading

Bilingualism

Educational Approaches and Issues

LO4 Discuss approaches and issues related to education.

Approaches to Student Learning

Educational Issues

International Comparisons

Private Schools and Home Education

Children with Disabilities

LO5 Identify different types of disabilities and discuss issues relating to their education.

Learning Disabilities

Attention Deficit Hyperactivity Disorder (ADHD)

Autism Spectrum Disorders

Physical Disabilities

Children's Disabilities and the Family

Educational Issues

"I have never let my schooling interfere with my education."

—MARK TWAIN, NINETEENTH-CENTURY AMERICAN WRITER

Courtesy of World Literacy Canada.

Gandhi's Glasses

Do we see the world differently when we put on glasses? What if those glasses were ones that had been worn by the famous peace advocate Mahatma Gandhi, the man who said, "Be the change you want to see in the world"? Inspired by the project The Gandhi Way: Engaging Youth in Global Citizenship, 15 teachers in 15 different schools guided 300 elementary school children from Toronto's Model School for Inner Cities program to write and illustrate a children's book. The book, *Gandhi's Glasses*, addresses social justice and equity issues that the children identified—issues such as recycling, violence, poverty, and gender discrimination.

The young authors decided the hero would be a little girl named Asha and that she would be confronted by all these concerns in one school day. At first, Asha thought she was "too busy" to help the boy who did not have enough bus fare, or to do anything about the backpacks blocking the wheelchair access ramp or all the litter on the playground. She thought she was "too little" to do anything about the way boys were not including girls in basketball games. Certainly she was "too little" to do anything about the bulldozing of the local park.

Then, she found a pair of Gandhi's glasses and she saw the world differently. She realized that indeed, in a peaceful way, she could make a difference. As the young authors say, "Whatever you do will be insignificant, but it's important that you do it." "Seeing ourselves as citizens of the globe, we have to always be fair." Another author reminded that "In a gentle way, you can change the world," to which two more added, "An eye for an eye will lead to blindness."

The Canadian International Development Agency (CIDA), World Literacy Canada (WLC), and the Toronto District School Board (TDSB) partnered to engage children to write and illustrate ways that global citizenship could be achieved in their own lives. Please refer to the World Literacy Canada Web site http://www.worldlit.ca/programs-history/gandhi-way-2/ for more information.

Imagine for a moment that you were engaged in writing and illustrating this book. What might you have learned? The collaborative efforts and dedication of those who guided the making of *Gandhi's Glasses* illustrate many of the concepts, theories, and approaches about cognitive development, intelligence, and education that you will be reading about in this chapter.

Physical Changes and Health

LO1 Describe physical changes and health in middle and late childhood

Body Growth and Change

How do children's bodies change in middle and late childhood? Physical growth during the elementary school years is relatively slow, but consistent. It is a period of relative calm before the rapid changes that occur during adolescence. During the public school years, children grow 5 to 7.5 cm a year until, at the age of 11, the average girl is 1.48 m tall, and the average boy is 1.45 m tall. During this time, children gain about 2.3 to 3.2 kg a year. The weight increase is due mainly to increases in the size of the skeletal and muscular systems and the size of some body organs. Muscle mass and strength gradually increase as "baby fat" decreases. The loose movements and knock-knees of early childhood give way to improved muscle tone. Thanks to both heredity and exercise, children double their strength capabilities during these years. Because of their greater number of muscle cells, boys are usually stronger than girls.

Proportional changes are among the most pronounced physical changes during this time. Head circumference and waist circumference decrease in relation to body height (Kliegman et al., 2007). A less noticeable physical change is that bones continue to ossify during middle and late childhood.

The Brain

The development of brain-imaging techniques such as magnetic resonance imaging (MRI) has led to an increase in research on the changes in the brain during middle and late childhood, and how these brain changes are linked to improvements in cognitive development (Diamond, 2009; Diamond, Casey, & Munakata, 2011). The total brain volume stabilizes by the end of middle and late childhood, but significant changes in various structures and regions of the brain continue to occur. In particular, the brain pathways and circuitry involving the prefrontal cortex, the highest level in the brain, continue to increase in middle and late childhood (Durston & Casey, 2006) (see Figure 9.1) These advances in the prefrontal cortex are linked to children's improved attention, reasoning, and cognitive control (Crone et al., 2009). Leading developmental neuroscientist Mark Johnson and his colleagues (2009) recently proposed that the prefrontal cortex likely orchestrates the functions of many other brain regions during development. As part of this neural leadership, organizational role, the prefrontal cortex may provide an advantage to neural networks and connections that include the prefrontal cortex. In their view, the prefrontal cortex coordinates the best neural connections for solving a problem at hand.

Changes also occur in the thickness of the cerebral cortex (cortical thickness) in middle and late childhood (Toga, Thompson, & Sowell, 2006). One study used brain scans to assess cortical thickness in 5- to 11-year-old children (Sowell et al., 2004). Cortical thickening across a two-year time period was observed in the temporal and frontal lobe areas that function in language, which may reflect improvements in language abilities such as reading.

As children develop, activation of some brain areas increases while others decrease (Diamond, Casey, & Munakata, 2011; Nelson, 2011). One shift in activation that occurs as children develop is from diffuse larger areas to more focal smaller areas (Turkeltaub et al., 2003). This shift is characterized by synaptic pruning, in which areas of the brain not being used lose synaptic connections and those being used show an increase in connections. In a recent study, researchers found less diffusion and more focal activation in the prefrontal cortex from 7 to 30 years of age (Durston et al., 2006). The activation change was accompanied by increased efficiency in cognitive performance, especially in cognitive control, which involves flexible and effective controlling attention, reducing interfering thoughts, inhibiting motor actions, and being flexible in switching between competing choices (Diamond, Casey, & Munakata, 2011).

Body Growth and Change

The Brain

Motor Development

Exercise

Health, Illness, and Disease

developmental **connection**

The Brain

Figure 9.1

The Prefrontal Cortex

The brain pathways and circuitry involving the prefrontal cortex (shaded in purple) show significant advances in development during middle and late childhood. **What cognitive processes are these changes in the prefrontal cortex linked to?**

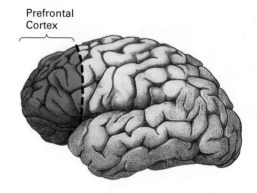

Prefrontal Cortex

Motor Development

During middle and late childhood, children's gross motor skills become much smoother and more coordinated than they were in early childhood. For example, only one child in a thousand can hit a tennis ball over the net at three years of age, yet by 10 or 11, most children can learn to play the sport. As well, most children enjoy running, riding a bike, swimming, and playing sports such as baseball and soccer. In gross motor skills, boys usually outperform girls.

Increased myelination of the central nervous system is reflected in the improvement of fine motor skills during middle and late childhood. Children can more adroitly use their hands as tools. Six-year-olds can hammer, paste, tie shoes, and fasten clothes. By seven years of age, children's hands have become steadier. At this age, children prefer a pencil to a crayon for printing, and reversal of letters is less common. Printing becomes smaller. Between 8 and 10 years of age, children can use their hands independently with more ease and precision. Fine motor coordination develops to the point at which children can write rather than print words. Cursive letter size becomes smaller and more even. At 10 to 12 years of age, children begin to show manipulative skills similar to the abilities of adults. The complex, intricate, and rapid movements needed to produce fine-quality crafts or to play a difficult piece on a musical instrument can be mastered. Girls usually outperform boys in fine motor skills.

------- **critical** thinking -------

Print is the format used by technology, such as word processing, email, and text messaging. As a result, many wonder whether cursive writing is becoming obsolete. How often do you use cursive writing in your personal life? As a student, are you able to submit your work using cursive writing? Do you think cursive writing is becoming obsolete? If so, should it be dropped from the curriculum?

Exercise

According to Active Healthy Kids Canada, physical activity is linked positively to physical, socio-emotional, and cognitive development. Not only is physical activity associated with better health and physical skills, but it also fosters creativity, problem solving, executive brain functioning, academic performance, self-esteem, and social skills such as sharing, turn taking, and negotiation. So much positive gain is linked to physical activity, whether it is structured or unstructured, that it is dismaying to learn that 88 percent of children and youth do not meet the Canadian guidelines of 90 minutes of vigorous physical activity a day. Instead of physical activity, children are spending an average of 7 hours and 48 minutes daily in sedentary screen activities such as watching television, playing video games, or chatting online with friends. This is far in excess of the Canadian Paediatric Society's recommendation that children's television viewing be limited to one or two hours daily (Active Healthy Kids Canada, 2012). Active play has been replaced by sedentary play, which, in the words of Dr. Tremblay, "It (sedentary play) is seductive, it's convenient, and it's cheaper than a baby-sitter, but it's really bad for their health" (Picard, 2012).

What are the statistics reported in the Active Healthy Kids Canada 2012 report card?

- 46 percent of Canadian children and youth are getting a mere three hours or less of active play each week (including weekend days)
- Children are spending 63 percent of their free time after school and on weekends being sedentary
- 92 percent of Canadian children said that, if given the choice, they would choose to play with friends over watching TV
- The proportion of Canadian children who play outside after school dropped 14 percent over the last decade
- At lunch and after school, children are getting only 24 minutes of moderate-to-vigorous-intensity physical activity out of a possible four hours

Why is this? Like their children, most Canadian adults fail to meet the guideline of 150 minutes of physical activity per week. Busy work schedules and safety concerns are the two primary reasons for the lack of physical activity. Parents report that as children, their physical activity levels were considerably higher than those of their children. A generation ago, children ran loose and were more free to explore the world around them.

Increasing children's exercise levels has positive outcomes (Beets & Foley, 2008; Corbin et al., 2008). For example, a recent study revealed that a high-intensity resistance training program

Does playing on a team guarantee vigorous physical activity?

decreases children's body fat and increases their muscle strength (Benson, Torode, & Fiatarone Singh, 2008). Another study found that 45 minutes of moderate physical activity and 15 minutes of vigorous physical activity daily were related to decreased odds of children being overweight (Wittmeier, Mollard, & Kriellaars, 2008). And recent research has shown that aerobic exercise is linked to increases in important cognitive activity—planning—in overweight nine-year-old children (Davis et al., 2007).

In light of the problem of child inactivity, many organizations are promoting an active lifestyle among Canada's young people. Among these groups are Right to Play, and Active Healthy Kids Canada and Canadian Olympian Silken Laumann has been an active advocate in their formation. You can find more information about these organizations on Connect at www.mcgrawhillconnect.ca.

Health, Illness, and Disease

Do Canadian children maintain a healthy diet? Is obesity really a big problem? What are the other major public health concerns? For the most part, middle and late childhood is a time of excellent health. Disease and death are less prevalent at this time than during other periods in childhood and in adolescence.

Balanced or Unbalanced Diet?

A healthy diet promotes normal growth and development and contributes to overall health. Surveys conducted by Health Canada, the Canada Food Guide, and other associations provide an assessment of our diets. Recent findings from Health Canada (2012) contrast with the findings of the Canadian Community Health Survey of 2004; the 2004 survey indicated that many Canadian children were not eating the balanced diet suggested by Canada's Food Guide, with fewer than 40 percent of 9- to 13-year-olds getting enough vegetables and fruit daily. Moreover, 61 percent of boys and 83 percent of girls aged 10 to 16 were not taking in enough milk products daily. At the same time, the percentage of calories from fat for children aged 5 to 11 dropped between 1972 and 2004 (Garriguet, 2007), probably indicating awareness about childhood obesity. Health Canada 2012 reports the diet of children between one and eight years of age provided adequate amounts of most vitamins and minerals. However, the survey found that one in five children took in more energy than they expended, and that 75 percent of children took in more sodium than recommended (Health Canada, 2012).

Obesity

According to the World Health Organization (WHO), nearly one-third (31.5 percent) of Canadian children between 5 and 17 years of age are overweight, and off that group, 11.6 percent are obese (Statistics Canada, 2012a). What can be done about childhood obesity? Parents play an important role in preventing children from becoming overweight and helping them lose weight if they become overweight (Wofford, 2008). They can encourage healthy eating habits in children by eating more family meals together, making healthy foods available, and not keeping sugar-sweetened beverages and other unhealthy foods in the home. They can also help reduce the likelihood that their children will become overweight by reducing children's screen time (both computer and TV), getting children involved in sports and other physical activities, and being healthy, physically active role models themselves (Salmon, Campbell, & Crasford, 2006).

Diets and exercise are certainly important for a successful weight-loss program for overweight children. Exercise increases the lean body mass, which in turn increases the resting metabolic rate. This results in more calories being burned in the resting state. Parents can find suggestions for physical activities from physicians, Health Canada, or health organizations such as the Canadian Association for Health, Physical Education, Recreation, and Dance.

Many experts recommend a combination of diet, exercise, and behaviour modification. In a typical behaviour modification program, children are taught to monitor their own behaviour, such as keeping a food diary. The diary records not only the type and amount of food eaten, but also when, with whom, and where it was eaten. For example, do children eat in front of the TV by themselves, or because they are angry or depressed? Such a diary identifies behaviours that need to be changed.

critical thinking

Mothers reported having more than twice as much daily outdoor play than their children when they were children. What are some of the factors that might account for this decline? What are some strategies for increasing children's physical activity?

critical thinking

The research shows that parents are important role models for their children. What advice would you give to parents who want to ensure that their children get enough exercise and eat a nutritious diet? How do you incorporate healthy nutrition and exercise into your lifestyle? If you are not already a parent, what changes, if any, might you want to make in your lifestyle once you become a parent?

Obese children who are embarrassed by their peers or parents may choose to lose weight to the extent of becoming anorexic (Johnston, 2004). As well, research indicates a link between disordered eating and girls who have been subjected to violence. The research concludes that eating disorders may be a form of resistance to further violation for some, and for others it may be a way to purge feelings of shame and guilt. The context for each individual girl or woman shapes the meaning and significance of their particular experience (Moore et al., 2009). Further, thinness in itself may become a goal as it is often perceived as a sign of interpersonal and economic success (Moore et al., 2009).

Striving for Thinness

Children's desire for thinness is as important a health issue as obesity (Johnston, 2004). In fact, Chapter 11 will show you how an obsession with dieting and anorexia nervosa is affecting many Canadian teens. However, the trend often starts in the pre-teen years.

A longitudinal study in Australia reported that over 40 percent of girls as young as five to eight years of age wanted to be thinner (Dohnt & Tiggemann, 2006). This desire for thinness foreshadowed the lowered self-esteem experienced by young girls a year later, highlighting the relationship of body weight and psychological well-being. A study from the University of Calgary found a link between disordered eating and an external locus of control (i.e., a belief of outside influence on one's environment) (Fouts & Vaughan, 2002). Peer pressure, family pressure, and media messages of thinness being good are some of the outside influences.

Because an obsession with thinness among school-age children may lead them to disordered eating behaviour—such as unnecessary fasting—that can damage their health in both the short term and the long term, parents should be aware of their children's desire to be thin and the underlying reasons for this desire. In some instances, such as those involving abuse, finding the underlying cause may be difficult and outside counselling may be helpful. Research reveals that for over 90 percent of girls who have survived sexual abuse, the onset of eating disorders occurs after their first abuse (Moore et al., 2009). Promoting a sense of competence in their children, listening to youngsters' concerns about not being as good as their peers, and explaining the unrealistic and unhealthy aspects of the media's portrayal of thinness may help children develop a positive body image.

Accidents and Injuries

Unintentional injuries and accidents are the leading cause of hospitalization and death during middle and late childhood. The most common cause of injury and death is motor vehicle accidents, either as a pedestrian or as a passenger (Wilson & Hocken-Berry, 2008). Other serious injuries involve bicycles, skateboards, roller skates, falls, and drowning (Birkin et al., 2006). Research also indicates that a higher level of injury-related mortality occurs in urban neighbourhoods of lower socio-economic status, indicating that an injury prevention strategy is needed (Birkin et al., 2006).

Many children suffer injuries and even death in preventable accidents. Most accidents occur at or near the child's home or school. One reason for these accidents is unnecessary risk taking. A study at the University of Guelph in Ontario showed that boys are more willing to take risks in everyday activities than girls (Morrongiello & Dawber, 2004). Another Canadian study found that boys were more likely to play sports and had played for more years by the ages of 11 to 14 years (Bowker, 2006). Together, these findings partly explain why boys are more likely than girls to experience injuries.

The most effective prevention strategy is to educate children about the proper use of equipment and the hazards of risk taking (Beta & Sowden, 2008). Safety helmets, protective eye and mouth shields, and protective padding are recommended for children who engage in active sports (Briem et al., 2004).

Cancer

Although childhood cancers account for less than one percent of all cancers diagnosed in Canada, cancer is the second leading cause of death in children between 1 and 14 years of age (PHAC, 2009b). Cancers are characterized by an uncontrolled proliferation of abnormal cells. Adult cancers are typically carcinomas that primarily attack glands and tissues that line organs such as lungs, colon, breast, prostate, and pancreas. Carcinomas are rare in children; childhood cancers are more likely to be rapid-growing tumours that primarily attack white blood and lymphatic systems. Leukemia, which accounts for one-third of all childhood cancers, is a disease in which the bone marrow makes an abundance of white blood cells that do not function properly. They invade the bone marrow and crowd out normal cells, making the child susceptible to bruising and infection. Brain and spinal tumours account for 20 percent of childhood cancers, and 12 percent are either Hodgkin (cancer of the lymph nodes) or non-Hodgkin lymphoma (cancer of the fighting cells) (PHAC, 2009b).

To this point, we have studied physical changes and health in middle and late childhood. For a review, see the **Reach Your Learning Objectives** section at the end of this chapter.

Cognitive Development

LO2 Explain cognitive changes in middle and late childhood.

Piaget's Concrete Operational Stage

According to Piaget (1952), the preschool child's thought is preoperational. Preschool children can form stable concepts and they have begun to reason, but their thinking is flawed by egocentrism and magical belief systems. As we discussed in Chapter 7, however, most researchers agree that Piaget underestimated children's abilities (Cherry, 2012). First we will cover the characteristics of concrete operational thought and evaluate Piaget's portrait of this stage, then we will do a critical analysis to evaluate Piaget's theory.

The Concrete Operational Stage

Piaget proposed that the concrete operational stage lasts approximately from 7 to 11 years of age. In this stage, children can perform concrete operations, and they can reason logically as long as reasoning can be applied to specific or concrete examples. Remember that *operations* are mental actions that allow children to do mentally what they have done physically before.

One of the most important developments in this stage is *reversibility*; that is, an understanding or awareness that actions can be reversed. The conservation tasks described in Chapter 7 indicate whether children are capable of concrete operations. For example, recall that in one task involving conservation of matter, the child is presented with two identical balls of clay. The experimenter rolls one ball into a long, thin shape; the other remains in its original ball shape. The child is then asked if there is more clay in the ball or in the long thin piece of clay. To answer this problem correctly, children have to imagine the clay rolling back into a ball. This type of imagination involves a reversible mental action applied to a real, concrete object. Concrete operations allow the child to consider several characteristics rather than focus on a single property of an object. In this example, the preoperational child is likely to focus on height or width. The concrete operational child coordinates information about both dimensions. As well, in this stage the child is able to understand and reverse the order of relationships and mental categories (Cherry, 2012). For example, a child might recognize and categorize various kinds of dinosaurs.

As shown in Figure 9.2, the concrete operational child also has the ability to classify things into different sets or subsets and to consider their interrelationships. Another example of this ability to deal with relations between objects is **seriation**, *the concrete operation that involves ordering stimuli along a quantitative dimension (such as length)*. To see if students can serialize, a teacher might haphazardly place eight sticks of different lengths on a table. The teacher then asks the students to arrange the sticks by length. Many young children end up with small groups of "big" sticks or "little" sticks, rather than a correct ordering by length. Another mistaken strategy they may use is to line up the tops of the sticks but ignore the bottoms. In contrast, the concrete operational thinker simultaneously understands that each stick must be longer than the one that precedes it and shorter than the one that follows it.

Piaget's Concrete Operational Stage

Information Processing

Intelligence

seriation The concrete operation that involves ordering stimuli along a quantitative dimension (such as length).

Figure 9.2

Classification

A family tree of four generations (I to IV) (Furth & Wachs, 1975): The preoperational child has trouble classifying the members of the four generations; a concrete operational child can classify the members within a generation and across different generations. For example, the concrete operational child understands that a family member can be a son, a brother, and a father, all at the same time.

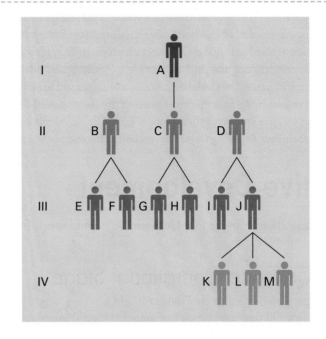

transitivity In concrete operational thought, a mental concept that underlies the ability to combine relations logically in order to understand certain conclusions.

Another aspect of reasoning about the relations between objects is **transitivity**, *the ability to combine relations logically in order to understand certain conclusions.* In this case, consider three sticks (A, B, and C) of differing lengths. In Piaget's view, concrete operational thinkers understand that if A is longer than B and B is longer than C, then A is longer C; preoperational thinkers do not. A summary of the characteristics of concrete operational thought is shown in Figure 9.3.

Evaluating Piaget's Theory

Piaget proposed some important ideas in cognitive development. Psychologists owe him the vision of children as active, constructive thinkers (Vidal, 2000). He also showed us how children need to make their experiences fit their schemas (cognitive frameworks) and likewise adapt their schemas to experience. But has Piaget's portrait of the concrete operational child stood the test of research?

According to Piaget, various aspects of a stage should emerge at the same time. In fact, however, some concrete operational abilities do not appear in synchrony. For example, children do not learn to conserve at the same time they learn to cross-classify. Additionally, some cognitive abilities emerge at a different time than Piaget thought. For example, conservation of numbers occurs as early as age three, not age seven as Piaget suggested. On the other hand, many adults still think in concrete operational ways.

Furthermore, education and culture exert stronger influences on children's development than Piaget reasoned (Holzman, 2009; Irvine & Berry, 2010). Some preoperational children can be

Figure 9.3

Characteristics of Concrete Operational Thought

Can use operations, mentally reversing action; shows conservation skills	Classification skills — can divide things into sets and subsets and reason about their interrelations	Not abstract — cannot imagine steps in algebraic equation, for example	Logical reasoning replaces intuitive reasoning, but only in concrete circumstances

trained to reason at a concrete operational stage. The age at which children acquire skills is related to how much practice their culture provides in these skills. Recall that in Chapters 2 and 7 we discussed Vygotsky, who offers an alternative to Piaget. Like Piaget, Vygotsky held that children construct their knowledge of the world. But Vygotsky did not propose stages of cognitive development; rather, he emphasized the importance of social interaction, the social contexts of learning, and the child's use of language to plan, guide, and monitor behaviour (Holzman, 2009).

Neo-Piagetians agree that although Piaget was a giant in the field of developmental psychology his theory needs considerable revision. Recall in Chapter 2 that we discussed how the Dynamic Systems Theory (DST) proposed by Esther Thelen brought new approaches to Piaget's stages. Thelen's experiments supported the theory that learning takes place through the interaction among the nervous system, the rest of the body, and the surrounding environment (Fausto-Sterling, 2011). Neo-Piagetians give more emphasis to how children use attention, memory, and strategies to process information (Case & Mueller, 2001). They especially believe that a more accurate portrayal of children's thinking requires attention to children's strategies, the speed at which children process information, the particular task involved, and the division of problems into smaller, more precise steps (Morra et al., 2008). These issues are addressed by the information-processing approach.

Information Processing

If instead of analyzing the type of thinking that children display we examine how they handle information during middle and late childhood, what do we find? During these years, most children dramatically improve their ability to sustain and control attention. As discussed in Chapter 7, they pay more attention to task-relevant stimuli than to salient stimuli. Other changes in information processing during middle and late childhood are those involving memory, thinking, and metacognition.

Memory

In Chapter 7, we concluded that short-term memory increases considerably during early childhood, but does not show as much increase after the age of seven. On the other hand, **long-term memory** *is a relatively permanent and unlimited type of memory that increases with age during middle and late childhood.* In part, improvements in memory reflect children's increased knowledge and their increased use of strategies. Keep in mind that it is important not to view memory in terms of how children add something to it but rather to underscore how children actively construct their memory (Ornstein, Coffman, & Grammer, 2009; Ornstein et al., 2010).

Knowledge and Expertise

Much of the research on the role of knowledge in memory has compared experts and novices. *Experts* have acquired extensive knowledge about a particular content area; this knowledge influences what they notice and how they organize, represent, and interpret information. This in turn affects their ability to remember, reason, and solve problems. When individuals have expertise about a particular subject, their memory also tends to be good regarding material related to that subject (Martinez, 2010).

For example, one study found that 10- and 11-year-olds who were experienced chess players ("experts") were able to remember more information about chess pieces than university students who were not chess players ("novices") (Chi, 1978) (see Figure 9.4). In contrast, when presented with other stimuli, university students were able to remember them better than the children were. Thus, the children's expertise in chess gave them superior memories, but only in chess. In general, there are developmental changes in expertise (Blair & Somerville, 2009). Older children usually have more expertise about various subjects than younger children do, and this can partially explain their better memory.

Strategies

If we know anything at all about long-term memory, it is that long-term memory depends on the learning activities individuals engage in when learning and remembering information (Ashcraft & Radvansky, 2010). Recall from Chapter 7 that strategies consist of deliberate mental activities to

Piaget with his wife and three children; he often used his observations of his children to provide examples of his theory.

long-term memory A relatively permanent and unlimited type of memory that increases with age during middle and late childhood.

Figure 9.4

The Role of Expertise in Memory

When 10- to 11-year-old children and university students were asked to remember a string of random numbers that had been presented to them, the university students fared better. However, the children who were chess "experts" had better memory for the location of chess pieces on a chess board than university students with no chess experience ("novices") (Chi, 1978).

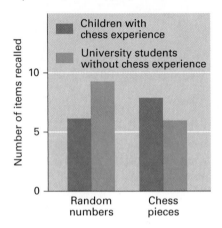

elaboration An important strategy that involves engaging in more extensive processing of information.

fuzzy trace theory States that memory is best understood by considering two types of memory representations: (1) verbatim memory trace, and (2) gist. In this theory, older children's better memory is attributed to fuzzy traces created by extracting the gist of information.

improve the procession of information. They do not occur automatically, but require effort and work. The following are some effective strategies adults can use to help children improve their memory skills.

Encourage children to engage in mental imagery. Mental imagery can help even young school-children to remember pictures. However, for remembering verbal information, mental imagery works better for older children than for younger children (Schneider, 2004).

- *Motivate children to remember material by understanding it rather than by memorizing it.* Children will remember information better over the long term if they understand the information rather than just rehearse and memorize it. Rehearsal works well for encoding information into short-term memory, but when children need to retrieve the information from long-term memory, it is much less efficient. For most information, encourage children to understand it, give it meaning, elaborate on it, and personalize it. Give children concepts and ideas to remember and then ask them how they can relate the concepts and ideas to their own personal experiences and meanings. Give them practice on elaborating a concept so they will process the information more deeply.
- *Repeat with variation on the instructional information and link early and often.* These are memory development research expert Patricia Bauer's (2009) recommendations to improve children's consolidation and reconsolidation of the information they are learning. Variations on a lesson theme increase the number of associations in memory storage and linking expands the network of associations in memory storage; both strategies expand the routes for retrieving information from storage.
- *Embed memory-relevant language when instructing children.* Teachers vary considerably in how much they use memory-relevant language that encourages students to remember information. In recent research that involved extensive observations of a number of first-grade teachers in the classroom, Peter Ornstein and his colleagues (Ornstein, Coffman, & Grammer, 2009; Ornstein et al., 2007, 2010) found that for the time segments observed the teachers rarely used strategy suggestions or metacognitive (thinking about thinking) questions. In this research, when lower-achieving students were placed in classrooms in which teachers were categorized as "high-mnemonic teachers" who frequently embedded memory-relevant information in their teaching, their achievement increased (Ornstein, Coffman, & Grammer, 2007).

Fuzzy Trace Theory

Might something other than knowledge and strategies be responsible for the improvement in memory during the elementary school years? Charles Brainerd and Valerie Reyna (1993; Reyna, 2004) argue that fuzzy traces account for much of this improvement. Their **fuzzy trace theory** *states that memory is best understood by considering two types of memory representations: (1) verbatim memory trace, and (2) gist.* The verbatim memory trace consists of the precise details of the information, whereas gist refers to the central idea of the information. When gist is used, fuzzy traces are built up. Although individuals of all ages extract gist, young children tend to store and retrieve verbatim traces. At some point during the early elementary school years, children begin to use gist more. According to the theory, this contributes to the improved memory and reasoning of older children because fuzzy traces are more enduring and less likely to be forgotten than verbatim traces. An example of how this might work might be found in the way you study for an exam. If you were asked to explain Piaget's concept of transitivity, something you recently read about or heard your professor explain, would you repeat the definition almost verbatim, or would you remember that "transit" was in the word and that it had something to do with sticks? Fuzzy trace is illustrated by the second example.

Fuzzy trace also influences decision making. For example, imagine that one hot summer day, a child thinks he or she would like to take his/her very first dive off one of the diving boards, and is deciding what kind of dive and whether it'll be the high or low board. What factors are likely to influence the decision? The child has watched older children dive, so knows what a dive looks like. The child has also seen a diver get hurt. So, not knowing or recalling any "verbatim" information about the depth of the water, how to position the body, the height of the diving board, or safety warnings, the child decides to jump, rather than dive, from the lower board. Having succeeded, the child may later try a jump from the high board. Here, the child is making decisions based on the "gist" of diving, rather than on specific detailed information.

Thinking

Three important aspects of thinking are being able to think critically, creatively, and scientifically.

CRITICAL THINKING   Psychologists and educators are currently very interested in critical thinking (Bonny & Sternberg, 2010; Fairweather & Cramond, 2011). **Critical thinking** *involves thinking reflectively and productively, and evaluating evidence.* In this book, the Critical Thinking questions challenge you to think critically about a topic or an issue related to the discussion. According to Ellen Langer (2005), mindfulness—being alert, mentally present, and cognitively flexible while going through life's everyday activities and tasks—is an important aspect of thinking critically. Mindful children and adults maintain an active awareness of the circumstances in their life and are motivated to find the best solutions to tasks. Mindful individuals create new ideas, are open to new information, and operate from a single perspective. By contrast, mindless individuals are entrapped in old ideas, engage in automatic behaviour, and operate from a single perspective.

Jacqueline and Martin Brooks (2001) lament that few schools really teach students to think critically and develop a deep understanding of concepts. Deep understanding occurs when students are stimulated to rethink previously held ideas. In the view of Brooks and Brooks, schools spend too much time getting students to give a single correct answer in an imitative way, rather than encouraging them to expand their thinking by coming up with new ideas and rethinking earlier conclusions. They observed that too often teachers ask students to recite, define, describe, state, and list, rather than to analyze, infer, connect, synthesize, criticize, create, evaluate, think, and rethink. Many successful students complete their assignments, do well on tests, and get good grades, yet they don't ever learn to think critically and deeply. They think superficially, staying on the surface of problems rather than stretching their minds and becoming deeply engaged in meaningful thinking.

CREATIVE THINKING   Cognitively competent children think not only critically, but also creatively (Rickards, Runco, & Moger, 2009). **Creative thinking** *is the ability to think in novel and unusual ways and to come up with unique solutions to problems.* Thus, intelligence and creativity are not the same thing. This difference was recognized by J. P. Guilford (1967), who distinguished between **convergent thinking**, *which produces one correct answer and characterizes the kind of thinking required on conventional tests of intelligence,* and **divergent thinking**, *which produces many different answers to the same question and characterizes creativity.* For example, a typical item on a conventional intelligence test is "How many quarters will you get in return for 60 dimes?" In contrast, the following question has many possible answers: "What image comes to mind when you hear the phrase 'sitting alone in a dark room' or 'some unique uses for a paper clip'?" It is important to recognize that children will show more creativity in some domains than others (Rickards, Runco, & Moger, 2009; Sternberg, 2009b). A child who shows creative thinking skills in mathematics may not exhibit these skills in art, for example.

How can children's creativity be improved? One way is brainstorming. In **brainstorming**, *individuals try to come up with ideas and play off each idea.* This can be done alone or in a group. The more ideas children produce, the better their chance is of creating something unique (Runco, 2000). Secondly, adults can provide activities that stimulate children's interest in finding insightful solutions to problems. Internal motivation should also be promoted: creative children's motivation is the satisfaction generated by the work itself (Amabile & Hennessey, 1992). Flexible thinking should be encouraged. Adults should also allow children to select their interests and support their inclinations, as this is less likely to destroy their natural curiosity than dictating which activities children should engage in (Csikszentmihalyi, 2000). Finally, children can also be introduced to creative people like poets and scientists. The Connecting Development to Life feature examines some recommendations for ways to accomplish this goal.

"For God's sake, think! Why is he being so nice to you?"
Copyright © The New Yorker Collection 1998 Sam Gross from cartoonbank.com. All Rights Reserved.

critical thinking Thinking reflectively and productively, and evaluating the evidence.

creative thinking The ability to think in novel and unusual ways and to come up with unique solutions to problems.

convergent thinking Produces one correct answer and is characteristic of the kind of thinking required on conventional tests of intelligence.

divergent thinking Produces many answers to the same question and is characteristic of creativity.

brainstorming A technique in which individuals try to come up with ideas and play off each idea. This can be done alone or in a group.

Strategies for Increasing Children's Creative Thinking

The following are some strategies for increasing children's creative thinking.

Encourage Brainstorming

Brainstorming is a technique in which people are encouraged to come up with creative ideas in a group, play off each other's ideas, and say practically whatever comes to mind that seems relevant to a particular issue. Facilitators usually tell participants to hold off from criticizing others' ideas at least until the end of the brainstorming session.

Provide Environments That Stimulate Creativity

Some environments nourish creativity, others inhibit it. Parents and teachers who encourage creativity often rely on children's natural curiosity. They provide exercises and activities that stimulate children to find insightful solutions to problems, rather than ask a lot of questions that require rote answers (Beghetto & Kaufman, 2011; Skiba et al., 2010; Sternberg, 2010d). Teachers also encourage creativity by taking students on field trips to locations where creativity is valued. Science, discovery, and children's museums offer rich opportunities to stimulate creativity.

Don't Overcontrol Children

Teresa Amabile (1993) says that telling children exactly how to do things leaves them feeling that originality is a mistake and exploration is a waste of time. Instead of dictating which activities they should engage in, teachers and parents who let children select their interests and who support their inclinations are less likely to destroy their natural curiosity (Hennessey, 2011; Hennessey & Amabile, 2010).

Encourage Internal Motivation

Parents and teachers should avoid excessive use of prizes, such as gold stars, money, or toys, which can stifle creativity by undermining the intrinsic pleasure students derive from creative activities (Hennessey, 2011). Creative children's motivation is the satisfaction generated by the work itself.

Build Children's Confidence

To expand children's creativity, teachers and parents should encourage children to believe in their own ability to create something innovative and worthwhile. Building children's confidence in their creative skills aligns with Bandura's (2008, 2009b, 2010) concept of self-efficacy, the belief that one can master a situation and produce positive outcomes.

Guide Children to Be Persistent and Delay Gratification

Parents and teachers need to be patient and understand that most highly successful creative products take years to develop. Most creative individuals work on ideas and projects for months and years without being rewarded for their efforts.

Encourage Children to Take Intellectual Risks

Parents and teachers should encourage children to take intellectual risks. Creative individuals take intellectual risks and seek to discover or invent something never before discovered or invented. Creative people are not afraid of failing or getting something wrong (Beghetto & Kaufman, 2011).

Introduce Children to Creative People

Teachers can invite creative people to their classrooms and ask them to describe what helps them become creative or to demonstrate their creative skills. A writer, poet, musician, scientist, and many others can bring their props and productions to the class, turning it into a theatre for stimulating students' creativity.

You learned that it is important to recognize that children will show more creativity in some domains than others. Choose one of the strategies mentioned above and describe how you would implement it differently to encourage creativity in writing, science, math, and art in children in middle and late childhood.

SCIENTIFIC THINKING   Like scientists, children ask fundamental questions about reality and seek answers to problems that seem utterly trivial or unanswerable to other people (such as why is the sky blue?). Do children generate hypotheses, perform experiments, and reach conclusions about their data in ways resembling those of scientists? Scientific reasoning often is aimed at identifying causal relations. Like scientists, children place a great deal of emphasis on causal mechanisms. Their understanding of how events are caused weighs more heavily in their causal inferences than even such strong influences as whether the cause happened immediately before the effect.

There also are important differences between the reasoning of children and the reasoning of scientists. Children are more influenced by happenstance events than by an overall pattern, and tend to maintain their old theories regardless of the evidence (Kuhn et al., 2008). Instead, they tend to bias the experiments in favour of whatever hypothesis they began with. Sometimes they see the results as supporting their original hypothesis even when the results directly contradict it.

Too often, the skills scientists use—such as careful observation, graphing, self-regulatory thinking, and knowing when and how to apply one's knowledge to solve problems—are not routinely taught in schools. Children have many concepts that are incompatible with science and reality. Good teachers perceive and understand a child's underlying scientific concepts, then use the concepts as a scaffold for learning (Fraser-Abder, 2011; Peters & Stout, 2011). Effective science teaching helps children distinguish between fruitful errors and misconceptions, and detect plainly wrong ideas that need to be replaced by more accurate conceptions (Bass, Contant, & Carin, 2009). Many science teachers help their students construct their knowledge of science through discovery and hands-on laboratory investigations (Victor, Kellough, & Tai, 2008). Constructivist teaching emphasizes that children need to build their own scientific knowledge and understanding. Keep in mind, though, that it is important that students not be left completely on their own to construct scientific knowledge independent of science content. Students' inquiry should be guided (Moyer, Hackett, & Everett, 2007). It is important for teachers—at a minimum—to initially scaffold students' science learning, extensively monitor their progress, and ensure that they are learning science content. Thus, in pursuing science investigations, students need to learn inquiry skills and science content (Gallagher, 2007).

How might experiences in families, economic conditions, and culture be linked to children's science achievement? A recent study of more than 107,000 students in 41 countries examined this question (Chiu, 2007). Students had higher science achievement scores when their schools had more resources, and when they lived in two-parent families, experienced more family involvement, lived with fewer siblings, lived in wealthier countries, or lived in countries with more equal distribution of household income.

Metacognition

Metacognition *is cognition about cognition, or knowing about knowing* (Flavell, 2004). The majority of developmental studies classified as "metacognitive" have focused on metamemory, or knowledge about memory (DeMarie, Abshier, & Ferron, 2001). This includes general knowledge about memory, such as knowing that recognition tests are easier than recall tests. It also encompasses knowledge about one's own memory, such as a student's ability to monitor whether he or she has studied enough for a test.

Young children do have some general knowledge about memory (Harris et al., 2010). By five or six years of age, children usually already know that unfamiliar items are harder to learn than familiar ones, that short lists are easier than long ones, that recognition is easier than recall, and that forgetting is more likely to occur over time (Lyon & Flavell, 1993). However, in other ways, young children's metamemory is limited. They don't understand that related items are easier to remember than unrelated ones, and that remembering the gist of a story is easier than remembering the piece verbatim (Kreutzer, Leonard, & Flavell, 1975). By Grade 5, students understand that gist recall is easier than verbatim recall.

Young children also have limited knowledge about their own memory abilities. For example, in one study, a majority of young children predicted that they would be able to recall all 10 items on a list, but none of them managed this feat when tested (Flavell, Friedrichs, & Hoyt, 1970). Throughout the elementary school years, children give more realistic evaluations of their memory skills (Schneider & Pressley, 1997).

In addition to metamemory, metacognition includes knowledge about strategies (White, Fredrikson, & Collins, 2010). In the view of Michael Pressley (2003, 2007), the key to education

What do you mean, "What is it?" It's the spontaneous, unfettered expression of a young mind not yet bound by the restraints of narrative or pictorial representation. **Science Cartoons Plus. Used with permission.**

As the Canada Research Chair and Professor in Developmental Cognitive Neuroscience in the Department of Psychiatry at the University of British Columbia, Professor Adele Diamond studies how executive functions can be modified by the environment, modulated by genetics and neurochemistry, and become derailed in certain disorders, effective interventions and ways to prevent disorders, and educational implications. Her work has helped change medical practice for the treatment of PKU (phenylketonuria) and for the inattentive type of ADHD. She helped found the field of developmental cognitive neuroscience and her current research is changing our understanding of the dopamine system in prefrontal cortex and of gender differences in that.

metacognition Cognition about cognition, or knowing about knowing

is helping students learn a rich repertoire of strategies that result in solutions to problems. Good thinkers routinely use strategies and effective planning to solve problems. Good thinkers also know when and where to use strategies. Understanding when and where to use strategies often results from monitoring the learning situation (Pressley & McCormick, 2007; Serra & Metcalfe, 2010).

Pressley and his colleagues (Pressley 2003, 2007; Pressley et al., 2001, 2004) have spent considerable time in recent years observing strategy instruction by teachers and strategy use by students in elementary and secondary school classrooms. They conclude that strategy instruction is far less complete and intense than what students need in order to learn how to use strategies effectively. They argue that education needs to be restructured so that students are provided with more opportunities to become competent strategic learners.

Intelligence

The word "intelligence" conjures up many notions ranging from a brilliant physicist to the counter-intelligence spies found in *The Bourne Identity*. Indeed, defining and understanding intelligence is one of the most engaging areas of research affecting society's largest institutions: government, education, and health care. Governments rely on research to formulate policies; education relies on research to ensure that classroom activities foster learning for each participant; and health care responds to the needs of people who have special needs. Here we define **intelligence** as *problem-solving skills and the ability to learn from and adapt to life's everyday experiences*. But even this broad definition doesn't satisfy everyone.

Robert Sternberg (2008a, b; 2009a, d) proposes that practical know-how should be considered part of intelligence. In his view, intelligence involves weighing options carefully and acting judiciously, as well as developing strategies to improve shortcomings. Also, a definition of intelligence based on a theory such as Vygotsky's, which we discussed more fully in Chapters 2 and 7, would have to include the ability to use the tools of the culture with help from more skilled individuals. Because intelligence is such an abstract, broad concept, it is not surprising that there are so many different ways to define it.

Interest in intelligence has often focused on individual differences and assessment. **Individual differences** *are the stable, consistent ways in which people are different from each other*. We can talk about individual differences in personality or any other domain, but it is in the domain of intelligence that the most attention has been directed at individual differences. For example, an intelligence test purports to inform us about whether a student can reason better than others who have taken the test.

The Stanford-Binet Tests

Over a century ago, public education became mandated in most of North America and Europe. Creating a system that could accommodate the large number of students was, and still is, a major challenge. In 1904, psychologist Alfred Binet was asked by the French Ministry to design a test that would help distinguish those children who could benefit from public education from those who needed special education. School officials wanted to reduce crowding by placing students who did not benefit from regular classroom teaching in special schools. Binet and his student Theophile Simon developed the first intelligence test to meet this request.

Binet also developed the concept of **mental age (MA)**, *an individual's level of mental development relative to others*. Not much later, in 1912, William Stern created the concept of **intelligence quotient (IQ)**, *a person's mental age divided by chronological age (CA), multiplied by 100*. That is:

$$IQ = \frac{MA}{CA} \times 100$$

Since 1904, Binet's test has been modified many times at Stanford University in California to take into account new research related to intelligence. In 2004, the test—now called the Stanford-Binet 5—was revised to analyze an individual's response in five content areas: fluid reasoning, knowledge, quantitative reasoning, visual-spatial reasoning, and working memory. A

intelligence Problem-solving skills and the ability to learn from and adapt to life's everyday experiences.

individual differences The stable, consistent ways in which people are different from each other.

mental age (MA) Binet's measure of an individual's level of mental development compared with that of others.

intelligence quotient (IQ) A person's mental age divided by chronological age, multiplied by 100. Depending on the mental age and the chronological age, a person's IQ can be above, equal to, or below 100.

Figure 9.5

The Normal Curve and Stanford-Binet IQ Scores

The distribution of IQ scores approximates a normal curve. Most scores fall in the middle range. Extremely high and extremely low scores are very rare. Slightly more than two-thirds of the scores fall between 84 and 116. Only about one in 50 individuals has an IQ of more than 132, and only about one in 50 individuals has an IQ of less than 68.

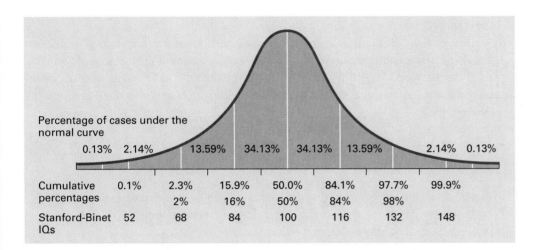

Percentage of cases under the normal curve								
0.13%	2.14%	13.59%	34.13%	34.13%	13.59%	2.14%	0.13%
Cumulative percentages 0.1%	2.3%	15.9%	50.0%	84.1%	97.7%	99.9%	
	2%	16%	50%	84%	98%		
Stanford-Binet IQs 52	68	84	100	116	132	148	

general composite score also is still obtained. The Stanford-Binet continues to be one of the most widely used tests to assess intelligence (Naglieri, 2000). Figure 9.5 illustrates the normal curve and Stanford-Binet IQ scores.

The Wechsler Scales

Another set of widely used tests to assess intelligence is the Wechsler scales developed by David Wechsler, who defined intelligence as "the global capacity of the individual to act purposefully, think rationally, and deal effectively with his environment" (Salovey & Mayer, 1990). The Wechsler scales provide an overall IQ as well as verbal and performance IQs. Verbal IQ is based on six verbal subscales, ranging from vocabulary to comprehension, word reasoning, general knowledge or information, and word similarities. Performance IQ is based on five performance subscales including block design, picture coding, object assembly, picture arrangement, and picture completion; this allows the examiner to see patterns of strengths and weaknesses in different areas of intelligence.

Types of Intelligence

Is it more appropriate to think of intelligence as a general ability or as a number of specific abilities? Sternberg, Gardner, and Mayer, Salovey, and Caruso have proposed influential theories oriented toward this viewpoint.

STERNBERG'S TRIARCHIC THEORY   Robert J. Sternberg (1986, 2004, 2007a, b, 2009a, d, 2010b, c) developed the **triarchic theory of intelligence**, *which states that intelligence comes in three forms: (1) analytical intelligence*—the ability to analyze, judge, evaluate, compare, and contrast; *(2) creative intelligence*—the ability to create, design, invent, originate, and imagine; and (3) *practical intelligence*—the ability to use, apply, implement, and put ideas into practice.

Sternberg (2009a, c; 2010b, c) says that children with different triarchic patterns perform differently in school (Sternberg, 2002). Students with high analytic ability tend to be favoured in conventional schooling. They often do well under direct instruction, in which the teacher lectures and

"You can't build a hut, you don't know how to find edible roots and you know nothing about predicting the weather. In other words, you do terribly on our I.Q. test." Copyright © 1992 by Sidney Harris. Reprinted with permission.

triarchic theory of intelligence Sternberg's theory that intelligence comes in three forms: analytical, creative, and practical.

Howard Gardner, here working with a young child, developed the view that intelligence comes in the forms of these eight kinds of skills: verbal, mathematical, spatial, bodily-kinesthetic, musical, intrapersonal, interpersonal, and naturalist.

gives objective tests. They often are considered "smart" students who get good grades, show up on high-level tracks, do well on traditional tests of intelligence, and get admitted into competitive programs in colleges and universities.

In contrast, children who are high in creative intelligence often are not "top students." They may not conform to their teachers' expectations of how assignments should be done, and may give unique answers to questions. Instead of giving conformist answers, they give unique answers, for which they might get reprimanded or marked down. No teacher wants to discourage creativity, but Sternberg stresses that too often a teacher's desire to improve students' knowledge suppresses creative thinking.

Like children who are high in creative intelligence, children who are practically intelligent often do not relate well to the demands of school. However, many of these children do well outside of the classroom's walls. They may have excellent social skills and common sense. As adults, some become successful managers, entrepreneurs, or politicians, in spite of having undistinguished school records.

GARDNER'S EIGHT FRAMES OF MIND

Howard Gardner (1983, 1993, 2002) believes there are eight types of intelligence:

- *Verbal skills:* the ability to think in words and to use language to express meaning
- *Mathematical skills:* the ability to carry out mathematical operations
- *Spatial skills:* the ability to think three-dimensionally
- *Bodily-kinesthetic skills:* the ability to manipulate objects and be physically skilled
- *Musical skills:* sensitivity to pitch, melody, rhythm, and tone
- *Interpersonal skills:* the ability to understand and effectively interact with others
- *Intrapersonal skills:* the ability to understand oneself and effectively direct one's life
- *Naturalist skills:* the ability to observe patterns in nature and understand natural and human-made systems

"You're wise, but you lack tree smarts."
© The New Yorker Collection, 1988, Donald Reilly from cartoonbank.com. All Rights Reserved.

MAYER-SALOVEY-CARUSO EMOTIONAL INTELLIGENCE (EI)

Professors John D. Mayer, Peter Salovey, and David R. Caruso propose that emotional intelligence represents an ability to validly reason with emotions and to use emotions to enhance thought. EI includes the abilities to 1) accurately perceive emotions, 2) reason with emotions, that is to access and generate emotions so as to assist thought—to ask "what if?" 3) to understand emotions, and emotional knowledge, and 4) to reflectively regulate and manage emotions so as to promote emotional and intellectual growth (Cherry, K., 2012; Mayer, 2004). Because emotions are one of the primary forms of information that we process, EI is important. People who score high on emotional intelligence tests find establishing relationships and avoiding conflict relatively easy. Emotionally intelligent people are more likely to have positive interactions with others, enjoy strong social support, and be particularly good at understanding the ingredients of psychologically healthy living (Mayer, 2004).

EVALUATING THE MULTIPLE INTELLIGENCE APPROACHES

The Sternberg, Gardner, and Mayer-Salovey-Caruso approaches have much to offer. They have stimulated educators to think more broadly about what makes up children's competencies and to develop programs that instruct students in multiple domains. In addition, they have contributed to interest in assessing intelligence and learning in innovative ways, such as by evaluating student portfolios (Moran & Gardner, 2006, 2007). One innovative program in Canada is Learning Through the Arts™ (LTTA). In this program, artists work with students and teachers receive training on arts education. In a sequential study (see Chapter 2), Queen's University researchers found that Grade 6 students with three years of LTTA participation did better in mathematics than their peers in other schools (Upitis, Smithrim, Patteson, MacDonald, & Finkle, 2003). The children also showed more positive attitudes toward their schools. Because students in schools with or without LTTA started out with similar academic performance and attitudes, the improvements might have come from the greater commitment, motivation, and discipline that arts fostered in LTTA schools.

Still, doubts about multiple-intelligence approaches persist. A number of psychologists think that the multiple-intelligence approaches have taken the concept of specific intelligences too far (Reeve & Charles, 2008). Some argue that a research base to support the three intelligences of Sternberg, the eight intelligences of Gardner, or the emotional intelligence proposed by Mayer, Salovey, and Caruso has not yet emerged. One expert on intelligence, Nathan Brody (2007), observes that people who excel at one type of intellectual task are likely to excel in others. Thus, individuals who do well at memorizing lists of digits are also likely to be good at solving verbal problems and spatial layout problems. If musical skill reflects a distinct type of intelligence, ask other critics, why not label the skills of outstanding chess players, prizefighters, painters, and poets as types of intelligence?

The argument between those who support the concept of general intelligence and those who advocate the multiple-intelligence view is ongoing (Brody, 2007; Horn, 2007; Sternberg, 2008a, b; Sternberg 2009a, c). Sternberg (2009a, c; 2010b, c) actually accepts that there is a general intelligence for the kinds of analytical tasks that traditional IQ tests assess, but thinks that the range of tasks those tests measure is far too narrow.

Music and Intelligence

Can music affect intelligence? Research on this question has followed two lines of approach, one dealing with the impact of taking music lessons and the other focusing on the effects of listening to music (Schellenberg, 2004).

In one study on the former, Glenn Schellenberg of the University of Toronto randomly assigned six-year-olds to either voice lessons, music keyboard lessons, drama lessons, or no lessons—the last two groups being the control groups—for 36 weeks. The IQs for children in all four groups rose at the end of the study, but the changes were slightly higher in the music groups than in the control groups in almost every subtest of the Wechsler scale used, suggesting improvement in general intelligence due to music training. The changes are small, however, and may be even smaller over the long term. In a subsequent study, Schellenberg (2006) found that for school-age children a rise of two IQ points was related to one year of music training, but for university students the same two-point increase was associated with six years of playing music regularly in their younger years.

How can the causal link between taking music lessons and improved IQ performance be explained? One possibility is the similarity between skills developed in learning music and skills promoting cognitive development such as memorization of long pieces, persistent practice, and understanding visual symbols (Schellenberg, 2006).

Another approach to examining music and intelligence is to see if listening to music changes people's performance in cognitive tasks. This approach tackles the so-called Mozart effect—a short-term improvement on performance of spatial tasks after listening to Mozart's music (Jones, West, & Estell, 2006; Schellenberg, 2006). Research suggests that the ability for spatial tasks (such as imagining what a piece of paper would look like after cutting and folding) is probably not enhanced by the characteristics of Mozart's music per se; instead, any improvement is likely a result of arousal or a happy mood in an individual because of exposure to a favourite audio stimulus (Jones et al., 2006; Schellenberg, 2006), whether it be Mozart or Lady Gaga.

In sum, learning and listening to music can improve performance on intelligence tasks, but the impact is small.

The Influence of Genetics

How strong is the effect of genetics on intelligence? The concept of heritability attempts to tease apart the effects of heredity and environment in a population. **Heritability** *is the fraction of the variance in a population that is attributed to genetics.*

heritability The fraction of variance in a population that is attributed to genetics and is computed using correlational techniques.

connecting development to life ⟵-----------

The "Flynn Effect" among Kenyan Children

If intelligence or IQ scores are determined by both nature and nurture, do the variations in the environment, such as improvements in nutrition and increases in family income, change the IQ across generations? The answer is a clear yes.

Research in developed countries has found a five- to nine-point increase in IQ over a decade (Daley, Whaley, Sigman, Espinosa, & Neumann, 2003). This change, called the Flynn effect, has been given a few explanations (Daley et al., 2003). First, healthier diets may have improved children's attention and intellectual functioning. Growing exposure to computers and the like may also have stimulated children's cognitive skills. Also, smaller family sizes, coupled with higher parental income, likely provided children with more resources in learning. Moreover, longer schooling in later generations may also have enhanced children's intellectual skills.

Can the Flynn effect also happen in developing nations? After all, incremental changes in family well-being and nutrition are proportionally more significant among those who start with little. Daley

and colleagues (2003) compared the IQ results and the environment of two cohorts in rural Kenya. Both cohorts were about 7.4 years old at the time of measurements in 1984 and 1998.

Overall, the IQ score of the latter cohort was 11 points higher than that of the earlier sample. These cohorts differed in a number of environmental factors. Compared with the 1984 sample, subjects in 1998 enjoyed diets with higher energy and protein, had parents with more education, and lived in smaller families with a higher likelihood of TV ownership. These changes may have contributed to the rise in IQ over the 14-year period. Better health and fewer siblings enabled children to learn better and to benefit more from better-educated parents and greater television exposure.

Because of the children's young age, the effect of schooling could not be examined in Daley's (2003) study. However, one can imagine that children's better health status and family environment may help them tackle academic problems, thus improving their IQ further in the years to come.

Most research on heredity and environment does not include environments that differ radically. Thus, it is not surprising that many genetic studies show environment to be a fairly weak influence on intelligence (Fraser, 1995).

The heritability index has several flaws. It is only as good as the data entered into its analysis and the interpretation made from them (Sternberg, Kaufman, & Grigorenko, 2008). The data are virtually all from traditional IQ tests, which some experts think are not always the best indicator of intelligence (Sternberg, 2008a, b). Also, the heritability index assumes that we can treat genetic and environmental influences as factors that can be separated, with each part contributing a distinct amount of influence. As we discussed in Chapter 2, genes and the environment interact: genes always exist in an environment and the environment shapes their activity.

Today, most researchers agree that genetics and environment interact to influence intelligence (Gottlieb, 2007; Sternberg, 2009a, c). For most people, this means that modifications in environment can change their IQ scores considerably, as illustrated in Schellenberg's research about music and intelligence. Although genetic endowment may always influence a person's intellectual ability, the environmental influences and opportunities we provide children and adults do make a difference (Campbell, 2007; Sternberg, 2009a, c).

Environmental Influences

The *nature vs. nurture* debate is nowhere more evident than in discussions about intelligence. For example, one of the first very heated arguments a young couple may have upon learning that their newborn child is learning delayed may be about whose family had the genetic liability. Susan Cain (2012) suggests that rather than asking which part is nature, which is nurture, and which is free will, we might ask how these factors are intertwined. Schooling clearly influences intelligence (Gustafsson, 2007). The biggest effects have been found when large groups of children have been deprived of formal education for an extended period, resulting in lower intelligence (Ceci & Gilstrap, 2000). Another possible effect of education can be seen in rapidly increasing IQ test scores around the world (Flynn, 1999, 2007). IQ scores have been increasing so fast that a high percentage of people regarded as having average intelligence at the turn of the century would now be considered below average in intelligence. If a representative sample of people today took the Stanford-Binet test version used in 1932, about 25 percent would be defined as having very superior intelligence, a label usually accorded to fewer than 3 percent of the population. Because the increase has taken place in a relatively short time, it can't be due to heredity. Rather, it may be due to increasing levels of education attained by a much greater percentage of the world's population, or to other environmental factors such as the explosion of information, including information about nutrition, to which people are exposed.

The worldwide increase in intelligence test scores that has occurred over a short time frame has been called the *Flynn effect* after the researcher who discovered it, James Flynn. For more about the Flynn effect, see the Connecting Development to Life feature.

Researchers are increasingly concerned about improving the early environment of children who are at risk for impoverished intelligence (Barajas, Philipsen, & Brooks-Gunn, 2008). For various reasons, many low-income parents have difficulty providing an intellectually stimulating environment for their children. Programs that educate parents to be more sensitive caregivers and better teachers, as well as support services such as quality child care programs, can make a difference in a child's intellectual development (Coltrane et al., 2008). Thus, the efforts to counteract a deprived early environment's effect on intelligence emphasize prevention rather than remediation.

A review of the research on early interventions concluded that (1) high-quality child care centre–based interventions are associated with increases in children's intelligence and school achievement; (2) the interventions are most successful with poor children and children whose parents have little education; (3) the positive benefits continue through adolescence, but are not as strong as in early childhood or the beginning of elementary school; and (4) the programs that continue into middle and late childhood have the best long-term results (Brooks-Gunn, 2003).

CULTURE AND INTELLIGENCE   Differences in conceptions of intelligence occur not only among psychologists but also among cultures (Zhang & Sternberg, 2011). What is viewed as intelligent in one culture may not be thought of as intelligent in another. For example, people in Western cultures tend to view intelligence in terms of reasoning and thinking skills, whereas people in Eastern cultures see intelligence as a way for members of a community to engage successfully in social roles (Nisbett, 2003).

CREATING CULTURE-FAIR TESTS   **Culture-fair tests** *are tests of intelligence that are intended to be free of cultural bias.* Two types of culture-fair tests have been devised.

The first includes items that are familiar to children from all socio-economic and ethnic backgrounds, or items that at least are familiar to the children taking the test. For example, a child might be asked how a bird and a dog are different, on the assumption that all children have been exposed to birds and dogs.

The second type of culture-fair test has no verbal questions. Figure 9.6 shows a sample question from the Raven's Progressive Matrices Test. Even though tests such as Raven's are designed to be culture-fair, people with more education still score higher on them than do those with less education.

Why is it so hard to create culture-fair tests? Most tests tend to reflect what the dominant culture thinks is important (Matsumoto & Juang, 2008). The language and context used favour one group over another. If tests have time limits, that will bias the test against groups not concerned with time. If languages differ, the same words might have different meanings for different language groups. Even pictures can produce bias because some cultures have less experience with drawings and photographs (Anastasi & Urbina, 1996).

Within the same culture, different subgroups could have different attitudes, values, and motivation, and this could affect their performance on intelligence tests. For example, Aboriginal children in New Brunswick had lower performance in science, reading, and writing tests than other children in Grade 6 (Ma & Klinger, 2000). The researchers speculated that Native students' weaker

culture-fair tests Tests of intelligence that are intended to be free of cultural bias.

Figure 9.6 -

Sample Item from the Raven Progressive Matrices Test

Individuals are presented with a matrix arrangement of symbols, such as the one at the top of this figure, and must then complete the matrix by selecting the appropriate missing symbol from a group of symbols, such as the ones at the bottom. Simulated item similar to those found in the Raven's Progressive Matrices.

Copyright © 1998 by Harcourt Assessment, Inc. Reproduced with permission. All rights reserved.

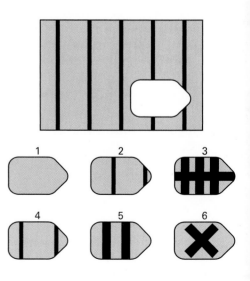

A child with Down syndrome. **What causes a child to develop Down syndrome? In which major classification of mental retardation does the condition fall?**

---- **critical** thinking ----

Patrick Lenon of L'Arche Lethbridge, Alberta, spoke at the Second Annual International Conference on Intellectual Disabilities/Mental Retardation in Bangkok, Thailand, and made two prominent points: disability is a way of life, not a medical condition, and all of us at times in our lives have special needs, and we need to move from seeing that we are service providers to recognizing that persons with an intellectual disability have gifts that the world needs—gifts of the heart that draw us into vulnerability and relationships.

Would you agree with Mr. Lenon that disability is a way of life? If so, why; if not, why not? What are some of the special needs all of us may have at times in our lives? What "gifts of the heart" might persons with intellectual disabilities give us?

cultural-familial intellectual disability A mental deficit in which no evidence of organic brain damage can be found; IQs range from 50 to 70.

performance was due to their lack of assimilation into the mainstream culture. This emphasis on environmental influence is consistent with other research findings.

Canadian children tend to score higher in some conventional intelligence tests than their American peers (Saklofske, Caravan, & Schwartz, 2000). Given the ethnic diversity, educational levels, and standard of living in both countries, heredity-based arguments cannot explain this difference in intelligence. Because of the difficulties in creating culture-fair tests, Robert Sternberg and his colleagues (Sternberg, 2010a; Zhang & Sternberg, 2011) conclude that there are no culture-fair tests, only *culture-reduced tests*.

It is important to consider that what is viewed as intelligent can be specific to a culture (Lonner, 1990; Serpell, 2000). In most Western cultures, children are considered intelligent if they are both smart and fast. By contrast, in the Buganda culture in Uganda, children who are slow in thought and say the socially correct things are considered intelligent. In the Caroline Islands in the Pacific Ocean, one of the most important dimensions of intelligence is the ability to navigate by the stars.

THE USE AND MISUSE OF INTELLIGENCE TESTS   Like any psychological test, intelligence tests are tools, and their effectiveness depends on the knowledge, skill, and integrity of the user. The following are some cautions on the use of information from IQ tests.

Scores on an IQ test easily can lead to stereotypes and expectations. It is crucial not to develop the expectation that because a child scored low on an IQ test, the child is not capable of learning, or conversely, because the child scored high, the child is gifted. An IQ test should always be considered a measure of current performance, not a measure of fixed potential, because maturational changes and environmental experiences can influence a person's intelligence. Moreover, it is wise to think of intelligence as consisting of a number of domains, such as creative and practical skills, which are not reflected in the test scores. Keep in mind the different types of intelligence described by Sternberg, Gardner, and Mayer, Salovey, and Caruso. Remember that, by considering the different domains of intelligence, you can find that every child has at least one or more strengths.

The Extremes of Intelligence

Intelligence tests have been used to discover indications of the extremes of intelligence. Here we examine both the low and the high extremes.

INTELLECTUAL DISABILITY OR DEVELOPMENTAL DELAY   These two terms refer to conditions of limited mental ability in which an individual has a low IQ, usually below 70 on a traditional intelligence test, and has difficulty adapting to everyday life. Intellectual disability is technically distinct from developmental delay. Developmental delay refers to a delay in a child's physical or mental growth before the age of five years. Intellectual disability refers to cognitive limitations due to the presence of a developmental delay in people over four years of age, and includes such conditions as Down's syndrome, autism, or mental impairment. An estimated 0.7 percent to about 3 percent of Canadians are affected (Crawford, 2008).

About 90 percent of people diagnosed with developmental delay fall into the mild category, with IQs of 55 to 70. About 6 percent are classified as moderately disabled, with IQs of 40 to 54. People in this category can attain skills at a Grade 2 level and may be able to support themselves as adults through some types of labour. About 3.5 percent are in the severe category, with IQs of 25 to 39; these individuals learn to talk and engage in very simple tasks, but require extensive supervision. Fewer than one percent have IQs below 25; they are profoundly mentally retarded and need constant supervision. More boys than girls are reported to have either intellectual or developmental delay conditions; of those, over 60 percent have more than one disability and 10 percent have 6 or more disabilities (Statistics Canada, 2003).

Cultural-familial intellectual disability *is a mental condition in which no evidence of organic brain damage can be found; IQs range from 50 to 70.* Psychologists suspect that such mental deficits result from the normal variation along the range of intelligence scores above 50, combined with growing up in a below-average intellectual environment.

GIFTEDNESS Dr. Joan Freeman, Founding President of the European Council for High Ability, has studied gifted and non-gifted children, noting their similarities and differences. She conducted the only longitudinal study of 20 people who were identified as gifted, tracking their lives over a period of 35 years. **Gifted** *children were identified as children who, according to tests, have a mental age considerably higher than their chronological age.* For example, a gifted three-year-old's vocabulary and understanding of concepts and subtle nuances of meaning may be on par with that of a first grader. Dr. Freeman identified four characteristics of gifted children: a lively mind, a keen sense of awareness, the ability to learn, and independence (Freeman, 2009).

As you have read, Gardner, Sternberg, and Mayer, Salovey, and Caruso have proposed that there are many types of intelligence. This being the case, it follows logically that there would be many types of giftedness and being gifted would pose challenges as well as opportunities. Dr. Freeman points out that "Success in school did not predict success outside of it." Most of the world's highest achievers, she points out, were never identified as gifted children. A gifted child is just one who has advanced beyond his or her peers; it takes drive, application, perseverance, and insight to turn that potential into exceptional adult success (Freeman, 2009). Deliberate practice is an important characteristic of individuals who become experts in a particular domain (Balchin, Hymer, & Matthews, 2009; Sternberg, 2009d).

An increasing number of experts argue that the education of children who are gifted requires a significant overhaul (Sternberg, 2009d; Webb et al., 2007). Ellen Winner (1996, 2006) argues that too often children who are gifted are socially isolated and under-challenged in the classroom. When it comes to programs for the gifted, school systems select students who have intellectual superiority and academic aptitude, whereas children who are talented in the visual and performing arts (arts, drama, dance), athletics, or other special aptitudes tend to be overlooked (Horowitz, 2009; Liben, 2009; Winner, 2009). In fact, according to educationalist Sir Ken Robinson (2009) and Dr. Freeman (2009), the school system, an industrial-age concept, cannot possibly address the needs of every child and often is unable to nurture the creative minds of students.

To this point, we have examined a number of ideas about cognitive development in middle and late childhood. For a review, see the **Reach Your Learning Objectives** section at the end of this chapter.

gifted Refers to children whose scores on IQ tests indicate that their mental age is considerably higher than their chronological age.

---

critical thinking

Internationally recognized educator Sir Ken Robinson argues that schools can do more to foster creativity if they transform the curriculum dramatically by eliminating the existing hierarchy of subjects. By that, Robinson argues that all fields of study be given equal importance; that is, the arts—for example, dance—should be given as much academic weight as the sciences—for example, physics. Each has an equal and central contribution to make to enabling students with diverse talents. Further, he argues that all subjects have much in common, so dividing learning into subjects undermines their fluid and dynamic interdisciplinary nature. Robinson also makes the point that learning is a personal process which happens in the minds and hearts of individuals, not in results on standardized or multiple-choice tests (Robinson, 2009). What do you think of Robinson's ideas? What changes would you recommend, if any, and why? If none, why not? What worked for you in school, and why? What did you learn outside the classroom, and how has this learning shaped your life?

Language Development

LO3 Discuss language development in middle and late childhood.

Language skills continue to develop during middle and late childhood, so that by the time children enter elementary school, learning to read and write is possible. They are able to use language about things that are not physically present, learn what a word is, and know how to recognize and talk about sounds (Berko-Gleason, 2003). They also learn the *alphabetic principle*, that the letters of the alphabet represent sounds of the language. Here we examine the changes in vocabulary, grammar, and reading, as well as the issue of bilingualism.

Vocabulary, Grammar, and Metalinguistic Awareness

Reading

Bilingualism

Vocabulary, Grammar, and Metalinguistic Awareness

During middle and late childhood, a change occurs in the way children think about words. When asked to say the first word that comes to mind when they hear a word, young children typically provide one that often follows the word in a sentence. For example, when asked to respond to "dog," the young child may say "barks." At about seven years of age, children begin to respond with a word that is the same part of speech as the stimulus word. For example, a child may now respond to the word "dog" with "cat" or "horse." This is evidence that children now have begun to categorize their vocabulary by parts of speech.

The process of categorizing becomes easier as children increase their vocabulary. Children's vocabulary increases from an average of about 14,000 words at age 6 to an average of 40,000 words by age 11.

Children make similar advances in grammar (Tager-Flusberg & Zukowski, 2009). During the elementary school years, children's improvement in logical reasoning and analytical skills helps them to understand such constructions as the appropriate use of comparatives (*shorter, deeper*) and subjectives ("If you were Prime Minister. . ."). As well, children become increasingly able to understand and use complex grammar, such in "The boy who kissed his mother wore a hat." They also learn to use language in a more connected way, producing connected discourse. They become able to relate sentences to one another to produce descriptions, definitions, and narratives that make sense. Children must be able to do these things orally before they can be expected to deal with them in written assignments.

These advances in vocabulary and grammar during the elementary school years are accompanied by the development of **metalinguistic awareness**, *which is knowledge about language, such as knowing what a preposition is or the ability to discuss the sounds of a language.* Metalinguistic awareness allows children "to think about the language, understand what words are, and even define them" (Berko-Gleason, 2009, p. 4). This understanding improves considerably between Grades 1 and 6 (Pan & Uccelli, 2009). Defining words becomes a regular part of classroom discourse, and children increase their knowledge of syntax as they study and talk about the components of sentences such as subjects and verbs (Meltzi & Ely, 2009).

Children also make progress in understanding how to use language in culturally appropriate ways, called *pragmatics* (Bryant, 2009; Siegal & Surian, 2010). By the time they enter adolescence, most children know the rules for the use of language in everyday contexts—that is, what is appropriate and inappropriate to say.

Reading

Before learning to read, children learn to use language to talk about things that are not present; they learn what a word is, and they learn how to recognize sounds and talk about them. Children who begin elementary school with robust vocabulary have an advantage when it comes to learning (Paris & Paris, 2006). A fluent vocabulary helps readers access word meaning effortlessly (Beaty, 2009; Cunningham & Hall, 2009).

How should children be taught to read? Debate currently focuses on the whole-language approach versus the phonics approach (Combs, 2010; Tompkins, 2011).

The **whole-language approach** *stresses that reading instruction should parallel children's natural language learning.* In some whole-language classes, beginning readers are taught to recognize whole words or even entire sentences, and to use the context of what they are reading to guess at the meaning of words. Reading materials that support the whole-language approach are whole and meaningful; that is, children are given material in its complete form, such as stories and poems. In this way, say the whole-language advocates, children learn to understand language's communicative function. Reading is connected to writing skills. Although there are variations in whole-language programs, most share the premise that reading should be integrated with other skills and subjects, such as science and social studies, and that it should focus on real-world material. Thus, a class might read newspapers, magazines, or books, and then write about and discuss them.

By contrast, the **basic-skills-and-phonetics approach** *emphasizes that reading instruction should teach phonetics and its basic rules for translating written symbols into sounds.* Early phonics-centred reading instruction should involve simplified materials. Only after children have learned correspondence rules that relate spoken phonemes to the letters of the alphabet that represent them should children be given complex reading materials, such as books and poems. Advocates of this approach often point to low reading achievement scores occurring as an outgrowth of the recent emphasis on holistic, literature-based instruction and the consequent lack of attention to basic skills and phonetics (Cunningham & Hall 2009; Mayer, 2008).

Which approach is better? Research suggests that children can benefit from both approaches, but instruction in phonics needs to be emphasized (Meltzi & Ely, 2009; Tompkins, 2011). An increasing number of experts in the field of reading now conclude that direct instruction in phonics is a key aspect of learning to read (Mayer, 2008).

metalinguistic awareness Knowledge about language, such as knowing what a preposition is or the ability to discuss the sounds of language.

whole-language approach An approach to reading instruction based on the idea that instruction should parallel children's natural language learning. Reading materials should be whole and meaningful.

basic-skills-and-phonetics approach An approach to reading instruction that stresses phonetics and basic rules for translating written symbols into sounds. Early reading instruction should involve simplified materials.

In a longitudinal study following children from Grade 1 to Grade 6, Linda Phillips and her colleagues at the University of Alberta (Phillips, Norris, Osmond, & Maynard, 2002) found some stability in reading skills. They classified children as below-average, average, and above-average readers and found that roughly 70 percent of children stayed in the same category in Grade 1 and Grade 6. However, a change of category membership in the remaining 30 percent of children does suggest that reading skills are not immune to change. Interestingly, both below-average readers and above-average readers had a good chance of moving to the average level. It is the large number of average readers who were most likely to remain in the same category. This finding of convergence of reading skills was partially supported by those from another longitudinal study at the University of Alberta: While good readers were likely to remain "good" from Grade 1 to Grade 5, poor readers showed signs of catching up over time (Parrila, Aunola, Leskinen, Nurmi, & Kirby, 2005).

Children's reading is a complex process. **What kinds of information-processing skills are involved?**

Bilingualism

Canada has been officially bilingual since the *Constitution Act* in 1867. This status has generated a demand for bilingual education and has produced some excellent research in language education. For example, Wallace Lambert and his colleagues at McGill University developed a number of French immersion programs for English-speaking children that have become models for various jurisdictions in Canada and abroad (Fraser, 2001).

French immersion programs use French as the instructional language for most subjects, not just language or literature. Contrary to what some people fear, students in these programs do not show a decline in their performance of their first language when they are part of the language majority in the community in which the programs are offered. Children in immersion programs also seem to have greater tolerance for people from other language backgrounds.

As a group, bilingual children tend to do better in language and cognitive tasks than monolingual children. Ellen Bialystok of York University in Toronto has shown that fluently bilingual children perform better than their single-language counterparts on tests of attentional control, concept formation, analytical reasoning, cognitive flexibility, and cognitive complexity (Bialystok, 1999). They also are more conscious of spoken and written language structure and better at noticing errors of grammar and meaning, skills that are important for reading (Bialystok, 1993, 1997). Furthermore, bilingual children in a number of countries do better than monolingual children on tests of intelligence (Lambert et al., 1993).

Can some of the bilingual children's advantages in non-linguistic tasks be attributed to the characteristics of either of the languages they know? For example, research has shown superior mathematical performances in Chinese-speaking children, including counting skills in preschoolers, compared to English-speaking American children, prompting some to wonder if the numbering structure in Chinese helped these children. A team from the University of Alberta studied this matter (Rasmussen, Ho, Nicoladis, Leung, & Bisanz, 2006) and found that Chinese–English bilingual preschoolers counted better in their dominant language, whether it was English or Chinese. Therefore, it is the everyday practice of the language users, not the peculiarities of a language, that affects children's counting. At the same time, because a language encompasses many different characteristics, research is always needed to test if any of these characteristics helps the speaker in specific cognitive tasks.

When is the best time to learn a new language? There appears to be no definitive answer to this question. Recent research indicates the complexity: sensitive periods likely vary across different language systems (Thomas & Johnson, 2008). Thus, for late language learners, such as adolescents and adults, new vocabulary is easier to learn than new sounds or new grammar (Neville, 2006). For example, children's ability to pronounce words with a native-like accent in a second language typically decreases with age, with an especially sharp drop occurring after the age of about 10 to 12. The way children and adults learn a second language differs somewhat. Compared with adults, children are less sensitive to feedback, less likely to use explicit strategies, and more likely to learn a second language from large amounts of input (Thomas & Johnson, 2008).

To this point, we have discussed a number of ideas about language development in middle and late childhood. For a review, see the **Reach Your Learning Objectives** section at the end of this chapter.

Second language acquisition can be exciting—and useful.

Educational Approaches and Issues

LO4 Discuss approaches and issues related to education.

constructivist approach A learner-centred approach that emphasizes the importance of individuals actively constructing their knowledge and understanding with guidance from the teacher.

direct instruction approach A structured, teacher-centred approach that is characterized by teacher direction and control, maximum time spent on learning tasks, and efforts to keep negative affect to a minimum.

Approaches to Student Learning

For most children, entering grade 1 ushers in a more mature student role and provides new standards by which they judge themselves. Certainly school exerts more influence on children than the transfer of knowledge. Controversy swirls about the best way to teach children and how to hold schools and teachers accountable (Johnson et al., 2011; Parkay & Stanford, 2010). Two prominent approaches, the constructivist approach and the direct instruction approach are at the centre of this controversy.

The **constructivist approach** *is a learner-centred approach that emphasizes the importance of individuals actively constructing their knowledge and understanding.* In this view, teachers carefully guide and monitor opportunities for children to explore, discover, collaborate, reflect and think critically about the world around them (Eby, Herrell, & Jordan, 2006; Eggen & Kauchak, 2006; Pontecorvo, 2004). The intention of the constructivist approach is to enable children to grasp deeper meaning of ideas with an open mind to different approaches and perspectives. In this type of classroom, desks are often arranged in a circle so that students can see each other when they share ideas, and initiate activities. Shelly Wright's high school class in Moosejaw, Saskatchewan illustrates this approach. Under her guidance, students decided they wanted to help war-orphaned children in Uganda. After doing some research, they developed plans, set goals, and initiated fund-raising activities. With the help of social media, students surpassed their goals; not only did they raise over $22,000 for aid, but they also launched a multi-media campaign against modern day slavery and created a Holocaust museum (Wright, S. 2013).

By contrast, the **direct instruction approach** *is characterized by teacher direction and control, maximum time spent by students on academic tasks, and efforts by the teacher to keep negative affect to a minimum.* An important goal in this approach is maximizing student learning time. In the traditional classroom where the directive approach dominates, desks may be set up in rows and the teacher sets the pace and explains the subject in ways that will capture student attention and motivate learning usually from the front of the classroom. Students may ask questions and seek guidance. Most university lecture halls illustrate this approach.

Which approach is better? Advocates of the constructivist approach argue that the direct instruction approach turns children into passive learners and does not adequately challenge them to think critically and creatively (Abruscato & DeRosa, 2010; Eby, Herrell, & Jordan, 2011). The direct instruction enthusiasts say that the constructivist approaches are too relativistic and vague, and do not give sufficient attention to disciplines such as history and science. Author Susan Cain (2012) argues that the focus on collaboration often disadvantages the introverted child who prefers to learn independently. She contends that one or two usually more extroverted children may dominate; consequently, the contributions of the shy or the introverted child may be overlooked (Cain, 2012).

Some experts in educational psychology believe that many effective teachers use both approaches, depending on the circumstances (Bransford et al., 2006). Some aspects of the curriculum may call more for a constructivist approach while others, such as teaching students who have a reading or writing disability, may lend themselves more to a direct instruction approach (Berninger, 2006).

critical thinking

Some of us are naturally more extraverted or introverted than others. Introverted children tend to become inspired when working independently; on the other hand, extraverted children excel when working in groups and often assume leadership roles in group activities. Because the introverted child is reluctant to speak up, his or her ideas often go unsaid, and when voiced, are often voiced quietly and therefore ignored. Whether using the constructivist approach or the direct instruction approach, how can teachers accommodate different learning styles of students? Would you define yourself as an introvert or an extravert? What behaviours lead you to define yourself? In what classroom situations are you most comfortable, and why?

spotlight on social policy ←-------------------------------

Educating Gifted Children Is No Simple Matter

In 2004, a mother in Ontario fought her local school board over the lack of special education for her gifted daughter. This case highlights the concern that gifted children do not always benefit from the public school system. Some experts argue that many gifted children may lose interest in schoolwork because of the lack of challenges (Mills, 2003). In addition, there may be teacher characteristics that do not help gifted children achieve success.

Recently, Carol Mills (2003), a prominent researcher in special education, used the Myers-Briggs Type Indicator, a widely used personality measure, on ordinary high school teachers and effective teachers in gifted classes. Those who excelled in teaching gifted classes showed greater preference for abstract reasoning and flexible thinking than did ordinary teachers. This preference is similar to the cognitive style of many gifted students. Interestingly, two-thirds of the special education teachers in this sample did not have a teaching certificate, and almost 80 percent had not received any education in training gifted children.

A few policy implications come out of Mills's findings. First, because of the different thinking styles between gifted students and many teachers in ordinary classrooms, these students should be offered special classes so they can benefit from interactions with teachers with a similar preference for innovative thinking. Second, the hiring and assignment of teachers should be related to their characteristics, not just their credentials. Teachers who are well-versed in an academic field and are flexible in thinking may be better educators for gifted children than teachers who have the papers but not the personality. Finally, even in ordinary classrooms, teachers should be made aware of gifted children's cognitive styles and be willing to accommodate their needs.

Educational Issues

We have discussed some of the challenges facing educators in developing curriculum and classroom approaches that would improve critical thinking, creativity, as well as address the different learning styles and aptitudes of students. Social issues such as poverty, ethnicity, and international comparisons further complicate these critical issues.

Poverty

Canada has no clear-cut definition of poverty; however, according to UNICEF"s report card 14% of Canadian children live in poverty; and according to Campaign 2000's report card released in November of 2012, nearly 1 in 7 children live in poverty (UNICEF, 2012). Further, the National Food Bank reports that although children and youth make up 21% of the population, they comprise 38% of those helped by food banks (Food Banks Canada, 2012). When a child pretends he or she has forgotten lunch or doesn't have shoes for gym, or can't go on school trips, poverty may be at the root. According to the Canadian Teachers' Federation (CTF) (2009), children with disabilities as well as children from families that are racialized, aboriginal, or new to Canada are at a greater risk of living in poverty. Because parents are unable to pay the rent, children from poor families are more likely to move, change schools frequently. Academic performance is diminished considerably as children are hungry, ashamed, and suffer from lowered self-esteem. Not only is academic performance adversely affected, so is student behaviour and school retention (CTF, 2009; Ferguson, 2009).

Many schools in rural areas, especially in First Nations communities are in disrepair and lack educational facilities such as gyms and libraries. The drop out rate among First Nations youth close to 60% (Mendleson, 2008). Frequently portables rather than proper buildings serve as schools. To quote once again the Hon. Jim Prentice, former Minister of Indian and Northern Affairs Canada, in his speech to the House of Commons upon introduction of the First Nations Jurisdiction Over Education in British Columbia Act: "First Nation children, frankly, have been the only children in Canada who have lacked an education system." (Mendelson, 2008).

How do low-income children in Canada fare in school? According to Health Canada (1999), elementary school children from families with the lowest socio-economic status (SES) were more

The local school in Pikangikum.

likely than other children to repeat a grade or to be enrolled in remedial classes. In contrast, children from families with the highest SES were more likely than their peers to be in gifted classes. Moreover, fewer than 15 percent of children with the top 20 percent of mathematics scores came from the lowest SES families, while over 25 percent came from the highest SES households.

In addition, research has demonstrated a link between family SES and behavioural adjustment in children. In a study at McMaster University, family SES was found to be more strongly related to conduct problems and hyperactivity than with emotional problems (Boyle & Lipman, 2002), suggesting children's behaviour may be more vulnerable to poor income or occupational status (which compose SES) than their feelings.

Campaign 2000's 2012 Report Card further notes that poverty costs $72 to $86 billion per year and impairs national interests. This means that over their life time, children who grow up in poverty experience compromised mental and physical health, productivity, and opportunity. Twice as many children in Prince Edward Island (22.5%) as Alberta (11.3%) live in poverty. As noted above, children of First Nations parents, immigrants, lone parents, racialized groups, and those with a disability are more vulnerable to poverty (Campaign 2000, 2012).

Recall that the microsystem in Bronfenbrenner's bio-ecological approach includes the neighbourhood in which we live. Two psychologists, Boyle and Lipman (2002), examined the immediate neighbourhood characteristics, such as percentage of unemployed people, percentage of neighbourhood income from the government, etc. They speculated that areas with a high number of families living in poverty were characterized by a lack of community involvement and high parental stress, which are detrimental to children's social development. Interestingly, within a neighbourhood, a higher family SES predicted less difficulty in child behaviour, suggesting that a relatively advantageous socio-economic position among peers may be conducive to children's adjustment.

Ethnicity in Schools

Children from immigrant or Aboriginal backgrounds have the additional stress of trying to adjust to the mainstream culture, conflicting values and i learning either official language.

IMMIGRANT CHILDREN Immigrant face a multitude of challenges in addition to the obvious ones such as food, climate, and social norms. Language poses a challenge which affects many dimensions of adjustment. Possibly neither the child nor the parents speak either one of Canada's two national languages, health and ability issues may go undetected as the behaviour or the learning delay may be assumed to be related exclusively to language.. Further, in addition to financial hardship, children may face discrimination, racism, and adverse peer relations such as bullying (Chang, 2010). Despite various challenges, children of recent immigrants fare better than children in general in psychological well-being and are less likely to experience situations that lead to poor school performance—hyperactivity, conduct disorder, emotional disorder, family dysfunction, and hostile parenting behaviour. Furthermore, even though immigrant children whose first language was not English or French had poorer mathematics, reading, and writing skills in the early elementary school years, their performance caught up with that of the rest of the class by age 10 or 11 (Statistics Canada, 2008). The reasons for these achievements range from cultural values for education to the motivating experience of having to start from zero in a new country.

ABORIGINAL CHILDREN Addressing poverty and all the related issues associated with poverty—housing, nutrition, health, and education is enormously complex, perhaps even more so in First Nations Reserves. Although attempts have been made, progress is sadly lacking. In other words, more children are living in poverty today than five years ago and the drop out rate among First Nations youth has not decreased in decades. Given their unique historical and cultural experiences some Aboriginal children, particularly those whose parents, grandparents, and other family

developmental **connection**

Bronfenbrenner's Bio-Ecological Theory

members may have been forced to attend a Residential School, may experience difficulty adjusting to mainstream schools. According to Eileen Antone (2000) of the University of Toronto, Aboriginal children often feel a sense of alienation due to the school's lack of understanding of and respect for the world views, spirituality, and other aspects of their cultures.

The chronological history of Canadian Residential Schools spans more than century. The Civilization Act of 1857 sought to assimilate Aboriginal peoples into Canadian culture To accomplish this, children were removed from their home, forced into labour, and denied the right to speak their language or practice their religion. Many other abuses occurred, and gradually the schools were closed, the last one as late as 1996; however, according to Aboriginal Affairs and Northern Development Canada (2010), the consequences of this policy has had a damaging negative impact on Aboriginal culture, heritage, and language. In July of 2008, Prime Minister Steven Harper made a formal apology on behalf of Canada to the students, their families, and communities (Truth and Reconciliation Commission of Canada, 2012). Approximately 80,000 former students are living today and are able to share their experiences (AANDC, 2010).

In response to the needs of Aboriginal children, some educators advocate the use of their native languages and Aboriginal teachers. The establishment of the Eva Bereti Cree Leadership Academy at Our Lady of Peace Elementary School in Edmonton illustrates this approach. This centre allows students to get involved in the Cree culture and language, as well as leadership training (Gonzalez, 2007). As for preparing Aboriginal teachers, a number of training initiatives, such as Saskatchewan's Urban Native Teacher Education Program, have been established. An additional recommendation is that the school officials maintain open dialogue with Aboriginal parents and children to ensure understanding of each other's perspective on issues such as definition of success and barriers faced by the children. The school administration should also train staff and students to be aware of cultural differences (Mattson & Caffrey, 2001).

International Comparisons

According to a report on industrialized countries in the Organisation for Economic Co-operation and Development (OECD; OECD, 2003), five-year-olds in Canada can expect 15.7 years of full-time schooling ahead, which is 4.2 years more than children in Turkey and 3.5 years fewer than those in Finland.

During their long academic journey, Canadian children face a different school environment than those of their peers in many countries. Think about the Harry Potter movies. Other than witchcraft, what else about Harry's school is different from many Canadian schools? (The school uniforms, for one!) In addition, as many immigrant children and parents point out, the school curricula in their home countries are often more rigorous than those in Canada. Furthermore, as an immigrant from Grenada has noted, religion is part of the daily school life in his home country, but it is a taboo in public schools in Canada (Cato, 2004).

Private Schools and Home Education

A large number of Canadian children are receiving private school education and home schooling. According to Statistics Canada (2001c), private school enrollment jumped by almost 24 percent throughout the 1990s. In contrast, the student population in public schools increased by 3.2 percent in the same period. As for home schooling, which is legal in all provinces, the student population can be as high as 80,000 (Basham, 2001).

Many people believe that private-school students come from wealthy families, but Statistics Canada data show otherwise. Children from families with an annual income of $100,000 or over and children from families with an annual income of less than $50,000 made up the same proportion of the private-school population (Lipps & Corak, 2001).

critical thinking

Have you or someone you know experienced home schooling or private schooling? What are the advantages and disadvantages of each to a child's development? What approach to education would you choose for your own children? Why?

What happens is that many parents make huge sacrifices to finance their children's education. Among the reasons parents do so are compatibility between family and school values, the opportunity to provide parental input, and small classes (Dexter, 2001). Also, some parents are disillusioned by the sometimes antagonistic relationships between school boards and teachers' unions.

Recognizing parents' sacrifice, some schools or organizations offer financial support to families with children in private schools. For example, Children First: School Choice Trust provides need-based bursaries to children in private elementary schools in Calgary and Ontario. Information about this organization and life in private schools is available on Connect at www.mcgrawconnect.ca.

Home-schooling families share many characteristics with private-school families. Wilfrid Laurier University's Bruce Arai (2000) has noted that family income and parental education vary greatly among home-schooling parents. These parents have to make sacrifices, such as giving up paid employment, finding appropriate instructional materials, and enduring the stigma of being antisocial (Brown, 2003). Still, many parents choose home schooling for their children because of religion, the need for a tailored curriculum for a gifted child, and fear of undesirable socialization in schools (Arai, 2000). Many home-schooling parents do not dislike public education; they just find home schooling more suited to their needs. Research in Canada and the United States justifies their efforts: Home-schooled children had higher-than-average performances (Basham, 2001).

Are home-schooled children loners with no social skills? In reality, many home-schooled children have regular interactions with peers during sporting activities, trips, and religious gatherings. Just like other children, whether or not these children develop good social skills depends on their personality, the parents, and the peer groups.

What are the implications of the popularity of private schools and home schooling? First, tax breaks or subsidies would help low-income families who choose these forms of education. After all, they pay taxes while saving tax dollars by not enrolling children in publicly funded schools. Secondly, provinces can ease home-school parents' burden by providing suggestions for educational materials.

To this point, we have studied a number of ideas about educational approaches and issues in middle and late childhood. For a review, see the **Reach Your Learning Objectives** section at the end of this chapter.

Children with Disabilities

LO5 Identify different types of disabilities and discuss issues relating to their education.

What are disabilities? Most of the provinces have accepted the definition of the Canadian Learning Disabilities Association, which in 2002 defined learning disabilities as "a cognitive processing disorder or condition with processing deficits" (Kozey & Siegel, 2008). The Learning Disabilities Association of Ontario (LDAO) refers to a variety of disorders that affect the "acquisition, retention, understanding, organization, or use of verbal and/or non-verbal information" in its definition (LDAO, 2010). The World Health Organization's (WHO) definition of learning disabilities is "a state of arrested or incomplete development of mind," and emphasizes that LD are not diseases, nor are they mental or physical illnesses. Rather they are a diagnosis used to identify people who have some type of intellectual impairment or social or adaptive dysfunction. Learning disabilities can be identified in childhood, or may be acquired in later life as the result of illness or accident.

Learning Disabilities

Children with a **learning disability** *(1) are of normal intelligence or above, (2) have difficulties in at least one academic area and usually several, and (3) have a difficulty that is not attributable to any other diagnosed problem or disorder.* The global concept of learning disabilities includes problems in listening, concentrating, speaking, and thinking. A comprehensive definition of learning disabilities is available on Connect at www.mcgrawhillconnect.ca.

Approximately 80 percent of children with a learning disability have a reading problem (Shaywitz, Gruen, & Shaywitz, 2007). **Dyslexia** *is a category that is reserved for individuals who have a severe impairment in their ability to read and spell* (Harley, 2009; Reid et al., 2009).

Learning disabilities are life-long and are characterized by difficulty with certain relatively specific skills such as language skills, attention, coordination, and self-control. They may affect many aspects of a person's life: family, peer relationships, daily routines, school, community, and work. Learning disabilities are not the result of major physical impairments, low socio-economic status, culture, language, low motivation, or instruction; however, these conditions may aggravate the situation (Kozey & Siegel, 2008). Statistics Canada (2003) reports that 12.4 percent of our population has disabilities. This figure does not include Yukon, Northwest Territories, and Nunavut. Further, the Statistics Canada definition is inclusive of a broad range of learning disabilities ranging from hearing, seeing, mobility, dexterity, learning, and developmental delay (physical, intellectual, or other) to developmental disorders such as Down syndrome, autism, or mental impairment, psychological disorders, and chronic disorders (heart condition or disease, epilepsy, cerebral palsy, spina bifida, fetal alcohol effect, etc.). Statistics Canada (2003) also reports that more than 10 percent of school-age children with disabilities have disabilities in 6 or more areas.

Diagnosing whether a child has a learning disability is often a difficult task (Bender, 2008; Fritschmann & Solari, 2008). Unlike in the United States, where national guidelines are established, in Canada each province and territory sets its own educational policies, including guidelines for responding to needs of children with learning disabilities. Saskatchewan has the most comprehensive policy, and is one of the only three provinces (along with Ontario and Quebec) to refer to learning disabilities in its educational policies (Kozey & Siegel, 2008). As a result, the same child may be diagnosed as having a learning disability in one province, but not in another. Although school-aged children with learning disabilities are relatively well served, diagnostic practices and services vary within provinces as well as between provinces. Canada has two official languages (French and English), as well as large Aboriginal and multicultural populations. Where special needs arise, poverty has an impact on the education and services that children with learning disabilities can access (Wiener & Siegel, 2010).

The precise causes of learning disabilities have not yet been determined (Bender, 2008; Hallahan, Kauffman, & Pullen, 2009). However, some possible causes have been proposed. Learning disabilities tend to run in families with one parent having a disability such as dyslexia, although the specific genetic transmission of learning disabilities has not been established (Petrill et al., 2006). Some leading researchers argue that some reading disabilities are likely due to genetics, but that a majority are the result of environmental influences (Shaywitz, Morris, & Shaywitz, 2008).

Researchers also use brain imaging techniques, such as magnetic resonance imaging, to reveal any regions of the brain that might be involved in learning disabilities (Shaywitz, Lyon, & Shaywitz, 2006) (see Figure 9.7). These techniques indicate it is unlikely that learning disabilities reside in a single specific brain location. Learning disabilities are more likely due to problems with integrating information from multiple brain regions or subtle difficulties in brain structures and functions.

Many interventions have focused on improving the child's reading ability (Bender, 2008; Lyytinen & Erskine, 2009). Intensive instruction over a period of time by a competent teacher can help many children (Berninger, 2006). For example, a recent brain-imaging study of 15 children with severe reading difficulties who had not shown adequate progress in response to reading instruction in Grade 1 were given an intensive eight weeks of instruction in phonological decoding skills and then another intensive eight weeks of word recognition skills (Simos et al., 2007). Significant improvement in a majority of children's reading skills and changes in brain regions involved in reading occurred as a result of the intensive instruction.

Frustration with learning in the classroom may affect how children with learning disabilities interact with their peers. A Canadian study found lower altruism scores, higher anxiety/emotional disorder scores, and higher aggression scores among children with learning disabilities than among other children. However, once family functioning had been taken into account, the discrepancies

learning disability A disability that involves (1) normal intelligence or above, (2) difficulties in at least one academic area and usually several, and (3) no other problem or disorder, such as mental retardation, that can be determined as causing the difficulty.

dyslexia A category of learning disabilities involving a severe impairment in the ability to read and spell.

---

developmental **connection**

The Brain

Figure 9.7

Brain Scans and Learning Disabilities

An increasing number of studies are using MRI brain scans to examine the brain pathways involved in learning disabilities. Shown here is nine-year-old Patrick Price, who has dyslexia. Patrick is going through an MRI scanner disguised by drapes to look like a child-friendly castle. Inside the scanner, children must lie virtually motionless as words and symbols flash on a screen, and they are asked to identify them by clicking different buttons.

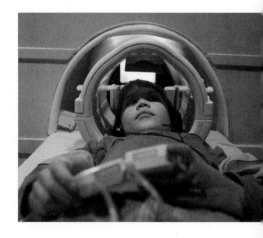

dropped (Milan, Hou, & Wong, 2006). These findings indicate that a supportive family environment is important for the social development of children with learning disabilities.

Attention Deficit Hyperactivity Disorder (ADHD)

attention deficit hyperactivity disorder (ADHD) A disability in which children consistently show one or more of the following characteristics over a period of time: (1) inattention, (2) hyperactivity, and (3) impulsivity.

Attention deficit hyperactivity disorder (ADHD) *is a disability in which children consistently show one or more of the following characteristics over a period of time: (1) inattention, (2) hyperactivity, and (3) impulsivity.* Children who are inattentive have such difficulty focusing on any one thing that they may get bored with a task after only a few minutes—or seconds. Children who are hyperactive show high levels of physical activity, seeming to be in almost constant motion. Children who are impulsive have difficulty curbing their actions and reactions: they do not do a good job of thinking carefully before acting. Depending on the characteristics that children with ADHD display, they can be diagnosed as (1) ADHD with predominantly inattention, (2) ADHD with predominantly hyperactivity/impulsivity, or (3) ADHD with both inattention and hyperactivity/impulsivity.

The number of children diagnosed and treated for ADHD has increased substantially in recent decades, by some estimates doubling in the 1990s. The disorder occurs as much as four to nine times more often in boys than in girls.

Definitive causes of ADHD have not been found. However, a number of causes have been proposed (Biederman, 2007). Some children likely inherit a tendency to develop ADHD from their parents (Goos, Ezzatian, & Schachar, 2007). According to the Association of Chief Psychologists with Ontario School Boards (ACPOSB, 2004), children whose siblings have ADHD are five to seven times more likely to have the same condition. Other children likely develop ADHD because of damage to their brain during prenatal or postnatal development (Banerjee, Middleton, & Faraone, 2007). Among early possible contributors to ADHD are cigarette and alcohol exposure during prenatal development and low birth weight (Greydanus, Pratt, & Patel, 2007).

There is controversy, however, about the diagnosis of ADHD (Taylor, Smiley, & Richards, 2009; Zentall, 2006). Some attribute the increase mainly to heightened awareness of the disorder. Others are concerned that many children are being incorrectly diagnosed. In fact, the renowned psychologist Jerome Kagan and educationalist Sir Ken Robinson both contend that there is no such diagnosis as ADHD. Diagnosing children with ADHD, they argue, stigmatizes the child and undermines the child's creative nature and prevents him or her from finding his element—which often is at odds with expectations in the classroom (Kagan, 2013; Robinson, 2009).

Still others are concerned about the social impact of ADHD on an individual. Many 10- to 15-year-olds with ADHD reported feeling "left out" in schools (Canadian Council on Social Development, 2003). Health Canada (1999) warned that "aggression, early school leaving, and perhaps later substance abuse" could occur if families and schools are unable to handle a child's ADHD.

As with learning disabilities, the development of brain-imaging techniques is leading to better understanding of ADHD (Shaw et al., 2007). A recent study revealed that peak thickness of the cerebral cortex occurred three years later (10.5 years of age) in children with ADHD than in children without ADHD (7.5 years of age) (Shaw et al., 2007). The delay was more prominent in the prefrontal regions of the brain that are especially important in attention and planning (see Figure 9.8).

Stimulant medication such as Ritalin or Adderall (which has fewer side effects than Ritalin) is effective in improving the attention of many children with ADHD, but it usually does not improve their attention to the same level as children who do not have ADHD (Pliszka, 2007). Researchers have often found that a combination of medication and behaviour management improves the behaviour of children with ADHD better than medical or behaviour management alone, although this is not true in every case (Jensen et al., 2007). Other drugs, such as the stimulant called mixed amphetamine salts extended release (MAS XR) and the non-stimulant Strattera (atomoxetine), are currently being studied in the treatment of children with ADHD. Early findings involving these drugs are promising (Bhatara & Aparasu, 2007; Faraone, 2007).

Critics like Kagan and Robinson argue that many physicians are too quick to prescribe stimulants for children with milder forms of ADHD (Kagan, 2013; Robinson, 2009). Although

critical thinking

You may know someone with a learning disability, perhaps a family member. What supports are available to the child and to the family? What are some of challenges to the daily routines experienced by the individual and by family and friends? What are the lifetime challenges facing the individual who has been diagnosed with a learning disability? What challenges might the child who is one of the 10 percent diagnosed with multiple disabilities?

developmental connection

The Brain

stimulants may help, they do carry potential risks for children, including loss of appetite, weight loss, and sudden death. The Canadian Paediatric Society, the Canadian Cardiovascular Society, and the Canadian Academy of Child and Adolescent Psychiatry recommend a thorough physical examination to identify potential risk factors for sudden death prior to prescribing stimulant medication (Goldman, 2010).

Recent studies have also focused on the possibility that exercise might reduce ADHD (Tantillo et al., 2002). Some mental health experts now recommend that children with ADHD exercise several times a day, and speculate that the increased rates of ADHD have coincided with the decline in children's activity levels (Ratey, 2006).

Autism Spectrum Disorders

Autism spectrum disorders (ASD), *also called pervasive developmental disorders, range from the severe disorder labelled autistic disorder to the milder disorder called Asperger syndrome.* Autism spectrum disorders are characterized by problems in social interaction, problems in verbal and non-verbal communication, and repetitive behaviours (Boucher, 2009; Hall, 2009; Simpson & LaCava, 2008). Children with these disorders may also show atypical responses to sensory experiences (National Institute of Mental Health, 2008). Autism spectrum disorders can often be detected in children as young as one to three years of age (Chapman, 2009). According to Statistics Canada, the number of persons with autism or any other developmental disorder was about one in 450 Canadians. The rate seems to be higher for school children. Preliminary results of an epidemiological study conducted at Montreal Children's Hospital found the rate to be one per 147 children (Norris, Paré, & Starkey, 2006).

Autistic disorder *is a severe developmental autism spectrum disorder that has its onset in the first three years of life.* It includes deficiencies in social relationships, abnormalities in communication, and restricted, repetitive, and stereotyped patterns of behaviour. Boys are three to four times more likely to have an autistic disorder than girls (Norris, Paré, & Starkey, 2006).

Asperger syndrome is a relatively mild autism spectrum disorder in which the child has relatively good verbal language, milder non-verbal language problems, and a restricted range of interests and relationships (Bennett et al., 2007; Norris, Paré, & Starkey, 2006). Children with Asperger syndrome often engage in obsessive repetitive routines and preoccupations with a particular subject (South, Ozonoff, & McMahon, 2005). For example, a child may be obsessed with baseball scores or railroad timetables.

What causes the autism spectrum disorders? The current consensus is that autism is a brain dysfunction with abnormalities in brain structure and neurotransmitters (Lainhart, 2006). Genetic factors likely play a role in the development of the autism spectrum disorders (Katzov, 2007). A recent study revealed that mutations—missing or duplicated pieces of DNA on chromosome 16—can raise a child's risk of developing autism 100-fold (Weiss et al., 2008). There is no evidence that family socialization causes autism (Rutter & Schopler, 1987). Mental retardation is present in some children with autism; others show average or above-average intelligence (McCarthy, 2007).

Children with autism benefit from a well-structured classroom, individualized instruction, and small-group instruction (Pueschel et al., 1995). As with children who are mentally retarded, behaviour modification techniques are sometimes effective in helping autistic children learn (Hall, 2009).

Physical Disabilities

Physical disabilities tend to be visible and often are a risk factor for academic as well as psychological problems. Data from the NLSCY show that having an "activity-limiting" condition is linked to poor academic performance through weakened problem solving and memory (King et al., 2005). This is likely a result of the difficulty in participating in play and other activities that promote cognitive skills that are important for academic performance. To alleviate this problem, physical and personnel assistance such as hearing aids and teacher aides should be available and accessible to these children.

Figure 9.8 - - - - - - - - - - - - - - - - -

Regions of the Brain in which Children with ADHD Had a Delayed Peak in the Thickness of the Cerebral Cortex

Note: The greatest delays occurred in the prefrontal cortex.

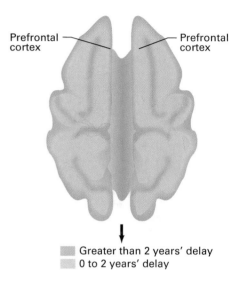

Prefrontal cortex — — Prefrontal cortex

▮ Greater than 2 years' delay
▮ 0 to 2 years' delay

autism spectrum disorders (ASD) Also called pervasive developmental disorders, they range from the severe disorder labelled autistic disorder to the milder disorder called Asperger syndrome. Children with these disorders are characterized by problems in social interaction, verbal and non-verbal communication, and repetitive behaviours.

autistic disorder A severe developmental autism spectrum disorder that has its onset in the first three years of life and includes deficiencies in social relationships, abnormalities in communication, and restricted, repetitive, and stereotyped patterns of behaviour.

Asperger syndrome A relatively mild autism spectrum disorder in which the child has relatively good verbal language, milder non-verbal language problems, and a restricted range of interests and relationships.

Children's Disabilities and the Family

A child's disabilities can cause much stress in parents. As indicated in Charlotte Johnston's paper on ADHD, most parents look for information on the disorder from books and medical professionals to decide what treatment to use or to discontinue (Johnston et al., 2005). Similarly, according to a research team from Dalhousie University, factors such as finding time and money to meet the needs of the child and fulfilling one's own and society's expectations of taking care of a sick child can place a heavy burden on parents of children with chronic medical problems (Burton, Lethbridge, & Phipps, 2006).

Parents do have the power to advocate for their children and some exert power to create change. In 2004, the parents of four autistic children appealed to the Supreme Court of Canada under the *Charter of Rights and Freedoms*, asserting that the failure of British Columbia to provide Lovaas treatments for their autistic children was a violation of their equality rights. The Lovaas treatment is an intensive applied behavioural analysis that costs between $45,000 and $60,000 per year, an expense the families had incurred. Although British Columbia had provided other treatments, it did not provide this one. The Supreme Court ruled in favour of the parents, directing the province to fund the Lovaas therapy and awarding damages to each of the adult petitioners (Tiedemann, 2008).

Advocacy of this magnitude can be exhilarating when the outcome is so positive. But the day-to-day advocacy that parents assume in their communities, in schools, and even within their nuclear and extended families can be a source of chronic stress. The Dalhousie research team found that caring for a child with a chronic condition was associated with maternal depression. Significantly, a mother with a chronically ill child had a lower probability of good health than one who smoked but did not have such a child (Burton, Lethbridge, & Phipps, 2006).

Educational Issues

The provision of special education in Canada has gone through significant changes. Before the early 1900s, the education system did not accept people with disabilities. Then, public schools began to accept exceptional students, but segregated them from ordinary students. Children with more severe disabilities, however, were institutionalized. For decades the movement toward inclusion has been challenging Canadian schools (Lupart, 1998). The 1970s saw parents' efforts to open the public school system to all children with disabilities. Subsequent provincial legislation promising access to public education for all children demonstrates the success of parents' efforts.

Despite all the changes, some wonder whether **mainstreaming**—*educating a child with special education needs in a regular classroom*—is, indeed, the best approach to teaching students with disabilities. Some experts believe that separate programs may be more effective and appropriate for children with disabilities because segregated classrooms can provide individualized instructions to meet students' special needs.

Even when the merits of mainstreaming are accepted, other issues can arise. As a survey with teachers in Nova Scotia shows, schools and the government sometimes do not provide enough personnel, time, and training for teachers to handle the diverse needs of special-education students in the mainstreamed classroom (Macmillan & Meyer, 2006). This has led to a sense of guilt among teachers who find themselves unable to meet the professional standard they set for themselves.

In addition, students who need special support do not always get it. In a national survey of parents with children with special needs, 31 percent reported problems accessing appropriate help, with parents of boys more likely to report this difficulty than those of girls (Uppal, Kohen, & Khan, 2006). The parents noted problems such as inadequate staff and learning aids, lack of services in the local area, and difficulty in communicating with the school and in getting an assessment.

In sum, mainstreaming or not, there should be appropriate support and training for teachers, and schools should have enough learning materials (such as talking books) to accommodate students with special needs.

To this point, we have discussed children with disabilities in middle and late childhood. For a review, see the **Reach Your Learning Objectives** section at the end of this chapter.

mainstreaming Educating a child with special education needs in a regular classroom.

Some experts suggest that mainstreaming children with disabilities is important. **What do you think?**

reach your **learning objectives**

Physical Changes and Health

LO1 Describe physical changes and health in middle and late childhood.

Body Growth and Change	■ During middle and late childhood, children grow an average of 5 to 7.5 cm a year. Muscle mass and strength gradually increase.
	■ Among the most pronounced changes are decreases in head circumference, waist circumference, and leg length in relation to body height.
The Brain	■ Advances in the prefrontal cortex are linked to children's improved attention, reasoning, and cognitive control.
	■ Temporal and frontal lobe development in childhood are reflected by improved language abilities such as reading.
Motor Development	■ Motor development becomes much smoother and more coordinated.
	■ Boys tend to develop gross motor skills earlier than girls; girls tend to develop fine motor skills earlier than boys.
	■ Increased myelination of the central nervous system is reflected in improved motor skills.
Exercise	■ Exercise plays an important role in children's growth and development.
	■ The sedentary lifestyle of children is a cause of concern for educators and policy makers in many parts of the world.
	■ Higher incidence of screen time, (television, computer games, texting, etc.) has been linked with being overweight and less physically fit, as well as with health issues such as diabetes and higher levels of cholesterol. Mothers report that when they were children, they experienced much higher levels of outdoor play activity than their children.
Health, Illness, and Disease	■ Nearly one of every three children (31.5 percent) are overweight. More boys than girls are obese and 36.2 percent of First Nations children living on reserves are obese.
	■ Children's low activity level and high-fat diets are the main reasons for the rise in obesity.
	■ Treatment of obesity focuses mainly on diet, exercise, and behaviour modification.
	■ An obsession with thinness among young girls can affect their psychological well-being.
	■ Unintentional accidents are the primary cause of hospitalization and death in middle and late childhood.
	■ Childhood cancers have a different profile from adult cancers and are the second leading cause of death in children between 1 and 14 years of age.

Cognitive Development

LO2 Explain cognitive changes in middle and late childhood.

Piaget's Concrete Operational Stage	■ Concrete operational thought involves operations, conservation, classification, seriation, and transitivity.
	■ Critics question Piaget's estimates of competence at different developmental levels, his stage concept, and other ideas.

Information Processing	■ Changes in information processing during middle and late childhood involve the following:
	1. Increased short- and long-term memory, which reflects increased knowledge and expertise.
	2. Increased application of strategies, including creative, critical, and scientific thinking skills.
	3. Increased metacognition (cognition about cognition), which further enhances a child's ability to process information.
Intelligence	■ Intelligence is defined as problem-solving skills and the ability to learn from and adapt to life's everyday experiences.
	■ The Stanford-Binet test and the Wechsler scales are widely used IQ tests.
	■ Sternberg proposed a triarchic theory of intelligence: analytical, creative, and practical.
	■ Gardner's eight types of intelligence include verbal, mathematical, spatial, movement, self-insight, insight about others, musical skills, and naturalist skills.
	■ Mayer-Salovey-Caruso propose that emotional intelligence has four primary elements: perceiving, using, understanding, and managing emotions.
	■ Music training is related to small increases in IQ.
	■ Most researchers agree that genetics, environment, and free will interact to influence intelligence.
	■ The Flynn effect refers to the worldwide increase in intelligence scores that has occurred over a short time. This increase is thought to be the result of improved educational opportunities.
	■ Culture-fair tests are those that are free of cultural bias.
	■ Several levels of intellectual disability or developmental delay exist, and may be organic or cultural-familial in nature.
	■ Giftedness refers to people who have higher than average intelligence and/or superior talent for something.
	■ Caution and care must be taken when using intelligence tests scores, as they do not measure different domains of intelligence.

Language Development

LO3 Discuss language development in middle and late childhood.

Vocabulary, Grammar, and Metalinguistic Awareness	■ Children become more analytical in their approach to words and grammar.
	■ Metalinguistic awareness, knowledge about language and the ability to discuss language, accompanies advances in vocabulary and grammar.
Reading	■ Current debate focuses on the whole-language approach versus the basic skills and phonetics approach.
	■ Metalinguistic awareness, knowledge about language and the ability to discuss language, accompanies advances in vocabulary and grammar.
	■ Effective reading instruction involves a balance of the two approaches and a positive classroom atmosphere.
	■ Many children weak in reading make good progress throughout the elementary school years even without remedial instruction.
Bilingualism	■ Many positive outcomes have been associated with knowledge of a second language.
	■ Success in learning a second language may be related to age.

Educational Approaches And Issues

LO4 Discuss approaches and issues related to education.

Approaches to Student Learning	■ Debate exists between which is more effective in teaching children: the constructivist approach or the direct instruction approach.
Educational Issues	■ Poverty is a major factor in school performance: children from low-income families tend to fare poorer academically and behaviourally.
	■ Ethnicity also influences school performance; children from immigrant or Aboriginal backgrounds are faced with additional challenges including poverty, bullying, value differences, and language.
	■ Immigrant children catch up with their classmates by age 10 or 11.
	■ Aboriginal children may experience a feeling of alienation due to the school's lack of understanding and respect for the world-views, spirituality, and other aspects of their culture.
International Comparisons	■ Canadian children face a different school environment than those of their peers in many countries, such as the number of years a child will attend school, the use of school uniforms, the role of religion, and academic performance.
Private Schools and Home Education	■ Many Canadian children are being educated in private schools or through home schooling, which is legal in all 10 provinces.
	■ Not all private-school children come from wealthy families.
	■ The reasons for enrolling children in these forms of education include family values and parents' discomfort with specific aspects of public schools.

Children with Disabilities

LO5 Identify different types of disabilities and discuss issues relating to their education.

Learning Disabilities	■ Children with a learning disability are of normal intelligence or above, have difficulties in at least one academic area and usually several, and have a difficulty that is not attributable to another diagnosed problem or disorder.
	■ The most common learning disability in children involves reading. Dyslexia is a severe impairment in the ability to read and spell.
	■ Diagnosis of a learning disability is often a difficult task, as diagnostic practices and services vary within and between provinces.
	■ The precise causes of learning disabilities have yet to be determined; however, they tend to run in families. Both genetics and environmental factors come into play.
	■ Children with learning disabilities show more anxiety and aggression and less altruism than other children.
Attention Deficit Hyperactivity Disorder (ADHD)	■ ADHD is a condition in which children consistently show problems in one or more of inattention, hyperactivity, and impulsivity.
	■ Considerable controversy surrounds the diagnosis and treatment of ADHD.
Autism Spectrum Disorders	■ Autism spectrum disorders range from severe developmental autism spectrum disorder to the relatively milder Asperger syndrome.
Physical Disabilities	■ Physical disabilities are often visible and pose a risk factor for academic performance, particularly when the disability is "activity-limiting."

Children's Disabilities and the Family	■ Issues such as finding appropriate treatments for the child and fulfilling expectations to take care of a sick child add stress to parents' lives.
Educational Issues	■ The old approach to educating children with disabilities was to segregate them from ordinary classrooms. Since the 1960s, some professionals have been promoting mainstreaming of those children.
	■ Lack of training and support for teachers and lack of learning aids are concerns in the education of special needs children.

McGraw-Hill Connect

McGraw-Hill Connect provides you with a powerful tool for improving academic performance and truly mastering course material. You can diagnose your knowledge with pre- and post-tests, identify the areas where you need help, search the entire learning package, including the eBook, for content specific to the topic you're studying, and add these resources to your personalized study plan. CONNECT for *Life-Span Development*, fifth Canadian edition, offers the following:

- chapter-specific online quizzes
- groupwork
- presentations
- writing assignments
- case studies
- and much more!

Visit CONNECT today!

review ---→ *connect* ---→ reflect

review

Characterize the changes that occur in the brain's development during middle and late childhood. **LO1**

How does Piaget's stage of concrete operational thought differ from the earlier preoperational stage? **LO2**

What are some of the different types of intelligence? **LO2**

What is metalinguistic awareness? **LO3**

What are some of the major issues in education that affect academic performance? **LO4**

connect

In this chapter, you read about the role of exercise and nutrition on children's health. With this information in mind, design a child's day that would optimize his or her health and development. What would the child have for meals and snacks? In addition to school, in what activities would you engage the child?

reflect *Your Own Personal Journey of Life*

Consider Gardner's Eight Frames of Mind. Create a list that puts in order your strengths and weaknesses, putting your major strength on top, and your major weakness on the bottom. What activities do you enjoy the most? How do these activities compare with your list of strengths and weaknesses?

CHAPTER 10

Socio-Emotional Development in Middle and Late Childhood

CHAPTER OUTLINE

"Children need models rather than critics."

—JOSEPH JOUBERT, NINETEENTH-CENTURY FRENCH ESSAYIST

Ladybug Brings Hope to the Homeless

In the century since The Empire Club of Canada was established, many distinguished speakers have shared their insights with society's elite. The list of speakers includes the Queen Mother, the Dalai Lama, prominent industrialists such as John C. Eaton, David Rockefeller, and Bill Gates . . . and the founder of the Winnipeg-based Ladybug Foundation, Ms. Hannah Taylor (Taylor, 2005).

The Ladybug Foundation raises money to help the homeless across the country. As Ms. Taylor said in her speech, homeless people "are great people, wrapped in old clothes with sad hearts" (p. E1). Ms. Taylor's presentation certainly touched her audience of business executives. One exclaimed, "Wow! Who said bankers don't cry?" (p. E9).

What impressed the audience more: her speech or her age? At the time of the Empire Club presentation in 2005, Ms. Taylor—or should we say, Hannah—was only nine years old. Her charity work began when she saw a homeless man eating food from the garbage when she was five years old. She started using baby food containers—the ladybug jars—for donations. With her father, she also started the Big Boss Lunches to raise money from the business community. Over the past few years, The Ladybug Foundation has raised over $1 million (Perkins, 2006).

Hannah's kind work parallels that of Ryan Hreljac, a six-year-old from the Ottawa area who heard about the lack of drinkable water in parts of Africa. Thinking that building a well in Africa would cost $70, he told his parents he would do household chores to raise the money. This began a fundraising campaign that would eventually become Ryan's Well Foundation, which finances the construction of wells in Africa.

Hannah's and Ryan's experiences not only show us how kindness and determination can help others, they also illustrate some of the topics in this chapter: moral development, prosocial behaviour, social cognition, and self-esteem. We will also examine other issues related to school-age children: family and school lives, poverty, and resilience.

To learn more about Hannah and Ryan, visit their Web sites: http://www.ladybugfoundation.ca/ and http://www.ryanswell.ca/.

Emotional and Personality Development

LO1 Discuss emotional and personality development in middle and late childhood.

In this section we will explore how the self continues to develop during middle and late childhood and the emotional changes that occur during these years. We will also explore the child's moral development and the role of gender during these years.

The Self

Emotional Development

The Self

What is the nature of the child's self-understanding and self-esteem in the elementary school years? What role do self-efficacy and self-regulation play in children's achievement?

The Development of Self-Understanding

In middle and late childhood, especially between ages 8 and 11, children increasingly define themselves through psychological traits and characteristics in contrast to the more concrete descriptions of younger children. Elementary school children also are more likely to define themselves in terms of social characteristics and social comparisons, such as smart, popular, or dumb (Harter, 2006).

In addition to the increase in psychological characteristics in self-definition, social aspects of the self also increase at this point in development. In one investigation, elementary school children often included references to social groups in their self-descriptions. For example, some children referred to themselves as part of a sports team or member of a science group.

Diane Ruble (2010) investigates children's acquisition of a sense of self and noted the use of social comparison in their self-evaluations. Between 8 and 12 years of age, children become increasingly aware of race, religion, authority roles, gender, and other social categories. They often evaluate themselves, sometimes quite harshly, based on what they think others may think of them. For example, a child might say, "No one will like me with this stupid haircut" (Kennedy-Moore, 2012). In sum, in middle and late childhood self-description increasingly involves psychological and social characteristics, including social comparison.

UNDERSTANDING OTHERS In middle and late childhood, children show an increase in **perspective taking**, *the ability to assume other people's perspectives and understand their thoughts and feelings.* Perspective taking is thought to be important in whether children develop prosocial or anti-social attitudes and behaviour (Davis-Kean, Jager, & Collins, 2009). In terms of prosocial behaviour, taking another's perspective improves children's likelihood of understanding and sympathizing with others (Eisenberg, Fabes, & Spinrad, 2006).

In Chapter 8, we indicated that four-year-old children show some skepticism of others' claims. In middle and late childhood, children become increasingly skeptical of some sources of information about psychological traits. For example, in one study, 10- to 11-year-olds were more likely to reject other children's self-reports that they were *smart* and *honest* than were 6- to 7-year-olds (Heyman & Legare, 2005). In a recent cross-cultural comparison of 6- to 11-year-olds from the United States and China, older children showed increased skepticism of others' self-reports concerning value-laden traits, such as *honest, smart*, and *nice*, but did not show increased skepticism about less value-laden characteristics, such as *outgoing, likes salty food*, and *likes the colour red* (Heyman, Fu, & Lee, 2007). Older Chinese children were more likely to expect others to show modesty when talking about themselves than were their U.S. counterparts.

developmental **connection**

Maslow

critical thinking

Recall Maslow's hierarchy of needs discussed in Chapter 2. Where on the hierarchy would you place the people who Hannah and Ryan are helping? Where would you place Hannah and Ryan? What are some of the contexts or realities of their lives that account for the different placement on the hierarchy?

perspective taking The ability to assume other people's perspectives and understand their thoughts and feelings.

Self-Esteem and Self-Concept

self-esteem The global evaluative dimension of the self; also referred to as self-worth or self-image.

self-concept Domain-specific evaluations of the self.

High self-esteem and a positive self-concept are important for children's well-being (Harter, 2006). **Self-esteem** *refers to global evaluations of the self; it is also referred to as self-worth or self-image.* For example, a child may perceive that she is not merely a person but a good person. Of course, not all children have an overall positive image of themselves. **Self-concept** *refers to domain-specific evaluations of the self.* Children can make self-evaluations in many domains of their lives—academic, athletic, appearance, and so on. In sum, self-esteem refers to global self-evaluations, and self-concept to more domain-specific evaluations.

Self-esteem reflects perceptions that do not always match reality (Baumeister et al., 2003). A child's self-esteem might reflect a belief about whether he or she is intelligent and attractive, for example, but that belief is not necessarily accurate. Thus, high self-esteem may refer to accurate, justified perceptions of one's worth as a person and one's successes and accomplishments, but it can also refer to an unwarranted sense of superiority over others (Krueger, Vohs, & Baumeister, 2008). In the same manner, low self-esteem may reflect either an accurate perception of one's shortcomings, or a distorted—even pathological—insecurity and inferiority.

Variations in self-esteem have been linked with many aspects of children's development. However, much of the research is *correlational* rather than *experimental*. Recall from Chapter 1 that correlation does not equal causation. Thus, if a correlational study finds an association between children's low self-esteem and low academic achievement, low academic achievement could cause the low self-esteem as much as low self-esteem causes low academic achievement. In fact, there are only moderate correlations between school performance and self-esteem, and these correlations do not suggest that high self-esteem produces better school performance (Baumeister et al., 2003)

critical thinking

What are some of the traits that shape your self-concept? How did you come to understand these strengths and weaknesses? How have your strengths and weaknesses shaped your overall self-esteem? Do you think parents and educators are overly concerned with children's self-esteem?

Children with high self-esteem have greater initiative, but this can produce positive or negative outcomes (Baumeister et al., 2003). These children are prone to both prosocial and antisocial actions (Krueger, Vohs, & Baumeister, 2008). A recent study revealed that over time, aggressive children with high self-esteem increasingly valued the rewards that aggression can bring and belittled their victims (Menon et al., 2007).

Children have the highest self-esteem when they perform competently in domains that are important to them. These areas might include academic skills, sports, social acceptance, and physical attractiveness. Anne Bowker, of Carleton University in Ottawa, studied how self-esteem and physical competence/appearance might be related in late childhood and early adolescence (2006). Noticeable physical changes and society's emphasis on fitness may cause children in this age period to be rather sensitive to their appearance. While both physical skills and appearance are important components of self-esteem, Bowker found that girls who are not athletic placed less importance on physical competence and treated appearance as an important criterion in determining their self-esteem.

Emotional support and social approval from others can also influence children's self-esteem. Some children with low self-esteem come from conflicted families or conditions in which they experience abuse or neglect—situations in which support was unavailable. In some cases, alternative sources of support can be implemented either informally through the encouragement of a teacher, a coach, or another significant adult, or more formally through such programs as Big Brothers and Big Sisters.

Self-Efficacy

self-efficacy The belief that one can master a situation and produce favourable outcomes.

Self-efficacy *is the belief that one can master a situation and produce favourable outcomes.* Albert Bandura (2001, 2008, 2009a, b; 2010), whose social cognitive theory we described in Chapter 2, states that self-efficacy is a critical factor in whether or not students achieve. Self-efficacy is the belief that "I can"; helplessness is the belief that "I cannot." Students with high self-efficacy endorse such statements as, "I know that I will be able to learn the material in this class" and "if others can do this, so can I."

Dale Schunk (2011) has applied the concept of self-efficacy to many aspects of students' achievement. In his view, self-efficacy influences a student's choice of activities. Students with low self-efficacy for learning may avoid many learning tasks, especially those that are challenging. By contrast, high-self-efficacy counterparts eagerly work at learning tasks (Schunk, 2011). Students with high self-efficacy are more likely to expend effort and persist longer at a learning task than are students with low self-efficacy.

Self-Regulation

One of the most important aspects of the self in middle and late childhood is the increased capacity for self-regulation. This increased capacity is characterized by deliberate efforts to manage one's behaviour, emotions, and thoughts, leading to increased social competence and achievement (Thompson, 2009a). A recent study found that self-control increased from 4 years of age to 10 years of age and that high self-control was linked to lower levels of deviant behaviour (Vazsonyi & Huang, 2010). In this study, parenting characterized by warmth and positive affect predicted the developmental increase in self-control. Another recent study revealed that children from low-income families who had a higher level of self-regulation made better grades in school than their counterparts who had a lower level of self-regulation (Buckner, Mezzacappa, & Beardslee, 2009).

Recall from our discussion in Chapter 9 that the increased capacity for self-regulation is linked to increased focal activation in the prefrontal cortex. This development is linked to improved cognitive control, which includes self-regulation (Diamond, Casey, & Munakata, 2011; Durston et al., 2006).

developmental **connection**

Erikson

Industry versus Inferiority

In Chapter 2, we described Erik Erikson's (1968) eight stages of human development. His fourth stage, *industry versus inferiority*, appears during middle and late childhood. The term "industry" expresses a dominant theme of this period: children become interested in how things are made and how they work. When children are encouraged to make, build, and work—whether building a model airplane, constructing a tree house, fixing a bicycle, solving an addition problem, or making pancakes—their sense of industry increases. However, parents who see their children's efforts at making things as "making a mess" may contribute to children's development of a sense of inferiority.

Children's social worlds beyond their families also contribute to a sense of industry. School becomes especially important in this regard. Consider children who are slightly below average in intelligence. They are too bright to be in special classes but not bright enough to be in gifted classes. They fail frequently in their academic efforts, developing a sense of inferiority. By contrast, consider children whose sense of industry is derogated at home. A series of sensitive and committed teachers may revitalize their sense of industry (Elkind, 1970).

Alfred Adler (1927) believed that realization of the ideal and behaviour toward that goal were likely formed in the first few months of life. During this time, the infant senses and responds to joy and sorrow. Upon this foundation, the child develops a primitive sense of well-being. Multiple factors influence the child's development—family, peers, television, community, schools, teachers—all of which set up boundaries intended to help the child regulate his or her behaviour. Like adults, children learn to wriggle their way around these boundaries in an attempt to attain a particular goal, be it a feeling of dominance or achievement. In so doing, the child's sense of the ideal directs this activity and often leads to a sense of inferiority, as we can not always achieve our ideal. Adler believed that much behaviour, prosocial or otherwise, is compensating for feelings of inferiority.

What characterizes Erikson's stage of industry versus inferiority?

developmental **connection**

Adler

Emotional Development

In Chapter 8, we saw that preschoolers become more and more adept at talking about their own and others' emotions. They also show a growing awareness about controlling and managing emotions to meet social standards. In middle and late childhood, children further develop their understanding and self-regulation of emotion (Cunningham, Kliwer, & Garner, 2009; Saarni et al., 2006).

Developmental Changes

The following important developmental changes in emotions occur during the elementary school years (Denham, Bassett, & Wyatt, 2007; Kuebli, 1994; Thompson, 2009a; Thompson & Goodvin, 2005); these changes are illustrated by nine-year-old Hannah's speech to the Empire Club that you read about in the chapter-opening vignette.

- An increased ability to understand complex emotions such as pride and shame; these emotions become less tied to the reactions of other people and more internalized and integrated with a sense of personal responsibility.
- Increased understanding that more than one emotion can be experienced in a particular situation. A third-grader, for example, may realize that achieving something might involve both anxiety and joy.
- An increased tendency to take into account the events leading to emotional reactions. A fourth-grader may become aware that her sadness today is influenced by her friend moving to another town last week.
- Marked improvement in the ability to suppress or conceal negative emotional reactions. A fifth-grader has learned to tone down his anger better than he used to when one of his classmates irritates him.
- The use of self-initiated strategies for redirecting feelings. In the elementary school years, children become more reflective about their emotional lives and increasingly use strategies to control their emotions. They become more effective at cognitively managing their emotions, such as soothing oneself after an upset.
- A capacity for genuine empathy. For example, a fourth-grader feels sympathy for a distressed person and experiences vicariously the sadness the distressed person is feeling.

Emotional Intelligence (EI)

emotional intelligence A form of social intelligence that involves the ability to monitor one's own and others' feelings and emotions, to discriminate among them, and to use this information to guide one's thinking and action.

As you read in Chapter 9, **emotional intelligence** *is a form of social intelligence that involves the ability to monitor one's own and others' feelings and emotions, to discriminate among them, and to use this information to guide one's thinking and action* (Cherry, K., 2012; Mayer, 2004).

Many schools have introduced social and emotional learning so that children can learn to recognize and manage emotions, care about others, make good decisions, behave ethically and responsibly, develop positive relationships, and avoid negative behaviours (Zins, 2004). One elementary school in a Toronto suburb organized a series of 13 workshops in June 2000 dealing with feeling-related issues, such as empathy, anger management, and friendship (Griffin, 2001).

Other schools in North America have implemented a class called "self science." The contents for self science match up with many of the components of emotional intelligence. The topics include developing self-awareness (in the sense of recognizing feelings and building a vocabulary for them); seeing the links among thoughts, feelings, decisions, and reactions; managing emotions and realizing what is behind a feeling (such as the hurt that triggers anger); and learning how to listen, cooperate, and negotiate. Names for these classes range from "social development" to "life skills" to "social and emotional learning." Their common goal is to raise every child's emotional competence through regular education. Schools that have instituted such programs report significant success (Zins, 2004). In 2006, The Faculty of Education at the University of British Columbia launched the first Social and Emotional Learning Practicum to graduate students so that educators can integrate social-emotional learning concepts and strategies into the curriculum (UBC, 2010).

Coping with Stress

An important aspect of children's emotional lives is learning how to cope with stress (Swearer, Givens, & Frerichs, 2010). As children get older, they more accurately appraise a stressful situation and determine how much control they have over it. Older children generate more coping alternatives to stressful conditions and use more cognitive coping strategies (Saarni et al., 2006). They are better than younger children at intentionally shifting their thoughts to something that is less stressful,

What are some changes in emotion during the middle and late childhood years?

seeing another perspective and reframing, or changing their perception of a stressful situation. For example, a younger child may be very disappointed that a teacher did not say hello when the child arrived in the classroom. An older child may reframe the situation and think, "My teacher may have been busy with other things and just forgot to say hello."

By 10 years of age, most children are able to use these cognitive strategies to cope with stress (Saarni, 1999). However, in families characterized by turmoil or trauma, children may be so overwhelmed by stress that they do not use such strategies (Klingman, 2006).

News events such as Hurricane Sandy, wars, or personal family or neighbourhood events such as a 911 call to rush a family member to the hospital raise special concerns about how to help children cope with stressful events (Kar, 2009). Researchers have offered some recommendations for parents, teachers, and other adults caring for children (Gurwitch et al., 2001, pp. 4–11):

- Reassure children (numerous times, if necessary) of their safety and security.
- Allow children to retell events and be patient in listening to them.
- Encourage children to talk about any disturbing or confusing feelings, reassuring them that such feelings are normal after a stressful event.
- Protect children from re-exposure to frightening situations and reminders of the trauma—for example, by limiting discussion of the event in front of the children.
- Help children make sense of what happened, keeping in mind that children may misunderstand what took place. For example, young children "may blame themselves, believe things happened that did not happen, believe that terrorists are in the school, etc. Gently help children develop a realistic understanding of the event" (p. 10).

Traumatic events may cause individuals to think about the moral aspects of life. Hopelessness and despair may short-circuit moral development when a child is confronted by the violence of war zones and impoverished inner cities (Nader, 2001).

To this point, we have discussed a number of ideas about emotional and personality development in middle and late childhood. For a review, see the **Reach Your Learning Objectives** section at the end of this chapter.

Moral Development and Gender

LO2 Describe moral development and gender development.

Recall our description of Piaget's view of moral development from Chapter 8. Piaget proposed that younger children are characterized by *heteronomous* morality—but that, by 10 years of age, they have moved into a higher stage called *autonomous* morality. According to Piaget, older children consider the intentions of the individual, believe that rules are subject to change, and are aware that punishment does not always follow wrongdoing.

A second major perspective on moral development was proposed by Lawrence Kohlberg (1958, 1986). Piaget's cognitive stages of development serve as the underpinnings for Kohlberg's theory, but Kohlberg suggested there are six stages of moral development. These stages, he argued, are universal. Development from one stage to another, said Kohlberg, is fostered by opportunities to take the perspective of others and to experience conflict between one's current stage of moral thinking and the reasoning of someone at a higher stage.

Moral Development

Gender

developmental **connection**

Piaget

Moral Development

Kohlberg arrived at his view after 20 years of using a unique interview technique with children. In the interview, children were presented with a series of stories in which characters face moral dilemmas. The following is the most well-known Kohlberg dilemma:

In Europe, a woman was near death from a special kind of cancer. There was one drug that the doctors thought might save her. It was a form of radium that a druggist in the same town had

Lawrence Kohlberg, the architect of a provocative cognitive developmental theory of moral development. **What is the nature of his theory?**

internalization The developmental change from behaviour that is externally controlled to behaviour that is controlled by internal standards and principles.

preconventional reasoning The lowest level in Kohlberg's theory of moral development. The individual shows no internalization of moral values—moral reasoning is controlled by external rewards and punishment.

conventional reasoning The intermediate level in Kohlberg's theory of moral development. Individuals abide by certain standards (internal), but they are the standards of others (external), such as parents or society.

postconventional reasoning The highest level in Kohlberg's theory of moral development. Morality is completely internalized and is not based on others' standards.

recently discovered. The drug was expensive to make, but the druggist was charging ten times what the drug cost him to make. He paid $200 for the radium and charged $2,000 for a small dose of the drug. The sick woman's husband, Heinz, went to everyone he knew to borrow the money, but he could only get together $1,000, which is half of what it cost. He told the druggist that his wife was dying and asked him to sell it cheaper or let him pay later. But the druggist said, "No, I discovered the drug, and I am going to make money from it." So, Heinz got desperate and broke into the man's store to steal the drug for his wife (Kohlberg, 1969, p. 379).

This story is one of 11 that Kohlberg devised to investigate the nature of moral thought. After reading the story, the interviewee answers a series of questions about the moral dilemma. Should Heinz have stolen the drug? Is it a husband's duty to steal the drug for his wife if he can get it no other way? Did the druggist have the right to charge that much when there was no law setting a limit on the price? Why, or why not? It is important to note that whether the individual says to steal the drug or not is not important in identifying the person's moral stage. What is important is the individual's moral reasoning behind the decision.

From the answers interviewees gave for this and other moral dilemmas, Kohlberg proposed three levels of moral development, each of which is characterized by two stages. A key concept in understanding moral development in his proposal is **internalization**, *the developmental change from behaviour that is externally controlled to behaviour that is controlled by internal standards and principles.* As children and adolescents develop, their moral thoughts become more internalized.

Kohlberg's Level 1: Preconventional Reasoning

Preconventional reasoning *is the lowest level in moral development. At this level, the individual shows no internalization of moral values—moral reasoning is controlled by external rewards and punishments.*

- Stage 1: *Heteronomous morality.* At this stage, moral thinking is often tied to punishment.
- Stage 2: *Individualism, instrumental purpose, and exchange.* At this stage, individuals pursue their own interests but also let others do the same. Thus, what is right involves an equal exchange. People are nice to others so that others will be nice to them in return.

Kohlberg's Level 2: Conventional Reasoning

At the **conventional reasoning** *level, internalization is intermediate. Individuals abide by certain standards (internal), but they are the standards of others (external), such as parents or society.*

- Stage 3: *Mutual interpersonal expectations, relationships, and interpersonal conformity.* At this stage, individuals value trust, caring, and loyalty to others as the basis of moral judgments. Children and adolescents often adopt their parents' moral standards at this stage, seeking to be thought of by their parents as a "good girl" or a "good boy."
- Stage 4: *Social systems morality.* At this stage, moral judgments are based on understanding the social order, law, justice, and duty. For example, adolescents may say that for a community to work effectively, it needs to be protected by laws that are adhered to by its members.

Kohlberg's Level 3: Postconventional Reasoning

Postconventional reasoning *is the highest level in Kohlberg's theory of moral development. At this level, morality is completely internalized and is not based on others' standards.* The individual recognizes alternative moral courses, explores the options, and then decides on a personal moral code.

- Stage 5: *Social contract or utility and individual rights.* At this stage, individuals reason that values, rights, and principles transcend the law. Laws and social systems can be examined in terms of the degree to which they preserve and protect fundamental human rights and values.
- Stage 6: *Universal ethical principles.* At this stage, the person has developed a moral standard based on universal human rights. When faced with a conflict between law and conscience, the person will follow conscience even though the decision might involve personal risk.

Kohlberg maintained that these levels and stages occur in a sequence and are age-related: before age nine, most children use level 1, preconventional reasoning based on external rewards and punishments, when they consider moral choices. By early adolescence, their moral reasoning is increasingly based on the application of standards set by others. Most adolescents reason at stage 3, with some signs of stages 2 and 4. By early adulthood, a small number of individuals reason in postconventional ways.

In support of this description of development, a 20-year longitudinal investigation found that use of stages 1 and 2 decreased with age (Colby et al., 1983) (see Figure 10.1). Stage 4, which did not appear at all in the moral reasoning of 10-year-olds, was reflected in the moral thinking of 62 percent of the 36-year-olds. Stage 5 did not appear until age 20 to 22 and never characterized more than 10 percent of the individuals.

Thus, the moral stages appeared somewhat later than Kohlberg initially envisioned, and reasoning at the higher stages, especially stage 6, was rare. Although stage 6 has been removed from the Kohlberg moral judgment scoring manual, it still is considered to be theoretically important in the Kohlberg scheme of moral development.

Influences on the Kohlberg Stages

What factors influence movement through Kohlberg's stages? Although moral reasoning at each stage presupposes a certain level of cognitive development, Kohlberg argued that advances in children's cognitive development did not ensure development of moral reasoning. Instead, moral reasoning also reflects children's experiences in dealing with moral questions and moral conflict.

Several investigators have tried to advance individuals' levels of moral development by having a model present arguments that reflect moral thinking one stage above the individuals' established levels. This approach applies the concepts of equilibrium and conflict that Piaget used to explain cognitive development. By presenting arguments slightly beyond the children's level of moral reasoning, the researchers created a disequilibrium that motivated the children to restructure their moral thought. The upshot of studies using this approach is that virtually any plus-stage discussion, for any length of time, seems to promote more advanced moral reasoning.

Figure 10.1

Kohlberg's Three Levels and Six Stages of Moral Development

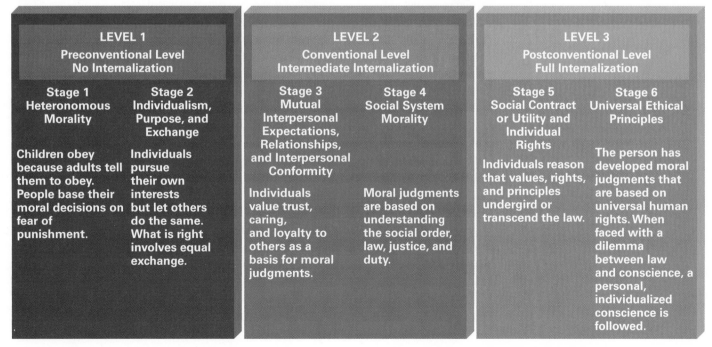

Kohlberg emphasized that peer interaction and perspective taking are critical aspects of the social stimulation that challenges children to change their moral reasoning. Whereas adults characteristically impose rules and regulations on children, the give-and-take among peers gives children an opportunity to take the perspective of another person and to generate rules democratically. Kohlberg stressed that in principle, encounters with any peers can produce perspective-taking opportunities that may advance a child's moral reasoning. A recent research review of cross-cultural studies involving Kohlberg's theory revealed strong support for a link between perspective-taking skills and more advanced moral judgments (Gibbs et al., 2007).

Kohlberg's Critics

Kohlberg's theory of moral development has not gone unchallenged (Gibbs, 2009; Narvaez & Lapsley, 2009; Walker & Frimer, 2011). Key criticisms involve the link between moral thought and moral behaviour, inadequate consideration of culture's role and the family's role in moral development, and the significance of concern for others.

MORAL THOUGHT AND MORAL BEHAVIOUR   Kohlberg's theory has been criticized for placing too much emphasis on moral thought and not enough emphasis on moral behaviour (Walker, 2004). Moral reasons can sometimes be a shelter for immoral behaviour. Corrupt CEOs and politicians endorse the loftiest of moral virtues in public before their own behaviour is exposed. Whatever the latest public scandal, you will probably find that the culprits displayed virtuous thoughts but engaged in immoral behaviour. No one wants a nation of cheaters and thieves who can reason at the postconventional level. Heinous actions can be cloaked in a mantle of moral virtue.

Social cognitive theorist Albert Bandura (1998, 2002) argues that people usually do not engage in harmful conduct until they have justified the morality of their actions to themselves. Immoral conduct is made personally and socially acceptable by portraying it as serving socially worthy or moral purposes, or even as doing God's or Allah's will. As for research on moral behaviour, one area where children are often studied is **altruism**, *an unselfish interest in helping someone else*. Ryan and Hannah in our opening vignette illustrate altruism. Acts of altruism are plentiful—the hardworking labourer who places $5 in a Salvation Army kettle; the Imam who visits dying patients; the child who takes in a wounded cat and cares for it, and so on.

CULTURE AND MORAL DEVELOPMENT   According to Kohlberg, stages of moral reasoning are universal, but some critics argue that his theory is culturally biased (Gibbs, 2009; Miller, 2007). Both Kohlberg and his critics may be partially correct.

One review of 45 studies in 27 cultures around the world, mostly non-European, provided support for the universality of Kohlberg's first four stages (Gibbs et al., 2007; Snarey, 1987). Individuals in diverse cultures developed through these four stages, in sequence, as Kohlberg predicted. More recent research revealed support for the qualitative shift from stage 2 to stage 3 across cultures (Gibbs et al., 2007). Stages 5 and 6, however, were not found in all cultures (Gibbs et al., 2007; Snarey, 1987). Furthermore, this review found that Kohlberg's scoring system does not recognize the higher-level moral reasoning of certain cultures, thus making his system more culture-specific than he envisioned (Snarey, 1987). In sum, although Kohlberg's approach does capture much of the moral reasoning voiced in various cultures around the world, critics point out that his approach misses or misconstrues some important moral concepts in particular cultures (Gibbs, 2009).

The Connecting through Research feature describes a Canadian researcher's findings on cultural differences and their effect on children's moral judgments.

FAMILY AND MORAL DEVELOPMENT   Kohlberg believed that family processes are essentially unimportant in children's moral development. He argued that parent–child relationships are usually power-oriented and provide children with little opportunity for mutual give-and-take or perspective taking. Rather, Kohlberg said that such opportunities are more likely to be provided by children's peer relations.

critical thinking

Frequently, someone on the Internet circulates something that may be considered offensive because of a racist, sexist, political, or religious/anti-religious message. Is there a line between being funny and being offensive? Have you received emails that cross that line? How do you handle emails you find offensive? Do you alert the sender? If so, what do you say? If not, why not?

←

altruism Unselfish interest in helping another person.

Morality and Modesty

Kang Lee of the University of Toronto has extensively studied cultural differences in child behaviour. In one study, school-age children in Canada and the People's Republic of China were asked to rate a hypothetical character's prosocial or antisocial behaviour and subsequent admission or denial of the behaviour (Lee, Cameron, Xu, Fu, & Board, 1997). Although children in both countries believed it was a good thing to admit one's guilt and a bad thing to deny wrongdoing in the antisocial conditions, there was a difference in the prosocial situations. Not admitting a good deed was rated positively by Chinese children, but not by Canadian children. Because modesty is highly valued in the Chinese culture, these findings show that children's moral judgment may be strongly related to culture.

Similarly, a more recent study (Fu, Xu, Cameron, Heyman, & Lee, 2007) found that Canadian children aged 9 and 11 were more willing to lie to help a friend or themselves than to lie to help a group, while Chinese children showed the opposite pattern. In fact, the older Chinese children were more willing to lie for a group than their younger peers, indicating increasing internalization of cultural values in their moral understanding in this age group.

While the description and explanation of cultural differences are interesting, a practical issue here is what to do with the information. Perhaps more awareness, particularly among educators, may foster understanding helpful to immigrant children trying to learn social mainstream expectations.

In contrast, most experts on children's moral development conclude that parents' moral values and actions influence children's developing moral thoughts (Laible & Thompson, 2007; Walker & Frimer, 2011). Nonetheless, most developmentalists agree with Kohlberg and Piaget that peers play an important role in the development of moral reasoning.

GENDER AND THE CARE PERSPECTIVE   The most publicized criticism of Kohlberg's theory has come from Carol Gilligan (1982, 1992, 1996), who argues that Kohlberg's theory reflects a gender bias. According to Gilligan, Kohlberg's theory is based on a male norm that puts abstract principles above relationships and concern for others. Kohlberg's **justice perspective** *puts justice at the heart of morality by positioning the individual as standing alone and independently making moral decisions.* In contrast to Kohlberg's view, Gilligan proposes a **care perspective**, *which is a moral perspective that views people in terms of their connectedness with others and emphasizes interpersonal communication, relationships with others, and concern for others.* According to Gilligan, Kohlberg greatly underplayed the care perspective, perhaps because he was a male, because most of his research was with males rather than females, and because he used male responses as a model for his theory.

In extensive interviews with girls from 6 to 18 years of age, Gilligan and her colleagues found that girls consistently interpret moral dilemmas in terms of human relationships and base these interpretations on listening to and watching other people (Gilligan, 1992; Gilligan et al., 2003). However, questions have also been raised about Gilligan's gender conclusions (Walker & Frimer, 2009a, 2011). For example, a meta-analysis (a statistical analysis that combines the results of many different studies) casts doubt on Gilligan's claim of substantial gender differences in moral judgment (Jaffee & Hyde, 2000). And a recent review concluded that girls' moral orientations are "somewhat more likely to focus on care for others than on abstract principles of justice, but they can use both moral orientations when needed (as can boys . . .)" (Blakemore, Berenbaum, & Liben, 2009, p. 132).

Other research, though, has revealed differences in how boys and girls tend to interpret some aspects of moral situations (Eisenberg, Fabes, & Spinrad, 2006). In support of this idea, one study found that females rated prosocial dilemmas (those emphasizing altruism and helping) as more significant than males did (Wark & Krebs, 2000). Another study revealed that young adolescent girls used more care-based reasoning about dating dilemmas than boys did (Weisz & Black, 2002).

SOCIAL CONVENTIONAL REASONING   Some theorists and researchers argue that Kohlberg did not adequately distinguish between moral reasoning and social conventional reasoning (Smetana, 2006; Turiel, 2006). **Social conventional reasoning** *focuses on conventional rules that have been*

justice perspective Focuses on the rights of the individual; individuals independently make moral decisions.

care perspective Views people in terms of their connectedness with others and emphasizes interpersonal communication, relationships, and concern for others.

social conventional reasoning Conventional rules that have been established by social consensus to control behaviour and maintain the social system.

established by social consensus to control behaviour and maintain the social system. The rules themselves are arbitrary, such as using a fork at meals and raising your hand in class before speaking.

In contrast, **moral reasoning** *focuses on ethical issues and rules of morality.* Unlike conventional rules, moral rules are not arbitrary. They are obligatory, widely accepted, and somewhat impersonal (Smetana, 2006; Turiel, 2006). Rules pertaining to lying, cheating, stealing, and physically harming another person are moral rules because violation of these rules affronts ethical standards that exist apart from social consensus and convention. Moral judgments involve concepts of justice, whereas social conventional judgments are concepts of social organization (Killen, Rutland, & Jampol, 2009; Killen & Smetana, 2010).

moral reasoning Rules that focus on ethical issues and morality. They are obligatory, widely accepted, and somewhat impersonal.

Prosocial Behaviour

Whereas Kohlberg's and Gilligan's theories focus primarily on the development of moral reasoning, the study of prosocial moral behaviour places more emphasis on the behavioural aspects of moral development (Eisenberg et al., 2009). Children engage in both immoral antisocial acts, such as lying and cheating, and prosocial moral behaviour, such as showing empathy or acting altruistically (Gasser & Keller, 2009; Heyman & Sweet, 2009). Even during the preschool years, children may care for others or comfort others in distress, but prosocial behaviour occurs more often in adolescence than in childhood (Eisenberg et al., 2009).

Children's sharing becomes a more complex sense of what is just and right during middle and late childhood. By the start of the elementary school years, children begin to express objective ideas about fairness (Eisenberg, Fabes, & Spinrad, 2006). For example, most four-year-olds are not selfless saints, and understanding that they have an obligation to share does not necessarily govern behaviour. However, use of the word "fair" as synonymous with equal or same is common among six-year-olds. By the mid- to late-elementary school years, children believe that equity sometimes means people with special merit or special needs deserve special treatment.

A study in the Montreal area (Benenson, Markovits, Roy, & Denko, 2003) examined the toy-sharing behaviour of 6-year-olds and 10-year-olds. Toy sharing was related to age and the likelihood of peers' detection of selfish behaviour. Older children split the time of using a toy more equally than did the younger subjects. Furthermore, when selfish behaviour was not likely to be detected— for example, when a toy did not make a sound to signal turn taking—children at both ages had a higher tendency to monopolize the use of the toy. Hence, children's sharing behaviour is affected by both developmental factors and the immediate environment.

Moral Personality

Beyond the development of moral reasoning and specific moral feelings and prosocial behaviours, do children also develop a pattern of moral characteristics that is distinctively their own? In other words, do children develop a moral personality, and if so, what are its components? Researchers have focused attention on three possible components: (1) moral identity, (2) moral character, and (3) moral exemplars (Walker & Frimer, 2009b, 2011; Walker, Frimer, & Dunlop, 2010).

- *Moral identity.* Individuals have a moral identity when moral notions and moral commitments are central to their lives. They construct the self with reference to moral categories. Violating their moral commitment would place the integrity of their self at risk.
- *Moral character.* A person with moral character has the willpower, desires, and integrity to stand up to pressure, overcome distractions and disappointments, and behave morally. A person of good moral character displays moral virtues such as "honesty, truthfulness, and trustworthiness, as well as those of care, compassion, thoughtfulness, and considerateness. Other salient traits revolve around virtues of dependability, loyalty, and conscientiousness" (Walker, 2002, p. 74).
- *Moral exemplars.* Moral exemplars are people who have lived exemplary moral lives. Their moral personality, identity, character, and set of virtues reflect moral excellence and commitment.

In sum, moral development is a multifaceted, complex concept. Included in this complexity are thoughts, feelings, behaviours, and personality.

Gender

As we discussed in Chapter 8, preschool children display a gender identity and gender-typed behaviour that reflects biological, cognitive, and social influences. Here we will examine the pervasive influence of gender stereotypes, gender similarities and differences, and gender-role classification.

Gender Stereotypes

According to the old ditty, boys are made of "frogs and snails and puppy dog tails" and girls are made of "sugar and spice and all that is nice." In the past, a well-adjusted boy was supposed to be independent, aggressive, and powerful. A well-adjusted girl was supposed to be dependent, nurturing, and uninterested in power. These notions reflect **gender stereotypes**, *which are broad categories that reflect general impressions and beliefs about females and males.*

Recent research has found that gender stereotypes are, to a great extent, still present in today's world, both in the lives of children and adults (Best, 2010; Martin & Ruble, 2010). Gender stereotyping continues to change during middle and late childhood and adolescence (Blakemore, Berenbaum, & Liben, 2009). By the time children enter elementary school, they have considerable knowledge about which activities are linked with being male or female. By five years of age, both boys and girls stereotype boys as powerful and in more negative terms, such as mean, and girls in more positive terms, such as nice (Martin & Ruble, 2010). Across the elementary school years, children become more flexible in their gender attitudes (Trautner et al., 2005).

A recent study of children from 3 to 10 years old revealed that girls and older children used a higher percentage of gender stereotypes (Miller et al., 2009). In this study, appearance stereotypes were more prevalent on the part of girls while activity (sports, for example) and trait (aggressive, for example) stereotyping was more commonly engaged in by boys. Researchers also have found that boys' gender stereotypes are more rigid than girls' (Blakemore, Berenbaum, & Liben, 2009).

Gender Similarities and Differences

Let us now examine some of the similarities and differences between the sexes, keeping in mind that (a) the differences are averages—not all females versus all males; (b) even when differences are reported, there is considerable overlap between the sexes; and (c) the differences may be due primarily to biological factors, socio-cultural factors, or both.

BRAIN STRUCTURE Does gender matter when it comes to brain structure and function? Human brains are much alike, whether the brain belongs to a male or a female (Halpern, 2007; Halpern et al., 2007). However, researchers have found some differences in the brains of males and females (Hofer et al., 2007a, b). However, many of these differences are either small or the research is inconsistent. Also, when sex differences in the brain have been revealed, in many cases they have not been directly linked to psychological differences (Blakemore, Berenbaum, & Liben, 2009). Although research on sex differences in the brain is still in its infancy, it is likely that there are far more similarities than differences in the brains of females and males.

COGNITIVE DEVELOPMENT No gender differences in general intelligence have been revealed but some gender differences have been found in some cognitive areas (Blakemore, Berenbaum, & Liben, 2009). Research in this area fuels the nature versus nurture debate: Are anatomical sex differences in the brain due to the biological origins of these differences? Do our brains reflect the traditional roles we have played? For example, are women more attuned to social situations than men because they give birth and nurture their babies? Have men developed more visuospatial skills because of their roles in providing for and protecting their family? What role is played by behavioural experiences, which underscores the brain's continuing plasticity? For example, will focused practice enhance ability? Or are our brains shaped by a combination of these factors? Figure 10.2 illustrates differences in visuospatial performance in males and females.

gender stereotypes Broad categories that reflect general impressions and beliefs about females and males.

Figure 10.2

Visuospatial Ability of Males and Females

Note that although the average male's visuospatial ability is higher than the average female's, the overlap between the sexes is substantial. Not all males have better visuospatial ability than all females—the substantial overlap indicates that although the average score of males is higher, many females outperform many males on such tasks.

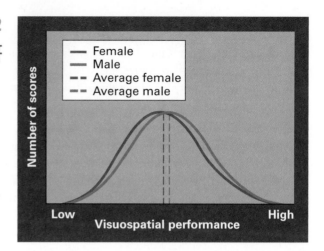

developmental **connection**

Freud

critical thinking

What do you think? Do men have better spatial skills? Are they better at sports and driving a car? Are men better at science and math? Are women more attuned to social situations? If so, are these traits hard-wired in the brain or has evolution and social context influenced the brain's development? The research is as complex as it is inconclusive, but what do you think? What role has your gender played in your behaviour? Academic performance? Your choices, including career choices? Have your choices been consistent with societal expectations?

On the other hand, elementary school girls score an average of 32 points higher than boys on reading tests, and boys have more difficulties in language and learning (Booth et al., 2009). Although most children do not fall behind, a Quebec study reports that more boys than girls repeat a grade in elementary school, and the gap increases considerably in secondary school (Pellitier, 2004). In addition to gender differences, *State of Learning in Canada: No Time for Complacency* (Canadian Council on Learning, 2007) further reports that economically disadvantaged children have more difficulty with learning (Booth et al., 2009).

One interesting area of gender differences in cognition is risk taking. In her study of elementary school children, Barbara Morrongiello of the University of Guelph found that boys were more likely than girls to select riskier options in everyday recreational activities (Morrongiello & Dawber, 2004). Girls' decision making was largely determined by concerns for safety, while boys' was influenced by fun, competence, and convenience as well as safety. This difference in thinking may reflect different environmental influences on the cognitive development of girls and boys. Girls tended to believe their choices were the same as the ones their parents would want them to select; on the other hand, most boys said their parents would want them to pick a safer option than the ones they had chosen.

SOCIO-EMOTIONAL DEVELOPMENT

Three areas of socio-emotional development in which gender similarities and differences have been studied extensively are aggression, emotion, and prosocial behaviour.

Aggression One of the most consistent gender differences is that boys are more physically aggressive than girls (Baillargeon et al., 2007; Tremblay, 2009). The difference occurs in all cultures and appears very early in children's development (White, 2001). The aggression difference is especially pronounced when children are provoked. Once again, both biological and environmental factors may account for these differences. Biological factors include heredity and hormones. Environmental factors include cultural expectations, adult and peer models, and social agents who reward aggression in boys and punish aggression in girls.

Emotion Girls are more likely to express their emotions openly and intensely than are boys, especially in displaying sadness and fear (Blakemore, Berenbaum, & Liben, 2009). Girls also are better at reading others' emotions and more likely to show empathy than are boys (Blakemore, Berenbaum, & Liben, 2009). Males usually show less self-regulation of emotion than females, and this low self-control can translate into behavioural problems (Eisenberg, Spinrad, & Smith, 2004).

Prosocial Behaviour Females view themselves as more prosocial and empathic (Eisenberg & Morris, 2004). Across childhood and adolescence, females engage in more prosocial behaviour (Hastings, Utendale, & Sullivan, 2007). The biggest gender difference occurs for kind and considerate behaviour, with a smaller difference in sharing.

Emotional development is multifaceted in that a variety of factors influence growth. In addition to gender, other factors include the cutoff dates to enter school or sports programs, which were originally established so that children in classes or on playing fields would be about the same age. However, when a child must be five years old by January 1 to enter kindergarten or to play a sport, that child may be almost a year older or younger than other children in the same group. Researchers have identified **relative age** *as the differences among children of the same age group,* and **relative age effect (RAE)** *as the consequence of relative age* (Musch & Grodin, 2001). Because a child's physical, socio-emotional, and cognitive abilities differ, the older children are advantaged. Consequently, they perform much better both academically and athletically and are, in fact, even less likely to be classified as learning disabled (Musch & Grodin, 2001). Through effort and hard work, the academic differences tend to level off. However, the same is not true of sports. The older children are often recipients of special supports such as better coaching because they are on the "rep" teams, easier access to ice time for hockey, and so on. As a result, they continue to outperform the younger members of the cohort right into adulthood, as measured by the birth dates of professional hockey, soccer, football, and baseball players in Europe and North America. Both physical and psychological factors are at work (Gladwell, 2008; Musch & Grodin, 2001).

Gender-Role Classification

In the 1970s, some researchers proposed that individuals could have both masculine and feminine traits. This thinking led to the development of the concept of **androgyny**, *the presence of masculine and feminine characteristics in the same person* (Bem, 1977; Spence & Helmreich, 1978).

Gender experts such as Sandra Bem argue that androgynous individuals are more flexible, competent, and mentally healthy than their masculine or feminine counterparts. To some degree, though, which gender-role classification is best depends on the context involved. For example, in close relationships, feminine and androgynous orientations might be more desirable. One study found that girls and individuals high in femininity showed a stronger interest in caring than did boys and individuals high in masculinity (Karniol, Grosz, & Schorr, 2003). However, masculine and androgynous orientations might be more desirable in traditional academic and work settings because of the achievement demands in these contexts.

Despite talk about the "sensitive male," William Pollack (1999) argues that little has been done to change traditional ways of raising boys. He says that the "boy code" tells boys that they should show little if any emotion and should act tough. Boys learn the boy code in many contexts—sandboxes, playgrounds, schoolrooms, camps, hangouts. The result, according to Pollack, is a "national crisis of boyhood." Pollack and others suggest that boys would benefit from being socialized to express their anxieties and concerns and to better regulate their aggression.

Measures have been developed to assess androgyny. One of the most widely used is the Bem Sex-Role Inventory. To check whether your gender-role classification is masculine, feminine, or androgynous, see Figure 10.3.

Gender in Context

Both the concept of androgyny and gender stereotypes talk about people in terms of personality traits such as "aggressive" or "caring." However, which traits people display may vary with the situation (Leaper & Friedman, 2007). Thus, the nature and extent of gender differences may depend on the context (Blakemore, Berenbaum, & Liben, 2009).

Consider prosocial behaviour, for example. The stereotype is that females are better than males at helping. Often the situation dictates who will be most helpful. Females are more likely than males to volunteer their time to engage in caregiving behaviour. However, in situations that involve danger, males are more likely than females to help (Eagly & Crowley, 1986). For example, a male is more likely than a female to stop and help a person stranded by the roadside with a flat tire. Indeed, one study documented that males are more likely to help when the context is masculine in nature (MacGeorge, 2003).

The importance of considering gender in context is nowhere more apparent than when examining what is culturally prescribed behaviour for females and males in different countries around

relative age The differences in development among children of the same age group.

relative age effect The consequences of developmental differences among children of the same age group.

critical thinking

Were you surprised to read about relative age and relative age effect (RAE)? Do you think RAE may be a factor in your development or the development of people you know? If so, how? If you have found RAE to be a factor in development, what effect do you think RAE may have on an individual's self-esteem and self-concept? Why do you think the RAE levels off academically but not athletically?

androgyny The presence of masculine and feminine characteristics in the same individual.

Figure 10.3

The Bem Gender-Role Inventory: Are You Androgynous?

Reproduced by special permission of the Distributor, Mind Garden, Inc., 1690 Woodside Road #202, Redwood City, CA 94061 USA www.mindgarden.com from the Bem Sex Role Inventory by Sandra Bem. Copyright 1978 by Consulting Psychologists Press, Inc. All rights reserved. Further reproduction is prohibited without the Distributor's written consent.

The following items are from the Bem Sex-Role Inventory. When taking the BSRI, a person is asked to indicate on a seven-point scale how well each of the 60 characteristics describes herself or himself. The scale ranges from 1 (never or almost never true) to 7 (always or almost always true).

EXAMPLES OF MASCULINE ITEMS	EXAMPLES OF FEMININE ITEMS
Defends open beliefs	Does not use harsh language
Forceful	Affectionate
Willing to take risks	Loves children
Dominant	Understanding
Aggressive	Gentle

Scoring: The items are scored on independent dimensions of masculinity and feminity as well as androgyny and undifferentiated classifications.

the world (Matlin, 2008). Although there has been greater acceptance of androgyny and similarities in male and female behaviour in some countries such as Canada and Australia, roles have remained very gender-specific in others. For example, in many Middle Eastern countries, the division of labour between males and females is dramatic. Males are socialized and schooled to work in the public sphere, females in the private world of home and childrearing.

To this point, we have studied a number of ideas about moral development and gender in middle and late childhood. For a review, see the **Reach Your Learning Objectives** section at the end of this chapter.

Families

LO3 Describe developmental changes in parent–child relationships and child maltreatment.

What are some of the most important parent–child issues in middle and late childhood?

Developmental Changes in Parent–Child Relationships

Recall Urie Bronfenbrenner's bio-ecological systems outlined in Chapter 2. The family, nuclear and extended, is a primary element of the microsystem and shapes a child's understanding of communication (both verbal and non-verbal), roles, activities, what's funny, what's sad, and even common sense. Bronfenbrenner asserted that each child deserves and needs a champion to help navigate the various systems, such as school, health care, community, and special organizations that the child encounters. In this microsystem, the process of interaction takes into account all participants. Other systems—chrono, macro, exo, and meso—exert enormous pressures on individual families; consequently, changes in the family mirror changes in the outer systems.

Bronfenbrenner expressed concern that economic demands and work responsibilities usurped so much parental time and attention that it could potentially undermine the family's interactive

Developmental Changes in Parent–Child Relationships

Child Maltreatment

developmental **connection**

Bronfenbrenner

processes (Bronfenbrenner, 1979). Bronfenbrenner's concerns were well-founded, for today, instead of engaging in conversation and mutually rewarding activities, often exhausted and stressed parents may leave children to watch television or play computer games while they deal with dinner and the pressures of their day. Although parents spend less time with their children in middle and late childhood than in early childhood, parents continue to be extremely important in their children's lives. In a recent analysis of the contributions of parents in middle and late childhood, the following conclusion was reached: "Parents serve as gatekeepers and provide scaffolding as children assume more responsibility for themselves and . . . regulate their own lives" (Huston & Ripke, 2006, p. 422). At this stage particularly, parents play an important role in supporting and stimulating children's academic achievement (Gupta, Thornton, & Huston, 2008; Huston & Ripke, 2006). The value parents place on education can mean the difference in the child's academic performance. Additionally, whether children participate in such activities as sports, music, and other activities is heavily influenced by the extent to which parents sign children up for such activities and encourage their participation (Simpkins et al., 2006).

During middle and late childhood, some control is transferred from parent to child. The process is gradual, and it produces coregulation rather than control by either the child or the parent alone. Parents continue to exercise general supervision and control, while children are allowed to engage in moment-to-moment self-regulation. The major shift to autonomy does not occur until about the age of 12 or later. A key developmental task as children move toward autonomy is learning to relate to adults outside the family on a regular basis—adults who interact with the child much differently than parents, such as teachers.

Parents as Managers

Parents can play important roles as managers of children's opportunities, as monitors of their behaviour, and as social initiators and arrangers (Parke & Buriel, 2006; Gauvain & Parke, 2010a). Mothers are more likely than fathers to engage in a managerial role in parenting.

Researchers have found that family management practices are related positively to students' grades and self-responsibility, and negatively to school-related problems (Eccles, 2007; Taylor & Lopez, 2005). Among the most important family management practices in this regard are maintaining a structured and organized family environment, such as establishing routines for homework, chores, bedtime, and so on, and effectively monitoring the child's behaviour, including the child's *screen time*—that is, the time spent watching TV, playing computer games, or on the Internet.

Stepfamilies or Blended Families

As noted in Chapter 8, nearly half a million Canadian families are stepfamilies. This new family is considerably more complex (McCloskey, 2004). It takes time for parents to marry, have children, get divorced, and then remarry. Consequently, there are far more elementary and secondary school children than infant or preschool children living in stepfamilies.

Remarried parents face the unique tasks of defining and strengthening their marriage and at the same time renegotiating the biological parent–child relationships and establishing stepparent–stepchild and stepsibling relationships (Coleman, Ganong, & Fine, 2004). The complex histories and multiple relationships make adjustment difficult (Hetherington & Stanley-Hagan, 2002).

In some cases, the stepfamily may have been preceded by the death of a spouse. However, by far the largest number of stepfamilies are preceded by divorce rather than death (Pasley & Moorefield, 2004). Three common types of stepfamily structure are (1) stepfather, (2) stepmother, and (3) blended or complex. In stepfather families, the mother typically has custody of the children and remarries, introducing a stepfather into her children's lives. In stepmother families, the father usually has custody and remarries, introducing a stepmother into his children's lives. In a blended or complex stepfamily, both parents bring children from previous marriages to live in the newly formed stepfamily.

As in divorced families, children in stepfamilies show more adjustment challenges, such as lower self-esteem and lower academic performance, than children in non-divorced families (Hetherington

& Kelly, 2002). However, it is important to recognize that a majority of children in stepfamilies do not have problems. In fact, in E. Mavis Hetherington's (2006) most recent longitudinal analysis, children and adolescents who had been in a simple stepfamily (stepfather or stepmother) for a number of years were adjusting and were functioning well in comparison to children and adolescents in conflicted nondivorced families and children and adolescents in complex (blended) stepfamilies. More than 75 percent of the adolescents in long-established simple stepfamilies described their relationships with their stepparents as "close" or "very close." Hetherington (2006) concluded that in long-established simple stepfamilies adolescents seem to eventually benefit from the presence of a stepparent and the resources provided by the stepparent.

Adolescence is an especially difficult time for the formation of a stepfamily (Gosselin, 2010). This may occur because becoming part of a stepfamily exacerbates normal adolescent concerns about identity, sexuality, and autonomy.

Parents with Mental Disorders

Living with a parent who has a mental disorder can be stressful. However, little research has been conducted to learn how children cope. In one of the pioneering studies, a team from the University of Alberta examined the adjustment of 13 adolescents who had a parent suffering from schizophrenia (Valiakalayil, Paulson, & Tibbo, 2004). These teens expressed a desire for information on mental illness and support; fear and confusion of parents' symptoms and behaviour; and feelings of sadness, frustration, fear, and resentment. They also experienced a lack of guidance. In terms of coping, many talked to friends and relatives, prayed, and reflected quietly. If adolescents can have a difficult time adjusting to their parent's mental illnesses, young children may find the parent's situation more frightening and confusing because of less understanding of mental issues, weaker communication skills, inability to express their feelings, and smaller support circles. Also, young children's trauma and confusion may intensify if the parent's illness results in being placed in another home.

Some programs have been developed to help children and adolescents cope with the mental illness of a parent. One such intervention is the SMILES Program (Simplifying Mental Illness plus Life Enhancement Skills). This program, designed for children between the ages of 8 and 16, includes activities, information about mental illness, and training in life skills to help children express themselves and handle negative feelings. Canadian and Australian participants in the program have reported improvement in their adjustment (Pitman & Matthey, 2004). Although it is still early to say what caused the improvement, at least we can say that there is help.

Child Maltreatment

Child maltreatment is a serious public health issue with far-reaching and multidimensional implications, ranging from health, economics, education, and to the justice system (Jack, 2011). The National Clearinghouse on Family Violence defines *child maltreatment* as harm or risk of harm a child or young person may experience while in the care of a person they trust such as a parent, older sibling, relative, teacher, or neighbour. Five categories of maltreatment include physical abuse or assault, sexual abuse, neglect, emotional harm, and exposure to family violence (Jack et al., 2006).

The prevalence of child maltreatment is difficult to ascertain. The World Health Organization (WHO) estimates that globally 57,000 deaths of children under 15 years of age can be attributed to homicide, and the majority of those are children under four years of age (WHO 2006). Canada has no community-based data collection, nor do reported numbers reflect all the incidents of police investigation. Approximately one-half of the 235,315 cases investigated in 2003 were substantiated; however, this is thought to be the tip of the iceberg as many go unreported (Jack et al., 2006). Child maltreatment frequently involves a combination of types. For example, emotional harm is linked with neglect, physical abuse, and exposure to family violence (Jack et al., 2006).

Child neglect is by far the most common form of child maltreatment. In every country where relevant data have been collected, neglect occurs up to three times as often as abuse (Benoit, Coolbear, & Crawford, 2008).

connecting through socio-cultural worlds of development

Adopting Internationally

The 2010 earthquake in Haiti called international attention to the plight of children left parentless not only in Haiti but also in other parts of the world. Natural disasters such as tsunamis and earthquakes, plus conditions such as war and poverty, motivate many to consider adoption. Recently, for example, the Canadian government agreed to permit the adoption of approximately 150 children from Haiti (CBC News, January, 17, 2010). Canadian parents adopt approximately 2,000 children annually. More than 40 percent are adopted from China, where a one-child policy is in effect (Adoption Council of Canada, 2003). Adopting children poses unique challenges requiring considerable thought; parents often do not foresee the problems they may encounter when they adopt (Ames, 1997).

International adoptees experience many of the same issues as local adoptees: adjustment to a new family, separation from biological siblings, curiosity about biological parents, search for an identity, and so on. At the same time, the child must learn a new language and adjust to a new culture. Further, the child may have experienced severe trauma or spent some time in an orphanage. Research conducted on Romanian children by Elinor Ames of the University of British Columbia (1997) found that the more time a child had spent in an orphanage, the more problems the child would likely have.

Parents also have to adjust to their foreign adoptees. For example, they need to decide what role the child's home culture will play in the family's life. If it is an interracial adoption, parents may find a need to discuss race and racism. Interestingly, the age when children start to ask questions about their adoptive status—four to five years—is also the time when they become aware of the presence of racial differences (Lee, Grotevant, Hellerstedt, Gunnar, & the Minnesota International Adoption Project Team, 2006); consequently, parents need to be prepared to deal with both the adoption and race discussions at the same time.

Ames identified four key areas that may require professional help: externalizing behavioural problems, below-average IQs, insecure attachment, and withdrawn, internalizing behaviours, such as rocking or staring into space. Adoptive parents had not anticipated these problems and found them stressful. The chief concern of adoptive parents had been health-related problems; however, within one year of living in the adoptive home, children's health problems were resolved. Why do some children make the adjustment so well, while others experience difficulty? The factors for success are related to the length of time and the quality of the orphanage from which the child was adopted, whether one or two children were adopted, the age of the parents, and the socio-economic status of the family. Older parents and those with better socio-economic means have greater success than parents who are younger and not as well-established economically. Older parents have greater advocacy skills and are better able to access resources (Ames, 1997).

Echoing Ames's study, a Swedish study followed a group of adoptees for 30 years and found that the majority of foreign adoptees function well in society. However, some experienced more physical, social, and economic difficulties than the general population (Lindblad, Hjern, & Vinnerljung, 2003). Foreign adoptees had higher odds for psychiatric care, substance abuse, and long-term sick leave than their own non-adopted siblings and immigrants. Compared to the general population, internationally adopted women were more likely to be single mothers and internationally adopted men were less likely to live with their own children, suggesting relationship difficulty with a significant romantic partner. Also, adoptees were more likely to have long-term dependence on welfare than their siblings. The authors did caution that a government and potential adoptive parents should be prepared to offer appropriate preventive or remedial support to those adoptees who may need help. Ames recommends that parents considering adoption should carefully examine their capacity in terms of time, energy, community, and family supports and resources, as well as their willingness to work with the various systems with which they may interact.

The Context of Maltreatment and Abuse

No single factor causes child maltreatment (Cicchetti, 2011; Cicchetti et al., 2010; Cicchetti & Toth, 2011). A combination of factors, including the culture, family, and developmental characteristics of the child, likely contribute to child maltreatment (Appleton & Stanley, 2009; Prinz et al., 2009).

According to a general survey conducted in 2009, immigrants and visible minorities are considerably less likely to report incidents of family violence. The survey was conducted in English and French, so immigrants who do not speak one of Canada's national languages were unable to participate (Sinha, 2012). Additionally, new Canadian women may not be aware of Canadian laws and may not appreciate the implications of a police investigation. For example, a recent immigrant from Uganda called the police to stop her husband, who was quite intoxicated at the time, from beating her. She was shocked to learn that the police not only took him away, but also issued a restraining order which forbade him from seeing her or their children. She called because she just wanted him to stop beating her. This case is consistent with the World Health Organization's (WHO) report linking alcohol and abuse. According to WHO, alcohol or drug abuse was a factor in 34 percent of the child welfare cases reported in Canada (WHO, 2006).

Social media, including the extensive violence that takes place in games or on TV, are reflected in the occurrence of violence in the family (Durrant, 2008). The family itself is obviously a key part of the context of abuse (Kennedy, 2009; Macmillan et al., 2009). The interactions of all family members need to be considered, regardless of who performs the violent acts against the child. For example, even though the father may be the one who physically abuses the child, the behaviour of the mother, the child, and siblings also should be evaluated.

Were parents who abuse children abused by their own parents? About one-third of parents who were abused themselves when they were young go on to abuse their own children (Cicchetti & Toth, 2006). Thus, some—but not a majority of—parents are involved in an intergenerational transmission of abuse.

Developmental Consequences of Maltreatment

Among the consequences of child maltreatment in childhood and adolescence are poor emotion regulation, attachment problems, problems in peer relations, difficulty in adapting to school, and other psychological problems such as depression and delinquency. Maltreated young children in foster care were more likely to show abnormal stress hormone levels than middle-SES young children living with their birth family (Gunnar, Fisher, & the Early Experience, Stress, and Prevention Network, 2006). In this study, the abnormal stress hormone levels were mainly present in the foster children who were neglected, best described as "institutional neglect" (Fisher, 2005). Abuse also may have this effect on young children (Gunnar & Fisher, 2006). Adolescents who experienced abuse or neglect as children are more likely than adolescents who were not maltreated as children to engage in violent romantic relationships, delinquency, sexual risk taking, and substance abuse (Shin, Hong, & Hazen, 2010; Wekerle et al., 2009).

In adolescence, youth who were subjected to maltreatment in their homes often leave, finding the street a safer place than home. Approximately 65,000 Canadian youth are homeless and these youth are five times more likely to have experienced sexual abuse than youth remaining in their homes. Another cause for youth leaving their homes is parental violence, particularly violence perpetrated by their mothers (Goldstein, Amiri, Vilhena, Wekerle, Thornton, & Tonmyr, 2012).

Later, during the adult years, individuals who were maltreated as children often have difficulty in establishing and maintaining healthy intimate relationships (Dozier, Stovall-McClough, & Albus, 2009). As adults, maltreated children are also at higher risk for violent behaviour toward other adults—especially dating partners and marital partners—as well as for substance abuse, anxiety, and depression (Miller-Perrin, Perrin, & Kocur, 2009). Clare MacMartin (2004) argues that sexual abuse may be the most traumatic because of social stigma. A common result of sexual abuse in childhood is repressed memory. Is it true that people can hide traumatic memories from their conscious mind? A recent study showed that over 80 percent of the victims could recall their experiences 13 years later, and that abuse that occurred after age five was more likely to be recalled than if it occurred at a younger age (Goodman et al., 2003). The pain of sexual abuse thus can be felt for a lifetime.

What can be done to prevent or reduce the incidence of child maltreatment? In one study of maltreating mothers and their one-year-olds, two treatments were effective in reducing child maltreatment: (1) home visitation that emphasized improved parenting, coping with stress, and increasing support for the mother; and (2) parent–infant psychotherapy that focused on improving maternal–infant attachment (Cicchetti, Toth, & Rogosch, 2005).

To this point we have discussed a number of ideas about families in middle and late childhood. For a review, see the **Reach Your Learning Objectives** section at the end of this chapter.

Peers, Bullying, and Social Media

LO4 Identify changes in peer relationships, the roles in bullying and its impact and the influence of social media on growth and development in middle and late childhood.

During middle and late childhood, children spend an increasing amount of time in peer interaction. As you will see in this section, friends are important for many reasons. You may also see your own experience with friends in the descriptions here.

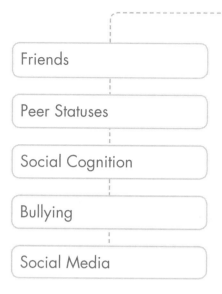

- Friends
- Peer Statuses
- Social Cognition
- Bullying
- Social Media

Friends

Having positive relationships with peers is especially important in middle and late childhood (Asher & McDonald, 2009; Bukowski, Motzoi, & Meyer, 2009). Engaging in positive interactions, resolving conflicts in nonaggressive ways, and having quality friendships in middle and late childhood not only have positive outcomes, but also are linked to more positive relationship outcomes in adolescence and adulthood (Huston & Ripke, 2006). For example, in one longitudinal study being popular with peers and engaging in low levels of aggression at 8 years of age were related to higher levels of occupational status at 48 years of age (Huesmann et al., 2006). Another study found that peer competence (a composite measure that included social contact with peers, popularity with peers, friendship, and social skills) in middle and late childhood was linked to having better relationships with coworkers in early adulthood (Collins & van Dulmen, 2006).

As noted earlier, between ages 8 and 12 children become increasingly aware of other perspectives; consequently, their concept of friendship matures. Robert Selman proposed a five-level framework illustrating this growth. He suggested that between 3 and 6, friendships are momentary. Between 5 and 9, friendships develop around other children who do something nice for them. Between 7 and 12, friendship takes on more of a quid pro quo nature. In other words, friendships are based on the rule that one friend does something nice for the other, and that nice favour will be returned. Should that not happen, the friendship is compromised. Gradually, in adolescence, this "play-by-the-rules" friendship matures to one in which compromise is possible, and children become friends through "thick and thin."

Like adult friendships, children's friendships are typically characterized by similarity (Giordano, 2009). Throughout childhood, friends are more similar than dissimilar in terms of many factors including age, sex, and race. Friends often share similar attitudes toward school as well as similar interests, tastes in music and fashion, and enjoyment of activities. Why are children's friendships important? Willard Hartup (1983, 1996, 2009) has studied peer relations and friendship for more than three decades. He recently concluded that friends can be cognitive and emotional resources from childhood through old age. Friends can foster self-esteem and a sense of well-being.

More specifically, children's friendships can serve six functions (Gottman & Parker, 1987):

- *Companionship.* Friendship provides children with a familiar partner and playmate, someone who is willing to spend time with them and join in collaborative activities.
- *Stimulation.* Friendship provides children with interesting information, excitement, and amusement.
- *Physical support.* Friendship provides time, resources, and assistance.
- *Ego support.* Friendship provides the expectation of support, encouragement, and feedback, which helps children maintain an impression of themselves as competent, attractive, and worthwhile individuals.
- *Social comparison.* Friendship provides information about where the child stands vis-à-vis others, and whether the child is doing okay.
- *Intimacy and affection.* Friendship provides children with a warm, close, trusting relationship with another individual in which self-disclosure takes place.

Friends also seem to have similar risk-taking tendencies. At the University of Guelph, Barbara Morrongiello's work shows that 53 percent of the dyads of best friends in her elementary school sample "fairly frequently" did risky things—"meaning that someone could get hurt"—together (Morrongiello & Dawber, 2004). In fact, the two children in each dyad expected their best friends to choose the same risky/safe action as they did in various situations. If both of them could not agree on an action, the success of persuading the other to follow along depended on the quality of the friendship.

Similarity happens in terms of age and sex, as well as race. For example, a study in Montreal (Aboud, Mendelson, & Purdy, 2003) showed that throughout the elementary school years, same-race friendships become more prevalent and cross-race friendships become rarer. Although children still socialize with peers of other races in school and some maintain a strong friendship with each other, "the shift away from cross-race friendships is observable" (p. 171). The researchers suggest that this shift may be a result of the older children's search for an identity, for which one's own race is an important issue.

Intimacy in friendships *is self-disclosure and the sharing of private thoughts.* Research reveals that intimate friendships may not appear until early adolescence (Berndt & Perry, 1990). By spending time with one another, finding common interests, and developing and showing trust, children can start the path of building friendships that will allow them to share their deep thoughts and feelings.

While face-to-face interactions are important for intimacy in friendships, researchers have come to wonder if online communication may reduce the intimacy levels with friends. As shown in a recent survey, "on an average school day," 33 percent to 86 percent of Canadian children from Grade 4 to Grade 11 email or use instant messaging with friends (Media Awareness Network, 2005). This high level of online communication may change the nature of modern friendships.

A recent study in the Netherlands highlighted two competing views on this issue (Valkenburg & Peter, 2007). The *reduction hypothesis* focuses on the communication partners on the Internet and argues that intimacy with existing friends drops when people engage in more and more online communication. The online environment distracts them from existing friendships and encourages them to form superficial connections with strangers. On the other hand, the *stimulation hypothesis* focuses on the communication process on the Internet and proposes that self-disclosure is easier online than offline. This allows people to develop intimacy with existing friends. In this study, the stimulation hypothesis was supported. Online communication with close friends had a positive correlation with closeness with these friends. Even lonely and socially anxious children found self-disclosure easier online than face-to-face, although they did not engage in more online communication than their peers. Maybe these children's social adjustment can be improved by learning to develop new friendships with peers face-to-face, and then to strengthen these friendships through online and offline communication.

Peer Statuses

Which children are likely to be popular with their peers? Developmentalists address this and similar questions by examining *sociometric status*, a term that describes the extent to which children are liked or disliked by their peer group (Cillessen, 2009). Sociometric status is typically assessed by asking children to rate how much they like or dislike each of their classmates. It can also be assessed by asking children to nominate the children they like the most and those they like the least.

Developmentalists have distinguished five peer statuses (Wentzel & Asher, 1995):

- *Popular children* are frequently nominated as a best friend and are rarely disliked by their peers.
- *Average children* receive an average number of both positive and negative nominations from their peers.
- *Neglected children* are infrequently nominated as a best friend but are not disliked by their peers.
- *Rejected children* are infrequently nominated as someone's best friend and are actively disliked by their peers.
- *Controversial children* are frequently nominated both as someone's best friend and as being disliked.

intimacy in friendships Self-disclosure and the sharing of private thoughts.

Popular children have the social skills that contribute to their being well-liked. They give out reinforcements, listen carefully, maintain open lines of communication with peers, are happy, control their negative emotions, act like themselves, show enthusiasm and concern for others, and are self-confident without being conceited.

Neglected children engage in low rates of interaction with their peers, who often describe them as shy. Rather than shy, however, they may be introverted, or perhaps a combination of introversion and shyness. The goal of many training programs for neglected children is to help them attract attention from their peers in positive ways and to hold that attention by asking questions, by listening in a warm and friendly way, and by saying things about themselves that relate to the peers' interests. They also are taught to enter groups more effectively.

Rejected children often have more serious adjustment problems later in life than do neglected children (Bukowski, Brendgen, & Vitaro, 2007; Dishion, Piehler, & Myers, 2008). One study found that in kindergarten, children who were rejected by their peers were less likely to engage in classroom participation, more likely to express a desire to avoid school, and more likely to report being lonely than children who were accepted by their peers (Buhs & Ladd, 2001). The combination of being rejected by peers and being aggressive forecasts problems. The best predictor of whether rejected children would engage in delinquent behaviour or drop out of school later during adolescence was aggression toward peers in elementary school. A recent study revealed that over the course of elementary school, children were less likely to engage in classroom participation during periods of peer rejection, but during times when they were not rejected they participated more in class (Ladd, Herald-Brown, & Reiser, 2008).

John Coie (2004, pp. 252–253) provides three reasons why aggressive peer-rejected boys have problems in social relationships:

First, the rejected, aggressive boys are more impulsive and have problems sustaining attention. As a result, they are more likely to be disruptive of ongoing activities in the classroom and in focused group play.

Second, rejected, aggressive boys are more emotionally reactive. They are aroused to anger more easily and probably have more difficulty calming down once aroused. Because of this they are more prone to become angry at peers and attack them verbally and physically. . . .

Third, rejected children have fewer social skills in making friends and maintaining positive relationships with peers.

Not all rejected children are aggressive (Rubin, Cheah, & Menzer, 2010). Although aggression and its related characteristics of impulsiveness and disruptiveness underlie rejection about half the time, approximately 10 to 20 percent of rejected children are shy.

How can rejected children be trained to interact more effectively with their peers? Rejected children may be taught to more accurately assess whether the intentions of their peers are negative (Bierman & Powers, 2009). They may be asked to engage in role playing or to discuss hypothetical situations involving negative encounters with peers, such as when a peer cuts into a line ahead of them. In some programs, children are shown videotapes of appropriate peer interaction and asked to draw lessons from what they have seen (Ladd, Buhs, & Troop, 2004).

One intervention program was successful in increasing social acceptance and self-esteem and decreasing depression and anxiety in peer-rejected children (DeRosier & Marcus, 2005). Students participated in the program once a week (50 to 60 minutes) for eight weeks. The program included instruction in how to manage emotions, how to improve prosocial skills, how to become better communicators, and how to compromise and negotiate.

Social Cognition

A boy accidentally trips and knocks another boy's soft drink out of his hand. That boy misinterprets the encounter as hostile, which leads him to retaliate aggressively against the boy who tripped. Through repeated encounters of this kind, the aggressive boy's classmates come to perceive him as habitually acting in inappropriate ways.

This encounter demonstrates the importance of *social cognition*—thoughts about social matters, such as the aggressive boy's interpretation of an encounter as hostile and his classmates' perception of his behaviour as inappropriate (Prinstein et al., 2009). Children's social cognition about their peers becomes increasingly important for understanding peer relationships in middle and late childhood. Of special interest are the ways in which children process information about peer relations and their social knowledge (Bukowski, Laursen, & Rubin, 2009; Dodge, Coie, & Lynam, 2006).

Kenneth Dodge (1983) argues that children go through five steps in processing information about their social world. They decode social cues, interpret, search for a response, select an optimal response, and then act. Dodge found that aggressive boys are more likely to perceive another child's actions as hostile when the child's intention is ambiguous. When aggressive boys search for cues to determine a peer's intention, they respond more rapidly, less efficiently, and less reflectively than do non-aggressive children. These are among the social cognitive factors believed to be involved in the nature of children's conflicts.

Social knowledge is also involved in children's ability to get along with peers. Children need to know what scripts to follow to get other children to be their friends. For example, as part of the script for getting friends, it helps to know that saying nice things, regardless of what the peer does or says, will make the peer like the child more.

Bullying

Nearly half, 47 percent, of Canadian parents report having a child victim of bullying (CIHR, 2012a). Bullying has been defined in many ways, but the Canadian Public Health Association (CPHA) defines bullying as the intentional use of power by one person over another; bullying takes four forms: physical, verbal, social, and electronic (CPHA, 2004). Some popular criteria are the intention to hurt, repetition of an action, lack of clear provocation, imbalance in power, and impact on the victim. Bullying is usually not physical; in fact, most bullying is verbal or relational, as in cyberbullying and social rejection and/or isolation.

Three roles are involved: the *bully*, the *bullied*, and the *bystander*. A fourth role, identified by Shelagh Dunn of the University of Alberta, is the *upstander*. The upstander refers to children whose empathy with the victimized child led them to employ intervention strategies. The children who intervene model Gandhi's famous quote, "Be the change you want to see" (Dunn, 2009).

Social contexts also influence bullying (Schwartz et al., 2010). Recent research indicates that 70 to 80 percent of victims and their bullies are in the same school classroom (Salmivalli & Peets, 2009); however, most bullying behaviour, because it is not physical, goes under the radar. Classmates are often aware of incidents and in many cases witness bullying. The larger social context of the peer group plays an important role in bullying (Salmivalli & Peets, 2009). In many cases, bullies torment victims to gain higher status in the peer group and bullies need others to witness their power displays. Many bullies are not rejected by their peer group; in fact, according to author, speaker, and professor Barbara Coloroso, many bullies have excellent leadership skills and are quite popular (2012, interview). In one study, bullies were rejected only by peers for whom they were a potential threat (Veenstra et al., 2010). In another study, bullies often affiliated with each other or in some cases maintained their position in the popular peer group (Wivliet et al., 2010). According to Public Safety Canada (2009), more boys than girls between the ages of 4 and 11 reported bullying others; the numbers increase to 42 percent for boys and 23 percent for girls in Grades 6, 7, and 8.

Recently, increased interest has been shown in relational aggression, which involves harming someone by manipulating a relationship (Crick et al., 2009; Salmivalli & Peets, 2009). Girls are much more likely than boys to engage in what is called **relational aggression**, *which involves such behaviours as trying to make others dislike a certain child by spreading malicious rumours about the child or ignoring another child when angry with him or her* (Underwood, 2004). Technology has provided an arena for relational aggression as children bully each other or hurt each other through text-messaging and the Internet.

Relational aggression increases in middle and late childhood (Dishion & Piehler, 2009). Mixed findings have characterized research on whether girls show more relational aggression than boys,

What are some characteristics of bullying? What are some strategies to reduce bullying?

relational aggression Such behaviours as trying to make others dislike a certain child by spreading malicious rumours about the child or ignoring another child when angry with him or her.

but one consistency in findings is that relational aggression comprises a greater percentage of girls' overall aggression than is the case for boys (Putallaz et al., 2007). And a recent research review revealed that girls engage in more relational aggression than boys in adolescence but not in childhood (Smith, Rose, & Schwartz-Mette, 2010). A recent study found links between parenting and children's relational aggression (Kuppens et al., 2009). In this study, parents' psychological control was linked to a higher incidence of relational aggression in their children.

The Impact of Bullying

"Sticks and stones may break my bones, but names will never hurt me!" Is this true? Studies indicate no; this is definitely not true. Bullying hurts and the psychological effects can be long-lasting. Children who were bullied report symptoms of depression and anxiety, loss of self-esteem, and sometimes increased aggressive behaviour. Bullied children also report more physical ailments, are absent from school more frequently, and have more thoughts of suicide. These problems may continue into adulthood (Public Safety Canada, 2009). As well, a disturbing number of Canadian children have committed suicide as a result of prolonged victimization by peers (Pepler et al., 2011). One of the tragic cases was the suicide of Mitchell Wilson, a boy with muscular dystrophy, brutally beaten by a boy who wanted his iPhone. Wilson took his life at age 11 when he learned he would have to face the boy who had victimized him in court (Mayer, 2011).

According to Dr. Tracy Vaillancourt, there are two types of children who bully: the habitual and the really impulsive. About 10 percent who bully are really impulsive children with poor emotional control. Not only are these children easily identified, they are likely already known to teachers, principals, and neighbours. On the other hand, the child who bullies habitually is not as easily identified as he or she is usually popular, able to manipulate people, and may have others who assist him or her (Coloroso, 2011; Vaillancourt, 2011).

Bullying is not only an issue for victims; it can indicate a serious problem for the bully. Those who bully tend to be hyperactive, disruptive, and impulsive. Boys tend to be physically strong, whereas the girls who bully tend to be physically weaker. Bullies show little sympathy or remorse for their victims (Public Safety Canada, 2009). Those who engage in bullying behaviours often report health problems such as anxiety, headaches, and depression. As the bullying child enters adolescence, he or she is more prone to antisocial and risk-taking behaviours and five to seven times more likely to consume alcohol and illegal substances (Pepler et al., 2011).

WHO IS LIKELY TO BE BULLIED?   In the study just described, boys and younger middle school students were most likely to be affected (Nansel et al., 2001). Children who said they were bullied reported more loneliness and difficulty in making friends, while those who did the bullying were more likely to have low grades and to smoke and drink alcohol. Researchers have found that anxious, socially withdrawn, and aggressive children are often the victims of bullying (Hanish & Guerra, 2004). Anxious and socially withdrawn children may be victimized because they are nonthreatening and unlikely to retaliate if bullied, whereas aggressive children may be the targets of bullying because their behaviour is irritating to bullies (Rubin, Bukowski, & Parker, 2006).

WHO IS LIKELY TO BULLY?   Bullying behaviour presumes a position of power. In families, perhaps one or both of the parents may bully their children, and in turn these children may victimize others who they deem to be less powerful (Coloroso, 2011; Pepler et al., 2011). Sources of power may stem from size, social status, or systemic advantage; that is, the societal power that marginalizes groups such as people with disabilities, racial or cultural groups, economically disadvantaged peoples, and/or sexual minorities. The child who bullies may use direct or indirect forms of victimization. Direct bullying strategies include insults, threats, physical aggression and/or intimidation, and racial and/or sexual slurs. Indirect strategies are social relational in nature and include gossiping, spreading rumours, and excluding the victimized person. Does the lack of social skills result in the use of aggression to resolve conflicts, or does a good understanding and interaction with others help bullies to manipulate peers to support their bullying (Larke, 2006)?

Distinguishing indirect bullying, such as isolating a victim, from direct physical bullying, Ian Larke (2006) of the University of Calgary proposes that good social skills are needed for indirect bullying. Hence, some bullies are good manipulators of peers and adults, while others lack social skills and use direct aggression to handle social interactions. Either way, each bullying incident reinforces the individual's sense of power; hence, bullying behaviour is repetitive (Pepler et al., 2011).

Cyberbullying

cyberbullying Verbal and written assault through cellphones, Web sites, webcams, chat rooms, email, online profiles, and MUD rooms, as well as altered sexual photographs.

Technology has brought with it new ways of to humiliate, intimidate, spread rumours, and exclude others: cyberbullying (Pepler et al., 2011). According to Shaheen Shariff (2005) of McGill University, **cyberbullying** *includes verbal and written assault through "cellphones, Web sites, Web-cams, chat rooms, and email" (p. 469), plus online profiles and MUD rooms, as well as altered sexual photographs.* Qing Li (2005) of the University of Calgary found in a sample of Grade 7 students that a quarter of them had been victims of cyberbullying. Furthermore, about 15 percent of the students admitted that they had cyberbullied someone. Interestingly, half of the students knew someone having been cyberbullied, but few reported the incidents to adults (Li, 2005), which may reflect a lack of trust in the adults' commitment to help (Li, 2006).

Although cyberbullying does not involve physical confrontation, the effects on the victims can still be very negative (Shariff, 2005). For one thing, a threatening message can cause much stress, including suicide. Moreover, gossip and sexual materials intended to degrade a victim can be sent to a multitude of individuals. Third, bullies can hide behind an Internet identity, leaving victims to wonder constantly whom in their life is—or are—targeting them. More information about cyberbullying is available on Connect at www.mcgrawhill.connect.ca.

Reducing Bullying

How can bullying be reduced? A recent research review revealed mixed results for school-based intervention (Vreeman & Carroll, 2007). School-based interventions vary greatly, ranging from involving the whole school in an antibullying campaign to individualized social skills training.

According to Debra Pepler and Wendy Craig of York University, bullying is a relationship problem in which the bully learns to appreciate his or her power, the victim becomes increasingly powerless, and the bystander often aligns him or herself with the aggressor. Relationship solutions are needed to stop bullying. Each participant in the relationship needs help: the child who bullies, the one who is bullied, and the ones who stand by. All three need to build confidence in their social skills and the supports need to be tailored to the individual situation. The overriding principle is that children depend on adults to help them in the development of relationship capacity (Pepler, 2009).

THE THREE R'S: RESTITUTION, RESOLUTION, AND RECONCILIATION Barbara Coloroso (CBC, 2012) recommends employing the "three R's":

- *Restitution:* The person who acted as a bully and the one/s who acted as bystander/s admits to the wrongdoing and recognizes the harm they have caused.
- *Resolution:* In an effort to mitigate the harm inflicted, those who assumed the roles of bully and bystander/s identify what they will and won't do.
- *Reconciliation:* The persons who inflicted harm directly through bullying behaviour or indirectly as a bystander attempt to talk to the person who was targeted, who may or may not be ready to accept an apology. If the targeted person chooses not to be friends, he or she can request that the behaviour stop. Once verbal confirmation is given, the targeted person can agree to move on and not hold a grudge. It may take a while, even a lifetime, for the targeted person to forgive and forget, let alone become friends with those who have inflicted pain, whether physical or relational.

STEPS TO RESPECT This bullying program consists of three steps: (1) establishing a school-wide approach, such as creating antibullying policies and determining consequences for bullying;

(2) training staff and parents to deal with bullying; and (3) teaching students to recognize, not tolerate, and handle bullying. In this third step, teachers provide skills training, such as how to be assertive, and information about bullying to students in Grades 3 through 6. The skills training by teachers occurs over a 12- to 14-week period. A recent study found that Steps to Respect was successful in reducing bullying and argumentativeness in Grade 3 through Grade 6 students (Frey et al., 2005). More information about Steps to Respect is available on Connect at www. mcgrawhill.connect.ca.

Social Media

For some children, screen time—time spent watching TV or playing computer games—has become their best friend, replacing school or neighbourhood friendships. Educators, parents, and researchers are all concerned about the negative effect that television and computer games may have on children. As Figure 10.4 illustrates, children spend a considerable amount of time engaged in computer games. The more-rapid-than-life action of television and of computer games triggers the release of dopamine, the neurotransmitter in the brain associated with pleasure. This creates a desire for more and faster action, and ultimately can lead to addiction (Doidge, 2007).

Another concern is whether children internalize the images on advertisements and in games. For example, does the media portrayal of young girls as sexual creatures influence the way young girls see themselves, or the way young boys see them? Is there a link between violence and aggression in children and the violence and aggression illustrated on television and in video games? Are these media contributing to obesity? Does school work suffer because of these media? Is targeting advertisements to children effective? Although there are positive applications and outcomes from both computer games and television, research supports these causes for concern.

Figure 10.4

How Wired Are Canadian Children?

Highlights from *Young Canadians in a Wired World Phase II: Student Survey* (Media Awareness Network, 2005)

- In Grade 4, 6 percent of children have a cell phone and 20 percent have their own computer with Internet access. These percentages rise to 46 percent and 51 percent, respectively, in Grade 11.

- Playing games is the top reason for boys using the Internet "on an average school day" from Grade 4 to grade 10, losing to instant messaging in Grade 11.

- Playing games is also the number one reason for girls getting online from Grade 4 to Grade 6, but is replaced by schoolwork and instant messaging in upper grades.

- Children spend roughly 45 minutes playing games "on an average school day" throughout these grades.

- The time spent on communicating with friends, downloading/listening to music, doing homework, and blogging rises from 21–37 minutes in Grade 4 to 31–68 minutes in Grade 11. It must be mentioned, though, some of these activities are performed at the same time.

- Children in all grades prefer the Internet to library books for homework projects.

- Parents have more rules on Internet use for girls and children in lower grades than for boys and children in higher grades. Adults were more likely to set these rules in 2005 than in 2001.

reach your **learning objectives**

Emotional and Personality Development

LO1 **Discuss emotional and personality development in middle and late childhood.**

The Self
- The internal self, the social self, and the socially comparative self become more prominent in middle and late childhood.
- Self-esteem refers to global evaluations of the self; self-esteem is also referred to as self-worth or self-image. Self-concept refers to domain-specific self-evaluations.
- Self-efficacy is the belief that one can master a situation and produce favourable outcomes.
- Erikson's fourth stage, industry versus inferiority, occurs in the elementary school years.
- Adler believed that a multitude of factors lead to varying degrees of inferiority and that the goal of behaviour, prosocial and otherwise, is to reduce or eliminate feelings of inferiority.

Emotional Development
- Increased understanding, reasoning, and controlling of emotions occur in middle and late childhood.
- Emotional intelligence is a form of social intelligence that involves the ability to monitor one's own and others' feelings and emotions, to discriminate among them, and to use this information to guide one's own thinking and action.
- A child's ability to assess and cope with stress becomes more competent as the child matures.

Moral Development and Gender

LO2 **Describe moral development and gender development.**

Moral Development
- Kohlberg developed a theory of moral reasoning with three levels—preconventional, conventional, and postconventional—and six stages (two at each level). Increased internalization characterizes movement to levels 2 and 3.
- Criticisms of Kohlberg's theory include the claims that Kohlberg overemphasized cognition and underemphasized behaviour, underestimated culture's role as well as the family's role, inadequately considered the significance of concern for others and the universality of the stages (e.g., stages 5 and 6 may not be found in all cultures).
- A moral personality has three possible components: moral identity, moral character, and moral exemplars.

Gender
- Using stereotypes, including gender stereotypes, helps people simplify the complexity of everyday life.
- Some differences in brain structure exist between boys and girls, but the link to behaviour is complex and inconclusive.
- Some experts, such as Hyde, argue that cognitive differences between females and males have been exaggerated.
- Current research reports that boys have more difficulty learning, particularly reading, than girls, and are more likely to repeat a grade than girls.
- In terms of socio-emotional differences, boys are more physically aggressive and active, while girls are more likely to better regulate their emotions and show more relational aggression. Prosocial behaviour, although linked to stereotyped behaviours, is contextual.
- Androgyny means having both masculine and feminine characteristics.
- Context plays an important role in gender classification and roles.

Families

LO3 Describe developmental changes in parent–child relationships and child maltreatment.

Developmental Changes in Parent–Child Relationships	■ New parent–child issues emerge in middle and late childhood years. Parents spend less time with their children in this stage, though parents continue to be extremely important in their children's lives. Some control is transferred from parent to child and becomes more coregulatory.
	■ Parents take on a role of manager, monitoring their children's behaviour and organizing their environment.
	■ Stepfamilies or blended families are common.
	■ Children who have parents with mental disorders may experience confusion and fear about the situation.
Child Maltreatment	■ Child maltreatment has serious health, justice, educational, and educational ramifications. Forms of child maltreatment include neglect, physical abuse, emotional abuse, sexual abuse, and exposure to family violence.
	■ Emotional abuse is linked with most other kinds of abuse.
	■ Neglect is the most common form of abuse.
	■ Most cases of maltreatment are thought to go unreported.
	■ Child maltreatment has long-term effects that impair an individual's functioning in adolescence and adulthood.

Peers, Bullying, and Social Media

LO4 Identify changes in peer relationships, the roles in bullying and its impact and the influence of social media on growth and development in middle and late childhood.

Friends	■ Children's friendships serve six functions: companionship, stimulation, physical support, ego support, social comparison, and intimacy/affection.
	■ Intimacy and similarity are common characteristics of friendships.
Peer Statuses	■ Five peer statuses have been identified: popular, average, neglected, rejected, and controversial.
Social Cognition	■ Social information-processing skills and social knowledge are two important dimensions of social cognition in peer relations.
Bullying	■ Bullying can result in short-term and long-term negative effects, including suicide, for the victim.
	■ Children who bully often engage in risk-taking behaviours in adolescence such as excessive alcohol and substance use.
	■ Most children who bully have excellent social skills and use these skills in relational bullying, such as isolating a victim, gossiping, texting.
	■ Children may engage in one or more of these four categories: bully, bullied, bystander, upstander.
	■ There is some overlap between offenders and victims of traditional and cyberbullying.
	■ Parents and educators are engaging in strategies to address bullying.
Social Media	■ Although screen time—television and computer games—may offer interesting and educational content, research supports the negative impacts on child development.

McGraw Hill Education connect®

McGraw-Hill Connect provides you with a powerful tool for improving academic performance and truly mastering course material. You can diagnose your knowledge with pre- and post-tests, identify the areas where you need help, search the entire learning package, including the eBook, for content specific to the topic you're studying, and add these resources to your personalized study plan. CONNECT for *Life-Span Development*, fifth Canadian edition, offers the following:

- chapter-specific online quizzes
- groupwork
- presentations
- writing assignments
- case studies
- and much more!

Visit CONNECT today!

review ----→ *connect* ----→ reflect

review

What impact does socio-economic status, ethnicity, and culture have in contributing to the development of Erikson's fourth stage of development, *industry versus inferiority*? **LO1**

How does Kohlberg's theory of moral development differ from Gilligan's? **LO2**

What are some of the factors that contribute to gender identity? **LO2**

How do parent–child relationships change in middle and late childhood? **LO3**

Describe child maltreatment and identify some of the long-term consequences to socio-emotional development. **LO3**

What are the roles and long-term impacts of bullying? **LO4**

Connect

More children are using food banks than ever before, and of the children using food banks many have disabilities and/or come from backgrounds that are racialized, Aboriginal, or new to Canada. What is the impact of poverty on identity, self-esteem, self-concept, and learning?

reflect *Your Own Personal Journey of Life*

In this chapter, you read that nearly half—47 percent—of Canadian parents report having a child who is a victim of bullying. Such a high percentage would indicate that most, if not all, of us have in some way been involved, either as the bully, the victim, the bystander, or perhaps the upstander. How is bullying defined, and what strategies could be put in place to encourage more children to be the upstander?

CHAPTER 11 Physical and Cognitive Development in Adolescence

CHAPTER OUTLINE

> "*In youth, we clothe ourselves with rainbows, and go brave as the zodiac.*"
>
> —RALPH WALDO EMERSON, NINETEENTH-CENTURY AMERICAN POET AND ESSAYIST

Adolescence: A Time of Firsts

Childhood is often romanticized as a relatively carefree period, free from adult responsibilities. Adolescence, on the other hand, is often characterized as a period of moodiness, temptation, and rebellion, during which we move away from the shelter of our family to the companionship of our friends.

The adolescent's world is filled with possibilities inconceivable 20 years ago. Twenty years ago very few families had computers, and even fewer were connected to the World Wide Web. Facebook, Twitter, blogs, avatars, virtual communities, text-messaging, and smartphones are very recent developments, altering communication patterns for all. New technologies or applications appear daily. Growing up with these communication tools, adolescents are highly adept at using them for entertainment, retrieving information, and socializing with friends (either two time zones or two houses away), and often spend considerable time doing so.

Like toddlerhood, adolescence is a period of "firsts"; however, instead of first steps and first words cheered on by delighted parents, teenagers often experience their first dance, first unchaperoned party, first kiss, first wet dream, and first menstrual period, often without the same degree of parental guidance. Unlike toddlerhood, our teenage "firsts" are (1) remembered, (2) often accomplished away from parents, and (3) usually shared with peers, rather than parents.

New responsibilities accompany a teen's developing sense of independence. Demands related to homework, part-time jobs, household chores, and other extracurricular activities are made even more complicated by demands such as choosing a career direction, getting good grades, keeping up with friends, and dating. Adolescence is a time of evaluation, independent decision making, commitment, and carving a place in the world.

Bodily changes converge with a heightened concern for body image. The desire to belong and to fit in fashions the teen's taste in a range of things, such as musical preferences, friendships, hairstyle, and even language. "Fitting in" is a must, for as one 12-year-old boy exclaimed, "If you're a guy and you don't fit in, you'll get pounded!" For many youngsters, "fitting in" may jeopardize health; for example, 12- and 13-year-old girls may share information about diet pills, rather than nutrition. Planning for the future, challenging authority, identifying hypocrisy, and breaking curfews are aspects of behaviour and thinking that may leave parents scratching their heads in puzzlement, or pulling out their hair in frustration. Most parents realize their child's desire for independence and strive for an appropriate balance between being overly protective and not protective enough.

Children whose childhoods were riddled with various kinds of abuse and neglect will find the teenage years particularly painful. Coming to terms with these experiences, dealing with continued abuse, and possibly having fewer social supports may lead to risky behaviour and feelings of isolation, which jeopardize the transition to adulthood. Media bombardments of sex and violence, plus the availability of alcohol, pornography, illicit drugs, and gambling, offer some teens permanent avenues for escape, rather than temporary detours for adventure and experimentation. For most, parental pressures and adolescent adventures may collide frequently as teens seek identity and independence.

This chapter focuses on the physical and cognitive development of adolescents, including puberty, adolescent sexuality, health challenges, risks and wellness, cognition, and education.

The Nature of Adolescence

LO1 Analyze the life stage of adolescence.

As in childhood development, genetic, biological, environmental, and social factors influence adolescent development (Berger, 2011). During their childhood years of development, adolescents experienced thousands of hours of interactions with parents, peers, and teachers. However, now they face dramatic biological changes, new experiences, and new developmental tasks. Relationships with parents take a different form, moments with peers become more intimate, and dating occurs for the first time, as do sexual exploration and possibly intercourse. The adolescent's thoughts are more abstract and idealistic. Biological changes trigger a heightened interest in body image (Polan & Taylor, 2011).

The issue of social change is relevant in the conceptualization of youth mainly because of the direct effect upon youth of changes in social institutions, and changes in the youth's relations (White, Wyn, & Albanese, 2011). Widespread agreement exists among social scientists that the last quarter-century has witnessed significant social changes that affect the experience of adolescence. Furlong and Cartmel (2007) conclude that the experiences of young people developing in a contemporary world are quite different from those encountered by the youth of previous generations. That is, current adolescents construct different meanings, and they make sense of the social conditions in ways that adolescents from previous generations did not.

An adolescent's enthusiasm for trying on new identities and enjoying moderate amounts of outrageous behaviour does not equate with hostility toward parental and societal standards. Acting out and boundary testing are time-honoured ways in which adolescents move toward integrating, rather than rejecting, parental values. However, in matters of taste and manners, the young people of every generation have seemed unnervingly radical and different from adults—different in how they look, in how they behave, in the music they enjoy, in their hairstyles, and in the clothing they choose. Although most adolescents negotiate the lengthy path to adult maturity successfully, too large a group does not (Lerner, Boyd, & Du, 2008). Ethnic, cultural, gender, socio-economic, age, and lifestyle differences influence the actual life trajectory of every adolescent (Patterson & Hastings, 2007). Different portrayals of adolescence emerge, depending on the particular group of adolescents being described (Balsano et al., 2008). Today's adolescents are exposed to a complex menu of lifestyle options, and the rate of adolescent drug use in Canada remains higher than a generation ago.

Too many adolescents are not provided with adequate opportunities and support to become competent adults (Eccles, Brown, & Templeton, 2008). In many ways, today's adolescents are presented with a less stable environment than adolescents of a decade or two ago. The explosion of technology and the war on terrorism, combined with economic pressures, higher divorce rates, youth crime, teen pregnancy, and increased geographic mobility of families, contribute to this lack of stability.

To this point, we have discussed a number of ideas about the nature of adolescence. For a review, see the **Reach Your Learning Objectives** section at the end of this chapter.

Physical Changes during Puberty

LO2 Describe the physical changes that occur during puberty.

One father remarked that the problem with his teenage son was not that he grew, but that he did not know when to stop growing. As we will see, there is considerable variation in the timing of the adolescent growth spurt.

Puberty is the most important marker of the beginning of adolescence, but it is not the same as adolescence. Great variations among individuals occur in the timing of puberty. Strong evidence argues for environmental and physiological effects and at the same time supports secular trends. One example is the earlier onset of menstruation. Considerable progress has been made in identifying genes that regulate the timing of puberty onset (Gajdos, Hirschhorn, & Palmert, 2009).

---

critical thinking

According to the research, teens who have secure attachments and good relationships with their parents are more likely to make a smoother transition from childhood to adolescence. Think of your high school years. What was your transition to adolescence like? Compare and contrast your own transition to adolescence to that of two of your peers. Outline particularly relevant influences that affected your transition to adolescence. Observe a few adolescents in a movie theatre or a shopping mall. What specific behaviours do you observe to suggest these adolescents might be struggling with their identity?

Sexual Maturation, Height, and Weight

Hormonal Changes

Body Image

Teen Perspectives on Maturity

The Brain

Furthermore, estrogen-like endocrine disrupting chemicals (EEDC), found in various plastic products needed for daily use as well as pesticides, have exerted the greatest effects on puberty (Roy, Chakraborty, & Chakraborty, 2009). For most, puberty ends long before adolescence does; the average age for puberty is between 8 and 15, and may take on average from 1.5 to 6 years for completion. What is puberty? **Puberty** *is not a single, sudden event, but rather a period of rapid physical maturation involving hormonal and bodily changes that occur primarily during early adolescence.* Pinpointing the beginning and the end is difficult; but the most notable changes are signs of sexual maturation, height, and weight (Polan & Taylor, 2011).

puberty A period of rapid skeletal and sexual maturation involving hormonal and bodily changes that occur primarily in early adolescence.

Sexual Maturation, Height, and Weight

Think back to the onset of puberty. Of the striking changes that were taking place in your body, what was the first to occur? Researchers have found that male pubertal characteristics typically develop in this order: increase in penis and testicle size, appearance of straight pubic hair, minor voice change, first ejaculation (which usually occurs through masturbation or a wet dream), appearance of kinky pubic hair, onset of maximum growth in height and weight, growth of hair in armpits, more detectable voice changes, and, finally, growth of facial hair.

What is the order of appearance of physical changes in females? First, either the breasts enlarge or pubic hair appears. Later, hair appears in the armpits. As these changes occur, the female grows in height and her hips become wider than her shoulders. **Menarche**—*a girl's first menstruation*—comes rather late in the pubertal cycle. Initially, her menstrual cycles may be highly irregular (Belsky, 2013). For the first several years, she may not ovulate every menstrual cycle; some girls do not ovulate at all until a year or two after menstruation begins. No voice changes comparable to those in pubertal males occur in pubertal females. By the end of puberty, the female's breasts have become more fully rounded. Figure 11.1 illustrates a comparison of the median ages at menarche in different countries.

menarche A girl's first menstruation.

What are some of the differences in the ways girls and boys experience pubertal growth?

Marked weight gains coincide with the onset of puberty (Jasik & Lustig, 2008). During early adolescence, girls tend to outweigh boys, but by about age 14 boys begin to surpass girls. Similarly, at the beginning of the adolescent period, girls tend to be as tall as or taller than boys of their age, but by the end of the middle school years most boys have caught up or, in many cases, surpassed girls in height.

As indicated in Figure 11.2, the growth spurt occurs earlier in girls than it does in boys. Boys grow 10 to 30 cm while girls grow 5 to 20 cm during this period. Increases in weight follow increases in height, both of which are related to increases in fat, bone, and muscle tissue (Polan & Taylor, 2011).

Figure 11.1

Median Ages at Menarche in Selected Northern European Countries and North America from 1845 to 1969

Notice the steep decline in the age at which girls experienced menarche in four northern European countries and North America from 1845 to 1969. Recently, the age at which girls experience menarche has been levelling off.

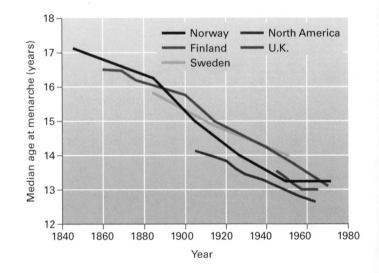

Hormonal Changes

Behind the first whisker in boys and the widening of hips in girls is a flood of **hormones,** *powerful chemical substances secreted by the endocrine glands and carried through the body by the bloodstream.* The endocrine system's role in puberty involves the interaction of the hypothalamus, the pituitary gland, and the gonads (sex glands). The **hypothalamus** *is a structure in the higher portion of the brain that monitors eating, drinking, and sex.* The **pituitary gland** *is an important endocrine gland that controls growth and regulates other glands.* The **gonads** *are the sex glands—the testes in males, the ovaries in females.*

How do the gonads, or sex glands, work? The pituitary sends a signal via *gonadotropins* (hormones that stimulate the testes or ovaries) to the appropriate gland to manufacture the hormone. Then, the pituitary gland, through interaction with the hypothalamus, detects when the optimal level of hormones is reached and responds by maintaining gonadotropin secretion (Yoo et al., 2006).

Not only does the pituitary gland release gonadotropins that stimulate the testes and ovaries, but the pituitary gland also secretes hormones, through interaction with the hypothalamus. These hormones either directly lead to growth and skeletal maturation, or produce growth effects through interaction with the thyroid gland, located at the base of the throat.

The concentrations of certain hormones increase dramatically during adolescence (Herbison et al., 2008). *Testosterone* is a hormone associated in boys with the development of genitals, an increase in height, and a change in voice. *Estradiol* is a hormone associated in girls with breast, uterine, and skeletal development. Note that both testosterone and estradiol are present in the hormonal makeup of both boys and girls, but testosterone dominates in male pubertal development and estradiol dominates in female pubertal development (Richmond & Rogol, 2007).

The same influx of hormones that puts hair on a male's chest and imparts curvature to a female's breast may contribute to psychological development (DeRose & Brooks-Gunn, 2008; Vermeersch et al., 2008). In one study of 108 boys and girls ranging in age from 9 to 14, a higher concentration of testosterone was present in boys who rated themselves more socially competent (Nottelmann et al., 1987). However, hormonal effects by themselves do not account for adolescent development (Dorn et al., 2006; Graber, 2008). For example, in one study, social factors were much better predictors of young adolescent girls' depression and anger than hormonal factors (Brooks-Gunn & Warren, 1989). Behaviour and moods also can affect hormones (DeRose & Brooks-Gunn, 2008). Stress, eating patterns, exercise, sexual activity, tension, and depression can activate or suppress various aspects of the hormonal system (Foster & Brooks-Gunn, 2008; Sontag et al., 2008). In sum, the hormone–behaviour link is complex.

Timing and Variations in Puberty

In North America—where children mature up to a year earlier than children in European countries—the average age of menarche has declined significantly since the mid-nineteenth century (refer to Figure 11.1). Fortunately, however, we are unlikely to see pubescent toddlers, since what has happened in the past century is likely the result of improved nutrition and health.

Why do the changes of puberty occur when they do, and how can variations in their timing be explained? The basic genetic program for puberty is wired into the species (Divall & Radovick, 2008), but nutrition, health, and other environmental factors also affect puberty's timing and makeup (Hermann-Giddens, 2006, 2007; Ji & Chen, 2008; McDowell, Brody, & Hughes, 2007).

Evolutionary psychologists argue that harmonious relationships with parents, particularly the quality of fathers' investment in the family, are associated with later pubertal timing of the daughter. Conversely, dysfunctional and harsh family relations have been linked with early onset of puberty.

For most boys, the pubertal sequence may begin as early as age 10 or as late as 13, and may end as early as age 13 or as late as 17. Thus the normal range is wide enough that, given two boys of the same chronological age, one might complete the pubertal sequence before the other one has begun it. For girls, menarche is considered within the normal range if it appears between the ages of 8 and 15.

Figure 11.2 - - - - - - - - - - - - - - -

Pubertal Growth Spurt

On average, the growth spurt that characterizes pubertal change occurs two years earlier for girls (10½) than for boys (12½).

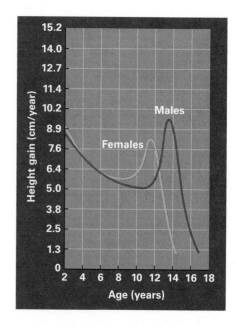

hormones Powerful chemical substances secreted by the endocrine glands and carried through the body by the bloodstream.

hypothalamus A structure in the higher portion of the brain that monitors eating, drinking, and sex.

pituitary gland An important endocrine gland that controls growth and regulates other glands.

gonads The sex glands—the testes in males and the ovaries in females.

- developmental **connection** - - - - - - - - -

Evolutionary Psychology

Body Image

One psychological aspect of physical change in puberty is certain: adolescents are preoccupied with their bodies and develop individual images of what their bodies are like (Allen et al., 2008; Jones, Bain, & King, 2008). Perhaps you looked in the mirror on a daily—and sometimes even on an hourly basis—to see if you could detect anything different about your changing body. Preoccupation with one's body image is strong throughout adolescence, but it is especially acute during puberty, a time when adolescents are more dissatisfied with their bodies than in late adolescence (Graber & Brooks-Gunn, 2002).

Gender Differences in Body Image

In general, girls are less happy with their bodies and have more negative body images than boys throughout puberty (Bearman et al., 2006). As pubertal change proceeds, girls often become more dissatisfied with their bodies, probably because their body fat increases. In addition, early- and late-maturing girls have different perceptions of body image, depending on their age. Early maturers are more likely to have a positive body image when they are young, and late maturers are more likely to have a positive body image when they are older. In contrast, boys become more satisfied as they move through puberty, probably because their muscle mass increases (Bearman et al., 2006). Here is a sampling of recent research on body image in adolescence:

- *Appearance.* Adolescent males who evaluated their appearance more positively and who said appearance was very important to them were more likely to engage in risky sexy behaviour, whereas adolescent females who evaluated their appearance more positively were less likely to engage in risky behaviour (Gillen, Lefkowitz, & Shearer, 2006).
- *Physical and mental health problems.* A longitudinal study of more than 2,500 adolescents found that lower body satisfaction placed them at risk for poorer overall health (Neumark-Sztainer et al., 2006). Another study indicated that 12- to 17-year-old female patients in psychiatric hospitals who had a negative body image were more depressed, anxiety-prone, and suicidal than same-aged female patients who were less concerned about their body image (Dyl et al., 2006).
- *Best and worst aspects of being a boy or a girl.* The negative aspects of puberty for girls appeared in a study that explored 400 middle school boys' and girls' perceptions of the best and worst aspects of being a boy or a girl (Zittleman, 2006). In the views of the middle school students, at the top of the list of the worst things about being a girl was the biology of being female, which included such matters as childbirth, PMS, periods, and breast cancer. The middle school students said that aspects of discipline (such as getting into trouble and being blamed more than girls even when they were not at fault) are the worst things about being a boy. However, another aspect of physical development was at the top of the students' list of the best things about being a girl—appearance (which included choosing clothes, hair styles, and beauty treatments). Students said the best thing about being a boy was playing sports.

Although we have described gender differences in the body images of adolescents, emphasizing that girls tend to have more negative body images than boys, keep in mind that there is considerable variation. Many adolescent girls have positive body images and many adolescent boys have negative body images.

Teen Perspectives on Maturity

Canadian researchers Barker and Galambos (2005) explored conceptions of maturity held by 170 adolescents in Grades 7 and 10. These adolescents were asked at what age they expected to reach adulthood, experience the greatest freedom, and have the most fun. The results specified that adolescents expect to have fun at an earlier age than they expect freedom or adulthood. Further, the adolescents cited the gaining of independence as critical to their expectations for the ages of adulthood (71 percent) and freedom (74 percent). Meanwhile, certain chronological transitions, such as reaching driving age (41 percent) and acquiring independence (41 percent), were associated with the expected age for fun. These adolescents who felt older than their age, and who admitted to

---

critical thinking

Think back to your own experience of entering puberty. Compare photos of yourself from elementary school and high school. Illustrate a few incredible changes that occurred for you during puberty. What are some of some of the beliefs regarding pubertal changes held by the adolescent in the Western culture as compared to the non-Western cultures?

engaging in more problem behaviours, but were low on psychological maturity, were more likely than other adolescents to cite chronological transitions as indicative of freedom. These findings suggest that establishing independence or autonomy—a key developmental task of adolescence—is especially important to all adolescents. The finding also indicates that adolescents hold the widespread conception that independence is a positive feature of growing up (Arnett & Galambos, 2003).

Another study by Galambos and her researchers (2005) examined the relationships between cognitive performance and psychosocial maturity among 48 adolescents in Grades 9 and 12. These findings suggest that cognitive abilities are in fact related to psychosocial maturity. The concept of psychosocial maturity encompasses attainments in several domains, including independent functioning, effective interpersonal communication and interaction, and social responsibility (Galambos, Barker, & Tilton-Weaver, 2003). Many teens effectively balance their work and play activities and get along easily with others. Teens who are maturity-focused tend to prefer the presence of others who are similarly focused (Galambos et al., 2003).

Body Art

An increasing number of adolescents are obtaining tattoos and getting parts of their body pierced (Mayers & Chiffriller, 2008). Many youth engage in such body modification to be different, to stamp their identity as unique. In one study of adolescents, 60 percent of the students with tattoos had academic grades of As and Bs (Armstrong, 1995). In this study, the average age at which the adolescents got their first tattoo was 14 years of age. Some studies indicate that tattoos and body piercings are markers for risk taking in adolescence (Deschesnes, Fines, & Demers, 2006). A recent study revealed that having multiple body piercings is especially a marker for risk-taking behaviour (Suris et al., 2007). However, other researchers argue that body art is increasingly used to express individuality and self-expression, rather than rebellion (Armstrong et al., 2004).

The Brain

Along with the rest of the body, the brain continues to change during adolescence; but the study of adolescent brain development is in its infancy. As advances in technology take place, significant strides will also likely be made in charting developmental changes in the adolescent brain (Giedd, 2008; McAnarney, 2008; Steinberg, 2009). What do we know now?

Using functional magnetic resonance imaging studies (fMRI) brain scans, scientists have recently discovered that adolescents' brains undergo significant structural changes (Casey, Getz, & Galvan, 2008; Toga, Thompson, & Sowell, 2006). The *corpus callosum*, where fibres connect the brain's left and right hemispheres, thickens in adolescence, and this improves adolescents' ability to process information (Giedd et al., 2006). We described advances in the development of the *prefrontal cortex*—the highest level of the frontal lobes involved in reasoning, decision making, and self-control—in Chapters 8 and 10. The prefrontal cortex doesn't finish maturing until the emerging adult years, approximately 18 to 25 years of age or later, but the *amygdala*—the seat of emotions such as anger—matures earlier than the prefrontal cortex. Figure 11.3 shows the locations of the corpus callosum, prefrontal cortex, and amygdala.

Perry (2003), the Senior Fellow of the Child Trauma Academy, has served as the Director of Provincial Programs in Children's Mental Health for the province of Alberta. He contends that traumatic experiences from early childhood affect long-term behaviour. In fact, traumatic events in childhood actually increase the risk for a host of social problems including teenage pregnancy, adolescent drug use, and certain medical problems (Perry, 2003). Perry's ideas are supported by neurological studies indicating that severe maltreatment during childhood is related to molecular and neurobiological damage in the emotional and memory parts of the brain that are still growing (Child Welfare Information Gateway, 2009). Perry's research is supported by Dr. Ruth Lanius of the University of Western Ontario. Using functional magnetic resonance imaging studies, she has investigated whether individuals who experience traumatic events use different regions of the brain when they recall events (Lanius et al., 2004). It has been established that different brain areas are, in fact, used by those who had experienced post-traumatic stress disorder (PTSD) compared to those who did not have PTSD.

Figure 11.3

Developmental Changes in the Adolescent Brain

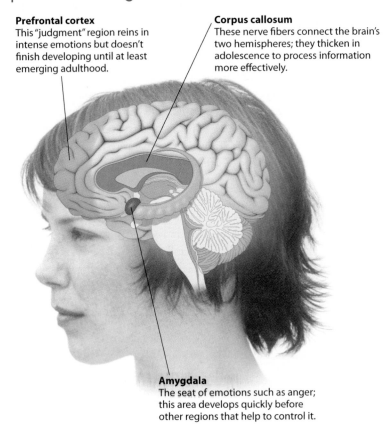

Prefrontal cortex
This "judgment" region reins in intense emotions but doesn't finish developing until at least emerging adulthood.

Corpus callosum
These nerve fibers connect the brain's two hemispheres; they thicken in adolescence to process information more effectively.

Amygdala
The seat of emotions such as anger; this area develops quickly before other regions that help to control it.

Other researchers have found that both the amygdala and hippocampus increase in volume during adolescence. Both structures are involved in emotion and are part of the group of structures sometimes called the limbic system. Changes in the limbic system during puberty may lead adolescents to seek novelty and to need higher levels of stimulation in order to experience pleasure (Spear, 2004). However, because of the relatively slow development of the prefrontal cortex, which is still maturing during adolescence, adolescents may lack the cognitive skills to effectively control their pleasure seeking (Toga, Thompson, & Sowell, 2006). This developmental disjunction between the limbic system and prefrontal cortex may account for an increase in risk taking and other problems in adolescence.

Leading researcher Charles Nelson (2003) points out that although adolescents are capable of very strong emotions, their prefrontal cortex hasn't adequately developed to the point where they can control these passions. It is as if their brain doesn't have the brakes to slow down their emotions. Or consider this interpretation of the development of emotion and cognition in adolescents: "early activation of strong 'turbo-charged' feelings with a relatively un-skilled set of 'driving skills' or cognitive abilities to modulate strong emotions and motivations" (Dahl, 2004, p. 18).

Of course, a major issue involves which comes first, biological changes in the brain or experiences that stimulate these changes (Lerner, Boyd, & Du, 2008). Consider a recent study in which the prefrontal cortex thickened and more brain connections formed when adolescents resisted peer pressure (Paus et al., 2008). Scientists have yet to determine whether the brain changes come first or whether the brain changes are the result of experiences with peers, parents, and others. Once again, we encounter the nature/nurture issue that is so prominent in examining development through the life span.

Are there implications for taking drugs and the legal system as a result of what we now know about changes in the adolescent's brain? According to leading expert Jay Giedd (2007, pp. D1–2), "Biology doesn't make teens rebellious or have purple hair or take drugs. It does not mean you are going to do drugs, but it gives you more of a chance to do that." Also, can the recent brain research we have just discussed be used to argue that because the adolescent's brain, especially the higher-level prefrontal cortex, is still developing, adolescents who commit crimes should not be tried as adults? Leading expert Elizabeth Sowell (2004) says that scientists can't just do brain scans on adolescents and make decisions regarding legal age.

To this point, we have discussed a number of ideas about physical changes during puberty. For a review, see the **Reach Your Learning Objectives** section at the end of this chapter.

Adolescent Sexuality

LO3 Describe adolescent sexuality, sexual identity, and risk factors related to intimate sexual behaviour.

Adolescence not only is characterized by substantial changes in physical growth and the development of the brain, but also is a bridge between the asexual child and the sexual adult (Kelly, 2008; Strong et al., 2008). Every society gives some attention to adolescent sexuality. In some societies, adults clamp down and protect adolescent females from males by chaperoning them. Other societies promote very early marriage. Yet other societies allow some sexual experimentation, such as many parts of Europe and North America, where sexual culture is widely available through television, videos, magazines, lyrics of popular music, computer games, and Web sites. Considerable controversy exists about just how far sexual experimentation should be allowed to go.

How might watching sex on television be linked to adolescents' behaviour? One study of 1,762 12- to 17-year-olds found that watching more sexually explicit TV shows was linked with an increased likelihood of initiating sexual intercourse in the next 12 months (Collins et al., 2004). Adolescents in the highest 10 percent of viewing sexually explicit TV shows were twice as likely to engage in sexual intercourse as those in the lowest 10 percent. The results held regardless of whether the TV programs involved actual sexual behaviour or just talk about sex. Another recent study revealed that more frequent viewing and stronger identification with popular TV characters were related to greater levels of sexual activity in one's peers (Ward & Friedman, 2006).

The *Canadian Youth, Sexual Health and HIV/AIDS Study: Factors Influencing Knowledge, Attitudes and Behaviours* is a comprehensive study undertaken by the Council of Ministers of Education, Canada (CMEC, 2003) to increase understanding of the factors contributing to adolescent sexual knowledge, attitudes, and behaviour. The study uses the World Health Organization's definition of sexual health: "the integration of the physical, emotional, intellectual, and social aspects of sexual being, in ways that are positively enriching and that enhance personality, communication, and love."

Researchers from four Canadian universities (Acadia, Alberta, Laval, and Queen's) surveyed over 11,000 students in Grades 7, 9, and 11 from each province and territory with the exception of Nunavut. Both positive and negative findings were reported. On the plus side, students reported:

- very little use of illicit substances
- a happy home
- school as an important source of sex education

But, on the negative side, students reported:

- peer pressure to party and engage in rebellious activities as a way of becoming popular
- widespread use of alcohol and drunkenness
- lower level of sexual knowledge than 15 years ago

Further, the researchers noted the following:

- Girls with low self-esteem are more likely to engage in risky sexual behaviour.
- Students who are not involved in school are more likely to engage in risky sexual behaviour.
- Half of the sexually active girls in Grades 9 and 11 who have also been pregnant report having four or more sexual partners.

Developing a Sexual Identity

The Timing of Adolescent Sexual Behaviours

Risk Factors and Sexual Problems

Adolescent Pregnancy and Health

Healthy sexual development in adolescence is the outgrowth of healthy development from infancy through childhood. Many behaviour patterns, including values related to gender roles and power, are formed well before adolescence. Positive childhood experiences help develop the self-confidence, trust, and autonomy a young person needs to handle peer pressure and navigate the sensual and sexual feelings natural to the teenage years. Conversely, healthy growth may be inhibited by destructive sexual attitudes, media images, and physical, emotional, and sexual abuse or neglect that may occur at this age. Behaviour patterns influence choices and affect the risk of pregnancy and sexually transmitted infections (STIs) and HIV/AIDS. Despite some media reports, most adolescents have healthy sexual attitudes and engage in sexual practices that will not compromise their development (CMEC, 2003). The *Canadian Guidelines for Sexual Health Education* focus on the importance of providing youth with the knowledge, motivation, and behavioural skills they need in order to make informed as well as responsible sexual decisions to enhance their sexual health. These guidelines, which are sensitive to diverse needs of youth, are intended to equip them with current and accurate information on reducing specific-risk taking behaviours including the proper use of contraceptives (PHAC, 2008a).

Developing a Sexual Identity

Sexual identity can be broadly defined as the recognition, acceptance, and expression of numerous aspects of one's sexuality and that includes aspects such as individual sexual values, behaviours, and desires, as well as sexual orientation. Actually defining and identifying one's sexual identity can be particularly challenging (Morgan, 2012). Specifically, sexual orientation refers to one's sexual attraction and/or behavioural predispositions toward one or both sexes (Morgan, 2012). In fact, achieving sexual identity can be a life-long task because, in part, societal standards keep on changing (Berger, 2011). Several researchers have proposed that most heterosexual individuals do not think about their sexual identity. In fact, heterosexuality is frequently understood as a silent and unmarked identity (Konik & Stewart, 2004). Actually, the invisibility of sexuality is especially prominent for men whose heterosexuality has been mandated from a young age through rigid masculine roles (Frankel, 2005).

Even though some adolescents who are attracted to individuals of the same sex fall in love with these individuals, others claim that their same-sex attractions are purely physical (Savin-Williams, 2006, 2008). A commonly held belief is that most gay males and lesbians quietly struggle with same-sex attractions in childhood, do not engage in heterosexual dating, and gradually recognize that they are a gay male or a lesbian in mid to late adolescence (Savin-Williams & Diamond, 2004). Many youth do follow this developmental pathway, but others do not (Bos et al., 2008; Diamond, L., 2008). For example, many youth have no recollection of early same-sex attractions and experience a more abrupt sense of their same-sex attraction in late adolescence (Savin-Williams, 2006).

Gay male and lesbian youth have diverse patterns of initial attraction, often have bisexual attractions, and may have physical or emotional attraction to same-sex individuals but do not always fall in love with them (Diamond, L., 2008; Savin-Williams & Cohen, 2007; Savin-Williams & Ream, 2007). In Canada, the literature reveals that exclusion, isolation, and fear remain realities for Canadian lesbian, gay, bisexual, transgendered, intersexed, and questioning queer (LGBTIQ) adolescents. They face greater risks related to their health and well-being than their heterosexual age-mates (Dysart-Gale, 2010).

The McGill University Sexual Identity Centre (MUSIC) provides specialized mental health care to all individuals. Couples and families with sexual orientation issues are particularly welcome (Sexual Identity Centre, 2012). In Chapter 13, "Physical and Cognitive Development in Early Adulthood," we will further explore same-sex and heterosexual attraction.

The Timing of Adolescent Sexual Behaviours

Sexual behaviour is a major determinant of sexual and reproductive health. In fact, early sexual intercourse, unprotected sex, and having multiple sexual partners put youth at risk of sexually transmitted infections (STIs) (Rotermann, 2012). Most Canadian youth have their first experience of

One important aspect of developing a sexual identity involves sexual orientation. These two individuals have a lesbian orientation. **What are some of the stigmas that adolescents who are homosexual face?**

Figure 11.4

Percentage of Canadian Youth Aged 15–17, 18–19 Reporting Ever Having Sexual Intercourse

Age Group	1996/1997	2003	2005	2009/2010
15–17	32%	30%	29%	30%
18–19	70%	68%	65%	68%

Source: Rotermann, M. (2012) Sexual behaviours and condom use of 15- to 24-year-olds in 2003 and 2009/2010. Health Reports 23(1), 1–5.

sexual intercourse during their teenage years (SIECCAN, 2012). In fact, 9 percent of 15- to 24-year-olds reported in 2009/2010 that they had their first sexual intercourse when they were younger than 15, and about 25 percent had had intercourse for the first time at age 15 or 16. Interestingly, in 2003 similar percentages of males and females reported having had sexual intercourse before age 15, but in 2009/2010 this was less common among females (8 percent) than males (10 percent) (Rotermann, 2012). Figure 11.4 shows the reported rates among youth ages 15 to 19.

Many adolescents are not emotionally prepared to handle sexual experiences, especially in early adolescence. Early sexual activity is linked with risky behaviours such as drug use, delinquency, and school-related problems (Armour & Haynie, 2007; Dryfoos & Barkin, 2006). In a longitudinal study of individuals from 10 to 12 years of age to 25 years of age, early sexual intercourse and affiliation with deviant peers were linked to substance use disorders in emerging adulthood (Cornelius et al., 2007). Adolescents who engage in sex before age 16 and experience a number of partners over time are the least effective users of contraception, and are at risk for early, unintended pregnancy and for sexually transmitted infections.

A recent study revealed that not feeling close to their parents, having low self-esteem, and watching television extensively were linked to adolescents being sexually active at 15 years of age (Hyde & Price, 2007). And a recent research review found that earlier onset of sexual intercourse was linked to living with other than two biological parents and a lower level of parental monitoring (Zimmer-Gembeck & Helfand, 2008). Absent fathers has also been linked to early sexual activity among girls.

Risk Factors and Sexual Problems

Dating Violence

According to the National Clearinghouse on Family Violence (2006), dating violence is a significant and widespread social problem. Dating violence is expressed in a range of harmful behaviours—from threats, to emotional maltreatment, to physical and sexual aggression. It is difficult to determine how many adolescents are affected by dating violence because many incidents of such violence go unreported. However, it is estimated from several studies that up to one-third of all adolescents may experience this type of abuse during an intimate partner relationship (Wolfe et al., 2009). Prevention is key to eliminating dating violence and promoting health, and so the process of well-being among adolescents can move forward (Runciman, 2012; Wekerle & Tanaka, 2010). Research on dating violence is of special importance because violence during adolescent dating relationships is often the catalyst for a pattern of abuse in later adult relationships (Marquart, Nannini, Edwards, Stanley & Wayman, 2007).

Contraceptive Use

Sexual activity carries with it considerable risks if appropriate safeguards are not taken (Carroll, 2007; Strong et al., 2008). Young people encounter two kinds of risks: unintended unwanted pregnancy and sexually transmitted infections. Both of these risks can be reduced significantly if contraception is used. Adolescents who engage in sex before age 16 and experience a number of partners over time are the least effective users of contraception, and are at risk for early, unintended pregnancy and for sexually transmitted infections (Cavanagh, 2004). Although adolescent contraceptive use is increasing, many sexually active adolescents still do not use contraceptives, or they use them inconsistently.

Gay and lesbian youth who do not experiment with heterosexual intercourse are spared the risk of pregnancy, but like their heterosexual peers they still face the risk of sexually transmitted diseases.

Sexually Transmitted Infections (STIs)

sexually transmitted infections (STIs)
Infections and diseases that are contracted primarily through sexual contact, which is not limited to sexual intercourse. Oral–genital and anal–genital contact also can transmit STIs and STDs.

Sexually transmitted infections (STIs) *are contracted primarily through sexual contact, which is not limited to sexual intercourse. Oral–genital and anal–genital contact can also transmit STIs and STDs.*

Sexually active adolescents are at greater risk than non–sexually active adolescents to contract sexually transmitted infections. Physiologically speaking, the cervix of an adolescent girl is composed of columnar epithelial cells that are more susceptible to STIs, especially human papillomavirus (HPV) and chlamydia infection. The immune systems of the adolescents tend to contribute to the increased risk because adolescents have not had the opportunity to develop sufficient resistance to these organisms (Kollar, Jordan, & Wilson, 2013).

According to the *Canadian Youth, Sexual Health and HIV/AIDS Study* (CMEC, 2003), between 22 and 24 percent of students in Grade 9 and 17 to 20 percent of students in Grade 11 reported that they would be too embarrassed to see a physician if they contracted a sexually transferred infection. However, the overwhelming majority of students, 77 to 88 percent, reported that they would tell their partners. According to the Canadian Council on Learning (CCL, 2009), more than two-thirds of reported cases of chlamydia, the most commonly reported STI in Canada, occur among young people aged 15 to 24. Between 1997 and 2004, a 55 percent increase was noted in the rate of reported chlamydia infections among 15- to 19-year-olds; a 77 percent increase occurred among 20- to 24-year-olds. In 2009, the reported rates of chlamydia among ages 15 to 19 and 20 to 24 increased, with females having higher increases (PHAC, 2011e). Geographic variations were observed, with the highest chlamydia rates being reported in Nunavut, the Northwest Territories, and Yukon (PHAC, 2012a). Regarding gonorrhea, females between the ages 14 to 24 and males between the ages of 20 and 24 accounted for the highest rates (PHAC, 2012a).

Human Papillomavirus (HPV)

HPV, a virus that can infect many different parts of the body, is thought to be one of the most commonly transmitted STIs. Over 100 types of HPV have been identified, and they can cause anogenital warts and cancer. HPV causes 70 percent of all cervical cancers and is linked to other cancers in both men and women. The virus is transmitted by oral, vaginal, and anal sex, as well as by intimate skin-to-skin contact with an infected individual. Fortunately, since 2006, a vaccine, Gardasil, has been approved for immunization for females and males between 9 and 26 years of age. The vaccine provides protection against four HPV types: two that cause approximately 70 percent of all cervical cancers (HPV-16 and HPV-18), and two others that cause approximately 90 percent of all anogenital warts in males and females (HPV-6 and HPV-11). A second vaccine, Cervarix, has been approved for use in females aged 10 to 25. This vaccine provides protection against the two HPV types that cause approximately 70 percent of all cervical cancer (HPV-16 and HPV-18) (PHAC, 2011f).

The vaccine protects against some high-risk types of HPV, but will not have an impact on an existing infection or existing precancerous conditions. Nor does the vaccine protect against all types of HPV. Side effects related to pregnancy and breastfeeding are unknown.

Adolescent Pregnancy and Health

Although the social stigma once attached to pregnancy out of wedlock has diminished, the health problems associated with adolescent pregnancies are serious and affect both the mother and the baby. The young mother runs the risk for anemia, hypertension, renal disease, and depressive disorders. A newborn's chances of survival are closely related to birth weight. Babies weighing less than 2,500 grams have significant health risks (Statistics Canada, 2007). Infants born to adolescent mothers are more likely to have low birth weights—a prominent factor in infant mortality—as well as neurological problems and childhood illnesses. Second and subsequent babies born to a teenage woman are more likely to be at risk due to low birth weight (Statistics Canada, 2007).

Rates of Adolescent Pregnancy in Canada

The rate of live births by mothers aged 15 to 17 decreased steadily between 1999 and 2005, from 11.0 to 7.4 per 1,000 females. The rate of live births increased to 8.2 per 1,000 females in 2008 (PHAC, 2012b). This initial decreasing rate of pregnancy was probably due to an increased access to various forms of contraception, such as condom use (Langille, 2007). It is important to prevent unplanned and unwanted pregnancies, which would be expected to have negative consequences on a teenager's health and future. For example, pediatricians must be able to provide adequate and acceptable birth control or at least know where to refer their clients in need (Yen & Martin, 2013).

Adolescent Pregnancy: Global Comparisons

Langille (2007) states that because rates of teenage pregnancy vary by country, reporting differences and making international comparisons can be difficult. In the United States, adolescent birth rates have declined in general, but they remain relatively high in certain groups, especially among Black and Hispanic teens and in the southern states, compared to those in other developed countries (CDC, 2011).

In examining adolescent pregnancy data from the Guttmacher Institute (2006), the number of adolescent pregnancies in Malawi, Uganda, and Ghana are similar. That is, in the 15- to 19-year-olds, approximately one-third do not want their last birth at all, and many want the birth at a later date.

The World Health Organization (2012b) states that about 16 million girls aged 15–19 years give birth annually (11 percent of births worldwide). Approximately 90 percent of such pregnancies occur in developing countries. Generally, however, the characteristics of young mothers are similar: little education, rural dwelling, low income, and marginalization. In addition, the risk of dying from a pregnancy-related cause is twice as high for adolescents aged 15–19, compared to older women. In low and middle income countries, complications of pregnancy and childbirth are the leading cause of death in women aged 15–19. In 2008, an estimated 3 million unsafe abortions occur each year throughout the world among 15–19 year olds.

Figure 11.5 illustrates socio-economic deprivation, both a cause and consequence of adolescent pregnancy (World Development Report, 2006; World Bank, 2006).

Consequences of Adolescent Pregnancy

The consequences of a high adolescent pregnancy rate are cause for great concern (Miller et al., 2003); of equal concern is the poverty that surrounds many young pregnant women. In the United States, where teen pregnancy is highest among the industrialized countries in the study reported in Figure 11.5, 80 percent of the teenage mothers were living at or near poverty levels well before they became pregnant (Glick, 2004). Factors of poverty are related to education and an individual's outlook for her future. Adolescent mothers often drop out of school. Although many resume their education later in life, breaking the cycle of poverty is difficult, and they generally do not catch up economically with women who postpone childbearing until their twenties.

Reducing Adolescent Pregnancy

Recommendations for reducing the high rate of adolescent pregnancy include (1) sex education and family planning, (2) access to contraceptive methods, (3) the life options approach, (4) abstinence, especially for young adolescents, and (5) broad community involvement and support. Eni

critical thinking

Urie Bronfenbrenner viewed each individual at the centre of an expanding circle of environmental influences. Discuss whether it is the early maturity of girls, or their environmental influences, that is the prime factor in teenage pregnancy. How might environmental influences be factors in teenage pregnancy? Design an adolescent-oriented sex-education program for your province or territory to focus on providing information on contraception.

Figure 11.5

Socio-Economic Deprivation

Source: World Health Organization. Preventing early and unwanted pregnancy and pregnancy related mortality and morbidity in adolescents—Training Course in Sexual and Reproductive Health Research, Geneva 2012, p. 9

and Phillips-Beck (2013) report that policy development is imperative to work with teen pregnancy. For example, a support system is necessary as well as safe-sex guidelines and family planning goals.

According to the Canadian Paediatric Society (2003), teens most as risk are those who:

- are experiencing family problems
- were born to adolescent mothers
- undergo early puberty
- have been sexually abused
- have frequent absenteeism and/or lack vocational goals
- have siblings who were pregnant during adolescence
- use alcohol, drugs, and tobacco
- live in group homes, detention centres, or on the street

The Canadian Paediatric Society (2003) believes that physicians, especially primary-care physicians, should discuss decision making with their young clients from an early age. The role of abstinence, the level of sexual activity, and increased use of contraceptives all play a role in the rate of teenage pregnancy. Education also plays a vital role (Langille, 2007).

To this point, we have discussed a number of ideas about adolescent sexuality. For a review, see the **Reach Your Learning Objectives** section at the end of this chapter.

Adolescent Health Problems and Wellness

LO4 Compare and contrast adolescent health issues related to eating disorders, substance use, and depression.

Adolescence is a critical juncture in the adoption of health-related behaviours (Park et al., 2008; Sirard & Barr-Anderson, 2008). Good nutrition, exercise, and adequate sleep are the foundations of good health. Many of the behaviours linked to poor health habits and early death in adults begin during adolescence. Conversely, the early formation of healthy behaviour patterns, such as regular exercise and a preference for foods low in fat and cholesterol, not only have immediate health benefits, but also help in adulthood to delay or prevent disability and mortality from heart disease, stroke, diabetes, and cancer (Schiff, 2009).

Nutrition, Exercise, and Sleep
Nutrition and Exercise

Exercise and good nutrition are proven ingredients for health and intellectual performance. This fact is supported by studies within Canada and across the globe linking fitness and active living to positive academic performance. According to the Active Healthy Kids Canada *Report Card on Physical Activity for Children and Youth* (2012), comprehensive approaches to fitness are linked to improved brain activity and memory, along with increased self-esteem, self-confidence, and self-image. In addition, young people who are engaged in physical fitness activities have reduced behavioural problems and feel more connected to their schools.

Evident disparities in access to organized sports and activities are a cause of concern. Young people from lower socio-economic backgrounds and those with disabilities are disadvantaged either by the costs of sports programs or access to them. These young people are missing out on the benefits (Active Healthy Kids Canada, 2012).

According to a report released by federal, provincial, and territorial ministers concerned with sport and physical activity (CFLRI, 2005) and Human Resources and Skills Development Canada (HRDC) (2010), approximately 50 percent of teenagers are at least moderately active. However, only

Sidebar

Nutrition, Exercise, and Sleep

Eating Disorders

Risk and Vulnerability

Substance Use and Addiction

Teen Depression

critical thinking

The Canadian Fitness and Lifestyle Research Institute (2005) defines three classifications of activity: active, moderately active, and inactive. An individual who walks at least one hour every day would be considered active; a half-hour a day, moderately active; a quarter-hour or less each day, inactive (CFLRI, 2005). Where would you place your activity level? If you placed your activity as either moderate or inactive, what could you do to improve it? In what way can you help a community to plan exercise programs? What steps would you include in planning an activity program?

about one in five are active enough to meet international guidelines for optimal growth and development. In this group, teenage boys are twice as likely to be active than girls (CFLRI, 2005). The Ministers have made an increase in physical activity and fitness a goal; consequently, more federal funding will flow through to assist local schools and municipalities meet this goal (CFLRI, 2005; Active Healthy Kids Canada, 2009).

Although peers are a factor in the amount of exercise in which a teen engages, parents may be the most effective role models for children and teens in terms of participating in healthy amounts of exercise.

Nutrition is essential to good health at all ages, but the adolescent body is undergoing so many changes that nutrition is particularly important. Canada's food guide offers guidelines for healthy eating. Snack foods often contain high levels of trans fats, which are unhealthy and may lead to cholesterol and heart problems later in adulthood. A good breakfast fuels the brain and body so that performance in school can be optimized, yet many teens skip breakfast.

Sleep Patterns and Circadian Rhythms

Like nutrition and exercise, sleep is an important influence on well-being. There recently has been a surge of interest in adolescent sleep patterns (Liu et al., 2008; Loessi et al., 2008). Mary Carskadon and her colleagues found that when given the opportunity, adolescents will sleep an average of 9 hours and 25 minutes a night. Especially during the week, most get six to seven hours of sleep, considerably less than the needed nine and a half hours. This shortfall creates a sleep deficit, which adolescents often attempt to make up for on the weekend (Carskadon, 2004, 2005, 2006).

Sleep patterns influence the hours during which adolescents learn most effectively in school (National Sleep Foundation, 2006). Further, according to Ontario researchers, evidence is mounting that indicates academic achievement and social competence are significantly compromised by sleep problems in adolescents (Gibson et al., 2006).

A **circadian rhythm** refers to *behavioural, physical, and mental changes that occur over roughly 24 hours.* A biological clock, which is located in nerve cells in the brain, controls the circadian rhythm. Circadian rhythms can change sleep–wake cycles, hormone release, body temperature, and other bodily functions such as elimination and hunger. Carskadon and her colleagues found that older adolescents tend to be sleepier during the day than younger adolescents. Their research suggests that adolescents' biological clocks, influencing the circadian rhythm, undergo a shift as they get older, delaying their period of wakefulness by about one hour. A delay in the nightly release of the sleep-inducing hormone melatonin, which is produced in the brain's pineal gland, seems to underlie this shift. Melatonin is secreted at about 9:30 p.m. in younger adolescents and approximately an hour later in older adolescents (Carskadon, 2004, 2005, 2006).

circadian rhythm Behavioural, physical, and mental changes that occur over roughly 24 hours.

When Gibson and his colleagues conducted a survey of 3,235 Ontario high school students from two school boards, they found similar adolescent sleep patterns. Seventy percent of the participating students reported having less than 8.5 hours of sleep on weeknights. Between 58 and 68 percent of students reported feeling "really sleepy" between 8 and 10 a.m. Another 27 percent reported feeling sleepy between 10 and 12 p.m. School records showed that students are often late for school and are involved in fewer extracurricular activities. Furthermore, nearly one-quarter (23 percent) of the students attributed a drop in their grades to sleepiness. The study recommends that educational and health communities develop strategies to address adolescent sleep deprivation and daytime sleepiness (Gibson et al., 2006).

Carskadon suggests that early school starting times may cause grogginess, inattention in class, and poor performance on tests. Based on her research, school officials in Edina, Minnesota, decided to start classes at 8:30 a.m. rather than 7:25 a.m. Since then, there have been fewer referrals for discipline problems, and the number of students who report being ill or depressed has decreased. The school system reports that test scores have improved for high school students, but not for middle school students. Many Canadian school boards are reviewing these findings that support Carskadon's belief that early start times are likely to be more stressful for older than for younger adolescents.

Eating Disorders

Not only are adolescents not getting enough sleep, but the number of adolescents who are overweight and getting insufficient exercise continues to increase. The obesity rates in Canadian children are increasing, as are the numbers of youth who suffer from hypertension and diabetes (Canadian Paediatric Society, 2004; Statistics Canada, 2003). Fast food consumption has also increased, as has "screen time" (i.e., watching television, playing computer games, general use of computers and videos). Rates of obesity and being overweight for both boys and girls who engage in moderate active physical activity are considerably lower than for those who do not. Teens who spent 30 or more hours in front of a screen were more likely to be obese that those who did not (Shields & Tremblay, 2008).

Eating disorders which involve serious disturbances in eating behaviour have become increasingly common among adolescents (Kirsch et al., 2007; Stice et al., 2007). Although anorexia nervosa is most common among adolescent girls, boys tend to exhibit a substantial high incidence of binge eating disorders (PHAC, 2011c).

A limited quantity of empirical research exists for males, but that situation is rapidly changing with gender differences and similarities being more frequently demonstrated (Weltzin, Cornella-Carlson, Fitzpatrick, Kennington, Bean, & Jefferies, 2012). Findings from one recent research study indicate that both the clinical significance and level of impairment caused by eating issues are similar for men and women (Striegel, Bedrosian, Wang, & Schwartz, 2012). Other researchers have found men, compared to women, present to treatment at a later age of onset, are more likely to have had a history of overweight, showed a higher BMI, and are less likely to have attempted suicide (Gueguen et al., 2012). Some evidence exists that younger and heavier gay men are at a higher risk for eating disorders (Boisvert & Harrell, 2009).

Individuals with anorexia nervosa or bulimia nervosa are similar, first in terms of their own disturbed perception of their body shape and weight, and second in their dissatisfaction with their bodies and their fear of gaining weight. Students who have eating disorders often have a perfectionistic attitude toward school or work and they tend to show low self-esteem (Statistics Canada, 2012c). Although the precise causes of developing an eating disorder are not yet known, a variety of factors related to adolescent eating disorders are involved:

- *Body image.* In general, adolescents are dissatisfied with their bodies, with males wanting to increase their upper body and females wanting to decrease the overall size of their body (Ata, Ludden, & Lally, 2007).
- *Parenting.* Adolescents who report observing more healthy eating patterns and exercise by their parents have more healthy eating patterns and exercise more themselves (Pakpreo et al., 2005). Family stress of any type may become a significant factor in the development of an eating disorder (Mayo Clinic, 2012).
- *Role models.* Watching commercials with idealized thin female images increased adolescent girls' dissatisfaction with their bodies (Hargreaves & Tiggemann, 2004). A recent study of adolescent girls revealed that frequently reading magazine articles about dieting and weight loss is linked with unhealthy weight-control behaviours five years later such as fasting, skipping meals, and smoking more cigarettes (van den Berg et al., 2007).
- *Screen time.* Adolescents who watch TV or are on their computers for more than two hours a day are more likely to be overweight than their counterparts (Shields & Tremblay, 2008).
- *Genetic or biological factors:* These factors may make some teens more likely to develop eating disorders (Mayo Clinic, 2012).

Eating disorders are common, with up to 5 percent of young women experiencing an eating disorder prior to entering adulthood. In addition, the ratio of adolescent women to women experiencing an eating disorder is ten to one (NEDIC, 2008). Researchers have consistently discovered that the onset of anorexia nervosa and bulimia nervosa occurs in adolescence, and that their onset in adulthood is rare (Striegel-Moore & Bulik, 2007). They have also found that eating disorders, including anorexia nervosa and bulimia nervosa, are far more prevalent in females than males (Hoek, 2006); however, more men than women report anabolic steroid use (NEDIC, 2008).

Anorexia Nervosa

Anorexia nervosa (AN) *is a life-threatening eating disorder that involves the relentless pursuit of thinness through starvation.* Anorexia nervosa can eventually lead to death; in fact, an estimated 10 percent of those with AN die within 10 years of diagnosis. Approximately 1.5 percent of teenage girls in Canada have had anorexia nervosa (National Eating Disorder Information Centre, 2008).

Three main characteristics apply to people suffering from anorexia nervosa: (1) they weigh less than 85 percent of what is considered normal for their age and height; (2) they have an intense fear of gaining weight that does not decrease with weight loss; and (3) they have a distorted image of their body shape (Rigaud et al., 2007). Even when they are extremely thin, they see themselves as too fat. They never think they are thin enough, especially in the abdomen, buttocks, and thighs. They usually weigh themselves frequently, often take their body measurements, and gaze critically at themselves in mirrors.

Anorexia nervosa typically begins in the early to middle teenage years, but is increasingly recognized in prepubertal children, often following an episode of dieting and the occurrence of some type of life stress. Most people with anorexia are white adolescent or young adult females from well-educated, middle- and upper-income families; further, they are usually competitive and high-achieving (Schmidt, 2003). They set high standards, become stressed about not being able to reach these standards, and are intensely concerned about how others perceive them. Unable to meet these high expectations, they turn to something they can control: their weight. Offspring of mothers with anorexia nervosa are at higher risk for becoming anorexic themselves (Striegel-Moore & Bulik, 2007). Problems in family functioning are increasingly being found to be linked to the appearance of anorexia nervosa in adolescent girls (Benninghoven et al., 2007), and a recent research review indicated that family therapy is often the most effective treatment of adolescent girls with anorexia nervosa (Bulik et al., 2007).

The fashion image in the North American culture that emphasizes "thin is beautiful" contributes to the incidence of anorexia nervosa (Striegel-Moore & Bulik, 2007). The media portray thin as beautiful in their choice of fashion models, whom many adolescent girls want to emulate. A recent study of adolescent girls revealed that friends often share similar body image and eating problems (Hutchinson & Rapee, 2007). In this study, an individual girl's dieting and extreme weight-loss behaviour could be predicted from her friends' dieting and extreme weight-loss behaviour.

Bulimia Nervosa

People with anorexia control their eating by restricting it. Most people with bulimia do not. **Bulimia nervosa (BN)** *is an eating disorder in which the individual consistently follows a binge-and-purge eating pattern.* The bulimic individual goes on an eating binge and then purges by self-induced vomiting or by using laxatives. Although many people binge and purge occasionally and some experiment with it, a person is considered to have a serious bulimic disorder only if the episodes occur at least twice a week for three months.

One recent study of adolescent girls found that increased dieting, pressure to be thin, exaggerated importance of appearance, body dissatisfaction, symptoms of depression, low self-esteem, and low social support predicted binge eating two years later (Stice, Presnell, & Spangler, 2002). About 70 percent of individuals who develop bulimia nervosa eventually recover from the disorder (Agras et al., 2004).

Obesity

Obesity *is having too much fatty tissue as measured by the ratio of weight and height, which is called the* **body mass index (BMI).** Obesity affects health, life expectancy, and quality of life. The World Health Organization defines obesity as having a BMI of 30 or more. A healthy BMI is between 18 and 24; a BMI between 25 and 29 indicates the individual is overweight. A BMI under 18 (anorexia nervosa) and over 30 are causes for serious concern. An estimated 50 percent of Canadians are overweight, and 15 percent fall in the category of obese (CIHR, 2006). For the first time in history, researchers are warning that obesity may overtake tobacco as the leading cause of death, and our life expectancy may decrease because of obesity.

anorexia nervosa (AN) An eating disorder that involves the relentless pursuit of thinness through starvation.

Anorexia nervosa has become an increasing problem for adolescent girls and young adult women. **What are some possible causes of anorexia nervosa? How does Urie Bronfenbrenner's theory that we are intensified by our environment factor in? Where on Maslow's hierarchy of needs would a person with anorexia nervosa fit? Why?**

bulimia nervosa (BN) An eating disorder in which the individual consistently follows a binge-and-purge eating pattern.

obesity Having too much fatty tissue as measured by the ratio of weight and height, which is called the body mass index (BMI).

Because adolescents are very concerned with their body image, those who are obese face both health and psychological problems. Health risks include type 2 diabetes, hypertension, cardiovascular disease, and cancer. Like younger children, teens who are overweight, especially those who are obese, are subjected to more name calling, bullying, and verbal and relational abuse (being excluded). Overweight and obese teens, particularly boys, are more likely to be bullies themselves as well as victims of bullying (Canadian Institute for Health Information CIHI, 2004).

Researchers have linked genetic factors to obesity, but note that environmental, economic, and social factors play a large role. Fast foods and reduced activity levels are also part of the picture (CIHI, 2004).

Risk and Vulnerability

For generations, adolescents have taken risks; in fact, risk taking is one of the ways teens challenge themselves and define their identity. Each individual has a unique definition of "risky" behaviour. To one teen risk may be trying out for the math team, while for another it's flying over ravines on a mountain bike. Whatever the definition, taking some risks is normal and healthy, according to psychiatrist Lynn Ponton, author of *The Romance of Risk* (1997).

Unfortunately, some risk taking is harmful and can lead to permanent problems and even death. The leading cause of death for teenagers is automobile accidents. Nearly half of all deaths in adolescents are due to accidents, and most of those, especially among older adolescents, involve motor vehicles. According to Mothers Against Drunk Driving (MADD) (2012), an estimate of over 5 percent of 16- to 17-year-olds and 15 percent of 18- to 20-year-olds were reported to be driving under the influence of alcohol in the past year.

Suicide is the second leading cause of teenage death. Suicide has increased five-fold for adolescent boys and three-fold for girls (Statistics Canada, 2010c). Gay and lesbian adolescents are also more likely to think about and attempt suicide, and suicide rates are five to eight times higher among First Nations and Inuit teens.

Self-injury is any attempt to alter one's mood by inflicting pain sufficient to cause tissue damage on one's self. Cutting has become a more common method of deliberate self-injury. Other injurious behaviours include burning, biting, and scratching. Such behaviours are deliberate, usually done in private and covered up. Wright, Briggs, and Behringer (2005) provide qualitative evidence that self-injuring adolescents report greater discomfort and dislike of their bodies than do adolescents who do not self-injure. In addition, these self-injuring adolescents experience the body as being "out of control" relative to non-suicidal injury (NSSI) youth. Muehlenkamp and Brausch (2012) found that body image may represent a necessary, but not sufficient, risk factor for (NSSI) in adolescents. Furthermore, the treatment for NSSI should consider targeting body-related pathology in addition to emotional regulation. Hooley, Ho, Slater, and Lockshin (2010) reported that community-based adolescents with NSSI histories had significantly higher pain tolerance thresholds.

A special concern involves teens who begin using drugs early in adolescence or even in childhood (King & Chassin, 2007). Scientists at the Mount Sinai School of Medicine and Columbia University have discovered that people who start using illicit substances in their early teen years are more likely to experience psychiatric disorders, especially depression, in their late twenties. A recent study revealed that individuals who began drinking alcohol before 14 years of age were more likely to become alcohol dependent than their counterparts who began drinking alcohol at 21 years of age or older (Hingson, Heeren, & Winter, 2006). A longitudinal study of individuals from 8 to 42 years of age also found that early onset of drinking was linked to increased risk of heavy drinking in middle age (Pitkanen, Lyyra, & Pulkkinen, 2005).

Another major risk factor in the use of illicit substances is that it increases the potential of criminal activity. Although most drug-related charges are for possession of marijuana, 7 percent of youth court cases are related to drug offences (Statistics Canada, 2004b). Violent crimes are associated with cocaine, gangs, trafficking, or settling debts (Statistics Canada, 2004b).

Substance Use and Addiction

In 2007, the police-reported rate of drug offences in Canada had reached its highest point in 30 years. Part of the increase in this overall rate is attributed to an increase in the rate of youths being accused of drug offences, which, in fact, doubled over the past decade. In recent years, however, most youths accused of drug offences have been cleared by means other than by formal charges by police. Examples include police discretion or referral to a diversion program (Canada Statistics, 2009).

Substance use by young people is a constantly evolving phenomenon. Recent Canadian surveys indicate that tobacco, alcohol, and cannabis are the substances most frequently used by youth (Canada Centre on Substance Use, 2007).

According to *Cross-Canada Report on Student Alcohol and Drug Use* (CCSA, 2011), among students in Grades 7 to 12 (those approximately 11 to 18 years of age) alcohol use was twice as prevalent as cannabis use (46 to 62 percent of students reported alcohol use and 17 to 32 percent) reported cannabis use in the past year. Aside from alcohol and cannabis, ecstasy was the most prevalent drug used (CCSA, 2011).

According to the report *Substance Abuse in Canada: Youth in Focus* (CCSA, 2007), "Early substance use has consistently been linked to negative consequences, including regular heavy use, dependence, and physical and social problems during young adulthood."

Cigarette Smoking

The prevalence of current smokers in Grades 6 to 9 significantly decreased between 2008 and 2009 (3 percent) and 2010 and 2011 (2 percent). No difference was detected in the prevalence of current smokers between male and female. However, among youth in Grades 10 to 12, 10 percent reported that they were current smokers, which is a significant decrease from 2008/09 (13 percent). At the same time there was a significantly greater proportion of male current smokers (11 percent) than female current smokers (9 percent) within this age group (Health Canada, 2012c).

Prescription and Non-Prescription Drugs

An alarming trend is the use of prescription painkillers and over-the-counter drugs by adolescents. A growing percentage of adolescents are using Vicodin and OxyContin, two highly addictive narcotics. A study conducted at the Ontario Institute for Studies in Education (OISE) in Toronto reported women with eating disorders also abused sleeping pills, diet pills, and prescription medications.

"Club drugs" are so labelled because they are popular at nightclubs and all-night dance parties called raves. The main club drugs are ecstasy and Rohypnol. Ecstasy is a methamphetamine, but it also has hallucinogenic properties. Although ecstasy use rose sharply among adolescents in the late 1990s, its use declined from 6 percent in 2001 to 4.1 percent in 2003 (CAMH, 2003) (see Figure 11.6).

The perception of risk of harm and the disapproval of trying ecstasy are higher in 2011 than estimates seen a decade ago. Present-day youth seem to be more aware of the potential for physical harm that ecstasy can cause (CAMH, 2011).

Recently, high-caffeine energy drinks have become a special concern among the medical community, which has called for restrictions on their labelling, sales, and marketing; many restrictions have been sanctioned. Energy-drink consumption is particularly popular among adolescents. In fact, half (50 percent) of all youth assessed last year use energy drinks (ranging from 34 percent of seventh-graders to almost 60 percent of twelfth-graders) (CAMH, 2011).

Prevention efforts regarding the use of drugs should include components which target the beliefs and attitudes that youth hold about drugs, specifically the risk of physical harm. For example, den Hollander and colleagues (2012) investigated whether the hippocampal volume of chronic ecstasy users is reduced when compared with healthy polydrug-using controls, as an indicator of hippocampal damage. It was found that the hippocampal volume in the ecstasy-using group was, on average, 10.5 percent smaller than hippocampal volume in the control group.

Dopamine in the Brain

Dopamine, *one of the key brain chemicals that carries and influences messages between nerve cells,* is heavily involved in the pleasure–reward circuit of the brain. Dopamine is excited when we do

dopamine One of the key brain chemicals that carry and influence messages between nerve cells.

Figure 11.6

Ecstasy and the Adolescent Brain

(a) In recent years, the use of ecstasy by adolescents has become increasingly popular at nightclubs and all-night dance parties called raves. (b) Ecstasy stimulates the release of the neurotransmitter serotonin in the brain, producing a euphoric high that lasts for several hours. However, ecstasy also destroys nerve cells and affects areas of the brain responsible for learning and memory. These images show a brain scan of a normal brain (left) and a brain under the influence of ecstasy (right). Note the dramatic differences in cerebral activity in the two brains as reflected in their different colouring in the brain scans.

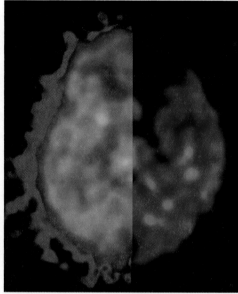

something that makes us feel good, for example, quenching our thirst on a hot summer day or having sex. According to the Canadian Institutes of Health Research (CIHR, 2004), more recent data suggest that the environment associated with the reward, without the reward itself even having to be present, triggers the release of dopamine. In other words, dopamine's "incentive value" may be responsible for a whole set of behaviours designed to obtain the reward.

The Canadian Centre on Substance Abuse (2007) states that many significant realizations have been obtained concerning the nature of drug abuse and how it affects the brain. The fact is that drugs produce their euphoric effects by acting on "specific" receptors in the brain yielding the highly sought effects. Initial periods of drug ingestion appear to have long-lasting effects that increase the person's vulnerability for future drug use resulting in psychiatric disorders such as depression. These behavioural and psychological changes seem to reflect changes within those pathways of the brain that regulate the user's responses to rewards and risks. Interesting enough the changes go beyond the receptor level and involve intricate alterations to the complexity inside the brain cells. In addition, environmental factors such as early traumatic experiences can further aggravate the development of these changes.

Thrill-seeking, novelty, and pleasure-seeking activities trigger dopamine, heightening its effects and sustaining its effects longer (Perry, 2002). It is possible that we are born with different levels of dopamine and are genetically primed to seek or avoid a wide variety of risk-taking activities. On the other hand, environmental factors may predispose individuals to substance abuse and dependence. In other words, researchers think some teens may have more of a built-in urge to experience life on the edge than others. Children with attentive, nurturing caregivers, who live in safe homes and communities, tend to be more resilient and less vulnerable to drug dependency (Perry, 2002).

Gambling

Despite the fact that minors in Canada are prohibited from legalized gambling, adolescents commonly engage in both legalized (lottery products, video lottery terminals) and self-organized (cards, sports betting, dice) gambling activities both at home and at school. The lifetime prevalence rates of

Dr. Roger Tonkin, Pioneer and Visionary in Adolescent Health Care

Dr. Roger Tonkin is a true visionary in the field of health care. His research, community initiatives, and government consulting work have influenced youth health practices and policies not only in British Columbia, but also all over the world. His treatment of youth with eating disorders, his medical practice, as well as his research have brought him international acclaim.

Born in Montreal in 1936, Tonkin studied at the University of Toronto and McGill University. He joined the University of British Columbia's Department of Paediatrics in 1968, and specializes in adolescent medicine and eating disorders. In addition to serving as Chair of the McCreary Centre Society, Dr. Tonkin is also a member of the Canadian Association for Adolescent Health, the Canadian Paediatric Society, and the Society for Adolescent Medical Council. Since 1994, he has served as president of the International Association for Adolescent Health. Tonkin was the driving force behind Vancouver's groundbreaking International Youth Health Assembly that included 500 young people and 1,100 health professionals from 50 countries.

As a pioneer in the field of adolescent medicine, Tonkin extended the range of health services to youth. For example, he founded

REACH Centre, a multidisciplinary community health centre that provides specialized service to a large number of transient youth. To promote a healthier lifestyle and encourage normal levels of activity and eating habits for young people, he conceived, built, and ran Camp Elsewhere on Gabriola Island. His unique approach to treating eating disorders has gained international attention and has served as a model for other countries.

In 1977, Tonkin founded the McCreary Centre Society, a small, non-profit agency concerned with the health of young people in British Columbia. The McCreary Centre Society's mission is to foster wider understanding of the importance of youth health, increase knowledge about youth health needs and issues, advocate for continuing commitment to youth issues, and initiate and implement innovative projects that directly address unmet health needs of young people.

Dr. Tonkin's work has not gone unnoticed. In 1998, he received the Order of British Columbia. More recently, in June 2010 the Canadian Paediatric Society awarded Dr. Tonkin the prestigious Ross Award. Both awards were given in recognition of his life-long work that has influenced health care standards for adolescents, both nationally and internationally (SPA, 2010).

---

pathological gambling for adults range from 1 percent to 2 percent and existing data suggest that the prevalence among adolescents may be two to four times higher (Canadian Paediatric Society, 2012).

Rates of gambling participation and problem gambling by youth vary among provinces and territories. The gambling rates of youth in Canada are very similar to those reported in the United States and elsewhere, suggesting that the majority of adolescents have gambled with similar prevalence of problem gambling (Volberg, Gupta, Griffiths, Olason, & Delfabbro, 2010). For example, of the students (Grades 7 through 12) taking part in a survey by the Centre for Addictions and Mental Health in Ontario, 42 percent reported involvement in at least one gambling activity in the previous year. Gambling participation increased with age and was more common among males. In this survey, it is indicated that 2.8 percent met criteria for pathological gambling (Problem Gambling Institute of Ontario, 2010).

Combating Substance Abuse

All three levels of government—local, provincial/territorial, and federal—as well as the National Native Alcohol and Drug Addictions Program (NNADAP) have mounted important strategies and campaigns against drug usage.

Since its origins in the 1970s, the goal of the program has been to help First Nations and Inuit communities to set up and operate programs aimed at reducing high levels of alcohol, drug, and solvent abuse in on-reserve populations (Health Canada, 2013).

The Centre for Addiction and Mental Health (CAMH) is Canada's largest mental health and addiction teaching hospital. In addition, it is one of the world's most respected research centres

What is the pattern of alcohol consumption among adolescents?

regarding addiction and mental health. CAMH combines clinical care, research, education, policy development, and health promotion to help transform the lives of people affected by mental health and addiction issues. In June 2012, CAMH launched *VISION 2020: Tomorrow, Today,* an eight-year strategic plan to build on the legacy of their founding organizations and core values. A few of their strategic directions are to enhance recovery by improving access to integrated care and social support, drive social change, and build an environment that supports recovery. In essence, this plan offers hope to those individuals and their families who are in need (CAMH, 2013).

Parents, peers, social support, and educational success can play important roles in preventing adolescent drug abuse. Positive relationships with parents and others can reduce adolescents' drug use (Wood et al., 2004). In one study, parental control and monitoring were linked with a lower incidence of problem behaviour by adolescents, including substance abuse (Fletcher, Steinberg, & Williams-Wheeler, 2004). A recent study also revealed that adolescents who averaged fewer than two family dinners a week were more likely to drink alcohol, smoke cigarettes, and abuse prescription drugs than their adolescent counterparts who averaged five or more family dinners a week (CASA, 2007). Another recent study of more than 5,000 middle school students revealed that having friends in their school's social network and having fewer friends who use substances were related to a lower level of substance use (Ennett et al., 2006). Researchers have also recently found that educational success—getting good grades, not dropping out of school, being connected to their school—has a protective role in reducing adolescents' drug use (Bachman et al., 2008).

Teen Depression

What is the nature of depression in adolescence? What causes an adolescent to commit suicide? Do depression and suicide run in families? Is depression genetically caused or a product of environment? According to the World Health Organization (WHO, 2009), depression is the leading cause of disability in developed nations, and the second most cited reason for visits to family doctors in Canada. Depression is more likely to occur in adolescence than in childhood, but causes and treatments remain undefined. Whether some people are more prone to depression by virtue of genetic makeup or whether environmental conditions play a determining role is not fully understood. What is known is that just as a young person undergoes pubescence and a tremendous physiological growth spurt, his or her brain undergoes massive reconstruction, or exuberance, which, combined with socio-cultural factors, sets the stage for mood swings and depression.

In 2004, Nancy Galambos and Erin T. Barker of the University of Alberta and Bonnie J. Leadbeater of the University of Victoria conducted a longitudinal study of 1,322 teenagers between 12 and 19 years of age to investigate gender differences in and risk factors for depressive symptoms. For this study, **depression** *was defined as experiencing over a prolonged period of time, a range of symptoms, including fatigue, irritability, inability to make decisions, sleeping problems, lack of interest in daily activities, and suicidal thoughts.* They found that boys were half as likely as girls to experience depression; in fact, in Galambos's words, the study revealed "a startling number of young women (25 percent) who should be identified as depressed and treated."

The study investigated four predictors of depressive symptoms: social support, body image, smoking, and physical activity. Although the results are inconclusive, no link was found between physical activity and depression among the teens; however, the study reported a link between smoking, social relationships, and body image with depression, although the link is not necessarily causal. Adolescents from families with a depressed parent may be at risk for both depression and smoking.

Reasons given for the higher rate of depression among adolescent girls include the following:

- Females tend to internalize emotions.
- Females tend to ruminate in their depressed mood and amplify it.
- Females' self-images, especially their body images, are more negative than those of males.
- Females face more discrimination than do males (Real, 1997).

Some specific factors may make an adolescent more prone to depression than others. Parents who divorce or have high marital conflict while their children are teens, and parents who are

critical thinking

Statistically, Aboriginal Canadians have suicide rates that are six times the national average for adolescents. Consider the social contexts of Aboriginal youth, on reserves, in small towns, and in urban areas. What factors do you think account for this alarmingly high rate? In what ways can the government provide educational plans for the prevention of suicide? What steps of suicidal prevention would you include in an educational program?

depression Experiencing, over a prolonged period of time, a range of symptoms, including fatigue, irritability, inability to make decisions, sleeping problems, lack of interest in daily activities, and suicidal thoughts.

depressed or emotionally unavailable or who are experiencing financial problems place adolescents at risk for developing depression. Poor peer relationships are also associated with adolescent depression. Not having a close relationship with a best friend, having less contact with friends, and experiencing peer rejection all increase depressive tendencies in adolescents.

Just as genetic factors are associated with depression, they are also associated with suicide. The closer a person's genetic relationship to someone who has committed suicide, the more likely that person will also commit suicide.

Woodgate (2006), an internationally renowned Canadian researcher, conducted a phenomenological study to gain an understanding of what it is like to be an adolescent living with depression. Thematic statements representative of the adolescent's lived experience were identified based upon interviews and field notes. The statement "living in the shadow" emerged as the essence of the adolescents' lived experiences. These experiences ultimately came to define what it was like to live with depression. The shadow of fear was associated not only with the fear of the return of "bad" feelings related to depression, but fear of not being able to receive help to manage those feelings. On top of that was the fear of having to do all the "hard work" in overcoming the bad feelings. Woodgate (2006) advocates that adolescents with depression need adequate resources and support throughout the illness trajectory, including those periods when their depression is under control.

To this point, we have discussed many ideas about adolescent health problems and wellness. For a review, see the **Reach Your Learning Objectives** section at the end of this chapter.

connecting development to life ‹------------,

Suicide

According to Kollar, Jordan, and Wilson (2013), suicide is defined as the deliberate act of self-injury with the intent that the injury results in death. In 2009, 202 Canadian teenagers aged 15–19 committed suicide. In the same year, suicide was rated as the second leading cause of death among teenagers, preceded only by accidents (Statistics Canada, 2012d). Each year, nearly 300 Canadian youths complete suicide. Many more attempt suicide. Suicide rates are five to seven times more prevalent among Aboriginal youth than for non-Aboriginal youth. Inuit youth suicide rates are among the highest in the world, at 11 times the national average (CIHR, 2012a). Suicide rates vary widely, however, among Aboriginal communities, and the maintenance of cultural continuity and support systems might be influential in offsetting the suicide rates (Chandler & LaLonde, 2008; Harder, Rash, Holyk, Jovel, & Harder, 2012).

While youth complete suicide at a lower rate than any other age group, the dramatic increase in the youth suicide rate over the past 40 years has made this group a special concern to health professionals (Roher & Casement, 2011). A retrospective analysis of standardized suicide rates using Statistics Canada mortality data for the period from 1980 to 2008 was conducted by Skinner & McFaull (2012). They analyzed the data by sex and by suicide method, over time for two age groups: 10- to 14-year-olds (children) and 15- to 19-year-olds (adolescents). The findings revealed a gradual increase in suicide by suffocation among female children and adolescents. In addition, the researchers found a decrease in suicides involving poisoning and firearms during the study period. The investigators conclude that suicide rates in Canada are increasing among female children and adolescents and decreasing among male children and adolescents.

Among adolescents, cyberbullying has become an increasing reality. Research indicates that these youth who have been bullied are at a higher risk, notably not only for suicide ideation and thoughts, but also for suicide attempts and completed suicides (Centre for Suicide Prevention, 2012). Due to the pervasive nature of social media sites, it has become more difficult than ever for victims to escape from their tormentors. It can happen anywhere—at home, at school, or at any time of the day or night (Brown, Cassidy, & Jackson, 2006). Victims, in extreme cases, frequently become aggressive and fight back, or they become depressed and attempt suicide. Youth who have experienced cyberbullying are almost twice as likely to attempt suicide compared to those who were not subjected to cyberbullying (Patchin & Hinduja, 2010).

Regarding suicide in rural and urban areas, Rhodes et al. (2008) noted that in many countries, including Canada, suicide rates tend to be higher in rural areas than in urban areas. It is well known that suicide rates in British Columbia's rural areas are much higher generally for Aboriginal compared to non-Aboriginal groups (Chandler & LaLonde, 2008).

White, Wyn, and Albanese (2011) argue that the reason for the rising rates of suicide in the Western world might be that society is failing young people. Even though many opportunities are available to them, youth feel adrift once they leave home and try to be successful in the world. It becomes important to acknowledge that the demise of traditional belief systems and narratives of meaning has made their journey more difficult. Such a result inevitably may leave some youth without a clear sense of connection.

Risk Factors: Suicide is a complex process. Causal basis for suicides can seldom be attributed to one single factor, such as a family breakup or homelessness (Centre for Suicide Prevention, 2012). It may be a routine incident or an overwhelming event that overloads a youth's coping mechanism (CMHA, 2013). Mental disorders seem to be the most important risk factor for adolescent suicide. Other common precursors to suicide include the presence of addictions, mood disorders, interpersonal problems with parents, conduct disorders, or a previous suicide attempt (Friedman, 2006). Substance abuse, for example, can impair judgment and exacerbate impulsivity. An impulsive teen might act speedily on suicidal thoughts (Kostenuik & Ratnapalan, 2010). For certain teens, suicide becomes the final pathway for release from their psychiatric and social problems (Kollar, Jordan, & Wilson, 2013). One other factor includes contagion or copycat suicide, terms that refer to the spread of suicidal activity. An increase in youth suicide is at times found after the suicide of one teenager is publicized in the community (Gould, Greenberg, Velting, & Shaffer, 2003). Gay, lesbian, and bisexual adolescents are at particularly high risk for suicide attempts. These attempts seem to occur

especially among those who have been raised in an environment devoid of adequate support systems (Saewyc et al., 2007).

Interventions: Strategies for suicide prevention frequently focus on risk factors. Public education campaigns, for example, are aimed at the improvement of the recognition of suicide risk and to increasing the understanding of causes and risk factors for suicidal behaviour, especially mental disorders (Mann et al., 2005). Other specific education strategies aimed at youth in particular include school and community programs (Gould et al., 2003). Promising school-based programs emphasize the process of screening students for mental health problems, and to referring them to health care professionals (Kutcher & Szumilas, 2008).

Other strategies include providing teachers with "gatekeeper" training to recognize depression; learning procedures for referral to mental health services; and developing peer-helper programs and crisis debriefing interventions aimed at youth (Kutcher & Szumilas, 2008). Appropriate emotional and psychological supports from friends and families appear to safeguard against suicide (Kostenuik & Ratnapalan, 2010). The media can help suicide prevention efforts by being a path for public education; on the other hand, media can hinder certain preventive efforts by glamorizing suicide, or by promoting it as a solution for life problems (Mann et al., 2005).

Adolescent Cognition

LO5 Explain cognitive development in adolescence and the influence of schools on adolescent cognition.

Adolescents' developing power of thought opens up new cognitive and social horizons.

Piaget's Theory

Recall from Chapter 9 that Piaget proposed children enter the *concrete operational stage* of cognitive development at about 7 years of age. At this stage they can reason logically about events and objects, categorizing them and identifying relationships. This stage lasts until about 11 years of age, when, according to Piaget, the fourth and final stage of cognitive development begins.

The Formal Operational Stage

How does formal operational thought differ from concrete operational thought? One major difference is that *formal operational thought* is more abstract than concrete operational thought. Adolescents are no longer limited to thinking about concrete experiences; they can imagine hypothetical possibilities or abstract propositions. Further, they can reason logically about them.

The abstract quality of the adolescent's thought at the formal operational level is evident in the adolescent's verbal problem-solving ability. Whereas the concrete operational thinker needs to see the concrete elements A, B, and C to be able to make the logical inference that if A=B and B=C, then A=C, the formal operational thinker can solve this problem merely through verbal presentation.

Accompanying the abstract nature of formal operational thought in adolescence are thoughts full of idealism and possibilities. While children frequently think in concrete ways, or in terms of what is real and limited, adolescents begin to engage in extended speculation about ideal characteristics—qualities they desire in themselves and in others. Such thoughts often lead adolescents to compare themselves with others in regard to such ideal standards. During adolescence, the thoughts of individuals are often fantasy flights into future possibilities.

At the same time that adolescents have increased ability to think more logically, they are less likely to use trial and error to figure out problems. Adolescents begin to think more scientifically, devising plans to solve problems and systematically testing solutions. This type of problem solving requires **hypothetical-deductive reasoning**, *in which an individual creates a hypothesis, deduces implications, and tests implications*. Thus, formal operational thinkers develop hypotheses, or best guesses, about ways to solve problems, then they systematically figure out and determine the best path to follow in solving the problem.

For adolescents who become formal operational thinkers, *assimilation* (incorporating new information into existing knowledge) dominates the initial development of formal operational thought, and the world is perceived subjectively and idealistically. Later in adolescence, as intellectual balance is restored, these individuals *accommodate* (adjust to new information) to the cognitive upheaval that has occurred. Figure 11.7 summarizes the characteristics of formal operational thought.

Evaluating Piaget's Theory

Some of Piaget's ideas on formal operational thought have been challenged (Byrnes, 2008). Those who have challenged Piaget's ideas argue that individual variation is greater than Piaget envisioned. Only about one in three young adolescents is a formal operational thinker, and many adults never think in this way. Furthermore, education in science and mathematics employs the scientific method and thereby fosters articulation of the types of responses that are thought to be evidence of formal operational thought.

Culture and education exert stronger influences on cognitive development than Piaget believed (Rogoff et al., 2007). Most contemporary developmentalists agree that cognitive development is not as stage-like as Piaget thought (Kellman & Arterberry, 2006). Furthermore, children can be trained to reason at a higher cognitive stage, and some abilities emerge earlier than Piaget thought (Scholnick, 2008).

Ethologists *are scientists who research the connections between animal and human behaviours,* as described in Chapter 2. Ethologists distinguish between biologically primary and secondary

hypothetical-deductive reasoning A type of problem solving in which an individual creates a hypothesis, deduces implications, and tests implications.

developmental **connection**

Ethologists

ethologists Scientists who research the connections between animal and human behaviours.

Figure 11.7

Characteristics of Formal Operational Thought

Adolescents begin to think in more abstract, idealistic, and logical ways than when they were children.

Abstract	Idealistic	Logical
Adolescents think more abstractly than children. Formal operational thinkers can solve abstract algebraic equations, for example.	Adolescents often think about what is possible. They think about ideal characteristics of themselves, others, and the world.	Adolescents begin to think more like scientists, devising plans to solve problems and systematically testing solutions. Piaget called this type of logical thinking "hypothetical-deductive reasoning."

abilities, defining the biologically primary abilities as those which are learned universally, at approximately the same age. Biologically secondary abilities, or higher-level abilities, are those which are not learned easily and require effort. Ethologists suggest that Piaget's early stages—sensorimotor, preoperational, and concrete operational—rely on biologically primary abilities because they are learned universally at approximately the same age. Walking, conservation, and seriation are learned whether a child is in a classroom environment or not. Secondary abilities are those abilities which are not universal and take more effort to obtain. Examples include participation in complex oral traditions such as storytelling, piano-playing, or agricultural skills. Within a singular culture, greater variation of achievement exists. Children who grow up in Eastern Ontario may become bilingual as a matter of course. Adults who move into the region may have to expend considerable effort and time learning French or English. Ethologists cite the lack of universality of biologically secondary abilities as a major flaw in Piaget's formal operational stage (Genovese, 2003).

Despite these critiques, Piaget can still be credited with the current field of cognitive development as he developed a long list of comprehensive and useful concepts of enduring influence. These include his theories of assimilation, accommodation, object permanence, egocentrism, conservation, and others. The current paradigm of children as active, constructive thinkers rather than passive receptacles of knowledge is attributed to him.

Piaget's theoretical ability was complemented by his adept skills of observation. His careful observations demonstrated inventive ways to discover how children act on and adapt to their world. He showed us that children simultaneously conceptualize their experiences in a way that fits their schematic view of the world while they adjust their world-view to account for new information and experiences. Piaget also revealed how cognitive change is likely to occur if the context is structured to allow gradual movement to the next level. Mature concepts do not emerge suddenly, but instead develop through a series of partial accomplishments that lead to increasingly comprehensive understandings (Gelman & Kalish, 2006).

In addition to thinking more logically, abstractly, and idealistically, characteristics of Piaget's formal operational thought stage, adolescent egocentrism plays an important role in adolescent thinking.

Adolescent Egocentrism

Recall from Chapter 7 that egocentrism in preschoolers was the child's belief that everyone could see the same things that the child sees. **Adolescent egocentrism** shifts to a *heightened self-awareness and self-consciousness*. David Elkind (1976) believed that adolescent egocentrism has two key components: the imaginary audience and personal fable.

Imaginary audience *involves adolescents' belief that others are as interested in them as they themselves are*. It may include the belief that everyone notices them as well as behaviours intended to attract attention, or exaggerated attempts not to be noticed. Adolescents, especially young adolescents, sense that they are "on stage," believing they are the main actors and all others are the audience.

According to Elkind, the **personal fable** *is the part of adolescent egocentrism that involves a sense of uniqueness and invincibility*. Adolescents' sense of *personal uniqueness* gives them the sense that no one else, especially parents, can understand how they really feel. As part of their effort to retain a sense of personal uniqueness, adolescents might craft a story about the self that is filled with fantasy, immersing themselves in a world that is far removed from reality. Personal fables frequently show up in adolescent diaries or in the names they use in computer games. Some teens create *avatars*, virtual representatives or caricatures of themselves, for use on the Internet. Avatars appeal greatly to the adolescent's personal fable because they can remain anonymous yet experience aspects of life, or alter-life, in the virtual world not available to them in the real world. They can attend lectures, art galleries, cafés, parties, etc. They can meet friends and carry on friendships in the virtual world.

Adolescents also often show a sense of *invincibility*, believing that nothing horrible can happen to them. Life is new, and they are young, so being in an automobile accident, getting caught shoplifting, becoming pregnant, or developing diseases caused by smoking happen to someone else.

Many adolescent girls spend long hours in front of the mirror, depleting cans of hairspray, tubes of lipstick, and jars of cosmetics. **How might this behaviour be related to changes in adolescent cognitive and physical development?**

adolescent egocentrism The heightened self-consciousness of adolescents.

imaginary audience Adolescents' belief that others are as interested in them as they themselves are.

personal fable The part of adolescent egocentrism that involves an adolescent's sense of uniqueness and invincibility.

A recent study of Grade 6 through 12 students examined whether aspects of the personal fable were linked to various aspects of adolescent adjustment (Aalsma, Lapsley, & Flannery, 2006). A sense of invincibility or invulnerability was linked to engaging in risky behaviours, such as smoking cigarettes, drinking alcohol, and delinquency, whereas a sense of personal uniqueness was related to depression and suicidal thoughts.

Information Processing

According to Deanna Kuhn (Kuhn & Franklin, 2006), the most important cognitive change in adolescence is improvement in *executive functioning*, which involves higher-order cognitive activities such as reasoning, making decisions, monitoring thinking critically, and monitoring one's cognitive progress. Improvements in executive functioning permit more effective learning and an improved ability to determine how attention will be allocated, to make decisions, and to engage in critical thinking.

Decision Making

Adolescence is a time of increased decision making—career choices, education, dating, and so on (Keating, 2007; Rivers, Reyna, & Mills, 2008; Sunstein, 2008). Adolescents are increasingly more likely to set realistic goals, anticipate consequences, and determine strategies for reaching their goals as they age. Compared with children, young adolescents are more likely to generate different options, examine a situation from a variety of perspectives, anticipate the consequences of decisions, and consider the credibility of sources.

For older adolescents and adults, the ability to make competent decisions does not guarantee that they will be made in everyday life, where breadth of experience often comes into play. For example, driver-training courses improve adolescents' cognitive and motor skills to levels equal to, or sometimes superior to, those of adults. However, driver training has not been effective in reducing adolescents' high rate of traffic accidents, although recently researchers have found that implementing a graduated driver licensing (GDL) program can reduce crash and fatality rates for adolescent drivers (Keating, 2007). GDR components include a learner's holding period, practice driving certification, night driving restriction, and passenger restriction.

Interestingly, some personality traits, such as introversion, extraversion, conscientiousness, and agreeableness may influence decision making. Most people make better decisions when they are calm rather than emotionally aroused (Dahl, 2004). That may be especially true for adolescents, who have a tendency to be emotionally intense. The same adolescent who makes a wise decision when calm may make an unwise decision when emotionally aroused (Giedd, 2008; Steinberg, 2009). In the heat of the moment, emotions may overwhelm decision-making ability.

The social context plays a key role in adolescent decision making. For example, adolescents' willingness to make risky decisions is more likely to occur in contexts where substances and other temptations are readily available (Gerrard et al., 2008; Reyna & Rivers, 2008). Recent research reveals that the presence of peers in risk-taking situations increases the likelihood that adolescents will make risky decisions (Steinberg, 2008). In one study of risk taking involving a simulated driving task, the presence of peers increased an adolescent's decision to engage in risky driving by 50 percent, but had no effect on adults (Gardner & Steinberg, 2005). One view is that the presence of peers activates the brain's reward system, especially dopamine pathways (Steinberg, 2008).

Critical Thinking

The development of critical-thinking skills is essential when adolescents enter formal education (Marin & Halpern, 2011). One need for the ability to think critically for the adolescent is that it is essential for success in the contemporary world where the rate of creation of new knowledge is accelerating rapidly each day (Gainer, 2012). Instruction that compels critical thought in the adolescent can be accomplished either by threading critical thinking skills into the content matter, or through explicit instruction specifically designed to provide guidance in the essentials of critical thinking skills (Marin & Halpern, 2011). For example, assignments designed to developing critical

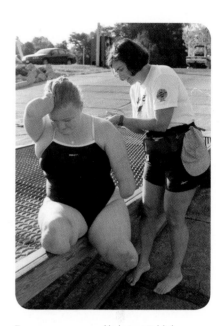

Teenagers are more likely to establish realistic goals and identify strategies to meet those goals. **What strategies do you think Ashley may have put in place to realize her dream of swimming across Lake Erie? What obstacles might she have faced? What role did her parents play in helping her realize her goals?**

thinkers have been designed by Brookfield (2011). These assignments encourage adolescents to reason in a reflective manner and process information more efficiently.

If fundamental skills (such as literacy and math skills) are not developed during childhood, critical-thinking skills are unlikely to mature in adolescence. For the subset of adolescents who lack such fundamental skills, potential gains in adolescent thinking are unlikely. For other adolescents, however, cognitive changes that allow improved critical thinking in adolescence include the following: (1) increased speed, automaticity, and capacity of information processing, which free cognitive resources for other purposes; (2) more breadth of content knowledge in a variety of domains; (3) increased ability to construct new combinations of knowledge; and (4) a greater range and more spontaneous use of strategies or procedures for applying or obtaining knowledge, such as planning, considering alternatives, and cognitive monitoring (Gathercole, Pickering, Ambridge, & Wearing, 2004).

The Brain

Neuroscientist Jay Giedd and his collaborators from UCLA, Harvard, the Montreal Neurological Institute, and other institutions found that of all parts of the brain, the frontal lobe undergoes the most complex change during adolescence (Giedd, Blumenthal, Jeffries, et al., 1999). Sometimes called the CEO, or chief executive officer, the frontal lobe is our head office, monitoring our decisions. It helps us plan ahead, resist impulses, understand consequences, focus attention, set priorities, and engage in other decision-making activities. Giedd's longitudinal study found the frontal lobe to be the last section of the brain to develop. During puberty, as the brain produces more neural connections it starts to specialize, pruning back to the essentials. This allows the brain to function more efficiently, but what gets pruned away is largely determined by the choices the teen makes. According to Giedd, because the frontal lobe of the brain is still under construction, "it's sort of unfair to expect them to have adult levels of organizational skills or decision making before their brain is finished being built" (Giedd, 2008).

Education

Nowhere is the convergence of the three processes of life-span development more evident than in high school. Changing hormones, restructuring of the brain, worrying about body image, developing emotional control, and managing time and money as well as relationships are very much a part of the teen's world. As anyone who has ever been in junior high or high school or who has watched *Degrassi High* knows, the classroom and homework frequently play a secondary role to other life situations.

The changing demographics are driving a need for teachers to know how to best assess and teach those students whose primary language is not English (Brice, Miller, & Brice, 2006). Strategies need to be developed to assist those English language learners (ELL) to adjust and become successful in their learning (Mastropieri & Scruggs, 2004).

A great many of today's high school students have grown up with the social spaces created by technology. They are tweeting and chatting on blogs, on Facebook, and in other virtual spaces. Many teachers and school administrators may be just learning these technologies in an effort to keep up with their students. Knowing how to use technology and manage information in itself transforms the classroom; no longer is the teacher the only or primary source of knowledge and skill. A major challenge facing education today is preparing students to manage all the information that is available to them (Silverslides, 2012).

Service-Learning

service-learning A form of education intended to promote social responsibility and service to the community.

Service-learning *is a form of education intended to promote social responsibility and service to the community.* In service-learning, students engage in activities such as tutoring, helping older adults, working in a hospital, assisting at a child-care centre, or cleaning up a vacant lot to make a play area. Thus, service-learning takes education out into the community (Hart, Atkins, & Donnelly, 2006; Reinders & Youniss, 2006).

In 1999, Ontario introduced a mandatory requirement of 40 hours of participation in community service as a way to build self-esteem and encourage a life-long commitment to community service. Students participate in a variety of projects such as tutoring, working in nursing homes or shelters, raising money and collecting clothes for those in need of them, recycling, cleaning, and other safety activities. A key feature of service-learning is that it benefits both the student volunteers and the recipients of their help (Hamilton & Hamilton, 2004).

Researchers have found student improvement in four important ways: grades, self-esteem, agency (belief in their ability to influence outcomes), and problem-solving skills (Meinhard, Foster, & Wright, 2006). Meinhard and Foster's study of Toronto high school students (2006) indicates a positive long-term effect on participants.

Katimavik, the Inuit word for "meeting place," is the name for a government program organized in 1977. Since its implementation, Katimavik has enabled over 30,000 youth between 17 and 21 years of age to work, live, and learn together in 2,000 communities across Canada. The primary goal of Katimavik is to enhance personal development by enabling young people to meet, live with, work with, and learn from each other (Katimavik, 2010). During three trimester experiences spread over nine months, participants live in three different Canadian communities and work with three different groups of like-minded young people. A trained group leader liaises among the groups and the non-profit partners for which the groups provide a variety of volunteer services. Helping a child learn to read, assisting with administrative work, accompanying seniors on outings, or building hiking trails are some of the community service activities engaged in by the participants (Katimavik, 2010).

Effective Schools

Schools that are most effective in responding to adolescent needs do far more than teach basic skills of reading, writing, and math. They offer an environment that is accountable and responsive to public scrutiny. While some schools buckle under increasing public criticism and dwindling resources, others form collaborative relationships within the community. Effective leadership, clear academic goals, a safe and orderly climate, expectation of minimum mastery of skills by all students, testing for program evaluation and redirection, parental involvement, and collegiality are the trademarks of effective schools (Bonell et al., 2013).

The Manitoba School Improvement Program (MSIP) cites strong community ties as essential to better schools (MSIP, 2011). Schools with open and respectful communication and an environment that builds confidence and academic enthusiasm among students foster effective learning. Additionally, shared vision and academic focus, combined with an ethic of caring, enables students to make a successful transition from elementary school to middle or junior high school to high school. These ingredients contribute to the **hidden curriculum,** *the moral atmosphere that is communicated through the school's rules, regulations, deportment, and moral orientation.* In this way, every school and classroom within a school infuses a value system. When students make the transition from one school to the next, and from one classroom to the next, they must figure out and adjust to this often unspoken curriculum.

As discussed throughout the chapter, the transition to middle or junior high school takes place at a time when many changes—in the individual, in the family, and in school—are occurring simultaneously. When students make the transition to middle or junior high school they experience the *top-dog phenomenon,* moving from being the oldest, biggest, and most powerful students in the elementary school to being the youngest, smallest, and least powerful students in the middle or junior high school.

There can also be positive aspects to the transition to middle or junior high school. Students are more likely to feel grown up, have more subjects from which to select, have more opportunities to spend time with peers and locate compatible friends, and enjoy increased independence from direct parental monitoring. They also may be more challenged intellectually by academic work.

Ministries of education across Canada have introduced innovative curriculum to prepare students for further education and work. Recall that Piaget and Kohlberg suggested that a child's

critical thinking

Recently, a student was suspended for putting derogatory remarks about his high school principal on his blog, and a college student was expelled for putting threatening remarks about another student on her blog. Many students in both high school and university use a blog. Write three policy statements that you think students should be required to follow in using their blogs. How do you suggest these policies be regulated? Other than a blog, what other social media sites can students use for messaging?

hidden curriculum The moral atmosphere communicated through the school's rules, regulations, deportment, and moral orientation.

developmental **connection**

Piaget and Kohlberg

moral development moves steadily from being externally controlled by the rewards associated with pleasing parents, teachers, and other adults to being internally controlled by the intrinsic rewards associated with making decisions that serve the common good of the community. On the basis of these theories, much curriculum, such as service learning, prejudice reduction, and emotional intelligence (EI), has been developed to address various moral concerns.

Technology has brought about another radical transformation to our concept of education. Computers and high-speed Internet access have been altering the nature of learning ever since their introduction. Rather than simply absorbing information, the technologies allow students to access original-source materials and discover truths for themselves. The classroom has become globalized as well, linking communities with Internet access across the world. This may help expand Canadian students' multicultural experiences to international frontiers.

Dropping Out of High School

In the last 50 years, school completion rates for Canadians have increased from 50 percent to 80 percent; however, no school can meet the needs of every student uniformly. As well, even the most effective schools can fail to meet the needs of some students altogether. Although the completion rates are encouraging, the number of young people who drop out remains the Achilles heel of our high schools (Richards, 2009). Dropout rates vary from province to province, with British Columbia having the lowest dropout rate. Although many return to finish later, fewer than half of the boys in Montreal French-language public schools complete high school. The Prairie provinces, with high concentrations of Aboriginal peoples, along with Newfoundland, have high dropout rates as well. Special challenges face francophone youth from Quebec and Aboriginal youth both on and off reserves.

Along with British Columbia, Nova Scotia, Prince Edward Island, and New Brunswick have high rates of completion. Graduation rates remain stable in Ontario (Statistics Canada, 2005c). Almost 50 percent of those who leave return by the age of 20 and complete their high school education (Statistics Canada, 2000).

To this point, we have discussed a number of ideas about adolescent cognition. For a review, see the **Reach Your Learning Objectives** section at the end of this chapter.

The transition from elementary to middle or junior high school occurs at the same time as a number of other developmental changes. **What are some of these other developmental changes?**

reach your learning objectives

The Nature of Adolescence

LO1 Analyze the life stage of adolescence.

- Biological, emotional, and environmental factors influence adolescent development.
- Adolescence is a period of idealistic and abstract thinking.
- Risks and temptations are more numerous than in previous generations.
- Although adolescence is a vulnerable period, most, especially those who report good family relationships, make the transition fairly smoothly.
- Although risk-taking is part of identity formation, for some the experimentation with sex, alcohol, drugs, and gambling lead to permanent problems in adulthood.
- Adolescents today have a less stable environment than they did a decade ago.

Physical Changes during Puberty

LO2 Describe the physical changes that occur during puberty.

Sexual Maturation, Height, and Weight	■ Puberty is a rapid change to physical maturation involving hormonal and bodily changes that occur primarily during early adolescence. ■ The onset of puberty can occur anytime between the ages of 8 and 15 and last from 1.5 to six years. ■ Menarche, the female menstrual cycle, occurs toward the end of the puberty period. ■ Growth spurts occur about two years earlier in girls than boys.
Hormonal Changes	■ Hormones are powerful chemical substances secreted by the endocrine glands and carried throughout the body in the bloodstream. ■ The concentration of testosterone in boys and estradiol in girls dominate pubertal development. ■ Individual variation is puberty is extensive.
Body Image	■ Adolescents show considerable interest in their body image. ■ Young adolescents are more preoccupied and less satisfied with their body image than are late adolescents. ■ Girls have more negative body images throughout puberty than boys do; however, there is widespread individual variation. ■ Puberty for girls comprises the best and worst of two worlds: menstrual cycles, PMS, breast cancer, etc. are among the worst; fashion choices and sports are among the best. Boys often identify playing sports as the best aspect of being a boy.
Teen Perspectives on Maturity	■ Research indicates that establishing independence or autonomy is a key developmental task of adolescence. ■ In adolescence cognitive abilities are related to psychosocial maturity.
The Brain	■ During adolescence, the brain undergoes a rapid transformation called exuberance. ■ The frontal lobe, or executive branch of the brain, is last to develop, making individuals more prone to respond with "gut" reactions to emotional stimuli. ■ Because the frontal lobe is last to develop, adolescents are more likely to take risks than are adults.

Adolescent Sexuality

LO3 Describe adolescent sexuality, sexual identity, and risk factors related to intimate sexual behaviour.

Developing a Sexual Identity	■ Mastering emerging emotions and forming a sense of sexual identity are multifaceted. ■ An adolescent's sexual identity involves sexual orientation, activities, interests, and styles of behaviour.
The Timing of Adolescent Sexual Behaviours	■ The percentage of teens who report they have had intercourse has declined; however, age, gender, and jurisdiction are factors. ■ Those who decide not to have sexual intercourse report a variety of reasons, including feelings of not being ready, self-respect, religious beliefs, and not being in love. ■ Those who decide to engage in sexual activity do so because they are in a serious relationship; however, peer pressure, alcohol, and drugs also play a role in their decision. ■ A small percentage (9 percent) report having intercourse before the age of 15. These youth are most vulnerable to risk factors including school problems, pregnancy, and STIs.

Risk Factors and Sexual Problems	■ Use of contraceptives has increased.
	■ Human papillomavirus (HPV) is thought to be the most commonly transmitted STI. Two types of vaccine are now available in Canada for protection against HPV.
	■ Rates of pregnancy vary by country; international comparisons can be difficult.
	■ Adolescent pregnancy increases health risks for both the mother and the offspring.
	■ Adolescent mothers have difficulty breaking the cycle of poverty as they are more likely to drop out of school and have lower-paying jobs as adults than adolescent girls who do not bear children.
Adolescent Pregnancy and Health	■ Strategies to reduce adolescent pregnancy include sex education and family planning, access to contraception, life options, community involvement and support, and abstinence.
	■ Aboriginal community policy initiatives provide emotional support, safe-sex guidelines, and family planning goals.

Adolescent Health Problems and Wellness

LO4 Compare and contrast adolescent health issues related to eating disorders, substance use, and depression.

Nutrition, Exercise, and Sleep	■ Adolescence is a critical juncture in the development of healthy or unhealthy patterns.
	■ Adolescent sleep patterns shift so that older teens are likely to be more wakeful at night than during the day.
	■ Researchers have found that adolescents report getting approximately eight hours of sleep, which is less than the nine hours and 25 minutes of sleep they report they would like to get.
	■ Grades and moods are adversely affected by daytime sleepiness.
Eating Disorders	■ Anorexia nervosa is the relentless pursuit of thinness through starvation and is most common among girls.
	■ Bulimia nervosa is the use of a binge-and-purge pattern of eating; boys exhibit a high incidence of binge eating disorder
	■ Obesity is having too much fatty tissue, as measured by the ratio of weight and height called the body mass index (BMI).
Risk and Vulnerability	■ Research indicates that people who start using illicit substances in their early teens are more likely to experience psychiatric disorders, especially depression, in their late twenties.
	■ Another major risk of the use of illicit substances is the potential for criminal activity.
	■ The effects of the increased and widespread use of alcohol are not yet known.
	■ Most teen experimentation tends to level off in the transition from adolescence to early adulthood.
	■ Positive relationships with parents and others are critical in reducing drug and alcohol use.
Substance Use and Addiction	■ Canadian surveys indicate that tobacco, alcohol, and cannabis are substances most often used by youth.
	■ Research shows that ecstasy produces euphoric effects by acting on "specific" receptors in the brain.

- Although drunk driving rates have decreased, impaired driving remains a major cause of death and injury; alcohol use has increased.
- High-caffeine energy drinks are a concern affecting adolescents' health.
- Rates of problem gambling continue to rise.

Teen Depression
- Depression is experiencing a wide range of symptoms, such as fatigue, irritability, sleeping problems, lack of interest, and suicidal thoughts over a long period of time.
- Adolescents have a higher rate of depression than children.
- Female adolescents are more likely to experience depression than males.
- A recent study found that 25 percent of teenage girls between 12 and 19 should be identified and treated for depression.

Suicide
- A study regarding adolescent depression found that adolescents need adequate support and resources.
- Adolescent suicide is on the rise.
- Mental disorders are the most important risk factor.
- Public education program regarding suicidal prevention are important.
- Appropriate psychological support is needed for the adolescent contemplating suicide.

Adolescent Cognition

LO5 Explain cognitive development in adolescence and the influence of schools on adolescent cognition.

Piaget's Theory
- Formal operational thought involves the ability to reason about what is possible and hypothetical, as opposed to what is real, and the ability to reflect on one's own thoughts.
- Abstraction and idealism, as well as hypothetical-deductive reasoning, are characteristic of formal operational thought.
- Two phases occur in the formal operational thought stage: assimilation in which reality is overwhelmed (early adolescence) and accommodation in which intellectual balance is restored through a consolidation of formal operational thought (middle adolescence).
- Ethologists argue that Piaget's earlier stages (sensorimotor, preoperational, and concrete operational) are biologically primary abilities that are universally learned.
- Ethologists believe that formal operational skills have to be studied and are not universally learned because they are not innate to the human mind; therefore, these skills are biologically secondary skills.
- Piaget did not consider the extensive individual variation.
- Many young adolescents are not formal operational thinkers, but rather are consolidating their concrete operational thought.

Adolescent Egocentrism
- Elkind proposed that adolescents, especially young adolescents, develop an egocentrism that involves both the construction of an imaginary audience and personal fable.
- Imaginary audience involves the belief that others are as preoccupied with the adolescent as the adolescent is with himself or herself.
- Personal fable is the sense of personal uniqueness and vulnerability.

Information Processing
- Two primary characteristics of information processing are decision making and information processing.
- Adolescence is a time of increased decision making.

- The ability to make competent decisions does not guarantee that such decisions will be made in everyday life, especially where breadth of experience comes into play.

- The section of the teen brain undergoing complex change and the last to fully develop is the frontal lobe, the decision-making section of the brain. The frontal lobe helps us plan ahead, focus attention, set priorities, resist impulse, and understand consequences. It helps us engage in decision making and monitor those decisions.

- Adolescence is an important transitional period in critical thinking because of such cognitive changes as increased speed, automaticity, and capacity of information processing; more breadth of content knowledge; increased ability to construct new combinations of knowledge; and greater range and spontaneous use of strategies.

- The activities in which a teen engages will shape his or her brain.

Education

- Transitions from elementary to middle or junior high school, and later to high school, are stressful because of the convergence of all three life-span development processes, biological, socio-emotional, and cognitive, and because of the "top-dog" phenomenon.

- Service-learning promotes social responsibility by engaging students in community activities, such as tutoring or working in hospitals.

- Katimavik, which has enabled over 30,000 youth between 17 and 21 years of age to meet each other in over 2,000 communities across Canada, is an example of service learning.

- Effective schools are characterized by their academic focus and open environment conducive to learning.

- Innovative curriculum is developed and reviewed in partnership with parents, police, community members, and students, and is responsive to social needs and technology.

- The hidden curriculum is the moral atmosphere infused by the school through its policies and deportment.

- Fewer Canadians are leaving high school before completion than a generation ago.

- Francophone and Aboriginal youth have the lowest high school completion rates and face unique challenges.

review ----> *connect* ----> reflect

review

What characterizes adolescent development? **LO1**

What are several key aspects of puberty? **LO2**

What factors affect the timing of puberty? **LO2**

What are some important aspects of adolescent sexuality? **LO3**

How effective are the *Canadian Guidelines for Sexual Health Education* for adolescents? **LO3**

What are the key aspects of eating disorders? **LO4**

What are a few important aspects of information processing in adolescence? **LO5**

connect

Peers exert both positive and negative pressure. How do they exert negative pressure in our society today?

reflect *Your Own Personal Journey of Life*

Reflect on your adolescence. Was it a time of stress and storm or a time of transition into young adulthood? Explain.

McGraw Hill Education connect®

McGraw-Hill Connect provides you with a powerful tool for improving academic performance and truly mastering course material. You can diagnose your knowledge with pre- and post-tests, identify the areas where you need help, search the entire learning package, including the eBook, for content specific to the topic you're studying, and add these resources to your personalized study plan. CONNECT for *Life-Span Development*, fifth Canadian edition, offers the following:

- chapter-specific online quizzes
- groupwork
- presentations
- writing assignments
- case studies
- and much more!

Visit CONNECT today!

CHAPTER 12

Socio-Emotional Development in Adolescence

CHAPTER OUTLINE

Self-Esteem and Identity Development

LO1 Describe self-esteem, the changes in the self and identity, and several of the prominent theories.

Self-Esteem

Identity

Identity: Family, Religion, Race, Ethnicity, Culture, and Sexual Orientation

LO2 Compare and contrast how family, religion, race, ethnicity, culture, and sexual orientation influence adolescent development.

Families

Religion

Racial, Ethnic, and Cultural Identity

Traditions and Changes in Adolescence around the World

Sexual Orientation and Identity

Friendship

LO3 Outline the changes that occur in peer relations and dating during adolescence.

Adolescent Groups versus Children's Groups

Peer Groups

Dating and Romantic Relationships

Adolescent Problems

LO4 Analyze adolescent problems in socio-emotional development, and the causes of the problems.

Young Offenders

Causes of Delinquency

Successful Prevention and Intervention Programs

LO5 Design strategies for helping adolescents with problems.

"*We are not just our future . . . we are also our present.*"

—HARINI SHIVALINGAM, CANADIAN YOUTH REPRESENTATIVE TO THE UNITED NATIONS WORLD CONFERENCE AGAINST RACISM, RACIAL DISCRIMINATION, XENOPHOBIA, AND RELATED INTOLERANCE (WCAR)

The Challenges of Being an Adolescent

As we discussed in Chapter 11, no two people are alike. However, the transition from childhood to adulthood encompasses similar milestones in both physical and cognitive development. The same applies to socio-emotional development, where significant changes occur during adolescence. The mainstay of the changes includes increased efforts for self-understanding and increased searching for an identity. Changes also occur in the social contexts of adolescents' lives, with transformations occurring in relationships with families and peers and other cultural contexts, such as schools, health care facilities, communities, and even countries. Some adolescents may develop socio-emotional problems, such as delinquency and depression. The scenarios below are a snapshot of some of the variations and unique contexts shaping an individual's choices and decisions.

THIRTEEN: *Amelia* worries that something is wrong with her because all her friends wear bras, have begun to menstruate, and are interested in boys. She wonders if these events will ever happen to her. *Spencer* and his friends attend a private school where laptops for each student are part of the tuition. They create a re-enactment of Louis Riel for their history project. Virtual world avatars are used as actors because their school has created a "controlled" account for all students.

FOURTEEN: When *Renée* isn't riding horses, she is studying. Ever since she can remember, she has wanted to be a veterinarian. She has a small circle of friends and isn't too interested in boys, although she does "swoon" whenever she sees Cal. *Joe* avoids everyone. He is attracted to other boys and is afraid if he shows this side of him, he will be beaten up. He knows that he is the subject of gossip and rumours.

FIFTEEN: *Carl* played on the football team last year in another high school and tried out for the team this year in his new high school. When he checks the board to see who had made the team, he sees that he has been cut. He loses his temper, kicks his locker, shouts profanities, and stomps out of the school angrily. On Tuesdays, Thursdays, and Sunday afternoons, *Samantha* babysits her neighbour's three-year-old daughter, Lisa, a child with Down syndrome. Samantha loves Lisa, and has learned so much from her that she thinks she'd like to become a teacher of children with special needs.

SIXTEEN: As soon as she got her licence, *Michelle* borrowed her father's car. With great pride, she picked up her best friend and they went for a ride. Michelle was very careful not to speed and to return the car on time because she doesn't want to jeopardize her father's trust. With a fake passport in his hand, *Sallieu* left Sierra Leone, landing at Toronto's Pearson International Airport. He learns that he is in Canada when he sees the signs that read, "Welcome to Canada." He has no money and nowhere to stay. Sallieu is one of hundreds of thousands of adolescents who flee their war-torn country of origin to seek what they hope will be a healthier and more peaceful environment.

SEVENTEEN: Because she was failing all her courses, *Jessica*, who has attention deficit disorder, dropped out of school. Much to her parents' dismay, she got a job at Tim Hortons. Three months later she quit, and hasn't worked since. She moved out of the family home because she "can't put up with their nagging anymore." *Philip* sends his university application in to three universities. He really isn't sure what he wants to study, and keeps changing his mind between medicine, international law, and child psychology.

EIGHTEEN: *Lynne* was referred to a nutritional counsellor after her hospitalization for anorexia nervosa. Her first appointment is for after school at 4:30, and she is dreading it. She knows what the counsellor will say; after all, she has been through this before. She snorts a line of coke to brace herself for her counselling appointment. *Jason's* avatar, Jake, meets Jude, another avatar, at a virtual café where they share anecdotes about their parents, classmates, and teachers. They leave the café and go to a bar. Although you are supposed to be 18 to have an Avatar account, Jason and a friend opened accounts a couple of years ago and created macho body images of themselves that they thought would appeal to the girls.

NINETEEN: *Evan* is excited about his first year at Carleton University. Although he has been looking forward to the freedom of living away from home, now that the time has come, he is worried about who his roommates will be. *Janice* has applied to participate in Katimavik because she isn't sure what she wants to do now that she has finished high school. She is tired of working in retail stores and wants to learn more about Canada.

Each scenario illustrates some of the milestones, challenges, and problems facing adolescents. Like the teens in this vignette, during adolescence each individual grapples with identity in a manner very different from childhood. As you can see from these snapshots, and as you may remember from your own adolescent years, the integrative physical, cognitive, and socio-emotional processes of development are strongly at play in the search for identity and the development of self-esteem.

Self-Esteem

Identity

Self-Esteem and Identity Development

LO1 Describe self-esteem, the changes in the self and identity, and several of the prominent theories.

Recall from Chapter 10 that *self-esteem* is the overall way we evaluate ourselves, and it is also referred to as self-image or self-worth. Controversy characterizes the extent to which self-esteem changes during adolescence and whether there are gender differences in adolescents' self-esteem (Harter, 2006). In one recent study, both boys and girls had particularly high self-esteem in childhood, but their self-esteem dropped considerably during adolescence (Robins et al., 2002). Another study also found that the self-esteem of girls declined during early adolescence, but the self-esteem of boys increased in early adolescence (Baldwin & Hoffman, 2002). In this study, adolescent self-esteem was related to positive family relationships.

Self-Esteem

Does self-esteem in adolescence foreshadow adjustment and competence in adulthood? A New Zealand longitudinal study assessed self-esteem at 11, 13, and 15 years of age, and adjustment and competence of the same individuals when they were 26 years old (Trzesniewski et al., 2006). The results revealed that adults characterized by poorer mental and physical health, worse economic prospects, and higher levels of criminal behaviour were more likely to have low self-esteem in adolescence than their better adjusted, more competent adult counterparts.

Recent research also indicates that self-esteem is often implicated in the development of adolescent behaviour, with high self-esteem serving as a role of positive adaptation (Boden, Fergusson, & Horwood, 2008). Conversely, low self-esteem has been considered an important factor in relation to manifestations of depression, both in adolescents and in adult samples (Bos, Huijding, Muris, Vogel, & Biesheuvel, 2010).

Self-esteem is a large part of adolescents' self-understanding; it is likely to be a fluctuating and dynamic construct, susceptible to internal and external influences during adolescence (Erol & Orth, 2011).

A question often raised is why would the self-esteem of girls decline during early adolescence? Girls are found to suffer from a greater number of emotional problems in adolescence than do boys. This gender difference seems to increase in middle to late adolescence (Essau, Lewinsohn, Seely, & Sasagawa, 2010). One explanation involves the greater interest young adolescent girls take in social relationships and society's failure to reward that interest (Impett, Schooler, Tolman, Sorsoli, & Henson, 2008).

The trend in research findings has been that male adolescents have shown higher self-esteem than females do (Moksnes, Moljord, Espnes, & Byrne, 2010). However, in a study by Erol and Orth (2011), no significant gender difference in the level of self-esteem was discovered. These findings also indicate that self-esteem increases and continues to increase slowly during the adolescent years. Actually, adolescent self-esteem changes more strongly than in young adulthood (Erol & Orth, 2011).

Identity

Who am I? What am I all about? What am I going to do with my life? What is different about me? How can I make it on my own? These questions, captured in the snapshot scenarios in the opening vignette, reflect the search for an identity. **Identity** *refers to our self-portraits that develop over our lifetime and are made up of many components, including negations and affirmations of various roles and characteristics.* By far the most comprehensive and provocative theory of identity development is Erik Erikson's. In this section, we examine his views on identity. We also discuss contemporary research on how identity develops and how social contexts influence that development.

identity Our self-portraits that develop over our lifetime and are made up of many components, including negations and affirmations of various roles and characteristics.

Identity is a self-portrait composed of many pieces. These pieces include:

- The career and work path a person wants to follow (vocational/career identity)
- Whether a person is conservative, liberal, or a centrist (political identity)
- A person's spiritual beliefs (religious identity)
- Whether a person is single, married, divorced, and so on (relationship identity)
- The extent to which the person is motivated to achieve and is intellectual (achievement, intellectual identity)
- Whether a person is heterosexual, homosexual, or bisexual (sexual identity)
- The part of the world or country a person is from and how intensely the person identifies with his/her cultural heritage (cultural/ethnic identity)
- The kinds of things a person likes to do, which may include sports, music, hobbies, and so on (interests)
- The individual's personality characteristics, such as being introverted or extraverted, anxious or calm, friendly or hostile, and so on (personality)
- The individual's body image (physical identity)

Synthesizing the identity components can be a long and drawn-out process, with many negations and affirmations of various roles and characteristics. Identity development gets done in bits and pieces. Decisions are not made once and for all, but have to be made again and again. Identity development does not happen neatly, and it does not happen cataclysmically (Kroger, 2007; Orbe, 2008; Phinney, 2008).

-- developmental **connection** --------

Erikson

Erik Erikson

By far the most comprehensive and provocative theory of identity development is Erik Erikson's. Erikson's psychosocial development theory is epigenetic, suggesting a synchrony between individual growth and social expectations. At each of eight chronological periods in the life span, physical changes occur to which one's social environment responds with particular expectations and supports in the form of cultural practices and institutions (Marcia & Josselson, 2013).

It was Erikson who first understood how central questions about identity are to understanding adolescent development. As you may remember from Chapter 2, identity versus identity confusion, the fifth of Erikson's eight stages, occurs at about the same time as adolescence. Erikson believed adolescence to be a time when individuals are interested in finding out who they are, what they are all about, and where they are headed in life. In fact, according to Erikson (1968), developing a coherent and synthesized sense of identity is one of the primary developmental tasks of the transition to adulthood.

The search for an identity during adolescence is aided by a **psychosocial moratorium,** *which is Erikson's term for the gap between childhood security and adult autonomy.* During this period, society leaves adolescents relatively free of responsibilities and free to try out different identities. Adolescents in effect search their culture's identity files, experimenting with different roles and personalities. They may want to pursue one career one month (lawyer, for example) and another career the next month (doctor, actor, teacher, social worker, or astronaut, for example). They may change their handwriting or signature daily. This experimentation is a deliberate effort on the part of adolescents to find out where they fit in the world.

Youth who successfully cope with conflicting identities emerge with a new sense of self that is both refreshing and acceptable. Adolescents who do not successfully resolve this identity crisis suffer what Erikson calls identity confusion. The confusion takes one of two courses: individuals withdraw, isolating themselves from peers and family, or they immerse themselves in the world of peers and lose their identity in the crowd.

psychosocial moratorium Erikson's term for the gap between childhood security and adult autonomy that adolescents experience as part of their identity exploration.

Identity Development

Contemporary views of identity development suggest several important considerations. First, identity development is a lengthy process; in many instances, it is a more gradual, less cataclysmic transition than Erikson's term "crisis" implies. Second, identity development is extraordinarily complex.

Identity formation neither begins nor ends with adolescence; rather, it is a life-long process. Identity formation begins with the appearance of attachment, the development of a sense of self, and the emergence of independence in infancy, and it reaches its final phase with a life review and integration in old age. What is important about identity in adolescence, especially late adolescence, is that for the first time, physical development, cognitive development, and social development advance to the point at which the individual can sort through and integrate childhood identities and identifications to construct a reasonable pathway toward adult maturity. Resolution of the identity issue at adolescence does not mean that identity will be stable throughout the remainder of one's life. A person who develops a healthy identity is flexible, adaptive, and open to changes in society, in relationships, and in careers. This openness assures numerous reorganizations of identity features throughout the life of the person who has achieved identity.

Identity formation does not happen neatly, and it usually does not happen suddenly; in addition, identities are developed in bits and pieces. At the bare minimum, identity involves commitment to a vocational direction, an ideological stance, and a sexual orientation. Decisions are not made once and for all, but have to be made again and again. The number of decisions may seem overwhelming at times: whom to date, whether or not to break up, whether or not to have intercourse, whether or not to take drugs, whether to go to college or university after high school or get a job, which major to choose, whether to study or whether to play, whether or not to be politically active, and so on. Over the years of adolescence, identity is a critical development task during the transition to adulthood in Western societies (Schwartz et al., 2011).

James Marcia's Identity Statuses and Development

How do individual adolescents go about the process of forming an identity? Eriksonian researcher James Marcia (1980, 1994) reasons that Erikson's theory of identity development contains four statuses of identity, or ways of resolving the identity crisis: identity diffusion, identity foreclosure, identity moratorium, and identity achievement. What determines an individual's identity status? Marcia classifies individuals based on the existence or extent of their crisis or commitment (see Figure 12.1). **Crisis** *is defined as a period of identity development during which the individual is exploring alternatives.* Most researchers use the term *exploration* rather than crisis. **Commitment** *is personal investment in identity.* Marcia viewed exploration as the process underlying identity development and viewed commitment as the outcome of the process. Newer models now view both exploration and commitment as processes. These newer models have also been used empirically to extract identity statuses that strongly resemble and extend those proposed by Marcia (Crocetti, Rubini, Luyckx, & Meeus, 2008). Interestingly, in demonstrating that identity statuses can be empirically derived from continuous measures of identity processes, strong evidence is provided that the status model does indeed capture the process of identity development (Schwartz et al., 2011).

The four statuses of identity are described as the following:

- **Identity diffusion** *occurs when individuals have not yet experienced a crisis (that is, they have not yet explored meaningful alternatives) or made any commitments.* Not only are they undecided about occupational and ideological choices, but they are also likely to show little interest in such matters.

crisis Marcia's term for a period of identity development during which the individual is exploring alternatives.

commitment Personal investment in identity.

identity diffusion Marcia's term for individuals who have not yet experienced a crisis (they have not explored meaningful alternatives) or made any commitments.

Figure 12.1 ---

Marcia's Four Statuses of Identity

Position on Occupation and Ideology	Identity Status			
	Identity diffusion	Identity foreclosure	Identity moratorium	Identity achievement
Crisis	Absent	Absent	Present	Present
Commitment	Absent	Present	Absent	Present

- **Identity foreclosure** *occurs when individuals have made a commitment but have not yet experienced a crisis*. This occurs most often when parents hand down commitments to their adolescents, usually in an authoritarian manner. In these circumstances, adolescents have not had adequate opportunities to explore different approaches, ideologies, and vocations on their own.
- **Identity moratorium** *occurs when individuals are in the midst of a crisis but their commitments are either absent or only vaguely defined.*
- **Identity achievement** *occurs when individuals have undergone a crisis, and have made a commitment.*

Emerging Adulthood and Beyond

A consensus is developing that the key changes in identity are more likely to take place in emerging adulthood (18 to 25 years of age) or later than in adolescence (Kroger, 2007; Luyckx et al., 2008a; Cote, 2009).

One of emerging adulthood's themes is not having many social commitments, which gives individuals considerable independence in developing a life path (Arnett, 2006). James Cote (2009) argues that because of this freedom, developing a positive identity in emerging adulthood requires considerable self-discipline and planning. Without this self-discipline and planning, emerging adults are likely to drift and not follow any particular direction. Cote also stresses that emerging adults who obtain a higher education are more likely to be on a positive identity path. Those who don't obtain a higher education, he says, tend to experience frequent job changes, not because they are searching for an identity, but rather because they are just trying to eke out a living in a society that rewards higher education. Phinney (2008) states that the increased complexity in the reasoning skills of college students, combined with a wide range of new experiences that highlight contrast between home and college, and between themselves and others, stimulates students to reach a higher level of ability to integrate various dimensions of their identity.

Resolution of the identity issue during adolescence and emerging adulthood does not mean that identity will be stable through the remainder of life. Many individuals who develop positive identities follow what are called **MAMA cycles;** that is, *their identity status changes from moratorium to achievement to moratorium to achievement* (Marcia, 1994). These cycles may be repeated throughout life (Francis, Fraser, & Marcia, 1989). Marcia (2002) points out that the first identity is just that—it is not, and should not be expected to be, the final product.

In short, questions about identity come up throughout life. An individual who develops a healthy identity is flexible and adaptive, and open to changes in society, in relationships, and in careers. This openness assures numerous reorganizations of identity throughout the individual's life.

Elkind's Age Dynamisms

As adolescents reconcile their sense of self, they often employ what Elkind calls "age dynamisms"; that is, they wish to put as much distance between their more sophisticated teenage self and their childish or juvenile self of the past. Yet, in doing so, individuals recognize a certain level of continuity about themselves—they still have the same birthmark or eye colouring, for example. Research indicates that as children move through Piaget's stages of cognitive development, they become more sophisticated in understanding the persistence or continuity of their personal identities and the identities of others. This understanding is strongly influenced by cultural background. When individuals belong to a cultural group that realizes that their heritage has been ravaged by war, disruption, dislocation, and its future is dismal, they may fail to see their own personal continuity and feel a loss of identity. Consequently, Lalonde, Chandler, Hallett, and Paul (2001) believe that Aboriginal youth run higher risks of suicide because in their quest for personal identity, their past and present narratives reflect not only the typical struggle, but also the loss of a culture that has been scorned and devalued.

To this point, we have studied a number of ideas about self-esteem and identity development in adolescence. For a review, see the **Reach Your Learning Objectives** section at the end of this chapter.

identity foreclosure Marcia's term for individuals who have made a commitment but have not experienced a crisis.

identity moratorium Marcia's term for individuals who are in the midst of a crisis, but their commitments are either absent or vaguely defined.

identity achievement Marcia's term for individuals who have undergone a crisis and have made a commitment.

---

critical thinking

Think about your development and the development of one or two close friends from high school in the following areas: vocational/career, political, religious, sexual, ethnic/cultural, and physical/sport. Compare and contrast ways in which Marcia's identity statuses (diffused, foreclosed, moratorium, or achieved) relate to you and friends in each of these areas. In what ways have you or someone you know shifted from one identity status to one another? What suggestions would you make to a friend who seems stuck in either a moratorium or foreclosed status, to assist him or her to shift to an achievement identity status? How would you apply Marcia's identity statuses to the teens portrayed in the opening vignette? What suggestions do you have for them to progress to an identity achievement status?

MAMA cycles The identity status changes from moratorium, to achievement, to moratorium, to achievement that are repeated throughout life.

connecting development to life

Child or Adult? The Case of Omar Khadr

Adolescence is the transition from childhood to adulthood, marked by dramatic changes in all three processes: biological changes occur as the young person goes through puberty; cognitive changes occur as the adolescent develops more abstract and hypothetical thinking patterns and is better equipped to think logically; and socio-emotional changes occur as the young person moves further and further from his or her family and begins navigating social systems such as friends, school, jobs, and community more independently. Just when is this transition complete? When is an individual considered an adult? This is more than a philosophical question—it is also a question of law. When should person be tried in a juvenile court? When should a person be tried in an adult court, where sentencing is much farther-reaching?

This question was at the heart of the debate surrounding a Canadian citizen, Omar Khadr. In 2002, 15-year-old Omar Khadr was arrested by the U.S. government and imprisoned in Guantanamo Bay (Steinberg, 2009). He was accused of killing a U.S. soldier in Afghanistan, war crimes, and supporting terrorism. His defence attorney argued that he was a boy soldier, a minor at the time of his crime, and therefore should not be tried in an adult court. They pointed out that he is the first child-soldier ever tried by the U.S. for war crimes (Steinberg, 2009).

Omar's family background further exacerbated his situation. His older brother is incarcerated in Toronto on charges related to terrorism, and another brother was also arrested on charges related to ties with the terrorist group Al-Qaeda. Omar's father is believed to be a friend and major financer of Osama Bin Laden, the man who masterminded the 9/11 attacks on the United States. The family's travels between Egypt, Afghanistan, Pakistan, and Canada since 1980 have attracted the attention of national security agencies in both Canada and the U.S. (CBC News, April 29, 2010). In October 2010, Khadr pleaded guilty to the charges as part of a plea bargain with the U.S. government. He was sentenced to 40 years in prison, but will serve only eight years due to the pretrial plea deal (CBC News, November 1, 2010). On September 29, 2012, at the hands of the American government, Omar Khadr was flown off the U.S. naval base from Guantanamo Bay, Cuba, to a maximum-security prison in Eastern Ontario with little chance of rehabilitation or parole for at least two years. His status is scheduled for review in December 2014 (Shepherd, 2012).

Neuroscientists who study the brain and the nervous system have shown through magnetic resonance imaging (MRI) that the adolescent brain is undergoing rapid changes, and that the prefrontal cortex, the executive branch that factors in consequences when making decisions and determining goals, is the last part of the brain to develop (Steinberg, 2009). This finding is important because it verifies what many already knew: adolescents tend to respond to situations with emotion, or with their gut feelings, whereas, adults, whose prefrontal cortex has developed, tend to use more logic and less emotion when making decisions. This finding could have been useful in mounting Khadr's defence.

Consider some of the theories you have learned about so far: Bronfenbrenner, Erikson, Freud, Kohlberg, Marcia, Maslow, Piaget, Vygotsky. How might each theorist explain Omar Khadr's behaviour? What are some of the many pieces that may be part of Khadr's identity resolution? What arguments would you make if you were the prosecuting attorney for the U.S. government? What arguments would you make if you were Khadr's defence attorney? What concepts and theories would you use to support your position?

Identity: Family, Religion, Race, Ethnicity, Culture, and Sexual Orientation

- Families
- Religion
- Racial, Ethnic, and Cultural Identity
- Traditions and Changes in Adolescence around the World
- Sexual Orientation and Identity

LO2 Compare and contrast how family, religion, race, ethnicity, culture, and sexual orientation influence adolescent development.

As indicated earlier, identity is very complex. Family, cultural and ethnic heritage, and sexual orientation all affect the development of an adolescent's identity. Another major contributory factor is socio-economic status, which underpins opportunities and access to resources and further shapes identity. This section will discuss areas where socio-economic status comes into play.

Families

Like people, families come in all sizes and shapes. Some families are lone-parent, while others, extended families, may have three or more generations under the same roof. Some families live in the same communities, while continents separate others. Some families are rich, others are middle-class, and many are poor. No matter the configuration, families provide the first source of information about the world. The family into which the adolescent was born shapes sense of humour, understanding of right and wrong, notions of common sense, and sense of self. Families provide models that the emerging adult considers, accepts, or rejects. Attachment, autonomy, and conflict are typical as adolescents assert their independence from their families.

Family Influences

In addition to studying parenting styles, researchers have also examined the roles of individuality and connectedness in the development of identity. According to Cooper and Grotevant (1989), **individuality** *consists of self-assertion, the ability to have and communicate a point of view, and separateness, the use of communication patterns to express how one is different from others.* **Connectedness** *consists of two dimensions: mutuality, sensitivity to and respect for others' views, and permeability, openness to others' views.* Parents are important figures in the adolescent's development of identity (Beyers & Goossens, 2008; Cooper, Behrens, & Trinh, 2008; Luyckx et al., 2007, 2008b; Schacter & Ventura, 2008). Relationships between parents and adolescents affect every aspect of adolescent development.

In general, research findings reveal that identity formation is enhanced by family relationships that are both individuated, which encourage adolescents to develop their own point of view, and connected, which provide a secure base from which to explore the widening social worlds of adolescence. When connectedness is strong and individuation weak, adolescents often have an identity foreclosure status. When connectedness is weak, adolescents often reveal identity confusion.

Research has demonstrated that parental behaviours and the quality of parent–child relationships related to empathy and prosocial behaviour are important correlates of youth development. Yoo, Feng, and Day (2013) found that parental behaviours, parental solicitation, and parental psychological control are particularly associated with empathy and prosocial behaviour in adolescents. Such influences are brought about through the degree of balanced connectedness (the balanced state of closeness and autonomy) in the parent–adolescent relationships. Another recent research study utilized an observational coding scheme to identify parenting behaviour which reflected psychological control and the granting of autonomy. Their study examined relations between these parenting dimensions and certain indices of child and family functioning. The findings identified particular patterns of psychological control and autonomy that undermine youth adjustment (Hauser Kunz & Grych, 2013). In fact, these findings suggest that the way in which parents respond to bids for greater independence by their children have implications for the child's psychological health in early adolescence. Parkin & Kuczynski (2012) examined 32 adolescents regarding their perspectives on parental expectations and on their own strategies for expressing resistance. It was found that adolescents described their strategies for expressing resistance as multifaceted, consisting of overt behavioural strategies and covert cognitive strategies that reflect autonomous and relational motives. In essence, adolescents thrive when they have superior executive functioning and can thoughtfully direct their own lives (Urban, Lewin-Bizan, & Lerner, 2010).

One emerging field of study focuses on the adolescent as thriving, especially in supportive relationships with parents. In fact, the facilitation of high levels of student engagement in their schooling has been suggested to be an important outcome in their development (Furlong et al., 2003). Further, thriving adolescents flourish when they succeed academically and, at the same time, are connected to school (Lewis, Huebner, Malone, & Valois, 2011). Extracurricular activities provide a key context for youth development, and the interest and participation of thriving adolescents has been linked with positive developmental outcomes. For example, the effect of having an interest in music, arts, and even sports is deemed vital and each interest can be enhanced if nurtured by caring adults (Scales, Benson, & Roehlkepartain, 2011). These ideas coincide with Diana Baumrind's (1971, 1991) authoritative parenting style, which was discussed in Chapter 8, "Socio-Emotional Development in Early Childhood."

individuality Self-assertion, the ability to have and communicate a point of view, and separateness, the use of communication patterns to express how one is different from others.

connectedness Comprises two dimensions: mutuality, sensitivity to and respect for others' views, and permeability, openness to others' views.

developmental **connection**

Baumrind

developmental **connection**

Bowlby and Ainsworth

←--------------------------→

With most adolescents, parents are likely to find themselves engaged in a delicate balancing act, weighing competing needs for autonomy and control, for self-assertion and commitment.

Autonomy and Attachment

Recall from Chapter 6 that one of the most widely discussed aspects of socio-emotional development in infancy is secure attachment to caregivers. In the past decade, researchers have explored whether secure attachment also might be an important concept in adolescents' relationships with their parents (Collins & Steinberg, 2006). Normative changes in thoughts, feelings, and behaviours do occur during adolescence; such changes can serve to "activate" the attachment system in ways that parallel the physical separation from caregivers during infancy. This activation can serve as a signal to parents and adolescents, as well, that adjustments need to be made within the parent–adolescent relationship. It was imperative that particular adjustments need to be made to accommodate adolescent needs. Both the parental sensitivity that typically accompanies secure attachment and the level of openness and flexibility between parents and adolescents with regard to evaluating and re-evaluating the attachment relationship can increase the probability that securely attached teens and their parents can successfully recognize and adapt to the ongoing developmental changes. In fact, a secure parent–adolescent relationship should, first acknowledge the teen's efforts as she or he strives for autonomy and, secondly, provide support the adolescent needs while maintaining the relationship (Boykin McElhaney, Allen, Stephenson & Hare, 2006). For example, Joseph Allen and his colleagues (Allen, Kuperminc, & Moore, 2005) found that securely attached adolescents were less likely than those who were insecurely attached to join gangs, become offenders, or use drugs.

Clearly, secure attachment with parents can be an asset for the adolescent, fostering the trust to engage in close relationships with others and laying the foundation for skills in close relationships. But a significant minority of adolescents from strong, supportive families nonetheless struggle in peer relations for a variety of reasons, such as being physically unattractive, maturing late, and experiencing cultural and socio-economic status (SES) discrepancies. On the other hand, some adolescents from troubled families find a positive, fresh start with peer relations that can compensate for their problematic family backgrounds (Berger, 2011).

The adolescent's push for autonomy and responsibility may puzzle many parents. Parents who see their teenager slipping from their grasp may have an urge to take stronger control as the adolescent seeks autonomy and responsibility. Heated emotional exchanges may ensue, with either side calling names, making threats, and doing whatever seems necessary to gain control. Parents may seem frustrated because they expect their teenager to heed their advice, to want to spend time with the family, and to grow up to do what is right. Some bickering may indicate a healthy family, since close relationships almost always include some level of conflict (Smetana, Metzger, & Campione-Barr, 2004).

The ability to attain autonomy and gain control over one's behaviour in adolescence is acquired through appropriate adult reactions to the adolescent's desire for control (Collins & Steinberg, 2006; Soenens et al., 2007). At the onset of adolescence, the average individual does not have the knowledge to make appropriate or mature decisions in all areas of life. As the adolescent pushes for autonomy, the wise adult relinquishes control in those areas in which the adolescent can make reasonable decisions, but continues to guide the adolescent to make reasonable decisions in areas in which the adolescent's knowledge is more limited. Gradually, adolescents acquire the ability to make mature decisions on their own.

Research in many countries has found that teens who remain closely attached to their parents are more likely to be academically successful and enjoy good peer relations (Mayseless & Scharf, 2007). Even while teens are becoming more autonomous they need their parents to provide a safe psychological base.

Balancing Freedom and Control

We have seen that parents play very important roles in adolescent development (Collins & Steinberg, 2006). Although adolescents are moving toward independence, they still need to stay connected with families (Hair et al., 2008).

In adolescence, parental and peer relationships are important sources of support and self-evaluation. These relationships are influential even though they change considerably as the adolescent matures, becomes increasingly independent, and comes to rely on parents and friends in ways different than before. Parental and peer relationships are shaped, as well, by broad cultural values that serve to define family relationships and their importance to the development of self. Whereas many youth in Western societies perceive peer relationships as increasingly important for establishing independence from the family, parents in many non-Western societies remain important sources of adolescent self-evaluations and may even surpass peer influence according to Song, Thompson, and Ferrer (2009).

Cultural studies of close relationships and their impact on adolescent psychological development, particularly those encountered in non-Western societies, can contribute to understanding more closely how social values help to define the significance to the developing person of these relationships. The study by Song, Thompson, and Ferrer (2009) examined age and gender differences related to the quality of attachment with mothers, fathers, and peers. The association of attachment were coupled with measures of self-evaluation among 584 Chinese adolescents in junior high, high school, and university. The findings revealed that in a context of considerable consistency of findings with Western studies, parent–child attachment in adolescents is also influenced by culture-specific practices that influence parent–youth relationships and their meaning to the child.

One philosophical variation among cultures is **locus of control,** *or the perceived extent to which individuals believe they have control over the events that affect them.* Some cultures favour an **external locus of control,** *wherein events that affect individuals are considered to be the result of fate or higher powers.* The community exerts considerable influence such that decisions are made that are for the common good of the family and the community. Those cultures, such as North American, with an **internal locus of control,** *believe that the individual can control life events.* This orientation holds that individuals can control outcomes and should be self-reliant.

The range from a strong external to a strong internal locus of control falls on a broad continuum and shapes behaviour and decisions (Giger & Davidhizar, 2004). For example, in a culture where the locus of control is external, individuals may believe that an illness is the result of fate and must be surrendered to honourably. In another culture, where the orientation is more toward an internal locus of control, individuals may believe they have control over and can cure the disease. Such orientations influence parenting styles as well as the communication patterns between parents and their children. Their optimism affects their health in many ways (Geers, Kosbab, Helfer, Weiland, & Wellman, 2007).

Parent–Adolescent Conflict

The classical Greek philosopher Socrates (469 BC to 399 BC) said, "Children today are tyrants" who "contradict their parents, gobble their food, and terrorize their teachers" (Bibby, 2010). This stereotype of teen behaviour and parent–adolescent conflict has a long history and abounds today. Rarely, however, do the conflicts involve major dilemmas such as drugs or delinquency. Project Canada, 2008, reports that 80 percent of the teens surveyed rate trust and honesty as extremely important. Sixty percent rate politeness and concern for others as very important to them. Most (80 percent) report that they try to stay out of trouble and that they have never been in trouble with the police (Bibby, 2010). So the stereotype really does not fit most teens, in spite of appearances, media reports, and fashion trends such as piercing and body art.

Conflict exists, and much of it involves the everyday events of family life, such as keeping a bedroom clean, dressing neatly, getting home by a certain time, not talking forever on the phone, and not spending so much time on the computer. Such conflict with parents often escalates during early adolescence, remains somewhat stable during the high school years, and then lessens as the adolescent reaches 17 to 20 years of age (Berger, 2011).

The everyday conflicts that characterize parent–adolescent relationships may actually serve a positive developmental function. These minor disputes and negotiations facilitate the adolescent's transition from being dependent on parents to becoming an autonomous individual. For example,

locus of control The perceived extent to which individuals believe they have control over the events that affect them.

external locus of control Events that affect individuals are considered to be the result of fate or higher powers.

internal locus of control The belief that the individual can control life events.

--- **critical** thinking ---

Currently, ease with technology characterizes the differences between many parents and their children. Parents may not be familiar with the social media their teenaged son or daughter visit regularly. On the other hand, some parents are equally savvy. For example, one mother uncovered her son's "anonymous" name and signed into Facebook to carry on a discussion with him and his peers. She believed she was able to understand her son better. When her son learned of her activity, he was furious and accused her of invading his privacy. Did the mother invade her son's privacy, or is Facebook a public space? What can she do to resolve the conflict? In what ways would a family meeting be helpful?

Parent–adolescent conflict may serve a positive developmental function in the adolescent's transition to adulthood.

one of the more consistent findings in the adolescent attachment literature is that when adolescents hold secure attachment states of mind, their interactions with their parents are characterized by healthy autonomy support. That is, the adolescents engage in productive problem-solving discussions that allow divergent opinions to be expressed while remaining engaged in the discussions. Meanwhile, those who are insecure tend to withdraw and disengage from parents when faced with the challenge of adapting to new demands of autonomy (Boykin McElhaney, Allen, Stephenson, & Hare, 2006). It is interesting to note that the socialization field has moved from parent-centred deterministic models to models that assign children an agentic role to direct their own socialization. Children are coming to be viewed as acting in purposeful ways that reflect their ability to interpret and evaluate parental messages and consequently evade intrusions into their personal lives (Parkin & Kuczynski, 2012).

However, no developmentalist would argue that the roles of communication and support are helpful, even essential, in parent–child relationships. The complexity is that some adolescents happily tell their parents about their activities, while others are secretive (Vieno, Nation, Pastore & Santinello, 2009). Meanwhile, most adolescents remain selectively noncommunicative in sharing aspects along with which their parents probably would not approve (Brown & Bakken, 2011). Does the question of secure attachment prevail in these instances?

The old model of parent–adolescent relationships suggested that as adolescents mature, they detach themselves from parents and move into a world of autonomy apart from parents. The old model also suggested that parent–adolescent conflict is intense and stressful throughout adolescence. The new model emphasizes that parents serve as important attachment figures and support systems while adolescents explore a wider, more complex social world. The new model also emphasizes that, in most families, parent–adolescent conflict is moderate rather than severe, and that the everyday negotiations and minor disputes not only are normal, but can also serve the positive developmental function of helping the adolescent make the transition from childhood dependency to adult independence (see Figure 12.2).

It is noteworthy that in some cultures, there is less parent–adolescent conflict than in others. American psychologist Reed Larson (Larson and Verma, 1999) recently spent six months in India studying middle socio-economic status adolescents and their families. He observed that in India, where the orientation to locus of control is external, there seems to be little parent–adolescent conflict, and many families likely would be described as "authoritarian" in Baumrind's categorization. Larson also observed that in India, adolescents do not go through a process of breaking away from their parents, and that parents choose their youths' marital partners.

Peers

Peers play powerful roles in the lives of adolescents (Allen & Antonishak, 2008; Brown et al., 2008). When you think back to your own adolescent years, you probably recall many of your most enjoyable moments as experiences shared with peers. Peer relations undergo important changes in adolescence, including changes in friendships and in peer groups and the beginning of romantic

Figure 12.2

Old and New Models of Parent–Adolescent Relationships

Old Model		New Model
Autonomy, detachment from parents; parent and peer worlds are isolated Intense, stressful conflict throughout adolescence; parent-adolescent relationships are filled with storm and stress on virtually a daily basis		Attachment and autonomy; parents are important support systems and attachment figures; adolescent-parent and adolescent-peer worlds have some important connections Moderate parent-adolescent conflict is common and can serve a positive developmental function; conflict greater in early adolescence

relationships. In middle and late childhood, as we discussed in Chapter 10, the focus of peer relations is on being liked by classmates and being included in games or lunchroom conversations. Being overlooked or, worse yet, being rejected can have damaging effects on children's development that sometimes is carried forward to adolescence (Bukowski, Velasquez, & Brendgen, 2008). We will take a closer look at the role peers play a bit later in the chapter.

Religion

Erikson was especially sensitive to the role of culture in identity development. He pointed out that throughout the world, ethnic groups have struggled to maintain their cultural identities while blending into the dominant culture (Erikson, 1968). Erikson said that this struggle for an inclusive identity, or identity within the larger culture, has been the driving force in the founding of churches, empires, and revolutions throughout history.

Religious and Spiritual Development

In Chapter 11, we described the many positive benefits of service-learning. A number of studies have found that adolescents who are involved in religious institutions are more likely to engage in service-learning than their counterparts who don't participate in religious institutions. Let's explore adolescents' concepts of religion and spirituality, as well as their religious and spiritual experiences.

Religious issues are important to many adolescents, but Reginald Bibby, Director of Project Teen, reports that surveys show a downward trend in religious interest among Christian adolescents. In fact, since 1984, those who self-identify as Christian have decreased by 50 percent, while those who identify as atheists have increased considerably in the same time frame (from 6 to 16 percent), as have the number of teens who say they have no faith at all (up from 12 to 32 percent). In contrast, those self-identifying as Muslim and "other" religions, which include Islam, Hinduism, and Buddhism, have also increased five times since 1984 (Bibby, 2009). According to Statistics Canada (2006a), immigrants comprise 20 percent of the population, and a large percentage are from the Middle East and Asia (Bibby, 2009). In spite of this downward trend, most (85 percent) of the teens interviewed said they would follow religious traditions, particularly those associated with rites of passage such as marriage and death (Bibby, 2010).

The findings of Project Teen illustrate Marcia's statuses in developing religious identity. The Canadian findings also mirror a U.S. developmental study which revealed that religiousness declines between 14 and 20 years of age (Koenig, McGue, & Iacono, 2008). In this study, religiousness was assessed with items such as frequency of prayer, frequency of discussing religious teachings, frequency of deciding moral actions for religious reasons, and the overall importance of religion in everyday life.

Analysis of the World Values Survey of 18- to 24-year-olds revealed that emerging adults in less developed countries were more likely to be religious than their counterparts in more developed countries (Lippman & Keith, 2006). For example, emerging adults' reports of religion being very important in their lives ranged from a low of 0 in Japan to 93 percent in Nigeria, and the belief in God ranged from a low of 40 percent in Sweden to a high of 100 percent in Pakistan.

Religion and Identity Development

As we saw earlier in this chapter, identity development becomes a central focus of adolescence and emerging adulthood (Kroger, 2007). As part of their search for identity, adolescents and emerging adults begin to grapple in more sophisticated, logical ways with such questions such as, "Is there really a God or higher spiritual being, or have I just been believing what my parents and the church imprinted in my mind?" and "What really are my religious views?" In Bibby's words, teens are "post-religious and pre-spiritual" (Bibby, 2010). A recent analysis of the link between identity and spirituality concluded that adolescence and adulthood can serve as gateways to a spiritual identity that "transcends, but not necessarily excludes, the assigned religious identity in childhood" (Templeton & Eccles, 2006, p. 261).

developmental **connection**

Erikson

critical thinking

Religion—whether Buddhist, Christian, Islam, Jewish, Muslim, or other—is a core factor of how we identify ourselves. Quite often religion shapes a number of very important aspects of family life as well as life decisions, including whom we may or may not marry. During adolescence, an individual might question the beliefs and traditions of his or her family, and may choose not to participate or to visit other places of worship. How might Marcia's identity statuses be applied to religious identity in adolescence? How might the MAMA effect be applied to religious identity during one's life? What effects would the adolescent's behaviour have upon the family? Suggest strategies the family can implement to accept such behaviours from the adolescent.

The Positive Role of Religion in Adolescents' Lives

Researchers have found that various aspects of religion are linked with positive outcomes for adolescents (Benson, Roehlkepartain, & Hong, 2008; Good & Willoughby, 2008; Lerner, Roeser, & Phelps, 2008). Religion also plays a role in adolescents' health and whether they engage in problem behaviours (Cotton et al., 2006). For example, in a recent national random sample of more than 2,000 11- to 18-year-olds, those who were higher in religiosity were less likely to smoke, drink alcohol, use marijuana, skip school, participate in delinquent activities, and be depressed than their low-religiosity counterparts (Sinha, Cnaan, & Gelles, 2007). A recent study of Indonesian Muslim 13-year-olds revealed that their religious involvement was linked to their social competence, including positive peer relations, academic achievement, emotional regulation, prosocial behaviour, and self-esteem (French et al., 2008).

Many religious adolescents also internalize their religion's message about caring and concern for people (Ream & Savin-Williams, 2003). For example, in one survey, religious youth were almost three times as likely to engage in community service as non-religious youth (Youniss, McLellan, & Yates, 1999).

MORAL DEVELOPMENT   Moral judgments are influenced both indirectly and directly by parents. Moral development is especially fostered by the openness and emphatic responses of parents to the adolescents (Polan & Taylor, 2011). Adolescents, using learned standards as a guide, learn to form decisions on which to direct their behaviour. During early adolescence, teens are usually at the conventional level of moral development (Polan & Taylor, 2011). They become more rule-oriented, and they begin to care about others. Following this stage of development, adolescents begin to question everything and everyone, which often places them in direct conflict with persons of authority. However, one of the benefits of this transition is that adolescents begin to try out their own values in relationships. By the time they reach adolescence, young people can reason at a higher plane if they have reached Piaget's stage of formal operations (Feldman & Landry, 2014).

- - - - - - developmental **connection** - - - -

Context, Culture, and Ethnicity

←- -

Racial, Ethnic, and Cultural Identity

Each family's socio-economic status, priorities, educational levels, religious beliefs, and even ideas of what is humorous, what is common sense, and what constitutes acceptable behaviour for males and females—these are some of the ingredients of the family's shared understanding of the world around them. Recall from Chapter 1 that context is the setting in which development occurs. This setting is influenced by historical, political, economic, geographic, social, and cultural factors. All of these aspects of socio-cultural contexts influence identity. Not only is each family unique, but individuals within the family unit are also unique. Personal contexts such as genetics, health, interests, talents, perspective, and position within the family are part of the factors that make one sibling different from another. For individuals of differing races, ethnicities, and cultures, adolescence and emerging adulthood are often special junctures in their development (Phinney, 2008; Syed & Azmitia, 2008; Umana-Taylor et al., 2008; Way et al., 2008). Although children are aware of some differences, most individuals consciously confront these aspects of their identities for the first time in adolescence (Statistics Canada, 2012i).

Adolescence is more than a stage of development; it represents a unique culture with common values, challenges, and characteristics. For example, adolescents share specific behavioural aspects associated with culture including their shared language, music, and rituals (Nelson & Nelson, 2010).

As you may recall from Chapter 1, ethnicity and cultural have very different meanings, as does race. **Race** *refers to physical features such a skeletal structure, the shape of the skull, the texture of the hair, and the colour of the skin.* The Canadian census uses the term **visible minority** for people to *identify themselves as neither Aboriginal nor Caucasian.* A person who identifies as a member of a visible minority may be of Asian, African, or Irish decent, and may be Muslim, Christian, or Islamic. **Ethnicity** *is based on cultural heritage, nationality characteristics, race, religion, and language.* One who identifies as Native Canadian or Aboriginal may be Iroquois, Métis, or Inuit. **Culture** *refers to*

race Physical features such a skeletal structure, the shape of the skull, the texture of the hair, and the colour of the skin.

visible minority The term used by the Canadian census for people who are neither Native nor Caucasian.

ethnicity Based on cultural heritage, nationality characteristics, race, religion, and language.

culture The behaviour patterns, beliefs, transmitted values, norms, and life practices of a particular group.

the behaviour patterns, beliefs, transmitted values, norms, and life practices of a particular group. These patterns of behaviours guide decision making and are passed on from generation to generation (Kozier et al., 2010).

For example, although both are Canadian, people from the East Coast have a shared history and understanding of the world that differs from people who live in the Prairie provinces of Alberta, Manitoba, and Saskatchewan. Location, employment histories, and settlement issues are among the factors unique to each area.

Like a very complex symphony, Canada is composed of people from all racial groups and hundreds of ethnic and cultural groups who were either born here or immigrated here. Toronto, one of the most multicultural cities in the world, boasts over 200 distinct ethnic groups and over 140 languages and dialects are spoken (City of Toronto, 1998–2010). As people interact with each other, their personal world-views and their personal identities are challenged. Such integration can be overwhelming at times and may lead to confusion and conflict. Many adolescents resolve this choice by developing a **bicultural identity:** *they identify in some ways with their cultural group and in other ways with the mainstream culture* (Phinney, 2006).

bicultural identity The way adolescents identify in some ways with their cultural group and in other ways with the mainstream culture.

There is growing evidence today that research indicates bicultural individuals who are able to form, strong positive multi-ethnic identities have better self-esteem, fewer mental health problems, and higher academic achievement than their peers with less developed singular (monoculture) ethnic identities (Fuligni, Witkow, & Garcia, 2005; Smokowski & Bacallao, 2007). In fact, developing ethnic and racial identities, whether with mixed ethnic and racial ancestry or across multiple cultural contexts (home and school), is a dynamic life-long process (Marks, Patton, & Garcia Coll, 2011).

Social Exclusion, Assimilation, and Multiculturalism

One of the more important social determinants of health is social exclusion (Mikkonen & Raphael, 2010). Social exclusion refers to situations in which specific groups are denied participation in Canadian life. Social exclusion practices exerted upon recent immigrants are well documented. It creates undesirable living conditions and personal experiences that endanger health. Social exclusion creates in the victims a sense of powerlessness, hopelessness, and depression, all of which further diminish the possibility of inclusion and assimilation into a given society (Mikkonen & Raphael, 2010).

According to Macionis and Gerber (2011), **assimilation** *is a process through which minorities adapt patterns of the dominant culture in a gradual way thus becoming increasingly more similar to the dominant group.* Assimilation involves changing modes of dress, values, religion, language, and even friends. Assimilation involves changes in ethnicity—not race.

assimilation A process by which immigrant groups adapt patterns of dominant groups. It involves changing the mode of dress and values as examples.

Fortunately, Canada embraces the ideal of **multiculturalism,** *recognition of cultural heterogeneity, and mutual respect among culturally diverse groups* (Macionis & Gerber, 2011).

multiculturalism The coexistence of distinct ethnic and cultural groups in the same society.

Canada's policy of multiculturalism preserves the right of choice, leading to what many identify as the Canadian mosaic. In other words, individuals can choose the aspects of their heritage they wish to leave behind and those they wish to preserve. The kind of controversy that can arise is illustrated by the cultural practice of some Islamic women who choose to wear *burqas*, outer garments that cover the entire body except for the eyes and hands. Those who support assimilation might argue that the burqa should not be worn, whereas those who hold a multiculturalist viewpoint are more likely to argue that wearing a burqa is a matter of personal choice. Whether we are talking about patterns of location, intermarriage, youth conflict, or employment equity, issues of race, ethnicity, and culture are in the forefront (Kozier et al. 2010).

People who identify as being a visible minority cite racism, discrimination, and bigotry as substantial problems influencing their relationships with authority figures, such as police, and their ability to find employment. Often these problems lead to feelings of alienation and health problems. For example, Aboriginal youths experience six times the national rates for suicide and drug addiction. Young immigrants voice the belief that Canada's tolerance lessens the problems of racism, but feel that efforts to promote tolerance and understanding should focus on schools and be aimed at staff, administrators, and teachers, as well as students.

Part of the development of a sense of self is the acquisition of an ethnic identity. Some adolescents achieve this by learning the customs of their heritage.

The indicators of identity change often differ for each succeeding generation (Phinney & Ong, 2007). First-generation immigrants are likely to be secure in their identities and unlikely to change much; they may or may not develop a new identity. The degree to which they begin to feel "Canadian" appears to be related to whether or not they learn English, develop social networks beyond their ethnic group, and become culturally competent in their new country. Second-generation immigrants are more likely to think of themselves as "Canadians," possibly because citizenship is granted at birth. Their ethnic identity is likely to be linked to retention of their language of origin and social networks. In the third and later generations, the issues become more complex. Historical, contextual, and political factors that are unrelated to acculturation may affect the extent to which members of later generation retain their ethnic identities. Racism and discrimination may further influence how ethnic identity is retained.

Researchers are increasingly finding that a positive ethnic identity is linked to positive outcomes for adolescents (Umana-Taylor, 2006). For example, in one study ethnic identity was related to higher school engagement and lower aggression (Van Buren & Graham, 2003). In a recent study, Navajo adolescents' affirmation and belonging to their ethnic heritage was linked to higher self-esteem, school connectedness, and social functioning (Jones & Galliher, 2007). Another study found that exploration was an important part of establishing a secure sense of one's ethnic identity, which in turn was linked to a positive attitude toward one's own group and other groups (Whitehead, Ainsworth, Wittig, & Gadino, 2009).

Ethnicity, Race, and Socio-Economic Status

Much of the research related to ethnicity and socio-economic status has shown a levelling out of economic well-being among ethnic groups, especially those of English and European heritage (Gee & Prus, 2000). What does stand out, however, is that visible minorities and immigrant groups are overrepresented in the lower socio-economic levels of society (Gee & Prus, 2000; Healey, 2009; Rowley, Kurtz-Costes, & Cooper, 2009).

Not all visible minority or immigrant families are poor; however, poverty contributes to the stressful life experiences of many (Leon-Guerrero, 2009). Thus, many adolescents experience multiple disadvantages: (1) prejudice, discrimination, and bias, and (2) the stressful effects of poverty.

Although some visible minority youth have middle-income backgrounds, economic advantage does not entirely enable them to escape the prejudice, discrimination, and bias associated with being a member of a minority group (Banks, 2008; Harris & Graham, 2007). Many visible minority youth report incidents of racial profiling while shopping or in interactions with the police.

Rites of Passage

rite of passage A ceremony or ritual that marks an individual's transition of from one status to another.

Culture plays an important role in identity. Many cultures signal the transition from childhood to adulthood by a **rite of passage,** *a ceremony or ritual that marks an individual's transition from one status to another.* Some societies have elaborate ceremonies that signal the adolescent's move to maturity and achievement of adult status (Kottak, 2004). Most rites of passage focus on the transition to adult status. To a Canadian youth, such a rite of passage might be a religious celebration, such as the Jewish bar or bat mitzvah, or Catholic confirmation. Such events as obtaining a driver's licence, being of legal age to drink alcohol, being of legal age to vote, or getting married are fairly universal indicators of the increasing responsibility associated with the transition to adulthood. Graduations from high school, college, or university are other culture-wide celebrations of maturity.

In some cultures, rites of passage are the avenue through which adolescents gain access to sacred adult practices, knowledge, and sexuality. These rites often involve dramatic practices intended to facilitate the adolescent's separation from the immediate family, especially the mother. The transformation is usually characterized by some form of ritual death and rebirth, or by means of contact with the spiritual world. In some cases, bonds are forged between the adolescent and the adult instructors through shared rituals, hazards, and secrets which allow the adolescent to enter the adult world. This kind of ritual provides a forceful and discontinuous entry into the adult world at a time when the adolescent is perceived to be ready for the change.

An especially rich tradition of rites of passage for adolescents has prevailed in African cultures, especially sub-Saharan Africa. Recall Sallieu, the adolescent in the opening vignette. Although well-educated, part of his decision to leave Sierra Leone was related to the rite of passage his father insisted on to prove the youth's transition from boyhood to manhood. In Sallieu's particular ethnic tribe, part of the rite of passage included the cutting of the backs of young men with knives (Dainkeh, 2010, interview). Under the influence of Western industrialized culture, many of these rites are disappearing today, although they are still prevalent especially in locations where formal education is not readily available.

Traditions and Changes in Adolescence around the World

Today, countless variations of expectations of adolescent behaviour are evident around the world. For example, North American culture encourages individuals to accentuate the positive (Kim, Schimmack, & Oishi, 2012). Meanwhile, self-enhancement is less pronounced in East Asian culture (Tsai, Levenson, & McCoy, 2006). Alternatively, however, we can observe many similar cultural practices around the world—walking on the streets of Seoul, South Korea, Kuala Lumpur, Malaysia, or Cairo, Egypt, we see young people wearing jeans, listening to familiar pop music, and reading ads for many of the same products used in Canada (Macionis & Gerber, 2011). English is rapidly emerging as the preferred second language around the world. Satellite-based communication enables individuals to experience sights and sounds of events taking place tens of thousands of kilometres away—often they happen at home, too (Macionis & Gerber, 2011). Are similar happenings occurring to adolescents as well? It is important to note that whether it is text-messaging, using Facebook, or tweeting, adolescents are always on the cutting edge of technology (Nelson & Nelson, 2010).

Thus, depending on the culture being observed, adolescence may involve many different experiences (Strohmeier & Schmitt-Rodermund, 2008). Some cultures have retained their traditions regarding adolescence, but rapid global change is altering the experience of adolescence in many places, presenting new opportunities and challenges to young people's health and well-being. Around the world, adolescents' experiences differ.

Health

Adolescent health and well-being have improved in some respects, but not in others. Overall, fewer adolescents around the world die from infectious diseases and malnutrition now than in the past (UNICEF, 2008). However, a number of adolescent health-compromising behaviours (especially illicit drug use and unprotected sex) are increasing in frequency (Blum & Nelson-Mmari, 2004). Extensive increases in the rates of HIV in adolescents have occurred in many sub-Saharan countries (UNICEF, 2008).

Gender

Around the world, the experiences of male and female adolescents continue to be quite different (Brown & Larson, 2002). Except for a few regions, such as Japan, the Philippines, and Western countries, males have far greater access to educational opportunities than females (UNICEF, 2008). In many countries, adolescent females have less freedom than males to pursue a variety of careers and engage in various leisure activities. Gender differences in sexual expression are widespread, especially in India, Southeast Asia, Latin America, and Arab countries, where there are far more restrictions on the sexual activity of adolescent females than on males. These gender differences do appear to be narrowing over time. Contemporary adolescents often have friends of the other sex who are not their lovers (Berger, 2010). More recently, a large Dutch study of high school students found that 1 in 12 teens stated that they were attracted to individuals of the same sex as themselves (Bos, Sandfort, de Bruyn & Hakvoort, 2008).

These Congolese Kota boys painted their faces as part of a rite of passage to adulthood. **What kinds of rites of passage do Canadian adolescents have?**

critical thinking

Immigration from one country to another is a complex and challenging endeavour. Not only do individuals and families have to make considerable adjustments, so too do our urban and rural communities. What are some of the adjustments immigrants must make? How have communities responded to the needs of newcomers? Outline a welcoming program for immigrant families in a rural community. What resources would you be able to offer such families?

In some countries, educational and career opportunities for women are expanding, and control over adolescent girls' romantic and sexual relationships is weakening. As well, the laws that exist in Canada today that are intended to protect women from spousal abuse and rape do not exist in many parts of the world.

Family

Several researchers have focused specifically on the parent–child differences between young people in Hong Kong and the United States or Australia. In every culture, adolescents seem to benefit from increasing autonomy, but parents in the United States allow more independence than do parents in Hong Kong (Qin, Pomerantz, & Wang, 2009). By age 18, many teenagers appreciate their parents, who have learned to allow more independence (Masche, 2010). Furthermore, in the United States, Hong Kong, and Australia alike, parent–adolescent communication and encouragement benefit the youths, insulating them somewhat from depression, suicide, and low self-esteem and assisting them to have high achievements and aspirations (Kwok & Shek, 2010).

Education

The ratio of school enrollment attendance for both girls and boys in primary and secondary schools has rising dramatically in recent years. As might be expected, greater enrollment rates are found among girls. The enrollment gap between boys and girls is actually narrowing around the world. In Latin America and the Caribbean, this gap is virtually eliminated. However, in other countries, such as India and Ethiopia, the enrollment of boys is higher (Murphy & Carr, 2007). Unfortunately, two-thirds of children in Africa do not attend secondary school (UNESCO, 2011). Almost everywhere, education is compulsory until at least the age of 12 (UNESCO, 2008). School attendance is an important developmental variable. Studies of classroom-level influences suggest that development is optimized when students are provided with emotionally and cognitive challenging tasks in a supportive environment (Eccles & Roesner, 2006).

Work

There is a trend for youth to stay longer in school. From age 16 it now takes students 8 years to complete the transition from high school to regular employment (Franke, 2003). Global economic work depends upon highly educated workers. Partly because political leaders recognize that educated adults advance national wealth and health, every nation is increasing the number of students in secondary schools (Berger, 2014). However, there are certain stipulations in Canada. For example, an adolescent may not work more than 2 hours on a school day, not more than 8 hours on a non-school day, and not between 9:00 p.m. and 6:00 a.m. (Government of Alberta, 2011).

Peers

Some cultures give peers a stronger role in adolescence than others (Brown et al., 2008). In most Western nations, peers figure prominently in adolescents' lives, in some cases taking on roles that are otherwise assumed by parents. Among street youth in South America, the peer network serves as a surrogate family that supports survival in dangerous and stressful settings. In other regions of the world, such as in Arab countries, peer relations are restricted, especially for girls (Booth, 2002).

Watkins, Larson, and Sullivan (2008) have examined how adolescents spend their time in work, play, and developmental activities such as school. What North American adolescents have in greater quantities than adolescents in other industrialized countries is discretionary time (Larson & Wilson, 2004). About 40 to 50 percent of an adolescent's waking hours (not counting summer vacations) is spent in discretionary activities, compared with 25 to 35 percent in East Asia and 35 to 45 percent in Europe. Whether this additional discretionary time is a liability or an asset for adolescents, of course, depends on how the time is used.

Although relaxation and social interaction are important aspects of life, spending large numbers of hours per week in unchallenging activities is unlikely to foster cognitive and socio-emotional development. Structured voluntary activities may provide more promise for adolescent development than unstructured time, especially if adults give responsibility to adolescents, challenge them, and provide competent guidance in these activities (Larson et al., 2007; Watkins, Larson, & Sullivan, 2008).

In sum, adolescents' lives are characterized by a combination of change and tradition. Researchers have found both similarities and differences in the experiences of adolescents in different countries (Larson & Wilson, 2004).

Sexual Orientation and Identity

Freud and Erikson believed that during adolescence, individuals make the transition from sexual latency to mature sexual behaviour. For heterosexuals, social and educational supports are in place. Role models, course materials, peer validation, and media portrayals mirror and support the heterosexual, non-transgendered and non-intersexed young person's emerging sexual identity. For the homosexual, intersexual, or transsexual youth, the supports are quite different, or in many rural areas, non-existent. Additionally, the young person may feel that the act of accessing whatever supports may be available would pose great personal risk.

Sexual identity *is the individual's inner conviction about his or her male or femaleness.* **Sexual orientation** *is related to the individual's sexual interests.* That is, no accepted explanation currently exists why some adolescents develop a heterosexual orientation. Most experts believe that sexual orientation develops out of a complex interplay of genetic, physiological, and environmental factors (LeVay & Valente, 2003).

Gender identity *refers to the individual's sense of belonging to a particular sexual category (male, female, lesbian, gay, and so on).* Gender roles or scripts refer to behaviours that meet widely shared expectations about how members of a particular sexual category are supposed to behave (Brym, Roberts, Lie, & Rytina, 2013).

An individual who is either *transgendered* or *intersexed* develops a more complex schemata, in that all the imposed messages don't quite fit the individual's self-understanding. The transgendered individual is anatomically male or female; however, they often feel they are "trapped" in the wrong body. They may undergo surgeries and hormonal therapies to obtain the body with which they most identify emotionally, psychologically, and socially. Recall from Chapter 4 that approximately 4 percent of the population is intersexed, born with male and female features (Ontario Human Rights Commission, 2006–2007). They will feel pressured to be male or female, or perhaps parents will make the decision for them before the intersexed individuals know what is best for themselves. Many adolescents who are attracted to individuals of the same sex are well adjusted as well as society accepts them. Homosexuality is no longer considered a psychological disorder by any of the major psychological or medical associations (Davison, 2005; van Wormer & McKinney, 2003). Meanwhile, many who are confused about their sexuality try to hide their identity. Binge drinking, drug addiction, and suicidal thoughts are more common (MMWR, 2011). Gay and lesbian teens may be rejected by their family or peers or even be assaulted by others (Koh & Ross, 2006; Lester, 2006).

To this point, we have explored a number of ideas about family, religion, race, ethnicity, culture, and sexual orientation in adolescence. For a review, see the **Reach Your Learning Objectives** section at the end of this chapter.

sexual identity An individual's inner conviction about his or her male or femaleness.

sexual orientation An individual's sexual interests; that is, whether or not a person is sexually and romantically attracted to others of the same sex, the opposite sex, or both sexes.

gender identity Refers to the individual's sense of belonging to a particular sexual category.

Friendship

LO3 Outline the changes that occur in peer relations and dating during adolescence.

In Chapter 10, we discussed the fact that children spend more time with their peers in middle and late childhood than in early childhood. Friendships become increasingly important in middle and late childhood, and relationships with peers are a strong motivation for most children. Advances in cognitive development during middle and late childhood also enable children to take the perspective of their peers and friends more readily, and their social skills increase.

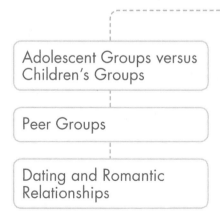

Adolescent Groups versus Children's Groups

Peer Groups

Dating and Romantic Relationships

Figure 12.3

Developmental Changes in Self-Disclosing Conversations

Self-disclosing conversations with friends increased dramatically in adolescence while declining in an equally dramatic fashion with parents. However, self-disclosing conversations with parents began to pick up somewhat during the college years. The measure of self-disclosure involved a five-point rating scale completed by the children and youth with a higher score representing greater self-disclosure. The data shown represent the means for each age group.

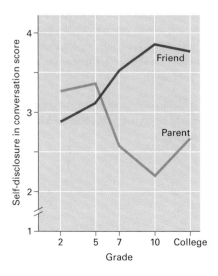

Remember leaving elementary school full of confidence and self-assurance, only to enter junior high school full of trepidation? This reflects the "top-dog" phenomenon discussed in Chapter 11. The swing from feeling great to feeling just plain terrible could occur within seconds, depending on the interactions that may have influenced the individual. Peers play an important role by helping each other to fit in, not be alone, and negotiate their way through high school. As you just read, for adolescents whose sexual orientation is homosexual, lesbian, or bisexual, and for those whose sexual identity is transsexual or intersexed, the socialization process and the pressure to fit in may be quite painful due to homophobic behaviours and feelings that heterosexual youth, sorting out their sexual identities, may have.

Adolescent Groups versus Children's Groups

Children's groups differ from adolescent groups in several important ways. The members of children's groups often are friends or neighbourhood acquaintances, and their groups usually are not as formalized as many adolescent groups. During the adolescent years, groups tend to include a broader array of members. In other words, adolescents other than friends or neighbourhood acquaintances often are members of adolescent groups. New friendships emerge.

Harry Stack Sullivan (1953) was the most influential theorist to discuss the importance of adolescent friendship. He believed that friends are important in shaping development. Everyone has basic social needs, such as the need for tenderness (secure attachment), playful companionship, social acceptance, intimacy, and sexual relations. Whether or not these needs are fulfilled largely determines our emotional well-being. For example, if the need for playful companionship goes unmet, then we become bored and depressed; if the need for social acceptance is not met, we suffer a lowered sense of self-worth (Sullivan, 1953; Buhrmester, 2005).

Many of Sullivan's ideas have withstood the test of time (Buhrmester, 2005). For example, adolescents report disclosing intimate and personal information to their friends more often than do younger children (Buhrmester, 1998) (see Figure 12.3). Adolescents also say they depend more on friends than on parents to satisfy their needs for companionship, reassurance of worth, and intimacy. The ups and downs of experiences with friends shape adolescents' well-being (Berndt, 2002).

The characteristics of friends have an important influence on adolescent development (Crosnoe et al., 2008; Rubin, Fredstrom, & Bowker, 2008). A recent study revealed that friends' grade-point averages were important positive attributes (Cook, Deng, & Morgano, 2007). Friends' grade-point averages were a consistent predictor of positive school achievement and also were linked to a lower level of negative behaviour in areas such as drug abuse and acting out.

Although most adolescents develop friendships with individuals who are close to their own age, some adolescents become best friends with younger or older individuals. Do older friends encourage adolescents to engage in delinquent behaviour or early sexual behaviour? A recent study also revealed that over time, from Grade 6 through Grade 10, girls were more likely to have older male friends, which places some girls on a developmental trajectory for engaging in problem behaviour (Poulin & Pedersen, 2007). Many aspects of the search for identity have become more arduous than when Erikson first described them. Developmentalists still believe that teens struggle through the identity crisis, but it now seems that attaining autonomy and achieving identity before the age of 18 is somewhat unlikely (Kroger, Martinussen, & Marcia, 2010).

Adolescents have embraced online social networking. Many teens make themselves vulnerable to embarrassment and damage their credibility or even become victims because of unwise online postings (Patchin & Hinduja, 2010). However, on a positive note, emerging identity is an important aspect of every adolescent's development. Using social networking sites allows adolescents to assert their identity in a unique way, checking out what their friends think of their creative endeavours (Clarke, 2009).

Peer Groups

Peers exert both positive and negative pressure. One the one hand, teens join school clubs, community organizations, and teams in which they work toward a common goal, perhaps raising money for a charitable organization or putting on a school play. On the other hand, young girls may want to be thin and young boys may want to be muscular. Some may fear being bullied or may become bullies.

According to PHAC (2012d), bullying is a relationship problem. Bullying is a form of repeated aggression in which a young person is intentionally harassed or harmed. Bullying can impact the physical, emotional, and social health of a young person (Lemstra, Nielson, Rogers, Thompson, & Moraros, 2012). Numerous cases have been reported in the media in which suicide, or attempted suicide, has been attributed to bullying (Klomek, Sourander, & Gould, 2010). Many categories of bullying exist, such as physical, relational, verbal, and electronic (CCL, 2008). Electronic, or "cyber" bullying is similar to relational and verbal bullying, but it occurs online. The Internet has become the new playground, and there are no limits. Victimization on the Internet through cyberbullying is increasing in frequency and scope; electronic bullies can remain "virtually" anonymous (Enough-Is-Enough, 2009–2013). On an international scale, of 35 countries, Canada has the 9th highest rate of bullying among 13-year-olds (CCL, 2008). Recently, reports indicate that at least one in three adolescent students have reported being bullied (CIHR, 2012a).

A large Canadian study found, in a sample of school children after they had participated in a school-based anti-bullying program (Totten, 2004), that educational interventions consisting of lectures and videos, although easy to administer, simply do not work. What appears to be somewhat effective are whole-school interventions that include sanctions, teacher training, classroom curriculum, conflict resolution training, and individual counselling (Vreeman & Carroll, 2007).

Peer Pressure

Peers can be more helpful than harmful especially in early and middle adolescence. During that time the biological and social stresses can be overwhelming (Nelson & DeBecker, 2008). A recent study revealed that 14 to 18 years of age is an especially important time for developing the ability to stand up for what one believes in and resist peer pressure to do otherwise (Steinberg & Monahan, 2007). Monahan, Steinberg, and Cauffman argue that after age 20 the impact of peers disappears because individuals become increasingly resistant to peer influence. Dumas, Ellis, and Wolfe (2012) conducted a study to examine identity development as a moderator of the relation between peer group pressure and control, and adolescents' engagement in risk behaviours. These investigators concluded that in more controlling peer groups, adolescents with greater identity commitment engaged in fewer risk behaviours than adolescents with lower identity commitment. Therefore, identity development may be an appropriate agent to discourage the negative effects of peer pressure in high-risk adolescents. The importance of identity development for adolescents cannot be overestimated. Identity development can be fostered with supportive families that encourage adolescent individuality and who, through quality interactions, encourage opinion-sharing and expose youth to different perspectives on important issues (Perosa, Perosa, & Tam, 2002). In fact, Oyserman and Destin (2010) have demonstrated that the identity construction of adolescents can be modified through short term in-class and after-school intervention programs.

Cliques and Crowds

Cliques exist in schools, creating tension between the adolescent's desire to belong and his or her desire to be an individual. The conflict between conformity and individualism is demonstrated in tastes in fashion, music, language, and behaviour, and often is dictated by the clique (Brown, 2003). The focus of the clique may be sports, popularity, drugs, rowdy behaviour, academics, or friendship emerging from childhood. Pressures to diet, smoke, drink, have sex, drive recklessly, join a club, or go to a particular movie or concert are all part of the powerful influence of cliques.

A crowd is a larger group of adolescents who share common interests. Cliques and crowds provide social control and social support, via comments, admiration, and isolation. For instance, one study in the Midwest United States found that "tough" and "alternative" crowds felt that teenagers should behave as they want to, whereas the "prep" crowd thought that parental authority carried most weight (Daddis, 2010).

Figure 12.4

Age of Onset of Romantic Activity

In this study, announcing that "I like someone" occurred earliest, followed by going out with the same person three or more times, having an exclusive relationship for over two months, and finally planning an engagement or marriage (which characterized only a very small percentage of participants by Grade 12) (Buhrmester, 2001).

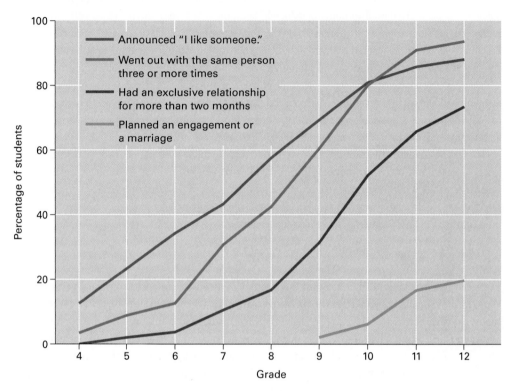

Dating and Romantic Relationships

Adolescents spend considerable time either dating or thinking about dating (Furman & Simon, 2008). Dating can be a form of recreation, a source of status, a setting for learning about close relationships, as well as a way of finding a mate. Regardless of racial, cultural, or ethnic backgrounds or gender, romantic relationships in adolescence form the initial steps toward the development of intimacy and commitments that characterize adult relationships (Connolly & McIsaac, 2009).

Developmental Changes in Dating

Can you remember confiding to a friend in middle school or junior high that you "liked" someone? Or what it was like when you first had an exclusive relationship with someone, "going out" with that person and only that person? Around Grade 10, half of adolescents had a romantic relationship that lasted two months or longer. By Grade 12, a quarter of adolescents still had not had a romantic relationship that lasted two months or longer (see Figure 12.4). One study found that 35 percent of 15- to 16-year-olds and almost 60 percent of 17- and 18-year-olds had had dating relationships that endured for 11 months or longer (Carver, Joyner, & Udry, 2003).

The functions of dating and romantic relationships also tend to change over the course of adolescence. Young adolescents are likely to see romantic relationships not as a way of fulfilling attachment or sexual needs, but as a context for exploring how attractive they are, how they should romantically interact with someone, and how all of this looks to the peer group (Brown, 1999). In fact, romantic relationships form an integral part of adolescent development. Awakening sexuality and passionate attraction are experienced for the first time in adolescence, and are markers of the healthy transition from childhood to adulthood (Connolly & McIsaac, 2009).

Cyberdating

In their early exploration of romantic relationships, today's adolescents often find comfort in numbers and begin hanging out together in mixed-sex groups (O'Sullivan et al., 2007). Sometimes they just hang out at someone's house or get organized enough to get someone to drive them to a mall or a movie. Or they may try *cyberdating*—"dating" over the Internet—as another alternative to traditional dating. Cyberdating is popular especially among middle school students. Of course, cyberdating can be dangerous, since one does not really know who is at the other end of the computer link. By the time they reach high school and are able to drive, most adolescents are more interested in real-life dating.

Recently, the term "sexting" came to existence. This term refers to a combination of sex and texting (SIECCAN Newsletter, 2011). Many young people choose to display information about their sexuality and sexual lives by indicating their sexual orientation on their social networking profile. They post stories and poems about sexual desires and experiences on blogs. In addition, some share nude or semi-nude images of themselves. They use either social networking sites or mobile phones ("sexting") (Brown, Keller, & Stern, 2009). Realistically, certain forms of sexting may violate Canadian child pornography laws, when it involves nude images of individuals under the age of 18 (SIECCAN Newsletter, 2011).

More worrisome is the possibility that the display of sexual content online can lead to an increased probability of teens being victimized online. Studies show that sex partners who meet online tend to engage in high-risk sexual behaviours, and are more vulnerable in acquiring sexually transmitted infections than are partners who meet through conventional means (McFarlane, Ross, & Elford, 2004). However, despite the high level of public concerns about sexting, very little research has been conducted into the contexts in which sexting actually occurs (Albury & Crawford, 2012).

Socio-Cultural Contexts and Dating

The socio-cultural context exerts a powerful influence on adolescents' dating patterns. Values and religious beliefs of people of various cultures often dictate the age at which dating begins, how much freedom is allowed in dating, whether dates must be chaperoned by adults or parents, and the roles of males and females in dating. For example, parents of Indian and Islamic cultures have more conservative standards regarding adolescent dating than parents in Canadian culture. Dating may be a source of cultural conflict for many immigrants and their families who have come from cultures in which dating is non-existent, begins at a later age, allows little freedom in dating, requires that dates are chaperoned, or especially restricts adolescent girls' dating.

Dating and Adjustment

Researchers have linked dating and romantic relationships with various measures of how well-adjusted adolescents are (Friedlander et al., 2007). Not surprisingly, one study of Grade 10 adolescents found that those who dated were more likely than those who did not date to be accepted by their peers and to be perceived as more physically attractive (Furman, Ho, & Low, 2005). Another recent study of 14- to 19-year-olds found that adolescents who were not involved in a romantic relationship had more social anxiety than their counterparts who were dating or romantically involved (La Greca & Harrison, 2005).

Dating and romantic relationships at an unusually early age have been linked with several problems. Early dating and "going with" someone is associated with adolescent pregnancy and problems at home and school (Florsheim, Moore, & Edgington, 2003). However, Grade 10 adolescents who dated also had more externalized problems, such as delinquency, and engaged in substance use (as well as genital sexual behaviour) more than their counterparts who did not date (Furman, Ho, & Low, 2005). A recent study of adolescent girls revealed that a higher frequency of dating was linked to having depressive symptoms and emotionally unavailable parents (Steinberg & Davila, 2008). Another recent study of adolescent girls found that those who engaged in co-rumination (excessive discussion of problems with friends) were more likely to be involved in a romantic relationship, and together co-rumination and romantic involvement predicted an increase in depressive symptoms (Starr & Davila, 2008).

To this point, we have discussed a number of ideas about friendship in adolescence. For a review, see the **Reach Your Learning Objectives** section at the end of this chapter.

Adolescent Problems

LO4 Analyze adolescent problems in socio-emotional development, and the causes of the problems.

In Chapter 11, we described adolescent problems: substance abuse, sexually transmitted infections and diseases, and eating disorders. Here, we will examine the problems of youth violence and gangs, as well as some of the causes and some of the solutions. First, however, we will examine the recent research on brain development in adolescence, as it may help explain why most teens do a few stupid things, while only a few get into serious trouble.

Young Offenders

Images from American newspaper accounts and movies have strongly influenced the way the phenomenon of youth violence and gangs is defined in Canada. However, the youth gang problem in the United States bears little resemblance to what is going on in most Canadian communities. The Youth Criminal Justice Act, which replaced the Young Offenders Act in 2003, is a key part of Canada's Youth Justice Renewal Initiative. The principles of the youth criminal justice system are to prevent crime, to rehabilitate and reintegrate offenders into society, and to ensure meaningful consequences for offences committed by young people. These principles underline the values, rights, and responsibilities of both society and young people in relation to youth crime.

young offenders Young people between the ages of 12 and 18 who commit criminal acts.

Young offenders *are those young people between the ages of 12 and 18 who commit criminal acts.* The Youth Criminal Justice Act defines a youth as an individual who, in the absence of evidence to the contrary, appears to be between 12 and 18 years of age. A child is defined as any person who, in the absence of evidence to the contrary, appears to be under 12. If the Crown successfully applies to the court, children between the ages of 10 and 12 who commit criminal acts may be dealt with as young criminals and be sentenced under this Act; as well, young people 14 years of age or more who are convicted of offences punishable by more than two years in jail may receive adult sentences. Violent crimes that fall into this category include murder, attempted murder, manslaughter, and aggravated sexual assault (Youth Criminal Justice Act, 2003). The range of crimes is extensive, from harassment, threatening, theft, "swarming" (which involves groups of young people victimizing individuals, often stealing items of clothing, such as shoes or jackets), or "wilding" (which involves indiscriminate acts of violence perpetrated by groups of young people). Date rape, sexual assault, and hate/bias crimes can range from verbal or psychological to physical threats or a combination of all three.

Youth Violence

Youth violence is a special concern. Gangs exist in every Canadian city, with the average age of gang members being 17 to 18 years. Gangs often engage in violent and criminal activities and use these activities as an indication of gang identity and loyalty. Between 1990 and 1999, the number of girls participating in gangs doubled (Ambert, 2007). A distinction is made between early-onset—before age 11—and late-onset—after 11—antisocial behaviour. Early-onset antisocial behaviour is associated with more negative developmental outcomes than late-onset antisocial behaviour (Schulenberg & Zarrett, 2006). Early-onset antisocial behaviour is more likely to persist into emerging adulthood and is associated with more mental health and relationship problems (Loeber et al., 2007).

Street Youth

Street youth are young people who have left home and live "on the street," in shelters or abandoned buildings ("squats"), primarily because the street seems a safer place than the home. Many migrate to cities from smaller communities. Not all are homeless; some live with their families at least part of the time. According to the McCreary Centre Society, street youth in Vancouver have, at some time, experienced physical or sexual abuse, and most either have run away or been kicked out of the home. About half the youth have addiction problems, and about 25 percent are involved in the sex trade. The problems that lead youth to the street begin long before adolescence.

Key findings of the McCreary Centre Society's report (2001), *No Place to Call Home: A Profile of Street Youth in British Columbia*, include:

- Over one-quarter of street youth have attempted suicide in the past year.
- Over one-third have been in government care, including foster care or group homes, and nearly one-half have spent time in a custody centre.
- Two-thirds say they are currently attending school, although most street youth have been expelled or suspended from school at some time.

Despite their apparent alienation from school and family, many street youth continue to have hope for a better life and reach out to adults for guidance.

Immigrant and refugee youth may face a double challenge in the transition from adolescence to adulthood. Not only are they confronted with the adjustment to adulthood, but they also must deal with the complexities of adapting to a new culture, one which may have been harsh to their self-esteem. Some of these young people may choose to join gangs to satisfy their unmet emotional, psychological, or social needs. Gangs often target those who are, or are thought to be, homosexual or lesbian.

Causes of Delinquency

Researchers have proposed many causes of delinquency, including heredity, identity problems, community influences, and family experiences. Erik Erikson (1968), for example, points out that adolescents whose development has restricted them from acceptable social roles or made them feel that they cannot measure up to the demands placed on them may choose a negative identity. Adolescents with a negative identity may find support for their delinquent image among peers, reinforcing the negative identity. For Erikson, delinquency is an attempt to establish an identity, although a negative one.

Economic realities may play a part in antisocial behaviours. Canada has a growing number of working-poor families where the parent or parents are working several part-time jobs to make ends meet, leaving little time and energy left for their family (Dodge, Coie, & Lynam, 2006; Farrington, 2004; Flannery et al., 2003). Among the risk factors that increase the likelihood an adolescent will become a gang member are disorganized neighbourhoods characterized by economic hardship, having other family members in a gang, drug use, lack of family support, and peer pressure (Ambert, 2007). Furthermore, adolescents in communities with high crime rates observe many models who engage in criminal activities (Loeber et al., 2007). These communities may be characterized by poverty, unemployment, and feelings of alienation toward the rest of society (Byrnes et al., 2007). Quality schooling, educational funding, and organized neighbourhood activities may also be lacking in these communities (Molnar et al., 2007).

Certain characteristics of family support systems are also associated with delinquency (Cavell et al., 2007; Feinberg et al., 2007). Parents of delinquents are less skilled in discouraging antisocial behaviour and in encouraging skilled behaviour than are parents of non-delinquents. Parental monitoring of adolescents is especially important in determining whether an adolescent becomes a delinquent (Ambert, 2007; Laird et al., 2008). Family discord and inconsistent and inappropriate discipline are also associated with delinquency (Bor, McGee, & Fagan, 2004). A recent study revealed that being physically abused in the first five years of life was linked to a greater risk of delinquency in adolescence (Lansford et al., 2007).

An increasing number of studies have found that siblings can have a strong influence on delinquency (Bank, Burraston, & Snyder, 2004). In one study, high levels of hostile sibling relationships and older sibling delinquency were linked with younger sibling delinquency in both brother and sister pairs (Slomkowski et al., 2001). Finally, having delinquent peers greatly increases the risk of becoming delinquent (Bukowski, Brendgen, & Vitaro, 2007). For example, a study found that peer rejection and having deviant friends at 7 to 13 years of age were linked with increased delinquency at 14 to 15 years of age (Vitaro, Pedersen, & Brendgen, 2007). Also, another recent study revealed that association with deviant peers was linked to a higher incidence of delinquency in male African American adolescents (Bowman, Prelow, & Weaver, 2007).

Other causes of problematic and delinquent behaviour are thought to include the swift rise in visual media, including violent computer games, materialism, and consumerism (Ambert, 2007).

developmental **connection**

Erikson

Figure 12.5

The Antecedents of Becoming a Young Offender

Antecedent	Association with Delinquency	Description
Identity	Negative identity	Erikson believes delinquency occurs because the adolescent fails to resolve a role identity. This failure is connected to a variety of factors in the person's life, not the least of which is relationship with family.
Self-control	Low degree	Some children and adolescents fail to acquire the essential controls that others have acquired during the process of growing up.
Age	Early initiation	Early appearance of antisocial behaviour is associated with serious offences later in adolescence. However, not every child who acts out becomes a delinquent.
Sex	Males	Boys engage in more antisocial behaviour than girls do, although the number of girls participating in gangs doubled between 1990 and 1999.
Expectations for education and school grades	Low expectations and low grades	Adolescents who become delinquents often have low educational expectations and low grades. Their verbal abilities are often weak. Due to a variety of circumstances such as poverty, for example, the teen may not see a bright future for him or herself.
Parental influences	Monitoring (low), support (low), discipline (ineffective)	Young offenders often come from families in which parents rarely monitor their adolescents, provide them with little support, and discipline them ineffectively.
Peer influences	Heavy influence, low resistance	Having peers who break the law greatly increases the risk of breaking the law.
Socio-economic status	Low	Serious offences are committed more frequently by lower-class males who, because of the stress of poverty, may not see a bright future for themselves.
Neighbourhood quality	Urban, high crime, high mobility	Communities often breed crime. Living in a high-crime area, which also is characterized by poverty and dense living conditions, increases the probability that a child will become a young offender. These communities often have grossly inadequate schools.

developmental **connection**

Bandura

critical thinking

Recall Bandura's social cognitive theory from Chapter 2. How might personal cognitive factors, behaviour, and environment interact and contribute to the delinquency of a younger sibling? In what ways is role modelling involved in developing delinquent behaviour? In what ways can the delinquent adolescent build a strong sense of socially acceptable self-efficacy?

Changing perceptions of male and female personality traits, increased divorce, and a reduction of interest in religion are thought to be contributing factors (Ambert, 2007). Also, a recent study found that peer rejection, doing poorly in school, and engaging in antisocial behaviour were linked with whether or not middle school students were members of a gang.

Cognitive factors, such as low self-control, low intelligence, and lack of sustained attention, also were implicated in delinquency. For example, a recent study revealed that low-IQ serious delinquents were characterized by low self-control (Koolhof et al., 2007). Another study found that at age 16, non-delinquents were more likely to have a higher verbal IQ and engage in sustained attention than delinquents (Loeber et al., 2007).

Attitudes surrounding youth and their involvement in Canada's justice system have transformed and evolved over many years. Under the current legislation, the Youth Criminal Justice Act, emphasis is placed on diverting youth (ages 12 to 17) accused of minor, non-violent offences from the formal court system using diversionary and extrajudicial measures. In 2010/2011, the number of cases completed in youth court declined for the second year in a row. Interestingly, the majority of cases completed in 2010/2011 involved non-violent cases (73 percent) in youth court. Violent cases accounted for the remaining 27 percent of youth court cases (Statistics Canada, 2012j). Figure 12.5 discusses some antecedents of becoming a young offender.

To this point, we have studied a number of ideas about adolescent problems. For a review, see the **Reach Your Learning Objectives** section at the end of this chapter.

Successful Prevention and Intervention Programs

LO5 Design strategies for helping adolescents with problems.

We have described some of the major adolescent problems in this and the preceding chapter: substance abuse; juvenile delinquency; school-related problems, such as dropping out of school; adolescent pregnancy; and sexually transmitted diseases.

The most at-risk adolescents have more than one problem. Researchers are increasingly finding that problem behaviours in adolescence are interrelated (Tubman & Windle, 1995). For example, heavy substance abuse is related to early sexual activity, lower grades, dropping out of school, and delinquency. Delinquency is related to early sexual activity, early pregnancy, substance abuse, and dropping out of school. Repeated pregnancies are associated with intimate violence. People with anorexia nervosa frequently take illicit drugs. Many, but not all, of these very high-risk youth "do it all."

In addition to understanding that many adolescents engage in multiple problem behaviours, it also is important to understand that all behaviour is motivated by something. Maslow and Rogers would say that individuals who commit antisocial acts are trying to improve themselves in some way. Until the multidimensional causes are understood, developing programs that reduce adolescent problems is difficult. An all-out effort by youth, parents, communities, police, and governments is essential; understanding the causes can be helpful in finding solutions.

Effective Interventions

Provincial and municipal governments across Canada have mounted successful campaigns and interventions, all of which include a broad range of partnerships within their jurisdictions. The campaign against bullying is an example of one recent large-scale campaign mounted in both Canada and the United States. There are many other interesting and effective interventions:

- *British Columbia:* The Active Youth Network, composed of representatives from various youth-serving agencies, including local police, the B.C. Transit Police, school officials, Probation Services, and the local Crown counsel, are analyzing criminal activity and surveillance. Their goal is to facilitate improved, consistent, and ongoing communication with all agencies and representatives of the justice system who work with active, high-risk youth.
- *Calgary:* Community Resources has been developed in concert with a number of police-initiated youth-at-risk activities to address concerns about youth violence.
- *Edmonton:* The Step Up and Step In program aims to reduce and prevent youth violence.
- Winnipeg: Project OASIS (New Directions for Children, Youth, Adults and Families) supports youth and their families who come from countries of political strife. Refugee youth are considered at risk of youth gang involvement.
- *Toronto:* Breaking the Cycle of Violence Program, developed by the Canadian Training Institute with Youth Link-Inner City Youth in Toronto, focuses on self-awareness, systemic roots of violence, and cognitive behavioural role modelling.

The Minister of Justice and Attorney General of Canada announced that the Government of Canada will continue to provide funding to support youth justice services in the provinces and territories. Effective April 1, 2013, the Youth Justice Service Funding program will be funded a level of $141.7M annually (Department of Justice Canada, 2013).

critical thinking

Suicide has often been thought of as an attention-getting behaviour; however, nothing could be farther from the truth. A suicide attempt is a "cry for help" from an individual who feels surrounded by hopelessness and has been unable to obtain relief from his or her impossible situation. This person may well be a successful repeater. What would you do? In what ways can you help an adolescent who is contemplating suicide? What community resources would you use for references?

developmental **connection**

Maslow and Rogers

Other strategies to reduce youth violence include training parents in authoritative parenting strategies. Some of the techniques suggested include:

- *One-word signals.* Because teens have short attention spans and tune out adult nagging or perceived nagging quickly, one-word reminders are more effective than lectures.
- *Reflective questioning strategies.* Ask questions that help the adolescent understand what they stand to lose, what they stand to gain, and what action plan might be useful in obtaining the goal they want. The follow-up question is to determine how the parent can assist the teen in obtaining the goal.
- *Choose your arguments carefully.* As one parent said, "Because I only have so many "no's" they better be ones I can enforce and that will make a difference; this rules out tattooing, body piercing, and fashion whims, but rules in respect for property, integrity, and accountability." Arguing with a teenager is an invitation for disaster, as their increased critical thinking skills and sense of invincibility will give them responses for every point an adult makes.
- *Listen. Listen. Listen.* Keep your mouth shut and listen. Use questions to help teens answer their own moral dilemmas.
- *Praise when earned.* Provide praise at every opportunity at which achievement can be acknowledged. Remember, it takes at least seven positive interactions to overcome the barriers of one negative interaction!

To this point, we have studied a number of ideas about successful prevention and intervention programs in adolescence. For a review, see the **Reach Your Learning Objectives** section at the end of this chapter.

reach your **learning objectives**

Self-Esteem and Identity Development

LO1 Describe self-esteem, the changes in the self and identity, and several of the prominent theories.

Self-Esteem	■ An individual's self-evaluation of his/her overall sense of self-worth.
Identity	■ Identity is a self-portrait composed of many pieces.
	■ Identity formation is extraordinarily complex.
	■ Erikson's theory is the most comprehensive view of identity development. Identity versus identity confusion is the stage in which the individual comes to terms with many aspects of his/her identity central to his/her being. Aspects of identity include career, political, religious, vocational, and sexual orientation.
	■ Marcia proposed four statuses of identity: diffusion, foreclosure, moratorium, and achievement. Achievement is attained when thought and commitment are present.
	■ Recent research indicates no significant gender differences in level of self-esteem.
	■ According to Elkind, age dynamism is the desire of adolescents to distance themselves from younger adolescents or children.

Identity: Family, Religion, Race, Ethnicity, Culture, and Sexual Orientation

LO2 Compare and contrast how family, religion, race, ethnicity, culture, and sexual orientation influence adolescent development.

Families	▪ Parental responses and behaviour influence adolescent development. ▪ The internal struggle for autonomy and the restraining tug of attachment may vary according to gender and cultural influences. ▪ Parental conflicts emerge as the struggle for autonomy competes with attachment needs. ▪ The family's culture may reflect an orientation to either external or internal locus of control.
Religion	▪ Religion is important to adolescent identity. ▪ Research findings in both Canada and the U.S. illustrate emerging religious identity in adolescence.
Racial, Ethnic, and Cultural Identity	▪ Erikson believed that ethnic groups struggle to maintain their heritage, while at the same time blend into the dominant culture. ▪ During adolescence, individuals interpret their racial, ethnic, and cultural backgrounds for the first time. ▪ Racial, ethnic, and cultural aspects of identity are enduring, basic factors of the self that include a sense of membership in a group or groups and the attitudes and feelings related to that membership. ▪ Immigrant youth in Canada may have a bicultural identity because they identify with both the land of their birth and with Canada. ▪ Socio-economic status (SES), particularly poverty, may adversely affect identity development. ▪ Rites of passage are ceremonies that mark an individual's transition from one status to another, especially to adulthood.
Traditions and Changes in Adolescence around the World	▪ As in other periods of development, culture influences adolescents' development. ▪ Cultural traditions around the world affect health, gender, family, peers, school, and work. ▪ Canadian youth who attend school assume an adult-like workweek of approximately 50 hours per week. This is more than any other teenage group surveyed.
Sexual Orientation and Identity	▪ Erikson and Freud both believed adolescence to be a critical period in understanding sexual orientation and identity. ▪ Sexual identity is an individual's innermost understanding of his/her maleness or femaleness. ▪ Sexual orientation is related to an individual's sexual interests. ▪ Gender identity refers to an individual belonging to a particular sexual category. ▪ Transgender or intersexed individuals can either adjust in society or risk problems. ▪ Homophobia is the intense fear, prejudice, and willingness to cause harm to anyone not heterosexual. ▪ Symbols related to sexual orientation and identity are internalized at an early age and may jeopardize an individual's self-esteem.

Friendship

LO3 Outline the changes that occur in peer relations and dating during adolescence.

Adolescent Groups versus Children's Groups	■ Children's groups are less formal, less heterogeneous, and less heterosexual than adolescent groups.
	■ During adolescence, groups tend to include a broader array of members. New friendships emerge.
	■ Harry Stack Sullivan was the most influential theorist to discuss the importance of friendship. He argued that there is a dramatic increase in the psychological importance and intimacy of close friends in early adolescence.
Peer Groups	■ The nature of groups broadens in adolescence.
	■ The pressure to conform to peers is strong during adolescence, especially during Grades 8 and 9.
	■ Adolescents experience tension between their desire to belong to a clique and their desire for independence. Clique membership becomes less important to older teens who have a clearer sense of identity than younger teens who have a greater need to fit in. A teen with low self-esteem is more apt to seek membership in a clique. A crowd may have merit to the adolescent.
Dating and Romantic Relationships	■ Dating takes on added importance in adolescence, and it can have many functions. Younger adolescents often begin to "hang out" together in heterosexual groups.
	■ Emotions are heavily involved in adolescent dating and romantic relationships.
	■ Culture can exert a powerful influence on adolescent dating.
	■ Dating and romantic relationships are linked to how well-adjusted adolescents are. Those who date are more accepted by their peers.
	■ Social networking, which includes cyberdating and sexting, has increased among adolescents in society.

Adolescent Problems

LO4 Analyze adolescent problems in socio-emotional development, and the causes of the problems.

Young Offenders	■ A young offender is an adolescent who breaks the law or engages in conduct that is considered illegal.
Causes of Delinquency	■ Multiple factors contribute to delinquency, including heredity, identity problems, family experiences, economic realities, and the swift rise in visual media including violent computer games.
	■ Researchers are increasingly finding that problem behaviours in adolescence are interrelated.

Successful Prevention and Intervention Programs

LO5 Design strategies for helping adolescents with problems.

	■ Researchers have found a number of common components in successful programs designed to prevent or reduce adolescent problems. Broad-based partnerships, a specific program focus, training, and educational curricula and resources are the keys to effective interventions.

review ---> *connect* ---> reflect

review

What are several changes in self-esteem that occur during adolescence? **LO1**

How does identity develop in adolescence? **LO1**

What characterizes religious and spiritual development in adolescence? **LO2**

How does ethnicity influence adolescent development? **LO2**

What is the nature of adolescent dating and romantic relationships? **LO3**

What features of peer groups are important for the adolescent? **LO3**

What is juvenile delinquency? Identify several contributing factors to juvenile delinquency. **LO4**

What are a few components of successful prevention/intervention programs for adolescents? **LO5**

connect

Adolescence is identified as the second time in the life of an individual when seeking independence is especially strong. From your own memories, when do you think that first time occurred? What characterized it?

reflect *Your Own Personal Journey of Life*

Reflect on your adolescence and your relationships with your parents. What was a source of conflict with your parents? How intense was your conflict? Would you behave differently toward your own adolescent than your parents did with you? If so, in what ways?

McGraw-Hill Connect provides you with a powerful tool for improving academic performance and truly mastering course material. You can diagnose your knowledge with pre- and post-tests, identify the areas where you need help, search the entire learning package, including the eBook, for content specific to the topic you're studying, and add these resources to your personalized study plan. CONNECT for *Life-Span Development*, fifth Canadian edition, offers the following:

- chapter-specific online quizzes
- groupwork
- presentations
- writing assignments
- case studies
- and much more!

Visit CONNECT today!

CHAPTER 13
Physical and Cognitive Development in Early Adulthood

CHAPTER OUTLINE

"*Or perhaps you have spent too long in the chalkfield of education, filling in the blanks. Memorize this or mark that.*
The poem is writing a multiple choice exam.
Which of the above."

—FROM "DRIVING IN THE BLIZZARD" IN *HARM'S WAY*, BY MAUREEN HYNES, CANADIAN POET

"*Whatever you can do, or dream you can, begin it. Boldness has genius, power, and magic.*"

—JOHANN WOLFGANG VON GOETHE, NINETEENTH-CENTURY GERMAN PLAYWRIGHT AND NOVELIST

Winning Gold: Canada's Women's Hockey Team, Olympics 2010

Early adulthood is an exciting time for work, dreams, play, and love. Finding our place in adult society and committing to the work required to attain our goals can take longer and be more difficult than we imagined. At times, we may doubt ourselves and wonder if we're on the right path, or if it isn't enough to just be. Sex and love are powerful passions—at times angels of light, and at other times fiends of torment. But at some point, the challenges of our goals force us to become realistic and more pragmatic. In this way, through our efforts and perseverance, the dreams of our childhood weave their way into the texture of our adult lives. The women of Canada's 2010 Olympic team illustrate this transition.

Most psychologists consider the ages between 18 and 40 as early adulthood. The women on the Olympic team fall into this category. The average age was 26 years and 10 months; the youngest player was 18, and the oldest, a mother of two sons, was 34. All were filled with the dreams of their childhood and had dedicated enormous time and effort to reach their goal.

What does it take to become a member of an Olympic team? First, of course, is desire and ability. Each woman had to want to play hockey and had to learn the skills involved. Then, after logging thousands of hours of skill-building practice and game playing, each woman had to put herself on the line and compete for her place by trying out. Once on the team, the women continued to train and play an ambitious schedule of games. Right before the Vancouver Games, they engaged in a rigorous "boot camp" where they began each day at 7 a.m. with a long-distance run, followed by yoga, weight training, kick-boxing, and on-ice training. They retired, or perhaps collapsed, nightly at 9:30 p.m. Through this boot camp experience, they not only got to appreciate each other's talents and dedication, but they also were able to build the trust essential for a fully functional team. Natural athletic ability was combined with desire, goals, and dedicated practice.

Their preparation brought proud results. The team capped a 15-game winning streak by defeating their arch competitors, the U.S. team, and winning the gold medal. After shaking hands, singing "O Canada," and sharing their emotions with reporters, the team retired to their lockers. However, in the exuberance of their celebration, they spontaneously returned to the ice with champagne, beer, and cigars, illustrating a youthful sense of fun. Winning gold made headlines, of course; but the on-ice celebration made even greater headlines. Considerable controversy was raised when the IOC (International Olympic Committee) made inquiries and the women apologized for any embarrassment it may have caused to either the IOC or the COC (Canadian Olympic Committee). To quote one player, "instead of talking about our gold medals, we were talking about the on-ice celebration" (CBC Sports, 2010).The team illustrates many aspects of early adulthood: peak physical strength, and the ability to make a commitment, set goals, and plan ahead. And, last, but not least, to the delight of many and the consternation of a few, the team demonstrated youthful spontaneity. It was a proud and joyful moment for women's hockey in Canada.

The Transition from Adolescence to Adulthood

The Criteria for Becoming an Adult

The Transition from High School to College, University, or Work

LO1 Outline the transition from adolescence to early adulthood.

For most individuals, becoming an adult involves a lengthy transition period. Recently, the transition from adolescence to adulthood has been referred to as *emerging adulthood*, which occurs from approximately 18 to 25 years of age (Arnett, 2006, 2007). Experimentation and exploration characterize the emerging adult. Choosing a career path, deciding where to live, and determining a lifestyle (for example, single, cohabiting, or married) are among the wide-ranging choices the young person makes. These decisions are connected to the type of life the individual has had.

Consider the changing life of Michael Maddaus (Broderick, 2003; Masten, Obradovic, & Burt, 2006). Growing up as a child and adolescent, Michael's mother drank heavily and his stepfather abused him. He coped by spending an increasing amount of time on the streets. He was arrested more than 20 times for his delinquency, frequently placed in detention centres, and rarely went to school. At 17, he joined the Navy and the experience helped him to gain self-discipline and hope. After his brief stint in the Navy, he completed high school through an adult learning centre, and began taking community college classes. However, he continued to have some setbacks with drugs and alcohol. A defining moment came when he delivered furniture to a surgeon's home. The surgeon became interested in helping Michael, and his mentorship led to Michael volunteering at a rehabilitation centre, then to a job with a neurosurgeon. Eventually, he obtained his undergraduate degree, went to medical school, got married, and started a family. Today, Michael Maddaus is a successful surgeon. One of his most gratifying volunteer activities is telling his story to troubled youth.

In a longitudinal study, Ann Masten and her colleagues (2006) found that emerging adults who became competent after experiencing difficulties while growing up were more intelligent, experienced higher parenting quality, and were less likely to grow up in poverty or low-income circumstances than their counterparts who did not become competent as emerging adults. A further analysis focused on individuals who were still showing maladaptive patterns in emerging adulthood, but who had gotten their lives together by the time they were in their late twenties and early thirties. The three characteristics shared by these "late-bloomers" were support by adults, ability to plan ahead, and the development of positive aspects of autonomy. In some cases, " . . . military service, marriage and romantic relationships, higher education, religion affiliations, and work opportunities may provide turning-point opportunities for changing the life course during emerging adulthood" (Masten, Obradovic, & Burt, 2006, p. 179).

The Criteria for Becoming an Adult

Around the world, youth are increasingly delaying their entry into adulthood, largely because contemporary society requires more education and skills than earlier generations (Clark, 2009). Thus, the transition is likely to be longer than previous generations. In addition to staying in school longer, economic factors contribute to the delay, including the increase in part-time employment and the rising costs of housing (Clark, 2009). How is adulthood determined? Statistics Canada (Clark, 2009) identifies five markers of the transition to adulthood:

- Left school
- Left parental home
- Has full-time full-year work
- Is in a conjugal union
- Has children who live with them

Jeffrey Arnett (2006) has recently labelled the age range from 18 to 25 as **emerging adulthood**. He says that during this time frame, *individuals have left the dependency of childhood, but have not yet entered the enduring responsibilities of adulthood*. They are at a point when they are exploring a variety of possible directions in what they want to do with their lives, especially in the areas of work and love.

critical thinking

The three common factors that Ann Masten and her colleagues found that late-bloomers shared were support from an adult, the ability to plan ahead, and the development of positive aspects of autonomy. In what ways do you think these three factors are important? You very likely know of someone who is a late-bloomer, or perhaps you, yourself, are a late-bloomer. What event do you think might motivate someone to "bloom"? How can a dramatic event, such as becoming a parent, motivate change? What barriers to change might late-bloomers encounter when attempting change?

emerging adulthood Arnett's description of young people between the ages of 18 and 25 who have left the dependency of childhood, but have not yet fully assumed the enduring responsibilities of adulthood.

Arnett (2006) describes five features of emerging adulthood:

- *Identity exploration, especially in love and work.* As we saw in Chapter 12, emerging adulthood is the time during which key changes in identity take place for many individuals (Cote, 2006; Kroger, 2007).
- *Instability.* Residential changes peak during early adulthood, a time during which there also is often instability in love, work, and education.
- *Self-focused.* According to Arnett (2006, p. 10), emerging adults "are self-focused in the sense that they have little in the way of social obligations, little in the way of duties and commitments to others, which leaves them with a great deal of autonomy in running their own lives."
- *Feeling in-between.* Many emerging adults don't consider themselves adolescents or full-fledged adults.
- *The age of possibilities, a time when individuals have an opportunity to transform their lives.* Arnett (2006) describes two ways in which emerging adulthood is the age of possibilities: (1) many emerging adults are optimistic about their future; and (2) for emerging adults who have experienced difficult times while growing up, emerging adulthood presents an opportunity to direct their lives in a more positive direction (Schulenberg & Zarett, 2006).

Taking responsibility for oneself is an important marker of adult status. In a recent study, both parents and college students agreed that taking responsibility for one's actions and developing emotional control are important aspects of becoming an adult (Nelson et al., 2007). However, parents and college students didn't always agree on other aspects of what it takes to become an adult.

In many countries, marriage is often a significant marker for entry into adulthood; however, getting married and starting a family is becoming less common. More couples cohabit and many young people return home in between relationships (Arnett, 2004; Clark, 2009). For example, in 1971, 65 percent of men and 80 percent of women were in or had been in a conjugal relationship by age 25; by 2001, these percentages had dropped by almost half to 34 percent and 49 percent, respectively (Clark, 2009).

The new freedoms and responsibilities of emerging adulthood represent major changes in individuals' lives. Keep in mind, though, that considerable continuity still glues adolescence and adulthood together. What determines an individual's well-being in the transition to adulthood? In a review of research, three types of assets were especially important to well-being during this transition: intellectual (academic success, ability to plan, anticipation, and good decision-making skills); psychological (mental health, mastery motivation, confidence in one's competence, identity, values, and community contributions); and social (connectedness to others through friendship and positive peer relations) (Eccles & Goodman, 2002). In one study of individuals from 18 to 26 years of age, succeeding rather than stalling in developmental tasks such as work, romantic involvement, and citizenship was linked to a positive trajectory of well-being. On the other hand, emotional health across the transition from late adolescence to young adulthood may be compromised in young people as they struggle to adapt to new social roles and responsibilities (Schulenberg, Bryant, & O'Malley, 2004).

The Transition from High School to College, University, or Work

Just as the transition from elementary school to middle or junior high school involves change and possible stress, so does the transition from high school to college or university, or the transition from school to work. In many instances, there are parallel changes in the transitions. Going from being a senior in high school to being a first-year student in college or the youngest person in the work group replays the "top-dog" phenomenon that occurred at the start of high school.

The transition from high school to college or university involves movement to a larger, more impersonal school structure; interaction with peers and new friends tend to include students from a broader range of geographical and cultural backgrounds. Another difference is the increased focus on achievement and assessment. Students are more likely to feel grown up, and have more subjects from which to select, more time to spend with peers, and more opportunities to explore different

critical thinking

What are some of the criteria being considered to qualify as an adult? Which criterion do you think is the most important? State why you think so. Do adolescents suddenly become adults at 19, or does the term "emerging adulthood," which suggests that individuals become adults over a period of years, make more sense to you? What makes you think so? Reflect on your own life. What events contributed to your "emerging adulthood"?

The transition from high school to college or university often involves positive as well as negative features. Loneliness, academic and work pressures, children, and other family members are all factors affecting the transition from high school to college or university. **What was your transition like?**

lifestyles and values. In addition, students have greater independence from parental guidance and monitoring. Challenges in academic work tend to be greater than those experienced before this point (Santrock & Halonen, 2006). The same holds true of those who enter the work force full-time. They, too, are likely to feel more grown up and explore different lifestyles and values. Plus, they also experience greater independence from parental guidance and monitoring.

Stress

Each year, more than 100,000 students enter college and university. Some live at home, and others live in residence (McIntyre, 2009). The advantage of living at home is that changes in behaviour that signal depression may be noticed by someone in the family. The same signals may not be noticed in students living away from home. For example, in a survey of students at Simon Fraser University in British Columbia, 18 percent reported that their academic performance is compromised by feelings of hopelessness, depression, anxiety, and seasonal affective disorder (Whiting, 2007). This study echoes the U.S. study of more than 300,000 freshmen at more than 500 colleges and universities, which found that postsecondary students experience more stress and are more depressed than in the past (Pryor et al., 2007). In 2005, 27 percent (up from 16 percent in 1985) said they frequently "felt overwhelmed with what I have to do." College females were twice as likely as their male counterparts to feel overwhelmed. The pressure to succeed in college, get a great job, and make lots of money were pervasive concerns of these students. The personal circumstances that caused the most stress for students were intimate relationships, finances, parental conflicts and expectations, and roommate conflicts.

Stress can be dealt with both negatively and positively. Negative ways to cope with stress include such things as repressing your feelings, projecting your frustration and anger on others, keeping your feelings bottled up inside, denying your feelings, and eating and/or drinking more.

Fortunately, there are positive ways to help cope with stress. The Canadian Mental Health Association (2010) recommends these tips:

- Keep things in perspective. Try not to get flustered by one bad mark or one period when things aren't going well.
- Talk to someone about what's bothering you.
- Identify what helps you relax and practise doing it.
- Take a break from what is causing you stress and try meditation, tai chi, or yoga.
- Get enough sleep by going to bed at a reasonable time every night.
- Exercise regularly and make time for fun in your life.
- Watch your diet, especially your intake of caffeine and sugar.

As we learn more about healthy lifestyles and how they contribute to a longer life span, emerging and young adults are increasingly interested in learning about physical performance, health, nutrition, exercise, and addiction.

To this point, we have studied a number of ideas about the transition from adolescence to adulthood. For a review, see the **Reach Your Learning Objectives** section at the end of this chapter.

Health

Eating and Weight

Regular Exercise

Substance Abuse

Physical Development, Health, and Wellness

LO2 Describe physical changes and health considerations for emerging adults.

Most of us reach our peak physical performance under the age of 30, often between the ages of 19 and 26. This peak of physical performance occurs not only for the average young adult, but for outstanding athletes as well (Feldman & Landry, 2014). Different types of athletes, however, reach their peak performances at different ages. Most swimmers and gymnasts reach their peak performance in their late teens. Golfers and marathon runners tend to peak in their late twenties. In other areas of athletics, peak performance is often in the early to mid-twenties.

Not only do we reach our peak in physical performance during early adulthood, but it is also during this age period that we begin to decline in physical performance. Muscle tone and strength usually begin to show signs of decline around the age of 30. Sagging chins and protruding abdomens also may begin to appear for the first time. The lessening of physical abilities is a common complaint among the just-turned thirties. Sensory systems show little change in early adulthood, but the lens of the eye loses some of its elasticity and becomes less able to change shape and focus on near objects. Hearing peaks in adolescence, remains constant in the first part of early adulthood, and then begins to decline in the last part of early adulthood. And in the mid- to late-twenties, the body's fatty tissue increases. The health profile of emerging and young adults can be improved by decreasing the incidence of certain health-impairing lifestyles, such as overeating, and alternatively, by engaging in health-improving practices that include healthy eating habits and regular exercise patterns, and by not abusing drugs (Waldron & Dieser, 2010). For example, the Canadian Society for Exercise Physiology indicates that to achieve health benefits adults should be required to accumulate at least 150 minutes of moderate- to vigorous-intensity aerobic physical activity per week, in bouts of 10 minutes or more (CSEP, 2012).

Health

Emerging adults have more than twice the mortality rate of adolescents (Park et al., 2006). Although emerging adults have a higher death rate than adolescents, emerging adults have few chronic health problems, and they have fewer colds and respiratory problems than when they were children (Rimsza & Kirk, 2005). Although most college students know what it takes to prevent illness and promote health, they don't fare very well when it comes to applying this information to themselves (Murphy-Hoefer, Alder, & Higbee, 2004). Many postsecondary students, it seems, have the same sense of invincibility they had in adolescence, and have overly optimistic beliefs about their future health status. A longitudinal study revealed that most bad health habits engaged in during adolescence increased in emerging adulthood. Inactivity, diet, obesity, substance use, reproductive health care, and health care access worsened between the ages of 19 and 25 (Harris et al., 2006).

The health profile of our nation's young adults can be improved by reducing the incidence of health-impairing lifestyle, such as overeating, and by engaging in a health-improving lifestyle that includes good eating habits, exercising regularly, and not abusing drugs (Robbins, Powers, & Burgess, 2008; Teague et al., 2009).

Eating and Weight

In earlier chapters, we explored obesity in childhood (Chapters 7 and 9) and examined the eating disorders of anorexia nervosa and bulimia nervosa in adolescence (Chapter 11). Now, we turn our attention to obesity in the adult years and the extensive preoccupation that many adults have with dieting.

Obesity

Obesity is a serious and pervasive health problem for many individuals (Corbin et al., 2008; Hahn, Payne, & Lucas, 2009). Information about weight and obesity is based on self-reporting, a practice that tends to underestimate the prevalence of obesity. Recall from Chapter 11 that the Canadian Institute of Health Research reported that an estimated 50 percent of Canadians are overweight, and that 15 percent of those who are overweight fall into the category of obese as defined by the World Health Organization (WHO) (CIHR, 2006). Although rates of obesity are rising in men, a higher percentage of women are morbidly obese (a body mass index (BMI) of 40 or more). Figure 13.1 demonstrates how BMI is calculated.

Obesity is linked to increased risk of hypertension, diabetes, and cardiovascular disease (Hahn, Payne, & Lucas, 2009). As indicated in Chapter 11, obesity is overtaking tobacco as the leading cause of death. For individuals who are 30 percent overweight, the probability of dying in middle adulthood increases by about 40 percent. What factors are involved in obesity? The possible culprits include heredity, leptin, set point, and metabolism and environmental factors and gender.

obesity According to the World Health Organization (WHO), obesity is defined as having a body mass index (BMI) equal to or more than 30.

Figure 13.1

Figure 13.1

Figuring Your Body Mass Index

Body mass index is a measure of weight in relation to height. Anyone with a BMI of 25 or more is considered overweight. People who have a body mass index of 30 or more (a BMI of 30 is roughly 30 pounds over a healthy weight) are considered obese (Kirk, Tytus, Tsuyuki, & Sharma, 2012). BMI has some limitations: it can overestimate body fat in people who are very muscular, and it can underestimate body fat in people who have lost muscle mass, such as the elderly.

Weight (pounds)

Height	120	130	140	150	160	170	180	190	200	210	220	230	240	250
4'6"	29	31	34	36	39	41	43	46	48	51	53	56	58	60
4'8"	27	29	31	34	36	38	40	43	45	47	49	52	54	56
4'10"	25	27	29	31	34	36	38	40	42	44	46	48	50	52
5'0"	23	25	27	29	31	33	35	37	39	41	43	45	47	49
5'2"	22	24	26	27	29	31	33	35	37	38	40	42	44	46
5'4"	21	22	24	26	28	29	31	33	34	36	38	40	41	43
5'6"	19	21	23	24	26	27	29	31	32	34	36	37	39	40
5'8"	18	20	21	23	24	26	27	29	30	32	34	35	37	38
5'10"	17	19	20	22	23	24	26	27	29	30	32	33	35	36
6'0"	16	18	19	20	22	23	24	26	27	28	30	31	33	34
6'2"	15	17	18	19	21	22	23	24	26	27	28	30	31	32
6'4"	15	16	17	18	20	21	22	23	24	26	27	28	29	30
6'6"	14	15	16	17	19	20	21	22	23	24	25	27	28	29
6'8"	13	14	15	17	18	19	20	21	22	23	24	25	26	28

Underweight   Healthy weight   Overweight   Obese

HEREDITY   Until recently, the genetic component of obesity had been underestimated by scientists (Jamshidi et al., 2007). Some individuals inherit a tendency to be overweight. Researchers have documented that animals can be inbred to have a propensity for obesity (Liu et al., 2005). Further, identical human twins have similar weights, even when they are reared apart (Collaku et al., 2004).

LEPTIN   Leptin (from the Greek word *leptos,* which means "thin") is a protein that is involved in satiety (the condition of being full to satisfaction) and released by fat cells, resulting in decreased food intake and increased energy expenditure. Leptin acts as an anti-obesity hormone. In humans, leptin concentrations have been linked with weight, percentage of body fat, weight loss in a single diet episode, and cumulative percentage of weight loss (de Luis et al., 2007). Some scientists are interested in the possibility that leptin might help obese individuals lose weight.

SET POINT   The amount of stored fat in your body is an important factor in your set point, the weight you maintain when you make no effort to gain or lose weight. Fat is stored in what are called adipose cells. When these cells are filled, you do not get hungry. When people gain weight—because of genetic predisposition, childhood eating patterns, or adult overeating—their number of fat cells increases, and they might not be able to get rid of them. A normal-weight individual has 30 to 40 billion fat cells. An obese individual has 80 to 120 billion fat cells. Some scientists have proposed that these fat cells can shrink but might not go away.

ENVIRONMENTAL FACTORS   Environmental factors play an important role in obesity (Wardlaw & Smith, 2009). The human genome has not changed markedly in the last century, yet obesity has noticeably increased (Li et al., 2007). The dramatic increase in obesity is likely due to greater availability of food (especially food high in fat), energy-saving devices, and declining physical activity.

Socio-cultural factors are involved in obesity, which is six times more prevalent among women with low incomes than among women with high incomes. Americans also are more obese than Europeans and people in many other areas of the world (Williams, 2005).

A Word about Dietary Fats

Dietary fats are both a necessary and unavoidable part of our diets. Some fats, such as those found in avocados and other such vegetables, are healthy; but the fats found in french fries, doughnuts, and fast foods are dangerous to health because they contain high levels of trans fats. Canadians spend about one-third of their food budgets on restaurant foods, which is where the trans fat levels are the highest. Called the *silent killer* by nutritionists, trans fats wreak havoc with the body's ability to regulate cholesterol and increase the risk of heart disease exponentially. A number of food manufacturers are currently taking steps to remove trans fats from their products, and soon legislation will require accurate labelling of fats for both store-bought and restaurant foods.

Dieting

Ironically, while obesity is on the rise, dieting has become an obsession with many (Schiff, 2009). Although many people regularly embark on a diet, few are successful in keeping weight off long term. A recent research review of the long-term outcomes of calorie-restricting diets revealed that overall one-third to two-thirds of dieters regain more weight than they lost on their diets (Mann et al., 2007).

Many divergent interests are involved in the topic of dieting. These include the public, health professionals, policy makers, the media, and the powerful diet and food industries. On one side are the societal norms that promote a very lean, aesthetic body. This ideal is supported by billions of dollars spent annually on diet books, programs, videos, foods, and pills. On the other side are health professionals and a growing minority of the press. Although they recognize the alarmingly high rate of obesity, they are frustrated by high relapse rates and the obsession with excessive thinness that can lead to chronic dieting and serious health risks. However, some individuals do lose weight and maintain the loss (Applebaum, 2008; Herman, van Strien, & Polivy, 2008). How often this occurs and whether some diet programs work better than others are still open questions.

What we do know about losing weight is that the most effective programs include exercise (Fahey, Insel, & Roth, 2009; Wardlaw & Hampl, 2007). Exercise not only burns up calories, but continues to elevate the person's metabolic rate for several hours *after* exercising. A recent study found that exercising 30 minutes a day, planning meals, and weighing themselves daily were the main strategies used by successful dieters compared with unsuccessful dieters (Kruger, Blanck, & Gillespie, 2006) (see Figure 13.2). Another recent study also revealed that daily weigh-ins are linked to maintaining weight loss (Wing et al., 2007).

Even when diets do produce weight loss, they can place the dieter at risk for other health problems (Cunningham & Hyson, 2006). One main concern focuses on weight cycling—yo-yo dieting—in which the person is in a recurring cycle of weight loss and weight gain (Janacek et al., 2005). Also, liquid diets and other very low-calorie strategies are linked with gallbladder damage.

With these problems in mind, when overweight people diet and maintain their weight loss, they do become less depressed and reduce their risk for a number of health-impairing disorders (Daubenmier et al., 2007; Mensah & Brown, 2007).

Restrained Eating

One area related to dieting that psychologists have studied is restrained eating. Too many people live their lives as one big long diet, interrupted by occasional hot fudge sundaes or chocolate chip cookies. **Restrained eaters** *are individuals who chronically restrict their food intake to control their weight. Restrained eaters often are on diets, are very conscious of what they eat, and tend to feel guilty after splurging on sweets* (de Lauzon-Guillain et al., 2006; Johnson & Wardle, 2005; Roefs et al., 2005). An interesting characteristic of restrained eaters if that when they stop dieting, they tend to binge eat—that is, eat large quantities of food in a short time. Also, when under stress, restrained eaters tend to increase their food intake, while unrestrained eaters tend to decrease their food intake (Lowe & Kral, 2005, 2006).

Figure 13.2

Comparison of Strategies in Successful and Unsuccessful Dieters

restrained eaters Individuals who chronically restrict their food intake to control their weight. Restrained eaters are often on diets, are very conscious of what they eat, and tend to feel guilty after splurging on sweets.

Regular Exercise

One of the main reasons why health experts want people to exercise is that it helps to prevent heart disease, diabetes, and other diseases (Anspaugh, Hamrick, & Rosato, 2009; Hoeger & Hoeger, 2008). Although exercise designed to strengthen muscles and bones or to improve flexibility is important to fitness, many health experts have stressed aerobic exercise. **Aerobic exercise** *is sustained exercise—jogging, swimming, or cycling, for example—that stimulates heart and lung activity.*

According to Health Canada, as little as one hour of light to moderate activity weekly, equivalent to a brisk walk, can improve health. This hour can be broken into parts; that is, a daily 10-minute brisk walk six times a week produces a health benefit. Only 36 percent of Canadians over 18 years of age are active enough to gain health benefits. In other words, 64 percent are not sufficiently active, down a bit from 20 years ago when over 70 percent of us were insufficiently active. Research on the benefits of exercise suggests that both moderate and intense activities produce important physical and psychological gains (Gostic, 2005). Some people enjoy rigorous, intense exercise. Others enjoy more moderate exercise routines (see Figure 13.3).

Researchers have found that exercise benefits not only physical health, but mental health as well. In particular, exercise improves self-concept and reduces anxiety and depression. Meta-analyses have shown that exercise can be as effective in reducing depression as psychotherapy. The enjoyment and pleasure we derive from exercise, added to its aerobic benefits, make exercise one of life's most important activities (Insel & Roth, 2008).

Substance Abuse

In Chapter 11, we explored substance abuse in adolescence. Fortunately, by the time individuals reach their mid-twenties, many have reduced their use of alcohol and drugs. That is the conclusion reached by Jerald Bachman and his colleagues (2002) in a longitudinal analysis of more than 38,000 individuals who were evaluated from the time they were high school seniors through their twenties. Recent national studies indicate that individuals who don't go to college are more likely to take drugs than college students and college-educated adults, except for one substance—alcohol—which college students are more likely to use (Johnston et al., 2007). Also, as in adolescence, male college students and young adults are more likely to take drugs than their female counterparts (Johnston et al., 2007).

Let's take a closer look at the use of alcohol and nicotine by young adults and at the nature of *addiction.*

Alcohol

Alcohol is widely consumed around the world and frequently linked to injuries, impaired driving, unprotected sexual activity, sexually transmitted infections (STIs), and HIV (Mundt et al., 2009; WHO, 2005). The World Health Organization noted another interesting co-relation: the rate of deaths from alcohol and from HIV in eight countries that were studied (Kenya, South Africa, Zambia, Belarus, Romania, Russian Federation, India, and Mexico) was very close (WHO, 2005). Approximately one-third of Canadian undergraduates report a pattern of heavy drinking, and 16.1 percent report drinking excessively more than four times a week. According to WHO, there are five patterns linking alcohol use and sexual behaviour:

1. construction of maleness in terms of alcohol use
2. denial and neglect of risk as a way of coping with life
3. use of alcohol-serving venues as contact paces for sexual encounters
4. use of alcohol at/during sexual encounters
5. the promotion of alcohol use in pornographic materials

More information, including a country-by-country breakdown, is available on Connect at www. mcgrawhillconnect.ca.

BINGE DRINKING   Heavy binge drinking often increases in college and university, and it can take its toll on students (Kinney, 2009; Wu et al., 2007).

---

aerobic exercise Sustained exercise (such as jogging, swimming, or cycling) that stimulates heart and lung activity.

Figure 13.3

Moderate and Vigorous Physical Activities

Moderate
Walking, briskly (7 to 9 kph)
Cycling, for pleasure or transportation (≤22 km)
Swimming, moderate effort
Conditioning exercise, general calisthenics
Racquet sports, table tennis
Golf, pulling cart or carrying clubs
Canoeing, leisurely (~5 kph)
Home care, general cleaning
Mowing lawn, with power mower
Home repair, painting

Vigorous
Walking, briskly uphill or with a load
Cycling, fast or racing (>16 km)
Swimming, fast treading crawl
Conditioning exercise, stair ergometer or ski machine
Racquet sports, singles tennis or racquetball
Golf, practise at driving range
Canoeing, rapidly (≥7 kph)
Moving furniture
Mowing lawn, with hand mower
Home repair, fix-up projects

Students reported that they drank to get drunk, to celebrate, to forget their worries, and to feel good. "Although the number of times per week students drink is not particularly high, the amount they drink at one time is significant cause for concern," noted Louis Gliksman, associate professor at the University of Western Ontario, and lead researcher of a study of drinking patterns among university students. One study considers heavy drinking to be drinking eight or more drinks for men and five or more for women on four or more days a month (Mundt et al., 2009). Academic performance is adversely affected because memory retrieval after an evening of binge drinking has been found to be significantly impaired the next morning. As well, students are more likely to miss classes, have trouble with the police, and engage in unprotected sex (Verster et al., 2003; WHO, 2005).

Drinking games, catalysts for binge drinking, are popular in colleges and universities; however, student associations oppose restrictions to reduce drinking, such as raising the legal age of drinking or increasing the cost of alcohol at campus pubs.

Many colleges and universities across Canada have initiated strategies to educate and help students who have problems with alcohol and drugs. Researchers also want to raise awareness of the hazards associated with alcohol abuse and to educate pub staff to recognize problem drinking and stop selling drinks to those who are overindulging. A longitudinal study revealed that binge drinking peaks at about 21 to 22 years of age and then declines through the remainder of the twenties (Bachman et al., 2002).

ALCOHOLISM   **Alcoholism** is *a disorder that involves long-term, repeated, uncontrolled, compulsive, and excessive use of alcoholic beverages.* Further, this pattern impairs the drinker's health, work, and social relationships. One in nine individuals who drink continues the path to alcoholism (Redgrave et al., 2007). Family studies consistently reveal a high frequency of alcoholism in the first-degree relatives of alcoholics (Conway, Swendsen, & Merikangas, 2003). Indeed, researchers have found that heredity likely plays a role in alcoholism, although the precise hereditary mechanism has not been found (Miles & Williams, 2007). An estimated 50 to 60 percent of individuals who become alcoholics are believed to have a genetic predisposition for it.

alcoholism A disorder that involves long-term, repeated, uncontrolled, compulsive, and excessive use of alcoholic beverages.

Although studies reveal a genetic influence on alcoholism, they also show that environmental factors play a role (Ksir, Hart, & Ray, 2008). The large cultural variations in alcohol use mentioned earlier also underscore the environment's role in alcoholism.

The prolonged sense of invincibility in young adults may lead them to believe that they would never become alcoholics; but this may be naive. Social norms on campuses support binge drinking, and many students who drink frequently and excessively may find they have a chemical or psychological dependency by the time they leave school.

Cigarette Smoking

Converging evidence from a number of studies underscores the dangers of smoking or being around those who smoke (Akhter et al., 2007). For example, smoking is linked to 30 percent of cancer deaths, 21 percent of heart disease deaths, and 82 percent of chronic pulmonary disease deaths. Second-hand smoke is implicated in as many as 9,000 lung cancer deaths a year. Children of smokers are at special risk for respiratory and middle-ear diseases (Wallace-Bell, 2003).

Fewer people smoke today than in the past, and according to the *Report on the State of Public Health in Canada,* people in middle age are the heaviest smokers (PHAC, 2011c). However, Canadians are starting to smoke at a slightly younger age, and more young smokers are females. The earlier an individual starts smoking, the greater the health risks are for that individual. The effects of smoking are both long-term, as noted above, and short-term. In the short term, smokers develop more colds and infections such as bronchitis and pneumonia. Smokers also consume more alcohol, develop a smoker's cough (related to chronic lung irritation), and suffer more after-effects such as headaches and hangovers than non-smokers.

Most adult smokers would like to quit, but their addiction to nicotine often makes quitting a challenge. Nicotine, the active drug in cigarettes, is a stimulant that increases the smoker's energy and alertness, a pleasurable and reinforcing experience. Nicotine also stimulates neurotransmitters that have a calming or pain-reducing effect.

Four main methods are used to help smokers overcome their addiction to nicotine: (1) using a substitute source of nicotine, such as nicotine gum and the nicotine patch; (2) taking an antidepressant such as Zyban; (3) controlling stimuli associated with smoking—for example, sensitizing the smoker to social cues that are linked to smoking, such as a social drink; and (4) going "cold turkey," that is, simply stopping smoking without making any major changes in their lifestyle. Lighter smokers usually have more success with going "cold turkey" than heavy smokers.

Studies indicate that when people do stop smoking, their risk of cancer is reduced. For example, a recent study revealed a decrease in lung cancer deaths after smoking cessation (Wakai et al., 2007). In this study, earlier cessation of smoking resulted in a lower rate of lung cancer.

Addiction

addiction A physical and/or psychological dependence on a drug.

Addiction *is a physical and/or psychological dependence on a drug.* Experts on drug abuse use the term *addiction* to describe either physical and/or psychological dependence on the drug (CAMH, 2011). Like drug and alcohol abusers, gamblers become completely preoccupied with gambling and pursue it compulsively despite adverse consequences. Run-ins with the law often accompany drug and alcohol addiction. Although gambling is a legally sanctioned government-run activity, individuals who gamble compulsively often experience financial ruin and exhibit antisocial behaviours. Eight percent of young adults between 15 and 24 years of age report dependency on alcohol or illicit drugs. One out of every ten aged 15 and over (about 2.6 million people) report symptoms consistent with alcohol or illicit drug dependence. In Ontario, 3.8 percent or about 340,000 adults are classified as having moderate or severe gambling problems (Statistics Canada, 2003a).

According to Holden (2012), addiction is a maladaptive response to an underlying condition such as the nonspecific inability to cope with the world. Addiction does not meet the criteria specified for a core disease entity, such as the presence of a primary measurable deviation from an anatomical or physiological norm. In fact, medicalizing addiction has not led to any management advances at the individual level. The requirement for facilitating help with addiction is but a social problem that requires social intervention (Holden, 2012).

Alcohol consumption is responsible for substantial increases in morbidity, mortality, and social problems in both developing and developed countries (Rehm et al., 2010). For Canada, the mortality burden attributable to alcohol consumption is large, as well as unnecessary. This mortality burden could be substantially reduced in a short period of time if effective public health policies were implemented (Shield, Taylor, Kehoe, Patra, & Rehm, 2012). Because of the considerable harm caused by alcohol consumption, during the 63rd World Health Assembly held in May 2010 the World Health Organization agreed to a global strategy for reducing the harmful use of alcohol. The strategy focused on strengthening reliable information about alcohol consumption and that alcohol-related harms be recognized, and on effective dissemination of this information. Each member country, such as Canada, has the responsibility to monitor its own alcohol consumption. The progress of the strategy will be assessed at the 66th World Health Assembly in 2013 (WHO, 2010).

Addiction affects many people. One such group that has not received much attention is the affected family members (AFM) who are at a high risk of ill health (Orford, Velleman, Natera, Templeton, & Copello, 2013). It is evident that AFMs bear substantial personal and household family costs. A study of more than 25,000 AFMs in the United States found that these people contributed to significantly higher health care costs over a two-year period compared to family members of individuals who had illnesses such as asthma or diabetes (Ray, Mertens, & Weisner, 2009).

Recovery from alcohol addiction is often unpredictable. Terrion (2013), a Canadian researcher at the University of Ottawa, explored aspects of the academic experience of postsecondary students in recovery. Several variables were explored including the identity formation process, development or relationships, and the use of support services. The researcher concluded that social and personal relationships are important to both abstinence and academic success for students in recovery. For example, positive and supportive relationships—with peers in school, with peers and family members outside of school, with professors, and with members of support groups such as Alcoholics Anonymous (AA)—appeared to be central to the experience of both recovery and post-secondary education for the participants in this study (Terrion, 2013).

One of the main treatment modalities is Alcoholics Anonymous (AA), a movement that has experienced unmeasured success. AA is a fellowship of men and women who share their experiences, strengths, and hopes with each other so that each may help others to solve their common problems and help others to recover from alcoholism (Alcoholics Anonymous, 2013).

Gambling problems often go undetected. Despite their increasing prevalence, most of those addicted do not receive help for their addiction. The social stigma associated with making personal disclosures is a primary factor deterring compulsive gamblers from seeking help. Public education, risk-reduction policies, socially responsible programs within the gambling industry, decreased access to underage access to gambling products, and early intervention programs may be useful strategies to prevent the development of problem gambling (PHAC, 2011c).

Relapses, broadly defined as episodes or events that disrupt the overall effort to stop an addiction, are common. During one study, 92 percent of recovering gamblers relapsed at least once during a 12-month follow-up period. Complete abstinence may be too rigid a criterion for successful recovery. Knowledge of relapse cessation may help develop comprehensive treatment models that further the goals of abstinence. The trans-theoretical model identifies strategies individuals use to bring about both long-term (maintenance) and short-term (relapse termination) behavioural changes. Situational, interpersonal, physical, emotional, and cognitive factors offer a wide range of

critical thinking

Do you abuse drugs? Respond yes or no to the following items:

Yes   No

_____ _____ I have gotten into problems because of using drugs.

_____ _____ Using alcohol or other drugs has made my college or university life unhappy at times.

_____ _____ Drinking alcohol or taking other drugs has been a factor in my losing a job.

_____ _____ Drinking alcohol or taking other drugs has interfered with my studying for exams.

_____ _____ Drinking alcohol or taking drugs has jeopardized my academic performance.

_____ _____ My ambition is not as strong since I've been drinking a lot or taking drugs.

_____ _____ Drinking or taking drugs has caused me to have difficulty sleeping.

_____ _____ I have felt remorse after drinking or taking drugs.

_____ _____ I crave a drink or other drugs at a definite time of the day.

_____ _____ I want a drink or another drug the next morning.

_____ _____ I have had a complete or partial loss of memory as a result of drinking or using other drugs.

_____ _____ Drinking or using other drugs is affecting my reputation.

_____ _____ I have been in the hospital or another institution because of my drinking or taking drugs.

College and university students who responded yes to items similar to these on the Rutgers Collegiate Abuse Screening test were more likely to be substance abusers than those who answered no. If you responded yes to just one of the 13 items on this screening test, consider going to your health or counselling centre for further screening.

variables that motivate people to terminate relapse, and may provide a multifaceted range of interventions that would help individuals meet their goals (Thygesen & Hodgins, 2003).

To this point, we have studied a number of ideas about physical development, health, and wellness in early adulthood. For a review, see the **Reach Your Learning Objectives** section at the end of this chapter.

Sexuality

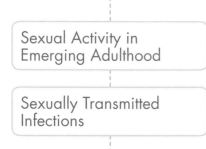

Sexual Activity in Emerging Adulthood

Sexually Transmitted Infections

Violence against Women

LO3 Examine the concept of sexuality in young adults.

Sexual awareness, feelings, and expressions—as fundamental to health as rest, nutrition, and exercise—develop over the life span. This is true for all of us, regardless of age, gender, sexual orientation, culture, career choices, or any other components that form our identities. Intimacy, commitments, marriage, and children are primary concerns for young adults.

In earlier chapters, we explored elements of childhood cognition. We learned that children develop self-esteem, learn to think critically, and make decisions. Positive early childhood development has a profound impact on healthy adult sexuality, attitudes, and activity. Freedom from harmful physical, emotional, and sexual abuse, combined with good nurturing and positive social interaction, contribute to the child's ability to make a successful transition from childhood to adolescence.

Similarly, a healthy transition from adolescence to adulthood is fostered by positive social interactions (Polan & Taylor, 2011). Media gender-role stereotyping, the linkage of violence and sex, unrealistic body images, combined with the prevalence of homophobia, complicate the adolescent transition to adulthood by creating a climate of fear, fascination, excitement, and temptation. Developmental milestones in cognition, including the ability to see other perspectives, reason abstractly, communicate effectively, and develop relationships with peers and adults, occur against a backdrop of mixed messages (Polan & Taylor, 2011). In addition, the young adult faces challenging realities, such as sexual orientation, unwanted pregnancies, miscarriages, addictions, infertility, poverty, violence (including sexual violence), artificial insemination and other reproductive technologies, infertility, and reproductive diseases (including cancer and endometriosis), which are rudely added to the experience of young adults as they are launched from the family home (Berger, 2014).

Sexual Activity in Emerging Adulthood

At the beginning of emerging adulthood (age 18), surveys indicate that slightly more than 60 percent of individuals have experienced sexual intercourse; by the end of emerging adulthood (age 25), most (80 percent) individuals have had sexual intercourse (Lefkowitz & Gillen, 2006; Statistics Canada, 2005c). The number of teens between the ages of 15 and 19 who report having had sexual intercourse at least once declined from 47 percent in 1996/1997 to 43 percent in 2005. By age 19, however, the number doubles (Rotermann, 2008). Teens in Quebec report higher rates of intercourse (58 percent) than other provinces, and Ontario the lowest at 37 percent (Rotermann, 2008). Although young women in Quebec and the eastern provinces report higher rates of sexual activity, overall the number of women reporting sexual intercourse has declined. The number of young men has remained constant (Rotermann, 2008; Statistics Canada, 2005c). Having more than one sexual partner is more common among men than women, and increases for both in emerging adulthood (Rotermann, 2008).

Sexual Orientation

Until the end of the nineteenth century, it was generally believed that people were either heterosexual or homosexual. Today, it is more accepted to view sexual orientation not as an either/or dichotomy, but as a continuum from exclusive male–female relations to exclusive same-sex relations (Strong et al., 2008) (see Figure 13.4). Some individuals are also *bisexual;* that is, sexually attracted to people of both sexes.

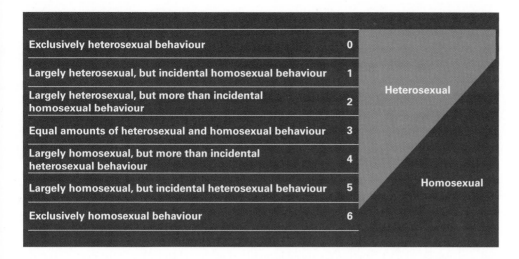

Exclusively heterosexual behaviour	0	
Largely heterosexual, but incidental homosexual behaviour	1	Heterosexual
Largely heterosexual, but more than incidental homosexual behaviour	2	
Equal amounts of heterosexual and homosexual behaviour	3	
Largely homosexual, but more than incidental heterosexual behaviour	4	
Largely homosexual, but incidental heterosexual behaviour	5	Homosexual
Exclusively homosexual behaviour	6	

Figure 13.4

The Continuum of Sexual Orientation

The continuum ranges from exclusive heterosexuality, which Kinsey and associates (1948) rated as 0, to exclusive homosexuality (6). People who are about equally attracted to both sexes (ratings 2 to 4) are bisexual.

Attitudes and laws related to homosexuality today reflect a history of controversy and struggle. In 1948, Canada ruled that homosexual activity was illegal. In the mid-50s, homosexuality was considered to be a psychological disorder; that designation was discontinued in the 1970s. In 1968, former Prime Minister Pierre Elliott Trudeau decriminalized homosexual intimacy when he decreed, "The government has no business in the bedrooms of the nation." In the early 1990s, gay activists fought hard to obtain legal status for their unions, and in 2006, the Canadian government proclaimed same-sex marriages to be legal.

All people, regardless of their sexual orientation, have similar physiological responses during sexual arousal and seem to be aroused by the same types of tactile stimulation. Investigators typically find no differences among lesbian, gay, and bisexuals (LGBs) and heterosexuals in a wide range of attitudes, behaviours, and adjustments (Peplau & Fingerhut, 2007). One recent review did find a higher prevalence of mental disorders in lesbians, gay men, and bisexuals than in heterosexuals, and concluded that the difference was due to the stress associated with stigma, prejudice, and discrimination (Meyer, 2003). The McCreary Centre Society (1999) reported "worries about my sexual orientation" as the third most common reason for a suicide attempt among gay adolescents.

Recently, researchers have explored the possible biological basis of same-sex relations (James, 2005). The results of hormone studies have been inconsistent. If gay males are given male sex hormones (androgens), their sexual orientation doesn't change; their sexual desire merely increases. A very early prenatal critical period might influence sexual orientation (James, 2005). If this critical-period hypothesis turns out to be correct, it would explain why clinicians have found that sexual orientation is difficult, if not impossible, to modify.

An individual's sexual orientation—same-sex, heterosexual, or bisexual—is most likely determined by a combination of genetic, hormonal, cognitive, and environmental factors (Berger, 2014). Most experts on same-sex relations believe that no one factor alone causes sexual orientation, and the relative weight of each factor can vary from one individual to the next.

In effect, no one knows exactly why some individuals are lesbian, gay, or bisexual. Nevertheless, scientists have discounted some of the myths. For example, children raised by gay or lesbian parents or couples are no more likely to be LGB than are children raised by heterosexual parents. There also is no evidence that being a gay male is caused by a dominant mother or a weak father, or that being a lesbian is caused by girls choosing male role models.

What likely determines an individual's sexual preference?

Attitudes and Behaviour of Lesbians and Gay Males

Many gender differences that appear in heterosexual relationships occur in same-sex relationships (Savin-Williams, 2008; Savin-Williams & Ream, 2007). For example, like heterosexual women, lesbians have fewer sexual partners than gay men, and lesbians have less permissive attitudes about casual sex outside a primary relationship than gay men (Peplau & Fingerhut, 2007). In a study that compared same-sex couples with opposite-sex dating, engaged, and married dyads, no differences were found in attachment security (Roisman et al., 2008). In this study, one difference between dyads was that lesbians were the most effective at working together in positive ways during laboratory observations.

A special concern involving sexual-minority individuals involves the hate crimes and stigma-related experiences they encounter. In a recent study, approximately 20 percent of sexual-minority adults reported that they had experienced a person or property crime related to their sexual orientation, about 50 percent said they had experienced verbal harassment, and more than 10 percent said they had encountered employment or housing discrimination (Herek, 2008).

Sexually Transmitted Infections

sexually transmitted infections (STIs) Diseases and infections that are contracted primarily through sexual contact.

Sexually transmitted infections (STIs) *are diseases and infections that are contracted primarily through sexual contact.* This contact is not limited to vaginal intercourse, but includes oral–genital and anal–genital contact as well. STIs are an increasing health problem. Among the main STIs individuals can get are bacterial infections (such as gonorrhea and syphilis), chlamydia, and two STIs caused by viruses—genital herpes and AIDS (acquired immune deficiency syndrome). Some infections are asymptomatic, especially in the early stages.

Human Papillomavirus (HPV)

HPV A virus (human papillomavirus) that causes warts on people; a few types of the virus cause warts on the genitals.

Recall from Chapter 11 that **HPV** is thought to be the most common sexually transmitted disease. Many types have been identified, some leading to cancer, others to anogenital warts. Fortunately a vaccine is now available and recommended to non-pregnant women who are not sexually active. This vaccine offers protection against the type of HPV responsible for 70 percent of cervical cancers. An estimated 75 percent of Canadians will have at least one HPV infection in their lifetime (Health Canada, 2007c). HPV is thought of as the silent infection, as the symptoms may go unnoticed and there are no obvious signs of infection, which may be either active or inactive. Consultation with a physician is important for treating anogenital warts. Having routine Pap (Papanicolaou) tests, practising safer sex, and reducing the number of partners are important in screening for and reducing the risk of HPV (Health Canada, 2007c). HPV, even when treated, is generally thought not to go away.

Gonorrhea

gonorrhea Reported to be one of the most common STIs in Canada, this sexually transmitted disease is caused by a bacterium called *Gonococcus,* which thrives in the moist mucous membranes lining the mouth, throat, vagina, cervix, urethra, and anal tract.

Gonorrhea, commonly called the "drip" or the "clap," is the second most commonly reported STI (PHAC, 2010d). Like HPV, most men and women do not experience symptoms. Gonorrhea is caused by a bacterium from the *Gonococcus* family, which thrives in the moist mucous membranes lining the mouth, throat, vagina, cervix, urethra, and anal tract. The bacterium is spread by contact between the infected moist membranes of one individual and the membranes of another (PHAC, 2010d).

Gonorrhea can be successfully treated in its early stages with penicillin or other antibiotics. Reported rates more than doubled between 2000 and 2008, from 6,189 to 12,723 cases (PHAC, 2010d).

Syphilis

syphilis A sexually transmitted disease caused by the bacterium *Treponema pallidum,* a member of the spirochete family.

Syphilis *is a sexually transmitted disease caused by the bacterium* Treponema pallidum, *a member of the spirochete family.* Like other STIs, it too has increased in incidence, from 174 cases reported in 2000 to 1,394 cases in 2008, with more males than females contracting the disease (PHAC, 2010d). The spirochete needs a warm, moist environment to survive, and it is transmitted by penile–vaginal, oral–genital, or anal contact. It can also be transmitted from a pregnant woman to her fetus after the fourth month of pregnancy. If the mother is treated before this time with penicillin, the syphilis will not be transmitted to the fetus.

In its early stages, syphilis can be effectively treated with penicillin. In its advanced stages, syphilis can cause paralysis or even death.

Chlamydia

Chlamydia, one of the most common of all sexually transmitted diseases, is named for *Chlamydia trachomatis*, an organism that spreads by sexual contact and infects the genital organs of both sexes. The number of reported cases of chlamydia increased from 46,439 in 2000 to 82,919 in 2008 (PHAC, 2010d). This STI is highly infectious, and women run a 70 percent risk of contracting it in a single sexual encounter. The male risk is estimated at between 25 and 50 percent. The greatest number of infections is found in individuals 15 to 24 years old (SOGC, 2011).

Males with chlamydia often get treatment because of noticeable symptoms in the genital region; however, females are asymptomatic. Therefore, many females go untreated and the chlamydia spreads to the upper reproductive tract where it can cause pelvic inflammatory disease (PID). The resultant scarring of tissue in the fallopian tubes can result in infertility or ectopic pregnancies (tubal pregnancies, or a pregnancy in which the fertilized egg is implanted outside the uterus). Some researchers suggest that chlamydia is the number-one preventable cause of female infertility (SOGC, 2011).

Genital Herpes

Genital herpes *is a highly contagious sexually transmitted disease caused by a large family of viruses with many different strains.* The actual number of cases is not known, but the risk factors include unprotected oral, genital, and anal intercourse (Li et al., 2008). These strains produce other, non–sexually transmitted diseases, such as chicken pox and mononucleosis. Herpes is the single most prevalent STI, affecting one in five Canadians. Three to five days after contact, itching and tingling can occur, followed by an eruption of sores and blisters. The attacks can last up to three weeks and may recur in a few weeks or a few years.

Although such drugs as acyclovir can be used to alleviate symptoms, there is no known cure for herpes. Therefore, people infected with herpes often experience severe emotional distress in addition to considerable physical discomfort. The virus can be transmitted through non-latex condoms and foams, making infected individuals reluctant to engage in sex, angry about the unpredictability of their lives, and fearful that they will not be able to cope with the pain of the next attack. For these reasons, support groups for victims of herpes have been established.

HIV and AIDS

No single STI has had a greater impact on sexual behaviour, or created more public fear in the last several decades, than infection with the human immunodeficiency virus (HIV) (Strong et al., 2008). HIV is a sexually transmitted infection that destroys the body's immune system. Once infected with HIV, the virus breaks down and overpowers the immune system, which leads to **AIDS** (acquired immune deficiency syndrome). HIV is transmitted through unprotected sexual intercourse and needle-sharing, and through pregnancy, delivery, and from an infected mother to her breast-fed child. An individual sick with AIDS has such a weakened immune system that a common cold can be life threatening. Medications can enhance the quality of life for patients with AIDS, but if left untreated, AIDS is fatal (Health Canada, 2010).

By the end of 2005, an estimated 58,000 Canadians were living with HIV infection, including AIDS. Of these, about 27 percent were not aware of their infection (PHAC, 2007). The incidence of HIV and AIDS has decreased in Canada generally; however, the numbers in First Nations and Inuit populations, where injection drug use continues to be a key mode of HIV transmission, are steadily increasing. As well, Aboriginal people are being affected at younger age than the general population. Although the number of women contracting the disease is increasing, street youth, especially those men who have sex with men and those who inject drugs, are most vulnerable (PHAC, 2010d).

---

critical thinking

Caroline contracted genital herpes from her boyfriend, whom she had been dating for the past three years. After breaking off that relationship and spending some time on her own, Caroline began dating Charles. Before becoming sexually involved with him, Caroline told Charles about her herpes infection, thinking that it was the right thing to do. Charles seemed accepting of the news, but soon after the discussion began treating Caroline differently. He became distant and cold toward her and eventually broke off their relationship saying that it "just wasn't working." Caroline firmly believed it was because she had told him about the herpes.

Caroline later met Jeff, whom she really liked and wanted to start dating. As they became closer to developing a sexual relationship, Caroline felt that she should tell Jeff about the herpes, but she was afraid that he also would abandon her. She thought that if she arranged it so that they never had sexual contact when she had herpes blisters (the time when infecting someone else is most likely to occur), she could protect him. She also thought that if they used latex condoms for protection, he would be safe, even though condoms can break.

Is Caroline making the right decision? If Caroline came to you for advice, what advice would you give? What should Caroline say, if anything, to Jeff? If Caroline did tell Jeff, and he did end their relationship, would telling him have been a mistake? Does Jeff have a right to know? Does Caroline have a right to privacy?

---

chlamydia The most common STD. Named for *Chlamydia trachomatis,* an organism that spreads by sexual contact and infects the genitals of both sexes.

genital herpes A highly contagious sexually transmitted disease caused by a large family of viruses of different strains. These strains also produce other, non–sexually transmitted diseases, such as chicken pox and mononucleosis.

AIDS Acquired immune deficiency syndrome; a primarily sexually transmitted disease caused by HIV, which destroys the body's immune system.

Globally, the total number of individuals with HIV reached 40 million in 2005 (UNAIDS, 2006). The greatest concern about AIDS is in sub-Saharan Africa, where it has reached epidemic proportions (Stephen Lewis, 2006: UNAIDS, 2006). Because of education and the development of more-effective drug treatments, deaths due to AIDS in North America have begun to decline. Contrast the figures in Canada, where an estimated 2,300 to 4,500 new HIV infections occurred in 2005, with the figures in Africa, where about 1.9 million people contracted the disease in 2008, and more than four million people had AIDS in 2000 (UNAIDS, 2006). According to Statistics Canada, the national population is estimated to be 33,930,000 as of January 1, 2010. Should the plague be of this magnitude in Canada, whole cities would be wiped out; for example Montreal, the second largest city in Canada, has an estimated population of a little over 1.6 million people. This is just a bit more than the number of people who died of AIDS in sub-Saharan Africa, where 1.4 million people died in 2008.

Protecting against STIs

Just asking a date about his or her sexual behaviour does not guarantee protection from HIV and other sexually transmitted diseases. For example, in one investigation, 655 students were asked to answer questions about lying and sexual behaviour (Cochran & Mays, 1990). Of the 422 respondents who said they were sexually active, 34 percent of the men and 10 percent of the women said they had lied so that their partner would have sex with them. Much higher percentages—47 percent of the men and 60 percent of the women—said they had been lied to by a potential sexual partner. When asked what aspects of their past they would be most likely to lie about, more than 40 percent of the men and women said they would understate the number of their sexual partners. Twenty percent of the men, but only 4 percent of the women, said they would lie about their results from an AIDS blood test.

The following are some good strategies for protecting against HIV and other sexually transmitted infections:

- *Know your and your partner's risk status.* Anyone who has had previous sexual activity with another person might have contracted an STI without being aware of it. Spend time getting to know a prospective partner before you have sex. Use this time to inform the other person of your STI status and inquire about your partner's. Remember that many people lie about their STI status.
- *Obtain medical examinations.* Many experts recommend that couples who want to begin a sexual relationship should have a medical checkup to rule out STIs before they engage in sex. If cost is an issue, contact your campus health service or a public health clinic.
- *Have protected, not unprotected, sex.* When correctly used, latex condoms help to prevent many STIs from being transmitted. Condoms are most effective in preventing gonorrhea, syphilis, chlamydia, and HIV. They are less effective against the spread of herpes (Norton, Fisher, Amico, Dovidio, & Johnson, 2012).
- *Do not have sex with multiple partners.* One of the best predictors of getting an STI is having sex with multiple partners. Having more than one sex partner elevates the likelihood that you will encounter an infected partner.

Violence against Women

Over the past three decades, the Federal-Provincial-Territorial Ministers Responsible for the Status of Women have shared a common vision to end violence against women. Violence against women in Canada is a serious and pervasive problem that crosses every social boundary; it affects essentially all communities across the country. Violence remains a significant barrier to women's equality, and it has devastating impacts on the lives of women, children, and families and on Canadian society as a whole.

The report *Assessing Violence against Women: A Statistical Profile* was released in 2002 and was followed by *Measuring Violence against Women: Statistical Trends 2006*. The 2006 report expanded the analysis into new areas, such as presenting information on Aboriginal women and women living in Canada's territories. This current report maintains this important focus and also includes information on dating violence, violence against girls, and violence that occurs outside of the intimate partner/family context. It also shows trends over time and provides data at national, provincial/territorial, and census metropolitan area levels (Statistics Canada, 2013a).

Sexual Assault

The term **sexual assault** *refers to all incidents of unwanted sexual activity including sexual attacks and sexual touching*. Too often, sex involves the exercise of power (Clark & Carroll, 2008). Research suggests that many victims continue to perceive sexual victimization as a private matter and most do not disclose their victimization to any source (Sable, Danis, Mauzy, & Gallagher, 2006). Youth and students may have higher rates of sexual assault because of lifestyle factors. A few factors include engaging more frequently in recreational activities and interacting with more individuals at any given time (Cass, 2007).

The National Violence against Women Survey (2004) estimated that 1.7 million Canadian women have been involved in at least one incident of sexual or physical assault by a date or boyfriend since the age of 16. In a national survey of 3,124 Canadian college and university students, 45 percent of female students reported incidents of sexual abuse since leaving high school. Thirty-five percent of female students said they had been physically assaulted in a dating relationship. Seventeen percent of the males admitted they had been physically violent toward a date since leaving high school. Women under 25 years of age are the most at risk. Eighty percent of the women who are abused by their partners continue to date the abusive partner.

Why is violence in a dating relationship so prevalent? The Nova Scotia Advisory Council on the Status of Women (2013) cites four contributing factors:

- *Patriarchal theory:* Men are socialized to exhibit dominance in relationships. Despite changing gender values, there are still some men who feel it is their right to punish, control, or batter their partners.
- *Peer pressure:* Boys often feel pressure from their peers to be sexually aggressive, which can contribute to sexually abusive behaviour and date rape.
- *Intergenerational violence:* Children who are victims of family violence or who witness abuse in the home often repeat abusive patterns in adolescence and adulthood. These young people often believe violence is an acceptable, or at least tolerable, means of resolving conflict.
- *Social learning theory:* The media bombard today's youth with violent and sexist images that convey the notion that violence is acceptable.

Sexual Harassment

Sexual harassment takes many forms—from sexist remarks and covert physical contact (patting, brushing against the body) to blatant propositions, stalking, and sexual assaults (Leaper & Brown, 2008; Mitchell, Koien, & Crow, 2008). It is a manifestation of power and the domination of one person by another, and millions of women experience such harassment each year in work and educational settings. The elimination of such exploitation requires the creation of work and academic environments that provide equal opportunities to develop a career and obtain an education in a climate free of sexual harassment (Das, 2008; Rospenda, Richman, & Shannon, 2008). Although sexual harassment of men by women occurs less frequently than the sexual harassment of women by men, it has equally devastating consequences.

To this point, we have discussed a number of ideas about sexuality in early adulthood. For a review, see the **Reach Your Learning Objectives** section at the end of this chapter.

critical thinking

Has violence, particularly dating violence, become so prevalent that it is considered the norm? What would you do if you or someone you know experienced violence or rape? What strategies could be put in place in your school to address violence against women and sexual harassment? What role does the Internet play in this? Outline a campaign against dating violence that could be implemented in a high school. What benefits and drawbacks might be encountered in such a program?

Violence against Women—A Continuing Outrage

"All women grow up in the context that includes the threat of violence, particularly sexualized violence . . . The exposure of violence in women's lives and its psychological effect on everyone, not only the direct victims, has intensified over the past ten years," wrote Jean Baker Miller in 1986 (Miller, 1986). Almost 20 years later, in March 2004, The United Nations (UN) issued its Declaration on the Elimination of Violence against Women, launching a two-year campaign to stop such violence. The Declaration defined "any act of gender-based violence that results in, or is likely to result in, physical, sexual, or psychological harm or suffering to women, including threats of such acts, coercion, or arbitrary deprivation of liberty, whether occurring in public or in private life," as violence against women. The UN further proclaimed that violence against women is a "manifestation of historically unequal power relations between men and women. . .one of the crucial social conventions by which women are forced into subordinate positions compared with men" (United Nations, 2004).

Violence against women starts before the woman is born and takes many forms, including those already mentioned as well as economic and educational opportunities (United Nations, 2006). The fact that preference for male babies exists to the extent that female fetuses are aborted and female babies are abandoned throughout the world is convincing evidence of the devaluing of female life. This practice, accompanied by neglect of girls, is prevalent in South and East Asia, North Africa, and the Middle East. Between 40 percent and 70 percent of female murder victims are killed by husbands or boyfriends in Australia, Canada, Israel, South Africa, and the United States (United Nations, 2006).

Using the UN's definition, Amnesty International (AI) tracks and reports incidents of violence around the world and categorizes three types of violence: domestic, community, and state (Amnesty International, 2004). AI reports astonishing levels of violence against women, ranging from battering and murder by intimate partners, sexual abuse of young girls, and dowry-related violence, to female genital mutilation, harassment and assault at work, forced prostitution, and sexual assault. Abuses by armed forces are well documented, as are violent acts of commission and omission, or acts condoned by police and government officials around the world. In fact, women are often subjected to violence, particularly sexual violence, while in police custody (United Nations, 2006).

In North America violence against women is illegal, yet Indigenous women in Canada are five times more likely than other women of the same age to die as the result of violence. Over half the women in Europe, North America, and Australia with physical disabilities have experienced physical abuse, compared to one-third of non-disabled women. Fear of violence often puts women at risk for STIs, unwanted pregnancies, and HIV and AIDS (United Nations, 2006). The acceptance and complexity of violence against women is illustrated by dating violence and the treatment of prostitutes.

Depression is one of the most common consequences of violence. Women subjected to violence are more likely to abuse alcohol and drugs, attempt suicide, and suffer symptoms of post-traumatic stress syndrome (PTSD). In 2005, Farley, Lynne, and Cotton reported their findings of a study of 100 women prostitutes in Vancouver. Seventy-two percent of the women interviewed met the criteria for PTSD. Fifty-two percent were First Nations women, most of whom reported a history of childhood sexual abuse by an average of four perpetrators. Many of the women had experienced homelessness and substance abuse. Ninety-five percent said they wanted to leave prostitution (Farley, Lynne, & Cotton, 2005).

In Canada, the cost of violence against women, including court, police, and counselling costs, was more than $1 billion in 1995. On average, women who are in a violent relationship leave seven times before leaving the relationship permanently. They stay because ending a relationship is threatening, they think their partner will change, they believe they understand him, and/or they may think they were to blame or somehow deserved the abuse.

Cognitive Development

LO4 Analyze the cognitive changes that occur in early adulthood.

Are young adults more advanced in their thinking than adolescents are? Let's examine what Piaget and others have said about this intriguing question.

Piaget's View

Creativity

Piaget's View

Piaget believed that an adolescent and an adult think *qualitatively* in the same way. That is, Piaget argued that formal operational thought (more logical, abstract, and idealistic than the concrete operational thinking of 7- to 11-year-olds) is entered into in early adolescence at approximately

11 to 15 years of age. Piaget believed that young adults are more *quantitatively* advanced in their thinking in the sense that they have more knowledge than adolescents. He also believed, as do information-processing psychologists, that adults especially increase their knowledge in a specific area, such as a physicist's understanding of physics or a financial analyst's knowledge of finance.

Some developmentalists believe many individuals do not consolidate their formal operational thinking until adulthood. That is, they may begin to plan and hypothesize about intellectual problems in adolescence, but they become more systematic and sophisticated at this as young adults. Nonetheless, many adults do not think in formal operational ways at all (Keating, 2004).

Realistic and Pragmatic Thinking

Other developmentalists believe that the idealism that Piaget described as part of formal operational thinking decreases in early adulthood. This occurs especially as young adults move into the world of work and face the constraints of reality (Labouvie-Vief, 1986).

K. Warner Schaie and Sherry Willis (2000) proposed a related perspective of adult cognitive change. They concluded that it is unlikely that adults go beyond the powerful methods of scientific thinking characteristic of the formal operational stage. However, Schaie argued that adults do progress beyond adolescents in their use of intellect. For example, he said that in early adulthood, individuals often switch from acquiring knowledge to applying knowledge. This occurs especially as individuals pursue long-term career goals and attempt to achieve success in their work.

Reflective and Relativistic Thinking

William Perry (1999) also described some changes in cognition that take place in early adulthood. He said that adolescents often view the world in terms of polarities—right/wrong, we/they, good/bad. As youth move into adulthood, they gradually move away from this type of absolute thinking as they become aware of the diverse opinions and multiple perspectives of others. Thus, in Perry's view, the absolute, dualistic thinking (either/or) of adolescence gives way to the reflective, relativistic thinking of adulthood. Other developmentalists also observe that reflective thinking is an important indicator of cognitive change in young adults (Fischer & Bidell, 2006).

Expanding on Perry's view, Gisela Labouvie-Vief (2006) recently proposed that the increasing complexity of cultures in the past century has generated a greater need for reflective, more complex thinking that takes into account the changing nature of knowledge and challenges. She also emphasizes that key aspects of cognitive development in emerging adulthood include deciding on a particular world-view, recognizing that the world-view is subjective, and understanding that diverse world-views should be acknowledged. In her perspective, considerable individual variation characterizes the thinking of emerging adults, with the highest level of thinking attained only by some. She argues that the level of education emerging adults achieve especially influences the likelihood that they will maximize their thinking potential.

As we see next, some theorists have pieced together some of these different aspects of thinking and proposed a new qualitative stage of cognitive development.

Is There a Fifth, Postformal Stage?

Postformal thought is qualitatively different from Piaget's formal operational thought (Moshman, 2006). **Postformal thought** involves understanding that the correct answer to a problem requires reflective thinking and can vary from one situation to another, and that the search for truth is often an ongoing, never-ending process (Kitchener, King, & DeLuca, 2006). Also part of postformal thought is the belief that solutions to problems need to be realistic and that emotion and subjective factors can influence thinking.

What is postformal thought like in practice? As young adults engage in more reflective judgment when solving problems, they might think deeply about many aspects of politics, their career and work, relationships, and other areas of life (Labouvie-Vief & Diehl, 1999). They might understand that what might be the best solution to a problem at work (with a co-worker or boss) might not be the best solution at home (with a romantic partner). Many young adults also become more skeptical about the

postformal thought Involves understanding that the correct answer to a problem requires reflective thinking and can vary from one situation to another, and that the search for truth is often an ongoing, never-ending process.

existence of a single truth, and often are not willing to accept an answer as final. They also often recognize that thinking can't just be abstract, but rather has to be realistic and pragmatic. And many young adults understand that emotions can play a role in thinking—for example, that they are likely to think more clearly when they are in a calm and collected state than when they are angry and highly aroused.

How strong is the research evidence for a fifth, postformal stage of cognitive development? Researchers have found that young adults are more likely to engage in this postformal thinking than adolescents are (Commons & Bresette, 2006). The fifth stage is controversial, however, and some critics argue that the research evidence has yet to be provided to document it as a qualitatively more advanced stage than formal operational thought. Another criticism is that rather than a discrete way of thinking, postformal thought may be a collection of attitudes about knowledge.

Creativity

Young adulthood is a time of great creativity for some people. At the age of 30, Thomas Edison invented the phonograph, Hans Christian Anderson wrote his first volume of fairy tales, and Mozart composed *The Marriage of Figaro*.

More recently, researchers have found that creativity peaks in adulthood and then declines, but that the peak often occurs in the forties. However, qualifying any conclusion about age and creative accomplishments are (1) the magnitude of the decline in productivity, (2) contrasts across creative domains, and (3) individual differences in lifetime output (Simonton, 1996).

Even though a decline in creative contributions is often found in the fifties and later, the decline is not as great as commonly thought. An impressive array of creative accomplishments occurs in late

In 2006, **Dr. Susan Tighe**, Ph.D., P.Eng., a professor of civil and environmental engineering at the University of Waterloo, was recognized as one of the top 40 under 40 in Canada for her creative work in civil engineering. Then, in 2007, she was awarded one of the Top 40 under 40 Awards for Vision and Leadership. In 2008, Tighe was identified as one of Canada's 80 Women to Watch by *Chatelaine* magazine. And in 2009, Tighe was selected as one of the Region of Waterloo's inaugural Top 40 under 40. She won the Ontario Premier's Excellence award for her research in infrastructure management, pavement, and transportation. Safety and environment concerns frame her work; for example, she is working to develop environmentally quiet pavements from recycled tires.

Sarah Polley played the lead in *Road to Avonlea* when she was a child, won a Gemini Award for her performance in the TV series *Straight Up* in 1996, and has starred in many films, including *The Sweet Hereafter*. She has shunned Hollywood, choosing to participate in non-commercial, independent projects. She received critical acclaim for her debut direction of *Away from Her*, based on a short story written by Alice Munro. *Away from Her* won best director and best feature film of 2006 at the Directors Guild of Canada Awards. In between directing *Take this Waltz*, a romantic drama, Polly starred in the science fiction movie *Splice*, about gene-combining experiments. Of her varied choices, Polly says, "I think my only criteria for choosing a role is if it's in a film I would want to go see."

Nikki Yanofsky, a musical prodigy, debuted at the Montreal International Jazz Festival in 2006, at the age of 16. Both a singer and a composer, she sang "I Believe" in the closing ceremonies of the 2010 Olympics and the opening ceremony of the Paralympics. In addition to her music career, Nikki is an ambassador for the Montreal Children's Hospital, the Children's Wish Foundation, and Music Counts. She has raised money for Haiti and to assist organizations such as War Child and World Vision Canada. What is evident to the listener, whether to her music or an interview, is her engaging enthusiasm. To learn more about Nikki, go to Connect at www.mcgrawhillconnect.ca.

adulthood. One of the most remarkable examples of creative accomplishment in late adulthood can be found in the life of Henri Chevreul. After a distinguished career as a physicist, Chevreul switched fields in his nineties to become a pioneer in gerontological research. He published his last research paper just a year prior to his death—at the age of 103!

Any consideration of decline in creativity with age requires consideration of the domain involved. In such fields as philosophy and history, older adults often show as much creativity as when they were in their thirties and forties. By contrast, in such fields as lyric poetry, abstract math, and theoretical physics, the peak of creativity is often reached in the twenties or thirties.

Pictured here are three notables whose creative talents have made an impact on three diverse fields: Dr. Susan Tighe (engineering), Sarah Polley (film), and Nikki Yanofsky (music).

There also is extensive individual variation in the lifetime output of creative individuals. Typically, as illustrated by these three examples, the most productive creators in any field are far more prolific than their least productive counterparts. However, those whom society recognizes or who become icons of their generation are as much a product of social and political factors as of talent. For example, the great writers of the Harlem Renaissance, all of whom were black, were not widely read by mainstream Americans until the middle or late 1970s. Now, no course in contemporary literature would exclude the writings of Langston Hughes and Zora Neale Hurston. As well, women authors and artists traditionally have not received the same recognition as their male counterparts. Pop icons such as Céline Dion, Avril Lavigne, and Nickelback are very much the products of aggressive marketing strategies.

To this point, we have studied a number of ideas on cognitive development in early adulthood. For a review, see the **Reach Your Learning Objectives** section at the end of this chapter.

developmental **connection**

Context

Careers and Work

LO5 Explain the key dimensions of careers and work in early adulthood.

At age 23, Joel graduated from university and accepted a job as a teacher at a Montreal high school. At 35, Marianne graduated from a community college and took a job as a computer programmer. At 25, Al and Shaohua graduated from nursing school and took part-time jobs in hospitals in Nova Scotia and Saskatoon. At 36, Anna has been contracted to teach English in both colleges and universities for each semester for the past six years; she would like a permanent job. Earning a living, choosing an occupation, establishing a career, and developing a career are important themes of early adulthood.

Developmental Changes

Values and Careers

The Occupational Outlook

The Impact of Work

Developmental Changes

Children have idealistic fantasies about what they want to be when they grow up. For example, young children might want to be a superhero, a sports star, or a movie star. In the high school years, they often have begun to think about careers on a somewhat less idealistic basis. In their late teens and early twenties, career decision making usually turns more serious and practical as they explore different career possibilities and settle on the career they want to enter. Going to college or university often means choosing a major or specialization that is designed to lead to work in a particular field. From the mid-twenties through the remainder of early adulthood, individuals often seek to establish their emerging career in a particular field. They may work hard to move up the career ladder and improve their financial standing.

Values and Careers

An important aspect of choosing a career is that it matches up with your values. When people know what they value most—what is important to them in life—they can refine their career choice more effectively. For example, one person values working in a career that involves helping others, and

critical thinking

Take a few minutes and think about the career you want to pursue. What do you think the profile of an ideal job candidate in this career field would be? What would be the profile of a co-worker with whom you would like to work? How have your career decisions evolved? If you had an opportunity would you make any career changes?

connecting through social policy ←--------

Dr. Samantha Nutt

Nothing affects policies, particularly economic policies, like disasters and war. To North Americans war brings about changes in economies and erosion of civil liberties, but to people who experience warfare in their homelands, such as the people of Sierra Leone, Iraq, Colombia, Ethiopia, and Darfur, war cripples economies, causes or contributes to famine, and contaminates resources. Further, war causes widespread psychological trauma. According to Dr. Samantha Nutt, war has "horrific implications for millions of people," and she wishes people could see military action through the eyes of a child (Hass, 2001; Nutt, 2007).

Can one Canadian influence change? Dr. Nutt believes that collectively we can make a difference to the lives of people affected by wars. To increase awareness of what happens to these women, children, and their families, Dr. Nutt tells their stories because she believes the "lessons of peace are best told through the stories of war" (Nutt, 2007). She tells the heart-wrenching story of how pre-adolescent boys find acquiring guns easier than obtaining water, or of a mother shot down in a pool of blood before her family and neighbours.

Dr. Nutt is a medical doctor with over a decade's experience working in war zones. Her work has always been aimed at improving the lives of women and children devastated by war. She believes that youth can effect change, and encourages students who want to do humanitarian work to get experience by working with or volunteering with international causes

By dedicating every day to raising awareness and providing relief and support for women and children harmed by the atrocities of war in the world, University of Toronto professor and family physician Samantha Nutt aligns her values with her work-life.

because, "once you have been in a war zone, your life changes, your perspective changes. It is impossible not to acknowledge that your life has been fundamentally altered." She is founder and executive-director of War Child, an educational and fundraising forum. When in Canada, she practises medicine with new immigrants, refugees, the poor, and young women (Hass, 2001). She has been awarded many prestigious designations, from being named one of Ten Great Canadian Women to Know by *Homemakers* magazine to National Trailblazer by Global TV. She was chosen as Personnalité de la Semaine by *La Presse* and CBC Radio Canada, and one of 200 Young Global Leaders in the World by the *World Economic Forum*.

Dr. Nutt concludes her essay "The Lessons of Peace" by saying, "War has taught me to place my trust in peace, and I believe that all citizens of the world deserve the right, and the opportunity, to live without violence. I believe it will be possible, some day, for war—and all the death, destruction, and unfathomable hardship that war brings—to be a footnote in the history of humankind. At the very least, I believe, it is incumbent upon us to try" (2007).

More information about Dr. Nutt's work is available on Connect at www.mcgrawhillconnect.ca.

another prefers a career in which creativity is essential. Among the values that some individuals think are important in choosing a career are working with people they like, working in a career with prestige, making a lot of money, being happy, not having to work long hours, being mentally stimulated, having plenty of time for leisure pursuits, working in the right geographical location, and working where physical and mental health are important.

Other values that some individuals think are important when they make choices about their work life are related to the contribution they may make to society at large. They may join Doctors, Engineers, or Teachers Without Borders, or other organizations dedicated to improving the lives of others. Dr. Samatha Nutt's passion for the welfare of children in war-torn countries led her not only to visit countries and experience first-hand the devastation caused by war, but also to bring her awareness to the public arena by organizing her professional life in Canada in ways that engage others. This chapter's Connecting through Social Policy features Dr. Nutt and the organization she founded, War Child.

The Occupational Outlook

As you explore the type of work you are likely to enjoy and in which you can succeed, it is important to be knowledgeable about different fields and companies. Occupations may have many job openings one year but few in another year as economic conditions change. Thus, it is critical to keep up with the occupational outlook in various fields. On way, you can monitor your future by keeping up with the occupational outlook in various fields and enhancing your skill sets accordingly. An excellent source is *Canada WorkInfoNet*, which is revised every two years.

What characteristics are employers looking for? According to a survey conducted by the Conference Board of Canada, employers are looking for people who possess a combination of academic experience, personal management, and teamwork skills to form the foundation of a high-quality Canadian workforce. Academic skills include the ability to communicate effectively, think critically, and engage in lifelong learning. Personal management skills include positive attitudes and behaviours, such as confidence, honesty, ethics, willingness to learn, as well as initiative, energy, and persistence. Teamwork skills include the ability to work with others, make cooperative decisions, and respect the thoughts and opinions of others in the group.

The combination of these skills, attitudes, and behaviours provides the foundation to get, keep, and progress in a job and to achieve the best results. More information is available on Connect at www.mcgrawhillconnect.ca.

critical thinking

Every dream and vision you might develop about your future can be broken down into specific goals and time frames. Keeping your career dreams in focus, write some of the specific educational and career goals you have for the next 20, 10, and 5 years. Be as concrete and specific as possible. In making up goals, start from the farthest point—20 years—and work backward. If you go the other way, you run the risk of adopting goals that are not precisely and clearly related to your dream. Compare and contrast your educational career goals after you have completed your work.

The Impact of Work

Work plays a powerful role in our lives. It defines people in fundamental ways (Blustein, 2008; Fouad & Bynner, 2008). As Dr. Samantha Nutt illustrates, people identify with their work, and that work shapes their identity and self-concept. In many ways, the relationship between a person and his or her work is quite reciprocal in that as the worker shapes the workplace, at the same time he or she is shaped by that working environment. Most individuals spend between 30 and 50 percent of their lives at work. The average workweek is between 35 and 40 hours, but almost 20 percent of us work over 50 hours a week. Work is an important influence on an individual's financial standing, housing, leisure activities, friendships, and health (Warr, 2004). Further, work creates a structure and rhythm to life that often is missed when individuals do not work for an extended period of time. When unable to work, many individuals experience emotional distress and low self-esteem.

Many adults have changing expectations about work, yet employers often are not meeting these expectations (Moen, 2007; Orrange, 2007). For example, current policies and practices were designed for a single breadwinner, a traditionally male workforce, and an industrial economy, making these policies and practices out of step with a workforce of women and men, and of single parents and dual earners. Many workers today want flexibility and greater control over the time and timing of their work, and yet most employers offer little flexibility even though policies like flextime and job-sharing may be "on the books."

Work during Postsecondary Education

We know that past demographic trends and changes in postsecondary participation rates have had a tremendous impact on postsecondary enrolments over the past half century. For example, when the early Boomers reached their late teens in the late 1960s, postsecondary enrolments greatly expanded as a result of both increased numbers of young adults and increases in postsecondary participation rates that continued through to the mid-1980s. Growth in postsecondary enrolments slowed somewhat during the late 1980s and early 1990s, reflecting both a decline in the number of young adults (the baby-bust cohort of the 1970s) and stagnation in the rate of postsecondary participation. However, by the late 1990s the children of the Boomer cohort (born 1980 to 1995) started to exert pressure on the postsecondary system once again. Berger, Motte, and Parkin (2007) state that one recent report from the Canada Millennium Scholarship Foundation warns postsecondary institutions to refocus enrolment strategies because enrolment is expected to peak in about 2013 and then begin to decline. Immigration has also had an impact on enrolment (Statistics Canada, 2007d).

Tuition fees have become an issue; unfortunately, students' wages have not kept pace with rising tuition costs, further decreasing accessibility and increasing debt loads (CCL, 2006). Students tend to work at low-paying jobs in service, retail, food, and tourism (Roberts et al., 2004). Additionally, many are working well over 15 or 20 hours a week, to the detriment of their studies. An example of the impact of tuition increases was revealed in a study conducted by the Canadian Medical Association. Over the 10-year period between 1990 and 2000 when tuition increased, enrolment in medical school for students from low-income families dropped from 22.6 percent to 15 percent. Other universities that have increased their tuition since deregulation in the mid-90s report similar findings. For example, when annual tuition rose from $3,500 to $10,000 at the University of Western Ontario, students from families whose incomes were under $40,000 dropped by approximately 10 percent from 17.3 percent to 7.7 percent. Even students in the five provinces (Alberta, Saskatchewan, Manitoba, Quebec, and Newfoundland and Labrador) where tuition has been frozen find the costs of attending university higher. Currently, British Columbia, Ontario, and Nova Scotia have set limits on tuition increases (CCL, 2006).

Statistics Canada (2003c) reports indicate that the dropout rate for high school students who worked more than 30 hours a week was 2.4 percent higher than for those who worked between 1 and 20 hours. Interestingly, Statistics Canada (2003c) reports that students who did not work at all were 1.5 times more likely to drop out than those who worked moderately. Further, a study of high school students who work 15 hours or less reported that students not only gained experience, which enhanced their future earning potential, but also developed a positive attitude toward work (Naylor, 1999). The trends identified among high school students are repeated in postsecondary students. Those who work long hours are more likely to abandon their studies. Working long hours may not be a causal factor for students leaving school, but the overwhelming weight of evidence suggests that students who wish to complete their educations need to avoid devoting too many hours to paid employment (CCL, 2006).

Unemployment

Unemployment produces stress, regardless of whether the job loss is temporary, cyclical, or permanent. Researchers have found that unemployment is related to physical problems (such as heart attack and stroke), mental problems (such as depression and anxiety), marital difficulties, and homicide (Gallo et al., 2006). A 15-year longitudinal study of more than 24,000 adults found that life satisfaction dropped considerably following unemployment and increased after becoming re-employed, but did not completely return to the life satisfaction level previous to being unemployed (Lucas et al., 2004). A recent study also revealed that immune system functioning declined with unemployment and increased with new employment (Cohen et al., 2007).

Stress comes not only from a loss of income and the resulting financial hardships, but also from decreased self-esteem. Individuals who cope best with unemployment have financial resources to rely on, often savings or the earnings of other family members. The support of understanding, adaptable family members also helps individuals cope with unemployment. Job counselling and self-help groups can provide practical advice on job searching, résumés, and interviewing skills, and also give emotional support.

Dual-Career Couples

Dual-earner couples may have particular problems finding a balance between work and the rest of life (Pitt-Catsouphes, Kossek, & Sweet, 2006). Balancing family life, work, and leisure is a challenge for many young dual-career couples (Pitt-Catsouphes, Kossek, & Sweet, 2006). When both partners are working, the tasks of managing home and family can tax the relationship. An additional complication arises when one or both of the people are working from home.

In heterosexual unions, men are taking increased responsibility for maintaining the home and caring for children, and women are taking increased responsibility for providing economic support. In same-sex unions, individuals divide the labour outside of the prescribed and internalized gender roles.

In spite of shifting roles, women in heterosexual unions perform a far greater proportion of household tasks than their husbands, even when they earn more money or their husband is unemployed (Greenstein, 2000). Women continue to do traditionally ascribed work such as cooking, laundry, and housecleaning, and men still do yard work, take out the garbage, and do auto maintenance. Thus, an important issue for many young relationships is juggling career and family work (Milke & Peltola, 2000).

Another issue that dual-career couples face focuses on compatible job schedules and/or locations. One individual might work primarily during the day, the other in the evening or at night, in which case they rarely see each other. If one spouse receives a job offer in another geographical location, the issues of whose career takes priority or whether the couple should consider a long-distance relationship are raised.

To this point, we have studied a number of ideas about careers and work in early adulthood. For a review, see the **Reach Your Learning Objectives** section at the end of this chapter.

reach your **learning objectives**

The Transition from Adolescence to Adulthood

LO1 Outline the transition from adolescence to early adulthood.

The Criteria for Becoming an Adult	■ Statistics Canada identifies five criteria of adulthood:
	  – Left parental home
	  – Left school
	  – Has full-time full-year work
	  – Is in a conjugal union
	  – Has children who live with them
	■ An emerging adult is one between ages 18 and 25 who has not yet assumed all the responsibilities of adulthood.

The Transition from High School to College, University, or Work	■ The challenges of emerging adulthood are many and may cause stress as well as bring happiness. ■ Finding positive ways to deal with stress is important to successful transitioning.

Physical Development, Health, and Wellness

LO2 Describe physical changes and health considerations for emerging adults

Health	■ Peak physical status is often reached between 18 and 30 years of age. There is a hidden hazard in this time period as this is when bad health habits are often formed. ■ Toward the latter part of early adulthood, a detectable slowdown in physical development is apparent for most individuals.

Eating and Weight	■ Obesity is a serious problem, with about 12 percent of Canadians overweight enough to be at increased health risk.
	■ Heredity, leptin, set point, and basal metabolism are biological factors involved in obesity. Environmental factors and culture also influence obesity.
	■ Many divergent interests are involved in the topic of dieting.
	■ For those who diet (Weight Watchers), exercise is usually an important component. Depending on the diet, dieting can be harmful; however, when overweight people diet and maintain their weight loss, it can have positive effects.
Regular Exercise	■ Both moderate and intense exercise produce important physical and psychological gains, such as lowered risk of heart disease and lowered anxiety.
Substance Abuse	■ Although some reduction in alcohol use has occurred among college and university first-year students, binge drinking is still a major concern. By the mid-twenties a reduction in both alcohol and drug use often occurs.
	■ A number of strategies, such as nicotine substitutes, have shown some success in getting smokers to quit, but quitting is difficult because of the addictive properties of nicotine.
	■ Addiction is a maladaptive response to an underlying condition such as a nonspecific inability to cope with the world. Alcohol consumption is responsible for substantial increase in morbidity, mortality, and social problems.

Sexuality

LO3 Examine the concept of sexuality in young adults.

Sexual Activity in Emerging Adulthood	■ Sexual awareness, attitudes, and expressions develop over the life span and are critical to healthy adult life.
	■ Media influence, which is often negative toward women and links sex and violence, is powerful.
	■ Although homophobia is still prevalent today, most Canadians take a live-and-let live attitude and believe that homosexuals should have the right to marry. This attitude is reflected in current legislation.
	■ Reproductive disease and manipulations are challenges faced by today's young adults.
	■ The generally accepted view of sexual orientation is along a continuum from exclusively heterosexual to exclusively homosexual.
Sexually Transmitted Infections	■ Sexually transmitted infections, or STIs (also called STDs, sexually transmitted diseases), are contracted primarily through sexual contact.
	■ Gonorrhea, syphilis, chlamydia, genital herpes, and HPV are among the most common STIs.
	■ Many STIs may be asymptomatic.
	■ The STI that has received the most attention in the last several decades is AIDS (acquired immune deficiency syndrome), which is caused by HIV, a virus that destroys the body's immune system.
	■ Some good strategies for protecting against AIDS and other STIs are to (1) know your own and your partner's risk status, (2) obtain medical examinations, (3) have only protected sex, and (4) not have sex with multiple partners.
Violence against Women	■ Sexual assault is a term referring to all incidents of unwanted sexual activity including sexual attacks and sexual touching.
	■ Occurs when one person uses his or her power over another individual in a sexual manner.

Cognitive Development

LO4 Analyze the cognitive changes that occur in early adulthood.

Piaget's View	■ Formal operational thought, entered into at age 11 to 15, is Piaget's final cognitive stage.
	■ Piaget said that adults are quantitatively more knowledgeable than adolescents, but that adults do not enter a new, qualitatively different stage.
	■ Some experts argue that the idealism of Piaget's formal operational stage declines in young adults and is replaced by more realistic, pragmatic thinking.
	■ Perry said that adolescents often engage in dualistic, absolute thinking, while young adults are more likely to engage in reflective, relativistic thinking.
	■ Postformal thought involves understanding that the correct answer might require reflective thinking and might vary from one situation to another, and that the search for truth is often never-ending.
	■ The postformal stage includes the understanding that solutions to problems often need to be realistic and that emotion and subjective factors can be involved in thinking.
Creativity	■ Creativity peaks in adulthood, often in the forties, and then declines. However, (a) the magnitude of the decline is often slight, (b) the creativity–age link varies by domain, and (c) there is extensive individual variation in lifetime creative output.

Careers and Work

LO5 Explain the key dimensions of careers and work in early adulthood.

Developmental Changes	■ Many young children have idealistic fantasies about a career. By the late teens and early twenties, their career thinking has usually turned more serious.
	■ By their early to mid-twenties, many individuals have completed their education or training and started in a career. In the remainder of early adulthood, they seek to establish their emerging career and start moving up the career ladder.
Values and Careers	■ It is important to match up a career to your values. There are many different values, ranging from the importance of money to working in a preferred geographical location.
	■ Service-producing industries will account for the most jobs in the next decade. Employment in the computer industry is projected to grow rapidly.
	■ Jobs that require a postsecondary education will be the fastest growing and highest paying.
The Occupational Outlook	■ The Conference Board of Canada reports that employers want a combination of academic, personal management, and teamwork skills.
	■ Canadian employers seek employees who have excellent generic skills, including computer and communication skills, plus the ability to work effectively on teams.
The Impact of Work	■ Work defines people in fundamental ways and is a key aspect of their identity. Most individuals spend about one-third of their adult life at work.
	■ The relationship between the workplace and the individual is reciprocal in that the worker shapes the workplace and the workplace shapes the individual's identity.
	■ Many workers would like more flexibility through policies such as flextime and job-sharing.
	■ College and university students work in an effort to cover increasing tuition costs.
	■ Increasing tuition costs have reduced access for students from lower income families.
	■ Unemployment creates stress and is related to health, mental health, marital problems, and homicide.
	■ Dual-career couples find balancing work and the rest of their lives challenging.

Mc Graw Hill Education **connect®**

McGraw-Hill Connect provides you with a powerful tool for improving academic performance and truly mastering course material. You can diagnose your knowledge with pre- and post-tests, identify the areas where you need help, search the entire learning package, including the eBook, for content specific to the topic you're studying, and add these resources to your personalized study plan. CONNECT for *Life-Span Development,* fifth Canadian edition, offers the following:

- chapter-specific online quizzes
- groupwork
- presentations
- writing assignments
- case studies
- and much more!

Visit CONNECT today!

review ----> *connect* ----> reflect

review

What are two main criteria for becoming an adult? **LO1**

What causes physical performance to peak and then slow down in early adulthood? **LO2**

What are some benefits of exercise? **LO2**

What characterizes the sexual activity of emerging adults? **LO3**

What are sexually transmitted infections? **LO3**

What changes in the cognitive development of young adults have been identified? **LO4**

What are some developmental changes in careers and work? **LO5**

connect

How does one's gender affect work opportunities and work environment for the young adult?

reflect *Your Own Personal Journey of Life*

If you are an emerging young adult, what career do you want to pursue? How many years of education will your career of choice require? If you have a young family and reside in a rural area, what resources are available for you, as a woman, if you wish to work?

CHAPTER 14 Socio-Emotional Development in Early Adulthood

CHAPTER OUTLINE

Stability and Change from Childhood to Adulthood

LO1 Examine stability and change in temperament, and summarize adult attachment styles.

Temperament

Attachment

Attraction, Love, and Close Relationships

LO2 Identify three key aspects of attraction, love, and close relationships.

Attraction

The Faces of Love

Falling Out of Love

Friendship

Loneliness

Intimate Relationships: Marriage and the Family Life Cycle

LO3 Describe intimate relationships such as marriage, the family life cycle, and cultural influences on family life.

Marital Trends in Canada

Social Contexts

Making Marriage Work

Benefits of a Good Marriage

The Family Life Cycle

Parenting Myths and Realities

The Diversity of Adult Lifestyles

LO4 Compare and contrast the diversity of adult lifestyles.

Single Adults

Cohabiting Adults

Divorced Adults

Remarried Adults

Parenting Adults

Lone-Parent Adults

Gay and Lesbian Adults

Gender, Relationships, and Moral Development

LO5 Summarize moral development and gender development.

Moral Development

Women's Development

Men's Development

> " . . . *love is only possible between two equals.*"
>
> —GUY VANDERHAEGHE, CONTEMPORARY CANADIAN AUTHOR

Variations: Do Any of These Scenarios Resemble Someone You Know?

As in Chapter 12, these snapshots are tiny glimpses into some of the challenges and milestones facing young adults.

THE SINGLE: Remaining single is a life choice for many young adults, such as Jerry. He is beginning to understand that many advantages exist in living the single lifestyle. For example, one such advantage is freedom to make autonomous decisions and pursue his own schedule and interests, which he really likes to do. A disadvantage of the single life is confronting his loneliness. But Jerry is active. He has many friends, and does not see loneliness as being an issue for him. What must become a concern for Jerry is pressure from society, around the age of 30, to settle down and get married. However, Jerry knows that at that time he can make a conscious decision to either marry or remain single.

THE ARRANGED MARRIAGE: Mehri is proud and happy that her father was able to arrange her marriage before he died of terminal cancer. She says the husband her father chose for her when she was 14 is perfect. He is kind, generous, and a good father to their two sons, who are now 8 and 10 years old.

LIVING APART: Dawit, a refugee to Canada, fled his homeland leaving behind a wife and child. He looks forward to the time when his family can be reunited. In the meantime, he sends as much money as he can to the wife and child he loves and misses.

SPOUSAL ABUSE: Jen had hoped that having a baby would bring them closer together and that Emanuel would soften. Emanuel, exhausted from working two part-time jobs and stressed with financial worries, took out his frustrations yet again, verbally abusing and threatening Jen. Jen, fearful for her safety, moved into a shelter with her four-month-old son. She is determined not to subject herself or her son to further abuse.

SAME-SEX MARRIAGE: Since their marriage, Sandra and Barb have been busy renovating their new house in addition to working full time. They also are the parents of an 11-year-old girl and an 8-year-old boy from Barb's first marriage, which ended in divorce once she came to terms with her lesbian status.

COHABITATING UNION: Melanie and James have lived together for 12 years. They enjoy their home and a wide circle of friends. James has a bipolar condition, which limits his ability to work. Melanie enjoys travelling, although James can rarely join her. Every year they privately renew their commitment to each other, and part of their commitment to each other is to value each other's freedom and autonomy.

POLYGAMOUS MARRIAGE: Sasha and Merianna pass themselves off as sisters to those who do not know them well. As far as the government is concerned, that is the status which allowed their husband, Ahmed, to bring them to Canada. To those they know well and trust, Sasha and Merianna are Ahmed's polygamous wives.

FEAR OF COMMITMENT: After a six-month period during which Gwenna gave Greg the emotional space he needed to sort out his ambivalence and doubt about their relationship, Greg requested more time to make up his mind. At this time, Gwenna took the painful—but ultimately empowering—step of ending the relationship.

EQUALITY IN MARRIAGE: Once their first child was born, traditional fixed gender roles seeped into their marriage, although they had consciously vowed to reject these well-indoctrinated scripts. George, feeling the pressure to provide for his family's economic future, thought Noreen should take over the responsibility for household chores. Needless to say, Noreen, who had a career of her own, did not agree.

EARLY ENDING OF A MARRIAGE: At 38 years of age, Jason finds himself the widowed father of two young children, Mary, age 10, and Bobby, age 8. His wife succumbed to breast cancer after a two-year battle. He feels alone and lost and has no idea where to begin.

Psychologist and philosopher Erich Fromm equates love to art, pointing out that love takes patience and practice (Fromm, 1956). Certainly, most would agree that love is central to our lives; so, finding a way to fit patience and practice into our busy schedules is sometimes overlooked until we find ourselves alone, like Jason in the above scenario. As these scenarios illustrate, relationships are complex and unique. Into each relationship, people carry their personal contexts, their unique factors of identity: family traditions, social and political attitudes, religious beliefs, and their ambitions for the future. Social contexts of class, ethnicity, gender, and race add further complexities, as no two individuals, no matter how superficially similar they are, share the same values and attitudes.

How do you think the individuals described above will negotiate their present or future relationships?

Stability and Change from Childhood to Adulthood

LO1 Examine stability and change in temperament, and summarize adult attachment styles.

For adults, socio-emotional development revolves around "the adaptive integration of emotional experience into satisfying daily life and successful relationships with others" (Thompson & Goodvin, 2005, p. 402). Young adults must make "choices of occupation, partners, and other activities" that will create lifestyles that are "emotionally satisfying, predictable, and manageable." They do not come to these tasks as blank slates, but do their decisions and actions simply reflect the person they had already become when they were 5 years old or 10 years old or 20 years old? Young adults around the world face challenges; however, many overcome them and continue their personal growth.

Current research shows that the first 20 years of life are not meaningless in predicting an adult's socio-emotional life (Caspi & Shiner, 2006). And there is every reason to believe that experiences in the early adult years are important in determining what the individual will be like later in adulthood. A common finding is that the smaller the time intervals over which we measure socio-emotional characteristics, the more similar an individual will look from one measurement to the next. Thus, if we measure an individual's self-concept at the age of 20 and then again at the age of 30, we will probably find more stability than if we measured the individual's self-concept at the age of 10 and then again at the age of 30.

In trying to understand the young adult's socio-emotional development, looking at an adult's life only in the present tense, ignoring the unfolding of social relationships and emotions, would be misleading. It would also be a mistake to only search through a 30-year-old's first 5 to 10 years of life when trying to understand why he or she is having difficulty in a close relationship.

Temperament

How stable is temperament? Recall that *temperament* is an individual's behavioural style and characteristic emotional responses. In early adulthood, most individuals assume greater responsibilities, foresee consequences, plan ahead, and are more even-keeled than in adolescence (Caspi, 1998). Along with these signs of general change in temperament, researchers also find links between some dimensions of childhood temperament and adult personality.

Is temperament in childhood linked with adjustment in adulthood? Here is what we know on the basis of the few longitudinal studies that have been conducted on this topic (Caspi, 1998). Recall from Chapter 6 the distinction between an easy and a difficult temperament. In one longitudinal study, children who had an easy temperament at 3 to 5 years of age were likely to be well adjusted as young adults (Chess & Thomas, 1987). In contrast, many children who had a difficult temperament at 3 to 5 years of age were not well-adjusted as young adults. Also, other researchers have found that boys with a difficult temperament in childhood are less likely as adults to continue their formal education, whereas girls with a difficult temperament in childhood are more likely to experience marital conflict as adults (Wachs, 2000).

Inhibition is a temperament characteristic that has been studied extensively by Jerome Kagan (2000, 2002, 2008). Kagan concluded that individuals with an inhibited temperament in childhood are less likely as adults to be assertive or to experience social support and more likely to delay entering a stable job track. A longitudinal study revealed that the 15 percent most inhibited girls and boys at four to six years of age were rated by their parents as inhibited, and they were actually delayed in establishing a stable partnership and in finding their first full-time job by 23 years of age (Asendorph, Denissen, & van Aken, 2008). Further, in the Uppsala (Sweden) Longitudinal Study shyness/inhibition in infancy/childhood was linked to social anxiety at 21 years of age (Bohlin & Hagekull, 2009). These researchers found unexpected gender differences as well. Williams and his

Temperament

Attachment

developmental **connection** - - - - - - - -

Stability vs. Change

researchers (2010) found that formerly inhibited boys were more likely than the average adolescent to use drugs. Conversely, inhibited girls were less likely to use drugs.

Ability to control one's emotions (a dimension in Mary Rothbart's and John Bates's analysis of temperament) has also been studied. In one longitudinal study, when three-year-old children showed good control of their emotions and were resilient in the face of stress, they were likely to continue to handle emotions effectively as adults (Block, 1993). By contrast, when three-year-olds had low emotional control and were not very resilient, they were likely to show problems in these areas as young adults.

In sum, a small number of studies reveal some continuity between certain aspects of temperament in childhood and adjustment in early adulthood. More research is needed to verify these linkages. Indeed, Theodore Wachs (1994, 2000) recently proposed ways that linkages between temperament in childhood and personality in adulthood might vary depending on the intervening contexts in individuals' experience (see Figure 14.1). Many aspects of the environment—including gender, culture, parenting, and general goodness of fit—may influence the persistence of aspects of a child's temperament through life. Previous studies indicate that temperament is also genetically influenced from childhood through adolescence. For example, new genes may be activated with puberty, causing changes in reactions and behaviours (Ganiban, Saudino, Ulbricht, Neiderhiser, & Reiss, 2008). One interesting note is that studies that do not include twins tend to generate lower heritability estimates for temperament (Loehlin, Neiderhiser, & Reiss, 2003).

Attachment

---- developmental **connection** --,

Attachment Theory

‹--------------------

Like temperament, attachment appears during infancy and plays an important part in socio-emotional development (Cassidy, 2009; Weinfield et al., 2009). We discussed its role in infancy, childhood, and adolescence. Attachment continues to shape development in early adulthood (Crowell et al., 2002; Feeney & Thrush, 2010). The Connecting through Research box illustrates how Susan Johnson has applied attachment theory to counselling couples.

Figure 14.1

Temperament in Childhood, Personality in Adulthood, and Intervening Contexts

Varying experiences with caregivers, the physical environment, peers, and schools can modify links between temperament in childhood and personality in adulthood. The example given here is for inhibition.

Initial Temperament Trait: Inhibition	
Child A	**Child B**
Intervening Context	
Caregivers Caregivers (parents) who are sensitive and accepting, and let the child set his or her own pace.	Caregivers who use inappropriate "low level control" and attempt to force the child into new situations.
School's Environment Presence of "stimulus shelters" or "defensible spaces" that the child can retreat to when there is too much stimulation.	Child continually encounters noisy, chaotic environments that allow no escape from stimulation.
Peers Peer groups consist of other inhibited children with common interests, so the child feels accepted.	Peer groups consist of athletic extroverts, so the child feels rejected.
Schools School is macro-managed so inhibited children are more likely to be tolerated and feel they can make a contribution.	School is micro-managed so inhibited children are less likely to be tolerated and more likely to feel undervalued.
Personality Outcomes	
As an adult, individual is closer to extroversion (outgoing, sociable) and is emotionally stable.	As an adult, individual is closer to introversion and has more emotional problems.

connecting through research

Dr. Susan Johnson, Psychologist, Counsellor, Researcher, and Co-Developer of Emotionally Focused Therapy

Married couples normally experience stressful periods that threaten the stability of their relationship. When this happens, couples may seek professional guidance, most of which is based on behavioural theories that use communication strategies to modify behaviour and seek solutions to problems.

Dr. Susan Johnson, believing many counselling strategies provided short-term relief from marital stress, partnered with Dr. Les Greenberg in the early 1980s to originate Emotionally Focused Couple Therapy (EFT). Based on John Bowlby's attachment theory, EFT "depathologizes dependency" by telling couples they are emotionally dependent on each other. Breaches of attachment, called "attachment injuries," between partners occur when one partner is experiencing insecurity because the other is either unsupportive or emotionally unavailable. EFT legitimizes vulnerability and encourages couples to listen for and respond to the childlike dependencies in our spouses and ourselves.

This novel and uniquely Canadian approach has an unprecedented track record of success: 70 to 75 percent of marriages stabilize once couples go through EFT counselling. The *Journal*

Visit Dr. Susan Johnson's Emotionally Focused Therapy Web site at www.iceeft.com.

of Marital and Family Therapy calls EFT ". . .one of the major advances in marital and family therapy of the last decade."

Dr. Johnson is the Director of the International Centre for Excellence in Emotionally Focused Therapy where training in EFT occurs. As well, she is a Distinguished Research Professor at Alliant University in San Diego, California, and Professor of Clinical Psychology at the University of Ottawa. Johnson's interest with couples and relationships began as a child as she observed people in an English pub. "I grew up in an English pub," she says, and observing people sparked a fascination about how couples connect, disconnect, and communicate in general. What better place than a pub to observe all that? Not only is she the author of numerous books, articles, and research on couples therapy, she delivers EFT workshops all over the world. She was the recipient of the American Association of Marriage and Family Therapy Award in 2000, and the recipient of the YMCA Women of Distinction Award in 2001 for her work in health and well-being.

Although relationships with romantic partners differ from those with parents, romantic partners fulfill some of the same needs for adults as parents do for their children (Mikulincer & Shaver, 2007, 2009). Recall from Chapter 6 that *securely attached* infants are defined as those who use the caregiver as a secure base from which to explore the environment. Similarly, adults may count on their romantic partners to be a secure base to which they can return and obtain comfort and security in stressful times (Feeney, 2009; Zeifman & Hazan, 2009).

Hazan and Shaver (1987, p. 515) measured attachment styles using the following brief assessment, where individuals are asked to read each paragraph and then place a check mark next to the description that best describes them:

1. I find it relatively easy to get close to others and I am comfortable depending on them and having them depend on me. I don't worry about being abandoned or about someone getting too close to me.

2. I am somewhat uncomfortable being close to others. I find it difficult to trust them completely and to allow myself to depend on them. I get nervous when anyone gets too close to me and it bothers me when someone tries to be more intimate with me than I feel comfortable with.

3. I find that others are reluctant to get as close as I would like. I often worry that my partner doesn't really love me or won't want to stay with me. I want to get very close to my partner, and this sometimes scares people away.

These items correspond to three attachment styles—secure attachment (option 1) and two insecure attachment styles (avoidant—option 2, and anxious—option 3):

- *Secure attachment style.* Securely attached adults have positive views of relationships, find it easy to get close to others, and are not overly concerned with or stressed out about their

What are some key dimensions of attachment in adulthood? How are they related to relationship patterns and well-being?

romantic relationships. These adults tend to enjoy sexuality in the context of a committed relationship and are less likely than others to have one-night stands.

- *Avoidant attachment style.* Avoidant individuals are hesitant about getting involved in romantic relationships, and once in a relationship, they tend to distance themselves from their partner.
- *Anxious attachment style.* These individuals demand closeness, are less trusting, and are more emotional, jealous, and possessive.

However, the majority of adults (about 60 to 80 percent) describe themselves as securely attached, and not surprisingly adults prefer having a securely attached partner (Shaver & Mikulincer, 2007; Zeifman & Hazan, 2009).

Researchers are studying links between adults' current attachment styles and many aspects of their lives (Feeney, 2009; Feeney & Monin, 2009; Mikulincer & Shaver, 2009). For example, securely attached adults are more satisfied with their close relationships than insecurely attached adults, and the relationships of securely attached adults are more likely to be characterized by trust, commitment, and longevity (Feeney, 2009; Feeney & Collins, 2007). Securely attached adults also are more likely than insecurely attached adults to provide support when they are distressed, and more likely to give support when their partner is distressed (Rholes & Simpson, 2007). Securely attached individuals are fully open to love. They are able to allow their partners to have space in their relationship and yet are firmly committed. They become animated when talking about their partner. The joy that is in their love for the other is well demonstrated. Decades of studies exploring different attachment styles indicate that insecurely attached adults have difficulty with their relationships. Meanwhile, securely attached individuals are more successful in the world of love (Belsky, 2013). A recent study of 18- to 20-year-olds revealed that recent secure attachment to parents was linked to ease in forming friendships in college (Parade, Leerkes, & Blankson, 2010).

One study found that adults with avoidant and anxious attachment styles were more likely to be depressed than securely attached adults (Hankin, Kassel, & Abela, 2005). Another research review of 10,000 adult attachment interviews revealed that attachment insecurity is linked to depression (Bakermans-Kranenburg & van Lizendoorn, 2009).

A study revealed that women with anxious or avoidant attachment styles and men with an avoidant attachment style are more likely to have unwanted but consensual sexual experiences than securely attached adults (Gentzler & Kerns, 2004). And a recent study of young women revealed a link between having an avoidant attachment pattern and a lower incidence of female orgasm (Cohen & Belsky, 2008). Recent interest in adult attachment has focused on ways that genes can affect ways in which adults can experience the environment (Diamond, 2009). Another study examined the link between the serotonin transporter gene (5-HTTLPR) and adult unresolved attachment (Caspers et al., 2009). In an attachment interview, unresolved attachment was assessed by listening to certain specific speech patterns giving excessive detail about the death of a parent, indicating that the deceased parent continued to play a major role in the adult's life. In this study, parental loss in early childhood was more likely to result in unresolved attachment in adulthood especially for individuals who had the shorter version of the gene. The long version of the gene apparently provided some protection from the negative psychological effects of parental loss.

Susan Johnson of the University of Ottawa and Les Greenberg of York University have developed a successful approach to therapy for couples called Emotionally Focused Therapy, or EFT, based on the findings of British psychiatrist John Bowlby, whom many acclaim as the "father of attachment theory." Bowlby, who was commissioned by the World Health Organization to study the psychological adjustment of babies and children orphaned during World War II, concluded that children have attachment needs of trust and security that must be met by at least one caregiver. Bowlby believed that adults transfer these needs to a romantic partner. Applying Bowlby's theories to intimate adult relationships, Greenberg and Johnson's EFT is based on the premise that romantic partners must meet each other's innate needs for attachment for the relationship to succeed. Greenberg and Johnson believe that we should treat our partners as adults, but in so doing we must tap into and respond to our partner's needs with the same care and concern we would give to a child. They claim that "attachment injuries" result when our innate needs are not met, and intimate partners can respond to each other in such a way that old "injuries" are healed and new ones averted (Makinen & Johnson, 2006).

A research review and conceptualization of attachment by leading experts Mario Mikulincer and Phillip Shaver (2007) concluded the following about the benefits of secure attachment. Individuals who are securely attached have a well-integrated sense of self-acceptance, self-esteem, and self-efficacy. They have the ability to control their emotions, are optimistic, and are resilient. Facing stress and adversity, they activate cognitive representations of security, are mindful of what is happening around them, and mobilize effective coping strategies.

Mikulincer and Shaver's (2007) review also concluded that attachment insecurity places couples at risk for relationship problems. For example, when an anxious individual is paired with an avoidant individual, the anxious partner's needs and demands frustrate the avoidant partner's preference for distance in the relationship; the avoidant partner's need for distance causes stress for the anxious partner's need for closeness. The result: both partners are unhappy in the relationship and the anxious–avoidant pairing can produce abuse or violence when a partner criticizes or tries to change the other's behaviour. Researchers also have found that when both partners have an anxious attachment pattern, the pairing usually produces dissatisfaction with the marriage and can lead to a mutual attack and retreat in the relationship (Feeney, 2009). When both partners have an anxious attachment style, they feel misunderstood and rejected, excessively dwell on their own insecurities, and seek to control the other's behaviour (Mikulincer & Shaver, 2007, 2009). It also is important to note that although attachment insecurities are linked to relationship problems, attachment style makes only a moderate-size contribution to relationship functioning and other factors contribute to relationship satisfaction and success (Mikulincer & Shaver, 2007, 2009). Later in the chapter, we will discuss such factors in our coverage of marital relationships.

To this point, we have discussed stability and change from childhood to adulthood. For a review, see the **Reach Your Learning Goals** section at the end of this chapter.

Attraction, Love, and Close Relationships

LO2 Identify three key aspects of attraction, love, and close relationships.

One question has intrigued philosophers, poets, and songwriters for centuries: What is love? Is it lustful and passionate? According to Erich Fromm, "The affirmation of one's own life, happiness, growth, freedom is rooted in one's capacity to love, i.e., in care, respect, responsibility and knowledge. If an individual is able to love productively, he loves himself too; if he can love only others, he cannot love at all" (Fromm, 1956, p. 60).

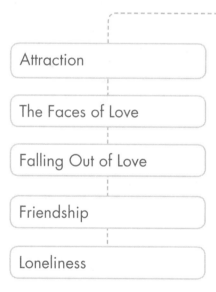

Attraction

The Faces of Love

Falling Out of Love

Friendship

Loneliness

Attraction

What attracts us to others and motivates us to spend more time with them? Does just being around someone increase the likelihood a relationship will develop? Are we more likely to associate with those who are similar to us? How important is physical attraction in a relationship?

Familiarity and Similarity

Social psychologists have found that for a close relationship to develop familiarity is a necessary condition. According to Berscheid and Regan (2011), the most basic principle of attraction is familiarity. In fact, the core concept of interpersonal attraction is the principle of familiarity. For the most part, friends and lovers are individuals who have been around each other for a long time. For example, they may have grown up together, gone to high school or university together, worked together, or attempted to go to the same social events.

The saying "birds of a feather do, indeed, flock together" helps to somewhat explain attraction. Guerrero, Anderson, and Afifi (2011) state that, overall, friends and lovers tend to be more alike than not alike. They appear to have the same attitudes, lifestyles, and physical attractions.

consensual validation An explanation of people's attraction to others who are similar to them; our own attitudes and behaviour are supported when someone else's attitudes and behaviour are similar to ours.

David Roche, keynote speaker, humorist, and performer, is pictured here with his wife, Marlena Blavin. **Have you ever been shocked by someone's appearance at first but come to appreciate his or her inner strength and beauty?**

- - - - - - - developmental **connection** - -

Erikson

←- ┘

Why are people attracted to others who have similar attitudes, values, and lifestyles? **Consensual validation,** which *provides an explanation of people's attraction to others who are similar to them, is one reason. Our own attitudes and behaviour are supported when someone else's attitudes and behaviour are similar to ours*—their attitudes, tastes, and values validate ours. People tend to shy away from the unknown. We might tend, instead, to prefer people whose attitudes and behaviour we can predict. Similarity implies that we will enjoy doing things with the other person, which often requires a partner who likes the same things and has similar attitudes.

Recently, it has come to the forefront that attractions occur not only in person, but also over the Internet (Park, 2010). Some critics argue that online romantic relationships never gain the interpersonal connection, while others state that the Internet may actually benefit anxious or shy individuals who find it difficult to meet potential partners in person (Rosenfeld & Thomas, 2012). Although online dating has become a popular strategy in finding a romantic partner, academic research into the antecedents of online dating are scarce. Valkenburg and Peter (2007) conducted a study using participants who were between 18 and 60 years of age. They found that respondents between 30 and 50 years of age were the most active online daters. Researchers have actually found that romantic relationships initiated on the Internet are more likely than those relationships that were initiated in person to last for more than two years (Bargh & McKenna, 2004).

Physical Attraction

As important as familiarity and similarity may be, they do not explain the spark that often ignites a romantic relationship: physical attractiveness. How important is physical attractiveness in relationships? Psychologists do not consider the link between physical beauty and attraction to be as clear-cut as advertisers would like us to believe. For example, heterosexual men and women across many cultures differ on the importance they place on good looks when they seek an intimate partner. Women tend to rate as most important such traits as considerateness, honesty, dependability, kindness, and understanding; men prefer good looks, cooking skills, and frugality (Eastwick & Finkel, 2008).

Although physical attractiveness may contribute to the early formation of relationships, as they endure physical attraction probably assumes less importance. David Roche, keynote speaker, humorist, and performer, pictured with his wife Marlena Blavin, is a case in point. He describes his face as a gift that makes him unique and has helped him learn that every person has feelings of being disfigured, or different, or unacceptable. David had to understand his own inner strength to face the difficulties of peer relations during childhood and adolescence.

The Faces of Love

Once we are initially attracted to another person, other opportunities exist that may deepen the relationship to love. Love refers to a vast and complex territory of human behaviour, spanning a range of relationships that includes friendship, romantic love, affectionate love, and consummate love (Berscheid, 2010). In most of these types of love, one recurring theme is intimacy (Weis & Sternberg, 2008).

Intimacy

Self-disclosure and the sharing of private thoughts are the hallmarks of intimacy. As we discussed in Chapter 12, adolescents have an increased capacity and need for intimacy. At the same time, they are engaged in the essential tasks of developing an identity and establishing their independence from their parents. Juggling the competing demands of intimacy, identity, and independence also becomes a central task of adulthood.

ERIKSON'S STAGE: INTIMACY VERSUS ISOLATION   Recall from our discussion in Chapter 12 that Erik Erikson (1968) believes *identity versus identity confusion*—pursuing who we are, what we are all about, and where we are going in life—is the most important issue to be negotiated in adolescence. According to Erikson, in early adulthood, after individuals are well on their way to establishing stable and cohesive identities, they enter the sixth developmental stage, *intimacy versus isolation*. Erikson describes intimacy as finding oneself, yet losing oneself in another person, and it requires a commitment to another person. If young adults form healthy friendships and an intimate relationship with another individual, intimacy will be achieved. If not, isolation will result.

An inability to develop meaningful relationships with others can harm an individual's personality. It may lead individuals to repudiate, ignore, or attack those who frustrate them. Such circumstances account for the shallow attempts of youth to merge themselves with a leader. Many youth want to be apprentices or disciples of leaders and adults who will shelter them from the harm of the "out-group" world. If this fails, and Erikson believes that it must, sooner or later the individuals recoil into a self-search to discover where they went wrong. This introspection sometimes leads to painful depression and isolation. It also may contribute to a mistrust of others.

Contemporary psychologists who have investigated the development of girls and women point out that a relationship can be only as strong as its weakest link. Relationships formed on equality will be much stronger than those where one partner is deemed stronger or more powerful than the other. Love, sexuality, and the desire for intimacy are important features from birth until death (Hatfield, Rapson, & Martel, 2007). The experience of love is centrally important to close relationships (Graham, 2011).

INTIMACY AND INDEPENDENCE   Development in early adulthood often involves balancing intimacy and commitment on the one hand, and independence and freedom on the other. At the same time as individuals are trying to establish an identity, they face the difficulty of having to cope with increasing their independence from their parents, developing an intimate relationship with another individual, and increasing their friendship commitments. They also face the task of being able to think for themselves and do things without always relying on what others say or do.

The extent to which young adults develop autonomy has important implications. Young adults who have not sufficiently moved away from parental ties may have difficulty in both interpersonal relationships and career development. Consider a son or daughter who is overprotected by his or her parents and continues to depend on them for financial support in early adulthood. He or she may have difficulty developing mature intimate relationships and a career. When an opportunity comes up that involves more responsibility and possibly more stress, he or she may turn it down. When things do not go well in his or her relationship, he or she may respond inappropriately.

The balance between intimacy and commitment, on the one hand, and independence and freedom, on the other, is delicate. Some individuals are able to experience a healthy independence and freedom along with an intimate relationship. Keep in mind that intimacy and commitment, and independence and freedom, are not just concerns of early adulthood. They are important themes of development that are worked and reworked throughout the adult years.

Romantic Love

Romantic love, *also called passionate love or eros, has strong components of sexuality and infatuation, and often predominates in the early part of a love relationship* (Berscheid, 2010; Regan, 2008). Poets, playwrights, and musicians through the ages have lauded the fiery passion of romantic love—and lamented the searing pain when it fails.

A complex intermingling of different emotions goes into romantic love—including such emotions as passion fear, anger, sexual desire, joy, and jealousy (Regan, 2008).

Affectionate Love

Love is more than just passion. **Affectionate love,** *also called companionate love, is the type of love that occurs when individuals desire to have the other person near and have a deep, caring affection for the person.*

Consummate Love

So far, we have discussed two types of love: romantic (or passionate) and affectionate (or companionate). According to Dr. Robert J. Sternberg (1986, 1988, 2004), these are not the only forms of love. Sternberg proposed a **triangular theory** *in which love can be thought of as having three main dimensions: passion, intimacy, and commitment.* Intimacy relates to the emotional feelings of warmth, closeness, and sharing in a relationship. Commitment is the cognitive appraisal of the relationship and the intent to maintain the relationship, even in the face of problems.

romantic love Also called "passionate love" or "eros," romantic love has strong components of sexuality and infatuation and often predominates in the early part of a love relationship.

affectionate love Also called companionate love, this is the type of love that occurs when individuals desire to have the other person near and have a deep, caring affection for the other person.

triangular theory of love Sternberg's theory that love can be thought of as having three main dimensions: passion, intimacy, and commitment.

In Sternberg's theory, the strongest, fullest form of love is *consummate love*, which involves all three dimensions (see Figure 14.2). If passion is the only ingredient in a relationship (with intimacy and commitment low or absent), we are merely *infatuated*. However, a fraction of couples (1 in 10 people) manage to stay passionate for years (Acevedo & Aron, 2009). An affair or a fling, or a teenage "crush" in which there is little intimacy, knowledge, and even less commitment, is an example. A relationship marked by intimacy and commitment but low or lacking in passion is called *affectionate love*, a pattern often found among couples who have been married for many years. If passion and commitment are present but intimacy is not, Sternberg calls the relationship *fatuous love*, as when one person worships another from a distance. But if couples share all three dimensions—passion, intimacy, and commitment—they experience consummate love (Sternberg & Sternberg, 2010).

In Western cultures love is seen as possible, acceptable, and desirable. In fact, the virtues of passion are extolled in music, song, theatre, television, and film. Young adults are primed and ready to experience love in their lives (Florsheim, 2003).

The readiness for love is not global across cultures. In many diverse cultures, passionate romantic love is a foreign concept. Marriages are frequently arranged on the basis of economic and status considerations. The concept of "love" was invented during the Middle Ages, when a few social philosophers first suggested that love ought to be a requirement for marriage (Feldman & Landry, 2014). The goal was to provide an alternative to the raw sexual desire that had served as the primary basis for marriage in earlier times (Haslett, 2004).

Falling Out of Love

The collapse of a close relationship may feel tragic. In the long run, however, our happiness and personal development may benefit from getting over being in love and ending a close relationship.

In particular, falling out of love may be wise if you are obsessed with a person who repeatedly betrays your trust; if you are involved with someone who is draining you emotionally or financially; or if you are desperately in love with someone who does not return your feelings. Being in love when love is not returned can lead to depression, obsessive thoughts, sexual dysfunction, inability

---

Figure 14.2

Sternberg's Triangle of Love

Sternberg identified three types of love: passion, intimacy, and commitment. Various combinations of these types of love result in these patterns of love: infatuation, affectionate love, fatuous love, and consummate love.

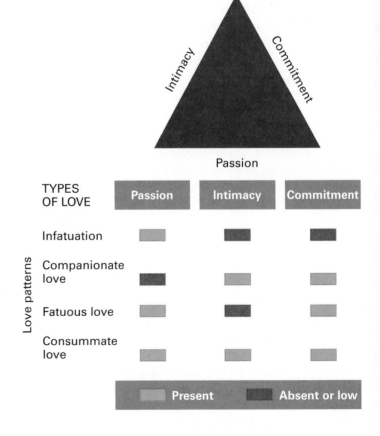

Personal Growth Following a Romantic Relationship Breakup

Studies of romantic breakups have mainly focused on their negative aspects (Kato, 2005; Kurdek, 1997). Few studies have examined the possibility that a romantic breakup might lead to positive changes.

One study assessed the personal growth that can follow the breakup of a romantic relationship (Tashiro & Frazier, 2003). The participants were 92 undergraduate students who had experienced a relationship breakup in the past nine months. They were asked to describe "what positive changes, if any, have happened as a result of your breakup that might serve to improve your future romantic relationships" (p. 118).

Self-reported positive growth was common following a romantic breakup. Changes were categorized in terms of person, relational, and environmental changes. The most commonly reported types of growth were person changes, which included feeling stronger and more self-confident, more independent, and better off emotionally. Relational positive changes included gaining relational wisdom, and environmental positive changes included having better friendships because of the breakup. Figure 14.3 provides examples of these positive changes. Women reported more positive growth than did men.

Figure 14.3

Examples of Positive Changes in the Aftermath of a Romantic Breakup

Change category	Exemplars of frequently mentioned responses
Person positives	1. "I am more self-confident." 2. "Through breaking up I found I could handle more on my own." 3. "I didn't always have to be the strong one, it's okay to cry or be upset without having to take care of him."
Relational positives	1. "Better communication." 2. "I learned many relationship skills that I can apply in the future (for example, the importance of saying you're sorry)." 3. "I know not to jump into a relationship too quickly."
Environmental positives	1. "I rely on my friends more. I forgot how important friends are when I was with him." 2. "Concentrate on school more: I can put so much more time and effort toward school." 3. "I believe friends' and family's opinions count—will seek them out in future relationships."

to work effectively, difficulty in making new friends, and self-condemnation. Thinking clearly in such relationships is often difficult, because our thoughts are so coloured by arousing emotions.

Some people get taken advantage of in relationships (Metts & Cupach, 2007; Tafoya & Spitzberg, 2007). For example, without either person realizing it, a relationship can evolve in a way that creates dominant and submissive roles. Detecting this pattern is an important step toward learning either to reconstruct the relationship or to end it if the problems cannot be worked out. To read further about breakups of romantic relationships, see Connecting through Research.

Friendship

Increasingly researchers are finding that friendship plays an important role in development throughout the human life span (Rawlins, 2009). As we saw in Chapter 8, friendship can serve many functions—companionship, intimacy/affection, support, and a source of self-esteem. In some cases, friends can provide a better buffer from stress and be a better source of emotional support than family members. This might be because friends choose each other, whereas family ties are obligatory. Individuals often select a friend in terms of such criteria as loyalty, trustworthiness, and support. Thus, it is not surprising that in times of stress, individuals turn to their friends for emotional support (Rawlins, 2009).

critical thinking

Gender roles are clearly defined throughout our lives—so well-defined that men and women have been indoctrinated and may follow them unconsciously, even when, like Noreen and George in the opening vignette, they consciously refute them. Traditionally, men earned the money and, therefore, made many or most of the decisions and women "obeyed" their husband's wishes. Obedience was tied to dependency on spousal economic support. Although the word "obey" has been removed from most marriage ceremonies, these traditional roles are well-ingrained. What are the traditional gender roles and how do they define our most intimate relationships? Do they still hold true? Why or why not? In your culture what are the traditional gender roles? In what ways do they not hold true?

As with children, adult friends usually come from the same age group. For many individuals, friendships formed in their twenties often continue through the twenties and into the thirties, although some new friends may be made in the thirties and some may be lost because of moving or other circumstances. Adulthood brings opportunities for new friendships as individuals relocate and may establish new friends in their neighbourhood or place of work (Blieszner, 2009).

Although it is unlikely that the phenomenon of "friends with benefits" relationships (FWBRs) is new, research on this type of relationship has emerged primarily within the last decade. FWBRs involve ongoing sexual activity occurring between partners who do not identify the relationships as romantic (Hughes, Morrison, & Asada, 2005). These relationships appear to be more common among today's youth and young adults than in previous generations (Bisson & Levine, 2009). In fact, Bogle (2008) argues that a shift has occurred from the predominant dating script to the hook-up script, which comprises many forms of casual dating relationships including FWBRs. One positive aspect of FWBRs is easy access to sex; a negative aspect is that of ruining the friendship (MacDonald, MacKeigan, & Weaver, 2011).

Gender Differences in Friendships

As in the childhood years, there are gender differences in adult friendships (Lauer & Lauer, 2007). Compared with men, women have more close friends and their friendships involve more self-disclosure and exchange of mutual support (Dow & Wood, 2006). Women are more likely to listen at length to what a friend has to say and be sympathetic, and women have been labelled as "talking companions" because talk is so central to their relationship (Dow & Wood, 2006). Women's friendships tend to be characterized not only by depth, but also by breadth: Women share many aspects of their experiences, thoughts, and feelings.

When female friends get together, they like to talk, but male friends are more likely to engage in activities, especially outdoors. Thus, the adult male pattern of friendship often involves keeping one's distance while sharing useful information. Men are less likely than women to talk about their weaknesses with their friends, and men want practical solutions to their problems rather than sympathy. Also, adult male friendships are more competitive than those of women. For example, male friends disagree with each other more often than women friends do (Felmlee, Sweet, & Sinclair, 2012).

Friendships between Women and Men

Cross-gender friendships can provide both opportunities and problems (Rawlins, 2009). The opportunities involve learning more about common feelings and interests and shared characteristics, as well as acquiring knowledge and understanding of beliefs and activities that historically have been typical of one gender.

Problems can arise in cross-gender friendships because of different expectations. Females appear to hold higher expectations for same-sex friends than for males (Flannagan, Marsh, & Fuhrman, 2005).

Loneliness

Recall that Erik Erikson (1968) believed that intimacy versus isolation is the key developmental issue for young adults to resolve. Social isolation can result in loneliness.

Each of us has times in our lives when we feel lonely, but for some people loneliness is a chronic condition. More than just an unwelcome social situation, chronic loneliness is linked with impaired physical and mental health. Chronic loneliness can even lead to an early death.

Weiss (1973) was one of the first researchers to conceptualize loneliness in a multidimensional way. He differentiated emotional and social loneliness as distinct states with different provisions. For example, emotional loneliness is due to an absence of an attachment and close intimate relationships. On the other hand, social loneliness is one result of a lack of social reassurance, and it acts as a response to social deficiencies. Findings on attachment styles, as disclosed by Hazan and Shaver (1987), indicate that individuals with specific attachment styles show differences in their perceived loneliness. Secure attachment styles seem to be consistently associated with lower levels of loneliness, whereas a positive relationship was found between insecure attachment and feelings of loneliness (DiTommaso, Brannen-McNulty, Ross, & Burgess, 2003; Wiseman, Mayseless, & Sharabany, 2006).

critical thinking

What are the factors that contribute to loneliness in individuals? To what extent do the gender differences described here reflect your own observations of loneliness? To what extent is social media a factor in promoting loneliness? What are four strategies that you could use with a colleague who confides in you that he/she is lonely?

How is adult friendship different among female friends, male friends, and cross-gender friends?

To this point, we have discussed many ideas about attraction, love, and close relationships. For a review, see the **Reach Your Learning Objectives** section at the end of this chapter.

Intimate Relationships: Marriage and the Family Life Cycle

LO3 Describe intimate relationships such as marriage, the family life cycle, and cultural influences on family life.

Until about 1950, a stable marriage was widely accepted as the endpoint of adult development. In the last 75 years, however, personal fulfillment both inside and outside marriage has emerged as a goal that competes with marital stability (Skolnick, 2007). The changing norm of male–female equality in marriage has produced marital relationships that are more fragile and intense than they were earlier in the twentieth century.

Marital Trends in Canada

The nuclear family is no longer the norm in Canada. In fact, the nuclear family that typified Canadian households of 50 years ago has changed into a complex and diverse web of family ties involving living alone, re-marriage, stepchildren, empty-nesters, and multiple generations living together and sharing a home ("Census Shows," 2012). What is interesting is that for the first time in 2011, Statistics Canada (2011b) measured the number of stepfamilies in the country, indicating that at present 1 in 10 children lives in some sort of reconstituted arrangement. Despite a growing population, the

Marital Trends in Canada

Social Contexts

Making Marriage Work

Benefits of a Good Marriage

The Family Life Cycle

Parenting Myths and Realities

number of married couples declined by 132,715 over the past decade (Statistics Canada, 2011b). Lone-parent families and multiple-family households, on the other hand, were on the rise. Same-sex couples were also on the steep incline, up 42.4 percent from 2006. In Canada's first-ever national count of foster children, the agency indicated that there were 29,590 of them under the age of 14 in 2011, with the highest rate in the province of Manitoba, where there is a high First Nations population ("Census Shows," 2012).

As elsewhere in the world, the face of the Canadian family continues to evolve in terms of age, size and configuration, and longevity. Canadian men and women are waiting until their late twenties to marry, and are not starting their families until they are well into their thirties and even early forties. One constant, however, is the level of stress people report. For example, married people report lower levels of extreme stress than singles. A recent national survey revealed that a higher percentage of singles (58 percent) reported they experienced extreme stress in the past month than married (52 percent) and divorced individuals (48 percent) (American Psychological Association, 2007).

Social Contexts

Contexts within a culture and across cultures are powerful influences on marriage (Karney & Bradbury, 2005). The traits that people look for in a marriage partner vary around the world.

Domesticity is also valued in some cultures, but not in others. In this study, adults from the Zulu culture in South Africa, Estonia, and Colombia placed a high value on housekeeping skills in their marital preference. By contrast, adults in the United States, Canada, and all Western European countries except Spain said that housekeeping skill was not an important trait in their partner.

Religion plays an important role in marriage in many cultures. However, in the United States, longitudinal studies have reported mixed findings concerning the relationship between religiosity and marital satisfaction (Mahoney, 2010). In a longitudinal study with a community sample of couples who were followed for 10 years, the religiosity of the wives predicted marital satisfaction but the religiosity of husbands did not (Clements, Stanley, & Markman, 2004). For example, Islam stresses the honour of the male and the purity of the female. It also emphasizes the woman's role in childbearing, childrearing, educating children, and instilling the Islamic faith in their children. Interfaith relationships can be very difficult; further, parental and family pressures may prohibit an interfaith relationship. In India, more than 70 percent of marriages continue to be arranged. However, as more women enter the workforce in India and move from rural areas to cities, these Indian women are increasingly resisting arranged marriage (Purnell, 2013).

In Scandinavian countries, cohabitation is popular among young adults; however, most Scandinavians eventually marry (Popenoe, 2007). In Sweden, on average women delay marriage until they are 31 years of age, while men delay marriage until they are 33. Some countries, such as Hungary, encourage early marriage and childbearing to offset declines in the population. Like Scandinavian countries, Japan has a high proportion of unmarried young people. However, rather than cohabiting as the Scandinavians do, unmarried Japanese young adults live at home longer with their parents before marrying. In 2002, the average age for Canadian women to marry was 31.5 years, and for men the average age was 34 (CCHD, 2006).

Making Marriage Work

John Gottman (1994, 2006; Gottman & Gottman, 2009; Gottman, Gottman, & Declaire, 2006) has been studying married couples' lives since the early 1970s. He uses extensive methods to study what makes marriages work. Gottman interviews couples about the history of their marriage, their philosophy about marriage, and how they view their parents' marriages. He videotapes them talking to each other about how their day went, and evaluates what they say about the good and bad times of their marriages. Gottman also uses physiological methods to measure their heart rate, blood flow, blood pressure, and immune functioning moment by moment. He checks back in with the couples every year to see how their marriages are faring. Gottman's research represents the most extensive assessment of marital relationships available. Currently, he and his colleagues are following up with 700 couples in seven different studies.

In his research, Gottman has found that seven main principles determine whether a marriage will work or not:

- *Establishing love maps.* Individuals in successful marriages have personal insights and detailed maps of each other's life and world. They are not psychological strangers. In good marriages, partners are willing to share their feelings with each other. They use these "love maps" to express not only their understanding of each other, but also their fondness and admiration.
- *Nurturing fondness and admiration.* In successful marriages, partners sing each other's praises. More than 90 percent of the time, when couples put a positive spin on their marriage's history, the marriage is likely to have a positive future.
- *Turning toward each other instead of away.* In good marriages, spouses are adept at turning toward each other regularly. They see each other as friends, and this friendship acts as a powerful shield against conflict. The friendship does not keep arguments from occurring, but it can prevent differences of opinion from overwhelming a relationship. In these good marriages, spouses respect each other and appreciate each other's point of view, even though they might not agree with it.
- *Letting your partner influence you.* Bad marriages often involve one spouse who is unwilling to share power with the other or be influenced by their ideas or desires. Although power mongering is more common in husbands, some wives also show this problem. A willingness to share power and to respect the other person's view is a prerequisite to compromising.
- *Solving solvable conflicts.* Gottman has found two types of problems that occur in marriage: (1) perpetual, and (2) solvable. Perpetual problems include spouses differing on whether to have children, one spouse wanting sex far more frequently than the other, or differing political or religious views. Solvable problems can be worked out and may include such things as not helping each other reduce daily stresses, or perhaps being more verbally affectionate. Unfortunately, more than two-thirds of marital problems fall into the perpetual category. Fortunately, marital therapists have found that couples often don't have to solve their perpetual problems for the marriage to work. Couples may decide to respect each other's autonomy rather than try to convince each other to change.

    Work, stress, in-laws, money, sex, housework, a new baby—these are among the typical areas of marital conflict, even in happy marriages. When there is conflict in these areas, it usually means that a husband and wife have different ideas about the tasks involved, their importance, or how they should be accomplished. If the conflict is perpetual, no amount of problem-solving expertise will fix it. The tension will decrease only when both partners feel comfortable living with the ongoing difference. However, when the issue is solvable, the challenge is to find the right strategy for dealing with it.
- *Overcoming gridlock.* One partner wants the other to attend church, and the other is an atheist. One partner is a homebody, while the other wants to go out and socialize a lot. Such problems often produce gridlock. Gottman believes the key to ending gridlock is not to try to solve the problem, but to move from gridlock to dialogue and to be patient.
- *Creating shared meaning.* The more the partners can speak candidly and respectfully with each other, the more likely it is that they will create shared meaning in their marriage. This also includes sharing goals with one's spouse and working together to achieve each other's goals.

In his research, Gottman has found that to resolve conflicts, couples should start out with a soft rather than a harsh approach, try to make and receive "repair attempts," regulate their emotions, compromise, and be tolerant of each other's faults. Conflict resolution is not about one person making changes; it is about negotiating and accommodating each other.

In addition to Gottman's view, other experts on marriage argue that such factors as forgiveness and commitment are important aspects of a successful marriage (Fincham, Stanley, & Beach, 2007). These factors function as self-repair processes in healthy relationships. For example, spouses may have a heated argument that has the potential to harm their relationship (Amato, 2007). After calming down, they may forgive each other and repair the damage. Also, spouses who have a strong

What makes marriages work? What are the benefits of having a good marriage?

-- **critical** thinking ------------

According to experts on marriage and family life, not every problem or conflict has a solution. One such problem may be views on church and religion. What are other possible perpetual problems? How do you think successful couples deal with conflicts such as these? What would be the consequences of conflict if it did not get resolved? What may happen to the couple?

commitment to each other may sacrifice their personal self-interest in times of conflict for the benefit of the marriage. Commitment especially becomes important when a couple is not happily married and can help them get through hard times with the hope that the future will involve more positive changes in the relationship.

"Marriages start to crack early," says Gottman's colleague, Robert Levenson, "and they are very hard to repair." Disagreements and arguments occur with regularity over money, raising children, work, and so forth. The major indicators that a marriage is "cracking" include contempt, aggression, stonewalling, avoiding, and anticipating the worst. Gottman's research indicates, "It's not the fight that does the damage—even the healthiest couples argue and disagree, and often never resolve perpetual problems—but what counts is the way the fight goes, and how well the couple succeeds at 'managing the conflict.'"

Benefits of a Good Marriage

Now that you know the early signs of a marriage "cracking" and what makes a marriage work, what are the benefits to having a good marriage? Individuals who are happily married live longer, healthier lives than either divorced individuals or those who are unhappily married (Karasu, 2007; Wilson & Smallwood, 2008). A recent study assessed 94,000 Japanese, 40 to 79 years of age, on two occasions: at the beginning of the study and approximately 10 years later (Ikeda et al., 2007). Compared with never-married individuals, those who were married had a lower risk of dying in the 10-year period. In another study, women in happy marriages had lower levels of biological and cardiovascular risk factors—such as blood pressure, cholesterol levels, and body mass index—and lower levels of depression, anxiety, and anger than women in unhappy marriages (Gallo et al., 2003). And a recent study indicated that the longer women were married, the less likely they were to develop a chronic health condition, and the longer that men were married, the lower their risk was of developing a disease (Dupre & Meadows, 2007).

What are the reasons for these benefits of a happy marriage? People in happy marriages likely feel less physically and emotionally stressed, which puts less wear and tear on a person's body. Such wear and tear can lead to numerous physical ailments, such as high blood pressure and heart disease, as well as psychological problems such as anxiety, depression, and substance abuse.

For some couples, an active choice is made not to have children (Blackstone & Stewart, 2012). Childfree adults do not universally reach the decision to remain so at the same stage of life or in the same way. When examining why some adults remain voluntarily childless, explanations may range from the impact of macro-level forces such as women's increasing labour force participation to micro-level motivations such as autonomy and freedom (Agrillo & Netini, 2008).

The Family Life Cycle

Intimacy, as Erikson points out, is the major crisis of young adulthood. The process of forming intimate relationships, leaving the parental home, and establishing a new home poses many challenges and many moments of tremendous joy. Although young people are staying single longer, cohabiting much more commonly, and are forming same-sex unions more openly, the ebb and flow of the family life cycle permeates the activities and decisions. Whatever lifestyle young adults choose, challenges posed by family life will emerge. As we go through life, we are at different points in the family life cycle.

Figure 14.4 shows a summary of these stages in the family life, along with key aspects of emotional processes involved in the transition from one stage to the next, and changes in family status required for developmental change to take place (Carter & McGoldrick, 2005).

Leaving Home and Becoming a Single Adult

Leaving home and becoming a single adult *is the first stage in the family life cycle and involves launching.* **Launching** *is the process by which youths move into adulthood and exit their family of origin.* Adequate completion of launching requires that the young adult separate from the family of origin

Figure 14.4

The Family Life Cycle

FAMILY LIFE-CYCLE STAGE	EMOTIONAL PROCESS OF TRANSITION: KEY PRINCIPLES
6. The family in later life	Accepting the shifting of generational roles
5. The family at mid-life	Accepting a multitude of exits from and entries into the family system
4. The family with adolescents	Increasing flexibility of family boundaries to include children's independence and grandparents' frailties
3. Becoming parents and families with children	Accepting new members into the system
2. The joining of families through marriage: the new couple	Commitment to new system
1. Leaving home; Single young adults	Accepting emotional and financial responsibility for self

leaving home and becoming a single adult The first stage in the family life cycle, which involves launching.

launching The process by which youths move into adulthood and exit their family of origin.

without cutting off ties completely or reactively fleeing to find some form of substitute emotional refuge. The launching period is a time for youth and young adults to formulate personal life goals, to develop an identity, and to become more independent before joining with another person to form a new family. This is a time for young people to sort out emotionally what they will take along from the family of origin, what they will leave behind, and what they will create for themselves.

The shift to adult-to-adult status between parents and children requires a mutually respectful and personal form of relating in which young adults can appreciate parents as they are, needing neither to make them into what they are not nor to blame them for what they could not be. In addition, young adults do not need to comply with parental expectations and wishes at their own expense.

The Joining of Families through Marriage: The New Couple

The **new couple** *is the second stage in the family life cycle, in which two individuals from separate families of origin unite to form a new family system.* This stage involves not only the development of a new marital system, but also an often complex realignment with extended families and friends. Women's changing roles, the increasingly frequent marriage of partners from divergent cultural backgrounds, and the increasing physical distances between family members are currently placing a much greater burden on couples to define their relationships for themselves than was true in the past. Marriage is usually described as the union of two individuals, but in reality, it is the union of two entire family systems and the development of a new, third system.

new couple The second stage in the family life cycle, in which two individuals from separate families of origin unite to form a new family system.

Becoming Parents and a Family with Children

Becoming parents and a family with children *is the third stage in the family life cycle that requires adults to move up a generation and become caregivers to the younger generation.* For many young adults, parental roles are well planned, coordinated with other roles in life, and developed with the individual's economic situation in mind. For others, the discovery that they are about to become parents is a startling surprise. In either event, the prospective parents may have mixed emotions and romantic illusions about having a child.

becoming parents and a family with children The third stage in the family life cycle that requires adults to move up a generation and become caregivers to the younger generation.

The Family with Adolescents

The **family with adolescents** *represents the fourth stage of the family life cycle, in which adolescents push for autonomy and seek to develop their own identity.* This involves a lengthy process of self-discovery, which transpires over at least 10 to 15 years. During this period, parents and their adolescent children may find themselves at a crossroads of sorts as the adolescent struggles to develop a mature autonomy and identity. Managing time and resources may cause family disagreements as teens take their first jobs, determine how to spend the money they earn, choose how much time to spend on homework, and so on. We discussed adolescent development and the family with adolescents in Chapter 12.

family with adolescents The fourth stage of the family life cycle in which adolescents push for autonomy and seek to develop their own identities.

Launching Children and Moving On

Launching children and moving on *is the fifth stage in the family cycle, a time of launching children, playing an important role in linking generations, and adapting to mid-life changes in development.* Until about a generation ago, most families were involved in raising their children for much of their adult lives until old age. Because of the lower birth rate and longer life of most adults, parents now launch their children about 20 years before retirement, which frees many mid-life parents to pursue other activities. Many emerging and young adults live at home much longer than a generation ago, so the final launching may be delayed by several years. Planning for retirement and menopause are two challenges for the family in mid-life. We will discuss mid-life families in greater detail in Chapter 16.

launching children and moving on The fifth stage in the family life cycle, a time of launching children, playing an important role in linking generations, and adapting to mid-life changes in development.

The Family in Later Life

The **family in later life** *is the sixth and final stage in the family life cycle, when retirement alters a couple's lifestyle, requiring adaptation. Grandparenting also characterizes many families in this stage.* With the increase in dual family earners and divorce, more and more grandparents are helping to

family in later life The sixth and final stage in the family life cycle, when retirement alters a couple's lifestyle, requiring adaptation. Grandparenting also characterizes many families in this stage.

raise grandchildren. Health concerns become more challenging to the family in later life. We will discuss the family in later life in Chapter 18.

Parenting Myths and Realities

The needs and expectations of parents have stimulated many myths about parenting (DeGenova & Rice, 2008), including:

- The birth of a child will save a failing marriage.
- As a possession or extension of the parent, the child will think, feel, and behave like the parents did in their childhood.
- Having a child gives the parents a "second chance" to achieve what they should have achieved.
- Parenting is an instinct and requires no training.

Parenting requires a number of interpersonal skills and imposes emotional demands, yet there is little in the way of formal education for this task. Most parents learn parenting practices from their own parents—some they accept, some they discard. Unfortunately, when methods of parents are passed on from one generation to the next, both desirable and undesirable practices are perpetuated. Adding to reality of the task of parenting, husbands and wives may bring different parenting practices to the marriage. The parents, then, may struggle with each other about which is a better practice to interact with a child. The task or challenge facing new parents is to form a united leadership style for their new family.

Moving successfully through this lengthy stage requires a commitment of time as a parent, understanding the roles of parents, and adapting to developmental changes in children. Problems that emerge when a couple first assumes the parental role include struggles with each other about taking responsibility, as well as a refusal or inability to function as competent parents to children. We extensively discussed this stage of the family life cycle in Chapters 6, 8, and 9.

To this point, we have discussed a number of ideas about intimate relationships: marriage and the family life cycle. For a review, see the **Reach Your Learning Objectives** section at the end of this chapter.

The Diversity of Adult Lifestyles

LO4 Compare and contrast the diversity of adult lifestyles.

Today's adult lifestyles are increasingly being reshaped. Adults may choose from many lifestyle options and form different types of families (Benokraitis, 2008). One of the most striking social changes in recent decades is the decreased stigma attached to people who do not maintain what were long considered conventional families. They may choose to live alone, cohabit, marry, divorce, remarry, or live with someone of the same sex. Let's explore each of these lifestyles and how they affect adults.

Single Adults

Many single adults live alone and many, particularly those in their twenties, live with their parents. In Canada, 41 percent of young adults in their twenties live with their parents, an increase from 27 percent in 1981 (Statistics Canada, 2003). The economy is a primary factor in young people living with parents. Other aspects of the decision to live at home include that young people are staying in school longer, waiting later to marry, and are fearful of divorce. Young people are delaying marriage at greater rates; for example, the proportion of adults not living in any type of union decreased from 64 percent to 45 percent for men, and 73 percent to 57 percent for women (Ambert, 2005).

Even when singles enjoy their lifestyles and are highly competent, they often are stereotyped (Schwartz & Scott, 2007). Stereotypes associated with being single range from the "swinging

Single Adults

Cohabiting Adults

Divorced Adults

Remarried Adults

Parenting Adults

Lone-Parent Adults

Gay and Lesbian Adults

single" to the "desperately lonely, suicidal" single. Of course, most single adults are somewhere between these extremes. Common problems of single adults may include forming intimate relationships with other adults, confronting loneliness, and finding a niche in a society that is marriage-oriented. Advantages of being single include having time to make decisions about one's life course, time to develop personal resources to meet goals, freedom to make autonomous decisions and pursue one's own schedule and interests, opportunities to explore new places and try out new things, and privacy.

Adults who reach the age of 30 may experience increasing pressure to settle down and get married. At this point, many single adults make a conscious decision to marry or to remain single. A recent national survey revealed that a higher percentage of singles (58 percent) reported they experienced extreme stress in the past month than married (52 percent) and divorced individuals (48 percent) (American Psychological Association, 2007).

Cohabiting Adults

Cohabitation refers to living together in an emotional and sexual relationship without being married. Cohabitation is perceived as being a freer lifestyle (Ambert, 2005; Casper & Bianchi, 2007; Cherlin, 2007; Popenoe, 2008). Cohabiting couples make up a growing proportion of all families in Canada. Over 1.3 million couples, or 16 percent of all couples, cohabit. In Quebec, the rate is almost double: 30 percent of all couples cohabit. Quebec's rate is about the same as in Sweden, where cohabitation rates are also high. The cohabitation rate in Norway is 24 percent; Finland, Mexico, New Zealand, France, and Canada follow in that order. The cohabitation rate in the United States is reported to be 8.2 percent (Ambert, 2005).

Who cohabits? Research has identified that younger adult couples are more likely to cohabit. Among older adults, cohabiting couples are often divorced. Males who cohabit tend to have lower income and educational levels than men who marry. Cohabiters tend to be less traditional in their outlook than their parents. Women who cohabit are more likely to have given birth to a child without a live-in partner than those who marry. A higher proportion of women who cohabit are older and often earn more than their partners compared to married women. This description applies to Canadian but not to European couples. Most couples who cohabit end up getting married (Ambert, 2005). A longitudinal study found that the timing of cohabitation is a key factor in marital outcomes (Kline et al., 2004).

More children are being raised in common-law unions than before. In 2001, 8.2 percent of children under 14 lived in cohabiting households, excluding Quebec, where the rate is 29 percent. When reconstituted families are factored in and the age limit is removed, the rate is estimated to be as high as 46 percent (Ambert, 2005).

Canada does not have accurate statistics on the stability of cohabitation, as many go unreported; however, based on the research available, cohabitation relationships are quite unstable. In fact, more than 50 percent dissolve within five years of the union, a rate far higher than the divorce rate of 30 percent (Ambert, 2005). Women whose first union was common-law were twice as likely to experience the dissolution of their relationship than women whose first union was marriage (Statistics Canada, 2003).

A longitudinal study found that the timing of cohabitation is a key factor in marital outcomes (Kline et al., 2004). Couples who cohabitated before they became engaged were at greater risk for poor marital outcomes than those who cohabited only after becoming engaged. Further, a recent study revealed that post-divorce cohabitation of any type (with the future spouse or with someone else) was linked with a lower level of remarital happiness (Xu, Hudspeth, & Bartkowski, 2006).

One advantage of cohabitation is poverty reduction, especially for lone-parents; however, the disadvantage is the instability of cohabiting relationships. Abuse, both physical and sexual, is more common in cohabiting relationships than in marriages (Ambert, 2005). In sum, researchers have not found that cohabitation leads to greater marital happiness and success. Rather, they have discovered either that it leads to no differences, or that cohabitation is not good for a marriage (Ambert, 2005).

Divorced Adults

Divorce rates are increasing, but the statistics reported are often confusing and misleading. To interpret the statistics, we need to know both how they are derived and their context. Are they based on total population, including children and singles, or are they based on the number of marriages? If they are based on the number of marriages, are these marriages new marriages or all marriages? Marriages for the sole purpose of citizenship usually end in divorce and become part of the statistics. Additionally, the population is aging, which means that there are not as many people in the vulnerable first five years of marriage, the peak time for divorce unless the individuals were previously married. As well, an unknown number of couples separate but never legally divorce. Despite all this, experts predict that if the present divorce rate continues, one in four Canadian couples will divorce before reaching their thirtieth wedding anniversary (Statistics Canada, 2007c).

If a divorce is going to occur, it usually takes place early in a marriage, peaking between the fifth and tenth year of marriage (Ambert, 1998) (see Figure 14.5). Although divorce has increased for all socio-economic groups, those in some groups have a higher incidence of divorce. Youthful marriage, low educational level, low income, not having a religious affiliation, having parents who are divorced, and having a baby before marriage are factors that are associated with increases in divorce (Popenoe, 2007; Rodrigues, Hall, & Fincham, 2006).

Dealing with Divorce

Both partners experience challenges after a marriage dissolves (Amato, 2006; Feeney & Monin, 2009). Both divorced women and divorced men complain of loneliness, diminished self-esteem, anxiety about the unknowns in their lives, and difficulty in forming satisfactory new intimate relationships (Hetherington, 2006). A recent study revealed that following marital dissolution, both men and women were more likely to experience an episode of depression than individuals who remained with a spouse over a two-year period (Rotermann, 2007). The challenges of divorce differ somewhat for custodial and non-custodial parents and for men and women (Rotermann, 2007; Sayer, 2006). Research shows this to be one of the most stressful aspects of divorce. Custodial parents have concerns about childrearing and overload in their lives. Non-custodial parents register complaints about alienation from or lack of time with their children.

If a marriage doesn't work, what happens after divorce? Psychologically, one of the most common characteristics of divorced adults is difficulty in trusting someone else in a romantic relationship. Following a divorce, though, people's lives can take diverse turns (Tashiro, Frazier, & Berman, 2006). In E. Mavis Hetherington's research, men and women took six common pathways in exiting divorce (Hetherington & Kelly, 2002, pp. 98–108):

- *The enhancers.* Accounting for 20 percent of the divorced group, most were females who "grew more competent, well adjusted, and self-fulfilled" following their divorce (p. 98). They were

Figure 14.5

The Divorce Rate in Relation to Number of Years Married

Shown here is the percentage of divorces as a function of how long couples have been married. Note that most divorces occur in the early years of marriage, peaking between the fifth and tenth year of marriage.

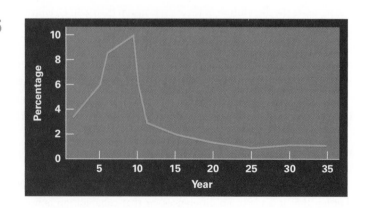

competent in multiple areas of life, showing a remarkable ability to bounce back from stressful circumstances and create something meaningful out of problems.

- *The good-enoughs.* The largest group of divorced individuals was described as average people coping with divorce. They showed some strengths and some weaknesses, some successes and some failures. When they experienced a problem, they tried to solve it. Many of them attended night classes, found new friends, developed active social lives, and were motivated to get higher-paying jobs. However, they were not as good at planning and were less persistent than the enhancers. Good-enough women usually married men who educationally and economically were similar to their first husbands, often going into a new marriage that was not much of an improvement over the first one.
- *The seekers.* These individuals were motivated to find new mates as soon as possible. "At one year post-divorce, 40 percent of the men and 38 percent of women had been classified as seekers. But as people found new partners or remarried, or became more secure or satisfied in their single life, this category shrank and came to be predominated by men" (p. 102).
- *The libertines.* People in this category often spent more time in singles bars and had more casual sex than their counterparts in the other divorce categories. However, by the end of the first year post-divorce, they often grew disillusioned with their sensation-seeking lifestyle and wanted a stable relationship.
- *The competent loners.* These individuals, who made up only about 10 percent of the divorced group, were "well-adjusted, self-sufficient, and socially skilled." They had a successful career, an active social life, and a wide range of interests. However, "unlike enhancers, competent loners had little interest in sharing their lives with anyone else" (p. 105).
- *The defeated.* Some of these individuals had problems before their divorce, and these problems increased after the breakup when "the added stress of a failed marriage was more than they could handle. Others had difficulty coping because divorce cost them a spouse who had supported them, or in the case of a drinking problem, restricted them" (p. 106).

Wright and Leahey (2013) state the developmental issues for the divorced family members. One such issue is adapting to living apart. Another is to deal with the extended family.

Remarried Adults

On average, divorced adults remarry within four years of their divorce, with men doing so sooner than women. Blended families come in many sizes and forms (Anderson & Sabatelli, 2007). The custodial and non-custodial parents and stepparent all might have been married and divorced, in some cases more than once. These parents might have residential children from prior marriages and a large network of grandparents and other relatives. Researchers have found that remarried adults are more likely to have higher levels of depressive symptoms than adults in intact, never-divorced families (Barrett & Turner, 2005).

Why do remarried adults with families find it so difficult to stay married? For one thing, many remarry not for love but for financial reasons, for help in rearing children, and to reduce loneliness. They also might carry into the blended family negative relationship patterns that resulted in the failure of an earlier marriage. Remarried couples also experience more stress in rearing children than do parents in never-divorced families (Ganong, Coleman, & Hans, 2006).

Parenting Adults

Like marriage, the age at which individuals have children has been increasing. In 2005, the average age at which women gave birth for the first time was a record high 25.2 years of age, up from 21 years of age in 2001 (Joint Economic Committee, 2007). Research findings from *A Profile of Mothers and Fathers in Canada: 1971–1996* commissioned by the Policy Division of Health Canada reported that first-time parents today are better educated and have relatively higher incomes than first time parents of the 1970s.

critical thinking

What are some of the variations in family structure with which you are familiar? What might be some of the unique tasks for each? What challenges must blended or reconstituted families overcome to ensure a successful adjustment? How do the tasks differ for each member; for example, how are the tasks of the custodial parent different from that of stepparent–stepchild? What are some of the adjustment tasks for siblings? for extended family members such as grandparents, cousins, aunts, and uncles? A lone-parent family may be headed by a single, separated, divorced, or widowed adult. What challenges and tasks face the lone-parent family? How does the context influence each scenario?

As birth control has become common practice, many individuals consciously choose when they will have children and how many children they will rear; as well, the number of one-child families is increasing. Several new trends are becoming apparent:

- By giving birth to fewer children and reducing the demands of child care, women free up a significant portion of their life spans for other endeavours.
- Men are apt to invest a greater amount of time in fathering.
- Parental care is often supplemented by institutional care (child care, for example).

As more women show an increased interest in developing a career, they are not only marrying later, but also having fewer children and having them later in life. Some of the advantages of having children early (in the twenties) are that the parents are likely to have more physical energy (for example, they can cope better with such matters as getting up in the middle of the night with infants and waiting up until adolescents come home at night). As well, the mother is likely to have fewer medical problems with pregnancy and childbirth, and the parents may be less likely to build up expectations for their children, as do many couples who have waited many years to have children. There are also advantages to having children later (in the thirties): the parents will have had more time to consider their goals in life, such as what they want from their family and career roles; the parents will be more mature and will be able to benefit from their life experiences to engage in more competent parenting; and the parents will be better established in their careers and have more income for childrearing expenses.

For many, economic pressures facing young families has necessitated that both parents work. In 2003, the Canadian Council on Social Development reported that 72 percent of Canadian mothers of children under 16 were in the workforce either part- or full-time (CCSD, 2006). Raising a child is expensive, particularly in the first year when expenses from birth to age one are estimated to be $10,000. Costs per year per child decline, but then rise again as the child enters the teen years (CCSD, 2006).

As a result of their increased time in the workplace, are mothers spending less time in caring for their children? A recent study reported on time allocation by parents from 1965 to 2000 (Bianchi, Robinson, & Milkie, 2006). The results indicated that fathers are increasing their participation in household chores, with mothers reducing their housework but not their child care. Parents now keep time with children high through effective time management and multi-tasking, spending more of their leisure time with children than in the past, and curtailing time with spouse, extended family, and friends.

In earlier times, motherhood and making a home for her family were considered a full-time occupation and the natural occupation for women. Nurturing children and having a career were thought to be incompatible. We have come to recognize that the balance between caring and achieving, nurturing and working—although difficult to manage—can be accomplished.

Lone-Parent Adults

Lone-parent families are those families headed by adults who are either single, separated, divorced, or widowed. Nationally, 25.8 percent of families with children are lone-parent families. Alberta, at 14.5 percent, has the lowest rate, while Nunavut, with 27.6 percent, has the highest rate (Statistics Canada, 2006b).

Although the number of men who head lone-parent families has increased, over 80 percent are headed by women, and their economic well-being is considerably more fragile than male lone parents. The average female lone parent earns $34,357. By comparison, the average male lone parent earns $48,248 (CCSD, 2006; Statistics Canada, 2001b).

Who are lone parents, aside from unmarried adolescents? Approximately 45 percent of lone parents are under 45 years of age, and many became single parents through divorce. For example, Marion, a 43-year-old teacher, found herself on her own with three teenagers, aged 15, 17, and 19, all in high school and all wanting to go to university. Her ex-husband provided no financial support; consequently, both she and her children incurred debt and delays while the children finished their education. On the other hand, Alicia, with two teenagers, was working part-time at the time of her

Dual-income families are an economic reality as well as an indicator of the changing roles for both men and women. What are some of the challenges dual-income parents face as they shape the emotional climate of the home? What strategies would you suggest a couple put in place to deal with these challenges?

divorce, and the children's father agreed to support the children financially until they finish their undergraduate work. Tina fits the profile of adolescent single parents described in Chapter 12. She had her first baby when she was 16, and her second at 19. In both cases, the child's father was older and abusive. Now, at 22, Tina has entered a community college to get the training she needs to, in her words, ". . . get off welfare and support myself and my children." Tina struggles to balance day-care, a part-time job, her studies, and her social life.

Another interesting phenomenon is the number of women in their mid-thirties who have decided to have and raise children as lone parents. They may have in vitro fertilization or adopt, but in either case, these women, who often have successful careers, decide to have and raise children on their own.

Gay and Lesbian Adults

Researchers have found that gay and lesbian relationships are similar—in their satisfactions, loves, joys, and conflicts—to heterosexual relationships (Mohr, 2009; Peplau & Fingerhut, 2007). For example, like heterosexual couples, gay and lesbian couples need to find a balance in their relationships that is acceptable to both partners in terms of romantic love, affection, how much autonomy is acceptable, and how egalitarian the relationship will be (Kurdek, 2006).

There are a number of misconceptions about homosexual couples (Kurdek, 2007; Peplau & Fingerhut, 2007). Contrary to stereotypes, one partner rarely takes the "masculine" counterpart to the other partner's "feminine" function. Only a small segment of the gay male population have a large number of sexual partners, and multiple partners is uncommon among lesbians as well. Researchers have found that lesbian and gay men prefer long-term, committed relationships (Peplau & Fingerhut, 2007). One aspect of relationships in which heterosexual and homosexual couples differ involves the obstacles that make it difficult to end a relationship (Peplau & Beals, 2002). In this regard, although same-sex marriages are lawful in Canada, laws surrounding divorce of same-sex couples remain unclear (Green & Mitchell, 2009; Weston, 2007).

Increasingly, gay and lesbian couples are creating families that include children (Bos, van Balen, & van den Boom, 2008). Researchers have found that children growing up in gay or lesbian families are just as well-liked as their peers, and there are no differences in the adjustment and mental health of children living in these families compared to children in heterosexual families.

To this point, we have discussed the diversity of adult lifestyles. For a review, see the **Reach Your Learning Objectives** section at the end of this chapter.

What are the research findings regarding the development and psychological well-being of children raised by gay and lesbian couples?

Gender, Relationships, and Moral Development

LO5 Summarize moral development and gender development.

In Chapter 10, we discussed Kohlberg and Gilligan's theories on moral development. In this section, we will look at another theory of moral development put forward by Urie Bronfenbrenner, whose bio-ecological theory was outlined in Chapter 2. Building on the discussion of gender roles in Chapters 8, 10, and 12, an overview of women and men's development also follows.

Moral Development

Urie Bronfenbrenner, whose bio-ecological theory of development you read about in Chapter 2, proposed five moral orientations based on an individual's context rather than on individual's passing through stages (see Figure 14.6). Individuals may move forward and backward in these orientations depending on the culture, an individual's exposure to differing values, the situation, and personal contexts.

Movement between orientations two, three, and four (authority, peer, and collective orientations) are related to the role religion, obedience to an authority, and peers play in an individual's

Moral Development

Women's Development

Men's Development

developmental **connection**

Bronfenbrenner

Figure 14.6

Bronfenbrenner's Five Moral Orientations

Orientation	Description
1. Self-oriented morality	An individual's personal needs take precedence over everyone else's needs. Others are considered only insofar as they can assist or hinder the individual.
2. Authority-oriented morality	Compliance to those who have authority or power, such as parents, teachers, police, and religious and political leaders.
3. Peer-oriented morality	Making choices about what is right and what is wrong based on what one's peers think, say, and do.
4. Collective-oriented morality	Making moral choices based on duty or obligation to family, country, etc.
5. Objectively oriented morality	Belief that universal principles have a morality of their own.

culture. For example, an individual whose religious views are fundamentalist Christian may make decisions based on his or her understanding of religious beliefs. These moral choices would differ from those made by an individual who does not adhere to any faith group, or one who adheres to the Muslim faith, for example. Another example would be voicing political dissent. Speaking against a government may be far more difficult, perhaps dangerous, in a country where compliance to authority means agreeing with the present government. And, another example would be the number of children a couple may decide to have. In one country such a decision is a matter of choice, whereas in another it's a matter of law.

Movement among orientations three, four, or five (peer, collective, and objective orientations) occurs when an individual is exposed to values that conflict, at least in part, with his or her own. For example, moving to Canada where women are not circumcised may cause parents to rethink their views. Moving from Canada to a country where women do not show their arms and legs in public may cause a woman to rethink her wardrobe.

Movement within the first four orientations involves situations where concern for others takes precedence over concern for self. For example, the service education adopted by Ontario schools is based on the notion that students who do volunteer work will develop a lasting concern for others. Through participation with others, an individual learns differing perspectives and develops empathy and altruism.

At any time in a person's life, adverse events may cause the individual to move to self-oriented morality as a matter of self-preservation. For example, an individual or family member who, because of economic upheaval, is thrust into poverty may experience the potential threat of losing his or her home. This person may make decisions and behave in ways he or she would not in other circumstances. Once economic stability is regained, the individual's decision making and behaviour may change again. In any case, the person's understanding of the world is influenced by these experiences.

Bronfenbrenner believed that very few people sustained objectively oriented morality. He thought that the hectic pace of modern life poses a threat second only to poverty and unemployment. The hectic pace of life may result in parents making hasty decisions that adversely affect the children and the harmony of the home. This deprives children of what he believed to be the development of their birthright virtues, such as honesty, responsibility, compassion, and integrity.

Women's Development

Jean Baker Miller's (1986) writings have been important in stimulating the examination of psychological issues from a female perspective. She believed that the study of women's psychological development opens up paths to a better understanding of all psychological development, male or female. She also concluded that when researchers examine what women have been doing in life, a large part of it is active participation in the development of others. According to Miller, women often try to interact with others in ways that will foster the other person's development along many dimensions—emotional, intellectual, and social.

Most experts believe it is important for women not only to maintain their competency in relationships, but to be self-motivated, too (Hyde, 2007; Matlin, 2008). Miller believed that through increased self-determination, coupled with already-developed relationship skills, many women would gain greater power in the North American culture. And, as Harriet Lerner (1989) concludes in her book *The Dance of Intimacy,* it is important for women to bring to their relationships nothing less than a strong, assertive, independent, and authentic self. She believes competent relationships are those in which the separate "I-ness" of both persons can be appreciated and enhanced while still staying emotionally connected to each other.

In sum, Miller, Lerner, Gilligan, and other gender experts believe that women are more relationship-oriented than men—and that this relationship orientation should be prized as a skill in our culture more than it currently is. Critics of this view of gender differences in relationships contend that it is too stereotypical (Dindia, 2006; Hyde, 2005, 2007; Matlin, 2004). They argue that there is greater individual variation in the relationship styles of men and women than this view acknowledges (Dindia, 2006; Hyde, 2007).

"You have no idea how nice it is to have someone to talk to.
Copyright © 1964 Don Orehek.

Men's Development

According to Joseph Pleck's (1995) *role-strain view,* male roles are contradictory and inconsistent. Men not only experience stress when they violate men's roles, they also are harmed when they do act in accord with men's roles (Levant, 2002). The following are some of the areas in which men's roles can cause considerable strain (Levant, 2002):

- *Health.* Men's life span is shorter than women's. They have higher rates of stress-related disorders, alcoholism, car accidents, and suicide. Men are more likely than women to be the victims of homicide. In sum, the male role is hazardous to men's health.
- *Male–female relationships.* Too often, the male's role involves images that men should be dominant, powerful, and aggressive, and should control women. "Real men," according to many traditional definitions of masculinity, look at women in terms of their bodies, not their minds and feelings, have little interest in rapport talk and relationships, and do not consider women equal to men in work or many other aspects of life. Thus the traditional view of the male role encourages men to disparage women, be violent toward women, and refuse to have equal relationships with women. As noted in Chapter 12, the social construct of maleness is a factor in sexual abuse and date rapes.
- *Male–male relationships.* Too many men have had too little interaction with their fathers, especially fathers who are positive role models. Nurturing and being sensitive to others have been considered aspects of the female role and not the male role. In addition, the male role emphasizes competition, rather than cooperation. All of these aspects of the male role have left men with inadequate positive emotional connections with other males.

Psychologist Ron Levant (2002) estimates that close to 80 percent of North American men are mildly or severely unable to express their feelings. Such emotional numbing is linked to depression. As a result, boys and young men are more likely to externalize their depression by engaging in risk behaviours twice as frequently as women, who are raised to pull pain inward, to blame themselves, and to be compliant rather than disruptive. Twice as many men as women take drugs, gamble, drink excessively, and so forth. To reconstruct their masculinity in more positive ways, Levant (2002) suggests every man should (1) re-examine his beliefs about manhood, (2) separate out the valuable aspects of the male role, and (3) get rid of those parts of the masculine role that are destructive. All of this involves becoming more "emotionally intelligent"—that is, becoming more emotionally self-aware, managing emotions more effectively, reading emotions better (one's own emotions and others'), and being motivated to improve close relationships.

To this point, we have discussed a number of ideas about gender, relationships, and moral development. For a review, see the **Reach Your Learning Objectives** section at the end of this chapter.

What are some changes in men's roles in home and family matters in the last 40 years?

reach your learning objectives

Stability and Change from Childhood to Adulthood

LO1 Examine stability and change in temperament, and summarize adult attachment styles.

Temperament
- The issue of stability versus change is a factor in both temperament and attachment.
- The first 20 years are important in predicting an adult's personality, but so, too, are continuing experiences in the adult years; the question is whether or not our core temperament changes as a result of our experiences.
- Previous studies indicate that temperament is genetically influenced from childhood to adolescence.
- In early adulthood, most individuals assume greater responsibilities, foresee consequences, plan ahead, and are more even-keeled than in adolescence.

Attachment
- Attachment patterns in young adults are linked to their attachment history, although attachment styles can change in adulthood as adults experience relationships.

Attraction, Love, and Close Relationships

LO2 Identify three key aspects of attraction, love, and close relationships.

Attraction
- Familiarity precedes a close relationship. We like to associate with people who are similar to us. The principles of consensual validation and matching can explain this.
- Physical attraction is usually more important in the early part of a relationship; criteria of physical attractiveness vary across cultures and historical time.

The Faces of Love
- Erikson theorized that intimacy versus isolation is the key developmental issue in early adulthood. There is a delicate balance between intimacy and commitment on the one hand, and independence and freedom on the other.
- Romantic love, also called passionate love, is involved when we say we are "in love." It includes passion, sexuality, and a mixture of emotions, not all of which are positive.
- Affectionate love, also called companionate love, usually becomes more important as relationships mature.
- Sternberg's triangular theory of love includes passion, intimacy, and commitment. When all three are present, Sternberg called this consummate love.

Falling Out of Love
- In the long run, the collapse of a relationship may be beneficial to one's health and future happiness.
- Dysfunctional relationships are those in which one person exploits another emotionally, financially, and/or physically.
- Women report more positive growth after a relational breakup than men.

Friendship
- Friendship plays an important role in adult development, especially in terms of emotional support.
- Female, male, and female–male friendships often have different characteristics. For example, self-disclosure and support is more common in female friendships.
- Friends with benefits relationships have emerged primarily within the last decade.

Loneliness	■ Loneliness often emerges when people make life transitions, and so it is not surprising that loneliness is common among first-year college and university students.
	■ Social loneliness results from an unsatisfying network of friends, whereas emotional loneliness is the product of unsatisfactory romantic or family relationships. Social loneliness is strongly linked to mental and physical health.
	■ Secure attachment experiences in childhood enable young adults to initiate and sustain relationships, resolve conflicts, and overcome loneliness.

Intimate Relationships: Marriage and the Family Life Cycle

LO3 Describe intimate relationships such as marriage, the family life cycle, and cultural influences on family life.

Marital Trends in Canada	■ Even though adults are remaining single longer and the divorce rate is high, we still show a strong predilection for marriage.
	■ The age at which individuals marry, expectations about what the marriage will be like, and the developmental course of marriage may vary not only across historical time within a culture, but also across cultures.
Social Contexts	■ Cultural and religious backgrounds influence the characteristics desired in a partner.
	■ The average age for marriage in Canada is early thirties.
Making Marriage Work	■ Gottman has conducted the most extensive research on what makes marriages work.
	■ In his research, these principles characterize good marriages: establishing love maps, nurturing fondness and admiration, turning toward each other instead of away, letting your partner influence you, solving solvable conflicts, overcoming gridlock, and creating shared meaning.
Benefits of a Good Marriage	■ Better mental and physical health and a longer life are benefits of marriage.
The Family Life Cycle	■ There are six stages in the family life cycle: leaving home and becoming a single adult; the joining of families through marriage—the new couple; becoming parents and a family with children; the family with adolescents; launching children and moving on; and the family in later life.
Parenting Myths and Realities	■ For some, the parental role is well planned and coordinated. For others, it is a surprise and sometimes chaotic.
	■ Some of the many myths about parenting include the following: the birth of a child will save a failing marriage; having a child gives the parents a "second chance" to achieve what they should have achieved; parenting is an instinct and requires no training.

The Diversity of Adult Lifestyles

LO4 Compare and contrast the diversity of adult lifestyles.

Single Adults	■ The economy, increased levels of education, and fear of divorce are some of the reasons young adults are waiting longer to marry.

Cohabiting Adults	■ Most young people who cohabit intend to marry.
	■ Cohabiting relationships are not as stable as married relationships.
	■ Although cohabitation is more prevalent today than a generation ago, no evidence supports that it is beneficial to marriage.
Divorced Adults	■ One in four marriages end in divorce by 30 years of marriage, with the greater number of divorces occurring within the first 5 to 10 years of marriage.
	■ Divorce brings unique challenges, including custodial arrangements.
Remarried Adults	■ On average, divorced adults remarry within four years.
	■ Blended or reconstituted families present unique challenges.
Parenting Adults	■ The advantages and disadvantages of adults becoming a parent in their twenties differ from those in their thirties.
	■ Managing time for child care, along with busy work schedules, is a priority for most parenting adults.
	■ Fathers are taking a greater role in parenting.
Lone-Parent Adults	■ Lone-parent families are headed by single, separated, divorced, and widowed adults.
	■ Poverty is the primary challenge to lone-parent families headed by young single women.
	■ More single women in their thirties and older who have completed their education and have stable jobs are deciding to become parents through in vitro fertilization or adoption.
Gay and Lesbian Adults	■ Gay and lesbian unions face the same challenges as heterosexual unions.
	■ The stereotypes of one partner taking the masculine role and the other taking the female role are erroneous.

Gender, Relationships, and Moral Development

LO5 Summarize moral development and gender development.

Moral Development	■ Urie Bronfenbrenner proposed five moral orientations that may vary according to the individual's context.
Women's Development	■ Many experts believe that it is important for females to retain their competence and interest in relationships, but also to direct more effort to self-development.
Men's Development	■ Despite concurrent achievement, the male role involves considerable strain.
	■ Talking about "the male experience" masks the diversity among males.

review ----> *connect* ----> reflect

review

How stable is temperament from childhood to adulthood? **LO1**

Which styles of attachment characterize adults? How are these styles of attachment linked to relationship outcomes? **LO1**

What are the three types of love? **LO2**

What makes a marriage work? **LO3**

Which stage in the family life cycle pertains to early adulthood? **LO3**

What similarities can be seen between homosexual and heterosexual relationships? **LO4**

What are several differences in the ways in which men and women communicate? **LO5**

connect

What may be several effects that divorce and remarriage can have on the children in those families?

reflect *Your Own Personal Journey of Life*

Which type of lifestyle are you living today? What, for you, are the advantages and disadvantages of this lifestyle? If you could have a different lifestyle, would you change it? Why?

Mc Graw Hill Education | **connect**

McGraw-Hill Connect provides you with a powerful tool for improving academic performance and truly mastering course material. You can diagnose your knowledge with pre- and post-tests, identify the areas where you need help, search the entire learning package, including the eBook, for content specific to the topic you're studying, and add these resources to your personalized study plan. CONNECT for *Life-Span Development*, fifth Canadian edition, offers the following:

- chapter-specific online quizzes
- groupwork
- presentations
- writing assignments
- case studies
- and much more!

Visit CONNECT today!

CHAPTER 15 Physical and Cognitive Development in Middle Adulthood

CHAPTER OUTLINE

The Nature of Middle Adulthood

LO1 Explain how midlife is changing, and define middle adulthood.

Changing Midlife

Physical Development

LO2 Discuss physical changes in middle adulthood.

Physical Changes

Health Concerns and Wellness Strategies

Culture, Relationships, and Health

Mortality Rates

Sexuality

Cognitive Development

LO3 Identify cognitive changes in middle adulthood.

Intelligence

Information Processing

Careers, Work, and Leisure

LO4 Characterize career development, work, and leisure in middle adulthood.

Work in Midlife

Career Challenges and Changes

Leisure

Meaning in Life

LO5 Explain the roles of meditation, religion, and spirituality in understanding meaning in life during middle adulthood.

Meditation, Religion, and Spirituality

Meaning in Life

Health and Well-Being

"*The event of creation did not take place many aeons ago. Astronomically or biologically speaking, creation is taking place every moment of our lives.*"

—DAVID SUZUKI, CONTEMPORARY CANADIAN SCIENTIST, ENVIRONMENTALIST, AND BROADCASTER

Middle Age

How do we know we're in middle age? Is it a few wrinkles around our eyes, our laugh lines, or the first grey hair? What are the boundaries—that is, when does it start? When does it end? Social determinants such as place of birth, date of birth, gender, health factors, economic security, job security, working conditions, hardiness, social networks, and educational background are critical determinants that contribute to how individuals in middle adulthood are able to balance the gains and losses at midlife.

Life expectancy is a measure of the overall quality of life in a country (Central Intelligence Agency, 2010). Thanks to access to extraordinarily good natural resources, education, health care, social networks, government supports, and generally good living conditions, life expectancy for Canadians is approximately 81 years: 79 for men and 83 for women (Statistics Canada, 2010a). Here, middle age might be considered to be somewhere between 35 and 65; however, in places where the health determinants are not readily accessible, the picture is quite different. For example, for First Nations peoples, particularly those living in rural areas or on reserves, such as the Inuit populations whose life expectancy is 64 for men and 73 for women, the boundaries for middle adulthood might be proportionately lowered to about ages 25 to 50 (Statistics Canada, 2010a). And, were we to be born in some African countries such as Zambia and Angola, where life expectancy is less than 40, middle adulthood might occur as early as 15 or 17 (Central Intelligence Agency, 2010).

As you have read in the previous chapters, early adulthood is vastly different today than a generation ago. The milestones that were once associated with the twenties—completing education, procuring secure employment, getting married, starting a family, purchasing a home—are now milestones associated with the thirties, if they occur at all. In fact, young adults are living at home longer, or returning to their homes after a relationship failure or a job loss; consequently, parents in middle adulthood find themselves supporting their children economically and emotionally through these events while concurrently working full- or part-time and perhaps providing care to failing parents.

A paradigm shift for early adulthood creates a paradigm shift for middle adulthood. One obvious example is that age boundaries for both have shifted. No longer is the age bracket for middle adulthood 35 to 55 years of age. In fact, one study found that almost half of individuals 65 to 69 years of age consider themselves middle-aged (National Council on Aging, 2000), and another study found a similar pattern: half of 60- to 75-year-olds view themselves as being middle-aged (Lachman, Maier, & Budner, 2000). Also, some individuals consider the upper boundary of midlife as the age at which they make the transition from work to retirement. Since mandatory retirement is no longer lawful and economic realities are demanding, many choose to postpone retirement, thus shifting the upper boundary even further.

The families young adults are creating are far more diverse: more lone parents; more intercultural and biracial unions; more same-sex relationships; as well as more blended families. This diversity sometimes challenges the assumptions of the older generations, who may or may not welcome such changes. Another critical aspect affecting families today involves the economic realities. Today's cost of living demands dual incomes; consequently, more and more grandparents are engaged in full- or part-time caregiving or grandparenting activities than in previous generations. At the same time, the average age of becoming a grandparent is now 55, approximately a decade older than previous generations (Edwards & Sterne, 2005). Hence, people in middle adulthood experience both the joy of becoming a grandparent and the toll of demanding responsibilities as they wish to help their children get established.

Fortunately, many of today's 50-year-olds are in better shape and more alert than their 40-year-old counterparts from a generation or two earlier. More people lead healthier lifestyles and medical discoveries help to stave off the aging process. Although people in middle adulthood are healthier than previous generations, they are constantly reminded that they are aging. All those outward signs—wrinkles, greying hair, declining strength, receding hairlines, declining vision, declining hearing—are constant reminders. The unwelcome onset of chronic diseases, many associated with stress—such as hypertension and cardiovascular disease as well as hormonal changes—also accompany and complicate middle adulthood. Thus, although people in middle adulthood are generally healthier and more able to help raise their grandchildren, care for their elderly parents, work full- or part-time, all this activity requires considerable juggling and problem solving. In the words of David Suzuki, people in middle adulthood are in the midst of the complicated process of creation: building a future for the next generation.

The Nature of Middle Adulthood

LO1 Explain how midlife is changing, and define middle adulthood.

As the opening vignette illustrates, midlife today is much different from a generation ago. How can middle adulthood be defined, and what are some of its main characteristics?

Changing Midlife

Compared with previous decades and centuries, an increasing percentage of the population is made up of middle-aged and older adults (Uhlenberg & Dannefer, 2007). When Carl Jung studied midlife transitions early in the twentieth century, he referred to midlife as the "afternoon of life" (Jung, 1933). Midlife serves as an important preparation for late adulthood, the "evening of life" (Lachman, 2004, p. 306). But "midlife" came much earlier in Jung's time. As a much greater percentage of the population lives to an older age, the midpoint of life and what constitutes middle age or middle adulthood are getting harder to pin down (Staudinger & Bluck, 2001).

In the past, the age structure of the population could be represented by a pyramid, with the largest percentage of the population in the childhood years. Today, the percentages of people at different ages in the life span are more similar, creating what is called the "rectangularization" of the age distribution (a vertical rectangle) (Himes, 2009a). This rectangularization has been created by health advances that promote longevity, low fertility rates, and the aging of the baby-boom cohort (Moen, 2007).

Middle adulthood *is generally considered to be the developmental period beginning at approximately 40 years of age and extending to about 60 or 65 years of age.*

Defining Middle Adulthood

The median age in Canada is 39.5, which means that half the population is older and the other half younger (Statistics Canada, 2006e). In 1966, the median age was only 25.4 years. The rising median age is one of the many indicators that the nation's population is aging, and has many implications for the labour force, economy, social services, and health care. So just how is middle adulthood defined today?

As you read in the opening in the opening vignette, the age boundaries are not set in stone; however, we will consider middle adulthood as the developmental period that begins at approximately 40 to 45 years of age and extends to about 60 to 65 years of age. For many people, middle adulthood is a time of declining physical skills and expanding responsibility; a period in which people become more conscious of the young–old polarity and the shrinking amount of time left in life; a point when individuals seek to transmit something meaningful to the next generation; and a time when people hope to reach and maintain satisfaction in their careers. In sum, middle adulthood involves "balancing work and relationship responsibilities in the midst of the physical and psychological changes associated with aging" (Lachman, 2004, p. 305).

In midlife, as in other age periods, individuals make choices, selecting what to do, how to invest time and resources, and evaluating what aspects of their lives they need to change. In midlife,

Changing Midlife

middle adulthood Generally considered to be the developmental period beginning at approximately 40 years of age and extending to about 60 or 65 years of age.

"a serious accident, loss, or illness" may be a "wake-up call" and produce "a major restructuring of time and a reassessment" of life's priorities (Lachman, 2004, p. 310). And with an absence of seniority protections, many middle-aged adults experience unexpected job loss and/or are strongly encouraged to take early retirement packages (Sweet, Moen, & Meiksins, 2007).

The concept of gains (growth) and losses (decline) is an important one in life-span development. Middle adulthood is the age period in which gains and losses as well as biological and socio-cultural factors balance each other (Baltes, Lindenberger, & Staudinger, 2006). Although biological functioning declines in middle adulthood, socio-cultural supports such as education, career, and relationships may peak in middle adulthood (Willis & Schaie, 2005). Thus, middle adulthood may be a unique developmental period in which growth and loss balance each other for many individuals.

Remember from our discussion in Chapter 1 that individuals have not only a chronological age, but also biological, psychological, and social ages. Some experts conclude that compared with earlier and later periods, middle age is influenced more by socio-cultural factors (Willis & Martin, 2005).

For many increasingly healthy adults, middle age is lasting longer. Indeed, an increasing number of experts on middle adulthood describe the age period of 55 to 65 as late midlife (Deeg, 2005). Compared with earlier midlife, late midlife is more likely to be characterized by "the death of a parent, the last child leaving the parental home, becoming a grandparent, the preparation for retirement, and in most cases actual retirement. Many people in this age range experience their first confrontation with health problems" (Deeg, 2005, p. 211). Overall, then, although gains and losses may balance each other in early midlife, losses may begin to dominate gains for many individuals in late midlife (Baltes, Lindenberger, & Staudinger, 2006).

Keep in mind, though, that midlife is characterized by individual variations (Perrig-Chiello & Perren, 2005). As life-span expert Gilbert Brim (1992) commented, middle adulthood is full of changes, twists, and turns; the path is not fixed. People move in and out of states of success and failure.

To this point, we have discussed the nature of middle adulthood. For a review, see the **Reach Your Learning Objectives** section at the end of this chapter.

Physical Development

LO2 Discuss physical changes in middle adulthood.

Physical Changes

Unlike the rather dramatic physical changes that occur in early adolescence and the sometimes abrupt decline in late adulthood, physical changes in midlife are usually gradual. Although everyone experiences some physical change due to aging in the middle adulthood years, the rates of this aging vary considerably from one individual to another. Genetic makeup and lifestyle factors play important roles in whether chronic disease will appear and when. Middle age is a window through which we can glimpse later life while there is still time to engage in prevention and to influence some of the course of aging (Lachman, 2004). Let's now explore some of the physical changes of middle age. Turning 50 is a milestone for many, as is turning 30 or 40 or 60. As we leave one decade, we lose a small part of our youth and come closer to old age. Amusing hints of aging are that our children are older than we ever thought they'd be, and strangers start to address us more respectfully, calling us "sir" or "ma'am." Although many may laugh at these subtle indicators that life is marching on, many may spend much time, effort, and money trying to hide the visible signs of aging.

Visible Signs

One of the most visible signs of physical change in middle adulthood is appearance. The skin begins to wrinkle and sag because of a loss of fat and collagen in underlying tissues (Farage et al., 2009). Small, localized areas of pigmentation in the skin produce aging spots, especially in areas that are exposed to sunlight, such as the hands and face. Hair becomes thinner and greyer due to a lower

- Physical Changes
- Health Concerns and Wellness Strategies
- Culture, Personality, Relationships, and Health
- Mortality Rates
- Sexuality

Famous hockey player Wayne Gretzky in 1975 and in 2013. **What are some of the most noticeable signs of aging?**

replacement rate and a decline in melanin production. Fingernails and toenails develop ridges and become thicker and more brittle.

Since a youthful appearance is stressed in our culture, many individuals whose hair is greying, whose skin is wrinkling, whose bodies are sagging, and whose teeth are yellowing strive to make themselves look younger. Undergoing cosmetic surgery, dyeing hair, purchasing wigs, enrolling in weight reduction programs, participating in exercise regimens, and taking heavy doses of vitamins are common in middle age. As well, middle-aged adults have shown a strong interest in plastic surgery and Botox, which may reflect their desire to take control of the aging process.

Height and Weight

Individuals lose height in middle age, and many gain weight. On average, from 30 to 50 years of age, men lose about an inch in height, then may lose another inch from 50 to 70 years of age (Hoyer & Roodin, 2003). The height loss for women can be as much as two inches from 25 to 75 years of age. Note that there are large variations in the extent to which individuals become shorter with aging. The decrease in height is due to bone loss in the vertebrae. On average, body fat accounts for about 10 percent of body weight in adolescence; it makes up 20 percent or more in middle age.

Being overweight poses critical health problems and may even lead to premature death in middle adulthood (Himes, 2009b; Wyn & Peckham, 2010). For individuals who are 30 percent or more overweight, the probability of dying in middle adulthood increases by about 40 percent. Obesity increases the probability that an individual will suffer a number of ailments, among them hypertension and digestive disorders (Bazzano et al., 2010; Bloomgarden, 2010). According to Statistics Canada, 52 percent of adults between 35 and 45 report themselves to be overweight or obese in 2011. As adults age, the rates increase: 59.6 percent between ages 45 and 65 (Statistics Canada, 2012a). Although we have highlighted the health risks of being overweight or obese in middle adulthood, severe weight loss also can pose a risk in the case of acute diseases.

Strength, Joints, and Bones

As we saw in Chapter 13, maximum physical strength and functioning is usually attained in the twenties. The term *sarcopenia* is given to age-related loss of muscle mass and strength (Doran et al., 2009; Narici & Maffulli, 2010). A loss of strength especially occurs in the back and legs. Muscle loss with age occurs at a rate of approximately 1 to 2 percent per year past the age of 50 (Marcell, 2003). Exercise can reduce the decline involved in sarcopenia (Park, Park, Shephard, & Aoyagi, 2010). The cushions for the movement of bones (such as tendons and ligaments) become less efficient in the middle adult years, a time when many individuals experience joint stiffness and more difficulty in movement. Maximum bone density occurs by the mid to late thirties, from which point there is a progressive loss of bone. The rate of bone loss begins slowly, but accelerates in the fifties (Ryan & Elahi, 2007). Women experience about twice the rate of bone loss as men. By the end of midlife, bones break more easily and heal more slowly (Neer & SWAN Investigators, 2010; Ritchie, 2010).

Vision and Hearing

Accommodation of the eye—the ability to focus and maintain an image on the retina—experiences its sharpest decline between 40 and 59 years of age. In particular, middle-aged individuals begin to have difficulty viewing close objects, which means that many individuals have to wear glasses with bifocal lenses. The eye's blood supply also diminishes, although usually not until the fifties or sixties. The reduced blood supply may decrease the visual field's size and accounts for an increase in the eye's blind spot. At 60 years of age, the retina receives only one-third as much light as it did at 20 years of age, much of which is due to a decrease in the size of the pupil (Scialfa & Kline, 2007).

Hearing also can start to decline by the age of 40. Auditory assessments indicate that hearing loss occurs in as many as 50 percent of individuals 50 years and older (Fowler & Leigh-Paffenroth, 2007). Sensitivity to high pitches usually declines first, though the ability to hear low-pitched sounds does not seem to decline much in middle adulthood. Men usually lose their sensitivity to high-pitched sounds sooner than women do. However, this gender difference might be due to men's greater exposure to noise in occupations such as mining, automobile work, and so on (Kline & Scialfa, 1996).

Researchers are identifying new possibilities for improving the vision and hearing of people as they age. One way this is being carried out is through better control of glare or background noise (Natalizia et al., 2010). Further, recent advances in hearing aids have dramatically improved hearing for many individuals (Lewis, Goodman, & Bentler, 2010).

Cardiovascular System

Midlife is the time when high blood pressure and high cholesterol levels may come as an unexpected surprise (Lachman, 2004). Heart disease and stroke combined are second to cancer as the leading cause of death in Canada, and are a major cause of illness and disability (Statistics Canada, 2012). As we age, fatty deposits and scar tissue slowly accumulate in the linings of blood vessels, gradually reducing blood flow to various organs, including the heart and brain. Fatty deposits can begin in childhood, and thus eating food high in fat content and being overweight as a child may have serious health consequences later in life (Masoro, 2006).

The level of cholesterol in the blood increases through the adult years and in midlife begins to accumulate on the artery walls, increasing the risk of cardiovascular disease (Betensky, Contrada, & Leventhal, 2009; Yetukuri et al., 2010). The type of cholesterol in the blood, however, influences its effect (Khera & Rader, 2010; Whayne, 2009). Cholesterol comes in two forms: LDL (low-density lipoprotein) and HDL (high-density lipoprotein). LDL is often referred to as "bad" cholesterol because when the level of LDL is too high it sticks to the lining of blood vessels, which can lead to atherosclerosis (hardening of the arteries). HDL is often referred to as "good" cholesterol because when it is high and LDL is low, the risk of cardiovascular disease is lessened (Gao et al., 2009; Weissglas-Volkov & Pajukanta, 2010).

Blood pressure (hypertension), too, usually rises in the forties and fifties. At menopause, a woman's blood pressure rises sharply and usually remains above that of a man through life's later years (Taler, 2009). An increasing problem in middle and late adulthood is *metabolic syndrome,* a condition characterized by hypertension, obesity, and insulin resistance. Metabolic syndrome often leads to the development of diabetes and cardiovascular disease. A recent study revealed that individuals who had metabolic syndrome had an increased risk for early death of any cause (Hui, Liu, & Ho, 2010).

Exercise, weight control, and a diet rich in fruits, vegetables, and whole grains can often help to stave off many cardiovascular problems in middle age (O'Donovan et al., 2010). For example, cholesterol levels are influenced by heredity, but LDL can be reduced and HDL increased by eating food that is low in saturated fat and cholesterol and by exercising regularly (Masley et al., 2008). Weight loss and exercise are strongly recommended in the treatment of metabolic syndrome (Dupuy et al., 2007). A recent study of 60-year-old men and women revealed a strong link between low levels of leisure-time physical activity and the presence of metabolic syndrome (Halldin et al., 2007). On the other hand, recent study of postmenopausal women revealed that 12 weeks of aerobic exercise training improved their cardiovascular functioning (O'Donnell, Kirwan, & Goodman, 2009).

Sleep

Some aspects of sleep become more problematic in middle age (McCrae & Dubyak, 2009). The total number of hours slept usually remains the same as in early adulthood, but beginning in the forties, wakeful periods are more frequent and there is less of the deepest type of sleep (stage 4). The amount of time spent lying awake in bed at night begins to increase in middle age, and this can produce a feeling of being less rested in the morning. Sleep problems in middle-aged adults are more common in individuals who use a higher number of prescription and non-prescription drugs, are obese, have cardiovascular disease, or are depressed (Kaleth et al., 2007; Loponen et al., 2010).

sleep apnea A serious condition that prevents a person from sleeping; a temporary cessation of breathing caused when the airways become blocked.

Getting adequate sleep is essential to good health and good sleep is not necessarily measured in hours, although consistency is recommended by health practitioners. However, the busy lifestyles of middle-aged adults may mean that that sleep patterns may be interrupted for a variety of reasons, such as waiting for teenagers to come home, financial worries, and so on. Approximately 40 percent of adults report experiencing *insomnia,* the inability to get to sleep or fall back to sleep once awakened, at some point in their lives (Fallows, 2011). Jet lag, room temperature, or resolving short-term problems may result in occasional insomnia; however, illness, depression, pain, and stress may cause chronic insomnia, a serious condition that results in irritability, depression, loss of concentration, and inability to work (Fallows, 2011).

Another sleep disorder is **sleep apnea,** *a serious condition that prevents a person from sleeping. Apnea is a temporary cessation of breathing caused when the airways become blocked; this occurs repeatedly during sleep.* Men, women, and children who suffer from sleep apnea literally stop breathing when they sleep. In self-reported surveys, 3 percent of adults 18 years and over reported experiencing sleep apnea. The rate increased to 5 percent in adults over 45 years of age. Among adults reporting sleep apnea, 75 percent were over 45 years of age, with nearly twice as many men reporting the condition as women (PHAC, 2010e). Canadians reporting sleep apnea are more vulnerable to having diabetes, hypertension, heart disease, and mood disorders such as depression, bipolar disorder, mania, or dysthymia (PHAC, 2010e).

Lungs

Little change in lung capacity occurs through most of middle adulthood. However, at about the age of 55, the proteins in lung tissue become less elastic. This change, combined with a gradual stiffening of the chest wall, decreases the capacity of the lungs to shuttle oxygen from the air people breathe to the blood in their veins. As shown in Figure 15.1, the lung capacity of individuals who are smokers drops precipitously in middle age. However, if the individuals quit smoking, their lung capacity improves, although not to the level of individuals who have never smoked.

---------------------------------- **Figure 15.1**

The Relation of Lung Capacity to Age and Cigarette Smoking

Lung capacity shows little change through middle age for individuals who have not smoked. However, smoking is linked with reduced lung capacity in middle-aged and older adults. When individuals stop smoking, their lung capacity becomes greater than those who continue to smoke, but not as great as the lung capacity of individuals who have never smoked.

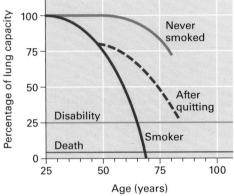

chronic disorders Conditions characterized by slow onset and long duration; are rare in early adulthood, increase in middle adulthood, and become common in late adulthood.

Health Concerns and Wellness Strategies
Health

In middle adulthood, the frequency of accidents declines, and individuals are less susceptible to colds and allergies than in childhood, adolescence, or early adulthood. Indeed, many individuals live through middle adulthood without having a disease or persistent health problem. However, for other individuals, disease and persistent health problems become more common in middle adulthood (Spiro, 2001).

Chronic disorders *are characterized by a slow onset and long duration. Chronic disorders are rare in early adulthood, increase in middle adulthood, and become common in late adulthood.* Arthritis is the leading chronic disorder in middle age, followed by hypertension.

Overall, arthritis is the leading chronic disorder in middle age followed by hypertension. The most common chronic disorders in middle age vary by gender (see Figure 15.2). Men have a higher incidence of fatal chronic conditions (such as coronary heart disease, cancer, and stroke); women have a higher incidence of non-fatal conditions (such as arthritis, varicose veins, and bursitis).

Stress and Disease

Stress is increasingly being found to be a factor in disease (Kahana, Kahana, & Hammel, 2009). The cumulative effect of stress often takes a toll on the health of individuals by the time they reach middle age. Stress is linked to disease through both the immune system and cardiovascular disease (Bauer, Jeckel, & Luz, 2009; Ho et al., 2010). For example, people who have had major life changes, such as loss of a spouse or a job, have an increased incidence of cardiovascular disease and early death.

THE IMMUNE SYSTEM AND STRESS   The immune system keeps us healthy by recognizing foreign materials such as bacteria, viruses, and tumours and then destroying them. Its machinery consists of billions of white blood cells located in the circulatory system. The number of white blood cells and their effectiveness in killing foreign viruses or bacteria are related to stress levels. When a person is under stress, viruses and bacteria are more likely to multiply and cause disease. One recent study in young and middle-aged adults revealed that persistently unemployed individuals had lower natural killer (NK) cell levels than their previously unemployed counterparts who became re-employed (Cohen et al., 2007). NK cells are a type of white blood cell that is more likely to be present in low-stress circumstances. The term *immunosenescence* is used to describe the progressive decline of immune system function with aging (Shah & Ershler, 2007).

STRESS AND THE CARDIOVASCULAR SYSTEM   Sometimes the link between stress and cardiovascular disease is indirect. For example, people who live in a chronically stressed condition are more likely to take up smoking, start overeating, and avoid exercising. All of these stress-related behaviours are linked with the development of cardiovascular disease by altering underlying physiological processes (Phillips & Hughes, 2010; Serido & Totenhagen, 2009). In addition, however, researchers have found that stress and negative emotions can affect the development and course of cardiovascular disease by altering underlying physiological processes (Das & O'Keefe, 2006). All of these stress-related behaviours are linked with the development of cardiovascular disease (Betensky, Contrada, & Leventhal, 2009; Tomiyama et al., 2010).

You may have heard someone say something like, "It's no wonder she died of a heart attack with all of the stress he put her through." But is it true that emotional stress can cause a person to have a heart attack? A clear link between emotional stress and having a heart attack has not been found, but chronic emotional stress is associated with high blood pressure, heart disease, and early death (Kiecolt-Glaser et al., 2002). And a recent study revealed that negative emotional events and anger at work were linked with the occurrence of acute coronary syndrome, a severe, sudden heart condition that has not yet developed into a heart attack (Lipovetzky et al., 2007). Apparently the surge in adrenaline caused by severe emotional stress causes the blood to clot more rapidly, and blood clotting is a major factor in heart attacks (Fogoros, 2001).

Poverty and Health

Evidence clearly links poverty to lower health status. Further, longer durations of poverty result in more serious health consequences. Canadians most vulnerable to poverty, and consequently more vulnerable to poor health, are lone mothers, Aboriginal peoples, new Canadians, racialized individuals, and people in the Atlantic provinces. These groups have consistently poorer health than the general population. For further information, read Connecting Development to Life, "The Thin Door."

In 1997, Jeff Reading, head of the Institute of Aboriginal Peoples' Health, said, "Raising the standard of living is the single most important factor to improve health status." Although improvements have been made in recent years, the gap remains between the health among Aboriginal people when compared to other Canadian groups remains a significant challenge (Health Canada 2012). While poverty is a major contributor, the reasons are more complex than poverty alone. The British Columbia Ministry of Aboriginal Health cites multi-generational experiences of racism, colonialism, residential schools, loss of culture, and loss of political institutions as contributing factors. These factors are at the heart of the Idle No More movement.

Mental Health

In Chapter 10, you read about the challenges of being a child whose parent has a mental health problem or illness. One of the issues for both the child and the adult is the stigma and fear attached to mental illness. Yet all of us either have suffered or are suffering from a mental illness or know someone who has—a family member, a friend, a colleague. According to the Mental Health Commission of Canada and the Centre for Addiction and Mental Health (CAMH), in any given year one in five Canadians experience mental health problems or illness. In fact, mental illness is the second leading cause of disability and premature death in Canada (CAMH, 2013).

Figure 15.2

Leading Chronic Disorders for Women and Men in Middle Age

Women	Men
1. Arthritis	1. Hypertension
2. Hypertension	2. Arthritis
3. Sinus problems	3. Hearing impairments

critical thinking

As you have read, poverty plays an important role in health. Consider the life map for an infant born into and growing up in poverty. Visualize the place of birth, the parent or parents, and the living accommodations. Visualize the individual going to public school, to high school, entering adulthood, and so on. What are the factors affecting the individual's health throughout the life span, and how does poverty play a role? What specific data should be gathered and resources developed to provide assistance to those who live in poverty? Must individuals change their economic situation to improve their health? How would the life map you've created differ in a rural and in an urban setting?

connecting development to life ←------------------

The Thin Door

I want to inspire and engage Canadians, from all walks of life, to empathize and respond to the injustice of homelessness in their community and motivate them to become involved in calling for the solution—a national housing program.

Cathy Crowe, nurse, educator, and social activist, on receiving the Atkinson Economic Justice Award, January 2004

Crowe's words are truer today than ever before, as the economic downturn that began in 2008 has left many households struggling to make ends meet. Imagine losing your job in your fifties when you have a mortgage, utilities, and taxes to pay, as well as children wishing to go to college or university. You may not be able to remain in the home you and your spouse have worked so hard to get. You may not be able to support your children as you had hoped. Or, imagine you are a single mother juggling two contract jobs.

Meaningful work and contributing to family and society are vital factors of self-esteem and identity, as well as family security. Those at the top of the economic chain are doing well, but the rest of Canadians, 10 million households, are struggling to make ends meet. More people are working, and they are doing so based on need. Many middle-income families are "cash-strapped" because incomes have stagnated (Statistics Canada, 2010b). If you adjust for inflation, typical workers earn 10 cents more an hour than they did in 1991.

According to Statistics Canada (2010b), 9.4 percent of Canadians—or more than 3 million—have seen their incomes drop by 9.1 percent over the last 25 years (McFeet, 2008; Statistics Canada, 2010b). About 606,000 of the people affected by low income are children under 17 years of age, and about one-third of this group is headed by female lone parents (Statistics Canada, 2010b)—many, if not all, of whom need safe housing. Families with only one wage earner are at greater risk of poverty, and the risk increases with the number of dependants in the family. Recent immigrants, regardless of their educational backgrounds, are earning considerably less than everyone else, averaging 63 cents for every dollar (McFeet, 2008).

Add to this the harsh psychological and economic consequences of layoffs. Most workers who are laid off find work, but their hourly income decreases by more than 20 percent in the majority of cases. Finding a job after being laid off in 2008 was even more difficult (Statistics Canada, 2010b). Contract work, outsourcing, and job loss account for some of the difficulty in finding stable, full-time work. Contract work offers no benefits, no pension, and further, some have rigid rules and little flexibility. For example, a person may work for an agency that contracts cleaning services with schools or hospitals. The terms of the contract may mean that, at the agency's discretion, no work will be done on any given day; therefore, the employees will not receive pay for that day, even though the contract stipulates that they be ready and willing to work. If the worker does not work the day before and the day after a holiday—Christmas, for example—that worker will lose holiday pay as well as pay for those two days of work. Additionally, contract or low-income workers are not unionized, so have no voice to argue for job security and benefits; consequently individuals work even when sick, and avoid costly trips to the dentist and expensive prescriptions when ill.

Education is no longer the route to job security. The census also shows that incomes for younger workers, well-educated or not, between 25 and 29 years of age have fallen (Statistics Canada, 2010b). One of the consequences is that many newly trained professionals, such as nurses and teachers, are contract workers struggling to make ends meet, often by juggling two or more contracts.

These data, coupled with the cost of housing, create an unsettling environment, one in which the security of owning a home, the family's primary asset, and/or meeting rental agreements thins the door between having a place of one's own to live or not. Aboriginal people, people of colour, people with disabilities, seniors, and women with children who head up the majority of low-income households are most at risk (Murphy et al., 2012).

The cycle of poverty is difficult to break and easy to fall into. Struggling to find good jobs, affordable housing, and to make ends meet has an enormous impact on adults and children alike, interfering with health, work, school, and social supports. For many who are struggling, a very thin door separates them from having a roof over their head and homelessness. The cost of chronic poverty is high, and may include costs beyond the immediately obvious. Pat Capponi, who drew from personal battles with poverty and mental health when she wrote *Dispatches from the Poverty Line* in 1997, noted what was as core to experiencing poverty then as it is today: "The hardest thing is keeping your sense of self . . . I fear the loss of self" (Capponi, 1997, p. 40).

The onset of 70 percent of mental health problems and illnesses occurs in childhood or adolescence. CAMH reports that at least half a million people are unable to work due to mental illness and that much worker absenteeism is related to mental health issues; consequently, those in the lowest income group are three to four times more likely to report fair to poor mental health (CAMH, 2013).

The prevalence of mental illness and the impact on the workplace have led to the introduction of a standard called Psychological Health and Safety in the Workplace in February 2013. The standard was developed by the Mental Health Commission of Canada in collaboration with the Bureau de normalisation du Quebec and the non-profit Canada Standards Association Group (CSA). According to Louise Bradley, president and CEO of the Mental Health Commission of Canada, the purpose of this initiative is to reduce the stigma associated with mental health issues, to promote mental health in the workplace, and to provide support for employees dealing with mental health issues (Bradley, 2012).

These Inuit people are attending a course on nutrition and heart health. **Why are Aboriginal people more susceptible to disease?**

Culture, Relationships, and Health

Emotional stability, a support network of family, friends, neighbours, and colleagues are related to health in middle adulthood. Let us now explore the role of culture in cardiovascular disease and two personality profiles that are associated with health and illness.

Culture and Cardiovascular Disease

Culture plays an important role in coronary disease. Cross-cultural psychologists believe that studies of immigrant groups help shed light on the role culture plays in health. As ethnic groups migrate, the health practices dictated by their cultures change, while their genetic predispositions to certain disorders remain constant (Ilola, 1990; Jorgensen, Borch-Johnsen, & Bjerregaard, 2006).

In 2010, Canada admitted 280,000 permanent residents and an additional 250 temporary visitors including international students and asylum seekers. Research shows that immigrants from the Philippines, China, and India, the three countries from which most immigrants come, are overrepresented in the prevalence of chronic disease. Language and cultural adjustment as well as overcoming or coping with feelings of isolation are perhaps the biggest barriers to health. Studies indicate that Chinese Canadians had higher rates of cancer and lower rates of cardiovascular disease than the general population, and that the longer South Asians live in Canada the more prone they are to factors, such as obesity, that lead to heart disease (Taylor, 2012).

critical thinking

Identify some of the causes of stress in middle adulthood. How might people alleviate stress in their lives? What strategies would you recommend for coping with stress? Identify the sources of stress in childhood, adolescence, and young adulthood. What are the similarities? What are the differences? How might the coping strategies be similar and how might they differ?

Mortality Rates

Infectious disease was the main cause of death until the middle of the twentieth century. As infectious disease rates declined, and more individuals lived through middle age, chronic disorders increased (Kelley-Moore, 2009). Chronic diseases are now among the main causes of death for individuals in middle adulthood (Merrill & Verbrugge, 1999) (see Figure 15.3).

Cancer has overtaken circulatory diseases as the leading cause of death in Canada, according to the Canadian Cancer Society (CCS). The CCS also estimates that 124 new cases of cancer are diagnosed daily (CCS, 2010). Eighty percent of people diagnosed with cancer are in their fifties or older. The Canadian Cancer Society predicts that the disease is on the rise nationwide as the population ages (CCS, 2010). Lung cancer is the most prevalent of cancers, followed by prostate and breast cancers. These three cancers account for over 54 percent of all cancer deaths.

Sexuality

What kinds of changes characterize the sexuality of women and men as they go through middle age? **Climacteric** *is a term that is used to describe the midlife transition in which fertility declines.* Let us explore the substantial differences in the climacteric of women and men.

climacteric A term used to describe the midlife transition in which fertility declines.

Menopause

Menopause *is the time in middle age, usually in the late forties or early fifties, when a woman's menstrual periods completely cease.* The average age at which women have their last period is 51, however there is large variation in the age at which menopause occurs—from 39 to 59 years of age. Virtually all women are postmenopausal by 60 years of age (Gosden, 2007). Later menopause is linked with increased risk for breast cancer (Mishra et al., 2009).

menopause The time in middle age, usually in the late forties or early fifties, when a woman's menstrual periods completely cease.

Figure 15.3

Leading Causes of Death in Canada

Cause of Death	%
Cancer	29%
Heart disease and other circulatory diseases (cerebrovascular, chronic obstructive pulmonary diseases and allied conditions, and diseases of arteries, arterioles, and capillaries)	28%
Unintentional injuries	4%

Source: Adapted from Statistics Canada, "Causes of Death," 84-208-XIE 2010001 2006. Released May 4, 2010.

Researchers have found that almost 50 percent of Canadian and American women have occasional hot flashes, but Taiwanese women report no significant effect of menopause. **What factors might account for these variations?**

Recall from Chapter 11, "Physical and Cognitive Development in Adolescence," that the timing of *menarche,* a girl's first menstruation, significantly decreased in the twentieth century, occurring as much as four years earlier in some countries (Susman & Dorn, 2009). Has there been a similar earlier onset in the occurrence of menopause? No, there hasn't, and there is little or no correlation between the onset of menarche and the onset of menopause (Gosden, 2007).

Perimenopause is the transitional period from normal menstrual periods to no menstrual periods at all, which often takes up to 10 years (De Franciscis et al., 2007; Seritan et al., 2010). Perimenopause is most common in the forties, but can occur in the thirties. A study of 30- to 50-year-old women found that depressed feelings, headaches, moodiness, and palpitations were the symptoms that women in perimenopause most frequently discussed with health care providers (Lyndaker & Hulton, 2004).

Heredity and experience influence the onset of menopause (Gosden, 2007; Liu et al., 2010). Multiple genes also influence menopause. Menopause occurs one to two years earlier in women who smoke cigarettes on a regular basis because tobacco smoke and tar can damage ovaries (Gosden, 2007). One study revealed that menopausal symptoms increased in women who smoked cigarettes, drank alcohol, were currently using oral contraceptives, were depressed, and ate high-sugar-content foods (Sabia et al., 2008). And a recent eight-year longitudinal study of women in their forties and fifties found that walking regularly one hour a day, five days a week, was linked to fewer symptoms of anxiety and depression as women made the transition from having regular menstrual periods to menopause (Nelson et al., 2008).

Not only the timing but also the side effects of menopause vary greatly. In menopause, production of estrogen by the ovaries declines dramatically, and this decline produces uncomfortable symptoms in some women: hot flashes, nausea, fatigue, and rapid heartbeat, for example (Cooper, Mishra, Clennell, Guralnik, & Kuh, 2008). Cross-cultural studies reveal wide variations in the menopause experience (Freeman & Sherif, 2007). For example, hot flashes are uncommon in Mayan women (Beyene, 1986). Asian women also report fewer hot flashes than women in Western societies. It is difficult to determine the extent to which these cross-cultural variations are due to genetic, dietary, reproductive, or cultural factors. Also, a study in Taiwan found no significant effect of menopausal transition on women's quality of life (Cheng et al., 2007).

HORMONE REPLACEMENT THERAPIES   One common treatment for menopausal discomforts approved by Health Canada has been hormone replacement therapy (HRT). HRT augments the declining levels of reproductive hormone production by the ovaries. If women take HRT for short-term relief of symptoms, the benefits may outweigh the risks (Schindler, 2006). However, the recent evidence of risks associated with HRT suggests that long-term hormone therapy should be seriously reevaluated (Warren, 2007).

The National Institutes of Health (U.S.) recommends that women with a uterus who are currently taking hormones should consult with their doctor to determine whether they should continue the treatment. One likely positive benefit of estrogen therapy is that it may help to protect against cognitive aging in women. A recent research review concluded that estrogen has protective effects on verbal memory and working memory when it is initiated soon after menopause begins—but when administered many years following menopause, there is no cognitive protection, and it can even be harmful when initiated later (Sherwin, 2007). A study of HRT's effects was halted as evidence emerged that participants who were receiving HRT faced an increased risk of stroke (National Institutes of Health, 2004). Recent analyses confirmed that combined estrogen and progestin hormone therapy poses an increased risk of cardiovascular disease (Toh et al., 2010). Estrogen alone increased the risk of stroke by about the same amount as estrogen combined with progestin. Preliminary data also indicated a trend toward increased risk of dementia (deterioration of mental functioning) among those receiving HRT. Because of the potential negative effects of HRT, many middle-aged women are seeking alternatives such as regular exercise, dietary supplements, herbal remedies, relaxation therapy, acupuncture, and nonsteroidal medications (Cardini et al., 2010; Gosden, 2007). For example, one recent study revealed that acupuncture and relaxation therapy reduced the number of hot flashes middle-aged women experienced (Zaborowska et al., 2007).

Hormonal Changes in Middle-Aged Men

Is there a male menopause? During middle adulthood, most men do not lose their capacity to father children, although there usually is a modest decline in their sexual hormone level and activity. Men experience hormonal changes in their fifties and sixties (Kohler et al., 2008). Testosterone production begins to decline about one percent a year during middle adulthood, and sperm count usually shows a slow decline, but men do not lose their fertility in middle age (Harman, 2007). The gradual decline in men's testosterone levels in middle age can reduce their sexual drive (Goel et al., 2009). A recent study of Taiwanese men revealed a testosterone deficiency that increased with age and this deficiency was higher in men who were obese and/or diabetic (Liu et al., 2009).

A common development in middle-aged men is **erectile dysfunction,** *the inability to adequately achieve and maintain an erection that results in satisfactory sexual performance* (De Berardis et al., 2009). According to a recent Canadian study, approximately 49.4 percent of men between the ages of 40 and 88 experience erectile dysfunction (ED); the rate increases with age (Grover et al., 2006). Middle-aged men's erections are less full and less frequent, and require more stimulation to achieve them. Researchers once attributed these changes to psychological factors, but increasingly they find that as many as 75 percent of the erectile dysfunctions in middle-aged men stem from physiological problems. Smoking, diabetes, hypertension, and elevated cholesterol levels are at fault in many erectile problems in middle-aged men (Laumann et al., 2007).

erectile dysfunction The inability to adequately achieve and maintain an erection that results in satisfactory sexual performance.

The male brain contains estrogen receptors too, so the interplay between hormones and the brain is the subject of further study. What has been referred to as "male menopause," then, probably has less to do with hormonal change than with the psychological adjustment men must make when they are faced with declining physical energy and with family and work pressures. Testosterone therapy has not been found to relieve such symptoms, suggesting that they may not be induced by hormonal change (Harman, 2007).

Treatment for men with erectile dysfunction has focused on the drug Viagra and similar drugs, such as Levitra and Cialis (Althof et al., 2010; Sperling et al., 2010). These drugs allow increased blood flow into the penis, which produces an erection. Their success rate is in the range of 60 to 85 percent (Pavone et al., 2008). The possible side effects of Viagra are headaches in 1 in 10 men, blackouts (Viagra can trigger a sudden drop in blood pressure), and seeing blue (because the eyes contain an enzyme similar to the one on which Viagra works in the penis, about 3 percent of users develop temporary vision problems ranging from blurred vision to a blue or green halo effect). Viagra should not be taken by men using nitroglycerin for the treatment of cardiovascular disease because the combination can significantly lower blood pressure and lead to fainting or even death in some men. Scientists do not know the long-term effects of taking the drug, although in short-term trials it appears to be a relatively safe drug. Studies continue to show that a high percentage of men who take Viagra, Levitra, or Cialis for erectile dysfunction are highly satisfied with the effectiveness of the drug (Abdo et al., 2008; McCullough et al., 2008; Rubio-Aurioles et al., 2008; Sharlip et al., 2008).

Lifestyle also plays a role in erectile dysfunction. Obesity, a sedentary lifestyle, and misuse of alcohol and drugs significantly increase the risk of erectile dysfunction (Heidelbaugh, 2010). A recent study revealed that low testosterone levels were related to the presence of metabolic syndrome and a high level of triglycerides (Corona et al., 2009). In another recent study, middle-aged men were randomly assigned to one of two treatment groups: (1) An experimental group that was given detailed, individualized information about the importance of reducing body weight, improved quality of diet, and increased physical activity in reducing erectile dysfunction, and (2) a control group that was provided general information about healthy food choices and increasing physical activity (Esposito et al., 2009). After two years of intervention, the men in the experimental group were more successful in improving their lifestyles and had a greater reduction in erectile dysfunction.

Sexual Attitudes and Behaviour

People vary tremendously in their sexual desire, and our sex lives are a complex and intricate combination of factors: desire, time, energy, opportunity, stress, privacy or lack of it, along with our feelings about our partners, about ourselves, and about our bodies. Although the ability of men and women to function sexually shows little biological decline in middle adulthood, sexual activity usually occurs less frequently than in early adulthood (Stones & Stones, 2007). Career interests, family matters, energy level, and routine may contribute to this decline.

In a survey of 10,000 people across 15 countries conducted by Durex, a condom manufacturer, four dimensions of sexual intimacy were ranked: partner's satisfaction, safer sex (condom always used with a casual partner), frequency of sex ranking, and average per year (Durex, 2006). Canada ranked number one in placing their partner's satisfaction above their own. A repeat of the survey in 2007 revealed that sex education from parents or health care professionals, satisfactory socio-economic status, and age are contributors to general confidence in sexual behaviour. Even in the healthiest relationships, partners' sexual interests may be out of sync at times. How often a couple makes love is not a major determinant of the health of their sex life; however, a couple's perception of and feelings about their compatibility in their love life are very important.

Sexually Transmitted Infections

Chlamydia, gonorrhea, syphilis, and AIDS have no age boundaries and can be contracted in middle age as easily as in early adulthood or the teenage years. Studies show that a woman is more likely to practise "safe sex" the first time she has intercourse or oral sex with her partner, but as time goes by and the relationship becomes more established, she is less likely to practise safe sex (Fang et al., 2010). The risk, however, is the same several weeks into the relationship as it is on the first night. Mary is a typical example. After 15 years of marriage, Mary separated from her husband and started to date. She had not been intimate with any other man for 17 years. After a few drinks, Mary had intercourse with her date. Just as a teenaged girl would be astonished to find she was pregnant, Mary was astonished to find she had contracted chlamydia. No age group is invincible.

To this point, we have discussed a number of ideas about physical development in middle adulthood. For a review, see the **Reach Your Learning Objectives** section at the end of this chapter.

Cognitive Development

LO3 Identify cognitive changes in middle adulthood.

In Chapter 13, we saw that cognitive abilities are very strong in early adulthood. Do they decline as we enter and move through middle adulthood? To answer this question, we will explore the possibility of cognitive changes in intelligence and information processing.

Intelligence

Our exploration of possible changes in intelligence in middle adulthood focuses on the concepts of fluid and crystallized intelligence, the Seattle Longitudinal Study, and cohort effects.

Fluid and Crystallized Intelligence

Cognitive psychologist John Horn believes that some abilities begin to decline in middle age while others increase (Horn & Donaldson, 1980). Horn maintains that **crystallized intelligence**, *an individual's accumulated information and verbal skills, continue to increase in the middle adulthood years*, whereas **fluid intelligence**, *one's ability to reason abstractly, begins to decline in the middle adulthood years* (see Figure 15.4).

Horn's data were collected in a cross-sectional manner. Recall from Chapter 1 that this involves assessing individuals of different ages at the same point in time. For example, a cross-sectional study might assess the intelligence of different groups of 40-, 50-, and 60-year-olds in a single evaluation, such as the one conducted in 2010. The average 40-year-old and the average 60-year-old were born in different decades, which produced different economic and educational opportunities. For example the 60-year-olds, born in the 1950s, had no cell phones or Internet access until they were

Intelligence

Information Processing

developmental **connection**

Research Methodologies

crystallized intelligence An individual's accumulated information and verbal skills, which continue to increase in the middle adulthood years.

fluid intelligence An individual's ability to reason abstractly, which begins to decline in the middle adulthood years.

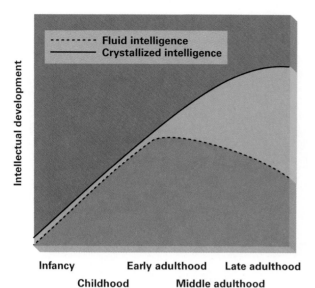

Figure 15.4

Fluid and Crystallized Intellectual Development across the Life Span

According to Horn, crystallized intelligence (based on cumulative learning experiences) increases throughout the life span, but fluid intelligence (the ability to perceive and manipulate information) steadily declines from middle adulthood.

45 or 50. However, the 40-year-olds, born in the 1970s, likely had cell phones and Internet access by the time they were age 25. Thus, if we find differences between 40- and 60-year-olds on intelligence tests when they are assessed cross-sectionally, these differences might be due to cohort effects related to technological differences rather than to age.

By contrast, recall that in a longitudinal study, the same individuals are studied over a period of time. Thus, a longitudinal study of intelligence in middle adulthood might consist of giving the same intelligence test to the same individuals when they are 40, 50, and 60 years of age. As we see next, whether data on intelligence are collected cross-sectionally or longitudinally can make a difference in what is found about intellectual decline (Abrams, 2009; Schaie, 2009).

The Seattle Longitudinal Study

For over half a century, Dr. K. Warner Schaie, along with Dr. Sherry L. Willis who joined him as a principal co-investigator in 1983, has conducted the most extensive study in human growth and development. Over 5,600 people have participated in this study, and the oldest participant in the 2011 wave was 103; the youngest was 36. New waves of participants have been added periodically; however, 26 of the original 500 individuals tested in 1956 are still participating (University of Washington Medicine, 2011). The main focus of this study is to understand change and stability in intellectual activities and abilities during the adulthood. To do this, a psychometric, measurement-based approach such as the one described in Chapter 9 has been used to test individuals at seven-year intervals (1956, 1963, 1970, etc.).

The main mental abilities tested include:

- Vocabulary (ability to understand ideas expressed in words)
- Verbal memory (ability to encode and recall meaningful language units, such as a list of words)
- Number (ability to perform simple mathematical computations, such as addition, subtraction, and multiplication)
- Spatial orientation (ability to visualize and mentally rotate stimuli in two- and three-dimensional space)
- Inductive reasoning (ability to recognize and understand patterns and relationships in a problem and use this understanding to solve other instances of the problem)
- Perceptual speed (ability to quickly and accurately make simple discriminations in visual stimuli)

K. Warner Schaie is a professor of human development and psychology at Pennsylvania State University, where he teaches and conducts research on adult development and aging. He also directs the Gerontology Center there. He is one of the pioneering psychologists who helped create the life-span perspective. He is the author or editor of more than 25 books and more than 250 journal articles and book chapters on adult development and aging. Dr. Schaie conducted the Seattle Longitudinal Study of Intellectual Development, a major research investigation that revealed that many intellectual skills are maintained or even increase during the years of middle age.

Life-span developmentalist K. Warner Schaie (right) with two older adults who are actively using their cognitive skills.

Figure 15.5

Longitudinal Changes in Six Intellectual Abilities from Age 25 to Age 67

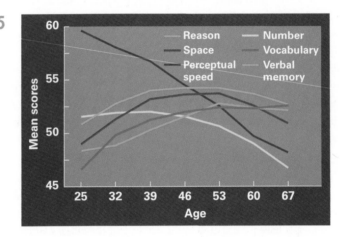

As shown in Figure 15.5, the highest level of functioning for four of the six intellectual abilities occurs in the middle adulthood years (Willis & Schaie, 1999). For both women and men, peak performance on vocabulary, verbal memory, inductive reasoning, and spatial orientation is attained in middle age. For only two of the six abilities—numerical ability and perceptual speed—are there declines in middle age. Perceptual speed shows the earliest decline, beginning in early adulthood. Notice, too, in Figure 15.6 that decline in functioning for most cognitive abilities began to steepen in the sixties, although the decline in verbal ability did not steepen until the mid-seventies. From the mid-seventies through the late eighties, all cognitive abilities showed considerable decline.

When Schaie and Willis (1994) assessed intellectual abilities both cross-sectionally and longitudinally, they found decline more likely in the cross-sectional than in the longitudinal assessments. For example, as shown in Figure 15.6, when assessed cross-sectionally inductive reasoning shows a consistent decline in the middle adulthood years. In contrast, when assessed longitudinally, inductive reasoning increases until toward the end of middle adulthood, when it begins to show a slight decline. In Schaie's (2008, 2009, 2010a, 2010b, 2011) view, it is in middle adulthood, not early adulthood, that people reach a peak in their cognitive functioning for many intellectual skills.

The results from Schaie's study that have been described so far focus on average cognitive stability, or change for all participants across the middle adulthood years. Schaie and Willis (Schaie,

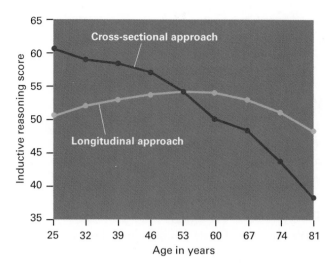

Figure 15.6

Cross-Sectional and Longitudinal Comparisons of Intellectual Change in Middle Adulthood

2005; Willis & Schaie, 2005) examined individual differences for the participants in the Seattle study and found substantial individual variations. They classified participants as "decliners," "stable," and "gainers" for three categories—number ability, delayed recall (a verbal memory task), and word fluency—from 46 to 60 years of age. The largest percentage of decline (31 percent) or gain (16 percent) occurred for delayed recall; the largest percentage with stable scores (79 percent) occurred for numerical ability. Word fluency declined for 20 percent of the individuals from 46 to 60 years of age.

Might the individual variations in cognitive trajectories in midlife be linked to cognitive impairment in late adulthood? In Willis and Schaie's analysis, cognitively normal and impaired older adults did not differ on measures of vocabulary, spatial orientation, and numerical ability in middle adulthood. However, declines in memory (immediate recall and delayed recall), word fluency, and perceptual speed in middle adulthood were linked to neuropsychologists' ratings of the individuals' cognitive impairment in late adulthood.

Interestingly, in terms of John Horn's ideas, middle age is a time of peak performance, both for some aspects of crystallized intelligence (vocabulary) and for fluid intelligence (spatial orientation and inductive reasoning) for the participants in the Seattle Longitudinal Study. Thus, in Schaie's view, people in middle adulthood may reach their peak functioning for many cognitive skills.

Evaluating Schaie and Willis

Some researchers disagree with Schaie and Willis's theory that middle adulthood is the time when the level of functioning in a number of cognitive domains is maintained or even increases (Finch, 2009). For example, psychologist Timothy Salthouse (2009a), who has specialized in cognitive aging, recently concluded that cross-sectional research on aging and cognitive functioning should not be dismissed and that this research indicates reasoning, memory, spatial visualization, and processing speed begin declining in early adulthood and show further decline in the fifties. Salthouse (2009a) does agree that cognitive functioning involving accumulated knowledge, such as vocabulary and general information, does not show early age-related decline and increases at least until 60 years of age.

Salthouse (2009a) argued that a lower level of cognitive functioning in early and middle adulthood is likely due to age-related neurobiological decline. Cross-sectional studies have shown that these neurobiological factors decline in the twenties and thirties: regional brain volume, cortical thickness, synaptic density, some aspects of myelination, the functioning of some aspects of neurotransmitters such as dopamine and serotonin, blood flow in the cerebral cortex, and the accumulation of tangles in neurons (Del Tredici & Braak, 2008; Erixon-Lindroth et al., 2005; Finch, 2009; Hsu et al., 2008; Pieperhoff et al., 2008; Salat et al., 2004).

Schaie (2009, 2010a, 2010b, 2011) continues to emphasize that longitudinal studies hold the key to determining age-related changes in cognitive functioning and that middle age is the time during which many cognitive skills actually peak. In the next decade, expanding research on age-related neurobiological changes and their possible links to cognitive skills should further refine our knowledge about age-related cognitive functioning in the adult years (Finch, 2009).

Information Processing

In our discussion of theories of development in Chapter 2 and in a number of child development and adolescence chapters (7, 9, and 11), we examined the information-processing approach to cognition. Among the information-processing changes that take place in middle adulthood are those involved in the speed of processing information, memory, expertise, and practical problem-solving skills.

Speed of Information Processing

As we saw in the Seattle Longitudinal Study, perceptual speed begins declining in early adulthood and continues to decline in middle adulthood. A common way to assess speed of information is through a reaction-time task, in which individuals simply press a button as soon as they see a light. Middle-aged adults are slower to push the button when the light appears than are young adults. However, the decline is not dramatic—under one second in most investigations. A current interest focuses on possible causes for the decline in speed of processing information in adults (Salthouse, 2009a). The causes may occur at different levels of analysis, such as cognitive ("maintaining goals, switching between tasks, or preserving internal representations despite distraction"), neuroanatomical ("changes in specific brain regions, such as the prefrontal cortex"), and neurochemical ("changes in neurotransmitter systems") such as dopamine (Hartley, 2006, p. 201).

Memory

According to the Seattle Longitudinal Study (Schaie, 1996), verbal memory peaked in the fifties. However, in some other studies, verbal memory shows a decline in middle age, especially when assessed in cross-sectional studies. For example, in several studies, when asked to remember lists of words, numbers, or meaningful prose, younger adults outperformed middle-aged adults (Salthouse & Skovronek, 1992). Although there is still some controversy about whether memory declines in the middle adulthood years, most experts conclude that it does (Hoyer & Roodin, 2009; Salthouse, 2009a). However, some experts argue that studies that have concluded there is a decline in memory during middle age often have compared young adults in their twenties with older middle-aged adults in their late fifties, and even have included some individuals in their sixties (Schaie, 2000). In this latter view, memory decline in the early part of middle age is either non-existent or minimal and does not occur until the latter part of middle age or late adulthood (Backman, Small, & Wahlin, 2001).

Cognitive aging expert Denise Park (2001) argues that starting in late middle age, more time is needed to learn new information. The slowdown in learning new information has been linked to changes in **working memory,** *the mental "workbench" where individuals manipulate and assemble information when making decisions, solving problems, and comprehending written and spoken language* (Baddeley, 2007a, b). In this view, in late middle age working memory capacity—the amount of information that can be immediately retrieved and used—becomes more limited (Leonards, Ibanez, & Giannakopoulos, 2002). Think of this situation as an overcrowded desk with many items in disarray. As a result of the overcrowding and disarray, long-term memory becomes less reliable, more time is needed to enter new information into long-term storage, and more time is required to retrieve the information. Thus, Park believes that much of the blame for declining memory in late middle age is a result of information overload that builds up as we go through the adult years.

Memory decline is more likely to occur when individuals don't use effective memory strategies, such as organization and imagery (Sugar, 2007). By organizing lists of phone numbers into different categories, or imagining the phone numbers as representing different objects around the house, many individuals can improve their memory in middle adulthood.

working memory The mental "workbench" where individuals manipulate and assemble information when making decisions, solving problems, and comprehending written and spoken language.

- - - - - - - **critical** thinking - - - - - - -

Design a working memory workbench. What might you include? Expertise, problem solving, and creativity are generally at their strongest in middle adulthood. Why is that? What role might technology play? What challenges might technology present to people in middle adulthood?

Expertise

Because it takes so long to attain, expertise often shows up more in middle adulthood than in the early adulthood years (Kim & Hasher, 2005). **Expertise** *involves having an extensive, highly organized knowledge and understanding of a particular domain.* Developing expertise and becoming an "expert" in a field usually is the result of many years of experience, learning, and effort.

Strategies that distinguish experts from novices include the following:

- Experts are more likely to rely on their accumulated experience to solve problems.
- Experts often process information automatically and analyze it more efficiently when solving a problem in their domain than novices do.
- Experts have better strategies and shortcuts to solving problems in their domain than novices do.
- Experts are more creative and flexible in solving problems in their domain than novices are (Csikszentmihalyi, 1997).

Practical Problem Solving

Everyday problem solving is another important aspect of cognition (Margrett & Deshpande-Kamat, 2009). Nancy Denney (1986, 1990) observed circumstances such as how young and middle-aged adults handled a landlord who would not fix their stove and what they did if a bank failed to deposit a cheque. She found that the ability to solve such practical problems improved through the forties and fifties as individuals accumulated practical experience. However, since Denney's research, other studies on everyday problem-solving and decision-making effectiveness across the adult years have been conducted (Margrett & Deshpande-Kamat, 2009). A recent meta-analysis of these studies indicated that everyday problem-solving and decision-making effectiveness remain stable in early and middle adulthood, then decline in late adulthood (Thornton & Dumke, 2005).

Creativity

Creativity *is the process of divergent thinking that requires encounters with the world and a degree of intensity and absorption.* Through encounters with the world, the individual gains a heightened consciousness of possibilities and limitations; in this manner, creative contributions are realistic, constructive, and achievable. Recall from Chapter 13 that creativity peaks along some domains in early adulthood, while others are more likely to peak in middle adulthood; in fact, most creative contributions are completed by age 50 (Lehman, 1960). The contemporary guru of creativity, Mihaly Csikszentmihalyi, believes everyone is capable (see Connecting through Research).

Existential psychologist Rollo May wrote, "Creativity is the process of bringing something new into being." He noted further that creativity requires passion, commitment, and courage. Creativity brings to our awareness what was previously hidden and points to new life. The experience is one of heightened consciousness—ecstasy." In his book *The Courage to Create* (1975), May argued that the ultimate betrayal is not to listen to our own original ideas. Listening to and acting upon our own ideas requires commitment and courage, both vital to finding innovative patterns on which society can be built.

Dr. Walter De Brouwer illustrates both Csikszentmihalyi's and May's theory as he became passionately absorbed in a challenge, then listened and acted upon his convictions. His five-year-old son's fall and subsequent months in intensive care heightened De Brouwer's consciousness of possibilities and limitations. He wondered why most homes, like his, had only a thermometer when access to more information would be so much more helpful and vital in emergencies (De Brouwer, 2012). This encounter led to the foundation in 2011 of Scanadu, a company that develops medical technology applications for consumers, and the launch in 2012 of Scout, a device that when held to a person's temple for 10 seconds can wirelessly monitor five different vital signs (temperature, heart rate, blood oxygenation level, pulse, respiratory rate) and transmit results to the person's smartphone. Scout currently is pending government approval, and once approved will become available to consumers. Scout, along with existing and future social networking sites for patients, will be key

expertise Having extensive, highly organized knowledge and understanding of a particular domain.

Stephen Hawking is a world-renowned expert in physics. Hawking authored the best-selling book *A Brief History of Time*. Hawking has a neurological disorder that has rendered him unable to walk or talk. He communicates with the aid of a voice-equipped computer. **What distinguishes experts from novices?**

creativity The process of divergent thinking that requires encounters with the world and a degree of intensity and absorption.

Mihaly Csikszentmihalyi

Mihaly Csikszentmihalyi is Director of the Quality of Life Research Center (QLRC), a non-profit institute that studies "positive psychology," the study of happiness, optimism, creativity, intrinsic motivation, and responsibility. He is one of the main architects of changing psychology's focus from the negative to the positive, believing that for too long the field has studied the dark side of life and that it is high time psychologists started focusing more on the good aspects of people. Often described as the guru of creativity, Csikszentmihalyi is best known for his concept of "flow," the mental state of joy or effortlessness individuals feel when they are "in the zone." Flow is characterized by having clear attainable goals and feedback. He has conducted a study of highly creative people in different walks of life—business, arts, science—to discover what they are thinking, feeling, and doing when they come up with their most creative insights (Csikszentmihalyi, 1995). Csikszentmihalyi

Mihaly Csikszentmihalyi, in the setting where he gets his most creative ideas. **When and where do you get your most creative thoughts?**

(1997, 2000) believes everyone is capable of achieving flow. One thing he found was that certain settings are more likely to stimulate creativity than others. Csikszentmihalyi offers a number of tips that involve a daily change in behaviour such as finding something new and surprising, surprising someone by doing something unpredictable, keeping a diary or notes of these surprises, following what captures your interest and curiosity, setting daily goals, organizing and taking charge of your daily schedule, and recognizing when you are most creative and productive. In 2000, the Dana Alliance, a non-profit organization of neuroscientists, awarded its first Thinker of the Year Award to Mihaly Csikszentmihalyi, in recognition of his life-long contribution to the field of positive psychology (Needle, 2001). Through his research methods, his dedication, and his own creative courage, Csikszentmihalyi has contributed an innovative pattern for understanding human motivation.

factors in revolutionizing the health care field, as patients will have access to more information and be more able to monitor their health. To listen to De Brouwer discuss how health care may be revolutionized, follow this link: http://www.youtube.com/watch?v=BSZJjN7o8Ck.

To this point, we have studied a number of ideas about cognitive development in middle adulthood. For a review, see the **Reach Your Learning Objectives** section at the end of this chapter.

Careers, Work, and Leisure

LO4 Characterize career development, work, and leisure in middle adulthood.

Are middle-aged workers as satisfied with their jobs as young adult workers?

- Work in Midlife
- Career Challenges and Changes
- Leisure

Work in Midlife

The role of work—whether one works in a full-time career or a part-time job, as a volunteer, or as a homemaker—is central during the middle years. Middle-aged adults may reach their peak in position and earnings. They may also be saddled with multiple financial burdens such as rent or mortgage, child care, home repairs, college tuition, loans to family members, or caregiving expenses. For many people, midlife is a time of evaluation, assessment, and reflection in terms of the work they do and want to do in the future (Moen, 2009a). Important considerations are job satisfaction and the quality of employment. An International Task Force headed by Canada, with participation from the United Nations (UN) and the International Labour Organization (ILO), identified the following factors as key to employment quality: job safety, both financial and non-financial remuneration, working hours, work–life balance, job stability, social dialogue, skills development, and job satisfaction. An analysis of the Canadian labour force indicated that immigrant workers ranked lower on

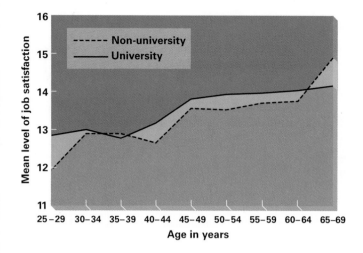

Figure 15.7

Age and Job Satisfaction

Job satisfaction increases with age for both college/university and non–college/university-educated adults. Among the reasons for increased satisfaction are more income, higher-status jobs, greater job security, and stronger job commitment.

From *Men in Their Forties: The Transition to Middle Age*, by Lois M. Tamir, 1982. Springer Publishing Co. Used by permission of the author.

each of these dimensions than non-immigrant workers, particularly those newest to Canada. As noted by the International Task Force, when an individual's values and job security are aligned with his or her work, satisfaction increases notably (see Figure 15.7) (Gilmore, 2009).

According to Statistics Canada, the economic downturn that began in 2008 adversely affected both Aboriginal workers and new Canadians the hardest and the longest (Gilmore, 2009; Usalcas, 2011). Creating an inclusive working environment and engaging in non-discriminatory practices, often systemic in nature, continues to be a challenge for employers (Human Resources and Skills Development Canada, 2012a).

Career Challenges and Changes

The current middle-aged worker faces several important challenges (Blossfeld, 2009). These include the globalization of work, rapid developments in information technologies, restructuring, downsizing, and privatization of organizations, as well as early retirement and concerns about pensions and health care. Some midlife career changes are self-motivated; others are the consequence of these challenges which may result in losing one's job (Moen, 2009a). Some individuals decide that they don't want to do the same work they have been doing for the rest of their lives (Hoyer & Roodin, 2009). Reconciling the dreams they may have had in their youth with the challenges of providing for their families and their future is often a critical source of stress. If individuals perceive that they are behind schedule, if their goals are unrealistic, they don't like the work they are doing, or their job has become too stressful, they could become motivated to change jobs.

The decline in defined-benefit pensions and increased uncertainty about the fate of health insurance are decreasing the sense of personal control for middle-aged workers. As a consequence, many are delaying retirement plans. In addition, couples increasingly have both spouses in the workforce who are expecting to retire. Historically retirement has been a male transition, but today far more couples have to plan two retirements (Moen & Altobelli, 2007; Moen, Kelly, & Magennis, 2008).

Approximately two-thirds (66.8 percent) of women with children under six years of age are employed outside the home (Human Resources and Skills Development Canada, 2012a). Balancing family and work responsibilities is particularly challenging. In addition to finding suitable and affordable daycare and before- and after-school care programs, women may find that parental leaves have interrupted their skill levels and networking aspects of career development. Further, women remain the primary caregivers of needy family members such as a sister who has been diagnosed with breast cancer or a parent suffering from congestive heart failure; hence, workers often experience intense conflict between work and family responsibilities (Human Resources and Skills Development Canada, 2012c). Another challenge to employers is to address the needs of workers to balance work and family life. Shortly following the turn of the century, Statistics Canada projected that nearly 1.1 million of the 16-million-person workforce would be looking for employment. That projection might be

critical thinking

Globalization strategies are shifting the work from expensive, unionized North American labour sources to cheaper sources elsewhere in the world. Particularly hard hit have been textile workers; in fact, finding products made in Canada is more challenging today than just a decade ago, as more and more garments are made outside of Canada. How might the impact differ in urban and rural settings? What might be the impact of job loss on an individual? on his or her family? What steps can a person take to help prepare for unexpected job loss in the future?

Reprinted with special permission of North American Syndicate.

even higher today, especially for those who work in the lumber or cattle-farming sectors. As noted earlier in the chapter in "The Thin Door," many jobs are being filled by contract workers who often do not receive benefits or vacation pay (Statistics Canada, 2007). More than a quarter-million of those seeking work are men and women between ages 45 and 64. Most older workers who lose their jobs because of globalization or restructuring want to find another full-time job; however, Human Resources and Skills Development Canada (HRSDC) reports that they face four major barriers: (1) lower educational levels, (2) outdated skills, (3) lack of job-seeking know-how, and (4) negative stereotyping by employers about their abilities, ambitions, and productivity. When laid-off workers are able to return to work, they do so at disproportionately lower wages. Many feel a sense of failure, become discouraged, give up looking for work, and are no longer included in the statistical count.

Leisure

Not only must adults learn how to work well, but they also need to learn how to relax and enjoy leisure (Gibson, 2009). **Leisure** refers to *the pleasant times after work when individuals are free to pursue activities and interests of their own choosing*—hobbies, sports, or reading, for example. In one analysis of research on what adults regret the most, not engaging in more leisure was one of the top six regrets (Roese & Summerville, 2005).

Vacations are important. In one study, 12,338 men 35 to 57 years of age were assessed each year for five years regarding whether they took vacations or not (Gump & Matthews, 2000). Then, the researchers examined the medical and death records over nine years for men who lived for at least a year after the last vacation survey. Compared with those who never took vacations, men who went on annual vacations were 21 percent less likely to die over the nine years and 32 percent less likely to die of coronary heart disease.

Adults at midlife need to begin preparing psychologically for retirement. Constructive and fulfilling leisure activities in middle adulthood are an important part of this preparation (Danigelis, 2007). If an adult develops leisure activities that can be continued into retirement, the transition from work to retirement can be less stressful.

Meaning in Life

LO5 Explain the roles of meditation, religion, and spirituality in understanding meaning in life during middle adulthood.

What role do meditation, religion, and spirituality play in our development as adults? Is meaning of life an important theme for many middle-aged adults?

Meditation, Religion, and Spirituality

Recall that Piaget believed that, starting in adolescence, people engage in the *formal operation stage* and that in this stage we are more capable of abstract thought that is both idealistic and logical. As

Sigmund Freud once commented that the two things adults need to do well to adapt to society's demands are to work and to love. To his list we add "to play and laugh." In our fast-paced society, it is all too easy to get caught up in the frenzied, hectic pace of our achievement-oriented work world and ignore leisure and play. Imagine your life as a middle-aged adult. **What would be the ideal mix of work and leisure? What leisure activities do you want to enjoy as a middle-aged adult? Why do you think laughter is important?**

leisure The pleasant times after work when individuals are free to pursue activities and interests of their own choosing.

Meditation, Religion, and Spirituality

Meaning in Life

Health and Well-Being

well, recall that in Kohlberg's highest stage of moral reasoning, the *postconventional stage*, morality becomes completely internalized and is not based on the ideas of others. Core to these concepts is human nature's quest to try to understand and explain the origin of the universe, our purpose in life, as well as gain confidence to cope with life's ups and downs. Many turn to meditation or religion for understanding, while others turn to spirituality. In many ways these approaches may be similar and even overlapping, but they do differ. Each one is defined differently depending on determinants such as culture, gender, age, and general well-being; thus, the following definitions are intended to provide a brief overview.

Meditation

"To meditate" means to think about something. In this context, **meditation** *refers to a variety of practices intended to foster clarity of thought, well-being, and relief from stress by focusing attention with calmness and concentration.* Once understood, practitioners can apply this stylized mental technique and meditate anyplace for as much time as they have. It is both restful and silent. Religions, particularly Eastern religions, have used meditation widely and have reported profound changes in how an individual perceives him- or herself, and thus alters his or her world-view (Shapiro & Walsh, 2008).

meditation A variety of practices intended to foster clarity of thought, well-being, and relief from stress by focusing attention with calmness and concentration.

Religion

Religion *is an organized set of beliefs about how the universe originated, as well as the nature and the purpose of the universe.* Religions also provide rituals, rites of passage, celebratory festivals, and a code of conduct that governs behaviour. The largest religious groups are Buddhism, Christianity, Hinduism, Islam, and Judaism. Within each large group are many sub-groups as well as many interpretations related to the nature of the universe and our roles. Indeed, within a family one may find as many views or interpretations as there are members of the family.

religion An organized set of beliefs about how the universe originated, as well as the nature and the purpose of the universe.

Statistics Canada combines four dimensions of religion—affiliation, attendance, personal practices, and importance of religion—to arrive at a *religiosity index*, which determines how religious a person is. Using these criteria, 40 percent of Canadians have a low degree of religiosity, 31 percent are moderately religious, and 29 percent are highly religious. Those in the highly religious group tend to be those in older age groups. Immigrants, especially those from South East Asia (e.g., the Philippines) and the Caribbean and Central America, as well as women, tend to have higher religiosity (Clark & Schellenberg, 2006). People in the Atlantic provinces are more likely to participate in religious practices than those in British Columbia, and immigrants are more likely than Canadian-born people to engage in such activities. Overall, 44 percent report that religion is important to their lives. In 2004, 48 percent of Canadians between the ages of 15 and 59 reported either no religious affiliation or not attending religious services; however, 53 percent engage in private religious practices such as prayer or meditation privately at least once monthly (Clark & Schellenberg, 2006).

Spirituality

Although the *Oxford English Dictionary* defines **spirituality** *as the quality or condition of being spiritual and an attachment or regard for things of the spirit as opposed to material or worldly interests,* there are so many definitions of spirituality that one may wonder whether it can be defined (Greenberg, 2008). Three characteristics of spirituality are an emotional response to the world, a cognitive context or set of beliefs about oneself and the world, and a spiritual practice. Spiritual practices vary considerably and may include prayer, observance of silence, reciting mantras, and acts of charity toward humans and animals (Jain et al., 2013).

spirituality The quality or condition of being spiritual and an attachment or regard for things of the spirit as opposed to material or worldly interests.

A growing number of people self-identify either as **atheist,** *a person who does not believe in the existence of any higher power,* or as **agnostic,** *a person who isn't sure whether or not a higher power exists.* Atheists and agnostics are more likely than not to look for scientific evidence in support of the existence a higher power. Internationally, Canada ranks number 10 of the top 20 countries surveyed

atheist A person who does not believe in the existence of God.

agnostic A person who isn't sure whether or not God exists.

critical thinking

In a recent book, provocatively titled *The God Delusion*, atheist and biologist Richard Dawkins articulates the view that clashes of religion are responsible for a great deal of conflict the world over. He argues that religious claims should be subject to the same burden of proof to which other claims (such as scientific theories) are subject (Dawkins, 2006). Some might argue that faith, intuition, or sensing something without empirical evidence is an important aspect of religion, while others support Dawkins's assertions. What do you think? Is God or some kind of higher power a delusion? Can or should the existence of a higher power be subjected to the burden of scientific proof? What role does religion play in clashes and wars that exist today? What are some, if any, other contributing factors?

What roles do meditation, religion, and spirituality play in the lives of middle-aged adults?

-------- developmental **connection** --

Evolutionary Psychology; Darwin; Natural Selection

intelligent design The belief that the origin and existence of life and the wondrous miracles of nature are the plan of a supreme intelligence or creator.

for the number of people who identify as either agnostic or atheist (Zukerman, 2005); however, determining the number of atheists is difficult as Census Canada does not request that information. As a result, we rely on estimates, which range from 19 percent to 23 percent (Zukerman, 2005; Trottier, 2010).

Meaning in Life

Austrian psychiatrist Victor Frankl's mother, father, brother, and wife died in the concentration camps and gas chambers in Auschwitz. Frankl survived the concentration camp and went on to write about meaning in life. In his book *Man's Search for Meaning* (1984), Frankl emphasized each person's uniqueness and the finiteness of life. He believes that examining the finiteness of our existence and the certainty of death adds meaning to life. If life were not finite, says Frankl, we might spend our life doing just about whatever we please because time would continue forever.

Frankl said that the three most distinct human qualities are spirituality, freedom, and responsibility. Spirituality, in his view, does not have a religious underpinning. Rather, it refers to a human being's uniqueness—to spirit, philosophy, and mind. Frankl proposed that people need to ask themselves such questions as why they exist, what they want from life, and what the meaning of their life is.

In middle adulthood, individuals begin to be faced with death, perhaps for the first time. They may experience the deaths of parents, older relatives, and friends. Also, faced with the prospect of their own morality in a more immediate way than early adulthood, and recognizing changes in their own aging bodies, many individuals in middle age begin to ask and evaluate the questions that Frankl proposed.

Roy Baumeister and Kathleen Vohs (2002, pp. 610–611) argue that the quest for a meaningful life can be understood in terms of four main needs for meaning that guide how people try to make sense of their lives:

- *Need for purpose.* Present events draw meaning from their connection with future events. Purposes can be divided into (1) goals, and (2) fulfillments. Life can be oriented toward a future anticipated state, such as living happily ever after or being in love.
- *Need for values.* This can lend a sense of goodness or positive characterization of life and justify certain courses of action. Values help people to determine whether certain acts are right or wrong. Frankl's (1984) view of meaning in life emphasized value as the main form of meaning that people need.
- *Need for a sense of efficacy.* This involves the belief that one can make a difference. A life with purposes and values but no efficacy might consist of a person knowing what is desirable but who is unable to do anything with that knowledge. With a sense of efficacy, people believe that they can control their environment, which has positive physical and mental health benefits (Bandura, 2001).
- *Need for self-worth.* Most individuals want to be good, worthy persons. Self-worth can be pursued individually, such as finding out that one is very good at doing something, or collectively, as when people find self-esteem from belonging to a group or category of people.

Intelligent Design

One contemporary debate is that of intelligent design versus the theory of *natural selection* and evolution as proposed by Darwin. Those who believe in **intelligent design** postulate that *the origin and existence of life and all the wondrous miracles of nature, including natural processes, are the plan of a supreme intelligence or creator, who is external to the world in which we live*. Specifically, this external creator is the God of Christianity. Many biologists, physicists, philosophers, and others argue that the origin of the universe is uncertain; furthermore, in time, rigorous scientific investigation may provide explanations for the wondrous mysteries.

Health and Well-Being

The World Health Organization (WHO) defines health as more than the absence of disease. WHO includes positive physical, social, psychological, mental, and spiritual aspects as ingredients to overall well-being (Jain et al., 2013). This definition is used not only by WHO, but also by neuroscientists who are examining the impact of prayer and meditation on the brain. Isabelle Raynauld's documentary *Mystical Brain,* put out by the National Film Board of Canada, reports the findings of neuroscientists from the University of Montreal and from the University of Wisconsin–Madison. Doctors have viewed and recorded brain activity (theta waves) of people skilled in prayer and meditation—Carmelite nuns in Montreal and monks in Wisconsin—during prayer or meditation. In both studies, researchers report a robust impact of prayer or meditation on the brain. Further, they have also observed positive physical and psychological responses in new practitioners within three months of practice (Raynauld, 2013). Do spirituality, religion, and meditation contribute to our overall well-being? Scientists who are expanding the field of neuroscience to explore areas of spirituality and theology would emphatically say that yes, prayer and meditation do contribute to peace of mind, and that today's technology enables us to gain an appreciation for how the brain influences our overall health and well-being.

While it is true that some cults and religious sects encourage behaviours that are damaging to health, such as ignoring sound medical advice, for individuals in the religious mainstream there is generally either no link between religion and physical health or a positive effect (Koenig, 2007; Williams & Sternthal, 2007). Meditation is used with success as a therapy in treating psychiatric disorders as well as hypertension (Shapiro & Walsh, 2008). Researchers have found that religious commitment helps to moderate blood pressure and hypertension, and that religious attendance is linked to a reduction in hypertension (Gillum & Ingram, 2007). Also, a number of studies have confirmed a positive association between religious participation and longevity (Oman & Thoresen, 2006). A common thread or goal of spirituality is to restore the brain and bodily imbalances caused by a host of internal and external factors. Researchers have found that those who define themselves as spiritual have experienced favourable responses to illness, including cardiovascular diseases. Many also have attributed their recovery from illness to their belief in spirituality (Jain et al., 2013).

To this point, we have discussed a number of ideas about meaning in life in middle adulthood. For a review, see the **Reach Your Learning Objectives** section at the end of this chapter.

reach your **learning objectives**

The Nature of Middle Adulthood

LO1 Explain how midlife is changing, and define middle adulthood.

Changing Midlife
- Middle age is generally between the ages of 40 and 60; however, the age boundaries of middle age are not set in stone.
- As more people live to an older age, what we think of as middle age seems to be occurring later.
- Developmentalists are beginning to study middle age more in response to the number of people in middle adulthood.

Physical Development

LO2 Discuss physical changes in middle adulthood.

Physical Changes	■ Physical changes in midlife are gradual. Genetic and lifestyle factors play important roles in whether chronic diseases will appear and when.
	■ Among the physical changes are outwardly noticeable changes in appearance (wrinkles, age spots); decreases in height; increases in weight; decreases in strength; deterioration of joints and bones; and changes in vision, hearing, cardiovascular system, and sleep.
Health Concerns and Wellness Strategies	■ Major health and wellness concerns include arthritis, hypertension, and obesity.
	■ Men have more fatal chronic disorders and women more non-fatal disorders in middle age.
	■ Accidents, colds, and allergies decline in number.
	■ Mental illness is the second leading cause of disability and premature death.
Culture, Relationships, and Health	■ Culture plays an important role in incidence of coronary disease.
	■ Poverty plays a critical role in health. Aboriginal people are poorer and have proportionately more health problems than any other group.
	■ Language is a primary health barrier for new Canadians.
	■ Health in middle age is linked to the current quality of social relationships.
Mortality Rates	■ Obesity is the silent killer, contributing to an increasing number of deaths and health concerns.
	■ Cancer has overtaken heart and cerebrovascular diseases as the number one cause of death in Canada.
Sexuality	■ Climacteric is the midlife transition in which fertility declines.
	■ Menopause is a natural part of aging for women and signals the end of childbearing.
	■ Hormone replacement therapy (HRT) has more risks than benefits if taken for over five years, causing cancer, heart disease, blood clots, and dementia.
	■ Although men may continue to father children in middle age, they experience physiological changes resulting in lower testosterone levels.
	■ Sex occurs less frequently, primarily due a variety of constraints.
	■ Middle-aged adults, particularly those who are sexually active, are vulnerable to STIs.

Cognitive Development

LO3 Identify cognitive changes in middle adulthood.

Intelligence	■ Horn argued that crystallized intelligence (accumulated information and verbal skills) continues to increase in middle adulthood, whereas fluid intelligence (ability to reason abstractly) declines.
	■ The Seattle Longitudinal Study, initiated by K. Warner Schaie over half a century ago and now conducted by Schaie and his partner Sherry L. Willis, found that intellectual abilities are less likely to be found to decline and more likely to be found to improve when assessed longitudinally than when assessed cross-sectionally in middle adulthood.
	■ The highest levels of four intellectual abilities (vocabulary, verbal memory, inductive reasoning, and spatial ability) occur in middle age.

Information Processing	■ Speed of information processing, often assessed through reaction time, declines in middle adulthood.
	■ Problem-solving skills remain relatively stable in early and middle adulthood, and then decline in late adulthood.
	■ Although Schaie found that verbal memory increased in middle age, some researchers have obtained results that contradict this.
	■ Memory is more likely to decline in middle age when individuals do not use effective strategies.
	■ Expertise involves having extensive, highly organized knowledge and understanding of a domain. Expertise often increases in the middle adulthood years.
	■ On the basis of interviews with leading experts in different domains, Csikszentmihalyi charted the way creative people go about living a creative life, such as waking up every morning with a mission and spending time in settings that stimulate their creativity.

Careers, Work, and Leisure

LO4 Characterize career development, work, and leisure in middle adulthood.

Work in Midlife	■ Work is central to identity in midlife.
	■ Individuals may reevaluate the type of work they are doing in midlife and make changes.
	■ Balancing work and family life is a major challenge of work in midlife.
Career Challenges and Changes	■ The current middle-aged worker faces such challenges as the globalization of work, rapid developments in information technologies, downsizing of organizations, economic downturn, and early retirement.
	■ People who are laid off realize both psychological and economic setbacks, from which recovery may be difficult or impossible.
	■ Career development for women is often interrupted by parental leave and the need to provide care for aging parents.
	■ Midlife job or career changes can be self-motivated or forced on individuals.
Leisure	■ Leisure refers to the pleasant times after work when individuals are free to pursue activities and interests of their own choosing—hobbies, sports, or reading, for example.
	■ Vacations and preparation for retirement are important in midlife.

Meaning in Life

LO5 Explain the roles of meditation, religion, and spirituality in understanding meaning in life during middle adulthood.

Meditation, Religion and Spirituality	■ Meditation, religion, and spirituality are approaches to understanding the meaning and purpose of life.
	■ The religiosity index is comprised of affiliation, practice, attendance, and importance.
	■ Many sub-groups exist within religious groups and offer different interpretations.
	■ Many people self-identify as either agnostic or atheist.
Meaning in Life	■ Frankl believes that examining the finiteness of our existence leads to exploration of meaning in life.
	■ Faced with the death of older relatives and less time to live themselves, many middle-aged individuals increasingly examine life's meaning.
	■ To make sense of their lives, individuals have four needs: purpose, values, efficacy, and self-worth.
	■ Intelligent design is the belief that a higher power is responsible for the creation of the universe.
Health and Well-Being	■ The World Health Organization defines health to include a positive physical, social, psychological, mental, and spiritual as ingredients to overall well-being.
	■ In mainstream religions, religion usually shows either a positive association or no association with physical health; however, those who engage in meditation, religion, or spirituality report improved well-being.

review ---→ *connect* ---→ reflect

McGraw-Hill Education connect

McGraw-Hill Connect provides you with a powerful tool for improving academic performance and truly mastering course material. You can diagnose your knowledge with pre- and post-tests, identify the areas where you need help, search the entire learning package, including the eBook, for content specific to the topic you're studying, and add these resources to your personalized study plan. CONNECT for *Life-Span Development*, fifth Canadian edition, offers the following:

■ chapter-specific online quizzes
■ groupwork
■ presentations
■ writing assignments
■ case studies
■ and much more!

Visit CONNECT today!

review

Identify key physical and cognitive changes in middle adulthood. **LO1, LO2**

What role do poverty and culture play in the health concerns of middle age? **LO1, LO2, LO3**

What are some of the key factors of procession information in middle adulthood? **LO2**

What are some approaches to understanding meaning in life? **LO3**

The International Task Force identified several factors key to the quality of employment. What are these factors and what are the major challenges facing workers today? **LO4**

How do meditation, religion, and spirituality contribute to an individual's sense of well-being? **LO5**

connect

In this chapter, you read about career challenges and changes. What are some of the challenges you might face? How might you prepare for these challenges?

reflect *Your Own Personal Journey of Life*

One of the signs of aging is the vulnerability of the body to illness. What strategies might you put in place to maintain overall health?

CHAPTER 16

Socio-Emotional Development in Middle Adulthood

CHAPTER OUTLINE

"*I remember when I was a boy, I watched my grandfather carve for me a whistle from the red willow. Blowing that whistle was not that amusing to me at the time. What was amusing was the way he worked with his hands. My grandfather had such sure hands. To me, he was a great creator and his hands were like his little helpers . . . I feel so happy that I was able to watch and learn from this man, my "Grandfather," because he taught me the meaning of 'Creating.'*"

—DALE AUGER, CREE ARTIST, 1991

Ahhh, We Made It: Middle Adulthood

Ahhh. Middle adulthood! The most wonderful, joyous period of our lives—the one in which we live happily ever after, the one in which we cheerfully provide all our resources, leadership, energy, and support to our perfect families, our secure workplaces, and our beautiful communities. We have come a long way:

- When we were children trying to understand our place in the world, we looked up to our parent(s), teachers, and all the other adults, wishing to be one of them someday so we could make the rules about what to eat for supper, what to wear to school, what to watch on TV, and what time to go to bed. We did all this without the help of the Internet and without video games.
- When we were in our teens, we saw adults quite differently—they became "so last year"; they really did not know what was going on and we couldn't tell them, either, because they just wouldn't understand. Even if we did want to talk, fat chance someone was there when we needed them.
- When we finished high school and tried to figure out what to do with the rest of our lives, and with whom to fall in love and live happily ever after, we took for granted that the adults around us might be helpful from time to time. After all, they were supposed to! If we were lucky, they might help us pay for our education or let us drive the family car once in a while, and so on. Then, as we got older and finally started our own families, they often helped out by babysitting so we could work, manage our lives, and make ends meet. The adults around us, our parents, grandparents, and so on, were really good about getting us all together for various holiday celebrations and traditions—even though someone usually got drunk, and tension often filled the air.

Now, we're finally here—in middle adulthood. And what do we do? Well, in between working and managing the household, we try to help our kids understand their place in the world. We try to help our teens fit in and behave responsibly. We try to help our young adults with their educational goals and support them through relationship starts and stops. We do the best we can. Then, we do some more: we cook, clean, go on the warpath to get our kids away from the TV or their iPhones and pick up their rooms; we coach sports teams; we supply the workforce; we do volunteer work; we help our friends and neighbours; we vote.

Oh! And we also help our parents, as they are now getting older, more frail, and less able to take care of themselves. If they need to move to an assisted living facility, we argue with our siblings and children over what is best, and then we manage and arrange it. They need us more and more now, but although they raised us and managed their own lives they really can't possibly understand all we're dealing with—and we can't talk to them, because we don't want them to worry. Very few of us had computers at home when we were growing up, so our parents did not have to deal with all we're trying to cope with—monitoring kids' Internet activities, trying to protect them from cyberbullying—not to mention that our jobs are not secure and there's no such thing as a stay-at-home mom anymore. On top of this we're transporting kids to their music lessons and hockey games, all while trying to figure out how we might be able to afford these activities. All this in between work demands, community supports, and our own social life—if we even have one.

Is it any wonder we're so tired? But, maybe by working through all these realities, we'll leave a reasonable legacy and develop the wisdom we need to face our own old age—as we sense it is fast approaching.

Personality Theories and Development in Middle Adulthood

LO1 Describe personality theories and development in middle adulthood.

What is the best way to conceptualize middle age? Is it a stage or a crisis? How pervasive are midlife crises? How extensively is middle age influenced by life events? Is personality linked with the contexts, such as the point in history at which individuals go through midlife, their culture, and their gender?

Stages of Adulthood

The Life-Events Approach

Stress in Midlife

Contexts of Midlife Development

Stages of Adulthood

Adult stage theories have been plentiful, and they have contributed to the view that midlife is a crisis in development. Two prominent adult stage theories are Erik Erikson's life-span view and Daniel Levinson's seasons of a man's life.

Erikson's Stage of Generativity versus Stagnation

Erikson (1968) proposed that middle-aged adults face a significant issue in the seventh stage of the life span—generativity versus stagnation. Generativity encompasses adults' desires to leave legacies to the next generation (Peterson, 2002). Through these legacies, adults achieve a kind of immortality. By contrast, *stagnation* (sometimes called self-absorption) develops when individuals sense they have done nothing for the next generation. A sense of boredom and apathy characterize the feeling of having lived an unfulfilled life.

By middle adulthood, the individual may have resolved the conflicts of earlier stages. With the successful resolution of the identity crisis, the virtue of *fidelity* emerges, enabling the person to sustain loyalties freely pledged in spite of value differences and contradictions. To resolve the crisis of early adulthood, intimacy versus isolation, young adults confront affiliations with partners, friends, gender, competition, and cooperation. Love is the virtue that can emerge from this stage. In middle age, as the conflict of *generativity versus stagnation* is resolved, the virtue of care emerges. According to Erikson, care is "the widening concern for what has been generated by love, necessity, or accident; it overcomes the ambivalence adhering to irreversible obligation" (Tonks, 1992). With the emergence of care, the individual is able to shift his or her perspective away from self and toward others. Erikson believed that generativity is the link between generations by which adults find renewal and concern for the following generation, especially their own children.

Middle-aged adults can develop generativity in a number of ways. Through biological generativity, adults have offspring. Through parental generativity, adults nurture and guide children. Through work generativity, adults develop skills that are passed down to others. And through cultural generativity, adults create, renovate, or conserve some aspect of culture that ultimately survives.

Adults promote and guide the next generation by parenting, teaching, leading, and doing things that benefit the community (Pratt et al., 2008a, b). In George Vaillant's (2002) longitudinal studies of aging in middle age, generativity (defined in this study as "taking care of the next generation") was more strongly related than intimacy to whether individuals would have an enduring and happy marriage at 75 to 80 years of age. One of the participants in Vaillant's studies said: "From 20 to 30, I learned how to get along with my wife. From 30 to 40, I learned how to be a success at my job, and at 40 to 50, I worried less about myself and more about the children" (Vaillant, 2002, p. 114).

Generative adults commit themselves to the continuation and improvement of society as a whole through their connection to the next generation. Generative adults develop a positive legacy of the self and then offer it as a gift to the next generation. Two examples of generative adults are Cathy Crowe, street nurse, and René Lévesque, politician.

critical thinking

Erik Erikson believed that if the crisis of generativity versus stagnation is successfully resolved, the middle-aged adult develops the virtue of care; if unresolved, the middle-aged adult develops a lack of caring for others, sometimes called self-absorption. How do you think the resolution of earlier stages contributes to the successful or unsuccessful completion of Erikson's seventh stage? Consider people you know, perhaps your parents or grandparents. In what ways have they developed generativity or stagnation? Do men and women develop generativity differently? If so, how and why? What tips or words of advice would you give to someone you thought was stagnating?

Cathy Crowe, street nurse and social justice advocate, believes that small acts, when multiplied by millions of people, can transform the world. Arguing that "Housing is a prerequisite for health," she has worked tirelessly to advocate for the homeless, declaring the homeless problem a national disaster.

René Lévesque (1922–1987), one of the most popular political leaders in Quebec, was a journalist before he entered Quebec provincial politics in 1960. Eight years later, at the age of 46, he created the Parti Québecois. *Option Québec*, Levesque's best-selling book, published in 1968, sets out the political, cultural, and psychological arguments for Quebec sovereignty (Morton & Weinfeld, 1998).

Figure 16.1

Items Used to Assess Generativity and Identity Certainty

These items were used to assess generativity and identity certainty in the longitudinal study of Smith College women (Stewart, Ostrove, & Helson, 2001). In the assessment of identity certainty, five of the items involved reverse scoring. For example, if an individual scored high on the item "Searching for who I am," it was an indication of identity uncertainty rather than identity certainty.

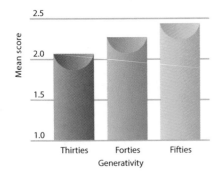

Does research support Erikson's theory that generativity is an important dimension of middle age? Yes, it does (Coleman & Podolskij, 2007; Gramling, 2007; Pratt et al., 2008a, b).

One recent study revealed that parents' generativity was linked to young adult offsprings' successful development (Peterson, 2006). In this study, generative parents had young adult children who were conscientious and agreeable. A longitudinal study of individuals from their college years through age 43 revealed that Erikson's stage of generativity versus stagnation showed a pattern of slow but steady increase in becoming more generative (Whitbourne, Sneed, & Sayer, 2009).

In another study, Carol Ryff (1984) examined the views of women and men at different ages and found that middle-aged adults especially were concerned about generativity. In yet another study, generative women with careers found gratification through work; generative women who had not worked in a career experienced gratification through parenting (Peterson & Stewart, 1996). And in a longitudinal study of Smith College women, generativity increased from the thirties through the fifties (Stewart, Ostrove, & Helson, 2001; Zucker, Ostrove, & Stewart, 2002). Figure 16.1 describes the items that were used to assess generativity and identity certainty in the Smith College Study.

Levinson's Seasons of a Man's Life

In *The Seasons of a Man's Life* (1978), clinical psychologist Daniel Levinson reported the results of extensive interviews with 40 middle-aged men who worked as hourly workers, business executives, academics, and novelists. Levinson bolstered his conclusions with information from the biographies of famous men and the development of memorable literary characters. Although Levinson's major interest focused on midlife change, he described a number of stages and transitions during the period from 17 to 65 years of age, as shown in Figure 16.2. Levinson emphasizes that developmental tasks must be mastered at each stage.

In early adulthood, the two major tasks to be mastered are exploring the possibilities for adult living and developing a stable life structure. From about the ages of 28 to 33, the man goes through a transition period in which he must face the more serious question of determining his goals. During his thirties, he usually focuses on family and career development. In the later years of this period, he enters a phase of *Becoming One's Own Man* (or BOOM, as Levinson calls it). By age 40, he has reached a stable location in his career, has outgrown his earlier, more tenuous attempts at learning to become an adult, and now must look forward to the kind of life he will lead as a middle-aged adult.

According to Levinson, the transition to middle adulthood lasts about five years (ages 40 to 45) and requires the adult male to come to grips with four major conflicts that have existed in his life

Figure 16.2

Levinson's Periods of Adult Development

At the end of one's teens, according to Levinson, a transition from dependence to independence should occur. This transition is marked by the formation of a dream—an image of the kind of life the youth wants to have, especially in terms of a career and marriage. Levinson sees the twenties as a *novice phase* of adult development. It is a time of reasonably free experimentation and of testing the dream in the real world. In early adulthood, the two major tasks to be mastered are exploring the possibilities for adult living and developing a stable life structure.

Era of late adulthood:
60 to ?

Late adult transition: Age 60 to 65

Culminating life structure for middle adulthood:
55 to 60

Age 50 transition:
50 to 55

Entry life structure for middle adulthood:
45 to 50

Middle adult transition: Age 40 to 45

Culminating life structure for early adulthood:
33 to 40

Age 30 transition:
28 to 33

Entry life structure for early adulthood:
22 to 28

Early adult transition: Age 17 to 22

since adolescence: (1) being young versus being old, (2) being destructive versus being constructive, (3) being masculine versus being feminine, and (4) being attached to others versus being separated from them. Seventy to 80 percent of the men Levinson interviewed found the midlife transition tumultuous and psychologically painful, as many aspects of their lives came into question. According to Levinson, the success of the midlife transition rests on how effectively the individual reduces the polarities and accepts each of them as an integral part of his being.

Because Levinson interviewed middle-aged males, the data about middle adulthood is considered more reliable than the data about early adulthood. When individuals are asked to remember information about earlier parts of their lives, they may distort and forget things. The original Levinson data included no females, although Levinson (1996) reported that his stages, transitions, and the crisis of middle age hold for females as well as males. Levinson's work did not include statistical analysis. The quality and quantity of the Levinson biographies make them outstanding examples of the clinical tradition.

How Pervasive Are Midlife Crises?

Levinson (1978) views midlife as a crisis, arguing that the middle-aged adult is suspended between the past and the future, trying to cope with this gap that threatens life's continuity. George Vaillant (1977) has a different view. Vaillant's study—called the "Grant Study"—involved Harvard University men in their early thirties and in their late forties who initially had been interviewed as undergraduates. He concludes that just as adolescence is a time for detecting parental flaws and discovering the truth about childhood, the forties are a decade of reassessing and recording the

critical thinking

Levinson's study was conducted in 1978. Since then, young adults have been staying in school longer and living at home longer. How might this change affect Levinson's theory? Levinson focused his study on men in middle adulthood; however, he believed that the stages, transitions, and crisis of middle age apply to women as well. Why, or why not, might this be true? What are the four conflicts Levinson believed men had to come to terms with? Are these conflicts as true today as Levinson thought in 1978? Are they equally true for men and for women? Are Levinson's transitions in line with your experience and observations?

---- developmental **connection** --

Research Methods

---- **Figure 16.3**

Age and Well-Being

In one study, six dimensions of well-being (self-acceptance, positive relations, personal growth, purpose in life, environmental mastery, and autonomy) were assessed in three different age groups of individuals (young adults, middle-aged adults, and older adults) (Keyes & Ryff, 1998). An increase or little change in most of the dimensions of well-being occurred during middle adulthood.

Dimensions of well-being
— Self-acceptance
— Purpose in life
— Positive relations
— Environmental mastery
— Personal growth
— Autonomy

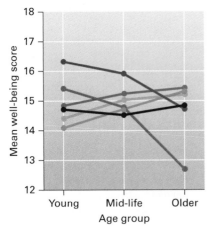

contemporary life-events approach Emphasizes that how life events influence the individual's development depends not only on the life event, but also on mediating factors, the individual's adaptation to the life event, the life-stage context, and the socio-historical context.

---- developmental **connection** --

Bronfenbrenner

truth about the adolescent and adulthood years. However, whereas Levinson sees midlife as a crisis, Vaillant believes that only a minority of adults experience a midlife crisis.

As with adolescent turmoil, midlife crises are uncommon in community samples. During middle adulthood, the significance of our lives is made even more complicated as we experience a heightened awareness of our mortality when we witness the death of friends, acquaintances, and our parents. The death of our parents is a clear signal that we are approaching old age and that our own mortality is imminent. We experience loss of youth, youthful strength, and healing capacities. Introspective appraisals of our values, behaviours, successes, as well as our failures, may contrast sharply with youthful dreams. The successful resolution of our midlife period is related to the legacy we may leave behind, the contribution we have made to our spouses, our children, our workplace, and our communities. The nature of our reflection helps us define the path we will take in our late adult years.

Adult development experts are virtually unanimous in their belief that midlife crises have been exaggerated (Brim, Ryff, & Kessler, 2004; Lachman, 2004; Wethington, Kessler, & Pixley, 2004). For most people, midlife is not a crisis (Pudrovska, 2009). On the contrary, a study found that adults experienced a peak of personal control and power in middle age. A study of individuals described as young (average age 19), middle-aged (average age 46), and older (average age 73) adults found that their ability to master their environment, autonomy, and personal relations improved during middle age (Keyes & Ryff, 1998) (see Figure 16.3). As we saw in Chapter 15, many cognitive skills such as vocabulary, verbal memory, and inductive reasoning peak in midlife, and many individuals reach the height of their career success in midlife. Further, reports of general well-being and life satisfaction tend to be high in midlife (Martin, Grünendahl, & Martin, 2001).

Individual Variations

Stage theories focus on the universals of adult personality development as they try to pin down stages that typify adult lives. These theories do not adequately address individual variations in adult development. According to the individual variations view, middle-aged adults interpret, shape, alter, and give meaning to their lives (Arpanantikul, 2004). Some may experience a crisis in some aspects of their lives but not others (Lachman, 2004). For example, in one-third of the cases in which individuals have reported having a midlife crisis, the "crisis is triggered by life events such as a job loss, financial problems, or illness" (Lachman, 2004, p. 315). How do events in life affect midlife development?

The Life-Events Approach

Age-related stages represent one major way to examine adult personality development. A second major way to conceptualize adult personality development is to focus on life events (Serido, 2009). In the early version of the life-events approach, life events were viewed as taxing circumstances for individuals, forcing them to change their personalities (Holmes & Rahe, 1967). Such events as the death of a spouse, divorce, marriage, and so on were believed to involve varying degrees of stress, and therefore were likely to influence the individual's development.

Today's life-events approach is more sophisticated. The **contemporary life-events approach** *emphasizes that how life events influence the individual's development depends not only on the life event, but also on mediating factors (physical health, family supports), the individual's adaptation to the life event (appraisal of the threat, coping strategies), the life-stage context, and the socio-historical context* (see Figure 16.4). If individuals are in poor health, for example, and have little family support, life events are likely to be more stressful. A divorce may be more stressful after many years of marriage, when adults are in their fifties, than when they have been married only a few years and are in their twenties, indicating that the life-stage context of an event makes a difference. The socio-historical context, as Bronfenbrenner's bio-ecological theory suggests, also makes a difference. For example, adults may be able to cope more effectively with divorce today than in the 1950s because divorce has become more common and accepted in today's society. Whatever the context or mediating variables, however, one individual may perceive a life event as highly stressful, whereas another individual may perceive the same event as a challenge.

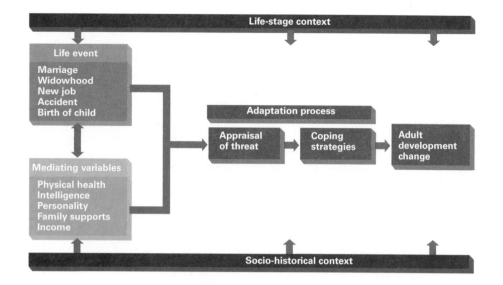

Figure 16.4

A Contemporary Life-Events Framework for Interpreting Adult Development Change

Although the life-events approach is a valuable addition to understanding adult development, like other approaches to adult development, it has its drawbacks. One of the most significant drawbacks is that the life-events approach places too much emphasis on change. It does not adequately recognize the stability that, at least to some degree, characterizes adult development.

Another drawback of the life-events approach is that it may not be life's major events that are the primary sources of stress, but rather our daily experiences (O'Connor et al., 2009). Enduring a boring but tense job or marriage and living in poverty do not show up on scales of major life events. Yet the everyday pounding we take from these living conditions can add up to a highly stressful life and eventually illness.

Some psychologists conclude that we can gain greater insight into the source of life's stresses by focusing less on major events and more on daily hassles and daily uplifts (McIntosh, Gillanders, & Rodgers, 2010; Neupert, Almeida, & Charles, 2007). In one study, the most frequent daily hassles of middle-aged adults were concerns about weight and the health of a family member, while their most frequent daily uplifts involved relating well with a spouse or lover, or a friend (see Figure 16.5). Middle-aged adults were more likely than college students to report that their daily hassles involved economic concerns (rising prices and taxes, for example). Critics of the daily hassles approach argue that some of the same problems involved with life-events scales occur when daily hassles are assessed. For example, knowing about an adult's daily hassles tells us nothing about physical changes, about how the individual copes with hassles, or about how the individual perceives hassles.

Stress in Midlife

Canadian psychologist Hans Selye, the "father of modern stress theory," defined **stress** as *"the non-specific response of the body to any demand made upon it"* and advanced the theory that stress plays a role in every disease (Pomfrey, 2012; Selye, 2013). Stress can be episodic or chronic, positive or negative in nature. **Episodic stress** *is related to an event which, once coped with, is over.* Such stress can be positive because it is motivational. One such stress would be final exams; another might be competing in a sporting event. **Chronic stress** *is negative, persistent, and as such can be crippling.* Selye believed that if stress continues unabated, the body will eventually shut down and not be able to rebound. Stress affects the immune system, making an individual vulnerable to illness and disease.

Many immigrants and racialized individuals—that is, individuals who experience racism by dominant groups—often experience chronic stress related to an abundance of daily hassles. Language is a chief, but not the only, source of stress. First- and second-generation individuals reported different responses to daily hassles in a recent study of South Asian people. Second-generation individuals from South Asia reported significantly more hassles with members of their own ethnic group and marginally lower self-esteem than first-generation immigrants. For

critical thinking

Discrimination and harassment on the basis of race, creed, ethnic origin, gender, sexual orientation, age, or physical or mental ability are in violation of the Canadian Human Rights Code. Nevertheless, Canadians experience almost daily harassment, either directly or indirectly. Harassment can be in the form of racist or sexist slurs or other demeaning behaviours, including email jokes. Demeaning behaviours, intended or unintended, make individuals feel unwelcome and not valued in their place of employment. This situation creates a hostile or poisoned environment that affects not only the quality of work, but also people's personal lives. Who might be most vulnerable to experiencing the behaviours associated with a poisoned environment? Why? What behaviours might the victim have to experience? What steps could a bystander or an individual subjected to discrimination or harassment take to address this situation? What have you experienced or observed, both inside and outside of work settings?

critical thinking

Identify some of the daily hassles and uplifts that face adolescents and early adults. How might these hassles be similar and how might they differ from those faced in middle adulthood?

stress The non-specific response of the body to any demand made upon it.

episodic stress Stress that is related to an event which, once coped with, is over.

chronic stress Stress that is negative, persistent, and as such can be crippling.

Figure 16.5

The Ten Most Frequent Daily Hassles and Uplifts of Middle-Aged Adults over a Nine-Month Period

How do these hassles and uplifts compare with your own?

Daily Hassles	Percentage of Times Checked	Daily Uplifts	Percentage of Times Checked
Concerns about weight	52.4	Relating well with your spouse or lover	76.3
Health of family member	48.1	Relating well with friends	74.4
Rising prices of common goods	43.7	Completing a task	73.3
Home maintenance	42.8	Feeling healthy	72.7
Too many things to do	38.6	Getting enough sleep	69.7
Misplacing or losing things	38.1	Eating out	68.4
Yardwork/outside home maintenance	38.1	Meeting your responsibilities	68.1
Property, investment, or taxes	37.6	Visiting, phoning, or writing someone	67.7
Crime	37.1	Spending time with family	66.7
Physical appearance	35.9	Home (inside) pleasing to you	65.5

first-generation individuals, hassles with members of their own ethnic groups predicted lower self-esteem, and hassles with people outside their own groups predicted greater depression (Abouguendia & Noels, 2001).

Racialized individuals report experiencing racism and discrimination. One study of the Chinese community in Toronto found that perceived discrimination correlated with various psychological symptoms, such as nervousness, sleep problems, headaches, moodiness, and worry (Health Canada, 2002). Profiling on the basis of race by police and officials at border crossings serve as documented and public examples of the type of stress related to racism and discrimination.

As noted in Chapter 15, single-parent families, especially those headed by women, and Aboriginal families have persistently low incomes and experience more than double the national rate of poverty. Consequently, they are subject to more daily stresses.

Do middle-aged adults experience stress differently than young adults and older adults? One study using daily diaries over a one-week period found that both young and middle-aged adults had more stressful days "and more days with multiple stresses than older adults" (Almeida & Horn, 2004). The study further reported that, although young adults experienced daily stressors more frequently than middle-aged adults, middle-aged adults experienced more "overload" stressors that involve juggling too many activities at once (Almeida & Horn, 2004). A recent study also revealed that middle-aged and older adults showed a smaller increase in psychological distress to interpersonal stressors than younger adults, and middle-aged adults were less physically reactive to work stressors than were younger adults (Neupert, Almeida, & Charles, 2007).

To what extent do middle-aged adults perceive that they can control what happens to them? Researchers have found that, on average, a sense of personal control decreases as adults become older (Lachman, 2006). In one study, approximately 80 percent of the young adults (25 to 39 years of age), 71 percent of the middle-aged adults (40 to 59 years of age), and 62 percent of the older adults (60 to 75 years of age) reported that they were often in control of their lives (Lachman & Firth, 2004). However, some aspects of personal control increase with age while others decrease (Lachman, 2006). For example, middle-aged adults feel they have a greater sense of control over their finances, work, and marriage than younger adults, but less control over their sex life and their children (Lachman & Firth, 2004).

Contexts of Midlife Development

As illustrated by the stories in the opening of this chapter, people live through middle age in a variety of contexts and each is unique. Bronfenbrenner's bio-ecological theory described in Chapter 2 provides an overview of how such things as historical contexts (cohort effects), gender, and culture influence the individual. Like Bronfenbrenner's theory, the contemporary life-events approach highlights the importance of the complex settings of our lives—of everything from our income and family supports to our socio-historical circumstances.

Historical Contexts (Cohort Effects)

Some developmentalists argue that changing historical times and different social expectations influence how different cohorts—groups of individuals born in the same year or time period—move through the life span. Bernice Neugarten (1986) argues that our values, attitudes, expectations, and behaviours are influenced by the period in which we live. For example, people born before 1985 grew up without smartphones, iPods, virtual social spaces, Twitter, and Facebook. In vitro fertilization (IVF) was not an option to people who wanted but were unable to have children, nor would a single woman choose to become a mother either through IVF or adoption. Science and social change enable more choices.

Neugarten (1986) holds that the social environment of a particular age group can alter its **social clock**—the timetable according to which individuals are expected to accomplish life's tasks, such as getting married, having children, or establishing themselves in a career and retiring. Social clocks provide guides for our lives; individuals whose lives are not synchronized with these social clocks find life to be more stressful than those who are on schedule, says Neugarten. She argues that today there is much less agreement than in the past on the right age or sequence for the occurrence of major life events. One study found that between the late 1950s and the late 1970s, there was a dramatic decline in adult's beliefs in a "right age" for major life events and achievements (Passuth, Maines, & Neugarten, 1984) (see Figure 16.6).

When Canadian couples were asked about the right age to become a grandmother, women who responded said the ideal age was between 48 and 52, depending on whether or not they were already grandmothers. Non-grandmothers typically gave a higher age than grandmothers (Peterson, 1996). As you read in Chapter 15, the average age for a becoming a grandparent in Canada is 55 (Edwards & Sterne, 2005).

Trying to tease out universal truths and patterns about adult development from one birth cohort is complicated because the findings may not apply to another birth cohort. Most of the individuals studied by Levinson and Vaillant, for example, were born before or during the Great Depression. What was true for these individuals may not be true for today's 40-year-olds born in the optimistic aftermath of World War II, or for the post-baby-boom generation as they approach the midlife transition during the War on Terror and economic uncertainty.

Gender Contexts

Critics say that the stage theories of adult development have a male bias (Deutsch, 1991). For example, the central focus of stage theories is on career choice and work achievement, which historically have dominated men's life choices and life changes more than women's. The stage theories do not adequately address women's concerns about relationships, interdependence, and caring (Gilligan, 1982). The adult stage theories also have placed little importance on childbearing and childrearing. Women's roles are often more complex, as the balance of career and family life usually is not experienced as intensely by men. Furthermore, the type of stressors experienced by middle-aged women and men may differ. One recent study revealed that middle-aged women had more interpersonal stressors, whereas their male counterparts had more self-focused stressors (Almeida & Horn, 2004).

Many women who are now at midlife and beyond experienced a role shift in their late twenties, thirties, or beyond (Fodor & Franks, 1990). As they were engaging in traditional roles, the women's movement began and changed the lives of a substantial number of traditionally raised women and

social clock The timetable according to which individuals are expected to accomplish life's tasks, such as getting married, having children, or establishing themselves in a career and retiring.

---

critical thinking

Review the dates in Figure 16.6. How do the appropriate age ranges of the late 1950s and the late 1970s compare with those of today? If you were to survey your friends and classmates, what differences might you find? How do you account for the changes? What additional changes might occur in 2020? Are economics and technology factors in creating change? If so, how?

Figure 16.6

Individuals' Conceptions of the Right Age for Major Life Events and Achievements: Late 1950s and Late 1970s

How have these conceptions for the "right" age changed? Do the ages indicated match your views, and what role does culture play?

ACTIVITY/EVENT	APPROPRIATE AGE RANGE	% WHO AGREE (late '50s study)		% WHO AGREE (late '70s study)	
		MEN	WOMEN	MEN	WOMEN
Best age for a man to marry	20–25	80	90	42	42
Best age for a woman to marry	19–24	85	90	44	36
When most people should become grandparents	45–50	84	79	64	57
Best age for most people to finish school and go to work	20–22	86	82	36	38
When most men should be settled on a career	24–26	74	64	24	26
When most men hold their top jobs	45–50	71	58	38	31
When most people should be ready to retire	60–65	83	86	66	41
When a man has the most responsibilities	35–50	79	75	49	50
When a man accomplishes most	40–50	82	71	46	41
The prime of life for a man	35–50	86	80	59	66
When a woman has the most responsibilities	25–40	93	91	59	53
When a woman accomplishes most	30–45	94	92	57	48

Critics say the stage theories of adult development have a male bias by emphasizing career choice and achievement, and that they do not adequately address women's concerns about relationships, interdependence, and caring. The stage theories assume a normative sequence of development, but as women's roles have become more varied and complex, determining what is normative is difficult. **What kinds of changes have taken place in middle-aged women's lives in recent years?**

their families. Changes are still occurring for many midlife women (George, 2006; Moen & Spencer, 2006). Basic changes in social attitudes regarding labour force participation, families, and gender roles have begun to broaden the opportunities available to women in middle adulthood, as well as other life-span periods (Moen & Wethington, 1999). The effects of these changes are the most far-reaching for the baby-boom cohort now entering midlife. Employment patterns across the life span for women in their middle adult years now more closely resemble those of males (Contemporary Research Press, 1993).

Is midlife and beyond to be feared by women as a loss of youth and opportunity, a time of decline? Or is it a new prime of life, a time for renewal, for shedding preoccupations with a youthful appearance and body, and for seeking new challenges, valuing maturity, and enjoying change? In one study, the early fifties were indeed a new prime of life for many women (Mitchell & Helson, 1990). In a sample of 700 women aged 26 to 80, women in their early fifties most often described their lives as "first-rate." Conditions that distinguished the lives of women in their early fifties from those of women in other age periods included more "empty nests," better health, higher income, and more concern for parents. Women in their early fifties showed confidence, involvement, security, and breadth of personality.

In sum, the view that midlife is a negative age period for women is stereotypical, as are so many perceptions of age periods (Aldwin & Levenson, 2001; Huyck, 1999). Midlife is a diversified, heterogeneous period for women, just as it is for men.

connecting development to life

‹-------------

Immigrants Define Canada: "The Land of the Second Chance"—
Nellie McClung (1873–1951)

In 1915, Nellie McClung, pioneer of women's rights in Canada, described her vision of Canada's future in "The Land of the Second Chance" as

> a land of the Fair Deal, where every race, colour, and creed will be given exactly the same chance; where no person can 'exert influence' to bring about his personal ends; where no man or woman's past can ever rise up to defeat them; where no crime goes unpunished; where every debt is paid; where no prejudice is allowed to masquerade as reason; where honest toil will insure an honest living; where the man who works receives the reward of his labour. (Morton & Weinfeld, 1998)

A bountiful landscape, plentiful water supply, peaceful elections and accessible education, health care, social supports, as well as guaranteed personal freedoms make Canada an enticing destination. Newcomers arrive with a spirit of adventure and optimism, sprinkled with a bit of anxiety. Expectations collide with stark realities. Where else can one meet such a diverse population, hear so many different languages, taste such diverse cuisines, and experience such changeable weather? Treatment of pets, superstitions, sports, fashion, and even the national anthem are wrought with cognitive dissonance. Language schools, social policies, and settlement programs are all designed to facilitate integration into Canadian life. McClung's vision has often been tarnished by our policies and practices.

Immigration policies and practices are constantly under review in an effort to be fair and to provide alternate routes for immigrants, refugees, and investors. The process not only takes considerable time, but is also expensive, financially, socially, and emotionally. For refugees, leaving their homeland often means leaving in desperation, without family, possessions, or sometimes even identification documents. For all newcomers, maintaining a sense of self and personal values while grappling with and adapting to a new cultural context and a new language entails an extraordinarily complex set of skills and experiences.

Statistics indicate that economic settlement into Canadian life takes approximately 10 years. Members of racialized groups are the most vulnerable to economic fluctuation and prejudice, and may require considerably more time (Lye, 1995; Pendakur, 2000). An individual's way of understanding the world around him or her is complicated by Canadian norms, family life, work, health, and leisure in addition to the day-to-day challenges of tending to a family, finding a home, a job, and making new friends. Hard work, exhaustion, nostalgia, painful searches for an orderly sense of self, intergenerational and marital conflicts, embarrassing or damaging misunderstandings of the new culture, racism, rejection, and humiliation are all on the list of the newcomer's varied experiences.

Challenging decisions have to be made about which traditions to hold on to and which to leave behind. "Do we arrange our child's marriage?" "Do I wear my traditional clothes?" "How can I practice my religion?" "How safe am I? Will those from whom I escaped when I sought asylum be able to find and harm me here?" Skills and training are frequently not recognized or are underutilized. The doctor from China works as a security guard in Vancouver, while the lawyer from Sri Lanka goes back to school to study nursing in Toronto. With both hope and hardship, immigrants have built Canada's bridges, roads, churches, and institutions, whether they arrived 5 years ago or 305 years ago. Fleeing wars, persecution, and poverty, people come to Canada to build a better way of life for their families and, in so doing, they have irrevocably altered the country's cultural landscape.

According to writer Oscar Handlin: "The history of immigration is the history of alienation and its consequences . . . For every freedom won, a tradition lost. For every second generation assimilated, a first generation in one way or another spurned. For the gains of goods and services, an identity lost, and uncertainty found" (Lye, 1995). While not perfect, multiculturalism in Canada works because newcomers integrate by the generosity, benevolence and sincerity of the national character. Newcomers of all backgrounds settle very nicely in this easygoing country (Hussain, 2013).

Cultural Contexts

In many cultures, though, especially non-industrialized cultures, the concept of middle age is not very clear, or in some cases is absent. Non-industrialized societies commonly describe individuals as young or old, but not as middle-aged (Grambs, 1989). Some cultures have no words for "adolescent," "young adult," or "middle-aged adult." In countries where life expectancy is in the mid-fifties, or where girls are promised in marriage by age 12, an age of 35 is considered old. The life course for men and women in Third World countries differs considerably from that of North Americans. For example, the chart below illustrates how the African Gusii culture, located south of the equator in Kenya, divides the life course for females and males (LeVine, 1979):

Females	Males
1. Infant	1. Infant
2. Uncircumcised girl	2. Uncircumcised boy
3. Circumcised girl	3. Circumcised boy warrior
4. Married woman	4. Male elder
5. Female elder	

Thus, movement from one status to the next is due primarily to life events, not age, in the Gusii culture. Although the Gusii do not have a clearly labelled midlife transition, some of the Gusii adults do reassess their lives around the age of 40. At this time, these Gusii adults examine their current status and the limited time they have remaining in their lives. Their physical strength is decreasing, and they know they cannot farm their land forever; so, they seek spiritual powers by becoming ritual practitioners or healers. As in North American culture, however, a midlife crisis in the Gusii culture is the exception, rather than the rule.

What is middle age like for women in other cultures? It depends on the modernity of the culture and the culture's view of gender roles (Dittmann-Kohli, 2005). Some anthropologists believe that middle age has more advantages in many non-industrialized societies than in the industrialized nations, such as the United States and Canada (Brown, 1985). First, they are often freed from cumbersome restrictions that were placed on them when they were younger. For example, in middle age, they may enjoy greater geographical mobility. Child care has ceased or can be delegated, and domestic chores are reduced. Commercial opportunities, visiting relatives living at a distance, and religious opportunities provide an opportunity to venture forth from the village. A second major change brought on by middle age is a woman's right to exercise authority over specified younger kin. Middle-aged women can extract labour from younger family members. The work of the middle-aged woman tends to be administrative, delegating tasks and making assignments to younger women. The middle-aged woman also makes important decisions for certain members of the younger generation: what a grandchild is to be named, who is ready to be initiated, and who is eligible to marry whom. A third major change brought on by middle age in non-industrialized societies is the eligibility of the woman for special statuses, and the possibility that these may provide recognition beyond the household. These statuses include the vocations of midwife, curer, holy woman, and matchmaker.

On the other hand, middle-aged women in many countries find themselves raising their grandchildren because their own children succumbed to the AIDS pandemic. These women have limited mobility, increased child care responsibilities, and their authority may be challenged by the whims of nature.

To this point, we have studied a number of ideas about personality theories and development in middle adulthood. For a review, see the **Reach Your Learning Objectives** section at the end of this chapter.

Stability and Change

LO2 Discuss stability and change in development during middle adulthood, including longitudinal studies.

Recall from Chapter 1 that an important issue in life-span development is the extent to which individuals show stability in their development versus the extent to which they change. A number of longitudinal studies have addressed the stability–change issue as they assess individuals at different points in their adult lives. In other words, are traits such as extraversion and conscientiousness consistent over time? Can an individual be conscientious during childhood, for example, and disorganized in young adulthood? Introverted in adolescence and outgoing in middle age?

Gusii dancers perform on habitat day in Nairobi, Kenya. Movement from one status to another in the Gusii culture is due primarily to life events, not age. The Gusii do not have a clearly labelled midlife transition.

Longitudinal Studies

Conclusions

Longitudinal Studies

We will examine four longitudinal studies to help understand the extent to which there is stability or change in adult development: Costa and McCrae's Baltimore Study, the Berkeley Longitudinal Studies, Helson's Mills College Study, and George Vaillant's Grant Study.

Costa and McCrae's Baltimore Study

A major study of adult personality development continues to be conducted by Paul Costa and Robert McCrae (McCrae & Costa, 2003, 2006; McCrae, Costa, et al., 1998). They focus on what are called the **big five factors of personality**, *which consist of openness to experience, conscientiousness, extraversion, agreeableness, and neuroticism (emotional stability)*. They are described in Figure 16.7. (Notice that if you create an acronym from these factor names, you will get the word OCEAN.) A number of research studies point toward these factors as important dimensions of personality (McCrae & Costa, 2003, 2006; McCrae, Costa, et al., 1998).

Using their five-factor personality test, Costa and McCrae (1995, 2000) studied approximately 1,000 university-educated men and women aged 20 to 96, assessing the same individuals over a period of many years. Data collection began in the 1950s to the mid-1960s and is ongoing. Costa and McCrae concluded that considerable stability occurs in the five personality factors—openness, conscientiousness, extraversion, agreeableness, and neuroticism (emotional stability). However, one study found that conscientiousness continued to develop in late adulthood (Roberts, Walton, & Bogg, 2005), and another study revealed that older adults were more conscientious and agreeable than middle-aged and younger adults (Allemand, Zimprich, & Hendriks, 2008).

A recent meta-analysis of personality stability and change organized according to the big-five framework included 87 longitudinal studies spanning 10 to 101 years of age (Roberts, Walton, & Viechtbauer, 2006):

- Results for extraversion were complex until it was subdivided into social dominance (assertiveness, dominance) and social vitality (talkativeness, sociability). Social dominance increases from adolescence through middle adulthood, whereas social vitality increases in adolescence and then decreases in early and late adulthood.
- Agreeableness and conscientiousness increase in early and middle adulthood.
- Neuroticism decreases in early adulthood.
- Openness to experience increases in adolescence and early adulthood, and then decreases in late adulthood. In general, personality traits change most during early adulthood.

developmental **connection**

Research Methods

Stability vs. Change

big five factors of personality Consist of openness to experience, conscientiousness, extraversion, agreeableness, and neuroticism (emotional stability) (acronym: OCEAN).

critical thinking

How would you describe yourself on Costa and McCrae's big five personality factors? According to research findings, personality traits can change over the life span with the greatest changes occurring in early adulthood. Is this true of you? If so, how? Have you observed some of the other changes indicated by the studies?

Figure 16.7

The Big Five Factors of Personality

Each of the broad super traits encompasses more narrow traits and characteristics. Use the acronym OCEAN to remember the big five personality factors (openness, conscientiousness, extraversion, agreeableness, neuroticism).

Openness	**C**onscientiousness	**E**xtraversion	**A**greeableness	**N**euroticism (emotional stability)
• Imaginative or practical	• Organized or disorganized	• Sociable or retiring	• Softhearted or ruthless	• Calm or anxious
• Interested in variety or routine	• Careful or careless	• Fun-loving or sombre	• Trusting or suspicious	• Secure or insecure
• Independent or conforming	• Disciplined or impulsive	• Affectionate or reserved	• Helpful or uncooperative	• Self-satisfied or self-pitying

Further studies to understand the big-five framework are being conducted in an effort to investigate various aspects. Professor Daniel Paulhus of British Columbia, for example, has conducted studies to determine the reliability of self-reported traits to actual behaviour as well as the universality of these traits. One study reported that cultural contexts influence self-reporting; for example people from East Asia are more ambivalent and dialectical in their self-description than North Americans, hence a person from East Asia is more likely to describe him or herself as being "outgoing but shy" (Hamamura, Heine, & Paulhus, 2008). In another study, the test was translated into 29 languages and administered to over 17,000 participants in 57 countries. The study noted ambivalence in both East Asian and African respondents, but nevertheless reported significant replication of the big five personality traits (Schmitt et al., 2007). Analysis of the big-five framework is also being investigated to determine how much of an individual's personality may be revealed in Facebook posts or in tweets.

Berkeley Longitudinal Studies

By far the longest-running longitudinal inquiry is the series of analyses called the Berkeley longitudinal studies. Initially, more than 500 children and their parents were studied in the late 1920s and early 1930s. The book *Present and Past in Middle Life* (Eichorn et al., 1981) profiles these individuals as they became middle-aged. The results from early adolescence through a portion of midlife did not support either extreme in the debate over whether personality is characterized by stability or change. Some characteristics were more stable than others, however. The most stable characteristics were the degree to which individuals are intellectually oriented, self-confident, and open to new experiences. The characteristics that changed the most include the extent to which the individuals are nurturing or hostile, and whether they have good self-control or not.

John Clausen (1993), one of the researchers in the Berkeley longitudinal studies, believes that too much attention has been given to discontinuities for all members of the human species, as exemplified in the adult stage theories. Rather, he believes that some people experience recurrent crises and change a great deal over the life course, while others have more stable, continuous lives and change far less.

Helson's Mills College Study

Another longitudinal investigation of adult personality development was conducted by Ravenna Helson and her colleagues (Helson, 1997; Helson & Wink, 1992; Stewart, Ostrove, & Helson, 2001). They initially studied 132 women who were seniors at Mills College in California in the late 1950s. In 1981, when the women were 42 to 45 years old, they were studied again. Helson and her colleagues distinguished three main groups among the Mills women: family-oriented, career-oriented (whether or not they also wanted families), and those who followed neither path (women without children who pursued only low-level work).

Despite their different college profiles and their diverging life paths, the women in all three groups experienced some similar psychological changes over their adult years. Between the ages of 27 and the early forties, there was a shift toward less traditionally feminine attitudes, including greater dominance, greater interest in events outside the family, and more emotional stability. This may have been due to societal changes from the 1950s to the 1980s, rather than due to age changes. Women in the third group (women without children who pursued low-level work) changed less than those committed to career or family.

During their early forties, many of the women shared the concerns that stage theorists, such as Levinson, found in men: concern for young and old, introspectiveness, interest in roots, and awareness of limitations and death. However, the researchers in the Mills College study concluded that rather than being in a midlife crisis, what was being experienced was *midlife consciousness*. They also indicated that commitment to the tasks of early adulthood—whether to a career or family (or both)—helped women learn to control their impulses, develop interpersonal skills, become independent, and work hard to achieve goals. Women who did not commit themselves to one of these lifestyle patterns faced fewer challenges and did not develop as fully as the other women (Rosenfeld & Stark, 1987).

In the Mills study, some women moved toward becoming "pillars of society" in their early forties to early fifties. Menopause, caring for elderly parents, and an empty nest were not associated with an increase in responsibility and self-control (Helson & Wink, 1992). The identity certainty and awareness of aging of the Mills College women increased from their thirties through their fifties (Stewart, Ostrove, & Helson, 2001).

George Vaillant's Studies

Longitudinal studies by George Vaillant help us examine a somewhat different question than the studies described so far: Does personality at middle age predict what a person's life will be like in late adulthood? Vaillant (2002) conducted three longitudinal studies of adult development and aging: (1) a sample of 268 socially advantaged Harvard graduates born about 1920 (called the Grant Study); (2) a sample of 456 socially disadvantaged inner-city men born about 1930; and (3) a sample of 90 middle-SES, intellectually gifted women born about 1910. These individuals have been assessed numerous times (in most cases, every two years), beginning in the 1920s to 1940s and continuing today for those still living. The main assessments involve extensive interviews with the participants, their parents, and teachers.

Vaillant categorized 75- to 80-year-olds as "happy–well," "sad–sick," and "dead" (see Figure 16.8). He used data collected from these individuals when they were 50 years of age to predict which categories they were likely to end up in at 75 to 80 years of age. Alcohol abuse and smoking at age 50 were the best predictors of which individuals would be dead at 75 to 80 years of age. Other factors at age 50 were linked with being in the "happy–well" category at 75 to 80 years of age: getting regular exercise, avoiding being overweight, being well-educated, having a stable marriage, being future-oriented, being thankful and forgiving, empathizing with others, being active with other people, and having good coping skills.

Wealth and income at age 50 were not linked with being in the "happy–well" category at 75 to 80 years of age. Generativity in middle age (defined as "taking care of the next generation") was more strongly related than intimacy to whether individuals would have an enduring and happy marriage at 75 to 80 years of age (Vaillant, 2002). Further, when individuals at 50 years of age were not

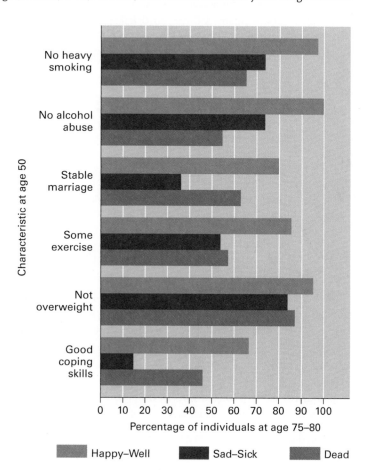

Figure 16.8

Links between Characteristics at Age 50 and Health and Happiness at Age 75 to 80

In a longitudinal study, the characteristics shown above at age 50 were related to whether individuals were happy–well, sad–sick, or dead at age 75 to 80 (Vaillant, 2002).

heavy smokers, did not abuse alcohol, had a stable marriage, exercised, maintained a normal weight, and had good coping skills, they were more likely to be alive and happy at 75 to 80 years of age.

Conclusions

What can we conclude about stability and change in personality development during the middle adult years?

According to a recent research review by leading researchers Brent Roberts and Daniel Mroczek (2008), there is increasing evidence that personality traits continue to change during the adult years, even into late adulthood. However, in the recent meta-analysis of 92 longitudinal studies described earlier, the greatest change in personality traits occurred in early adulthood—from about 20 to 40 years of age (Roberts, Walton, & Viechtbauer, 2006).

Thus, people show greater stability in their personality when they reach midlife than when they were younger adults. These findings support what is called a *cumulative personality model* of personality development, which states that with time and age, people become more adept at interacting with their environment in ways that promote the stability of personality (Caspi & Roberts, 2001). However, this does not mean that change is absent throughout midlife. Ample evidence shows that social contexts, new experiences, and socio-historical changes can affect personality development.

In sum, recent research contradicts the old view that stability in personality begins to set in at about 30 years of age (McAdams & Olson, 2010; Roberts & Mroczek, 2008; Roberts, Wood, & Caspi, 2008; Roberts et al., 2009). Although there are some consistent developmental changes in the personality traits of large numbers of people, at the individual level people can show unique patterns of personality traits—and these patterns often reflect life experiences related to themes of their particular developmental period (Roberts & Mroczek, 2008). For example, researchers have found that individuals who are in a stable marriage and have a solid career track become more socially dominant, conscientious, and emotionally stable as they go through early adulthood (Roberts & Wood, 2006). And for some of these individuals, there is greater change in their personality traits than for other individuals (McAdams & Olson, 2010; Roberts & Mroczek, 2008; Roberts et al., 2009).

To this point, we have discussed a number of ideas about stability and change in middle adulthood. For a review, see the **Reach Your Learning Objectives** section at the end of this chapter.

Close Relationships

LO3 Identify some important aspects of close relationships in middle adulthood.

There is a consensus among middle-aged Americans that a major component of well-being involves positive relationships with others, especially parents, spouse, and offspring (Lachman, 2004; Markus et al., 2004). To begin our examination of midlife relationships, let's explore love and marriage in middle-aged adults.

Love and Marriage at Midlife

Recall from Chapter 14 that two major forms of love are romantic love and affectionate love. The fires of romantic love are strong in early adulthood. Affectionate or companionate love increases during middle adulthood. That is, physical attraction, romance, and passion are more important in new relationships, especially in early adulthood. Security, loyalty, and mutual emotional interest become more important as relationships mature, especially in middle adulthood (see Figure 16.9).

Marital Trends

According to Statistics Canada (2007c), the portrait of marriage and the family is undergoing dramatic shifts. This portrait includes the following trends:

- For the first time in history, more than half (51.5 percent) of the Canadian population was unmarried in 2006.

Love and Marriage at Midlife

The Empty Nest and Its Refilling

Sibling Relationships and Friendships

Grandparenting

Intergenerational Relationships

- The number adults over the age of 15 who are unmarried has increased from just fewer than 50 percent to slightly over 50 percent.
- For the first time in Canadian history, slightly more married couples do not have children living at home.
- In July 2005, Canada legalized gay marriage, and in 2006, for the first time in its history, Statistics Canada included gay marriages in its national census.
- Married couples are more likely to have children than common-law couples.
- The number of single-parent families has increased.
- The proportion of common-law relationships has also risen in most of Canada, but soared by more than 20 percent in Quebec, where common-law has been a defining characteristic of family patterns.
- More people, particularly those who have divorced, are choosing to cohabit rather than marry.
- The number of one-person households has increased by over 10 percent.

Numerous factors have contributed to these changes. Not only are people waiting longer to marry, but those considering marriage may also have experienced the divorce of their own parents. This experience may create additional caution. Those who have divorced may choose more informal arrangements than marriage. Further, as economic self-sufficiency for both women and men has taken on greater importance, marriage may no longer be viewed as the primary rite of passage into adulthood.

A recent study revealed that marital satisfaction increased in middle age (Gorchoff, John, & Helson, 2008). Even some marriages that were difficult and rocky during early adulthood turn out to be better adjusted during middle adulthood. Although the partners may have lived through a great deal of turmoil, they eventually discover a deep and solid foundation on which to anchor their relationship.

Marriage and Divorce

Even some marriages that were difficult and rocky during early adulthood turn out to be better adjusted during middle adulthood. Partners who engage in mutually pleasing activities usually view their marriage as more positive at this time. In 2010/2011, the national divorce rates declined by 2% in every province except British Columbia where the rate increased by 4%. The decline in divorce rates since 2006 was 22%, in Nova Scotia where a couple's chances of reaching their 30th wedding anniversary are great. The rate of divorce declines with each additional year of marriage (Kelly, 2013). In Quebec, where the rate of divorce is highest, about 50 percent of those who marry can anticipate sharing their 30th wedding anniversary. The risk of divorce prior to the 30th wedding anniversary for Canadian couples is 38 percent, and for U.S. couples, the rate is 44 percent (Ambert, 2005).

Are there any differences in the factors that predict whether couples will divorce in midlife rather than as younger adults? In Chapter 14, "Socio-Emotional Development in Early Adulthood," we described John Gottman's extensive research on the factors that make a successful marriage. In a 14-year longitudinal study, Gottman and Robert Levenson (2000) found that couples who divorce in midlife tend to have a relationship characterized as cool and distant, with suppressed emotions. The midlife divorcing couples were alienated and avoidant; it is a distant relationship with little or no laughter, love, or interest in each other. One of the divorcing midlife partners often feels that his or her life is "empty." The researchers found that when divorce occurs among younger adults (often in the first five years of a marriage), it is characterized by heated emotions that tend to burn out the marriage early. The young divorcing couples frequently were volatile and expressive, full of disappointment that they let each other know about.

Divorce in middle adulthood may be more positive in some ways and more negative in others than divorce in early adulthood. For mature individuals, who may have more resources at their disposal, the perils of divorce can be fewer and less intense than for younger individuals. Their children are adults and may be able to cope better with their parents' divorce. The partners may have attained a better understanding of themselves, and may be searching for changes that could include ending a poor marriage.

In contrast, the emotional and time commitment to a marriage that has existed for so many years may not be lightly given up. Many midlife individuals perceive divorce as a failure in what they

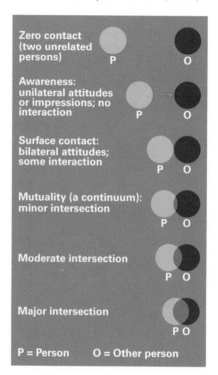

Figure 16.9

The Development of Relationships

One view of how close relationships develop states that we begin a relationship with someone at a zero point of contact (*top*), and then gradually move from a surface relationship into more intense, mutual interaction, sharing ourselves more and more with the other person as the relationship develops. At the final stage, a major intersection, we are probably experiencing affectionate or companionate love (*bottom*).

Divorce rates in Canada, although considerably lower than those in the United States, are the third highest in the world. Approximately 30 percent of Canadians divorce; the most vulnerable period for a marriage is the fifth year, when the rate is highest. On the basis of what you have read in Chapters 14 and 16, your observations, and your experience, what are the factors that contribute to a lasting relationship? What factors do you believe can potentially destroy a relationship? What, if any, societal factors may influence decisions to marry? to remain in a marriage? to divorce? If you were a marriage counsellor, what advice would you give to a couple who came to you?

had hoped would be the best years of their lives. The divorcer might see the situation as an escape from an untenable relationship, but the divorced partner frequently sees it as a betrayal, the ending of a relationship that had been built up over many years and that involved a great deal of commitment and trust.

Studies reported by Anne-Marie Ambert (2005) indicate that the top three socio-cultural and demographic factors that put marriages at risk are:

- Youthful marriages (defined as those who marry before their personalities have stabilized)
- Low income and poverty
- Cohabitation prior to marriage—particularly cohabiting couples with children

According to Ambert, the reasons people give for relationship breakdown (alcoholism, adultery, violence, fell out of love) are related to North American cultural values such as individualism. She argues that some of the reasons given for divorce would be considered frivolous in some cultures where family solidarity is more deeply ingrained in the cultural values. In many countries, the only acceptable causes for marital dissolution are abandonment and abuse (Ambert, 2005).

A recent study found that women who initiated a divorce in midlife were characterized more by self-focused growth and optimism than women whose husbands initiated the divorce (Sakraida, 2005). Financial stress infiltrates relationships. Today, 85 percent of Canadian couples with children are dual income, and most are carrying a debt load equal to more than their combined incomes (Sauvé, 2005). The busy-ness of their lives, combined with financial burden, exact additional stress on relationships. Paul Gottman of the Gottman Institute (U.S.) who uses rigorous scientific observations to understand relationships, reports that the magic ratio of positivity (empathy, asking questions, showing affection, etc.) and negativity (criticism, blame, showing disdain or contempt) is an indicator of stability or instability in a relationship. For couples whose relationships are likely to succeed, there are more positive things going on than negative. In fact, he found the ratio be five to one. That is, there are five times as many positive than negative interactions. For couples heading for divorce the ratio is reversed—that is, there is more negativity than positivity (Gottman, 2007).

The Empty Nest and Its Refilling

Recall from Chapter 14 that the family at midlife, the fifth stage in Carter and McGoldrick's family life cycle, is characterized by multiple entries and exits. An important event in a family is the launching of a child into adult life, to a career, or to family independent of the family of origin. Parents face new adjustments as disequilibrium is created by a child's absence. In the **empty nest syndrome**, *marital satisfaction decreases because parents derive considerable satisfaction from their children, and the children's departure leaves parents with empty feelings.* For most parents, marital satisfaction does not decline; on the contrary, it increases during the years after childrearing (Fingerman, 2006; Fingerman & Lang, 2004). A recent study revealed that the transition to an empty nest increased marital satisfaction and this increase was linked to an increase in the quality of time—but not the quantity of time—spent with partners (Gorchoff, John, & Helson, 2008).

With the recent economic downturn, the refilling of the empty nest is becoming a common occurrence, as adult children return to live after several years of college or university, after graduating, or to save money after finding work (Merrill, 2009). Young adults may have to settle for contract or part-time work, or may return home after an unsuccessful career or a divorce. Some do not leave home until their middle to late twenties because they are unable to support themselves. Numerous labels have been applied to these young adults who return to their parents' homes to live, including "boomerang kids," and "B2B" (or back-to-bedroom) (Furman, 2005).

The middle generation has always provided support for the younger generation, even after the nest is bare. Through loans and monetary gifts for education and through emotional support, the middle generation continues to help the younger generation. Adult children appreciate the financial and emotional support their parents provide them at a time when they often feel considerable stress about their career, work, and lifestyle. And parents feel good that they can provide this support.

empty nest syndrome Occurs when marital satisfaction decreases because parents derive considerable satisfaction from their children, and the children's departure leaves parents with empty feelings.

Another study of 40- to 60-year-old parents revealed that they provided financial, practical, and emotional support on average every few weeks to each of their children over 18 years of age (Fingerman et al., 2009).

Some families are skillful at handling the multiple entries and exits, while others experience disequilibrium. When young adults remain at home, they need to be treated more like adults than children. Some parents who have difficulty letting go engage in "perma-parenting" or "helicoptering" (Paul, 2003). However well-intentioned these parents may be, most young adults will find them too intrusive; furthermore, close monitoring or hovering can slow the transition into adulthood. Another common complaint voiced by both adult children and their parents is a loss of privacy. The adult children complain that their parents restrict their independence. Parents often complain that their quiet home has become noisy, that they stay up late worrying when their adult children will come home, that meals are difficult to plan because of conflicting schedules, that their relationship as a married couple has been invaded, and that they have to shoulder too much responsibility for their adult children. In sum, when adult children return home to live a disequilibrium in family life is created, which requires considerable adaptation on the part of parents and their adult children.

Doonesbury   BY GARRY TRUDEAU

Doonesbury © 1991 G.B. Trudeau. Reprinted with permission of Universal Press Syndicate. All Rights Reserved.

Sibling Relationships and Friendships

Sibling relationships persist over the entire life span for most adults (Dunn, 2007). Eighty-five percent of today's adults have at least one living sibling. Sibling relationships in adulthood may be extremely close, apathetic, or highly competitive (Bedford, 2009). The advent of technology has made it easier for siblings to remain in contact. The majority of sibling relationships in adulthood have been found to be close (Cicirelli, 1991). Those siblings who are psychologically close to each other in adulthood tend to have been that way in childhood. It is rare for sibling closeness to develop for the first time in adulthood (Dunn, 1984). A recent study revealed that adult siblings often provide practical and emotional support to each other (Voorpostel & Blieszner, 2008).

Friendships and social networks continue to be important in middle adulthood, just as they were in early adulthood. It takes time to develop intimate friendships, and so friendships that have endured over the adult years are often deeper than those that have just been formed in middle adulthood; nevertheless, friendships provide a support system when problems arise.

Grandparenting

A major milestone in middle adulthood is becoming a grandparent. In the past, Canadians typically become grandparents in their late forties or early fifties (B.C. Council for Families, 2007); however, as you have read, people are becoming grandparents in their mid to late fifties (Edwards, & Sterne, 2005). Due to longevity, the relationship between children and grandparents lasts for 20 years, frequently more. In a survey, university students reported feeling close to their grandparents, exchanging visits, phone calls, and emails on a regular basis (B.C. Council for Families, 2007).

Grandparents continue to be major family resources: they provide babysitting and they pass on family folklore, history, traditions, and social values. Additionally, grandparents serve as confidants and role models (B.C. Council for Families, 2007). Although grandparents continue to serve these roles, as families have changed so too has grandparenting. Dual-earning families, increased divorce rates of the child's parents as well as of the grandparents themselves, custody arrangements, plus the divergent health and interests of individuals who become grandparents are some of the situations that can make grandparenting more challenging today than in the past. In some cases, grandparents may be step-grandparents; for example, one child explained to his class that he was very lucky because he had six grandparents who loved him. In addition, some grandparents provide as many as 60 or more hours of unpaid child care for their children (Fuller-Thomson & Minkler, 2001). Almost half of the grandparents who move in with their children are immigrants. Partly because women live longer than men, there are more grandmothers than grandfathers who live with their children. About 70 percent of the grandparents who move in with their children are grandmothers.

As we can see, grandparents play important roles in the lives of many grandchildren (Oberlander, Black, & Starr, 2007). Researchers have consistently found that grandmothers have more contact with grandchildren than grandfathers (Watson, Randolph, & Lyons, 2005). Perhaps women tend to define their role as grandmothers as part of their responsibility for maintaining ties between family members across generations. Men may have fewer expectations about the grandfather role and see it as more voluntary.

Grandparent Roles and Styles

The diversity of grandparent interaction with their grandchildren was apparent in an early investigation (Neugarten & Weinstein, 1964). For some, being a grandparent is a source of biological reward and continuity. For others, being a grandparent is a source of emotional self-fulfillment, generating feelings of companionship and satisfaction that may have been missing in earlier adult–child relationships. And for yet others, being a grandparent is a remote role, especially when the children and grandchildren have relocated. Fortunately, technology is enabling people to stay more connected.

An early study identified three styles of grandparent interaction with their grandchildren: dominant-formal, fun-seeking, and distant. In the formal style, the grandparent performed what was considered to be a proper and prescribed role. These grandparents showed a strong interest in their grandchildren, but were careful not to give childrearing advice. In the fun-seeking style, the grandparent was informal and playful. Grandchildren were a source of leisure activity; mutual satisfaction was emphasized. A substantial portion of grandparents were distant figures. In the distant-figure style, the grandparent was benevolent but interaction was infrequent. Grandparents who were over the age of 65 were more likely to display a formal style of interaction; those under 65 were more likely to display a fun-seeking style (Szinovacz, 2009).

According to tradition among Aboriginal peoples, "children are gifts from the spirit world and they have to be treated gently lest they become disillusioned. . . ." Elders play an important role in helping their children and grandchildren understand the interconnectedness and harmony or imbalance of aspects or elements within the universe. These things include the individual, the family, the community, the nation, as well as the natural and spiritual phenomena of the universe. A recent study revealed that grandparenting can provide a sense of purpose and a feeling of being valued during middle and late adulthood, when generative needs are strong (Thiele & Whelan, 2008).

The Changing Profile of Grandparents

An increasing number of grandchildren live with their grandparents (Silverstein, 2009). Not only are grandparents helping their adult children by babysitting, but the number of Canadian grandparents who have full custodial care of their grandchildren who are under 18 years of age rose by 20 percent between 1991 and 2001. Approximately one-third of Aboriginal grandparents have full custodial care of their grandchildren, and many of these grandparents are also caring for seniors. Divorce, adolescent pregnancies, and drug use by parents are the main reasons that grandparents are thrust

connecting development to life

Elders—The Glue That Binds

When asked what an Elder is, Nellie Makokis Carlson, from Saddle Lake Amiskwachly Academy, thought a moment before saying, "It's a lifetime of experience. What you have lived through, good and bad. Also, it's an experience where Elders have this wisdom which they can pass on to the young people" (Carlson, 2007). As we have discussed, the extended family is considerably more diverse than it once was. Young people relocate to urban areas, sometimes "getting into trouble" according to Elder Margaret Bear of Ochapowace First Nation (Interviews with Saskatchewan Elders, 2007). Consequently, family gatherings become less frequent and more complicated because people may have to travel considerable distances to attend.

Health, cultural dissonance, poverty, and the emotional burdens further exacerbate problems. Too often, Elders report that their grandchildren would rather play video games than learn about their heritage. Some community leaders discredit the Elders, accusing them of living in the past. Others revere the Elders, agreeing with Elder Maggie Auger that, "Elders are the glue that holds us all together. They hold what little tradition we have left" (Meili, 1994). Further, they argue that one of the most effective ways to mend family circles is to rekindle relationships with Elders who can offer much in the way of physical, mental, and spiritual healing, and who can serve to remind their families of spiritual beliefs, traditions, and history (Meili, 1994).

"My grandmother taught me everything I do has a consequence. Even if I break a twig or step on a flower, the world will never be the same again. I learned to think about everything I did," said Francis Tootoosis, a Cree grandfather (Meili, 1994). Grandparents have often faced trials and hardships in the past, and now have the time and patience to share and teach their grandchildren about their culture and traditions. Their stories are interesting and insightful. Elders may share their stories about survival through winter. For example, Elder Nancy Bitternose talks about melting snow and ice in the winter to wash her family's clothes (Interviews with Saskatchewan Elders, 2007).

Elders initiated the Aboriginal healing movement of the 1970s, which seeks a restoration of spiritual values and balance. Previously, many of the healing practices and ceremonies of Aboriginal people were made illegal by the newcomers to North America. According to one Native healer, "In order to preserve the culture and the old ways, sacred traditional 'bundles,' teachings and rituals were passed on behind closed doors and brought back to the surface near the start of the seventies. As the Euro-western world began to not only accept but also express an interest in Aboriginal views on life, acceptance became more widespread, even among the native culture" (Criger, interview, 2007).

---

back into the "parenting" role they thought they had shed. One study of grandparents raising their grandchildren found that stress was linked with three conditions: younger grandparents, grandchildren with physical and psychological problems, and low family cohesion (Sands & Goldberg-Glen, 2000). Poverty is also a major contributing factor (Fuller-Thomson & Minkler, 2005). A recent study of more than 12,000 50- to 80-year-old grandparents found that any negative effects on grandparent health were the exception rather than the rule (Hughes et al., 2007).

As divorce and remarriage have become more common, a special concern of grandparents is visitation privileges with their grandchildren. In the last 10 to 15 years, more laws have been passed giving grandparents the right to petition a court for visitation privileges with their grandchildren, even if a parent objects. Whether such forced visitation rights for grandparents are in the child's best interest is still being debated.

Intergenerational Relationships

Family is important to most people. When 21,000 adults aged 40 to 79 in 21 countries were asked, "When you think of who you are, you think mainly of _____," 63 percent said "family," 9 percent said "religion," and 8 percent said "work" (HSBC Insurance, 2007). In this study, in all 21 countries, middle-aged and older adults expressed a strong feeling of responsibility between generations in their family, with the strongest intergenerational ties indicated in Saudi Arabia, India, and Turkey. More than 80 percent of the middle-aged and older adults reported that adults have a duty to care for their parents (and parents-in-law) in time of need later in life.

Adults in midlife play important roles in the lives of the young and the old (Birditt et al., 2010; Ha & Ingersoll-Dayton, 2008; Fingerman et al., 2008, 2009). Middle-aged adults share their experience and transmit values to the younger generation (Swartz, 2008). They may be launching children and experiencing the empty nest, adjusting to their grown children returning home, or becoming grandparents. They also may be giving or receiving financial assistance, caring for a widowed or sick parent, or adapting to being the oldest generation after both parents have died (Silverstein, Gans, & Yang, 2006).

A valuable service that adult children can perform is to coordinate and monitor services for an aging parent who becomes disabled mentally, emotionally, physically, or a combination (Huyck, Ayalon, & Yoder, 2007). This might involve locating a nursing home and monitoring its quality, procuring medical services, arranging public service assistance, and handling finances. In some cases, adult children provide direct assistance with daily living, including such activities as eating, bathing, and dressing. Even less severely impaired older adults may need help with shopping, housework, transportation, home maintenance, and bill paying.

A recent study revealed that even when aging parents had health problems, they and their children generally described positive changes in their relationship in recent years (Fingerman et al., 2007). However, in most cases researchers have found that relationships between aging parents and their children are usually characterized by ambivalence (Birditt et al., 2010; Davey et al., 2009; Fingerman et al., 2008). Perceptions include love, reciprocal help, and shared values on the positive side and isolation, family conflicts and problems, abuse, neglect, and caregiver stress on the negative side. A dark side does exist, however. According to Statistics Canada, adult children are the biggest perpetrators of violence against seniors, which can take one or more of several forms including neglect, physical abuse, psychological/ emotional abuse, and economic/financial abuse (RCMP, 2012; Statistics Canada, 2012k).

With each new generation, personality characteristics, attitudes, and values are replicated or changed (Bengtson & Psouni, 2008). As older family members die, their biological, intellectual, emotional, and personal legacies are carried on in the next generation. Their children become the oldest generation and their grandchildren the second generation. For the most part, family members maintain considerable contact across generations (Miller-Day, 2004). However, a recent study found that married men and women have a lower incidence of intergenerational contact than never-married or divorced individuals (Sarkisian & Gerstel, 2008). In this study, married adults were less likely to live with their parents, keep in touch, and give or receive emotional, financial, or practical help. Nonetheless, another recent study revealed that when young adults have children, they are more likely to see their parents than if they don't have children (Bucx et al., 2008).

As we continue to stay connected with our parents and our children as we age, both similarity and dissimilarity across generations are found. For example, similarity between parents and an adult child is most noticeable in religion and politics; it is least noticeable in gender roles, lifestyle, and work orientation.

The following studies provide further evidence of the importance of intergenerational relationships in development.

- In a New Zealand study of the childrearing antecedents of intergenerational relations, supportive family environments and parenting in childhood (assessed when the children were 3 to 15 years of age) were linked with more positive relationships (in terms of contact, closeness, conflict, and reciprocal assistance) between the children and their middle-aged parents when the children were 26 years old (Belsky et al., 2001).
- The motivation of adult children to provide social support to their older parents was linked with earlier family experiences (Silverstein et al., 2002). Children who spent more time in shared activities with their parents and were given more financial support by them earlier in their lives provided more support to their parents when they became older.

What is the nature of intergenerational relationships?

- Recent Studies indicate that: Adult children of divorce who were classified as securely attached were less likely to divorce in the early years of their marriage than their insecurely attached counterparts (Crowell, Treboux, & Brockmeyer, 2009).
- Divorce in the grandparent generation was linked to less education and marital conflict in the grandchild generation (Amato & Cheadle, 2005). These links were mediated by these characteristics of the middle generation: less education, increased marital conflict, and more tension in early parent–child relationships.
- Parents who smoked early and often, and persisted in becoming regular smokers, were more likely to have adolescents who became smokers (Chassin et al., 2008).

Gender differences also characterize intergenerational relationships (Etaugh & Bridges, 2010; Nauck & Suckow, 2006). Women's relationships across generations are thought to be closer than other family bonds (Merrill, 2009). Also in this study, married men were more involved with their wife's kin than with their own. And maternal grandmothers and maternal aunts were cited twice as often as their counterparts on the paternal side of the family as the most important or loved relative. Also, a recent study revealed that mothers' intergenerational ties were more influential for grandparent–grandchild relationships than fathers' were (Monserud, 2008). Although researchers have documented that mothers and daughters in adulthood generally have frequent contact and mutually positive feelings, little is known about what mothers and daughters like about their relationship. For instance, how do mothers' and daughters' descriptions of enjoyable visits differ at different points in adult development?

Family Caregiving

While middle-aged adults are guiding and financially supporting their children through adolescence and early adulthood, they may also be providing emotional and financial support to elderly parents (Etaugh & Bridges, 2010; Pudrovska, 2009). These simultaneous pressures from adolescents or young adult children and aging parents may contribute to stress in middle adulthood; on the other hand, family caregiving may heighten the warmth and intimacy of relationships. Consequently, middle-aged adults have been described as the "sandwich" generation, and their situation has been labelled the "generation squeeze" or "generational overload." When adults immigrate to another country, intergenerational stress and dependency may also increase.

Demographically, the baby boomers have arrived. At the same time, health-care policy is shifting the responsibility for care from formal settings to informal caregivers. In other words, caring for the many seniors who remain in their home and require at least periodic care falls to neighbours, friends, and families. At the same time, families are smaller, more diverse, less stable, and more complex.

One of Canada's leading workplace health researchers, Dr. Linda Duxbury, reports that approximately 47 percent, or almost one in two adult Canadians, spend an average of two hours per week in caregiving-related activities. The essential care for family members who are chronically ill, physically or mentally challenged, or frail or elderly is often demanding and exhausting. The Canadian Caregiver Coalition describes the cost to informal caregivers in terms of " . . . lost time at work, reduced productivity, high stress levels, increased health problems, lack of free time, financial pressures, and . . . negative impact on relationships."

In response to this stressful challenge, provincial groups are calling attention to the needs of the caregiver as well as the needs of those in need of care. The Family Caregivers Association of Nova Scotia (FCgANS), organized in the early 1990s, is the first organization of its kind to respond to the needs of caregivers by offering a toll-free information line, a newsletter, and a database of services and products. In conjunction with the Canadian Caregiver Coalition, FCgANS attempts to raise awareness of caregiving issues and to influence policy.

To this point, we have discussed a number of ideas about close relationships in middle adulthood. For a review, see the **Reach Your Learning Objectives** section at the end of this chapter.

reach your learning objectives

Personality Theories and Development in Middle Adulthood

LO1 Describe personality theories and development in middle adulthood.

Stages of Adulthood	According to Erikson's theory: ■ The seventh stage of the human life span, generativity versus stagnation, occurs in middle adulthood. ■ Care is the virtue that emerges when the crisis of generativity versus stagnation is successfully resolved. ■ Four types of generativity are biologial, parental, work, and cultural. According to Levinson's theory: ■ Developmental tasks should be mastered at different points in development. ■ Changes in middle age focus on four conflicts: being young versus being old, being destructive versus being constructive, being masculine versus being feminine, and being attached to others versus being separated from them. Other research findings: ■ For the most part, midlife crises have been exaggerated. Most adults feel a greater sense of autonomy and mastery in middle adulthood. ■ Many who experience a crisis attribute it to a negative life event rather than age. ■ There is considerable individual variation in development during the middle adulthood years.
The Life-Events Approach	■ Life events influence the individual's development. ■ How life events influence the individual's development depends not only on the life event, but also on mediating factors, adaptation to the event, the life-stage context, and the socio-historical context.
Stress in Midlife	■ Stress can be positive or negative, episodic or chronic. ■ Chronic stress can affect an individual's immune system, causing distress and disease. ■ Poverty, discrimination, or family conflict may produce chronic stress. ■ Immigrants, Aboriginal people, lone parents, and seniors are more likely to experience daily hassles and stress related to racialized discrimination and/or poverty.
Contexts of Midlife Development	■ Historical, gender, and cultural are three midlife contexts. ■ Neugarten believed that the social environment of a particular cohort can alter its social clock, the timetable according to which individuals are expected to accomplish life's tasks, such as getting married, having children, and establishing a career. She noted a diminished agreement between the late 1950s and 1970s in the "right" time for events to occur. ■ Critics say that the adult stage theories are male-biased because they place too much emphasis on achievement and careers. The stage theories do not adequately address women's concerns about relationships. ■ Midlife is a heterogeneous period for women, as it is for men. For some women, midlife is the prime of their lives. ■ In many non-industrialized societies, a woman's status often improves in middle age. ■ In many cultures, where life expectancy is lower than in North America and social roles are prescribed at earlier ages, the concept of middle age is not clear. ■ Most cultures distinguish between young adults and old adults.

Stability and Change

LO2 Discuss stability and change in development during middle adulthood, including longitudinal studies.

Longitudinal Studies

Costa and McCrae's Baltimore study:
- The big five personality factors are openness to experience, conscientiousness, extraversion, agreeableness, and neuroticism.
- These factors show considerable stability; however, early adulthood is when most change occurs.

Berkeley Longitudinal Studies:
- The extremes in the stability–change argument were not supported.
- The most stable characteristics were intellectual orientation, self-confidence, and openness to new experiences.
- The characteristics that changed the most were nurturance, hostility, and self-control.

Helson's Mills College Study:
- In this study of women, there was a shift toward less traditional feminine characteristics from age 27 to the early forties, but this might have been due to societal changes.
- In their early forties, women experienced many of the concerns that Levinson described for men. However, rather than a midlife crisis, this is best called midlife consciousness.

George Vaillant's Grant Study:
- This study investigated whether or not personality in middle adulthood is a predictor of what the individual's life is like in late adulthood.
- Individuals who did not abuse tobacco or alcohol, who had stable marriages, exercised, and maintained a normal weight, and who had good coping skills were more likely to be alive and happy at ages 75 to 80 years.

Conclusions
- Amid change, there is still some underlying coherence and stability.
- Social context, experiences, socio-historical changes can influence personality development.

Close Relationships

LO3 Identify some important aspects of close relationships in middle adulthood.

Love and Marriage at Midlife
- Affectionate love increases in midlife, especially in marriages that have endured many years.
- A majority of middle-aged adults who are married say that their marriage is good or excellent.
- Researchers recently have found that couples who divorce in midlife are more likely to have a cool, distant, emotionally suppressed relationship, whereas divorcing young adults are more likely to have an emotionally volatile and expressive relationship.
- Divorce is a special concern. In one recent study, divorce in middle age had more positive emotional effects for women than for men, while marriage had more positive emotional effects for men than for women.

The Empty Nest and Its Refilling
- Rather than decreasing satisfaction as once thought, the empty nest increases it.
- An increasing number of young adults are returning home to live with their parents.

Sibling Relationships and Friendships
- Sibling relationships continue throughout life. Some are close, some are distant, and others are competitive.
- Friendships continue to be important in middle age.

Grandparenting	■ Becoming a grandparent is a major milestone of middle adulthood.
	■ Due to increasing divorce rates and the career and work life of parents, the role of grandparents is undergoing considerable change.
	■ Two contemporary trends are the role of grandparents raising their grandchildren and the visitation rights of grandparents in the event of parental divorce.
Intergenerational Relationships	■ Continuing contact across generations in families usually occurs.
	■ Mothers and daughters have the closest relationships.
	■ The middle-aged generation plays an important role in linking generations.
	■ The middle-aged generation has been called the "sandwich" or "squeezed generation" because it is caught between obligations to children and obligations to parents.
	■ The demands of family caregiving have both positive and negative implications for individual life-course development and for the family systems to which they belong.

McGraw-Hill Connect

McGraw-Hill Connect provides you with a powerful tool for improving academic performance and truly mastering course material. You can diagnose your knowledge with pre- and post-tests, identify the areas where you need help, search the entire learning package, including the eBook, for content specific to the topic you're studying, and add these resources to your personalized study plan. CONNECT for *Life-Span Development*, fifth Canadian edition, offers the following:

- chapter-specific online quizzes
- groupwork
- presentations
- writing assignments
- case studies
- and much more!

Visit CONNECT today!

review ---→ *connect* ---→ reflect

review

What activities in middle adulthood illustrate Erikson's stage of generativity versus stagnation? **LO1**

How have cohort effects influenced changes in the social clock? **LO2**

What are Costa and McCrae's big five factors of personality? **LO2**

How can love and marriage at midlife be characterized? **LO3**

How has the profile of grandparents changed? **LO3**

Explain how close relationships have an impact on aspects of personality development in middle adulthood. **LO3**

connect

What are the different kinds of stress and what role does stress play in our lives?

reflect *Your Own Personal Journey of Life*

What is the nature of your relationship with your grandparents? What legacy have they left? What are the intergenerational relationships like in your family?

CHAPTER 17   Physical and Cognitive Development in Late Adulthood

CHAPTER OUTLINE

> "*What continues to perplex me is that all these years of existence taught me so little. I had hoped for wisdom, but I don't even know what wisdom is. I hope it has something to do with putting the top of my car up when it rains hard, because I almost always do that.*"
>
> —JUNE CALLWOOD, CANADIAN JOURNALIST, AUTHOR, AND SOCIAL ACTIVIST, IN 2001 WHEN SHE WAS 75

Hallelujah—I'm Your Man: Leonard Cohen

The old are kind
but the young are hot.
Love may be blind
but Desire is not.
—Leonard Cohen

The iconic songwriter, poet, and singer Leonard Cohen was born in Montreal in 1934. In 2008, he was inducted into the Rock and Roll Hall of Fame; in 2010, he received a Grammy Award for Lifetime Achievement; and in 2013, Cohen received the Juno Award for Artist of the Year. His music has transcended generations, and today, at nearly 80 years of age, Cohen is still captivating audiences with his music, his lyrics, his poetry, and his humour.

After graduating from McGill University, where he studied poetry, Cohen moved to New York City, attending Columbia University in 1958. Here, he was awarded a grant that allowed him to travel the world and establish a residence on the Greek island of Hydra. After publishing four books of poetry and two novels, Cohen returned to the United States in 1966, where he took up songwriting in the hopes that he would be able to support himself financially (Rock Hall, 2013). Folk musicians such as Bob Dylan, Pete Seeger, Woody Guthrie, Joni Mitchell, Joan Baez, Simon and Garfunkel and many more gathered in the coffee houses of Greenwich Village to exchange ideas and compose and sing songs of social justice that shaped social consciousness and defined the decade. Here, amidst the active creative and political climate of the Village, rife with protests against the Vietnam War and in favour of desegregation, Cohen launched his musical career. Focusing on his favourite themes—romance, religion, and politics—Cohen composed and released music widely enjoyed today: songs such as "Suzanne" and "First We Take Manhattan" (Holden, 2013; Rock Hall, 2013).

He was less prolific in the 1970s and '80s, although one of his best known songs, "Hallelujah," was released in 1984. "Hallelujah" remains popular today, and has been recorded by many artists including k.d. lang, who performed it at the opening of the 2010 Olympics in Vancouver. In 1992, he released *The Future*, in which he sings the cynical line "Get ready for the future, it is murder." After this album was released, Cohen retreated to a Zen Buddhist monastery in an effort to deal with chronic depression. In 2008 he launched a world tour, and, accompanied by superb musicians, he has received standing ovations and requests for encore upon encore in Australia, Europe, and, naturally, Canada. He released *Old Ideas* in 2012, which provided further proof of his vibrancy. Cohen's artistic outlook might best be expressed in by the lyrics from his song "Anthem," which he wrote in 1992: "There is a crack, a crack in everything / That's how the light gets in" (Rock Hall, 2013). His poetry and lyrics endeavour to open up the cracks and shine some light on our sometimes confusing and disturbing lives.

Longevity and Biological Theories of Aging

LO1 Describe longevity and the biological theories of aging.

In his eighties, Linus Pauling argued that vitamin C slows the aging process. Aging researcher Roy Walford fasts two days a week because he believes undernutrition (not malnutrition) also slows the aging process. What do we really know about longevity?

Life Expectancy and Life Span

We are no longer a youthful society. In fact, the concept of a period called "late adulthood" is a recent one—until the twentieth century, most individuals died before they were 65. Life span and life expectancy are two different concepts. Recall from Chapter 1 that **life span** *is the upper boundary of life, the maximum number of years an individual can live*, whereas **life expectancy** *is the number of years that probably will be lived by the average person born in a particular year*. Improvements in medicine, nutrition, exercise, and lifestyle have increased our life expectancy by an average of 30 additional years since 1900.

In 2012, Statistics Canada reported that life expectancy is 79 for men, and 83 for women; interestingly, Statistics Canada also reported that people in British Columbia are likely to live a bit longer (80 for men and 84 for women) (Statistics Canada, 2012g). The Territories (Northwest Territories, Yukon, and Nunavut) together have the lowest life spans (76.3 years) (Statistics Canada, 2012g). This variation across the country is further illustrated by the percentage of an area's population over the age of 65. For example, 15.4 percent of Nova Scotia's population is over age 65, whereas in sharp contrast, only 2.8 percent of Nunavut's population is that age. In fact, approximately one-third of the population in Nunavut is under 15 years of age, representing the highest number of children relative to the rest of the Canadian population. The Atlantic provinces have proportionally more people over 65 and fewer people under 15 (15 percent) than the rest of the country (Statistics Canada, 2009).

Centenarians

In industrialized countries, the number of centenarians (individuals 100 years and older) is increasing at a rate of approximately 7 percent each year (Perls, 2007). According to Statistics Canada (2013), over 1,000 more centenarians were enumerated 2011 than five years earlier in 2006. In other words, 5,825 people over the age of 100 were enumerated in 2011, up from 4,635 in 2006 (Statistics Canada, 2013b). This represents a considerable increase since 1970, when the number of centenarians was 1,440 (Statistics Canada, 2006a). Projections by Statistics Canada are that the number will escalate to 17,000 by 2031, and be close to 80,000 by 2061 (Statistics Canada, 2013b). Women reaching 100 years of age outnumber men by five to one; that is, for every 100 men currently, there are approximately 500 women (Statistics Canada, 2013b).

As a consequence of this increase in numbers, centenarians are now being studied more often. For example, McGill University's Centre for Studies in Aging (MCSA) was established in 1985. Since then, it has become one of the world's leading research centres investigating age-related conditions including memory, cognition, and forms of dementia such as Alzheimer's disease (McGill Centre, 2013). One view is that "the older you get, the sicker you get." However, researchers are finding that could be a myth. Recent research on 100-year-olds reveals that many of them have been quite healthy in their old age (Terry et al., 2008; Xie et al., 2008). One recent study of 400 centenarians found that 32 percent of the males and 15 percent of the females have never been diagnosed with common age-associated diseases such as heart disease, cancer, and stroke (Evert et al., 2003). Another study of 93 centenarians revealed that despite some physical limitations, they have a low rate of age-associated diseases, and most have good mental health (Selim et al., 2005). Another

Life Expectancy and Life Span

The Young Old, the Old Old, and the Oldest Old

The Robust Oldest Old

Biological Theories of Aging

life span The upper boundary of life, the maximum number of years an individual can live. The maximum life span of human beings is about 120 years.

life expectancy The number of years that probably will be lived by the average person born in a particular year.

Living Longer in Okinawa

Individuals live longer on the Japanese island of Okinawa in the East China Sea than anywhere else in the world. In Okinawa, there are 34.7 centenarians for every 100,000 inhabitants, the highest ratio in the world. In comparison, Canada has about 14.7 centenarians for every 100,000 residents. The life expectancy in Okinawa is 81.2 years (86 for women, 78 for men), also the highest in the world.

What is responsible for such longevity in Okinawa? Some possible explanations include the following (Willcox, Willcox, & Suzuki, 2002; Willcox et al., 2007, 2008):

- *Diet.* Okinawans eat very healthy food, heavy on grains, fish, and vegetables, light on meat, eggs, and dairy products. The risk of dying of cancer is far lower among Okinawans than among Japanese and Canadians. About 100,000 Okinawans moved to Brazil and quickly adopted the eating regimen of their new home, one heavy on red meat. The result: the life expectancy of the Brazilian Okinawans is now 17 years lower than Okinawa's 81 years!

- *Low-stress lifestyle.* The easygoing lifestyle in Okinawa more closely resembles that of a laid-back South Sea island than that of the high-stress world on the Japanese mainland.

- *Caring community.* Okinawans look out for each other and do not isolate or ignore their older adults. If older adults need help, they don't hesitate to ask a neighbour. Such support and caring is likely responsible for Okinawa having the lowest suicide rate among older women in East Asia, an area noted for its high suicide rate among older women.

- *Activity.* Many older adults in Okinawa are active, engaging in such activities as taking walks and working in their gardens. Many older Okinawans also continue working at their jobs.

- *Spirituality.* Many older adults in Okinawa find a sense of purpose in spiritual matters. Prayer is commonplace and believed to ease the mind of stress and problems.

consideration of aging has to do with function; that is, how well people can perform activities of daily living (ADL). These activities include meal preparation, general housekeeping, ability to handle finances, social life, grocery shopping, heavy domestic work, and mobility outside the home (Doupe et al., 2011).

Although a disproportionate number of centenarians are women, men are more likely to be healthier than women (Terry et al., 2008). One explanation for this gender difference in centenarians' health is that to reach this exceptional age, men may need to be in excellent health (Perls, 2007). By contrast, women may be more adaptive to living with illnesses when they are older, and thus can reach an exceptional old age in spite of having a chronic disability.

Clearly, genes play an important role in surviving to an extremely old age; however, there is no single "longevity gene." Rather, a very complex combination of genetic factors contribute to longevity (Sebastiani et al., 2012). But there are also other factors at work, such as family history, health (weight, diet, smoking, and exercise), education, personality, and lifestyle (Rudin et al., 2007). Environmental factors play an important role in the life expectancy of Seventh-Day Adventists, a religious group whose life expectancy on average is 88, considerably higher than the overall Canadian average (Sebastiani et al., 2012).

What about you? What chance do you have of living to be 100? To find out, see Figure 17.1. According to the items in Figure 17.1, among the most important factors in longevity are heredity and family history, health (weight, diet, smoking, and exercise), education, personality, and lifestyle. To read further about living to a very old age, see the Connecting Development to Life feature.

The rapid growth in the 85- and 100-year-old age categories suggests that some potentially important changes might lie ahead:

- Even if it is still an option, retiring at 65 might be too young for many of tomorrow's older adults.
- Increasing health and longer productivity of the elderly might offset some of the economic burden that planners have long assumed will exist for a greying North America.
- Society's dismal view of old age might get a needed push toward a more positive image.

Figure 17.1

Can You Live to Be 100?

This test gives you a rough guide for predicting your longevity. The basic life expectancy for males is age 79, and for females is 83. Write down your basic life expectancy. If you are in your fifties or sixties, you should add ten years to the basic figure because you have already proved yourself to be a durable individual. If you are over age 60 and active, you can add another two years.

LIFE EXPECTANCY

Decide how each item applies to you and add or subtract the appropriate number of years from your basic life expectancy.

1. Family history

_____ Add five years if two or more of your grandparents lived to 80 or beyond.

_____ Subtract four years if any parent, grandparent, sister, or brother died of a heart attack or stroke before 50.

_____ Subtract two years if anyone died from these diseases before 60.

_____ Subtract three years for each case of diabetes, thyroid disorder, breast cancer, cancer of the digestive system, asthma, or chronic bronchitis among parents or grandparents.

2. Marital status

_____ If you are married, add four years.

_____ If you are over 25 and not married, subtract one year for every unmarried decade.

3. Economic status

_____ Add two years if your family income is over $60,000 per year.

_____ Subtract three years if you have been poor for the greater part of your life.

4. Physique

_____ Subtract one year for every ten pounds you are overweight.

_____ For each inch your girth measurement exceeds your chest measurement, deduct two years.

_____ Add three years if you are over 40 and not overweight.

5. Exercise

_____ Add three years if you exercise regularly and moderately (jogging three times a week).

_____ Add five years if you exercise regularly and vigorously (long-distance running three times a week).

_____ Subtract three years if your job is sedentary.

_____ Add three years if your job is active.

6. Alcohol

_____ Add two years if you are a light drinker (one to three drinks a day).

_____ Subtract five to ten years if you are a heavy drinker (more than four drinks per day).

_____ Subtract one year if you are a teetotaler.

7. Smoking

_____ Subtract eight years if you smoke two or more packs of cigarettes per day.

_____ Subtract two years if you smoke one to two packs per day.

_____ Subtract two years if you smoke less than one pack.

_____ Subtract two years if you regularly smoke a pipe or cigars.

8. Disposition

_____ Add two years if you are a reasoned, practical person.

_____ Subtract two years if you are aggressive, intense, and competitive.

_____ Add one to five years if you are basically happy and content with life.

_____ Subtract one to five years if you are often unhappy, worried, and often feel guilty.

9. Education

_____ Subtract two years if you have less than a high school education.

_____ Add one year if you attended four years of school beyond high school.

_____ Add three years if you attended five or more years beyond high school.

10. Environment

_____ Add four years if you have lived most of your life in a rural environment.

_____ Subtract two years if you have lived most of your life in an urban environment.

11. Sleep

_____ Subtract five years if you sleep more than nine hours a day.

12. Temperature

_____ Add two years if your home's thermostat is set at no more than 68°F.

13. Health care

_____ Add three years if you have regular medical checkups and regular dental care.

_____ Subtract two years if you are frequently ill.

_____ Your Life Expectancy Total

SECTION 9 | Late Adulthood   **477**

The Young Old, the Old Old, and the Oldest Old

Late adulthood, which begins in the sixties and extends to approximately 120 to 125 years of age, has potentially the longest span of any period of human development—50 to 60 years. The combination of the lengthy span and the dramatic increase in the number of adults living to older ages has led to increased interest in differentiating the late adulthood period. Most of the demarcations involve two sub-periods, although exact agreement on the age cut-offs for the sub-periods has not been reached. Some developmentalists distinguish between the *young old* (65 to 74 years of age) and the *old old* or *old age* (75 years and older) (Charness & Bosman, 1992). Yet others distinguish the *oldest old* (85 years and older) from younger older adults (65 to 84 years of age) (Dunkle, 2009). Many experts on aging, however, prefer to talk about such categories as the young old, old old, and oldest old in terms of function rather than age. In Chapter 1, we described age not only in terms of chronological age, but also in terms of biological age, psychological age, mental age, and social age. Thus, in terms of functional age—the person's actual ability to function—an 85-year-old might well be more biologically and psychologically fit than a 65-year-old.

Still, significant differences exist between adults in their sixties and seventies and those over 85 (Dunkle, 2009). As we discussed in Chapter 1, Paul Baltes and his colleagues (Baltes, 2003; Scheibe, Freund, & Baltes, 2007) argue that the oldest-olds (85 and over) face a number of problems, including sizable losses in cognitive potential and ability to learn; an increase in chronic stress; a sizable prevalence of physical and mental disabilities; high levels of frailty; increased loneliness; and the difficulty of dying with dignity at older ages. According to Baltes (2003; Scheibe, Freund, & Baltes, 2007), when compared with the oldest old, the young old have a substantial potential for physical and cognitive fitness, higher levels of emotional well-being, and more effective strategies for mastering the gains and losses of old age.

As noted earlier, the oldest old are much more likely to be female. They also have a much higher rate of morbidity and a far greater incidence of disability than do the young old. Today's oldest old are much more likely to be living in institutions, less likely to be married, and more likely to have low educational attainment. Their needs, capacities, and resources are often different from those in their sixties and seventies (Scheibe, Freund, & Baltes, 2007).

The Robust Oldest Old

A substantial portion of the oldest old function effectively. Society's preoccupation with the disability and mortality of the oldest old has concealed the fact that the majority of adults aged 80 and over continue to live in the community. Sixty-five percent of women over the age of 85 live outside institutions, while 77 percent of men in this age group live outside institutions. Twenty-two percent of seniors over the age of 85 live alone. Sixty-three percent rate their general health as good, 43 percent say they are independent in their daily living activities, and 95 percent rate their mental health as good (Shields & Martel, 2005). Shields and Martel found that exercise, moderate alcohol consumption, good nutrition, and low stress levels contribute significantly to positive physical and mental health ratings later in life and for speedy successful recovery from injury and illness.

Biological Theories of Aging

Even if we stay remarkably healthy throughout our adult lives, we begin to age at some point. Life-span experts even argue that biological aging actually begins at birth (Schaie, 2000). What are the biological explanations for aging? Intriguing explanations of why we age are provided by five biological theories: evolutionary theory, cellular clock theory, free-radical theory, mitochondrial theory, and hormonal stress theory.

Evolutionary Theory

Recall from Chapter 2 the view that the benefits conferred by evolutionary selection decrease with age (Baltes, 2003). In the evolutionary theory of aging, natural selection has not eliminated many harmful conditions and nonadaptive characteristics in older adults (Austad, 2009). Why? Because

(a) Frenchwoman Jeanne Louise Calment died at the age of 122. Greater ages have been claimed, but scientists say the maximum human life span is between 120 and 125. *(b)* Heredity is an important component of how long we will live. For example, in Figure 17.1 you were able to add five years to your life expectancy if two or more of your grandparents lived to 80 or beyond. And if you were born a female, you get to start out with a basic life expectancy that is seven years longer than if you were born a male. The three sisters shown above are all in their eighties.

- - - - - developmental **connection** - - - - -

Stability vs. Change and Continuity vs. Discontinuity

←- -

natural selection is linked to reproductive fitness, which is present only in the earlier part of adulthood. For example, consider Alzheimer's disease, an irreversible brain disorder, which does not appear until the late middle adulthood or late adulthood years. In evolutionary theory, if Alzheimer's disease occurred earlier in development, it may have been eliminated many centuries ago.

Cellular Clock Theory

In 1965, Leonard Hayflick observed a phenomenon: as cells aged, they divided more slowly until they were no longer able to divide. The Hayflick limit is the foundation of the **cellular clock theory:** *cells do not live forever. They divide a maximum of about 75 to 80 times, but as we age, our cells become increasingly less capable of dividing* until they can no longer divide. On the basis of the ways cells divide, Hayflick places the upper limit of the human life span at about 120 to 125 years of age (Clark, 2011; Hayflick, 1977).

In the last decade, scientists have tried to fill a gap in cellular clock theory (Liew & Norbury, 2009; Sahin & DePhinho, 2010; Zou et al., 2009). Hayflick did not know why cells die. The answer may lie at the tips of chromosomes, at telomeres, which are DNA sequences that cap chromosomes (Davoli, Denchi, & de Lange, 2010; Osterhage & Friedman, 2009). Each time a cell divides, the telomeres become shorter and shorter (see Figure 17.2). After about 70 or 80 replications, the telomeres are dramatically reduced and the cell no longer can reproduce. A recent study revealed that healthy centenarians had longer telomeres than unhealthy centenarians (Terry et al., 2008). Another recent study found that women with higher intakes of vitamins C and E had longer telomeres than women with lower intakes of these vitamins (Xu et al., 2009).

Injecting the enzyme telomerase into human cells grown in the laboratory has been found to substantially extend the life of the cells beyond the approximately 70 to 80 normal cell divisions (Aubert & Lansdorp, 2008). However, telomerase is present in approximately 85 percent of cancerous cells and thus may not produce healthy life extension of cells (Fakhoury, Nimmo, & Autexier, 2007). To capitalize on the high presence of telomerase in cancerous cells, researchers currently are investigating gene therapies that inhibit telomerase and lead to the death of cancerous cells while keeping healthy cells alive (Effros, 2009a; Skordalakes, 2009; Wu et al., 2009).

Free-Radical Theory

A second microbiological theory of aging is the **free-radical theory,** *which states that people age because, when cells metabolize energy, the by-products include unstable oxygen molecules known as free radicals* (Chehab et al., 2008). *These molecules ricochet around the cells, damaging DNA and other cellular structures* (Afanas'ev, 2009). The damage can lead to a range of disorders, including cancer and arthritis (Farooqui & Farooqui, 2009). Overeating is linked with an increase in free radicals, and researchers recently have found that calorie restriction—a diet restricted in calories although adequate in proteins, vitamins, and minerals—reduces the oxidative damage created by free radicals (Keijer & van Schothorst, 2008). And a recent study revealed a greater concentration of free radicals in 20- to 80-year-old smokers than in non-smokers (Thavanati et al., 2008).

Mitochondrial Theory

There is increasing interest in the role that mitochondria—tiny bodies within cells that supply energy for function, growth, and repair—might play in aging (Scheckhuber, 2009). **Mitochondrial theory** *states that aging is due to the decay of mitochondria. It appears that this decay is primarily due to oxidative damage and loss of critical micronutrients supplied by the cell* (Crane et al., 2010; Figueiredo et al., 2009).

How does this damage and loss of nutrients occur? Among the by-products of mitochondrial energy production are the free radicals we just described. According to the mitochondrial theory, the damage caused by free radicals initiates a self-perpetuating cycle in which oxidative damage impairs mitochondrial function, which results in the generation of even greater amounts of free radicals. The result is that over time, the affected mitochondria become so inefficient that they cannot generate enough energy to meet cellular needs. Defects in mitochondria are linked with cardiovascular

cellular clock theory Leonard Hayflick's theory that cells can divide a maximum of about 75 to 80 times, and that as we age, our cells become increasingly less capable of dividing.

Figure 17.2
Telomeres and Aging
The photograph shows actual telomeres lighting up the tips of chromosomes.

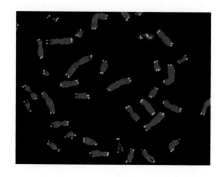

free-radical theory A microbiological theory of aging that states that people age because inside their cells' normal metabolism produces unstable oxygen molecules known as free radicals. These molecules ricochet around inside cells, damaging DNA and other cellular structures.

mitochondrial theory States that aging is due to the decay of mitochondria. It appears that this decay is primarily due to oxidative damage and loss of critical micronutrients supplied by the cell.

hormonal stress theory States that aging in the body's hormonal system can lower resilience to stress and increase the likelihood of disease.

- - - - - **critical** thinking - - - - -

As you have just read, more and more people are living to be centenarians and women outnumber men by five to one. Why do you think women live longer than men? Are there any societal changes that could be made to enable men to live longer? If so, what? Imagine that you live to be a centenarian. What do you think your life would be like? What might be some of the joys? Some of the challenges?

The Aging Brain

The Immune System

Physical Appearance and Movement

Sensory Development

The Circulatory System and Lungs

Sexuality

disease, neurodegenerative diseases such as dementia, and decline in liver functioning (Bueler, 2010; Kim, Wei, & Sowers, 2008). Mitochondria likely play important roles in neural plasticity (Mattson, 2007). However, it is not known whether the defects in mitochondria cause aging or are merely accompaniments of the aging process (Van Remmen & Jones, 2009).

Hormonal Stress Theory

The first four biological theories of aging—evolutionary, cellular clock, free-radical, and mitochondrial—focus on changes at the cellular level. A fifth biological theory of aging emphasizes changes at the hormonal level. **Hormonal stress theory** *states that aging in the body's hormonal system can lower resilience to stress and increase the likelihood of disease* (Finch & Seeman, 1999).

Normally, when people experience stressors, the body responds by releasing certain hormones. As people age, the hormones stimulated by stress remain at elevated levels longer than when people were younger. These prolonged, elevated levels of stress-related hormones are associated with increased risks for many diseases, including cardiovascular disease, cancer, diabetes, and hypertension (Epel, 2009; Wolkowitz et al., 2010).

Recently, a variation of hormonal stress theory has emphasized the contribution of a decline in immune system functioning with aging (Effros, 2009b; Swain & Nikolich-Zugich, 2009; Walston et al., 2009). Aging contributes to immune system deficits that give rise to infectious diseases in older adults (Suvas, 2008). The extended duration of stress and diminished restorative processes in older adults may accelerate the effects of aging on immunity.

Which of these biological theories best explains aging? That question has not yet been answered. It might turn out that all of these biological processes are involved in aging.

To this point, we have examined a number of ideas about longevity and biological theories of aging. For a review, see the **Reach Your Learning Objectives** section at the end of this chapter.

The Course of Physical Development in Late Adulthood

LO2 Describe and give examples of how a person's brain and body change in late adulthood.

The physical decline that accompanies aging usually occurs slowly, and sometimes even lost function can be restored. We'll examine the main physical changes behind the losses of late adulthood and describe ways that older adults can age successfully.

The Aging Brain

How does the brain change during late adulthood? Does it retain plasticity? The change in the brain's abilities to perceive sensations, process information, create and retain memories, and accommodate new information is very gradual, unless an individual suffers from a stroke or other debilitating disease or accident. The healthy brain can plan, analyze, and organize information skillfully; further, the healthy, albeit aging, brain is able to draw on a lifetime of experience in planning, analyzing, and organizing information and make wise and valid judgments. In this way, the aging brain may even gain a bit or outperform a more youthful brain (Sweeney, 2009).

The Shrinking, Slowing Brain

On average, the brain loses 5 to 10 percent of its weight between the ages of 20 and 90. Brain volume also decreases (Bondare, 2007). One recent study found that the volume of the brain was 15 percent less in older adults than younger adults (Shan et al., 2005). Scientists are not sure why these changes occur, but believe they might result from a decrease in dendrites, damage to the myelin sheath that covers axons, or simply the death of brain cells. However, the current consensus is that under normal conditions adults are unlikely to lose brain cells per se (Nelson, 2008).

Some areas shrink more than others (Raz et al., 2010). The prefrontal cortex is one area that shrinks with aging, and recent research has linked this shrinkage with a decrease in working memory and other cognitive activities in older adults (Pardo et al., 2007; Sakatini, Tanida, & Katsuyama, 2010).

A general slowing of function in the brain and spinal cord begins in middle adulthood and accelerates in late adulthood (Birren, 2002). This slowdown can affect physical coordination and intellectual performance. After age 70, many adults no longer show a knee-jerk reflex, and by age 90, most reflexes are virtually gone (Spence, 1989). The slowing of central nervous system functioning can impair the performance of older adults on intelligence tests, especially timed tests (Birren, Woods, & Williams, 1980). For example, one neuroimaging study revealed that older adults were more likely to be characterized by slower processing in the prefrontal cortex during retrieval of information on a cognitive task than were younger adults (Rypma, Eldreth, & Rebbechi, 2007).

Aging has also been linked to a reduction in the production of some neurotransmitters, including acetylcholine, dopamine, and gamma-aminobutyric acid (GABA) (Jagust & D'Esposito, 2009; Lester, Rogers, & Blaha, 2010). Some researchers believe that reductions in acetylcholine may be responsible for small declines in memory functioning, and even with the severe memory loss associated with Alzheimer's disease, which we discuss later in the chapter (Bentley, Driver, & Dolan, 2009; Daulatzai, 2010). Normal age-related reductions in dopamine may cause problems in planning and carrying out motor activities (Lester, Rogers, & Blaha, 2010). Severe reductions in the production of dopamine have been linked with age-related diseases characterized by a loss of motor control, such as Parkinson's disease (Brooks, 2010; Mena et al., 2009). GABA helps to control the preciseness of the signal sent from one neuron to another, decreasing "noise," and its production decreases with aging (Yuan, 2008).

The Adapting Brain

If the brain were a computer, this description of the aging brain might lead you to think that it could not do much of anything. However, unlike a computer, the brain has remarkable repair capability (Jessberger & Gage, 2010; Prakash, Snook, & Kramer, 2010). Even in late adulthood, the brain loses only a portion of its ability to function, and the activities older adults engage in can influence the brain's development (Erickson et al., 2009). For example, in a recent fMRI study, higher levels of aerobic fitness were linked with greater volume in the hippocampus, which translates into better memory (Erickson et al., 2009). Like other muscles, an exercise routine is vital to maintaining the brain's fitness; in fact, with exercise, the brain may actually improve with use (Sweeney, 2009).

Researchers have found that **neurogenesis,** *the generation of new neurons,* does occur in lower mammalian species, such as mice (Marlatt et al., 2010). Also, research indicates that exercise and an enriched, complex environment can generate new brain cells in mice, and that stress reduces their survival rate (Segovia, Arco, & Mora, 2009). Researchers recently have discovered that if rats are cognitively challenged to learn something, new brain cells survive longer (Shors, 2009).

It also is now accepted that neurogenesis can occur in humans (Aimone, Wiles, & Gage, 2009; Hagg, 2009). However, researchers have documented neurogenesis in only two brain regions: the hippocampus, which is involved in memory, and the olfactory bulb, which is involved in smell (Arenkiel, 2010; Zou et al., 2010). It also is not known what functions these new brain cells perform, and at this point researchers have documented that they last for only several weeks (Nelson, 2006). Researchers currently are studying factors that might inhibit and promote neurogenesis, including various drugs, stress, and exercise (Gil-Mohapel et al., 2010; van Praag, 2009). They also are examining how the grafting of neural stem cells to various regions of the brain, such as the hippocampus, might increase neurogenesis (Farin et al., 2009; Szulwach et al., 2010).

Dendritic growth can occur in human adults, possibly even in older adults (Eliasieh, Liets, & Chalupa, 2007). Recall from Chapter 4, "Physical Development in Infancy," that dendrites are the receiving portion of the neuron. One study compared the brains of adults at various ages (Coleman,

developmental **connection**

Stability vs. Change

neurogenesis The generation of new neurons.

---- **Figure 17.3**

The Decrease in Brain Lateralization in Older Adults

Younger adults primarily use the right prefrontal region of the brain (top left photo) during a recall memory task, while older adults use both the left and right prefrontal regions (bottom two photos) (Madden et al., 1999)

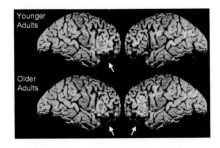

- - - developmental **connection** - -

Continuity vs. Discontinuity

---- **Figure 17.4**

The Brains of the Mankato Nuns

Sister Marcella Zachman (left) stopped teaching at age 97. At 99, she helps ailing nuns exercise their brains by quizzing them on vocabulary or playing a card game called Skip-Bo, at which she deliberately loses. Sister Mary Esther Boor (right), also 99 years of age, is a former teacher who stays alert by doing puzzles and volunteering to work the front desk. The nuns donate their brains for research that explores the effects of stimulation on brain growth.

1986). From the forties through the seventies, the growth of dendrites increased. However, in people in their nineties, dendritic growth no longer occurred. This dendritic growth might compensate for the possible loss of neurons through the seventies but not in the nineties. Lack of dendritic growth in older adults could be due to a lack of environmental stimulation and activity. Further research is needed to clarify what changes characterize dendrites during aging.

Stanley Rapaport (1994), chief of the neurosciences laboratory at the National Institute on Aging, demonstrated another way in which the aging brain can adapt. He compared the brains of younger and older people engaged in the same tasks. The older brains had rewired themselves to compensate for losses. If one neuron was not up to the job, neighbouring neurons helped to pick up the slack. Rapaport concluded that as brains age, they can shift responsibilities for a given task from one region to another.

Changes in lateralization may provide one type of adaptation in aging adults (Angel et al., 2009; Zhu, Zacks, & Slade, 2010). Recall that lateralization is the specialization of function in one hemisphere of the brain or the other. Using neuroimaging techniques, researchers recently found that brain activity in the prefrontal cortex is lateralized less in older adults than in younger adults when they are engaging in cognitive tasks (Cabeza, 2002; Rossi et al., 2005). For example, Figure 17.3 shows that when younger adults are given the task of recognizing words they have previously seen, they process the information primarily in the right hemisphere; older adults are more likely to use both hemispheres (Madden et al., 1999). The decrease in lateralization in older adults might play a compensatory role in the aging brain. That is, using both hemispheres may improve the cognitive functioning of older adults.

Of course, individual differences exist in how the brain changes in older adults (Raz et al., 2010). Consider the successful businessman 80-year-old T. Boone Pickens, who continues to lead a highly active lifestyle, regularly exercising and engaging in cognitively complex work. Pickens recently underwent an fMRI in cognitive neuroscientist Denise Park's laboratory, during which he was presented with various cognitive tasks. Instead of both hemispheres being active, his left hemisphere was still dominant, just as is the case for most younger adults (Helman, 2008). Indeed, as the cognitive tasks became more complex, the more Pickens used the left hemisphere of his brain (see Figure 17.3). Does staying intellectually challenged affect one's quality of life and longevity? To read further about aging and the brain, see Connections through Research.

The Immune System

Decline in the functioning of the body's immune system with aging is well documented (Agarwal & Busse, 2010). As we indicated earlier in our discussion of hormonal stress theory, the extended duration of stress and diminished restorative processes in older adults may accelerate the effects of aging on immunity (Zitvogel, Kepp, & Kroemer, 2010). Also, malnutrition involving low levels of protein is linked to a decrease in T-cells that destroy infected cells and hence to deterioration in the immune system (Hughes, 2010). Exercise can improve immune system functioning (De la Fuente & Gimenez-Llort, 2010; Sakamoto et al., 2009). Because of the decline in the functioning of their immune systems, vaccination against influenza is especially important in older adults (Maggi, 2010; Michel, 2010).

Physical Appearance and Movement

In Chapter 15, "Physical and Cognitive Development in Middle Adulthood," we pointed out some changes in physical appearance that take place. The changes are most noticeable in the form of facial wrinkles and age spots.

We also get shorter when we get older. Our weight usually drops after we reach 60 years of age. This likely occurs because we lose muscle, which also gives our bodies a more "sagging" look (Evans, 2010).

Older adults move more slowly than young adults, and this slowing occurs for movements with a wide range of difficulty (Sakuma & Yamaguchi, 2010). Even when they perform everyday tasks

Does Staying Intellectually Challenged Affect One's Quality of Life and Longevity?

The Nun Study, directed by David Snowdon, is an intriguing ongoing investigation of aging initiated in 1986 (Sweeney, 2009) (see Figure 17.4). Initially, 678 nuns residing in a convent in Mankato, Minnesota, participated; the nuns are the largest group of brain donors in the world. As of 2009, 50 of the original nuns, many centenarians, remain in the study (Sweeney, 2009). Examination of the nuns' donated brains, as well as others, has led neuroscientists to believe that the brain has a remarkable capacity to change and grow, even in old age. The Sisters of Notre Dame in Mankato led an intellectually challenging life and shared many commonalities. For example, they maintained detailed personal and collective records, ate a nutritious diet, were unmarried, had access to health care, and lived in a safe and clean environment (Sweeney, 2009). Brain researchers believe these factors contribute to their quality of life as older adults and possibly to their longevity.

Findings from the Nun Study so far include:

- Idea density, a measure of linguistic ability assessed early in the adult years (age 22), was linked with higher brain weight, fewer incidences of mild cognitive impairment, and fewer characteristics of Alzheimer's disease in 75- to 95-year-old nuns (Riley et al., 2005).
- Positive emotions early in adulthood were linked to longevity (Danner, Snowdon, & Friesen, 2001). Handwritten autobiographies from 180 nuns, composed when they were 22 years of age, were scored for emotional content. The nuns whose early writings had higher scores for positive emotional content were more likely to still be alive at 75 to 95 years of age than their counterparts whose early writings were characterized by negative emotional content.
- Sisters who had taught for most of their lives showed more moderate declines in intellectual skills than those who had spent most of their lives in service-based tasks, which supports the notion that stimulating the brain with intellectual activity keeps neurons alive and healthy (Snowdon, 2002).
- Sisters with high levels of folic acid showed little evidence of Alzheimer-like damage to their brain after death.

Analysis of the brains indicated that some showed signs of disease, yet the nuns did not exhibit symptoms of the disease while alive (Sweeney, 2009). This and other research provides hope that scientists will discover ways to tap into the brain's capacity to adapt in order to prevent and treat brain diseases. For example, scientists might learn more effective ways to help older adults recover from strokes (Carter et al., 2010; Saur et al., 2010). Even when areas of the brain are permanently damaged by stroke, new message routes can be created to get around the blockage or to resume the function of that area.

such as reaching and grasping, moving from one place to another, and continuous movement, older adults tend to move more slowly than when they were young (Mollenkopf, 2007).

Adequate mobility is an important aspect of maintaining an independent and active lifestyle in late adulthood (Clark et al., 2010; Webber, Porter, & Menec, 2010). One recent study of the functional ability of non-institutionalized individuals 70 years of age and older revealed that over an eight-year period, the most deterioration occurred in their mobility (Holstein et al., 2007). Another study revealed that obesity was linked to mobility limitation in older adults (Houston et al., 2009). The good news is that regular walking decreases the onset of physical disability in older adults (Newman et al., 2006). Also, exercise and appropriate weight lifting can help to reduce the decrease in muscle mass and improve the older person's body appearance (Peterson et al., 2009; Venturelli et al., 2010; Weiss et al., 2010). And a recent study revealed that it is not just physical exercise that is linked to preserving older adults' motor functions; in this study, engaging in social activities protected against loss of motor abilities (Buchman et al., 2009).

Sensory Development

Sensory changes in late adulthood involve vision, hearing, taste, smell, touch, and pain. These senses are linked to our ability to perform everyday activities (Cimarolli, 2009; Wood et al., 2010). This link was documented in a study of more than 500 adults 70 to 102 years of age, in which sensory acuity, especially vision, was related to whether and how well older adults bathed and groomed themselves, completed household chores, engaged in intellectual activities, and watched TV (Marsiske, Klumb, & Baltes, 1997). How do vision, hearing, taste, smell, touch, and pain change in late adulthood?

- - - **critical** thinking - - - - - - - - - - - - - - -

How does a person age gracefully? Think of the people you know who are in late adulthood. Would you classify their functioning levels as "young old," "old old," or "oldest old"? Why? Apart from physical exercise, what can you do to prepare for a positive experience of physical aging?

Vision

With aging, visual acuity, colour vision, and depth perception decline. Several diseases of the eye may emerge in aging adults. In late adulthood, the decline in vision that began for most of us in early or middle adulthood becomes more pronounced (Dillon et al., 2010; Lindenberger & Ghisletta, 2009). Night driving is especially difficult, to some extent because tolerance for glare diminishes (Babizhayev, Minasyan, & Richer, 2009; Wood et al., 2010). *Dark adaptation* is slower, meaning that older individuals take longer to recover their vision when going from well-lighted rooms to semi-darkness. The area of the visual field becomes smaller, suggesting that a stimulus's intensity in the peripheral area of the visual field needs to be increased if the stimulus is to be seen. Events taking place away from the centre of the visual field may not be detected (Stutts, 2007). Furthermore, colour vision and depth perception typically decline in late adulthood (Scialfa & Kline, 2007; Stutts, 2007).

This visual decline often can be traced to reduction in the quality or intensity of light reaching the retina. At 60 years of age, the retina receives only about one-third as much light as it did at 20 years of age (Scialfa & Kline, 2007). In extreme old age, these changes may be accompanied by degenerative changes in the retina, causing severe difficulty in seeing. Large-print books and magnifiers may be needed in such cases.

DISEASES OF THE EYE   Cataracts, glaucoma, and macular degeneration are three diseases that can impair the vision of older adults.

- *Cataracts* involve a thickening of the lens of the eye, which causes vision to become cloudy, opaque, and distorted (Sugimoto, Kuze, & Uji, 2008). By age 70, approximately 30 percent of individuals experience a partial loss of vision due to cataracts. If individuals have access, surgery to remove cataracts is usually very successful.
- *Glaucoma* involves damage to the optic nerve because of pressure created by a buildup of fluid in the eye (Fechtner et al., 2010; Jampel et al., 2009). If untreated, glaucoma can destroy vision. It is a problem for 1 percent of individuals in their seventies and 10 percent of individuals in their nineties (Musch et al., 2009). Special eye drops can be used to treat glaucoma.
- *Macular degeneration* is a disease involving deterioration of the retina that corresponds to the focal centre of the visual field. Individuals with macular degeneration may have relatively normal peripheral vision, but be unable to see clearly what is right in front of them (Ghosh et al., 2010; Rovner et al., 2009). This affects one in 25 individuals from 66 to 74 years of age, and one in six who are older. One study revealed that cigarette smoking is a contributing factor in macular degeneration (Schmidt et al., 2006). If the disease is detected early, it can be treated with laser surgery (Fleckenstein et al., 2010; Sorensen & Kemp, 2010). Macular degeneration is difficult to treat and is a leading cause of blindness in older adults.

Hearing

Although hearing impairment can begin in middle adulthood, it usually does not become much of an impediment until late adulthood (Fozard, 2000). In Canada, 55 percent of people over the age of 12 who have a hearing problem are over the age of 65 (Millar, 2005). Almost a quarter of those individuals over the age of 80 are hearing impaired. Hearing impairments are more common among senior men than women, at 12 percent versus 9 percent, respectively. Many older adults don't recognize that they have a hearing problem, while others deny that they have one or accept it as a part of growing old (Fowler & Leigh-Paffenroth, 2007). Older women are more likely to seek treatment for their hearing problem than are older men (Fowler & Leigh-Paffenroth, 2007).

Two devices can be used to minimize the problems linked to hearing loss in older adults: (1) hearing aids that amplify sound to reduce middle ear–based conductive hearing loss, and (2) cochlear implants that restore some hearing following neurosensory hearing loss (Pauley et al., 2008). Two-thirds of those with a hearing problem have some form of correction, while one-third either do not seek correction or have no current correction available (Millar, 2005). Researchers are currently exploring the use of stem cells as an alternative to the use of cochlear implants (Pauley et al., 2008).

Figure 17.5

Vision and Hearing Decline in Old Age and Late Old Age

Perceptual System	Old Age (65–74 Years)	Late Old Age (75 Years and Older)
Vision	There is a loss of acuity even with corrective lenses. Less transmission of light occurs through the retina (half as much as in young adults). Greater susceptibility to glare occurs. Colour discrimination ability decreases.	There is a significant loss of visual acuity and colour discrimination, and a decrease in the size of the perceived visual field. In late old age, people are at significant risk for visual dysfunction from cataracts and glaucoma.
Hearing	There is a significant loss of hearing at high frequencies and some loss at middle frequencies. These losses can be helped by a hearing aid. There is greater susceptibility for background noises to mask what is heard.	There is a significant loss at high and middle frequencies. A hearing aid is more likely to be needed than in old age.

Earlier, we indicated that life-span developmentalists are increasingly making distinctions between the young old or old age (ages 65 to 74) and the old old or late old age (75 years and older). This distinction is important when considering the degree of decline in various perceptual systems. As indicated in Figure 17.5, the decline in the perceptual systems of vision and hearing is much greater in late old age than in young old age (Charness & Bosman, 1992).

Smell and Taste

Most older adults lose some of their sense of smell or taste, or both (Roberts & Rosenberg, 2006). These losses often begin around 60 years of age (Hawkes, 2006). Researchers have found that older adults show a greater decline in their sense of smell than in their taste (Schiffman, 2007). Smell and taste decline less in healthy older adults than in their less-healthy counterparts.

Reductions in the ability to smell and taste can reduce enjoyment of food and life satisfaction (Rolls & Drewnowski, 2007). Also, a decline in the sense of smell can reduce the ability to detect smoke from a fire. If elderly individuals need to be encouraged to eat more, compounds that stimulate the olfactory nerve are sometimes added to food. However, many older adults compensate for their diminished taste and smell by eating sweeter, spicier, and saltier foods, which can lead to eating more low-nutrient, highly seasoned "junk food" (Hoyer & Roodin, 2009). Further, a recent study of 19 to 39, 40 to 59, and 60-year-old and older adults revealed that although adults' ability to detect a smell declines as they get older, the perceived pleasantness of a smell increases in the older group (Markovic et al., 2007).

Touch and Pain

Changes in touch and pain are also associated with aging (Gagliese, 2009; Schmader et al., 2010). One study found that with aging, individuals could detect touch less in the lower extremities (ankles, knees, and so on) than in the upper extremities (wrists, shoulders, and so on) (Corso, 1977). For most older adults, a decline in touch sensitivity is not problematic (Hoyer & Roodin, 2009). And a recent study revealed that older adults who are blind retain a high level of touch sensitivity, which likely is linked to their use of active touch in their daily lives (Legge et al., 2008).

Older adults are less sensitive to pain and suffer less from it than younger adults do (Harkins, Price, & Martinelli, 1986). Although decreased sensitivity to pain can help older adults cope with disease and injury, it can be harmful if it masks injury and illness that need to be treated.

critical thinking

Imagine yourself giving a talk to a group of people in middle adulthood about aging after age 60. Using the information you have just read, construct a list of the five key physical changes or occurrences you would tell them they were most likely to experience in late adulthood. What would you suggest they do to counteract any problems in these areas?

The Circulatory System and Lungs

Every seven minutes, someone in Canada dies of heart disease or stroke. As alarming as this may seem, the number represents a decline of over 40 percent in the last decade due to advances in research and improved surgical procedures, drug therapies, and prevention programs. What are cardiovascular diseases (CVD)? Cardiovascular diseases are diseases or injuries of the heart, the blood vessels in the heart, and the veins and arteries throughout the body and within the brain. Stroke, a form of CVD, is the result of a blood flow problem in the brain (Heart and Stroke Foundation, 2013). CVDs are chronic, lifelong diseases caused by the interaction of genetic predisposition, behaviours, and environment. These diseases increase in late adulthood (Ballard, 2010; PHAC, 2009d; Prystowsky et al., 2010). According to Public Health Agency of Canada (PHAC), approximately 14.8 percent of seniors between 65 and 74 years of age report having heart disease. For those over 75 years, the percentage climbs to 22.9 percent (PHAC, 2009d).

Today, most experts on aging recommend that consistent blood pressures above 120/80 should be treated to reduce the risk of heart attack, stroke, or kidney disease (Krakoff, 2008). Blood pressure can rise with age because of illness, obesity, anxiety, stiffening of blood vessels, or lack of exercise (Shizukuda, Plummer, & Harrelson, 2010). The longer any of these factors persists, the worse the individual's blood pressure gets (Miura et al., 2009). One recent study revealed that exercise capacity and walking were the best predictors of earlier death in older adults with heart problems (Reibis et al., 2010).

It is important to note that CVD can be prevented by not smoking, regular physical activity, healthy nutrition, healthy weight, early recognition of high blood pressure and high cholesterol, and effective stress management (PHAC, 2009d).

Lung capacity drops 40 percent between the ages of 20 and 80, even without disease (Fozard, 1992). Lungs lose elasticity, the chest shrinks, and the diaphragm weakens (Cherniack & Cherniack, 2007). The good news, though, is that older adults can improve lung functioning with diaphragm strengthening exercises. Severe impairments in lung functioning and death can result from smoking (Whincup et al., 2006).

Seniors are more vulnerable to respiratory infections caused by the influenza virus. Consequently, Health Canada advises that people, especially older adults, obtain flu vaccinations each fall and wash their hands carefully as safeguards to becoming infected. Vaccinations are recommended in the fall because the flu season is from November to April (PHAC, 2012).

Sexuality

In the absence of two circumstances—disease and stereotyping of seniors as asexual—sexuality can be lifelong (Woloski-Wruble et al., 2010). Aging does induce some changes in human sexual performance, more so in men than women (Bauman, 2008). Orgasm becomes less frequent in males, occurring in every second to third act of intercourse, rather than every time. More direct stimulation usually is needed to produce an erection.

A recent interview study of more than 3,000 adults 57 to 85 years of age revealed that many older adults are sexually active as long as they are healthy (Lindau et al., 2007). Sexual activity did decline through the later years of life: 73 percent of 57- to 64-year-olds, 53 percent of 65- to 74-year-olds, and 26 percent 75- to 85-year-olds reported that they were sexually active. Even in the sexually active oldest group (75 to 85), more than 50 percent said they still have sex at least two to three times a month. Fifty-eight percent of sexually active 65- to 74-year-olds and 31 percent of 75- to 85-year-olds said they engage in oral sex.

As with middle-aged and younger adults, older adults who did not have a partner were far less likely to be sexually active than those who had a partner. For older adults with a partner who reported not having sex, the main reason was poor health, especially the male partner's physical health. Various therapies for older adults who report sexual difficulties have been effective (Bain, 2010; Malatesta, 2007). Even when intercourse is impaired by infirmity, other relationship needs persist, among them closeness, sensuality, and being valued as a man or a woman (Brock & Jennings, 2007; Hurd Clarke, 2006).

developmental **connection**

Stability vs. Change

To this point we have discussed a number of ideas about the course of physical development in late adulthood. For a review, see the **Reach Your Learning Objectives** section at the end of this chapter.

Physical and Mental Health and Wellness

LO3 Identify factors of health and wellness in late adulthood.

How healthy are older adults? What types of health problems do they have? As we discuss the health of older adults, you will see that there are more healthy older adults than we used to imagine. As noted earlier in the chapter, seniors comprise a larger percentage of the population: 14 percent of us are over 65, up from 9 percent in the previous census. Immigrants account for 28 percent of the senior population, and Aboriginals 1 percent (Public Health Agency of Canada, 2010b). Although seniors experience the impact of chronic conditions, reduced mobility, and sensory functioning, 44 percent perceive their health to be excellent or very good, and 37 percent report taking action such as changing eating habits or increasing physical activity in order to improve their health (PHAC, 2010b).

Health Problems

In Chapter 15, "Physical and Cognitive Development in Middle Adulthood," we defined *chronic disorders* as disorders with a slow onset and a long duration. Chronic diseases are rare in early adulthood, increase in middle adulthood, and become more common in late adulthood.

In 2009, 89 percent of seniors had at least one chronic condition, with arthritis and rheumatism leading the way affecting 44 percent of seniors (PHAC, 2010b). Women were more likely to require assistance with daily activity than men, at 29 percent to 15 percent, respectively. In a study examining chronic pain, Ramage-Morin (2008) found 27 percent of seniors living in private households (as compared with 16 percent of those aged 18 to 64) reported chronic pain. Seniors living in long-term health care facilities were more likely to report chronic pain (38 percent) than seniors living in private households.

Women in late adulthood have a higher incidence of arthritis and hypertension, and are more likely to have visual problems but less likely to have hearing problems than are older men. Low income is also strongly related to health problems in late adulthood (Ferraro, 2006). Approximately three times as many poor as non-poor older adults report that their activities are limited by chronic disorders. Recent studies document links between low socio-economic status and health problems (Friedman & Herd, 2010; Yang & Lee, 2010). One study revealed that frailty increased for low-income older adults, regardless of their ethnicity (Szanton et al., 2010).

Causes of Death in Older Adults

More than two-thirds of all older adults die of heart disease, cancer, or cerebrovascular disease (stroke). Chronic lung diseases, pneumonia and influenza, and diabetes round out the six leading causes of death among older adults. If cancer, the leading cause of death in older adults, were completely eliminated, the average life expectancy would rise by only one to two years. However, if all cardiovascular (the second leading cause of death among seniors) and kidney diseases were eradicated, the average life expectancy of older adults would increase by approximately 10 years. Research following 2,400 seniors between 1994 and 2003 found that for the women in the study, psychological or financial stress were significant predictors of death within the eight-year period (Wilkins, 2006). For men, the two most significant predictors of death within the eight years were chronic disease or widowhood. Men who lived with their wives lived longer than those whose wives had died.

Health Problems

Exercise, Nutrition, and Weight

The Nature of Mental Health in Late Adulthood

Dementia, Alzheimer's Disease, and Related Disorders

Health Promotion

Arthritis

arthritis An inflammation of the joints accompanied by pain, stiffness, and movement problems.

Arthritis *is an inflammation of the joints accompanied by pain, stiffness, and movement problems.* Statistics Canada (2010) reported that in 2008, 50.6 percent of women over the age of 65 years experienced arthritis or rheumatism, while only 33.8 percent of men aged 65 and older did. Fifty-three percent of Aboriginal seniors living off reserve reported having arthritis or rheumatism (Turcotte & Schellenberg, 2007). Education, physical exercise, diet and weight control along with early recognition and appropriate medical treatment are key to reducing the impact of arthritis (PHAC 2010). Arthritis can affect hips, knees, ankles, fingers, and vertebrae. Individuals with arthritis often experience pain and stiffness, as well as problems in moving about and performing routine daily activities. There is no known cure for arthritis. However, the symptoms of arthritis can be reduced by drugs, such as aspirin, range-of-motion exercises for the afflicted joints, weight reduction, and, in extreme cases, replacement of the crippled joint with a prosthesis (Health Canada, 2003).

Osteoporosis

osteoporosis An aging disorder involving an extensive loss of bone tissue. It is the main reason many older adults walk with a marked stoop.

Normal aging involves some loss of bone tissue from the skeleton. However, in some instances, loss of bone tissue can become severe. **Osteoporosis** *is an aging disorder involving an extensive loss of bone tissue. It is the main reason many older adults walk with a marked stoop.* Women are especially vulnerable to osteoporosis, the leading cause of broken bones in women (Iacono, 2007).

According to the Osteoporosis Society of Canada, fractures, most often hip fractures (approximately 30,000 hip fractures annually), from osteoporosis are more common than heart attack, stroke, and breast cancer combined. At least one in three women and one in five men will suffer from an osteoporotic fracture in their lifetime, and more than 80 percent of all fractures in people over 50 years of age are caused by osteoporosis (Osteoporosis Canada, 2012).

This aging condition is related to deficiencies in calcium, vitamin D, estrogen depletion, and lack of exercise. To prevent osteoporosis, young and middle aged women should eat foods rich in calcium such as broccoli, dairy products, turnip greens, and kale; get more exercise; and avoid smoking (Cashman, 2008; Lanham-New, 2008). Alternatively, drugs, such as Fosamax, can be used to reduce the risk of osteoporosis (Suzuki et al., 2008), but Gillian Sanson (2003) suggests their effectiveness and possible side effects warrant careful reflection before use. Women in late adulthood should also get bone density checks. A program of regular exercise may have the potential to prevent osteoporosis (Schwab & Klein, 2008; Health Canada, 2008).

Accidents

In Canada, falls are the number one external cause of injury and the eighth leading cause of death among people aged 75 and over, sixth for those aged 65 to 74, and third for those aged 55 to 64 (Statistics Canada, 2005). The Public Health Agency of Canada estimates that one in three seniors is likely to fall at least once each year (PHAC, 2010b). Falls are related to risk factors such as disease, arthritis, Parkinson's disease, stroke, and blood pressure disorders as well as physical limitations. Cognitive impairment and alcohol consumption may also contribute to falls (PHAC, 2010b). Falls that occur at home and traffic accidents in which an older adult is the driver or an older pedestrian is hit by a vehicle are common (Aschkenasy & Rothenhaus, 2006). Falls account for 62 percent of all injury-related hospitalizations for seniors (Public Health Agency of Canada, 2005). Over 90 percent of all seniors who fracture their hip do so in a fall. Twenty percent of these hip fracture patients will die within the year as a result of their injury. Among adults who have a hip fracture, the median age is 80 (Carrière, 2007). Carrière found that slips, trips, or stumbles on "surfaces other than snow or ice" accounted for 53 percent of the hip fractures among seniors (p. 37). Seniors who are housebound or living alone are at greater risk for falls, particularly those who, lacking social networks, may undertake higher risk activities, such as climbing a ladder (PHAC, 2010b).

Exercise, Nutrition, and Weight

Can exercise slow the aging process? Can eating a nutritious but calorie-reduced diet increase longevity? Let's examine how exercise, nutrition, and weight might influence how healthily we age.

All we know about older adults indicates that they are healthier and happier when they are more active. Several decades ago, it was believed that older adults should be more passive and inactive to be well-adjusted and satisfied with life. In today's world, we believe that although older adults may be in the evening of their life span, they are not meant to passively live out their remaining years.

Exercise

The benefits of physical exercise for people in late adulthood have been clearly established (Shields et al., 2010; Edwards & Mawani, 2006). These benefits include improved physical and mental health and reduced risks for heart attacks, strokes, falls, injuries, colon and breast cancers, obesity, and back pain. In a recent assessment of fitness in Canadians aged 20 to 69, only 10 percent of men and less than 5 percent of women aged 60 to 69 were ranked as being in very good/excellent aerobic fitness condition (Shields, et al., 2010). Edwards and Mawani (2006) remark that seniors who are socially isolated, Aboriginal, living in institutions, female, from low economic and educational backgrounds, and/or seriously ill or disabled are more likely to have significantly lower activity levels.

In one study, exercise literally meant a difference in life or death for middle-aged and older adults. More than 10,000 men and women were divided into categories of low fitness, medium fitness, and high fitness (Blair et al., 1989). Then they were studied over a period of eight years. Sedentary participants (low fitness) were more than twice as likely to die during the eight-year time span of the study than those who were moderately fit, and they were more than three times as likely to die as those who were highly fit. The positive effects of being physically fit occurred for both men and women in this study. Further, another study revealed that 60-year-old and older adults who were in the lowest fifth in terms of physical fitness as determined by a treadmill test were four times more likely to die over a 12-year period than their counterparts who were in the top fifth of physical fitness (Sui et al., 2007). Also in this study, older adults who were physically fit but overweight had a lower mortality risk over the 12 years than their normal weight counterparts who were low in fitness (Sui et al., 2007). And a longitudinal study found that men who exercised regularly at 72 years of age had a 30 percent higher probability of still being alive at 90 years of age than their sedentary counterparts (Yates et al., 2008).

Gerontologists increasingly recommend strength training in addition to aerobic activity and stretching for older adults (Suetta et al., 2008). The average person's lean body mass declines with age—approximately three kilograms of lean muscle are lost each decade during the adult years. The rate of loss accelerates after age 45. The average percentage ratio of muscle to fat for a 60- to 70-year-old woman is 44 percent fat. In a 20-year-old woman, the ratio is 23 to 24 percent. Weight lifting can preserve and possibly increase muscle mass and bone density in older adults (Johnston, De Lisio, & Parise, 2008). A recent review of 62 research studies concluded that strength training can improve muscle strength and some aspects of functional limitation, such as gait speed, in older adults (Latham et al., 2004).

Researchers who study exercise and aging have discovered the following:

■ Exercise is linked to increased longevity. In a longitudinal study of Chinese women, those who exercised regularly were less likely to die over approximately a six-year time period (Matthews et al., 2007). A recent study also revealed that systolic blood pressure during exercise was linked to an increase in long-term survival of 75-year-olds (Hedberg et al., 2009). And in one analysis, energy expenditure by older adults during exercise that burns up at least 1,000 calories a week was estimated to increase life expectancy by about 30 percent, while burning up 2,000 calories a week in exercise was estimated to increase life expectancy by about 50 percent (Lee & Skerrett, 2001).

■ Exercise is related to prevention of common chronic diseases. Exercise can reduce the risk of developing cardiovascular disease, type 2 diabetes, osteoporosis, stroke, and breast cancer (Aizawa et al., 2010; Marks, Katz, & Smith, 2010; Yassine et al., 2009).

■ Exercise is associated with improvement in the treatment of many diseases. When exercise is used as part of the treatment, individuals with these diseases show improvement in symptoms: arthritis, pulmonary disease, congestive heart failure, coronary artery disease, hypertension, type 2 diabetes, obesity, and Alzheimer's disease (Coker et al., 2009; Rimmer et al., 2009).

■ Exercise improves older adults' cellular functioning. Researchers increasingly are finding that exercise improves cellular functioning in older adults (Boveris & Navarro, 2008). For example, two recent studies revealed that telomere length was greater in leukocytes (white blood cells) when older adults engaged in vigorous aerobic activity (Cherkas et al., 2008; LaRocca, Seals, & Pierce, 2010).

- Exercise improves immune system functioning in older adults. A recent study revealed that following exercise, a number of components of immune system functioning in older adult women improved (Sakamoto et al., 2009).
- Exercise can optimize body composition and reduce the decline in motor skills as aging occurs. Exercise can increase muscle mass and bone mass, as well as decrease bone fragility (Gu et al., 2009; Maimoun & Sultan, 2010). A recent study found that participation in exercise activities was linked to a delay in the onset and progression of frailty (Peterson et al., 2009).
- Exercise reduces the likelihood that older adults will develop mental health problems and can be effective in the treatment of mental health problems. For example, exercise reduces the likelihood that older adults will develop depression and can be effective in treating depression in older adults (Davidson, 2010; Deligiannidis & Freeman, 2010).
- Exercise is linked to improved brain and cognitive functioning in older adults. As we saw earlier in the chapter, exercise increases brain volume in older adults (Erickson et al., 2009). Also, exercise increases the information-processing skills of older adults (Williamson et al., 2009).

Despite the extensive documentation of exercise's power to improve older adults' health and quality of life, a recent national survey revealed that older adults have increased their exercise levels only slightly in recent years (Centers for Disease Control and Prevention, 2008). Possible explanations of older adults' failure to substantially increase their exercise focus on such factors as chronic illnesses, life crises (such as a spouse's death) that disrupt exercise schedules, embarrassment at being around others who are in better shape (especially if they haven't exercised much earlier in life), and the "why bother?" factor (not believing that exercise will improve their lives much) (Painter, 2008). But as we have seen, it is never too late to begin to exercise, and older adults can significantly benefit from regular exercise (Farrell et al., 2010; LaRocca, Seals, & Pierce, 2010; Reibis et al., 2010). We will further discuss the influence of exercise on older adults' cognitive functioning in Chapter 18.

In sum, exercise is an excellent way to maintain health. Researchers continue to document its positive effects in older adults (Deeny et al., 2008; Temple et al., 2008). The current recommended level of aerobic activity for adults 60 years of age and older is 30 minutes of moderately intense activity, such as brisk walking or riding a stationary bicycle, five or more days a week, and strength training on two or more days a week (Der Ananian & Prohaska, 2007). Flexibility and balance exercises also are recommended. More about researchers' investigations into exercise's positive benefits for health is shown in Figure 17.6.

Nutrition and Weight

Seventeenth-century English philosopher and essayist Francis Bacon was the first author to recommend scientific evaluation of diet and longevity. He advocated a frugal diet. Yet the proportion of seniors who are obese, as measured by body mass index (BMI), was estimated to be 29 percent in 2008. Approximately 18.5 percent are underweight (PHAC, 2010b). Poor nutritional habits among seniors can exacerbate health issues and aggravate symptoms of chronic diseases.

Scientists have accumulated considerable evidence that calorie restriction (CR) in laboratory animals (in most cases rats) can increase the animals' life span (Marques, Markus, & Morris, 2010; Minor et al., 2010; Vasunilashorn & Crimmins, 2009). Animals fed diets restricted in calories, although adequate in protein, vitamins, and minerals, live as much as 40 percent longer than animals given unlimited access to food (Jolly, 2005). Furthermore, chronic problems, such as kidney disease, appear at a later age (Fernandez, 2008). CR also delays biochemical alterations such as the age-related rise in cholesterol and triglycerides observed in both humans and animals (Fontana, 2009). Research also indicates that CR may provide neuro-protection for an aging central nervous system (Contestabile, 2009; Opalach et al., 2010). For example, a recent study revealed that following CR for three months, the verbal memory of older adults improved (Witte et al., 2009).

No one knows for certain how CR works to increase the life span of animals (Anderson & Weindruch, 2007). Some scientists believe it might lower the level of free radicals and reduce oxidative stress in cells (Lopez-Lluch et al., 2006). For example, one recent study found that calorie

Figure 17.6

The Jogging Hog Experiment

Jogging hogs reveal the dramatic effects of exercise on health. In one investigation, a group of hogs was trained to run approximately 165 km per week (Bloor & White, 1983). Then, the researchers narrowed the arteries that supplied blood to the hogs' hearts. The hearts of the jogging hogs developed extensive alternate pathways for blood supply, and 42 percent of the threatened heart tissue was salvaged, compared with only 17 percent in a control group of non-jogging hogs.

restriction slowed the age-related increase in oxidative stress (Ward et al., 2005). Others believe calorie restriction might trigger a state of emergency called "survival mode" in which the body eliminates all unnecessary functions to focus only on staying alive.

Whether similar very-low-calorie diets can stretch the human life span is not known (Mattison et al., 2007). In some instances, the animals in these studies ate 40 percent less than normal. In humans, a typical level of calorie restriction involves a 30 percent decrease, which translates into about 1,120 calories a day for the average woman and 1,540 for the average man. Malnutrition is estimated to be as high as 60 percent among seniors living in nursing homes or hospitals; however, seniors living alone are also more prone to malnutrition because they may not feel like cooking or make poor food choices (PHAC 2010b). Most nutritional experts do not recommend very-low-calorie diets for older adults; rather, they recommend a well-balanced, low-fat diet that includes the nutritional factors needed to maintain good health.

The Growing Controversy over Vitamins and Aging

For years, most experts on aging and health argued that a balanced diet was all that was needed for successful aging; vitamin supplements were not recommended. However, recent research suggests the possibility that some vitamin supplements—mainly a group called "antioxidants," which includes vitamin C, vitamin E, and beta-carotene—help slow the aging process and improve the health of older adults.

The theory is that antioxidants counteract the cell damage caused by free radicals, which are produced both by the body's own metabolism and by environmental factors, such as smoking, pollution, and bad chemicals in the diet (Flora, 2007; Ristow & Zarse, 2010). When free radicals cause damage (oxidation) in one cell, a chain reaction of damage follows. Antioxidants act much like a fire extinguisher, helping to neutralize free-radical activity.

Some research studies have found links between the antioxidant vitamins and health. For example, one study linked low blood vitamin C concentration in older adults with an earlier incidence of death (Fletcher, Breeze, & Shetty, 2003). However, recent large-scale studies of men revealed that taking vitamin C and vitamin E did not prevent cardiovascular disease or cancer (Gaziano et al., 2009; Sesso et al., 2008). And another recent study indicated that diet supplementation with vitamins C, E, and beta-carotene had no effect on cancer incidence or cancer death (Lin et al., 2009).

Long Canadian winters and lack of exposure to the sun have contributed to a deficiency in vitamin D, the sunshine vitamin (Schwalfenberg, 2013). Vitamin D deficiency contributes to cancerous melanoma and osteoporosis. Vitamin D enables the body to absorb calcium and is associated with offsetting several diseases including cancer, osteoporosis, autoimmune disease, cardiovascular disease, and infectious disease. Studies have also shown that people with adequate levels of vitamin D have lower risk of sun damage and of developing rheumatoid arthritis in women (Nordqvist, 2009; Sorenson, 2011).

There is no evidence that antioxidants can increase the human life span, but some aging and health experts believe they can reduce a person's risk of becoming frail and sick in the later adult years (Korantzopoulos et al., 2007). However, there are a lot blanks and uncertainties in what we know. That is, we do not know which vitamins should be taken, how large a dose should be taken, what the constraints are, and so on. Critics also argue that key experimental studies documenting the effectiveness of the vitamins in slowing the aging process have not been conducted. The studies in this area so far have been so-called population studies that are correlational, rather than experimental, in nature. Other factors—such as exercise, better health practices, and good nutritional habits—might be responsible for the positive findings about vitamins and aging, rather than vitamins per se. Also, the free radical theory is a theory and not a fact, and is only one of a number of theories about why we age.

Possible links between vitamins and cognitive performance in older adults also have been the focus of increased research attention. A recent review of cross-sectional and longitudinal research studies concluded that taking B vitamins, especially folate, B_6, and B_{12}, is positively related to cognitive performance in older adults (Wengreen et al., 2007). Some studies also have found that taking B vitamins is positively related to cognitive performance in older adults (Feng et al., 2006). However, other studies indicate that taking B vitamins and other supplemental vitamins has no effect on the cognitive functioning of older adults (McNeill et al., 2007).

The Nature of Mental Health in Late Adulthood

Although a substantial portion of the population can now look forward to a longer life, that life unfortunately may be hampered by a mental disorder in old age. Conn and other researchers (2006) state that 20 percent of seniors in Canada have a mental illness, similar to that of other age groups. What is important to note is that "80 to 90 percent of nursing home residents live with some form of mental illness and/or cognitive impairment" (p. S37). Mental disorders combined with declining physical strength make individuals increasingly dependent on the help and care of others. Depression and substance abuse often go hand in hand.

Depression

Major depression *is a mood disorder in which the individual is deeply unhappy, demoralized, self-derogatory, and bored. The individual with major depression does not feel well, loses stamina easily, has a poor appetite, and is listless and unmotivated.* Major depression has been called the "common cold" of mental disorders. Estimates of depression's frequency among older adults vary. Between 14.7 and 20 percent of Canadian senior citizens live with depression (Buchanan et al., 2006). Within hospitals and long-term care facilities, the percentage increases to 21 percent and 40 percent, respectively. While it is common, depression and aging do not necessarily go hand in hand; in fact, a recent review concluded that depression is less common among older adults than younger adults (Fiske, Wetherell, & Gatz, 2009). More than half of the cases of depression in older adults represents the first time these individuals have developed depression in their life (Fiske, Wetherell, & Gatz, 2009).

One study found that the lower frequency of depressive symptoms in older adults compared with middle-aged adults was linked to fewer economic hardships, fewer negative social interchanges, and increased religiosity (Schieman, van Gundy, & Taylor, 2004).

Other research indicates that older adults who engage in regular exercise, especially aerobic exercise, are less likely to be depressed, whereas those who are in poor health and experiencing pain are more likely to be depressed (Mavandadi et al., 2007).

Depressive symptoms increase in the oldest old (85 years and older), and this increase is associated with a higher percentage of women in the group, more physical disability, more cognitive impairment, and lower socio-economic status (Hybels & Blazer, 2004).

One recent longitudinal study found greater rates of depression in women than men at 50 and 60 years of age, but not at 80 years of age (Barefoot et al., 2001). Men showed increases in depressive symptoms from 60 to 80, but women did not. In this cohort, men may have undergone more profound role shifts after 60 years of age because they were more likely than women to have retired from active involvement in the work world. Thus, the absence of a gender difference in depression in older adults may be cohort specific and may not hold as women who have entered the workforce in greater numbers are assessed in late adulthood.

Among the most common predictors of depression in older adults are earlier depressive symptoms, poor health, disability, loss events such as the death of a spouse, and low social support (Lee & Park, 2008; Ng et al., 2010). Individuals living alone appeared to be more vulnerable to depression; however, good social support and being socially integrated in the community helped to buffer the effects of declining health on depression in these individuals (Hybels & Blazer, 2004). Insomnia is often overlooked as a risk factor for depression in older adults (Fiske, Wetherell, & Gatz, 2009). Curtailment of daily activities is a common pathway to late-life depression (Fiske, Wetherell, & Gatz, 2009). Often accompanying this curtailment of activity is an increase in self-critical thinking that exacerbates depression.

major depression A mood disorder in which the individual is deeply unhappy, demoralized, self-derogatory, and bored. The individual with major depression does not feel well, loses stamina easily, has a poor appetite, and is listless and unmotivated.

developmental **connection**

Continuity vs. Discontinuity

Depression is a treatable condition, not only in young adults but in older adults as well (Asghar-Ali & Braun, 2009; Lakey et al., 2008; Snowden, Steinman, & Frederick, 2008; Vahia et al., 2010). Unfortunately, as many as 80 percent of older adults with depressive symptoms receive no treatment at all. Combinations of medications and psychotherapy produce significant improvement in almost four out of five elderly adults with depression (Koenig & Blazer, 1996); as well, prayer and meditation have proven to be helpful (Raynauld, 2013).

Major depression can result not only in sadness, but also in suicidal tendencies (Bergman Levy et al., 2010). According to the Centre for Suicide Prevention Resource Toolkit (2012), seniors, particularly men, have the highest suicide rate of any group. The Centre paraphrases Dr. Leon Kagan, Director of Geriatric Psychiatry at the University of Alberta, who says that many seniors cope well with aging; it is when they begin to lose their independence they become at risk for depression (Centre for Suicide Prevention, 2012; Monette, 2012). Depression and deaths of seniors by suicide are often overlooked or difficult to determine. Economic pressures, isolation, and being unmarried and less educated are also thought to be contributing factors (Monette, 2012).

Substance Abuse

In many cases, older adults are taking multiple medications, which can increase the risks associated with consuming alcohol or other drugs. For example, when combined with tranquillizers or sedatives, alcohol use can impair breathing, produce excessive sedation, and be fatal.

Seniors are less likely to use alcohol on a regular basis than younger adults, with 48 percent of seniors drinking alcohol once a month or more versus 67 percent of those aged 25 to 54 (Turcotte & Schellenberg, 2007). Regular low to moderate use of alcohol has been associated with higher self-ratings of excellent or very good health, and may reduce the likelihood of developing certain diseases. However, heavy drinking is a potential major problem, both in the physical and psychological consequences and the apparent difficulty in diagnosing alcohol abuse or addiction among seniors. The belief is that substance abuse often goes undetected in older adults, and there is concern about older adults who abuse not only illicit drugs, but prescription drugs as well (Segal, 2007). Too often, screening questionnaires are not appropriate for older adults, and the consequences of alcohol abuse—such as depression, inadequate nutrition, congestive heart failure, and frequent falls—may erroneously be attributed to other medical or psychological conditions (Hoyer & Roodin, 2009).

Because of the dramatic increase anticipated in the number of older adults over the twenty-first century, substance abuse is likely to characterize an increasing number of older adults (Atkinson, Ryan, & Turner, 2001).

Late-onset alcoholism is the label used to describe the onset of alcoholism after the age of 65. Late-onset alcoholism is often related to loneliness, loss of a spouse, or a disabling condition.

In 2003, 12 percent of Canadian men between 65 and 74 (and 3 percent of women) were reported to be heavy drinkers, having five or more drinks on one occasion (Turcotte & Schellenberg, 2007). The conclusion of a cross-sectional study of older people living in Canadian community dwellings indicated that men suffering from loneliness and depression and lacking engagement in activities are the most vulnerable to alcohol abuse (St. John, Montgomery, & Tyas, 2008).

Researchers have especially found that moderate drinking of red wine is linked to better health and increased longevity (Das, Mukherjee, & Ray, 2010; Queen & Tollefsbol, 2010). Explanations for the benefits of red wine centre on its connection to lowering stress and reducing risk of coronary heart disease (Angelone et al., 2010). Increasing evidence supports the hypothesis that a chemical in red wine, resveratrol, plays a key role in red wine's health benefits, although consistent evidence for this link has yet to be found (Goswami & Das, 2009; Issuree et al., 2009; Kaeberlein, 2010; Marques, Markus, & Morris, 2010; Park et al., 2009). Scientists are exploring how resveratrol, as well as calorie restriction, increases SIRT1, an enzyme that is involved in DNA repair and aging (Lin et al., 2010; Morselli et al., 2010; Mukherjee et al., 2009).

critical thinking

Imagine that you suspect a parent or grandparent is suffering from depression or substance abuse. What are some of the behavioural signs that might raise this concern? How do you think you would respond? What would you do? What help might be available? How would this concern impact your well-being?

Dementia, Alzheimer's Disease, and Related Disorders

An estimated half-million Canadians suffer from the most debilitating of mental disorders: Alzheimer's disease or related forms of dementia such as multi-infarct dementia and Parkinson's disease (Canadian Health Care Association, 2012; Jellinger, 2009). Alzheimer's disease, the most common dementia, has been the focus of extensive attention.

Dementia

dementia A global term for any neurological disorder in which the primary symptoms involve a deterioration of mental functioning.

Dementia *is a global term for any neurological disorder in which the primary symptoms involve a deterioration of mental functioning.* Individuals with dementia often lose the ability to care for themselves and can lose the ability to recognize familiar surroundings and people (including family members) (Mast & Healy, 2009; Okura et al., 2010; Travers, Martin-Khan, & Lie, 2010).

The Alzheimer Society of Canada estimates that nearly 500,000 Canadians, or 1.5 percent of the Canadian population, currently have dementia (Dudgeon, 2010). Sixty-four percent of all dementias in Canada are Alzheimer's disease, and 60 percent of people in long-term-care facilities have Alzheimer's disease. Further, one in five people with Parkinson's disease will develop it (Alzheimer Society of Canada, 2013).

Alzheimer's Disease

Alzheimer's disease A fatal progressive, and irreversible disorder characterized by a gradual deterioration of memory, reasoning, language, and eventually, physical functioning.

As just noted, the most common form of dementia is **Alzheimer's disease,** *a fatal, progressive, and irreversible disorder characterized by a gradual deterioration of memory, reasoning, language, and eventually, physical functioning.* Although aging is a risk factor, Alzheimer's disease is not a normal part of aging (Alzheimer Society, 2013; MediResource, 2010–2011).

With a difference in onset, Alzheimer's is now also described as early-onset (initially occurring in individuals younger than 65 years of age) or late-onset (which has its initial onset in individuals 65 years of age and older). Early-onset Alzheimer's disease is rare (about 7 percent of all cases) and generally affects people 30 to 60 years of age (Dudgeon, 2010).

As Alzheimer's disease progresses, the brain deteriorates and shrinks. Figure 17.7 provides a comparison of the normally aging brain of a healthy individual and the brain of an individual with Alzheimer's disease.

CAUSES AND TREATMENTS   Alzheimer's disease involves a deficiency in the important brain messenger chemical acetylcholine, which plays an important role in memory (Alcaro et al., 2010; Mura et al., 2010; Rentz et al., 2010). Also, as Alzheimer's disease progresses, the brain shrinks and deteriorates (see Figure 17.7). The deterioration of the brain in Alzheimer's disease is characterized by the formation of amyloid plaques (dense deposits of protein that accumulate in the blood vessels) and neurofibrillary tangles (twisted fibres that build up in neurons) (Galimberti & Scarpini, 2010; Tabira, 2009; Tarawneh & Holtzman, 2010). Researchers are especially seeking ways to interrupt the progress of amyloid plaques and neurofibrillary tangles in patients with Alzheimer's disease (Miura et al., 2007). There is increasing interest in the role that oxidative stress might play in Alzheimer's disease (Bonda et al., 2010; Di Bona et al., 2010; Galasko et al., 2010). Oxidative stress occurs when the body's antioxidant defences don't cope with the free-radical attacks and oxidation in the body. Recall that earlier you read that free-radical theory is a major theory of biological aging.

developmental **connection**

Early Brain Development

Although scientists are not certain what causes Alzheimer's disease, age is an important risk factor, and genes also likely play an important role (Avramopoulos, 2009; Bettens, Sleegers, & Van Broeckhoven, 2010; Gomez Ravetti et al., 2010). The number of individuals with Alzheimer's disease doubles every five years after the age of 65. A gene called apolipoprotein E (apoE), which is linked to increasing presence of plaques and tangles in the brain, could play a role in as many as one-third of the cases of Alzheimer's disease (Golanska et al., 2010; Lane & He, 2009; Vemuri et al., 2010). One study of almost 12,000 pairs of twins in Sweden found that identical twins were both

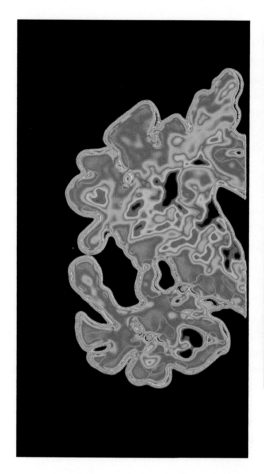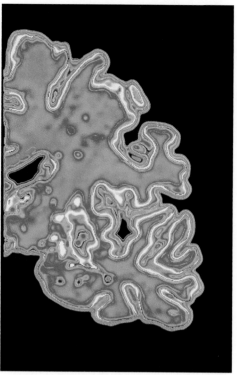

Figure 17.7

Two Brains: Normal Aging and Alzheimer's Disease

The brain image on the left is from a brain ravaged by Alzheimer's disease. The brain image on the right is from a brain of a normal aging individual. Note the deterioration and shrinking in the Alzheimer's brain.

more likely to develop Alzheimer's disease than fraternal twins, suggesting a genetic influence on the disease (Gatz et al., 2006). Another recent study revealed that the presence of the apoE gene lowers the age of onset of Alzheimer's disease (Sando et al., 2008).

Peter St. George-Hyslop (2012) of the University of Toronto has identified four genes that influence the inherited susceptibility to Alzheimer's disease. His pioneering work has led to the exploration of proteins that cause the death of nerve cells in the brain. Early detection, before any symptoms appear, and early treatment can be effective in reducing the disease, which once started is irreversible and leads to death. (St. George-Hyslop, 2012).

Although individuals with a family history of Alzheimer's disease are at greater risk, the disease is complex and likely caused by a number of factors, including lifestyles. For many years, scientists have known that a healthy diet, exercise, and weight control can lower the risk of cardiovascular disease. Now they are finding that these healthy lifestyle factors may also lower the risk of Alzheimer's disease. Researchers have revealed older adults with Alzheimer's disease are more likely to also have cardiovascular disease than are individuals who do not have Alzheimer's disease (Helzner et al., 2009; Reynolds et al., 2010). Recently, more cardiac risk factors have been implicated in Alzheimer's disease—obesity, smoking, atherosclerosis, high cholesterol and lipids (Abellan von Kahn et al., 2009; Florent-Bechard et al., 2009; Reynolds et al., 2010; Sonnen et al., 2009; Sottero et al., 2009). As with many problems associated with aging, exercise may also reduce the risk of Alzheimer's disease (Geda et al., 2010; Radak et al., 2010; Rolland, Abellan van Kahn, & Vellas, 2010). One recent study of more than 2,000 men 71 to 93 years of age revealed that those who walked less than 0.4 km a day were almost twice as likely to develop Alzheimer's disease as their male counterparts who walked more than 3 km a day (Abbott et al., 2004). And another study of older adults found that those who exercised three or more times a week were less likely to develop Alzheimer's disease over a six-year period than those who exercised less (Larson et al., 2006).

Cognitive exercise is also important. Ellen Bialystok (2007; Bialystok, Craik, & Ryan, 2006) suggests that evidence points to a protective influence of superior executive control process development, as a result of learning two languages earlier in life, serving to protect older adults from cognitive decline. In further study, Bialystok found that when compared to monolingual patients, those patients who were bilingual reported symptoms 5.1 years later and were diagnosed 4.3 years later than their monolingual counterparts. In this study, there were no differences in gender, formal education, or immigration status; in other words, they found that "lifelong bilingualism is a further factor contributing to cognitive reserve" (Craik, Bialystok, & Freedman, 2010).

EARLY DETECTION OF ALZHEIMER'S DISEASE   *Mild cognitive impairment (MCI)* represents a transitional state between the cognitive changes of normal aging and very early Alzheimer's disease and other dementias. MCI is increasingly recognized as a risk factor for Alzheimer's disease (Bombois et al., 2008).

Distinguishing between individuals who merely have age-associated declines in memory and those with MCI is difficult, as is predicting which individuals with MCI will subsequently develop Alzheimer's disease (Schwam & Xu, 2010; Vellas & Aisen, 2010). One effort in this regard is to have individuals with MCI undergo an fMRI (functional magnetic resonance imaging) brain scan (Pihlajamaki, Jauhiainen, & Soininen, 2009). If the scan shows that certain brain regions involved in memory are smaller than those of individuals without memory impairments, the individual is more likely to progress to Alzheimer's disease (Alzheimer's Association, 2010). Also, recent research indicates that individuals without MCI have a higher degree of cortical thickness than individuals with MCI (Wang et al., 2009). In addition, fMRI scans can detect changes in the brain that are fairly typical of early-Alzheimer's disease, even before symptoms develop (Matsuda, 2007). A recent research review indicated that fMRI measurement of neuron loss in the medial temporal lobe is a predictor of memory loss and eventually dementia (Vellas & Aisen, 2010).

Longitudinal studies have indicated that certain aspects of memory may provide indicators of subsequent dementia and Alzheimer's disease (Jessen et al., 2010; Johnson et al., 2009). In one study, performance on a short verbal recall memory task in individuals with no indication of the presence of Alzheimer's disease was linked to whether the disease was present in the individuals 10 years later (Tierney et al., 2005). In another study, older adults whose episodic memory was impaired in an initial assessment were more than twice as likely to develop Alzheimer's disease over a 10-year period than those with impairments in other cognitive domains such as semantic memory, working memory, and visual-spatial ability (Aggarwal et al., 2005).

DRUG TREATMENT OF ALZHEIMER'S DISEASE   Several drugs called cholinerase inhibitors are among those used to treat Alzheimer's disease. Three of these drugs are donepezil (Aricept), rivastigmine (Exelon), and galantamine (Reminyl). They are designed to improve memory and other cognitive functions by increasing levels of acetylcholine in the brain (Emre et al., 2010; Howland, 2010; Orhan et al., 2009; Pepeu & Giovannini, 2009). The drugs have been effective in slowing down the progression of Alzheimer's symptoms in mild to moderate stages of the disease, but they have not been approved for advanced stages of Alzheimer's disease. In 2003, memantine (Ebixa)— a drug that works differently than the cholinerase inhibitors—received conditional approval by Health Canada for use in treating moderate to severe Alzheimer's disease (Alzheimer Society of Canada, 2009b). Memantine is in the class of drugs called NMDA antagonists, and it regulates the information-processing activities of the neurotransmitter glutamate (Shah et al., 2008). Researchers have found that memantine improves cognitive and behavioural functioning in individuals with moderate to severe Alzheimer's disease (Farlow, Miller, & Pejovic, 2008).

Researchers are beginning to study how combinations of drugs might further reduce Alzheimer's symptoms. One recent review found that memantine combined with donepezil improved cognitive and behavioural functioning in individuals with moderate or severe Alzheimer's disease (Xiong & Doraiswamy, 2005). Keep in mind, though, that the drugs used to treat Alzheimer's disease only slow the downward progression of the disease; they do not treat its cause (Rafii & Aisen, 2009).

CARING FOR INDIVIDUALS WITH ALZHEIMER'S DISEASE Caring for Alzheimer's patients is a special concern (Iliffe et al., 2009; Kelsey, Laditka, & Laditka, 2010; Silverstein, Wong, & Brueck, 2010). Currently, 55 percent of Canadians aged 65 and over with dementia live in their own homes, with support from their spouse, family members, and/or community-based professionals (Dudgeon, 2010). With institutional bed shortages and the expected increase in the number of people with dementia, this percentage is forecast to rise to 62. Psychologists and other health care professionals believe that the family can be an important support system for the Alzheimer's patient, but this support can have costs for the family, which can become emotionally and physically drained by the extensive care required for a person with Alzheimer's. For example, depression has been reported in 50 percent of family caregivers to Alzheimer's patients (Redinbaugh, MacCallum, & Kiecolt-Glaser, 1995). A recent meta-analysis found that female caregivers reported providing more caregiving hours, higher levels of burden and depression, as well as lower levels of well-being and physical health than male caregivers (Pinquart & Sorensen, 2006).

Respite care has been developed to help people who have to meet the day-to-day needs of Alzheimer's patients. This type of care provides an important break away from the burden of providing chronic care. Caregivers can suffer from workload, depression, guilt, and exhaustion; therefore various types of respite care are designed to provide caregivers with temporary rest. Different types of respite care include out of home respite services and in-home care including the use of technology particularly for video chat services. More research is underway to understand the costs, caregiver training, and readiness to use respite care (Canadian Healthcare Association, 2012).

A different view of caring for a relative with Alzheimer's has been advanced by Geila Bar-David (1999). She explored the experiences of a small group of caregivers in southern Ontario looking after their spouse or a parent. Bar-David's approach was to view the intense experience of caring for a relative with Alzheimer's as a potential for the personal growth of the caregiver. The initial findings support her belief that given the opportunity to reflect on their experience "in relation to a constructive model of caregiving, they can better understand what they are going through, what they can expect, and how they can emerge from the experience with increasing integrity rather than despair."

Multi-Infarct Dementia

Multi-infarct dementia *involves a sporadic and progressive loss of intellectual functioning caused by repeated temporary obstruction of blood flow in cerebral arteries.* The result is a series of mini-strokes. The term "infarct" refers to the temporary obstruction of blood vessels. It is estimated that 15 to 25 percent of dementias involve the vascular impairment of multi-infarct dementia.

Multi-infarct dementia is more common among men with a history of high blood pressure. The clinical picture of multi-infarct dementia is different from that of Alzheimer's disease. Many patients recover from multi-infarct dementia, whereas Alzheimer's disease shows a progressive deterioration. The symptoms of multi-infarct dementia include confusion, slurring of speech, writing impairment, and numbness on one side of the face, arm, or leg (Hoyer & Roodin, 2009). However, after each occurrence, there usually is a rather quick recovery, although each succeeding occurrence is usually more damaging. Approximately 35 to 50 percent of individuals who have these transient attacks will have a major stroke within five years unless the underlying problems are treated. Especially recommended for these individuals are exercise, improved diet, and appropriate drugs, which can slow or stop the progression of the underlying vascular disease (Craft, 2009).

Parkinson's Disease

Another dementia is **Parkinson's disease,** *a chronic, progressive disease characterized by muscle tremors, slowing of movement, and partial facial paralysis.* Parkinson's disease is triggered by degeneration of dopamine-producing neurons in the brain (Swanson, Sesso, & Emborg, 2009). Dopamine is a neurotransmitter that is necessary for normal brain functioning. Why these neurons degenerate is not known. The main treatment for Parkinson's disease involves the drug L-dopa, which is converted by the brain into dopamine (Stowe et al., 2008; Yamamoto & Schapira, 2008). However, it is difficult to determine the correct level of dosage of this drug, as it loses its efficacy over time. Another treatment for advanced Parkinson's disease is deep brain stimulation (DBS), which involves implantation of

multi-infarct dementia Involves a sporadic and progressive loss of intellectual functioning caused by repeated temporary obstruction of blood flow in cerebral arteries.

Parkinson's disease A chronic, progressive disease characterized by muscle tremors, slowing of movement, and partial facial paralysis.

Canadian actor Michael J. Fox has become a leading spokesperson for Parkinson's disease since he was diagnosed with the condition.

electrodes within the brain (Ellrichmann, Harati, & Müller, 2008). The electrodes are then stimulated by a pacemaker-like device. Stem cell transplantation offers hope for the future in treating Parkinson's disease (Newman & Bakay, 2008; Wang et al., 2008). Two factors that are associated with a lower risk of developing Parkinson's disease are taking ibuprofen and drinking coffee (Chand & Litvan, 2007).

Health Promotion

What is the quality of nursing homes and other extended-care facilities for older adults? What is the nature of the relationship between older adults and health-care providers?

Care Options

In our society, only about 7 percent of adults 65 years of age and over reside in an institutional setting. Among adults 85 years of age and older, 32 percent live in nursing homes or other extended-care facilities. Institutionalization of this older age group of Canadians has decreased, falling from 38 percent in 1981 to 32 percent in 2001 (Turcotte & Schellenberg, 2007). Women are far more likely to be living in an institutional setting than men after the age of 65.

The quality of nursing homes and other extended-care facilities for older adults varies enormously and is a source of continuing national concern (Eskildsen & Price, 2009). Because of the inadequate quality of many nursing homes and the escalating costs for nursing home care, many specialists in the health problems of the aged stress that home health care, elder-care centres, and preventive medicine clinics are good alternatives (Katz et al., 2009). They are potentially less expensive than hospitals and nursing homes. They also are less likely to engender the feelings of depersonalization and dependency that occur so often in residents of institutions. Currently, there is an increased demand for, but shortage of, home-care workers because of the increase in population of older adults and their preference to stay out of nursing homes (Moos, 2007).

Prescription Drug Use

Seniors' use of prescribed drugs accounts for 40 percent of all purchases of prescribed medication, a larger share than any other single age group in Canada (Canadian Institute for Health Information, 2010). Inappropriate use of these medications may account for 30 percent of the hospitalizations of people over the age of 65. Multiple prescription drug use is common, with 53 percent of seniors living in institutions being given five or more drugs per day, while 13 percent of those residing in private dwellings take that many drugs per day (Ramage-Morin, 2009). The more drugs used, the greater the risk is for adverse effects. The Canadian Mental Health Association, Ontario (2010) reports that as many as 50 percent of seniors do not take their medications as prescribed, share their medication with spouses, and are unaware of the interaction between their prescription and alcohol.

Problems with eyesight and multiple and confusing instructions for taking the drugs add to the chance of making an error in use. Another potential source of danger is that seniors may be prescribed different and contraindicated drugs from various doctors whom they consult during the same time period. Even if they are taking compatible drugs, biological changes in the aging body alter the drugs' efficacy, absorption rates, and the length of time the drugs will remain in the body (usually for a longer period of time).

Therefore, it is critical that seniors and care providers carefully manage their use of prescribed medications. Taking regular inventories of the drugs and checking for contraindications, side effects, and interactions is highly recommended. One approach is referred to as the "brown bag" technique, in which the person places all the medication bottles in a brown bag (or other suitable container) and takes them to her/his physician during a regular visit.

Autonomy

An important factor related to health, and even survival, in a nursing home is the patient's feelings of control and self-determination. Older adults frequently find their autonomy compromised not only by health challenges, but also by societal prejudices. Early studies by Rodin

connecting through research ←-------

Ursula Franklin

Celebrated physicist, educator, author, peace advocate, Quaker, and humanitarian Ursula Franklin was born in Germany in 1921. As a young adult, she witnessed and experienced first-hand the Nazi work camps—where, because her mother was Jewish, she was imprisoned and forced to work repairing buildings. Upon completion of her Ph.D. at the technical university in Berlin in 1948 she immigrated to Canada, completed her post-doctoral work at the University of Toronto, and worked at the Ontario Research Foundation. She joined the faculty of the University of Toronto in 1967, becoming a full professor in 1973, and the first woman to be honoured with the title of university professor by the University of Toronto in 1984 (Ursula Franklin Academy [UFA], 2008–2013). Currently, she is a Professor Emerita in the department of metallurgy and material sciences and has been inducted into the Canadian Sciences Hall of Fame. Her many publications and her tireless advocacy have earned her several awards and honorary degrees, including a Companion of the Order of Canada, the Order of Ontario, and a Fellow of

the Royal Society of Canada (UFA, 2008–2013). Toronto honoured her dedication to education by naming one of the city's high schools after her, the Ursula Franklin Academy, where she continues to assume active participation and leadership, particularly in encouraging young women to enter the sciences and to broaden our understanding of the role of technology in our lives.

Franklin has turned her attention to how feminism, language, and social justice contribute to drafting the map that could lead us to peace (Franklin, 2006; Hirsh, 2008). Franklin points out that when an earthquake hits any part of the world, we find ways to help each other; however, when we create an enemy, we alienate each other and create war. In our responses to victims of floods or earthquakes, we integrate social justice and peace, and find peaceful maps (Hirsh, 2008). In her acceptance speech for the Pearson Peace Medal from the United Nations Association in Canada (2001), Franklin said, "Peace is not the absence of war. Peace is the presence of justice and the absence of fear" (Geary-Martin, 2013).

and Langer (1977) reported that being able to make decisions is important for seniors, including those living in nursing homes. Having some control over such things as when and what to eat, and who can visit and when, have been found to contribute to the overall alertness and well-being of residents. These early findings are consistent with the goals of contemporary approaches to care.

Meeting the Mental Health Needs of Older Adults

Older adults receive disproportionately fewer mental health services than the rest of the population (Conn, 2003). Mental health issues often are unrecognized and untreated, often masked by co-existing health conditions. Conn (2003) suggests as many as 55 percent of seniors with depression go untreated. Service availability varies widely across Canada and between urban and rural settings, with the former areas having greater access to mental health care (Conn, 2003; Keefe et al., 2004).

The Canadian Mental Health Association (2010) suggests that good mental health can be promoted by several means. Their recommendations for seniors include maintaining social contacts among peers, family members, and neighbours; eating a healthy diet; keeping a positive attitude; knowing the signs of depression and having regular medical check-ups; and engaging in enjoyable activity, both physical and mental. How can we better meet the mental health needs of the elderly? First, psychologists must be encouraged to include more older adults on their client lists, and the elderly must be convinced that they can benefit from therapy. Second, we must make mental health care accessible, including affordable.

-- **critical** thinking -------------

Good physical and mental health appear to share a number of common points. Using the information in this section, construct a six-point list of different ways to help an older adult maintain good mental health. How might you incorporate these points into your life now in an effort to ensure good health in your senior years?

The Older Adult and Health-Care Providers

Almost all seniors in Canada have a doctor (96 percent), and 88 percent had seen their doctor in the previous year (Rotermann, 2005). People over the age of 65 use physicians more than any other group, have more hospital admissions, and have generally longer stays than other age groups (Turcotte & Schellenberg, 2007). In 2003, 15 percent of those aged 65 and older received home care (Rotermann, 2005). Of this care, 57 percent received care from professional sources, 28 percent from friends and family members, and 15 percent from some combination of the two. In addition, a small percentage of seniors are seeking out alternative health care (Turcotte & Schellenberg, 2007). In 2003, just over 7 percent of seniors aged 65 to 74 sought out alternative health care practitioners, while less than 5 percent over the age of 74 did.

The attitudes of both the health-care provider and the older adult are important aspects of the older adult's health care (Greene & Adelman, 2001). Unfortunately, health-care providers too often share society's stereotypes and negative attitudes toward the elderly (Nussbaum, Pecchioni, & Crowell, 2001). In a health-care setting, these attitudes can take the form of avoidance, dislike, and begrudged tolerance, rather than positive, hopeful treatment. Health-care personnel are more likely to be interested in treating younger persons, who more often have acute problems with a higher likelihood of successful recovery. They often are less motivated to treat older persons, who are more likely to have chronic problems with a lower likelihood of successful recovery.

To this point, we have discussed a number of ideas about physical and mental health and wellness in late adulthood. For a review, see the **Reach Your Learning Objectives** section at the end of this chapter.

Cognitive Functioning in Older Adults

LO4 Describe the cognitive functioning of older adults.

At the age of 70, John Rock invented the birth control pill. At age 92, Hazel McCallion continued to serve as mayor of Mississauga, Ontario, having been re-elected or acclaimed each election since 1978. At age 80, Canadian author Robertson Davies wrote *The Cunning Man*, to add to his over 30 other works of fiction. Other internationally acclaimed Canadian authors now in their seventies and eighties and still actively engaged in their art are Margaret Atwood and Alice Munro. When Pablo Casals was 95, a reporter asked him why, as the greatest cellist who ever lived, he still practised six hours per day. Mr. Casals replied, "Because I feel like I am making progress" (Canfield & Hansen, 1995).

The Multi-Dimensional, Multi-Directional Nature of Cognition

In thinking about the nature of cognitive change in adulthood, it is important to consider that cognition is a multi-dimensional concept. It is also important to consider that while some dimensions of cognition might decline as we age, others might remain stable or even improve (Bucur & Madden, 2007).

Cognitive Mechanics and Cognitive Pragmatics

Paul Baltes (2003; Baltes, Lindenberger, & Staudinger, 2006) clarified the distinction between those aspects of the aging mind that show decline and those that remain stable or even improve. **Cognitive mechanics** *are the hardware of the mind and reflect the neurophysiological architecture of the brain developed through evolution. Cognitive mechanics involve the speed and accuracy of the processes involving sensory input, visual and motor memory, discrimination, comparison, and categorization.* Because of the

The Multi-Dimensional, Multi-Directional Nature of Cognition

Education, Work, and Health: Links to Cognitive Functioning

Promoting Cognitive Skills in Later Life: Use It or Lose It

Cognitive Neuroscience and Aging

cognitive mechanics The "hardware" of the mind, reflecting the neurophysiological architecture of the brain developed through evolution; involve the speed and accuracy of the processes involving sensory input, visual and motor memory, discrimination, comparison, and categorization.

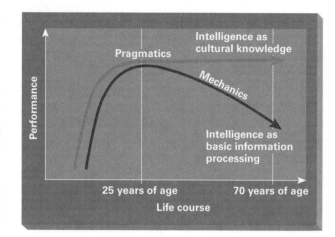

Figure 17.8

Theorized Age Changes in Cognitive Mechanics and Cognitive Pragmatics

Baltes argues that cognitive mechanics decline during aging, whereas cognitive pragmatics do not. Cognitive mechanics have a biological/genetic foundation; cognitive pragmatics have an experiential/cultural foundation.

strong influence of biology, heredity, and health on cognitive mechanics, their decline with aging is likely. Some researchers conclude that the decline in cognitive mechanics may begin as soon as early mid-life (Finch, 2009; Salthouse, 2009).

Conversely, **cognitive pragmatics** *are the culture-based software programs of the mind. Cognitive pragmatics include reading and writing skills, language comprehension, educational qualifications, professional skills, and also the type of knowledge about the self and life skills that help us master or cope with life.* Because of the strong influence of culture on cognitive pragmatics, their improvement into old age is possible. Thus, while cognitive mechanics may decline in old age, cognitive pragmatics may actually improve (see Figure 17.8).

The distinction between cognitive mechanics and cognitive pragmatics is similar to the one between fluid (mechanics) and crystallized (pragmatics) intelligence that was described in Chapter 15. Indeed, the similarity is so strong that some experts now use these terms to describe cognitive aging patterns: fluid mechanics and crystallized pragmatics (Lovden & Lindenberger, 2007).

What factors are most likely to contribute to the decline in fluid mechanics in late adulthood? Among the most likely candidates are processing speed, working memory capacity, and suppressing irrelevant information (inhibition) (Lovden & Lindenberger, 2007). Now that we have examined the distinction between fluid mechanics and crystallized pragmatics, let us explore some of the more specific cognitive processes that reflect these two general domains, beginning with these aspects of cognitive mechanics: sensory/motor and speed of processing.

cognitive pragmatics The culture-based "software programs" of the mind; include reading and writing skills, language comprehension, educational qualifications, professional skills, and also the type of knowledge about the self and life skills that help us master or cope with life.

Speed-of-Processing Dimensions

It is now well-accepted that the speed of processing information declines in late adulthood (Salthouse, 2009), although there is considerable individual variation in this ability (Hartley, 2006). Accumulated knowledge may compensate to some degree for slower processing speed in older adults. For example, one recent study found that knowledge was more important on a memory task for older adults than younger adults, and that older adults may rely on age-related increases in knowledge to partially compensate for a decline in processing speed (Hedden, Lautenschlager, & Park, 2005).

The decline in processing speed in older adults is likely due to a decline in functioning of the brain and central nervous system (Finch, 2009). Health and exercise may influence how much decline in processing speed occurs (Gerrotsen et al., 2003). Studies have found that aerobic exercise modestly increases attention and processing speed, executive function, and memory, although the effects on working memory are less consistent (Smith et al., 2010).

developmental **connection**

Information Processing Approach

Attention

Changes in attention are important aspects of cognitive aging (Commodari & Guarnera, 2008). Three aspects of attention that have been investigated in older adults are selective attention, divided attention, and sustained attention:

selective attention Focusing on a specific aspect of experience that is relevant while ignoring others that are irrelevant.

divided attention Concentrating on more than one activity at the same time.

sustained attention The state of readiness to detect and respond to small changes occurring at random times in the environment.

episodic memory The retention of information about the where and when of life's happenings.

semantic memory A person's knowledge about the world—including fields of expertise, general academic knowledge of the sort learned in school, and "everyday knowledge."

- **Selective attention** *is focusing on a specific aspect of experience that is relevant while ignoring others that are irrelevant.* An example of selective attention is the ability to focus on one voice among many in a crowded room or a noisy restaurant. Another is making a decision about which stimuli to attend to when making a left turn at an intersection. Generally, older adults are less adept at selective attention than younger adults are (Bucur & Madden, 2007). However, on simple tasks involving a search for a feature, such as determining whether a target item is present on a computer screen, age differences are minimal when individuals are given sufficient practice.

- **Divided attention** *involves concentrating on more than one activity at the same time.* When the two competing tasks are reasonably easy, age differences among adults are minimal or non-existent. However, the more difficult the competing tasks are, the less effectively older adults divide attention when compared to younger adults (Bucur & Madden, 2007). A study conducted by Erin I. Skinner and Myra A. Fernandes of the University of Waterloo investigated the effect of divided attention using study-list repetition. They found that younger adults made fewer errors, whereas older adults were more susceptible to erroneous recall (Skinner & Fernandes, 2009).

- **Sustained attention** *is the state of readiness to detect and respond to small changes occurring at random times in the environment.* Sometimes sustained attention is referred to as vigilance. On tests of simple vigilance, older adults usually perform as well as younger adults; however, older adults' performance usually drops on complex vigilance tasks (Bucur & Madden, 2007). For example, a recent study revealed that older adults showed less effective decision making on a complex laboratory task that required sustained attention than did younger adults (Isella et al., 2008).

Memory

Memory does change during aging, but not all memory changes with age in the same way (Barba, Attali, & La Corte, 2010). The main dimensions of memory and aging that have been studied include episodic memory, semantic memory, cognitive resources (such as working memory and perceptual speed), memory beliefs, and non-cognitive factors, such as health education and socio-economic factors.

EPISODIC MEMORY   **Episodic memory** *is the retention of information about the where and when of life's happenings* (Tulving, 2000)—for example, what it was like when your younger sister or brother was born, or what happened to you on your first date, or what you were doing when you heard that airplanes had struck the World Trade Center in New York.

Younger adults have better episodic memory than older adults (Cansino, 2009). A recent study of 18- to 94-year-olds revealed that increased age was linked to increased difficulty in retrieving episodic information, facts, and events (Siedlecki, 2007). Older adults report that they can remember older events better than more recent ones; however, the evidence of research contradicts this and reports that in older adults, the older the memory, the less accurate it is.

Autobiographical memory is the personal recollection of events and facts. Autobiographical memories are stored as episodic memories (Daselaar et al., 2008). A robust finding in autobiographical memory is called the reminiscence bump, in which adults remember more events from the second and third decades of their lives than from other decades (Bernstein & Rubin, 2002). The "bump" is found more for positive than negative life events. A recent study revealed that the "bump" was characterized not only by positive life events, but also by high perceived control over the event and high perceived influence of the event on one's later development (Gluck & Bluck, 2007).

SEMANTIC MEMORY   **Semantic memory** *is a person's knowledge about the world, including a person's fields of expertise* (such as knowledge of chess, for a skilled chess player), *general academic knowledge of the sort learned in school* (such as knowledge of geometry), *and "everyday knowledge" about meanings of words, famous individuals, important places, and common things* (such as information about Nelson Mandela, Mahatma Gandhi, and Pierre Trudeau). Semantic memory appears to be independent of an individual's personal identity with the past. For example, you can access a fact—such as "Kabul is the capital of Afghanistan"—and not have the foggiest idea of when and where you learned it.

Does semantic memory decline during aging? Among the tasks that researchers often use to assess semantic memory are vocabulary, general knowledge, and word identification (Bucur & Madden, 2007). Older adults do often take longer to retrieve semantic information, but usually they can ultimately retrieve it. However, the ability to retrieve very specific information (such as names) usually declines in older adults (Luo & Craik, 2008). For the most part, episodic memory declines more in older adults than semantic memory (Yoon, Cole, & Lee, 2009).

Although many aspects of semantic memory are reasonably well-preserved in late adulthood, a common memory problem for older adults is the *tip-of-the-tongue (TOT) phenomenon*, in which individuals can't quite retrieve familiar information but have the feeling that they should be able to retrieve it (Bucur & Madden, 2007). Researchers have found that older adults are more likely to experience TOT states than younger adults (Bucur & Madden, 2007).

COGNITIVE RESOURCES: WORKING MEMORY AND PERCEPTUAL SPEED   One view of memory suggests that a limited number of cognitive resources can be devoted to any cognitive task. Two important cognitive resource mechanisms are working memory and perceptual speed. Working memory is the concept currently used to describe short-term memory as a place for mental work. **Working memory** *is like a mental "workbench" that allows individuals to manipulate and assemble information when making decisions, solving problems, and comprehending written and spoken language* (Baddeley, 2007a). Researchers have found a decline in working memory during the late adulthood years.

Perceptual speed is another cognitive resource that has been studied by researchers on aging (Deary, Johnson, & Starr, 2010; Salthouse, 2009). Perceptual speed is the ability to perform simple perceptual-motor tasks, such as deciding whether pairs of two-digit or two-letter strings are the same or different. Perceptual speed shows considerable decline in late adulthood, and it is strongly linked with decline in working memory (Bopp & Verhaeghen, 2007). A recent study revealed that trial-to-trial variability in perceptual speed on a reaction time task signalled impending decline in cognitive performance in older adults (Lovden et al., 2007).

EXPLICIT AND IMPLICIT MEMORY   Researchers also have found that aging is linked to changes in explicit memory (Yoon, Cole, & Lee, 2009). **Explicit memory** *is memory of facts and experiences that individuals consciously know and can state.* Explicit memory also is sometimes called declarative memory. Examples of explicit memory include being at a grocery store and remembering what you wanted to buy, or recounting the events of a movie you have seen. **Implicit memory** *is memory without conscious recollection; it involves skills and routine procedures that are automatically performed.* Implicit memory is sometimes called procedural memory. Examples of implicit memory include unconsciously remembering how to drive a car, swing a golf club, or type on a keyboard.

Implicit memory is less likely to be adversely affected by aging than explicit memory (Howard et al., 2008). Thus, older adults are more likely to forget what items they wanted to buy at a grocery store (unless they wrote them down on a list and brought it with them) than they are to forget how to drive a car. Their perceptual speed might be slower in driving the car, but they remember how to do it.

SOURCE MEMORY   **Source memory** *is the ability to remember where one learned something.* Failures of source memory increase with age in the adult years and can create awkward situations, such as when an older adult forgets who told a joke and retells it to the source (Besken & Gulgoz, 2009; Glisky & Kong, 2008). Lynn Hasher (2003, p. 1301) argues that age differences are substantial in many studies of memory, such as resource memory, when individuals are asked "for a piece of information that just doesn't matter much. But if you ask for information that is important, old people do every bit as well as young adults . . . young people have mental resources to burn. As people get older, they get more selective in how they use their resources."

working memory The concept currently used to describe short-term memory as a place for mental work. Working memory is like a "workbench" where individuals can manipulate and assemble information when making decisions, solving problems, and comprehending written and spoken language.

implicit memory Memory without conscious recollection; it involves skills and routine procedures that are automatically performed.

explicit memory Memory of facts and experiences that individuals consciously know and can state.

source memory The ability to remember where one learned something.

prospective memory Involves remembering to do something in the future.

PROSPECTIVE MEMORY   **Prospective memory** *involves remembering to do something in the future,* such as remembering to take your medicine or remembering to do an errand. Although some researchers have found a decline in prospective memory with age, a number of studies show that whether there is a decline is complex and depends on such factors as the nature of the task and what is being assessed (Einstein & McDaniel, 2005; Marsh et al., 2007; Rendell et al., 2007). For example, age-related deficits occur more often in time-based (such as remembering to call someone next Friday) than in event-based (remembering to tell your friend to read a particular book the next time you see her) prospective memory tasks. Further, declines in prospective memory occur more in laboratory than real-life settings (Bisiacchi, Tarantino, & Ciccola, 2008). Indeed, in some real-life settings, such as keeping appointments, older adults' prospective memory is better than younger adults' (Luo & Craik, 2008).

BELIEFS, EXPECTATIONS, AND FEELINGS   Some studies have found that older adults' beliefs and expectancies about memory play a role in their actual memory (Lineweaver, Berger, & Hertzog, 2009; McDougall et al., 2009). It matters what people tell themselves about their ability to remember. Older adults' positive or negative beliefs or expectancies about their memory skills are related to their actual memory performance (Hess & Hinson, 2006). In one study, older adults were randomly assigned to read one of two mock newspaper articles at the beginning of a testing situation (Hess et al., 2003). One described the declines in memory that characterize aging; the other emphasized research on the preservation of memory skills in older adults. The older adults who read the pessimistic account of memory and aging remembered 20 to 30 percent fewer words than people who read about the ability to maintain memory in old age.

Attitudes and feelings also matter (Reese & Cherry, 2004). One study found that individuals with low anxiety about their memory skills and high self-efficacy regarding their use of memory in everyday contexts had better memory performance than their high-anxiety/low-self-efficacy counterparts (McDougall et al., 1999).

NON-COGNITIVE FACTORS   Health, education, and socio-economic status can influence an older adult's performance on memory tasks (Fritsch et al., 2007; Lachman et al., 2010; Noble et al., 2010). Although such non-cognitive factors as good health are associated with less memory decline in older adults, they do not eliminate memory decline. A recent study revealed that older adults with less education had lower cognitive abilities than those with more education (Lachman et al., 2010). However, for older adults with less education, frequently engaging in cognitive activities improved their episodic memory.

One criticism of research on memory and aging is that it has relied primarily on laboratory tests. The argument is that such tasks are contrived and do not represent the everyday cognitive tasks performed by older adults. A number of researchers have found that using more familiar tasks reduces age decrements in memory but does not eliminate them. Younger adults are better than older adults at remembering faces, routes through town, grocery items, and performed activities.

CONCLUSIONS ABOUT MEMORY AND AGING   Some, but not all, aspects of memory decline in older adults (Healey & Hasher, 2009). The decline occurs primarily in episodic and working memory, not in semantic memory. A decline in perceptual speed is associated with memory decline (Salthouse, 2009). Successful aging does not mean eliminating memory decline, but reducing it and adapting to it. As we will see later in this chapter, older adults can use certain strategies to reduce memory decline.

Decision Making

Despite declines in many aspects of memory, such as working memory and long-term memory, many older adults preserve decision-making skills reasonably well (Healey & Hasher, 2009). In some cases, though, age-related decreases in memory will impair decision making (Brand & Markowitsch, 2010). However, older adults especially perform well when decision making is not constrained by time pressures and when the decision is meaningful for them (Yoon, Cole, & Lee, 2009).

Wisdom

Does wisdom improve with age? If so, what is "wisdom"? **Wisdom** *is expert knowledge about the practical aspects of life that permits excellent judgment about important matters.* This practical knowledge involves exceptional insight into human development and life matters, good judgment, and an understanding of how to cope with difficult life problems. Thus, wisdom, more than standard conceptions of intelligence, focuses on life's pragmatic concerns and human conditions (Staudinger & Gluck, 2011). This practical knowledge system can take many years to acquire, accumulating through intentional, planned experiences and accidental experiences. One recent study on wisdom revealed that older adults engaged in higher-ordered reasoning about social conflicts than young or middle-aged adults (Grossman et al., 2010). The higher-order reasoning activities that older adults used included multiple perspectives, allowance for compromise, and recognizing the limits of one's knowledge.

In regard to wisdom, research by Baltes and his colleagues (Baltes & Kunzmann, 2007; Baltes & Smith, 2008) has found that:

- High levels of wisdom are rare. Few people, including older adults, attain a high level of wisdom. That only a small percentage of adults show wisdom supports the contention that it requires experience, practice, or complex skills.
- The time frame of late adolescence and early adulthood is the main age window for wisdom to emerge (Staudinger & Dorner, 2007; Staudinger & Gluck, 2011). No further advances in wisdom have been found for middle-aged and older adults beyond the level they attained as young adults.
- Factors other than age are critical for wisdom to develop to a high level. For example, certain life experiences, such as being trained and working in a field concerned with difficult life problems and having wisdom-enhancing mentors, contribute to higher levels of wisdom. Also, people higher in wisdom have values that are more likely to consider the welfare of others rather than their own happiness.
- Personality-related factors, such as openness to experience, generativity, and creativity, are better predictors of wisdom than cognitive factors such as intelligence.

Robert J. Sternberg (2000, 2009d), whose triarchic theory of intelligence we described in Chapter 8, argues that wisdom is linked to both practical and academic intelligence. In his view, academic intelligence is a necessary, but in many cases insufficient, requirement for wisdom. Practical knowledge about the realities of life is also needed for wisdom. For Sternberg, balance among self-interest, the interests of others, and contexts produces a common good. Thus, wise individuals don't just look out for themselves—they also need to consider others' needs and perspectives, as well as the particular context involved. Sternberg assesses wisdom by presenting problems to individuals that require solutions which highlight various intrapersonal, interpersonal, and contextual interests. He also emphasizes that these aspects of wisdom should be taught in schools. Sternberg's emphasis on using knowledge for the common good in a manner that addresses competing interests is what mainly differentiates it from Baltes and his colleagues' view of wisdom.

Traditional Native elders are carefully selected because one of the essential requirements of being an elder is the ability to use wisdom to guide others. The individual is selected for his or her keen compassion and perceptive abilities. Once selected, the individual goes through years of rigorous mentoring and training, which involves traditional teachings and ceremonies, to be given the combined experiences and accumulated wisdom of other elders (Criger, 2007, interview).

Education, Work, and Health: Links to Cognitive Functioning

Education, work, and health are three important influences on the cognitive functioning of older adults. They are also three of the most important factors involved in understanding why cohort effects need to be taken into account in studying the cognitive functioning of older adults. Indeed cohort effects are very important to consider in the study of cognitive aging (Margrett & Deshpande-Kamat, 2009).

wisdom Expert knowledge about the practical aspects of life that permits excellent judgment about important matters.

Education

Successive generations in Canada are better educated. More older adults have gone to college or university than their parents or grandparents; as well, more older adults are returning to college or university today to further their education than in past generations. Educational experiences are positively correlated with scores on intelligence tests and information-processing tasks, such as memory (Aiken Morgan, Sims, & Whitfield, 2010; Ganguli et al., 2010; Schaie, 2008; Wilson et al., 2009).

Older adults might seek more education for a number of reasons (Manheimer, 2007). They might want to better understand the nature of their aging. They might want to learn more about the social and technological advances that have produced dramatic changes in their lives. They might want to discover new knowledge and to learn relevant skills to cope with societal and job demands in later life. Finally, older adults may seek more education to enhance their self-discovery and the leisure activities that will enable them to make a smoother adjustment to retirement.

Work

Successive generations also have had work experiences that include a stronger emphasis on cognitively oriented labour (Elias & Wagster, 2007). Our great-grandfathers and grandfathers were more likely to be manual labourers than were our fathers, who are more likely to be involved in cognitively oriented occupations. As the industrial society continues to be replaced by the information society, younger generations will have more experience in jobs that require considerable cognitive investment. The increased emphasis on information processing in jobs likely enhances an individual's intellectual abilities (Kristjuhan & Taidre, 2010; Schooler & Kaplan, 2008).

Health

Successive generations have also been healthier in late adulthood, since better treatments for a variety of illnesses (such as hypertension) have been developed. Many of these illnesses have a negative impact on intellectual performance (Dahle, Jacobs, & Raz, 2009; Pressler et al., 2010). Hypertension has been linked to lower cognitive performance in a number of studies in both older, middle aged, and younger adults (Bucur & Madden, 2010).

K. Warner Schaie (1994) concluded that some diseases are linked to cognitive dropoffs—these diseases include heart disease, diabetes, and high blood pressure. Schaie does not believe the diseases directly cause mental decline. Rather, the lifestyles of the individuals with the diseases might be the culprits. For example, overeating, inactivity, and stress are related to both physical and mental decline (Lee et al., 2007). And researchers have found age-related cognitive decline in adults with mood disorders, such as depression (Chodosh et al., 2007; Gualtieri & Johnson, 2008).

A number of research studies have found that lifestyle and exercise are linked to improved cognitive functioning (Kramer & Morrow, 2009; Liu-Ambrose et al., 2010; Williamson et al., 2009). Researchers have found that aerobic exercise is related to improved memory and reasoning (Erickson et al., 2009). Walking or any other aerobic exercise appears to get blood and oxygen pumping to the brain, which can help people think more clearly (Studenski et al., 2006).

Studies have also documented that the mental health of older adults can influence their cognitive functioning. A recent study revealed that depressive symptoms predicted cognitive decline in older adults, and a six-year longitudinal study found that higher levels of anxiety and depression assessed at the beginning of the study were linked to poorer memory functioning six years later (van Hooren et al., 2005).

A final aspect of health that is important to consider in cognitive functioning in older adults is *terminal decline*. This concept emphasizes that changes in cognitive functioning may be linked more to distance from death or cognition-related pathology than distance from birth (Lovden & Lindenberger, 2007; Palgi et al., 2010). A recent study revealed that inconsistency in speed of processing was an early marker of impending death (Macdonald, Hultsch, & Dixon, 2008).

Promoting Cognitive Skills in Later Life: Use It or Lose It

Changes in cognitive activity patterns might result in disuse and consequent atrophy of cognitive skills. This concept is captured in the adage, "Use it or lose it." The mental activities that likely benefit the maintenance of cognitive skills in older adults are activities such as reading books, doing crossword puzzles, and going to lectures and concerts. Use it or lose it also is a significant component of the engagement model of cognitive optimization that emphasizes how intellectual and social engagement can buffer age-related declines in intellectual development (La Rue, 2010; Park et al., 2007; Stine-Morrow, 2007). The following studies support the use it or lose it concept and the engagement model of cognitive optimization:

- An analysis of middle-aged and older adults who participated in the Victoria Longitudinal Study found that participation in intellectually engaging activities served as a buffer against cognitive decline (Hultsch et al., 1999). Recent analyses of the participants in this study revealed that engagement in cognitively complex activities was linked to faster and more consistent processing speed (Bielak et al., 2007).
- In a longitudinal study of 801 Catholic priests 65 years and older, those who regularly read books, did crossword puzzles, or otherwise exercised their minds were 47 percent less likely to develop Alzheimer's disease than the priests who rarely engaged in these activities (Wilson et al., 2002).
- A recent study revealed that reading daily was linked to reduced mortality in men in their seventies (Jacobs et al., 2008).
- In another recent study, 488 individuals 75 to 85 years of age were assessed for an average of five years (Hall et al., 2009). At the beginning of the research, the older adults indicated how often they participated in six activities—reading, writing, doing crossword puzzles, playing card or board games, having group discussions, and playing music—on a daily basis. Across the five years of the study, the point at which memory loss accelerated was assessed and it was found that for each additional activity the older adult engaged in, the onset of rapid memory loss was delayed by .18 years. For older adults who participated in 11 activities per week compared to their counterparts who engaged in only 4 activities per week, the point at which accelerated memory decline occurred was delayed by 1.29 years.

If cognitive skills are atrophying in late adulthood, can they be retrained? An increasing number of research studies indicate that they can to a degree (Boron, Willis, & Schaie, 2007; Kramer & Morrow, 2009; Park & Reuter-Lorenz, 2009; Willis, Schaie, & Martin, 2009). There are essentially two main conclusions that can be derived from research: (1) training can improve the cognitive skills of many older adults; but (2) there is some loss in plasticity in late adulthood (Baltes, Lindenberger, & Staudinger, 2006).

A recent research review concluded that providing structured experience in situations requiring higher-level cognitive coordination of skills—such as playing complex video games, switching tasks, and dividing attention—can improve older adults' cognitive skills (Hertzog et al., 2009).

In an extensive recent study by Sherry Willis and her colleagues (2006), older adults were randomly assigned to one of four groups: those training in (1) reasoning, (2) memory, and (3) speed of processing; and (4) a control group that received no training. Each type of training showed an immediate effect in its domain—reasoning training improved reasoning, memory training improved memory, and speed of processing training improved speed of processing. However, the training effects did not transfer across cognitive domains, such that speed of processing training did not benefit the older adults' memory or reasoning, for example. The older adults who were given reasoning training did have less difficulty in the activities of daily living than a control group who did not receive this training. The activities of daily living that were assessed included how independently the older adults were able to prepare meals, do housework, do finances, go shopping, and engage in health maintenance. Each intervention maintained its effects on the specific targeted

critical thinking

Have you ever observed a cashier, sales clerk, or nurse address a senior as "dear" or "sweetie"? Have you ever been with or observed a situation where a parent or grandparent is seeking information only to have a service provider explain the information to you or another younger person with the senior but not to the older person? Why do you suppose this happens? What are some of the assumptions underlying this kind of behaviour? How do you think this makes the older person feel? How might it contribute to their sense of autonomy? Their sense of self?

ability across the five years of the study. However, neither memory nor speed of processing training benefited the older adults' activities of daily living.

Another recent study had older adults participate in a 20-week activity called Senior Odyssey, a team-based program involving creative problem solving that is derived from the Odyssey of the Mind program for children and emerging adults (Stine-Morrow et al., 2007). In a field experiment, compared with a control group who did not experience Senior Odyssey, the Senior Odyssey participants showed improved processing speed, somewhat improved creative thinking, and increased mindfulness. Mindfulness involves generating new ideas, being open to new information, and being aware of multiple perspectives (Langer, 2000, 2007).

In sum, the cognitive vitality of older adults can be improved through cognitive and fitness training (Kramer & Morrow, 2009). However, benefits have not been observed in all studies (Salthouse, 2006). Further research is needed to determine more precisely which cognitive improvements occur through cognitive and physical fitness training in older adults (Stine-Morrow, 2007).

Cognitive Neuroscience and Aging

On several occasions in this chapter, we have indicated that certain regions of the brain are involved in links between aging and cognitive functioning. Recall from Chapter 2 the substantial increase in interest in the brain's capacity to adapt to trauma, injury, and aging. The field of cognitive neuroscience has emerged as the major discipline that studies links between brain and cognitive functioning (Meeks & Jeste, 2009; Phillips & Andres, 2010; Schiavone et al., 2009; Voelcker-Rehage, Godde, & Staudinger, 2010). This field especially relies on brain imaging techniques, such as fMRI and PET, to reveal the areas of the brain that are activated when individuals are engaging in certain cognitive activities (Charlton et al., 2010; Erickson et al., 2009; Kennedy & Raz, 2009; Park & Reuter-Lorenz, 2009; Ystad et al., 2010). For example, as an older adult is asked to encode and then retrieve verbal materials or images of scenes, the older adult's brain activity is monitored by an fMRI brain scan. Recall that in Chapter 15 we discussed how this technique was used by neuroscientists from the University of Montreal and the University of Wisconsin to investigate the impact of prayer and meditation on the brain and broadening the field of neuroscience to include neurospirituality or neurotheology.

Changes in the brain can influence cognitive functioning, and changes in cognitive functioning can influence the brain. For example, aging of the brain's prefrontal cortex may produce a decline in working memory (Smith, 2007). And when older adults do not regularly use their working memory, neural connections in the prefrontal lobe may atrophy. Further, cognitive interventions that activate older adults' working memory may increase these neural connections.

Although in its infancy as a field, the cognitive neuroscience of aging is beginning to uncover some important links between aging, the brain, and cognitive functioning. These include the following:

- Neural circuits in specific regions of the brain's prefrontal cortex decline, and this decline is linked to poorer performance by older adults on complex reasoning tasks, working memory, and episodic memory tasks (Grady et al. 2006).
- Older adults are more likely than younger adults to use both hemispheres of the brain to compensate for aging declines in attention, memory, and language (Dennis & Cabeza, 2008).
- Functioning of the hippocampus declines less than the functioning of the frontal lobes in older adults.
- Patterns of neural differences with age are larger for retrieval than encoding (Gutchess et al., 2005).
- Compared with younger adults, older adults show greater activity in the frontal and parietal regions while they are engaging in tasks that require cognitive control processes such as attention (Park & Gutchess, 2005).
- Younger adults have better connectivity between brain regions than older adults. For example, a recent study revealed that younger adults had more connections between brain activations in

frontal, occipital, and hippocampal regions than older adults during a difficult encoding task (Leshikar et al., 2010).

■ An increasing number of cognitive and fitness-training studies include brain-imaging techniques, such as fMRI, to assess the results of this training on brain functioning (Erickson et al., 2009). In one study, older adults who walked one hour a day three days a week for six months showed increased volume in the frontal and temporal lobes of the brain (Colcombe et al., 2006).

Denise Park and Patricia Reuter-Lorenz (2009) recently proposed a neurocognitive scaffolding view of connections between the aging brain and cognition. In this view, increased activation in the prefrontal cortex with aging reflects an adaptive brain that is compensating to the challenges of declining neural structures and function, and declines in various aspects of cognition, including working memory and long-term memory. Scaffolding involves the use of complementary neural circuits to protect cognitive functioning in an aging brain. Among the factors that can strengthen brain scaffolding are cognitive engagement and exercise. In the next several decades, we are likely to see increased effort to uncover links among aging, the brain, and cognitive functioning.

To this point, we have discussed several ideas related to cognitive functioning in older adults. For a review, see the **Reach Your Learning Objectives** section at the end of this chapter.

Meditation, Religion, and Spirituality in Late Adulthood

LO5 Explain the role of meditation, prayer, and spirituality in the lives of older adults.

In Chapter 15, we described meditation, religion, and spirituality with a special focus on middle age, including links to health and well-being. Here, we continue our exploration by describing its importance in the lives of many older adults. In many societies around the world, the elderly are the spiritual leaders in their churches and communities. For example, Pope Francis, elected Pope of the Catholic Church in March 2013, was born in 1934; the 14th Dalai Lama was born in 1935.

The religious patterns of older adults are being increasingly studied (George, 2009; Krause, 2009; Levin, Chatters, & Taylor, 2010; Sapp, 2010). In 2005, 37 percent of Canadians over the age of 65 attended religious services at least once a week, as compared with 16 percent of people between 15 and 44 (Clark & Schellenberg, 2006). Forty-five percent of seniors over 65 who did not attend religious services engaged in personal religious activity, such as private prayer, meditation, or studying religious books. One recent study of rural older adults found that their spirituality/religiousness was linked to a lower incidence of depression (Yoon & Lee, 2007).

Older adults who derived a sense of meaning in life from religion had higher levels of life satisfaction, self-esteem, and optimism. A recent study revealed that religious attendance at least weekly was linked to a lower risk of mortality (Gillum et al., 2008). Religion can also provide some important psychological needs in older adults, including helping them face impending death, find and maintain a sense of meaningfulness and significance in life, and accept the inevitable losses of old age (Daaleman, Perera, & Studenski, 2004). In one study, although church attendance decreased in older adults in their last year of life, their feelings of religiousness and the strength or comfort they received from religion were either stable or increased (Idler, Kasl, & Hays, 2001). Socially, the religious community can provide a number of functions for older adults, such as social activities, social support, and the opportunity to assume teaching and leadership roles.

Throughout the text you have read about many studies demonstrating the interconnection between health and well-being and lifestyle. Dr. Mario Beauregard of the Neuroscience Research Centre at the University of Montreal proposes that the examination of the impact of consciousness on the brain is revolutionizing modern scientific worldviews as this research explores the

During late adulthood, many individuals increasingly engage in prayer. **How might this be linked with longevity?**

connection between philosophy and science without proposing a religious dogma of any type. In other words, the next frontier of science is an exploration of the mind and consciousness (Beauregard, 2012; Raynauld, 2013). Through neuroscience, researchers are examining the connection of prayer, meditation, activities such as Tai Chi or Qigong on the brain and seeing increases in neurotransmitters, such as serotonin and dopamine, which contribute to health and well-being. According to Dr. Herbert Benson, a cardiovascular specialist at Harvard Medical School and a pioneer in the field of mind/body medicine, the "relaxation response" occurs during periods of prayer and meditation. The body's metabolism decreases, the heart rate slows, blood pressure goes down, and we breathe more calmly and regularly (Schiffman, 2012). Beauregard notes the healing impact of placebo medication on patients with severe Parkinson's disease (Beauregard, 2012). Andrew Newberg, another pioneer in the study of religious and spiritual experiences on the brain, believes that these studies can help fill the gap between traditional science and spiritual practices in very practical ways. Newberg equates activities such as meditation and prayer to as fundamental to well-being as fitness training is to an athlete, regardless of the particular sport (Fowler & Rodd, 2013).

To this point, we have discussed a number of ideas about the role of meditation, prayer, and spirituality in late adulthood. For a review, see the **Reach Your Learning Objectives** section at the end of this chapter.

reach your **learning objectives**

Longevity and Biological Theories of Aging

LO1 Describe longevity and the biological theories of aging

Life Expectancy and Life Span	▪ Life expectancy refers to the number of years that probably will be lived by an average person born in a particular year. Life span is the maximum number of years any member of a species can live.
	▪ Life expectancy has increased dramatically in economically privileged regions. Life span, however, remains the same.
	▪ An increasing number of people are living to be 100 years or older.
	▪ Females live on average about six years longer than males do, likely due to biological and social factors; centenarian women outnumber men five to one.
The Young Old, the Old Old, and the Oldest Old	▪ The young old are 65 to 74 years of age, the old old are 75 years and older, and the oldest old are 85 years and older.
	▪ Significant numbers of the oldest old function effectively and are in good health. Negative stereotypes and social reactions combined with decreased abilities create challenges for people as they age.
	▪ A number of experts believe that when the terms "young old," "old old," and "oldest old" are used, they should refer to functional age, not chronological age. Some 85-year-olds function far better than some 65-year-olds.
The Robust Oldest Old	▪ Early portraits of the oldest old were too negative; there is cause for optimism in the development of new regimens and interventions.

| Biological Theories of Aging | ■ **Evolutionary Theory:** Natural selection has eliminated many of the of the harmful conditions to human life.
■ **Cellular Clock Theory:** Hayflick proposed that cells can divide a maximum of about 75 to 80 times, and that as we age, our cells become less capable of dividing. In the last decade, scientists have found that telomeres likely are involved in explaining why cells lose their capacity to divide.
■ **Free-Radical Theory:** People age because unstable oxygen molecules called free radicals are produced in cells.
■ **Mitochondria Theory:** Aging is due to the decay of mitochondria. It appears that this decay is primarily due to oxidative damage and loss of critical micronutrients supplied by the cell.
■ **Hormone Stress Theory:** Aging in the body's hormonal system can lower resilience to stress and increase the likelihood of disease. |

The Course of Physical Development in Late Adulthood

LO2 Describe and give examples of how a person's brain and body change in late adulthood.

The Aging Brain	■ The brain occupies less of the cranial cavity after 50 years of age. ■ The aging brain retains considerable plasticity and adaptiveness. ■ Growth of dendrites can take place in older adults. ■ The brain has the capacity to virtually rewire itself to compensate for loss in older adults.
The Immune System	■ A decline in immune system functioning with aging is well documented. ■ Exercise can improve immune system functioning.
Physical Appearance and Movement	■ The most obvious signs of aging are wrinkled skin and age spots on the skin. ■ People get shorter as they age, and their weight often decreases after age 60 due to loss of muscle.
Sensory Development	■ The visual system declines, but the vast majority of older adults can have their vision corrected so that they can continue to work and function in the world. ■ Hearing decline often begins in middle age, but usually does not become much of an impediment until late adulthood. Hearing aids can diminish hearing problems for many older adults. ■ Smell and taste can decline, although the decline is minimal in healthy older adults. ■ Changes in touch sensitivity are associated with aging, but this does not present a problem for most older adults. ■ Sensitivity to pain decreases in late adulthood.
The Circulatory System and Lungs	■ When heart disease is absent, the amount of blood pumped is the same, regardless of an adult's age. ■ Treatment for cardiovascular diseases (CVD) has improved as a result of research, improved surgical procedures, drug therapies, and prevention programs. ■ Lung capacity does drop, but older adults can improve lung functioning with diaphragm-strengthening exercises.
Sexuality	■ Aging in late adulthood does include some changes in sexual performance, more for males than females. Nonetheless, there are no known age limits to sexual activity.

Physical and Mental Health and Wellness

LO3 Identify factors of health and wellness in late adulthood.

Health Problems	<ul><li>As we age, our probability of disease or illness increases.</li><li>Chronic disorders are rare in early adulthood, increase in middle adulthood, and become common in late adulthood. The most common chronic problem is arthritis.</li><li>Nearly three-quarters of older adults die of heart disease, cancer, or stroke.</li><li>Arthritis is especially common in older adults.</li><li>Osteoporosis is the main reason why many older adults walk with a stoop; women are especially vulnerable.</li><li>Accidents are usually more debilitating to older adults than to younger adults.</li></ul>
Exercise, Nutrition, and Weight	<ul><li>The physical benefits of exercise have clearly been demonstrated in older adults.</li><li>Aerobic exercise and weightlifting are both recommended if the adults are physically capable.</li><li>Food restriction in animals can increase the animals' life span, but whether this works with humans is not known. In humans, being overweight is associated with an increased mortality rate.</li><li>Most nutritional experts recommend a well-balanced, low-fat diet for older adults, but do not recommend an extremely low-calorie diet.</li><li>Controversy focuses on whether vitamin supplements—especially the antioxidants, vitamin C, vitamin E, and beta-carotene—can slow the aging process and improve older adults' health.</li></ul>
The Nature of Mental Health in Late Adulthood	<ul><li>Twenty percent of seniors in Canada have a mental illness, similar to that of other age groups, while 80 to 90 percent of seniors living in nursing homes are diagnosed with some form of mental illness.</li><li>At least 10 percent of older adults have mental health problems sufficient to require professional help.</li><li>Depression has been called the "common cold" of mental disorders. However, a majority of older adults with depressive symptoms never receive mental health treatment.</li><li>Older people who are lonely are more vulnerable to late onset alcoholism and substance abuse.</li><li>Frequently depression and substance abuse are disregarded or go unnoticed.</li></ul>
Dementia, Alzheimer's Disease, and Related Disorders	<ul><li>Dementia is a global term for any neurological disorder in which the primary symptoms involve a deterioration of mental functioning.</li><li>Alzheimer's disease is by far the most common dementia. This progressive, irreversible disorder is characterized by gradual deterioration of memory, reasoning, language, and, eventually, physical functioning.</li><li>Special efforts are being made to discover the causes of Alzheimer's and effective treatments for it. Some experts believe Alzheimer's is a puzzle with many pieces.</li><li>Special brain scans, analysis of spinal fluids, and a sophisticated urine test are being used to detect Alzheimer's before its symptoms appear.</li><li>Alzheimer's disease involves a predictable, progressive decline.</li><li>An important concern is caring for Alzheimer's patients and the burdens this places on caregivers.</li><li>In addition to Alzheimer's disease, other types of dementia are multi-infarct dementia and Parkinson's disease.</li></ul>

Health Promotion	■ Although only 7 percent of adults over 65 reside in institutions, 32 percent of adults 85 and over do. The quality of nursing homes varies enormously.
	■ Simply giving nursing home residents options for control and teaching coping skills can change their behaviour and improve their health.
	■ The attitudes of both the health-care provider and the older adult patient are important aspects of the older adult's health care. Too often, health-care personnel share society's negative view of older adults.

Cognitive Functioning in Older Adults

LO4 Describe the cognitive functioning of older adults.

The Multi-Dimensional, Multi-Directional Nature of Cognition	■ Baltes emphasizes a distinction between cognitive mechanics (the neurophysiological architecture, including the brain) and cognitive pragmatics (the culture-based software of the mind).
	■ Cognitive mechanics are more likely to decline in older adults than are cognitive pragmatics.
	■ Researchers have found that the speed of processing dimensions declines in older adults.
	■ In selective attention, older adults fare more poorly than younger adults in general, but when tasks are simple and sufficient practice is given, age differences are minimal. Likewise, for divided attention, on simple tasks adult age differences are minimal, but on difficult tasks older adults do worse than younger adults.
	■ Older adults perform as well as middle-aged and younger adults on measures of sustained attention.
	■ Younger adults have better episodic memory than older adults.
	■ Older adults have more difficulty retrieving semantic information, but they usually can retrieve it eventually.
	■ Researchers have found declines in working memory and perceptual speed in older adults.
	■ Older adults are more likely to show a decline in explicit rather than in implicit memory.
	■ Prospective memory involves remembering what to do in the future; the relation of prospective memory to aging is complex.
	■ An increasing number of studies are finding that people's beliefs about memory play an important role in their memory performance, however some researchers are critical of these findings.
	■ Non-cognitive factors, such as health, education, and socio-economic status, are linked to memory in older adults.
	■ Wisdom is expert knowledge about the practical aspects of life that permits excellent judgments about important matters.
Education, Work, and Health: Links to Cognitive Functioning	■ Successive generations of Canadians have been better educated.
	■ Education is positively correlated with scores on intelligence tests. Older adults may return to education for a number of reasons.
	■ Successive generations have had work experiences that include a stronger emphasis on cognitively oriented labour. The increased emphasis on information processing in jobs likely enhances an individual's intellectual abilities.
	■ Poor health is related to decreased performance on intelligence tests in older adults.
	■ Exercise is linked to higher cognitive functioning in older adults.

Promoting Cognitive Skills in Later Life: Use It or Lose It	■ Researchers are finding that older adults who engage in cognitive activities, especially challenging ones, have higher cognitive functioning than those who do not use their cognitive skills.
	■ Two main conclusions can be derived from research on training cognitive skills in older adults: (1) there is plasticity, and training can improve the cognitive skills of many older adults; and (2) there is some loss in plasticity in late adulthood.
Cognitive Neuroscience and Aging	■ The field of cognitive neuroscience is uncovering important links between aging, the brain, and cognitive functioning.

Meditation, Religion, and Spirituality in Late Adulthood

LO5 Explain the role of meditation, religion, and spirituality in late adulthood.

■ Many elderly are spiritual leaders in their religious institutions and community.

■ Research has found that meditation, religion, and practices in spirituality have a robust impact on the brain. Understanding the interconnection among these practices, the brain, and overall well-being is thought to be the new frontier of neuroscience.

connect

McGraw-Hill Connect provides you with a powerful tool for improving academic performance and truly mastering course material. You can diagnose your knowledge with pre- and post-tests, identify the areas where you need help, search the entire learning package, including the eBook, for content specific to the topic you're studying, and add these resources to your personalized study plan. CONNECT for *Life-Span Development*, fifth Canadian edition, offers the following:

■ chapter-specific online quizzes
■ groupwork
■ presentations
■ writing assignments
■ case studies
· and much more!

Visit CONNECT today!

review ---→ *connect* ---→ reflect

review

Identify and define the five biological theories of aging. **LO1**

What are some of physical changes that occur in late adulthood? **LO2**

Identify health problems that face older people and the impact these may have on caregivers. **LO3**

How does education impact aging? **LO4**

What role do meditation, religion, and spirituality play in late adulthood? **LO5**

connect

In this section, we learned that older adults fare better when they are given more responsibility and control in their lives. At what other age stages is giving individuals more responsibility and control particularly important for their development? In what ways?

reflect *Your Own Personal Journey of Life*

What changes in your lifestyle now might help you age more successfully when you become an older adult?

CHAPTER 18
Socio-Emotional Development in Late Adulthood

"There's nothing pleasant in the realization that my time is running out. I like it here. In fact, I like almost everything about the place. I've been here all my life. Things fit."

—THOMAS SCOTT, CANADIAN POET, 2006

Dr. Herbert Clifford Belcourt

One satisfying aspect of aging is knowing that your life has positively affected the lives of others. Consider Bronfenbrenner's bio-ecological theory outlined in Chapter 2. Our first sphere of influence is close to home: ourselves, our family, and our friends. Beyond that, some people's sphere of influence extends to a wider community. Dr. Herb Belcourt has received many awards, including the Silver Medal for Community Service (1977), the Alberta Aboriginal Role Model Award (1996), the Queen's Golden Jubilee Medal (2003), and the Alberta Centennial Award (2005) for his commitment to making affordable housing available and education accessible for members of the Métis community.

Dr. Belcourt's convocation address at the University of Alberta in 2001 illustrates a life review, as he traced his roots and experiences for the audience. As the eldest of 10 children, his father nurtured his work ethic and entrepreneurial spirit. He worked at a range of occupations, such as logging and coal mining, and later started up an upholstery business. Having accumulated experience and sensing a niche market, he took an educated risk and started Belcourt Construction, one of the largest power line construction companies in Alberta (Belcourt, 2001).

As a successful businessman, Belcourt demonstrated his interest in helping people get ahead by starting Canative Housing Corporation in 1970, with his cousin Orval Belcourt and his friend Georges Brousseau. Canative's mission was to provide affordable housing and education to Métis people in Calgary and Edmonton. Many were skeptical about the venture, thinking that Belcourt was simply trying to line his own pockets; however, Belcourt had a vision, and his motives came from within. Belcourt says he is "here to do something to help people and not himself" (Stevens, 2006). In addition to affordable housing, Canative provided an Urban Skills Training Program that taught parenting, homemaking, health, and budgeting. Canative also provided daycare (Belcourt, 2001; Stevens, 2006).

Dr. Herb Belcourt overcame adversity to leave a legacy that will impact lives for generations to come.

In 2002, Dr. Belcourt liquidated Canative and invested $14 million to further the educational opportunities for people. Interest from the investment is used for bursaries and scholarships. He also donated a residence house for Métis post-graduate students at the University of Alberta. He chaired the first advisory board for the world's first online MBA program at Athabasca University. He was a member of Athabasca's Governing Council from 1997 to 2004, and was among the first to receive the Order of Athabasca in recognition of his exemplary service to the university and society. In 2001, he received an Honorary Doctorate of Law from the University of Alberta. In 2007, Dr. Belcourt was awarded an Honorary Diploma in Community Service from MacEwan College. Although "retired," he serves on many committees and boards in support and promotion of education for Aboriginal peoples.

In terms of Erikson's psychosocial stages of development, Dr. Belcourt in middle adulthood established a legacy that will go on for generations; as well, he can review his life with satisfaction. On a philosophical note, he ended the convocation address with this advice: "Keep positive. Trust yourself. Always remember family and community. Take pride in your heritage and remember where you came from. And once in a while, take an educated chance, because life is what you make of it."

Theories of Socio-Emotional Development

LO1 Discuss four theories of socio-emotional development and aging.

In this section we will look at the main theories of socio-emotional development that focus on late adulthood: Erikson's theory, activity theory, socio-emotional selectivity theory, and selective optimization with compensation theory. We also examine social determinants of health.

Erikson's Theory

We initially described Erik Erikson's (1968) eight stages of the human life span in Chapter 1, and as we explored different periods of development in this book, we have examined the stages in more detail. Here we will discuss his final stage.

Integrity versus despair *is Erikson's eighth and final stage of development, which individuals experience during late adulthood. This involves reflecting on the past and either piecing together a positive review or concluding that one's life has not been well spent.* Through many different routes, the older adult may have developed a positive outlook in each of the preceding periods. If so, retrospective glances and reminiscences will reveal a picture of a life well spent, and the older adult will be satisfied (integrity). However, if the older adult resolved one or more of the earlier stages in a negative way (being socially isolated in early adulthood or stagnated in middle adulthood, for example), retrospective glances about the total worth of his or her life might be negative (despair). Figure 18.1 portrays how positive resolutions of Erikson's eight stages can culminate in wisdom and integrity for older adults.

Life Review

Life review is prominent in Erikson's final stage of integrity versus despair. Life review involves looking back at one's life experiences, evaluating them, interpreting them, and often reinterpreting them (George, 2010; Robitaille et al., 2010). A leading expert on aging, Robert Butler, provides this perspective on life review: ". . . there are chances for pain, anger, guilt, and grief, but there are also opportunities for resolution and celebration, for affirmation and hope, for reconciliation and personal growth" (Butler, 2007, p. 72).

Butler (2007) states that the life review is set in motion as the person looks forward in time and realizes that death is not that far away. Sometimes the life review proceeds quietly; at other times it is intense, requiring considerable work to achieve some sense of personality integration. These thoughts may continue to emerge in brief, intermittent spurts or become essentially continuous. One 76-year-old man commented, "My life is in the back of my mind. It can't be any other way. Thoughts of the past play on me. Sometimes I play with them, encouraging and savouring them; at other times I dismiss them."

Life reviews can include socio-cultural dimensions, such as culture, ethnicity, and gender. Life reviews also can include interpersonal, relationship dimensions, including sharing and intimacy with family members or a friend (Cappeliez & O'Rourke, 2006). And life reviews can include personal dimensions, which might involve the creation and discovery of meaning and coherence. These personal dimensions might unfold in such a way that the pieces do or do not make sense to the older adult. In the final analysis, each person's life review is in some sense unique.

As the past marches by in review, the older adult surveys it, observes it, and reflects on it. Reconsideration of previous experiences and their meaning occurs, often with revision or expanded understanding taking place. This reorganization of the past may provide a more valid picture for the individual, providing new and significant meaning to one's life. It may also help prepare the individual for and reduce fear of death (Cappeliez, O'Rourke, & Chaudhury, 2005). A recent study revealed that one particular life-review course, "Looking for Meaning," reduced the depressive symptoms of middle-aged and older adults (Pot et al., 2010).

Erikson's Theory

Activity Theory

Socio-Emotional Selectivity Theory

Selective Optimization with Compensation Theory

Social Determinants of Health

integrity versus despair Erikson's eighth and final stage of development, which individuals experience in late adulthood; involves reflecting on the past and either piecing together a positive review or concluding that one's life has not been well spent.

Figure 18.1

Erikson's View of How Positive Resolution of the Eight Stages of the Human Life Span Can Culminate in Wisdom and Integrity in Old Age

In Erikson's view, each stage of life is associated with a particular psychosocial conflict and a particular resolution. In this chart, Erikson describes how the issues from each of the earlier stages can mature into the many facets of integrity and wisdom in old age. At left, Erikson is shown with his wife Joan, an artist.

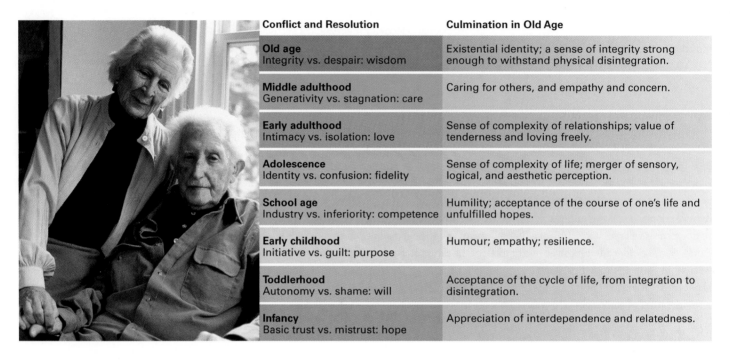

Conflict and Resolution	Culmination in Old Age
Old age Integrity vs. despair: wisdom	Existential identity; a sense of integrity strong enough to withstand physical disintegration.
Middle adulthood Generativity vs. stagnation: care	Caring for others, and empathy and concern.
Early adulthood Intimacy vs. isolation: love	Sense of complexity of relationships; value of tenderness and loving freely.
Adolescence Identity vs. confusion: fidelity	Sense of complexity of life; merger of sensory, logical, and aesthetic perception.
School age Industry vs. inferiority: competence	Humility; acceptance of the course of one's life and unfulfilled hopes.
Early childhood Initiative vs. guilt: purpose	Humour; empathy; resilience.
Toddlerhood Autonomy vs. shame: will	Acceptance of the cycle of life, from integration to disintegration.
Infancy Basic trust vs. mistrust: hope	Appreciation of interdependence and relatedness.

One aspect of life review involves identifying and reflecting on not only the positive aspects of one's life, but also on regrets as part of developing a mature wisdom and self-understanding (Choi & Jun, 2009). The hope is that by examining not only the positive aspects of one's life, but also what an individual has regretted doing, a more accurate vision of the complexity of one's life and possibly increased life satisfaction will be attained (King & Hicks, 2007).

The following is a sampling of recent studies on regrets in older adults:

■ For low-income older adults, regrets about education, careers, and marriage were common, but the intensity of regrets was greater for finance/money, family conflict and children's problems, loss and grief, and health (Choi & Jun, 2009). Common indications of pride involved children and parenting, careers, volunteering/informal caregiving, having a long/strong marriage, and personal growth.

■ Making downward social comparisons, such as "I'm better off than most people," was linked to a reduction in the intensity of regrets in older adults (Bauer, Wrosch, & Jobin, 2008).

■ Following the death of a loved one, resolving regrets was related to lower depression and improved well-being (Torges, Stewart, & Nolen-Hoeksema, 2008). In this study, older adults were more likely to resolve their regrets than were younger adults.

Some clinicians use reminiscence therapy with their older clients. Reminiscence therapy involves discussing past activities and experiences with another individual or group (Peng et al., 2009). The therapy may include the use of photographs, familiar items, and video/audio recordings. Researchers have found that reminiscence therapy improves the mood of older adults (Fiske, Wetherell, & Gatz, 2009). In fact, one study of institutionalized older adults revealed that reminiscence therapy increased their life satisfaction and decreased their depression and loneliness (Chiang et al., 2010).

Robert Peck's Reworking of Erikson's Final Stage

Robert Peck (1968) reworked Erikson's final stage of development, integrity versus despair, by describing three developmental tasks, or issues, that men and women face when they become old. **Differentiation versus role preoccupation** *is Peck's developmental task in which older adults must redefine their worth in terms of something other than work roles.* Adjustment to retirement involves identifying with new roles and quite often requires an adjustment in relationships as well. Peck believes older adults need to pursue a set of valued activities so that time previously spent in an occupation and with children can be filled. **Body transcendence versus body preoccupation** *is Peck's developmental task in which older adults must cope with declining physical well-being.* As older adults age, they may experience a chronic illness and considerable deterioration in their physical capabilities. For men and women whose identity has revolved around their physical well-being, the decrease in health and deterioration of physical capabilities may present a severe threat to their identity and feelings of life satisfaction. However, while most older adults experience illnesses, many enjoy life through human relationships that allow them to go beyond a preoccupation with their aging body. **Ego transcendence versus ego preoccupation** *is Peck's developmental task in which older adults must recognize that although death is inevitable and probably not too far away, they feel at ease with themselves by realizing that they have contributed to the future through the competent rearing of their children or through their vocation and ideas.*

Activity Theory

Activity theory *states that the more active and involved older adults are, the more likely they will be satisfied with their lives.* Researchers have found strong support for activity theory, beginning in the 1960s and continuing into the twenty-first century (Neugarten, Havighurst, & Tobin, 1968; Riebe et al., 2005). These researchers have found that when older adults are active, energetic, and productive, they age more successfully and are happier than if they disengage from society.

One recent large-scale longitudinal study of older adults in Manitoba examined the relation between everyday activities and indicators of successful aging, namely well-being, functioning, and mortality, over a six-year period (Menec, 2003). Participants were asked to fill out a 21-item activities checklist to indicate their participation in each of the activities within the past week. The activities were grouped into three categories: social activities (visiting family or relatives, for example), productive activities (volunteer work, doing light housework or gardening, for example), and solitary activities (collecting hobbies, for example). Well-being was assessed by asking participants how happy they were on a five-point scale ranging from happy and interested in life (1) to so unhappy that life is not worthwhile (5). Function was evaluated in terms of whether cognitive impairment or physical difficulties were present. The results of the study indicated that greater overall activity (but especially social and productive activity) was related to happiness, better functioning, and a lower mortality rate.

Activity theory suggests that many individuals will achieve greater life satisfaction if they continue their middle-adulthood roles into late adulthood. If these roles are stripped from them (as in early retirement), it is important for them to find substitute roles that keep them active and involved.

Socio-Emotional Selectivity Theory

Socio-emotional selectivity theory *states that older adults become more selective about their social networks. Because they place a high value on emotional satisfaction, older adults often spend more time with familiar individuals with whom they have had rewarding relationships.* Developed by Laura Carstensen (1998, 2006, 2008), this theory argues that older adults deliberately withdraw from social contact with individuals peripheral to their lives, while they maintain or increase contact with close friends and family members with whom they have had enjoyable relationships. This selective narrowing of social interaction maximizes positive emotional experiences and minimizes emotional risks as individuals become older.

differentiation versus role preoccupation Peck's developmental task in which older adults must redefine their worth in terms of something other than work roles.

body transcendence versus body preoccupation Peck's developmental task in which older adults must cope with declining physical well-being.

ego transcendence versus ego preoccupation Peck's developmental task in which older adults must recognize that although death is inevitable and probably not too far away, they feel at ease with themselves by realizing that they have contributed to the future through the competent raising of their children or through their vocation and ideas.

activity theory States that the more active and involved older adults are, the more likely they will be satisfied with their lives.

socio-emotional selectivity theory States that older adults become more selective about their social networks. Because they place a high value on emotional satisfaction, older adults often spend more time with familiar individuals with whom they have had rewarding relationships.

What are the main ideas involved in socio-emotional selectivity theory?

----- **critical** thinking -----

An eclectic view would suggest that we take the portions of different theories that are applicable to a given situation and combine them to assist someone to live a more positive life experience. From the theories about aging described in this portion of the chapter, construct an approach to successfully understand the current situation of someone you know who is over 65. Which elements of which theories did you take for your approach? Are there any problems in combining the particular aspects in terms of contradictions in advice to the aging person?

Socio-emotional selectivity theory challenges the stereotype that the majority of older adults are in emotional despair because of their social isolation (Charles & Carstensen, 2009, 2010; Scheibe & Carstensen, 2010). Rather, older adults consciously choose to decrease the total number of their social contacts in favour of spending increasing time in emotionally rewarding interaction with friends and family. That is, they systematically hone their social networks so that available social partners satisfy their emotional needs.

Is there research evidence to support life-span differences in the composition of social networks? Longitudinal studies reveal far smaller social networks for older adults than for younger adults (Charles & Carstensen, 2010). In one study of individuals 69 to 104 years of age, the oldest participants had fewer peripheral social contacts than the relatively younger participants, but about the same number of close emotional relationships (Lang & Carstensen, 1994). And a recent study revealed that compared with younger adults, older adults reported more intense positive emotions with family members, less intense positive emotions with new friends, and equally intense positive emotions with established friends (Charles & Piazza, 2007).

Socio-emotional selectivity theory also focuses on the types of goals that individuals are motivated to achieve (Charles & Carstensen, 2009, 2010). It states that two important classes of goals are (1) knowledge-related and (2) emotional. This theory emphasizes that the trajectory of motivation for knowledge-related goals starts relatively high in the early years of life, peaking in adolescence and early adulthood, and then declining in middle and late adulthood (see Figure 18.2). The emotion trajectory is high during infancy and early childhood, declines from middle childhood through early adulthood, and increases in middle and late adulthood.

One of the main reasons given for these changing trajectories in knowledge-related and emotion-related goals involves the perception of time (Carstensen, 2006). When time is perceived as open-ended, as it is when individuals are younger, people are more strongly motivated to pursue information, even at the cost of emotional satisfaction. But as older adults perceive that they have less time left in their lives, they are motivated to spend more time pursuing emotional satisfaction.

In one study, older adults said they experience less intense negative emotions with family members, established friends, and new friends than younger adults reported (Charles & Piazza, 2007). Consider also these two recent studies: in one study, older adults socialized more frequently

Figure 18.2

Idealized Model of Socio-Emotional Selectivity through the Life Span

According to Carstensen's theory of socio-emotional selectivity, the motivation to reach knowledge-related and emotion-related goals changes across the life span.

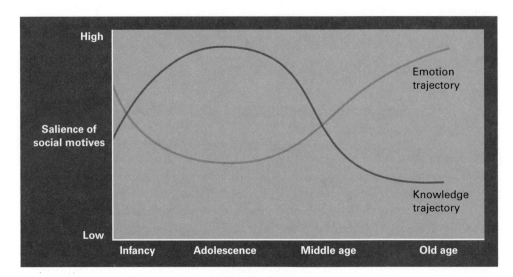

with their neighbours than middle-aged adults did (Cornwell, Laumann, & Schumm, 2008); in the other study, older adults described their own emotions and the emotions of others more positively than younger adults did (Lockenhoff, Costa, & Lane, 2008). Yet other studies have found that older adults are more inclined to engage in passive emotion self-regulation strategies (distracting oneself from the problem and suppressing feelings, for example) and are less inclined to express anger in dealing with interpersonal problems than younger adults are (Blanchard-Fields & Coats, 2007; Coats & Blanchard-Fields, 2008).

Thus, compared with younger adults, the feelings of older adults mellow (Schmidt & Schulz, 2007). Emotional life is on a more even keel with fewer highs and lows. It may be that although older adults have less extreme joy, they have more contentment, especially when they are connected in positive ways with friends and family. Next, we explore a recently proposed theory that, like socio-emotional selectivity theory, focuses on what is necessary for the realization of developmental goals.

developmental **connection**

Stability vs. Change

Selective Optimization with Compensation Theory

Selective optimization with compensation theory *states that successful aging is linked to three main factors: selection, optimization, and compensation (SOC).* The theory describes how people can produce new resources and allocate them effectively to the tasks they want to master (Freund & Lamb, 2011; Riediger, Li, & Lindenberger, 2006). *Selection* is based on the concept that older adults have a reduced capacity and loss of functioning, which require a reduction in performance in most life domains. *Optimization* suggests that it is possible to maintain performance in some areas through continued practice and the use of new technologies. *Compensation* becomes relevant when life tasks require a level of capacity beyond the current level of the older adult's performance potential. Older adults especially need to compensate in circumstances with high mental or physical demands, such as when thinking about and memorizing new material very fast, reacting quickly when driving a car, or running fast. When older adults develop an illness, the need for compensation is obvious.

Paul Baltes and his colleagues proposed the selective optimization with compensation theory (Baltes, 2003; Baltes, Lindenberger, & Staudinger, 2006). They describe the life of the late Arthur Rubinstein to illustrate their theory. When he was interviewed at 80 years of age, Rubinstein said that three factors were responsible for his ability to maintain his status as an admired concert pianist into old age. First, he mastered the weakness of old age by reducing the scope of his performances and playing fewer pieces (which reflects *selection*). Second, he spent more time practising than he had earlier in his life (which reflects *optimization*). Third, he used special strategies, such as slowing down before fast segments, thus creating the impression of faster playing (which reflects *compensation*).

The process of selective optimization with compensation is likely to be effective whenever people pursue successful outcomes (Freund & Lamb, 2011; Staudinger & Jacobs, 2011). What makes SOC attractive to aging researchers is that it makes explicit how individuals can manage and adapt to losses. By using SOC, they can continue to live satisfying lives, although in a more restrictive manner. Loss is a common dimension of old age, although there are wide variations in the nature of the losses involved. Because of this individual variation, the specific form of selection, optimization, and compensation likely will vary depending on the person's life history, pattern of interests, values, health, skills, and resources.

In Baltes's view (2003; Baltes, Lindenberger, & Staudinger, 2006), the selection of domains and life priorities is an important aspect of development. Life goals and priorities likely vary across the life course for most people. For many individuals, it is not just the sheer attainment of goals, but rather the attainment of meaningful goals that makes life satisfying.

In one cross-sectional study, the personal life investments of 25- to 105-year-olds were assessed (Staudinger, 1996) (see Figure 18.3). From 25 to 34 years of age, participants said that they personally invested more time in work, friends, family, and independence, in that order. From 35 to 54 and 55 to 65 years of age, family became more important than friends to them in

selective optimization with compensation theory States that successful aging is linked to three main factors: selection, optimization, and compensation (SOC).

Figure 18.3

Degree of Personal Life Investment at Different Points in Life

Shown here are the top four domains of personal life investment at different points in life. The highest degree of investment is listed at the top (for example, work was the highest personal investment from 25 to 34 years of age, family from 35 to 84, and health from 85 to 105).

25 to 34 Years	35 to 54 Years	55 to 65 Years	70 to 84 Years	85 to105 Years
Work	Family	Family	Family	Health
Friends	Work	Health	Health	Family
Family	Friends	Friends	Cognitive fitness	Thinking about life
Independence	Cognitive fitness	Cognitive fitness	Friends	Cognitive fitness

terms of their personal investment. Little changed in the rank ordering of persons 70 to 84 years old, but for participants 85 to 105 years old, health became the most important personal investment. Thinking about life showed up for the first time on the most important list for those who were 85 to 105 years old.

Social Determinants of Health

Our living conditions play a major role in health. Determinants such as income, education, social inclusion, and housing figure significantly in the health of all, and late adulthood is no exception (Davis, 2011). Poverty factors into each determinant for the young and for those in late adulthood. Among seniors, home ownership is the single most important asset; however, most low-income seniors are renters, and their rent may take up more than 40 percent of their total expenditures. Food accounts for another 20 percent, leaving 40 percent for everything else—transportation, utilities, Internet access, telephone, health care, entertainment, and so on. Those living in urban areas are more hard pressed as rents are higher and may account for a larger percentage (National Seniors Council, 2011). Each province has initiated policies in an effort to reduce poverty, yet the problem persists. The economic downturn has further exacerbated the issue.

Fortunately, most seniors are relatively healthy and often are providing care in the form of grandparenting activities for their children. However, as the population ages, and more become seniors—and do so often with less financial security in the form of pensions than today—elder care looms as a major policy issue for both the provinces and the federal government.

One point to note about the study just described is the demarcation of late adulthood into the subcategories of 70 to 84 and 85 to 105 years of age. This fits with our comments on several occasions that researchers increasingly do not study late adulthood as a homogeneous category.

To this point, we have studied a number of theories of socio-emotional development that pertain to late adulthood. For a review, see the **Reach Your Learning Objectives** section at the end of this chapter.

Personality, the Self, and Society

LO2 Describe links between personality and mortality, and identify changes in the self and society in late adulthood.

Is personality linked to mortality in older adults? Do self-perceptions and self-control change in late adulthood? How are older adults perceived and treated by society?

Personality

The Self

Older Adults in Society

Personality

Might certain personality traits be related to how long older adults live? Researchers have found that some personality traits are associated with the mortality of older adults (Mroczek, Spiro, & Griffin, 2006).

We described the "Big Five" factors of personality in Chapter 16, "Socio-Emotional Development in Middle Adulthood." Researchers have found that several of the Big Five factors of personality continue to change in late adulthood. For example, in one study conscientiousness continued to develop in late adulthood (Roberts, Walton, & Bogg, 2005), and in another study older adults were more conscientious and agreeable than middle-aged and younger adults (Allemand, Zimprich, & Hendriks, 2008).

Might certain personality traits be related to how long older adults live? Researchers have found that some personality traits are associated with the mortality of older adults. A longitudinal study of more than 1,200 individuals across seven decades revealed that the Big Five personality factor of conscientiousness predicted higher mortality risk from childhood through late adulthood (Martin, Friedman, & Schwartz, 2007). Another study found that two of the Big Five factors were linked to older adults' mortality, with low conscientiousness and high neuroticism predicting earlier death (Wilson et al., 2004). And in a five-year longitudinal study higher levels of conscientiousness, extraversion, and openness were related to higher mortality risk (Iwasa et al., 2008).

Following are the results of two other recent studies of the Big Five factors in older adults:

- One study examined developmental changes in the components of conscientiousness (Jackson et al., 2009). In this study, the transition into late adulthood was characterized by increases in these aspects of conscientiousness: impulse control, reliability, and conventionality.
- A study revealed that poor decision making in older adults was linked to the Big Five factor of neuroticism (Denburg et al., 2009).

Affect and outlook on life are also linked to mortality in older adults (Chida & Steptoe, 2008; Mroczek, Spiro, & Griffin, 2006). Older adults characterized by negative affect don't live as long as those who display more positive affect, and optimistic older adults who have a positive outlook on life live longer than their counterparts who are more pessimistic and have a negative outlook on life (Levy et al., 2002).

developmental **connection**

Research Methods: Longitudinal Research

The Self

Our exploration of the self focuses on changes in self-esteem and self-acceptance. In Chapter 12, we described how self-esteem drops in adolescence, especially for girls. How does self-esteem change in the adult years?

Self-Esteem

In a cross-sectional study of self-esteem, a very large, diverse sample of 326,641 individuals from ages 9 to 90 was assessed (Robins et al., 2002). About two-thirds of the participants were from the United States. The individuals were asked to respond to the item "I have high self-esteem" on the following five-point scale:

1	2	3	4	5
Strongly Disagree				Strongly Agree

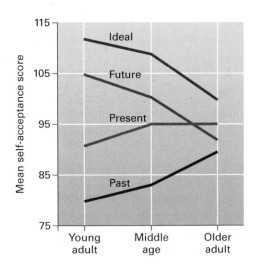

Figure 18.4

Changes in Self-acceptance across the Adult Years

Acceptance of ideal and future selves decreases with age, acceptance of past selves increases with age, and acceptance of present selves increases slightly in middle age and then levels off.

Self-esteem increased in the twenties, levelled off in the thirties and forties, rose considerably in the fifties and sixties, and then dropped significantly in the seventies and eighties (see Figure 18.4). Through most of the adult years, the self-esteem of males was higher than the self-esteem of females. However, in the seventies and eighties, the self-esteem of males and females converged.

Why might self-esteem decline in older adults? Explanations include deteriorating physical health and negative societal attitudes toward older adults, although these factors were not examined in the large-scale study just described. Researchers have found that in late adulthood, being widowed, institutionalized, or physically impaired, having a low religious commitment, and experiencing a decline in health are linked to low self-esteem (Giarrusso & Bengtson, 2007).

Is self-esteem more stable at some points in the life span than at others? A meta-analysis revealed that self-esteem was the least stable in early childhood (Trzesniewski, Donnellan, & Robins, 2003). One reason for this may be that young children don't completely understand the questions they are asked about their self-esteem, but rather provide responses based on their current mood. The stability of self-esteem increases in late adolescence and early adulthood. By late adolescence, individuals are experiencing less dramatic physical changes (compared to pubertal change, for example), and are able to better engage in self-control that likely contributes to the increase in stability of self-esteem. The stability of self-esteem decreases in late adulthood, a time during which dramatic life changes and shifting social circumstances (such as death of a loved one and deteriorating health) may occur.

Self-Acceptance

Another aspect of the self that changes across the adult years is self-acceptance. Self-acceptance is related to possible selves; that is, what individuals might become, what they would like to become, and what they are afraid of becoming (Hoppmann & Smith, 2007). As shown in Figure 18.4, young and middle-aged adults showed greater acceptance of their ideal and future selves than their present and past selves. However, in older adults there was little difference in acceptance of various selves because of decreased acceptance of ideal and future selves and increased acceptance of past selves (Ryff, 1991).

One recent study of older adults (mean age of 81) revealed that hope-related activities had more positive effect and a higher probability of survival over a 10-year period (Hoppmann et al., 2007). Also in this study, hoped-for selves were linked to more likely participation in these domains. Another study of older adults 70- to 100-plus years found that over time 72 percent of the older adults added new domains of hope and 53 percent added new fears (Smith & Freund, 2002). In this study, hopes and fears about health were reported more often than ones related to family and social relationships. Also, for some individuals, as middle-aged adults, their possible selves centre on attaining hoped-for selves, such as acquiring material possessions, but as older adults, they become more concerned with maintaining what they have and preventing or avoiding health problems and dependency (Smith, 2009).

Self-Control

Although older adults are aware of age-related losses, most still effectively maintain a sense of self-control (Lewis, Todd, & Xu, 2011). A recent survey across a range of 21 developed and developing countries revealed that a majority of adults in their sixties and seventies reported being in control of their lives (HSBC Insurance, 2007). In developed countries such as Denmark, the United States, and Great Britain, adults in their sixties and seventies said they had more control over their lives than their counterparts in their forties and fifties. Older adults in Denmark reported the highest self-control.

The negative effects of age-typical problems, such as a decline in physical and cognitive skills and an increase in illness, may be buffered by a flexible, accommodating control style. Researchers have found that accommodating control strategies (changing one's goals to fit a given circumstance) increase in importance and *assimilative control strategies* (changing a situation to meet one's goals) decrease in importance beginning in middle adulthood (Brandstädter & Renner, 1990).

However, it is important to consider not just general self-control, but how people self-regulate their behaviour in specific areas of their lives. One study examined individuals from 13 to 90 years of age. For the oldest group (60 to 90 years of age), self-control was lowest in the physical domain; for the youngest group (13 to 18 years of age), it was lowest in the social domain (Bradley & Webb, 1976). Other researchers have found a decline in perceived self-control in cognitive functioning in older adults (Bertrand & Lachman, 2003).

Older Adults in Society

Does society negatively stereotype older adults? What are some social policy issues in an aging society?

Stereotyping Older Adults

Ageism is a persistent and destructive prejudice and is fundamentally inconsistent with the values expressed in the Canadian Charter of Rights. **Ageism** *is prejudice against others because of their age, especially prejudice against older adults* (Leifheit-Limson & Levy, 2009). Persons in late adulthood are often perceived as incapable of thinking clearly, learning new things, enjoying sex, contributing to the community, or holding responsible jobs. Many older adults face painful discrimination and might be too polite or timid to attack it. Older adults might not be hired for new jobs or might be eased out of old ones because they are perceived as rigid or feeble-minded, or because employing older adults is not considered cost-effective.

ageism Prejudice against others because of their age, especially prejudice against older adults.

In addition, older adults could be shunned socially, possibly because they are perceived as senile or boring. At other times, they might be perceived as children and described with adjectives such as "cute" and "adorable." The elderly might be edged out of their family life by children who see them as sick and overly demanding. Reg MacDonald (National Advisory Council on Aging, 2001) notes that people over 65 "are more likely than other groups to be subject to a guardianship or adult protection" legal action, which cast doubts over the elder's mental competence. While giving control over someone's life to another person may be warranted to safeguard a person at risk, they may at times be sought as a result of stereotypical misconceptions over the true capacities of the older person.

The personal consequences of negative stereotyping about aging can be serious. A physician (60 years old himself) recently told an 80-year-old: "Well, of course, you are tired. You just need to slow down. Don't try to do so much. After all you are very old." Many older adults accept this type of advice, even though it is rooted in age stereotyping rather than medical records. Further, a longitudinal study of adults 70 years of age and older revealed that the older adults who had more negative aging stereotypes at the beginning of the study were more likely to experience hearing decline three years later (Levy, Slade, & Gill, 2006).

Ageism is widespread (Barnes et al., 2008; Tang, 2008). One study found that men were more likely to negatively stereotype older adults than were women (Rupp, Vodanovich, & Crede, 2005). Research indicates that the most frequent form is disrespect for older adults, followed by

critical thinking

Think of a person you know who is 65 or older. Quickly write down the first five or six words that come to mind when you think of this person. Now think of the older people in general and jot down the first five or six words that come to mind. Which list most closely resembles stereotypical images of people in late adulthood?

assumptions about ailments or frailty caused by age (Palmore, 2004). However, the increased number of adults living to an older age has led to active efforts to improve society's image of older adults, obtain better living conditions for older adults, and gain political clout.

The Canadian Association of Retired Persons (CARP) is dedicated to providing information, social networking, and political advocacy for all retired persons 50 years of age and older. Most provinces have a seniors' organization, such as the Alberta Council on Aging or the New Brunswick Senior Citizens Federation, the aims of which include addressing the needs of seniors, improving the quality of life for all older residents in the province, and advising all levels of government on policies and legislation affecting the aged. Most municipalities have seniors' organizations run through local parks and recreation departments as well. Local communities organize social networking, fitness activities, or special interest groups such as photography, hiking, bridge, or art for and by seniors.

Policy Issues in an Aging Society

As noted in Chapter 17, Canadians over the age of 65 constitute the fastest growing age group in Canada. To put this growth in perspective, consider that in the 1950s and 1960s, people over 65 accounted for less than 8 percent of the population. Today, 13.7 percent of the population is over 65, and the number is projected to grow to over 24 percent by 2036 (Turcotte & Schellenberg, 2007).

Policy issues about the well-being of older adults are reviewed as Canadians age. For example, in 2007, Canada eliminated mandatory retirement at a specific age, and regulations about individual registered retirement savings plans (RRSP) have been modified (Klassen, T. R. 2012; Taylor, P.S.2007). Other policy issues include the status of the economy and the viability of the social insurance system, sources of income, the provision of health care, supports for families who care for older adults, social activities, and generational inequity (Statistics Canada, 2007; Neugarten, 1988).

Health, wellness, and security are crucial elements in the quality of an individual's life and in successful aging (Browne & Braun, 2008; Kane, 2007; Special Senate Committee on Aging, 2009; Turcotte & Schellenberg, 2007). Escalating health-care costs are currently causing considerable concern. Across Canada, provinces have made cuts to the budgets of their ministries of health, and the federal government has made cuts in transfer payments to the provinces. The current view is that the increase in health-care costs is the result of an aging population, and that the future will see costs soar so high that maintaining the health system as it is will harm the nation financially. Older adults are seen as having more illnesses than younger people, even though most older adults view their health as good or very good. In a survey conducted in 2003, 37 percent of seniors reported themselves to be in excellent or very good health. This compares with the self-perception for 63 percent of individuals between 25 and 54 years (Turcotte & Schellenberg, 2007). Research shows that older adults do visit doctors more often (although we know very little about the nature of these visits), and are hospitalized more frequently and for longer periods of time than other age groups. As noted with other age groups, education and financial security are strong predictors of better health.

Although many raise the concern that health-care costs will rise because of the changing demographics, the Special Senate Committee on Aging (2009) suggested that this increase may not be as overwhelming as some pundits predict. The Committee believes that provinces can handle the costs through a careful integration of the various levels of care available to respond to health needs, including community-based home care, clinics, hospitals, and long-term facilities. This debate between the "common-sense" version of future health-care costs and the evidence from research into health-care costs is of major importance to Canadians. Some politicians lean toward the introduction of a two-tier health system, while the other perspective promotes the continuation of a universal, single-tier health system. The Commission on the Future of Health Care in Canada (Romanow, 2002) recommended a revitalized and sustainable universal health-care system for Canadians. The current federal government has indicated its desire to act on the Romanow report, although the shape of the future of universal health care in Canada is yet to be fully formed.

A special concern is that although many of the health problems of older adults are chronic rather than acute, the medical system is still based on a "cure" model, rather than a "care" model (Stone, 2006). Chronic illness is long-term, often lifelong, and requires long-term, if not life-term, management (Garasen, Windspoll, & Johnsen, 2008; Nutting et al., 2007). Chronic illness often follows a pattern of an acute period that may require hospitalization, followed by a longer period of remission, and then repetitions of this pattern. The patient's home, rather than the hospital, often becomes the centre of managing the patient's chronic illness. In a home-based system, a new type of cooperative relationship among doctors, nurses, patients, family members, and other service providers needs to be developed (May et al., 2004). Health-care personnel need to be trained and be made available to provide home services, sharing authority with the patient and perhaps yielding to patient authority over the long term.

Eldercare *is the physical and emotional caregiving for older members of the family, whether that care is day-to-day physical assistance or responsibility for arranging and overseeing such care.* An important issue involving eldercare is how it can best be provided (Beverly et al., 2010; Nabe-Nielsen et al., 2009). With so many women in the labour market, who will replace them as caregivers? An added problem is that many caregivers are in their sixties, and may not be in perfect health themselves. They may find the responsibility of caring for relatives who are in their eighties or nineties stressful.

Cranswick and Dosman (2008) reported that in 2002, a little more than two million family members and friends provided care to a senior "because of their long-term health condition" (p. 49). In 2007, this number of caregivers rose to 2.7 million people over the age of 45 providing informal care for seniors, with 75 percent of these care providers being between the ages of 45 and 64. Women constituted 57 percent of the informal caregivers, and they spent more time each week providing the care than did male caregivers. Women were more likely to care for more than one person at a time, as well as being the primary caregiver. Six of every ten care providers were tending to the needs of a parent or parent-in-law. Fewer than 10 percent said they were taking care of a spouse, but this number may be under representative as women tend not to report caring for an ill husband as caregiving. About one-third of caregivers were the person's friend, neighbour, or an extended family member.

Not all informal caregivers live in the same community as the person for whom they provide care. Vézina and Turcotte (2010) found 22 percent of those providing informal care lived more than an hour's travel time away from the parent they helped. Caring from a distance is difficult, as it might interfere with providing assistance for such necessary chores as grocery shopping, taking the parent to doctor's appointments, and the ease of checking in physically with the parent daily, if necessary. People providing care from a distance report having to take time off work (although women were more likely than men to do so), having higher costs in providing care, and not having other siblings with which to share the responsibility of caring for the parent.

Yet another policy issue involving aging is *generational inequity* (introduced in Chapter 1): the view that our aging society is being unfair to its younger members because older adults pile up advantages by receiving an inequitably large allocation of resources. Some authors have argued that generational inequity produces intergenerational conflict and divisiveness in the society at large (Longman, 1987). The generational equity issue raises questions about whether the young should be required to pay for the old (Svihula & Estes, 2008).

The generational equity issue sometimes takes the form of whether the "advantaged" old population is using up resources that should go to disadvantaged children. The argument is that older adults are advantaged because they have publicly provided pensions, health care, housing subsidies, tax breaks, and other benefits that younger age groups do not have. This distribution of wealth should not be viewed as one of generational equity, but rather as a major shortcoming of our broader economic and social policies.

Income

Many older adults are understandably concerned about their income (Holden & Hatcher, 2006). University of British Columbia economist Kevin Milligan (2008) found a significant drop in the number of elderly people living in poverty between the 1970s and the early 2000s (see also Myles & Picot, 2000). The improvement of pension funds, both government and private, accounts for much of this change. The median after-tax income for a senior couple was $41,400 in 2006, up 18 percent

eldercare The physical and emotional caregiving for older members of the family, whether that care is day-to-day physical assistance or responsibility for arranging and overseeing such care.

developmental **connection**

Attachment Theory

over 1996 (National Seniors Council, 2011). However, Milligan (2008) noted that people aged 55 to 64 who were struggling financially were more likely to experience poverty after age 64.

The National Seniors Council (NSC) reported that based on data gathered in 2007, the median after tax income of senior couples in 2006 was $41,400, an increase of 18 percent since 1996. The income for unattached seniors increased to $20,800 (NSC, 2011). The income gap between senior men and women closed significantly during the last two decades of the twentieth century, due largely to the increased participation by women in the paid workforce. With increased participation, more women became eligible for the Canadian Pension Plan or the Quebec Pension Plan (CPP/QPP), private pension plans through their employers, and their own retirement savings plans.

Canada Pension Plan and Old Age Security play a critical role in income security for seniors (NSC, 2011). In fact, the largest share of income for those over 65 comes from the Old Age Security (OAS) program. People with or without a high school diploma relied on OAS/GIS and CPP/QPP significantly more so than those with higher education (Human Resources and Skills Development Canada, 2008). Employer-sponsored pension plans (EPPs), registered retirement savings plans (RRSPs), and private retirement savings plans are three potentially additional sources of pension income after retirement. In 2008, 51 percent of men and 50 percent of women who could contribute to a private pension fund did so, compared to 56 percent and 52 percent in 1997, respectively (Moussaly, 2010). Contribution to an EPP remained the same throughout the period, at 32 percent of those tax filers age 15 and over. Morissette and Ostrovsky (2007) noted that EPPs declined in number from the mid 1980s through the 1990s, especially for men, as companies dropped plans. However, women during this period increased their level of access to EPPs with their larger representation within the workforce. RRSP contribution fell from 41 percent of tax filers in 1997 to only 34 percent in 2008 (Moussaly, 2010). Having a higher income level allows people to contribute maximum amounts to pensions, thus low income earners in mid-life are less likely to contribute and therefore will not have access to these pensions later in life.

In 2006, 5.4 percent of people aged 65 and older in Canada lived on what is called a "low income," which indicates they did not have enough money to meet expected monthly expenditures (National Seniors Council, 2011). This number spiked following the economic downturn of 2008 (Friesen, 2010). Women were nearly twice as likely to live below this level than were men, as 3.4 percent of men over 65 lived on a low income, compared with 7 percent of women aged 65 and over (Canada Year Book, 2008). Living with a partner reduced the chance of living on a low income to an estimated 1.4 percent, as compared with unattached individuals at 15.5 percent on a low income (14 percent of unattached senior men and 16.1 of unattached senior women). Thirteen percent of Aboriginal seniors lived in low income settings in 2000. For those living without a partner, 50 percent lived in a low income situation (Turcotte & Schellenberg, 2007). This rise in poverty among seniors poses an additional source of stress for their children who may be trying to ensure their parents have their basic needs met. This trend is particularly hard on new Canadians, many of whom have sponsored their parents to join them in Canada. This concern is especially pronounced in metropolitan areas, such as Montreal, Toronto, and Vancouver (Friesen, 2010). Those most at risk are those who have worked fewer than 10 years, recent immigrants, and Aboriginal peoples (NRC, 2011). The Conference Board of Canada notes that poverty among seniors in Canada is one of the lowest in the world. When compared to other countries, Canada ranks number 3. The Netherlands ranks number 1, with an elderly poverty rate of 1.7 percent, whereas in Australia nearly 40 percent of the elderly live in poverty. Both the Netherlands and Canada have universal pension plans. The Conference Board also notes that those most vulnerable are widows over the age of 75, largely due to pension allowances linked to employment history (Conference Board of Canada, 2013).

Workers may not accurately understand whether they have a workplace pension plan or how their plan is structured. Statistics Canada reports that 4 percent of employees in the private sector thought their workplaces had a registered pension plan, when, in fact, they did not (Morissette and Zhang, 2004). Schellenberg and Ostrovsky (2008a) reported that 16 percent of Canadians with EPP coverage preparing for retirement were unaware of what coverage they had. Within this group of workers, immigrants were twice as likely as native Canadians to be wrong in their knowledge about a company pension plan. University graduates, unionized workers, employees of large firms, and financial and insurance workers were more knowledgeable about their pension situation than other workers. Many employees confuse their registered retirement savings plan (RRSP) contributions with the company's registered pension plan (RPP).

Work and Retirement

What percentage of older adults continue to work? How productive are they? Who adjusts best to retirement? What is the changing pattern of retirement in Canada and around the world? These are some of the questions we will now examine.

WORK   At the beginning of the twenty-first century, the percentage of men over the age of 65 who continue to work full-time is an estimated 70 percent less than at the beginning of the twentieth century. The earlier trend in the 1990s, when workers appeared to be retiring early (at age 55 or 60), has reversed itself in the 2000s, with more wanting to stay employed after they reach 65 (Special Senate Committee on Aging, 2009). This new trend is creating an important change in older adults' work patterns: working part-time after retiring (Hardy, 2006; Schellenberg & Ostrovsky, 2008b). In 2001, 321,000 Canadian seniors were employed. This figure represents one in 12 of those over the age of 65, many of whom are working in an effort to make ends meet (Curry & Friesen, 2012; Duchesne, 2004). As noted earlier, mandatory retirement practices and policies are no longer legal. They were found to be discriminatory, and therefore, inconsistent with the Charter of Rights. In 2012, amendments to the Canadian Human Rights Act and the Canadian Labour Code prohibit federally regulated employers from setting a mandatory retirement age unless factors of age such as agility, eye-sight, strength, for example firefighters, prevent an individual from meeting an occupational requirement (Government of Canada, 2013). Prior to this change, in all sectors of government occupations (with the exclusion of elected officials) and in many organizations and businesses, maintaining employment after age 65 was very difficult. But, Schellenberg and Ostrovsky (2008b) state that most Canadians still set the age of 65 as their retirement mark and only a few keep working beyond it. Duchesne (2004) reports that employed seniors are more likely to be self-employed; 45 percent of employed seniors as compared with 12 percent of people aged 15 to 64. The Special Senate Committee on Aging (2009) heard evidence that most Canadian workers retire before their ability to work is impaired. Cognitive ability is one of the best predictors of job performance in the elderly. Older workers have lower rates of absenteeism, fewer accidents, and increased job satisfaction, compared with their younger counterparts (Warr, 2004). This means that the older worker can be of considerable value to a company, above and beyond the older worker's cognitive competence. Also, recall from our discussion earlier in the chapter that substantively complex work is linked to a higher level of intellectual functioning (Schooler, 2007). This likely is a reciprocal relation; that is, individuals with higher cognitive ability likely continue to work as older adults, and when they work in substantively complex jobs, this likely enhances their intellectual functioning.

An increasing number of middle-aged and older adults are embarking on a second or third career (Moen & Spencer, 2006). In some cases, this is an entirely different type of work or a continuation of previous work but at a reduced level. Many older adults also participate in unpaid work, as volunteers or active participants in voluntary associations. These options provide older adults with opportunities for productive activity, social interaction, and a positive identity.

RETIREMENT IN CANADA AND OTHER COUNTRIES   The retirement option for older workers is a late-twentieth-century phenomenon in North America (Atchley, 2007). During the economic recession in the 1990s, many older workers were encouraged to take early retirement (before age 65) to reduce the number of layoffs among younger workers or to cut operating costs for struggling organizations. The median retirement age in Canada for 2005 was 62.6 for men and 60 for women (Turcotte & Schellenberg, 2007). The decades following World War II saw the beginning of several pension plans, both private and government-initiated. University of Toronto economist Michael Baker notes that to draw on the maximum benefit of government pensions people ought to retire at age 60, for later retirement results in a loss.

For those who choose to retire, the number one reason is that it has become financially possible to leave work (Turcotte & Schellenberg, 2007). In cases where people leave involuntarily, poor health accounts for 44 percent of the retirements, compared with 20 percent of the voluntary retirements. Some retirees would continue working if they could reduce the number of days or hours they work, and if it didn't influence the pension they would receive when they fully retire.

------- developmental **connection** -------

Stability vs. Change

<-------------------------------

ADJUSTMENT TO RETIREMENT   Much of our identity is tied to the work we do. For example, a nurse, teacher, or electrician has internalized their profession into their sense of self; therefore, retirement is a process, not an event (Moen, 2007). Not surprisingly, research has found that people with higher incomes and good physical and emotional health adjust to retirement more successfully than those who are ill and have the burden of trying to make ends meet (Donaldson, Earl, & Muratore, 2010). A recent study revealed that retired married and remarried women reported being more satisfied with their lives and in better health than retired women who were widowed, separated, divorced, or had never been married (Price & Joo, 2005). Another recent study indicated that women spend less time planning for retirement than men do (Jacobs-Lawson, Hershey, & Neukam, 2005).

As noted above, retirees who adjust best to retirement are healthy, have adequate income, are active, are better educated, have an extended social network including both friends and family, and usually were satisfied with their lives before they retired (Raymo & Sweeney, 2006; Turcotte & Schellenberg, 2007). Older adults with inadequate income and poor health, and who must adjust to other stress that occurs at the same time as retirement, such as the death of a spouse, have the most difficult time adjusting to retirement (Reichstadt et al., 2007). Flexibility is also a key factor in whether individuals adjust well to retirement (Baehr & Barnett, 2007). A recent study also found that individuals who had difficulty adjusting to retirement had a strong attachment to work, including full-time jobs and a long work history, lack of control over the transition to retirement, and low self-efficacy (van Solinge & Henkens, 2005). Planning and then successfully carrying out the plan is an important aspect of adjusting well in retirement. A special concern in retirement planning involves women, who are likely to live longer than men and more likely to live alone (less likely to remarry and more likely to be widowed) (Moen, 2007). About two-thirds of Canadians do make financial plans for retiring during their work life, but this planning takes many forms and has varying degrees of thoroughness, from detailed investment for retirement to a review of what government pensions are available (Schellenberg & Ostrovsky, 2008a, b). Lower income earners and immigrants are more likely not to have an adequate understanding of their post-retirement needs and the government pension system.

Individuals who view retirement planning only in terms of finances don't adapt as well to retirement as those who have a more balanced retirement plan (Birren, 1996). It is important not only to plan financially for retirement, but to consider other areas of your life as well (Sener, Terzioglu, & Karabulut, 2007).

Technology and Social Media

The Internet plays an increasingly important role in access to information and communication among adults as well as youth (Cresci, Yarandi, & Morrell, 2010; Cutler, 2009; Rosenberg et al., 2009). A recent study revealed that older adults are clearly capable of being trained to learn new technologies (Hickman, Rogers, & Fisk, 2007).

Although older adults are less likely than younger adults to have a computer in their home and use the Internet, older adults are the fastest-growing segment of Internet users in Canada (Veenhof & Timusk, 2009). Forty-five percent of seniors age 65 to 74 were using the Internet in 2007, as compared with 11 percent in 2000. Those over 74 increased their use of the Internet from 5 percent in 2000 to 21 percent in 2007. Seniors' use of email was the most frequent Internet activity, followed by general browsing for information, and then gaming. Seniors spend more time playing games than people aged 45 to 64 (Veenhof & Timusk, 2009). Information on retirement and health issues is also sought over the Internet. As with children and younger adults, cautions about the accuracy of information on the Internet—in areas such as health care—always need to be kept in mind (Cutler, 2006).

Canadian seniors make fewer purchases over the Internet than those aged 45 to 64 (Veenhof & Timusk, 2009). About 40 percent of Canadian seniors using the Internet spent five or more hours per week online in 2007, about the same as people aged 45 to 65. They are especially interested in learning to use email and going online for health information (Westlake et al., 2007). Turcotte and Schellenberg (2007) found Aboriginal seniors were less likely to use the Internet than non-Aboriginal seniors and younger Aboriginals.

Living Arrangements

As noted earlier, housing is one of the primary determinants of health. Some 93 percent of seniors over the age of 65 live in private households (Clark, 2005). The remaining 7 percent live in nursing homes or hospitals, with those living in long-term care facilities being largely over the age of 85. Of those living in private households, 69 percent live in a house, 29 percent in an apartment, and 1 percent in a mobile home. However, for many seniors, housing poses a vulnerability. Seniors suffering from health problems, often related to housing and nutrition, require more formal care than those whose financial position is more secure. Additionally, the needs for seniors requiring more formal care often go unmet. The emotional, physical, and financial strain on the senior who may be isolated, and on his or her family, may impose undue hardship, and the need may go unmet altogether (Lobsinger, 2011).

Multi-generational living has always been a custom for new Canadians; however, this is gradually becoming more popular in response to increased housing prices and decreased job security. Today, 3.1 percent of Canadian households are multi-generational. Not only are children returning home, but on the flip side, many aging parents are moving in with their adult children and grandchildren (Tipper, 2011). Almost two-thirds of older adults live with family members—usually a spouse, but perhaps a child or a sibling, for example—while almost one-third live alone. The older people become, the greater is their chance of living alone. The majority of older adults living alone are widowed. Older adults living alone often report being more lonely than their counterparts who live with someone (Routasalo et al., 2006). Being lonely is not a given, however, for those who live alone. Older adults who can sustain themselves while living alone often have good health and few disabilities, and they may have regular social exchanges with relatives, friends, and neighbours.

The majority of the elderly adults in institutions are widows, many of whom cannot physically navigate their environment, are mentally impaired, or are incontinent (cannot control their excretory functions). Of seniors over age 85, 22 percent live on their own (Turcotte & Schellenberg, 2007). Over 50 percent of seniors live with a spouse, and of those between 75 and 85 who live alone, 43 percent are women. Becoming widowed or divorced can have serious financial implications, particularly for women. Widows are more likely to move after the death of a spouse (especially if living in an apartment) than seniors experiencing a divorce (Lin, 2005). But married couples move more often than widowed seniors; two out of five of the moves involving downsizing to a smaller home.

Most seniors live in urban settings, with 31 percent of Canadian seniors living in Toronto, Montreal, or Vancouver. The oldest (proportionally) communities in Canada are Victoria (British Columbia) and St. Catharines–Niagara (Ontario), both with 17 percent of the population over 65. Calgary (Alberta) has the lowest elderly population, at 9 percent (Turcotte & Schellenberg, 2007). Clark (2005) reports that seniors living in large urban areas and immigrants are more likely to have housing affordability problems than those living in smaller communities and people born in Canada, respectively. While many seniors live in urban areas, rural communities are experiencing the fastest growing increases in actual percentage of seniors to working age people (Alasia, 2010). In 2006, for every one person aged 65 and over living in a rural community, there were 4.3 working age people, compared with one senior to 5.6 working age people in urban areas. Alasia (2010) suggests this is the result of shifts in available job causing younger people to move to urban areas, and the restructuring of municipalities during the 1990s.

To this point we have discussed a number of issues relating to personality, the self, and society in late adulthood. For a review, see the **Reach Your Learning Objectives** section at the end of this chapter.

critical thinking

With another student in your class, brainstorm to generate a list of advantages and disadvantages of seniors living in facilities designed by and for them. Consider multi-generational homes. How might they be designed? What may be the advantages and disadvantages to families living in a multi-generational home? What would be the advantages and disadvantages to seniors living in senior residences?

Families and Social Relationships

LO3 Characterize the families and social relationships of aging adults.

What are the relationships of aging couples like? What roles do grandparents and great-grandparents play? What do friendships and social networks contribute to the lives of older adults?

The Aging Couple

The time from retirement until death is sometimes referred to as the "final stage in the marriage process." A recent study revealed that marital satisfaction was greater in older adults than middle-aged adults (Henry et al., 2007). In this study, older adults perceived their spouse to be less hostile than did middle-aged adults.

Retirement alters a couple's lifestyle, requiring adaptation (Higo & Williamson, 2009; Price & Nesteruk, 2010). The greatest changes occur in the traditional family in which the husband works and the wife is a homemaker, as each may need to re-learn their roles and help in the upkeep and management of their home. Marital happiness in older adults is also affected by each partner's ability to deal with personal conflict, including aging, illness, and eventual death (Field, 1996).

Seniors living with a spouse have more immediate access to support and financial security (Turcotte & Schellenberg, 2007). Individuals who are married or partnered in late adulthood are usually happier and live longer than those who are single (Manzoli et al., 2007). Marital satisfaction is greater for women than for men, possibly because women place more emphasis on attaining satisfaction through marriage than men do. However, as more women develop careers, this gender difference may not continue. A longitudinal study of adults 75 years of age and older revealed that individuals who were married were less likely to die across a span of seven years (Rasulo, Christensen, & Tomassini, 2005). Does cohabiting affect an individual's health? One study involving more than 8,000 51- to 61-year-old adults revealed that the health of couples who cohabited did not differ from the health of married couples (Waite, 2005). Another study, however, found that those who were over 50 and who cohabited were more depressed than their married counterparts (Brown, Bulanda, & Lee, 2005).

A recent study explored the quality of marriages in older adults and its link to loneliness (de Jong Gierveld et al., 2009). Two types of loneliness were studied: emotional (the affective state of feeling isolated) and social (a factor of integration in social networks that can provide a sense of connection with others). Approximately 20 to 25 percent of the older adults who were married felt moderate or strong emotional or social loneliness. Stronger emotional and social loneliness appeared in older adults whose spouse has health problems, who don't usually get emotional support from their spouse, who rarely converse with their spouse, who rate their sex life as not very pleasant or not applicable. Emotional loneliness was stronger in older adults in their second marriage and social loneliness was stronger in husbands with a disabled wife. Also, stronger emotional and social loneliness characterized older adults who had smaller social networks and less contact with their children.

Divorced and Remarried Older Adults

Rising divorce rates, increased longevity, and better health have led to an increase in remarriage by older adults (Ganong & Coleman, 2006). The majority of divorced older adults are women, due to their greater longevity and because men are more likely to remarry, thus removing themselves from the pool of divorced older adults (Peek, 2009). Divorce is far less common in older adults than younger adults, likely reflecting cohort effects rather than age effects since divorce was somewhat rare when current cohorts of older adults were young (Peek, 2009).

What happens when an older adult wants to remarry or does remarry? Reactions to older adults who choose to remarry range from raised eyebrows to outright rejection by adult children (Ganong & Coleman, 2006). As well, an increasing number of older adults cohabit (Mutchler, 2009). However, the majority of adult children support the decision of their older adult parents to remarry.

Not all older adults are or ever have been married. At least 8 percent of all individuals who reach the age of 65 have never been married. Contrary to the popular stereotype, older adults who have never been married seem to have the least difficulty coping with loneliness in old age. Many of them discovered long ago how to live autonomously and how to be self-reliant.

Romance and Sex in Older Adults' Relationships

Few of us imagine older couples taking an interest in sex or romantic relationships, but as Leonard Cohen pointed out, "The old are kind but the young are hot. Love may be blind but Desire is not." We might think of seniors as being interested in a game of bridge or a conversation on the porch, but not much else. In fact, a number of older adults date. The increased health and longevity of older adults have resulted in a much larger pool of active older adults. And the increased divorce rate has added more older adults to the senior dating pool.

Older adults may express their sexuality differently from younger adults, especially when engaging in sexual intercourse becomes difficult. Older adults especially enjoy touching and caressing as part of their sexual relationship. When older adults are healthy, they still may engage in sexual activities (Waite, Das, & Laumann, 2009; Waite et al., 2009). For example, a recent U.S. study found that among 75- to 85-year-olds, 40 percent of women and 78 percent of men reported having a stable sexual partner (Waite et al., 2009). The gender differential is likely due to women's higher likelihood of being widowed, age difference in spouses, and a consequence of their probability of living longer. With the increased use of drugs to treat erectile dysfunction, older adults can be expected to increase their sexual activity (Aubin et al., 2009; Chevret-Measson et al., 2009). However, companionship often becomes more important than sexual activity in older adults. Older couples often emphasize intimacy over sexual prowess.

Older Adult Parents and Their Adult Children

Parent–child relationships in later life differ from those earlier in the life span (Fingerman, Whiteman, & Dotterer, 2009; Fingerman, Miller, & Seidel, 2009; Merrill, 2009). They are influenced by a lengthy joint history and extensive shared experiences and memories.

Approximately 80 percent of older adults have living children, many of whom are middle-aged. About 10 percent of older adults have children who are 65 years or older. Adult children are an important part of the aging parent's social network. Researchers have found that older adults with children have more contacts with relatives than those without children (Johnson & Troll, 1992).

Increasingly, diversity characterizes older adult parents and their adult children (Pudrovska, Schieman, & Carr, 2006). Divorce, cohabitation, and non-marital childbearing are more common in the history of older adults today than in the past (Allen, Blieszner, & Roberto, 2000).

Gender plays an important role in relationships involving older adult parents and their children (Ward-Griffin et al., 2007). As noted earlier, adult daughters, rather than adult sons, are more likely to be the caregivers and as such are more involved in the lives of aging parents. An extremely valuable task that adult children can perform is to coordinate and monitor services for an aging parent who becomes disabled (Silverstein, 2009). This might involve locating a nursing home and monitoring its quality, procuring medical services, arranging public service assistance, and handling finances. In some cases, adult children provide direct assistance with daily living, including such activities as eating, bathing, and dressing. Even less severely impaired older adults may need help with shopping, housework, transportation, home maintenance, and bill paying.

Researchers have found that ambivalence characterized by both positive and negative perceptions is often present in relationships between adult children and their aging parents (Fingerman et al., 2007). These perceptions include love, reciprocal help, and shared values on the positive side, and isolation, family conflicts and problems, abuse, neglect, and caregiver stress on the negative side (Fowler, 1999). One study of 1,599 adult children's relationships with their older adult parents found that ambivalence was likely to be present when relationships involve in-laws, those in poor health, and adult children with poor parental relationships in early life (Wilson, Shuey, & Elder, 2003).

What roles can grandparents play in children's development?

Grandparenting and Great-Grandparenting

Let us explore aspects of grandparenting and great-grandparenting: How satisfying are these roles? How do they differ?

The Changing Profile of Grandparents

Earlier in the text, you read that people are waiting longer to marry and start families. Consequently, the ages of grandparenting and great-grandparenting have increased. Another interesting dynamic is that an increasing number of grandchildren live with their grandparents. This is particularly true in First Nations communities and where the grandmothers are not in the paid labour force (Fuller-Thomson, 2005).

Partly because women live longer, there are more grandmothers than grandfathers who live with their children. About 70 percent of the grandparents who move in with their children are grandmothers. Grandparent caregivers report a greater degree of closeness to their grandchildren than non-caregivers, and that the health and well-being of the children were similar to those children raised in their parent's home, in spite of poorer economic conditions (Fuller-Thomson, 2005). On the downside, however, studies of grandparents raising their grandchildren in the United States report that the grandparent, usually a grandmother, may also feel isolated, and experience limited physical strength and possible depression. No Canadian study has been conducted to see if this is also the case in Canada (Fuller-Thomson, 2005). More typically, grandmother caregivers live apart from their grandchildren and provide care when a crisis emerges, such as when the parent suffers from a mental illness, drug or alcohol addiction, incarceration, or is a teenager (Fuller-Thomson, 2005).

The extended family was most common in Nunavut (9.7 percent) and the Northwest Territories (5.4 percent), followed by British Columbia (4.9 percent) and Ontario (4.8 percent), and was least common in Quebec (1.6 percent). Fewer than 3 percent of people born in Canada were involved in a multi-generational household, as opposed to 7 percent of those born elsewhere. In Canada, Aboriginal children are far more likely to grow up in multi-generational households than non-Aboriginal children. Traditional Aboriginal cultural values promote extended families in the Northwest Territories and Nunavut. In Aboriginal communities, grandparents and elders are viewed as community assets, and as such are highly respected (Milan and Hamm, 2003). Turcotte and Schellenberg (2007) found the second most common extracurricular activity among Aboriginal children (after sports) was spending time with elders (35 percent reported this activity).

As you read in Chapter 16, grandparental visitation rights and privileges are also a special concern. Rosenthal and Gladstone (2000) report that a number of self-help and advocacy groups have formed in Canada to address these issues. Such groups as the Grandparents Requesting Access and Dignity (GRAND) society and the Canadian Grandparents Rights Association attempt to raise the public's awareness of child custody and access issues for grandparents, to advocate family law reform to include the rights of grandparents, and to support those involved in access or custody disputes.

Great-Grandparenting

Because of increased longevity, more grandparents today than in the past are also great-grandparents. At the turn of the twentieth century, the three-generation family was common, but now the four-generation family is common. One contribution of great-grandparents is to transmit family history by telling their children, grandchildren, and great-grandchildren where the family came from, what their members achieved, what they endured, and how their lives changed over the years (Harris, 2002).

There has been little research on great-grandparenting. One study examined the relationship between young adults and their grandparents and great-grandparents (Roberto & Skoglund, 1996). The young adults interacted with and participated in more activities with their grandparents than great-grandparents. They also perceived their grandparents to have a more defined role and as more influential in their lives than great-grandparents.

Lillian Troll (2000) has found that older adults who are embedded in family relationships have much less distress than those who are family deprived. Next, we will consider some other aspects of social relationships in late adulthood: friendship and social support.

Friendship

In early adulthood, friendship networks expand as new social connections are made away from home. In late adulthood, new friendships are less likely to be forged, although some adults do seek out new friendships, especially following the death of a spouse (Zettel-Watson & Rook, 2009). As noted earlier in the section on *socio-emotional selectivity theory*, older adults become more selective about their social networks. Noted expert in the field and founding director of the Stanford Center on Longevity, Laura Carstensen concluded in 1998 that people choose close friends over new friends as they grow older. And, as long as they have several close people in their network, they seem content. Supporting Carstensen's view, recall the recent study we described earlier in this chapter in which, compared with younger adults, older adults said they experienced less intense positive emotions with new friends and more intense positive emotions with established friends (Charles & Piazza, 2007).

In one study of 128 married older adults, women were more depressed than men if they did not have a best friend, and women who did have a friend reported lower levels of depression (Antonucci, Lansford, & Akiyama, 2001). Similarly, women who did not have a best friend were less satisfied with life than women who did have a best friend.

Three recent studies documented the importance of friendship in older adults:

- A study of almost 1,700 adults 60 years and older revealed that friendships are more important than family relationships in predicting mental health (Fiori, Antonucci, & Cortina, 2006). Even when the researchers controlled for health, age, income, and other factors, older adults whose social contacts were mainly restricted to their family members were more likely to have depressive symptoms. Friends likely provide emotional intimacy and companionship, as well as integration into the community (Antonucci, Akiyama, & Sherman, 2007).
- A recent longitudinal study of adults 75 years of age and older revealed that individuals with close ties with friends were less likely to die across a seven-year age span (Rasulo, Christensen, & Tomassini, 2005). The findings were stronger for women than men.
- A recent study revealed that unmarried older adults embedded in a friend-focused network fare better physically and psychologically than unmarried older adults in a restricted network with little friend contact (Fiori, Smith, & Antonucci, 2007).

At the beginning of the twentieth century, the three-generation family was common, but now the four-generation family is common as well. Thus, an increasing number of grandparents are also great-grandparents. The four-generation family shown here is the Jordans—author John Santrock's mother-in-law, daughter, granddaughter, and wife.

Fear of Victimization, Crime, and Elder Maltreatment

Some of the physical decline and limitations that characterize development in late adulthood contribute to a sense of vulnerability and fear among older adults. For some elderly adults, the fear of crime may become a deterrent to travelling, attending social events, and pursuing an active lifestyle. This said, seniors reported feeling more satisfied with their personal safety in 2004 than an earlier sample in 1999—92 percent compared to 89 percent, respectively (Ogrodnik, 2007).

Like child maltreatment, elder abuse can take several forms: neglect, physical abuse, psychological or emotional abuse, and economic or financial abuse, including fraud. In 2004, 10 percent of Canadian seniors experienced at least one act of victimization during the previous year (Ogrodnik, 2007). This was one-third the rate of victimization for non-seniors; and women are twice as vulnerable to violence than men. In terms of assaults, sexual assaults, and robberies, seniors experienced significantly less victimization than non-seniors. Theft of seniors' personal property was less than half that of people aged 55 to 64, and nearly eight times lower than 15- to 24-year-olds. Ogrodnik (2007) found that seniors experienced nearly three times fewer break-ins, automobile thefts, and acts of vandalism than non-seniors. Most often, seniors are victimized by a family member (Ogrodnik, 2007). For more information on elder abuse, see the Connecting through Research feature.

In this section we have discussed families and social relationships in late adulthood. For a review, see the **Reach Your Learning Objectives** section at the end of this chapter.

Elder Abuse

When we become elderly, we hope the principles outlined by the United Nations—independence, participation, care, self-fulfillment, and dignity—will govern our well-being. When these principles are not upheld, when the news reports a story or an exposé about victimization of seniors, for example, we are horrified. Elder abuse is a term that includes all types of mistreatment toward older people, whether an act of commission or omission, and whether intentional or unintentional. The abuse can be physical, psychological, or financial and results in unnecessary suffering, injury, pain, and decreased quality of life. Further, abuse violates the individual's human rights. Not reporting abuse or acknowledging it is a form of abuse in itself, as is neglect (Department of Justice, 2013).

It is not possible to know the extent of elder abuse, as families and institutions may not report incidents. Shame and guilt often prevent victims or families from reporting abuse. Caregivers in institutions may not be adequately trained, and institutions may not have policies and procedures in place or may turn a blind eye (Department of Justice, 2013). While much abuse goes unreported, police reports on family violence for 2007 represent one-third of the violent crimes against seniors. While family violence against seniors is lower than against those aged 55 to 64 and 25 to 34 (48 versus 104 and 406 per 100,000, respectively), its occurrence is still very troubling (Statistics Canada, 2009).

The types of abuse that are most common result from frustration and financial need. Senior women are more likely than senior men to be victims of family violence. Half of the police-reported cases of family violence against seniors do not result in physical injury, and when it does it tends to be minor injury (91 percent) (Statistics Canada, 2009). The psychological impact of family violence is not assessed in the police reports. Being frail, disabled, and/or suffering from dementia or Alzheimer's disease increases an individual's vulnerability to victimization (Turcotte & Schellenberg, 2007; CNPEA, 2006). Senior women are more likely to be abused by a spouse or adult children, while senior men are abused more often by adult children (Statistics Canada, 2009).

Elder abuse is not confined to Canada; in fact, it is a worldwide occurrence. In 2006, the United Nations, following up on a Plan of Action determined in 2002, declared June 15 World Elder Abuse Day. The Canadian Network for the Prevention of Elder Abuse (CNPEA) is an arm of the International Network (INPEA). Provincial networks are also linked; together, these networks work with governmental and non-governmental groups and individuals around the world to document abuses and provide educational materials in an effort to increase awareness and work toward prevention. For more information, visit the CPNEA's Web site at www.cnpea.ca. The site offers an overview of incidents that have been reported around the world, ranging from malnutrition in nursing homes in one country, to abandonment and neglect in another.

Social Integration

LO4 Describe social supports and social integration, and understand how altruism, ethnicity, gender, and culture are linked to aging.

What are the roles of altruism, gender, and ethnicity in aging? What are the social aspects of aging in different cultures?

Social Support and Social Integration

Social support and social integration play important roles in the physical and mental health of older adults (Antonucci et al., 2011; Birditt, 2009; Kahana, Kahana, & Hammel, 2009).

In the **convoy model of social relations,** *individuals go through life embedded in a personal network of individuals to whom they give and from whom they receive social support* (Antonucci, Birditt, & Akiyama, 2009; Antonucci et al., 2011). Social support can help individuals of all ages cope more effectively (Griffiths et al., 2007). In a study of friendships among Canadian seniors, Colin Lindsay (2008) found that 82 percent of people aged 75 and over said they had at least one close friend, compared with 88 percent of those between 65 and 74 and over 90 percent of those in younger age groups. The percentage of seniors aged 75 and over with two close friends was lower (just over 70 percent). Thus, some 18 percent of people over 75 do not report having a close friend.

Social support for an older adult is related to their physical and mental health. It is linked with a reduction in symptoms of disease, with the ability to meet one's own health-care needs, and with mortality (Rook et al., 2007). According to an analysis of Statistics Canada data, social supports also

Social Support and Social Integration

Altruism and Volunteerism

Gender

Ethnicity

Culture

convoy model of social relations According to this model, individuals go through life embedded in a personal network of individuals to whom they give and from whom they receive social support.

decrease the probability that an older adult will be institutionalized or isolated, and are also associated with a lower incidence of depression in older adults (Turcotte & Schellenberg, 2007).

Social Integration

Social integration also plays an important role in the lives of many older adults (Rohr & Lang, 2009; von Tilburg, 2009). Remember from our earlier discussion of socio-emotional selectivity theory that many older adults choose to have fewer peripheral social contacts and more emotionally positive contacts with friends and family (Charles & Carstensen, 2009, 2010). Thus, a decrease in the overall social activity of many older adults may reflect their greater interest in spending more time in the small circle of friends and families where they are less likely to have negative emotional experiences. Researchers have found that older adults tend to report being less lonely than younger adults and less lonely than would be expected based on their circumstances (Schnittker, 2007). Their reports of feeling less lonely than younger adults likely reflect their more selective social networks and greater acceptance of loneliness in their lives (Koropeckyj-Cox, 2009).

However, being lonely and socially isolated is a significant health risk factor in older adults (Cheung, Chau, & Yip, 2008; Mullins, 2007). In one longitudinal study, poor social connections, infrequent participation in social activities, and social disengagement predicted cognitive decline in older adults (Zunzunegui et al., 2003).

Researchers have found that a low level of social integration is linked with coronary heart disease in older adults (Loucks et al., 2006). Also, in one study, being part of a social network was related to longevity, especially for men (House, Landis, & Umberson, 1988). Being lonely and socially isolated is a significant health risk factor in older adults (Koropeckyj-Cox, 2009). For example, a recent study found that loneliness predicted increased blood pressure four years later in middle-aged and older adults (Hawkley et al., 2010).

What role does social support play in the health of the elderly?

Altruism and Volunteerism

Two billion hours of volunteer activity occur every year in Canada (Special Senate Committee on Aging, 2009). Just 11 percent of Canadians supply 77 percent of that activity. A common perception is that older adults need to be given help rather than give help themselves; however, the 2003 General Social Survey found that seniors are more likely than younger adults to participate in volunteer activity, contributing a greater number of hours than other age groups (Turcotte & Schellenberg, 2007). The reasons for participating include the desire to share skills, learn new ones, and to give back to their community, among others (Special Senate Committee on Aging, 2009). Researchers recently have found that when older adults engage in altruistic behaviour and volunteering they benefit from these activities. For example, a recent study revealed that volunteering was linked with less frailty in older adults (Jung et al., 2010). Almost 50 percent of the volunteering efforts of older adults are for services provided by religious organizations (Burr, 2009). Researchers also have found that volunteering as an older adult is associated with a number of positive outcomes (Harootyan, 2007).

A recent study of 21,000 individuals 50 to 79 years of age in 21 countries revealed that one-third give back to society, saying that they volunteer now or have volunteered in the past (HSBC Insurance, 2007). In this study, about 50 percent who volunteer reported that they do so for at least one-half day each week. And a recent study found that volunteering steadily increases from 57 to 85 years of age (Cornwell, Laumann, & Schumm, 2008). Among the reasons for the positive outcomes of volunteering are its provision of constructive activities and productive roles, social integration, and enhanced meaningfulness.

Even though they represent a significant proportion of volunteers, many Canadian seniors report that physical limitations and health prevent them from volunteering. Lack of time is the second most commonly cited reason for not volunteering for both seniors and younger people. Thirdly, seniors cite they have given time to the community over the years, and it is time for younger people to take on that role. Finally, many individuals prefer to donate money instead of making a long-term commitment (Turcotte & Schellenberg, 2007). The federal government has an initiative to encourage seniors to stay involved within their communities. The New Horizons for Seniors program offers grants up to $25,000 for the creation of community programs that integrate seniors' "skills, experiences and wisdom in support of their community" (Special Senate Committee on Aging, 2009). In its appraisal of the program, the Special Senate Committee on Aging noted the need to bring more young people into the volunteer sector. These grants are to help facilitate the interface of seniors as volunteers with younger people, in part as an effort to instill the value of volunteer activity in the younger group.

Gender

Do our gender roles change when we become older adults? Some developmentalists believe there is decreasing femininity in women and decreasing masculinity in men when they reach the late adulthood years (Gutmann, 1975). The evidence suggests that older men do become more feminine— nurturing, sensitive, and so on—but it appears that older women do not necessarily become more masculine—assertive, dominant, and so on (Turner, 1982). Keep in mind that cohort effects are especially important to consider in such areas as gender roles. As socio-historical changes take place and are assessed more frequently in life-span investigations, what were once perceived to be age effects may turn out to be cohort effects (Schaie, 2007).

A possible double jeopardy also faces many women—the burden of both ageism and sexism (Slack & Jensen, 2008). The poverty rate for older adult females is almost double that of older adult males. Not only is it important to be concerned about older women's double jeopardy of ageism and sexism, but special attention also needs to be devoted to female ethnic minority older adults (Leifheit-Limson & Levy, 2009). They face what could be described as triple jeopardy—ageism, sexism, and racism. Should the woman also have a disability, her life experience is further jeopardized—a quadruple jeopardy (Ontario Human Rights Commission, 2001). An important research and political agenda for the twenty-first century is increased interest in the aging and the rights of older adult women.

Ethnicity

In 2009, nearly one-third of seniors living in Canada were immigrants to the country (Turcotte & Schellenberg, 2007). One-quarter of these seniors were members of a visible minority. This is a significant increase over past Canadian demographics, both in terms of the percentage of people identified with a visible minority and the place of origin of immigrants to Canada. Only 3 percent of people aged 65 and over immigrating to Canada prior to 1991 were members of a visible minority, whereas since 1991 that percentage is 75.6 percent. As we learned earlier, immigrants who arrived in the 1990s have a lower likelihood of retiring before age 65, and when they do retire, their economic situation may be worse than that of Canadian-born seniors (Schellenberg & Ostrovsky, 2008b). The act of immigrating and the economy they joined at the time of their arrival limits their financial situation. In addition, their access to resources to plan for their retirement or to access community services is lower than for non-immigrants.

Sharon Koehn (2006) studied the health-care access of new immigrants in British Columbia. Her study found that immigrants needed more care than non-immigrants, and they had a harder time accessing health care. For those whose language was not English, interpreters (both family members and others) often proved unreliable and inaccurate in translation of health information both about the person's condition and the physician's response. Many immigrants were found to not expect much government provision of health care, and so did not seek it out.

The Aboriginal population in Canada is younger than any other of the country's ethnic groups. Turcotte and Schellenberg (2007) note that even Aboriginal seniors are younger (on average) than non-Aboriginal seniors. The percentage of Aboriginal seniors is expected to grow at a similar rate as the rest of Canada over the next two decades. There are differences between the three groups that constitute the name Aboriginal, the North American Indian, the Métis, and the Inuit. Inuit seniors live predominantly in Northern communities among other Inuit. Just over half of North American Indian seniors live on reservations where the majority of others are North American Indians. Métis seniors are more urbanized, but still less so than non-Aboriginals.

Apart from the problems and prejudices faced by the elderly, individuals from racialized groups may experience the full brunt of ageism, sexism, poverty, and racial or ethnic prejudice.

critical thinking

Consider your own cultural or ethnic group's attitudes toward aging. If you are not sure, talk with older family members about their recollections of how older members of the group were treated, what roles they held, restrictions they faced, and any special rights or responsibilities they had. Are there differences in attitudes about aging women and men? With these descriptions in mind, what part of that set of attitudes is positive, and which is potentially negative? How could you change a group's less positive views concerning its older members?

connecting through social policy

End-of-Life Decisions

People in late adulthood often think about death as loved ones, spouses, or friends pass on. When we are able to share the final stages of life with a loved one, we are able to share one of life's most powerful and intimate occasions: Death. The word alone conjures up a range of emotional responses, from fear, to loss, to love. Euthanasia or assisted suicide are hotly debated topics in Canada.

On the one hand, proponents of assisted suicide argue that people have the right to die with dignity and that assisted suicide should be a choice; moreover, to deny that choice is unconstitutional. Seven jurisdictions—The Netherlands, Belgium, Luxembourg, and Switzerland, plus the three U.S. states of Oregon, Washington State, and Montana—have legally sanctioned assisted suicide. Further, the laws in Wales and England have been clarified so that not all cases of assisted suicide will result in persecution (Schuklenk et al., 2011). However, according to Canada's Criminal Code, like suicide, assisted suicide is not legal, nor is it lawful to counsel a person to commit suicide.

Those who oppose assisted suicide argue that suicide, assisted or not, is a violation of religious beliefs. Additionally, those who oppose changes to the Criminal Code that would sanction assisted suicide fear that people with depression or disabilities may be counselled into assisted suicide. The purpose of the law, according to court rulings, is to protect those most vulnerable and to avert wrongful deaths (Fong, 2013).

The Civil Liberties Association in British Columbia is advocating for change. Gloria Taylor, a woman suffering from ALS, illustrated their argument. She wanted to end her life before it became more unbearable. She won her case in B.C. court by gaining a personal exemption from the Criminal Code. Ms. Taylor died unexpectedly in the fall of 2012 assisted by an unknown physician (Crawford, 2013; Fong, 2013).

Susan Griffiths of Winnipeg decided to travel to Switzerland, where medically assisted suicide is legal, because her multiple sclerosis has made her life unbearable. She would much prefer to die in her own home, surrounded by her family (Gallinger, 2013). The Parti Quebecois has pledged to introduce death with dignity legislation as a way to circumvent the Criminal Code (Crawford, 2013).

How do Canadians feel? According to the Royal Society of Canada expert panel on end-of-life decision making (ROS EOL Panel), comprised of experts in the fields of bioethics, clinical medicine, health law and policy, and philosophy, a substantial majority of Canadians support the decriminalization of assisted suicide because the issue is so contentious (Schuklenk et al., 2011). However, the panel notes that education is essential and that terms such as voluntary, competent, palliative sedation, advance directives, and others must be carefully defined.

Canada is a country of tremendous diversity; hence, responses to death and dying vary, not only from culture to culture but also from person to person. Approaches toward illness, discussions of prognosis, and locus of control vary. For example, one with an external locus of control may assert that the illness is "God's will"; others may believe that to discuss predictions about death and dying may bring it nearer. Other groups, such as Aboriginal groups, may prefer to use Aboriginal medicines (Schuklenk et al., 2011). The debate has been in the Canadian courts for more than 20 years, and is not likely to be resolved quickly and easily. Civil liberties groups will continue to argue in favour of a change in the Criminal Code, and the Alliance of People with Disabilities is likely to continue to argue to maintain the law as is (Fong, 2013). As one dying man said, "You never really know how you feel until the gun barrel of death is down your throat." People in late adulthood realize this is the last chapter of their lives.

Culture

What factors are associated with whether older adults are accorded a position of high status in a culture? Seven factors are most likely to predict high status for older adults in a culture (Sangree, 1989):

- Older persons have valuable knowledge.
- Older persons control key family/community resources.
- Older persons are permitted to engage in useful and valued functions as long as possible.
- There is role continuity throughout the life span.
- Age-related role changes involve greater responsibility, authority, and advisory capacity.
- The extended family is a common family arrangement in the culture, and the older person is integrated into the extended family.

In general, respect for older adults is greater in collectivistic cultures (such as China and Japan) than in individualistic cultures (such as Canada). However, some researchers are finding that this collectivistic/individualistic difference in respect for older adults is not as strong as it used to be, and that in some cases older adults in individualistic cultures receive considerable respect (Antonucci, Vandewater, & Lansford, 2000).

Cultures vary in the prestige they give to older adults. In the Inuit culture, older adults are especially treated with respect because of their wisdom and extensive life experience. **What are some other factors that are linked to respect for older adults in a culture?**

------ **critical** thinking ------

On the basis of all that you have read in Chapters 17 and 18, and what your professor has discussed, construct a multi-dimensional plan to ensure successful aging. Outline five features of positive aging in each of the following domains: physical, cognitive, and socio-emotional.

To this point, we have discussed several ideas about social integration in late adulthood. For a review, see the **Reach Your Learning Objectives** section at the end of this chapter.

Successful Aging

LO5 Explain how to age successfully.

For too long, the positive dimensions of aging were ignored (Charles & Carstensen, 2010; Depp & Jeste, 2010; Stirling, 2011). Throughout this book, we have called attention to the positive aspects of aging. There are many robust, healthy older adults (Willcox et al., 2008). With a proper diet, an active lifestyle, mental stimulation and flexibility, positive coping skills, good social relationships and support, and the absence of disease, many of our abilities can be maintained or, in some cases, even improved, as we get older (Antonucci et al., 2011; Hughes, 2010; Lachman et al., 2010). Even when individuals develop a disease, improvements in medicine mean that increasing numbers of older adults with diseases can still lead active, constructive lives.

Being active is especially important in successful aging (Erickson & Kramer, 2009). Older adults who get out and attend meetings, participate in church activities, go on trips, and exercise regularly are more satisfied with their lives than their counterparts who disengage from society (Reichstadt et al., 2007). Older adults who are emotionally selective, optimize their choices, and compensate effectively for losses increase their chances of aging successfully (Baltes & Smith, 2008; Scheibe & Carstensen, 2010; Staudinger & Jacobs, 2011).

Successful aging also involves perceived control over the environment (Bandura, 2010; HSBC Insurance, 2007). In Chapter 17, we described how perceived control over the environment had a positive effect on nursing home residents' health and longevity. In recent years, the term self-efficacy has often been used to describe perceived control over the environment and the ability to produce positive outcomes (Bandura, 2009, 2010). Researchers have found that many older adults are quite effective in maintaining a sense of control and have a positive view of themselves (Dunbar, Leventhal, & Leventhal, 2007).

For example, one recent study of centenarians found that many were very happy, and that self-efficacy and an optimistic attitude were linked to their happiness (Jopp & Rott, 2006). Examining the positive aspects of aging is an important trend in life-span development and is likely to benefit future generations of older adults (Antonucci et al., 2011; Carstensen & Charles, 2010; Stirling, 2011).

To this point, we have studied ideas about successful aging. For a review, see the **Reach Your Learning Objectives** section at the end of this chapter.

reach your **learning objectives**

Theories of Socio-Emotional Development

LO1 Discuss four theories of socio-emotional development and aging.

Erikson's Theory

- Erikson's eighth and final stage of development, which individuals experience in late adulthood, involves reflecting on the past and either integrating it positively or concluding that one's life has not been well spent.
- Life review is an important task for most seniors.
- Peck described three developmental tasks that older adults face: (1) differentiation versus role preoccupation, (2) body transcendence versus preoccupation, and (3) ego transcendence versus preoccupation.

Activity Theory	■ The theory that the more active and involved older adults are, the more likely they will be satisfied with their lives.
Socio-Emotional Selectivity Theory	■ The theory that older adults become more selective about their social networks. Because they place a high value on emotional satisfaction, they are motivated to spend more time with familiar individuals with whom they have had rewarding relationships.
	■ Knowledge-related and emotion-related goals change across the life span, with emotion-related goals being more important when individuals get older.
Selective Optimization with Compensation Theory	■ The theory that successful aging is linked to three main factors: (1) selection, (2) optimization, and (3) compensation. These are especially likely to be relevant when loss occurs.
Social Determinants of Health	■ Social determinants of health include income, education, social inclusion, and housing.

Personality, the Self, and Society

LO2 Describe links between personality and mortality, and identify changes in the self and society in late adulthood.

Personality	■ Low conscientiousness, high neuroticism, negative affect, pessimism, and a negative outlook on life are related to earlier death in late adulthood.
The Self	■ In one large-scale study, self-esteem increased through most of adulthood but declined in the seventies and eighties. The stability of self-esteem declines in older adults. Further research is needed to verify these developmental changes in self-esteem.
	■ Changes in types of self-acceptance occur through the adult years as acceptance of ideal and future selves decreases with age and acceptance of past selves increases.
	■ Most older adults effectively maintain a sense of self-control, although self-regulation may vary by domain. For example, older adults often show less self-regulation in the physical domain than younger adults.
Older Adults in Society	■ Ageism is prejudice against others because of their age. Too many negative stereotypes of older adults continue to exist.
	■ Policy issues in an aging society include the status of the economy and the provision of health care, eldercare, and generational inequity.
	■ The income gap between senior men and women has narrowed due to additional participation of women in the workforce.
	■ Of special concern are older adults who are in poverty. Poverty rates are especially high among older women who live alone and seniors from ethnic minority groups and Aboriginals.
	■ Workers, particularly immigrant workers, may not accurately understand their workplace pension plan or how it is structured.
	■ Today, the percentage of men over 65 who continue to work full-time is less than at the beginning of the twentieth century.
	■ An important change in older adults' work patterns is the increase in part-time work.
	■ Some individuals continue a life of strong work productivity throughout late adulthood.
	■ A retirement option for older workers is a late-twentieth-century phenomenon in Canada.

- Individuals who are healthy, have adequate income, are active, are better educated, have an extended social network of friends and family, and were satisfied with their lives before they retired adjust best to retirement.

- Older adults are less likely to have a computer in their home and less likely to use the Internet than younger adults, but they are the fastest-growing age segment of Internet users.

- Most older adults live in the community, not in institutions. Almost two-thirds of older adults live with family members, usually a spouse.

Families and Social Relationships

LO3 Characterize the families and social relationships of aging adults.

| The Aging Couple | - Retirement alters a couple's lifestyle and requires adaptation. Married older adults are often happier than single older adults. |

| Older Adult Parents and Their Adult Children | - Approximately 80 percent of older adults have living children, many of whom are middle-aged.
- Adult daughters are more likely than adult sons to be involved in the lives of aging parents. An important task that adult children can perform is to coordinate and monitor services for an aging parent who becomes disabled.
- Ambivalence can characterize the relationships of adult children with their aging parents. |

| Grandparenting and Great-Grandparenting | - Most grandparents are satisfied with their roles. There are different grandparent roles and styles. The profile of grandparents is changing due to such factors as divorce and remarriage.
- Because of increased longevity, more grandparents today are also great-grandparents. One contribution of great-grandparents is family history. |

| Friendship | - There is more continuity than change in friendship for older adults, although there is more change for males than for females. |

| Fear of Victimization, Crime, and Elder Maltreatment | - Seniors experience significantly less assault, sexual assault, robbery, theft, and acts of vandalism than non-seniors.
- Maltreatment can take several forms, ranging from neglect to physical abuse, psychological or emotional abuse, or economic or financial abuse, including fraud. |

Social Integration

LO4 Describe social supports and social integration, and understand how altruism, ethnicity, gender, and culture are linked to aging.

| Social Support and Social Integration | - Social support and social integration play important roles in both the physical and mental health of people in late adulthood.
- Being lonely and socially isolated is a significant health risk factor in late adulthood. |

| Altruism and Volunteerism | - Altruism and volunteerism are beneficial to people in late adulthood. |

Gender	■ There is stronger evidence that men become more feminine (nurturant, sensitive) as older adults than there is that women become more masculine (assertive).
	■ An individual with a physical, emotional, or cognitive disability may experience further prejudice.
Ethnicity	■ Individuals from racialized groups face special burdens, having to cope with the full brunt of racism, ageism, poverty, and, if they are female, sexism.
Culture	■ Historically, respect for older adults in China and Japan was high, but today their status is more variable.
	■ Factors that predict high status for the elderly across cultures range from their valuable knowledge to integration into the extended family.

Successful Aging

LO5 Explain how to age successfully.

Successful Aging	■ Increasingly, the positive aspects of older adults are being studied. Factors that are linked to successful aging include an active lifestyle, positive coping skills, good social relationships and support, and self-efficacy.

review ---→ *connect* ---→ reflect

review

Describe how issues of earlier stages mature into the many facets of integrity and wisdom in late adulthood. **LO1**

Define ageism and cite examples you have observed. **LO2**

How might loneliness be a factor in late adulthood, even for the aging couple? **LO3**

How are altruism, gender, ethnicity, and culture linked to social integration? **LO4**

What are some of the factors linked to successful aging? **LO5**

connect

In Chapter 16 you read about the Big Five personality factors, and in this chapter you read about how these factors, particularly low conscientiousness and high neuroticism, may be linked to mortality rates in late adulthood. Why do you think this may be true?

reflect *Your Own Personal Journey of Life*

How might your ability to age successfully as an older adult be related to what you are doing in your life now? What behaviours would you like to maintain? What might you change?

connect

McGraw-Hill Connect provides you with a powerful tool for improving academic performance and truly mastering course material. You can diagnose your knowledge with pre- and post-tests, identify the areas where you need help, search the entire learning package, including the eBook, for content specific to the topic you're studying, and add these resources to your personalized study plan. CONNECT for *Life-Span Development*, fifth Canadian edition, offers the following:

■ chapter-specific online quizzes

■ groupwork

■ presentations

■ writing assignments

■ case studies

■ and much more!

Visit CONNECT today!

CHAPTER OUTLINE

> *"Four parts to life: being born, being young, being a parent, and being dead. Death brings the fourth, the complete, the full, four makes it total, four makes it whole, and the final fourth is with us from birth."*
>
> —B.A.CAMERON (CAM HUBERT), CONTEMPORARY CANADIAN WRITER

National Mourning

They were young, as we are young,

They served, giving freely of themselves,

To them, we pledge, amid the winds of time,

To carry their torch and never forget.

We will remember them.

—DAKOTA BRANT, YOUTH DELEGATE, 2005 ABORIGINAL SPIRITUAL JOURNEY

People sat in their cars in the northbound lanes of Toronto's Don Valley Parkway, at the Don Mills exit. Headed home at the end of the day, they were stuck in the usual rush hour traffic. In the southbound lanes, traffic was typically dense, yet moving steadily. Then things changed. Four police motorcycles, lights flashing, appeared in the southbound lanes. They blocked off the nearby on-ramps. The traffic heading south dwindled to nothing, the road left empty. In a moment, five more police motorcycles, lights flashing in V-formation, were in the left-hand express lane of the barren stretch of highway. They were moving at high speed. No car moved in the northbound lanes. The motorcycles were followed by three police cars, lights flashing. A short distance back was a hearse containing a flag-draped coffin, followed by two black limousines, dark-tinted glass keeping the mourners inside free of the public's gaze. Another three police cars and four more motorcycles, all with lights flashing, brought up the rear. Behind them, southbound traffic moved like a tidal surge in a narrow gorge. The northbound traffic inched forward.

Another Canadian solider, killed in combat in Afghanistan, was being brought home for burial. Two days earlier, his flag-draped coffin had been carried aboard a military transport at the NATO airbase in Kandahar on the shoulders of members of his unit, his comrades in arms. Now, his family was preparing to bury their son; a wife, her husband; children, their father. Along a stretch of Ontario's Highway 401, the signs read "Highway of Heroes," for it is the section that leads from the Canadian Forces Base at Trenton to Toronto. Many of the fallen soldiers and their families have travelled this route on that final trip home. People, strangers to the deceased and their family, line the overpasses as these motorcades pass under. Flags wave, banners read "God Bless," hats are removed, veterans salute. Many of these solemn homecoming ceremonies are items on the nightly news. These ceremonies prompt further reflection on our losses, our role in this war, and the contrast between the nation's response to soldiers today and its response to those who died in previous wars.

The Canadian War Museum's chart contains the Canadian casualty figures for World Wars I and II, the Korean War, and Afghanistan. In 1917, at Vimy Ridge alone, more than 10,000 Canadian soldiers were killed or wounded. This battle was pivotal because it turned the course of the war (Cook, 2004). According to the *National Post* (Berthiaume, 2012), the total number of Canadian soldiers wounded in action during the mission from April 2002 to December 2011 was 635. The total number of Canadian soldiers killed was 158 (Berthiaume, 2012).

	Population	Served	Died	Wounded
World War I (1914–1918)	7,800,000	625,825	61,082	154,361
World War II (1939–1945)	11,500,000	1,086,343	42,042	54,414
Korean War (1950–53)	14,000,000	27,751	516	1,072
Afghanistan (2002–)	32,000,000	40,000	158	635

Instead of being flown home, soldiers in previous wars were buried on foreign soil. Many of Canada's war dead are buried in carefully maintained cemeteries in 75 different countries around the world; many still lie in unmarked graves. Every five years since 1985, the people of Apeldoorn, Netherlands, have held a parade honouring the Canadian forces that liberated their town from the Nazis in 1945 (Veteran Affairs Canada, 2010). Returning Canadian veterans are paraded through the town on vintage World War II vehicles, feted at dinners, and thanked for freeing the town by Dutch children eagerly waving Canadian flags. A service is held at the monument for the soldiers who died during the war. The numbers of veterans has declined steadily, and those who go back are now in their eighties and nineties. The parade of 2010 was the last, and from now on the town will remember the sacrifice Canadians made to free their village with an annual "liberation" street festival.

Death closes out the life span. This final chapter will help you explore a topic that many people find difficult.

Defining Death and Life/Death Issues

LO1 Evaluate issues in determining death and decisions regarding death.

Is there one point in the process of dying at which death takes place, or is death a more gradual process? What are some decisions individuals can make about life, death, and health care?

Issues in Determining Death

Issues in Determining Death

Decisions Regarding Life, Death, and Health Care

Thirty years ago, determining if someone was dead was more clear-cut than it is today. The end of certain biological functions, such as breathing and blood pressure, and rigidity of the body (rigor mortis) were considered to be clear signs of death. However, in the past several decades, defining death has become more complex (Kendall et al., 2007; Quesnel et al., 2007).

brain death *is a neurological definition of death, which states that a person is brain dead when all electrical activity of the brain has ceased for a specified period of time. A flat EEG (electroencephalogram) recording for a specified period of time is one criterion of brain death.* The higher portions of the brain often die sooner than the lower portions. Because the brain's lower portions monitor heartbeat and respiration, individuals whose higher brain areas have died may continue breathing and have a heartbeat. The definition of brain death currently followed by most physicians includes the death of both the higher cortical functions and the lower brain stem functions (Truog, 2007, 2008).

Some medical experts argue that the criteria for death should include only higher cortical functioning. If the cortical death definition were adopted, physicians could claim a person is dead when he or she has no cortical functioning, even though the lower brain stem is functioning. Supporters of the cortical death policy argue that the functions we associate with being human, such as intelligence and personality, are located in the higher cortical part of the brain. They believe that when these functions are lost, the "human being" is no longer alive. To date, the cortical definition of death is not a legal definition of death anywhere in Canada.

brain death A neurological definition of death, which states that a person is brain dead when all electrical activity of the brain has ceased for a specified period of time; a flat EEG recording for a specified period of time is one criterion of brain death.

Decisions Regarding Life, Death, and Health Care

In cases of catastrophic illness or emergency circumstances, patients might not be able to respond adequately to participate in decisions about their medical care, possibly being comatose or irrational. To prepare for this type of situation, some individuals make earlier choices.

Living Wills and Do Not Resuscitate Orders

For many patients in a coma, it is unclear what their wishes regarding termination of treatment might be if they still were conscious (Burck et al., 2007). Recognizing that terminally ill patients might prefer to die rather than linger in a painful or vegetative state, the organization Choice in Dying created the living will. This document is designed to be filled in while the individual can still think clearly; it expresses the person's desires regarding extraordinary medical procedures that might be used to sustain life when a person is terminally ill.

Physicians' concerns over malpractice suits and the efforts of people who support the living will concept have raised the profile of this issue across Canada. Excluding Nunavut, each Canadian province and territory provides a legal framework for a person to write instructions about the care they wish to receive (or not receive), should they lose their capacity to give informed consent (Vogel, 2011).

Where laws do not exist, the living will only serves as a request, which may or may not be followed. The actual terminology varies across the country. Ontario calls the document a "power of attorney for personal care." In other provinces, living wills are referred to as "health-care directives" or "advanced directives." In the province of Quebec, a person can file a mandate with a notary or have two witnesses oversee the signing of a living will to make it legally binding. Alberta

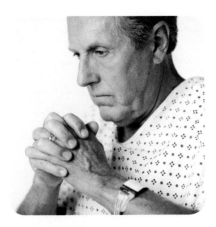

Advances in medical technology have complicated the definition of death. **What is the nature of the controversy about the criteria that should be used for determining when death occurs?**

has begun a program to have all advanced directives and living wills placed online so they are available to physicians if the person cannot speak when he or she appears in the emergency room (McLaren, 2009).

Within an institutional setting, the living will results in a do not resuscitate (DNR) order being placed on the person's medical chart. The DNR order first arose as a response to the accepted standard medical practice in the 1970s of giving cardiopulmonary resuscitation (CPR) to anyone having cardiopulmonary arrest (Ewanchuk & Brindley, 2006). The DNR order was created in the 1980s to prevent the use of CPR in terminal cases, and in time came to include any other treatment that might prolong a patient's life. Today's DNR order prevents the use of either specified means or all means to prolong the person's life or to resuscitate the person if his or her heart stops. In Ontario, DNR can now be kept with the person who is dying at home (Buchman, 2008). The DNR is necessary if 911 is called at the time of death, as emergency workers are obligated to start all life-maintaining activity when they arrive on scene. The DNR prevents what could be a very troubling experience for family and possibly for the patient, if resuscitated.

A DNR order can be arranged without a formal living will. In many cases, the patient and doctor decide that further treatment is futile and call for a DNR order to be written (Princess Margaret Hospital, 2005). If the patient is unable to speak, the decision rests with the family, and if there is no next of kin, the physician can make the choice to enter a DNR on the patient's chart. If they do not know what their family member would want, these decisions can be very hard for the next of kin.

Garrett, Tuokko, Stajduhar, Lindsay, and Buehler (2008), using data from the Canadian Study of Health and Aging, found the discussion and formalization of end-of-life care among older Canadians was influenced by regional differences, gender, and education level. People with higher education and females were more likely to contemplate, discuss, and formalize their wishes for end-of-life care. Apparently Ontarians were more likely to hold these discussions than people living in the Atlantic region. On the other hand, Goodridge (2010) examined data drawn from health record reviews of 310 adults who had died in three acute care facilities in a major urban centre of a Western Canadian health region. The researcher concludes that the findings demonstrate a significant gap between institutional EOL (end-of-life) care policies and practice in this particular health region. Furthermore, these findings challenge institutional decision makers and front-line health-care providers to collaborate more effectively to develop relevant clinical policies that enhance client care, especially at a particularly vulnerable time in their life.

Bravo and colleagues (2011) conducted a postal survey to estimate the frequency with which Canadians communicate the preferences about the health care provided to them, and any research which involves them, should they become incapacitated. These researchers surveyed five populations (older adults, informal caregivers, physicians, researchers in aging and research ethics, and board members) from the provinces of Nova Scotia, Ontario, Alberta, and British Columbia. One of the findings indicated that two out of three respondents had been advised to communicate their health-care preferences in advance. Verbal wishes were more frequent than were written wishes (69 percent versus 49 percent). The researchers concluded that even though advance planning has increased over the last two decades in Canada, further efforts are needed to encourage Canadians to voice their health-care and research preferences in the event of incapacity.

There still are ethical issues around using DNR orders. Ewanchuk and Brindley (2006) noted there can be a conflict between a DNR order and the surgical room standard of providing CPR to patients undergoing surgery. They suggest that the risks of surgery and the resulting need for CPR could at times set aside a DNR order if the surgery was to help the terminally ill person live more comfortably, or was addressing a medical issue not directly related to their terminal disease, such as repairing a fracture. Vanpee and Swine (2004) raised several concerns, including that DNRs reduce the level of care provided for the terminally ill person, and that frail elderly people may be targeted for DNRs more than other patients.

The absence of written instruction around whether or not to use "heroic" or simpler life-sustaining measures helped to foster the Terri Schiavo case. In 1990, Terri Schiavo suffered severe brain damage, leaving her in a "persistent vegetative state." At her husband's request, the State of

Florida ruled that the feeding tube could be removed. Without nourishment, Terri would die. Terri's parents challenged the court's decision, and the tube was reinserted. This occurred two more times before several courts, including the U.S. Court of Appeals, refused to permit the reinsertion of the feeding tube for a third time. In March 2005, within two weeks of the feeding tube's removal, Terri died. The Terri Schiavo case not only addresses the DNR issue, but it also falls into the next topic, euthanasia.

Euthanasia

euthanasia The act of painlessly ending the lives of individuals who are suffering from an incurable disease or severe disability.

passive euthanasia Occurs when a person is allowed to die by withholding available treatment, such as withdrawing a life-sustaining device.

active euthanasia Occurs when death is deliberately induced, as when a lethal dose of a drug is injected.

Euthanasia (*"easy death"*) *is the act of painlessly ending the lives of individuals who are suffering from an incurable disease or severe disability.* Sometimes euthanasia is called "mercy killing" or "physician-assisted suicide." Distinctions are made between two types of euthanasia: passive and active. **Passive euthanasia** *occurs when a person is allowed to die by withholding available treatment, such as withdrawing a life-sustaining device.* This might involve turning off a respirator or a heart-lung machine, or as in the Terri Schiavo case, the removal of a feeding tube. **Active euthanasia** *occurs when death is deliberately induced, as when a lethal dose of a drug is injected.*

Technological advances in life-support devices raise the issue of quality of life (Fenigsen, 2008; Georges et al., 2008). Should individuals be kept alive in undignified and hopeless states? The trend is toward acceptance of passive euthanasia in the case of terminally ill patients, as in the case of Terri Schiavo (Truog, 2008). The inflammatory argument that once equated this practice with suicide is rarely heard today. However, experts do not yet entirely agree on the precise boundaries or the exact mechanisms by which treatment decisions should be implemented (Asscher, 2008; Fenigsen, 2008). Can a comatose patient's life-support systems be disconnected when the patient has left no written instructions to that effect? Does the family of a comatose patient have the right to overrule the attending physician's decision to continue life-support systems? These are important questions with no simple or universally agreed-upon answers.

Discussion of euthanasia peaks when cases of active euthanasia are uncovered. One such case occurred in Halifax in November 1996, when Dr. Nancy Morrison was caring for a terminally ill patient. At the request of his family, all life supports were turned off, and doses of morphine and hydromorphone were administered to ease pain. Two hours later, the patient was still in great pain. It was alleged that Dr. Morrison administered potassium chloride, which caused the patient's death within moments. She was charged with first-degree murder, which was later reduced to manslaughter. Charges eventually were entirely dismissed due to lack of evidence. Dr. Morrison accepted a reprimand from her Provincial College of Physicians and Surgeons (Keatings & Smith, 2010).

The case of *Sue Rodriguez vs. British Columbia*, in which Sue Rodriguez sought the right to have a physician assist her to commit suicide, dominated the media headlines for weeks in 1993. She had amyotrophic lateral sclerosis and wished to end her life when the quality of that life was severely threatened. The case went all the way to the Supreme Court of Canada, which ruled against her claim. The justices stated, "given the concerns about abuse and the great difficulty in creating appropriate safeguards, the blanket prohibition on assisted suicide is not arbitrary or unfair" (Attorney-General, 1993). Although it was against the law, Sue Rodriguez did have help to commit suicide when she decided to end her life. No charges were laid, since no witness would come forward with information.

Less than two weeks after the Supreme Court ruling against Rodriguez in 1993, Robert Latimer suffocated his 12-year-old severely disabled daughter Tracy with exhaust fumes from the family pickup. When Latimer was tried for first-degree murder, the media focused on Tracy's disability and spoke of her father's action as mercy killing. The jury found him guilty of second-degree murder and recommended the minimum sentence of 10 years with the possibility of full parole in 2010. The case went to the Supreme Court of Canada on an appeal, in which the justices ruled against Latimer. As of November 2010, Latimer is on full parole. Robert Latimer will be allowed to go to the United Kingdom to take part in a panel debate on end-of-life issues. However, the organizers of a debate on assisted suicide and mercy killings say visa issues have kept Robert Latimer from attending their

Sue Rodriguez fought for the right to have a physician assist her to commit suicide. Although the Supreme Court of Canada ruled against her, she did commit suicide with assistance.

event in Britain. He currently lives in Victoria, B.C., but often travels back to a farm in Saskatchewan to be with his family (Canadian Broadcasting Company, 2012a, b).

Canadian researchers led by Keith Wilson (Wilson et al., 2007) surveyed 379 terminally ill cancer patients on the legalization of euthanasia and/or physician-assisted suicide. They found nearly 63 percent of the patients supported the legalization of one or both, just over 26 percent said no to both, and 11 percent were undecided. Of those 238 who supported one or the other option to end life, 22 patients "indicated a desire to receive a hastened death" (p. 321). Of this small group, 40 percent were assessed as clinically depressed. Wilson and colleagues (2007) noted that these depressed patients ought to be referred for counselling, while the 60 percent who were not depressed counter the often-used argument that only depressed people favour euthanasia or physician-assisted suicide. While loss of dignity was not a significant reason for supporting the hastened termination of life in this study, perceptions of being a burden on others was.

Although active euthanasia is legal in Belgium (in 2002), the Netherlands (in 2002), and Luxembourg (in 2009), it is a criminal offence in most countries, including Canada and in all states in the United States, except two—Oregon (in 1994) and Washington State (in 2009). Several attempts have been made since 1991 to make euthanasia and physician-assisted suicide legal in Canada by moving a bill thorough parliament (Eckstein, 2007). Bloc Québécois MP Francine Lalonde has tried twice, her first bill dying with the dissolution of the House in 2005. Her second effort, Bill C-384, was defeated on April 21, 2010, by a free vote of 228 to 59. Currently, the Canadian Medical Association (2007) states that, "Canadian physicians should not participate in euthanasia or assisted suicide" (p. 2). Orville Endicott (2003) prepared a report for the Council of Canadians with Disabilities in which he clearly laid out the reasons for not proceeding with the legalization of euthanasia or physician-assisted suicide, as it was a threat to disabled Canadians. Endicott noted the stigma and discrimination that faces disabled people in Canada, reducing the value of their lives in the eyes of many. The use of the term *mercy killing*, with its attended sense of "good" whenever public discussion of the death of a disabled or terminally ill person at the hands of another arises, also speaks to the mindset that would encourage the killing of disabled people.

A study on active euthanasia in Flanders, Belgium between June and November 2007 found that 2 percent of all deaths were the result of the administration of life-ending drugs to people who had asked to end their life (Chambaere, Bilsen, Cohen, Onwuteake-Philipsen, Mortier, & Deliens, 2010). They were mainly younger than age 80, had terminal cancer, were in a palliative mode of care, and were largely at home. The study also found that 1.8 percent of the deaths in this area of Belgium during the period were the result of life-ending drugs being given to patients who did not ask to be killed, who tended to be over 80, who did not have cancer, and who were in a hospital at the time of their death. Just over 70 percent were comatose, while 20 percent had dementia. Forty percent of the unrequested euthanized group had, according to the physician, favoured euthanasia in a previous conversation. The authors suggest the unrequested group represents a vulnerable population, people who cannot speak for themselves and need protection. They also suggest that advanced directives could be used to avoid the problem.

Yun and colleagues (2011), a group of Korean researchers, administered a questionnaire to four groups, one group being oncologists, regarding their attitudes toward end-of-life interventions. The interventions investigated included the following: active euthanasia, physician-assisted suicide, as well as withdrawal of futile life-sustaining treatment, active pain control, and withholding life sustaining measures. The findings revealed that the oncologists had more negative attitudes than those in the other groups toward actively ending life (euthanasia and physician-assisted suicide).

Needed: Better Care for Dying Individuals

The Canadian Hospice Society Palliative Care Association (CHPCA, 2010) states that between 16 and 30 percent of Canadians who die will have access to hospice palliative care depending on where they live in Canada. Interestingly, in two-mid size hospitals in a Canadian city, Cohen and colleagues (2011) used hospital charts of deceased clients to compare the services received by one group who received palliative care to a second group of deceased patients who had not received palliative care. The researchers also compared the care characteristics of both groups. The findings indicated that referral to palliative care services appeared to depend upon being admitted to the right hospital. Referral was strongly associated with clients having cancer and being younger. The results suggest that establishing palliative care units or teams of committed health care providers in every hospital could actually increase both referral rates and the equity of access to palliative care services. Collier (2011) states that although some jurisdictions have health centres that give palliative care fairly effectively, no single province or territory stands out as the gold standard for others to copy.

Kaufman (2005) indicates that scientific advances have sometimes made dying harder by delaying the inevitable. Even though analgesics are available, too many individuals experience severe pain during the last days and months of life (Lo & Rubenfeld, 2005). Many health-care providers are increasingly interested in helping individuals experience a "good death" (Brink & Smith, 2008; Lyall, 2007). However, many have not been trained to provide adequate end-of-life care or understand how important it is (Lofmark et al., 2008). End-of-life care should include respect for the goals, preferences, and choices of the patient and his or her family (Harrington & Smith, 2008; Mosenthal et al., 2008).

Chochinov (2007) is a Canadian researcher who is internationally known for his work on death and dying. He claims that health-care providers not only have an important task to conduct but also exert a profound effect on how clients experience their illness and on their sense of dignity. He developed a framework for caring to guide health-care professionals toward maintaining client dignity. This framework is called the A(attitude), B(behaviour), C(compassion), and D(dialogue) of dignity conserving care. For example, dialogue should be used routinely to acquaint the health-care providers with poignant moments and experiences of the client's life, with the intent of bolstering the client's sense of meaning and purpose.

Palliative care *is a humanized program committed to making the end of life as free from pain, anxiety, and depression as possible.* Whereas a hospital's goals are to cure illness and prolong life, hospice care emphasizes palliative care, which involves reducing pain and suffering and helping individuals die with dignity (Kaasa, 2008; Miyashita et al., 2008). A multidisciplinary team involving health-care and community professionals works together to treat the dying person's symptoms, make the individual as comfortable as possible, show interest in the person and the person's family, and help them cope with death (White et al., 2008). This approach tends to the physical, social, emotional, economic, and spiritual needs of the patient (Moss & Dobson, 2006).

The palliative care movement began toward the end of the 1960s in London, England, when a new kind of medical institution, St. Christopher's Hospice, opened. Little effort is made to prolong life at St. Christopher's—there are no heart-lung machines, and there is no intensive care unit, for example. A primary goal is to bring pain under control and to help dying patients face death in a psychologically healthy way. The hospice also makes every effort to include the dying individual's family; it is believed that this strategy benefits not only the dying individual, but family members as well, probably easing the process of grieving after the loved one's death. The first hospice program in Canada was established at St. Boniface Hospital in Winnipeg, in 1974.

The palliative care movement has grown rapidly in Canada, but advocates continue to under-score the need to develop palliative care options that are available to more Canadians (CHPCA, 2010). Effective palliative care can become possible through building on strengths in palliative care as well as on addressing existing barriers (Steinstra & Chochinov, 2012). This process involves, first, ensuring physically accessible hospice and palliative care locations, and second, critically thinking about how to include those individuals who have been excluded or stigmatized such as the vulnerable population. The vulnerable population includes disabled and incarcerated individuals, and the homeless, who also are in need of palliative care services. Carstairs (2010), in her report "Raising the Bar—A Roadmap for the Future of Palliative Care in Canada," states that at least 70 percent of Canadians do not have access to palliative care. She points out that Canadians are living longer, but with a multitude of complex health conditions. Further, Canadians who are

palliative care A humanized program committed to making the end of life as free from pain, anxiety, and depression as possible.

at end-of-life and their families need to have access to interdisciplinary health and social services, based on their needs. She claims, however, that for Canadians to have access to quality palliative care, five requirements are needed: a culture of care, sufficient capacity, support for caregivers, integrated services, and leadership. Goals are identified in the report for each requirement. In order to meet these goals 17 recommendations are stipulated to serve as a roadmap for the federal, provincial, and territorial governments as well as for the entire community. Palliative care, which is a whole-person health-care endeavour, is multi-disciplinary in nature, which can occur in any health-care setting whose aim is to relieve suffering and improve the quality of living and dying (Carstairs, 2010).

The Canadian Institute for Health Information (2007a) examined the percentage of deaths within hospital-based palliative care in 2003 and 2004 in the four western provinces. They found a range from 13 percent of deaths in Manitoba to 16 percent in Alberta were of people in hospital-based palliative care programs. There are just over 200 palliative care physicians in Canada, some of whom work in the community making house calls in their efforts to support people dying at home (CHPCA, 2010). Whether the hospice program is carried out in the dying person's home, through a combination of home and institutional care, or in an institution, often depends on medical needs and the availability of caregivers, including family and friends (Terry et al., 2006).

Researchers have found that family members provide a large proportion of end-of-life care for their loved ones (CHPCA, 2010). Although this experience can be very rewarding and serve as a source of strength in the time after the patient's death, it is also very demanding. Brazil, Thabane, Foster, and Bédard (2009) found gender differences in the nature of the care provided by family members and the impact providing the care had on them. Women were more likely to provide support in toileting-related activity than the males. Men, on the other hand, were more likely to be involved with mobility issues. When the person received care from a woman, they were less likely to receive care from other people.

In terms of stress, not only are physical and mental stress increased for the caregiver, but a recent study found that cognitive functioning can also be impaired (MacKenzie, Smith, Hasher, Leach, & Behl, 2007). A study of 209 Canadian palliative care nurses found the group reported lower levels of work stress when compared to other female workers (Fillion, Tremblay, Truchon, Côté, Struthers, & Dupuis, 2007). The main sources of stress were worry over self-efficacy, lack of resources, and interpersonal issues with other professionals. It appears that involvement with the person dying and his or her family and friends was generally not a source of stress, but instead was a place where job satisfaction was found.

The Canadian Virtual Hospice, an online resource, was developed to provide support and individualized information about palliative and end-of-life care. It is intended for clients, families, health-care providers, researchers, and educators (Canadian Virtual Hospice, 2013).

Halifax-based physicians Graeme Rocker and Daren Heyland (2003) called for research into the cost-effectiveness and the success of hospice palliative care providing better dying and death experiences. Research on cost-effectiveness has begun. Johnson, Abernathy, Howell, Brazil, and Scott (2009) found that the cost for delivering palliative home care to 434 patients for one year was $2.4 million, or $5,586.33 per patient. The average hospital stay time during the period was 64 days. They suggest that home care is cheaper than in-patient hospital care.

Researchers from Alberta and Quebec examined costs a little differently (Dumont, Jacobs, Fassbender, Anderson, Turcotte, & Harel, 2009). They looked at costs across settings and between those involved in care provision. They found, as expected, that the largest share of the cost was paid by the public health care system (71.3 percent); family costs were next (26.6 percent), followed by not-for-profit organizations (1.6 percent). Hospital costs and home care were the first and second most costly element in care provision, both paid for by the province. Time given by family was the third largest expense.

To this point, we have discussed a number of ideas about defining death and life/death issues. For a review, see the **Reach Your Learning Objectives** section at the end of this chapter.

critical thinking

Differentiate between active and passive euthanasia. What is your position regarding active and passive euthanasia? What are your arguments to defend your position on either active or passive euthanasia? Form a peer group where each member prepares one question and one observation on each type of euthanasia. Then, in group, compare and contrast similarities and differences of opinions. What recommendations would you offer for health authorities to implement a universal palliative care program?

Changing Historical
Circumstances

Death in Different Cultures

Death and Socio-Historical, Cultural Contexts

LO2 Analyze the death system within your personal, cultural, and historical ontexts.

When, where, and how people die have changed historically in North America, and attitudes toward death vary across cultures.

Changing Historical Circumstances

Until recent decades, the dying process and death were mainly the matter of private decisions made within specific cultures and/or religious frameworks. Currently, questions on how end-of-life decisions are made have become a matter of public policy and ethical debate (Blank, 2011). For example, two things promise to complicate end-of-life decisions in the future: the aging population in most developed countries, and an increasing incidence of AIDS and other chronic diseases in developing countries. Therefore, as a greater proportion of societal resources are exhausted at the life's end, the ethical and policy issues will gain increased momentum. The more we can understand, deliberate upon, and frame the issues right now, the greater will be our opportunities to deal effectively with their rising consequences (Blank, 2011).

Death in Different Cultures

Cultural variations characterize the experience of death and attitudes about death (Baglow, 2007; Walter, 2005). To live a full life and die with glory was the prevailing goal of the ancient Greeks. Individuals are more conscious of death in times of war, famine, and plague. Whereas we in North America are conditioned from early in life to live as though we are immortal, in much of the world this fiction cannot be maintained. Death crowds the streets of Calcutta daily, as it does the scrubby villages of Africa's Sahel. Children live with the ultimate toll of malnutrition and disease; mothers lose as many babies as survive into adulthood; and it is rare that a family remains intact for many years. Even in rural areas where life is better and health and maturity may be reasonable expectations, the presence of dying people in the house, the large attendance at funerals, and the daily contact with aging adults prepare the young for death and provide them with guidelines on how to die.

By contrast, in Canada it is not uncommon to reach adulthood without having seen someone die. Carleton University Professor John Baglow (2007) suggests that the invisibility of real death, which is tucked away in hospitals and handled by professionals, has "generated a proliferation of death discourses" (p. 227). We are more likely to see death in fictional television shows, movies, video games, and, closest to reality, through the lens of the news media.

Most societies throughout history had philosophical or religious beliefs about death, and most societies have a ritual that deals with death (Bruce, 2007) (see Figure 19.1). Death may be seen as a punishment for one's sins, an act of atonement, or a judgment of a just God. For some, death means loneliness; for others, death is a quest for happiness. For still others, death represents redemption, a relief from the trials and tribulations of earthly life. Some embrace death and welcome it; others abhor and fear it. For those who welcome it, death may be seen as the fitting end to a fulfilled life. In many Aboriginal cultures, for example, death is viewed as a natural part of life, as natural as the setting sun. Aboriginal children are not shielded from death; in fact, "It's a good day to die," sums up widespread traditional Aboriginal beliefs. From this perspective, how we depart from Earth is influenced by how we have lived. Care for the aging and dying is an emerging health issue in Canada; it affects Aboriginal peoples especially. Hampton and colleagues (2010) conducted a study with Aboriginal elders in Saskatchewan. Their findings add an interesting segment to the growing literature indicating that cultural beliefs, values, and needs are significantly important for dying individuals and for their family members.

Figure 19.1

A Ritual Associated with Death

Family Memorial Day at the national cemetery in Seoul, Korea.

In most societies, death is not viewed as the end of existence—though the biological body has died, the spirit is believed to live on (Morgan, 2003). This religious perspective is favoured by most Canadians as well. However, cultures differ in their perceptions of death and their reactions to it. In the Gond culture of India, death is believed to be caused by magic and demons. The members of the Gond culture react angrily to death. In the Tanala culture of Madagascar, death is believed to be caused by natural forces. The members of the Tanala culture show a much more peaceful reaction to death than those in the Gond culture. Other cultural variations in attitudes toward death include a belief in reincarnation, which is an important aspect of the Hindu and Buddhist religions (Dillon, 2003).

A descriptive cross-sectional study was conducted by Iranmanesh, Hosseini, and Esmaili (2011) to evaluate a good health concept from the bereaved Iranian's family member's perspective. Based on the results, the highest scores belonged to the domains "being respected as an individual," having a "natural death," "religious and spiritual comfort," and "control over the future." The domain perceived by family members as less important was "unawareness of death." The researchers conclude that providing a good death requires that professional caregivers be sensitive and pay attention to the preferences of each person's unique perspectives. Spiritual needs are essential to be considered in the provision of holistic care. In another study, which explored the Asian American Hindu (AIAH) cultural views related to death and dying, Gupta (2011) conducted interviews with three focus groups. The three groups consisted of senior citizens, middle-aged adults, and young adults. The results of this qualitative study indicate that all three generations were believers in the afterlife and the karmic philosophy. It is interesting to note, however, that the generations exhibited noticeable differences in the degree to which Hindu traditions surrounding death and bereavement have been influenced by the fact that they live in the United States.

Social norms and cultural values shape the meanings attached to values, beliefs, and practices for immigrants who are adapting to a new culture—especially if they are still attached to the beliefs of their country of origin (Gupta, 2011).

In many ways, we in Canada are death avoiders and death deniers. This denial can take many forms, including the following:

- the tendency of the funeral industry to gloss over death and fashion life-like qualities in the dead
- the adoption of euphemistic language for death—for example, "exiting," "passing on," "never say die," and "good for life," which implies forever
- the persistent search for a "fountain of youth"
- the rejection and isolation of the aged, who may remind us of death
- the adoption of the concept of a pleasant and rewarding afterlife, suggesting that we are immortal
- the medical community's emphasis on the prolongation of biological life, rather than on diminishing human suffering

To this point, we have discussed a number of ideas about death in socio-historical, cultural contexts. For a review, see the **Reach Your Learning Objectives** section at the end of this chapter.

A Developmental Perspective on Death

LO3 Outline death and attitudes from a life-span perspective.

Do the causes of death vary across the human life span? Do we have different expectations about death as we develop through the life span? What are our attitudes toward death at different points in our development?

critical thinking

What is your personal view of death? Discuss with a group of peers your family rituals associated with death. Design a plan indicating the rituals you would like associated with your own death. Compare and contrast the views of death held by cultures other than your own.

Causes of Death and Expectations about Death

Understanding Death from a Life-Span Perspective

Causes of Death and Expectations about Death

In 2009, a total of 238,418 people died in Canada, down 0.1 percent from 2008. Of the deaths in 2009, 120,311 were males and 118,107 were females (Statistics Canada, 2012b).

The two leading causes of death in Canada were cancer and heart disease. These two diseases were responsible for just over half (51 percent) of the 238,617 deaths in 2008. Interestingly, for the first time cancer was the leading cause of death in every province and territory. Heart disease was the second leading cause of death in every province and territory in 2008 except Nunavut, where suicide ranked second (Statistics Canada, 2010c). The other seven leading causes of death, ranked in order, were chronic respiratory diseases, accidents (unintentional injuries), diabetes, Alzheimer's disease, influenza and pneumonia, kidney disease, and suicide (Statistics Canada, 2010c).

One of the more interesting historical changes in death is the age group. The infant mortality rate has continued a long-term downward trend, declining from 6.4 infant deaths per 1,000 live births in 2001 to 4.9 in 2009. During the same period, the male infant mortality rate decreased from 6.9 to 5.1 deaths per 1,000 live births, while for females it decreased from 5.8 to 4.7 (Statistics Canada, 2012b). Life expectancy for seniors has shown an upward trend over the last 15 years. A senior in Canada at age 65 could expect to live an additional 20.2 years in 2007–2009, up 2.1 years from 1992–1994 (Statistics Canada, 2012b).

Considering the human life span, in infants death usually is the result of complications due to congenital malformations as well as chromosomal abnormalities (Statistics Canada, 2012f). Meanwhile, from 2000 to 2009, Alzheimer's disease in older adults had the largest relative increase (24.4 percent) in the number of deaths (Statistics Canada, 2012e).

In both Canada and the United States, three-quarters of all deaths were attributed to the 10 leading causes of death in 2009. However, there were some notable differences. For example, cancer led heart disease as the most common cause of death in Canada in 2009, while in the United States heart disease ranked first as the most common leading cause of death (Statistics Canada, 2012b).

More Aboriginal Canadians die at a younger age than non-Aboriginals. Aboriginal people living in regions where there is a high proportion of other Aboriginal people die at a younger age than those living in areas where there is a low proportion of Aboriginal people (Allard, Wilkins, & Berthelot, 2004). Tjepkema, Wilkins, Senécal, Guimond, and Penny (2009) found the life expectancy of Métis men and women age 25 or older was shorter by 3.3 and 5.5 years, respectively, than non-Aboriginals. The rates of cancer among Aboriginal peoples are lower than they are among non-Aboriginal people. Meanwhile, the incidence of heart disease is a leading cause of death for the Aboriginal people (Statistics Canada, 2011d).

Understanding Death from a Life-Span Perspective

The ages of children and adults influence the way they experience and think about death. A mature, adult-like conception of death includes an understanding that death is final and irreversible, that death represents the end of life, and that all living things die. Adults recognize that death comes to all living things, and that they know death is the final stage in the human life cycle. Four aspects of death that children and adults do not view in the same way are the following: irreversibility, finality, inevitability, and causality (Willis, 2002). The reality of death is that death is inevitable; it is caused by a breakdown in the functioning of the body (Slaughter, 2005). Most researchers agree that as children grow, they develop a more mature approach to death (Hayslip & Hansson, 2003). Recent research is in general agreement that death is first conceptualized by children as a biological event when they are about five or six years of age. At that time children begin to construct a biological model of how the human body functions to maintain "life" (Slaughter, 2005).

Childhood

Unfortunately, children frequently receive negative responses from their parents, other adults, or teachers when they talk about death. Such responses give young children the message that death is a negative concept which they are not to discuss. In fact, when it comes to talking about death, many parents respond in a way that is confusing and potentially harmful to children. It seems that their objective is not to teach, but to protect, their children (Willis, 2002). Most psychologists believe that honesty is the best strategy in discussing death with children.

A study conducted by Cox, Garrett, and Graham (2004–2005) examined the potential influence of Disney films on children's concepts of death. They concluded that certain films may serve as a catalyst to introduce the concept of death into discussions between children and adults or peers. For example, in the film *The Lion King* death is acknowledged and the young main character grieves and displays a range of typical grieving emotions from self-blame and anger to profound sadness. Lee, Lee, and Moon (2009) state that the concept of death, as a kind of social knowledge, should be included in social cultural contexts.

Death is not well understood during the preschool period. For these children the permanence and finality of death are somewhat problematic to understand. Consequently, death is viewed as an altered temporary state such as sleep (Hurwitz, Duncan, & Wolfe, 2004). Fortunately, the child is able to interpret meaning from words and images rather than depend solely upon physical interactions (Nielson, 2012). As children enter the school-age period their thoughts become more concrete, organized, and logical (Hurwitz, Duncan, & Wolfe, 2004). Children's perceptions are less egocentric and they are better able to understand the biological basis of death; they begin to comprehend its permanence (Poltorak & Glazer, 2006). This important shift in children's thinking about the biological world allows for a deeper and more detailed account of how the concept of death comes to be understood by childhood (Slaughter, 2005). A study was conducted by Slaughter and Griffiths (2007) to determine whether or not the developmental acquisition of a mature concept of death— that is, to understand death as a biological event—affects young children's fear of death. The results provided fairly strong empirical support for the widely held belief that discussing death and dying in biological terms is the best way to alleviate fear of dying in young children.

Discussing end-of-life issues with the dying child and his or her family can be difficult (Nielson, 2012). However, effective communication, characterized by compassion and openness, has been shown to improve client outcomes and to increase satisfaction (Levetown & American Academy of Pediatrics Committee on Bioethics, 2008). This type of communication must be cognitively informative, and at the same time sensitive to the needs of the client and his or her family. A shift is occurring, with the adoption of the family-centred care model, to include clients, family members, as well siblings in communication efforts regarding end-of-life matters (Harrison, 2010).

An expert on death and dying, Robert Kastenbaum (2007), takes a different view on developmental dimensions of death and dying. He believes, as attachment theorist John Bowlby (1980) does, that even very young children are acutely aware of and concerned about separation and loss. Kastenbaum (2007) also says that many children work hard at trying to understand death. Thus, instead of viewing young children as having illogical perceptions of death, Kastenbaum thinks a more accurate stance is to view them as having concerns about death and striving to understand it.

The following clarification of children's experience with the death of others was provided by Bert Hayslip and Robert Hansson (2003). They concluded that "experiences with the deaths of grandparents, friends, heroes (sports figures, rock stars), and parents are particularly powerful influences on children's awareness of death, as are culturally relevant experiences . . ." (Hayslip & Hansson, 2003, p. 440). School shootings such as the one that occurred at Virginia Tech, the Air India tragedy, and the deaths of such public figures as Kurt Cobain and Princess Diana bring children to a closer understanding of death.

The death of a parent is especially difficult for children (Sood et al., 2006). When a child's parent dies, the child's school performance and peer relationships often worsen. For some children, as well as adults, a parent's death can be devastating and result in a hypersensitivity about death, including a fear of losing others close to the individual. In some cases, loss of a sibling can result in similar negative outcomes (Sood et al., 2006). However, a number of factors, such as the quality of the relationship and type of death (whether due to an accident, long-standing illness, suicide, or murder, for example), can influence the individual's development following the death of a person

developmental **connection**

Piaget's Cognitive Development Theory and Bowlby's Attachment Theory

close to him or her. Stikkelbroek and colleagues (2012) examined the association between parental death during childhood and psychopathology during adulthood. They found that the majority of children overcome the loss of a parent during childhood without experiencing increased mental health problems, reduced functional limitations, or an increased need for mental health services during adulthood.

It is not unusual for terminally ill children to distance themselves from their parents as they approach the final phase of their illness. The distancing may be due to the depression that many dying patients experience, or it may be a child's way of protecting parents from the overwhelming grief they will experience at the death. Most dying children know they have a terminal illness. Their developmental level, social support, and coping skills influence how well they cope with knowing they will die.

Adolescence

During the adolescent years, concepts of death further evolve. However, the understanding of death even among older adolescents may still be more ambiguous and less mature than that of adults (Poltorak & Glazer, 2006). The subject of death may be avoided, glossed over, kidded about, neutralized, and controlled by a cool, spectator-like orientation. This perspective is typical of the adolescent's self-conscious thought; however, some adolescents do show a concern for death, both in trying to fathom its meaning and in confronting the prospect of their own demise (Linebarger, Sahler, & Egan, 2009).

developmental **connection**

Erikson's Theory of Identity vs. Role Confusion

Deaths of friends, siblings, parents, or grandparents bring death to the forefront of adolescents' lives. Deaths of peers who commit suicide "may be especially difficult for adolescents who feel . . . guilty for having failed to prevent the suicide or feel that they should have died, or . . . feel they are being rejected by their friends who hold them responsible for the death" (Hayslip & Hansson, 2003, p. 441). Deaths that result from gang fighting or a random school shooting create fear and trauma, and can lead to depression and anxiety. The adolescent's ability to focus and concentrate on school, jobs, extracurricular activities, and family gatherings may be compromised and counselling may be required.

Adolescents develop more abstract conceptions of death than do children. For example, adolescents describe death in terms of darkness, light, transition, or nothingness (Nielson, 2012). They also develop religious and philosophical views about the nature of death and whether there is life after death.

developmental **connection**

Piaget's Theory of Formal Operations

Recall the concepts of adolescent egocentrism and personal fable from Chapter 11, "Physical and Cognitive Development in Adolescence"—adolescents' preoccupation with themselves and their belief that they are invincible and unique. It is not unusual for adolescents to think that they are somehow immune to death and that death is something that happens to other people but not to them.

Adulthood

Death is the irreversible cessation of all bodily and mental functions. Death is universal for all mankind. Beyond understanding the objective meaning of death, a subjective meaning of death exists at the individual level. These personal meanings of death are constructed by the individual and they are primarily cognitive interpretations of objects and events associated with death that are derived from the personal experiences of the individual. Even though meanings are unique to the individual, certain meanings may be shared with others (Cicirelli, 2001; King, Hicks, Krull, & Del Gaiso, 2006). Meaning in life has been found to be an essential part of the folk concept (Scollon & King, 2004).

Young adults are more realistic about personal mortality than adolescents are. Reactions of young adults to death are influenced by the experience of death of loved ones, as well as whether or not the death was sudden, or had been anticipated. For example, the sudden loss of a loved one appears to shake a young adult's belief in their unique invulnerability. Such an experience can be more traumatic for younger, rather than older adults (Liu & Aaker, 2007). The most frustrating aspect of the grieving process for adults seems to be situations where they have lost a loved one through a violent crime and are unable to find meaning in the event (Currier, Holland, & Neimeyer, 2006). Often, the survivors of loved ones who have been murdered become involved in community or national organizations that support crime victims and survivors of murdered loved ones or those that seek to prevent violence (Stetsone, 2002).

An increase in consciousness about death accompanies individuals' awareness that they are aging, which usually intensifies in middle adulthood. In our discussion of middle adulthood, we indicated that mid-life is a time when adults begin to think more about how much time is left in their lives. Research indicates that middle-aged adults are most fearful of death (Cicirelli, 2006). The inevitability of death has been accepted, and many anxieties are focused on how death will come about. The fact is that to an older person, death is highly important, but it is apparently not as frightening as it was at mid-life. Older adults, though, think about death more and talk about it more in conversation with others than do middle-aged and young adults. They also have more direct experience with death as their friends and relatives become ill and die (Hayslip & Hansson, 2003). Older adults are forced to examine the meaning of life and death more frequently than are younger adults.

In old age, one's own death may take on an appropriateness it lacked in earlier years. Some of the increased thinking and conversing about death, and an increased sense of integrity developed through a positive life review, may help older adults accept death. Older adults are less likely to have unfinished business than are younger adults. They usually do not have children who need to be guided to maturity, their spouses are more likely to be dead, and they are less likely to have work-related projects that require completion. Lacking such anticipations, death may be less emotionally painful to them. Even among older adults, however, attitudes toward death are sometimes as individualized as the people holding them. One 82-year-old woman declared that she had lived her life and was now ready to see it come to an end. Another 82-year-old woman declared that death would be a regrettable interruption to her participation in activities and relationships.

To this point, we have discussed a developmental perspective on death. For a review, see the **Reach Your Learning Objectives** section at the end of this chapter.

developmental **connection**

Erikson's Three Stages of Adult Development

critical thinking

According to the text, our understanding of and attitudes toward death change as we age. How have your ideas about dying and death changed during your lifetime? Has experience played a role in how you now think about death? If you have had no personal experience with death, then where have you gained your information about the topic? Suppose you decide to write your own eulogy to be shared by others at your celebration of life. What would you have the reader of your eulogy say? In what ways might your life experiences change the eulogy you prepared for yourself?

Facing One's Own Death

LO4 Differentiate the psychological aspects involved in facing one's own death within the contexts in which most people die.

Most dying individuals want an opportunity to make some decisions regarding their own life and death (Kastenbaum, 2007). Some individuals want to complete unfinished business; they want time to resolve problems and conflicts and to put their affairs in order.

A recent study examined the concerns of 36 dying individuals from 38 to 92 years of age with a mean age of 68 (Terry et al., 2006). The three areas of concern that consistently appeared were (1) privacy and autonomy, mainly in regard to their families; (2) inadequate information about physical changes and medication as they approached death; and (3) the motivation to shorten their life, which was indicated by all patients.

Kübler-Ross's Stages of Dying

Perceived Control and Denial

The Contexts in Which People Die

Kübler-Ross's Stages of Dying

Elisabeth Kübler-Ross (1969) divided the behaviour and thinking of dying persons into five stages: denial and isolation, anger, bargaining, depression, and acceptance. **Denial and isolation** *is Kübler-Ross's first stage of dying, in which the person denies that death is really going to take place.* The person may say, "No, it can't be me. It's not possible." This is a common reaction to terminal illness. However, denial is usually only a temporary defence, and eventually it is replaced by increased awareness when the person is confronted with such matters as financial considerations, unfinished business, and worry about surviving family members.

denial and isolation Kübler-Ross's first stage of dying, in which the person denies that death is really going to take place.

anger Kübler-Ross's second stage of dying, in which the dying person recognizes that denial can no longer be maintained. Denial often gives way to anger, resentment, rage, and envy.

bargaining Kübler-Ross's third stage of dying, in which the person develops the hope that death can somehow be postponed or delayed.

depression Kübler-Ross's fourth stage of dying, in which the dying person comes to accept the certainty of death. At this point, a period of depression or preparatory grief may appear.

acceptance Kübler-Ross's fifth stage of dying, in which the person develops a sense of peace, an acceptance of one's fate, and, in many cases, a desire to be left alone.

- - - - - - - - - - - - - - - - - - - **Figure 19.2**

Kübler-Ross's Stages of Dying

According to Elisabeth Kübler-Ross, we go through five stages of dying: denial and isolation, anger, bargaining, depression, and acceptance. **Does everyone go through these stages or go through them in the same order? Explain.**

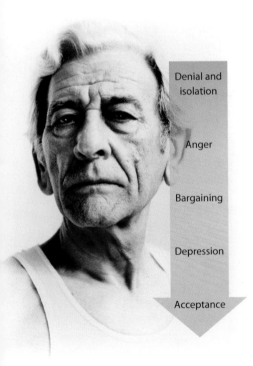

Denial and isolation

Anger

Bargaining

Depression

Acceptance

Anger *is Kübler-Ross's second stage of dying, in which the dying person recognizes that denial can no longer be maintained. Denial often gives way to anger, resentment, rage, and envy.* The dying person's question is, "Why me?" At this point, the person becomes increasingly difficult to care for, since anger may become displaced and projected onto physicians, nurses, family members, and even God. The realization of loss is great, and those who symbolize life, energy, and competent functioning are especially salient targets of the dying person's resentment and jealousy.

Bargaining *is Kübler-Ross's third stage of dying, in which the person develops the hope that death can somehow be postponed or delayed.* Some persons enter into bargaining or negotiation—often with God—as they try to delay their death. Psychologically, the person is saying, "Yes, me, but . . ." In exchange for a few more days, weeks, or months of life, the person promises to lead a reformed life dedicated to God or to the service of others.

Depression *is Kübler-Ross's fourth stage of dying, in which the dying person comes to accept the certainty of death. At this point, a period of depression or preparatory grief may appear.* The dying person may become silent, refuse visitors, and spend much of the time crying or grieving. This behaviour should be perceived as normal in this circumstance, and is actually an effort to disconnect the self from all love objects. Attempts to cheer up the dying person at this stage should be discouraged, says Kübler-Ross, because the dying person has a need to contemplate impending death.

Acceptance *is Kübler-Ross's fifth stage of dying, in which the person develops a sense of peace, an acceptance of one's fate, and, in many cases, a desire to be left alone.* In this stage, feelings and physical pain may be virtually absent. Kübler-Ross describes this fifth stage as the end of the dying struggle, the final resting stage before death. A summary of Kübler-Ross's dying stages is presented in Figure 19.2.

What is the current evaluation of Kübler-Ross's approach? According to psychology death expert Robert Kastenbaum (2004), there are some problems with the theory:

- The existence of the five-stage sequence has not been demonstrated by either Kübler-Ross or independent research.
- The stage interpretation neglects the patients' total life situations, including relationship support, specific effects of illness, family obligations, and institutional climate in which they were interviewed.

Because of the criticisms of Kübler-Ross's stages of dying, some psychologists prefer to describe them not as stages, but rather as potential reactions to dying. At any one moment, a number of emotions may wax and wane. Hope, disbelief, bewilderment, anger, and acceptance may come and go as individuals try to make sense of what is happening to them. However, we should not forget Kübler-Ross's pioneering efforts. Her contribution was important in calling attention to people who are attempting to cope with life-threatening illnesses. She did much to encourage giving needed attention to the quality of life for dying persons and their families.

In 1980, Kübler-Ross publicly proclaimed her belief in a life after death. Adding this element to her writing and workshops concerning care for the dying made some of her peers uncomfortable. Some even rejected her work entirely, claiming she was no longer objective. Many people find her thoughts on life after death comforting and simply an extension of her earlier work, which places death in the context of an entire life.

The extent to which people have found meaning and purpose in their lives is linked with how they approach death. A study of 160 individuals with less than three months to live revealed that those who had found purpose and meaning in their lives felt the least despair in the final weeks, while dying individuals who saw no reason for living were the most distressed and wanted to hasten death (McClain, Rosenfeld, & Breitbart, 2003). In this and other studies, spirituality helped to buffer dying individuals from severe depression (Smith, McCullough, & Poll, 2003).

Perceived Control and Denial

Perceived control and denial may work together as an adaptive strategy for some older adults who face death. When individuals are led to believe they can influence and control events—such as prolonging their lives—they may become more alert and cheerful. Even when death is close, a few people never let go for their zest for life. We must respect their denial and follow their lead about what in the moment is vital in their lives (Zerwekh, 2006).

Denial also may be a useful way for some individuals to approach death; it can be adaptive or maladaptive. Denial can be used to avoid the destructive impact of shock by delaying the necessity of dealing with one's death. Denial can also insulate the individual from having to cope with intense feelings of anger and hurt. However, if denial keeps a person from having a life-saving operation, it clearly is maladaptive. Denial is neither good nor bad; its adaptive qualities need to be evaluated on an individual basis.

The Contexts in Which People Die

Hospitals offer several important advantages to the dying individual—professional staff members are readily available, and the medical technology present may prolong life. Yet, a hospital may not be the best place for many people to die. Population surveys have indicated that most individuals say they would rather die at home (Stajduhar, Allan, Cohen, & Heyland, 2008). In examining patient and family preferences for place of dying, Stajduhar and colleagues (2008) found only half preferred home death, while the others preferred to be in a hospital. Further, they found over half of the patients and their families disagreed on where the best place for them to die would be. Stenekes and Streeter (2010) suggest that conversations on the advantages and hurdles each location presents must occur within families, with their loved ones. If available, community-based palliative care can provide necessary supports, in most cases to allow the pending death to take place in the person's home.

To this point, we have discussed a number of ideas about facing one's own death. For a review, see the **Reach Your Learning Objectives** section at the end of this chapter.

critical thinking

To explore your own death and dying, respond to the following questions and discuss your answers with several friends or family members. How would you prefer to die, if you have a choice? What are your thoughts about being cremated or buried following your own death? If you were to choose now between cremation or burial following your own death, which would you choose? Why?

Coping with the Death of Someone Else

LO5 Identify ways to cope with the death of another person.

Loss can come in many forms in our lives—divorce, a pet's death, loss of a job. However, no loss is greater than that which comes with the death of a person we love and care for—a parent, sibling, spouse, relative, or friend. In ratings of life's stresses that require the most adjustment, death of a spouse is given the highest number. How should we communicate with a dying individual? How do we cope with the death of someone we love?

Communicating with a Dying Person

Most psychologists believe that it is best for dying individuals and their significant others to know that they are dying so that they can interact and communicate with each other on the basis of this mutual knowledge (Banja, 2005). What are some of the advantages of this open awareness context for the dying individual? The client's hopes can be discussed while anticipation of and preparation for future health states and treatment plans are examined. Developing an understanding of the client's values and beliefs is essential to assist health professionals deliver appropriate client-centred care. The challenges associated with engaging clients and families in meaningful discussions can be made more meaningful by promoting honesty, rapport, trust, and respect (Moore, 2007). In fact, Tulsky (2005) suggests the following for providers: 1) acknowledge the effect, for example "this must be overwhelming for you"; 2) identify loss, for example "it must be difficult to discuss your dependence"; 3) legitimize feelings, for example "being sad is normal under the circumstances"; 4) explore, for example "what scares you most about the future?" Direct discussion and validation of

Communicating with a Dying Person

Grieving

Making Sense of the World

Losing a Life Partner

Forms of Mourning, the Funeral, and Celebration of Life

Figure 19.3

Effective Strategies for Communicating with a Dying Person

1. Establish your presence and be at the same eye level. Do not be afraid to touch the dying person—dying individuals are often starved for human touch.

2. Eliminate distraction—for example, ask if it is okay to turn off the TV. Realize that excessive small talk can be a distraction.

3. Dying individuals who are very frail often have little energy. If the dying person you are visiting is very frail, you may not want to visit for very long.

4. Do not insist that the dying person feel acceptance about death if the dying person wants to deny the reality of the situation; on the other hand, do not insist on denial if the dying individual indicates acceptance.

5. Allow the dying person to express guilt or anger; encourage the expression of feelings.

6. Do not be afraid to ask the person what the prognosis (expected outcome) for their illness is. Discuss alternatives and unfinished business.

7. Sometimes dying individuals do not have access to others; ask the dying person if there is anyone he or she would like to see that you can contact.

8. Encourage the dying individual to reminisce, especially if you have memories in common.

9. Talk with the individual when she or he wishes to talk. If this is impossible, make an appointment and keep it.

10. Express your regard for the dying individual, do not be afraid to express love, and do not be afraid to say good-bye.

emotion in a supportive way can be highly effective. It is most helpful if health professionals are particularly aware of their own nonverbal behaviour.

In addition to an open communication system, what are some other suggestions for conversing with a dying individual? Some experts believe that conversation should not focus on mental pathology or preparation for death, but should focus on strengths of the individual and preparation for the remainder of life. Since external accomplishments are not possible, communication should be directed more at internal growth. Caring and support for a dying person does not have to come from a mental health professional only; a concerned nurse, an attentive physician, a sensitive spouse, or an intimate friend can provide an important support system (DeSpelder & Strickland, 2005). Figure 19.3 presents some effective strategies for communicating with a dying person.

Grieving

Our exploration of grief focuses on dimensions of grieving, as well as cultural diversity in healthy grieving.

Dimensions of Grieving

grief The emotional numbness, disbelief, separation anxiety, despair, sadness, and loneliness that accompany the loss of someone we love.

Grief *is the emotional numbness, disbelief, separation anxiety, despair, sadness, and loneliness that accompany the loss of someone we love.* Grief is not a simple emotional state, but rather it is a complex, evolving process with multiple dimensions (Lund, 2007). In this view, pining for the lost person is one important dimension. Pining or yearning reflects an intermittent, recurrent wish or need to recover the lost person. A recent study revealed that the death of a loved one is most frequently followed by yearning and acceptance, with most of the negative feelings associated with the death diminishing by six months after the death (Maciejewski et al., 2007). In this study, yearning was more common than depression following a loved one's death. Another important dimension of grief is separation anxiety, which not only includes pining and preoccupation with thoughts of the deceased person, but also focuses on places and things associated with the deceased; there is crying or sighing as a type of suppressed cry. Grief may also involve despair and sadness, which include a sense of hopelessness and defeat, depressive symptoms, apathy, loss of meaning for activities that used to involve the person who is gone, and growing desolation. In fact, depression and despair are predictable dimensions of grief (Zerwekh, 2006).

These feelings occur repeatedly shortly after a loss (Moules et al., 2004). As time passes, pining and protest over the loss tend to diminish, although episodes of depression and apathy may remain or increase. The sense of separation anxiety and loss may continue to the end of one's life, but most of us emerge from grief's tears, turning our attention once again to productive tasks and regaining a more positive view of life (Carrington & Bogetz, 2004).

The grieving process is more like a roller-coaster ride than an orderly progression of stages with clear-cut time frames (Lund, 2007). The ups and downs of grief often involve rapidly changing emotions, meeting the challenges of learning new skills, detecting personal weaknesses and limitations, creating new patterns of behaviour, and forming new friendships and relationships (Feldon, 2003). For most individuals, grief becomes more manageable over time, with fewer abrupt highs and lows. But many grieving spouses still report that even though time has brought them some healing, they have never gotten over the loss; they have just learned to live with it.

Cognitive factors are involved in the severity of grief after a loved one has died. One study focused on 329 adults who had suffered the loss of a close relative (Boelen, van den Bout, & van den Hout, 2003). The more negative beliefs and self-blame the adults had, the more severe were their symptoms of traumatic grief, depression, and anxiety.

Long-term grief is sometimes masked and can predispose individuals to become depressed and even suicidal (Kastenbaum, 2007). Good family communication can help reduce the incidence of depression and suicidal thoughts. It is important to remember that each individual processes and recovers from grief in different ways (Zerwekh, 2006). An estimated 80 to 90 percent of survivors experience normal or uncomplicated grief reactions that include sadness and even disbelief or considerable anguish. By six months after their loss, they accept it as a reality, are more optimistic about the future, and function competently in their everyday lives. However, six months after their loss, approximately 10 to 20 percent of survivors have difficulty moving on with their life, feel numb or detached, believe their life is empty without the deceased, and feel that the future has no meaning. Initially referred to as complicated grief, leading expert Holly Prigerson and her colleagues (Boelen & Prigerson, 2007; Maciejewski et al., 2007) recently have advocated use of the term **prolonged grief** to describe this *type of grief that involves enduring despair and is still unresolved over an extended period of time*. Prolonged grief usually has negative consequences on physical and mental health (Bonanno et al., 2007; Piper et al., 2007; Wortman & Boerner, 2007). A person who loses someone he or she was emotionally dependent on is often at greatest risk for developing prolonged grief (Johnson et al., 2007). A study found that therapy focused on motivational interviewing, emotion coping, and communication skills was effective in reducing prolonged grief (Zuckoff et al., 2006).

prolonged grief Grief that involves enduring despair and is still unresolved over an extended period of time.

Another type of grief is *disenfranchised grief*, which describes an individual's grief over a deceased person that is a socially ambiguous loss that can't be openly mourned or supported (Read & Elliott, 2007; Reilly et al., 2008). Examples of disenfranchised grief include a relationship that isn't socially recognized such as an ex-spouse, a hidden loss such as an abortion, and circumstances of the death that are stigmatized such as death because of AIDS. Disenfranchised grief may intensify an individual's grief because it cannot be publicly acknowledged. This type of grief may be hidden or repressed for many years, only to be reawakened by later deaths.

Dual-Process Model of Coping with Bereavement

The **dual-process model of coping with bereavement** *consists of two main dimensions: (1) loss-oriented stressors and (2) restoration-oriented stressors* (Stroebe, Schut, & Stroebe, 2005, p. 50). Loss-oriented stressors focus on the deceased individual and can include grief work, as well as positive (such as "relief at the end of suffering") and negative reappraisal ("yearning and rumination") of the meaning of the loss. Restoration-oriented stressors involve the secondary stressors that emerge as indirect outcomes of bereavement. They can include a changing identity (such as from "wife" to "widow") and mastering skills (such as dealing with finances). Restoration rebuilds "shattered assumptions about the world and one's own place in it."

dual-process model of coping with bereavement Consists of two main dimensions: (1) loss-oriented stressors and (2) restoration-oriented stressors.

In the dual-process model, effective coping with bereavement often involves an oscillation between coping with loss and coping with restoration (Wijngaards-de Meij et al., 2008). Earlier

In this final chapter, we talk about the ending of life, dying and death. Of the six billion people on Earth, the vast majority do not believe that the death of the human body is the end of the human being. The world's five major religions, Christianity, Islam, Judaism, Buddhism, and Hinduism, all postulate the continuation of existence after death. Of course, within each major religion, there are differences of practice and belief among subgroups, called sects. Overall, Christians, Muslims, and Jews speak of a resurrection of the person's soul at some point after death. Although each of these three religions offers a different understanding of when and how this resurrection happens, the overall common thread is a day of judgment when the person's life will be reviewed by God. Those who have lived appropriately will enter heaven (a place of comfort and peace) and those who have sinned will be punished (in a place of great pain and sorrow). In the beliefs of some sects of Christianity, the punishment may be temporary, while in others it is permanent. In the Jewish faith, concerns about a life after death are not frequently discussed, as the faith calls its members to focus on living appropriately in the present and to leave to God what will come after life. The Islamic faith is similar to Christianity in tying daily actions with the reward or punishment awaiting their followers after death.

Hinduism and Buddhism approach the idea of life after death in an entirely different way. Both religions see this life as simply one of many that the spirit passes through on its journey of enlightenment. Rather than a day of judgment, these faiths believe that each life you live is connected to what you did or failed to do in the last life or what you need to learn in the present. While Buddhism and Hinduism are different in many respects, the ultimate goal for each is for the spirit to escape the physical ties of the world we know. For Buddhists, this is to escape the ties of pain and desire that the human body has and to reach the state of "Nirvana," or extinction. For Hindus, the goal is to leave the material cycle and become one with Brahman, who is everything physical, spiritual, and conceptual.

Apart from the world's major religions, there are other spiritual or religious practices. Aboriginal cultures around the globe hold beliefs about the existence of spirits after death, whose connection with the living world may be strongly tied to their own behaviours during life or those of the people they left behind. In the past 20 years a "new age" spirituality has arisen in the Western world, which rejects the formal religions and promotes an individualistic approach to spiritual growth. These new age sects often borrow beliefs and practices from a variety of sources, and many believe in a continuation of the spirit after death.

In a text that has offered scientific research to support what is stated about human life-span development, there is little scientific evidence to support what religions or spiritual beliefs say about life after death. Instead, the person is asked to have faith in what their religious or spiritual leader tells them.

Whatever religion or spiritualism people follow can deeply affect the way in which they respond to dying and death. The religions of the world all have specific rituals to perform for the dying person and the dead, to help them transform into whatever comes next. These ceremonies also offer solace and social support for the bereaved.

models often emphasized a sequence of coping with loss through such strategies as grief work as an initial phase, followed by restoration efforts. However, in the dual-process model, coping with loss and engaging in restoration can be carried out concurrently (Richardson, 2007). According to this model, the person coping with death might be involved in grief group therapy while settling the affairs of the loved one. Oscillation might occur in the short term during a particular day as well as across weeks, months, and even years. Although loss and restoration coping can occur concurrently, over time there often is an initial emphasis on coping with loss, followed by greater emphasis on restoration over time (Milberg et al., 2008).

Coping and Type of Death

The impact of death on surviving individuals is strongly influenced by the circumstances under which the death occurs (Hansson & Stroebe, 2007; Wortman & Boerner, 2007). Deaths that are sudden, untimely, violent, or traumatic are likely to have more intense and prolonged effects on surviving individuals and make the coping process more difficult for them (Murphy et al., 2003; Sveen & Walby, 2008). Such deaths often are accompanied by post-traumatic stress disorder (PTSD) symptoms, such as intrusive thoughts, flashbacks, nightmares, sleep disturbance, problems in concentrating, and others (Raphael, Taylor, & McAndrew, 2008). Beliefs about life after death can also impact how individuals cope with death. The Connecting through Research feature explores different views of life after death.

Cultural Diversity in Healthy Grieving

Contemporary orientations toward grieving emphasize the importance of breaking bonds with the deceased and the return of survivors to autonomous lifestyles.

In the Jewish community, mourning is divided into graduated time periods, each with its appropriate practices (Olyan, 2004). The observance of these practices is required of the spouse and the immediate kin of the deceased. The first period is *aninut*, the period between death and burial. The next two periods make up *avelut*, or mourning proper. The first of these is *shivah*, a period of seven days, which commences with the burial. This is followed by *sheloshim*, the 30-day period following the burial, including shivah. At the end of sheloshim, the mourning process is considered over for all but one's parents. In this case, mourning continues for 11 months, although observances are minimal. The seven-day period of the shivah is especially important in mourning in traditional Judaism.

Grief and mourning rituals are influenced by many factors. Tony Walter (2005) found that in Western Europe and North America, the dominant religious beliefs, type of government and its rules around death and internment of the dead, and the commercial nature of the handling of the dead all influence the nature of the mourning rituals practised. Local variations crop up with the additional influence of sub-cultures and variation in geography and immigration patterns. Thus, while an overall general pattern of grief and bereavement might be suggested for any cultural group, local individual variations will at times create significant differences. This was further examined by Ronald Marshall and University of Toronto Professor Patsy Sutherland (2008), who found that the influence of religion, immigrant culture, and the history of oppression via slavery produced unique local variations in grief and mourning in Jamaica, Trinidad, Grenada, and Barbados. Not only were there differences between the islands, but also within each one.

In summary, people grieve in a variety of ways. The diverse grieving patterns are culturally embedded practices. Thus, there is no one right, ideal way to grieve. There are many different ways to feel about a deceased person, and no set series of stages that the bereaved must pass through to become well adjusted. The stoic widower may need to cry out over his loss at times. The weeping widow may need to put her husband's wishes aside as she becomes the financial manager of her estate. What is needed is an understanding that healthy coping with the death of a loved one involves growth, flexibility, and appropriateness within a cultural context.

Making Sense of the World

Grieving is a healthy and necessary process that individuals must go through to be able to move on with their lives (Heidrich, 2007). Fortunately, most people adapt to bereavement successfully, and such adaptation can even be associated with improving coping, personal growth, and acquiring a new appreciation of life (Dutton & Zisook, 2005). One recent study found that mourners who expressed positive themes of hope for a positive future showed better adjustment than those who focused on negative themes of pain and suffering (Gamino & Sewell, 2004).

An interesting phenomenon is the near-death experience which is marked by an altered state of consciousness. It generally results from oxygen deprivation, severe trauma, or any number of life-threatening conditions. Individuals who have had near-death experiences often do not fear death (Zerwekh, 2006).

Each individual may offer a piece of death's puzzle. "When I saw him last Saturday, he looked as though he was rallying," says one family member. "Do you think it might have had something to do with his sister's illness?" remarks another. "I doubt it, but I heard from an aide that he fell going to the bathroom that morning," comments yet another. "That explains the bruise on his elbow," says the first individual. "No wonder he told me that he was angry because he could not seem to do anything right," chimes in a fourth family member. So it goes in the attempt to understand why someone who was rallying on Saturday was dead on Wednesday.

When a death is caused by an accident or a disaster, the effort to make sense of it is pursued more vigorously. As pieces of news come trickling in, they are integrated into the puzzle. The bereaved want to put the death into a perspective that they can understand—divine intervention, a curse from

---

critical thinking

Suppose a friend or relative told you that they were having trouble dealing with the death of a loved one. Using the material in this chapter, what would you do to help them? How will you know whether or not you are helping a grieving family? Compare and contrast strategies you would use if the family's loved one was a child, a young adult, or an older adult. What measures would you take to help the family grieve after you leave the relationship?

a neighbouring tribe, a logical sequence of cause and effect, or whatever it may be. A recent study of more than 1,000 postsecondary students found that making sense was an important factor in their grieving of a violent loss by accident, homicide, or suicide (Currier, Holland, & Neimeyer, 2006).

Losing a Life Partner

Those left behind after the death of an intimate partner suffer profound grief and often endure financial loss, loneliness, increased physical illness, and psychological disorders, including depression (Kowalski & Bondmass, 2008; Zisook & Kendler, 2007). How they cope with the crisis varies considerably (Ott et al., 2007). A study that included data from 3 years pre-death to 18 months post-death revealed that nearly half of surviving spouses experienced low levels of distress consistently over the four years (Bonanno, Wortman, & Nesse, 2004). Another study found that widowed individuals were more likely to increase their religious and spiritual beliefs following the death of a spouse, and this increase was linked with a lower level of grief (Brown et al., 2004). And a recent study concluded that chronic grief was more likely to characterize bereaved spouses who were highly dependent on their spouse (Ott et al., 2007).

One in two Canadian women over the age of 65 will experience widowhood. Only one in eight Canadian men in the same age group will become widowers. Widowed women are probably the poorest group in North America, despite the myth of huge insurance settlements. Many widows are lonely (Lund, 2007). The poorer and less educated they are, the lonelier they tend to be. The bereaved are also at increased risk for many health problems, including death (Ajdacic-Gross et al., 2008; Elwert & Christakis, 2008).

Optimal adjustment after a death depends on several factors. Women do better than men largely because, in our society, women are responsible for the emotional life of the couple, whereas men usually manage the finances and material goods (Fry, 2001). Thus, women have better networks of friends, closer relationships with relatives, and more experience in taking care of themselves psychologically (Antonucci, Akiyama, & Sherman, 2007). Older widows do better than younger widows, perhaps because they are more prepared for the death of a partner. Men who are widowed usually have more money than their female counterparts, and are much more likely to remarry.

Older adults, however, have unique needs during bereavement. These needs may predispose them to a variety of problems including increased morbidity and mortality (Kowalski & Bondmass, 2008; Stroebe, Schut, & Stroebe, 2007). Finding balance in their completely changed lives is of utmost importance for bereaved caregivers. Re-establishing a balance is a primary objective as they navigate their way through coping with grief and new life circumstances within a complex psychosocial context (Holtslander & Duggleby, 2010). Holtslander, Bally, and Steeves (2011) studied ways in which caregivers who survive the loss of their spouse to cancer find balance in their lives. It was found that bereaved caregivers should be assessed for their risk of losing control of balance, their level of support, and the impact of a difficult caregiving experience. Additional research is required to identify the needs of a wide range of cultural groups, ages, disease states, caregiving experiences, and in varying geographical locations such as the rural areas.

Social supports help both widows and widowers adjust to the death of a spouse (Schulz, Hebert, & Boerner, 2008; Walsh, 2008; Wortman & Boerner, 2007). Local resources, professional, voluntary, or self-help-oriented programs are available to assist people as they work through their grief. The Bereaved Families of Ontario has chapters across the province providing information, newsletters, social activities, as well as group discussion and support sessions. This organization has a grassroots foundation of people who share their experiences dealing with grief and loss.

Researchers have found that religiosity and coping skills are related to well-being following the loss of a spouse in late adulthood (Leighton, 2008). Further, a recent study revealed that compared with continually married counterparts, 50-year-old and older adults who experienced the death of a spouse reported a higher participation in volunteer work several years after the death (Li, 2007). The volunteer work helped to protect the spouses from depressive symptoms, and an increase in volunteer hours enhanced their self-efficacy. Another recent study also found that when older adults helped others following the death of a spouse, they experienced an accelerated decline in depressive symptoms (Brown et al., 2008).

How might grieving vary across individuals and cultures?

Personalizing Funerals

War has a way of creating new technologies, often ones to more efficiently kill people. World War I saw its share of new killing technologies, such as tanks, poisonous gases, and improved machine guns. While not invented for or during the war, the airplane made its first combat flight during the conflict. Used in the early months as a means of reconnaissance, it quickly took on machine guns to fight other aircraft and dropped bombs on enemy positions. Flying these machines was not the safest profession, and many of the pilots and crew died after being shot down by enemy aircraft or in crashes due to mechanical problems. According to Florian Schnurer (2008), the public funerals of the pilots took on an overriding political nature as they were used to transmit nationalistic sentiments to the public to sustain the war effort. The political leaders who appeared at these media events became the focus of news reporters' stories, rather than the family of the fallen "hero." Schnurer (2008) claims this was true across Europe; as the war raged on into 1916, every nation used the pilots' funerals as opportunities to communicate with the masses.

At first what took place at the pilots' funerals might seem unnatural, or even offensive. A funeral being used to reinforce a message that a powerful person or persons want the people to believe in does not seem proper. Yet, how we dispose of our dead has always conveyed messages about order and disorder and how to maintain or re-establish the former, and survive or minimize the latter. In the past, religious or spiritual rituals have dominated and shaped the nature of funerals and the mourning process in most cultures in the world (Kastenbaum, 2004; Lynch, 2004). But this is changing.

In the past several decades, funeral directors, clergy, and others have noticed a secularization of the funeral (Emke, 2002; Kastenbaum, 2004, 2007; Lynch, 2004). *Secularization* refers to the removal or downplaying of religious practices within the funeral service. In the place of religion is a *personalization* of the funeral service, focusing on the deceased person's life. Many reasons have contributed to this change. As we learned in Chapter 15, fewer people attend religious services and therefore may not know a clergy member to officiate at a funeral. The funeral home can offer to arrange for clergy to lead the service, but the family might ask them to tone down the religious element (Wishart, 2006). Secularization crept into funerals as death was professionalized, with doctors pronouncing it, and

funeral directors preparing the body, supplying the location for visitation, the funeral service, and the wake after internment. The customer (the person planning the funeral) is confronted with a line of products to provide "after-death care" to their loved one and to memorialize their life. The marking of a death can be a sizable commercial event.

Robert Kastenbaum (2004) laments this change, suggesting that past death rituals had significant power in marking the endpoint of a life and the starting of a new life for the survivors. Religious services connected the grievers to each other and transferred the deceased from the realm of the living to that of the dead. Today, funeral directors are planning funerals with families that celebrate the individual's life and focus on moving through the event with a minimum of discomfort and pain. Many funeral directors are no longer lowering the casket into the grave in front of the family, seeing it as causes much anguish. Others suggest that lowering the casket is important in accepting the reality of death. The personalization of funerals has been hailed as a most positive innovation, allowing families to make a meaningful memorial service for the deceased. In this service, who they were is talked about, their accomplishments hailed, and the personal sense of loss is acknowledged for each of those in attendance.

Today you can pre-arrange your funeral, pay a flat fee for the service, and when you die your family will only need to call the funeral home. Lynch (2004) notes that this is an interesting idea (one in four people over age 60 have made such pre-arrangements), but wonders how it will be received by the children who attend the funeral Mom or Dad planned for themselves and not the one they would have designed for them.

What types of funerals have you attended? How did they seem to you? Were they meaningful? joyous? sad? If you were to plan your own funeral, what would it be like? Would religion or spirituality have a prominent role, or would eulogies by your friends and family dominate? Take a moment and think through these questions. As you do, consider this: some people (for example Kastenbaum, 2007; Wishart, 2006) say that death makes us review all of the deceased person's life and often all of our life up to that point in time. As you think about funerals, yours or another's, what does your life review tell you? It might be interesting to compare notes on funeral plans with your family, friends, or fellow classmates.

Forms of Mourning, the Funeral, and Celebration of Life

In some cultures, a ceremonial meal is arranged; in others, a black armband is worn for one year following a death. Cultures vary in how they practise mourning.

The funeral is an important aspect of mourning in many cultures. One consideration involves what to do with the body. In Canada, approximately 56 percent of corpses are cremated, while the remaining 44 percent are buried in either the ground or in a vault in a mausoleum (Memorial Society of British Columbia, 2004). Cremation is more popular in British Columbia (at 78 percent) and less popular in Prince Edward Island (at 13 percent). Cremation also is more popular in Canada than in the United States, and most popular of all in Japan and many other Asian countries. The Connecting Development to Life feature discusses the impact of personalizing funerals.

The funeral industry has been the source of controversy in recent years. Funeral directors and their supporters argue that the funeral provides a form of closure to the relationship with the deceased, especially when there is an open casket. Their dissenters, however, stress that funeral directors are just trying to make money; they further argue that the art of embalming is grotesque. One way to avoid being exploited, since bereavement makes us vulnerable to being talked into purchasing more expensive funeral arrangements, is to purchase them in advance. However, most of us do not follow this procedure.

To this point, we have discussed a number of ideas about coping with the death of someone else. For a review, see the **Reach Your Learning Objectives** section at the end of this chapter.

critical thinking

Think about the personalization of the funeral service, either your own or that of someone else. In what ways would a celebration of life be appealing to you? On the other hand, what would not be appealing about a celebration of life?

reach your **learning objectives**

Defining Death and Life/Death Issues

LO1 Evaluate issues in determining death and decisions regarding death.

Issues in Determining Death	▪ Twenty-five years ago, death was assessed and defined in simpler ways.
	▪ Brain death is a neurological definition of death, which states that a person is brain dead when all electrical activity of the brain has ceased for a specified period of time. Medical experts debate whether this should mean both the higher and lower brain functions, or just the higher cortical functions.
Decisions Regarding Life, Death, and Health Care	▪ Living wills and DNRs are increasingly used.
	▪ Euthanasia is the act of painlessly ending the life of a person who is suffering from an incurable disease or disability. Distinctions are made between active and passive euthanasia.
	▪ The need for more humanized care for the dying person includes the development of palliative care.

Death and Socio-Historical, Cultural Contexts

LO2 Analyze the death system within your personal, cultural, and historical contexts.

Changing Historical Circumstances	▪ When, where, and why people die have changed historically. Today, death occurs most often among the elderly.
	▪ Our exposure to death in the family has been minimized.
	▪ Most societies throughout history have had philosophical or religious beliefs about death, and most societies have rituals that deal with death.
Death in Different Cultures	▪ Most cultures do not view death as the end of existence—spiritual life is thought to continue.
	▪ Canadian culture has been described as a death-denying and death-avoiding culture.

A Developmental Perspective on Death

LO3 Outline death and attitudes from a life-span perspective.

Causes of Death and Expectations about Death	■ Although death is more likely to occur in late adulthood, death can come at any point in development.
	■ The deaths of some people, especially children and younger adults, often are perceived to be more tragic than those of others, such as very old adults who have had an opportunity to live a long life.
	■ In children and younger adults, death is more likely to occur because of accidents; in older adults it is more likely to occur because of chronic diseases.
Understanding Death from a Life-Span Perspective	■ Infants do not have a concept of death.
	■ Preschool children also have little concept of death, often showing little or no upset feelings at the sight of a dead animal or person. Preschool children sometimes blame themselves for a person's death.
	■ In the elementary school years, children develop a more realistic orientation toward death.
	■ Most psychologists believe honesty is the best strategy for helping children cope with death.
	■ Death may be glossed over in adolescence. Adolescents have more abstract, philosophical views of death than children do.
	■ There is no evidence that a special orientation toward death emerges in early adulthood.
	■ Middle adulthood is a time when adults show a heightened consciousness about death and death anxiety.
	■ Older adults often show less death anxiety than middle-aged adults, but older adults experience and converse about death more frequently.
	■ Attitudes about death may vary considerably among adults of any age.

Facing One's Own Death

LO4 Differentiate the psychological aspects involved in facing one's own death within the contexts in which most people die.

Kübler-Ross's Stages of Dying	■ Kübler-Ross proposed five stages: denial and isolation, anger, bargaining, depression, and acceptance.
	■ Not all individuals go through the same sequence, and some individuals may struggle to the end.
Perceived Control and Denial	■ Perceived control and denial may work together as an adaptive orientation for the dying individual.
	■ Denial can be adaptive or maladaptive, depending on the circumstances.
The Contexts in Which People Die	■ Most deaths in Canada occur in hospitals; this has advantages and disadvantages.
	■ Many individuals say they would rather die at home, but they worry that they will be a burden and about the lack of medical care.

Coping with the Death of Someone Else

LO5 Identify ways to cope with the death of another person.

Communicating with a Dying Person	■ Most psychologists recommend an open communication system; this system should not dwell on pathology or preparation for death, but should emphasize the dying person's strengths.
Grieving	■ Grief is the emotional numbness, disbelief, separation anxiety, despair, sadness, and loneliness that accompany the loss of someone we love.
	■ Grief is multi-dimensional and in some cases may last for years.
	■ Complicated grief involves enduring despair that is still unresolved after an extended period of time.
	■ In the dual-process model of coping with bereavement, oscillation occurs between two dimensions: (1) loss-oriented stressors and (2) restoration-oriented stressors.
	■ Grief and coping vary with the type of death.
	■ There are cultural variations in grieving.
Making Sense of the World	■ The grieving process may stimulate individuals to strive to make sense of their world; each individual may contribute a piece to death's puzzle.
Losing a Life Partner	■ Usually the most difficult loss is the death of a spouse.
	■ The bereaved are at risk for many health problems.
	■ Social support benefits widows and widowers.
Forms of Mourning, the Funeral, and Celebration of Life	■ Mourning and funerals vary from culture to culture.
	■ The most important aspect of mourning in most cultures is the funeral. In recent years, the funeral industry has been the focus of controversy, possibly being replaced with a celebration of life.

connect
McGraw Hill Education

McGraw-Hill Connect provides you with a powerful tool for improving academic performance and truly mastering course material. You can diagnose your knowledge with pre- and post-tests, identify the areas where you need help, search the entire learning package, including the eBook, for content specific to the topic you're studying, and add these resources to your personalized study plan. CONNECT for *Life-Span Development*, fifth Canadian edition, offers the following:

- chapter-specific online quizzes
- groupwork
- presentations
- writing assignments
- case studies
- and much more!

Visit CONNECT today!

review ----> *connect* ----> reflect

review

What are some issues regarding the determination of death? **LO1**

What is your personal understanding of death within your own cultural context? **LO2**

What are some variations of death in different cultures? **LO2**

What are some attitudes about death at different points throughout the life span? **LO3**

What is the sequence of stages that an individual goes through when facing death, according to Kübler-Ross? **LO3**

What may be some of your own personal reactions when you face your own death? **LO4**

How would you cope with the pending death of a loved one? **LO5**

connect

What are the important aspects that you found in the Canadian report on palliative care called "Raising the Bar"?

reflect *Your Own Personal Journey of Life*

You and your family had a discussion regarding life directives. Have you signed one yet? Explain.

Glossary

A

acceptance Kübler-Ross's fifth stage of dying, in which the person develops a sense of peace, an acceptance of one's fate, and, in many cases, a desire to be left alone.

accommodation In Piaget's theory, individuals adjust to new information.

active (niche-picking) genotype–environment correlations Exist when children seek out environments they find compatible and stimulating.

active euthanasia Occurs when death is deliberately induced, as when a lethal dose of a drug is injected.

activity theory States that the more active and involved older adults are, the more likely they will be satisfied with their lives.

addiction A physical and/or psychological dependence on a drug.

adolescent egocentrism The heightened self-consciousness of adolescents.

aerobic exercise Sustained exercise (such as jogging, swimming, or cycling) that stimulates heart and lung activity.

affectionate love Also called companionate love, this is the type of love that occurs when individuals desire to have the other person near and have a deep, caring affection for the other person.

afterbirth The third stage of birth when the placenta, umbilical cord, and other membranes are detached and expelled.

ageism Prejudice against others because of their age, especially prejudice against older adults.

agnostic A person who isn't sure whether or not God exists.

AIDS Acquired immune deficiency syndrome; a primarily sexually transmitted disease caused by HIV, which destroys the body's immune system.

alcoholism A disorder that involves long-term, repeated, uncontrolled, compulsive, and excessive use of alcoholic beverages.

altruism Unselfish interest in helping another person.

Alzheimer's disease A fatal, progressive, and irreversible disorder characterized by a gradual deterioration of memory, reasoning, language, and eventually, physical functioning.

amnion A life-support system that is like a bag or envelope containing a clear fluid in which the developing embryo floats.

androgyny The presence of masculine and feminine characteristics in the same individual.

anger Kübler-Ross's second stage of dying, in which the dying person recognizes that denial can no longer be maintained. Denial often gives way to anger, resentment, rage, and envy.

anger cry Similar to the basic cry, with more excess air forced through the vocal chords.

animism The belief that inanimate objects have "lifelike" qualities and are capable of action.

anorexia nervosa (AN) An eating disorder that involves the relentless pursuit of thinness through starvation.

Apgar scale A widely used method to assess the health of newborns at one and five minutes after birth; evaluates infants' heart rate, respiratory effort, muscle tone, body colour, and reflex irritability.

arthritis An inflammation of the joints accompanied by pain, stiffness, and movement problems.

Asperger syndrome A relatively mild autism spectrum disorder in which the child has relatively good verbal language, milder non-verbal language problems, and a restricted range of interests and relationships.

assimilation A process by which immigrant groups adapt patterns of dominant groups. It involves changing the mode of dress, values as examples; in Piaget's theory, individuals incorporate new information into their existing knowledge.

atheist A person who does not believe in the existence of God.

attachment A close emotional bond between two people.

attention The focusing of mental resources on select information.

attention deficit hyperactivity disorder (ADHD) A disability in which children consistently show one or more of the following characteristics over a period of time: (1) inattention, (2) hyperactivity, and (3) impulsivity.

authoritarian parenting A restrictive, punitive style in which parents exhort the child to follow their directions and to respect work and effort.

The authoritarian parent places firm limits and controls on the child and allows little verbal exchange.

authoritative parenting A style in which parents encourage their children to be independent but still place limits and controls on their actions. Extensive verbal give-and-take is allowed, and parents are warm and nurturing toward the child.

autism spectrum disorders (ASD) Also called pervasive developmental disorders, they range from the severe disorder labelled autistic disorder to the milder disorder called Asperger syndrome. Children with these disorders are characterized by problems in social interaction, verbal and non-verbal communication, and repetitive behaviours.

autistic disorder A severe developmental autism spectrum disorder that has its onset in the first three years of life and includes deficiencies in social relationships, abnormalities in communication, and restricted, repetitive, and stereotyped patterns of behaviour.

autonomous morality The second stage of moral development, displayed by older children (about 10 years of age and older). The child becomes aware that rules and laws are created by people and that in judging an action one should consider the actor's intentions as well as the consequences.

B

bargaining Kübler-Ross's third stage of dying, in which the person develops the hope that death can somehow be postponed or delayed.

basal metabolism rate (BMR) The minimum amount of energy a person uses in a resting state.

basic cry A rhythmic pattern usually consisting of a cry, a briefer silence, a shorter inspiratory whistle that is higher pitched than the main cry, and then a brief rest before the next cry.

basic-skills-and-phonetics approach An approach to reading instruction that stresses phonetics and basic rules for translating written symbols into sounds. Early reading instruction should involve simplified materials.

Bayley Scales of Infant Development Scales developed by Nancy Bayley and widely used in the assessment of infant development. The current version has five scales: cognitive, language, motor, socio-emotional, and adaptive.

becoming parents and a family with children The third stage in the family life cycle that requires adults to move up a generation and become caregivers to the younger generation.

behavioural and social cognitive approach The theory that behaviour, environment, and person/cognitive factors are important in understanding development.

bicultural identity The way adolescents identify in some ways with their cultural group and in other ways with the mainstream culture

big five factors of personality Consist of openness to experience, conscientiousness, extraversion, agreeableness, and neuroticism (emotional stability) (acronym: OCEAN).

bio-ecological approach Focuses on five environmental systems: microsystem, mesosystem, exosystem, macrosystem, and chronosystem.

biological age A person's age in terms of biological health.

biological processes Changes in an individual's physical nature.

blastocyst The inner mass of cells that develops during the germinal period. These cells later develop into the embryo.

body mass index (BMI) A measure of weight in relation to height.

body transcendence versus body preoccupation Peck's developmental task in which older adults must cope with declining physical well-being.

bonding Close contact, especially physical, between parents and their newborn in the period shortly after birth.

brain death A neurological definition of death, which states that a person is brain dead when all electrical activity of the brain has ceased for a specified period of time; a flat EEG recording for a specified period of time is one criterion of brain death.

brainstorming A technique in which individuals try to come up with ideas and play off each idea. This can be done alone or in a group.

Brazelton Neonatal Behavioral Assessment Scale (NBAS) A test given 24 to 36 hours after birth to assess newborns' neurological development, reflexes, and reactions to people and objects.

breech position The baby's position in the uterus that causes the buttocks to be the first part to emerge from the vagina.

Broca's area An area in the brain's left frontal lobe involved in producing words.

bulimia nervosa (BN) An eating disorder in which the individual consistently follows a binge-and-purge eating pattern.

C

caesarean delivery The baby is removed from the mother's uterus through an incision made in her abdomen.

care perspective Views people in terms of their connectedness with others and emphasizes interpersonal communication, relationships, and concern for others.

case study An in-depth look at a single individual.

cellular clock theory Leonard Hayflick's theory that cells can divide a maximum of about 75 to 80 times, and that as we age, our cells become increasingly less capable of dividing.

centration The focusing, or centring, of attention on one characteristic to the exclusion of all others.

cephalocaudal pattern The sequence in which the greatest growth in size, weight, and feature differentiation gradually works down from top to bottom.

child-centred kindergarten Education that involves the whole child and includes concern for the child's physical, cognitive, and social development.

child-directed speech This type of speech has a higher-than-normal pitch and involves the use of simple words and sentences.

chlamydia The most common STD. Named for *Chlamydia trachomatis,* an organism that spreads by sexual contact and infects the genitals of both sexes.

chromosomes Threadlike structures that are made up of deoxyribonucleic acid, or DNA.

chronic disorders Conditions characterized by slow onset and long duration; are rare in early adulthood, increase in middle adulthood, and become common in late adulthood.

chronic stress Stress that is negative, persistent, and as such can be crippling.

chronological age The number of years that has elapsed since a person's birth; what is usually meant by "age."

circadian rhythm Behavioural, physical, and mental changes that occur over roughly 24 hours.

climacteric A term used to describe the midlife transition in which fertility declines.

cognitive mechanics The "hardware" of the mind, reflecting the neurophysiological architecture of the brain developed through evolution; involve the speed and accuracy of the processes involving sensory input, visual and motor memory, discrimination, comparison, and categorization.

cognitive pragmatics The culture-based "software programs" of the mind; include reading and writing skills, language comprehension, educational qualifications, professional skills, and also the type of knowledge about the self and life skills that help us master or cope with life.

cognitive processes Changes in an individual's thought, intelligence, and language.

cognitive theories Emphasize conscious thoughts.

cohort effects Occur due to a person's time of birth or generation but not to actual age.

commitment Personal investment in identity.

congruence The relationship between a person's ideal self and real self as determined by self-selected descriptors.

connectedness Comprises two dimensions: mutuality, sensitivity to and respect for others' views, and permeability, openness to others' views.

consensual validation An explanation of people's attraction to others who are similar to them; our own attitudes and behaviour are supported when someone else's attitudes and behaviour are similar to ours.

conservation Awareness that altering an object's or a substance's appearance does not change its basic properties.

constructivist approach A learner-centred approach that emphasizes the importance of individuals actively constructing their knowledge and understanding with guidance from the teacher.

contemporary life-events approach Emphasizes that how life events influence the individual's development depends not only on the life event, but also on mediating factors, the individual's adaptation to the life event, the life-stage context, and the socio-historical context.

context The settings, influenced by historical, political, economic, social, and cultural factors, in which development occurs.

continuity–discontinuity issue Regards whether development involves gradual, cumulative change (continuity) or distinct stages (discontinuity).

conventional reasoning The intermediate level in Kohlberg's theory of moral development. Individuals abide by certain standards (internal), but they are the standards of others (external), such as parents or society.

convergent thinking Produces one correct answer and is characteristic of the kind of thinking required on conventional tests of intelligence.

convoy model of social relations According to this model, individuals go through life embedded in a personal network of individuals to whom they give and from whom they receive social support.

coordination of secondary circular reactions Piaget's fourth sensorimotor substage, which develops between eight and 12 months of age. Actions become more outwardly directed, and infants coordinate schemes and act with intentionality.

correlational research The goal is to describe the strength of the relationship between two or more events or characteristics.

creative thinking The ability to think in novel and unusual ways and to come up with unique solutions to problems.

creativity The process of divergent thinking that requires encounters with the world and a degree of intensity and absorption

crisis Marcia's term for a period of identity development during which the individual is exploring alternatives.

critical period A period of time in each of Freud's psychosexual stages during which an individual resolves conflicts between sources of pleasure and the demands of reality.

critical thinking Thinking reflectively and productively, and evaluating the evidence.

cross-cultural studies Comparisons of one culture with one or more other cultures; provide information about the degree to which children's development is similar, or universal, across cultures, and the degree to which it is culture-specific.

cross-sectional approach A research strategy in which individuals of different ages are compared at one time.

crystallized intelligence An individual's accumulated information and verbal skills, which continue to increase in the middle adulthood years.

cultural-familial intellectual disability A mental deficit in which no evidence of organic brain damage can be found; IQs range from 50 to 70.

culture The behaviour patterns, beliefs, and all other products of a group that are passed on from generation to generation.

culture-fair tests Tests of intelligence that are intended to be free of cultural bias.

cyberbullying Verbal and written assault through cellphones, Web sites, webcams, chat rooms, email, online profiles, and MUD rooms, as well as altered sexual photographs.

D

deferred imitation Imitation that occurs after a time delay of hours or days.

dementia A global term for any neurological disorder in which the primary symptoms involve a deterioration of mental functioning.

denial and isolation Kübler-Ross's first stage of dying, in which the person denies that death is really going to take place.

depression (1) Experiencing, over a prolonged period of time, a range of symptoms, including fatigue, irritability, inability to make decisions, sleeping problems, lack of interest in daily activities, and suicidal thoughts. (2) Kübler-Ross's fourth stage of dying, in which the dying person comes to accept the certainty of death. At this point, a period of depression or preparatory grief may appear.

descriptive research Has the purpose of observing and recording behaviour.

developmentally appropriate practice Education based on knowledge of the typical development of children within an age span (age appropriateness) and the uniqueness of the child (individual appropriateness).

differentiation versus role preoccupation Peck's developmental task in which older adults must redefine their worth in terms of something other than work roles.

difficult child Tends to react negatively and cry frequently, engages in irregular daily routines, and is slow to accept new experiences.

direct instruction approach A structured, teacher-centred approach that is characterized by teacher direction and control, high teacher expectations for students' progress, maximum time spent by students on academic tasks, and efforts by the teacher to keep negative affect to a minimum.

dishabituation The increase in responsiveness after a change in stimulation.

divergent thinking Produces many answers to the same question and is characteristic of creativity.

divided attention Concentrating on more than one activity at the same time.

DNA (deoxyribonucleic acid) A molecule in the shape of a double helix; contains genetic information.

dopamine One of the key brain chemicals that carry and influence messages between nerve cells.

doula A caregiver who provides continuous physical, emotional, and educational support to the mother before, during, and after childbirth.

dual-process model of coping with bereavement Consists of two main dimensions: (1) loss-oriented stressors and (2) restoration-oriented stressors.

dynamic systems theory The perspective on motor development that seeks to explain how motor behaviours are assembled for perceiving and acting.

dyslexia A category of learning disabilities involving a severe impairment in the ability to read and spell.

E

easy child Generally is in a positive mood, quickly establishes regular routines in infancy, and adapts easily to new experiences.

eclectic theoretical orientation An orientation that does not follow any one theoretical approach, but rather selects the best features from each theory.

ego According to Freud, the "executive branch" of the psyche, used for reasoning and decision making.

ego transcendence versus ego preoccupation Peck's developmental task in which older adults must recognize that although death is inevitable and probably not too far away, they feel at ease with themselves by realizing that they have contributed to the future through the competent raising of their children or through their vocation and ideas.

egocentrism The inability to distinguish between one's own perspective and someone else's perspective.

elaboration An important strategy that involves engaging in more extensive processing of information.

eldercare The physical and emotional caregiving for older members of the family, whether that care is day-to-day physical assistance or responsibility for arranging and overseeing such care.

embryonic period Prenatal development that occurs two to eight weeks after conception, during which the rate of cell differentiation intensifies, support systems for the cells form, and organs appear.

emerging adulthood Arnett's description of young people between the ages of 18 and 25 who have left the dependency of childhood, but have not yet fully assumed the enduring responsibilities of adulthood.

emotion Feeling, or affect, that occurs when a person is in a state or an interaction that is important to him or her, especially to his or her well-being.

emotion regulation Effectively managing arousal to adapt to and reach a goal.

emotional intelligence A form of social intelligence that involves the ability to monitor one's own and others' feelings and emotions, to discriminate among them, and to use this information to guide one's thinking and action.

empty nest syndrome Occurs when marital satisfaction decreases because parents derive considerable satisfaction from their children, and the children's departure leaves parents with empty feelings.

epigenetics The study of ongoing, bidirectional interchange of biological and environmental factors that result in heritable modifications, but which do not alter DNA, our genetic code.

episodic memory The retention of information about the where and when of life's happenings.

episodic stress Stress that is related to an event which, once coped with, is over.

equilibration A mechanism that Piaget proposed to explain how children shift from one stage of thought to the next.

erectile dysfunction The inability to adequately achieve and maintain an erection that results in satisfactory sexual performance.

Erikson's theory Eight stages of psychosocial development unfold throughout the human life span. Each stage consists of a unique developmental task that confronts individuals with a crisis that must be faced.

ethnicity A characteristic based on cultural heritage, nationality characteristics, race, religion, and language.

ethologists Scientists who research the connections between animal and human behaviours.

ethology The study of animals to discover their responses to the environment, their physiological makeup, their communication abilities, and their evolutionary aspects.

euthanasia The act of painlessly ending the lives of individuals who are suffering from an incurable disease or severe disability.

evocative genotype–environment correlations Exist when the child's genotype elicits certain types of physical and social environments.

evolutionary psychology A contemporary approach that emphasizes that behaviour is a function of mechanisms, requires input for activation, and is ultimately related to survival and reproduction.

executive attention Action planning, allocating attention to goals, error detection and compensation, monitoring progress on tasks, and dealing with novel or difficult circumstances.

experiment A carefully regulated procedure in which one or more of the factors believed to influence the behaviour being studied are manipulated, while all other factors are held constant.

expertise Having extensive, highly organized knowledge and understanding of a particular domain.

explicit memory Memory of facts and experiences that individuals consciously know and can state.

external locus of control Events that affect individuals are considered to be the result of fate or higher powers.

F

family in later life The sixth and final stage in the family life cycle, when retirement alters a couple's lifestyle, requiring adaptation. Grandparenting also characterizing many families in this stage.

family with adolescents The fourth stage of the family life cycle in which adolescents push for autonomy and seek to develop their own identities.

fertilization The process that, in humans, begins when a female gamete (ovum) fuses with a male gamete (sperm) to create a zygote.

fetal period Prenatal development that begins two months after conception and lasts for seven months, on average.

fine motor skills Motor skills that involve more finely tuned movements, such as finger dexterity.

first habits and primary circular reactions Piaget's second sensorimotor substage, which develops between one and

four months of age. In this substage, the infant coordinates sensation and two types of schemes: habits and primary circular reactions.

fluid intelligence An individual's ability to reason abstractly, which begins to decline in the middle adulthood years.

free-radical theory A microbiological theory of aging that states that people age because inside their cells normal metabolism produces unstable oxygen molecules known as free radicals. These molecules ricochet around inside cells, damaging DNA and other cellular structures.

Freud's five psychosexual stages Freud postulated that as children grow up, their focus of pleasure and sexual impulses shifts from the oral stage to the anal stage, followed by the phallic stage, the latency period, and finally the genital stage.

fuzzy trace theory States that memory is best understood by considering two types of memory representations: (1) verbatim memory trace, and (2) gist. In this theory, older children's better memory is attributed to fuzzy traces created by extracting the gist of information.

G

gender The social and psychological dimensions of being male or female.

gender identity Refers to the individual's sense of belonging to a particular sexual category; the sense of being male or female, which most children acquire by the time they are three years old.

gender role A set of expectations that prescribe how females or males should think, act, and feel.

gender schema theory The idea that gender-typing emerges as children gradually develop gender schemas of what is gender-appropriate and gender-inappropriate in their culture.

gender stereotypes Broad categories that reflect general impressions and beliefs about females and males.

generational inequity An aging society's unfairness to its younger members due to older adults piling up advantages by receiving inequitably large allocations of resources.

genes Units of hereditary information composed of DNA; act as a blueprint for cells to reproduce themselves and manufacture the proteins that maintain life.

genital herpes A highly contagious sexually transmitted disease caused by a large family of viruses of different strains. These strains also produce other, non–sexually transmitted diseases, such as chicken pox and mononucleosis.

genotype A person's genetic heritage; the actual genetic material.

germinal period Prenatal development in the first two weeks after conception; includes the creation of the zygote, continued cell division, and the attachment of the zygote to the uterine wall.

gifted Refers to children whose scores on IQ tests indicate that their mental age is considerably higher than their chronological age.

gonads The sex glands—the testes in males and the ovaries in females.

gonorrhea Reported to be one of the most common STIs in Canada, this sexually transmitted disease is caused by a bacterium called *Gonococcus*, which thrives in the moist mucous membranes lining the mouth, throat, vagina, cervix, urethra, and anal tract.

grasping reflex A neonatal reflex that occurs when something touches the infant's palm; the infant responds by grasping tightly.

grief The emotional numbness, disbelief, separation anxiety, despair, sadness, and loneliness that accompany the loss of someone we love.

gross motor skills Involve large muscle activities, such as moving one's arms and walking.

H

habituation Decreased responsiveness to a stimulus after repeated presentations of the stimulus.

heritability The fraction of variance in a population that is attributed to genetics and is computed using correlational techniques.

heteronomous morality The first stage of moral development in Piaget's theory, occurring from approximately four to seven years of age. Justice and rules are conceived of as unchangeable properties of the world, removed from the control of people.

hidden curriculum The moral atmosphere communicated through the school's rules, regulations, deportment, and moral orientation.

hormonal stress theory States that aging in the body's hormonal system can lower resilience to stress and increase the likelihood of disease.

hormones Powerful chemical substances secreted by the endocrine glands and carried through the body by the bloodstream.

HPV A virus (human papillomavirus) that causes warts on people; a few types of the virus cause warts on the genitals.

humanists Psychologists who believe people work hard to become the best they can possibly become.

hypothalamus A structure in the higher portion of the brain that monitors eating, drinking, and sex.

hypotheses Specific assumptions and predictions that can be tested to determine their accuracy.

hypothetical-deductive reasoning A type of problem solving in which an individual creates a hypothesis, deduces implications, and tests implications.

I

id According to Freud, the element of personality consisting of instincts, which are an individual's reservoir of psychic energy.

identity Our self-portraits that develop over our lifetime and are made up of many components, including negations and affirmations of various roles and characteristics.

identity achievement Marcia's term for individuals who have undergone a crisis and have made a commitment.

identity diffusion Marcia's term for individuals who have not yet experienced a crisis (they have not explored meaningful alternatives) or made any commitments.

identity foreclosure Marcia's term for individuals who have made a commitment but have not experienced a crisis.

identity moratorium Marcia's term for individuals who are in the midst of a crisis, but their commitments are either absent or vaguely defined.

imaginary audience Adolescents' belief that others are as interested in them as they themselves are.

imminent justice The concept that if a rule is broken, punishment will be meted out immediately.

implicit memory Memory without conscious recollection; it involves skills and routine procedures that are automatically performed.

incongruity The gap between the real self (the "I am") and the ideal self (the "I should be").

individual differences The stable, consistent ways in which people are different from each other

individuality Self-assertion, the ability to have and communicate a point of view, and separateness, the use of communication patterns to express how one is different from others.

indulgent parenting A style in which parents are highly involved with their children but place few demands or controls on them.

infinite generativity The ability to produce a seemingly endless number of meaningful sentences using a finite set of words and rules.

information-processing approach Emphasizes that individuals manipulate information, monitor it, and strategize about it. Central to information processing are the processes of memory and thinking.

insecure avoidant babies Show insecurity by avoiding the caregiver.

insecure disorganized babies Show insecurity by being disorganized and disoriented.

insecure resistant babies Often cling to the caregiver, then resist by fighting against the closeness, perhaps by kicking or pushing away.

integrity versus despair Erikson's eighth and final stage of development, which individuals experience in late adulthood; involves reflecting on the past and either piecing together a positive review or concluding that one's life has not been well spent.

intelligence Problem-solving skills and the ability to learn from and adapt to life's everyday experiences.

intelligence quotient (IQ) A person's mental age divided by chronological age, multiplied by 100. Depending on the mental age and the chronological age, a person's IQ can be above, equal to, or below 100.

intelligent design The belief that the origin and existence of life and the wondrous miracles of nature are the plan of a supreme intelligence or creator.

intermodal perception The ability to relate and integrate information from two or more sensory modalities, such as vision and hearing.

internal locus of control The belief that the individual can control life events.

internalization The developmental change from behaviour that is externally controlled to behaviour that is controlled by internal standards and principles.

internalization of schemes Piaget's sixth and final sensorimotor substage, which develops between 18 and 24 months of age. In this substage, the infant develops the ability to use primitive symbols.

intimacy in friendships Self-disclosure and the sharing of private thoughts.

intuitive thought substage Occurs between approximately four and seven years of age, when children begin to use primitive reasoning and want to know the answers to all sorts of questions.

J

justice perspective Focuses on the rights of the individual; individuals independently make moral decisions.

K

kwashiorkor A condition caused by a deficiency in protein, in which the child's abdomen and feet swell with water.

L

laboratory A controlled setting where many of the complex factors of the "real world" are absent.

language A form of communication, whether spoken, written, or signed, that is based on a system of symbols.

language acquisition device (LAD) A biological endowment that enables the child to detect certain language categories, such as phonology, syntax, and semantics.

lateralization Specialization of function in one hemisphere of the cerebral cortex or the other.

launching The process by which youths move into adulthood and exit their family of origin.

launching children and moving on The fifth stage in the family life cycle, a time of launching children, playing an important role in linking generations, and adapting to mid-life changes in development.

learning disability A disability that involves (1) normal intelligence or above, (2) difficulties in at least one academic area and usually several, and (3) no other problem or disorder, such as mental retardation, that can be determined as causing the difficulty.

leaving home and becoming a single adult The first stage in the family life cycle, which involves launching.

leisure The pleasant times after work when individuals are free to pursue activities and interests of their own choosing.

life expectancy The average age a child born in a given year can expect to live to, based on specific mortality rates calculated for a given year; the number of years that probably will be lived by the average person born in a particular year.

life span The upper boundary of life, the maximum number of years an individual can live. The maximum life span of human beings is about 120 years.

life-span development The pattern of change that begins at conception and continues through the life cycle.

life-span perspective The view that development is lifelong, multidimensional, multidirectional, plastic, contextual, and multidisciplinary and involves growth, maintenance, and regulation.

locus of control The perceived extent to which individuals believe they have control over the events that affect them.

longitudinal approach A research strategy in which the same individuals are studied over a period of time, usually several years or more.

long-term memory A relatively permanent and unlimited type of memory that increases with age during middle and late childhood.

low-birth-weight infant Born after a regular period of gestation (the length of time between conception and birth) of 38 to 42 weeks but who weighs less than 2.5 kg.

M

mainstreaming Educating a child with special education needs in a regular classroom.

major depression A mood disorder in which the individual is deeply unhappy, demoralized, self-derogatory, and bored. The individual with major depression does not feel well, loses stamina easily, has a poor appetite, and is listless and unmotivated.

MAMA cycles The identity status changes from moratorium, to achievement, to moratorium, to achievement that are repeated throughout life.

marasmus A wasting away of body tissues in the infant's first year, caused by severe protein-calorie deficiency.

meditation A variety of practices intended to foster clarity of thought, well-being, and relief from stress by focusing attention with calmness and concentration.

meiosis The process of cellular division that divides sex cells and produces four daughter cells, each with 23 single chromosomes.

menarche A girl's first menstruation.

menopause The time in middle age, usually in the late forties or early fifties, when a woman's menstrual periods completely cease.

mental age (MA) Binet's measure of an individual's level of mental development compared with that of others; an individual's ability to solve problems on a diagnostic instrument relative to others of the same chronological age.

metacognition Cognition about cognition, or knowing about knowing

metalinguistic awareness Knowledge about language, such as knowing what a preposition is or the ability to discuss the sounds of language.

middle adulthood Generally considered to be the developmental period beginning at approximately 40 years of age and extending to about 60 or 65 years of age.

midwife A responsible and accountable professional who works in partnership with women to give the necessary support, care, and advice during pregnancy, labour, and the postpartum period.

mitochondrial theory States that aging is due to the decay of mitochondria. It appears that this decay is primarily due to oxidative damage and loss of critical micronutrients supplied by the cell.

mitosis The process of cellular division during which cellular material is duplicated and two daughter cells are formed.

Montessori approach An educational philosophy in which children are given considerable freedom and spontaneity in choosing activities.

moral development Thoughts and feelings regarding standards of right and wrong and behaviours regarding rules and conventions about what people should do in their interactions with others.

moral reasoning Rules that focus on ethical issues and morality. They are obligatory, widely accepted, and somewhat impersonal.

Moro reflex A neonatal startle response that occurs in reaction to a sudden, intense noise or movement. When startled, the newborn arches its back, throws its head back, and flings out its arms and legs. Then the newborn rapidly draws its arms and legs close to the centre of the body.

multiculturalism The coexistence of distinct ethnic and cultural groups in the same society.

multi-infarct dementia Involves a sporadic and progressive loss of intellectual functioning caused by repeated temporary obstruction of blood flow in cerebral arteries.

myelination The process in which nerve cells are covered and insulated with a layer of fat cells, increasing the speed at which information travels through the nervous system.

N

natural childbirth Developed in 1914 by Dick-Read, this method attempts to reduce the mother's pain by decreasing her fear through education about childbirth and relaxation techniques during delivery.

naturalistic observation Observing behaviour in real-world settings, making no effort to manipulate or control the situation.

neglectful parenting A style in which the parent is very uninvolved in the child's life.

Neonatal Intensive Care Unit Network Neurobehavioral Scale (NNNS) Provides a more comprehensive analysis of the newborn's behaviour, neurological and stress responses, and regulatory capacities; an offspring of the NBAS.

neurogenesis The generation of new neurons.

neuron Nerve cell that handles information processing at the cellular level.

neuroscience Scientific study of the brain, the nervous system, and the spinal cord in an effort to understand how these organs and systems work as well as how to respond when they malfunction.

new couple The second stage in the family life cycle, in which two individuals from separate families of origin unite to form a new family system.

nonshared environmental experiences The child's own unique experiences, both within the family and outside the family, that are not shared by another sibling. Thus, experiences occurring within the family can be part of the "nonshared environment."

O

obesity Having too much fatty tissue as measured by the ratio of weight and height, which is called the body mass index (BMI).

object permanence The Piagetian term for one of an infant's most important accomplishments: understanding that objects and events continue to exist even when they cannot directly be seen, heard, or touched.

observation A systematic and scientific inquiry into behaviour that may be conducted in a natural environment or a laboratory setting.

operations In Piaget's theory, an internalized set of actions that allow a child to do mentally what before he or she did physically.

organization Piaget's concept of grouping isolated behaviours and thoughts into a higher-order system.

organogenesis Organ formation that takes place during the first two months of prenatal development.

osteoporosis An aging disorder involving an extensive loss of bone tissue. It is the main reason many older adults walk with a marked stoop.

P

pain cry A sudden appearance of loud crying without preliminary moaning and a long initial cry followed by an extended period of breath holding.

palliative care A humanized program committed to making the end of life as free from pain, anxiety, and depression as possible.

Parkinson's disease A chronic, progressive disease characterized by muscle tremors, slowing of movement, and partial facial paralysis.

passive euthanasia Occurs when a person is allowed to die by withholding available treatment, such as withdrawing a life-sustaining device.

passive genotype–environment correlations Exist when the natural parents, who are genetically related to the child, provide a rearing environment for the child.

perception The interpretation of what is sensed.

personal fable The part of adolescent egocentrism that involves an adolescent's sense of uniqueness and invincibility.

perspective taking The ability to assume other people's perspectives and understand their thoughts and feelings.

phenotype The way an individual's genotype is expressed in observed and measurable characteristics.

phonology The study of how sounds are organized and used.

Piaget's theory Children actively construct their understanding of the world and go through four stages of cognitive development.

pituitary gland An important endocrine gland that controls growth and regulates other glands.

placenta A life-support system that consists of a disc-shaped group of tissues in which small blood vessels from the mother and offspring intertwine but do not join.

plasticity Refers to the capacity for change.

positive psychology This approach contends that understanding happiness can facilitate human grown and development.

postconventional reasoning The highest level in Kohlberg's theory of moral development. Morality is completely internalized and is not based on others' standards.

postformal thought Involves understanding that the correct answer to a problem requires reflective thinking and can vary from one situation to another, and that the search for truth is often an ongoing, never-ending process.

postpartum depression A major depressive episode that typically occurs about four weeks after delivery. Women with postpartum depression have such strong feelings of sadness, anxiety, or despair, that for at least a two-week period they have trouble coping with daily tasks.

postpartum period Occurs after childbirth when the mother adjusts, both physically and psychologically, to the process of child-birth; lasts for about six weeks or until her body has completed its adjustment and returned to a near pre-pregnant state.

preconventional reasoning The lowest level in Kohlberg's theory of moral development. The individual shows no internalization of moral values—moral reasoning is controlled by external rewards and punishment.

preoperational stage Piaget's second stage, lasting from two to seven years of age, during which children begin to represent the world with words, images, and drawings. They form stable concepts and begin to reason.

prepared childbirth A childbirth strategy similar to natural childbirth but that includes a special breathing technique to control pushing in the final stages of labour and a more detailed anatomy and physiology course; developed by Fernand Lamaze.

preterm infant Born prior to 38 weeks after conception.

primary emotions Present in humans and other animals and emerge early in life; examples are joy, anger, sadness, fear, and disgust.

prolonged grief Grief that involves enduring despair and is still unresolved over an extended period of time.

prospective memory Involves remembering to do something in the future.

proximodistal pattern The sequence in which growth starts at the centre of the body and moves toward the extremities.

psychoanalytic approach Development is primarily unconscious and heavily coloured by emotion. Behaviour is merely a surface characteristic. It is important to analyze the symbolic meanings of behaviour. Early experience is important to development.

psychoanalytic theory of gender Derived from Freud's view that the preschool child develops a sexual attraction to the opposite-sex parent, renounces this attraction by approximately five or six years of age because of anxious feelings, and subsequently identifies with the same-sex parent, unconsciously adopting the same-sex parent's characteristics.

psychological age An individual's adaptive capacities compared with those of other individuals of the same chronological age.

psychosocial moratorium Erikson's term for the gap between childhood security and adult autonomy that adolescents experience as part of their identity exploration.

puberty A period of rapid skeletal and sexual maturation involving hormonal and bodily changes that occur primarily in early adolescence.

R

race (1) A classification of people according to real or imagined biological characteristics, such as skin colour and blood group. (2) Physical features such a skeletal structure, the shape of the skull, the texture of the hair, and the colour of the skin.

reciprocal socialization The idea that children socialize parents, just as parents socialize children.

reflexes Built-in reactions to stimuli; they govern the newborn's movements, which are automatic and beyond the newborn's control.

reflexive smile Does not occur in response to external stimuli. It happens during the month after birth, usually during irregular patterns of sleep.

relational aggression Such behaviours as trying to make others dislike a certain child by spreading malicious rumours about the child or ignoring another child when angry with him or her

relative age The differences in development among children of the same age group.

relative age effect The consequences of developmental differences among children of the same age group.

religion An organized set of beliefs about how the universe originated, as well as the nature and the purpose of the universe.

REM (rapid eye movement) sleep A recurring sleep stage during which vivid dreams commonly occur.

restrained eaters Individuals who chronically restrict their food intake to control their weight. Restrained eaters are often on diets, are very conscious of what they eat, and tend to feel guilty after splurging on sweets.

rite of passage A ceremony or ritual that marks an individual's transition of from one status to another.

romantic love Also called "passionate love" or "eros," romantic love has strong components of sexuality and infatuation and often predominates in the early part of a love relationship.

rooting reflex When the infant's cheek is stroked or the side of the mouth is touched, the infant turns its head toward the side that was touched in an apparent effort to find something to suck.

rules of morphology The study of the structure and form of words, including inflection, derivation, and compound words.

S

scaffolding In cognitive development, Vygotsky used this term to describe the changing support over the course of a teaching session, with the more-skilled person adjusting the amount of guidance to fit the child's current performance level.

scheme In Piaget's theory, a cognitive structure that helps individuals organize and understand their experiences.

secondary circular reactions Piaget's third sensorimotor substage, which develops between four and eight months of age. In this substage, the infant becomes more object-oriented, moving beyond preoccupation with the self.

securely attached babies Use the caregiver as a secure base from which to explore the environment.

selective attention Focusing on a specific aspect of experience that is relevant while ignoring others that are irrelevant.

selective optimization with compensation theory States that successful aging is linked to three main factors: selection, optimization, and compensation (SOC).

self-actualization The individualized expression of self in terms of reaching one's fullest potential without concern for praise or rewards.

self-concept Domain-specific evaluations of the self.

self-conscious emotions Require self-awareness, especially consciousness and a sense of "me"; examples include jealousy, empathy, and embarrassment.

self-efficacy The belief that one can master a situation and produce favourable outcomes.

self-esteem The global evaluative dimension of the self; also referred to as self-worth or self-image.

self-understanding The child's cognitive representation of self, the substance and content of self-conceptions.

semantic memory A person's knowledge about the world—including fields of expertise, general academic knowledge of the sort learned in school, and "everyday knowledge."

semantics The meaning of words.

sensation Occurs when a stimulus reaches sensory receptors—the eyes, ears, tongue, nostrils, and skin.

separation protest An infant's crying when the caregiver leaves.

sequential approach A combined cross-sectional, longitudinal design.

seriation The concrete operation that involves ordering stimuli along a quantitative dimension (such as length).

service-learning A form of education intended to promote social responsibility and service to the community.

sexual identity An individual's inner conviction about his or her male or femaleness.

sexual orientation An individual's sexual interests; that is, whether or not a person is sexually and romantically attracted to others of the same sex, the opposite sex, or both sexes.

sexually transmitted infections (STIs) Infections and diseases that are contracted primarily through sexual contact, which is not limited to sexual intercourse. Oral–genital and anal–genital contact also can transmit STIs and STDs.

shared environmental experiences Children's common environmental experiences that are shared with their siblings, such as their parents' personalities and intellectual orientation, the family's social class, and the neighbourhood in which they live.

short-term memory The memory component in which individuals retain information for 15 to 30 seconds, assuming there is no rehearsal.

simple reflexes Piaget's first sensorimotor substage, which corresponds to the first month after birth. In this substage, sensation and action are coordinated primarily through reflexive behaviours.

sleep apnea A serious condition that prevents a person from sleeping; a temporary cessation of breathing caused when the airways become blocked.

slow-to-warm-up child Has a low activity level, is somewhat negative, shows low adaptability, and displays a low intensity of mood.

small-for-date infants Born with birth weight below normal when length of the pregnancy is considered; may be preterm or full-term; also called *small-for-gestational-age infants*.

social age Social roles and expectations related to a person's age.

social clock The timetable according to which individuals are expected to accomplish life's tasks, such as getting married, having children, or establishing themselves in a career and retiring.

social cognitive theory of gender Explains that children's gender development occurs through observing and imitating what other people say and do, and through being rewarded and punished for gender-appropriate and gender-inappropriate behaviour.

social constructivist approach An approach that emphasizes that both learning and the construction of knowledge occur in social contexts.

social conventional reasoning Conventional rules that have been established by social consensus to control behaviour and maintain the social system.

social policy A national government's course of action designed to influence the welfare of its citizens.

social referencing Involves "reading" emotional cues in others to help determine how to act in a particular situation.

social role theory A theory that gender differences result from the contrasting roles of men and women.

social smile Occurs in response to an external stimulus, which, early in development, typically is a face

socio-emotional processes Changes in an individual's relationships with other people, emotions, and personality.

socio-emotional selectivity theory States that older adults become more selective about their social networks. Because they place a high value on emotional satisfaction, older adults often spend more time with familiar individuals with whom they have had rewarding relationships.

source memory The ability to remember where one learned something.

spirituality The quality or condition of being spiritual and an attachment or regard for things of the spirit as opposed to material or worldly interests.

stability–change issue Regards whether development is best described as involving stability or as involving change; involves the degree to which we become older renditions of our early experience or, instead, develop into someone different from who we were at an earlier point in development.

standardized test Has uniform procedures for administration and scoring.

Strange Situation An observational measure of infant attachment that requires the infant to move through a series of introductions, separations, and reunions with the caregiver and an adult stranger in a prescribed order.

stranger anxiety An infant's fear and wariness of strangers; it tends to appear in the second half of the first year of life.

stress The non-specific response of the body to any demand made upon it.

sucking reflex A newborn automatically sucks an object placed in its mouth.

sudden infant death syndrome (SIDS) A condition that occurs when an infant stops breathing, usually during the night, and suddenly dies without apparent cause.

superego According to Freud, the moral branch of the personality, which takes into account whether something is right or wrong.

sustained attention Focused and extended engagement with an object, task, event, or other aspect of the environment; the state of readiness to detect and respond to small changes occurring at random times in the environment.

symbolic function substage Piaget's first substage of preoperational thought, in which the child gains the ability to mentally represent an object that is not present (occurs between two and four years of age).

syntax The formation of grammatically correct sentences.

syphilis A sexually transmitted disease caused by the bacterium *Treponema pallidum*, a member of the spirochete family.

T

telegraphic speech The use of short and precise words to communicate.

temperament An individual's behavioural style and characteristic way of emotionally responding.

teratogen Any agent that causes a birth defect or negatively alters cognitive and behavioural outcomes. The field of study that investigates the causes of birth variations is called *teratology*. From the Greek word *tera*, meaning "monster."

tertiary circular reactions, novelty, and curiosity Piaget's fifth sensorimotor substage, which develops between 12 and 18 months of age. In this substage, infants become intrigued by the many properties of objects and by the many things that they can make happen to objects.

theory An interrelated, coherent set of ideas that help explain and make predictions.

theory of mind The awareness of one's own mental processes and the mental processes of others.

transitivity In concrete operational thought, a mental concept that underlies the ability to combine relations logically in order to understand certain conclusions.

triangular theory of love Sternberg's theory that love can be thought of as having three main dimensions: passion, intimacy, and commitment.

triarchic theory of intelligence Sternberg's theory that intelligence comes in three forms: analytical, creative, and practical.

trophoblast The outer layer of cells that develops in the germinal period to provide nutrition and support for the embryo.

U

umbilical cord A life-support system containing two arteries and one vein that connects the baby to the placenta.

V

visible minority The term used by the Canadian census for people who are neither Native nor Caucasian.

Vygotsky's theory A socio-cultural cognitive theory that emphasizes developmental analysis, the role of language, and social relations.

W

Wernicke's area A region of the brain's left hemisphere involved in language comprehension

whole-language approach An approach to reading instruction based on the idea that instruction should parallel children's natural language learning. Reading materials should be whole and meaningful.

wisdom Expert knowledge about the practical aspects of life that permits excellent judgment about important matters.

working memory The concept currently used to describe short-term memory as a place for mental work. Working memory is like a "workbench" where individuals can manipulate and assemble information when making decisions, solving problems, and comprehending written and spoken language.

Y

young offenders Young people between the ages of 12 and 18 who commit criminal acts.

Z

zone of proximal development Vygotsky's term for the range of tasks too difficult for a child to master alone but that can be learned with the guidance and assistance of adults or more-skilled children.

zygote A single cell formed when an ovum is fertilized by a sperm.

References

A

Aalsma, M., Lapsley, D. K., & Flannery, D. (2006). Narcissism, personal fables, and adolescent adjustment. *Psychology in the Schools, 43,* 481–491.

Abbott, R. D., White, I. R., Ross, G. W., Masaki, K. H., Curb, J. D., & Petrovitch, H. (2004). Walking and dementia in physically capable elderly men. *Journal of the American Medical Association, 292,* 1447–1453.

Abdo, C. H., Afif-Abdo, J., Otani, F., & Machado, A. C. (2008). Sexual satisfaction among patients with erectile dysfunction treated with counseling, sildenafil, or both. *Journal of Sexual Medicine, 5*(7), 1720–1726.

Abellan van Kan, G., Rolland, Y., Nourhashemi, F., Coley, N., Andrieu, S., & Vellas, B. (2009). Cardiovascular disease risk factors and progression of Alzheimer's disease. *Dementia and Geriatric Cognitive Disorders, 27,* 240–246.

Aboriginal Affairs and Northern Development Canada (AANDC). (2010). Statement of apology: Prime Minister Harper offers full apology on behalf of Canadians for the Indian Residential Schools system. Retrieved from http://www.aadnc-aandc.gc.ca/eng/1100100015644/1100100015649

Aboud, F. E., Mendelson, M. J., & Purdy, K. T. (2003). Cross-race peer relations and friendship quality. *International Journal of Behavioral Development, 27*(2), 165–173.

Abouguendia, M., & K. A. Noels. (2001). General and acculturation-related daily hassles and psychological adjustment in first- and second-generation South Asian immigrants to Canada. *International Journal of Psychology, 36*(3), 163–173.

Abrams, L. (2009). Exploring the generality of retest effects: Commentary on "When does age-related cognitive decline begin?" *Neurobiology of Aging, 30,* 525–527.

Abruscato, J. A., & DeRosa, D. A. (2010). *Teaching children science: A discovery approach* (7th ed.). Boston: Allyn & Bacon.

Accornero, V. H., Amado, A. J., Morrow, C. E., Xue, L., Anthony, J. C., & Bandstra, E. S. (2007). Impact of prenatal cocaine exposure on attention and response inhibition as assessed by continuous performance tests. *Journal of Developmental and Behavioral Pediatrics, 28,* 195–205.

Acevedo, B., & Aron, A. (2009). Does a long term relationship kill romantic love? *Review of General Psychology, 13,* 59–65.

Active Healthy KidsCanada. (2012). *Is active play extinct? The Active Healthy Kids Canada 2012 Report Card on Physical Activity for Children and Youth.* Toronto: Active Healthy Kids Canada.

Adler, A. (1927). *The Practice and Theory of Individual Psychology.*

Adolph, K. E. (2008). Motor and physical development: Locomotion. In M. M. Haith & J. B. Benson (Eds.), *Encyclopedia of infant and early childhood development.* Oxford, UK: Elsevier.

Adolph, K. E., & Joh, A. S. (2007). Motor development: How infants get into the act. In A. Slater & M. Lewis (Eds.), *Infant Development.* New York: Oxford University Press.

Adolph, K. E., & Joh, A. S. (2008). Multiple learning mechanisms in the development of action. In A. Needham & A. Woodward (Eds.), *Learning and the infant mind.* New York: Oxford University Press.

Adoption Council of Canada. (2003). Canadians adopt almost 20,000 children from abroad.

Afanasev, I. (2009). Superoxide and nitric oxide in senescence and aging. *Frontiers in Bioscience, 14,* 3899–3912.

Agarwal, S., & Busse, P. J. (2010). Innate and adaptive immunosenescence. *Annals of Allergy, Asthma, and Immunology, 104,* 183–190.

Aggarwal, N. T., Wilson, R. S., Beck, T. L., Bienias, J. L., Berry-Kravis, E., & Bennett, D. A. (2005). The apolipoprotein E epsilon4 allele and incident Alzheimer's disease in persons with mild cognitive impairment. *Neurocase, 11,* 3–7.

Agras, W. S., et al. (2004). Report of the National Institutes of Health workshop on overcoming barriers to treatment research in anorexia nervosa. *International Journal of Eating Disorders, 35,* 509–521.

Agrelo, R., & Wutz, A. (2010). Context of change—X inactivation and disease. *EMBO Molecular Medicine, 2,* 6–15.

Agrillo, C., & Netini, C. (2008). Childfree by choice: A review. *Journal of Cultural Geography, 25*(3), 347–363.

Aguiar, A., & Baillargeon, R. (2002). Development in young infants' reasoning about occluded objects. *Cognitive Psychology, 45,* 267–336.

Ahrons, C. (2004). *We're still family.* New York: HarperCollins.

Ahrons, C. (2007). Family ties after divorce: Long-term implications for children. *Family Process, 46,* 53–65.

Aiken Morgan, A. T., Sims, R. C., & Whitfield, K. E. (2010). Cardiovascular health and education as sources of individual variability in cognitive aging among African Americans. *Journal of Aging and Health, 22,* 477–503.

Aimone, J. B., Wiles, J., & Gage, F. H. (2009). Computational influence of adult neurogenesis on memory encoding. *Neuron, 61,* 187–202.

Ainsworth, M. D. S. (1979). Infant-mother attachment. *American Psychologist, 34,* 932–937.

Aizawa, K., Shoemaker, J. K., Overend, T. J., & Petrella, R. J. (2010). Longitudinal changes in central artery stiffness with lifestyle modification, washout, and drug treatment in individuals at risk for cardiovascular disease. *Metabolic Syndrome and Related Disorders,8*(4), 323.

Ajdacic-Gross, V., Ring, M., Gadola, E., Lauber, C., Bopp, M., Gutzwiller, F., & Rossler, W. (2008). Suicide after bereavement: An overlooked problem. *Psychology and Medicine, 38,* 673–676.

Akhtar, N., & Herold, K. (2008). Pragmatic development. In M. M. Haith & J. B. Benson (Eds.), *Encyclopedia of infant and early childhood development.* Oxford, UK: Elsevier.

Akhter, M., Nishino, Y., Nakaya, N., Kurashima, K., Sato, Y., Kuriyama, S., et al. (2007). Cigarette smoking and the risk of colorectal cancer among men: A prospective study in Japan. *European Journal of Cancer Prevention, 16,* 102–107.

Alasia, A. (2010). Population change across Canadian communities 1981–2006. *Rural and Small Town Canada Analysis Bulletin, 8*(4), 1–32.

Albury, K., & Crawford, K. (2012). Sexting, consent and young people's ethics: Beyond Megan's story. *Continuum: Journal of Media and Cultural Studies, 26*(3), 463–473.

Alcaro, S., et al. (2010). Simple choline esters as potential anti-Alzheimer agents. *Current Pharmaceutical Design, 16,* 692–697.

Alcoholics Anonymous. (2013). *Information on A.A.* Retrieved from http://www.aa.org/

Aldwin, C. M., & Levenson, M. R. (2001). Stress, coping, and health at midlife: A developmental perspective. In M. E. Lachman (Ed.), *Handbook of midlife development.* New York: John Wiley.

Allard, Y., Wilkins, R., & Berthelot, J. (2004). Premature mortality in health regions with high Aboriginal populations. *Health Reports, 15*(1), 51–60.

Allemand, M., Zimprich, D., & Hendriks, A. A. J. (2008). Age differences in five personality domains across the life span. *Developmental Psychology, 44,* 758–770.

Allen, J. P., & Antonishak, J. (2008). Adolescent peer influences: Beyond the dark side. In M. J. Prinstein & K. A. Dodge (Eds.), *Understanding peer influence in children and adolescents.* New York: Guilford.

Allen, J. P., Kuperminc, G. P., & Moore, C. (2005, April). *Stability and predictors of change in attachment security across adolescence.* Paper presented at the meeting of the Society for Research on Child Development, Atlanta.

Allen, K. L., Byrne, S. M., McLean, N. J., & Davis, E. A. (2008). Overconcern with weight and shape is not the same as body dissatisfaction: Evidence from a prospective study of pre-adolescent boys and girls. *Body Image, 5*(3), 261–270.

Allen, K. R., Blieszner, R., & Roberto, K. A. (2000). Families in middle and later years: A review and critique of research in the 1990s. *Journal of Marriage and the Family, 62,* 911–926.

Allen, M. C. (2008). Neurodevelopmental outcomes of preterm infants. *Current Opinion in Neurology, 21,* 123–128.

Alleyne, R. (2010, May 16). Lying children will grow up to be successful citizens. *The Telegraph.* Retrieved from http://www.telegraph.co.uk/science/7730522/Lying-children-will-grow-up-to-be-successful-citizens.html

Alm, B., Lagercrantz, H., & Wennergren, G. (2006). Stop SIDS—sleeping solitary supine, sucking smoother, stopping smoking substitutes. *Acta Paediatrica, 95,* 260–262.

Almeida, D., & Horn, M. (2004). Is daily life more stressful during middle adulthood? In G. Brim, C. D. Ryff, & R. Kessler (Eds.), *How healthy are we? A national study of well-being in midlife.* Chicago: University of Chicago Press.

Al-Sahab, B., Saqib, M., Hauser, G., & Tamim, H. (2010). Prevalence of smoking during pregnancy and associated risk factors among Canadian women: A national survey. *BMC Pregnancy and Childbirth, 10*(24), 1–9.

Althof, S. E., Rubio-Aurioles, E., Kingsberg, S., Zeigler, H., Wong, D. G., & Burns, P. (2010). Impact of tadalafil once daily in men with erectile dysfunction—including a report of the partner's evaluation. *Urology, 75*(6), 1358–1363.

Altimer, L. (2008). Shaken baby syndrome. *Journal of Perinatal and Neonatal Nursing, 22,* 68–76.

Alvarez, A., & del Rio, P. (2007). Inside and outside the zone of proximal development: An eco-functional reading of Vygotsky. In H. Daniels, J. Wertsch, & M. Cole (Eds.), *The Cambridge companion to Vygotsky.* New York: Cambridge University Press.

Alzheimer Society of Canada. (2009a). Alzheimer disease. Retrieved from http://www.alzheimer.ca/english/disease/whatisit-intro.htm

Alzheimer Society of Canada. (2009b). Treatment: Drug treatments. Retrieved from http://www.alzheimer.ca/

Alzheimer Society of Canada. (2013). Alzheimer's disease. Retrieved from http://www.alzheimer.ca/en/About-dementia/Alzheimer-s-disease/What-is-Alzheimer-s-disease

Alzheimer's Association. (2010). 2010 Alzheimer's disease facts and figures. *Alzheimer's and Dementia, 6,* 158–194.

Amabile, T. M. (1993). Commentary. In D. Goleman, P. Kaufman, & M. Ray, *The creative spirit.* New York: Plume.

Amabile, T. M., & Hennessey, B. A. (1992). The motivation for creativity in children. In A. K. Boggiano & T. S. Pittman (Eds.), *Achievement and motivation.* New York: Cambridge University Press.

Amato, P. R. (2006). Marital discord, divorce, and children's well-being: Results from a 20-year longitudinal study of two generations.

In A. Clarke-Stewart & J. Dunn (Eds.), *Families count.* New York: Cambridge University Press.

Amato, P. R. (2007). Transformative processes in marriage: Some thoughts from a sociologist. *Journal of Marriage and the Family, 69,* 305–309.

Amato, P. R., & Cheadle, J. (2005). The long reach of divorce: Divorce and child well-being across three generations. *Journal of Marriage and the Family, 67,* 191–206.

Amato, P. R., & Dorius, C. (2010). Fathers, children, and divorce. In M.E. Lamb (Ed.), *The role of the father in child development* (5th ed.). New York: Wiley.

Ambert, A. (1998). *Divorce: Facts, figures, and consequences.* Vanier Institute of the Family: Child and Family Canada.

Ambert, A. (2003). The negative social construction of adoption: Its effects on children and parents.

Ambert, A. (2005). *Divorce, facts, causes & consequences.* The Vanier Institute of the Family. Retrieved from http://www.vifamily.ca/library/cft/divorce_05.html#What_causes

Ambert, A. M. (2007). *The rise in the number of children and adolescents who exhibit problematic behaviours: Multiple causes.* Vanier Institute of the Family.

Amed, S., Daneman, D., Mahmud, F. H., & Hamilton, J. (2010). Type 2 diabetes in children and adolescents. *Expert Review of Cardiovascular Therapy, 8,* 393–406.

American Psychological Association. (2007). *Stress in America.* Washington, DC: Author.

American Public Health Association. (2006). *Understanding the health culture of recent immigrants to the United States.* Retrieved from http://www.apha.org/

Ames, E. A. (1997, January 1). *The development of Romanian orphanage children adopted to Canada: Final report.* Simon Fraser University.

Amsterdam, B. K. (1968). *Mirror behavior in children under two years of age.* Unpublished doctoral dissertation, University of North Carolina, Chapel Hill.

Anastasi, A., & Urbina, S. (1996). *Psychological testing* (7th ed.). Upper Saddle River, NJ: Prentice Hall.

Anderson, R. M., & Weindruch, R. (2007). Metabolic reprogramming in dietary restriction. *Interdisciplinary Topics in Gerontology, 35,* 18–38.

Anderson, S. A., & Sabatelli, R. M. (2007). *Family interaction* (4th ed.). Boston: Allyn & Bacon.

Anetzberger, G. J., & Teaster, P. B. (2010). Future directions for social policy and elder abuse: Through the looking glass of generational characteristics. *Journal of Elder Abuse and Neglect, 22,* 207–215.

Angel, L., Fay, S., Bourazzaoui, B., Granjon, L., & Isingrini, M. (2009). Neural correlates of cued recall in young and older adults: An event-related potential study. *Neuroreport, 20,* 75–79.

Angelone, T., et al. (2010). Distinct signaling mechanisms are involved in the dissimilar myocardial and coronary effects elicited by quercetin and myricetin, two red wine flavonoids. *Nutrition, Metabolism, and Cardiovascular Diseases, 21*(5), 362–71.

Anspaugh, D. J., Hamrick, M. H., & Rosato, F. D. (2009). *Wellness* (7th ed.). New York: McGraw-Hill.

Antone, E. M. (2000). Empowering Aboriginal voice in Aboriginal education. *Canadian Journal of Native Education, 24,* 92–101.

Antonucci, T. C., Akiyama, H., & Sherman, A. M. (2007). Social networks, support, and integration. In J. E. Birren (Ed.), *Encyclopedia of gerontology* (2nd ed.). San Diego: Academic Press.

Antonucci, T. C., Birditt, K. S., & Akiyama, H. (2009). Convoys of social relations: An interdisciplinary approach. In V. L. Bengtson, D. Gans, N. M. Putney, & M. Silverstein (Eds.), *Handbook of theories of aging* (2nd ed.). New York: Springer.

Antonucci, T. C., Fiori, K. L., Birditt, K., & Jackey, L. M. H. (2011). Convoys of social relations: Integrating life-span and life-course perspectives. In R.M. Lerner, W. F. Overton, A. M. Freund, & M. E. Lamb (Eds.), *Handbook of life-span development.* New York: Wiley.

Antonucci, T. C., Lansford, J. E., & Akiyama, H. (2001). The impact of positive and negative aspects of marital relationships and friendships on the well-being of older adults. In J. P. Reinhardt (Ed.), *Negative and positive support.* Mahwah, NJ: Erlbaum.

Antonucci, T. C., Vandewater, E. A., & Lansford, J. E. (2000). Adulthood and aging: Social processes and development. In A. Kazdin (Ed.), *Encyclopedia of psychology.* Washington, DC: American Psychological Association and Oxford University Press.

Applebaum, M. (2008). Why diets fail—expert diet advice as a cause of diet failure. *American Psychologist, 63,* 200–202.

Appleton, J. V., & Stanley, N. (2009). Editorial: Childhood outcomes. *Child Abuse Review, 18,* 1–5.

Arai, A. B. (2000). Reasons for home schooling in Canada. *Canadian Journal of Education, 25*(3), 204–217.

Arenkiel, B. R. (2010). Adult neurogenesis supports short-term olfactory memory. *Journal of Neurophysiology, 103*(6), 2935–2937.

Armour, S., & Haynie, D. L. (2007). Adolescent sexual debut and later delinquency. *Journal of Youth and Adolescence, 36,* 141–152.

Armstrong, M. L. (1995). Adolescent tattoos: Educating and pontificating. *Pediatric Nursing, 21*(6), 561–564.

Armstrong, M. L., Roberts, A. E., Owen, D. C., & Koch, J. R. (2004). Contemporary college students and body piercing. *Journal of Adolescent Health, 35,* 58–61.

Arnett, J., & Galambos, N. (2003). Culture and conceptions of adulthood. In J. Arnett & N. Galambos (Eds.), *New directions for*

child and adolescent development: Exploring cultural conceptions of the transition to adulthood (No. 100, pp. 63–76). San Franscisco: Jossey-Bass.

Arnett, J. J. (2004). *Emerging adulthood.* New York: Oxford University Press.

Arnett, J. J. (2006). Emerging adulthood: Understanding the new way of coming of age. In J. J. Arnett & J. L. Tanner (Eds.), *Emerging adults in America.* Washington, DC: American Psychological Association.

Arnett, J. J. (2007). Socialization in emerging adulthood. In J. E. Grusec & P. D. Hastings (Eds.), *Handbook of socialization.* New York: Guilford.

Aron, A., Aron, E., & Coupos, E. (2008). *Statistics for the behavioral and social sciences.* Upper Saddle River, NJ: Prentice Hall.

Aronson, S., & Huston, A. (2004). The mother-infant rerlationship in single, cohabiting, and married families: A case for marriage? *Journal of Family Psychology, 18*(1), 5–18.

Arpanantikul, M. (2004). Midlife experiences of Thai women. *Journal of Advanced Nursing, 47,* 49–56.

Arshad, S. H. (2005). Primary prevention of asthma and allergy. *Journal of Allergy and Clinical Immunology, 116,* 3–14.

Aschkenasy, M. T., & Rothenhaus, T. C. (2006). Trauma and falls in the elderly. *Emergency Clinics of North America, 24,* 413–432.

Asendorph, J. B. (2008). Shyness. In M. M. Haith & J. B. Benson (Eds.), *Encyclopedia of infant and early childhood development.* Oxford, UK: Elsevier.

Asendorph, J., Denissen, J., & van Aken, M. (2008). Inhibited and aggressive preschool children at 23 years of age: Personality and social transition into adulthood. *Developmental Psychology, 44,* 997–1011.

Asghar-Ali, A., & Braun, U. K. (2009). Depression in geriatric patients. *Minerva Medica, 100,* 105–113.

Ashcraft, M. H., & Radvansky, G. A. (2010). *Cognition* (5th ed.). Upper Saddle River, NJ: Pearson.

Asher, S. R., & McDonald, K. L. (2009). The behavioral basis of acceptance, rejection, and perceived popularity. In K. H. Rubin, W. M., Bukowski, & B. Laursen (Eds.), *Handbook of peer interactions, relationships, and groups.* New York: Guilford.

Aslin, R. N., & Lathrop, A. L. (2008). Visual perception. In M. M. Haith & J. B. Benson (Eds.), *Encyclopedia of infant and early childhood development.* Oxford, UK: Elsevier.

Asscher, J. (2008). The moral distinction between killing and letting die in medical cases. *Bioethics, 22*(5), 278–285.

Association of Chief Psychologists with Ontario School Boards (ACPOSB). (2004). *Attention deficit hyperactivity disorder.* Retrieved from http://www.acposb .on.ca/ADHD.html

Ata, R. N., Ludden, A. B., & Lally, M. M. (2007). The effect of gender and family, friend, and media influences on eating behaviors and body image during adolescence. *Journal of Youth and Adolescence, 36,* 1024–1037.

Atchley, R. C. (2007). Retirement. In J. E. Birren (Ed.), *Encyclopedia of gerontology* (2nd ed.). San Diego: Academic Press.

Atkinson, A. P., & Wheeler, M. (2004). The grain of domains: The evolutionary-psychological case against domain-general cognition. *Mind and Language, 19,* 147–176.

Atkinson, L., Raval, V., Benoit, D., Poulton, L., Gleason, K., Goldberg, S., et al. (2005). On the relation between maternal state of mind and sensitivity in the prediction of infant attachment security. *Developmental Psychology, 41*(1), 42–53.

Atkinson, R. M., Ryan, S. C., & Turner, J. A. (2001). Variation among aging alcoholic patients in treatment. *American Journal of Geriatric Psychiatry, 9,* 275–282.

Attorney-General. (1993). Decisions: Supreme Court judgments. *Rodriguez v. British Columbia (Attorney General),* [1993] 3 S.C.R. 519.

Aubert, G., & Lansdorp, P. M. (2008). Telomeres and aging. *Physiological Review, 88,* 557–579.

Aubin, S., Heiman, J. R., Berger, R. E., Murallo, A. V., & Yung-Wen, L. (2009). Comparing Sildenafil alone vs. Sildenafil plus brief couple therapy on erectile dysfunction and couples' sexual and marital quality of life: A pilot study. *Journal of Sexual and Marital Therapy, 35,* 122–143.

Aubrey, T., Klodawsky, F., & Coulombe, D. (2012). Comparing the housing trajectories of different classes within a diverse homeless population. *American Journal of Community Psychology, 49,* 142–155.

Aucoin, K. J., Frick, P. J., & Bodin, S. D. (2006). Corporal punishment and child adjustment. *Journal of Applied Developmental Psychology, 27,* 527–541.

Audesirk, G., Audesirk, T., & Byers, B. E. (2011). *Biology* (9th ed.). Upper Saddle River, NJ: Benjamin Cummings.

Austad, S. (2009). Comparative biology of aging. *Journals of Gerontology Series A: Biological Sciences and Medical Services, 64A*(2), 199–201.

Autism Society of Canada. (2004). *Canadian autism research agenda and Canadian autism strategy: A white paper.* Ottawa: Autism Society of Canada.

Auyeung, B., Baron-Cohen, S., Ashwin, E., Knickmeyer, R., Taylor, K., Hackett, G., et al. (2009). Fetal testosterone predicts sexually differentiated childhood behavior in girls and in boys. *Psychological Science, 20,* 144–148.

Avramopoulos, D. (2009). Genetics of Alzheimer's disease: Recent advances. *Genome Medicine, 27,* 34.

Avent, N. D., Plummer, Z. E., Madgett, T. E., Maddocks, D. G., & Soothill, P. W. (2008). Post-genomic studies and their application to non-invasive prenatal diagnosis. *Seminars in Fetal and Neonatal Medicine, 13,* 91–98.

B

B.C. Council for Families. (2007). Quick facts on grandparenting.

Babizhayev, M. A., Minasyan, H., & Richer, S. P. (2009). Cataract halos: A driving hazard in aging populations: Implications of the Halometer DG test for assessment of intraocular light scatter. *Applied Ergonomics, 40,* 545–553.

Bachman, J. G., O'Malley, P. M., Schulenberg, J. E., Johnston, L. D., Bryant, A. L., & Merline, A. C. (2002). *The decline of substance abuse in young adulthood.* Mahwah, NJ: Erlbaum.

Bachman, J. G., O'Malley, P. M., Schulenberg, J. E., Johnston, L. D., Freedman-Doan, P., & Messersmith, E. E. (2008). *The education-drug use connection.* Clifton, NJ: Psychology Press.

Backman, L., Small, B. J., & Wahlin, A. (2001). Aging and memory: Cognitive and behavioral processes. In J. E. Birren & K. W. Schaie (Eds.), *Handbook of the psychology of aging* (5th ed.). San Diego: Academic Press.

Baddeley, A. D. (2007a). *Working memory, thought and action.* New York: Oxford University Press.

Baddeley, A. D. (2007b). Working memory: Multiple models, multiple mechanisms. In H. L. Roediger, Y. Dudai, & S. M. Fitzpatrick (Eds.). *Science of memory: concepts.* New York: Oxford University Press.

Baehr, T. A., & Barnett, M. M. (2007). Examining retirement from a multi-level perspective. In K. S. Shultz & G. A. Adams (Eds.), *Aging and work in the 21st century.* Mahwah, NJ: Erlbaum.

Baglow, J. S. (2007). The rights of the corpse. *Mortality, 12*(3), 223–239.

Bahrick, L. (2006). Development of intermodal perception. *Encyclopedia of Cognitive Science.* Retrieved from http://www. onlinelibrary.wiley.com/

Bahrick, L. E., & Hollich, G. (2008). Intermodal perception. In M. M. Haith & J. B. Benson (Eds.), *Encyclopedia of infant and early childhood development.* Oxford, UK: Elsevier.

Bailes, C. N., Erting, C. J., Erting, L. C., & Thumann-Prezioao, C. (2009). Language and literacy acquisition through parental mediation in American Sign Language. *Sign Language Studies, 9*(4), 417–456.

Bailey, H. N., Moran, G., Pederson, D. R., & Bento, S. (2007). Understanding the transmission of attachment using variable- and relationship-centered approaches. *Development and Psychopathology, 19,* 313–343.

Baillargeon, R. (2004). Infants' reasoning about hidden objects: Evidence for event-general and event-specific expectations. *Developmental Science, 7*(4), 391–424.

Baillargeon, R. H., Zoccolillo, M., Keenan, K., Cote, S., Perusse, D., Wu, H. X., et al. (2007). Gender differences in physical aggression: A prospective population-based survey of children before and after two years of age. *Developmental Psychology, 43,* 13–26.

Bain, J. (2010). Testosterone and the aging male: To treat or not to treat? *Maturitas, 66*(1), 16–22.

Baker, D. A. (2007). Consequences of herpes simplex virus in pregnancy and their prevention. *Current Opinions in Infectious Diseases, 20,* 73–76.

Bakermans-Kranenburg, M., & van IJzendoorn, M. (2009). The first 10,000 attachment interviews: Distribution of adult attachment representations in clinical and non-clinical groups. *Attachment & Human Development, 11*(3), 223–263.

Bakermans-Kranenburg, M. J., Breddels-Van Bardewijk, F., Juffer, M. K., Velderman, M. H., & van IJzenddorn, M. H. (2007). Insecure mothers with temperamentally reactive infants. In F. Juffer, M. J. Bakermans-Kranenburg, & M. H. van IJzendoorn (Eds.), *Promoting positive parenting.* Mahwah, NJ: Erlbaum.

Balchin, T., Hymer, B., & Matthews, D. (Eds.). (2009). *International companion to gifted education.* London: Routledge.

Baldwin, S., & Hoffman, J. P. (2002). The dynamics of self-esteem: A growth curve analysis. *Journal of Youth and Adolescence, 31,* 101–113.

Ball, J. (2009). Supporting young indigenous children's language development in Canada: A review of research on needs and promising practices. *The Canadian Modern Language Review, 66*(1), 19–47.

Ballard, V. L. (2010). Stem cells for heart failure in the aging heart. *Heart Failure Reviews, 15*(5), 447–456.

Balsano, A., Phelps, E., Theokas, C., Lerner, J. V., & Lerner, R. M. (2008). Patterns of early adolescents' participation in youth developing programs having positive youth development. *Journal of Research on Adolescence, 19*(2), 249–259.

Baltes, P. B. (2003). On the incomplete architecture of human ontogeny: Selection, optimization, and compensation as foundation for development theory. In U. M. Staudinger & U. Lindenberger (Eds.), *Understanding human development.* Boston: Kluwer.

Baltes, P. B. (2006). Facing our limits: The very old and the future of aging. Unpublished manuscript, Max Planck Institute, Berlin.

Baltes, P. B. (2009). Aging and wisdom. In D. C. Park & N. Schwarz (Eds.), *Cognitive aging* (2nd ed.). Clifton, NJ: Psychology Press.

Baltes, P. B., & Kunzmann, U. (2007). Wisdom and aging: The road toward excellence in mind and character. In D. C. Park & N. Schwarz (Eds.), *Cognitive aging: A primer* (2nd ed.). Philadelphia: Psychology Press.

Baltes, P. B., & Smith, J. (2003). New frontiers in the future of aging: From successful aging of the young old to the dilemmas of the fourth age. *Gerontology, 49,* 123–135.

Baltes, P. B., Lindenberger, U., & Staudinger, U. (2006). Lifespan theory in developmental psychology. In W. Damon & R. Lerner (Eds.), Handbook of child psychology (6th ed.). New York: Wiley.

Baltes, P. B., & Smith, J. (2008). The fascination of wisdom: Its nature, ontogeny, and function. *Perspectives in Psychological Sciences, 3,* 56–64.

Baltes, P. B., Reuter-Lorenz, P., & Rösler, F. (Eds.). (2006). *Lifespan development and the brain.* New York: Cambridge University Press.

Bandura, A. (1977). *Social learning theory.* Englewood Cliffs, NJ: Prentice Hall.

Bandura, A. (1986). *Social foundations of thought and action: A social cognitive theory.* Englewood Cliffs, NJ: Prentice Hall.

Bandura, A. (1998, August). *Swimming against the mainstream: Accentuating the positive aspects of humanity.* Paper presented at the meeting of the American Psychological Association, San Francisco.

Bandura, A. (2001). Social cognitive theory. *Annual Review of Psychology.* Palo Alto, CA: Annual Reviews.

Bandura, A. (2002). Selective moral disengagement in the exercise of moral agency. *Journal of Moral Education, 31,* 101–119.

Bandura, A. (2004, May). *Toward a psychology of human agency.* Paper presented at the meeting of the American Psychological Society, Chicago.

Bandura, A. (2006). Going global with social cognitive theory: From prospect to paydirt. In S. I. Donaldson, D. E. Berger, & K. Pezdek (Eds.), *The rise of applied psychology: New frontiers and rewarding careers.* Mahwah, NJ: Erlbaum.

Bandura, A. (2007a). Self-efficacy. In S. Clegg & J. Bailey (Eds.), *International encyclopedia of organization studies.* Thousand Oaks, CA: Sage.

Bandura, A. (2007b). Social cognitive theory. In W. Donsbach (Ed.), *International encyclopedia of communication.* Thousand Oaks, CA: Sage.

Bandura, A. (2008). Reconstrual of "free will" from the agentic perspective of social cognitive theory. In J. Baer, J. C. Kaufman, & R. F. Baumeister (Eds.), *Are we free? Psychology and free will.* Oxford, UK: Oxford University Press.

Bandura, A. (2009a). Social and policy impact of social cognitive theory. In M. Mark, S. Donaldson, & B. Campell (Eds.), *Social psychology and program/policy evaluation.* New York: Guilford.

Bandura, A. (2009b). Self-efficacy. In D. Carr (Ed.), *Encyclopedia of the life course and human development.* Boston: Gale Cengage.

Bandura, A. (2010). Self-efficacy. In D. Matsumoto (Ed.), *Cambridge dictionary of psychology.* New York: Cambridge University Press.

Banerjee, T. D., Middleton, F., & Faraone, S. V. (2007). Environmental risk factors for attention-deficit hyperactivity disorder. *Acta Pediatrica, 96,* 1269–1274.

Banja, J. (2005). Talking to the dying. *Case Manager, 16,* 37–39.

Bank, L., Burraston, B., & Snyder, J. (2004). Sibling conflict and ineffective parenting as predictors of adolescent boys' antisocial behavior and peer difficulties: additive and interactive effects. *Journal of Research on Adolescence, 14,* 99–125.

Banks, J. A. (2008). *Introduction to multicultural education* (4th ed.). Boston: Allyn & Bacon.

Barajas, R. G., Philipsen, N., & Brooks-Gunn, J. (2008). Cognitive and emotional outcomes for children in poverty. In D. R. Crane & T. B. Heaton (Eds.), *Handbook of families and poverty.* Thousand Oaks, CA: Sage.

Bar-David, G. (1999). Three phase development of caring capacity in primary caregivers for relatives with Alzheimer's disease. *Journal of Aging Studies, 13*(2), 177–197.

Barba, G. D., Attali, E., & La Corte, V. (2010). Confabulation in healthy aging is related to interference of overlearned, semantically similar information on episodic memory recall. *Journal of Clinical and Experimental Neuropsychology,* 1–6.

Barbarin, O. A., & Miller, K. (2009). Developmental science and early education: An introduction. In O. A. Barbarian & B. H. Wasik (Eds.), *Handbook of child development and early education.* New York: Guilford.

Barefoot, J. C., Mortensen, E. L., Helms, J., Avlund, K., & Schroll, M. (2001). A longitudinal study of gender differences in depressive symptoms from age 50 to 80. *Psychology and Aging, 16,* 342–345.

Bargh, J., & McKenna, K. (2004). The Internet and social life. *Annual Review of Psychology* (Vol. 55). Palo Alto, CA: Annual Reviews.

Baringa, M. (2003, January 3). Newborn neurons search for meaning. *Science, 299,* 32–34.

Barker, E., & Galambos, N. (2005). Adolescents' implicit theories of maturity. *Journal of Adolescent Research, 20*(5), 557–576.

Barker, E. D., Boivin, M., Brendgen, M., Fontaine, N., Arseneault, L., Vitaro, F., et al. (2008). Predictive validity and early predictions of peer-victimization trajectories in preschool. *Archives of General Psychiatry, 65*(10), 1185–1192.

Barnes, K. (2003). *Pregnancy (Gestational) Diabetes: Health Canada.* Retrieved from http://www.hc-sc.gc.ca/pphb-dgspsp/ccdpc-cpcmc/diabetes-diabete/english/whatis/pregnancy.html

Barnes, L. L., de Leon, C. F., Lewis, T. T., Bienias, J. L., Wilson, R. S., & Evans, D. A. (2008). Perceived discrimination and mortality in a population-based study of older adults. *American Journal of Public Health, 98,* 1241–1247.

Barone, D., Hardman, D., & Taylor, J. (2006). *Reading first in the classroom.* Boston: Allyn & Bacon.

Barrett, A. E., & Turner, R. J. (2005). Family structure and mental health: The mediating effects of socioeconomic status, family process, and social stress. *Journal of Health and Social Behavior, 46,* 156–169.

Barrett, L. F., Mesquita, B., Ochsner, K. N., & Gross, J. J. (2007). The experience of emotion. *Annual Review of Psychology* (Vol. 58). Palo Alto, CA: Annual Reviews.

Barrett, T. M., Davis, E. F., & Needham, A. (2007). Learning about tools in infancy. *Developmental Psychology, 43*, 352–368.

Barron, J., Petrilli, F., Strath, L., & McCaffrey, R. (2007). Successful interventions for smoking cessation in pregnancy. *MCN American Journal of Maternal and Child Nursing, 32*, 42–47.

Bart, W. M., & Peterson, D. P. (2008). Stanford-Binet test. In N. J. Salkind (Ed.), *Encyclopedia of educational psychology.* Thousand Oaks, CA: Sage.

Bartlett, E. (2004). The effects of fatherhood on the health of men: A review of the literature. *Journal of Men's Health and Gender, 1*(2–3), 159–169.

Basaran, A. (2007). Progesterone to prevent preterm delivery: Enigma or ready? *American Journal of Obstetrics and Gynecology, 197*, 686.

Basham, P. (2001). Home schooling: From the extreme to the mainstream. *Public Policy Sources* (Vol. 51). Vancouver: The Fraser Institute.

Bass, J. E., Contant, T. L., & Carin, A. A. (2009). *Activities for leading science as inquiry* (7th ed.). Boston: Allyn & Bacon.

Bateman, B. T., & Simpson, L. L. (2006). Higher rate of stillbirth at the extremes of reproductive age: A large nationwide sample of deliveries in the United States. *American Journal of Obstetrics and Gynecology, 194*, 840–845.

Bates, J. E. & Pettit, G. S. (2007). Temperament, parenting, and socialization. In J. E. Grusec & P. D. Hastings (Eds.), *Handbook of socialization.* New York: Guilford.

Bauer, I., Wrosch, C., & Jobin, J. (2008). I'm better off than most people: The role of social comparisons for coping with regret in young adulthood and old age. *Psychology and Aging, 23*, 800–811.

Bauer, M. E., Jeckel, C. M., & Luz, C. (2009). The role of stress factors during aging of the immune system. *Annals of the New York Academy of Sciences, 1153*, 139–152.

Bauer, P. J. (2007). *Remembering the times of our lives.* Mahwah, NJ: Erlbaum.

Bauer, P. J. (2008). Learning and memory: Like a horse and carriage. In A. Netdham & A. Woodward (Eds.), *Learning and the infant mind.* New York: Oxford University Press.

Bauer, P. J. (2009). Neurodevelopmental changes in infancy and beyond: Implications for learning and memory. In O. A. Barbarin & B. H. Wasik (Eds.), *Handbook of child development and early education.* New York: Guilford.

Bauer, P. J., Wenner, J. A., Dropik, P. L., & Wewerka, S. S. (2000). Parameters of remembering and forgetting in the transition from infancy to early childhood. *Monographs of the Society of Research in Child Development, 65* (4, Serial No. 263).

Bauman, W. P. (2008). Sexuality in later life. In R. Jacoby, C. Oppenheimer, T. Dening, & A. Thomas (Eds.), *Oxford textbook of old age psychiatry.* Oxford, UK: Oxford University Press.

Baumeister, R. F., & Vohs, K. D. (2002). The pursuit of meaningfulness in life. In C. R. Snyder & S. J. Lopez (Eds.), *Handbook of positive psychology.* New York: Oxford University Press.

Baumeister, R. F., Campbell, J. D., Krueger, J. I., & Vohs, K. D. (2003). Does high self-esteem cause better performance, interpersonal success, happiness, or healthier lifestyles? *Psychological Science in the Public Interest, 4*(1), 1–44.

Baumrind, D. (1971). Current patterns of parental authority. *Developmental Psychology Monographs, 4*(1, Pt. 2).

Baumrind, D. (1991). Effective parenting during the early adolescent transition. In P. A. Cowan & E. M. Hetherington (Eds.), *Advances in family research* (Vol. 2). Hillsdale, NJ: Erlbaum.

Bauserman, R. (2002). Child adjustment in joint-custody versus sole-custody arrangements: A meta-analytical review. *Journal of Family Psychology, 16*, 91–102.

Bayley, N. (1969). *Manual for the Bayley Scales of infant development.* New York: Psychological Corporation.

Bayley, N. (1993). *Bayley Scales of infant development* (2nd ed.). San Antonio: The Psychological Corporation.

Bayley, N. (2005). *Bayley Scales of infant and toddler development* (3rd ed.) (Bayley—III). Upper Saddle River, NJ: Pearson.

Baysinger, C. L. (2010). Imaging during pregnancy. *Anesthesia and Analgesia, 110*, 863–867.

Bazzano, L. A., et al. (2010). Body mass index and risk of stroke among Chinese men and women. *Annals of Neurology, 67*, 11–20.

Beach, J., & Bertrand, J. (2009, December). Early childhood programs and the education system. *Paediatric Child Health, 14*(10), 666–668.

Beach, J., et al. (2009). *Early childhood education and care in Canada, 2008* (8th ed.). Child Care Canada: Childcare Resource and Research Unit.

Bearman, S. K., Presnall, K., Martinez, E., & Stice, E. (2006). The skinny on body dissatisfaction: A longitudinal study of adolescent girls and boys. *Journal of Youth and Adolescence, 35*, 217–229.

Beaty, J. J. (2009). *50 early childhood literacy strategies* (2nd ed.). Boston: Allyn & Bacon.

Beaty, J. J., & Pratt, L. (2011). *Early literacy in preschool and kindergarten* (3rd ed.). Boston: Allyn & Bacon.

Beaupré, P., & Cloutier, E. (2006). *Navigating family transitions: Evidence from the general social survey.* Ottawa: Social and Aboriginal Statistics Division, Statistics Canada.

Beauregard, M. (2012, May 4). The neuroscience of spiritual experiences. Psychiatry Department, McGill University.

Beck, C. T. (2006). Postpartum depression: It isn't just the blues. *American Journal of Nursing, 106*, 40–50.

Bedford, V. H. (2009). Sibling relationships: Adulthood. In D. Carr (Ed.), *Encyclopedia*

of the life course and human development. Boston: Gale Cengage.

Beeghly, M., Martin, B., Rose-Jacobs, R., Cahral, H., Heeren, T., Augustyn, M., et al. (2006). Prenatal cocaine exposure and children's language functioning at 6 and 9.5 years: Moderating effects of child age, birth weight, and gender. *Journal of Pediatric Psychology, 31*, 98–115.

Beets, M. W., & Foley, J. T. (2008). Association of father involvement and neighborhood quality with kindergartners' physical activity: A multilevel structural equation model. *American Journal of Health Promotion, 22*, 195–203.

Beghetto, R. A., & Kaufman, J. C. (2011). *Nurturing creativity in the classroom.* New York: Cambridge University Press.

Belic, Roko, Director. (2011) Happy . Retrieved from http://www.thehappymovie.com/film/ on Sept. 6, 2012.

Bell, M. A., & Wolfe, C. D. (2007). The cognitive neuroscience of early socioemotional development. In C. A. Brownell & C. B. Kopp (Eds.), *Socioemotional development in the toddler years.* New York: Guilford.

Belsky, J. (1981). Early human experience: A family perspective. *Developmental Psychology, 17*, 3–23.

Belsky, J. (2009). Social-contextual determinants of parenting. In R. E. Tremblay, R. deV Peters, M. Boivin, & R. G. Barr (Eds.), *Encyclopedia on early childhood development.* Montreal: Centre of Excellence for Early Childhood Development.

Belsky, J. (2010). *Experiencing the lifespan* (2nd ed.). New York: Worth.

Belsky, J. (2013). *Experiencing the lifespan* (3rd ed). New York: Worth.

Belsky, J., & Pasco Fearon, R. (2002a). Early attachment security, subsequent maternal sensitivity, and later child development: Does continuity in development depend on continuity of care-giving? *Attachment & Human Development, 4*, 361–387.

Belsky, J., Burchinal, M., McCartney, K., Vandell, D., Clarke-Stewart, K. & Owen, M. (2007). Are there long-term effects of early child care? *Child Development, 78*(2), 681–701.

Belsky, J., Jaffe, S., Hsieh, K., & Silva, P. (2001). Child-rearing antecedents of intergenerational relations in young adulthood: A prospective study. *Developmental Psychology, 37*, 801–813.

Bem, S. L. (1977). On the utility of alternative procedures for assessing psychological androgyny. *Journal of Consulting and Clinical Psychology, 45*, 196–205.

Bender, H. L., Allen, J. P., McElhaney, K. B., Antonishak, J., Moore, C. M., Kello, H. O., et al. (2007). Use of harsh physical discipline and developmental outcomes in adolescence. *Development and Psychopathology, 19*, 227–242.

Bender, W. N. (2008). *Learning disabilities* (6th ed.). Boston: Allyn & Bacon.

Benegbi, M. (2007, Winter). 45 years later . . . Where do we stand? *Canadian Journal of Clinical Pharmacology, 14*(1), e37–e39.

Benenson, J. F., & Heath, A. (2006). Boys withdraw more in one-on-one situations, whereas girls withdraw more in groups. *Developmental Psychology, 42,* 272–282.

Benenson, J. F., Apostoleris, N. H., & Parnass, J. (1997). Age and sex differences in dyadic and group interaction. *Developmental Psychology, 33,* 538–543.

Benenson, J. F., Markovits, H., Roy, R., & Denko, P. (2003). Behavioural rules underlying learning to share: Effects of development and context. *International Journal of Behavioral Development, 27,* 116–121.

Bengtson, H., & Psouni, E. (2008). Mothers' representations of caregiving and their adult children's representations of attachment: Intergenerational concordance and relations to beliefs about mothering. *Scandinavian Journal of Psychology, 49,* 247–257.

Benn, P. A., & Chapman, A. R. (2010). Ethical challenges in providing noninvasive prenatal diagnosis. *Current Opinion in Obstetrics and Gynecology, 22,* 128–134.

Bennett, T., Szatmari, P., Bryson, S., Volden, J., Zwaigenbaum, L., Vaccarella, L., et al. (2007). Differentiating autism and Asperger syndrome on the basis of language delay or impairment. *Journal of Autism and Developmental Disorders, 43*(4), 860–868.

Benninghoven, D., Tetsch, N., Kunzendorf, S., & Jantschek, G. (2007). Body image in patients with eating disorders and their mothers, and the role of family functioning. *Comprehensive Psychiatry, 48,* 118–123.

Benoit, D. (2009). Efficacy of attachment-based interventions. In R. E. Tremblay, R. deV Peters, M. Boivin, & R. G. Barr (Eds.), *Encyclopedia on early childhood development.* Montreal: Centre of Excellence for Early Childhood Development.

Benoit, D., Coolbear, J., & Crawford, A. (2008). Abuse, neglect, and maltreatment of infants. In M. M. Haith & J. B. Benson (Eds.), *Encyclopedia of infant and early childhood development.* Oxford, UK: Elsevier.

Benokraitis, N. (2008). *Marriages and families* (6th ed.). Upper Saddle River, NJ: Prentice Hall.

Benson, A. C., Torode, M. E., & Fiatarone Singh, M. A. (2008). The effects of high-intensity progressive resistance training on adiposity in children: A randomized controlled trial. *International Journal of Obesity, 31,* 1016–1027.

Benson, P. L., Roehlkepartain, E. C., & Hong, K. L. (2008). Spiritual development. *New Directions for Youth Development, 118.*

Bentley, P., Driver, J., & Dolan, R. J. (2009). Modulation of fusiform cortex activity by cholinesterase inhibition predicts effects on subsequent memory. *Brain, 132,* 2356–2371.

Benzies, K., Tough, S. W., Tofflemire, K., Frick, C., Faber, A., & Newburn-Cook, C. (2006). Factors influencing women's decisions about timing of motherhood. *Journal of Obstetric Gynecologic & Neonatal Nursing, 35*(5), 625–633.

Berger, J., Motte, A., & Parkin, A. (2007). *The price of knowledge 2006–7: Chapter 1—Why access matters.* Montreal: The Canadian Millennium Scholarship Foundation.

Berger, K. (2011). *The developing person through the life span* (8th ed.). New York: Worth.

Berger, K. (2014). *Invitation to the life span* (2nd ed). New York: Worth.

Berger, J. T. (2010). What about process? Limitations in advanced directives, care planning, and noncapacitated decision making. *American Journal of Bioethics, 10,* 33–34.

Bergeson, T. R., & Trehub, S. E. (2007). Signature tunes in mothers' speech to infants. *Infant Behavior & Development, 30,* 648–654.

Bergman Levy, T., Barak, Y., Sigler, M., & Aizenberg, D. (2010). Suicide attempts and burden of physical illness among depressed elderly patients. *Archives of Gerontology and Geriatrics, 52*(1), 115–117.

Berk, L. E., & Spuhl, S. T. (1995). Maternal interaction, private speech, and task performance in preschool children. *Early Childhood Research Quarterly, 10,* 145–169.

Berkowitz, R. L., Roberts, J., & Minkoff, H. (2006). Challenging the strategy of maternal age-based prenatal genetic counseling. *JAMA,* 1446–1448.

Berko-Gleason, J. (1958). The child's learning of English morphology. *Word, 14,* 150–177.

Berko-Gleason, J. (2003). Unpublished review of J. W. Santrock's *Life-span development* (9th ed.). New York: McGraw-Hill.

Berko-Gleason, J. (2009). The development of language: An overview. In J. Berko-Gleason & N. Ratner (Eds.), *The development of language* (7th ed.). Boston: Allyn & Bacon.

Berndt, T. J. (2002). Friendship quality and social development. *Current Directions in Psychological Science, 11,* 7–10.

Berndt, T. J., & Perry, T. B. (1990). Distinctive features and effects of early adolescent friendships. In R. Montemayor (Ed.), *Advances in adolescent research.* Greenwich, CT: JAI Press.

Berninger, V. W. (2006). Learning disabilities. In W. Damon & R. Lerner (Eds.), *Handbook of child psychology* (6th ed.). New York: Wiley.

Bernstein, A. (2012, March 7). If Canada's game is hockey, its science is stem cells. *The Globe and Mail.* Retrieved from http://www.theglobeandmail.com/commentary/if-canadas-game-is-hockey-its-science-is-stem-cells/article551653/

Bernstein, D., & Rubin, D. C. (2002). Emotionally charged autobiographical memories across the life span: The recall of happy, sad, traumatic, and involuntary memories. *Psychology and Aging, 17,* 636–652.

Berscheid, E. (2010). Love in the fourth dimension. *Annual Review of Psychology* (Vol. 61). Palo Alto, CA: Annual Reviews.

Berthiaume, L. (2012, Feb. 2). Over 2000 Canadians were wounded in Afghan mission: report. *The National Post.* Retrieved from http://www.news.nationalpost.com

Bertrand, R. M., & Lachman, M. E. (2003). Personality development in adulthood and old age. In I. B. Weiner (Ed.). *Handbook of psychology,* Vol. VI. New York: John Wiley.

Besken, M., & Gulgoz, S. (2009). Reliance on schemas in source memory: Age differences and similarities of schemas. *Neuropsychology, Development, and Cognition. Section B: Aging, Neuropsychology, and Cognition, 16,* 1–2.

Best, D. L. (2010). Gender. In M. H. Bornstein (Ed.), *Handbook of cultural developmental science.* New York: Oxford University Press.

Betensky, J. D., Contrada, R. J., & Leventhal, E. (2009). Cardiovascular disease. In D. Carr (Ed.), *Encyclopedia of the life course and human development.* Boston: Gale Cengage.

Bettens, K., Sleegers, K., & Van Broeckhoven, C. (2010). Current status on Alzheimer disease molecular genetics: From past, to present, to future. *Human Molecular Genetics, 19*(R1), R4–R11.

Beverly, C., Burger, S. G., Maas, M. L., & Specht, J. K. (2010). Aging issues: Nursing imperatives for healthcare reform. *Nursing Administration Quarterly, 34,* 95–109.

Beyene, Y. (1986). Cultural significance and physiological manifestations of menopause: A biocultural analysis. *Culture, Medicine and Psychiatry, 10,* 47–71.

Beyers, W., & Goossens, L. (2008). Dynamics of perceived parenting and identity formation in late adolescence. *Journal of Adolescence, 31,* 165–184.

Bezanson, K. (2010). The "great recession," families and social reproduction. *Transition: The Vanier Institute of the Family, 40*(1).

Bhatara, V. S., & Aparasu, R. R. (2007). Pharmacotherapy with atomoxetine for U.S. children and adolescents. *Annals of Clinical Psychiatry, 19,* 175–180.

Bialystok, E. (1993). Metalinguistic awareness: The development of children's representations in language. In C. Pratt & A. Garton (Eds.), *Systems of representation in children.* London: Wiley.

Bialystok, E. (1997). Effects of bilingualism and biliteracy on children's emerging concepts of print. *Developmental Psychology, 33,* 429–440.

Bialystok, E. (1999). Cognitive complexity and attentional control in the bilingual mind. *Child Development, 70,* 537–604.

Bialystok, E. (2007). Cognitive effects of bilingualism: How linguistic experience leads to cognitive change. *International Journal of Bilingual Education and Bilingualism, 10*(3), 210–223.

Bialystok, E., Craik, F., & Ryan, J. (2006). Executive control in a modified antisaccade task: Effects of aging and bilingualism. *Journal of Experimental Psychology, 32*(6), 1341–1354.

Bianchi, S., Robinson, J., & Milkie, M. (2006). *Changing rhythms of American family*

life (Rose series in sociology). New York: Russell Sage Foundation Publications.

Bianco, I. H., Carl, M., Russell, C., Clarke, J. D., & Wilson, S. W. (2008). Brain asymmetry is encoded at the level of axon terminal morphology. *Neural Development, 3*, 9.

Bibby, R. (2009, May). *Restless gods and restless youth: An update on the religious situation in Canada.* Paper presented at the Annual Meeting of the Canadian Sociological Association, Ottawa.

Bibby, R. (2010). Beyond the stereotypes—an inside look at Canada's emerging millennials. *Canadian Education Association.* Education Canada, Vol. 50(1).

Biederman, J. (2007). Advances in the neurobiology of ADHD. *CNS Spectrums, 12* (suppl. 4), S6–S7.

Bielak, A. A. M., Hughes, T. F., Small, B. J., & Dixon, R. A. (2007). It's never too late to engage in lifestyle activities: Significant concurrent but not change relationships between lifestyle activities and cognitive speed. *Journals of Gerontology B: Psychological Sciences and Social Sciences, 62*, P331–P339.

Bierman, K. L., & Powers, C. J. (2009). Social skills training to improve peer relations. In K. H. Rubin, W. M. Bukowski, & B. Laursen (Eds.), *Handbook of peer interactions, relationships, and groups.* New York: Guilford.

Bigelow, A. E. (2003). The development of joint attention in blind infants. *Development and Psychopathology, 15*, 59–275.

Billari, F., et al. (2011). Social age deadlines for the childbearing of women and men. *Human Reproduction, 26*(3), 616–622.

Binder, T., & Vavrinkova, B. (2008). Prospective randomized comparative study of the effect of buprenorphine, methadone, and heroin on the course of pregnancy, birthweight of newborns, early postpartum adaptation, and the course of neonatal abstinence syndrome (NAS). *Neuroendocrinology Letters, 29*, 80–86.

Biography.com. (2013). Leonard Cohen biography. Arts & Entertainment Network. Retrieved from http://www.biography.com/people/leonard-cohen-9252529

Birch, S. A. J. (2005). When knowledge is a curse: Childrens' and adults' reasoning about mental states. *Current Directions in Psychological Science, 14*, 25–29.

Birditt, K. S. (2009). Spousal caregiving. In D. Carr (Ed.), *Encyclopedia of the life course and human development.* Boston: Gale Cengage.

Birditt, K. S., Miller, L. M., Fingerman, K. L., & Lefkowitz, E. S. (2010). Tensions in the parent and adult child relationship: Links to solidarity and ambivalence. *Psychology and Aging, 24*(2): 287–295.

Birken, C., Parkin, P., To, T. & Macarthur C. (2006). Trends in the rates of death from unintentional injury among Canadian children in urban areas: Influence of socioeconomic status. *CMAJ, 175*(8), 867–868.

Birren, J. E. (2002). Unpublished review of J. W. Santrock's *Life-span development* (9th ed.). New York: McGraw-Hill.

Birren, J. E. (Ed.). (1996). *Encyclopedia of gerontology.* San Diego: Academic Press.

Birren, J. E. (Ed.). (2007). *Encyclopedia of gerontology* (2nd ed.). San Diego: Academic Press.

Birren, J. E., Woods, A. M., & Williams, M. V. (1980). Behavioral slowing with age: Causes, organization, and consequences. In L. W. Poon (Ed.), *Aging in the 1980s: Psychological issues.* Washington, DC: American Psychological Association.

Bisiacchi, P. S., Tarantino, V., & Ciccola, A. (2008). Aging and prospective memory: The role of working memory and monitoring processes. *Aging: Clinical and Experimental Research, 20*, 569–577.

Bisson, M., & Levine, T. (2009). Negotiating a friends with benefits relationship. *Archives of Sexual Behavior, 25*, 125–140.

Bjorklund, D. F. (2006). Mother knows best: Epigenetic inheritance, maternal effects, and the evolution of human intelligence. *Developmental Review, 26*, 213–242.

Bjorklund, D. F. (2007). *Why youth is not wasted on the young.* Malden, MA: Blackwell.

Bjorklund, D. F. (2008). Advances in memory in childhood: Strategies, knowledge, and meta cognition. In M. Courage & N. Cowan (Eds.), *The development of memory in infancy and childhood.* Philadelphia: Psychology Press.

Bjorklund, D. F., & Pellegrini, A. D. (2002). *The origins of human nature.* New York: Oxford University Press.

Black, E. (2003). *War against the weak: Eugenics and America's campaign to create a master race.* New York: Four Walls Eight Windows.

Black, M. M., & Lozoff, B. (2008). Nutrition and diet. In M. M. Haith & J. B. Benson (Eds.), *Encyclopedia of infant and early childhood development.* Oxford, UK: Elsevier.

Black, M. M., & Hurley, K. M. (2007). Helping children develop healthy eating habits. In R. E. Tremblay, R. G. Barr, R. Peters, & M. Boivin (Eds.), *Encyclopedia on early childhood development* (rev. ed.). Retrieved from www.child-encyclopedia.com/documents/Black-HurleyANGxp_rev-Eating.pdf

Blackstone, A., & Stewart, M. (2012). Choosing to be childfree: Research on the decision not to parent. *Sociology Compass, 6*(9), 718–727.

Blair, M., & Somerville, S. C. (2009). The importance of differentiation in young children's acquisition of expertise. *Cognition, 112*, 259–280.

Blair, S. N., Kohl, H. W., Paffenbarger, R. S., Clark, D. G., Cooper, K. H., & Gibbons, L. W. (1989). Physical fitness and all-cause mortality: A prospective study of healthy men and women. *Journal of the American Medical Association, 262*, 2395–2401.

Blakemore, J. E. O., Berenbaum, S. A., & Liben, L. S. (2009). *Gender development.* Clifton, NJ: Psychology Press.

Blakemore, S. J. (2010). The developing social brain: Implications for education. *Neuron, 65*, 744–747.

Blanchard-Fields, F., & Coats, A. (2007). *Emotions in everyday problems: Age differences in elicitation and regulation.* Paper submitted for publication. Atlanta: Department of Psychlogy, Georgia Tech University.

Blank, R. (2011). End-of-life decision making across cultures. *Journal of Law, Medicine & Ethics, 39*(2), 201–214.

Blieszner, R. (2009). Friendship, adulthood. In D. Carr (Ed.). *Encyclopedia of the life course and human development.* Boston: Gale Cengage.

Block, J. (1993). Studying personality the long way. In D. Funder, R. D. Parke, C. Tomlinson-Keasey, & K. Widaman (Eds.), *Studying lives through time.* Washington, DC: American Psychological Association.

Bloom, L. (1998). Language acquisition in developmental context. In W. Damon (Ed.), *Handbook of child psychology* (5th ed., Vol. 5). New York: Wiley.

Bloom, L., Lifter, K., & Broughton, J. (1985). The convergence of early cognition and language in the second year of life: Problems in conceptualization and measurement. In M. Barrett (Ed.), *Single word speech.* London: Wiley.

Bloomgarden, Z. T. (2010). Gestational diabetes mellitus and obesity. *Diabetes Care, 33*, e60–e65.

Bloor, C., & White, F. (1983). Unpublished manuscript. University of California at San Diego, LaJolla, CA.

Blossfeld, H-P. (2009). Globalization. In D. Carr (Ed.), *Encyclopedia of the life course and human development.* Boston: Gale Cengage.

Blum, J. W., Beaudoin, C. M., & Caton-Lemos, L. (2005). Physical activity patterns and maternal well-being in postpartum women. *Maternal and Child Health Journal, 8*, 163–169.

Blum, R., & Nelson-Mmari, K. (2004). Adolescent health from an international perspective. In R. Lerner & L. Steinberg (Eds.), *Handbook of adolescent psychology.* New York: Wiley.

Blustein, D. L. (2008). The role of work in psychological health and well-being. *American Psychologist, 63*, 228–240.

Boden, J., Fergusson, D. & Horwood, L. (2008). Does adolescent self-esteem predict later life outcomes? A test of the causal role of self-esteem. *Development and Psychopathology, 20*, 319–339.

Boelen, P. A., & Prigerson, H. G. (2007). The influence of symptoms of prolonged grief disorder, depression, and anxiety on quality of life among bereaved adults: A prospective study. *European Archives of Psychiatry and Clinical Neuroscience, 257*, 444–452.

Boelen, P. A., van den Bout, J., & van den Hout, M. A. (2003). The role of cognitive variables in psychological functioning after the death of a first degree relative. *Behavior Research and Therapy, 41*, 1123–1136.

Boerce, G. C. (2006). Carl Jung, 1987–1961. Retrieved from http://webspace.ship.edu/cgboer/jung.html

Boeving, C. A., & Forsyth, B. (2008). AIDS and HIV. In M. M. Haith & J. B. Benson (Eds.),

Encyclopedia of infant and early childhood development. Oxford, UK: Elsevier.

Bogle, K. (2008). *Hooking up: Sex, dating, and relationships on campus*. New York: University Press.

Bohlin, G., & Hagekull, B. (2009). Socioemotional development: From infancy to young adulthood. *Scandinavian Journal of Psychology, 50*, 592–601.

Boisvert, J., & Harrell, W. (2009). Homosexuality as a risk factor for eating disorder symptomology in men. *The Journal of Men's Studies, 17*, 210–225.

Bombois, S., Debette, S., Bruandt, A., Delbeuck, X., Delmaire, C., Leys, D., et al. (2008). Vascular subcortical hyperintensities predict conversion to vascular and mixed dementia MCI patients. *Stroke, 39*(7), 2046–2051.

Bonanno, G. A., Neria, Y., Mancini, A., Coiofman, K. G., Litz, B., & Insel, B. (2007). Is there more to complicated grief than depression and posttraumatic stress disorder? *Journal of Abnormal Psychology, 116*, 342–351.

Bonanno, G. A., Wortman, C. B., & Nesse, R. M. (2004). Prospective patterns of resilience and maladjustment during widowhood. *Psychology and Aging, 19*, 260–271.

Bonda, D. J., et al. (2010). Oxidative stress in Alzheimer's disease: A possibility for prevention. *Neuropharmacology, 59*(4–5), 290–294.

Bondare, W. (2007). Brain and central nervous system. In J. E. Birren (Ed.), *Encyclopedia of gerontology* (2nd ed.). San Diego: Academic Press.

Bonell, C., et al. (2013). The effects of school environment on student health: A systematic review of multi-level studies. *Health & Place, 21*, 180–191.

Bonny, C. R., & Sternberg, R. J. (2010). Teaching and learning to think critically. In R. E. Mayer & P. A. Alexander (Eds.), *Hand-book of research on learning and instruction*. New York: Routledge.

Bonvillian, J. (2005). Unpublished review of J. W. Santrock's *Topical life-span development* (3rd ed.). New York: McGraw-Hill.

Booth, A. (2006). Object function and categorization in infancy: Two mechanisms of facilitation. *Infancy, 10*, 145–169.

Booth, D., Elliott, S., & Bruce, F. (2009). Boys' literacy attainment: Research and related practice. Retrieved from from www.edu.gov. on.ca/eng/research/boys_literacy.pdf

Booth, M. (2002). Arab adolescents facing the future: Enduring ideas and pressures to change. In B. B. Brown, R. W. Larson, & T. S. Saraswathi (Eds.), *The world's youth*. New York: Cambridge University Press.

Bopp, K. L., & Verhaeghen, P. (2007). Age-related differences in control processes in verbal and visuospatial working memory: Storage, transformation, supervision, and coordination. *Journals of Gerontology B: Psychological Sciences and Social Sciences, 62*, P239–P246.

Bor, W., McGee, T. R., & Fagan, A. A. (2004). Early risk factors for adolescent antisocial behavior: An Australian longitudinal study. *Australian and New Zealand Journal of Psychiatry, 38*, 365–372.

Bornstein, M. H. (1975). Qualities of color vision in infancy. *Journal of Experimental Child Psychology, 19*, 401–409.

Bornstein, M. H. (2006). Parenting science and practice. In W. Damon & R. Lerner (Eds.), *Handbook of child psychology* (6th ed.). New York: Wiley.

Bornstein, M. H., & Zlotnik, D. (2008). Parenting styles and their effects. In M. M. Haith & J. B. Benson (Eds.), *Encyclopedia of infant and early childhood development*. Oxford, UK: Elsevier.

Boron, J. B., Willis, S. L., & Schaie, K. W. (2007). Cognitive training gain as a predictor of mental status. *Journals of Gerontology B: Psychological Sciences and Social Sciences, 62B*, P45–P52.

Bos, A., Huijding, J., Muris, P., Vogel, L., & Biesheuvel, J. (2010). Global, contingent and implicit self-esteem and psychopathological symptoms in adolescents. *Personality and Individual Differences, 48*, 311–316.

Bos, H. M. W., Sandfort, T. G. M., de Bruyn, E. H., & Hakvoort, E. M. (2008). Same-sex attraction, social relationships, psychosocial functioning, and school performance. *Developmental Psychology, 44*, 102–116.

Bos, H., van Balen, F., & van den Boom, D. (2005). Lesbian families and family functioning: an overview. *Patient Education and Counselling, 59*, 263–275.

Bouchard, T. J., Lykken, D. T., McGue, M., Segal, N. L., & Tellegen, A. (1990). Source of human psychological differences. The Minnesota Study of Twins Reared Apart. *Science, 250*, 223–228.

Boucher, J. (2009). *The autistic spectrum*. Thousand Oaks, CA: Sage.

Boukydis, C. F., & Lester, B. M. (2008). Mother-infant consultation during drug treatment: Research and innovative clinical practice. *Harm Reduction Journal, 5*(6).

Boveris, A., & Navarro, A. (2008). Brain mitochondrial dysfunction in aging. *IUBMB Life, 60*, 308–314.

Bowen, A., & Muhajarine, N. (2006). Prevalence of antenatal depression in women enrolled in an outreach program in Canada. *Journal of Obstetrics, Gynecologic and Neonatal Nursing, 35*(4), 491–498.

Bowen, A., Bowen, R., Maslany, G., & Muhajarine, N. (2008, July). Anxiety in a socially high-risk sample of pregnant women in Canada. *The Canadian Journal of Psychiatry, 53*(7), 435–440.

Bowker, A. (2006). Relationship between sports participation and self-esteem during early adolescence. *Canadian Journal of Behavioural Science, 38*, 214–229.

Bowlby, J. (1969). *Attachment and loss* (Vol. 1). London: Hogarth Press.

Bowlby, J. (1980). *Attachment and loss* (Vol. 3): Loss, sadness, and depression. New York: Basic Books.

Bowlby, J. (1989). *Secure and insecure attachment*. New York: Basic Books.

Bowman, M. A., Prelow, H. M., & Weaver, S. R. (2007). Parenting behaviors, association with deviant peers, and delinquency in African American adolescents: A mediated-moderation model. *Journal of Youth and Adolescence, 36*, 517–527.

Boyer, K., & Diamond, A. (1992). Development of memory for temporal order in infants and young children. In A. Diamond (Ed.), *Development and neural bases of higher cognitive function*. New York: New York Academy of Sciences.

Boykin McElhaney, K., Allen, J., Stephenson, C., & Hare, A. (2006). Attachment and autonomy during adolescence. In R. Lerner & L. Steinberg (Eds.), *Handbook of adolescent psychology* (3rd ed.) Vol. 1 (pp. 358–403). Hoboken, NJ: Wiley.

Boyle, M. H., & Lipman, E. L. (2002). Do places matter? Socioeconomic disadvantage and behavioral problems of children in Canada. *Journal of Consulting and Clinical Psychology, 70*, 378–389.

Bradley, L. (2012). Sharing my vision—Changing directions, changing lives: The mental health strategy for Canada unveiled. Mental Health Commission of Canada. Retrieved from http://www.mentalhealthcommission.ca/

Bradley, R. E., & Webb, R. (1976). Age-related differences in locus of control orientation in three behavior domains. *Human Development, 19*, 49–55.

Brain Canada Foundation. The news. (August, 2012). Retrieved from http://braincanada.ca on Sept. 12, 2012.

Brainerd, C. J., & Reyna, V. E. (1993). Domains of fuzzy-trace theory. In M. L. Howe & R. Pasnak (Eds.), *Emerging themes in cognitive development*. New York: Springer.

Braithwaite, D., Emery, J., Walter, F., Prevost, A. T., & Sutton, S. (2004, January 21). Psychological impact of genetic counseling for familial cancer: A systematic review and meta-analysis. *Journal of the National Cancer Institute, 96*(2), 122–133.

Brand, M., & Markowitsch, H. J. (2010). Mechanisms contributing to decision-making difficulties in late adulthood: Theoretical approaches, speculations, and empirical evidence. *Gerontology, 56*(4), 430–434.

Brandstädter, J., & Renner, G. (1990). Tenacious goal pursuit and flexible goal adjustment: Explication and age-related analysis of assimilative and accommodative strategies of coping. *Psychology and Aging, 5*, 58–67.

Brannen, C., Dyck, K., Hardy, C., & Mushquash, C. (2012). Rural mental health services in Canada: A model for research and practice. In J. Kulig & A. Williams (Eds.), *Health in rural Canada* (pp. 239–257). Vancouver: UBC Press.

Brannen, C., McGrath, P., Johnston, C., Dozois, D., Elgar, F., & Whitehead, M. (2006). Managing our mood (MOM): Distance treatment for post-partum depression in rural Nova Scotia. Paper presented at the Annual Conference of the Canadian Rural Health Research Society, Prince George, BC.

Bransford, J., et al. (2006). Learning theories in education. In P. A. Alexander & P. H. Winne (Eds.), *Handbook of educational psychology* (2nd ed.). Mahwah, NJ: Erlbaum.

Bravo, G., et al. (2011). Are Canadians providing advance directives about health care and research participation in the event of decisional incapacity? *The Canadian Journal of Psychiatry, 56*(4), 209–218.

Brazelton, T. B. (2004). Preface: The neonatal intensive care unit network neurobehavioral scale. *Pediatrics, 113* (Suppl.) S632–S633.

Brazil, K., Thabane, L., Foster, G., & Bédard, M. (2009). Gender differences among Canadian spousal caregivers at the end of life. *Health and Social Care in the Community, 17*(2), 159–166.

Breaslau, N., Paneth N. S., & Lucia, V. C. (2004). The lingering academic deficits of low birth weight children. *Pediatrics, 114,* 1035–1040.

Bredekamp, S. (2011). *Effective practices in early childhood education.* Upper Saddle River, NJ: Merrill.

Bremner, G. (2007). Perception and knowledge of the world. In A. Slater & M. Lewis (Eds.), *Introduction to infant development* (2nd ed.). Malden, MA: Blackwell.

Brice, A., Miller, K., & Brice, R. (2006). Language in the English as a second language and general education classrooms: A tutorial. *Communication Disorders Quarterly, 27,* 240–247.

Briem, V., Radeborg, K., Salo, I., & Bengtsson, H. (2004). Developmental aspects of children's behavior and safety while cycling. *Journal of Pediatric Psychology, 29,* 369–377.

Brim, G. (1992, December 7). Commentary, *Newsweek,* p. 52.

Brim, G., Ryff, C. D., & Kessler, R. (Eds.). (2004). *How healthy are we? A national study of well-being at midlife.* Chicago: University of Chicago Press.

Brink, P., & Smith, T. F. (2008). Determinants of home death in palliative home care: Using the interRAI palliative care to assess end-of-life care. *American Journal of Hospice and Palliative Medicine, 25*(4), 263–270.

Brislin, R. W. (2000). Cross-cultural training. In A. Kazdin (Ed.), *Encyclopedia of psychology.* Washington, DC: American Psychological Association and Oxford University Press.

Brock, L. J., & Jennings, G. (2007). Sexuality and intimacy. In J. A. Blackburn & C. N. Dulmas (Eds.), *Handbook of gerontology.* New York: Wiley.

Broderick, R. (2003, July/August). A surgeon's saga. *Minnesota: The Magazine of the University of Minnesota Alumni Association,* 26–31.

Brody, N. (2007). Does education influence intelligence? In P. C. Kyllonen, R. D. Roberts, & L. Stankov (Eds.), *Extending intelligence.* Mahwah, NJ: Erlbaum.

Bronfenbrenner, U. (1979). *The ecology of human development. Experiments by nature and design.* Cambridge, MA: Harvard University Press.

Bronfenbrenner, U. (1986). Ecology of the family as a context for human development: Research perspectives. *Developmental Psychology, 22,* 723–742.

Bronfenbrenner, U. (2000). Ecological theory. In A. Kazdin (Ed.), *Encyclopedia of psychology.* Washington, DC: American Psychological Association and Oxford University Press.

Bronfenbrenner, U. (2004). *Making human beings human.* Thousand Oaks. CA: Sage.

Bronfenbrenner, U., & Morris, P. (1998). The ecology of developmental processes. In W. Damon (Ed.), *Handbook of child psychology* (5th ed., Vol. 1). New York: Wiley.

Bronfenbrenner, U., & Morris, P. A. (2006). The ecology of human development. In W. Damon & R. Lerner (Eds.), *Handbook of child psychology* (6th ed.). New York: Wiley.

Bronstein, P. (2006). The family environment: Where gender role socialization begins. In J. Worell & C. D. Goodheart (Eds.), *Handbook of girl's and women's psychological health.* New York: Oxford University Press.

Brooker, R. (2011). *Biology* (2nd ed.). New York: McGraw-Hill.

Brookfield, S. (2011). *Teaching for critical thinking: Tools and techniques to help students question their assumptions.* San Francisco: Jossey-Bass.

Brooks, D. J. (2010). Imaging approaches to Parkinson's disease. *Journal of Nuclear Medicine, 51,* 596–609.

Brooks, J. G., & Brooks, M. (2001). *The case for constructivist classroom* (2nd ed.). Upper Saddle River, NJ: Erlbaum.

Brooks-Gunn, J. (2003). Do you believe in magic? What we can expect from early childhood programs. *Social Policy Report, Society for Research in Child Development, XVII* (No. 1), 1–13.

Brooks-Gunn, J., & Donahue, E. H. (2008). Introducing the issue. *Future of Children, 18*(1), 3–10.

Brooks-Gunn, J., & Warren, M. P. (1989). The psychological significance of secondary sexual characteristics in 9- to 11-year-old girls. *Child Development, 59,* 161–169.

Brown, B., & Bakken, J. (2011). Parenting and peer relationships: Reinvigorating research on family—peer linkages in adolescence. *Journal of Research and Adolescence, 21,* 153–165.

Brown, B. B. (1999). Measuring the peer environment of American adolescents. In S. L. Friedman & T. D. Wachs (Eds.), *Measuring environment across the life span.* Washington, DC: American Psychological Association.

Brown, B. B., & Larson, R. W. (2002). The kaleidoscope of adolescence: Experiences of the world's youth at the beginning of the 21st century. In B. B. Brown, R. W. Larson, & T. S. Saraswathi (Eds.), *The world's youth.* New York: Cambridge University Press.

Brown, B. B., Bakken, J. P., Amerigner, S. W., & Mahon, S. D. (2008). A comprehensive conceptualization of the peer influence process in adolescence. In M. J. Prinstein & K. A. Dodge (Eds.), *Understanding peer influence in children and adolescents.* New York: Guilford.

Brown, J. K. (1985). Introduction. In J. K. Brown & V. Kerns (Eds.), *In her prime: A new view of middle-aged women.* South Hadley, MA: Bergin & Garvey.

Brown, J. D., Keller, S., & Stern, S. (2009). Sex, sexuality, sexting and sexed: Adolescents and the media. *The Prevention Researcher, 16*(4), 12–16.

Brown, K., Cassidy, W., & Jackson, M. (2006). Cyber-bullying: Developing policy to direct responses that are equitable and effective in addressing this special form of bullying. *Canadian Journal of Educational Administration and Policy, 57.* Retrieved from http://www.umanaitoba.ca/publications/ cjeap/articles/brown_jackson_cassidy.html

Brown, M. (2003, July 10). Parents bring class home. *The Markham Economist & Sun,* 14–15.

Brown, S. L., Brown, R. M., House, J. S., & Smith, D. M. (2008). Coping with spousal loss: Potential buffering effects of self-reported helping behavior. *Personality and Social Psychology Bulletin, 34,* 849–861.

Brown, S. L., Bulanda, J. R., & Lee, G. R. (2005). The significance of nonmarital cohabitation: Marital status and mental health benefits among middle-aged and older adults. *Journals of Gerontology B: Psychological Sciences and Social Sciences, 60,* S21–S29.

Brown, S. L., Nesse, R. M., House, J. S., & Utz, R. L. (2004). Religion and emotional compensation: Results from a prospective study of widowhood. *Personality and Social Psychology Bulletin, 30,* 1165–1174.

Browne, C. V., & Braun, K. L. (2008). Globalization, women's migration, and the long-care workforce. *Gerontologist, 48,* 16–24.

Brownell, C. A., & Kopp, C. B. (Eds.). (2007). *Socioemotional development in the toddler years.* New York: Guilford.

Brownell, C. A., Ramani, G. B., & Zerwas, S. (2006). Becoming a social partner with peers: Cooperation and social understanding in one- and two-year-olds. *Child Development, 77,* 803–821.

Bruce, A. (2007). Time(lessness): Buddhist perspectives and end-of-life. *Nursing Philosophy, 8,* 151–157.

Bruck, M., Ceci, S. J., & Principe, G. F. (2006). The child and the law. In W. Damon & R. Lerner (Eds.), *Handbook of child psychology* (6th ed.). New York: Wiley.

Bruin, J., Gerstein, H., & Holloway, A. (2010). Long-term consequence of fetal and neonatal nicotine exposure: A critical review. *Toxicological Sciences, 116*(2), 364–374.

Brune, C. W., & Woodward, A. L. (2007). Social cognition and social responsiveness in 10-month-old infants. *Journal of Cognition and Development, 2,* 3–27.

Brunstein Klomek, A., Marrocco, F., Kleinman, M., Schofeld, I. S., & Gould, M. S. (2007). Bullying, depression, and suicidality in adolescents. *Journal of the American Academy of Child and Adolescent Psychiatry, 46,* 40–49.

Bryant, J. A. (Ed.). (2007). *The children's television community*. Mahwah, NJ: Erlbaum.

Bryant, J. B. (2009). Language in social contexts: Communication competence in the preschool years. In J. Berko Gleason & N. Ratner (Eds.), *The development of language* (7th ed.). Boston: Allyn & Bacon.

Brym, R., Roberts, L., Lie, J., & Rytina, S. (2013). *Sociology: Your compass for a new world*. Toronto: Nelson.

Buchanan, D., Tourigny-Rivard, M.-F., Cappeliez, P., Frank, C., Janikowski, P., Spanjevic, L., . . . & Herrmann, N. (2006). National guidelines for seniors' mental health: The assessment and treatment of depression. *The Canadian Journal of Geriatrics, 9*(supplement 2), S52–58.

Buchman, A. S., Boyle, P. A., Wilson, R. S. Fleischman, D. A., Leurgans, S., & Bennett, D. A. (2009). Association between late-life social activity and motor decline in older adults. *Archives of Internal Medicine, 169*, 1139–1146.

Buchman, S. (2008). *Do not resuscitate confirmation form*. Newsbriefs: The Ontario College of Family Physicians. Retrieved from http://www.ocfp.on.ca

Buckett, W. (2004). Are we becoming more infertile? Infertility Awareness Association of Canada. Retrieved from http://www.iaac.ca/

Buckner, J. C., Mezzacappa, E., & Beardslee, M. R. (2009). Self-regulation and its relations to adaptive functioning in low income youths. *American Journal of Orthopsychiatry, 79*, 19–30.

Bucur, B., & Madden, D. J. (2007). Information processing/cognition. In J. E. Birren (Ed.), *Encyclopedia of gerontology* (2nd ed.). San Diego: Academic Press.

Bucur, B., & Madden, D. J. (2010). Effects of adult age and blood pressure on executive function and speed of processing. *Experimental Aging Research, 36*, 153–168.

Bucx, F., van Wel, F., Knijn, T., & Hagendoorn, L. (2008). Intergenerational contact and the life course status of young adult children. *Journal of Marriage and the Family, 70*, 144–156.

Bueler, H. (2010). Mitochondrial dynamics, cell death, and the pathogenesis of Parkinson's disease. *Apoptosis, 15*, 1336–1353.

Bugental, D. B., & Grusec, J. E. (2006). Socialization processes. In W. Damon & R. Lerner (Eds.), *Handbook of child psychology* (6th ed.). New York: Wiley.

Buhrmester, D. (1998). Need fulfillment, interpersonal competence, and the developmental contexts of early adolescent friendship. In W. M. Bukowski & A. F. Newcomb (Eds.), *The company they keep: Friendship in childhood and adolescence:* New York: Cambridge University Press.

Buhrmester, D. (2005, April). *The antecedents of adolescents' competence in close relationships: A six-year-study*. Paper presented at the meeting of the Society for Research in Child Development, Atlanta.

Buhs, E. S., & Ladd, G. W. (2001). Peer rejection as antecedent of young children's school adjustment: An examination of mediating processes. *Developmental Psychology, 37*, 550–560.

Bukowski, W. M., Brendgen, M., & Vitaro, F. (2007). Peers and socialization: Effects on externalizing and internalizing problems. In J. E. Grusec & P. D. Hastings (Eds.), *Handbook of Socialization*. New York: Guilford.

Bukowski, W. M., Laursen, B., & Rubin, K. H. (Eds.). (2009). *Social and emotional development*. Clifton, NJ: Psychology Press.

Bukowski, W. M., Motzoi, C., & Meyer, F. (2009). Friendship as process, function, and outcome. In K. H. Rubin, W. M. Bukowski, & B. Laursen (Eds.), *Handbook of peer interactions, relationships, and groups*. New York: Guilford.

Bukowski, W. M., Velasquez, A. M., & Brendgen, M. (2008). Variation in patterns of peer influence: Considerations of self and other. In M. J. Prinstein & K. A. Dodge (Eds.), *Understanding peer influence in children and adolescents*. New York: Guilford.

Bulik, C. M., Berkman, N. D., Brownley, K. A., Sedway, J. A., & Lohr, K. N. (2007). Anorexia nervosa treatment: A systematic review of randomized controlled trials. *International Journal of Eating Disorders, 40*, 310–320.

Burck, J. R., Vena, M., Jolicoeur, M., & Jolicoeur, L. E. (2007). At a threshold: Making decisions when you don't have all the answers. *Physical Medicine and Rehabilitation Clinics of North America, 18*, 1–25.

Burney, R., & Leerkes, E. (2010). Links between mothers' and fathers' perception of infant temperament and coparenting. *Infant Behavior & Development, 33*, 125–135.

Burns, C., Dunn, A., Brady, M., Starr, N., & Blosser, C. (2013). *Pediatric primary care*. St. Louis: Elsevier.

Burns, L., Mattick, R. P., Lim, K., & Wallace, C. (2007). Methadone in pregnancy: Treatment retention and neonatal outcomes. *Addiction, 102*, 264–270.

Burr, J. (2009). Volunteering, later life. In D. Carr (Ed.), *Encyclopedia of the life course and human development*. Boston: Gale Cengage.

Burton, P., Lethbridge, L., & Phipps, S. (2006). Children with disabilities and chronic conditions and longer-term parental health. Retrieved from http://atlanticresearchdatacentre.dal.ca/

Burton, P., Phipps, S., & Curtis, L. (2005). *All in the family: A simultaneous model of parenting style and child conduct*. Ottawa: Family and Labour Studies Division, Statistics Canada.

Bushnik, T. (2006). *Child care in Canada*. Ottawa: Statistics Canada Cat. No. 89-599-MIE–No. 003.

Buss, D. M. (1999). *Evolutionary psychology: The new science of the mind*. Boston: Allyn & Bacon.

Buss, D. M. (2000). Evolutionary psychology. In A. Kazdin (Ed.), *Encyclopedia of psychology*. Washington, DC: American Psychological Association and Oxford University Press.

Buss, D. M. (2008). *Evolutionary psychology* (3rd ed.). Boston: Allyn & Bacon.

Buss, K. A., & Goldsmith, H. H. (2007). Biobehavioral approaches to early socioemotional development. In C. A. Brownell & C. B. Kopp (Eds.), *Socioemotional development in the toddler years*. New York: Guilford.

Bussey, K., & Bandura, A. (1999). Social cognitive theory of gender development and differentiation. *Psychological Review, 106*, 676–713.

Bustamante-Aragones, A., Gonzalez-Gonzalez, C., de Abla, M. R., Ainse, E., & Ramos, C. (2010). Noninvasive prenatal diagnosis using ccffDNA in maternal blood: State of the art. *Expert Review of Molecular Diagnostics, 10*, 197–205.

Butler, R. N. (2007). Life review. In J. E. Birren (Ed.), *Encyclopedia of gerontology* (2nd ed.). San Diego: Academic Press.

Byrnes, H. F., Chen, M. J., Miller, B. A., & Maguin, E. (2007). The relative importance of mothers' and youths' neighborhood perceptions for youth alcohol use and delinquency. *Journal of Youth and Adolescence, 36*, 649–659.

Byrnes, J. P. (2008). Piaget's cognitive developmental theory. In M. M. Haith & J. B. Benson (Eds.), *Encyclopedia of infant and early childhood development*. Oxford, UK: Elsevier.

C

Cabeza, R. (2002). Hemispheric asymmetry reduction in older adults: The HAROLD model. *Psychology and Aging, 17*, 85–100.

Cabrera, N., Hutchens, R., & Peters, H. E. (Eds.). (2006). *From welfare to childcare*. Mahwah, NJ: Erlbaum.

Cain, S. (2012). *Quiet—The power of introverts in a world that can't stop talking*. New York: Crown Publishers.

Caley, L., Syms, C., Robinson, L., Cederbaum, J., Henry, M., & Shipkey, N. (2008). What human service professionals know and want to know about fetal alcohol syndrome. *Canadian Journal of Clinical Pharmacology, 15*, e117–e123.

Calkins, S. D. (2007). The emergence of self-regulation: Biological and behavioral control mechanisms supporting toddler competencies. In C. A. Brownell & C. B. Kopp (Eds.), *Socioemotional development in the toddler years*. New York: Guilford.

Cameron, J. R., Hansen, R., & Rosen, D. (1989). Preventing behavioral problems in infancy through temperament assessment and parental support programs. In W. B. Carey & S. C. McDevitt (Eds.), *Clinical and education applications of temperament research*. Amsterdam: Swets & Zeitlinger.

Campaign 2000. (2009). Report card on child and family poverty in Canada: 1989–2009. Keep the Promise: Make Canada poverty-free. Retrieved from http://www.campaign2000.ca/reportcards.html

Campaign 2000. (2012). Needed: A federal action plan to end child and family poverty in Canada. Retrieved from http://www.campaign2000.ca/reportcards.html

Campanella, J., & Rovee-Collier, C. (2005). Latent learning and deferred imitation at 3 months. *Infancy, 7*(3), 243–262.

Campbell, D. A., Lake, M. F., Falk, M., & Backstrand, J. R. (2006). A randomized-controlled trial of continuous support by a lay doula. *Journal of Obstetrics and Gynecology: Neonatal Nursing, 35*, 456–464.

Campbell, D., Scott, K. D., Klaus, M. H., & Falk, M. (2007). Female relatives or friends trained as labor doulas: Outcomes at 6 to 8 weeks postpartum. *Birth, 34*, 220–227.

Campos, J. J. (2005). Unpublished review of J. W. Santrock's *Life-span development* (10th ed.). New York: McGraw-Hill.

Campos, J. J., Langer, A., & Krowitz, A. (1970). Cardiac responses on the visual cliff in prelocomotor human infants. *Science, 170*, 196–197.

Canada Centre on Substance Abuse. (2011). Cross-Canada report on student alcohol and drug use. Retrieved from http://www.ccsa.ca

Canada Statistics. (2009). *Trends in police-reported drug offence in Canada* (No. 85-002-X). Retrieved from http://www.statcan.gc.ca

Canada Year Book. (2008). *Income, pensions, spending and wealth*. Ottawa: Statistics Canada.

Canadian Association for Neuroscience. (2012). Canadian neuroscience news. Retrieved from http://www.can-acn.org/page/4

Canadian Blood Services. (2012). *Types and Rh system*. Retrieved from http://www.blood.ca/

Canadian Broadcasting Company (CBC). (2012, September 24). Barbara Coloroso on bullying. *Information Morning on CBC Fredrickton*. Retrieved on February 5, 2013 from http://www.cbc.cainformationmorningfredericton/2012/09/24/barbara-coloroso-on-bullying/

Canadian Broadcasting Company (CBC). (2012a, September 17). Robert Latimer gets OK to travel to U.K. for panel talk. Retrieved from http://www.cbc.ca/news

Canadian Broadcasting Company (CBC). (2012b, October 17). Robert Latimer visa problems scuttle U.K. trip, debate groups says. Retrieved from http://www.cbc.ca/news/

Canadian Cancer Society. (2010). Cancer: The leading cause of death in the country. Retrieved from http://www.cancer.ca/Quebec/About%20us/Media%20centre/QC-Media%20releases/QC-Quebec%20media%20releases/QC_StatistiquesCanadiennesCancer_2010.aspx?sc_lang=en

Canadian Child Care Federation. (2009). Ages and stages of numeracy development. Retrieved from http://www.ccf-fcsge.ca

Canadian Child Care Federation. (2013). About Canadian Child Care Federation (CCCF). Retrieved from http://www.cccf.fcsge.ca/

Canadian Council for Refugees. (2012). Family reunification. Retrieved from http://ccrweb.ca/en/family-reunification

Canadian Council on Learning (CCL). (2006). Working to learn: Meeting university and college costs. *Lessons in Learning*. Retrieved from http://www.ccl-cca.ca/

Canadian Council on Learning (CCL). (2007). State of learning in Canada: No time for complacency. Retrieved from http://www.ccl-cca.ca

Canadian Council on Learning (CCL). (2008). *Bullying in Canada: How intimidation affects learning*. Retrieved from http://www.cci-cca.ca/

Canadian Council on Learning (CCL). (2009). Learning about sex and sexual health. Retrieved from http://www.cci-cca.ca/

Canadian Council on Social Development (CCSD). (2002). Fact sheet on families. Retrieved from http://www.ccsd.ca/

Canadian Council on Social Development (CCSD). (2003). Persons with disabilities and medication uses. CCSD's disability information sheet (no. 11) [electronic version]. Retrieved from http://www.ccsd.ca/drip/research/dis11/dis11.pdf

Canadian Council on Social Development (CCHD). (2006). *Families: A Canadian profile*. Retrieved from http://www.ccsd.ca/

Canadian Fertility and Andrology Society. (2012). Fertility FAQ. Retrieved from http://www.cfas.ca/index.php?option=com_content&view=article&id=1126&Itemid=692

Canadian Fitness and Lifestyle Research Institute. (2005). CFLRI 2005 physical activity monitor. Retrieved from http://www.cflri.ca/pub_page/106

Canadian Healthcare Association. (2012) Respite care in Canada. Retrieved on September 15, 2013 from http://www.cha.ca/wp-content/uploads/2012/11Respite_Care_in_Canada_EN_web.pdf

Canadian Hospice Palliative Care Association (CHPCA). (2010). Fact sheet: Hospice palliative care in Canada. Retrieved from http://www.chpca.net/resource_doc_library/Fact_sheet_HPC_in-Canada.pdf

Canadian Institute for Health Information (CIHI). (2004). Chapter 4—Aboriginal peoples' health. *Improving the Health of Canadians*. Retrieved from http://www.cihi.ca

Canadian Institute for Health Information (CIHI). (2006). How healthy are rural Canadians? Ottawa: Author.

Canadian Institute for Health Information (CIHI). (2007a). *Health care use at the end of life in Western Canada*. Ottawa: CIHI.

Canadian Institute for Health Information (CIHI). (2010). *Drug use among seniors on public drug programs in Canada, 2002 to 2008*. Ottawa: CIHI.

Canadian Institute for Health Information (CIHI). (2011). Obesity in Canada.

Canadian Institutes of Health Research (CIHR). (2006). Improving the health of Canadians. Retrieved from http://www.cihi.ca

Canadian Institutes of Health Research (CIHR). (2012a). Fact sheet—Suicide prevention. Retrieved from http://www.cihr-irsc.gc.ca

Canadian Institutes of Health Research (CIHR). (2012b, June 30). Guidelines for human pluipotent stem cell research, June 29, 2007. Retrieved from http://www.cihr-irsc.gc.ca/

Canadian Institutes of Health Research, Natural Sciences and Engineering Research Council of Canada, and Social Sciences and Humanities Research Council of Canada. (2010). *Tri-Council policy statement: Ethical conduct for research involving humans*.

Canadian Medical Association (CMA). (2007). Euthanasia and assisted suicide (update 2007). Retrieved from http://policybase.cma.ca/dbtw-wpd/Policypdf/PD07-01.pdf

Canadian Mental Health Association (CMHA). (2010). Tip sheet for post-secondary students. Retrieved from http://acsm.ca

Canadian Mental Health Association (CAMH). (2012). Fast facts about mental illness. Retrieved on September 10, 2013 from http://www.cmha.ca/media/fast-facts-about-mental-illness/#.Ui83axYTu8o

Canadian Mental Health Association, Ontario. (2010). *Mental health and addictions issues for older adults: Opening the doors to a strategic framework*. Toronto: CMHA Ontario.

Canadian Midwifery Regulators Consortium. (2012). What is a Canadian registered midwife? Retrieved from http://cmrc-ccosf.ca/node/18

Canadian Nurses Association. (2009, June 10). *Federal contribution to reducing poverty in Canada*. Brief to the House of Commons Standing Committee on Human Resources, Skills and Scoial Development and the Status of Persons with Disabilities (HUMA). Ottawa.

Canadian Paediatric Society. (2003). Position statement: Adolescent pregnancy. Retrieved from http://www.cps.ca/documents/position/adolescent-pregnancy

Canadian Paediatric Society. (2012). Position statement: Gambling in children and adolescents. Retrieved from http://www.cps.ca/

Canadian Psychological Association. (2000). *Canadian Code of Ethics for Psychologists*, 3rd edition.

Canadian Public Health Association (CPHA). (2004). *Assessment toolkit for bullying: Harassment and peer relations at school: Definitions, Bullying, 2004*. Retrieved from http://www.cpha.ca

Canadian Teachers' Federation (CTF). (2009). Supporting education building Canada—Child poverty and schools. Retrieved from http://www.ctf-fce.ca/publications/Briefs/FINAL_Hilldayleavebehind_eng.pdf

Canadian Virtual Hospice. (2013). Canadian Virtual Hospice: Features and content. Retrieved from http://www.virtualhospice.ca/

Canfield, J., & Hansen, M. V. (1995). *A second helping of chicken soup for the soul*. Deerfield Beach, FL: Health Communications.

Canfield, R. L., & Haith, M. M. (1991). Young infants' visual expectations for symmetric and asymmetric stimulus sequences. *Developmental Psychology, 27*, 198–208.

Cansino, S. (2009). Episodic memory decay along the adult lifespan: A review of behavioral and neurophysiological evidence. *International Journal of Psychophysiology, 71,* 64–69.

Canterino, J. C., Ananth, C. V., Smulian, J., Harrigan, J. T., & Vintzileos, A. M. (2004). Maternal age and risk of fetal death in singleton gestation: United States, 1995–2000. *Obstetrics and Gynecology Survey, 59,* 649–650.

Cappeliez, P., & O'Rourke, N. (2006). Empirical validation of model of reminiscence and health in later life. *Journals of Gerontology B: Psychological and Social Sciences, 61,* P237–P244.

Cappeliez, P., O'Rourke, N., & Chaudhury, H. (2005). Functions of reminiscence and mental health in later life. *Aging and Mental Health, 9,* 295–301.

Capponi, P. (1997). *Dispatches from the poverty line.* Toronto: Penguin.

Cardini, F., et al. (2010). The use of complementary and alternative medicine by women experiencing menopausal symptoms in Bologna. *BMC Women's Health.*

Carolan, M., & Nelson, S. (2007). First mothering over 35 years: Questioning the association of maternal age and pregnancy risk. *Health Care for Women International, 28,* 534–555.

Carlson, S. M., & Zelazo, P. D. (2008). Symbolic thought. In M. M. Haith & J. B. Benson (Eds.), *Encyclopedia of infant and early childhood development.* Oxford, UK: Elsevier.

Carnagey, N. L., Anderson, C. A., & Bushman, B. J. (2007). The effect of video game violence on physiological desensitization to real-life violence. *Journal of Experimental Social Psychology, 43,* 489–496.

Carpendale, J., & Lewis, C. (2004). Constructing an understanding of mind: The development of children's social understanding within social interaction. *Behavioral and Brain Science, 27,* 79–96.

Carpendale, J., & Lewis, C. (2011). The development of social understanding: A relational perspective. In R.M. Lerner, W. F. Overton, A. M. Freund, & M. E. Lamb (Eds.), *Handbook of life-span development.* New York: Wiley.

Carpendale, J., Muller, U., & Bibok, M. B. (2008). Piaget's theory of cognitive development. In N. J. Salkind (Ed.), *Encyclopedia of educational psychology.* Thousand Oaks, CA: Sage.

Carrière, G. (2007). Hip fracture outcomes in the household population. *Health Reports, 18*(4), 37–42.

Carrington, N. A., & Bogetz, J. E. (2004). Normal grief and bereavement. *Journal of Palliative Medicine, 7,* 309–323.

Carroll, J. L. (2007). *Sexuality now* (2nd ed.). Belmont, CA: Wadsworth.

Carskadon, M. A. (2004). Sleep difficulties in young people. *Archives of Pediatrics and Adolescent Medicine, 158,* 597–598.

Carskadon, M. A. (2005). Sleep and circadian rhythms in children and adolescents: Relevance for athletic performance of young people. *Clinical Sports Medicine, 24,* 319–328.

Carskadon, M. A. (2006, March). *Too little, too late: Sleep bioregulatory processes across adolescence.* Paper presented at the meeting of the Society for Research on Adolescence, San Francisco.

Carstairs, S. (2010). Raising the bar: A roadmap for the future of palliative care in Canada.

Carstensen, L. L. (1998). A life-span approach to social motivation. In J. Heckhausen & C. Dweck (Eds.), *Motivation and self-regulation across the life span.* New York: Cambridge University Press.

Carstensen, L. L. (2006). The influence of a sense of time on human development. *Science, 312,* 1913–1915.

Carstensen, L. L. (2008, May). *Long life in the 21st century.* Paper presented at the meeting of the Association of Psychological Science, Chicago.

Carter, A. R., et al. (2010). Resting interhemispheric functional magnetic resonance imaging connectivity predicts performance after stroke. *Annals of Neurology, 67,* 365–375.

Carter, B., & McGoldrick, M. (2005). Overview: The expanded family life cycle, individual, family and social perspectives. In B. Carter & M. McGoldrick (Eds.). *The expanded family life cycle: Individual, family and social perspectives* (3rd ed.). Toronto: Pearson.

Carver, K., Joyner, K., & Udry, J. R. (2003). National estimates of romantic relationships. In P. Florsheim (Ed.), *Adolescent romantic relations and sexual behavior.* Mahwah, NJ: Erlbaum.

Carver, L. J., & Bauer, P. J. (2001). The dawning of a past: The emergence of long-term explicit memory in infancy. *Journal of Experimental Psychology: General, 130,* 726–745.

Carveth, D. (2006, October 22). *Sigmund Freud today: What are his enduring contributions?* Lecture presented to the Oraynu Congregation for Humanistic Judaism.

CASA. (2007, September). The importance of family dinners IV. Retrieved from http://www.casacolumbia.org/articlefiles/380-Importance%20of%20Family%20Dinners%20IV.pdf

Case, R., & Mueller, M. P. (2001). Differentiation, integration, and covariance mapping as fundamental processes in cognitive and neurological growth. In J. L. McClelland & R. S. Siegler (Eds.), *Mechanisms of cognitive development.* Mahwah, NJ: Erlbaum.

Casey, B. J., Getz, S., & Galvan, A. (2008). The adolescent brain. *Developmental Review, 28,* 42–77.

Casey, P. H. (2008). Growth of low birth weight preterm children. *Seminars in Perinatology, 32,* 20–27.

Cashman, K. D. (2008). Altered bone metabolism in inflammatory disease: Role for nutrition. *Proceedings of the Nutrition Society, 67,* 196–205.

Casper, L. M., & Bianchi, S. M. (2007). Cohabitation. In A. S. Skolnick & J. H. Skolnick (Eds.), *Family in transition* (14th ed.). Boston: Allyn & Bacon.

Caspers, K., et al. (2009). Association between the serotonin transporter polymorphism (5-HTTLPR) and adult unresolved attachment. *Developmental Psychology, 45,* 64–76.

Caspi, A. (1998). Personality development across the life course. In W. Damon (Ed.), *Handbook of child psychology* (Vol. 3). New York: Wiley.

Caspi, A., & Roberts, B. W. (2001). Personality development across the life course: The argument for change and continuity. *Psychological Inquiry, 12,* 49–66.

Caspi, A., & Shiner, R. L. (2006). Personality development. In W. Damon & R. Lerner (Eds.), *Handbook of child psychology* (6th ed.). New York: Wiley.

Cass, A. (2007). Routine activities and sexual assault: An analysis of individual- and school-level factors. *Journal of Violence and Victims, 22*(3), 350–364.

Cassidy, J. (2009). The nature of the child's ties. In J. Cassidy & P. R. Shaver (Eds.), *Handbook of attachment* (2nd ed.). New York: Guilford.

Cassidy, J., & Berlin, L. J. (1994). The insecure/ambivalent pattern of attachment: Theory and research. *Child Development, 65,* 971–991.

Cato, K. (2004, December 7). Learning lessons from Grenada. *Toronto Star,* p. A26.

Caulfield, R. A. (2001). *Infants and toddlers.* Upper Saddle River, NJ: Prentice Hall.

Cavanagh, S. E. (2004). The sexual debut of girls in early adolescence: The intersection of race, pubertal timing, and friendship group characteristics. *Journal of Research on Adolescence, 14,* 285–312.

CBC News. (2010, April 29). Omar Kadhr: Coming of age in a Guantanamo Bay jail cell. Retrieved from http://www.cbc.ca/world/story/2009/01/13/f-omar-khadr.html

CBC Newsworld. (2003). The life and times of Jean Chrétien. Canadian Broadcasting Corporation.

CBC Sports. (2010, February 26). IOC rep downplays women's hockey party; Hockey Canada apologizes for party on ice. Retrieved from http://www.cbc.ca/

Ceci, S. J. (2000). Bronfenbrenner, Urie. In A. Kazdin (Ed.), *Encyclopedia of psychology.* Washington, DC: American Psychological Association and Oxford University Press.

Ceci, S. J., & Gilstrap, L. L. (2000). Determinants of intelligence: Schooling and intelligence. In A. Kazdin (Ed.), *Encyclopedia of psychology.* Washington, DC: American Psychological Association and Oxford University Press.

Ceci, S. J., Kulkofsky, S., Klemfuss, J. Z., Sweeney, C. D., & Bruck, M. (2007). Unwarranted assumptions about children's testimonial accuracy. *Annual Review of Clinical Psychology, 3,* 311–328.

Census Shows New Face of the Canadian Family. (2012, September 19). *The Canadian Press.* Retrieved from http://www.cbc.ca/

Centers for Disease Control and Prevention (CDC). (2008). *National health interview study.* Atlanta: Author.

Centers for Disease Control and Prevention (CDC). (2011). Vital signs:

Teen pregnancy—United States 1991–2009, *Morbidity and Mortality Report Weekly Report, 60*(13), 414–420.

Central Intelligence Agency (CIA). (2010). Country comparison: Life expectancy at birth. *The world factbook.* Retrieved from https://www.cia.gov/

Centre for Addiction and Mental Health (CAMH). (2003). Press release: Ecstasy use down, cigarettes and LSD continue to decline, but heavy drinking remains a problem. Retrieved from http://www.camh.ca

Centre for Addiction and Mental Health (CAMH). (2011). Drug use among Ontario students, 1977–2011 (no. 33). Retrieved from http://www.camh.net

Centre for Addiction and Mental Health (CAMH). (2013). VISION 2020: Tomorrow. today. Retrieved from http://www.camh.ca/

Centre for Suicide Prevention. (2012). Teen suicide resource toolkit. Retrieved from http://www.suicideinfo.ca

Chalmers, B., & Wen, S. W. (2003). Perinatal care in Canada. In M. DesMeules & D. Stewart (Eds.), *Women's Health Surveillance Report.* Ottawa: Canadian Institute for Health Information. Retrieved from http://www.hc-sc.gc.ca/pphb-dgspsp/publicat/whsr-rssf/index.html

Chalmers, B., Kaczorowski, J., O'Brien, B., & Royle, C. (2012). *Birth, 39*(3), 203–210.

Chalmers, B., Levitt, C., Heaman, M., O'Brien, B., Sauve, R., & Kaczorowski, J. (2009). Breastfeeding rates and hospital feeding practices in Canada: A national survey of women. *Birth, 36*(2), 122–132.

Chambaere, K., Bilsen, J., Cohen, J., Onwuteake-Philipsen, B. D., Mortier, F., & Deliens, L. (2010). Physician-assisted deaths under the euthanasia law in Belgium: A population-based survey. *CMAJ* [online] doi:10.1503/cmaj.091876.

Chand, P., & Litvan, I. (2007). Parkinson's disease. In J. E. Birren (Ed.), *Encyclopedia of gerontology* (2nd ed.). San Diego: Academic Press.

Chandler, M., & LaLonde, C. (2008). Cultural continuity as a moderator of suicide risk among Canada's First Nations. In L. Kirmayer & G. Valaskakis (Eds.), *Healing traditions: The mental health of Aboriginal peoples in Canada* (pp. 221–248). Vancouver: UBC Press.

Chao, R., & Tseng, V. (2002). Parenting of Asians. In M. H. Bornstein (Series Ed.), *Handbook of parenting (vol. 4.): Social conditions and applied parenting* (2nd ed.). Mahwah, NJ: Erlbaum.

Chapman, T. (2009). Autism and its impact on child development. In R. E. Tremblay, R. deV Peters, M. Boivin, & R. G. Barr (Eds.), *Encyclopedia on early childhood development.* Montreal: Centre of Excellence for Early Childhood Development.

Charles, S. C., & Piazza, J. R. (2007). Memories of social interactions: Age differences in emotional intensity. *Psychology and Aging, 22,* 300–309.

Charles, S. T., & Carstensen, L. L. (2009). Socioemotional selectivity theory. In H. Reis & S. Specher (Eds.), *Encyclopedia of Human Relationships.* Thousand Oaks, CA: Sage.

Charles, S. T., & Carstensen, L. L. (2010). Social and emotional aging. *Annual Review of Psychology* (Vol. 61). Palo Alto, CA: Annual Reviews.

Charlton, R. A., Barrick, T. R., Lawes, N. C., Markus, H. S., & Morris, R. G. (2010). White matter pathways associated with working memory in normal aging. *Cortex, 46,* 474–489.

Charness, N., & Bosman, E. A. (1992). Human factors and aging. In F. I. M. Craik & T. A. Salthouse (Eds.), *The handbook of aging and cognition.* Hillsdale, NJ: Erlbaum.

Charpak, N., et al. (2005). Kangaroo mother care: 25 years after. *Acta Paediatrica, 94,* 514–522.

Chassin, L., Presson, C., Seo, D. C., Sherman, S. J., Macy, J., Wirth, R. J., et al. (2008). Multiple trajectories of cigarette smoking and the intergenerational transmission of smoking: A multigenerational, longitudinal study of a Midwestern community sample. *Health Psychology, 27,* 819–828.

Chatzimichael, A., Tsalkidis, A., Cassimos, D., Gardikis, S., Tripsianis, G., Defteros, S., et al. (2007). The role of breastfeeding and passive smoking on the development of severe bronchiolitis in infants. *Minerva Pediatrica, 59,* 199–206.

Chehab, O., Ouertani, M., Souiden, Y., Chaieb, K., & Mahdouani, K. (2008). Plasma antioxidants and human aging: A study on healthy elderly Tunisian population. *Molecular Biotechnology.*

Chen, X., et al. (2009). Interactions of IL-12A and IL-12B polymorphisms on the risk of cervical cancer in Chinese women. *Clinical Cancer Research, 15,* 400–405.

Chen, X., DeSouza, A. T., Chen, H., & Wang, L. (2006). Reticent behaviour and experiences in peer inteactions in Chinese and Canadian children. *Developmental Psychology, 42,* 656–665.

Chen, X., Hastings, P. D., Rubin, K. H., Chen, H., Cen, G., & Stewart, S. L. (1998). Child-rearing attitudes and behavioral inhibition in Chinese and Canadian toddlers: A cross-cultural study. *Developmental Psychology, 34,* 677–686.

Chen, X. K., Wen, S. W., Yang, Q., & Walker, M. C. (2007). Adequacy of prenatal care and neonatal mortality in infants born to mothers with and without antenatal high-risk conditions. *Australian and New Zealand Journal of Obstetrics and Gynecology, 47,* 122–127.

Chen, Z., & Siegler, R. E. (2000). Across the great divide: Bridging the gap between understanding of toddlers' and older children's thinking. *Monograph of the Society for Research in Child Development, 65*(2).

Cheng, M. H., Lee, S. J., Wang, S. J., Wang, P. H., & Fuh, J. L. (2007). Does menopausal transition affect the quality of life? A longitudinal study of middle-aged women in Kinmen. *Menopause, 14,* 885–890.

Cherkas, L. F., et al. (2008). The association between physical activity in leisure time and leukocyte telomore length. *Archives of Internal Medicine, 168,* 154–158.

Cherlin, A. J. (2007). The deinstitutionalization of marriage. In S. J. Ferguson (Ed.), *Shifting the center: Understanding contemporary families* (3rd ed.). New York: McGraw-Hill.

Cherniack, N. S., & Cherniack, E. P. (2007). Respiratory system. In J. E. Birren (Ed.), *Encyclopedia of gerontology* (2nd ed.). San Diego: Academic Press.

Cherry, K. (2012). Emotional intelligence? Definitions, history, and measures of intelligence. About.com/Psychology. Retrieved from http://psychology.about.com/od/personalitydevelopment/a/emotionalintell.htm

Chess, S., & Thomas, A. (1977). Temperamental individuality from childhood to adolescence. *Journal of Child Psychiatry, 16,* 218–226.

Chess, S., & Thomas, A. (1987). *Origins and evolution of behavior disorders.* Cambridge, MA: Harvard University Press.

Cheung, Y. T., Chau, P. H., & Yip, P. S. (2008). A revisit of older adults' suicides and severe acute respiratory syndrome (SARS) epidemic in Hong Kong. *International Journal of Psychiatry.*

Chevret-Measson, M., Lavallee, E., Troy, S., Arnould, B., Oudin, S., & Cuzin, B. (2009). Improvement in quality of sexual life in female partners of men with erectile dysfunction treated with sildenafil citrate: Findings of the Index of Sexual Life (ISL) in a couple study. *Journal of Sexual Medicine, 6,* 761–769.

Chi, M. T. (1978). Knowledge structures and memory development. In R. S. Siegler (Ed.), *Children's thinking: What develops?* Hillsdale, NJ: Erlbaum.

Chia, P., Sellick, K., & Gan, S. (2006). The attitudes and practices of neonatal nurses in the use of kangaroo care. *Australian Journal of Advanced Nursing, 23,* 20–27.

Chiang, K. J., et al. (2010). The effects of reminiscence therapy on psychological well-being, depression, and loneliness among the institutionalized aged. *International Journal of Geriatric Psychiatry, 25,* 380–388.

Chida, Y., & Steptoe, A. (2008). Positive psychological well-being and mortality: A quantitative review of prospective observational studies. *Psychosomatic Medicine, 70,* 741–756.

Chief Public Health Officer. (2009). *Report on the state of public health in Canada, 2009: Growing up well—Priorities for a healthy future.* Ottawa: Ministry of Public Health. Retrieved from http://publichealth.gc.ca/CPHOreport

Child Welfare Information Gateway. (2009). Understanding the effects of maltreatment on brain development. Retrieved from http://www.childtrauma.org.

Chiu, M. M. (2007). Families, economies, cultures, and science achievement in 41 countries: Country-, school-, and student-level analyses. *Journal of Family Psychology, 21,* 510–519.

Chochinov, H. (2007). Dignity and the essence of medicine: The A, B, C, and D of dignity conserving care. *British Medical Journal, 335,* 184–187.

Chodosh, J., Kado, D. M., Seeman, T. E., & Karlamangla, A. S. (2007). Depressive symptoms as a predictor of cognitive decline: MacArthur Studies of Successful Aging. *American Journal of Geriatric Psychiatry, 15,* 406–415.

Choi, N. G., & Jun, J. (2009). Life regrets and pride among low-income older adults: Relationships with depressive symptoms, current life stressors, and coping resources. *Aging and Mental Health, 13,* 213–225.

Chomsky, N. (1957). *Syntactic structures.* The Hague: Mouton.

Chow, J., Ateah, C., Scott, S., Ricci, S., & Kyle, T. (2013). *Canadian maternity and pediatric nursing.* Philadelphia: Lippincott Williams & Wilkins.

Christie, J. F., Vukelich, C., & Enz, B. J. (2007). *Teaching language and literacy.* Boston: Allyn & Bacon.

Christofides, A., Schauer, C., & Zlotkin, S. H. (2005). Iron deficiency and anemia prevalence and associated etiologic factors in First nations and Inuit communities in northern Ontario and Nunavut. *Canadian Journal of Public Health, 96,* 304–307.

Chuang, S., & Canadian Immigrant Settlement Sector Alliance (CISSA-ACSEI). (2010). New start for youth study: An examination of the settlement pathways of newcomer youth. CISSA-ACSEI. Toronto: Lexington Books

Chuang, S. S., Rasmi, S., & Friesen, C. (2011). Service providers' perspectives on the pathways of adjustment for newcomer children and youth in Canada. In S. S. Chuang & R. P. Moreno (Eds.), *Immigrant children: Change, adaptation, and cultural transformation* (pp. 149–170). Lanham, MD: Lexington Books.

CIA World Factbook. (2012). Retrieved from https://www.cia.gov/library/publications/the-world-factbook/geos/ca.html

Cicchetti, D. (2011). Developmental psychopathology. In R. M. Lerner, W. F. Overton, A. M. Freund, & M. E. Lamb (Eds.), *Handbook of life-span development.* New York: Wiley.

Cicchetti, D., & Toth, S. L. (2006). Developmental psychopathology and preventive intervention. In W. Damon & R. Lerner (Eds.), *Handbook of child psychology* (6th ed.). New York: Wiley.

Cicchetti, D., & Toth, S. L. (2011). Child maltreatment: The research imperative and the exploration of results to clinical contexts. In B. Lester & J. D. Sparrow (Eds.), *Nurturing children and families.* New York: Wiley.

Cicchetti, D., Rogosch, F. A., Gunnar, M. R., & Toth, S. L. (2010). The differential impacts of physical and sexual abuse and internalizing problems on daytime cortisol rhythm in school-aged children. *Child Development, 81,* 252–269.

Cicchetti, D., Toth, S. L. & Rogosch, F. A. (2005). A prevention program for child maltreatment. Unpublished manuscript. University of Rochester, Rochester, N.Y.

Cicirelli, V. (2001). Personal meanings of death in older adults and young adults in relations to their fears of death. *Death Studies, 25,* 663–683.

Cicirelli, V. (2006). Fear of death in mid-old age. *Journals of Gerontology: Series B: Psychological and Social Sciences, 61*(B), 75–81.

Cicirelli, V. G. (1991). Sibling relationships in adulthood. *Marriage and Family Review, 16,* 291–310.

CIHR (Canadian Institutes of Health Research). (2012). *Canadian bullying statistics.* Retrieved from http://www.cihr-irsc.gc.ca/

Cillessen, A. H. N. (2009). Sociometric methods. In K. H. Rubin, W. M. Bukowski, & B. Laursen (Eds.), *Handbook of peer interactions, relationships, and groups.* New York: Guilford.

Cimarolli, V. R. (2009). Sensory impairments. In D. Carr (Ed.), *Encyclopedia of the life course and human development.* Boston: Gale Cengage.

Clark W., & Schellenberg, G. (2006). Who's religious? Statistics Canada. Retrieved from http://www.statcan.gc.ca/pub/11-008-x/2006001/9181-eng.htm

Clark, D. J., Patten, C., Reid, K. F., Carabello, R. J., Phillips, E. M., & Fielding, R. A. (2010, in press). Impaired voluntary neuromuscular activation limits muscle power in mobility-limited older adults. *Journal of Gerontology A: Biological Sciences and Medical Sciences, 65*(5), 495–502.

Clark, E. (1993). *The lexicon in acquisition.* New York: Cambridge University Press.

Clark, J. (2011). Will the Hayflick limit keep us from living forever? How stuff works. Retrieved from http://science.howstuffworks.com/life/genetic/hayflick-limit.htm

Clark, M. D., & Carroll, M. H. (2008). Acquaintance rape scripts of women and men: Similarities and differences. *Sex Roles, 58,* 616–625.

Clark, M., Riben, P., & Nowgesic, E. (2002). The association of housing density, isolation and tuberculosis in Canadian First Nations communities. *International Journal of Epidemiology, 31,* 940–945.

Clark, W. (2005).What do seniors spend on housing? *Canadian Social Trends, 85*(Autumn), 2–7.

Clark, W. (2009). *Delayed transitions of young adults.* Ottawa: Statistics Canada.

Clark, W., & Schellenberg, G. (2006). Who's religious? *Canadian Social Trends, 81,* 2–9.

Clarke, B. (2009). Friends forever: How young adolescents use social-networking sites. *Society Online, 24*(6), 22–26.

Clarke-Stewart, A. K., & Miner, J. L. (2008). Child and day care, effects of. In M. M. Haith & J. B. Benson (Eds.), *Encyclopedia of infant and early childhood development.* Oxford, UK: Elsevier.

Clausen, J. A. (1993). *American lives.* New York: Free Press.

Claxton, L. J., Keen, R., & McCarty, M. E. (2003). Evidence of motor planning in infant reaching behavior. *Psychological Science, 14,* 354–356.

Clayson, M. (2007). Cigarette smoking and the effects on children. *Ezine Articles.* Retrieved from http://ezinearticles.com/?Cigarette-Smoking-and-the-Effects-on-Children&id=464003

Clements, M., Stanley, S., & Markman, H. (2004). Before they said "I do": Discriminating among marital outcomes over 13 years. *Journal of Personality and Social Psychology, 66,* 613–626.

Cleveland, L., Minter, M., Cobb, K., Scott, A., & German, V. (2008). Lead hazards for pregnant women and children: Part 2. *American Journal of Nursing, 108*(11), 40–47.

Coats, A., & Blanchard-Fields, F. (2008). Emotion regulation in interpersonal problems: The role of cognitive-emotional complexity, emotion regulation goals, and expressivity. *Psychology and Aging, 23,* 39–51.

Cochran, S. D., & Mays, V. M. (1990). Sex, lies, and HIV. *New England Journal of Medicine, 322*(11), 774–775.

Cohen, D., & Belsky, J. (2008). Avoidant romantic attachment and female orgasm: Testing an emotion-regulation hypothesis. *Attachment and Human Development, 10,* 1–10.

Cohen, F., Kemeny, M. E., Zegans, L. S., Johnson, P., Kearney, K. A., & Stites, D. P. (2007). Immune function declines with unemployment and recovers after stressor termination. *Psychosomatic Medicine, 69,* 225–234.

Cohen, J., Wilson, D., Thurston, A., Macleod, R. & Deliens, L. (2011). Access to palliative care services in hospital a matter of being in the right hospital: Hospital charts study in a Canadian city. *Palliative Medicine, 26*(1), 89–94.

Cohen, L. B., & Cashon, C. H. (2003). Infant perception and cognition. In I. B. Weiner (Ed.), *Handbook of psychology* (Vol. VI). New York: Wiley.

Coie, J. (2004). The impact of negative social experiences on the development of antisocial behavior. In J. B. Kupersmidt & K. A. Dodge (Eds.), *Children's peer relations: From development to intervention.* Washington, DC: American Psychological Association.

Coker, R. H., Williams, R. H., Kortebein, P. M., Sullivan, D. H., & Evans, W. J. (2009). Influence of exercise intensity on abdominal fat and adiponectin in elderly adults. *Metabolic Syndrome and Related Disorders, 94,* 4258–4266.

Colby, A., Kohlberg, L., Gibbs, J., & Lieberman, M. (1983). A longitudinal study of moral judgment. *Monographs of the Society for Research in Child Development* (Serial No. 201).

Colcombe, S. J., Erickson, K. I., Scalf, P. E., Kim, J. S., Prakash, R., McAuely, E., et al. (2006). Aerobic exercise training increase brain volume in aging humans. *Journals of Gerontology A: Medical Sciences, 61,* 1166–1170.

Cole, M. (2006). Culture and cognitive development in phylogenetic, histroical, and ontogenetic perspective. In W. Damon & R. Lerner (Eds.), *Handbook of child psychology* (6th ed.). New York: Wiley.

Cole, M., & Gajdamaschko, N. (2007). Vygotsky and culture. In H. Daniels, J. Wertsch, & M. Cole (Eds.), *The Cambridge companion to Vygotsky*. New York: Cambridge University Press.

Cole, P. M., Dennis, T. A., Smith-Simon, K. E., & Cohen, L. H. (2009). Preschoolers' emotion regulation strategy understanding: Relations with emotion socialization and child self-regulation. *Social Development, 18*(2), 324–352.

Coleman, M., Ganong, L., & Fine, M. (2004). Communication in stepfamilies. In A. L. Vangelisti (Ed.), *Handbook of family communication*. Mahwah, NJ: Erlbaum.

Coleman, P. D. (1986, August). *Regulation of dendritic extent: Human aging brain and Alzheimer's disease*. Paper presented at the meeting of the American Psychological Association, Washington, DC.

Coleman, P. G., & Podolskij, A. (2007). Identity loss and recovery in the life stories of Soviet World War II veterans. *Gerontologist, 47*, 52–60.

Collaku, A., Rankinen, T., Rice, T., Leon, A. S., Rao, D. C., Skinner, J. S., et al. (2004). A genome-wide linkage scan for dietary energy and nutrient intakes. *American Journal of Clinical Nutrition, 79*, 881–886.

Collier, R. (2011). Access to palliative care varies widely across Canada. *Canadian Medical Association Journal, 183*(2), E87–E88.

Collins, R. L., Elliott, M. N., Berry, S. H., Kanocouse, D. E., Kunkel, D., Hunter, S. B., et al. (2004). Watching sex on television predicts adolescent initiation of sexual behavior. *Pediatrics, 114*, e280–e289.

Collins, W. A., & Steinberg, L. (2006). Adolescent development in interpersonal context. In W. Damon & R. Lerner (Eds.), *Handbook of child psychology* (6th ed.). New York: Wiley.

Collins, W. A., & van Dulmen, M. (2006). The significance of middle childhood peer competence for work and relationships in early childhood. In A. C. Huston & M. N. Ripke (Eds.), *Developmental contexts in middle childhood*. New York: Cambridge University Press.

Coloroso, B. (2003). *The bully, the bullied, and the bystander*. Toronto: HarperCollins.

Coltrane, S. L., Parke, R. D., Schofield, T. J., Tsuha, S. J., Chavez, M., & Lio, S. (2008). Mexican American families and poverty. In D. R. Crane & T. B. Heaton (Eds.), *Handbook of families and poverty*. Thousand Oaks, CA: Sage.

Combs, M. (2006). *Readers and writers in the primary grades* (3rd ed.). Upper Saddle River, NJ: Prentice Hall.

Combs, M. (2010). *Readers and writers in the primary grades*. Boston: Allyn & Bacon.

Committee on Hospital care and Institute for Patient and Family-Centred Care. (2012). Patient and family-centred care and the pediatrician's role. *Pediatrics, 129*, 394–404.

Commodari, E., & Guarnera, M. (2008). Attention and aging. *Aging: Clinical and Experimental Research, 20*, 578–584.

Commoner, B. (2002). Unraveling the DNA myth: The spurious foundation of genetic engineering. *Harper's Magazine, 304*, 39–47.

Commons, M. L., & Bresette, L. M. (2006). Illuminating major creative scientific innovators with postformal stages. In C. Hoare (Ed.), *Handbook of adult development and learning*. New York: Oxford University Press.

Comstock, G., & Scharrer, E. (2006). Media and popular culture. In W. Damon & R. Lerner (Eds.), *Handbook of child psychology* (6th ed.). New York: Wiley.

Conference Board of Canada. (2013). Elderly poverty. Retrieved from http://www.conferenceboard.ca/hcp/details/society/elderly-poverty.aspx

Conn, D. (2003). Submission to the Standing Committee on Social Affairs, Science and Technology: Mental Health and Mental Illness: Seniors Roundtable June 4, 2003. Retrieved from http://www.ccsmh.ca/

Conn, D., et al. (2006). National guidelines for seniors' mental health: Introduction and project background. *The Canadian Journal of Geriatrics, 9*(supplement 2), S36–S41.

Connolly, J. A., & McIsaac, C. (2009). Romantic relationships in adolescence. In R. Lerner & L. Steinberg (Eds.), *Handbook of adolescent psychology* (3rd ed.). New Jersey: Wiley.

Connor, S. (2009, April). Fertility expert: "I can clone a human being." Controversial doctor filmed creating embryos before injecting them into wombs of women wanting cloned babies. Retrieved from http://www.independent.co.uk/news/science/fertility-expert-i-can-clone-a-human-being-1672095.html

Contemporary Research Press. (1993). *American working women: A statistical handbook*. Dallas: Author.

Contestabile, A. (2009). Benefits of caloric restriction on brain aging and related pathological states: Understanding mechanisms to devise novel therapies. *Current Medicinal Chemistry, 16*, 350–361

Conway, K. P., Swendsen, J. D., & Merikangas, K. R. (2003). Alcohol expectancies, alcohol consumption, and problem drinking: The moderating role of family history. *Addictive Behaviors, 28*, 823–836.

Conway, K. S., & Kutinova, A. (2006). Maternal health: Does prenatal care make a difference? *Health Economics, 15*, 461–488.

Cook, T. (2004). The Battle of Vimy Ridge, 9–12 April 1917. Canadian War Museum. Retrieved from http://www.warmuseum.ca/cwm/exhibitions/vimy/index_e.shtml

Cook, T. D., Deng, Y., & Morgano, E. (2007). Friendship influences during early adolescence: The special role of friends' grade point average. *Journal of Research on Adolescence, 17*, 325–356.

Cooper, A. R., & Moley, K. H. (2008). Maternal tobacco use and its preimplantation effects on fertility: More reasons to stop smoking. *Seminars in Reproductive Medicine, 26*, 204–212.

Cooper, C. R., & Grotevant, H. D. (1989, April). *Individuality and connectedness in the family and adolescent's self and relational competence*. Paper presented at the meeting of the Society for Research in Child Development, Kansas City.

Cooper, C. R., Behrens, R., & Trinh, N. (2008). Identity development. In R. A. Shweder, T. R. Bidell, A. C. Daily, S. D. Dixon, P. J. Miller, & J. Model (Eds.), *The Chicago companion to the child*. Chicago: University of Chicago Press.

Cooper, R., Mishra, G., Clennell, S., Guralnik, J., & Kuh, D. (2008). Menopausal status and physical performance in midlife: Findings from a British cohort study. *Menopause, 15*, 1079–1085.

Cope, M., & Allison, D. (2008). Critical review of the World Health Organization's 2007 report on "evidence of the long-term effects of breastfeeding: Systematic reviews and meta-analysis" with respect to obesity. *Obesity Reviews, 9*, 594–605.

Coplan, R. J., & Armer, M. (2005). Talking yourself out of being shy: Shyness, expressive vocabulary, and socioemotional adjustment in preschool. *Merrill-Palmer Quarterly, 51*, 20–41.

Coplan, R. J., Prakash, K., O'Neil, K., & Armer, M. (2004). Do you "want" to play? Distinguishing between conflicted shyness and social disinterest in early childhood. *Developmental Psychology, 40*(2), 244–258.

Corbin, C. B., Welk, G. J., Corbin, W. R., & Welk, K. A. (2008). *Concepts of physical fitness* (14th ed.). New York: McGraw-Hill.

Cordier, S. (2008). Evidence for a role of paternal exposure in developmental toxicity. *Basic and Clinical Pharmacology and Toxicology, 102*, 176–181.

Cornelius, J. R., Clark, D. B., Reynolds, M., Kirisci, L., & Tarter, R. (2007). Early age of first sexual intercourse and affiliation with deviant peers predict development of SUD: A prospective longitudinal study. *Addictive Behavior, 32*, 850–854.

Cornwell, B., Laumann, E. O., & Schumm, L. P. (2008). The social connectedness of older adults: A national profile. *American Sociological Review, 73*, 185–203.

Corona, G., et al. (2009). The age-related decline of testosterone is associated with different specific symptoms and signs in patients with sexual dysfunction. *International Journal of Andrology, 32*, 720–728.

Corsini, R. (1999). *The dictionary of psychology*. Philadelphia: Brunner/Mazel.

Corso, J. F. (1977). Auditory perception and communication. In J. E. Birren & K. W. Schaie (Eds.), *Handbook of the psychology of aging* (2nd ed.). New York: Van Nostrand Reinhold.

Cosmides, L. (2011). Evolutionary psychology. *Annual Review of Psychology* (Vol. 62). Palo Alto, CA: Annual Reviews.

Costa, P. T., & McCrae, R. R. (1995). Solid ground on the wetlands of personality: A reply to Black. *Psychological Bulletin, 117*, 216–220.

Costa, P. T., Jr., & McCrae, R. R. (2000). Contemporary personality psychology. In C. E. Coffey & J. L. Cummings (Eds.). *Textbook of geriatric neuropsychiatry*. Washington, DC: American Psychiatric Press.

Costa, R., & Figueiredo, B. (2011). Infant's psychophysiological profile and temperament at 3 and 12 months. *Infant Behavior & Development, 34*, 270–279.

Costanzo, M., et al. (2010). The genetic landscape of a cell. *Science, 327*, 425–431.

Cote, J. (2009). Identity formation and self development in adolescence. In R. M. Lerner & L. Steinberg (Eds.), *Handbook of adolescence psychology* (2nd ed.) (pp. 260–234). New York: Wiley.

Cote, J. E. (2006). Emerging adulthood as an institutionalized moratorium: Risks and benefits to identity formation. In J. J. Arnett & J. L. Tanner (Eds.), *Emerging adults in America*. Washington, DC: American Psychological Association.

Côté, S. M., Boivin, M., Nagin, D. S., Japel, C., Xu, Q., Zoccolillo, M., et al. (2007). The role of maternal education and nonmaternal care services in the provision of children's physical aggression problems. *Archives of General Psychiatry, 64*(11), 1305–1312.

Cotton, S., Zebracki, M. A., Rosenthal, S. L., Tsevat, J., & Drotar, D. (2006). Religion/spirituality and adolescent health outcomes: A review. *Journal of Adolescent Health, 38*, 472–480.

Council of Ministers of Education Canada (CMEC). (2003). Canadian youth sexual health & HIV/AIDS study: Factors influencing knowledge, attitudes and behaviours. Retrieved from http://www.cmec.ca/

Courage, M. L., & Richards, J. E. (2008). Attention. In M. M. Haith & J. B. Benson (Eds.), *Encyclopedia of infant and early childhood development*. Oxford, UK: Elsevier.

Courage, M. L., Reynolds, G. D., & Richards, J. E. (2006). Infants' attention to patterned stimuli: Developmental changes from 3 to 12 months of age. *Child Development, 77*(3), 680–695.

Courtin, C. (2000). The impact of sign language on the cognitive development of deaf children: The case of theories of mind. *Journal of Deaf Studies and Deaf Education, 5*, 201–219.

Cowan, C. P., & Cowan, P. A. (2000). *When partners become parents*. Mahwah, NJ: Erlbaum.

Cowan, P., Cowan, C., Ablow, J., Johnson, V. K., & Measelle, J. (2005). *The family context of parenting in children's adaptation to elementaly school*. Mahwah, NJ: Lawrence Erlbaum Associates.

Cox, J. (2006). Postnatal depression in fathers. *Lancet, 366*, 982.

Cox, M., Garrett, E., & Graham, J. (2004–2005). Death in Disney films: Implications for children's understanding of death. *Omega—Journal of Death and Dying, 50*(4), 267–280.

Craft, S. (2009). The role of metabolic disorders in Alzheimer disease and vascular dementia:

Two roads converged. *Archives of Neurology, 66*, 300–305.

Craik, F.I.M., Bialystok, E., & Freedman, M. (2010, November 9). Delaying the onset of Alzheimer disease—Bilingualism as a form of cognitive reserve. *Neurology, 75*(19), 1726–1729.

Crane, J. D., Devries, M. C., Safdar, A., Hamadeh, M. J., & Tarnopolsky, M. A. (2010). The effect of aging on human skeletal muscle mitochondrial and intramyocellular lipid ultrastructure. *Journal of Gerontology: Biological Sciences and Medical Sciences, 65*(A), 119–128.

Cranswick, K., & Dosman, D. (2008). Eldercare: What we know today. *Canadian Social Trends, 90*(Autumn), 48–56.

Crawford, A. (2013, March 9). How 20 years has changed the debate over assisted suicide. CBC News Politics. Retrieved from http://www.cbc.ca/

Crawford, C. (2008, March). *No place like home: A report on the housing needs of people with intellectual disabilities*. Canadian Association for Community Living. Retrieved from http://www.communitylivingbc.ca/wp-content/uploads/NoPlaceLikeHome.pdf

Cresci, M. K., Yarandi, H. N., & Morrell, R. W. (2010). The digital divide and urban older adults. *Computers, Informatics, Nursing, 28*, 88–94.

Creswell, J. W. (2008). *Educational research* (3rd ed.). Upper Saddle River, NJ: Prentice Hall.

Crick, N. R., Murray-Close, D., Marks, P. E. L., & Mohajeri-Nelson, N. (2009). Aggression and peer relationships in school-age children: Relational and physical aggression in group and dyadic contexts. In K. H. Rubin, W. M. Bukowski, & B. Laursen (Eds.), *Handbook of peer interactions, relationships, and groups*. New York: Guilford.

Crocetti, E., Rubini, M., Luyckx, K., & Meeus, W. (2008). Identity formation in early and middle adolescents from various ethinic groups: From three dimensions to five statuses. *Journal of Youth and Adolescence, 37*, 983–996.

Crocker, B., et al. (2011). Very high vitamin D supplementation rates among infants aged 2 months in Vancouver and Richmond, British Columbia, Canada. *BMC Public Health, 11*, 1–8.

Crompton, S., & Keown, L. (2009, Winter). Do parental benefits influence fertility decisions? *Canadian Social Trends, 88*, 46–53.

Crone, E. A., et al. (2009). Neurocognitive development of relational reasoning. *Developmental Science, 12*, 55–66.

Crosnoe, R., Riegle-Crumb, C., Field, S., Frank, K., & Muller, C. (2008). Peer group contexts of girls' and boys' academic experiences. *Child Development, 79*, 139–155.

Crouter, A. C. (2006). Mothers and fathers at work. In A. Clarke-Stewart & J. Dunn (Eds.), *Families count*. New York: Cambridge University Press.

Crowell, J. A., Treboux, D., & Brockmeyer, S. (2009). Parental

divorce and adult children's attachment representations and marital status. *Attachment and Human Development, 11*, 87–101.

Crowell, J. A., Treboux, D., Gao, Y., Fyffe, C., Pan, H., & Water, E. (2002). Assessing secure base behavior in adulthood: Development of a measure, links to adult attachment representations, and relations to couples' communication and reports of relationships. *Developmental Psychology, 38*, 679–693.

Crowley, K., Callahan, M. A., Tenenbaum, H. R., & Allen, E. (2001). Parents explain more to boys than to girls during shared scientific thinking. *Psychological Science, 12*, 258–261.

Croyle, R. T. (2000). Genetic counseling. In A. Kazdin (Ed.), *Encyclopedia of psychology*. Washington, DC: American Psychological Association and Oxford University Press.

CSEP. (2012). Canadian physical activity guidelines. Retrieved from http://www.csep.ca/

Csikszentmihalyi, M. (1995). *Creativity*. New York: HarperCollins.

Csikszentmihalyi, M. (1997). *Finding flow*. New York: Basic Books.

Csikszentmihalyi, M. (2000). Creativity: An overview. In A. Kazdin (Ed.), *Encyclopedia of psychology*. Washington, DC: American Psychological Association and Oxford University Press.

Cuevas, K., Rovee-Collier, C., & Learmonth, A. (2006). Infants form associations between memory representatives of stimuli that are absent. *Psychological Science, 17*, 543–549.

Cunningham, J. N., Kliwer, W., & Garner, P. W. (2009). Emotion socialization, child emotion understanding and regulation, and adjustment in urban African American families: Differential associations across child gender. *Development and Psychopathology, 21*, 261–283.

Cunningham, P. M., & Hall, D. P. (2009). *Making words first grade*. Boston: Allyn & Bacon.

Cunningham, W., & Hyson, D. (2006). The skinny on high-protein, low-carbohydrate diets. *Preventive Cardiology, 9*, 166–171.

Curran, K., Ducette, J., Eisenstein, J., & Hyman, I. A. (2001, August). *Statistical analysis of the cross-cultural data: The third year*. Paper presented at the meeting of the American Psychological Association, San Francisco.

Currier, J. M., Holland, J. M., & Neimeyer, R. A. (2006). Sense-making, grief, and the experience of violent loss: Toward a mediational model. *Death Studies, 30*, 403–428.

Curry, B., & Friesen, J. (2012, August 23). Low-income seniors threatened by changes to federal income support. *The Globe and Mail*. Retrieved from http://www.theglobeandmail.com/news/politics/low-income-seniors-threatened-by-changes-to-federal-income-support/article1315681/

Cutler, S. J. (2006). Technological change and aging. In R. H. Binstock & L. K. George (Eds.), *Handbook of aging and the social sciences* (6th ed.). San Diego: Academic Press.

Cutler, S. J. (2009). Media and technology use, later life. In D. Carr (Ed.), *Encyclopedia of the life course and human development*. Boston: Gale Cengage.

Cuzon, V. C., Yeh, P. W., Yanagawa, Y., Obata, K., & Yeh, H. H. (2008). Ethanol consumption during early pregnancy alters the disposition of tangentially migrating GAB Aergic interneurons in the fetal cortex. *Journal of Neuroscience, 28*, 1854–1864.

D

D'Entremont, B., & Hartung, C. (2003). A longitudinal investigation of joint attention, emotion regulation and attachment. Poster presentation at the Society for Research in Child Development, Tampa, FL.

Daaleman, T. P., Perera, S., & Studenski, S. A. (2004). Religion, spirituality, and health status in geriatric outpatients. *Annals of Family Medicine, 2*, 49–53.

Daddis, C. (2010). Adolescent peer crowds and patterns of belief in the boundaries of personal authority. *Journal of Adolescence, 33*, 699–708.

Dahl, R. E. (2004). Adolescent brain development: A period of vulnerabilities and opportunities. *Annals of the New York Academy of Sciences, 1021*, 1–22.

Dahle, C. L., Jacobs, B. S., & Raz, N. (2009). Aging, vascular risk, and cognition: Blood glucose, pulse pressure, and cognitive performance in healthy adults. *Psychology and Aging, 24*, 154–162.

Dainkeh, S. (2010, May). Interview.

Dakin, E., & Pearlmutter, S. (2009). Older women's perceptions of elder maltreatment and ethical dilemmas in adult protective services: A cross-cultural, exploratory study. *Journal of Elder Abuse and Neglect, 21*, 15–57.

Daley, A. J., Macarthur, C., & Winter, H. (2007). The role of exercise in treating postpartum depression: A review of the literature. *Journal of Midwifery & Women's Health, 52*, 56–62.

Daley, T. C., Whaley, S. E., Sigman, M. D., Espinosa, M. P., & Neumann, C. (2003). IQ on the rise: The Flynn effect in rural Kenyan children. *Psychological Science, 14*, 215–219.

Dalton, T. C., & Bergen, V. W. (2007). *Early experience, the brain, and consciousness*. Mahwah, NJ: Erlbaum.

Daltro, P., et al. (2010). Congenital chest malformations: A multimodality approach with emphasis on fetal MRI imaging. *Radiographics, 30*, 385–395.

The DANA Foundation. (2012) Brain Awareness Week. Retrieved from (http://dana.org/news/ Retrieved on Sept. 8, 2012.

Daniels, H. (2007). Pedagogy. In H. Daniels, J. Wertsch, & M. Cole (Eds.), *The Cambridge companion to Vygotsky*. New York: Cambridge University Press.

Danigelis, N. L. (2007). Leisure. In J. E. Birren (Ed.), *Encyclopedia of gerontology* (2nd ed.). San Diego: Academic Press.

Danne, T., & Becker, D. (2007). Pediatric diabetes: Achieving practical, effective insulin therapy in type 1 and 2 diabetes. *Acta Pediatrica, 96*, 1560–1570.

Danner D., Snowdon D., & Friesen W. (2001). Positive emotions in early life and longevity: Findings from the Nun Study. *Journal of Personality and Social Psychology, 80*(5), 814–813.

Darling-Hammond, L., & Bransford, J. (with LePage, P., Hammerness, K., & Duffy, H.). (2005). *Preparing teachers for a changing world: What teachers should learn and be able to do.* San Francisco: Jossey-Bass.

Darrah, J., Senthilselvan, A., & Magill-Evans, J. (2009). Trajectories of serial motor scores of typically developing children: Implications for clinical decision making. *Infant Behavior and Development, 32*, 72–78.

Das, A. (2008). Sexual harassment at work in the United States. *Archives of Sexual Behavior, 38*, 909–921.

Das, D. K., Mukherjee, S., & Ray, D. (2010). Resveratrol and red wine, healthy heart and longevity. *Heart Failure Reviews, 15*(5), 467–477.

Das, S., & O'Keefe, J. H. (2006). Behavioral cardiology: Recognizing and addressing the profound impact of psychosocial stress on cardiovascular health. *Current Atherosclerosis Reports, 8*, 111–118.

Daselaar, S. M., Rice, H. J., Greenberg, D. L., Cabeza, R., LaBar, K. S., & Rubin, D. C. (2008). The spatiotemporal dynamics of autobiographical memory: Neural correlates of recall, emotional intensity, and reliving. *Cerebral Cortex, 18*, 217–229.

Daubenmier, J. J., Weidner, G., Sumner, M. D., Mendell, N., Merritt-Worden, T., Studley, J., et al. (2007). The contribution of changes in diet, exercise, and stress management to changes in coronary risk in women and men in the multisite cardiac lifestyle intervention program. *Annals of Behavior Medicine, 33*, 57–68.

Daulatzai, M. A. (2010). Early stages of pathogenesis in memory impairment during normal senescence and Alzheimer's disease. *Journal of Alzheimer's Disease, 20*(2), 355–367.

Davey, A., Tucker, C. J., Fingerman, K. L., & Savla, J. (2009). Within-family variability in representations of past relationships with parents. *Journals of Gerontology: Social Sciences, 69*, 125–136.

Davidson, J. R. (2010). Major depressive disorder treatment guidelines in America and Europe. *Journal of Clinical Psychiatry, 71* (Suppl. E1), E04.

Davidson, M. R., London, M. L., & Ladewig, P. A. (2008). *Olds' maternal-newborn nursing and women's health across the lifespan* (8th ed.). Upper Saddle River, NJ: Prentice Hall.

Davies, G. A. L., Wolfe, L. A., Mottola, M. F., & MacKinnon, C. (2003). Joint SOGC/CSEP clinical practice guideline: Exercise in pregnancy and the post partum period. *Canadian Journal of Applied Physiology, 28*(3), 329–341.

Davis, C. L., Tomporowski, P. D., Boyle, C. A., Waller, J. L., Miller, P. H., Nagieri, J. A., et al. (2007). Effects of aerobic exercise on overweight children's cognitive functioning: A randomized controlled trial. *Research Quarterly for Exercise and Sport, 78*, 510–519.

Davis, K. (2011, May 13). Social determinants of health in Canada: A treadmill of progress. *Ontario Health Promotion E-Bulletin No. 708.* Retrieved from http://www.ohpe.ca/node/12295

Davis-Kean, P. E., Jager, J., & Collins, W. A. (2009). The self in action: An emerging link between self-beliefs and behaviors in middle childhood. *Child Development Perspectives, 3*, 184–188.

Davison, G. (2005). Issues and nonissues in the gay affirmative treatment of patients who are gay, lesbian, or bisexual. *Clinical Psychology: Science and Practice, 12*, 25–28.

Davoli, T., Denchi, E. L., & de Lange, T. (2010). Persistent telomere damage induces bypass of mitosis and tetraploidy. *Cell, 141*, 81–93.

Daws, D. (2000). *Through the night.* San Francisco: Free Association Books.

Day, N. L., Goldschmidt, L., & Thomas, C. A. (2006). Prenatal marijuana exposure contributes to the prediction of marijuana use at age 14. *Addiction, 101*, 1313–1322.

De Berardis, G., Pellegrini, F., Franciosi, M., Pamparana, F., Morelli, P., & Togoni, G. (2009). Management of erectile dysfunction in general practice. *Journal of Sexual Medicine, 6*, 1127–1134.

De Brouwer, W. (2012). Life meets trek: Walter De Brouwer at TEDxSanJoseCA 2012. Retrieved from http://www.youtube.com/watch?v=BSZJjN7o8Ck

De Franciscis, P., Cobellis, L., Fornaro, F., Sepe, E., Torella, M., & Colarcurci, N. (2007). Low-dose hormone therapy in the perimenopause. *International Journal of Gynecology and Obstetrics, 98*, 138–142.

de Haan, M., & Martinos, M. (2008). Brain function. In M. M. Haith & J. B. Benson (Eds.), *Encyclopedia of infant and early childhood development.* Oxford, UK: Elsevier.

de Jong Gierveld, J., Broese van Groenou, M., Hoogendoorn, A. W., & Smit, J. H. (2009). Quality of marriages in later life and emotional and social loneliness. *Journals of Gerontology B: Psychological Sciences and Social Sciences, 64*(B), 497–506.

De la Fuente, M., & Gimenez-Llort, L. (2010). Models of aging of neuroimmunomodulation: Strategies for its improvement. *Neuroimmunomodulation, 17*, 213–216.

de Lauzon-Guillain et al. (2006). Is restrained eating a risk factor for weight gain in a general population? *American Journal of Clinical Nutrition, 83*(1), 132–138.

de Luis, D. A., Aller, R., Izaola, O., Gonzales Sagrado, M., Bellioo, D., & Conde, R. (2007). Effects of a low-fat versus a low-carbohydrate diet on adipocytokines in obese adults. *Hormone Research, 67*, 296–300.

de Rosnay, M., Cooper, P. J., Tsigaras, N., & Murray, L. (2006). Transmission of social anxiety from mother to infant: An experimental study using a social referencing paradigm. *Behavior Research and Therapy*, *44*, 1165–1175.

Deary, I. J., Johnson, W., & Starr, J. M. (2010). Are processing speed tasks biomarkers of aging? *Psychology and Aging, 25*, 219–228.

DeCasper, A. J., & Spence, M. J. (1986). Prenatal maternal speech influences newborn's perception of speech sounds. *Infant Behavior and Development, 9*, 133–150.

Declercq, E., Cunningham, D. K., Johnson, C., & Sakala, C. (2008). Mothers' reports of postpartum pain associated with vaginal and cesarean deliveries: Results of a national survey. *Birth, 35*, 16–24.

Deeg, D. J. H. (2005). The development of physical and mental health from late midlife to early old age. In S. L. Willis & M. Martin (Eds.), *Middle adulthood*. Thousand Oaks, CA: Sage.

Deeny, S. P., et al. (2008). Exercise, APOE, and working memory: MEG and behavioral evidence for benefit of exercise in epsilon4 carriers. *Biological Psychology, 78*(2), 179–187.

DeGenova, M. K., & Rice, F. P. (2008). *Intimate relationships, marriages, and families* (7th ed.). New York: McGraw-Hill.

Del Tredici, K., & Braak, H. (2008). Neurofibrillary changes of the Alzheimer type in very elderly individuals: Neither inevitable nor benign. Commentary on no disease in the brain of a 115-year-old woman. *Neurobiology of Aging, 29*, 1133–1136.

dela Cruz, A. M., & McCarthy, P. (2010). Alberta Aboriginal head start in urban and northern communities: Longitudinal study pilot phase. *Chronic Diseases in Canada, 30*(2), 40–45.

Deligiannidis, K. M., & Freeman, M. P. (2010). Complementary and alternative medicine for the treatment of depressive orders in women. *Psychiatric Clinics of North America, 33*, 441–463.

DeMarie, D., Abshier, D. W., & Ferron, J. (2001, April). *Longitudinal study of predictors of memory improvement over the elementary school years: Capacity, strategies, and metamemory revisited.* Paper presented at the meeting of the Society for Research in Child Development, Minneapolis.

Dempster, F. N. (1981). Memory span: Sources of individual and developmental differences. *Psychological Bulletin, 80*, 63–100.

den Hollander, B., et al. (2012). Preliminary evidence of hippocampal damage in chronic users of ecstasy. *Journal of Neurology Neurosurgery and Psychiatry, 83*, 83–85.

Denburg, N. L., et al. (2009). Poor decision making among older adults is related to elevated levels of neuroticism. *Annals of Behavioral Medicine, 37*, 164–172.

Denham, S. A., Bassett, H. H., & Wyatt, T. (2007). The socialization of emotional competence. In J. E. Grusec & P. D. Hastings (Eds.), *Handbook of socialization*. New York: Guilford.

Denmark, F. L., Rabinowitz, V. C., & Sechzer, J. A. (2005). *Engendering psychology: Women and gender revisited* (2nd ed.). Boston: Allyn & Bacon.

Denney, N. W. (1986, August). *Practical problem solving*. Paper presented at the meeting of the American Psychological Association, Washington, DC.

Denney, N. W. (1990). Adult age differences in traditional and practical problem solving. *Advances in Psychology, 72*, 329–349.

Dennis, N. A., & Cabeza, R. (2008). Neuroimaging of healthy cognitive aging. In F. I. M. Craik & T. A. Salthouse (Eds.), *Handbook of aging and cognition* (3rd ed.). Mahwah, NJ: Erlbaum.

Department of Indian and Northern Affairs Canada. (1996). *A Word from Commissioners*. Royal Commission on Aboriginal Peoples. Retrieved from http://www.iainc-inac.gc.ca/

Department of Justice Canada. (2013). *Government of Canada announces continued support to youth justice services*. Retrieved from http://www.justice.gc.ca/

Depp, C., & Jeste, D. V. (2010). Successful aging. *Annual Review of Clinical Psychology* (Vol. 6). Palo Alto, CA: Annual Reviews.

Der Ananian, C., & Prohaska, T. R. (2007). Exercise and physical activity. In J. E. Birren (Ed.), *Encyclopedia of gerontology* (2nd ed.). San Diego: Academic Press.

Derbyshire, E. (2007a). Nutrition in pregnant teenagers: How nurses can help. *British Journal of Nursing, 16*, 144–145.

Derbyshire, E. (2007b). The importance of adequate fluid and fiber intake during pregnancy. *Nursing Standard, 21*, 40–43.

DeRose, L., & Brooks-Gunn, J. (2008). Pubertal development in early adolescence: Implications for affective processes. In N. B. Allen & L. Sheeber (Eds.), *Adolescent emotional development and the emergence of depressive disorders*. New York: Cambridge University Press.

DeRosier, M. E. & Marcus, S. R. (2005). Building friendships and combating bullying: Effectiveness of S. S. Grin at one-year follow-up. *Journal of Clinical Child and Adolescent Psychology, 34*, 140–150.

Deschesnes, M., Fines, P., & Demers, S. (2006). Are tattooing and body piercing indicators of risk-taking behaviours among high school students? *Journal of Adolescence, 29*, 379–393.

DesMeules, M., Pong, R. W., Read Guernsey, J., Wang, F., Luo, W., & Dressler, M. P. (2012). Rural health status and determinants in Canada. In J. C. Kulig & A. M. Williams (Eds.), *Health in Rural Canada* (pp. 23–43). Vancouver: UBC Press.

DeSpelder, L. A., & Strickland, A. L. (2005). *The last dance: Encountering death and dying* (6th ed., rev. update). Mountain View, CA: Mayfield.

Deutsch, F. M. (1991). Women's lives: The story not told by theories of development. *Contemporary Psychology, 36*, 237–238.

Dexter, B. (2001, August 23). More parents opting for private schools. *Toronto Star*.

Di Bona, D., et al. (2010). Immune-inflammatory responses and oxidative stress in Alzheimer's disease: Therapeutic implications. *Current Pharmaceutical Design, 16*, 684–691.

Diamond, A. (2001). A model system for studying the role of dopamine in the prefrontal context during early development in humans: Early and continuously treated phenylketonuria. In C. Nelson & M. Luciana (Eds.), *Handbook of developmental cognitive neuroscience*. Cambridge, MA: MIT Press.

Diamond, A. (2009). The interplay of biology and the environment broadly defined. *Developmental Psychology, 45*, 1–8.

Diamond, A. D. (2007). Interrelated and interdependent. *Developmental Science, 10*, 152–158.

Diamond, A., Casey, B. J., & Munakata, Y. (2011). *Developmental cognitive neuroscience*. New York: Oxford University Press.

Diamond, L. M. (2008). Female bisexuality from adolescence to adulthood: Results from a 10-year longitudinal study. *Developmental Psychology, 44*, 5–14.

Dietz, P., et al. (2010). Estimates of nondisclosure of cigarette smoking among pregnant and nonpregnant women of reproductive age in the United States. *American Journal of Epidemiology, 173*(3), 355–359.

Dillon, C. F., Gu, Q., Hoffman, H. J., & Ko, C. W. (2010). Vision, hearing, balance, and sensory impairment in Americans aged 70 years and over: United States, 1999–2006. *NCHS Data Brief, 31*, 1–8.

Dillon, J. (2003). Reincarnation: The technology of death. In C. D. Bryant (Ed.), *Handbook of death and dying*. Thousand Oaks, CA: Sage.

Dindia, K. (2006). Men are from North Dakota, women are from South Dakota. In K. Dindia & D. J. Canary (Eds.), *Sex differences and similarities in communication*. Mahwah, NJ: Erlbaum.

Dishion, T. J., & Piehler, T. F. (2009). Deviant by design: Peer contagion in development, interventions, and schools. In K. H. Rubin, W. M. Bukowski, & B. Laursen (Eds.), *Handbook of peer interactions, relationships, and groups*. New York: Guilford.

Dishion, T. J., Piehler, T. F., & Myers, M. W. (2008). Dynamic and ecology of adolescent peer influence. In M. J. Prinstein & K. A. Dodge (Eds.), *Understanding peer influence in children and adolescents*. New York: Guilford.

DiTommaso, E., Brannen-McNulty, C., Ross, L. & Burgess, M. (2003), Attachment styles, social skills and loneliness in young adults. *Personality and Individual Differences, 35*, 303–312.

Dittmann-Kohli, F. (2005). Middle age identity in cultural and lifespan perspective. In S. L. Willis & M. Martin (Eds.), *Middle adulthood*. Thousand Oaks, CA: Sage.

Divall, S. A., & Radovick, S. (2008). Pubertal development and menarche. *Annals of the New York Academy of Sciences, 1135*, 19–28.

Dixon, D. (2008). Informed consent or institutionalized eugenics? How the medical profession encourages abortion of fetuses with Down Syndrome. *Issues in Law & Medicine, 24*(1), 3–59.

Doblado, M., & Moley, K. H. (2007). Glucose metabolism in pregnancy and embryogenesis. *Current Opinion in Endocrinology, Diabetes, and Obesity, 14,* 488–493.

Dodge, K. A. (1983). Behavioral antecedents of peer social status. *Child Development, 54,* 1386–1399.

Dodge, K. A., Coie, J. D., & Lynam, D. R. (2006). Aggression and antisocial behavior in youth. In W. Damon & R. Lerner (Eds.), *Handbook of child psychology* (6th ed.). New York: Wiley.

Doherty, M. (2008). *Theory of mind.* Philadelphia: Psychology Press.

Doherty, T., Chopra, M., Nkonki, L., Jackson, D., & Greiner, T. (2006). Effects of the HIV epidemic on infant feeding in South Africa: "When they see me coming with the tins they laugh at me." *Bulletin of the World Health Organization, 84,* 90–96.

Doherty, W. J., & Beaton, J. A. (2004). Mothers and fathers parenting together. In A. Vangelisti (Ed.), *Handbook of family communication.* Mahwah, NJ: Lawrence Erlbaum.

Dohnt, H. & Tiggemann, M. (2006). The contribution of peer and media influences to the development of body satisfaction and self-esteem in young girls: A prospective study. *Developmental Psychology, 42,* 929–936.

Doidge, N. (2007). *The brain that changes itself.* Toronto: James H. Silberman Books.

Doidge, N. (2006, May 8). The doctor is totally in. *Maclean's,* pp. 40–42.

Donaldson, T., Earl, J. K., & Muratore, A. M. (2010). Extending the integrated model of retirement adjustment: Incorporating mastery and retirement planning. *Journal of Vocational Behavior, 77*(2), 279–289. Retrieved from http://www.sciencedirect.com/science/article/pii/S0001879110000679

Dondi, M., Simion, F., & Caltran, G. (1999). Can newborns discriminate between their own cry and the cry of another newborn infant? *Developmental Psychology, 35*(2), 418–426.

Dontigny, L., Arsenault, M. Y., Martel, M. J., Biringer, A., Cormier, J., Delaney, M., et al. (2008). Rubella in pregnancy. *Journal of Obstetrics and Gynecology Canada, 30,* 152–168.

Doran, P., Donoghue, P., O'Connell, K., Gannon, J., & Ohlendieck, K. (2009). Proteomics of skeletal muscle aging. *Proteomoics, 9,* 989–1003.

Dorn, L. D., Dahl, R. E., Woodward, H. R., & Biro, F. (2006). Defining the boundaries of early adolescence: A user's guide to assessing pubertal status and pubertal timing in research with adolescents. *Applied Developmental Science, 10,* 30–56.

Dorval, V., Ritchie, K., & Gruslin, A. (2007). Screening HIV in pregnancy. *Canadian Journal of Public Health, 98*(5), 379–382.

Doty, R. L., & Shah, M. (2008). Taste and smell. In M. M. Haith & J. B. Benson (Eds.), *Encyclopedia of infant and early childhood development.* Oxford, UK: Elsevier.

Doupe, M., Fransoo, R., Chateau, D., Dik, N., Burchill, C., Soodeen, R. A., Bozat-Emre, S., Guenette, W., & Holden, M. (2011). Planning for older adult care in Manitoba. University of Manitoba Faculty of Medicine & Community Health Sciences. Retrieved from http://mchp-appserv.cpe.umanitoba.ca/reference/LOC_4_pager_WEB.pdf

Dow, B. J., & Wood, J. (Eds.). (2006). *The Sage handbook of gender and communication.* Thousand Oaks, CA: Sage.

Dowbiggin, I. R. (1997). *Keeping America safe: Psychiatry and eugenics in the United States and Canada 1880–1940.* Ithaca, NY: Cornell University Press.

Dowling, J. (2004). *The great debate: Nature or nurture?* Washington, DC: Joseph Henry Press.

Dozier, M., Stovall-McClough, K. C., & Albus, K. E. (2009). Attachment and psychopathology in adulthood. In J. Cassidy & P. R. Shaver (Eds.), *Handbook of attachment* (2nd ed.). New York: Guilford.

Draghi-Lorenz, R. (2007, July). *Self-conscious emotions in young infants and the direct perception of self and others in interaction.* Paper presented at the meeting of the International Society for Research on Emotions, Sunshine Coast, Australia.

Draghi-Lorenz, R., Reddy, V., & Costall, A. (2001). Rethinking the development of "nonbasic" emotions: A critical review of existing theories. *Developmental Review, 21,* 263–304.

Dryfoos, J. G., & Barkin, C. (2006). *Growing up in America today.* New York: Oxford University Press.

Dube, S., Boily, M. C., Mugurungi, O., Mahomva, A., Chikhata, F., & Gregson, F. (2008). Estimating vertically acquired HIV infections and the impact of the prevention of mother-to-child transmission program in Zimbabwe: Insights from decision analysis models. *Journal of Acquired Immune Deficiency Syndrome, 48*(1), 72–81.

Dubois, J., Dehaene-Lambertz, G., Perrin, M., Mangin, J. F., Cointepas, Y., Duchesnay, E., et al. (2007). Asynchrony of the early maturation of white matter bundles in healthy infants: Quantitative landmarks revealed noninvasively by diffusion tensor imaging. *Human Brain Mapping, 29,* 14–27.

Duchesne, D. (2004). More seniors at work. *Perspectives on Labour and Income, 5*(2), 5–17.

Duczkowska, A., et al. (2010). Magnetic resonance imaging in the evaluation of fetal spinal canal contents. *Brain Development, 33,* 10–20.

Dudgeon, G. (2010). *Rising tide: The impact of dementia on Canadian society.* Toronto: Alzheimer Society of Canada.

Duffy, T. M., & Kirkley, J. R. (Eds.) (2004). *Learner-centered theory and practice in distance education.* Mahwah, NJ: Erlbaum.

Dumas, T. M., Ellis, W. E., & Wolfe, D. A. (2012). Identity development as a buffer of adolescent risk behaviors in the context of peer group pressure and control. *Journal of Adolescence, 35,* 917–927.

Dumont, S., Jacobs, P., Fassbender, K., Anderson, D., Turcotte, V., & Harel, F. (2009). Costs associated with resource utilization during the palliative phase of care: A Canadian perspective. *Palliative Medicine, 23*(8), 708–717.

Dunbar, L., Leventhal, H., & Leventhal, E. A. (2007). Self-regulation, health, and behavior. In J. E. Birren (Ed.), *Encyclopedia of gerontology* (2nd ed.). San Diego: Academic Press.

Dunkle, R. E. (2009). Oldest old. In D. Carr (Ed.), *Encyclopedia of the life course and human development.* Boston: Gale Cengage.

Dunn, J. (2005). Commentary: Siblings in their families. *Journal of Family Psychology, 19,* 654–657.

Dunn, J. (2007). Siblings and socialization. In J. E. Grusec & P. D. Hastings (Eds.), *Handbook of socialization.* New York: Guilford.

Dunn, S. (2009). Upstanders could bring peace to playgrounds everywhere. University of Alberta news archives. Retrieved from http://www.archives.expressnews.ualberta.ca/article/2009/04/10146.html

Dupre, M. E., & Meadows, S. O. (2007). Disaggregating the effects of marital trajectories on health. *Journal of Family Issues, 28,* 623–652.

Dupuy, A. M., Jaussent, I., Lacroux, A., Durant, R., Cristol, J. P., & Delcourt, C. (2007). Waist circumference adds to the variance in plasma C. reactive protein levels in elderly patients with metabolic syndrome. *Gerontology, 53,* 91–101.

Durrant, J. E. (2008). Physical punishment, culture, and rights: Current issues for professionals. *Journal of Developmental and Behavioral Pediatrics, 29,* 55–66.

Durston, S., & Casey, B. J. (2006). What have we learned about cognitive development from neuroimaging. *Neuropsychologia, 44,* 2149–2157.

Durston, S., Davidson, M. C., Tottenham, N. T., Galvan, A., Spicer, J., Fossella, J. A., et al. (2006). A shift from diffuse to focal cortical activity with development. *Developmental Science, 9,* 1–8.

Dutton, Y., & Zisook, S. (2005). Adaptation to bereavement. *Death Studies, 29*(10), 877–903.

Dyl, J., Kittler, J., Phillips, K. A., & Hunt, J. I. (2006). Body dysmorphic disorder and other clinically significant body image concerns in adolescent psychiatric inpatients: Prevalence and clinical characteristics. *Child Psychiatry and Human Development, 36,* 369–382.

Dysart-Gale, D. (2010). Social justice and social determinants of health: Lesbian, gay, bisexual, transgendered, intersexed, and queer youth in Canada. *Journal of Child and Adolescent Psychiatric Nursing, 23*(1), 23–28.

E

Eagly, A. H. (2001). Social role theory of sex differences and similarities. In J. Worell (Ed.), *Encyclopedia of women and gender*. San Diego: Academic Press.

Eagly, A. H. (2009). Gender roles. In J. Levine & M. Hogg (Eds.), *Encyclopedia of group processes and intergroup relations*. Thousand Oaks, CA: Sage.

Eagly, A. H., & Crowley, M. (1986). Gender and helping behavior: A meta-analytic review of the social psychological literature. *Psychological Bulletin, 100*, 283–308.

Eagly, A. H., & Fischer, A. (2009). Gender inequalities in power in organizations. In B. van Knippenberg & D. Tjosvold (Eds.), *Power and interdependence in organizations*. New York: Cambridge University Press.

Eagly, A. H., & Sczesny, S. (2009). Stereotypes about women, men, and leaders: Have times changed? In M. Barreto, M. Ryan, & M. Schmitt (Eds.), *Barriers to diversity: The glass ceiling after 20 years*. Washington, DC: APA Books.

Eastwick, P. W., & Finkel, E. J. (2008). Sex differences in mate preferences revisited: Do people know what they initially desire in a romantic partner? *Journal of Personality and Social Psychology, 94*, 245–264.

Eby, J. W., Herrell, A. L., & Jordan, M. L. (2011). *Teaching in elementary school: A reflective approach* (6th ed.). Boston: Allyn & Bacon.

Eccles, J., & Roesner, R. (2009). Schools, academic motivation, and stage–environment fit. In R. Lerner & L. Steinberg (Eds.), *Handbook of adolescent psychology* (3rd ed.) (Vol. 1) (pp. 404–434). New York: Wiley.

Eccles, J. S. (2007). Families, schools, and development achievement-related motivation and engagement. In J. E. Grusec & P. D. Hastings (Eds.), *Handbook of socialization*. New York: Guilford.

Eccles, J. S., & Goodman, J. (Eds.). (2002). *Community programs to promote youth development*. Washington, DC: National Academy Press.

Eccles, J. S., Brown, B. V., & Templeton, J. (2008). A developmental framework for selecting indicators of well-being during the adolescent and young adult years. In B. V. Brown (Ed.), *Key indicators of child and youth well-being*. Clifton, NJ: Psychology Press.

Echevarría, J. M., & Avellón, A. (2006). Hepatitis B virus genetic diversity. *Journal of Medical Virology, 78* (Suppl. 1), S36–42.

Eckstein, C. (2007). History of euthanasia in Canada, part II. Compassionate Healthcare Network International. Retrieved from http://www.chninternational.com/history_of_euthanasia_in_canada%20part2.htm

Edin, F., Macoveanu, J., Olesen, P., Tegner, J., & Klingberg, T. (2007). Stronger synaptic connectivity is a mechanism behind development of working memory-related brain activity during childhood. *Journal of Cognitive Neuroscience, 19*, 750–760.

Edwards, P., & Mawani, A. (2006). *Healthy aging in Canada: A new vision, a vital investment from evidence to action—A background paper*. Prepared for the Federal, Provincial and Territorial Committee of Officials (Seniors).

Edwards, P., & Sterne, M. J. (2005). Grandparenting in the twenty-first century: The times they are a changin'. Ontario Health Promotion E-Bulletin. Retrieved from http://www.ohpe.ca/epublish/1/434

Effros, R. B. (2009a). Kleemeier Award lecture 2008—The canary in the coal mine: Telomeres and human healthspan. *Journals of Gerontology A: Biological Sciences and Medical Sciences, 64*(A), 511–515.

Effros, R. B. (2009b). The immunological theory of aging revisited. In V. L. Bengtson, D. Gans, N. M. Putney, & M. Silverstein (Eds.), *Handbook of theories of aging* (2nd ed.). New York: Springer

Egeland, B. (2009). Attachment-based interventions on the quality of attachment among infants and young children. In R. E. Tremblay, R. deV Peters, M. Boivin, & R. G. Barr (Eds.), *Encyclopedia on early childhood development*. Montreal: Centre of Excellence for Early Childhood Development.

Eggen, P. D., & Kauchak, D. P. (2006). *Strategies and models for teachers: Teaching content and critical thinking* (5th ed.). Boston: Allyn & Bacon.

Eichorn, D. H., Clausen, J. A., Haan, N., Honzik, M. P., & Mussen, P. H. (Eds.). (1981). *Present and past in middle life*. New York: Academic Press.

Einarson, A., & Ito, S. (2007). Re: Use of contemporary antidepressants during breastfeeding: A proposal for a specific safety index. *Drug Safety, 30*, 643.

Einstein, G. O., & McDaniel, M. A. (2005). Prospective memory. *Current Directions in Psychological Science, 14*, 286–290.

Eisenberg, N., & Morris, A. S. (2004). Moral cognitions and social responding in adolescence. In R. Lerner & L. Steinberg (Eds.), *Handbook of adolescent psychology*. New York: Wiley.

Eisenberg, N., Fabes, R. A., & Spinrad, T. L. (2006). Prosocial development. In W. Damon & R. Lerner (Eds.), *Handbook of child psychology* (6th ed.). New York: Wiley.

Eisenberg, N., Fabes, R. A., Guthrie, I. K., & Reiser, M. (2002). The role of emotionality and regulation in children's social competence and adjustment. In L. Pulkkinen & A. Caspi (Eds.), *Paths to successful development*. New York: Cambridge University Press.

Eisenberg, N., Morris, A. S., McDaniel, B., & Spinrad, T. L. (2009). Moral cognitions and prosocial responding in adolescence. In R. M. Lerner & L. Steinberg (Eds.), *Handbook of adolescent psychology* (3rd ed.). New York: Wiley.

Eisenberg, N., Spinrad, T. L., & Smith, C. L. (2004). Emotion-related regulation: Its conceptualization, relations to social functioning, and socialization. In P. Philippot & R. S. Feldman (Eds.), *The regulation of emotion*. Mahwah, NJ: Erlbaum.

Ekeblad, S. (2010). Islet cell tumors. *Advances in Experimental Medicine and Biology, 654*, 771–789.

Elder, G. H., & Shanahan, M. J. (2006). *The life course and human development*. New York: John Wiley & Sons.

Elias, J. W., & Wagster, M. V. (2007). Developing context and background underlying cognitive intervention/training studies in older populations. *Journals of Gerontology B: Psychological Sciences and Social Sciences, 62*, 5–10.

Eliasieh, K., Liets, L. C., & Chalupa, L. M. (2007). Cellular reorganization in the human retina during normal aging. *Investigative Ophthalmology and Visual Science, 48*, 2824–2830.

Elkind, D. (1970, April 5). Erik Erikson's eight ages of man. *New York Times Magazine*.

Elkind, D. (1976). *Child development and education: A Piagetian perspective*. New York: Oxford University Press.

Elliott, V. S. (2004). Methamphetamine use increasing. Retrieved from www.amaasson.org/

Ellrichmann, G., Harati, A., & Müller, T. (2008). Deep brain stimulation improves performance of complex instrumental paradigms. *European Neurology, 60*, 32–36.

Else-Quest, N. Hyde, J., Goldsmith, H., & Van Hulle, C. (2006). Gender differences in temperament: A meta-analysis. *Psychological Bulletin, 132*(1), 33–72.

Eltis, K. (2007, Summer). Genetic determinism and discrimination: A call to re-orient prevailing human rights discourse to better comport with the public implications of individual genetic testing. *The Journal of Law, Medicine & Ethics, 35*(2), 282–294.

Elwert, F., & Christakis, N. A. (2008). The effect of widowhood on mortality by the causes of death of both spouses. *American Journal of Public Health, 98*(11), 2092–2098.

Emke, I. (2002). Why the sad face? Secularization and the changing function of funerals in Newfoundland. *Mortality, 7*(3), 269–284.

Emre, M., et al. (2010). Drug profile: Transdermal rivastigmine patch in the treatment of Alzheimer disease. *CNS Neuroscience and Therapeutics, 16*(4), 246–253.

Endicott, O. (2003). Legalizing physician-assisted death: Can safeguards protect the interests of vulnerable persons? Council of Canadian with Disabilities. Retrieved from http://www.ccdonline.ca/en/humanrights/endoflife/euthanasia/lpad

Engler, A. J., Ludington-Hoe, S. M., Cusson, R. M., Adams, R., Bahnsen, M., Brumbaugh, E., et al. (2002). Kangaroo care: National survey of practice, knowledge, barriers, and perceptions. *American Journal of Maternal/Child Nursing, 27*, 146–153.

Eni, R., & Phillips-Beck, W. (2013). Teenage pregnancy and parenthood perspectives of First Nation Women. *The International Indigenous Policy Journal, 4*(1). Retrieved from http://www.ir.lib.uwo.ca/

Ennett, S. T., Bauman, K. E., Hussong, A., Faris, R., Foshee V. A., & Cai, L. (2006). The peer context of adolescent substance use: Findings from social network analysis. *Journal of Research on Adolescence, 16*, 159–186.

Enough-Is-Enough. (2009–2013). Online bullying. Retrieved from http://www.internetsafety101.org/

Ensembl Human. (2010). Explore the homo sapiens genome. Retrieved from www.ensembl.org/Homo_sapiens/index.html

Ensor, R., Spencer, D., & Hughes, C. (2010). You feel sad? Emotional understanding mediates effects of verbal ability and mother-child mutuality on prosocial behaviors: Findings from 2 to 4 years. *Social Development, 20*, 93–110.

Epel, E. S. (2009). Psychological and metabolic stress: A recipe for accelerated cellular aging. *Hormones, 8*, 7–22.

Erickson, K. I., & Kramer, A. F. (2009). Aerobic exercise effects on cognitive and neural plasticity in older adults. *British Journal of Sports Medicine, 43*, 22–24.

Erickson, K. I., et al. (2009). Aerobic fitness is associated with hippocampal volume in elderly humans. *Hippocampus, 19*, 1030–1039.

Erikson, E. H. (1968). *Identity: Youth and crisis.* New York: W. W. Norton.

Erixon-Lindroth, N., Farde, L., Robins Whalin, T. B., Sovago, J., Halldin, C., & Backman, L. (2005). The role of the striatal dopamine transporter in cognitive aging. *Psychiatry Research: Neuroimaging, 138*, 1–12.

Erol, R., & Orth, U. (2011). Self-esteem development from age 14 to 30 years: A longitudinal study. *Journal of Personality and Social Psychology, 101*, 607–609.

Escobar-Chaves, S. L., & Anderson, C. A. (2008). Media and risky behavior. *Future of Children, 18*(1), 147–180.

Eskildsen, M., & Price, T. (2009). Nursing home care in the USA. *Geriatrics and Gerontology, 9*, 1–6.

Esposito, K., et al. (2009). Effects of intensive lifestyle changes on erectile dysfunction in men. *Journal of Sexual Medicine, 6*, 243–250.

Essau, C., Lewinsohn, P., Seeley, J., & Sasagawa, S. (2010). Gender differences in the development course of depression. *Journal of Affective Disorders, 127*, 185–190.

Etaugh, C., & Bridges, J. S. (2010). *Women's lives* (2nd ed.). Boston: Allyn & Bacon.

Evanoo, G. (2007). Infant crying: A clinical conundrum. *Journal of Pediatric Care, 21*, 333–338.

Evans, S. E. (2004). *Forgotten crimes: The Holocaust and people with disabilities.* Chicago: Ivan R. Dee.

Evans, W. J. (2010). Skeletal muscle loss: Cachexia, sarcopenia, and inactivity. *American Journal of Clinical Nutrition, 91*, S1123–S1127.

Evert, J., Lawler, E., Bogan, H., & Perls, T. (2003). Morbidity profiles of centenarians: Survivors, delayers, and escapers. *Journals of Gerontology A: Biological Sciences and Medical Sciences, 58*, 232–237.

Ewanchuk, M., & Brindley, P. G. (2006). Ethics review: Perioperative do-not-resuscitate orders—doing "nothing" when "something" can be done. *Critical Care, 10*(219) [online] doi:10.1186/cc4929.

F

Fagan, J. F. (1992). Intelligence: A theoretical viewpoint. *Current Directions in Psychological Science, 1*, 82–86.

Fagan, J., Holland, C., & Wheeler, K. (2007). The prediction from infancy, of adult IQ and achievement. *Intelligence, 35*(3), 225–231.

Fagot, B. I., Rogers, C. S., & Leinbach, M. D. (2000). Theories of gender socialization. In T. Eckes & H. M. Trautner (Eds.), *The developmental social psychology of gender.* Mahwah, NJ: Erlbaum.

Fahey, T. D., Insel, P. M., & Roth, W. T. (2009). *Fit and well* (8th ed.). New York: McGraw-Hill.

Fair, D., & Schlaggar, B. L. (2008). Brain development. In M. M. Haith & J. B. Benson (Eds.), *Encyclopedia of infant and early childhood development.* Oxford, UK: Elsevier.

Fairweather, E., & Cramond, B. (2011). Infusing creative and critical thinking into the classroom. In R. A. Beghetto & J. C. Kaufman (Eds.), *Nurturing creativity in the classroom.* New York: Cambridge University Press.

Fakhoury, J., Nimmo, G. A., & Autexier, C. (2007). Harnessing telomerase in cancer therapeutics. *Anti-cancer Agents in Medicinal Chemistry, 7*, 475–483.

Falbo, T., & Poston, D. L. (1993). The academic, personality, and physical outcomes of only children in China. *Child Development, 64*, 18–35.

Fallows, M. (2011, April). Insomnia: How do I beat it? *The Teacher, 49*(6), 6. Retrieved from http://www.nstu.ca/images/pklot/wellteacherAPR11.pdf

Fang, L., Oliver, A., Gayatri, J. C., & Wong, T. (2010). Trends in age disparities between younger and middle -aged adults among reported rates of chlamydia, gonorrhea, and infectious syphillis infections in Canada: Findings from 1997 to 2007. *Sexually Transmitted Diseases, 37*(1) 18–25. Retrieved on September 10, 2013 from http://journals.lww.com/stdjournal/Abstract/2010/01000/Trends_in_Age_Disparities_Between_Younger_and.4.aspx

Fantz, R. L. (1963). Pattern vision in newborn infants. *Science, 140*, 296–297.

Farage, M. A., Miller, K. W., Berardesca, E., & Malbach, H. I. (2009). Clinical implications of aging skin: Cutaneous disorders in the elderly. *American Journal of Clinical Dermatology, 10*, 73–86.

Faraone, S. V. (2007). Stimulant therapy in the management of ADHD: Mixed-amphetamine salts (extended release). *Expert Opinion on Pharmacotherapy, 8*, 2127–2134.

Farin, A., Liu, C. Y., Langmoen, I. A., & Apuzzo, M. L. (2009). The biological restoration of central nervous system architecture and function: Part 2-emergence of the realization of adult neurogenesis. *Neurosurgery, 64*, 581–600.

Farley, M., Lynne, J., & Cotton, A. J. (2005). Prostitution in Vancouver: Violence and the colonization of First Nations Women. *Transcultural Psychiatry, 42*(2), 242–271.

Farlow, M. R., Miller, M. L., & Pejovic, V. (2008). Treatment options in Alzheimer's disease: Maximizing benefit, managing expectations. *Dementia and Geriatric Cognitive Disorders, 25*, 408–422.

Farooqui, T., & Farooqui, A. A. (2009). Aging: An important factor for the pathogenesis of neurogenerative diseases. *Mechanisms of Aging and Development, 130*, 203–215.

Farrell, S. W., Fitzgerald, S. J., McAuley, P., & Barlow, C. E. (2010). Cardiorespiratory fitness, adiposity, and all-cause mortality in women. *Medicine and Science in Sports and Exercise, 42*(11), 2006–2012.

Farrington, D. P. (2004) Criminological psychology in the 21st century. *Criminal Behaviour and Mental Health, 14*, 152–166.

Fausto-Sterling, A. (2011). In praise of Esther Thelen. *Psychology Today.* Retrieved from http://www.psychologytoday.com/blog/sexing-the-body/201106/in-praise-esther-thelen

Fechtner, R. D., et al. (2010). Prevalance of ocular surface complaints in patients with glaucoma using topical intraocular pressure-lowering medications. *Cornea, 29*(6), 618–621.

Feeney, B. C., & Collins, N. L. (2007). Interpersonal safe haven and secure base caregiving processes in adulthood. In W. S. Rholes & J. A. Simpson (Eds.), *Adult attachment.* New York: Guilford.

Feeney, J. A. (2009). Adult romantic attachment: Developments in the study of couple relationships. In J. Cassidy & P. R. Shaver (Eds.), *Handbook of attachment* (2nd ed.). New York: Guilford.

Feeney, J. A., & Monin, J. K. (2009). An attachment theoretical perspective on divorce. In J. Cassidy & P. R. Shaver (Eds.), *Handbook of attachment* (2nd ed.). New York: Guilford.

Feinberg, M. E., Button, T. M., Neiderhiser, J. M., Reiss, D., & Hetherington, E. M. (2007). Parenting and antisocial behavior and depression: Evidence of genotype x parenting environment interaction. *Archives of General Psychiatry, 64*, 457–465.

Feldman, R., & Eidelman, A. (2003). Skin-to-skin contact (kangaroo care) accelerates autonomic and neuro-behavioral maturation in preterm infants. *Developmental Medicine and Child Neurology, 45*, 274–281.

Feldman, R., & Eidelman, A. I. (2007). Maternal postpartum behavior and the emergence of infant-mother and infant-father synchrony in preterm and full-term infants: The role of neonatal vagal tone. *Developmental Psychobiology, 49*, 290–302.

Feldman, R., & Landry, O. (2014). *Discovering the lifespan* (Canadian ed.). Don Mills, ON: Pearson.

Feldman, R. (2007). Parent-infant synchrony. *Current Directions in Psychological Science, 16*, 340–345.

Feldman, R., Weller, A., Sirota, L., & Eidelman, A. I. (2003). Testing a family intervention hypothesis: The contribution of mother-infant skin-to-skin (kangaroo care)

to family interaction, proximity, and touch. *Journal of Family Psychology, 17,* 94–107.

Feldon, J. M. (2003). Grief as a transformative experience: Weaving through different lifeworlds after a loved one has committed suicide. *International Journal of Mental Health Nursing, 12,* 74–85.

Felmlee, D., Sweet, E., & Sinclair, H. (2012). Gender rules: Same- and cross-gender friendships norms. *Sex Roles, 66,* 518–529.

Feng, L., Ng, T. P., Chuah, L., Niti, M., & Kua, E. H. (2006). Homocysteine, folate, and vitamin B-12 and cognitive performance in older Chinese adults: Findings from the Singapore Longitudinal Aging Study. *American Journal of Clinical Nutrition, 84,* 1506–1512.

Fenigsen, R. (2008). Other people's lives: Reflections on medicine, ethics, and euthanasia. *Issues in Law and Medicine, 23,* 281–297.

Ferber, S. G., & Makhoul, I. R. (2008). Neurobehavioral assessment of skin-to-skin effects on reaction to pain in preterm infants: A randomized, controlled within-subject trial. *Acta Pediatrica, 97,* 171–176.

Ferguson, D. M., Harwood, L. J., & Shannon, F. T. (1987). Breastfeeding and subsequent social adjustment in 6- to 8- year-old children. *Journal of Child Psychology and Psychiatry, 28,* 378–386.

Fernandez, G. (2008). Progress in nutritional immunology. *Immunologic Research, 40,* 244–261.

Ferraro, K. F. (2006). Health and aging. In R. H. Binstock & L. K. George (Eds.), *Handbook of aging and the social sciences* (6th ed.). San Diego: Academic Press.

Ferris, M. (2010). Voices from the field—Aboriginal children and obesity. In R.E. Tremblay, R. G. Barr, R. DeV. Peters, & M. Boivin (Eds.), *Encyclopedia on Early Childhood Development* [online]. Montreal, Quebec: Centre of Excellence for Early Childhood Development, (1–6). Retrieved from http://www.child-encyclopedia.com/documents/FerrisANGps.pdf

Field, D. (1996). Review of relationships in old age by Hansson & Carpenter. *Contemporary Psychology, 41,* 44–45.

Field, T. M. (2007). *The amazing infant.* Malden, MA: Blackwell.

Field, T. M. (2008). Breastfeeding and antidepressants. *Infant Behavior and Development, 31*(3), 481–487.

Field, T. M., & Hernandez-Reif, M. (2008). Touch and pain. In M. M. Haith & J. B. Benson (Eds.), *Encyclopedia of infant and early childhood development.* Oxford, UK: Elsevier.

Field, T. M., Hernandez-Reif, M., Feije, L., & Freedman, J. (2006). Prenatal, perinatal, and neonatal stimulation, *Infant Behavior and Development, 29,* 24–31.

Fiese, B. H., & Winter, M. A. (2008). Family influences. In M. M. Haith & J. B. Benson (Eds.), *Encyclopedia of infant and early childhood development.* Oxford, UK: Elsevier.

Figueiredo, P. A., Powers, S. K., Ferreira, R. M., Appell, H. J., & Duarta, J.

A. (2009). Aging impairs skeletal muscle mitochondrial bioenergetic function. *Journals of Gerontology A: Biological Sciences and Medical Sciences, 64,* 21–33.

Fillion, L., Tremblay, I., Truchon, M., Côté, D., Sutruthers, C. W., & Dupuis, R. (2007). Job satisfaction and emotional distress among nurses providing palliative care: Empirical evidence for an integrative occupational stress-model. *International Journal of Stress Management, 13*(1), 1–25.

Finch, C. E. (2009). The neurobiology of middle-age has arrived. *Neurobiology of Aging, 30,* 507–514.

Finch, C. E., & Seeman, T. E. (1999). Stress theories of aging. In V. L. Bengtson, & K. W. Schaie (Eds.). *Handbook of theories of aging.* New York: Springer.

Fincham, F. D., Stanley, S. M., & Beach, S. R. H. (2007). Transformative processes in marriage: An analysis of emerging trends. *Journal of Marriage and the Family, 69,* 275–292.

Fingerman, K. L., Hay, E. L., Kamp Dush, C. M., Cichy, K. E., & Hosteman, S. J. (2007). Parents' and offsprings' perceptions of change and continuity when parents transition to old age. *Advances in Life Course Research, 12,* 275–306.

Fingerman, K. L., Miller, L., & Seidel, A. J. (2009). Functions families serve in old age. In S. Qualls & S. Zarlt (Eds.), *Aging families and caregiving: A clinician's guide to research, practice, and technology.* New York: Wiley.

Fingerman, K. L., Pitzer, L., Lefkowitz, E. S., Birditt, K. S., & Moroczek, D. (2008). Ambivalent relationship qualities between adults and their parents: Implications for both parties' well-being. *Journals of Gerontology B: Psychological Sciences and Social Sciences, 63*(B), 362–371.

Fingerman, K. L., Whiteman, S. D., & Dotterer, A. M. (2009). Mother-child relationships in adolescence and old age. In H. T. Reis & S. K. Sprecher (Eds.), *Encyclopedia of human relationships.* Thousand Oaks, CA: Sage.

Finn, C. T., & Smoller, J. W. (2006). Genetic counseling in psychiatry. *Harvard Review of Psychiatry, 14*(2), 109–121.

Fiorentino, L., & Howe, N. (2004). Language competence, narrative ability, and school readiness in low-income preschool children. *Canadian Journal of Behavioural Science, 36,* 280–294.

Fiori, K. L., Antonucci, T. C., & Cortina, K. S. (2006). Social network typologies and mental health among older adults. *Journals of Gerontology B: Psychological Sciences and Social Sciences, 61,* P25–P32.

Fiori, K. L., Smith, J., & Antonucci, T. C. (2007). Social network types among older adults: A multidimensional approach. *Journals of Gerontology B: Psychological Sciences and Social Sciences, 62,* P322–P330.

FIRA. (2012). Brand new Canadian website for new dads. Retrieved from http://www.fira.ca/

Firbank, O. (2011). Framing home-care policy: A case study of reforms in a Canadian jurisdiction. *Journal of Aging Studies, 25,* 36–44.

Fischer, K. W., & Bidell, T. R. (2006). Dynamic development of action, thought, and emotion. In W. Damon & R. M. Lerner (Eds.), *Handbook of child psychology: Theoretical models of human development* (6th ed.). New York: Wiley.

Fischer, K. W., & Immordino-Yang, M. H. (2008). The fundamental importance of the brain and learning for education. *The Jossey-Bass reader on the brain and learning.* San Francisco: Jossey-Bass.

Fisher, M. (2001). Alfred Adler. Retrieved from http://www.muskingum.edu/~ psych/psycweb/history/adler.htm

Fisher, P. A. (2005, April). *Translational research on underlying mechanisms of risk among foster children: Implications for prevention science.* Paper presented at the meeting of the Society for Research in Child Development, Washington, DC.

Fiske, A., Wetherell, J. L., & Gatz, M. (2009). Depression in older adults. *Annual Review of Clinical Psychology* (Vol. 5). Palo Alto, CA: Annual Reviews.

Fitzgerald et al. (2004). Fish consumption and other environmental exposures and their associations with serum PCB concentrations among Mohawk women at Akwesasne. *Environmental Research, 94*(2), 160–170.

Flannagan, D., Marsh, D., & Fuhrman, R. (2005). Judgments about the hypothetical behaviors of friends and romantic partners. *Journal of Social and Personal Relationships, 22,* 797–815.

Flannery, D. J., Hussey, D., Biebelhausen, L., & Wester, K. (2003). Crime, delinquency, and youth gangs. In G. Adams & M. Berzonsky (Eds.), *Blackwell handbook of adolescence.* Malden, MA: Blackwell.

Flavell, J. H. (2004). Theory-of-mind development: Retrospect and prospect. *Merrill-Palmer Quarterly, 50,* 274–290.

Flavell, J. H., Friedrichs, A., & Hoyt, J. (1970). Developmental changes in memorization processes. *Cognitive Psychology, 1,* 324–340.

Flavell, J. H., Miller, P. H., & Miller, S. (2002). *Cognitive development* (4th ed.). Upper Saddle River, NJ: Prentice Hall.

Fleckenstein, M., et al. (2010). Tracking progression using spectral domain optical coherence tomography in geographic atrophy due to age-related macular degeneration. *Investigations in Ophthalmology and Vision Science, 51*(8), 3846–3852.

Flegal, W. A. (2007). Blood group genotyping in Germany. *Transfusion, 47* (Suppl. 1), S47–S53.

Fleming, L. M., & Tobin, D. J. (2005). Popular child-rearing books: Where is daddy? *Psychology of Men and Masculinity, 6,* 18–24.

Fletcher, A. C., Steinberg, L., & Williams-Wheeler, M. (2004). Parental influences on adolescent problem behavior: Revisiting Stattin and Kerr. *Child Development, 75,* 781–796.

Fletcher, A. E., Breeze, E., & Shetty, P. S. (2003). Antioxidant vitamins and mortality in older persons. *American Journal of Nutrition, 78,* 999–1010.

Flint, M. S., Baum, A., Chambers, W. H., & Jenkins, F. J. (2007). Induction of DNA damage, alteration of DNA repair, and transcriptional activation by stress hormones. *Psychoneuroen-docrinology, 32*, 470–479.

Flora, S. J. (2007). Role of free radicals and antioxidants in health and disease. *Cellular and Molecular Biology, 53*, 1–2.

Florent-Bechard, S., et.al. (2009). The essential role of lipids in Alzheimer's disease. *Biochimie, 91*, 804–809.

Florsheim, P. (2003). Adolescent romantic and sexual behavior: What we know and where we go from here. In P. Florsheim (Ed.), *Adolescent romantic relations and sexual behavior: Theory, research and practical implications.* Mahwah, NJ: Erlbaum.

Florsheim, P., Moore, D., & Edgington, C. (2003). Romantic relationships among pregnant and parenting adolescents. In P. Florsheim (Ed.), *Adolescent romantic relations and sexual behavior.* Mahwah, NJ: Erlbaum.

Flynn, J. R. (1999). Searching for justice: The discovery of IQ gains over time. *American Psychologist, 54*, 5–20.

Flynn, J. R. (2007). The history of the American mind in the 20th century: A scenario to explain IQ gains over time and a case for the relevance of g. In P. C. Kyllonen, R. D. Roberts, & L. Stankov (Eds.), *Extending intelligence.* Mahwah, NJ: Erlbaum.

Fodor, I. G., & Franks, V. (1990). Women in midlife and beyond. The new prime of life? *Psychology of Women Quarterly, 14*, 445–449.

Foege, W. (2000). *The power of immunization. The progress of nations.* New York: UNICEF.

Fogoros, R. N. (2001). *Does stress really cause heart disease?* Retrieved from http://www.about.com

Follari, L. (2007). *Foundations and best practices in early childhood education.* Upper Saddle River, NJ: Prentice Hall.

Fong, P. (2013, March 18). Protecting the vulnerable still the goal, says government lawyer in B.C. right-to-die case. *The Star.* Retrieved from http://www.thestar.com/

Fonseca, E. B., Celik, E., Parra, M., Singh, M., Nicolaides, K. H., & the Fetal Medicine Foundation Second Trimester Screening Group. (2007). Progesterone and the risk of preterm birth among women with a short cervix. *New England Journal of Medicine, 357*, 462–469.

Fontana, L. (2009). The scientific basis of caloric restriction leading to longer life. *Current Opinion in Gastroenterology, 25*, 144–150.

Food Banks Canada. (2012). Hunger count 2012. Retrieved from http://foodbankscanada.ca/getmedia/3b946e67-fbe2-490e-90dc-4a313dfb97e5/HungerCount2012.pdf.aspx

Forbes, J., et al. (2011). A national review of vertical HIV transmission. *AIDS, 26*, 757–763.

Forester, M. B., & Merz, R. D. (2007). Risk of selected birth defects with prenatal illicit drug use, Hawaii, 1986–2002. *Journal of Toxicology and Environmental Health, 70*, 7–18.

Forget-Dubois, N., Dionne, G., Lemelin, J-P., Perusse, D., Tremblay, R. E., &

Boivan, M. (2009). Early child language mediates the relation between home environment and school readiness. *Child Development, 80*, 736–749.

Foster, D. (2005). The formation and continuance of lesbian families in Canada. *CBMH/BCHM, 22*(2), 281–297.

Foster, H., & Brooks-Gunn, J. (2008). Role strain in the transition to adolescence: Pubertal timing associations with behavior problems by gender and race/ethnicity. *Developmental Psychology.*

Foster-Cohen, S., Edgin, J. O., Champion, P. R., & Woodward, L. J. (2007). Early delayed language development in very preterm infants: Evidence from the MacArthur-Bates CDI. *Journal of Child Language, 34*, 655–675.

Fouad, N. A., & Bynner, J. (2008). Work transitions. *American Psychologist, 63*, 241–251.

Fouts, G., & Vaughan, K. (2002). Locus of control, television viewing, and eating disorder symptomatology in young females. *Journal of Adolescence, 25*, 307–311.

Fowler, C. G., & Leigh-Paffenroth, E. D. (2007). Hearing. In J. E. Birren (Ed.), *Encyclopedia of gerontology* (2nd ed.). San Diego: Academic Press.

Fowler, G. (1999). *As we grow old: How adult children and their parents can face aging with candor and grace.* Valley Forge, PA: Judson Press.

Fowler, J., & Rodd, E. (Eds.). (2013). The neuroscience of religious experience: Andrew Newberg LIVE on Big Think. Retrieved from http://bigthink.com/

Fozard, J. (1992, December 6). Commentary in "We can age successfully." *Parade Magazine*, 14–15.

Fozard, J. L. (2000). Sensory and cognitive changes with age. In K. W. Schaie & M. Pietrucha (Eds.), *Mobility and transportation in the elderly.* New York: Springer.

Francis, D. D., Szegda, K., Campbell, G., Martin, W. D., & Insel, T. R. (2003). Epigenetic sources of behavioural differences in mice. *Nature Neuroscience, 6*, 445–446.

Francis, J., Fraser, G., & Marcia, J. E. (1989). *Cognitive and experimental factors in moratorium-achievement (MAMA) cycles.* Unpublished manuscript, Department of Psychology, Simon Fraser University, Burnaby, British Columbia.

Franke, S. (2003). Studying and working: The busy lives of students with paid employment (Cat. No. 11-008). *Canadian Social Trends, 68*(Spring), 22–25.

Frankel, L. (2005). An appeal for additional research about the development of heterosexual male sexual identity. *Journal of Psychology and Human Sexuality, 16*, 1–16. doi:10.1300/J056v16n04_01

Frankl, V. (1984). *Man's search for meaning.* New York: Basic Books.

Franklin, U. (2006). *The Ursula Franklin reader: Pacifism as a map.* Toronto: Between the Lines Publishing.

Fraser, G. (2001, September). Immersion schools: Wallace Lambert's Legacy. *Canadian Issues,* Fall 2011, p. 5.

Retrieved from http://connection.ebscohost.com/c/articles/74680261/immersion-schools-wallace-lamberts-legacy

Fraser, S. (Ed.). (1995). *The bell curve wars: Race, intelligence, and the future of America.* New York: Basic Books.

Fraser-Abder, P. (2011). *Teaching budding scientists.* Boston: Allyn & Bacon.

Frederick, I. O., Williams, M. A., Sales, A. E., Martin, D. P., & Killien, M. (2008). Pre-pregnancy body mass index, gestational weight gain, and other maternal characteristics in relation to infant birth weight. *Maternal Child Health Journal, 12*(5), 557–567.

Freeman, E. W., & Sherif, K. (2007). Prevalence of hot flushes and night sweats around the world: A systematic review. *Climacteric, 10*, 197–214.

Freeman, J. (2009) "Very young and gifted": Young gifted and talented web-site. CfBT Education Trust.

Freeman, R. (2011). Reggio Emilia, Vygotsky, and family childcare: Four American providers describe their pedagogical practice. *Child Care in Practice, 17*, 227–246.

French, D. C., Eisenberg, N., Vaughan, J., Purwono, U., & Suryanti, T. A. (2008). Religious involvement and the social competence and adjustment of Indonesian Muslim adolescents. *Developmental Psychology, 44*, 597–611.

Fretts, R. C., Zera, C., & Heffner, C. Z. (2008). Maternal age and pregnancy. In M. M. Haith & J. B. Benson (Eds.), *Encyclopedia of infancy and early childhood.* London, UK: Elsevier.

Freund, A. M., & Lamb, M. E. (2011). Introduction: Social and emotional development across the life span. In R. M. Lerner, W. F. Overton, A. M. Freund, & M.E. Lamb (Eds.), *Handbook of life-span development.* New York: Wiley.

Frey, K. S., Hirschstein, M. K., Snell, J. L., Van Schoiack Edstrom, L., MacKenzie, E. P., & Broderick, C. J. (2005). Reducing playground bullying and supporting beliefs: An experimental trial of the Steps to Respect Program. *Developmental Psychology, 41*, 479–490.

Friedlander, L., Connolly, J., Pepler, D., & Craig, W. (2007). Biological, familial, and peer influences on dating in early adolescence, *Archives of Sexual Behavior, 36*, 821–830.

Friedman, E. M., & Herd, P. (2010). Income, education, and inflammation: Differential associations in a national probability sample (the MIDUS study). *Psychosomatic Medicine, 72*(3), 290–300.

Friedman, R. (2006). Uncovering an epidemic—screening for mental illness in teens. *The New England Journal of Medicine, 355*(26), 2717–2719.

Friendly, M., & Prabhu, N. (2010). Can early childhood education and care help keep Canada's promise of respect for diversity? Toronto: Childcare Resource and Research Unit. Retrieved from http://www.childcarecanada.org

Friendly, M., Doherty, G., & Beach, J. (2006). Quality by design: What do we know about quality in early learning and child care, and what do we think? A literature review. Childcare Resource and Research Unit, University of Toronto. Retrieved from http://www.childcarequality.ca/wdocs/QbD_LiteratureReview.pdf

Friesen, J. (2010, November 25). Number of seniors living in poverty soars nearly 25%. *The Globe and Mail*. Retrieved from http://www.theglobeandmail.com/news/national/number-of-seniors-living-in-poverty-soars-nearly-25/article1315450/

Fritsch, T., McClendon, M. J., Smyth, K. A., Lerner, A. J., Friedland, R. P., & Larson, J. D. (2007). Cognitive functioning in healthy aging: The role of reserve and lifestyle factors early in life. *Gerontologist, 47*, 307–322.

Fritschmann, N. S., & Solari, E. J. (2008). Learning disabilities. In N. J. Salkind (Ed.), *Encyclopedia of educational psychology*. Thousand Oaks, CA: Sage.

Fromm, E. (1956). *The art of loving*. New York: Harper & Row Publishers.

Fry, P. S. (2001). The unique contribution of key existential factors to the prediction of psychological well-being of older adults following spousal loss. *The Gerontologist, 41*, 69–81.

Frye, D. (1999). Development of intention: The relation of executive function of theory of mind. In P. D. Zelazo, J. W. Astington, & D. R. Oison (Eds.), *Developing theories of intention: Social understanding and self-control*. Mahwah, NJ: Erlbaum.

Fu, G., Xu, F., Cameron, C. A., Heyman, G., & Lee, K. (2007). Cross-cultural differences in children's choices, categorizations, and evaluations of truths and lies. *Developmental Psychology, 43*, 278–293.

Fuligni, A. J., & Witkow, M. (2004). The postsecondary educational progress of youth from immigrant families. *Journal of Research on Adolescence, 14*, 159–183.

Fuligni, A.J., Witkow, M., & Garcia, C. (2005). Ethnic identity and the academic adjustment of adolescents from Mexican, Chinese, and European backgrounds. *Developmental Psychology, 41*, 799–811.

Fuller-Thomson, E. (2005). Grandparents raising grandchildren in Canada: Profile of a skipped generation. Social and economic dimensions of an aging population (SEDAP). Retrieved from http://socserv2.mcmaster.ca/sedap/p/sedap132.pdf

Fuller-Thomson, E., & Minkler, M. (2001). American grandparents providing extensive care to their grandchildren: Prevalence and profile. *The Gerontologist, 41*(2), 201–209.

Funai, E. F., Evans, M., & Lockwood, C. J. (2008). *High risk obstetrics*. Oxford, UK: Elsevier.

Furlong, A., & Cartmel, F. (2007). *Young people and social change: Individualism and risk in late modernity* (2nd ed). Buckingham: Open University.

Furlong, M., et al. (2003). Multiple contexts of school engagement: Moving toward a unifying framework for educational research and practice. *The California School Psychologist, 8*, 99–113.

Furman, E. (2005). *Boomerang nation*. New York: Fireside.

Furman, W. C., & Simon, V. A. (2008). Homophily in adolescent romantic relationships. In M. J. Prinstein & K. A. Dodge (Eds.), *Understanding peer influences in children and adolescents*. New York: Guilford.

Furman, W. C., Ho, M., & Low, S. (2005, April). *Adolescent dating experiences and adjustment*. Paper presented at the meeting of the Society for Research in Child Development, Atlanta.

Furth, H. G., & Wachs, H. (1975). *Thinking goes to school*. New York: Oxford University Press.

G

Gagliese, L. (2009). Pain and aging: The emergence of a new subfield of pain research. *Journal of Pain, 10*, 343–353.

Gainer, J. (2012). Critical thinking: Foundational for digital literacies and democracy. *Journal of Adolescent & Adult Literacy, 58*(1), 14–17.

Gajdos, Z., Hirschhorn, J., & Palmert, M. (2009). What controls the timing of puberty? An update on progress from genetic investigation. *Current Opinion in Endocrinology, Diabetes & Obesity, 16*, 16–24.

Galambos, N. L., Barker, E. T., & Tilton-Weaver, L. C. (2003). Who gets caught at maturity gap? A study of pseudomature, immature, and mature adolescents. *International Journal of Behavioural Development 2003, 27*(3), 253–263.

Galambos, N. L., Leadbeater, B. J., & Barker, E. T. (2004). Gender differences in and risk factors for depression in adolescence: A 4-year longitudinal study. *International Journal of Behavioural Development 2004, 28*(1), 16–25. Retrieved from http://www.tandf.co.uk/journals

Galambos, N., MacDonald, S., Naphtali, C., Cohen, S. A., & deFrias, C. (2005). Cognitive performance differentiates selected aspects of psychosocial maturity of adolescence. *Developmental Neuropsychology, 28*(1), 473–492.

Galasko, D., & Montine, T. J. (2010). Biomarkers of oxidative damage and inflammation in Alzheimer's disease. *Biomarkers in Medicine, 4*, 27–36.

Galimberti, D., & Scarpini, E. (2010). Treatment of Alzheimer's disease: Symptomatic and disease-modifying approaches. *Current Aging Science, 3*, 46–56.

Gallagher, J. J. (2007). *Teaching science for understanding*. Upper Saddle River, NJ: Prentice Hall.

Gallicano, G. (2010). Alcohol and its effect on fetal development: What do we know? *Pediatric Health, 4*(5), 459.

Gallo, L. C., Troxel, W. M., Matthews, K. A., & Kuller, L. W. (2003). Marital status and quality in middle-aged women: Associations with levels and trajectories of cardiovascular risk factors. *Health Psychology, 22*, 453–463.

Gallo, W. T., Bradley, E. H., Dubin, J. A., Jones, R. N., Falba, T. A., Teng, H. M., et al. (2006). The persistence of depressive symptoms in older workers who experience involuntary job loss: Results from the health and retirement survey. *Journal of Gerontology B: Psychological Sciences and Social Sciences, 61*, S221–S228.

Gamino, L. A., & Sewell, K. W. (2004). Meaning constructs as predictors of bereavement adjustment: A report from the Scott & White Grief Study. *Death Studies, 28*, 397–421.

Ganguli, M., Snitz, B. E., Lee, C. W., Vanderbilt, J., Saxton, J. A., & Chang, C. C. (2010). Age and education effects and norms on a cognitive test battery from a population-based cohort: The Monongahela-Youghiogheny Healthy Aging Team. *Aging and Mental Health, 14*, 100–107.

Ganiban, J., Saudino, K., Ulbricht, J., Neiderhiser, J., & Reiss, D. (2008). Stability and change in temperament across adolescence. *Journal of Personality and Social Psychology, 95*, 222–236.

Ganong, L., & Coleman, M. (2006). Obligations to step-parents acquired in later life: Relationship quality and acuity of needs. *Journals of Gerontology B: Psychological Sciences and Social Sciences, 61*, S80–S88.

Ganong, L., Coleman, M., & Hans, J. (2006). Divorce as prelude to stepfamily living and the consequences of re-divorce. In M. A. Fine & J. H. Harvey (Eds.), *Handbook of divorce and relationship dissolution*. Mahwah, NJ: Erlbaum.

Gao, L. L., Chan, S. W., & Mao, Q. (2009). Depression, perceived stress, and social support among first-time Chinese mothers and fathers in the postpartum period. *Research in Nursing and Health, 32*, 50–58.

Garasen, H., Windspoll, R., & Johnsen, R. (2008). Long-term patients' outcomes after intermediate care at a community hospital for elderly patients: 12-month follow-up of a randomized controlled trial. *Scandinavian Journal of Public Health, 36*, 197–204.

Garcia-Bournissen, F., Tsur, L., Goldstein, L., Staroselsky, A., Avner, M., Asrar, F., et al. (2008). Fetal exposure to isotretinoin—an international problem. *Reproductive Toxicology, 25*, 124–128.

Gardner, D. S., Hosking, J., Metcalf, B. S., An, J., Voss, L. D., & Wilkin, T. J. (2009). Contribution of early weight gain to childhood overweight and metabolic health: A longitudinal study (Early Bird 36). *Pediatrics, 123*, e67–e73.

Gardner, H. (1983). *Frames of mind*. New York: Basic Books.

Gardner, H. (1993). *Multiple intelligences*. New York: Basic Books.

Gardner, H. (2002). The pursuit of excellence through education. In M. Ferrari (Ed.), *Learning from extraordinary minds*. Mahwah, NJ: Erlbaum.

Gardner, M., & Steinberg, L. (2005). Peer influence on risk taking, risk preference, and risky decision making in adolescence and adulthood. *Developmental Psychology, 41,* 625–635.

Garolla, A., Pizzol, D., & Foresta, C. (2011). The role of human papillomavirus on sperm function. *Current Opinions in Obstetrics and Gynecology, 23,* 232–237.

Garrett, D. D., Tuokko, H., Stajduhar, K. I., Lindsay, J., & Buehler, S. (2008). Planning for end-of-life care: Findings from the Canadian Study of Health and Aging. *Canadian Journal of Aging, 27,* 11–21.

Garriguet, D. (2007). Canadians' eating habits. *Health Reports, 18,* 17–31.

Gartner, L. M., Morton, J., Lawrence, R. A., Naylor, A. J., O'Hare, D., & the American Academy of Pediatrics Section on Breastfeeding. (2005). Breastfeeding and the use of human milk. *Pediatrics, 115,* 496–506.

Gasser, L., & Keller, M. (2009). Are the competent morally good? Perspective taking and moral motivation of children involved in bullying. *Social Development, 18,* 798–816.

Gathercole, S., Pickering, S., Ambridge, B., & Wearing, H. (2004). The structure of working memory from 4 to 15 years of age. *Developmental Psychology, 40,* 177–190.

Gathercole, V. C. M., & Hoff, E. (2007). Input and the acquisition of language: Three questions. In E. Hoff & M. Shatz (Eds.), *Blackwell handbook of language development.* Malden, MA: Blackwell.

Gatz, M., Reynolds, C. A., Fratiglioni, L., Johansson, B., Mortimer, J. A., Berg, S., et al. (2006). Role of genes and environments for explaining Alzheimer's disease. *Archives of General Psychiatry, 63,* 168–174.

Gauvain, M. (2008). Vygotsky's sociocultural theory. In M. M. Haith & J. B. Benson (Eds.), *Encyclopedia of infant and early childhood development.* Oxford, UK: Elsevier.

Gauvain, M., & Parke, R. D. (2010a). Parenting. In M. H. Bornstein (Ed.), *Handbook of cultural developmental science.* New York: Psychology Press.

Gauvain, M., & Parke, R. D. (2010b). Socialization. In M. H. Bornstein (Ed.), *Handbook of cultural developmental science.* New York: Psychology Press.

Gauvain, M., & Perez, S. M. (2007). The socialization of cognition. In J. E. Grusec & P. D. Hastings (Eds.), *Handbook of socialization.* Mahwah, NJ: Erlbaum.

Gaziano, J. M., et al. (2009). Vitamins E and C in prevention of prostate and total cancer in men: The Physicians Health Study II randomized controlled trial. *Journal of the American Medical Association, 3001,* 52–62.

Geary, D. C. (2006). Evolutionary developmental psychology: Current status and future directions. *Developmental Review, 26,* 113–119.

Geary-Martin, C. (2013). Dr. Ursula M. Franklin, c.c. frsc. bronze. Retrieved from http://camie.ca/wordpress/galleries/commissions/ursula-franklin/

Geda, Y. E., et al. (2010). Physical exercise, aging, and mild cognitive impairment: A population-based study. *Archives of Neurology, 67,* 80–86.

Gee, E. M., & Prus. S. G. (2000). Income inequality in Canada: A "racial divide". In M. A. Kalbach, & W. E. Kalhach (Eds.). *Perspectives on ethnicity in Canada.* Toronto: Harcourt Canada.

Geers, A., Kosbab, K., Helfer, S., Weiland, P. & Wellman, J. (2007). Further evidence for individual differences in placebo responding: An interactionist perspective. *Journal of Psychosomatic Research, 62,* 563–570.

Geher, G., & Miller, G. (Eds.). (2007). *Mating intelligence.* Mahwah, NJ: Erlbaum.

Gelman, R. (1969). Conservation acquisition: A problem of learning to attend to relevant attributes. *Journal of Experimental Child Psychology, 7,* 67–87.

Gelman, S. A. (2009). Learning from others: Children's construction of concepts. *Annual Review of Psychology, 60,* 115–140.

Gelman, S. A., & Kalish, C. W. (2006). Conceptual development. In W. Damon & R. Lerner (Eds.), *Handbook of child psychology* (6th ed.). New York: Wiley.

Gelman, S. A., & Opfer, J. E. (2002). Development of the animate-inanimate distinction. In U. Goswami (Ed.), *Blackwell handbook of childhood cognitive development.* Malden, MA: Blackwell.

Genesee, F. (2001). Bilingual first language acquisition: Exploring the limits of the language faculty. In M. McGroarty (Ed.) *Annual Review of Applied Linguistics: Language and Psychology,* Vol. 21 (pp. 153–168). New York: Cambridge University Press.

Genome Canada. (2012). Did you know? Retrieved from http://www.genomecanada.ca/en/info/dna/know.aspx

Genovese, J. E. C. (2003, June). Piaget, pedagogy, and evolutionary psychology. *Evolutionary Psychology, 1,* 127–137. Retrieved from http://www.human-nature.com/ep

Gentzler, A. L., & Kerns, K. A. (2004). Associations between insecure attachment and sexual experiences. *Personal Relationships, 11,* 249–266.

Geoffroy, M., Côté, S. M., Parent, S., & Séguin, J. R. (2006, August). Daycare attendance, stress, and mental health. *Canadian Journal of Psychiatry, 51*(9), 607–615.

George, L. K. (2006). Perceived quality of life. In R. H. Binstock & L. K. George (Eds.), *Handbook of aging and the social sciences* (6th ed.). San Diego: Academic Press.

George, L. K. (2009). Religious and spirituality, later life. In D. Carr (Ed.), *Encyclopedia of the life course and human development.* Boston: Gale Cengage.

George, L. K. (2010). Still happy after all these years: Research frontiers on subjective well-being in later life. *Journals of Gerontology B: Psychological Sciences and Social Sciences, 65*(B), 331–339.

Georges, J. J., The, A. M., Onwuteaka-Philipsen, B. D., & van der Wal, G. (2008). Dealing with requests for euthanasia: A qualitative study investigating the experience of general practitioners. *Journal of Medical Ethics, 34,* 150–155.

Gerards, F. A., Twisk, J. W., Fetter, W. P., Wijnaendts, L. C., & van Vugt, J. M. (2008). Predicting pulmonary hypoplasia with 2-or-3 dimensional ultrasonography in complicated pregnancies. *American Journal of Gynecology and Obstetrics, 198,* e1–e6.

Gerrard, M., Gibbons, F. X., Houihan, A. E., Stock, M. L., & Pomery, E. A. (2008). A dual-process approach to health risk decision-making. *Developmental Review, 28,* 29–61.

Gerrotsen, M., Berg, I., Deelman, B., Visser-Keizer, A., & Jong, B. (2003). Speed of information processing after unilateral stroke. *Journal of Clinical and Experimental Neuropsychology, 25,* 1–13.

Gershoff, E. T. (2002). Corporal punishment by parents and associated child behaviors and experiences: A meta-analysis and theoretical review. *Psychological Bulletin, 128,* 539–579.

Gettler, L., McDade, T., Feranil, A., & Kuzawa, C. (2011). Longitudinal evidence that fatherhood decreases testosterone in human males. *Proceedings of the National Academy of Science, 108*(39), 16194–16199.

Ghetti, S., & Alexander, K. W. (2004). "If it happened, I would remember it": Strategic use of event memorability in the rejection of false autobiographical events. *Child Development, 75,* 542–561.

Ghosh, S., et al. (2010). Prospective randomized comparative study of macular thickness following phacoemulsification and manual small incision cataract surgery. *Acta Ophthalmologica, 88*(4).

Giannarelli, F., Sonenstein, E., & Stagner, M. (2006). Child care arrangements and help for low-income families with young children: Evidence from the National Survey of America's Families. In N. Cabrera, R. Hutchens, & H. E. Peters (Eds.), *From welfare to childcare.* Mahwah, NJ: Erlbaum.

Giarrusso, R., & Bengtson, V. L. (2007). Self-esteem. In J. E. Birren (Ed.), *Encyclopedia of gerontology* (2nd ed.). San Diego: Academic Press.

Gibbs, J. C. (2009). *Moral development and reality: Beyond the theories of Kohlberg and Hoffman* (2nd ed.). Boston: Allyn & Bacon.

Gibbs, J. C., Basinger, K. S., Grime, R. L., & Snarey, J. R. (2007). Moral judgment development across cultures: Revisiting Kohlberg's universality claims. *Developmental Review, 27,* 443–500.

Gibson, E. J. (2001). *Perceiving the affordances.* Mahwah, NJ: Erlbaum.

Gibson, E. J., & Walk, R. D. (1960). The "visual cliff." *Scientific American, 202,* 64–71.

Gibson, E. S., Powles, A. C. P., Thabane, L., O'Brien, S., Molnar, D.S., Trajanovic, N., et al. (2006). Sleepiness is serious in adolescence: Two surveys of 3235 Canadian students. *BMC Public Health, 6,* 116.

Gibson, H. J. (2009). Leisure and travel, adulthood. In D. Carr (Ed.), *Encyclopedia of the life course and human development.* Boston: Gale Cengage.

Giedd, J. N. (2008). The teen brain: Insights from neuroimaging. *Journal of Adolescent Medicine, 42,* 335–343.

Giedd, J. N. (2007, September). Commentary in S. Jayson "Teens driven to distraction." *USA Today*, pp. D1–2.

Giedd, J. N., et al. (2006). Puberty-related influences on brain development. *Molecular and Cellular Endocrinology, 25*, 154–162.

Giedd, J. N., Blumenthal, J., Jeffries, N. O., Castellanos, F. X., Liu, H., Zijdenbos, T. P., et al. (1999, October). Brain development during childhood and adolescence: A longitudinal MRI study. *Nature Neuroscience, 2*(10), 861–863.

Giger, J., & Davidhizar, R. (2004). Introduction to transcultural nursing. In M. S. Ledbetter (Ed.), *Transcultural nursing: Assessment and intervention* (4th ed.) (pp. 3–19). St. Louis: CV Mosby.

Giles, A., & Rovee-Collier, C. (2011). Infant long-term memory for associations formed during mere exposure. *Infant Behavior and Development, 34*, 3270338.

Gillen, M., Lefkowitz, E., & Shearer, C. (2006). Does body image play a role in risky sexual behavior and attitudes? *Journal of Youth and Adolescence, 35*, 230–242.

Gilligan, C. (1982, 1993). *In a different voice: Psychological theory and women's development*. Cambridge, MA: Harvard University Press.

Gilligan, C. (1996). The centrality of relationships in psychological development: A puzzle, some evidence, and a theory. In G. G. Noam & K. W. Fischer (Eds.), *Development and vulnerability in close relationships*. Hillsdale, NJ: Erlbaum.

Gilligan, C. (1992, May). *Joining the resistance: Girls' development in adolescence*. Paper presented at the symposium on development and vulnerability in close relationships, Montreal.

Gilligan, C., Spencer, R., Weinberg, M. K., & Bertsch, T. (2003). On the listening guide: A voice-centered relational model. In P. M. Carnic & J. E. Rhodes (Eds.), *Qualitative research in psychology* Washington, DC: American Psychological Association.

Gilliland, A. (2010). After praise and encouragement: Emotional support strategies used by birth doulas in the USA and Canada. *Midwifery, 27*, 525–531.

Gillum, R. F., & Ingram, D. D. (2007). Frequency of attendance at religious services, hypertension, and blood pressure: The third national health and nutrition examination survey. *Psychosomatic Medicine, 68*, 382–385.

Gillum, R. F., King, D. E., Obisesan, T. O., & Koenig, H. G. (2008). Frequency of attendance at religious services and mortality in a U.S. national cohort. *Annals of Epidemiology, 18*, 124–129.

Gil-Mohapel, J., Simpson, J. M., Titerness, A. K., & Christie, B. R. (2010). Characterization of the neurogenesis quiet zone in the rodent brain: Effects of age and exercise. *European Journal of Neuroscience, 31*, 797–807.

Gilmore, J. (2009). *The immigrant labour force analysis: The 2008 Canadian immigrant labour market—Analaysis of quality of employment*. Ottawa: Statistics Canada,

catalogue no. 71-606-X. Retrieved from http://www.statcan.gc.ca/pub/71-606-x/71-606-x2009001-eng.pdf

Giordano, P. C. (2009). Friendship, childhood and adolescence. In D. Carr (Ed.), *Encyclopedia of the life course and human development*. Boston: Gale Cengage.

Girling, A. (2006). The benefits of using the Neonatal Behavioral Assessment Scale in health visiting practice. *Community Practice, 79*, 118–120.

Gjerdingen, D., Katon, W., & Rich, D. E. (2008). Stepped care treatment of postpartum depression: A primary care-based management model. *Women's Health Issues, 18*, 44–52.

Gladwell, M. (2008). *The Outliers*. New York: Little, Brown and Company.

Glantz, J. C. (2005). Elective induction vs. spontaneous labor associations and outcomes. *Journal of Reproductive Medicine, 50*, 235–240.

Glick, G. C. (2004). On the demographic stratification in U.S. teenage pregnancy rates. Retrieved from http://artsci.drake.edu/dussj/2004/Glick.pdf

Gliori, G., Imm, P., Anderson, H. A., & Knobeloch, L. (2006). Fish consumption and advisory awareness among expectant women. *Wisconsin Medicine Journal, 105*, 41–44.

Glisky, E. L., & Kong, L. L. (2008). Do young and older adults rely on different processes in source memory tasks? A neuropsychological study. *Journal of Experimental Psychology: Learning, Memory, and Cognition, 34*, 809–822.

Gluck, J., & Bluck, S. (2007). Looking back across the life span: A life story account of the reminiscence bump. *Memory and Cognition, 35*, 1928–1939.

Glynn, L. M., Schetter, C. D., Hobel, C. J., & Sandman, C. A. (2008). Pattern of perceived stress and anxiety in pregnancy predicts preterm birth. *Health Psychology, 27*, 43–51.

Godding, V., Bonnier, C., Fiasse, L., Michel, M., Longueville, E., Lebecque, P., et al. (2004). Does in utero exposure to heavy maternal smoking induce nicotine withdrawal symptoms in neonates? *Pediatric Research, 55*, 645–651.

Goel, A., Sinha, R. J., Dalela, D., Sankhwar, S., & Singh, V. (2009). Andropause in Indian men: A preliminary cross-sectional study. *Urology Journal, 6*, 40–46.

Gogtay, N., & Thompson, P. M. (2010). Mapping gray matter development: Implications for typical development and vulnerability to psychopathology. *Brain and Cognition, 72*, 6–15.

Goh, V. I., & Koren, G. (2008). Folic acid in pregnancy and fetal outcomes. *Journal of Obstetrics and Gynecology, 28*, 3–13.

Goldberg, W. A., & Lucas-Thompson, R. (2008). Maternal and paternal employment, effects of. In M. M. Haith & J. B. Benson (Eds.), *Encyclopedia of infant and early childhood development*. Oxford, UK: Elsevier.

Goldenberg, R. L., & Culhane, J. F. (2007). Low birth weight in the United States.

American Journal of Clinical Nutrition, 85 (Suppl.), S584–S590.

Goldman, R. (2010, February). ADHD stimulants and their effect on height in children. *Canadian Family Physician*. Retrieved from http://www.cfp.ca/cgi/content/full/56/2/145

Goldschmidt, L., Richardson, G. A., Willford, J., & Day, N. L. (2008). Prenatal marijuana exposure and intelligence test performance at age 6. *Journal of the American Academy of Child and Adolescent Psychiatry*.

Goldsmith, H. H. (2011). Human development: Biological and genetic processes. *Annual Review of Psychology* (Vol. 62). Palo Alto, CA: Annual Reviews.

Goldstein, A. L., Amiri, T., Vilhena, N., Wekerle C., Thornton, T., & Tonmyr, L. (2012, December 13). Youth on the street and youth involvement in welfare: Maltreatment, mental health and substance use. Public Health Agency. Retrieved from http://www.phac-aspc.gc.ca/

Goldstein, M. H., King A. P., & West, M. J. (2003). Social interaction shapes babbling: Testing parallels between birdsong and speech. *Proceedings of the National Academy of Sciences, 100*(13), 8030–8035.

Gollnick, D. M., & Chinn, P. C. (2009). *Multicultural education in a pluralistic society* (8th ed.). Boston: Allyn & Bacon.

Golombok, S., & Tasker, F. (2010). Gay fathers. In M. E. Lamb (Ed.), *The role of the father in child development* (5th ed.). New York: Wiley.

Golombok, S., Rust, J., Zervoulis, K., & Croudace, T., Golding, J., & Hines, M. (2008). Developmental trajectories of sex-typed behavior in boys and girls: A longitudinal general population study of children aged 2.5–8 years. *Child Development, 79*, 1583–1593.

Gomez Ravetti, M., Rosso, O. A., Berretta, R., & Moscato, P. (2010). Uncovering molecular biomarkers that correlate cognitive decline with the changes of hippocampus' gene expression profiles in Alhzeimer's disease. *PLoS One, 5*, e10153.

Gonzalez, R. (2007, March 11). Aboriginal school to open in fall. *The Catholic Register*, p. 8.

González-del Angel, A., Cervera, M., Gómez, L., Pérez-Vera, P., Orozco, L., Carnevale, A., & Del Castillo, V. (2000). Ataxia-pancytopenia syndrome. *Am J Med Genet, 90*(3), 252–254.

Good, M., & Willoughby, T. (2008). Adolescence as a sensitive period for spiritual development. *Child Development Perspectives, 2*, 32–37.

Goodman, G. S., Ghetti, S., Quas, J. A., Edelstein, R. S., Alexander, K. W., Redlich, A. D., Cordon, I. M., & Jones, D. P. H. (2003). A prospective study of memory for child sexual abuse: New findings relevant to the repressed-memory controversy. *Psychological Science, 14*(2), 113–118.

Goodridge, D. (2010). End of life policies: Do they make a difference in practice? *Social Science & Medicine, 70*, 1166–1170.

Goos, L. M., Ezzatian, P., & Schachar, R. (2007). Parent-of-origin effects in attention-deficit hyperactivity disorder. *Psychiatry Research, 149,* 1–9.

Gorchoff, S. M., John, O. P., & Helson, R. (2008). Contextualizing change in marital satisfaction during middle age: An 18-year longitudinal study. *Psychological Science, 19,* 1194–1200.

Gordon, A. (2007, January 6). Time to let dads in. *Toronto Star,* pp. L1–L2.

Gore, K. (2009). Socialization, gender. In D. Carr (Ed.), *Encyclopedia of the life course and human development.* Boston: Gale Cengage.

Gosden, R. G. (2007). Menopause. In J. E. Birren (Ed.), *Encyclopedia of gerontology* (2nd ed.). San Diego: Academic Press.

Gosselin, J. (2010). Individual and family factors related to psychosocial adjustment in stepmother families with adolescents. *Journal of Divorce and Remarriage, 51,* 108–123.

Gostic, C. L. (2005). The crucial role of exercise and physical activity in weight management and functional improvement for seniors. *Clinical Geriatric Medicine, 21,* 747–756.

Goswami, S. K., & Das, D. K. (2009). Resveratrol and chemoprevention. *Cancer Letters, 284,* 1–6.

Gottlieb, G. (2007). Probabalistic epigenesis. *Developmental Science, 10,* 1–11.

Gottleib, G., Wahlsten, D., & Lickliter, R. (2006). The significance of biology for human development: A developmental psychobiological systems view. In W. Damon & R. Lerner (Eds.), *Handbook of child psychology* (6th ed.). New York: Wiley.

Gottman, J. M. (1994). *Why marriages succeed or fail.* New York: Simon & Schuster.

Gottman, J. M. (2006, April 29). Secrets of long term love. *New Scientist, 2549,* 40.

Gottman, J. M. (2007). The magic relationship ratio. Retrieved from http://www.youtube.com/watch?v=Xw9SE315GtA

Gottman, J. M. (2008). *Research on parenting.* Retrieved from http://www.gottman.com/parenting/research

Gottman, J. M., & Gottman, J. S. (2009). Gottman method of couple therapy. In A. S. Gurman (Ed.), *Clinical handbook of couple therapy* (4th ed.). New York: Guilford.

Gottman, J. M., & Levenson, R. W. (2000). The timing of divorce: Predicting when a couple will divorce over a 14-year period. *Journal of Marriage and the Family, 62,* 737–745.

Gottman, J. M., & Parker, J. G. (Eds.). (1987). *Conversations of friends.* New York: Cambridge University Press.

Gottman, J. M., Gottman, J. S., & Declaire, J. (2006). *10 lessons to transform your marriage: America's love lab experts share their strategies for strengthening your relationship.* New York: Random House.

Gould, M., Greenberg, T., Velting, D., & Shaffer, D. (2003). Youth suicide risk and preventative interventions: A review of the past 10 years. *Journal of the American Academy of Child and Adolescent Psychiatry, 42,* 386–405.

Goulet, C., Frappier, J., Fortin, S., Lampton, A., & Boulanger, M. (2009). Development and evaluation of a shaken baby syndrome prevention program. *Journal of Obstetric, Gynecologic and Neonatal Nursing, 38,* 7–21.

Government of Alberta. (2011). Employment standards: Adolescent and young persons. Retrieved from http://www.employment.alberta.ca/

Government of Canada. (2013) Eliminating mandatory retirement age. Canada's economic action plan. Retrieved on September 15, 2013 from http://actionplan.gc.ca/en

Government of Manitoba. (n.d.). *For the sake of the children: A supportive information program for parents experiencing separation and divorce.* Retrieved from http://www.gov.mb.ca /fs/childfam/ for_sake_ of_children.html

Graber, J. A. (2008). Pubertal and neuroendocrine development and risk for depressive disorders. In N. B. Allen & L. Sheeber (Eds.), *Adolescent emotional development and the emergence of depressive disorders.* New York: Cambridge University Press.

Graber, J. A., & Brooks-Gunn, J. (2002). Adolescent girls' sexual development. In G. M. Wingood & R. J. DiClemente (Eds.), *Handbook of women's sexual and reproductive health.* New York: Kluwer Academic/Plenum Publishers.

Grady, C. L., Springer, M. V., Hongwanishkul, D., McIntosh, A. R., & Winocur, G. (2006). Age-related changes in brain activity across the adult lifespan. *Journal of Cognitive Neuroscience, 18,* 227–241.

Graham, J. (2011). Measuring love in romantic relationships: A meta-analysis. *Journal of Social and Personal Relationships, 28*(6), 748–771.

Graham, S. (Ed.). (2006). Our children too: A history of the first 25 years of the Black caucus of the Society for Research in Child Development. *Monographs of the Society for Child Development, 71* (1, Serial No. 283).

Grambs, J. D. (1989). *Women over forty* (rev. ed.). New York: Springer.

Gramling, L. F. (2007). Women in young and mid-adulthood: Theory advancement and retroduction. *ANS Advances in Nursing Science, 30,* 95–107.

Gray, K. A., Day, N. L., Leech, S., & Richardson, G. A. (2005). Prenatal marijuana exposure: Effect on child depressive symptoms at ten years of age. *Neurotoxicology and Teratology, 27,* 439–448.

Gredler, M. E. (2008). Vygotsky's cultural historical theory of development. In N. J. Salkind (Ed.), *Encyclopedia of educational psychology.* Thousand Oaks, CA: Sage.

Green, R. J., & Mitchell, V. (2009). Gay and lesbian couples in therapy. In A. S. Gurman (Ed.), *Clinical handbook of couple therapy* (4th ed.). New York: Guilford.

Greenberg, N. (2008, October). Can spirituality be defined? University Studies Interdisciplinary Colloquy on Spirituality and Critical Inquiry. Retrieved from http://notes.utk.edu/bio/unistudy.nsf/935c0

d855156f9e08525738a006f2417/
bdc83cd10e58d14a852573b00072525d

Greene, M. G., & Adelman, R. D. (2001). Building the physician-older patient relationship. In M. L. Hummert & J. F. Nussbaum (Eds.), *Aging, communication, and health.* Mahwah, NJ: Erlbaum.

Greener, M. (2011). Thalidomide's shadow: Drug-induced teratogenicity. *Nurse Prescribing, 9*(5), 228–232.

Greenfield, P., Keller, H., Fuligni, A., & Maynard, A. (2003). Cultural pathways through universal development. *Annual Review of Psychology (54)* 461–490. Palo Alto, CA: Annual Reviews.

Greenough, A. (2007). Late respiratory outcomes after preterm birth. *Early Human Development, 83,* 785–788.

Greenstein, T. N. (2000). Economic dependence, gender, and the division of labor in the home: A replication and extension. *Journal of Marriage and the Family, 62,* 322–335.

Greer, F. R., Sicherer, S. H., Burks, A. W., & the Committee on Nutrition and Section on Allergy and Immunology. (2008). Effects of early nutritional interventions on the development of atopic disease in infants and children: The role of maternal dietary restriction, breast feeding, timing of introduction of complementary foods, and hydrolyzed formulas. *Pediatrics, 121,* 183–191.

Greydanus, D. E., Pratt, H. D., & Patel, D. R. (2007). Attention deficit, hyperactivity disorder across the lifespan: The child, adolescent, and adult. *Disease-A-Month, 53,* 70–131.

Griffin, K. (2001, June 7). Educators spread antibullying message to elementary level. *Economist & Sun/Tribune.*

Griffiths, R., Horsfall, J., Moore, M., Lane, D., Kroon, V., & Langdon, R. (2007). Assessment of health, well-being, and social connections: A survey of woman living in western Sydney. *International Journal of Nursing Practice, 13,* 3–13.

Grigoriadis, S., & Kennedy, S. H. (2002). Role of estrogen in the treatment of depression. *American Journal of Therapy, 9,* 503–509.

Groen, R., Bae, J., & Lim, K. (2012). Fear of the unknown: Ionizing radiation exposure during pregnancy. *American Journal of Obstetrics & Gynecology, 206*(6), 456–462.

Groer, M. W., & Morgan, K. (2007). Immune, health, and endocrine characteristics of depressed postpartum mothers. *Psychoneuroimmunology, 32,* 133–138.

Grossman, I., Na, J., Varnum, M. E., Park, D. C., Kitayama, S., & Nisbett, R. E. (2010). *Reasoning about social conflicts improves into old age.* Proceedings of the National Academy of Sciences U.S.A.

Grossman, K., & Grossman, K. E. (2009). The impact of attachment to mother and father at an early age on children's psychosocial development through early adulthood. In R. E. Tremblay, R. deV Peters, M. Boivin, & R. G. Barr (Eds.), *Encyclopedia on early childhood development.* Montreal: Centre of Excellence for Early Childhood Development.

Grover, S. A., Lowensteyn, I., Kaouche, M., Marchand, S., Coupal, L., DeCarolis, E., Zoccoli, J., & Defoy, I. (2006, January 23). The prevalence of erectile dysfunction in the primary care setting—Importance of risk factors in diabetes and vascular disease. *JAMA Internal Medicine Arch Intern Med, 166*(2), 213–219. doi:10.1001/archinte.166.2.213. Retrieved from http://archinte.jamanetwork.com/article.aspx?articleid=409589

Grusec, J. E. (2009). Parents' attitudes and beliefs: Their impact on children's development. In R. E. Tremblay, R. deV Peters, M. Boivin, & R. G. Barr (Eds.), *Encyclopedia of early childhood development.* Montreal: Centre of Excellence for Early Childhood Development.

Gu, D., Dupre, M. E., Sautter, J., Zhu, H., Liu, Y., & Yi, Z. (2009). Frailty and mortality among Chinese at advanced ages. *Journals of Gerontology A: Biological Sciences and Medical Sciences, 64,* 279–289.

Gualtieri, C. T., & Johnson, L. G. (2008). Age-related cognitive decline in patients with mood disorders. *Progress in Neuro-psychopharmacology and Biological Psychiatry.*

Gueguen, J., et al. (2012). Severe anorexia nervosa in men. Comparison with severe AN in women and analysis of mortality. *International Journal of Eating Disorders, 45*(4), 537–545.

Guelinckx, I., Devlieger, R., Beckers, K., & Vansant, G. (2008). Maternal obesity: Pregnancy complications, gestational weight gain, and nutrition. *Obesity Review, 9,* 140–150.

Guerrero, L., Anderson, P., & Afifi, W. (2011). *Close encounters: Communication in relationships* (3rd ed.). Thousand Oaks: Sage.

Guilford, J. P. (1967). *The structure of intellect.* New York: McGraw-Hill.

Gump, B., & Matthews, K. (2000, March). *Annual vacations, health, and death.* Paper presented at the meeting of American Psychosomatic Society, Savannah, GA.

Gunderson, E. P., Rifas-Shiman, S. L., Oken, E., Rich-Edwards, J. W., Kleinman, K. P., Taveras, E. M., et al. (2008). Association of fewer hours of sleep at 6 months postpartum with substantial weight retention at 1 year postpartum. *American Journal of Epidemiology, 167,* 178–187.

Gunnar, M. R., & Quevado, K. (2007). The neurobiology of stress and development. *Annual Review of Psychology* (Vol. 58). Palo Alto, CA: Annual Reviews.

Gunnar, M. R., Fisher, P. A., & the Early Experience, Stress, and Prevention Network. (2006). Bringing basis research on early experience and stress neurobiology to bear on preventive interventions for neglected and maltreated children. *Development and Psychopathology, 18,* 651–677.

Gupta, A., Thornton, J. W., & Huston, A. C. (2008). Working families should be poor—the New Hope Program. In D. R. Crane & T. B. Heaton (Eds.), *Handbook of families and poverty.* Thousand Oaks, CA: Sage.

Gupta, R. (2011). Death beliefs and practices from an Asian Indian American Hindu perspective. *Death Studies, 35,* 244–266.

Gupta, R. P., de Wit, M. L., & McKeown, D. (2007, October). The impact of poverty on the current and future health status of children. *Paediatric Child Health, 12*(8), 667–672.

Gurwitch, R. H., Silovsky, J. F., Schultz, S., Kees, M., & Burlingame, S. (2001). *Reactions and guidelines for children following trauma/disaster.* Norman, OK: Department of Pediatrics, University of Oklahoma Health Sciences Center.

Gustafsson, J. E. (2007). Schooling and intelligence: Effects of track of study on level and profile of cognitive abilities. In P. C. Kyllonen, R. D. Roberts, & L. Stankov (Eds.), *Extending intelligence.* Mahwah, NJ: Erlbaum.

Gutchess, A. H., Welsch, R. C., Hedden, T., Bangert, A., Minear, M., Liu, L. L., et al. (2005). Aging and the neural correlates of successful picture encoding: Frontal activations compensate for decreased medial-temporal activity. *Journal of Cognitive Neuroscience, 17,* 84–96.

Gutmann, D. L. (1975). Parenthood: A key to the comparative study of the life cycle. In N. Datan & L. Ginsberg (Eds.), *Life-span developmental psychology: Normative life crises.* New York: Academic Press.

Guttmacher Institute. (2006). Adolescents in Malawi, Uganda, and Ghana. Retrieved from http://www.guttmacher.org/

H

Ha, J. H., & Ingersoll-Dayton, B. (2008). The effect of widowhood on intergenerational ambivalence. *Journals of Gerontology B: Psychological Sciences and Social Sciences, 63,* S49–S58.

Hagg, T. (2009). From neurotransmitters to neurotrophic factors to neurogenesis. *Neuroscientist, 15,* 20–27.

Hahn, D. B., Payne, W. A., & Lucas, E. B. (2009). *Focus on health* (9th ed.). New York: McGraw-Hill.

Hahn, W. K. (1987). Cerebral lateralization of function: From infancy through childhood. *Psychological Bulletin, 101,* 376–392.

Hair, E. C., Moore, K. A., Garrett, S. B., Ling, T., & Cleveland, K. (2008). The continued importance of quality parent-adolescent relationships during late adolescence. *Journal of Research on Adolescence, 18,* 187–200.

Haith, M. M., Hazen, C., & Goodman, G. S. (1988). Expectation and anticipation of dynamic visual events by 3.5 month old babies. *Child Development, 59,* 467–479.

Halford, G. S. (2008). Cognitive developmental theories. In M. M. Haith & J. B. Benson (Eds.), *Encyclopedia of infancy and early childhood.*

Hall, C. B., Lipton, R. B., Sliwinski, M., Katz, M. J., Derby, C. A., & Verghese, J. (2009). Cognitive activities delay onset of memory decline in persons who develop dementia. *Neurology, 73,* 356–361.

Hall, L. (2009). *Autism spectrum disorders: From therapy to practice.* Boston: Allyn & Bacon.

Hallahan, D. P., Kauffman, J. M., & Pullen, P. C. (2009). *Exceptional learners* (11th ed.). Boston: Allyn & Bacon.

Halldin, M., Rosell, M., de Faire, U., & Hellenius, M. L. (2007). The metabolic syndrome: Prevalence and association to leisure-time and work-related physical activity in 60-year-old men and women. *Nutrition, Metabolism, and Cardiovascular Diseases, 17,* 349–357.

Halpern, D. F. (2007). The nature and nurture of critical thinking. In R. J. Sternberg, H. Roediger, & D. Halpern (Eds.), *Critical thinking in psychology.* New York: Cambridge University Press.

Halpern, D. F., Benbow, C. P., Geary, D. C., Gur, R. C., Hyde, J. S., & Gernsbacher, M. A. (2007). The science of sex differences in science and mathematics. *Psychological Science in the Public Interest, 8,* 1–51.

Halpern, I. F., & Brand, K. L. (1999, April). *The role of temperament in children's emotion reactions and coping responses to stress.* Paper presented at the meeting of Society for Research in Child Development, Albuquerque.

Hamamura, T., Heine, S. J., & Paulhus, D. L. (2008). Cultural differences in response styles: The role of the dialectical thinking. *Personality and Individual Differences, 44,* 932–942. Retrieved from http://www2.psych.ubc.ca/~ heine/docs/2008DialecticalResponses.pdf

Hamilton, M. A., & Hamilton, S. F. (2004). Designing work and service for learning. In S.F. Hamilton & M. A. Hamilton (Eds.), *The youth development handbook: Coming of age in American communities* (pp. 147–169). Thousand Oaks, CA: Sage.

Hamlin, J. K., Hallinan, E. V., & Woodward, A. L. (2008). Do as I do: 7-month-old infants selectively reproduce others' goals. *Developmental Science 11*(4), 487–94.

Hampton, et al. (2010). Completing the circle: Elders speak about end of life care with Aboriginal families in Canada. *Journal of Palliative Care, 6*(1), 6–14.

Han, W-J. (2009). Maternal employment. In D. Carr (Ed.). *Encyclopedia of the life course and human development.* Boston: Gale Cengage.

Hanish, L. D., & Guerra, N. G. (2004). Aggressive victims, passive victims, and bullies: Developmental continuity or developmental change? *Merrill-Palmer Quarterly, 50,* 17–38.

Hankin, B. L., Kassel, J. D., & Abela, J. R. (2005). Adult attachment dimensions and specificity of emotional distress symptoms: Prospective investigations of cognitive risk and interpersonal stress generation as mediating mechanisms. *Personality and Social Psychology Bulletin, 31,* 136–151.

Hannon, E., & Trehub, S. (2005). Tuning in to musical rhythms: Infants learn more readily than adults. *Proceedings of the National Academy of Science, 102,* 12639–12643.

Hansson, R. O., & Stroebe, M. S. (2007). *Bereavement in late life: Development, coping and adaptation*. Washington, DC: American Psychological Association.

Harder, G., Rash, J., Holyk, T., Jovel, E., & Harder, K. (2012). Indigenous youth suicide: A systematic review of the literature. *Pimatisiwin: A Journal of Aboriginal and Indigenous Community Health, 10*(1), 125–142.

Hardy, M. (2006). Older workers. In R. H. Binstock & L. K. George (Eds.), *Handbook of aging and the social sciences* (6th ed.). San Diego: Academic Press.

Hargreaves, D. A., & Tiggemann, M. (2004). Idealized body images and adolescent body image: "Comparing" boys and girls. *Body Image, 1*, 351–361.

Harkins, S. W., Price, D. D., & Martinelli, M. (1986). Effects of age on pain perception. *Journal of Gerontology, 41*, 58–63.

Harley, T. A. (2009). *The psychology of language*. Philadelphia: Psychology Press.

Harlow, H. F. (1958). The nature of love. *American Psychologist, 13*, 673–685.

Harman, S. M. (2007). Andropause. In J. E. Birren (Ed.), *Encyclopedia of gerontology* (2nd ed.). San Diego: Academic Press.

Harootyan, R. A. (2007). Volunteer activity in older adults. In J. E. Birren (Ed.), *Encyclopedia of gerontology* (2nd ed.). San Diego: Academic Press.

Harrington, S. E., & Smith, T. J. (2008). The role of chemotherapy at the end of life: "When is enough, enough?" *Journal of the American Medical Association, 299*, 2667–2678.

Harris, G. (2002). *Grandparenting: How to meet its responsibilities*. Los Angeles: The Americas Group.

Harris, K. M., Gorden-Larsen, P., Chantala, K., & Udry, J. R. (2006). Longitudinal trends in race/ethnic disparities in leading health indicators from adolescence to young adulthood. *Archives of Pediatrics and Adolescent Medicine, 160*, 74–81.

Harris, K. R., Graham, S., Brindle, M., & Sandmel, K. (2010). Metacognition and children's writing. In D. Hacker, J. Dunlosky, & A. Graesser (Eds.), *Handbook of metacognition in education*. Mahwah, NJ: Erlbaum.

Harris, P. L. (2000). *The work of the imagination*. Oxford: Oxford University Press.

Harris, P. L. (2006). Social cognition. In W. Damon & R. Lerner (Eds.), *Handbook of child psychology* (6th ed.). New York: Wiley.

Harris, Y. R., & Graham, J. A. (2007). *The African American child*. New York: Springer.

Harrison, T. (2010). Family-centred pediatric nursing care. State of the science. *Journal of Pediatric Nursing, 25*, 335–343.

Hart, D., Atkins, R., & Donnelly, T. M. (2006). Community service and moral development. In M. Killen & J. Smetana (Eds.), *Handbook of moral development*. Mahwah, NJ: Erlbaum.

Hart, S., & Carrington, H. (2002). Jealousy in 6-month-old infants. *Infancy, 3*, 395–402.

Harter, S. (2006). The self. In W. Damon & R. Lerner (Eds.), *Handbook of child psychology* (6th ed.). New York: Wiley.

Hartley, A. (2006). Changing role of the speed of processing construct in the cognitive psychology of human aging. In J. E. Birren & K. W. Schaie (Eds.), *Handbook of the psychology of aging* (6th ed.). San Diego: Academic Press.

Hartshorne, H., & May, M. S. (1928–1930). *Moral studies in the nature of character: Studies in the nature of character*. New York: Macmillan.

Hartup, W. W. (1983). The peer system. In P. H. Mussen (Ed.), *Handbook of child psychology* (4th ed., Vol. 4). New York: Wiley.

Hartup, W. W. (1996). The company they keep: Friendships and their development significance. *Child Development, 67*, 1–13.

Hartup, W. W. (2009). Critical issues and theoretical viewpoints. In K. H. Rubin, W. M. Bukowski, & B. Laursen (Eds.), *Handbook of peer interactions, relationships, and groups*. New York: Guilford.

Hartwig, S., et al. (2010). Genomic characterization of Wilms' tumor suppressor 1 targets in nephron progenitor cells during kidney development. *Development, 137*, 1189–1203.

Hasher, L. (2003, February 28). Commentary in "The wisdom of the wizened." *Science, 299*, 1300–1302.

Hass, J. (2001). Rocking in the real world. *Canadian Medical Association Journal, 165*(9), 1288.

Hastings, P. D., Utendale, W. T., & Sullivan, C. (2007). The socialization of prosocial development. In J. E. Grusec & P. D. Hastings (Eds.), *Handbook of socialization*. New York: Guilford.

Hatfield, E., Rapson, R., & Martel, L. (2007). Passionate love and sexual desire. In S. Kitayama & D. Cohen (Eds.), *Handbook of cultural psychology* (pp. 760–779). New York: Guilford Press.

Hauser Kunz, J., & Grych, J. (2013). Parental psychological control and autonomy granting: Distinctions and associations with child and family. *Science and Practice, 13*(2), 77–94.

Hawkes, C. (2006). Olfaction in neurogenerative disorder. *Advances in Otorhinolaryngology, 63*, 133–151.

Hawkley, L. C., Thisted, R. A., Masi, C. M., & Cacioppo, J. T. (2010). Loneliness predicts increased blood pressure: 5-year cross-lagged analyses in middle-aged and older adults. *Psychology and Aging, 25*, 132–141.

Hayflick, L. (1977). The cellular basis for biological aging. In C. E. Finch & L. Hayflick (Eds.), *Handbook of the biology of aging*. New York: Van Nostrand.

Hayslip, B., & Hansson, R. (2003). Death awareness and adjustment across the life span. In C. D. Bryant (Ed.), *Handbook of death and dying*. Thousand Oaks, CA: Sage.

Hazan, C., & Shaver, P. R. (1987). Romantic love conceptualized as an attachment process. *Journal of Personality and Social Psychology, 52*, 522–524.

He, C., Hotson, L., & Trainor, L. J. (2009). Development of infant mismatch responses to auditory pattern changes between 2 and 4 months of age. *European Journal of Neuroscience, 29*, 861–867.

Healey, J. F. (2009). *Race, ethnicity and class* (5th ed.). Thousand Oaks, CA: Sage.

Healey, M. K., & Hasher, L. (2009). Limitations to the deficit attenuation hypothesis: Aging and decision making. *Journal of Consumer Psychology, 19*, 17–22.

Health Canada. (1999). *Healthy development of children and youth: The role of the determinants of health*. Ottawa: Health Canada.

Health Canada. (2002). Healthy development of children and youth: The role of the determinants of health. Retrieved from www.hc-sc.gc.ca/dcadea/publications/healthy_dev_overview_e.html

Health Canada. (2005). Sudden infant death syndrome (SIDS). Retrieved from http://www.hc-sc.gc.ca/

Health Canada. (2007a). Eating well with Canada's Food Guide. Retrieved from http://www.hc-sc.gc.ca/

Health Canada. (2007c). Human papillomavirus (HPV). Retrieved from www.hc-sc.gc.ca/

Health Canada. (2008). Seniors and aging— Osteoarthritis. Retrieved May 5, 2010 from http://www.hc-sc.gc.ca/hl-vs/iyh-vsv/diseases-maladies/seniors-aines-ost-art-eng.php

Health Canada. (2010). Healthy Canadians: A federal report on comparable health indicators 2010. Retrieved from http://www.hc-sc.gc.ca/hcs-sss/pubs/system-regime/2010-fed-comp-indicat/index-eng.php

Health Canada. (2011a). Lead and health. Retrieved from http://www.hc-sc.gc.ca/

Health Canada. (2011b). Lead-based paint. Retrieved from http://www.hc-sc.gc.ca/

Health Canada. (2012). Nutrition for healthy term infants: Recommendations from birth to six months. Statement of the Infant Feeding Joint Working Group: Canadian Paediatric Society, Dietitians of Canada and Health Canada. Retrieved from http://www.hc-sc.gc.ca/fn-an/nutrition/infant-nourisson/recom/index-eng.php

Health Canada. (2012a). First Nations and Inuit health: Fetal alcohol syndrome/Fetal alcohol effects. Retrieved from http://www.hc-sc.gc.ca/

Health Canada. (2012b). Food and nutrition: Principles and recommendations for infant feeding from birth to six months. Retrieved from http://www.hc-sc.gc.ca/

Health Canada. (2012c). Summary of results of the 2010–2011 Youth Smoking Survey. Retrieved from http://www.hc-ps/

Health Canada (2012d, May). Brain: Canada's brain research fund. Factsheet. http://www.hc-sc.gc.ca/ahc-asc/media/nr-cp/_2012/2012-60fs-eng.php (retrieved September 8, 2012)

Health Canada. (2013). National native alcohol and drug abuse program. Retrieved from http://www.hc-sc.gc.ca/

Healthy Child Manitoba. (2012). *Position paper: Developing a national prevalence plan for FASD in Canada.* Retrieved from http://www.canfasd.ca/.

Heart and Stroke Foundation Canada. (2013). Statistics. Retrieved from http://www.heartandstroke.com/site/c.iklQLcMWJtE/b.3483991/k.34A8/Statistics.htm

Hedberg, P., Ohrvik, J., Lonnberg, I., & Nilsson, G. (2009). Augmented blood pressure response to exercise is associated with improved long-term survival in older people. *Heart, 95,* 1072–1078.

Hedden, T., Lautenschlager, G., & Park, D. C. (2005). Contributions of processing ability and knowledge to verbal memory tasks across the adult lifespan. *Quarterly Journal of Experimental Psychology, 58*(A), 169–190.

Heidrich, D. (2007). *The dying process.* In K. Kuebler, D. Heinrich, & P. Esper (Eds.), *Palliative and end-of-life-care* (2nd ed.) (pp. 33–45). St. Louis: Elsevier.

Heimann, M., Strid, K., Smith, L., Tjus, T., Ulvund, S. E., & Meltzoff, A. N. (2006). Exploring the relation between memory, gestural communication, and the emergence of language in infancy: A longitudinal study. *Infant and Child Development, 15,* 233–249.

Helman, C. (2008). Inside T. Boone Pickens' brain. *Forbes.* Retrieved from http://www.forbes.com/

Helson, R. (1997, August). *Personality change: When is it adult development?* Paper presented at the meeting of the American Psychological Association, Chicago.

Helson, R., & Wink, P. (1992). Personality change in women from the early 40s to early 50s. *Psychology and Aging, 7,* 46–55.

Helzner, E. P., et al. (2009). Contribution of vascular risk factors to the progression of Alzheimer disease. *Archives of Neurology, 66,* 343–348.

Henderson, A. J. (2008). The effects of tobacco smoke exposure on respiratory health in school-aged children. *Pediatric Respiratory Review, 9,* 21–28.

Hennessey, B. A. (2011). Intrinsic motivation and creativity: Have we come full circle? In R. A. Beghetto & J. C. Kaufman (Eds.), *Nurturing creativity in the classroom.* New York: Cambridge University Press.

Hennessey, B. A., & Amabile, T. M. (2010). Creativity. *Annual Review of Psychology* (Vol. 61). Palo Alto, CA: Annual Reviews.

Henriksen, T. B., Hjollund, N. H., Jensen, T. K., Bonde, J. P., Andersson, A. M., Kolstad, H., et al. (2004). Alcohol consumption at the time of conception and spontaneous abortion. *American Journal of Epidemiology, 160,* 661–667.

Henry, N. J. M., Berg, C. A., Smith, T. W., & Florsheim, P. (2007). Positive and negative characteristics of marital interaction and their association with marital satisfaction in middle aged and older couples. *Psychology and Aging, 22,* 428–441.

Hepper, P. (2007). The foundations of development. In A. Slater & M. Lewis, *Introduction to infant development* (2nd ed.). New York: Oxford University Press.

Herbison, A. E., Porteus, R., Paper, J. R., Mora, J. M., & Hurst, P. R. (2008). Gonadotropin-releasing hormone neuron requirements for puberty, ovulation, and fertility. *Endocrinology, 149,* 597–604.

Herek, G. M. (2008). Hate crimes and stigma-related experiences among sexual minority adults in the United States: Prevalence estimates from a national probability sample. *Journal of Interpersonal Violence, 24*(1), 54–74.

Herman, C. P., van Strien, T., & Polivy, J. (2008). Undereating or eliminating overeating. *American Psychologist, 63,* 202–203.

Hermann-Giddens, M. E. (2006). Recent data on pubertal milestones in United States children: The secular trend toward earlier development. *International Journal of Andrology, 29,* 241–246.

Hermann-Giddens, M. E. (2007). The decline in the age of menarche in the United States: Should we be concerned? *Journal of Adolescent Health, 40,* 201–203.

Hernandez-Reif, M. (2007). Unpublished review of J. W. Santrock, *Life-span development* (12th ed.). New York: McGraw-Hill.

Hernandez-Reif, M., Diego, M., & Field, T. (2007). Preterm infants show reduced stress behaviors and activity after 5 days of massage therapy. *Infant Behavior and Development, 30,* 557–561.

Hertzman, C. (2009, December). The state of child development in Canada: Are we moving toward, or away from, equity from the start? *Paediatric Child Health, 14*(10), 673–676.

Hertzog, C., Kramer, A. F., Wilson, R. S., & Lindenberger, U. (2009). Enrichment effects on adult cognitive development. *Psychological Perspectives in the Public Interest, 9,* 1–65.

Hertz-Picciotto, I., Park, H. Y., Dostal, M., Kocan, A., Trnovec, T., & Sram, R. (2008). Prenatal exposure to persistent and non-persistent organic compounds, and effects on immune system development. *Basic and Clinical Pharmacology and Toxicology, 102,* 146–154.

Hess, T. M., & Hinson, J. T. (2006). Age-related variation in the influences of stereotypes on memory in adulthood. *Psychology and Aging, 21,* 621–625.

Hess, T. M., Auman, C., Colcombe, S. J., & Rahhal, T. A. (2003). The impact of stereotype threat on age differences in memory performance. *Journals of Gerontology: Psychological and Social Sciences, 58*(B), P3–P11.

Hetherington, E. M. (2000). Divorce. In A. Kazdin (Ed.), *Encyclopedia of psychology.* Washington, DC: American Psychological Association and Oxford University Press.

Hetherington, E. M. (2006). The influence of conflict, marital problem solving, and parenting on children's adjustment in nondivorced, divorced, and remarried families. In A. Clarke-Stewart & J. Dunn (Eds.), *Families count.* New York: Oxford University Press.

Hetherington, E. M., & Kelly, J. (2002). *For better or for worse: Divorce reconsidered.* New York: Norton.

Hetherington, E. M., & Stanley-Hagan, M. (2002). Parenting in divorced and remarried families. In M. H. Bornstein (Ed.), *Handbook of parenting* (2nd ed., Vol. 3). Mahwah, NJ: Erlbaum.

Heyman, G. D., & Legare, C. H. (2005). Children's evaluation of sources of information about traits. *Developmental Psychology, 41,* 636–647.

Heyman, G. D., & Sweet, M. A. (2009). Children's reasoning about lie-telling and truth-telling in polite circumstances. *Social Development, 18*(3), 728–746.

Heyman, G. D., Fu, G., & Lee, K. (2007). Evaluating claims people make about themselves: The development of skepticism. *Child Development, 78,* 367–375.

Hickman, J. M., Rogers, W. A., & Fisk, A. D. (2007). Training older adults to use a new technology. *Journals of Gerontology B: Psychological Sciences and Social Sciences, 62* (Special Issue), P77–P84.

Higo, M., & Williamson, J. B. (2009). Retirement. In D. Carr (Ed.), *Encyclopedia of the life course and human development.* Boston: Gale Cengage.

Hill, M. A. (2007). Early human development. *Clinical Obstetrics and Gynecology, 50,* 2–9.

Himes, C. L. (2009a). Age structure. In D. Carr (Ed.), *Encyclopedia of the life course and human development.* Boston: Gale Cengage.

Himes, C. (2009b). Obesity. In D. Carr (Ed.), *Encyclopedia of the life course and human development.* Boston: Gale Cengage.

Hingson, R. W., Heeren, T., & Winter, M. R. (2006). Age at drinking onset and alcohol dependence: Age at onset, duration, and severity. *Archives of Pediatric and Adolescent Medicine, 160,* 739–746.

Hirsh, J. (2008, January 2). 3-D dialogue: Ursula Franklin and pacifism. Retrieved from http://www.youtube.com/

Hockenberry, M. (2010). *Wong's essentials of pediatric nursing* (8th ed.). New York: Elsevier.

Hockenberry, M., & Wilson, D. (2013). *Wong's essentials of pediatric nursing* (9th ed). St. Louis: Elsevier.

Hoeger, W. W. K., & Hoeger, S. A. (2008). *Principles and labs for physical fitness* (6th ed.). New York: McGraw-Hill.

Hoek, H. W. (2006). Incidence, prevalence and mortality of anorexia nervosa and other eating disorders. *Current Opinion in Psychiatry, 19,* 389–394.

Hoff, E., Laursen, B., & Tardif, T. (2002). Socioeconomic status and parenting. In M. H. Bornstein (Ed.), *Handbook of parenting* (2nd ed.). Mahwah, NJ: Erlbaum.

Hofheimer, J. A., & Lester, B. M. (2008). Neuropsychological assessment. In M. M. Haith & J. B. Benson (Eds.), *Encyclopedia of infancy and early childhood*. Oxford, UK: Elsevier.

Holden, K., & Hatcher, C. (2006). Economic status of the aged. In R. H. Binstock & L. K. George (Eds.), *Handbook of aging and the social science* (6th ed.). San Diego: Academic Press.

Holden, S. (2013, January 17). When they hammered out justice in the 60's—Greenwich Village: Music that defined a generation. *New York Times.* Retrieved from http://movies.nytimes.com/

Holden, T. (2012). Addiction is not a disease. *Canadian Medical Association Journal, 184*(6), 679.

Hollich, G., Newman, R. S., & Jusczyk, P. W. (2005). Infants' use of synchronized visual information to separate streams of speech. *Child Development, 76,* 598–613.

Hollier, L., & Wendel, G. (2008). Third trimester antiviral prophylaxis for preventing maternal genital herpes simplex virus (HSV) recurrences and neonatal infection. *Cochrane Database of Systematic Reviews, 1,* CD004946.

Holmes, L. (2011). Human teratogens: Update 2010. *Birth Defects Research (Part A), 91,* 1–7.

Holmes, T. H., & Rahe, R. H. (1967). The social readjustment rating scale. *Journal of Psychosomatic Research, 11,* 213–218.

Holstein, B. E., Due, P., Almind, G., & Avlund, K. (2007). Eight-year change in functional ability among 70- to 95-year-olds. *Scandinavian Journal of Public Health, 35,* 243–249.

Holtslander, L., & Duggleby, W. (2010). The hope experienced of older bereaved women who cared for a spouse with terminal cancer. *Qualitative Health Research, 19,* 388–400.

Holtslander, L., Bally, J., & Steeves, M. (2011). Walking a fine line: An exploration of the experience of findings balance for older persons bereaved after caregiving for a spouse with advanced cancer. *European Journal of Oncology Nursing, 15,* 254–259.

Holzman, L. (2009). *Vygotsky at work and play.* Clifton, NJ: Psychology Press.

Hooley, J., Ho, D. E., Slater, J., & Lockshin, A. (2010). Pain perception and non-suicidal self-injury. *Personality Disorder: Theory, Research, and Treatment, 1,* 170–179.

Hopkins, J. R. (2000). Erikson, E. H. (2000). In A. Kazdin (Ed.), *Encyclopedia of psychology.* Washington, DC: American Psychological Association and Oxford University Press.

Hoppmann, C. A., Gerstorf, D., Smith, J., & Klumb, P. L. (2007). Linking possible selves and behavior: Do domain-specific hopes and fears translate into daily activities in very old age? *Journals of Gerontology B: Psychological Sciences and Social Sciences, 62,* P104–P111.

Hoppmann, C., & Smith, J. (2007). Life-history related differences in possible selves in very old age. *International Journal of Aging and Human Development, 64,* 109–127.

Horn, J. (2007). Spearman, *g*, expertise, and the nature of human cognitive capacity. In P. C. Kyllonen, R. D. Roberts, & L. Stankov (Eds.), *Extending intelligence.* Mahwah, NJ: Erlbaum.

Horn, J. L., & Donaldson, G. (1980). Cognitive development II: Adulthood development of human abilities. In O. G. Brim & J. Kagan (Eds.), *Constancy and change in human development.* Cambridge, MA: Harvard University Press.

Horne, R. S., Franco, P., Adamson, T. M., Groswasser, J., & Kahn, A. (2002). Effects of body position on sleep and arousal characteristics in infants. *Early Human Development, 69,* 25–33.

Horney, K. (1967). *Feminine psychology.* New York: W.W. Norton & Company, Inc.

Horowitz, F. D. (2009). Introduction: A developmental understanding of giftedness and talent. In F. D. Horowitz, R. F. Subotnik, & D. J. Matthews (Eds.), *The development of giftedness and talent across the life span.* Washington, DC: American Psychological Association.

Horowitz, J. A., & Cousins, A. (2006). Postpartum depression treatment rates for at-risk women. *Nursing Research, 55* (Suppl. 2), S23–S27.

House, J. S., Landis, K. R., & Umberson, D. (1988). Social relationships and health. *Science, 241,* 540–545.

Houston, D. K., et al. (2009). Overweight and obesity over the adult life course and incident mobility limitation in older adults: The health, aging, and body composition study. *American Journal of Epidemiology, 169,* 927–936.

Howard, D. V., Howard, J. H., Dennis, N. A., LaVine, S., & Valentino, K. (2008). Aging and implicit learning of an invariant association. *Journals of Gerontology B: Psychological Sciences and Social Sciences, 63,* 100–P105.

Howe, M. L., & Courage, M. L. (2004). Demystifying the beginnings of memory. *Developmental Review, 24,* 1–5.

Howes, C. (2008). Friends and peers. In M. M. Haith & J. B. Benson (Eds.), *Encyclopedia of infant and early childhood development.* Oxford, UK: Elsevier.

Howland, R. H. (2010). Drug therapies for cognitive impairment and dementia. *Journal of Psychosocial Nursing and Mental Health Services, 48*(4), 11–14.

Hoyer, W. J., & Roodin, P. A. (2003). *Adult development and aging* (5th ed.). New York: McGraw-Hill.

Hoyer, W. J., & Roodin, P. A. (2009). *Adult development and aging* (6th ed.). New York: McGraw-Hill.

Hoyer, W. J., Rybash, J. M., & Roodin, P. A. (1999). *Adult development and aging* (4th ed.). New York: McGraw-Hill.

Hoyert, D. L., Mathews, T. J., Menacker, F., Strobino, D. M., & Guyer, B. (2006). Annual summary of vital statistics: 2004, *Pediatrics, 117,* 168–183.

HSBC Insurance. (2007). *The future of retirement: The new old age-global report.* London: Author.

Hsu, H. C. (2004). Antecedents and consequences of separation anxiety in first-time mothers: Infant, mother, and social-contextual characteristics. *Infant Behavior and Development, 27,* 113–133.

Hsu, J. L., et al. (2008). Gender differences and age-related white matter changes of the human brain: A diffusion tensor imaging study. *NeuroImage, 39,* 566–577.

Hu, H., et al. (2006). Fetal lead exposure at each stage of pregnancy as a predictor of infant mental development. *Environmental Health Perspectives, 114,* 1730–1735.

Huesmann, L. R., Dubow, E. F., Eron, L. D., & Boxer, P. (2006). Middle childhood family-contextual and personal factors as predictors of adult outcomes. In A. G. Huston & M. N. Ripke (Eds.), *Developmental contexts in middle childhood: Bridges to adolescence and adulthood.* New York: Cambridge University Press.

Huesmann, L. R., Moise-Titus, J., Podolski, C., & Eron, L. D. (2003). Longitudinal relations between children's exposure to TV violence and their aggressive and violent behavior in young adulthood: 1977–1992. *Developmental Psychology, 39,* 201–221.

Hughes, C., & Ensor, R. (2010). Do early social cognition and executive function predict individual differences in preschoolers' prosocial and antisocial behavior? In B. Sokol, U. Muller, J. Carpendale, A. Young, & G. Iarocci (Eds.), *Self- and social-regulation.* New York: Oxford University Press.

Hughes, M. E., Waite, L. J., LaPierre, T. A., & Luo, Y. (2007). All in the family: The impact of caring for grandchildren on grandparents' health. *Journals of Gerontology B: Psychological Sciences and Social Sciences, 62,* S108–S119.

Hughes, M., Morrison, K., & Asada, K. (2005). What's love got to do with it? Exploring the impact of maintenance rules, love attitudes, and network support of friends with benefits relationships. *Western Journal of Communication, 69,* 49–66.

Hughes, T. F. (2010). Promotion of cognitive health through cognitive activity in the aging population. *Aging and Health, 6,* 111–121.

Hui, W. S., Liu, Z., & Ho, S. C. (2010). Metabolic syndrome and all-cause mortality: A meta-analysis of prospective cohort studies. *European Journal of Epidemiology, 25*(6), 375–384.

Huizink, A. C., & Mulder, E. J. (2006). Maternal smoking, drinking, or cannibis use during pregnancy and neurobehavioral and cognitive functioning in human offspring. *Neuroscience and Biobehavioral Research, 30,* 24–41.

Hultsch, D. F., Hertzog, C., Small, B. J., & Dixon, R. A. (1999). Use it or lose it: Engaged lifestyle as a buffer of cognitive decline in aging? *Psychology and Aging, 14,* 245–263.

Human Cloning Foundation. (2012). Welcome to the official website of the

Human Cloning Foundation. http://www. humancloning.org

Human Genome Project Information. (2009). Cloning fact sheet. U.S. Department of Energy Office of Science, Office of Biological and Environmental Research, Human Genome Program. Retrieved from http://www.ornl.gov/

Human Resources and Skills Development Canada. (2008). *Special reports—What difference does learning make to financial security?* Retrieved from http://www4.hrsdc.gc.ca/.3ndic.1t.4r@-eng.jsp?iid=54

Human Resources and Skills Development Canada. (2012a). *Chapter 2—The new economy, a changing society and a renewed agenda for labour standards.* Ottawa: Author. Retrieved from http://www.hrsdc.gc.ca/eng/labour/employment_standards/fls/final/page07.shtml

Human Resources and Skills Development Canada. (2012b). *Family life—Age of mother at childbirth.* Retrieved from http://www4.hrsdc.gc.ca/

Human Resources and Skills Development Canada. (2012c). *Indicators of well-being in Canada: Work–employment rate.* Retrieved from http://www4.hrsdc.gc.ca/.3ndic.1t.4r@-eng.jsp?iid=13#M_7

Hunt, C. E., & Hauck, F. (2006, June 20). Sudden infant death syndrome. *Canadian Medical Association Journal, 174*(13), 1861–1869.

Hurd Clarke, L. (2006). Older women and sexuality: Experiences in marital relationships across the life course. *Canadian Journal of Aging, 25,* 129–140.

Hurt, H., Brodsky, N. L., Roth, H., Malmud, F., & Giannetta, J. M. (2005). School performance of children with gestational cocaine exposure. *Neurotoxicology and Teratology, 27,* 203–211.

Hurwitz, C., Duncan, J., & Wolfe, J. (2004). Caring for the child with cancer at the close of life. *Journal of the American Medical Association, 292,* 2141–2149.

Huston, A. C., & Ripke, M. N. (2006). Experiences in middle childhood and children's development: A summary and integration of research. In A. C. Huston & M. N. Ripke (Eds.), *Developmental contexts in middle childhood.* New York: Cambridge University Press.

Hutchinson, D. M., & Rapee, R. M. (2007). Do friends share similar body image and eating problems? The role of social networks and peer influences in early adolescence. *Behavior Research and Therapy, 45,* 1557–1577.

Huyck, M. H. (1999). Gender roles and gender identity in midlife. In S. L. Willis & J. D. Reid (Eds.), *Life in the middle.* San Diego: Academic Press.

Huyck, M. H., Ayalon, L., & Yoder, J. (2007). Using mixed methods to evaluate the use of caregiver strain measure to assess outcomes of a caregiver support program for caregivers of older adults. *International Journal of Geriatrics and Psychiatry, 22,* 160–165.

Hybels, C. F., & Blazer, D. G. (2004). Epidemiology of the late-life mental disorders. *Clinical Geriatric Medicine, 19,* 663–696.

Hyde, J. S. (2005). The gender similarities hypothesis. *American Psychologist, 60,* 581–592.

Hyde, J. S. (2007a). *Half the human experience* (7th ed.). Boston: Houghton Mifflin.

Hyde, J. S. (2007b). New directions in the study of gender similarities and differences. *Current Directions in Psychological Science, 16,* 259–263.

Hyde, J. S., & Price, M. (2007, November). *When two isn't better than one: Predictors of early sexual activity in adolescence using a cumulative risk model.* Paper presented at the meeting of the Society for the Scientific Study of Sexuality, Indianapolis.

Hyman, I. E., & Loftus, E. F. (2001). False childhood memories and eye-witness errors. In M. L. Eisen, J. A. Quas, & G. S. Goodman (Eds.), *Memory and suggestibility in the forensic interview.* Mahwah, NJ: Erlbaum.

Hyson, M. C., Copple, C., & Jones, J. (2006). Early childhood development and education. In W. Damon & R. Lerner (Eds.), *Handbook of child psychology* (6th ed.). New York: Wiley.

I

Iacoboni, M., & Dapretto, M. (2006). The mirror neuron system and the consequences of its dysfunction. *Nature Reviews: Neuroscience, 7,* 942–951.

Iacono, M. V. (2007). Osteoporosis: A national public health priority. *Journal of Perianesthesia Nursing, 223,* 175–180.

ICM. (2011). ICM international definition of the midwife. The Hague: International Confederation of Midwives.

Idler, E. L., Kasl, S. V., & Hays, J. C. (2001). Patterns of religious practice and belief in the last year of life. *Journals of Gerontology B: Psychological Sciences and Social Sciences, 56,* S326–S334.

Ikeda, A., et al. (2007). Marital status and mortality among Japanese men and women: The Japanese Collaborative Cohort Study. *BMC Public Health, 7,* 73.

Iliffe, S., et al. (2009). Primary care and dementia: 1. Diagnosis, screening, and disclosure. *International Journal of Geriatric Psychiatry, 24,* 895–901.

Ilola, L. M. (1990). Culture and health. In R. W. Brislin (Ed.), *Applied cross-cultural psychology.* Newbury Park, CA: Sage.

Imada, T., Zhang, Y., Cheour, M., Taulu, S., Ahonen, A., & Kuhl, P. K. (2007). Infant speech perception activates Broca's area: A developmental magnetoencephalography study. *Neuroreport, 17,* 957–962.

Impett, E. A., Schooler, D., Tolman, L., Sorsoli, L., & Henson, J. M. (2008). Girls' relationship authenticity and self-esteem across adolescence. *Developmental Psychology, 44,* 722–733.

Insel, P. M., & Roth, W. T. (2008). *Core concepts in health* (10th ed.). New York: McGraw-Hill.

International Clearinghouse for Birth Defects Monitoring Systems. (2001). *Annual Report.* Rome, Italy.

Ip, S., Chung, M., Raman, G., Chew, P., Magula, N., Devine, D., et al. (2007). Breastfeeding and maternal and infant health outcomes in developed countries. *Evidence Report/Technology Assessment, 153,* 1–86.

Iranmanesh, S., Hosseini, H., & Esmaili, M. (2011). Evaluating the "good death" concept from Iranian bereaved family members' perspective. *The Journal of Supportive Oncology, 9*(2), 59–63.

Irvine, S. H., & Berry, J. W. (Eds.). (2010). *Human abilities in cultural contexts.* New York: Cambridge University Press.

Isella, V., Mapelli, C., Morielli, N., Pelati, O., Franceschi, M., Appollonio, I. M. (2008). Age-related quantitative and qualitative changes in decision-making ability. *Behavioral Neurology, 19,* 59–63.

Issuree, P. D., Pushparaj, P. N., Pervaiz, S., & Melendez, A. J. (2009). Resveratrol attenuates C5a-induced inflammatory responses in vitro and in vivo by inhibiting phospholipase D and sphingosine kinase activities. *FACEB Journal, 23,* 2412–2424.

Iwasa, H., Masui, Y., Gondo, Y., Inagaki, H., Kawaal, C., & Suzuki, T. (2008). Personality and all-cause mortality among older adults dwelling in a Japanese community: A five-year population-based prospective cohort study. *American Journal of Geriatric Psychiatry, 16,* 399–405.

J

Jack, S., et al. (2006). Child maltreatment in Canada: Overview paper. Public Health Agency of Canada.

Jack, S. (2011). Child maltreatment in Canada. National Clearinghouse on Family Violence. Public Health Agency of Canada. Retrieved from http://www.phac-aspc.gc.ca/ncfv-cnivf/pdfs/nfnts-2006-maltr-eng.pdf

Jackendoff, R., & Pinker, S. (2005). The nature of the language faculty and its implications for evolution of language (reply to Fitch, Hauser, & Chomsky). *Cognition, 97*(2), 211–225.

Jackson, J. J., et al. (2009). Not all conscientiousness scales change alike: A multimethod, multisample study of age differences in the facets of conscientiousness. *Journal of Personality and Social Psychology, 96,* 446–459.

Jackson, S. L. (2008). *Research methods.* Belmont, CA: Wadsworth.

Jacobs, J. M., Hammerman-Rozenberg, R., Cohen, A., & Stressman, J. (2008). Reading daily predicts reduced mortality among men from a cohort of community-dwelling 70-year-olds. *Journals of Gerontology B: Psychological Sciences and Social Sciences, 63,* S73–S80.

Jacobs-Lawson, J. M., Hershey, D. A., & Neukam, K. A. (2005). Gender differences in factors that influence time spent planning for retirement. *Journal of Women and Aging, 16,* 55–69.

Jaeggi, S. M., Berman, M. G., & Jonides, J. (2009). Training attentional processes. *Trends in Cognitive Science, 37,* 644–654.

Jaffee, S., & Hyde, J. S. (2000). Gender differences in moral orientation: A meta-analysis. *Psychological Bulletin, 126,* 703–726.

Jagust, W., & D'Esposito, M. (Eds.). (2009). *Imaging the human brain.* Oxford, UK: Oxford University Press.

Jain, M. M., Joshi, A., Tayade, N. G., Jaiswar, S. R., & Thakkar, K. B. (2013, January 16). Knowledge, attitude, and practices regarding "The role of spirituality in current medical practice amongst medical professionals" in a tertiary care hospital. *Journal of Medical and Dental Sciences.* Retrieved from http://www.jemds.com/

James, A. H., Brancazio, L. R., & Price, T. (2008). Aspirin and reproductive outcomes. *Obstetrical and Gynecological Survey, 63,* 49–57.

James, W. H. (2005). Biological and psychosocial determinants of male and female human sexual orientation. *Journal of Biosocial Science, 37,* 555–567.

Jampel, H., et al. (2009). Retinal thickness in eyes of older normal individuals and its implication for the diagnosis of glaucoma. *Journal of Glaucoma, 18,* 37–43.

Jamshidi, Y., Snieder, H., Ge, D., Spector, T. D., & O'Dell, S. D. (2007). The SH2B gene is associated with serum leptin and body fat in normal female twins. *Obesity, 15,* 5–9.

Janacek, R. J., Anderson, N., Liu, M., Zheng, S., Yang, Q., & Tso, P. (2005). Effects of yo-yo diet, caloric restriction, and olestra on tissue distribution of hexachlorobenzene. *American Journal of Physiology and Gastrointestinal Liver Physiology, 288,* G292–G299.

Janssen, P., Saxell, M., Page, L., Klein, M., Liston, R., & Lee, S. (2009). Outcomes of planned home births with registered midwife versus planned hospital birth with midwife or physician. *Canadian Medical Association Journal, 181*(6–7), 377–383.

Jasik, C. B., & Lustig, R. H. (2008). Adolescent obesity and puberty: The "perfect storm." *Annals of the New York Academy of Sciences, 1135,* 265–279.

Jaswal, V. K., & Neely, L. A. (2006). Adults don't always know best: Preschoolers use past reliability over age when learning new words. *Psychological Science, 17,* 757–758.

Javo, C., Rønning, J. A., & Heyerdahl, S. (2004). Child-rearing in an indigenous Sami population in Norway: A cross-cultural comparison of parental attitudes and expectations. *Scandinavian Journal of Psychology, 45,* 67–78.

Jellinger, K. A. (2009). Significance of brain lesions in Parkinson disease dementia and Lewy body dementia. *Frontiers of Neurology and Neuroscience, 24,* 114–25.

Jensen, P. S., et al. (2007). Three-year follow-up of the NIMH MTA study. *Journal of the American Academy of Child and Adolescent Psychiatry, 46,* 989–1002.

Jessberger, S., & Gage, F. H. (2008). Stem-cell-associated structural and functional plasticity in the aging hippocampus. *Psychology and Aging, 23,* 684–691.

Jha, A. (2012, October 14). Childhood stimulation key to brain development, study finds. *Special Needs Digest, 20*(5), 530–537.

Ji, C. Y., & Chen, T. J. (2008). Secular changes in stature and body mass index for Chinese youth in sixteen major cities, 1950s–2005. *American Journal of Human Biology, 67*(2), 387–395.

Jiao, S., Ji, G., & Jing, Q. (1996). Cognitive development of Chinese urban only children and children with siblings. *Child Development, 67,* 387–395.

Johansson, E. (2006). Children's morality: Perspectives and research. In B. Spodak & N. Saracho (Eds.), *Handbook of research on the education of young children* (2nd ed.). Mahwah, NJ: Erlbaum.

Johnson, A. P., Abernathy, T., Howell, D., Brazil, K., & Scott, S. (2009). Resource utilization and costs of palliative cancer care in an interdisciplinary health care model. *Palliative Medicine, 23,* 448–459.

Johnson, C. L., & Troll, L. E. (1992). Family functioning in late life. *Journals of Gerontology, 47,* S66–S72.

Johnson, F., & Wardle, J. (2005). Dietary restraint, body dissatisfaction, and psychological distress: a prospective analysis. *Journal of Abnormal Psychology, 114*(1), 119.

Johnson, G. B., & Losos, J. (2010). *The living world* (6th ed.). New York: McGraw-Hill.

Johnson, H. L., Erbelding, E. J., & Ghanem, K. G. (2007). Sexually transmitted infections during pregnancy. *Current Infectious Disease Reports, 9,* 125–133.

Johnson, J. A., Musial, D. L., Hall, G. E., & Gollnick, D. M. (2011). *Foundations of American education* (15th ed.). Upper Saddle River, NJ: Prentice Hall.

Johnson, J. G., Zhang, B., Greer, J. A., & Prigerson, H. G. (2007). Parental control, partner dependency, and complicated grief among widowed adults in the community. *Journal of Nervous and Mental Disease, 195,* 26–30.

Johnson, K., & Daviss, B. (2005). Outcomes of planed home births with certified professional midwives: Large prospective study in North America. *BMJ 330*(7505), 1416.

Johnson, S. (2004), *The practice of emotionally focused marital therapy: Creating connections* (2nd ed.). New York: Brunner/Mazel.

Johnson, S. (2007). Cognitive and behavioral outcomes following very preterm birth. *Seminars in Fetal and Neonatal Medicine, 12,* 363–373.

John-Steiner, V. (2007). Vygotsky on thinking and speaking. In H. Daniels, J. Wertsch, & M. Cole (Eds.), *The Cambridge companion to Vygotsky.* New York: Cambridge University Press.

Johnston, A. M., Barnes, M. A., & Desrochers, A. (2008). Reading comprehension: Developmental processes, individual differences, and interventions. *Canadian Psychology, 49*(2), 125–132.

Johnston, A. P., De Lisio, M., & Parise, G. (2008). Resistance training, sarcopenia, and the mitochondrial theory of aging. *Applied Physiology, Nutrition, and Metabolism, 33,* 191–199.

Johnston, B. B. (2008). Will increasing folic acid in fortified grain products further reduce neural tube defects without causing harm? Consideration of the evidence. *Pediatric Research, 63,* 2–8.

Johnston, C., Seipp, C., Hommersen, P., Hoza, B., & Fine, S. (2005). Treatment choices and experiences in attention deficit and hyperactivity disorder: Relations to parents' beliefs and attributions. *Child: Care, Health & Development, 31,* 669–677.

Johnston, L. D., O'Malley, P. M., Bachman, J. G., & Schulenberg, J. E. (2007). *Monitoring the future national survey results on drug use, 1975–2006. Vol. II: College students and adults ages 19–45* (NIH Publication No. 07-6206). Bethesda, MD: National Institute on Drug Abuse.

Joint Economic Committee. (2007, February). *Investing in raising children.* Washington, DC: U.S. Senate.

Jolley, S. N., Ellmore, S., Barnard, K. E., & Carr, D. B. (2007). Dysregulation of the hypothalamic-pituitary-adrenal axis in postpartum depression. *Biological Research for Nursing, 8,* 210–222.

Jolly, C. A. (2005). Diet manipulation and prevention of aging, cancer, and autoimmune disease. *Current Opinions in Clinical Nutrition and Metabolic Care, 8,* 382–387.

Jones, D. C., Bain, N., & King, S. (2008). Weight and muscularity concerns as longitudinal predictors of body image among early adolescent boys: A test of the dual path model. *Body Image, 5,* 195–204.

Jones, M. D., & Galliher, R. V. (2007). Ethnic identity and psychosocial functioning in Navajo adolescents. *Journal of Research on Adolescence, 17,* 683–696.

Jones, M. H., West, S. D., & Estell, D. B. (2006). The Mozart effect: Arousal, preference, and spatial performance. *Psychology of Aesthetics, Creativity, and the Arts, 5,* 26–32.

Jopp, D., & Rott, C. (2006). Adaptation in very old age: Exploring the role of resources and attitudes for centenarians' happiness. *Psychology and Aging, 21,* 266–280.

Jordan, S. J., et al. (2008). Serious ovarian, fallopian tube, and primary peritoneal cancers: A comprehensive epidemiological analysis. *International Journal of Cancer.*

Jorgensen, M. E., Borch-Johnsen, K., & Bjerregaard, P. (2006). Lifestyle modifies obesity-associated risk of cardiovascular disease in a genetically homogeneous population. *American Journal of Clinical Nutrition, 84,* 29–36.

Joseph, J. (2006). *The missing gene.* New York: Algora.

Joseph, K., Allen, A., Dodds, L., Turner, L., Scott, H., & Liston, R. (2005). The perinatal effects of delayed childbearing. *Obstetrics & Gynecology, 105,* 1410–1418.

Joshi, S., & Kotecha, S. (2007). Lung growth and development. *Early Human Development, 83*, 789–794.

Judy, H. (2003–2004). Yours, mine and ours: New boundaries for modern stepfamilies. *Transition Magazine, 33*(4) [online] http://www.vifamily.ca/

Juffer, F., Bakermans-Kranenburg, M. J., & van IJzendoorn, M. H. (2007). *Promoting positive parenting.* Mahwah, NJ: Erlbaum.

Jung, C. (1933). *Modern man in search of a soul.* New York: Harcourt Brace.

Jung, Y., Gruenewald, T. L., Seeman, T. E., & Sarkisian, C. A. (2010). Productive activities and development of frailty in older adults. *Journals of Gerontology B: Psychological Sciences and Social Sciences, 65*(B), 256–261.

Jylhava, J., et al. (2009). Genetics of C-reactive protein and complement factor H have an epistatic effect on carotid artery compliance: The Cardiovascular Risk in Young Finns Study. *Clinical and Experimental Immunology, 155*, 53–58.

K

Kaasa, S. (2008). Editorial: Palliative care research—Time to intensify international collaboration. *Palliative Medicine, 22*, 301–302.

Kaeberlein, M. (2010). Reseveratrol and rapamycin: Are they anti-aging drugs? *Bioessays, 32*, 96–99.

Kagan, J. (1987). Perspectives on infancy. In J. D. Osofsky (Ed.), *Handbook on infant development* (2nd ed.). New York: Wiley.

Kagan, J. (2000). Temperament. In A. Kazdin (Ed.), *Encyclopedia of psychology.* Washington, DC: American Psychological Association and Oxford University Press.

Kagan, J. (2002). Behavioral inhibition as a temperamental category. In R. J. Davidson, K. R. Scherer, & H. H. Goldsmith (Eds.), *Handbook of affective sciences.* New York: Oxford University Press.

Kagan, J. (2008). Fear and wariness. In M. M. Haith & J. B. Benson (Eds.), *Encyclopedia of infant and early childhood development.* Oxford, UK: Elsevier.

Kagan, J. (2013). Temperamental contributions to inhibited and uninhibited profiles. In P. D. Zelazo (Ed.), *Oxford handbook of developmental psychology.* New York: Oxford University Press.

Kagan, J., Snidman, N., Kahn, V., & Towsley, S. (2007). The preservation of two infant temperaments into adolescence. *Monographs of the Society for Research in Child Development, 72*(2), 1–75.

Kagitcibasi, C. (2007). *Family, self, and human development across cultures.* Mahwah, NJ: Erlbaum.

Kahana, A., Kahana, B., & Hammel, R. (2009). Stress in later life. In D. Carr (Ed.), *Encyclopedia of the life course and human development.* Boston: Gale Cengage.

Kail, R. V. (2007). Longitudinal evidence that increases in processing speed and working

memory enhance children's reasoning. *Psychological Science, 18*, 312–313.

Kaleth, A. S., Chittenden, T. W., Hawkins, B. J., Hargens, T. A., Guill, S. G., Zedalis, D., et al. (2007). Unique cardiopulmonary exercise test responses in overweight middle-aged adults with obstructive sleep apnea. *Sleep Medicine, 8*, 160–168.

Kamerman, S. B. (1989). Child care, women, work, and the family: An international overview of child-care services and related policies. In J. S. Lande, S. Scarr, & N. Gunzenhauser (Eds.), *Caring for children: Challenge to America.* Hillsdale, NJ: Erlbaum.

Kamerman, S. B. (2000a). Parental leave policies. *Social Policy Report of the Society for Research in Child Development, XIV* (No. 2), 1–15.

Kamerman, S. B. (2000b). From maternity to paternity child leave policies. *Journal of the Medical Women's Association, 55*, 98–99.

Kane, R. L. (2007). Health care and services. In J. E. Birren (Ed.), *Encyclopedia of gerontology* (2nd ed.). San Diego: Academic Press.

Kar, N. (2009). Psychological impact of disasters on children: Review of assessment and interventions. *World Journal of Pediatrics, 5*, 5–11.

Karasu, S. R. (2007). The institution of marriage: Terminable or interminable? *American Journal of Psychotherapy, 61*, 1–16.

Karney, B. R., & Bradbury, T. N. (2005). Contextual influences on marriage. *Current Directions in Psychological Science, 14*, 171–175.

Karniol, R., Grosz, E., & Schorr, I. (2003). Caring, gender-role orientation, and volunteering. *Sex Roles, 49*, 11–19.

Kastenbaum, R. J. (2004). *Death, society, and human experience* (8th ed.). Boston: Allyn & Bacon.

Kastenbaum, R. J. (2007). *Death, society, and human experience* (9th ed.). Boston: Allyn & Bacon.

Katimavik. (2010). http://www.katimavik.org/

Kato, T. (2005). The relationship between coping with stress due to romantic break-ups and mental health. *Japanese Journal of Social Psychology, 20*, 171–180.

Katz, P. R., Karuza, J., Intrator, O., & Mor, V. (2009). Nursing home physician specialists: A response to the workforce crisis in long-term care. *Annals of Internal Medicine, 150*, 411–413.

Katzov, H. (2007). New insights into autism from a comprehensive genetic map. *Clinical Genetics, 72*, 186–187.

Kaufman, S. R. (2005). *And a time to die.* New York: Scribner.

Kavsek, M. (2004). Predicting IQ from infant visual habituation and dishabituation: A meta-analysis. *Journal of Applied Developmental Psychology, 25*, 369–393.

Keating, D. P. (2004). Cognitive and brain development. In R. Lerner & L. Steinberg (Eds.), *Handbook of Adolescent Psychology.* New York: Wiley.

Keating, D. P. (2007). Understanding adolescent development: Implications for driving safety. *Journal of Safety Research, 38*, 147–157.

Keatings, M., & Smith, O. (2010). *Ethical & legal issues in Canadian nursing* (3rd ed.). Toronto: Mosby.

Keefe, J., Fancey, P., Keating, N., Frederick, J., Eales, J., & Dobbs, B. (2004). *Caring contexts of rural seniors: Phase I—Technical Report.* Retrieved from http://www.msvu.ca/site/media/msvu/RuralSeniorsTechnicalReportEXECUTIVESUMMARY.pdf

Keen, R. (2005). Unpublished review of J. W. Santrock's *Topical life-span development* (3rd ed.). New York: McGraw-Hill.

Keijer, J., & van Schothorst, E. M. (2008). Adipose tissue failure and mitochondria as a possible target for improvement by bioactive food components. *Current Opinion in Lipidology, 19*, 4–10.

Keller, H. (2002). Culture and development: Developmental pathways to individualism and interrelatedness. In W. J. Lonner, D. L. Dinnel, S. A. Hayes, & D. N. Sattler (Eds.), *Online readings in psychology and culture* (Unit 11, Chapter 1). Bellingham, Washington: Center for Cross-Cultural Research, Western Washington University. Retrieved from http://www.wwu.edu/

Keller, H., Yovsi, R., Borke, J., Kartner, J., Jensen, H. & Papligoura, Z. (2004a). Developmental Consequences of early parenting experiences: Self-recognition and self-regulation in three cultural communities. *Child Development, 75*(6), 1745–1760.

Keller, H., et al. (2004b). The bio-culture of parenting: Evidence from five cultural communities. *Parenting: Science and Practice, 4*, 25–50.

Kelley-Moore, J. (2009). Chronic illness, adulthood and later life. In D. Carr (Ed.), *Encyclopedia of the life course and human development.* Boston: Gale Cengage.

Kellman, P. J., & Arterberry, M. E. (2006). Infant visual perception. In W. Damon & R. Lerner (Eds.), *Handbook of child psychology* (6th ed.). New York: Wiley.

Kelly, G. F. (2008). *Sexuality today* (9th ed.). New York: McGraw-Hill.

Kelly, L., et al. (2009). Palliative care of First Nations people: A qualitative study of bereaved family members. *Canadian Family Physician, 55*, 394–395.

Kelly, M. B. (2013). Divorce cases in civil court 2010/2011. Statistics Canada (2013). Retrieved on September 13, 2013 from http://statcan.gc.ca/pub/85-002-x/2012001/article/11634-eng.htm

Kelsey, S. G., Laditka, S. B., & Laditka, J. N. (2010). Caregiver perspectives on transitions in assisted living and memory care. *American Journal of Alzheimer's Disease and Other Dementias, 25*(3), 255–264.

Kendall, M., Harris, F., Boyd, K., Sheikh, A., Murray, S. A., Brown, D., et al. (2007). Key challenges and ways forward in researching the "good death": Qualitative in-depth interview and focus group study. *British Medical Journal, 334*, 485–486.

Kennedy, K. M., & Raz, N. (2009). Aging white matter and cognition: Differential effects of regional variations in diffusion properties of memory, executive functioning, and speed. *Europsycholgia, 47*, 916–927.

Kennell, J. H. (2006). Randomized controlled trial of skin-to-skin contact from birth versus conventional incubator for physiological stabilization in 1200 g to 2199 g newborns. *Acta Paediatica (Sweden), 95*, 15–16.

Keon, W. J. (2009, December). Early childhood education and care: Canada's challenges and next steps. *Paediatric Child Health, 14*(10), 660–661.

Kevles, D. J. (1985). *In the name of eugenics: Genetics and the uses of human heredity.* Los Angeles: University of California Press.

Keyes, C. L. M., & Ryff, C. D. (1998). Generativity in adult lives: Social structure contours and quality of life consequences. In D. P. McAdams & E. de St. Aubin (Eds.), *Generativity and adult development: How and why we care for the next generation.* Washington, DC: American Psychological Association.

Khalil, A., & O'Brien, P. (2010). Alcohol and pregnancy. *Obstetrics, Gynaecology and Reproductive Medicine, 20*(10), 311–313.

Khera, A. V., & Rader, D. J. (2010). Future therapeutic directions in reverse cholesterol transport. *Current Atherosclerosis Reports, 12*, 73–81.

Kiecolt-Glaser, J. K., McGuire, L., Robles, T. F., & Glaser, R. (2002). Psychoneuro-immunology and psychosomatic medicine: Back to the future. *Psychosomatic Medicine, 64*, 15–28.

Killen, M., & Smetana, J. G. (2010). Social development in the context of social justice. *Social Development, 19*, 642–657.

Killen, M., Rutland, A., & Jampol, N. S. (2009). Social exclusion in childhood and adolescence. In K. H. Rubin, W. M. Bukowski, & B. Laursen (Eds.), *Handbook of peer interactions, relationships, and groups.* New York: Guilford.

Kim, H., Schimmack, U., & Oishi, S. (2012). Cultural differences in self- and other-evaluations and well-being: A study of European and Asian Canadians. *Journal of Personality and Social Psychology, 102*(4), 856–873. doi:10.1037/a0026803.

Kim, J. A., Wei, Y., & Sowers, J. R. (2008). Role of mitochondrial dysfunction in insulin resistance. *Circulation Research, 102*, 401–414.

Kim, S. Y., Su, J., Yancurra, L., & Yee, B. (2009). Asian American and Pacific Islander families. In N. Tewari & A. Alvarez (Eds.), *Asian American psychology.* Clifton, NJ: Psychology Press.

Kim, S., & Hasher, L. (2005). The attraction effect in decision making: Superior performance by older adults. *Quarterly Journal of Experimental Psychology, 58A*, 120–133.

King, G., McDougall, J., DeWit, D., Hong, S., Miller, L., Offord, D., et al. (2005). Pathways to children's academic performance and prosocial behaviour: Roles of physical health status, environmental, family, and child

factors. *International Journal of Disability, Development, and Education, 52*, 313–344.

King, K. M., & Chassin, L. (2007). A prospective study of the effects of age of initiation of alcohol and drug use on young adult substance dependence. *Journal of Studies on Alcohol and Drugs, 68*, 256–265.

King, L. A., & Hicks, J. A. (2007). Whatever happened to "What might have been?" Regrets, happiness, and maturity. *American Psychologist, 62*, 625–636.

King, L., Hicks, J., Krull, J., & Del Gaiso, A. (2006). Positive affect and the experience of meaning in life. *Journal of Personality and Social Psychology, 90*(1), 174–196.

King, W. J., MacKay, M., Sirnick, A., & Canadian Shaken Baby Study Group. (2003). Shaken baby syndrome in Canada: Clinical characteristics and outcomes of hospital cases. *Canadian Medical Association Journal, 168*(2), 155–159.

Kingston, N. (2008). Standardized tests. In N. J. Salkind (Ed.), *Encyclopedia of educational psychology.* Thousand Oaks, CA: Sage.

Kini, S., Morrell, D., Thong, K. J., Kopakaki, A., Hillier, S., & Irvine, D. S. (2010). Lack of impact of semen quality on fertilization in assisted conception. *Scottish Medicine, 55*, 20–23.

Kinney, J. (2009). *Loosening the grip* (9th ed.). New York: McGraw-Hill.

Kirk, R. E. (2003). Experimental design. In I.B. Weiner (Ed.), *Handbook of psychology* (Vol. II). New York: John Wiley.

Kirsch, G., McVey, G., Tweed, S., & Katzman, D. K. (2007). Psychosocial profiles of young, adolescent females seeking treatment for an eating disorder. *Journal of Adolescent Health, 40*, 351–356.

Kisilevsky, B. S., Hains, S. M., Jacquet, A. Y., Granier-Deferre, C., & Lecanuet, J. P. (2004). Maturation of fetal responses to music. *Developmental Science, 7*, 550–559.

Kisilevsky, B. S., Hains, S. M., Lee, K., Xie, X., Huang, H., Ye, H. H., et al. (2003). Effects of experience on fetal voice recognition. *Psychological Science, 14*, 220–224.

Kitchener, K. S., King, P. M., & DeLuca, S. (2006). The development of reflective judgment in adulthood. In C. Hoare (Ed.), *Handbook of adult development and learning.* New York: Oxford University Press.

Klassen, T. R. (2012, February). The future of mandatory contractual retirement in South Korea. Canadian Labour Market and Skills Research Network. Retrieved on September 15 from http://www.clsrn.econ.ubc.ca/workingpapers/CLSRN%20Working%20Paper%20no.%2093%20-%20Klassen.pdf

Klieger, C., Pollex, E., & Koren, G. (2008). Treating the mother—protecting the newborn: The safety of hypoglycemic drugs in pregnancy. *Journal of Maternal-Fetal and Neonatal Medicine, 21*, 191–196.

Kliegman, R. M., Behrman, R. E., Jenson, H. B., & Stanton, B. F. (2007). *Nelson textbook of pediatrics* (18th ed.). London: Elsevier.

Klimes-Dougan, B., & Zeman, J. (2007). Introduction to the special issue of social development: Emotion socialization

in childhood and adolescence. *Social Development, 16*, 203–209.

Kline, D. W., & Scialfa, C. T. (1996). Visual and auditory aging. In J. E. Birren & K. W. Shaie (Eds.), *Handbook of the psychology of aging* (5th ed.). San Diego: Academic Press.

Kline, G. H., Stanley, S. M., Markman, H. J., Olmos-Gallo, P. A., S. Peters, M., Whitton, S. W., et al. (2004). Timing is everything: Pre-engagement cohabitation and increased risk for poor marital outcomes. *Journal of Family Psychology, 18*, 311–318.

Klingman, A. (2006). Children and war trauma. In W. Damon & R. Lerner (Eds.), *Handbook of child psychology* (6th ed.). New York: Wiley.

Klodawsky, F. (2006). Landscapes on the margin: Gender and homelessness in Canada. *Gender Place and Culture, 13*, 365–381.

Klomek, A. B., Sourander, A., & Gould, M. (2010). The association of suicide and bullying in childhood to young adulthood: A review of cross-sectional and longitudinal research findings. *Canadian Journal of Psychiatry, 55*(5), 282–288.

Klug, W. S., Cummings, M. R., Spencer, C., & Palladino, M. A. (2010). *Essentials of genetics* (7th ed.). Upper Saddle River, NJ: Benjamin Cummings.

Knight, B. G., & Sayegh, P. (2010). Cultural values and caregiving: The updated sociocultural stress and coping model. *Journal of Gerontology: Psychological Sciences, 65*(B), 5–13.

Kochanska, G., & Aksan, N. (2007). Conscience in childhood: Past, present, and future. *Merrill-Palmer Quarterly, 50*, 299–310.

Kochanska, G., Aksan, N., Prisco, T. R., & Adams, E. E. (2008). Mother-child and father-child mutually responsive orientation in the first two years and children's outcomes at preschool age: Mechanisms of influence. *Child Development, 79*, 30–44.

Kochanska, G., Barry, R. A., Jimenez, N. B., Hollatz, A. L., & Woodard, J. (2009). Guilt and effortful control: Two mechanisms that prevent disruptive developmental trajectories. *Journal of Personality and Social Psychology, 97*, 322–333.

Koehn, S. (2006). Ethnic minority seniors face a "double whammy" in health care access. *GRC News, 25*(2), 1–2.

Koenig, H. G. (2007). Religion and remission of depression in medical inpatients with heart failure/pulmonary disease. *Journal of Nervous and Mental Disease, 195*, 389–395.

Koenig, H. G., & Blazer, D. G. (1996). Depression. In J. E. Birren (Ed.), *Encyclopedia of gerontology* (Vol. 1). San Diego: Academic Press.

Koenig, L. B., McGue, M., & Iacono, W. G. (2008). Stability and change in religiousness during emerging adulthood. *Developmental Psychology, 44*, 523–543.

Koerner, M. V., & Barlow, D. P. (2010). Genomic imprinting—an epigenetic regulatory model. *Current Opinion in Genetics & Development, 20*(2), 164–170.

Koh, A., & Ross, L. (2006). Mental health issues. A comparison of lesbian, bisexual,and heterosexual women. *Journal of Homosexuality, 51*, 33–57.

Kohlberg, L. (1958). The development on modes of moral thinking and choice in the years 10 to 16. Unpublished doctoral dissertation, University of Chicago.

Kohlberg, L. (1969). Stage and sequence: The cognitive-developmental approach to socialization. In D. A. Goslin (Ed.), *Handbook of socialization theory and research*. Chicago: Rand McNally.

Kohlberg, L. (1986). A current statement of some theoretical issues. In S. Modgil & C. Modgil (Eds.), *Lawrence Kohlberg*. Philadelphia: Falmer.

Kohler, T. S., Kim, J., Feia, K., Bodi, J., Johnson, M., Makhlouf, A., et al. (2008). Prevalence of androgen deficiency in men with erectile dysfunction. *Urology, 71*, 693–697.

Kollar, L., Jordan, K., & Wilson, D. (2013). Health problems of school-age children and adolescents. In M. Hockenberry & D. Wilson (Eds.), *Wong's Essential of pediatric nursing* (9th ed.) (pp.498–535). Philadelphia: Elsevier.

Konik, J., & Stewart, A. (2004). Sexual identity development in the context of compulsory heterosexuality. *Journal of Personality, 72*, 815–844. doi:10.1111/j.0022-3506.2004.00281.x

Koolhof, R., Loeber, R., Wei, E. H., Pardini, D., & D'escury, A. C. (2007). Inhibition deficits of serious delinquent boys of low intelligence. *Criminal Behavior and Mental Health, 17*, 274–292.

Kopp, C. B. (2008). Self-regulatory processes. In M. M. Haith & J. B. Benson (Eds.), *Encyclopedia of infant and early childhood development*. Oxford, UK: Elsevier.

Kopp, C. B. (2011). Social-emotional development in the early years: Socialization and consciousness. *Annual Review of Psychology* (Vol. 62). Palo Alto, CA: Annual Reviews.

Korantzopoulos, P., Kolettis, T. M., Galaris, D., & Goudevenos, J. A. (2007). The role of oxidative stress in the pathogenesis and perpetuation of arterial fibrillation. *International Journal of Cardiology, 115*, 135–143.

Korat, O. (2009). The effect of maternal teaching talk on children's emergent literacy as a function of type of activity and maternal education level. *Journal of Applied Developmental Psychology, 30*, 34–42.

Koropeckyj-Cox, T. (2009). Singlehood. In D. Carr (Ed.), *Encyclopedia of the life course and human development*. Boston: Gale Cengage.

Korrick, S. A., & Sagiv, S. K. (2008). Polychlorinated biphenyls, organopesticides, and neurodevelopment. *Current Opinion in Pediatrics, 20*, 198–204.

Kostelnik, M. J., Soderman, A. K., & Whiren, A. P. (2011). *Developmentally appropriate curricula* (5th ed.). Upper Saddle River, NJ: Merrill.

Kostenuik, M., & Ratnapalan, M. (2010). Approach to adolescent suicide prevention. *Canadian Family Physician, 56, 755–760.*

Kotovsky, L., & Baillargeon, R. (1994). Calibration-based reasoning about collision events in 11-month-old infants. *Cognition, 51*, 107–129.

Kottak, C. P. (2004). *Cultural anthropology* (10th ed.). New York: McGraw-Hill.

Koukoura, O., Sifakis, S., Stratoudakis, G., Manta, N., Kaminopetros, P., & Koumantakis, E. (2006). A case report of recurrent anencephaly and literature review. *Clinical and Experimental Obstetrics and Gynecology, 33*, 185–189.

Kowalski, S. D., & Bondmass, M. D. (2008). Physiological and psychological symptoms of grief in widows. *Research in Nursing and Health, 31*, 23–30.

Kozey, M., & Siegel, L. (2008). Definitions of learning disabilities in Canadian provinces and territories.

Kozier, et al. (2010). *Fundamentals of Canadian nursing* (2nd Canadian ed.). Toronto: Pearson.

Krakoff, L. R. (2008). Older patients need better guidelines for optimal treatment of high blood pressure: 1 size fits few. *Hypertension, 51*, 817–818.

Kramer, A. F., & Morrow, D. (2009). Cognitive training and expertise. In D. Park & N. Schwartz (Eds.), *Cognitive aging* (2nd ed.). Clifton, NJ: Psychology Press.

Kramer, L., & Bank, L. (2005). Sibling relationship contributions to individual and family wellbeing: Introduction to the special issue. *Journal of Family Psychology, 19*, 483–485.

Kramer, M., et al. (2008). Effects of prolonged and exclusive breastfeeding on child behaviour and maternal adjustment: Evidence from a large, randomized trial. *Pediatrics, 121*, e435–e440.

Kraska, M. (2008). Quantitative research methods. In N. J. Salkind (Ed.), *Encyclopedia of educational psychology*. Thousand Oaks, CA: Sage.

Krause, N. (2009). Deriving sense of meaning in late life: An overlooked forum for the development of interdisciplinary theory. In V. L. Bengtson, D. Gans, N. M. Putney, & M. Silverstein (Eds.), *Handbook of theories of aging* (2nd ed.). New York: Springer.

Kreutzer, M., Leonard, C., & Flavell, J. H. (1975). An interview study of children's knowledge about memory. *Monographs of the Society for Research in Child Development, 40*(1, Serial No. 159).

Kriebs, J. M. (2009). Obesity as a complication of pregnancy and labor. *Journal of Perinatal and Neonatal Nursing, 23*(1), 15–22.

Krimer, L. S., & Goldman-Rakic, P. S. (2001). Prefrontal microcircuits. *Journal of Neuroscience, 21*, 3788–3796.

Kristjuhan, U., & Taidre, E. (2010). Postponed aging in university teachers. *Rejuvenation Research, 13*(2–3), 353–355.

Kroger, J. (2007). *Identity development: Adolescence through adulthood*. Thousand Oaks, CA: Sage.

Kroger, J., Martinussen, M., & Marcia, J. (2010). Identity status change during adolescence and young adulthood: A metanalysis. *Journal of Adolescence, 33*, 683–698.

Krueger, J. I., Vohs, K. D., & Baumeister, R. F. (2008). Is the allure of self-esteem a mirage after all? *American Psychologist, 63*, 64.

Kruger, J., Blanck, H. M., & Gillespie, C. (2006). Dietary and physical activity behaviors among adults successful at weight loss management. *International Journal of Behavioral Nutrition and Physical Activity, 3*, 17.

Ksir, C. J., Hart, C. L., & Ray, O. S. (2008). *Drugs, society, and human behavior* (12th ed.). New York: McGraw-Hill.

Kübler-Ross, E. (1969). *On death and dying*. New York: Macmillan.

Kuebli, J. (1994, March). Young children's understanding of everyday emotions. *Young Children*, 36–48.

Kuhl, P. K. (2007). Is speech learning "gated" by the social brain? *Developmental Science, 10*, 110–120.

Kuhn, D., & Franklin, S. (2006). The second decade: What develops (and how)? In W. Damon & R. Lerner (Eds.), *Handbook of child psychology* (6th ed.). New York: Wiley.

Kuhn, D., Iordanou, K., Pease, M., & Wirkala, C. (2008). Beyond control variables: What needs to develop to achieve skilled scientific knowledge? *Cognitive Development, 23*, 435–451.

Kulkofsky, S., & Klemfuss, J. Z. (2008). What the stories children tell can tell about their memory: Narrative skill and young children's suggestibility. *Developmental Psychology, 44*, 1442–1456.

Kuppens, S., Grietens, H. Onghena, P., & Michiels, D. (2009). Relations between parental psychological control and childhood relational aggression: Reciprocal in nature? *Journal of Clinical Child and Adolescent Psychology, 38*, 117–131.

Kurdek, L. A. (1997). Adjustment to relationship dissolution in gay, lesbian, and heterosexual partners. *Personal Relationships, 4*, 145–161.

Kurdek, L. A. (2006). Differences between partners from heterosexual, gay, and lesbian cohabiting couples. *Journal of Marriage and the Family, 68*, 509–528.

Kurdek, L. A. (2007). The allocation of household labor between partners in gay and lesbian couples. *Journal of Family Issues, 28*, 132–148.

Kutcher, S., & Szumilas, M. (2008). Youth suicide prevention. *CMAJ, 178*(3), 282–285.

Kwok, S., & Shek, D. (2010). Hopelessness, parent-adolescent communication, and suicidal ideation among Chineses adolescents in Hong Kong. *Suicide and Life Threatening Behaviour, 40*, 224–233.

L

La Greca, A. M., & Harrison, H. M. (2005). Adolescent peer relations, friendships, and romantic relationships: Do they predict social anxiety and depression? *Journal of Clinical Child and Adolescent Psychology, 34*, 49–61.

LaRochelle-Côté, S., & Dionne, C. (2009, Autumn). Family working patterns. *Perspectives on Labour and Income, 9*, 15–26.

La Rue, A. (2010). Healthy brain aging: Role of cognitive reserve, cognitive stimulation, and cognitive exercises. *Clinics in Geriatric Medicine, 26*, 99–111.

Labouvie-Vief, G. (1986, August). *Modes of knowing and life-span cognition.* Paper presented at the meeting of the American Psychological Association, Washington, DC.

Labouvie-Vief, G. (2006). Emerging structures of adult thought. In J. J. Arnett & J. L. Tanner (Eds.), *Emerging adults in America.* Washington, DC: American Psychological Association.

Labouvie-Vief, G., & Diehl, M. (1999). Self and personality development. In J. C. Kavanaugh & S. K. Whitbourne (Eds.), *Gerontology: An interdisciplinary perspective.* New York: Oxford University Press.

Lachlan, R. F., & Feldman, M. W. (2003). Evolution of cultural communication systems. *Journal of Evolutionary Biology, 16*, 1084–1095.

Lachman, M. E. (2004). Development in midlife. *Annual Review of Psychology* (Vol. 55). Palo Alto, CA: Annual Reviews.

Lachman, M. E. (2006). Perceived control over aging-related declines. *Current Directions in Psychological Science, 15*, 282–286.

Lachman, M. E., & Firth, K. (2004). The adaptive value of feeling in control during midlife. In G. O. Brim., C. D. Ryff, & R. C. Kessler (Eds.), *How healthy are we? A national study of well-being at midlife.* Chicago: University of Chicago Press.

Lachman, M. E., Agrigoroaei, S., Murphy, C., & Tun, P. A. (2010). Frequent cognitive activity compensates for education differences in episodic memory. *American Journal of Geriatric Psychiatry, 18*, 4–10.

Lachman, M. E., Maier, H., & Budner, R. (2000). A portrait of midlife. Unpublished manuscript, Brandeis University, Waltham, MA.

LaCour, D., & Trimble, C. (2012). Humanpapillomavirus in infants: Transmission, prevalence, and persistence. *Journal of Pediatric Adolescent Gynecology, 25*, 93–97.

Lacroix, V., Pomerleau, A., Malcuit, G., Séguin, R., & Lamarre, G. (2001). *Canadian Journal of Behavioural Science, 33*(2), 65–76.

Ladd, G. W., Buhs, E., & Troop, W. (2004). School adjustment and social skills training. In P. K. Smith & C. H. Hart (Eds.), *Blackwell handbook of childhood social development.* Malden, MA: Blackwell.

Ladd, G. W., Herald-Brown, S. L., & Reiser, M. (2008). Does chronic peer rejection predict the development of children's classroom participation during the grade school years? *Child Development, 79*, 1001–1015.

Laible, D., & Thompson, R. A. (2007). Early socialization: A relationship perspective. In J. E. Grusec & P. D. Hastings (Eds.), *Handbook of socialization.* New York: Guilford.

Lainhart, J. E. (2006). Advances in autism neuroimaging research for the clinician and geneticist. *American Journal of Medical Genetics, C: Seminars in Medical Genetics, 142*, 33–39.

Laird, R. D., Criss, M. M., Pettit, G. S., Dodge, K. A., & Bates, J. E. (2008). Parents' monitoring knowledge attenuates the link between antisocial friends and adolescent delinquent behavior. *Journal of Abnormal Child Psychology, 36*, 299–310.

Lakey, S. L., Gray, S. L., Ciechanowski, P., Schwartz, S., & Logerfo, J. (2008). Antidepressant use in nonmajor depression: Secondary analysis of a program to encourage active, rewarding lives for seniors (PEARLS), a randomized controlled trial in older adults from 2000 to 2003. *American Journal of Pharmacotherapy, 6*, 12–20.

Lalonde, C., Chandler, M. J., Hallett, D., & Paul, D. (2001). Personal persistence, identity development, and suicide: A study of native and non-native North American adolescents. April 2003. *Monographs of the Society for Research in Child Development.*

Lamb, M., & Lewis, C. (2011). The role of parent-child relationships in two-parent families. In M. Bornstein & M. Lamb (Eds.), *Developmental science: An advanced textbook* (6th ed.), (pp. 469–517). New York: Taylor & Francis.

Lamb, M., & Lewis, C. (2010). The development and significance of father-child relationships in two-parent families. In M. Lamb (Ed.), *The role of the father in child development* (4th ed.), (pp. 94–153). Hoboken, NJ: Wiley.

Lamb, M. (2012). Mothers, fathers, families, and circumstances: Factors affecting children's adjustment. *Applied Developmental Science, 16*(2), 98–111.

Lamb, M. (Ed.). (2010). *The role of the father in child development* (5th ed.). Hoboken, NJ: Wiley.

Lamb, M. E. (1994). Infant care practices and the application of knowledge. In C. B. Fisher & R. M. Lerner (Eds.), *Applied developmental psychology.* New York: McGraw-Hill.

Lamb, M. E. (2005). Attachments, social networks, and developmental contexts. *Human Development, 48*, 108–112.

Lambert, W. E., Genesee, F., Holobow, N., & Chartrand, L. (1993). Bilingual education for majority English-speaking children. *European Journal of Psychology of Education, 8*, 3–22.

Lamont, R. F., & Jaggat, A. N. (2007). Emerging drug therapies for preventing spontaneous labor and preterm birth. *Expert Opinion on Investigational Drugs, 16*, 337–345.

Landau, L. I. (2008). Tobacco smoke exposure and tracking of lung function into adult life. *Pediatric Respiratory Reviews, 9*, 39–44.

Landry, S. H. (2009). The role of parents in early childhood learning. In R. E. Tremblay, R. deV Peters, M. Boivin, & R. G. Barr (Eds.), *Encyclopedia of early childhood development.* Montreal: Centre of Excellence for Early Childhood Development.

Lane, R. M., & He, Y. (2009). Emerging hypotheses regarding the influnces of butyrylcholinesterase-K variant, APOE epsilon4, and hyperhomocysteinemaia in neurogenerative dementias. *Medical Hypotheses, 73*, 230–250.

Lang, F. R., & Carstensen, L. L. (1994). Close emotional relationships in late life: Further support for proactive aging in the social domain. *Psychology and Aging, 9*, 315–324.

Langer, E. (2005). *On becoming an artist.* New York: Ballantine.

Langer, E. J. (2000). Mindful learning. *Current Directions in Psychological Science, 9*, 220–223.

Langer, E. J. (2007, August). *Counterclockwise: Mindfulness and aging.* Paper presented at the meeting of the American Psychological Association, San Francisco.

Langille, D. (2007). Teenage pregnancies: Trends, contributing factors and the physician's role. *CMAJ, 176*(11), 1601–1602.

Lanham-New, S. A. (2008). Importance of calcium, vitamin D, and vitamin K for osteoporosis prevention and treatment. *Proceedings of the Nutrition Society, 67*, 163–176.

Lanius, R. A., et al. (2004). The nature of traumatic memories: A 4-TfMRI functional connectivity analysis. *American Journal of Psychiatry, 161*(1), 36–44.

Lansford, J. E., Miller-Johnson, S., Berlin, L. J., Dodge, K. A., Bates, J. E., & Pettit, G. S. (2007). Early physical abuse and later violent delinquency: A prospective longitudinal study. *Child Maltreatment, 12*, 233–245.

Larke, I. (2006). The relationship between bullying and social skills in primary school students. *Issues in Educational Research, 16*, 38–51.

LaRocca, T. J., Seals, D. R., & Pierce, G. L. (2010). Leukocyte telomere length is preserved with aging in endurance exercise-trained adults and related to maximum aerobic capacity. *Mechanisms of Aging and Development, 131*, 165–167.

LaRochelle-Côté, S., Gougeon, P., & Pinard, D. (2009, October). Changes in parental work time and earnings. *Perspectives on Labour and Income, 10*(10). Catalogue no. 75-001-X.

Larson, F. B., Wang, L., Bowen, J. D., McCormick, W. C., Teri, L., Crane, P., et al. (2006). Exercise is associated with reduced risk for incident dementia among persons 65 years of age and older. *Annals of Internal Medicine, 144*, 73–81.

Larson, R. W., & Verma, S. (1999). How children and adolescents spend time across the world: Work, play, and developmental opportunities. *Psychological Bulletin, 125,* 701–736.

Larson, R. W., & Wilson, S. (2004). Adolescence across place and time: Globalization and the changing, pathways to adulthood. In R. Lerner & L. Steinberg (Eds.), *Handbook of adolescent psychology.* New York: Wiley.

Larson, R., Pearce, N., Sullivan, P., & Jarrett, R. L. (2007). Participation in youth programs as a catalyst for negotiation of family autonomy with connection. *Journal of Youth and Adolescence, 36*(1), 31–45.

Lasker, J. N., Coyle, B., Li, K., & Ortynsky, M. (2005). Assessment of risk factors for low birth weight deliveries. *Health Care for Women International, 26,* 262–280.

Latham, N. K., Bennett, D. A., Stretton, C. M., & Anderson, C. S. (2004). Systematic review of resistance strength training in older adults. *Journals of Geronotology A: Biological Sciences and Medical Sciences, 59,* M48–M61.

Lauer, R., & Lauer, J. C. (2007). *Marriage and family: The quest for intimacy* (6th ed.). New York: McGraw-Hill.

Laumann, E. O., West, S., Glasser, D., Carson, C., Rosen, R., & Kang, J. H. (2007). Prevalence and correlates of erectile dysfunction by race and ethnicity among men aged 40 or older in the United States: From the male attitudes regarding sexual health survey. *Journal of Sexual Medicine, 4,* 57–65.

Leahy-Warren, P., & McCarthy, G. (2011). Maternal parental self-efficacy in the postpartum period. *Midwifery, 27,* 802–811.

Leaper, C., & Brown, C. S. (2008). Perceived experience of sexism among adolescent girls. *Child Development, 79,* 685–704.

Leaper, C., & Friedman, C. K. (2007). The socialization of gender. In J. E. Grusec & P. D. Davidson (Eds.), *Handbook of socialization.* New York: Guilford.

Learning Disabilities Association of Ontario (LDAO). (2010). Definitions of LDs. Retrieved from http://www.ldao.ca

Lee, B. K., Glass, T. A., McAtee, M. J., Wand, G. S., Bandeen-Roche, K., Bolla, K. I., et al. (2007). Associations of salivary cortisol with cognitive function in the Baltimore Memory Study. *Archives of General Psychiatry, 64,* 810–818.

Lee, I. M., & Skerrett, P. J. (2001). Physical activity and all-cause mortality: What is the dose-response relation? *Medical Science and Sports Exercise, 33* (6 Suppl.), S459–S471.

Lee, J., Lee, J., & Moon, S. (2009). Exploring children's understanding of death concepts. *Asia Pacific Journal of Education, 29*(2), 251–264.

Lee, K. (2010). Does your child tell lies? Here are some answers about children's lies. *Child Development Research Group Institute of Child Study.*

Lee, K., Cameron, C. A., Xu, F., Fu, G., & Board, J. (1997). Chinese and Canadian children's evaluations of lying and truth telling: Similarities and differences in the context of pro- and antisocial behaviors. *Child Development, 68,* 924–934.

Lee, R. M., Grotevant, H. D., Hellerstedt, W. L., Gunnar, M. R., & the Minnesota International Adoption Project Team. (2006). Cultural socialization in families with internationally adopted children. *Journal of Family Psychology, 20,* 571–580.

Lee, Y., & Park, K. (2008). Does physical activity moderate the association between depressive symptoms and disability in older adults? *International Journal of Psychiatry, 23,* 249–256.

Lefkowitz, E. S., & Gillen, M. M. (2006). "Sex is just a normal part of life": Sexuality in emerging adulthood. In J. J. Arnett & J. L. Tanner (Eds.), *Emerging adults in America.* Washington, DC: American Psychological Association.

Legge, G. E., Madison, C., Vaughn, B. N., Cheong, A. M., & Miller, J. C. (2008). Retention of high tactile acuity throughout the lifespan in blindness. *Perception and Psychophysics, 70,* 1471–1488.

Lehman, H. C. (1960). The age decrement in outstanding scientific creativity. *American Psychologist, 15,* 128–134.

Leifheit-Limson, E., & Levy, B. (2009). Ageism/age discrimination. In D. Carr (Ed.), *Encyclopedia of the life course and human development.* Boston: Gale Cengage.

Leighton, S. (2008). Bereavement therapy with adolescents: Facilitating a process of spiritual growth. *Journal of Child and Adolescent Psychiatric Nursing, 21,* 24–34.

Lemstra, M. E., Nielsen, G., Rogers, M. R., Thompson, A. T., & Moraros, J. S. (2012). Risk indicators and outcomes associated with bullying in youth aged 9–15 years. *Canadian Journal of Public Health, 103*(1), 9–13.

Lennon, E. M., Gardner, J. M., Karmel, B. Z., & Flory, M. J. (2008). Bayley Scales of Infant Development. In M. M. Haith & J. B. Benson (Eds.), *Encyclopedia of infant and early childhood development.* Oxford, UK: Elsevier.

Lenroot, R. K., & Giedd, J. N. (2006). Brain development in children and adolescents: Insights from anatomical magnetic resonance imaging. *Neuroscience and Biobehavioral Reviews, 30,* 718–729.

Leonardi-Bee, J. A., Smyth, A. R., Britton, J., & Coleman, T. (2008). Environmental tobacco smoke and fetal health: Systematic review and analysis. *Archives of Disease in Childhood: Fetal and Neonatal Edition.*

Leonards, U., Ibanez, V., & Giannakopoulos, P. (2002). The role of stimulus type in age-related changes of visual working memory. *Experimental Brain Research, 146,* 172–183.

Leon-Guerrero, A. (2009). *Social problems* (2nd ed.). Thousand Oaks, CA: Sage.

Leppanen, J. M., Moulson, M., Vogel-Farley, V. K., & Nelson, C. A. (2007). An ERP study of emotional face processing in the adult and infant brain. *Child Development, 78,* 232–245.

Lerner, H. (1989). *The dance of intimacy.* New York: Harper & Row.

Lerner, H. (1998). *The mother dance: How children change your life.* New York: Harper Perennial.

Lerner, R. M., Boyd, M., & Du, D. (2008). Adolescent development. In I. B. Weiner & C. B. Craighead (Eds.), *Encyclopedia of psychology* (4th ed.). Hoboken, NJ: Wiley.

Lerner, R. M., Roeser, R. W., & Phelps, E. (Eds.). (2009). *Positive youth development and spirituality: From theory to research.* West Conshohocken, PA: Templeton Foundation Press.

Leshikar, E. D., Gutchess, A. H., Hebrank, A. C., Sutton, B. P., & Park, D. C. (2010). The impact of increased relational encoding demands in frontal and hippocampal function in older adults. *Cortex, 46,* 507–521.

Lester, B. (2000). Unpublished review of J. W. Santrock's *Life-span development* (8th ed.). New York: McGraw-Hill.

Lester, B. M., Tronick, E. Z., & Brazelton, T. B. (2004). The Neonatal Intensive Care Unit Network neurobehavioral scale procedures. *Pediatrics, 113* (Suppl.), S641–S667.

Lester, D. (2006). Sexual orientation and suicidal behaviour. *Psychological Reports, 99,* 923–924.

Lester, D. B., Rogers, T. D., & Blaha, C. D. (2010). Acetylcholine-dopamine interactions in the pathophysiology and treatment of CNS disorders. *CNS Neuroscience & Therapeutics, 16*(3), 137–162.

Letourneau, N. L., Hungler, K. M., & Fisher, K. (2005). Low-income Canadian Aboriginal and non-Aboriginal parent-child interactions. *Child: Care, Health & Development, 31,* 545–554.

Levant, R. F. (2002). Men and masculinity. In J. Worell (Ed.), *Encyclopedia of women and gender.* San Diego: Academic Press.

LeVay, S., & Valente, S. (2003). *Human sexuality.* Sunderland, MA: Sinauer Associates.

Levetown, M., & American Academy of Pediatrics Committee on Bioethics. (2008). Communicating with children and families: From everyday interactions to skill in conveying distressing information. *Pediatrics, 121,* e1441–e1460.

Levin, J., Chatters, L. M., & Taylor, R. J. (2010). Theory in religion, aging, and health: An overview. *Journal of Religion and Health, 50*(2), 389–406.

LeVine, S. (1979). *Mothers and wives: Gusii women of East Africa.* Chicago: University of Chicago Press.

Levinson, D. J. (1978). *The seasons of a man's life.* New York: Knopf.

Levinson, D. J. (1996). *Seasons of a woman's life.* New York: Alfred Knopf.

Levitt, C., Hanvey, L., Kaczorowski, J., Chalmers, B., Heaman, M., & Bartholomew, S. (2011). Breastfeeding policies and practices in Canadian hospitals: Comparing 1993 with 2007. *Birth, 38*(3), 228–237.

Levy, B. R., Slade, M. D., & Gill, T. (2006). Hearing decline predicted by elders' age stereotypes. *Journal of Gerontology B: Psychological Sciences and Social Sciences, 61,* P82–P87.

Levy, B. R., Slade, M. D., Kunkel, S. R., & Kasl, S. V. (2002). Longevity increased by positive self-perceptions of aging. *Journal of Personality and Social Psychology, 83,* 261–270.

Lewis, A., Huebner, E., Malone, P., & Valois, R. (2011). Life satisfaction and student engagement in adolescence. *Journal of Youth and Adolescence, 40,* 249–262.

Lewis, M. (2005). The child and its family: The social network model. *Human Development, 33,* 48–61.

Lewis, M. (2007). Early emotional development. In A. Slater & M. Lewis (Eds.), *Introduction to infant development* (2nd ed.). New York: Oxford University Press.

Lewis, M. D. (2000, January/February). The dynamic systems approaches for an integrated account of human development. *Child Development 71*(1), 36–43. Retrieved from http://www.psych.yorku.ca/adler/courses/4010/documents/LewisChDev2000.pdf on September 12, 2012.

Lewis, M. D. (2012) Memoirs of an addicted brain. Retrieved from http://www.youtube.com/watch?v=MBPBcJlZIsA on September 12, 2012.

Lewis, M. D., Todd, R., & Xu, X. (2011). The development of emotion regulation: A neuropsychological perspective. In R. M. Lerner, W. F. Overton, A. M. Fruend, & M. E. Lamb (Eds.), *Handbook of life-span development.* New York: Wiley.

Lewis, M., & Brooks-Gunn, J. (1979). *Social cognition and the acquisition of the self.* New York: Plenum.

Lewis, M., Feiring, C., & Rosenthal, S. (2000). Attachment over time. *Child Development, 71,* 707–720.

Lewis, R. (2010). *Human genetics* (9th ed.). New York: McGraw-Hill.

Lewis, R. (2012). *Human genetics* (10th ed.). New York: McGraw-Hill.

Lewis, T., & Maurer, D. (2009). Effects of early pattern deprivation on visual development. *Optometry and Vision Science, 86*(6), 640–646.

Li, C., Goran, M. I., Kaur, H., Nollen, N., & Ahluwalia, J. S. (2007). Developmental trajectories of overweight during childhood: Role of early life factors. *Obesity, 15,* 760–761.

Li, D. K., Willinger, M., Petitti, D. B., Odulil, R. K., Liu, L., & Hoffman, H.J. (2006). Use of a dummy (pacifier) during sleep and risk of sudden infant death syndrome (SIDS): Population based case-control study. *British Medical Journal, 332,* 18–22.

Li, Q. (2006). Cyberbullying in schools: A research of gender differences. *School Psychology International, 27,* 157–170.

Li, Q. (2005, April). *Cyberbullying in schools: Nature and extent of Canadian adolescents experience.* Paper presented at the conference of the American Education Research Association, Montreal.

Li, X., Kim, P., & Gilbert, M. (2008, June 19). Trends in herpes simplex virus cases in British Columbia 1992–2006: STI and HIV prevention and control. BC Centre of Disease Control. Retrieved from http://www.bccdc.ca/

Li, Y. (2007). Recovering from spousal bereavement in later life: Does volunteer participation play a role? *Journals of Gerontology B: Psychological Sciences and Social Sciences, 62,* S257–S266.

Liben, L. S. (2009). Giftedness during childhood: The spatial-graphic domain. In F. D. Horowitz, R. F. Subotnik, & D. J. Matthews (Eds.), *The development of giftedness and talent across the life span.* Washington, DC: American Psychological Association.

Lie, E., & Newcombe, N. (1999). Elementary school children's explicit and implicit memory of faces of preschool classmates. *Developmental Psychology, 35,* 102–112.

Liegeois, F., Connelly, A., Baldeweg, T., & Vargha-Khadem, F. (2008). Speaking with a single cerebral hemisphere: fMRI language organization after hemispherectomy in childhood. *Brain and Language, 106*(3), 195–203.

Lieven, E. (2008). Language development: Overview. In M. M. Haith & J. B. Benson (Eds.), *Encyclopedia of infant and early childhood development.* Oxford, UK: Elsevier.

Liew, L. P., & Norbury, C. J. (2009). Telomere maintenance: All's well that ends well. *Archives of Toxicology, 83,* 407–416.

Lin, J. (2005). The housing transitions of seniors. *Canadian Social Trends, 85* (Winter), 22–26.

Lin, J., et al. (2009). Vitamins C and E and beta carotene supplementation and cancer risk: A randomized controlled trial. *Journal of the National Cancer Institute, 101,* 14–23.

Lin, J. N., et al. (2010). Resveratrol modulates tumor cell proliferation and protein translation via SIRT1-dependent AMPK activation. *Journal of Agricultural and Food Chemistry, 58,* 1584–1592.

Lindau, S. T., Schumm, L. P., Laumann, E. O., Levinson, W., O'Muircheartaigh, C. A., & Waite, L. J. (2007). A study of sexuality and health among older adults in the United States. *New England Journal of Medicine, 357,* 762–774.

Lindblad, F., Hjern, A., & Vinnerljung, B. (2003). Intercountry adopted children as young adults—A Swedish cohort study. *American Journal of Orthopsychiatry, 73,* 190–202.

Lindenberger, U., & Ghisletta, P. (2009). Cognitive and sensory declines in old age: Gauging the evidence for a common cause. *Psychology and Aging, 24,* 1–16.

Linebarger, J., Sahler, O., & Egan, K. (2009). Coping with death. *Pediatrics in Review, 30,* 350–356.

Lineweaver, T. T., Berger, A. K., & Hertzog, C. (2009). Expectations about memory change across the life span are impacted by aging stereotypes. *Psychology and Aging, 24,* 169–176.

Lipovetzky, N., Hod, H., Roth, A., Kishon, Y., Sclarovksy, S., & Green, M. S. (2007). Emotional events and anger at the workplace as triggers for a first event of the acute coronary syndrome: A case-crossover study. *The Israel Medical Association Journal, 9,* 310–315.

Lippa, R. A. (2005). *Gender, nature, and nurture* (2nd ed.). Mahwah, NJ: Erlbaum.

Lippman, L. A., & Keith, J. D. (2006). The demographics of spirituality among youth: International perspectives. In E. Roehlkepartain, P. E. King, L. Wagener, & P. L. Benson (Eds.), *The handbook of spirituality in childhood and adolescence.* Thousand Oaks, CA: Sage.

Lipps, G., & Corak, M. (2001, July 4). Trends in the use of private education, 1987/88 to 1998/99. *The Daily.* Ottawa: Statistics Canada.

Liston, F., Allen, V., O'Connell, C., & Jangaard, K. (2008). Neonatal outcomes with caesarean delivery at term. *Arch Dis Child Fetal Neontal Ed, 93,* F176–F182.

Liu, A., Hu, X., Ma, G., Cui, Z., Pan, Y., Chang, S., et al. (2008). Evaluations of a classroom-based physical activity promoting program. *Obesity Reviews, 9* (Suppl. 1), S130–S134.

Liu, P., Lu, Y., Recker, R. R., Deng, H. W., & Dvornyk, V. (2010). ALOX12 gene is associated with the onset of natural menopause in white women. *Menopause, 17,* 152–156.

Liu, S., Liston, R., Joseph, K., Heaman, M., Sauve, R., & Kramer, M. (2007). Maternal mortality and severe morbidity associated with low-risk planned caesarian delivery versus planned vaginal delivery at term. *Canadian Medical Association, 176*(4) 455–460.

Liu, W., & Aaker, J. (2007). Do you look to the future or focus on today? The impact of life experiences on intertemporal decisions. *Organizational Behaviour and Human Decision Processes, 102,* 212–225.

Liu, Y. J., Xiao, P., Xiong, D. H., Recker, R. R., & Deng, H. W. (2005). Searching for obesity genes: Progress and prospects. *Drugs Today, 41,* 345–362.

Liu-Ambrose, T., et al. (2010). Resistance training and executive functions: A 12-month randomized controlled trial. *Archives of Internal Medicine, 170,* 170–178.

Lloyd, K., & Wise, K. (2004). Protecting children from exposure to environmental tobacco. *Nursing Times, 100,* 36–38.

Lo, B., & Rubenfeld, G. (2005). Palliative sedation in dying patients: "We turn to it when everything else hasn't worked." *Journal of the American Medical Association, 294,* 1810–1816.

Lobsinger, T. (2011, Spring). Eldercare: By seniors for seniors. *The Vanier Institute of the Family: Transition, 41*(1), 1.

Lockenhoff, C. E., Costa, P. T., & Lane, R. D. (2008). Age differences in descriptions of emotional experiences in oneself and others. *Journals of Gerontology B: Psychological Sciences and Social Sciences, 63,* P62–P99.

Loeber, R., Pardini, D. A., Stouthamer-Loeber, M., & Raine, A. (2007). Do cognitive, physiological, and psychosocial risk and promotive factors predict desistance from delinquency in males? *Development and Psychopathology, 19,* 867–887.

Loehlin, J. C. (2010). Is there an active gene-environment correlation in adolescent drinking behavior? *Behavior Genetics, 37*(3), 463–476.

Loehlin, J. C., Horn, J. M., & Ernst, J. L. (2007). Genetic and environmental influences on adult life outcomes: Evidence from the Texas adoption project. *Behavior Genetics, 37,* 463–476.

Loehlin, J., Neiderhiser, J., & Reiss, D. (2003). The behavior genetics of personality and the NEAD study. *Journal of Research in Personality, 37,* 373–387.

Loessi, B., Valerius, G., Kopasz, M., Hornyak, M., Riemann, D., & Voderholzer, U. (2008). Are adolescents chronically sleep-deprived? An investigation of sleep habits of adolescents in the Southwest of Germany. *Child Care Health and Development, 34*(5), 549–556.

Lofmark, R., et al. (2008). Physicians' experiences with end-of-life decision-making: Survey in six European countries and Australia. *BMC Medicine, 12,* 4.

Loiselle, C. G., Profetto-McGrath, J., Polit, D. F., & Beck, C.T. (2011). *Canadian essentials of nursing research* (3rd ed). New York: Wolters Kluwer Health/Lippincott, Williams & Wilkins.

Lombardo, P. A. (2008). *Three generations, no imbeciles: Eugenics, the Supreme Court, and Buck v. Bell.* Baltimore: Johns Hopkins University Press.

London, M. L., Ladewig, P. A., Ball, J. W., & Bindler, R. A. (2007). *Maternal and child nursing care* (2nd ed.). Upper Saddle River, NJ: Prentice Hall.

Longman, P. (1987). *Born to pay: The new politics of aging in America.* Boston: Houghton-Mifflin.

Lonner, W. J. (1990). An overview of cross-cultural testing and assessment. In R.W. Brislin (Ed.), *Applied cross-cultural psychology.* Newbury Park, CA: Sage.

Lopez-Lluch, G., et al. (2006). Calorie restriction induces mitochondrial biogenesis and bioenergetic efficiency. *Proceedings of the National Academy of Sciences USA, 103,* 1768–1773.

Loponen, M., Hublin, C., Kalimo, R., Manttari, M., & Tenkanen, L. (2010). Joint effect of self-reported sleep problems and three components of the metabolic syndrome on risk of coronary heart disease. *Journal of Psychosomatic Research, 68,* 149–158.

Lorenz, K. Z. (1965). *Evolution and the modification of behavior.* Chicago: University of Chicago Press.

Loutfy, M., et al. (2012). High prevalence of unintended pregnancies in HIV-positive women of reproductive age in Ontario, Canada: A retrospective study. *HIV Medicine, 13,* 107–113.

Lovden, M., & Lindenberger, U. (2007). Intelligence. In J. E. Birren (Ed.), *Encyclopedia of gerontology* (2nd ed.). San Diego: Academic Press.

Lowe, M., & Kral, T. (2005, 2006). Stress-induced eating in restrained eaters may not be caused by stress or restraint. *Appetite, 46,* 16–21.

Lu, M. C., & Lu, J. S. (2008). Prenatal care. In M. M. Haith & J. B. Benson (Eds.), *Encyclopedia of infancy and early childhood development.* Oxford, UK: Elsevier.

Lucas, R. E., Clark, A. E., Yannis, G., & Diener, E. (2004). Unemployment alters the setpoint for life satisfaction. *Psychological Science, 15,* 8–13.

Ludington-Hoe, S. M., Lewis, T., Morgan, K., Cong, X., Anderson, L., & Reese, S. (2006). Breast and infant temperatures with twins during kangaroo care. *Journal of Obstetric, Gynecologic, and Neonatal Nursing, 35,* 223–231.

Lumpkin, A. (2011). *Introduction to physical education, exercise science, and sport studies* (8th ed.). New York: McGraw-Hill.

Lunau, K. (2012). Campus crisis: the broken generation. *Maclean's.* Retrieved from http://www2.macleans.ca/2012/09/05/the-broken-generation/

Lund, D. A. (2007). Bereavement and loss. In J. E. Birren (Ed.), *Encyclopedia of gerontology* (2nd ed.). San Diego: Academic Press.

Luo, L., & Craik, F. I. M. (2008). Aging and memory: A cognitive approach. *Canadian Journal of Psychology, 53,* 346–353.

Luo, Z., Wilkins, R. R., Platt, R. W., & Kramer, M. S. (2004). Risks of adverse pregnancy outcomes among Inuit and North American Indian women in Quebec, 1985–97. *Paediatric and Perinatal Epidemiology, 18,* 40–50.

Luyckx, K., Soenens, B., Goossens, L., & Vansteenkiste, M. (2007). Parenting, identity formation, and college adjustment: A mediation model with longitudinal data. *Identity, 7,* 309–330.

Luyckx, K., Schwartz, S. J., Goossens, L., Soenens, B., & Beyers, W. (2008a). Developmental typologies of identity formation and adjustment in female emerging adults: A latent class growth analysis approach. *Journal of Research on Adolescence, 18*(4), 595–619.

Luyckx, K., Soenens, B., Vansteenkiste, M., Goossens, L., & Berzonsky, M. D. (2008c). Parental psychological control and dimensions of identity formation in emerging adulthood. *Journal of Family Psychology, 21,* 546–550.

Lyall, J. (2007). What is a good death? *Nursing Older People, 19,* 6–8.

Lye, J. (1995). Fiction and the immigrant experience. Brock University. Retrieved from http://www.brocku.ca/

Lykken, D. (2001). *Happiness: What studies on twins show us about nature, nurture, and the happiness set point.* New York: Golden Books.

Lynch, T. (2004). Funerals-R-Us: From funeral home to mega-industry. *Generations, 28*(2), 11–14.

Lyndaker, C., & Hulton, L. (2004). The influence of age on symptoms of perimenopause. *Journal of Obstetric, Gynecological, and Neonatal Nursing, 33,* 340–347.

Lyon, T. D., & Flavell, J. H. (1993). Young children's understanding of forgetting over time. *Child Development, 64,* 789–800.

Lyytinen, H., & Erskine, J. (2009). Early identification and prevention of reading problems. In R. E. Tremblay, R. deV Peters, M. Boivin, & R. G. Barr (Eds.), *Encyclopedia on early childhood development.* Montreal: Centre of Excellence for Early Childhood Development.

M

Ma, X., & Klinger, D. A. (2000). Hierarchical linear modelling of student and school effects on academic achievement. *Canadian Journal of Education, 25*(1), 41–55.

Maas, J. B. (1998). *Power sleep.* New York: Villard Books.

Maccoby, E. E. (1998). *The two sexes: Growing up apart, coming together.* Cambridge, MA: Harvard University Press.

Maccoby, E. E. (2002). Gender and group processes. *Current Directions in Psychological Science, 11,* 54–58.

Maccoby, E. E., & Martin, J. A. (1983). Socialization in the context of the family: Parent-child interaction. In P. H. Mussen (Ed.), *Handbook of child psychology* (4th ed., Vol. 4). New York: Wiley.

MacDonald, H., MacKeigan, K., & Weaver, A. (2011). Experiences and perceptions of young adults in friends with benefits relationships: A qualitative study. *The Canadian Journal of Human Sexuality, 20*(1–2), 41.

Macdonald, S. W., Hultsch, D. F., & Dixon, R. A. (2008). Predicting impending death: Inconsistency in speed is a selective and early marker. *Psychology and Aging, 23,* 595–607.

MacGeorge, E. L. (2003). Gender differences in attributions and emotions in helping contexts. *Sex Roles, 48,* 175–182.

Maciejewski, P. K., Zhang, B., Block, S. D., & Prigerson, H. G. (2007). An empirical examination of the stage theory of grief. *Journal of the American Medical Association, 297,* 716–723.

Macionis, J., & Gerber, L. (2011). *Sociology.* Toronto: Pearson.

Macionis, J., Jansson, S. W. & Benoit, C. (2013). *Society: The basics* (5th Canadian ed.). Toronto: Pearson.

MacKenzie, C. S., Smith, M. C., Hasher, L., Leach, L., & Behl, P. (2007). Cognitive functioning under stress: Evidence from informal caregivers of palliative patients. *Journal of Palliative Medicine, 10*(3), 749–758.

Mackoff, R., Iverson, E., Kicket, P., Dorey, F., Upperman, J., & Metzenberg, A. (2010). Attitudes of genetic counsellors towards genetic susceptibility testing in children. *Journal of Genetic Counselling, 19,* 402–416.

MacMartin, C. (2004). Judicial constructions of the seriousness of child sexual abuse. *Canadian Journal of Behavioural Science, 36,* 66–80.

Macmillan, H. L., Wathen, C. N., Barlow, J., Fergusson, D. M., Leventhal, J. M.,

& Taussig, H. N. (2009). Interventions to prevent child maltreatment and associated impairment. *Lancet, 373*, 250–266.

Macmillan, R., & Meyer, M. J. (2006). Inclusion and guilt: The emotional fallout for teachers. *Exceptionality Education Canada, 16*, 25–43.

Maconochie, N., Doyle, P., Prior, S., & Simmons, R. (2007). Risk factors for first trimester miscarriage—Results from a UK-population-based case-control study. *British Journal of Obstetrics and Gynecology, 114*, 170–176.

Mactier, H. (2011). The management of heroin misuse in pregnancy: Time for a rethink? *Arch Dis Child Fetal Neonatal Ed, 96*, F457–F460.

Madden, D. J., Gottlob, L. R., Denny, L. L., Turkington, T. G., Provenzale, J. M., Hawk. T. C., et al. (1999). Aging and recognition memory: Changes in regional cerebral blood flow associated with components of reaction time distributions. *Journal of Cognitive Neuroscience, II*, 511–520.

Mader, S. S. (2011). *Inquiry into life* (13th ed.). New York: McGraw-Hill.

Maggi, S. (2010). Vaccination and healthy aging. *Expert Review of Vaccines, 9* (Suppl. 3), S3–S6.

Magnuson, K. A., & Duncan, G. J. (2002). Parents in poverty. In M. H. Bornstien (Ed.), *Handbook of parenting* (2nd ed., Vol. 4). Mahwah, NJ: Erlbaum.

Mahler, M. (1979). *Separation-individuation* (Vol. 2). London: Jason Aronson.

Maimoun, L., & Sultan, C. (2010). Effects of physical activity on bone remodeling. *Metabolism, 60*(3), 373–388.

Maindonald, E. (2005). Sudden infant death syndrome (SIDS). *Nursing, 35*(7), 53.

Make Poverty History. (2010). End poverty in Canada. Retrieved from http://www .makepovertyhistory.ca/learn/issues/ end-poverty-in-canada

Makinen, J., & Johnson, S. (2006). Resolving attachment injuries in couples using emotionally focused therapy: Steps toward forgiveness and reconciliation. *Journal of Consulting and Clinical Psychology, 74*(6), 1055–1064.

Malamitsi-Puchner, A., & Boutsikou, T. (2006). Adolescent pregnancy and perinatal outcome. *Pediatric Endocrinology Reviews, 3* (Suppl. 1), 170–171.

Malatesta, V. J. (2007). Sexual problems, women, and aging: An overview. *Journal of Women and Aging, 19*, 139–154.

Mamtani, M., Patel, A., & Kulkarni, H. (2008). Association of the pattern of transition between arousal states in neonates with the cord blood lead level. *Early Human Development, 84*, 231–235.

Mandler, J. M. (2000). Unpublished review of J. W. Santrock's *Life-span development* (8th ed.). New York: McGraw-Hill.

Mandler, J. M. (2004). *The foundations of mind*. New York: Oxford University Press.

Mandler, J. M. (2006). Jean Mandler. Retrieved from http://cogsci.ucsd. edu/~jean/

Manheimer, R. J. (2007). Education and aging. In J. E. Birren (Ed.), *Encyclopedia of gerontology* (2nd ed.). San Diego: Academic Press.

Manitoba Scool Improvement Program (MSIP). (2011). Manitoba school improvement program: Annual report. Retrieved from http://www.msip.ca/

Mann, J., et al. (2005). Suicide prevention strategies A systematic review. *JAMA, 294*(16), 2064–2074.

Mann, T., Tomiyama, A. J., Westling, E., Lew, A-M., Samuels, B., & Chatman, J. (2007). Medicare's search for effective obesity treatments. *American Psychologist, 62*, 220–233.

Manzoli, L., Villari, P., Pirone, M., & Boccia, A. (2007). Marital status and mortality in the elderly: A systematic review and meta-analysis. *Social Science Medicine, 64*, 77–94.

Marcell, J. J. (2003). Sarcopenia: Causes, consequences, and preventions. *Journals of Gerontology A: Biological and Medical Sciences*, M911–M916.

Marcia, J., & Josselson, R. (2013). Eriksonian personality research and its implications for psychotherapy. *Journal of Personality*, doi:10,1111/jopy.12014.

Marcia, J. E. (1980). Ego identity development. In J. Adelson (Ed.), *Handbook of adolescent psychology*. New York: Wiley.

Marcia, J. E. (1994). The empirical study of ego identity. In H. A. Bosma, T. L. G. Graafsma, H. D. Grotevant, & D. J. De Levita (Eds.), *Identity and development*. Newbury Park, CA: Sage.

Marcia, J. E. (2002). Identity and psychosocial development in adulthood. *Identity, 2*, 7–28.

Margrett, J. A., & Deshpande-Kamat, N. (2009). Cognitive functioning and decline. In D. Carr (Ed.), *Encyclopedia of the life course and human development*. Boston: Gale Cengage.

Marin, L., & Halpern, D. (2011). Pedagogy for developing critical thinking in adolescents: Explicit instruction produces greatest gains. *Thinking Skills and Creativity, 6*, 1–13.

Markides, K. S., Rudkin, L., & Wallace, S. P. (2007). Ethnicity and minorities. In J. E. Birren (Ed.), *Encyclopedia of gerontology* (2nd ed.). San Diego: Academic Press.

Markovic, K., Reulbach, U., Vassiliadu, A., Lunkenheimer, J., Lunkenheimer, B. Spannenberger, R., et al. (2007). Good news for elderly persons: Olfactory pleasure increases at later stages of the life span. *Journals of Gerontology A: Biological Sciences and Medical Sciences, 62*, 1287–1293.

Marks, A. K., Patton, F., & García Coll, C. (2011). Being bicultural: A mixed-methods study of adolescents' implicitly and explicitly measured multiethnic identities. *Developmental Psychology, 47*(1), 270–288. doi:10.1037/ a0020730.

Marks, B. L., Katz, L. M., & Smith, J. K. (2009). Exercise and the aging mind: Buffing the baby boomer's body and brain. *The Physician and Sportsmedicine, 37*, 119–125.

Markus, H. R., Ryff, C. D., Curhan, K., & Palmersheim, K. (2004). In their own words: Well-being among high school and college-educated adults. In G. Brim, C. D. Ryff, & R. Kessler (Eds.), *How healthy are we? A national study of well-being in midlife*. Chicago: University of Chicago Press.

Marlatt, M. W., Lucassen, P. J., & van Pragg, H. (2010). Comparison of neurogenic effects of fluoxetine, duloxetine, and running in mice. *Brain Research, 1341*, 93–99.

Marlow, N., Hennessy, E. M., Bracewell, M. A., Wolke, D., & the EPICure Study Group. (2007). Motor and executive function at 6 years of age after extremely preterm birth. *Pediatrics, 120*, 793–804.

Marquart, B., Nannini, D., Edwards, R., Stanley, L., & Wayman, J. (2007). Prevalence of dating violence: Regional and gender differences. *Adolescence, 42*, 645–657.

Marques, F. Z., Markus, M. A., & Morris, B. J. (2010). The molecular basis of longevity, and clinical populations. *Maturitas, 65*, 87–91.

Marsh, H., Ellis, L., & Craven, R. (2002). How do preschool children feel about them selves? Unraveling measurement and multidimensional self-concept structure. *Developmental Psychology, 38*, 376–393.

Marsh, I., Keating, M., Punch, S., & Harden, J. (2009). *Sociology: Making sense of society*. (4th ed.) London: Pearson Education/Prentice-Hall.

Marsh, R. L., Hicks, J. L., Cook, G. I., & Mayhorn, C. B. (2007). Comparing older and younger adults in an event-based prospective memory paradigm containing an output monitoring component. *Neuropsychology, Development, and Cognition, Section B: Aging, Neuropsychology, and Cognition, 14*, 168–188.

Marshall, K. (2003). Parental leave: More time off for baby. *Canadian Social Trends*, Winter 2003, Statistics Canada Catalogue no. 11-008, 13–18.

Marshall, K. (2006). Converging gender roles. Statistics Canada Catalogue no. 11-010.

Marshall, K. (2008). Fathers' use of paid parental leave. Retrieved from http://www .statcan.gc.ca/pub/75-001-x/2008106/ article/10639-eng.htm

Marshall, R., & Sutherland, P. (2008). The social relations of bereavement in the Caribbean. *Omega (Westport), 57*(1), 21–34.

Marsiske, M., Klumb, P. L., & Baltes, M. M. (1997). Everyday activity patterns and sensory functioning in old age. *Psychology and Aging, 12*, 444–457.

Martell, L. (2003). Postpartum women's perceptions of the hospital environment. *Journal of Obstetric Gynecologic & Neonatal Nursing, 32*(4), 478–485.

Martin, C. L., & Ruble, D. (2004). Children's search for gender cues. *Current Directions in Psychological Science, 13*, 67–70.

Martin, C. L., & Ruble, D. N. (2010). Patterns of gender development/Gender-role development. *Annual Review of Psychology* (Vol. 61). Palo Alto, CA: Annual Reviews.

Martin, L. R., Friedman, H. S., & Schwartz, J. E. (2007). Personality and mortality risk across the life span: The importance of conscientiousness as a biopsychosocial attribute. *Health Psychology, 26,* 428–436.

Martin, M., Grünendahl, M., & Martin, P. (2001). Age differences in stress, social-resources, and well-being in middle and older age. *Journals of Gerontology: Psychological Sciences and Social Sciences, 56B,* P214–P222.

Martinez, M. E. (2010). *Learning and cognition.* Upper Saddle River, NJ: Merrill.

Masche, J. (2010). Explanation of normative declines in parent's knowledge about their adolescent children. *Journal of Adolescence, 33,* 271–284.

Masley, S. C., Weaver, W., Peri, G., & Phillips, S. E. (2008). Efficacy of lifestyle changes in modifying practical markers of wellness and aging. *Alternative Therapies in Health and Medicine, 14,* 24–29.

Maslow, A. H. (1954, 1968). *Toward a psychology of being.* Toronto: Van Nostrand Reinhold, Ltd.

Maslow, A. H (1968). *Toward a psychology of being* (2nd ed.). New York: D. Van Nostrand.

Maslow, A. H. (1970). *Motivation and personality.* New York: Harper and Row.

Masoro, E. J. (2006). Are age-associated diseases an integral part of aging? In E. J. Masoro & S. N. Austad (Eds.), *Handbook of the biology of aging* (6th ed.). San Diego: Academic Press.

Massey, Z., Rising, S. S., & Ickovics, J. (2006). Centering Pregnancy group prenatal care: Promoting relationship-centered care. *Journal of Obstetric, Gynecologic, and Neonatal Nursing, 35,* 286–294.

Mast, B. T., & Healy, P. J. (2009). Dementias. In D. Carr (Ed.), *Encyclopedia of the life course and human development.* Boston: Gale Cengage.

Masten, A. S., Obradovic, J., & Burt, K. B. (2006). Resilience in emerging adulthood: Developmental perspectives on continuity and transformation. In J. J. Arnett & J. L. Tanner (Eds.), *Emerging adults in America.* Washington, DC: American Psychological Association.

Mastropieri, M. & Scruggs, T. (2004). *The inclusive classroom: Strategies for effective instruction* (2nd ed). Upper Saddle River, NJ: Pearson.

Mathole, T., Lindmark, G., Majoko, F., & Ahlberg, B. M. (2004). A qualitative study of women's perspectives of antenatal care in rural areas of Zimbabwe. *Midwifery, 20,* 122–132.

Matlin, M. W. (2004). *The psychology of women* (5th ed.). Belmont, CA: Wadsworth.

Matlin, M. W. (2008). *The psychology of women* (6th ed.). Belmont, CA: Wadsworth.

Matsuda, H. (2007). The role of neuroimaging in mild cognitive impairment. *Journal of Nuclear Medicine, 48,* 1289–1300.

Matsumoto, D., & Juang, L. (2008). *Culture and psychology* (4th ed.). Belmont, CA: Wadsworth.

Matthews, C. E., Jurj, A. L., Shu, X. O., Yang, G., Li, Q., Gao, Y. T., et al. (2007). Influence of exercise, walking, cycling, and overall nonexercise physical activity on mortality in Chinese women. *American Journal of Epidemiology, 165,* 1343–1350.

Mattison, J. A., Roth, G. S., Lane, M. A., & Ingram, D. K. (2007). Dietary restriction in aging nonhuman primates. *Interdisciplinary Topics in Gerontology, 35,* 137–158.

Mattson, L., & Caffrey, L. (2001). *Barriers to equal education for Aboriginal learners: A review of the literature.* British Columbia Human Rights Commission.

Mattson, M. P. (2007). Mitochondrial regulation of neuronal plasticity. *Neurochemical Research, 32,* 707–715.

Mavandadi, S., et al. (2007). Effects of depression treatment on depressive symptoms in older adulthood: The moderating role of pain. *Journal of the American Geriatrics Association, 55,* 202–211.

May, F. B. (2006). *Teaching reading creatively: Reading and writing as communication* (7th ed.). Upper Saddle River, NJ: Prentice Hall.

May, R. (1975) *The courage to create.* New York: Bantam Books.

May, V., Onarcan, M., Oleschowski, C., & Mayron, Z. (2004). International perspectives on the role of home care and hospice in aging and long-term care. *Caring, 23,* 14–17.

Mayer, A. (2011, September 28). Interview: Who's a bully? Psychologist Tracy Vaillancourt on kids who bully and what parents can do. CBC News Canada. Retrieved from http://www.cbc.ca/news/canada/story/2011/09/28/f-bullying-q-and-a.html

Mayer, J. D. (2004). Who is emotionally intelligent—and how does it matter? Retrieved from http://www.unh.edu/emotional_intelligence/EI%20Assets/Reprints...EI%20Proper/EI2004MayerSaloveyCarusotarget.pdf

Mayer, J. D., Salovey, P., & Caruso, D. R. (2004). Emotional intelligence, theory, findings, and applications. *Psychological Inquiry, 15*(3), 197–215.

Mayer, R. E. (2008). *Curriculum and instruction* (2nd ed.). Upper Saddle River, NJ: Prentice-Hall.

Mayers, L. B., & Chiffriller, S. H. (2008). Body art (body piercing and tattooing) among university undergraduate students: "Then and now." *Journal of Adolescent Health, 42,* 201–203.

Mayeux, R. (2005). Mapping the new frontier: Complex genetic disorders. *Journal of Clinical Investigation, 115,* 1404–1407.

Mayo Clinic. (2012). Teen eating disorders: Tips to protect your teen. Retrieved from http://www.mayoclinic.com/

Mayseless, O., & Scharf, M. (2007). Adolescents' attachment representation and their capacity for intimacy in close relationships. *Journal of Research on Adolescence, 17,* 23–50.

Mbonye, A. K., Neema, S., & Magnussen, P. (2006). Treatment-seeking practices for malaria in pregnancy among rural women in Mukono district, Uganda. *Journal of Biosocial Science, 38,* 221–237.

McAdams, D. P., & Olson, B. D. (2010). Personality development: Continuity and change over the life course. *Annual Review of Psychology* (Vol. 61). Palo Alto, CA: Annual Reviews.

McAlister, A., & Peterson, C. (2007). A longitudinal study of child siblings and theory of mind development. *Cognitive Development, 22,* 258–270.

McAnarney, E. R. (2008). Editorial: Adolescent brain development: Forging new links? *Journal of Adolescent Health, 42,* 321–323.

McCall, J., & Vicol, L. (2011). HIV infection and contraception. *Journal of the Association of Nurses in AIDS Care, 22*(3), 193–201.

McCarthy, J. (2007). Children with autism spectrum disorders and intellectual disability. *Current Opinion in Psychiatry, 20,* 472–476.

McCartney, K. (2009). Current research on childcare effects. In R. E. Tremblay, R. deV Peters, M. Boivan, & R. G. Barr (Eds.), *Encyclopedia on early childhood development.* Montreal: Center of Excellence for Early Childhood Development.

McCartney, K., Dearing, E., Taylor, B. A., & Bub, K. L. (2007). Quality child care supports the achievement of low-income children: Direct and indirect pathways through caregiving and the home environment. *Journal of Applied Developmental Psychology, 28,* 411–426.

McClain, C. S., Rosenfeld, B., & Breitbart, W. S. (2003, March). *The influence of spirituality on end-of-life despair in cancer patients close to death.* Paper presented at the meeting of American Psychosomatic Society, Phoenix.

McClosky, D. (2003–2004, Winter). Introduction to Canada's stepfamilies. *Transition Magazine.* Vol. 33 No 4. Montreal: The Vanier Institite of the Family.

McCrae R. R., Costa P. T., et al. (1998). Age differences in personality across the adult lifespan: Parallels in five cultures. *Developmental Psychology, 35,* 466–477.

McCrae, C., & Dubyak, P. (2009). Sleep patterns and behavior. In D. Carr (Ed.), *Encyclopedia of the life course and human development.* Boston: Gale Cengage.

McCrae, R. R., & Costa, P. T. (2003). *Personality in adulthood* (2nd ed.). New York: Guilford.

McCrae, R. R., & Costa, P. T. (2006). Cross-cultural perspectives on adult personality trait development. In D. K. Mroczek & T. D. Little (Eds.), *Handbook of personality development.* Mahwah, NJ: Erlbaum.

McCreary Centre Society. (2001). *Street youth not just an urban issue in B.C.* www.msc.bc.ca

McCreary Centre Society. (1999, June 14). Press release: B.C. study shows gay youth face high suicide risk. Retrieved from www.mcs.bc.ca

McCullough, A. R., Steidle, C. P., Klee, B., & Tseng, L. J. (2008). Randomized, double-blind, cross-over trial of sildenafil in men with moderate erectile dysfunction: Efficacy at 8 and 12 hours postdose. *Urology, 71*, 686–692.

McDonald, S., et al. (2009). Preterm birth and low birth weight among in vitro fertilization singletons: A systematic review and meta-analyses. *European Journal of Obstetrics, Gynecology, and Reproductive Biology, 146*, 138–148.

McDonald, S. D., et al. (2010). Preterm birth and low birth weight among in vitro fertilization twins: A systematic review and meta-analyses. *European Journal of Obstetrics, Gynecology, and Reproductive Biology, 148*, 105–113.

McDougall, G. J., Strauss, M. E., Holston, E. C., & Martin, M. (1999, November). *Memory self-efficacy and memory-anxiety as predictors of memory performance in at-risk elderly.* Paper presented at the meeting of the Gerontological Society of America, San Francisco.

McDowell, M. A., Brody, D. J., & Hughes, J. P. (2007). Has age of menarche changed? Results from the National Health and Nutrition Examination Survey. *Journal of Adolescent Health, 40*, 227–231.

McElwain, N. L., & Booth-LaForce, C. (2006). Maternal sensitivity to infant distress and nondistress as predictors of infant-mother attachment security. *Journal of Family Psychology, 2*, 247–255.

McFarlane, M., Ross, M., & Elford, J. (2004). The Internet and HIV/STD prevention. *AIDS Care, 16*(8), 929–930.

McFeet, T. (2008, May). Income gaps grow, as Canada's have-nots get left behind. Retrieved from http://www.cbc.ca

McGuire, S. (2001). Are behavioral genetic and socialization research compatible? *American Psychologist, 56*, 171.

McHale, J. P., Kuersten-Hogan, R., & Rao, N. (2004). Growing points for coparenting theory and research. *Journal of Adult Development, 11*, 221–234.

McHale, J., Khazan, I., Erera, P., Rotman, T., DeCourcey, W., & McConnell, M. (2002). Coparenting in diverse family systems. In M. H. Bornstien (Ed.), *Handbook of parenting* (2nd ed., Vol. 3). Mahwah, NJ: Erlbaum.

McIntosh, E., Gillanders, D., & Rodgers, S. (2010). Rumination, goal linking, daily hassles, and life events in major depression. *Clinical Psychology and Psychotherapy, 17*, 33–43.

McIntyre, M. (2009). Universities must help students with depression. Children's Mental Health Ontario. Retrieved from www.kidsmentalhealth.ca/news_and_events/view_html_article.php?id=796#top

McKay, A. (2006). Trends in teen pregnancy in Canada with comparison to USA and England/Wales. *The Canadian Journal of Human Sexuality, 15*(3–4), 157–161.

McKenzie, B., & Bacon, B. (2002). Parent education after a separation: Results from a multi-site study on best practices. *Canadian Journal of Community Mental Health* (Special Supplement No. 4), 73–88.

McKeough, A., Bird, S., Tourigny, E., Romaine, A., Graham, S., Ottmann, J., et al. (2008). Storytelling as a foundation to literacy development for Aboriginal children: Culturally and developmentally appropriate practices. *Canadian Psychology, 49*(2), 148–154.

McLaren, A. (1990). *Our own master race: Eugenics in Canada, 1885–1945.* Toronto: McClelland & Stewart.

McLaren, C. (2009). Alberta creates electronic registry for personal directives. *CMAJ, 180*(7), 708.

McLeod, S. (2012). Carl Rogers. Simply Psychology. Retrieved from http://www.simplypsychology.org/carl-rogers.html on September 15, 2013.

McMahon, T. (2013, March 11). The smartphone will see you now–Putting medical technology in the hands of patients could revolutionize medicine. *McLean's.*

McMillan, J. H. (2008). *Educational research* (5th ed.). Boston: Allyn & Bacon.

McMillen, I. C., MacLaughlin, S. M., Muhlhausler, B. S., Gentili, S., Duffield, J. L., & Morrison, J. L. (2008). Developmental origins of adult health and disease: The role of periconceptional and fetal nutrition. *Basic and Clinical Pharmacology and Toxicology, 102*, 82–89.

McNamara, F., & Sullivan, C. E. (2000). Obstructive sleep apnea in infants. *Journal of Pediatrics, 136*, 318–323.

McNamara, F., Lijowska, A. S., & Thach, B. T. (2002). Spontaneous arousal activity in infants during NREM and REM sleep. *Journal of Physiology, 538*, 263–269.

McNeill, G., et al. (2007). Effect of multivitamin and multiple supplementation on cognitive function in men and women aged 65 years and over: A randomized controlled trial. *Nutrition Journal, 6*, 10.

McPherson, M., Weissman, G., Strickland, B., van Dyck, P., Blumberg, S., & Newacheck, P. (2004). Implementing community-based systems of services for children and youths with special health care needs: How well are we doing? *Pediatrics, 113*(5 supp.), 1538–1544.

McShane, K., & Hastings, P. (2004). Culturally sensitive approaches to research on child development and family practices in first peoples communities. *First Peoples Child and Family Review, 1*(1), 38–44.

McShane, K., Smylie, J., & Adomako, P. (2009). Health of First Nations, Inuit, and Métis children in Canada. In J. Smylie & P. Adomako (Eds.), *Indigenous children's health report: Health assessment in action.* Toronto: Centre for Research on Inner City Health, Keenan Research Center.

Meaney, M. J. (2010). Epigenetics and the biological definition of gene x environment interactions. *Child Development, 81*, 41–79.

Media Awareness Network. (2005). Young Canadians in a wired world Phase II: Student survey. Retrieved from www.media-awareness.ca/english/research/YCWW/phaseII/upload/YCWWII_Student_Survey.pdf

Medical News Today (2009, August 24) What is vitamin D? What are the benefits of vitamin D? *Medical News Today.* Retrieved on April 17, 2013 from http://www.medicalnewstoday.com/articles/161618.php

MediResource. (2010–2011). Alzheimer's disease. Canada.com MediResource Inc. Retrieved from http://bodyandhealth.canada.com/channel_condition_info_details.asp?disease_id=218&channel_id=11&relation_id=10899

Meeks, T. W., & Jeste, D. V. (2009). Neurobiology of wisdom: A literature review. *Archives of General Psychiatry, 66*, 355–365.

Meerlo, P., Sgoifo, A., & Suchecki, D. (2008). Restricted and disrupted sleep: Effects on autonomic function, neuroendocrine stress systems, and stress responsivity. *Sleep Medicine Review, 12*, 197–210.

Mehrotra, C. M., & Wagner, L. S. (2009). *Aging and diversity.* Clifton, NJ: Psychology Press.

Meinhard, A. G., Foster, M. K. & Wright, C. (2006, Winter). Rethinking school-based community service: The importance of a structured program. *The Philanthropist.*

Meltzi, G., & Ely, R. (2009). Language development in the school years. In J. B. Gleason & N. Ratner (Eds.), *The development of language* (7th ed.). Boston: Allyn & Bacon.

Meltzoff, A. N. (1988). Infant imitation and memory: Nine-month-old infants in immediate and deferred tests. *Child Development, 59*, 217–225.

Meltzoff, A. N. (2004). Imitation as a mechanism of social cognition: Origins of empathy, theory of mind, and the representation of action. In U. Goswami (Ed.), *Blackwell handbook of childhood cognitive development.* Malden, MA: Blackwell.

Meltzoff, A. N. (2005). Imitation. In B. Hopkins (Ed.), *Cambridge encyclopedia of child development.* Cambridge: Cambridge University Press.

Meltzoff, A. N. (2007). Infants' causal learning. In A. Gopnik & L. Schulz (Eds.), *Causal learning.* New York: Oxford University Press.

Meltzoff, A. N., & Moore, M. K. (1999). A new foundation for cognitive development: The birth of the representational infant. In E. K. Skolnick, K. Nelson, S. A. Gelman, & P. H. Miller (Eds.), *Conceptual development.* Mahwah, NJ: Erlbaum.

Meltzoff, A. N., & Williamson, R. A. (2008). Imitation and modeling. In M. M. Haith & J. B. Benson (Eds.), *Encyclopedia of infant and early childhood development.* Oxford, UK: Elsevier.

Memorial Society of British Columbia. (2004). Public health impact of crematoria. Retrieved from http://www.memorialsocietybc.org/c/g/cremation-report.html

Mena, M. A., Casarejos, M. J., Solano, R. M., & de Yebenes, J. G. (2009). Half a century of L-DOPA. *Current Topics in Medicinal Chemistry, 9,* 880–893.

Mendelson, M. (2008). Improving education on reserves: A First Nations education authority act. The Caledon Institute of Social Policy. Retrieved from http://www.caledoninst.org/publications/pdf/684eng.pdf

Menec, V. H. (2003). The relation between everyday activities and successful aging: A 6-year longitudinal study. *Journal of Gerontology B: Psychological Sciences and Social Sciences, 58,* 574–582.

Menias, C. O., Elsayes, K. M., Peterson, C. M., Huete, A., Gratz, B. I., & Bhalla, S. (2007). CT of pregnancy-related complications. *Emergency Radiology, 13,* 299–306.

Menn, L., & Stoel-Gammon, C. (2009). Phonological development: Learning sounds and sound patterns. In J. Berko Gleason (Ed.), *The development of language* (7th ed.). Boston: Allyn & Bacon.

Menon, M., Tobin, D. D., Corby, B. C., Menon, M., Hodges, E. V. E., & Perry, D. G. (2007). The developmental costs of high self-esteem in aggressive children. *Child Development, 78,* 1627–1639.

Mensah, G. A., & Brown, D. W. (2007). An overview of cardiovascular disease burden in the United States. *Health Affairs, 26,* 38–48.

Meristo, M., Falkman, K. W., Hjelmquist, E., Tedoldi, M., Surian, L., & Siegal, M. (2007). Language access and theory of mind reasoning: Evidence from deaf children in bilingual and oral environments. *Developmental Psychology, 43*(5), 1156–1169.

Merrill, D. M. (2009). Parent-child relationships: Later-life. In D. Carr (Ed.), *Encyclopedia of the life course and human development.* Boston: Gale Cengage.

Mesch, G., Talmud, I., & Quan-Haase, A. (2012). IM social networks: Individual, relational and cultural characteristics. *Journal of Social and Personal Relationships.* doi: 10.1177/0265407512448263

Messinger, D. (2008). Smiling. In M. M. Haith & J. B. Benson (Eds.), *Encyclopedia of infant and early childhood development.* Oxford, UK: Elsevier.

Metts, S., & Cupach, W. R. (2007). Responses to relational transgressions. In M. Tafoya & B. H. Spitzberg (Eds.), *The dark side of interpersonal communication.* Mahwah, NJ: Erlbaum.

Meyer, I. H. (2003). Prejudice, social stress, and mental health in gay, lesbian, and bisexual populations: Conceptual issues and research evidence. *Psychological Bulletin, 129,* 674–697.

Michel, J. P. (2010). Updated vaccine guidelines for aging and aged citizens of Europe. *Expert Review of Vaccines, 9* (Suppl. 3), S7–S10.

Mikkonen, J., & Raphael, D. (2010). *Social determinants of health: The Canadian facts.* Retrieved from http://www.thecanadianfacts.org/

Mikulincer, M., & Shaver, P. R. (2007). *Attachment in adulthood.* New York: Guilford.

Mikulincer, M., & Shaver, P. R. (2009). Adult attachment and affect regulation. In J. Cassidy & P. R. Shaver (Eds.), *Handbook of attachment* (2nd ed.). New York: Guilford.

Milan, A., & Hamm, B. (2003). Across the generations: Grandparents and grandchildren. *Canadian Social Trends, 71,* 2–7.

Milan, A., Hou, F., & Wong, I. (2006). Learning disabilities and child altruism, anxiety and aggression. *Canadian Social Trends* (Catalogue no. 11-008), 16–20.

Milberg, A., Olsson, E. C., Jakobsson, M., Olsson, M., & Friedrichsen, M. (2008). Family members' perceived needs for bereavement follow-up. *Journal of Pain and Symptom Management, 35,* 58–69.

Miles, M. F., & Williams, R. W. (2007). Meta-analysis for microarray studies of the genetics of complex traits. *Trends in Biotechnology, 25,* 45–47.

Milke, M. A., & Peltola, P. (2000). Playing all the roles: Gender and the work-family balancing act. *Journal of Marriage and the Family, 61,* 476–490.

Millar, W. J. (2005). Hearing problems among seniors. *Health Reports, 16*(4), 49–52.

Miller, B. C., Bayley, B. K., Christensen, M., Leavitt, S. C., & Coyl, D. D. (2003). Adolescent pregnancy and childbearing. In G. Adams & M. Berzonsky (Eds.), *Blackwell handbook of adolescence.* Malden, MA: Blackwell.

Miller, C. F., Lurye, L. E., Zusuls, K. M., & Ruble, D. N. (2009). Accessibility of gender stereotype domains: Developmental and gender differences in children. *Sex Roles, 60,* 870–881.

Miller, J. (2007). Cultural psychology of moral development. In S. Kitayama & D. Cohen (Eds.), *Handbook of cultural psychology.* New York: Guilford.

Miller, J. B. (1986). *Toward a new psychology of women* (2nd ed.). Boston: Beacon Press.

Miller, K., Couchie, R., Ehman, W., Graves, L., Grzybowski, S., & Medves, J. (2012). Joint position paper on rural maternity care. *Canadian Journal of Rural Medicine, 17*(4), 135–141.

Miller-Day, M. A. (2004). *Communication among grandmothers, mothers, and adult daughters.* Mahwah, NJ: Erlbaum.

Miller-Perrin, C. L., Perrin, R. D., & Kocur, J. L. (2009). Parental, physical, and psychological aggression: Psychological symptoms in young adults. *Child Abuse and Neglect, 33,* 1–11.

Milligan, K. (2008). The evolution of elderly poverty in Canada. *IDEAS, 34*(1), 79–94.

Milligan, K., Atkinson, L., Trehub, S. E., Benoit, D., & Poulton, L. (2003). Maternal attachment and the communication of emotion through song. *Infant Behavior & Development, 26,* 1–13.

Mills, C. J. (2003). Characteristics of effective teachers of gifted students: Teacher background and personality styles of students. *Gifted Child Quarterly, 47*(4), 272–281.

Mills, D., & Mills, C. (2000). *Hungarian kindergarten curriculum translation.* London: Mills Production.

Minde, K., & Zelkowitz, P. (2008). Premature babies. In M. M. Haith & J. B. Benson (Eds.), *Encyclopedia of infancy and early childhood development.* Oxford, UK: Elsevier.

Mindell, J., Sadeh, A., Wiegand, B., How, T., & Goh, D. (2010). Cross-cultural differences in infant and toddler sleep. *Sleep Medicine, 11,* 274–280.

Minister of Public Works and Government Services Canada. (2010). *The current state of multiculturalism in Canada and research themes on Canadian multiculturalism 2008–2010.* Ottawa: Citizenship and Immigration Canada. Retrieved from http://www.cic.gc.ca/english/pdf/pub/multi-state.pdf

Minnesota Centre for Twin Research. (2012). Sir Francis Galton and twin research. Retrieved from https://mctfr.psych.umn.edu/research/Sir%20Galton.html

Minor, R. K., Allarad, J. S., Younts, C. M., Ward, T. M., & de Cabo, R. (2010). Dietary interventions to extend life span and health span based on calorie restriction. *Journals of Gerontology A: Biological Sciences and Medical Sciences, 65*(7), 695–703.

Miranda, M. L. (2004). The implications of developmentally appropriate practices for the kindergarten general music classroom. *Journal of Research in Music Education, 52,* 43–53.

Mischel, W. (2004). Toward an integrative science of the person. *Annual Review of Psychology* (Vol. 55). Palo Alto, CA: Annual Reviews.

Mischel, W., Shoda, Y., & Ayduk, O. (2008). *Introduction to personality: Toward an integrative science of the person* (8th ed.). New York: Wiley.

Mishra, G. D., Cooper, R., Tom, S. E., & Kuh, D. (2009). Early life circumstances and their impact on menarche and menopause. *Women's Health, 5,* 175–190.

Mitchell, E. A., Stewart, A. W., Crampton, P., & Salmond, C. (2000). Deprivation and sudden infant death syndrome. *Social Science and Medicine, 51,* 147–150.

Mitchell, M. S., Koien, C. M., & Crow, S. M. (2008). Harassment: It's not (all) about sex! Part I: The evolving legal framework. *Health Care Management, 27,* 13–22.

Mitchell, V., & Helson, R. (1990). Women's prime of life: Is it the 50s? *Psychology of Women Quarterly, 14,* 451–470.

Miura, K., et al. (2009). Four blood pressure indexes and the risk of stroke and myocardial infarction in Japanese men and women: A meta-analysis of 16 cohort studies. *Circulation, 119,* 1892–1898.

Miura, Y., Yasuda, K., Yamamoto, K., Kopike, M., Nishida, Y., & Kobayashi, K. (2007). Inhibition of Alzheimer amyloid aggregation with sulfated glycopolymers. *Biomacromolecules, 8,* 2129–2134.

Miyashita, M., Sato, K., Morita, T., & Suzuki, M. (2008). Effect of a population-based educational intervention focusing on end-of-life home care, life-prolonging treatment, and knowledge about palliative care. *Palliative Medicine, 22,* 376–382.

Moen, P. (2007). Unpublished review of J. W. Santrock's *Life-span development* (12th ed.). New York: McGraw-Hill.

Moen, P. (2009a). Careers. In D. Carr (Ed.), *Encyclopedia of the life course and human development.* Boston: Gale Cengage.

Moen, P., & Altobelli, J. (2007). Strategic selection as a retirement project: Will Americans develop hybrid arrangements? In J. James & P. Wink (Eds.), *The crown of life: Dynamics of the early post retirement period.* New York: Springer.

Moen, P., & Spencer, D. (2006). Converging divergences in age, gender, health, and well-being: Strategic selection in the third age. In R. H. Binstock & L. K. George (Eds.), *Handbook of aging and the social sciences* (6th ed.). San Diego: Academic Press.

Moen, P., & Wethington, E. (1999). Midlife development in a life course context. In S. L. Willis & J. D. Reid (Eds.), *Life in the middle: Psychological and social development in middle age.* San Diego: Academic Press.

Moen, P., Kelly, E., & Magennis, R. (2008). Gender strategies: Social and institutional convoys, mystiques, and cycles of control. In M. C. Smith & T. G. Reio (Eds.), *Handbook of research on adult development and learning.* Mahwah: Erlbaum.

Mohr, J. J. (2009). Same-sex romantic attachment. In J. Cassidy & P. R. Shaver (Eds.), *Handbook of attachment* (2nd ed.). New York: Guilford.

Moise, K. J. (2005). Fetal RhD typing with free DNA I maternal plasma. *American Journal of Obstetrics and Gynecology, 192,* 663–665.

Moksnes, U., Moljord, I., Espnes, G., & Byrne, D. (2010). The association between stress and emotional states in adolescents: The role of gender and self-esteem. *Personality and Individual Differences, 49,* 430–435.

Mollenkopf, H. (2007). Mobility and flexibility. In J. E. Birren (Ed.), *Encyclopedia of gerontology* (2nd ed.). San Diego: Academic Press.

Molnar, B. E., Cerda, M., Roberts, A. L., & Buka, S. L. (2007). Effects of neighborhood resources on aggressive and delinquent behaviors among urban youths. *American Journal of Public Health, 98,* 1086–1093.

Mondloch, C., Geldart, S., Maurer, D., & Le Grand, R. (2003). Developmental changes in face processing skills. *Journal of Experimental Psychology, 86,* 67–84.

Monette, M. (2012). Senior suicide: An overlooked problem. *Canadian Medical Association Journal, 184*(17), E885–E886.

Monge, P., Wesseling, C., Guardado, J., Lundberg, II, Ahlbom, A., Cantor, K. P., et al. (2007). Parental occupation exposure to pesticides and the risk of childhood leukemia in Costa Rica. *Scandinavian Journal of Work, Environment, and Health, 33,* 293–303.

Monserud, M. A. (2008). Intergenerational relationships and affectual solidarity between grandparents and young adults. *Journal of Marriage and the Family, 70,* 182–195.

Moore, C. (2007). *Advance care planning and end-of-life decision making.* In K. Kuebler, D. Heidrich, & P. Esper (Eds.), *Palliative and end-of-life care* (2nd ed.) (pp. 49–62). St. Louis: Elsevier.

Moore, D'Aoust, Robertson, Savage, & Jiwani. (2009). Swallowing the hurt: Exploring the links between anorexia, bulimia and violence against women and girls. Public Health Agency of Canada (PHAC). Retrieved from http://www.phac-aspc.gc.ca/ncfv-cnivf/publications/femrav-eng.php

Moos, B. (2007, July 4). Who'll care for aging boomers? *Dallas Morning News,* A1–2.

Moos, M. K. (2006). Prenatal care: Limitations and opportunities. *Journal of Obstetric, Gynecologic, and Neonatal Nursing, 35,* 278–285.

Moran S., & Gardner, H. (2006). Extraordinary achievements. In W. Damon & R. Lerner (Eds.), *Handbook of child psychology* (6th ed.). New York: Wiley.

Moran, S., & Gardner, H. (2007). Hill, skill, and will: Executive function from a multiple intelligences perspective. In L. Meltzer (Ed.), *Executive function in education.* New York: Guilford.

Moreno, A., Posada, G. E., & Goldyn, D. T. (2006). Presence and quality of touch influence coregulation in mother-infant dyads. *Infancy, 9,* 1–20.

Morgan, E. (2012). Not always a straight path: College students' narratives of heterosexual identity development. *Sex Roles, 66*(1–2), 79–93.

Morgan, J. D. (2003). Spirituality. In C. D. Bryant (Ed.), *Handbook of death and dying.* Thousand Oaks, CA: Sage.

Morissette, R., & Ostrovsky, Y. (2007). Pensions and retirement savings of families. *Perspectives on Labour and Income* (Winter), 43–56.

Morra, S., Gobbo, C., Marini, Z., & Sheese, R. (2008). *Cognitive development: Neo Piagetian perspectives.* Mahwah, NJ: Erlbaum.

Morrison, G. S. (2008). *Fundamentals of early childhood education* (5th ed.). Upper Saddle River, NJ: Prentice Hall.

Morrissey, M. V. (2007). Suffer no more in silence: Challenging the myths of women's mental health in childbearing. *International Journal of Psychiatric Nursing Research, 12,* 1429–1438.

Morrongiello, B., & Dawber, T. (2004). Identifying factors that relate to children's risk-taking decisions. *Canadian Journal of Behavioural Science, 36,* 255–266.

Morrow, L. (2009). *Literacy development in the early years.* Boston: Allyn & Bacon.

Morselli, E., et al. (2010). The life-span prolonging effect of sirtuin-1 is mediated by autophagy. *Autophagy, 6,* 186–188.

Morton, D., & Weinfeld, M. (1998). *Who speaks for Canada? Words that shape a country.* Toronto: McClelland & Stewart.

Morton, J. (2003). Targeting generation X. *Public Relations Quarterly, 48*(4), 43–45.

Moschonis, G., Grammatikaki, E., & Manios, Y. (2008). Perinatal predictors of overweight at infancy and preschool childhood: The GENESIS study. *International Journal of Obesity, 32*(1), 39–47.

Mosenthal, A. C., Murphy, P. A., Barker, L. K., Lavery, R., Retano, A., & Livingston, D. H. (2008). Changing the culture around end-of-life care in the trauma intensive care unit. *Journal of Trauma, 64,* 1587–1593.

Moshman, D. (2006). Theories of adult development. In J. Demick & C. Andreoletti (Eds.), *Handbook of adult development* (pp. 42–60). New York: Springer.

Moss, E. L., & Dobson, K. S. (2006). Psychology, spirituality, and end-of-life care: An ethical integration? *Canadian Psychology, 47*(4), 284–299.

Moss, E., Cyr, C., Bureau, J. F., Tarabulsy, G. M., & Dubois-Comtois, K. (2005). Stability of attachment during the preschool period. *Developmental Psychology, 41,* 773–783.

Moss, K. (2003). Witnessing violence—Aggression and anxiety in young children. *Supplement to Health Reports, 14* (Catalogue 82-003). Ottawa: Statistics Canada.

Motherrisk. (2012). *Drugs in pregnancy.* Retrieved from http://www.motherrisk.org/

Mothers Against Drunk Drivers (MADD). (2012). Statistics. Retrieved from http://www.madd.org/

Moules, N. J., Simonson, K., Prins, M., Angus, P., & Bell, J. M. (2004). Making room for grief. *Nursing Inquiry, 11,* 99–107.

Moulson, M. C., & Nelson, C. A. (2008). Neurological development. In M. M. Haith & J. B. Benson (Eds.), *Encyclopedia of Infant and Early Childhood Development.* Oxford, UK: Elsevier.

Moussaly, K. (2010). *Participation in private retirement savings plans, 1997 to 2006.* Ottawa: Statistics Canada. Catalogue no. 13F0026M, no. 1.

Moyer, R. H., Hackett, J. K., & Everett, S. A. (2007). *Teaching science as investigations.* Upper Saddle River, NJ: Prentice Hall.

Mroczek, D. K., Spiro, A., & Griffin, P. W. (2006). Personality and aging. In J. E. Birren & W. Schaie (Eds.), *Handbook of the psychology of aging* (6th ed.). San Diego: Academic Press.

Muehlenkamp, J., & Brausch, A. (2012). Body image as a mediator of non-suicidal self-injury in adolescents. *Journal of Adolescence, 35*(1), 1–9.

Muir, D., & Hains, S. (1999). Young infants' perception of adult intentionality: Adult contingency and eye direction. In P. Rochat (Ed.), *Early social cognition: Understanding others in the first months of life* (pp. 155–188).

Muir, D., & Lee, K. (2003). The still-face effect: methodological issues and new application. *Infancy, 4,* 483–491.

Mukherjee, S., Lekli, I., Gurusamy, N., Bertelli, A. A., & Das, D. K. (2009). Expression of the longevity proteins by both red and white wines and their cardioprotective components, resveratrol, tyrosol, and hyrdoxytyrosol. *Free Radical Biology and Medicine, 46,* 573–578.

Mullins, L. (2007). Loneliness in old age. In J. E. Birren (Ed.), *Encyclopedia of gerontology* (2nd ed.). Oxford, UK: Elsevier.

Mullis, P. E., & Tonella, P. (2008). Regulation of fetal growth: Consequences and impact of being born small. *Best Practice Research:*

Clinical Endocrinology and Metabolism, 22, 173–190.

Mulvaney, M. K., & Mebert, C. J. (2007). Parental corporal punishment predicts behavior problems in early childhood. *Journal of Family Psychology, 21,* 389–397.

Mundt, M., Zaklestskaia, L., & Fleming, M. (2009). Extreme college drinking and alcohol-related injury risk. *Alcoholism: Clinical & Experimental Research, 33*(9), 1532–1538.

Munro, S., Kornelson, J., & Hutton, E. (2009). Decision-making in patient-initiated elective caesarean delivery: The influence of birth stories. *Journal of Midwifery & Women's Health, 54*(5), 373–379.

Mura, E., et al. (2010). Beta-amyloid: A disease target or a synaptic regulator affecting age-related neurotransmitter changes? *Current Pharmaceutical Design, 16,* 672–683.

Murray, J. P., & Murray, A. D. (2008). Television: Uses and effects. In M. M. Haith & J. B. Benson (Eds.), *Encyclopedia of infant and early childhood development.* Oxford, UK: Elsevier.

Murphy, B., Zhang, X., & Dionne, C. (2012). Low income in Canada: A multipline and multi-index persepctive. Catalogue no. 75F0002M–No. 001. Statistics Canada. Retrieved on September 10, 2013 from http://www.statcan.gc.ca/pub/75f0002m/75f0002m2012001-eng.pdf

Murphy, E., & Carr, D. (2007). *Powerful partners: Adolescent girls' education and delayed childbearing.* Retrieved from http://www.prb.org

Murphy, N., Carbone, P., & Council on Children with Disabilities. (2011). Parent-provider-community partnerships: Optimizing outcomes for children with disabilities. *Pediatrics, 128*(4), 795–802.

Murphy, S. A., Johnson, L. C., Chung, I., & Beaton, R. D. (2003). The prevalence of PTSD following the violent death of a child and predictors of change 5 years later. *Journal of Traumatic Stress, 16,* 17–25.

Murphy-Hoefer, R., Alder, S., & Higbee, C. (2004). Perceptions about cigarette smoking and risks among college students. *Nicotine and Tobacco Research, 6* (Suppl. 3), S371–S374.

Murray, C. S., Woodcock, A., Smillie, F. I., Cain, G., Kissen, P., & Castovie, A. (2004). Tobacco smoke exposure, wheeze, and atopy. *Pediatric Pulmonology, 37,* 492–498.

Murray, J. P. (2007). TV violence: Research and controversy. In N. Pecora, J. P. Murray, & E. A. Wartella (Eds.), *Children and television.* Mahwah, NJ: Erlbaum.

Musch, D. C., et al. (2009). Visual field progression in the Collaborative Initial Glaucoma Treatment Study: The impact of treatment and other baseline factors. *Ophthalmology, 116,* 200–207.

Musch, J., & Grodin, S. (2001). Unequal competition as an impediment to personal development: A review of the relative age effect in sport. *Developmental Review, 21,* 147–167.

Mustard, J. F. (2009, December). Canadian progress in early child development-putting

science into action. *Paediatric Child Health, 14*(10), 689–690.

Mutchler, J. E. (2009). Family and household structure, later life. In D. Carr (Ed.), *Encyclopedia of the life course and human development.* Boston: Gale Cengage.

Myles, J., & Picot, G. (2000). Poverty indices and policy analysis. *The Review of Income and Wealth, 46*(2), 161–179.

N

Nabe-Nielsen, K., et al. (2009). Differences between day and noonday workers in exposure to physical and psychological work factors in the Danish eldercare sector. *Scandinavian Journal of Work, Environment, and Health, 35,* 48–55.

Nabet, C., Lelong, N., Ancel, P. Y., Saurel-Cubizolles, M. J., & Kaminski, M. (2007). Smoking during pregnancy according to obstetric complications and parity: Results of the EUROPOP study. *European Journal of Epidemiology, 22,* 715–721.

Nader, K. (2001). Treatment methods for childhood trauma. In J. P. Wilson, M. J. Friedman, & J. Lindy (Eds.), *Treating psychological trauma and PTSD.* New York: Guilford Press.

Nagashima, J., et al. (2010). Three-month exercise and weight loss program improves heart rate recovery in obese persons along with cardiopulmonary function. *Journal of Cardiology.*

Naglieri, J. A. (2000). Stanford-Binet Intelligence Scale. In A. Kazdin (Ed.), *Encyclopedia of psychology.* Washington, DC: American Psychological Association and Oxford University Press.

Nakamura, K., Sheps, S., & Clara Arck, P. (2008). Stress and reproductive failure: Past notions, present insights, and future directions. *Journal of Assisted Reproduction and Genetics, 25*(2–3), 47–62.

Nakata, T., & Trehub, S. E. (2004). Infants' responsiveness to maternal speech and singing. *Infant Behavior & Development, 27,* 455–464.

Nakayama, H. (2010). Development of infant crying behavior: A longitudinal case study. *Infant behavior and Development, 33,* 463–471.

Nanovskaya, T. N., Nekhayeva, I. A., Hankins, G. D., & Ahmed, M. S. (2008). Transfer of methadone across the dually perfused preterm human placental lobule. *American Journal of Obstetrics and Gynecology, 198,* e1–e4.

Nansel, T. R., Overpeck, M., Pilla, R., Ruan, W., Simons-Morton, B., & Scheidt, P. (2001). Bullying behaviors among U.S. youth. *Journal of the American Medical Association, 285,* 2094–2100.

Narberhaus, A., Segarra, D., Caldu, X., Gimenez, M., Junque, C., Pueyo, R., et al. (2007). Gestational age at preterm birth in relation to corpus callosum and general cognitive outcome in adolescents. *Journal of Child Neurology, 22,* 761–765.

Narducci, A., Einarson, A., & Bozzo, P. (2012). Human papillomavirus vaccine and

pregnancy. *Canadian Family Physician, 58,* 268–269.

Narici, M. V. & Maffulli, N. (2010). Sarcopenia: Characteristics, mechanisms, and functional significance. *British Medical Bulletin, 95*(1), 139–159.

Narvaez, D., & Lapsley, D. (Eds.). (2009). *Moral personality, identity, and character: An interdisciplinary future.* New York: Cambridge University Press.

Natali, A., Pucci, G., Boldrini, B., & Schillaci, G. (2009). Metabolic syndrome: At the crossroads of cardiorenal risk. *Journal of Nephrology, 22,* 29–38.

Natalizia, A., Casale, M., Guglielmelli, E., Rinaldi, V., Vressi, F., & Savinelli, F. (2010). An overview of hearing impairment in older adults: Perspectives for rehabilitation with-hearing aids. *European Review for Medical and Pharmaceutical Sciences, 14,* 223–229.

National Aboriginal Health Organization. (2012). *Midwifery.* Retrieved from http://www.naho.ca/

National Advisory Council on Aging. (2001, Summer). Seniors and the law. *Bulletin of the National Advisory Council on Aging, 14*(3).

National Clearinghouse on Family Violence. (2006). *Violence in dating relationships.* Government of Canada, (No. HP20-3/2006E). Retrieved from http://www.phac-aspc.gc.ca/

National Council on Aging. (2000, March). *Myths and realities survey results.* Washington, DC: Author.

National Eating Disorder Information Centre (NEDIC). (2008). Understanding statistics on eating disorders. Retrieved from http://www.nedic.ca/knowthefacts/statistics.shtml

National Institutes of Health. (2004). *Women's health initiative hormone therapy study.* Bethesda, MD: National Institutes of Health.

National Institute of Mental Health. (2008). Autism spectrum disorders (pervasive developmental disorders). Retrieved from http://www.nimh.nih.gov/

National Sleep Foundation. (2006). Sleep in America poll. Washington, DC: Author.

Native Women's Association of Canada. (2010). *What their stories tell us: Research findings from the Sisters in Spirit Initiative.* Retrieved from http://www.nwac.ca/

Nauck, B., & Suckow, J. (2006). Intergenerational relations in cross-cultural comparison: How social networks frame intergenerational relations between mothers and grandmothers in Japan, Korea, China, Indonesia, Israel, Germany, and Turkey. *Journal of Family Issues, 27,* 1159–1185.

Nava-Ocampo, A. A., & Koren, G. (2007). Human teratogens and evidence-based teratogen risk counseling: The Motherisk approach. *Clinical Obstetrics and Gynecology, 50,* 123–131.

Naylor, C. (1999, May). How does working part-time influence secondary students' achievement and impact on their overall well-being? *BCTF Research Report.* Retrieved from http://www.bctf.ca/uploadedfiles/publications/research_reports/99ei02.pdf

Needham, A. (2008). Learning in infants' object perception, object-directed action, and tool use. In A. Needham & A. Woodward (Eds.), *Learning and the infant mind.* New York: Oxford University Press.

Needle, D. (2001, March 6). Website honors "Thinker of the Year." *Internetnews.com.*

Neer, R. M., & SWAN Investigators. (2010). Bone loss across menopausal transition. *Annals of the New York Academy of Sciences, 1192,* 66–71.

Nelson, C. A. (2003). Neural development and lifelong plasticity. In R. M. Lerner, F. Jacobs, & D. Wertlieb (Eds.), *Handbook of applied developmental science* (Vol. 1). Thousand Oaks, CA: Sage.

Nelson, C. A. (2006). Unpublished review of J. W. Santrock's *Topical life-span development* (4th ed.) New York: McGraw-Hill.

Nelson, C. A. (2008). Unpublished review of J. W. Santrock's *Topical life-span development* (5th ed.). New York: McGraw-Hill.

Nelson, C. A. (2009). Brain development and behavior. In A. M. Rudolph, C. Rudolph, L. First, G. Lister, & A. A. Gersohon (Eds.), *Rudolph's pediatrics* (22nd ed.). New York: McGraw-Hill.

Nelson, C. A. (2011). Brain development and behavior. In A. M. Rudolph, C. Rudolph, L. First, G. Lister, & A. A. Gersohon (Eds.), *Rudolph's pediatrics* (22nd ed.). New York: McGraw-Hill.

Nelson, C. A., Thomas, K. M., & de Haan, M. (2006). Neural bases of cognitive development. In W. Damon, R. Lerner, D. Kuhn, & R. Siegler (Eds.), *Handbook of child psychology* (6th ed., Vol. 2). New York: Wiley.

Nelson, C. A., Zeanah, C., & Fox, N. A. (2007). The effects of early deprivation on brain-behavioral development: The Bucharest Early Intervention Project. In D. Romer & E. Walker (Eds.), *Adolescent psychopathology and the developing brain: Integrating brain and prevention science.* New York: Oxford University Press.

Nelson, D. B., Sammel, M. D., Feeman, E. W., Lin, H., Gracia, C. R., & Schmitz, K. H. (2008). Effect of physical activity on menopausal symptoms among urban women. *Medicine and Science in Sports and Exercise, 40,* 50–58.

Nelson, R., & DeBecker, T. (2008). Achievement motivation in adolescents: The role of peer climate and best friends. *Journal of Experimental Education, 76,* 170–189.

Nelson, T. D., & Nelson, J. M. (2010). Evidence-based practice and the culture of adolescence. *Professional Psychology: Research and Practice, 41*(4), 305–311. doi:10.1037/a0020328.

Ness, A., Dias, T., Damus, K., Burd, I., & Berghella, V. (2006). Impact of recent randomized trials on the use of progesterone to prevent preterm birth: A 2005 follow-up survey. *American Journal of Obsterics and Gynecology, 195,* 1174–1179.

Neufeld, G., & Mate, G. (2004). *Hold on to your kids: Why parents matter.* Toronto: Knopf.

Neugarten, B. L. (1986). The aging society. In A. Pifer & L. Bronte (Eds.), *Our aging society: Paradox and promise.* New York: W. W. Norton.

Neugarten, B. L. (1988, August). *Policy issues for an aging society.* Paper presented at the meeting of the American Psychological Association, Atlanta.

Neugarten, B. L., & Weinstein, K. K. (1964). The changing American grandparent. *Journal of Marriage and the Family, 26,* 199–204.

Neugarten, B. L., Havighurst, R. J., & Tobin, S. S. (1968). Personality and patterns of aging. In B. L. Neugarten (Ed.), *Middle age and aging.* Chicago: University of Chicago Press.

Neupert, S. D., Almeida, D. M., & Charles, S. T. (2007). Age differences in reactivity to daily stressors: The role of personal control. *Journals of Gerontology: Psychological Sciences and Social Sciences, 62B,* P316–P225.

Neville, H. J. (2006). Different profiles of plasticity within human cognition. In Y. Munakata & M. H. Johnson (Eds.), *Attention and Performance XXI: Processes of change in brain and cognitive development.* Oxford, UK: Oxford University Press.

The New England centenarian study. (2012). Boston University School of Medicine New England Centenarian Study. Retrieved on April 20, 2013 from http://www.bumc .bu.edu/centenarian/

Newburg, D. S., & Walker, W. A. (2007). Protection of the neonate by the innate immune system of developing gut and of human milk. *Pediatric Research, 61,* 2–8.

Newcombe, N. (2008). The development of implicit and explicit memory. In N. Cowan & M. Courage (Eds.), *The development of memory in childhood.* Philadelphia: Psychology Press.

Newcombe, N. S. (2007). Developmental psychology meets the mommy wars. *Journal of Applied Developmental Psychology, 28,* 553–555.

Newell, K., Scully, D. M., McDonald, P. V., & Baillargeon, R. (1989). Task constraints and infant grip configurations, *Developmental Psychobiology, 22,* 817–832.

Newman, A. B., et al. (2006). Association of long-distance corridor walk performance with mortality, cardiovascular disease, mobility limitation, and disability. *Journal of the American Medical Association, 295,* 2018–2026.

Newman, M. B., & Bakay, R. A. (2008). Therapeutic potentials of human embryonic stem cells in Parkinson's disease. *Neurotherapeutics, 5,* 237–251.

Ng, T. P., Feng, L., Niti, M., & Yap, K. B. (2010). Low blood pressure and depressive symptoms among Chinese older subjects: A population-based study. *American Journal of Medicine, 123,* 342–349.

NICHD Early Child Care Research Network. (2005). Predicting individual differences in attention, memory, and planning in first graders from experiences at home, child care, and school. *Developmental Psychology, 41,* 99–114.

Nielson, D. (2012). Discussing death with pediatric patients: Implications for nurses. *Journal of Pediatric Nursing, 27,* e59–e64.

Nisbett, R. (2003). *The geography of thought.* New York: Free Press.

Noble, J. M., et al. (2010). Association of C-reactive protein with cognitive impairment. *Archives of Neurology, 67,* 87–92.

Nohr, E. A., Bech, B. H., Davies, M. J., Fryenberg, M., Henriksen, T. B., & Olsen, J. (2005). Prepregnancy obesity and fetal death: A study with the Danish National Birth Cohort. *Obstetrics and Gynecology, 106,* 250–259.

Noland, J. S., Singer, L. T., Short, E. J., Minnes, S., Arendt, R. E., Kirchner, H. L., et al. (2005). Prenatal drug exposure and selective attention in preschoolers. *Neurotoxicology and Teratology, 27,* 429–438.

Nordqvist, C. (2009, August 24). What is vitamin D? What are the benefits of vitamin D? *Medical News Today.* Retrieved from http://www.medicalnewstoday.com/articles/161618.php

Norgard, B., Puho, E., Czeilel, A. E., Skriver, M. V., & Sorensen, H. T. (2006). Aspirin use during early pregnancy and the risk of congenital abnormalities. *American Journal of Obstetrics and Gynecology, 192,* 922–923.

Norris, S., Paré, J-R., & Starkey, S. (2006). Childhood autism in Canada: Some issues relating to behavioural intervention. Library of Parliament. Parliamentary Information and Research Services. Retrieved from www2.parl .gc.ca/Content/LOP/ResearchPublications/prb0593-e.htm

Norton, W., Fisher, J., Amico, K., Dovidio, J., & Johnson, B. (2012). Relative efficacy of a pregnancy, sexually transmitted infection, or human immunodeficiency virus, prevention-focused interventions on changing sexual risk behavior among young adults. *Journal of American College Health, 60,* 574–582.

Nottelmann, E. D., Susman, E. J., Blue, J. H., Inoff-Germain, G., Dorn, L. D., Loriaux, D. L., et al. (1987). Gonadal and adrenal hormone correlates of adjustment in early adolescence. In R. M. Lerner & T. T. Foch (Eds.), *Biological-psychological interactions in early adolescence.* Hillsdale, NJ: Erlbaum.

Nova Scotia Advisory Council on the Status of Women. (2013). *Nova Scotia Advisory Council on the Status of Women.* Retrieved from http://women.gov.ns.ca/

Nowakowski, M. (2009). Temperament and joint attention: Stability, continuity, and predictive outcomes in children's socioemotional development (Doctoral Dissertation). Retrieved from Proquest Dissertation and Theses Database (AAT NR65903).

Nussbaum, J. F., Pecchioni, L., & Crowell, T. (2001). The older patient-health care provider relationship in a managed care environment. In M. L. Hummert & J. F. Nussbaum (Eds.), *Aging, communication, and health*. Mahwah, NJ: Erlbaum.

Nussbaum, R., McInnes, R., & Willard, H. (2007). *Thompson & Thompson: Genetics in medicine* (7th ed.). Philadelphia: Saunders Elsevier.

Nutt, S. (2007). Speech presented to the University Women's Club in Georgetown, ON, and from personal interview in May 2007.

Nutting, P. A., Dickinson, W. P., Dickinson, L. M., Nelson, C. C., King, D. K., Crabtree, B. F., et al. (2007). Use of chronic care model elements is associated with higher-quality care for diabetes. *Annals of Family Medicine, 5,* 14–20.

O

O'Brien, B., Chalmers, B., Fell, D., Heaman, M., Darling, E., & Herbert, P. (2011). The experience of pregnancy and birth with midwives: Results from the Canadian Maternity Experiences Survey. *Birth, 38*(3), 207–215.

O'Connor, A. B., & Roy, C. (2008). Electric power plant emissions and public health. *American Journal of Nursing, 108,* 62–70.

O'Connor, D. B., Conner, M., Jones, F., McMillan, B., & Ferguson, E. (2009). Exploring the benefits of conscientiousness: An investigation of the role of daily stressors and health benefits. *Annals of Behavioral Medicine, 37,* 184–196.

O'Connor, E., & McCartney, K. (2007). Attachment and cognitive skills: An investigation of mediating mechanisms. *Journal of Applied Developmental Psychology, 28,* 458–476.

O'Donnell, E., Kirwan, L. D., & Goodman, J. M. (2009). Aerobic exercise training in healthy postmenopausal women: Effects of hormone therapy. *Menopause, 16,* 770–776.

O'Donovan, G., et al. (2010). The ABC of physical activity for health: A consensus statement from the British Association of Sport and Exercise Science. *Journal of Sports Sciences, 28,* 573–591.

O'Neill, D. K., Main, R. M., & Ziemski, R. A. (2009). "I like Barney": Preschoolers' spontaneous conversational initiations with peers. *First Language, 29*(4), 401–425.

O'Sullivan, L. F., Cheng, M. M., Harris, K. M., & Brooks-Gunn, J. (2007). I wanna hold your hand: The progression of social, romantic, and sexual events in adolescent relationships. *Perspectives on Sexual and Reproductive Health, 39,* 100–107.

Oakes, L. M. (2008). Categorization skills and concepts. In M. M. Haith & J. B. Benson (Eds.), *Encyclopedia of infant and early childhood development*. Oxford, UK: Elsevier.

Oakes, L. M., Kannass, K. N., & Shaddy, D. J. (2002). Developmental changes in endogenous control of attention: The role of target familiarity on infants' distraction latency. *Child Development, 73,* 1644–1655.

Obenauer, S., & Maestre, L. A. (2008). Fetal MRI of lung hypoplasia: Imaging findings. *Clinical Imaging, 32,* 48–50.

Oberlander, S. E., Black, M. M., & Starr, R. H. (2007). African American adolescent mothers and grandmothers: A multigenerational approach to parenting. *American Journal of Community Psychology, 39,* 37–46.

Ogrodnik, L. (2007). *Seniors as victims of crime 2004 and 2005.* Canadian Centre for Justice Profile Series. Ottawa: Statistics Canada.

Okpik, A. (2005). *We call it survival: Nunavut Arctic College.*

Okura, T., et al. (2010). Prevalence of neuropsychiatric symptoms and their association with functional limitations in older adults in the United States: The aging, demographics, and memory study. *Journal of the American Geriatrics Society, 58*(2), 330–337.

Olson, H. C., King, S., & Jirikowic, T. (2008). Fetal alcohol spectrum disorders. In M. M. Haith & J. B. Benson (Eds.), *Encyclopedia of infancy and early childhood.* Thousand Oaks, CA: Sage.

Olyan, S. M. (2004). *Biblical mourning: Ritual and social dimension.* New York: Oxford Press.

Oman, D., & Thoresen, C. E. (2006). Do religion and spirituality influence health? In R. F. Paloutzian & C. L. Park (Eds.), *Handbook of the psychology of religion and spirituality.* New York: Guilford.

Ontario Government. (2010, February 19). Full-day learning for four- and five-year-olds: Premier's announcement. Retrieved from http://www.edu.gov.on.ca/earlylearning

Ontario Human Rights Commission. (2006–2007). *Discussion paper: Toward a commission policy on gender identity.* Appendix 2. Retrieved from www.ohrc.on.ca/en/

Opalach, K., Rangaraju, S., Madorsky, I., Leeuwenburgh, C., & Notterpek, L. (2010). Lifelong calorie restriction alleviates age-related oxidative damage on peripheral nerves. *Rejuvenation Research, 13,* 65–74.

Opitz, B., & Friederici, A. D. (2007). Neural basis of processing sequential and hierarchical structures. *Human Brain Mapping, 28,* 585–592.

Orbe, M. P. (2008). Theorizing multidimensional identity negotiation: Reflections on the lived experiences of first-generation college students. In M. Azmitia, M. Syed, & K. Radmacher (Eds.), *The intersections of personal and social identities. New Directions for Child and Adolescent Development, 120,* 81–95.

Orecchia, R., Lucignani, G., & Tosi, G. (2008). Prenatal irradiation and pregnancy: The effects of diagnostic imaging and radiation therapy. *Recent Results in Cancer Research, 178,* 3–20.

Orford, J., Velleman, R., Natera, G., Templeton, L., & Copello, A. (2013). Addiction in the family is a major but neglected contributor to the global burden of adult ill-health. *Social Science and Medicine, 78,* 70–77.

Organisation for Economic Co-operation and Development (OECD). (2003). *Education at a glance: OECD indicators 2003.* OECD.

Organisation for Economic Co-operation and Development (OECD). (2010). *Programme for International Student Assessment (PISA).* Retrieved from http://www.oecd.org/edu/school/programmeforinternationalstudentassessmentpisa/pathwaystosuccess-howknowledgeandskillsatage15shapefuturelivesincanada.htm

Orhan, G., Orhan, I., Subutay-Oztekin, N., Ak, F., & Sener, B. (2009). Recent anticholinesterase pharmaceuticals of natural origin and their synthetic analogues for the treatment of Alzheimer's disease. *Recent Patents on CNS Drug Discovery, 4,* 43–51.

Ornstein, P. A., Coffman, J. L., & Grammer, J. K. (2007, April). *Teachers' memory-relevant conversations and children's memory performance.* Paper presented at the biennial meeting of the Society for Research in Child Development, Boston.

Ornstein, P. A., Coffman, J. L., & Grammer, J. K. (2009). Learning to remember. In O. A. Barbarin & B. H. Wasik (Eds.), *Handbook of child development and early education.* New York: Guilford.

Ornstein, P. A., Coffman, J. L., Grammer, J. K., San Souci, P. P., & McCall, L. E. (2010). Linking the classroom context and the development of children's memory skills. In J. Meece & J. Eccles (Eds.), *The handbook of research on schools, schooling, and human development.* New York: Routledge.

Orrange, R. M. (2007). *Work, family, and leisure: Uncertainty in a risk society.* Boulder, CO: Rowman & Littlefield.

Osteoporosis Canada. (2012). Osteoporosis facts & statistics. Retrieved from http://www.osteoporosis.ca/osteoporosis-and-you/osteoporosis-facts-and-statistics/

Osterhage, J. L., & Friedman, K. L. (2009). Chromosome end maintenance by telomerase. *Journal of Biological Chemistry, 284,* 16061–16065.

Ostfeld, B., Esposito, L., Perl, H., & Hegyi, T. (2010). Concurrent risks in sudden infant death syndrome. *Pediatrics, 125*(3), 447–453.

Ott, C. H., Lueger, R. J., Kelber, S. T., & Prigerson, H. G. (2007). Spousal bereavement in older adults: Common, resilient, and chronic grief with defining characteristics. *Journal of Nervous and Mental Disease, 195,* 332–341.

Otto, B. W. (2010). *Language development in early childhood* (3rd ed.). Upper Saddle River, NJ: Prentice Hall.

Oyserman, D., & Destin, M. (2010). Identity-based motivation: implications for interventions. *The Counselling Psychologist, 38,* 1001–1043.

P

Pagani, L. S., Jalbert, J., Lapointe, P., & Hébert, M. (2006). Effects of junior kindergarten on emerging literacy in children from low-income and linguistic-minority families. *Early Childhood Education Journal, 33,* 209–215.

Painter, K. (2008, June 16). Older, wiser, but less active. *USA Today*, p. 4D.

Pakpreo, P., Ryan, S., Auinger, P., & Aten, M. (2005). The association between parental lifestyle behaviors and adolescent knowledge, attitudes, intentions, and nutritional and physical activity behaviors. *Journal of Adolescent Health, 34*, 129–130.

Palda, V. A., Guise, J. M., Wayhen, C. N., with the Canadian Task Force on Preventive Health Care. (2004). Interventions to promote breastfeeding: Applying the evidence in clinical practice. *Canadian Medical Association Journal, 170*, 976–978.

Palgi, Y., Shira, A., Ben-Ezra, M., Spalter, T., Shmoktkin, D., & Kave, G. (2010). Delineating terminal change in subjective well-being and subjective health. *Journals of Gerontology B: Psychological Sciences and Social Sciences, 65*(B), 61–64.

Palmore, E. B. (2004). Research note: Ageism in Canada and the United States. *Journal of Cross Cultural Gerontology, 19*, 41–46.

Pan, B. A., & Uccelli, P. (2009). Semantic development. In J. Berko Gleason & N. Ratner (Eds.), *The development of language* (7th ed.). Boston: Allyn & Bacon.

Panigrahy, A., Borzaga, M., & Blumi, S. (2010). Basic principles and concepts underlying recent advances in magnetic resonance imaging of the developing brain. *Seminars in Perinatology, 34*, 3–19.

Pannikar, V. (2003). The return of thalidomide: New uses and renewed concerns. *Leprosy Review, 74*(3), 286–288.

Parade, S., Leerkes, E., & Blankson, A. (2010). Attachment to parent, social anxiety and close relationships of female students over the transition to college. *Journal of Youth and Adolescence, 39*, 127–137.

Pardo, J. V., et al. (2007). Where the brain grows old: Decline in anterior cingulate and medial prefrontal function with normal aging. *Neuroimage, 35*, 1231–1237.

Paredes, I., Hidalgo, L., Chedraui, P., Palma, J., & Eugenio, J. (2005). Factors associated with inadequate prenatal care in Ecuadorian women. *International Journal of Gynecology and Obstetrics, 88*, 168–172.

Paris, S. G., & Paris, A. H. (2006). Assessments of early reading. In W. Damon & R. Lerner (Eds.), *Handbook of child psychology* (6th ed.). New York: Wiley.

Park, D. (2001). Commentary in Restak, R. *The secret life of the brain*. Washington, DC: Joseph Henry Press.

Park, D. C., & Gutchess, A. H. (2005). Long-term memory and aging: A cognitive neuroscience perspective. In R. Cabeza, L. Nyberg, & D. Park, (Eds.), *Cognitive neuroscience of aging: Linking cognitive and cerebral aging.* New York: Oxford University Press.

Park, D. C., & Reuter-Lorenz, P. (2009). The adaptive brain: Aging and neurocognitive scaffolding. *Annual Review of Psychology* (Vol. 60). Palo Alto, CA: Annual Reviews.

Park, D. C., & Schwarz, N. (Eds.). (2009). *Cognitive aging* (2nd ed.). Clifton, NJ: Psychology Press.

Park, D. C., Gutchess, A. H., Meade, M. L., & Stine-Morrow, E. A. L. (2007). Improving cognitive function in older adults: Nontraditional approaches. *Journals of Gerontology B: Psychological Sciences and Social Sciences, 62* (Special Issue I), P45–P52.

Park, D. W., Baek, K., Kim, J. R., Lee, J. J., Ryu, S. H., Chin, B. R., et al. (2009). Resveratrol inhibits foam cell formation via NADPH oxidase 1-mediated reactive oxygen species and monocyte chemotactic protein-1. *Experimental Molecular Medicine, 41*, 171–179.

Park, H., Park, S., Shephard, R. J., & Aoyagi, Y. (2010). Yearlong physical activity and sarcopenia in older adults: The Nakanojo Study. *European Journal of Applied Physiology, 109*(5), 953–961.

Park, M. J., Brindis, C. D., Chang, F., & Irwin, C. E. (2008). A midcourse review of the healthy people 2010: 21 critical health objectives for adolescents and young adults. *Journal of Adolescent Health, 42*, 329–334.

Parke, R. D., & Buriel, R. (2006). Socialization in the family: Ethnic and ecological perspective. In W. Damon & R. Lerner (Eds.), *Handbook of child psychology* (6th ed.). New York: Wiley.

Parke, R. D. (2004). Development in the family. *Annual Review of Psychology* (Vol. 55). Palo Alto, CA: Annual Reviews.

Parke, R. D., Leidy, M. S., Schofield, T. J., Miller, M. A., & Morris, K. L. (2008). Socialization. In M. M. Haith & J. B. Benson (Eds.), *Encyclopedia of infant and early childhood development*. Oxford, UK: Elsevier.

Parkin, C., & Kuczynski, L. (2012). Adolescent perspectives on rules and resistance within the parent-child relationship. *Journal of Adolescent Research, 27*(5), 632–658.

Parrila, R., Aunola, K., Leskinen, E., Nurmi, J. E., & Kirby, J. R. (2005). Development of individual differences in reading: Results from longitudinal studies in English and Finnish. *Journal of Educational Psychology, 97*, 299–319.

Parten, M. (1932). Social play among preschool children. *Journal of Abnormal and Social Psychology, 27*, 243–269.

Pasley, K., & Moorefield, B. S. (2004). Stepfamilies. In M. Coleman & L. Ganong (Eds.), *Handbook of contemporary families*. Thousand Oaks, CA: Sage.

Passuth, P. M., Maines, D. R., & Neugarten, B. L. (1984). *Age norms and age constraints twenty years later.* Paper presented at the annual meeting of the Midwest Sociological Society, Chicago.

Patchin, J.W., & Hinduja, S. (2010). Changes in adolescent online social networking behaviors from 2006 to 2009. *Computers in Human Behavior, 26*, 1818–1821. doi:10.1016/j.chb.2010.07.009

Patterson, C. J. (2009a). Lesbian and gay parents and their children: A social science perspective. *Nebraska Symposium on Motivation, 54*, 142–182.

Patterson, C. J. (2009b). Children of lesbian and gay parents: Psychology, law, and policy. *American Psychologist, 64*, 727–736.

Patterson, C. J., & Hastings, P. D. (2007). Socialization in the context of family diversity. In J. E. Grusec & P. D. Hastings (Eds.), *Handbook of socialization*. New York:

Patterson, M. L., & Werker, J. F. (2003). Two-month-old infants match phonetic information in lips and voice. *Developmental Science, 6*, 191–196.

Paul, P. (2003, September/October). The PermaParent trap. *Psychology Today, 36*(5), 40–53.

Pauley, S., Kopecky, B., Beisel, K., Soukup, G., & Fritzsch, B. (2008). Stem cells and molecular strategies to restore hearing. *Panminerva Medicine, 50*, 41–53.

Paulhus, D. L. (2008). Birth order. In M. M. Haith & J. B. Benson (Eds.), *Encyclopedia of infant and early childhood development*. Oxford, UK: Elsevier.

Paulson, J. F., Dauber, S., & Leiferman, J. A. (2006). Individual and combined effects of postpartum depression in mothers and fathers on parenting behavior. *Pediatrics, 118*, 659–668.

Paus, T., Toro, R., Leonard, G., Lerner, J. V., Lerner, R. M., Perron, M., et al. (2008). Morphological properties of the action-observation cortical network in adolescents with low and high resistance to peer influence. *Social Neuroscience, 3*(3–4), 303–316.

Pavone, C., Curto, F., Anello, G., Serretta, V., Almasio, P. L., & Pavone-Macaluso, M. (2008). Prospective, randomized crossover comparison of sublingual apopmorphine (3 mg) with oral sildenafil (50 mg) for male erectile dysfunction. *Journal of Urology, 179* (Suppl. 5), S92–S94.

Peck, R. C. (1968). Psychological developments in the second half of life. In B. L. Neugarten (Ed.), *Middle age and aging*. Chicago: University of Chicago Press.

Peek, M. K. (2009). Marriage in later life. In D. Carr (Ed.), *Encyclopedia of the life course and human development*. Boston: Gale Cengage.

Pelayo, R., Owens, J., Mindell, J., & Sheldon, S. (2006). Bed sharing with unimpaired parents is not an important risk for sudden infant death syndrome: Letter to the editor. *Pediatrics, 117*, 993–994.

Pellicano, E. (2010). Individual differences in executive function and central coherence predict developmental changes in theory of mind in autism. *Developmental Psychology, 46*, 530–544.

Pendakur. R. (2000, January–February). Immigrants and the labour force: Policy, regulation and impact. *Canadian Journal of Sociology Online*.

Peng, X. D., Huang, C. Q., Chen, L. J., & Lu, Z. C. (2009). Cognitive behavioral therapy and reminiscence techniques for the treatment of depression in the elderly: A systematic review. *Journal of International Medical Research, 37*, 975–982.

Pepeu, G., & Giovannini, M. G. (2009). Cholinesterase inhibitors and beyond. *Current Alzheimer Research, 6*, 86–96.

Peplau, L. A., & Beals, K. P. (2002). Lesbians, gays, and bisexuals in relationships. In J. Worrell (Ed.), *Encyclopedia of women and gender*. San Diego: Academic Press.

Peplau, L. A., & Fingerhut, A. W. (2007). The close relationships of lesbians and gay men. *Annual Review of Psychology* (Vol. 58). Palo Alto, CA: Annual Reviews.

Pepler, D. (2009). Bullying. No Way! Retrieved from www.bullyingnoway.com.au/talkout/profiles/ researchers/debraPepler.shtm

Pepler, D., et al. (2011, April). Why worry about bullying. *Health Care Quarterly, 14,* special issue. Retrieved from http://www.longwoods.com/articles/images/HQ_vol14_ChildHealth_Issue2_Pepler.pdf

Perez, S. M., & Gauvain, M. (2007). The sociocultural context of transitions in early socioemotional development. In C. A. Brownell & C. B. Kopp (Eds.), *Socioemotional development in the toddler years.* New York: Guilford.

Perkins, T. (2006, November 23).Give a little love, says Hannah. *Toronto Star,* p. C3.

Perlman, M., & Ross, H. S. (2005). If-then contingencies in children's sibling conflicts. *Merrill-Palmer Quarterly, 51,* 42–66.

Perls, T. T. (2007). Centenarians. In J. E. Birren (Ed.), *Encyclopedia of gerontology* (2nd ed.). San Diego: Academic Press.

Perner, J., Stummer, S., Sprung, M., & Doherty, M. (2002). Theory of mind finds its Piagetian perspective: Why alternative naming comes with understanding belief. *Cognitive Development, 17,* 1451–1472.

Perosa, L., Perosa, S., & Tam, H. (2002). Intergenerational system theory and identity development in young adult women. *Journal of Adolescent Research, 17,* 235–259.

Perrig-Chiello, P., & Perren, S. (2005). The impact of past transitions on well-being in middle age. In S. L. Willis & M. Martin (Eds.), *Middle adulthood.* Thousand Oaks, CA: Sage.

Perrin, J., et al. (2007). A family-centered, community-based system of services for children and youth with special health care needs. *Archives of Pediatric & Adolescent Medicine, 161*(10), 933–936.

Perry, B. (2003). Effects of traumatic events on children. Retrieved from http://www.childtrauma.org

Perry, B. D. (2002–2003). *Risk and vulnerability.* Kaiser Foundation. Retrieved from www.kaiserfoundation.ca/modules/document.asp?locid=414&docid=986

Perry, W. G. (1999). *Forms of ethical and intellectual development in the college years: A scheme.* San Francisco: Jossey Bass.

Peters, J. M., & Stout, D. L. (2011). *Science in elementary education* (11th ed.). Boston: Allyn & Bacon.

Peterson, B. E. (2002). Longitudinal analysis of midlife generativity, intergenerational roles, and caregiving. *Psychology and Aging, 17,* 161–168.

Peterson, B. E. (2006). Generativity and successful parenting: An analysis of young adult outcomes. *Journal of Personality, 74,* 847–869.

Peterson, B. E., & Stewart, A. J. (1996). Antecedents and contexts of generativity motivation at midlife. *Psychology and Aging, 11,* 21–33.

Peterson, C. (1996). The ticking of the social clock: Adults' beliefs about the timing of transition events. *International Journal of Aging and Human Development, 42,* 189–203.

Peterson, C. C., Garnett, M., Kelly, A., & Attwod, T. (2009). Everyday social and conversation applications of theory-of-mind understanding by children with autism-spectrum disorders or typical development. *European Child and Adolescent Psychiatry, 18,* 105–115.

Peterson, C., & McCabe, A. (1994). A social interactionist account of developing decontextualized narrative skill. *Developmental Psychology, 30*(6), 937–948.

Peterson, C., & Roberts, C. (2003). Like mother, like daughter: Similarities in narrative style. *Developmental Psychology, 39*(3), 551–562.

Peterson, C. C. (2005). Mind and body: Concepts of human cognition, physiology and false belief in children with autism or typical development. *Journal of Autism and Developmental Disorders, 35,* 487–497.

Peterson, C. C., Garnett, M., Kelly, A., & Attwod, T. (2009). Everyday social and conversation applications of theory-of-mind understanding by children with autism-spectrum disorders or typical development. *European Child and Adolescent Psychiatry, 18,* 105–115.

Petitto, L., & Marentette, P. (1991). Babbling in the manual mode: Evidence for the ontogeny of language. *Science, 251,* 1493–1496.

Petrill, S. A., Deater-Decklherd, K., Thompson, L. A., Dethorne, L. S., & Schatschneider, C. (2006). Reading skills in early readers: Genetic and shared environmental influences. *Journal of Learning Disabilities, 39,* 48–55.

Pfeifer, M., Goldsmoth, H. H., Davidson, R. J., & Rickman, M. (2002). Continuity and change in inhibited and uninhibited children. *Child Development, 73,* 1474–1485.

Phillipp, B., & Merewood, A. (2004). The baby-friendly was: The best breastfeeding start. *Pediatric Clinics North America, 51,* 761–783.

Phillips, A. C., & Hughes, B. M. (2010). Introductory paper. Cardiovascular reactivity at the crossroads: Where are we now? *Biological Psychology, 86*(2), 95–97.

Phillips, A. C., Burns, V. E., & Lord, J. M. (2007). Stress and exercise: Getting the balance right for aging immunity. *Exercise and Sport Sciences Reviews, 35,* 35–39.

Phillips, L. H., & Andres, P. (2010). The cognitive neuroscience of aging: New findings on compensation and connectivity. *Cortex, 46,* 421–424.

Phillips, L. M., Norris, S. P., & Anderson, J. (2008). Unlocking the door: Is parents' reading to children the key to early literacy development? *Canadian Psychology, 49*(2), 82–88.

Phillips, L. M., Norris, S. P., Osmond, W. C., & Maynard, A. M. (2002). Relative reading achievement: A longitudinal study of 187 children from first through sixth grades. *Journal of Education Psychology, 94,* 3–13.

Phinney, J. S. (2006). Ethnic identity exploration in emerging adulthood. In J. J. Arnett & J. L. Tanner (Eds.), *Emerging adults in America.* Washington, DC: American Psychological Association.

Phinney, J. S. (2008). Bridging identities and disciplines: Advances and challenges in understanding multiple identities. In M. Azmitia, M. Syed, & K. Radmacher (Eds.), *The intersections of personal and social identities. New Directions for Child and Adolescent Development, 120,* 81–95.

Phinney, S., & Ong, A. (2007). Ethnic identity in immigrant families. In J. Lansford, K. Deater-Deckard, & M. Bornstein (Eds), *Immigrant families in contemporary society* (pp. 51–68). New York: Guilford.

Phipps, S. (2003, June). *The impact of poverty on health: A scan of research literature.* Ottawa: Canadian Institute for Health Information. Retrieved from http://www.cihi.ca/

Piaget, J. (1932). *The moral judgment of the child.* New York: Harcourt Brace Jovanovich.

Piaget, J. (1952). *The origins of intelligence in children.* New York: International Universities Press.

Piaget, J. (1954). *The construction of reality in the child.* New York: Basic Books.

Piaget, J. (1962). *Play, dreams, and imitation.* New York: W. W. Norton.

Piaget, J., & Inhelder, B. (1969). *The child's conception of space* (F. J. Langdon & J. L. Lunger, Trans.). New York: W. W. Norton.

Pieperhoff, P., Homke, L., Schneider, F., Habel, U., Shah, N. J., Zilles, K., et al. (2008). Deformation field morphometry reveals age-related structural differences between the brains of adults up to 51 years. *Journal of Neuroscience 28,* 828–842.

Pihlajamaki, M., Jauhiainen, A. M., & Soininen, H. (2009). Structural and functional MRI in mild cognitive impairment. *Current Alzheimer Research, 6,* 179–185.

Pinette, M., Wax, J., & Wilson, E. (2004). The risks of underwater birth. *American Journal of Obstetrics and Gynecology, 190,* 1211–1215.

Ping, H., & Hagopian, W. (2006). Environmental factors in the development of type 1 diabetes. *Reviews in Endocrine and Metabolic Disorders, 7,* 149–162.

Pinheiro, R. T., Magalhaes, P. V., Horta, B. L., Pinheiro, K. A., da Silva, R. A., & Pinto, R. H. (2006). Is paternal postpartum depression associated with maternal postpartum depression? Population-based study in Brazil. *Acta Psychiatrica Scandinavia, 113,* 230–232.

Pinquart, M., & Sorensen, S. (2006). Gender differences in caregiver stressors, social resources, and health: An updated meta-analysis. *Journals of Gerontology B: Psychological Sciences and Social Sciences, 61,* P33–P45.

Piper, W. E., Ogrodniczuk, J. S., Joyce, A. S., Weideman, R., & Rosie, J. S. (2007). Group composition and group therapy for complicated grief. *Journal of Consulting and Clinical Psychology, 75,* 116–125.

Pitkanen, T., Lyyra, A. L., & Pulkkinen L. (2005). Age of onset of drinking and the use of alcohol in adulthood: A follow-up study from age 8–42 for females and males. *Addiction, 100,* 652–661.

Pitman, E., & Matthey, S. (2004). The SMILES program: A group program for children with mentally ill parents or siblings. *American Journal of Orthopsychiatry, 74,* 383–388.

Pitt-Catsouphes, M., Kossek, E. E., & Sweet, S. (Eds.). (2006). *The work and family handbook.* Mahwah, NJ: Erlbaum.

Pleck, J. H. (1995). The gender-role strain paradigm. In R. F. Levant & W. S. Pollack (Eds.), *A new psychology of men.* New York: Basic Books.

Pliszka, S. R. (2007). Pharmacologic treatment of attention deficit hyperactivity disorder: Efficacy, safety, and mechanisms of action. *Neuropsychology Review, 17,* 61–72.

Plomin, R. (2004). Genetics and developmental psychology. *Merrill-Palmer Quarterly, 50,* 341–352.

Plomin, R., DeFries, J. C., Craig, I. W., & McGuffin, P. (Eds.). (2003). *Behavioral genetics in the postgenomic era.* Washington, DC: APA Books.

Plomin, R., DeFries, J. C., & Fulker, D. W. (2007). Nature and nurture during infancy and early childhood. New York: Cambridge University Press.

Pohl, R. (2002, April). Poverty in Canada: Street Level Consulting and Counselling, Calgary, Alberta. Retrieved from http://www.streetlevelconsulting.ca/

Pohlhaus, et al. (2011). Sex differences in application, success, and funding rates for NIH extramural programs. *Academic Medicine, 86*(6), 759–767.

Polan, E., & Taylor, D. (2011). *Journey across the lifespan: Human development and health promotion* (4th ed.) Philadelphia: Davis.

Pollack, W. (1999). *Real boys.* New York: Owl Books.

Pollard, I. (2007). Neuropharmacology of drugs and alcohol in mother and fetus. *Seminars in Fetal and Neonatal Medicine, 12,* 106–113.

Poltorak, D., & Glazer, J. (2006). The development of children's understanding of death: Cognitive and psychodynamic considerations. *Child and Adolescent Psychiatric Clinics of North America, 15,* 567–573.

Pomerleau, A., Scuccumarri C., & Malcuit, G. (2003). Mother-infant behavioural interactions in teenage and adult mothers during the first six months postpartum: Relations with infant development. *Infant Mental Health Journal, 24,* 495–509.

Pomfrey, E. (2012). What is stress? Natural Health and Meditation Resource Page. Retrieved from http://www.tm.org/resource-pages/60-what-is-stress

Pontecorvo, C. (2004). Thinking with others: The social dimension of learning in families and schools. In A. Perret-Clermont, L. B. Resnick, C. Pontecorvo, T. Zittoun, & B. Burge (Eds.), *Joining society.* New York: Cambridge University Press.

Ponton, L. E. (1997). *The romance of risk: Why teenagers do the things they do.* New York: Basic Books.

Popenoe, D. (2007). *The state of our unions: 2007.* Piscataway, NJ: The National Marriage Project, Rutgers University.

Popenoe, D. (2008). *Cohabitation, marriage, and child wellbeing: A cross-national perspective.* Piscataway, NJ: The National Marriage Project, Rutgers University.

Poranganel, L., Titley, K., & Kulkarni, G. (2006). Establishing a dental home: A program for promoting comprehensive oral health starting from pregnancy through childhood. *Oral Health, 96,* 10–14.

Porterfield, S. (2011). Vertical transmission of human papillomavirus from mother to fetus: Literature review. *The Journal of Nurse Practitioners, 7*(8), 665–670.

Posada, G. (2008). Attachment. In M. M. Haith & J. B. Benson (Eds.), *Encyclopedia of infancy and early childhood.* Oxford, UK: Elsevier.

Posner, M. I., & Rothbart, M. K. (2007). *Educating the human brain.* Washington, DC: American Psychological Association.

Pot, A. M., et al. (2010). The impact of life review on depression in older adults: A randomized controlled trial. *International Psychogeriatrics, 22*(4), 572.

Poulin, F., & Pedersen, S. (2007). Developmental changes in gender composition of friendship networks in adolescent girls and boys. *Developmental Psychology, 43,* 1484–1496.

Poulin-Dubois, D., & Héroux, G. (1994). Movement and children's attributions of life properties. *International Journal of Behavioral Development, 17*(2), 329–347.

Prakash, A., Powell, A. J., & Geva, T. (2010). Multimodality noninvasive imaging for assessment of congenital heart disease. *Circulation. Cardiovascular Imaging, 3,* 112–125.

Prakash, R. S., Snook, M., & Kramer, A. F. (2010). Aerobic fitness is associated with gray matter volume and white matter integrity in multiple sclerosis. *Brain Research, 1341,* 41–51.

Pratt, M. W., Norris, J. E., Cressman, K., Lawford, H., & Hebblethwaite, S. (2008a). Parents' stories of grandparenting concerns in the three-generational family: Generativity, optimism, and forgiveness. *Journal of Personality, 76,* 581–604.

Pratt, M. W., Norris, J. E., Hebblethwaite, S., & Arnold, M. L. (2008b). Intergenerational transmission of values: Family generativity and adolescents' narratives of parent and grandparent value teaching. *Journal of Personality, 76,* 171–198.

Preece, M. (2003–2004). When lone parents marry: The challenge of stepfamily relationships. *Transition Magazine, 33*(4) [online] http://www.vifamily.ca/

Pressler, S. J., et al. (2010). Cognitive deficits in chronic heart failure. *Nursing Research, 59,* 127–139.

Pressley, M. (2003). Literacy and literacy instruction. In I. B. Weiner (Ed.), *Handbook of psychology* (Vol. VII). New York: Wiley.

Pressley, M. (2007). Achieving best practices. In L. B. Gambrell, L. M. Morrow, & M. Pressley, (Eds.), *Best practices in literary instruction.* New York: Guilford.

Pressley, M., & McCormick, C. B. (2007). Child and adolescent development for educators. New York: Guilford.

Pressley, M., Raphael, L., Gallagher, D., & DiBella, J. (2004). Providence–St. Mel School: How a school that works for African-American students works. *Journal of Educational Psychology, 96,* 216–235.

Pressley, M., Wharton-MacDonald, R., Allington, R., Block, C. C., Morrow, L., Tracey, D., et al. (2001). A study of effective first grade literacy instruction. *Scientific Studies of Reading, 15,* 35–58.

Preston, A. M., Rodriguez, C., Rivera, C. E., & Sahai, H. (2003). Influence of environmental tobacco smoke on vitamin C status in children. *American Journal of Clinical Nutrition, 77,* 167–172.

Price, C. A., & Joo, E. (2005). Exploring the relationship between marital status and women's retirement satisfaction. *International Journal of Aging and Human Development, 61,* 37–55.

Price, C. A., & Nesteruk, O. (2010). Creating retirement paths: Examples from the lives of women. *Journal of Women and Aging, 22,* 136–149.

Princess Margaret Hospital. (2005). Do not resuscitate orders. Caring to the End of Life Series. Toronto: University Health Network. Retrieved from http://www.caringtoeend.ca/body.php?id=515&cc=1

Prinstein, M. J., & Dodge, K. A. (Eds.). (2008). *Understanding peer influence in children and adolescents.* New York: Guilford.

Prinstein, M. J., Boivan, M., & Bukowski, W. M. (2009). Peer reputations and psychological adjustment. In K. H. Rubin, W. M. Bukowski, & B. Laursen (Eds.), *Handbook of peer interactions, relationships, and groups.* New York: Guilford.

Prinz, R. J., Sanders, M. R., Shapiro, C. J., Witaker, D. J., Lutzker, J. R. (2009). Population-based prevention of child maltreatment: The U.S. Triple P System Population Trial. *Prevention Science, 10,* 1–13.

Problem Gambling Institute of Ontario. (2010). Ontario youth gambling report: Data from the 2009 Ontario student drug use and health survey. Retrieved from http://www.problemgambling.ca

Promislow, D. E. L., Fedorka, K. M., & Burger, J. E. P. (2005). Evolutionary biology of aging: Future directions. In S. Austad & E. Masoro (Eds.), *The Handbook of the Biology of Aging* (6th ed.).

Pryor, J. H. Y., Hurtado, S., Harkness, J., & Korn, W. S. (2007). *The American* freshman: National norms for fall, 2007. Los Angeles: Higher Education Research Institute, UCLA.

Prystowsky, E. N., et al. (2010). The impact of new and emerging clinical data on treatment strategies for atrial fibrillation. *Journal of Cardiovascular Electrophysiology, 21*(8), 946–58.

Public Health Agency of Canada (PHAC). (2005). Report on seniors' falls in Canada.

Public Health Agency of Canada (PHAC). (2007, November). HIV/AIDS epi updates. Canada. Retrieved from http://www.phac-aspc .gc.ca/

Public Health Agency of Canada (PHAC). (2008a). *Canadian guidelines for sexual health education.* Ottawa. Retrieved from http://www.phac-aspc.gc.ca/publicat/ cgshe-ldnemss/

Public Health Agency of Canada (PHAC). (2008b). *Canadian perinatal health report 2008 edition.* Ottawa.

Public Health Agency of Canada (PHAC). (2009a). Breastfeeding & infant nutrition. Retrieved from http://www.phac-aspc.gc.ca/ dca-dea/prenatal/nutrition-eng.php

Public Health Agency of Canada (PHAC). (2009b). Childhood cancers: Ages 1–14. Retrieved from http://www.phac-aspc. gc.ca/

Public Health Agency of Canada (PHAC). (2009d). Tracking heart disease and stroke in Canada. Retrieved from http://www .phac-aspc.gc.ca/publicat/2009/cvd-avc/ summary-resume-eng.php

Public Health Agency of Canada (PHAC). (2009e). *What mothers say: The Canadian maternity experiences survey.* Retrieved from http://www.publichealth. gc.ca/mes

Public Health Agency of Canada (PHAC). (2010b). Chapter 3. *The health and well-being of Canadian seniors: The Chief Public Health Officer's report on the state of public health in Canada 2010.* Retrieved from http://www.phac-aspc.gc.ca/

Public Health Agency of Canada (PHAC). (2010d). *Report on sexually transmitted infections in Canada: 2008.* Retrieved from http://www.phac-aspc.gc.ca/

Public Health Agency of Canada (PHAC). (2010e). What is the impact of sleep apnea on Canadians? Retrieved from http://www.phac-aspc.gc.ca/cd-mc/ sleepapnea-apneesommeil/ff-rr-2009-eng. php

Public Health Agency of Canada (PHAC). (2011a). Joint statement on safe sleep: Preventing sudden infant deaths in Canada. Retrieved from http://www.phac-aspc.gc.ca

Public Health Agency of Canada (PHAC). (2011b). Shaken baby syndrome (SBS). Retrieved from http://www.phac-aspc.gc.ca

Public Health Agency of Canada (PHAC). (2011c). *The Chief Public Health Officer's report on the state of public health in Canada, 2011.* Retrieved from http://www.phac-aspc .gc.ca/

Public Health Agency of Canada (PHAC). (2011d). *HIV/AIDS epi updates—July 2010.* Retrieved from http://www.sogc.org/

Public Health Agency of Canada (PHAC). (2011e). Reported cases and rates of chlamydia by age group and sex, 1991 to 2009. Retrieved from http://www.phac-aspc .gc.ca/

Public Health Agency of Canada (PHAC). (2011f). Human papillomavirus (HPV) prevention and HPV vaccines: Questions and answers. Retrieved from http://www.phac-aspc .gc.ca/

Public Health Agency of Canada (PHAC). (2011g). *The sensible guide to a healthy pregnancy.* Retrieved from http://www .healthycanadians.ca/

Public Health Agency of Canada (PHAC). (2012a). Executive summary. *Report on sexually transmitted infections in Canada: 2009.* Retrieved from http://www.phac-aspc.gc.ca/

Public Health Agency of Canada (PHAC). (2012b). Canadian perinatal surveillance system. Retrieved from http://www.phac-aspc .gc.ca/

Public Health Agency of Canada (PHAC). (2012c). *Perinatal health indicators for Canada, 2011.* Retrieved from http://www .phac-asap.gc.ca/

Public Health Agency of Canada (PHAC). (2012d). *The health of Canada's young people: A mental health focus.* Retrieved from http://www.phac-aspc.gc/

Public Health Agency of Canada (PHAC). (2010). Life with arthritis in Canada: A personal and public health challenge. Retrieved on September 15, 2013 from http://www.phac-aspc.gc.ca/cd-mc/ arthritis-arthrite/lwaic-vaaac-10/4-eng. php#Sel

Public Safety Canada. (2009). Bullying prevention in schools. Retrieved from www .publicsafety.gc.ca/

Pudrovska, T. (2009). Midlife crises and transitions. In D. Carr (Ed.), *Encyclopedia of the life course and human development.* Boston: Gale Cengage.

Pudrovska, T., Schieman, S., & Carr, D. (2006). Strains of singlehood in later life: Do race and gender matter? *Journals of Gerontology B: Psychological Sciences and Social Sciences, 61,* S315–S322.

Pugh, (2004). CrossCurrents. Centre for Addiction and Mental Health (CAMH). Retrieved from http://www.camh.net/

Pujazon-Zazik, M., & Park, M. (2010). To tweet, or not to tweet: Gender differences and potential positive and negative health outcomes of adolescents' social Internet use. *American Journal of Men's Health, 4,* 77–85.

Purnell, L. (2013). *Transcultural health care: A culturally competent approach* (4th ed.). Philadelphia: Davis.

Putallaz, M., Grimes, C. L., Foster, K. J., Kupersmidt, J. B., Clie, J. D., & Dearing, K. (2007). Overt and relational aggression and victimization: Multiple perspectives within the school setting. *Journal of School Psychology, 45,* 523–547.

Putnam, S. P., Sanson, A. V., & Rothbart, M. K. (2002). Child temperament and parenting. In M. H. Bornstein (Ed.), *Handbook of parenting* (2nd ed.). Mahwah, NJ: Erlbaum.

Q

Qin, L., Pomerantz, E., & Wang, Q. (2009). Are gains in the decision-making autonomy during early adolescence beneficial for emotional functioning? The case of the United States and China. *Child Development, 80,* 1705–1721.

Queen, B. L., & Tollefsbol, T. O. (2010). Polyphenols and aging. *Current Aging Science, 3,* 34–42.

Quesnel, C., Fulgencio, J. P., Drie, C., Marro, B., Payen, L., Lembert, N., et al. (2007). Limitations of computed tomographic angiography in the diagnosis of brain death. *Intensive Care Medicine, 33,* 2129–2135.

Quinn, P. C., Bhatt, R. S., & Hayden, A. (2008). What goes with what: Development of perceptual grouping in infancy. In B. H. Ross (Ed.), *Motivation* (Vol. 49). London: Elsevier.

R

Raabe, A., & Muller, W. U. (2008). Radiation exposure during pregnancy. *Neurosurgery Review, 31*(3), 351–352.

Racine, T., & Carpendale, J. (2007). The role of shared practice in joint attention. *British Journal of Developmental Psychology, 25,* 3–25.

Radak, Z., Hart, N., Srga, L., Koltai, E., Atalay, M., Ohno, H., et al. (2010). Exercise plays a preventive role against Alzheimers disease. *Journal of Alzheimer's Disease, 20*(3), 777–83.

Rafii, M. S., & Aisen, P. S. (2009). Recent developments in Alzheimer's disease therapeutics. *BMC Medicine, 7,* 7.

Raghuveer, G. (2010). Lifetime cardiovascular risk of childhood obesity. *American Journal of Clinical Nutrition, 91*(5), 1514S-1519S.

Rajendran, G., & Mitchell, P. (2007). Cognitive theories of autism. *Developmental Review, 27,* 224–260.

Ram, N., Morelli, S., Lindberg, C., & Carstensen, L. L. (2008). From static to dynamic: The ongoing dialetic about human development. In K. W. Schaie & R. P. Abeles (Eds.), *Social structures and aging individuals: Continuing challenges.* Mahwah, NJ: Erlbaum.

Ramage-Morin, P. (2008). Chronic pain in Canadian seniors. *Health Reports, 19*(1), 1–16.

Ramage-Morin, P. (2009). Medication use among senior Canadians. Statistics Canada Catalogue no. 82-003-X. Retrieved from http://www.statcan.gc.ca/

pub/82-003-x/2009001/article/10801-eng.pdf

Rapaport, S. (1994, November 28). Interview. *U.S. News and World Report*, p. 94.

Raphael, B., Taylor, M., & McAndrew, V. (2008). Women, catastrophe, and mental health. *Australia and New Zealand Journal of Psychiatry, 42*, 13–23.

Raphael, D. (Ed.). (2010). *Health promotion and quality of life in Canada: Essential readings.* Toronto: Canadian Scholars' Press.

Rasmussen, C., Ho, E., Nicoladis, E., Leung, J., & Bisanz, J. (2006). Is the Chinese number-naming system transparent? Evidence from Chinese-English bilingual children. *Canadian Journal of Experimental Psychology, 60*, 60–67.

Rasulo, D., Christensen, K., & Tomassini, C. (2005). The influence of social relations on mortality in later life: A study on elderly Danish twins. *Gerontologist, 45*, 601–608.

Ratey, J. (2006, March 27). Commentary in L. Szabo, ADHD treatment is getting a workout. *USA Today*, 6D.

Ratzan, S. (2011). Our new "social" communication age in health. *Journal of Health Communication: International Perspectives, 16*(8), 803–804.

Raudenbush, S. W. (2001). Comparing personal trajectories and drawing causal inferences from longitudinal data. *Annual Review of Psychology, 52*, 501–25.

Raven, P. H. (2011). *Biology* (9th ed.). New York: McGraw-Hill.

Rawlins, W. K. (2009). *The compass of friendship.* Thousand Oaks, CA: Sage.

Ray, G., Mertens, J., & Weisner, C. (2009). Family members of people with alcohol or drug dependence: Health problems and medical cost compared to family members of people with diabetes and asthma. *Addiction, 104*, 203–214.

Raymo, J. M., & Sweeney, M. M. (2006). Work-family conflict and retirement preferences. *Journals of Gerontology B: Psychological Sciences and Social Sciences, 61*, S161–S169.

Raynauld, I. (Dir.). (2013). *Mystical brain.* National Film Board Canada.

Raz, N., Ghisletta, P., Rodrique, K. M., Kennedy, K. M., & Lindenberger, U. (2010). Trajectories of brain imaging in-middle-aged older adults: Regional and individual differences. *Neuroimage, 51*(2), 501–511.

Royal Canadian Mounted Police (RCMP). (2012). Elder abuse. Retrieved from http://www.rcmp-grc.gc.ca/

Read, S., & Elliott, D. (2007). Exploring a continuum of support for bereaved people with intellectual disabilities: A strategic approach. *Journal of Intellectual Disabilities, 11*, 167–181.

Real, T. (1997). *I don't want to talk about it: Overcoming the secret legacy of male depression.* New York: Simon and Schuster.

Ream, G. L., & Savin-Williams, R. (2003). Religious development in adolescence. In G. Adams & M. Berzonsky (Eds.), *Blackwell handbook of adolescence.* Malden, MA: Blackwell.

Redinbaugh, E. M., MacCallum, J., & Kiecolt-Glaser, J. K. (1995). Recurrent syndromal depression in caregivers. *Psychology and Aging, 10*, 358–368.

Reeb, B. C., Fox, N. A. Nelson, C. A., & Zeanah, C. H. (2008). The effects of early institutionalization of social behavior and underlying neural correlates. In M. de Haan & M. Gunnar (Eds.), *Handbook of social developmental neuroscience.* Malden, MA: Blackwell.

Reece, E. A. (2008). Obesity, diabetes, and links to congenital defects: A review of the evidence and recommendations for intervention. *Journal of Maternal-Fetal and Neonatal Medicine, 21*, 173–180.

Reese, C. M., & Cherry, K. E. (2004). Practical memory concerns in adulthood. *International Journal of Aging and Human Development, 59*, 235–253.

Reeve, C. L., & Charles, J. E. (2008). Survey of opinions on the primacy of g and social consequences of ability testing: A comparison of expert and non-expert views. *Intelligence, 36*, 681–688.

Regan, P. C. (2008). *The mating game* (2nd ed.). Thousand Oaks, CA: Sage.

Regev, R. H., Lusky, A., Dolfin, T., Litmanovitz, I., Arnon, S., Reichman, B., & Israel Neonatal Network. (2003). Excess mortality and morbidity among small-for-gestational-age premature infants: A population based study. *Journal of Pediatrics, 143*, 186–191.

Rehm, J., et al. (2010). The relation between different dimensions of alcohol consumption and burden of disease—an overview. *Addiction, 105*, 817–843.

Reibis, R. K., Treszi, A., Wegscheider, K., Ehrlich, B., Dissmann, R., & Voller, H. (2010). Exercise capacity is the most powerful predictor of 2-year mortality in patients with left ventricular systolic dysfunction. *Herz, 35*, 104–110.

Reichstadt, J., Depp, C. A., Palinkas, L. A., Folsom, D. P., & Jeste, D. V. (2007). Building blocks of successful aging: A focus group study of older adults' perceived contributors to successful aging. *American Journal of Geriatric Psychiatry, 15*, 194–201.

Reilly, D. E., Hastings, R. P., Vaughan, F. L., & Huws, J. C. (2008). Parental bereavement and the loss of a child with intellectual disabilities: A review of the literature. *Intellectual and Developmental Disabilities, 46*, 27–43.

Reinders, H., & Youniss, J. (2006). School-based required community service and civic development in adolescence. *Applied Developmental Science, 10*, 2–12.

Rendell, P. G., McDaniel, M. A., Forbes, R. D., & Einstein, G. O. (2007). Age-related effects in prospective memory are modulated by ongoing task complexity and relation to target cue. *Neuropsychology, Development, and Cognition, Section B: Neuropsychology and Cognition, 14*, 236–256.

Renner, P., Grofer Klinger, L., & Klinger, M. R. (2006). Exogenous and endogenous attention orienting in autism spectrum disorders. *Child Neuropsychology, 12*, 361–382.

Rentz, D. M., et al. (2010). Cognition, reserve, amyloid deposition in normal aging. *Annals of Neurology* (Vol. 67). Palo Alto, CA: Annual Reviews.

Reyna, V. F. (2004). How people make decisions that involve risk: A dual-process approach. *Current Directions in Psychological Science, 13*, 60–66.

Reyna, V. F., & Rivers, S. E. (2008). Current theories and rational decision making. *Developmental Review, 28*, 1–11.

Reynolds, C. A., Gatz, M., Prince, J. A., Berg, S., & Pedersen, N. L. (2010). Serum lipid levels and cognitive changes in late life. *Journal of the American Geriatrics Society, 58*, 501–509.

Reynolds, M. (2012). *The legacy of child abuse.* McGill Publications, Headway, Vol. 4., No. 1.

Rhodes, A., et al. (2008). The impact of rural residence on medically serious medicinal self-poisonings. *General Hospital Psychiatry, 30*(6), 552–60.

Rholes, W. S., & Simpson, J. A. (2007). Introduction: New directions and emerging issues in adult attachment. In W. S. Rholes & J. A. Simpson (Eds.), *Adult attachment.* New York: Guilford.

Richards, J. (2009). Dropouts: The Achilles Heel of Canada's school system. Commentary 298. Toronto: C.D. Howe Institute. Retrieved from http://www.cdhowe.org

Richardson, G. A., Goldschmidt, L., & Larkby, C. (2008). Effects of prenatal cocaine exposure on growth: A longitudinal analysis. *Pediatrics, 120*, e1017–e1027.

Richardson, G. A., Goldschmidt, L., & Willford, J. (2008). The effects of prenatal cocaine use on infant development. *Neurotoxicology and Teratology, 30*, 96–106.

Richardson, R., & Hayne, H. (2007). You can't take it with you: The translation of memory across development. *Current Directions in Psychological Science, 16*, 223–227.

Richardson, V. E. (2007). A dual process model of grief counseling: Findings from the Changing Lives of Older Couples (CLOC) Study. *Journal of Gerontological Social Work, 48*, 311–329.

Richmond, E. J., & Rogol, A. D. (2007). Male pubertal development and the role of androgen therapy. *Nature Clinical Practice: Endocrinology and Metabolism, 3*, 338–344.

Rickards, T., Runco, M. A., Moger, S. (Eds.). (2009). *The Routledge Companion to Creativity.* New York: Routledge.

Riebe, D., Garber, C. E., Rossi, J. S., Greaney, M. L., Nigg, C. R., Lees, F. D., et al. (2005). Physical activity, physical function, and stages of change in older adults. *American Journal of Health Behavior, 29*, 70–80.

Riediger, M., Li, S. C., & Lindenberger, U. (2006). Selection, optimization, and compensation as developmental mechanisms of adaptive resource allocation: Review and preview. In J. E. Birren & K. W. Schaie (Eds.), *Handbook of the psychology of aging* (6th ed.). San Diego: Academic Press.

Rifas-Shiman, S. L., Rich-Edwards, J. W., Willett, W. C., Kleinman, K. P., Oken, E., & Gillman, M. W. (2006). Changes in dietary intake from the first to the second trimester of pregnancy. *Pediatric and Perinatal Epidemiology, 20,* 35–42.

Rifkin, J. (2005, Spring). Ultimate therapy: Commercial eugenics in the 21st century. *Harvard International Review, 29*(1), 44–48.

Rigaud, D., Verges, B., Colas-Linhart, N., Petiet, A., Moukkaddem, M., Van Wymelbeke, V., et al. (2007). Hormonal and psychological factors linked to the increased thermic effect of food in malnourished fasting anorexia nervosa. *Journal of Clinical Endocrinology and Metabolism, 92,* 1623–1629.

Riley, K. P., Snowdon, D. A., Derosiers, M. F., & Markesbery, W. R. (2005). Early life linguistic ability, late life cognitive function, and neuropathology: Findings from the Nun Study. *Neurobiology of Aging, 26,* 341–347.

Rimmer, J. H., Rauworth, A. E., Wang, E. C., Nicola, T. L., & Hill, B. (2009). A preliminary study to examine the effects of aerobic and therapeutic (nonaerobic) exercise on cardiorespiratory fitness and coronary risk reduction in stroke survivors. *Archives of Physical Medicine and Rehabilitation, 90,* 407–412.

Rimsza, M. E., & Kirk, G. M. (2005). Common medical problems of the college student. *Pediatric Clinics of North America, 52,* 9–24.

Ristow, M., & Zarse, K. (2010). How increased oxidative stress promotes longevity and metabolic health: The concept of mitochondria hormesis (mitohormesis). *Experimental Gerontology, 45,* 410–418.

Ritchie, S., Maxwell, K. L., & Bredekamp, S. (2009). Rethinking early schooling: Using developmental science to transform children's early experiences. In O. A. Babarin & B. H. Wasik (Eds.), *Handbook of child development and early education.* New York: Guilford.

Rivers, S. E., Reyna, V. F., & Mills, B. (2008). Risk taking under the influence: A fuzzy-trace theory of emotion in adolescence. *Developmental Review, 28,* 107–144.

Robbins, G., Powers, D., & Burgess, S. (2008). *A fit way of life.* New York: McGraw-Hill.

Roberto, K. A., & Skoglund, R. R. (1996). Interactions with grandparents and great-grandparents: A comparison of activities, influences, and relationships. *International Journal of Aging and Human Development, 43,* 107–117.

Roberts, B. W., & Mroczek, D. (2008). Personality trait change in adulthood. *Current Directions in Psychological Science, 17,* 31–35.

Roberts, B. W., & Wood, D. (2006). Personality development in the context of the neo-socioanalytic model of personality. In D. Mroczek & T. Little (Eds.), *Handbook of personality development.* Mahwah, NJ: Erlbaum.

Roberts, B. W., Jackson, J. J., Fayard, J. V., Edmonds, G., & Meints, J. (2009). Conscientiousness. In M. Leary & R. Hoyle (Eds.), *Handbook of individual differences in social behavior.* New York: Guilford.

Roberts, B. W., Walton, K. E., & Bogg, T. (2005). Conscientiousness and health across the life course. *Review of General Psychology, 9,* 156–168.

Roberts, B. W., Walton, K. E., & Viechtbauer, W. (2006). Pattern of mean-level change in personality traits across the life course: A meta-analysis of longitudinal studies. *Psychological Bulletin, 132,* 1–25.

Roberts, B. W., Wood, D., & Caspi, A. (2008). Personality development. In O. P. John, R. W. Robins, & L. A. Pervin (Eds.), *Handbook of personality* (3rd ed.). New York: Guilford.

Roberts, D. F., Henrikson, L., & Foehr, V. G. (2004). Adolescents and the media. In R. Lerner & L. Steinberg (Eds.), *Handbook of adolescent psychology.* New York: Wiley.

Roberts, L. W., Clifton, R. A., Ferguson, B., Kampen, K., & Langlois, S. (Eds.). (2004). *Recent social trends in Canada, 1960–2000.* Montreal: McGill-Queen's University Press.

Roberts, S. B., & Rosenberg, I. (2006). Nutrition and aging: Changes in the regulation of energy metabolism with aging. *Physiology Review, 86,* 651–667.

Robins, R. W., Trzesniewski, K. H., Tracey, J. L., Potter, J., & Gosling, S. D. (2002). Age differences in self-esteem from age 9 to 90. *Psychology and Aging, 17,* 423–434.

Robinson, K. (2009). *The element: How finding your passion changes everything.* London, England: Penguin Books.

Robitaille, A., Cappeliez, P., Coulombe, D., & Webster, J. D. (2010). Factorial structure and psychometric properties of the reminiscence functions scale. *Aging and Mental Health, 14,* 184–192.

Rochlen, A. B., McKelley, R. A., Suizzo, M. A., & Scaringi, V. (2008). Predictors of relationship satisfaction, psychological well-being, and life-satisfaction among stay-at-home fathers. *Psychology of Men and Masculinity, 9,* 17–28.

Rock Hall. (2013). Leonard Cohen biography. Retrieved from http://rockhall.com/inductees/leonard-cohen/bio/

Rocker, G., & Heyland, D. (2003). New research initiatives in Canada for end-of-life and palliative care. *CMAJ, 169*(4), 300–301.

Rode, S. S., Chang, P., Fisch, R. O., & Sroufe, L. A. (1981). Attachment patterns of infants separated at birth. *Developmental Psychology, 17,* 188–191.

Rodin, J., & Langer, E. J. (1977). Long-term effects of a control-relevant intervention with the institutionalized aged. *Journal of Personality and Social Psychology, 35,* 397–402.

Rodrigues, A. E., Hall, J. H., & Fincham, F. D. (2006). What predicts divorce and relationship dissolution. In M. A. Fine & J. H. Harvey (Eds.), *Handbook of divorce and relationship dissolution.* Mahwah, NJ: Erlbaum.

Rodriguez, E. T., Tamis-LeMonda, C. S., Spellman, M. E., Pan, B. A., Riakes, H., Lugo-Gil, J., et al. (2009). The formative role of home literacy experiences across the first three years of life in children from low-income families. *Journal of Applied Developmental Psychology, 30*(6), 677–694.

Roefs, A., Herman, C. P., MacLeod, C. M., Smulders, F. T. Y., & Jansen, A. (2005). At first sight: How do restrained eaters evaluate high-fat palatable foods? *Appetite, 44,* 103–114.

Roese, N. J., & Summerville, A. (2005). What we regret most…and why. *Personality and Social Psychology Bulletin, 31,* 1273–1285.

Rogers, C. (1961 & 1965). *On becoming a person—A therapist's view of psychotherapy.* Boston: Houghton Mifflin.

Rogoff, B. (2001, April). *Examining cultural processes in developmental research.* Paper presented at the meeting of the Society for Research in Child Development, Minneapolis.

Rogoff, B., Moore, L., Najafi, B., Dexter, A., Correa-Chavez, M., & Solis, J. (2007). Children's development of cultural repertoires through participation in everyday routines and practices. In J. E. Grusec & P. D. Hastings (Eds.), *Handbook of socialization.* New York: Guilford.

Roher, E., & Casement, T. (2011). Suffering in silence: Teenagers and suicide. *Principal Connections, 15*(2), 9–11.

Rohr, M. K., & Lang, F. R. (2009). Aging well together—A mini-review. *Gerontology, 55,* 333–343.

Roisman, G. I., Clausell, E., Holland, A., Fortuna, K., & Elieff, C. (2008). Adult romantic relationships as contexts of human development: A multimethod comparison of same-sex couples with opposite-sex dating, engaged, and married dyads. *Developmental Psychology, 44,* 91–101.

Rolland, Y., van Kahn G.A., & Vellas, B. (2010). Healthy brain aging: Role of exercise and physical activity. *Clinics in Geriatric Medicine, 26,* 75–87.

Rolls, B. J., & Drewnowski, A. (2007). Diet and nutrition. In J. E. Birren (Ed.), *Encyclopedia of gerontology* (2nd ed.). San Diego: Academic Press.

Romano, A. M., & Lothian, J. A. (2008). Promoting, protecting and supporting normal birth: A look at the evidence. *Journal of Obstetric and Gynecological Neonatal Nursing, 37,* 94–105.

Romanow, R. J. (2002). *Building on values: The future of health care in Canada.* Retrieved from http://publications.gc.ca/site/eng/237274/publication.html

Romer, D., Duckworth, A. L., Sznitman, S., & Park, S. (2010). Can adolescents learn self-control? Delay of gratification in the development of control over risk taking. *Prevention Science, 11*(3), 319–330.

Rook, K. S., Mavandadi, S., Sorkin, D. H., & Zettel, L. A. (2007). Optimizing social relationships as a resource for health and wellbeing in later life. In C. M. Aldwin, C. L. Park, & A. Spiro (Eds.), *Handbook of health psychology and aging.* New York: Guilford.

Rosander, K., & von Hofsten, C. (2004). Infants' emerging ability to represent occluded object motion. *Cognition, 91*, 1–22.

Rosenberg, L., Kottorp, A., Winblad, B., & Nygard, L. (2009). Perceived difficulty in everyday technology use among older adults with or without cognitive deficits. *Scandinavian Journal of Occupational Therapy, 16*, 1–11.

Rosenberg, T. J., Garbers, S., Lipkind, H., & Chiasson, M. A. (2005). Maternal obesity and diabetes as risk factors for adverse pregnancy outcomes: Differences among 4 racial/ethnic groups. *American Journal of Public Health, 95*, 1545–1551.

Rosenblith, J. F. (1992). *In the beginning* (2nd ed.). Newbury Park, CA: Sage.

Rosenfeld, A., & Stark, E. (1987, May). The prime of our lives. *Psychology Today*, 62–72.

Rosenfeld, M., & Thomas, R. (2012). Searching for a mate: The rise of the internet as a social intermediary. *American Sociological Review, 77*(4), 523–547.

Rosenthal, C., & Gladstone, J. (2000, September 1). *Grandparenthood in Canada*. The Vanier Institute of the Family.

Rosnow, R. L., & Rosenthal, R. (2008). *Beginning behavioral research* (6th ed.). Upper Saddle River, NJ: Prentice Hall.

Rospenda, K. M., Richman, J. A., & Shannon, C. A. (2008). Prevalence and mental health correlates of harassment and discrimination in the workplace: Results from a national study. *Journal of Interpersonal Violence, 24*, 819–843.

Rossi, S., Miniussi, C., Pasqualetti, P., Babilioni, C., Rossini, P. M., & Cappa, S. F. (2005). Age-related functional changes of prefrontal cortex in long-term memory: A repetitive transcranial magnetic stimulation study. *Journal of Neuroscience, 24*, 7939–7944.

Roterman, M. (2005). Seniors' health care use. *Supplement to Health Reports, 16*, 33–45.

Rotermann, M. (2007). Marital breakdown and subsequent depression. *Health Reports, 18*, 33–44.

Rotermann, M. (2008). Trends in sexual behaviour and condom use. Components of Statistics Canada Catalogue no. 82-003-X. http://www.statcan.gc.ca/pub/82-003-x/2008003/article/10664-eng.pdf

Rotermann, M. (2012). Sexual behaviour and condom use of 15- to 24-year-olds in 2003 and 2009/2010. *Health Reports, 23*(1), 1–5 (No. 82-003-XPE). Retrieved from http://www.statcan.gc.ca

Rothbart, M. K. (2004). Temperament and the pursuit of an integrated developmental psychology. *Merrill-Palmer Quarterly, 50*, 492–505.

Rothbart, M. K. (2007). Temperament, development, and personality. *Current Directions in Psychological Science, 16*, 207–212.

Rothbart, M. K., & Bates, J. E. (2006). Temperament. In W. Damon & R. Lerner (Eds.), *Handbook of child psychology* (6th ed.). New York: Wiley.

Rothbart, M. K., & Gartstein, M. A. (2008). Temperament. In M. M. Haith & J. B. Benson (Eds.), *Encyclopedia of infant and early childhood development*. Oxford, UK: Elsevier.

Rothbart, M. K., & Putnam, S. P. (2002). Temperament and socialization. In L. Pulkkinen & A. Caspi (Eds.), *Paths to successful development*. New York: Cambridge University Press.

Rothbart, M. K., & Sheese, B. E. (2007). Temperament and emotion regulation. In J. J. Gross (Ed.), *Handbook of emotion regulation*. New York: Guilford Press.

Rothbaum, F., & Trommsdorff, G. (2007). Do roots and wings complement or oppose one another? The socialization of relatedness and autonomy in cultural context. In J. E. Grusec & P. D. Hastings (Eds.), *Handbook of socialization*. New York: Guilford.

Rothbaum, F., Kakinuma, M., Nagaoka, R., & Azuma., H. (2007). Attachment and Amae: Parent-child closeness in the United States and Japan. *Journal of Cross-Cultural Psychology, 38*(4), 465–486.

Rouse, D. J., et al. (2007). A trial of 17 alpha-hyroxyprogesterone caproate to prevent prematurity in twins. *New England Journal of Medicine, 357*, 454–461.

Routasalo, P. E., Savikko, N., Tilvis, R. S., Strandberg, T. E., & Pitkala, K. H. (2006). Social contacts and their relationship to loneliness among aged people—a population-based study. *Gerontology, 52*, 181–187.

Rovee-Collier, C. (1987). Learning and memory in children. In J. D. Osofsky (Ed.), *Handbook of infant development* (2nd ed.). New York: Wiley.

Rovee-Collier, C. (2008). The development of infant memory. In N. Cowan & M. Courage (Eds.), *The development of memory in childhood*. Philadelphia: Psychology Press.

Rovers, M. M., de Kok, I. M., & Schilder, A. G. (2006). Risk factors for otitis media: An international perspective. *International Journal of Otorhinolaryngology, 70*, 1251–1256.

Rovner, B. W., Casten, R. J., Leiby, B. E., & Tasman, W. S. (2009). Activity loss is associated with cognitive decline in age-related macular degeneration. *Alzheimer's and Dementia, 5*, 12–17.

Rowley, S. R., Kurtz-Costes, B., & Cooper, S. M. (2009). The role of schooling in ethnic minority achievement and attainment. In J. Meece & J. Eccles (Eds.), *Handbook of research on schools, schooling, and human development*. Clifton, NJ: Psychology Press.

Roy, J., Chakraborty, S. & Chakraborty, Y. (2009). Estrogen-like endocrine disrupting chemicals affecting puberty in humans—a review. *Medical Science Monitor: International Medical Journal of Experimental and Clinical Research, 15*(6), RA137–45.

Rubenstein, D. (2004). Language games and natural resources. *Journal of the Theory of Social Behavior, 34*, 55–71.

Rubin, K. H., Bukowski, W., & Parker, J. G. (1998). Peer interactions, relationships, and groups. In N. Eisenberg (Ed.), *Handbook of child psychology* (5th ed., Vol. 3). New York: Wiley.

Rubin, K. H., Cheah, C., & Menzer, M. M. (2010). Peers. In M. H. Bornstein (Ed.), *Handbook of cultural development science*. New York: Psychology Press.

Rubin, K., Fredstrom, B., & Bowker, J. (2008). Future directions in friendship in childhood and early adolescence. *Social Development*.

Rubio-Aurioles, E., Casabe, A., Torres, L. O., Quinzanos, L., Glina, S., Filimon, I., et al. (2008). Efficacy and safety of tadalafil in the treatment of Latin American men with erectile dysfunction: Results of integrated analysis. *Journal of Sexual Medicine, 5*(8), 1965–1976.

Ruble, D. (2010). Social development and achievement motivation. Retrieved from http://www.psych.nyu.edu/ruble/

Rudin, E., Rincon, M., Bauman, J., & Barzilai, N. (2007). Obesity. In J. E. Birren (Ed.), *Encyclopedia of gerontology* (2nd ed.). San Diego: Academic Press.

Rudy, D., & Grusec, J. (2006, March). Authoritairan parenting in individualist and collectivist groups: Associations with maternal emotion and cognition and children's self-esteem. *Journal of Family Psychology, 20*(1).

Rueda, M. R., Posner, M. I., & Rothbart, M. K. (2005). The development of executive attention: Contributions to the emergence of self-regulation. *Developmental Neuropsychology, 28*, 573–594.

Ruff, H. A., & Capozzoli, M. C. (2003). Development of attention and distractibility in the first 4 years of life. *Developmental Psychology, 39*, 877–890.

Ruffman, T., Slade, L., & Crowe, E. (2002). The relation between children's and mothers' mental state language and theory-of-mind understanding. *Child Development, 73*, 734–751.

Runciman, S. (2012). Breaking the cycle of violence: An exploration into dating violence prevention curriculum. (Master's thesis). Retrieved from http://www.qspace.library.queensu.ca

Runco, M. (2000). Research on the processes of creativity. In A. Kazdin (Ed.), *Encyclopedia of psychology*. Washington, DC: American Psychological Association and Oxford University Press.

Rupp, D. E., Vodanovich, S. J., & Crede, M. (2005). The multidimensional nature of ageism: Construct validity and group differences. *Journal of Social Psychology, 145*, 335–362.

Rusen, I. D., Liu, S., Sauve, R., Joseph, K. S., & Kramer, M. S. (2004). Sudden infant death syndrome in Canada: Trends in rates and risk factors, 1985–1998. *Chronic Diseases in Canada, 25*(1), 1–6.

Rusk, T. N., & Rusk, N. (2007, Winter). Not by genes alone: New hope for prevention. *Bulletin of the Menninger Clinic, 71*(1), 1–21.

Rutter, M., & Schopler, E. (1987). Autism and pervasive developmental disorders: Concepts and diagnostic issues. *Journal of Autism and Pervasive Developmental Disorders, 17*, 159–186.

Ruys, J. H., Jonge, G. A., Brand, R., Engelberts, A., & Semmekrot, B. A. (2007). Bed-sharing in the first four months of life: A risk factor for sudden infant death. *Acta Paediatric, 96*, 13099–1403.

Ryan, A. S., & Elahi, D. (2007). Body: Composition, weight, height, and build. In J. E. Birren (Ed.), *Encyclopedia of gerontology* (2nd ed.). San Diego: Academic Press.

Ryan-Harshman, M., & Aldoori, W. (2008). Folic acid in pregnancy of neural tube defects. *Canadian Family Physician, 54*, 36–38.

Ryff, C. D. (1984). Personality development from the inside: The subjective experience of change in adulthood and aging. In P. B. Baltes & O. G. Brim (Eds.), *Life-span development and behavior.* New York: Academic Press.

Ryff, C. D. (1991). Possible selves in adulthood and old age: A tale of shifting horizons. *Psychology and Aging, 6*, 286–295.

Rypma, B., Eldreth, D. A., & Rebbechi, D. (2007). Age-related differences in activation-performance relations in delayed-response tasks: A multiple component analyses. *Cortex, 43*, 65–76.

S

Saarni, C. (1999). *The development of emotional competence.* New York: Guilford.

Saarni, C., Campos, J., Camras, L. A., & Witherington, D. (2006). Emotional development. In W. Damon & R. Lerner (Eds.), *Handbook of child psychology* (6th ed.). New York: Wiley.

Sabbagh, M. A., Xu, F., Carlson, S. M., Moses, L. J., & Lee, K. (2006). The development of executive functioning and theory of mind: A comparison of Chinese and U.S. preschoolers. *Psychological Science, 17*, 74–81.

Sabeti, P. C., Varilly, P., Fry, B., Lohmueller, J., Hostetter, E., Cotsapas, C., et al. (2007, October 18). Genome-wide detection and characterization of positive selection in human populations. *Nature, 449*, 913–918. doi:10.1038/nature06250

Sabia, S., Fournier, A., Mesrine, S., Boutron-Rualt, M. C., & Clavel-Chapelon, F. (2008). Risk factors for onset of menopausal symptoms: Results from a large cohort study. *Maturitas, 60*, 108–121.

Sable, M., Danis, D., Mauzy, D., & Gallagher, S. (2006). Barriers to reporting sexual assault for women and men: Perspectives of college students. *Journal of American College Health, 55*(3), 157–161.

Sadeh, A. (2008). Sleep. In M. M. Haith & J. B. Benson (Eds.), *Encyclopedia of infant and early childhood development.* Oxford, UK: Elsevier.

Saewyc, E., et al. (2007). Suicidal ideation and attempts among adolescents in North American school-based surveys: Are bisexual youth at increasing risk? *Journal of LGBT Health Research, 3*, 25–36.

Saffran, J. R., Werker, J. F., & Werner, L. A. (2006). The infant's auditory world: Hearing, speech, and the beginning of language. In W. Damon & R. Lerner (Eds.), *Handbook of child psychology* (6th ed.). New York: Wiley.

Sahin, E., & DePhinho, R. A. (2010). Linking functional decline of telomeres, mitochondria

and stem cells during aging. *Nature, 464*, 520–528.

Sai, F. (2005). The role of the mother's voice in developing mother's face preference: Evidence for intermodal perception at birth. *Infant and Child Development, 14*, 29–50.

Sakamoto, Y., et al. (2009). Effect of exercise, aging, and functional capacity on acute secretory immunoglobulin A response in elderly people over 75 years of age. *Geriatrics and Gerontology International, 9*, 81–88.

Sakatini, K., Tanida, M., & Katsuyama, M. (2010). Effects of aging on activity in the prefrontal cortex and autonomic nervous system during mental stress task. *Advances in Experimental Medicine and Biology, 662*, 473–478.

Saklofske, D. H., Caravan, G., & Schwartz, C. (2000). Concurrent validity of the Wechsler Abbreviated Scale of Intelligence (WASI) with a sample of Canadian children. *Canadian Journal of School Psychology, 16*(1), 87–94.

Sakraida, T. J. (2005). Divorce transition differences of midlife women. *Issues in Mental Health Nursing, 26*, 225–249.

Salat, D. H., Buckner, R. K., Snyder, A. Z., Greve, D. N., Desikan, R. S. R., Busa, E., et al. (2004). Thinning of the cerebral cortex in aging. *Cerebral Cortex, 14*, 721–730.

Salkind, N. (2003). *Statistics for people who (think they) hate statistics.* Paperback, Revised.

Salmivalli, C., & Peets, K. (2009). Bullies, victims, and bully-victim relationships in middle childhood and adolescence. In K. H. Rubin, W. M. Bukowski, & B. Laursen (Eds.), *Handbook of peer interactions, relationships, and groups.* New York: Guilford.

Salmon, J., Campbell, K. J., & Crawford, D. A. (2006). Television viewing habits associated with obesity risk factors: A survey of Melbourne children. *Medical Journal of Australia, 184*, 64–67.

Salovey, P., & Mayer, J. D. (1990). Emotional intelligence. *Imagination, Cognition, and Personality, 9*, 185–211.

Salthouse, T. A. (2006). Mental exercise and mental aging: Evaluating the validity of the "use it or lose it" hypothesis. *Perspectives on Psychological Science, 1*, 68–87.

Salthouse, T. A. (2009a). Executive function. In D. C. Park & N. Schwarz (Eds.), *Cognitive aging* (2nd ed.). Clifton, NJ: Psychology Press.

Salthouse, T. A. (2009b). When does age-related cognitive decline begin? *Neurobiology of Aging, 30*, 507–514.

Salthouse, T. A., & Skovronek, E. (1992). Within context assessment of working memory. *Journal of Gerontology, 47*, P110–P117.

Sameroff, A. (2010). A unified theory of development: A dialectic integration of nature and nurture. *Child Development, 81*, 6–22.

Sando, S. B., et al. (2008). APOE epsilon4 lowers age at onset and is a high risk factor for Alzheimer's disease: A case-control study from central Norway. *BMC Neurology, 8*, 9.

Sands, R. G., & Goldberg-Glen, R. S. (2000). Factors associated with stress among

grandparents raising their grandchildren. *Family Relations, 49*, 97–105.

Sangree, W. H. (1989). Age and power: Life-course trajectories and age structuring of power relations in East and West Africa. In D. I. Kertzer & K. W. Schaie (Eds.), *Age structuring in comparative perspective.* Hillsdale, NJ: Erlbaum.

Sann, C., & Streri, A. (2007). Perception of object shape and texture in human newborns: Evidence from cross-modal tasks. *Developmental Science, 10*, 399–410.

Sanson, A., & Rothbart, M. K. (1995). Child temperament and parenting. In M. H. Bornstein (Ed.), *Handbook of parenting* (Vol. 4). Hillsdale, NJ: Erlbaum.

Sanson, G. (2003). The myth of osteoporosis. Canadian Women's Health Network.

Sapp, S. (2010). What have religion and spirituality to do with aging? Three approaches. *The Gerontologist, 50*(2), 271–275.

Sarkisian, N., & Gerstel, N. (2008). Till marriage do us part: Adult children's relationship with their parents. *Journal of Marriage and the Family, 70*, 360–376.

Sato, R. L., Li, G. G., & Shaha, S. (2006). Antepartum seafood consumption and mercury levels in newborn cord blood. *American Journal of Obstetrics and Gynecology, 194*(6), 1683–1688.

Saur, D., Ronneberger, O., Kummerer, D., Mader, I., Weiller, C., & Kloppel, S. (2010). Early functional magnetic resonance imaging activations predict language outcome after stroke. *Brain, 133*, 1252–1264.

Sauvé, R. (2002). *Connections: Tracking the links between jobs and family.* Ottawa: The Vanier Institute of the Family. Retrieved from www.vifamily.ca

Savin-Williams, R. C. (2006). *The new gay teenager.* Cambridge, MA: Harvard University Press.

Savin-Williams, R. C. (2008). Who's gay? It depends on how you measure it. In D. A. Hope (Ed.), *Nebraska Symposium on Motivation: Contemporary perspectives on lesbian, gay, and bisexual identities.* Lincoln, NE: University of Nebraska Press.

Savin-Williams, R. C., & Cohen, K. M. (2007). Development of same-sex attracted youth. In I. H. Meyer & M. E. Northridge (Eds.), *The health of sexual minorities: Public health perspectives on lesbian, gay, bisexual and transgender populations* (pp. 27–47). New York: Springer.

Savin-Williams, R. C., & Diamond, L. (2004). Sex. In R. Lerner & L. Steinberg (Eds.), *Handbook of adolescent psychology.* New York: Wiley.

Savin-Williams, R. C., & Ream, G. L. (2007). Prevalence and stability of sexual orientation components during adolescence and young adulthood. *Archives of Sexual Behavior, 36*, 385–394.

Sayal, K., Heron, J., Golding, J., & Emond, A. (2007). Prenatal alcohol exposure and gender differences in childhood mental health problems: A longitudinal population-based study. *Pediatrics, 119*, e426–e434.

Sayer, L. C. (2006). Economic aspects of divorce and relationship dissolution. In M. A.

Fine & J. H. Harvey (Eds.), *Handbook of divorce and relationship dissolution*. Mahwah, NJ: Erlbaum.

Scales, P., Benson, P., & Roehlkepartain, E. (2011). Adolescent thriving: The role of sparks, relationships, and empowerment, *Journal of Youth and Adolescence, 40*, 263–277.

Scarr, S. (1993). Biological and cultural diversity: The legacy of Darwin for development. *Child Development, 64*, 1333–1353.

Schacter, E. P., & Ventura, J. J. (2008). Identity agents: Parents as active and reflective participants in their children's identity formation. *Journal of Research on Adolescence, 18*, 449–476.

Schaie, K. W. (1994). The life course of adult intellectual abilities. *American Psychologist, 49*, 304–313.

Schaie, K. W. (1996). *Intellectual development in adulthood: The Seattle Longitudinal Study.* New York: Cambridge University Press.

Schaie, K. W. (2000). Unpublished review of J. W. Santrock's *Life-span development* (8th ed.). New York: McGraw-Hill.

Schaie, K. W. (2005). *Developmental influences on adult intelligence: The Seattle Longitudinal Study.* New York: Oxford University Press.

Schaie, K. W. (2007). Generational differences: The age-cohort period model. In J. E. Birren (Ed.), *Encyclopedia of gerontology* (2nd ed.). Oxford, UK: Elsevier.

Schaie, K. W. (2008). Historical processes and patterns of cognitive aging. In S. M. Hofer & D. F. Alwin (Eds.), *Handbook on cognitive aging: Interdisciplinary perspective.* Thousand Oaks, CA: Sage.

Schaie, K. W. (2009). When does age-related cognitive decline begin? Salthouse again reifies the "cross-sectional fallacy." *Neurobiology of Aging, 30*, 528.

Schaie, K. W. (2010a). Adult intellectual abilities. *Corsini encyclopedia of psychology.* New York: Wiley.

Schaie, K. W. (2010b). *Developmental influences on adult intellectual development.* New York: Oxford University Press.

Schaie, K. W. (2011). Historical influences on aging and behavior. In K.W. Schaie & S. L. Willis (Eds.), *Handbook of the psychology of aging* (7th ed.). New York: Elsevier.

Schaie, K. W., & Willis, S. L. (1994) Assessing the elderly. In C. B. Fisher & R. M. Lerner (Eds.), *Applied developmental psychology* (pp. 339–372). New York: McGraw Hill.

Schaie, K. W., & Willis, S. L. (2000). *Adult development and aging* (5th ed.). Upper Saddle River, NJ: Prentice Hall.

Schattschneider C., Fletcher, J. M., Francis, D. J., Carlson, C. D., & Foorman, B. R. (2004). Kindergarten prediction of reading skills: A longitudinal comparative analysis. *Journal of Educational Psychology, 96*, 265–282.

Scheckhuber, C. Q. (2009). Impact of mitochondrial dynamics on organismic aging. *Scientific World Journal, 9*, 282–286.

Scheibe, S., & Carstensen, L. L. (2010). Emotional aging: Recent findings and future trends. *Journal of Gerontology: Psychological Sciences, 65*(B), 135–144.

Scheibe, S., Freund, A. M., & Baltes, P. B. (2007). Toward a developmental psychology of *Sehnsucht* (life-longings): The optimal (utopian) life. *Developmental Psychology, 43*, 778–795.

Schellenberg, E. G. (2004). Music lessons enhance IQ. *Psychological Science, 15*, 511–514.

Schellenberg, E. G. (2006). Long-term positive associations between music lessons and IQ. *Journal of Experimental Psychology, 98*, 457–468.

Schellenberg, G., & Ostrovsky, Y. (2008a). The retirement retirement puzzle: Sorting the pieces. *Canadian Social Trends, 86*(Winter), 35–47.

Schellenberg, G., & Ostrovsky, Y. (2008b). The retirement plans and expectations of older workers. *Canadian Social Trends, 86*(Winter), 11–34.

Scher, A., & Harel, J. (2008). Separation and stranger anxiety. In M. M. Haith & J. B. Benson (Eds.), *Encyclopedia of infant and early childhood development.* Oxford, UK: Elsevier.

Schiavone, F., Charton, R. A., Barrick, T. R., Morris, R. G., & Markus, H. G. (2009). Imaging age-related cognitive decline: A comparison of diffusion tensor and magnetization transfer IMRI. *Journal of Magnetic Resonance Imaging, 29*, 23–30.

Schieman, S., van Gundy, K., & Taylor, J. (2004). The relationship between age and depressive symptons: A test of competing explanatory and suppression influences. *Journal of Aging Health, 14*, 260–285.

Schiff, W. J. (2009). *Nutrition for healthy living.* New York: McGraw-Hill.

Schiff, W. J. (2011). *Nutrition for healthy living* (2nd ed.). New York: McGraw-Hill.

Schiffman, R. (2012, January 18). Why people who pray are healthier than those who don't. *The Huffington Post.* Retrieved from http://www.huffingtonpost.com/ richard-schiffman/why-people-who-pray-are-heathier_b_1197313.html

Schiffman, S. S. (2007). Smell and taste. In J. E. Birren (Ed.), *Encyclopedia of gerontology* (2nd ed.). San Diego: Academic Press.

Schindler, A. E. (2006). Climacteric symptoms and hormones. *Gynecological Endocrinology, 22*, 151–154.

Schmader, K. E., et al. (2010). Treatment considerations for elderly and frail patients with neuropathic pain. *Mayo Clinic Proceedings, 85* (Suppl. 3), S26–S32.

Schmidt, K. L., & Schulz, R. (2007). Emotions. In J. E. Birren (Ed.), *Encyclopedia of gerontology* (2nd ed.). San Diego: Academic Press.

Schmidt, L., Fox, N., Perez-Edgar, K., & Hamer, D. (2009). Linking gene, brain, and behavior: DRD4, frontal asymmetry, and temperament. *Psychological Science, 20*, 831–837.

Schmidt, S., et al. (2006). Cigarette smoking strongly modifies the association of LOC387715 and age-related macular degeneration. *American Journal of Human Genetics, 78*, 852–864.

Schmidt, U. (2003). Aetiology of eating disorders in the 21st century: New answers to old questions. *European Child and Adolescent Psychiatry, 12* (Suppl. 1), 1130–1137.

Schmitt, D. P., Allik, J., McCrae, R., & Benet-Martinez, V. (2007). The geographic distribution of big five personality traits: Patterns and profiles of human self-description across 56 nations. *Journal of Cross-Cultural Psychology, 38*(2), 173–212. doi: 10.1177/0022022106297299. Retrieved from http://biculturalism.ucr.edu/ pdfs/Schmitt%20et%20al_JCCP2007.pdf

Schneider, W. (2004). Memory development in children. In U. Goswami (Ed.), *Blackwell handbook of childhood cognitive development.* Malden, MA: Blackwell.

Schneider, W., & Pressley, M. (1997). *Memory development from 2 to 20* (2nd ed.). Mahwah, NJ: Erlbaum.

Schnittker, J. (2007). Look (closely) at all the lonely people: Age and social psychology of social support. *Journal of Aging and Health, 19*, 659–682

Schnurer, F. (2008). "But in death he has found victory": The funeral ceremonies for the "knights of the sky" during the Great War as transnational media events. *European Review of History, 15*(6).

Scholnick, E. K. (2008). Reasoning in early development. In M. M. Haith & J. B. Benson (Eds.), *Encyclopedia of infant and early childhood development.* Oxford, UK: Elsevier.

Schooler, C. (2007). Use it—and keep it, longer, probably: A reply to Salthouse (2006). *Perspectives on Psychological Science, 2*, 24–29.

Schooler, C., & Kaplan, L. J. (2008). Them who have, get: Social structure, environmental complexity, intellectual functioning, and self-directed orientations in the elderly. In K. W. Schaie & R. P. Abeles (Eds.), *Social structures and aging individuals.* New York: Springer.

Schoppe-Sullivan, S. J., Mangelsdorf, S. C., Brown, G. L., & Sokolowski, M. S. (2007). Goodness-of-fit in family context: Infant temperament, marital quality, and early coparenting behavior. *Infant Behavior and Development, 30*, 82–96.

Schuklenk, U., Van Delden, J. J. M., Downie, J., McLean, S. A. M., Upshur, R., Weinstock, D. (2011, November 25). End-of-life decision-making in Canada: The report by the Royal Society of Canada expert panel on end-of-life decision-making. *Bioethics.* Retrieved from http://www.ncbi. nlm.nih.gov/pmc/articles/PMC3265521/

Schulenberg, J. E., & Zarett, N. R. (2006). Mental health during emerging adulthood: Continuity and discontinuity in courses, causes, and functions. In J. J. Arnett & J. L. Tanner (Eds.), *Emerging adults in America.* Washington, DC: American Psychological Association.

Schulenberg, J. E., Bryant, A., & O'Malley, P. (2004). Taking hold of some kind of life: How developmental tasks relate to trajectories of well-being during the transition to adulthood. *Development and Psychopathology, 16*, 1119–1140.

Schultz, T. R. (2010). Computational modeling of infant concept learning: The developmental shift from features to correlations. In L. Oakes,

C. Cashon, M. Casasola, & D. Rakison (Eds.), *Infant perception and cognition*. New York: Oxford University Press.

Schulz, R., Hebert, R., & Boerner, K. (2008). Bereavement after caregiving. *Geriatrics, 63*, 20–22.

Schunk, D. H. (2011). *Learning theories: An educational perspective* (5th ed.). Upper Saddle River, NJ: Prentice Hall.

Schuurmans, N., Senikas, V., & Lalonde, A. (2009). *Healthy beginnings: Giving your baby the best start from preconception to birth* (4th ed) Hoboken,NJ: Wiley.

Schwab, P., & Klein, R. F. (2008). Nonpharmacological approaches to improve bone health and reduce osteoporosis. *Current Opinion in Rheumatology, 20*, 213–217.

Schwalfenberg, G. (2013). Not enough vitamin D: Health consequences for Canadians. *Canadian Family Physician, 53*(5), 841–854. Retrieved from http://www.cfp.ca/content/53/5/841.abstract

Schwam, E., & Xu, Y. (2010). Cognition and function in Alzheimer's disease: Identifying the transitions from moderate to severe disease. *Dementia and Geriatric Cognitive Disorders, 29*, 309–316.

Schwartz, D., Kelly, B. M., Duong, M., & Badaly, D. (2010). Contextual perspective on intervention and prevention efforts for bully/victim problems. In E. M. Vernberg & B. K. Biggs (Eds.), *Preventing and treating bullying and victimization*. New York: Oxford University Press.

Schwartz, D. L., Lin, X., Brophy, J., & Bransford, J. D. (1999). Toward the development of flexibly adaptive instructional designs. In C. M. Reigelut (Ed.), *Instructional design theories and models* (Vol. II). Mahwah, NJ: Erlbaum.

Schwartz, M. A., & Scott, B. (2007). *Marriages and families* (5th ed.). Upper Saddle River, NJ: Prentice Hall.

Schwartz, S., et al. (2011). Examining the light and dark sides of emerging adults' identity: A study of identity status differences in positive and negative psychosocial functioning. *Journal of Youth and Adolescence, 40*, 839–859.

Scialfa, C. T., & Kline, D. W. (2007). Vison. In J. E. Birren (Ed.), *Encyclopedia of gerontology* (2nd ed.). San Diego: Academic Press.

Science Daily. (2008, January 15). *Human gene count tumbles again*, p. l.

Scollon, C., & King, L. (2004). Is the good life the easy life? *Social Indicators Research, 68*, 127–162.

Scourfield, J., Van den Bree, M., Martin, N., & McGuffin, P. (2004). Conduct problems in children and adolescents: A twin study. *Archives of General Psychiatry, 61*, 489–496.

Sebastian-Galles, N. (2007). Biased to learn language. *Developmental Science, 10*, 713–718.

Sebastiani P., et al. (2012). Genetic signatures of exceptional longevity in humans. *PLoS ONE, 7*(1): e29848. doi:10.1371/journal.pone.0029848. Retrieved

from http://www.plosone.org/article/info:doi/10.1371/journal.pone.0029848

Segal, B. (2007). Addiction: General. In J. E. Birren (Ed.), *Encyclopedia of gerontology* (2nd ed.). San Diego: Academic Press.

Segovia, A., Arco, A. D., & Mora, F. (2009). Environmental enrichment, prefrontal cortex, stress, and aging of the brain. *Journal of Neural Transmission, 116*, 1007–1016.

Selim, A. J., Fincke, G., Berlowitz, D. R., Miller, D. R., Qian, S. X., Lee, A., Cong, Z., Rogers, W., Sileim, B. J., Ren, X. S., Spiro, A., & Kazis, L. E. (2005). Comprehensive health status assessment of centenarians: Results from the 1999 Large Health Survey of Veteran Enrollees. *Journals of Gerontology A: Biological Sciences and Medical Sciences, 60*, 515–519.

"Selye, Dr. Hans." (2013). *Canadian Medical Hall of Fame*. Retrieved from http://www.cdnmedhall.org/dr-hans-selye

Semmler, C., Ashcroft, J., van Jaarsveld, C. H., Carnell, S., & Wardle, J. (2009). Development of overweight in children in relation to parental weight and socioeconomic status. *Obesity, 17*(4), 814–820.

Sener, A., Terzioglu, R. G., & Karabulut E. (2007). Life satisfaction and leisure activities during men's retirement: A Turkish sample. *Aging and Mental Health, 11*, 30–36.

Serido, J. (2009). Life events. In D. Carr (Ed.), *Encyclopedia of the life course and human development*. Boston: Gale Cengage.

Serido, J., & Totenhagen, C. (2009). Stress in adulthood. In D. Carr (Ed.), *Encyclopedia of the life course and human development*. Boston: Gale Cengage.

Seritan, A. L., Iosif, A. M., Park, J. H., DeatherageHand, D., Sweet, R. L., & Gold, E. B. (2010). Self-reported anxiety, depressive, and vasomotor symptoms: A study of perimenopausal women presenting to a specialized midlife assessment center. *Menopause, 17*, 410–415.

Serpell, R. (2000). Culture and intelligence. In A. Kazdin (Ed.), *Encyclopedia of psychology*. Washington, DC: American Psychological Association and Oxford University Press.

Serra, M. J., & Metcalfe, J. (2010). Effective implementation of metacognition. In D. J. Hacker, J. Dunlosky, & A. C. Graesser (Eds.), *Handbook of metacognition and education*. New York: Psychology Press.

Sesso, H. D., et al. (2008). Vitamins E and C in the prevention of cardiovascular disease in men: The Physicians Health Study II randomized controlled trial. *Journal of the American Medical Association, 300*, 2123–2133.

Sexual Identity Centre. (2012). Retrieved from http://www.mcgill.ca/cosum/

Shah, N. S., & Ershler, W. B. (2007). Immune system. In J. E. Birren (Ed.), *Encyclopedia of gerontology* (2nd ed.). San Diego: Academic Press.

Shah, R. S., Lee, H. G., Xiongwei, Z., Perry, G., Smith, M. A., & Catellani, R. J. (2008). Current approaches in the

treatment of Alzheimer's disease. *Biomedicine and Pharmacotherapy*.

Shan, Z. Y., Liu, J. Z., Sahgal, V., Wang, B., & Yue, G. H. (2005). Selective atrophy of left hemisphere and frontal lobe of the brain in older men. *Journals of Gerontology A: Biological Sciences and Medical Sciences, 60*, A165–A174.

Shapiro, D., & Walsh R. (Eds.). (2008). *Meditation: Classical and contemporary perspectives*. Rutgers, New Jersey: Aldine Transaction.

Shariff, S. (2005). Cyber-dilemmas in the new millennium: School obligations to provide student safety in a virtual school environment. *McGill Journal of Education, 40*, 467–487.

Sharlip, I. D., Shumaker, B. P., Hakim, L. S., Goldfischer, E., Natanegra, F., & Wong, D. G. (2008). Tadalafil is efficacious and well tolerated in the treatment of erectile dysfunction (ED) in men over 65 years of age: Results from multiple observations in men with ED in national tadalafil study in the United States. *Journal of Sexual Medicine, 5*, 716–725.

Shaughnessy, J. J., Zechmeister, E. B., & Zechmeister, J. S. (2003). *Research methods in psychology* (6th ed.). New York: McGraw-Hill.

Shaver, P. R., & Mikulincer, M. (2007). Attachment theory and research. In A. W. Kruglanski, & E. T. Higgins (Eds.), *Social psychology* (2nd ed.). New York: Guilford.

Shaw, P., Eckstrand, K., Sharp, W., Blumenthal, J., Lerch, J. P., Greenstein, D., et al. (2007). Attention-deficit/hyperactivity disorder is characterized by a delay in cortical maturation. *Proceedings of the National Academy of Sciences, 104*(49), 19649–19654.

Shaywitz, S. E., Gruen, J. R., & Shaywitz, B. A. (2007). Management of dyslexia, its rationale, and underlying neurobiology. *Pediatric Clinics of North America, 54*, 609–623.

Shaywitz, S. E., Morris, R., & Shaywitz, B. A. (2008). The education of dyslexic children from childhood to young adulthood. *Annual Review of Psychology, 59*. Palo Alto, CA: Annual Reviews.

Shea, A. K., & Steiner, M. (2008). Cigarette smoking during pregnancy. *Nicotine and Tobacco Research, 10*, 267–278.

Sheahan, S. L. & Free, T. A. (2005). Counseling parents to quit smoking. *Pediatric Nursing, 31*, 98–102, 105–109.

Shema, L, Ore, L., Ben-Shachar, M., Haj, M., & Linn, S. (2007). The association between breastfeeding and breast cancer occurrence among Jewish women: A case control study. *Journal of Cancer Research and Clinical Oncology, 133*, 903.

Shepherd, M. (2012). Omar Khadr repatriated to Canada. *The Star*. Retrieved from http://www.thestar.com

Sheridan, M., & Nelson, C. A. (2008). Neurobiology of fetal and infant development: Implications for mental health. In C. H. Zeanah (Ed.), *Handbook of infant mental health* (3rd ed.). New York: Guilford.

Sherwin, B. B. (2007). Does estrogen protect against cognitive aging in women? *Current Directions in Psychological Science, 16,* 275–279.

Shi, R., & Werker, J. (2001). Six-month-old infants' preference for lexical words. *Psychological Science, 12,* 70–75.

Shi, R., & Werker, J. F. (2003). The basis of preference for lexical words in 6-month-old infants. *Developmental Science, 6,* 484–488.

Shield, K., Taylor, B., Kehoe, T., Patra, J., & Rehm, J. (2012). *BMC Public Health, 12*(91), 1–12.

Shields, M., & Martel, L. (2005). Healthy living among seniors. *Supplement to Health Reports, 16,* 7–20.

Shields, M., & Tremblay, M. (2008, June). Sedentary behaviour and obesity. Catalogue no. 82-003-X Health Reports. Retrieved from http://www.statcan.gc.ca/pub/82-003-x/2008002/article/10599-eng.pdf

Shields, M., Tremblay, M. S., Laviolette, M., Craig, C. L., Janssen, I., & Gorber, S. C. (2010). Fitness of Canadian adults: Results from the 2007–2008 Canadian health measures survey. *Health Reports, 21*(1), 1–15.

Shin, S. H., Hong, H. G., & Hazen, A. L. (2010). Childhood sexual abuse and adolescence substance use: A latent class analysis. *Drug and Alcohol Dependence, 109*(1), 226–235.

Shiraev, E., & Levy, D. (2007). *Cross-cultural psychology* (3rd ed.). Boston: Allyn & Bacon.

Shizukuda, Y., Plummer, S. L., & Harrelson, A. (2010). Customized exercise echocardiography: Beyond detection of coronary artery disease. *Echocardiography, 27,* 186–194.

Shors, T. J. (2009). Saving new brain cells. *Scientific American, 300,* 46–52.

Shriver, T. (2007, November 9). Silent eugenics: Abortion & Down Syndrome. *Commonweal, 134,* 10–11.

Sick Kids. (2012). Paediatric Consultation Clinic (PCC). Retrieved from http://www.sickkids.ca/

SIECCAN. (2012). Trends in sexual intercourse experience among Canadian teens. Retrieved from http://www.sexualityandu.ca

SIECCAN Newsletter. (2011). Sexting: Considerations for Canadian youth. *The Canadian Journal of Human Sexuality, 20*(3), 111–113.

Siedlecki, K. L. (2007). Investigating the structure and age invariance of episodic memory across the adult life span. *Psychology and Aging, 22,* 251–268.

Siegal, M., & Surian, L. (2010). Conversational understanding in young children. In E. Hoff & M. Shatz (Eds.), *Blackwell handbook of language development.* New York: Wiley.

Siegler, I. C., Poon, L. W., Madden, D. J., Dilworth-Anderson, P., Schaie, K. W., Willis, S. L., et al. (2009). Psychological aspects of normal aging. In D. G. Blazer & D. Steffens (Eds.), *Textbook of geriatric psychiatry*

(4th ed.) Arlington, VA: American Psychiatric Publishing.

Siegler, R. S. (2006). Microgenetic analysis of learning. In W. Damon & R. Lerner (Eds.), *Handbook of child psychology* (6th ed.). New York: Wiley.

Siegler, R. S. (2007). Cognitive variability. *Developmental Science, 10,* 104–109.

Sigman, M., Cohen, S. E., & Beckwith, L. (2000). Why does infant attention predict adolescent intelligence? In D. Muir & A. Slater (Eds.), *Infant development: Essential readings.* Malden, MA: Blackwell.

Signal, T. L., Gander, P. H., Sangalli, M. R., Travier, N., Firestone, R. T., & Tuohy, J. F. (2007). Sleep duration and quality in healthy nulliparous and multiparous women across pregnancy and post-partum. *Australian and New Zealand Journal of Obstetrics and Gynecology, 47,* 16–22.

Silberg, J. L., Maes, H., & Eaves, L. J. (2010). Genetic and environmental influences on the transmission of parental depression to children's depression and conduct disturbance: An extended Children of Twins study. *Journal of Child Psychology and Psychiatry, 51*(6), 734–744.

Silverman, I. (2003). Confessions of a closet sociobiologist: Personal perspectives on the Darwinian movement in psychology. *Evolutionary Psychology, 1,* 1–9.

Silverslides, A. (2012). Blogging the nursing life. *Canadian Nurse, 108*(1), 22–27.

Silverstein, M. (2009). Caregiving. In D. Carr (Ed.), *Encyclopedia of the life course and human development.* Boston: Gale Cengage.

Silverstein, M., Conroy, S. J., Wang, H., Giarrusso, R., & Bengtsson, V. L. (2002). Reciprocity in parent-child relation over the adult life course. *Journals of Gerontology: Psychological Sciences and Social Sciences, 57*(B), S3–S13.

Silverstein, M., Gans, D., & Yang, F. M. (2006). Intergenerational support to aging parents. *Journal of Family Issues, 27,* 1068–1084.

Silverstein, N. M., Wong, C. M., & Brueck, K. E. (2010). Adult day health care for participants with Alzheimer's disease. *American Journal of Alzheimer's Disease and Other Dementias, 25*(3), 276–283.

Simonton, D. K. (1996). Creativity. In J. E. Birren (Ed.), *Encyclopedia of aging.* San Diego: Academic Press.

Simos, P. G., Fletcher, J. M., Sarkari, S., Billingsley, R. L., Denton, C., & Papanicolaou, A. C. (2007). Altering the brain circuits for reading through intervention: A magnetic source imaging study. *Neuropsychology, 21,* 485–496.

Simpkins, S. D., Fredricks, J. A., Davis-Kean, P. E., & Eccles, J. S. (2006). Healthy mind, healthy habits: The influence of activity involvement in middle childhood. In A. C. Huston & M. N. Ripke (Eds.), *Developmental contexts in middle childhood.* New York: Cambridge University Press.

Simpson, K. R. (2010). Reconsideration of the costs of convenience: Quality, operational,

and fiscal strategies to minimize elective labor induction. *Journal of Perinatal and Neonatal Nursing, 24*(1), 43–52.

Simpson, R. L., & LaCava, P. G. (2008). Autism spectrum disorders. In N. J. Salkind (Ed.), *Encyclopedia of educational psychology.* Thousand Oaks, CA: Sage.

Singer L., et al. (2004). Cognitive outcomes of preschool children with prenatal cocaine exposure. *JAMA, 291*(20). 2448–2456.

Singer, L., et al. (2012). Neurobehavioral outcomes of infants exposed to MDMA (ecstasy) and other recreational drugs during pregnancy. *Neurotoxicology and Teratology, 34*(3), 303–310.

Sinha, J. W., Cnaan, R. A., & Gelles, R. J. (2007). Adolescent risk behaviors and religion: Findings from a national study. *Journal of Adolescence, 30,* 231–249.

Sinha, M. (2012). Victimization among visible minority and immigrant populations. *National Clearing House on Family Violence E- Bulletin, February 2012.* Retrieved from http://www.phac-aspc.gc.ca/ncfv-cnivf/EB/2012/february-fevrier/1-eng.php#anchor1

Sirard, J. R., & Barr-Anderson, D. J. (2008). Editorial: Physical activity in adolescents: From associations to interventions. *Journal of Adolescent Health, 42,* 327–328.

Skinner, B. F. (1957). *Verbal behavior.* New York: Appleton-Century-Crofts.

Skinner, E. I., & Fernandes, M. (2009). Illusory recollection in older adults and younger adults under divided attention. *Psychology and Aging, 24*(1), 211–216. Retrieved from http://cogneurolab.uwaterloo.ca/publications/Erin_Skinner/Illusory_recollection_in_older_adults.pdf

Skinner, R., & McFaull, S. (2012). Suicide among children and adolescents in Canada: Trends and sex difference, 1980–2008. *Canadian Medical Association Journal, 184*(9), 1029–1034.

Skipper, J. I., Goldin-Meadow, S., Nusbaum, H. C., & Small, S. L. (2007). Speech-associated gestures, Broca's area, and the human mirror system. *Brain and Language, 101,* 260–277.

Skolnick, A. S. (2007). Grounds for marriage: How relationships succeed or fail. In A. S. Skolnick & J. H. Skolnick (Eds.), *Family in transition* (14th ed.). Boston: Allyn & Bacon.

Skordalakes, E. (2009). Telomerase structure paves the way for new cancer therapies. *Future Oncology, 5,* 163–167.

Slack, T., & Jensen, L. (2008). Employment hardship among older workers: Does residential and gender inequality extend into old age? *Journals of Gerontology B: Psychological Sciences and Social Sciences, 63,* S15–S24.

Slater, A. (2002). Visual perception in the newborn infant: Issues and debates. *Intellectica, 1*(34), 57–76.

Slaughter, V., & Griffiths, M. (2007). Death understanding and fear of death in young children. *Clinical Child Psychology and Psychiatry, 12*(4), 525–535.

Slaughter, V. (2005). Young children's understanding of death. *American Psychologists, 40*(3), 179–186.

Slomkowski, C., Rende, R., Conger, K. J., Simons, R. L., & Conger, R. D. (2001). Sisters, brothers, and delinquency: Social influence during early and middle adolescence. *Child Development, 72,* 271–283.

Smetana, J. (2006). Social domain theory. In M. Killen & J. G. Smetana (Eds.), *Handbook of moral development.* Mahwah, NJ: Erlbaum.

Smetana, J., Metzger, A., & Campione-Barr, N. (2004). African American late adolescents' relationships with parents: Developmental transitions and longitudinal patterns. *Child Development, 75,* 932–947.

Smith, A. D. (2007). Memory, In J. E. Birren (Ed.), *Encyclopedia of gerontology* (2nd ed.). San Diego: Academic Press.

Smith, B. (2007). *The psychology of sex and gender.* Boston: Allyn & Bacon.

Smith, D. L. (2008). Birth complications and outcomes. In M. M. Haith & J. B. Benson (Eds.), *Encyclopedia of infancy and early childhood. development* Oxford, UK: Elsevier.

Smith, E. (2005). Fathers of stem cell research win pretigious prize—Laker Award known as America's Nobel Prize. *University of Toronto News.*

Smith, J. (2009). Self. In D. Carr (Ed.), *Encyclopedia of the life course and human development.* Boston: Gale Cengage.

Smith, J., & Freund, A. M. (2002). The dynamics of possible selves in old age. *Journals of Gerontology B: Psychological Sciences and Social Sciences, 57,* P492–P500.

Smith, L. B., & Breazeal, C. (2007). The dynamic lift of developmental processes. *Developmental Science, 10,* 61–68.

Smith, L. M., LaGasse, L., Derauf, C., Grant, P., Shah, R., Arria, A., et al. (2008). Prenatal methamphetamine use and neonatal neurobehavioral outcome. *Neurotoxicology and Teratology, 30,* 20–28.

Smith, P. J., Blumenthal, J., Hoffman, B. M., Cooper, H., Strauman, T. A., Welsh-Bohmer, K., Browndyke, J. N., & Sherwood, A. (2010). Aerobic exercise and neurocognitive performance: A meta-analytic review of randomized controlled trials. *Psychosomatic Medicine: Journal of Biobehavioural Medicine.* Retrieved from http://www.psychosomaticmedicine.org/content/72/3/239.short

Smith, R. L., Rose, A. J., & Schwartz-Mette, R. A. (2010). Relational and overt aggression in childhood and adolescence: Clarifying mean-level gender differences and associations with peer acceptance. *Social Development, 19,* 243–269.

Smith, T. B., McCullough, M. E., & Poll, J. (2003). Religiousness and depression: Evidence for a main effect and the moderating influence of stressful life events. *Psychological Bulletin, 129,* 614–636.

Smithbattle, L. (2007). Legacies of advantage and disadvantage: The case of teen mothers. *Public Health Nursing, 24,* 409–420.

Smithers, L. (2012, August 7). Children's healthy diets lead to healthier IQ. University of Adelaide: Health Sciences, Media Release, Research Story. Retrieved from http://www.adelaide.edu.au/news/print55161.html

Smokowski, P. R., & Bacallao, M. (2007). Acculturation, internalizing mental health symptoms, and self-esteem: Cultural experiences of Latino adolescents in North Carolina. *Child Psychiatry and Human Development, 37*(3), 273–292.

Snarey, J. (1987, June). A question of morality. *Psychology Today,* pp. 6–8.

Snijders, B. E., et al. (2007). Breast-feeding duration and infant atopic manifestations, by maternal allergic status, in the first two years of life (KOALA study.) *Journal of Pediatrics, 151,* 347–351.

Snow, C. E., & Yang, J. Y. (2006). Becoming bilingual, biliterate, and bicultural. In W. Damon & R. Lerner (Eds.), *Handbook of child psychology* (6th ed.). New York: Wiley.

Snowden, M., Steinman, L., & Frederick, J. (2008). Treating depression in older adults: Challenges to implementing the recommendations of an expert panel. *Prevention of Chronic Disorders, 5,* A26.

Snowdon, D. A. (2002). *Aging with grace: What the Nun Study teaches us about leading longer, healthier, and more meaningful lives.* New York: Bantam.

Snyder, K. A., & Torrence, C. M. (2008). Habituation and novelty. In M. M. Haith & J. B. Benson (Eds.), *Encyclopedia of infant and early childhood development.* Oxford, UK: Elsevier.

Society of Obstetricians and Gynaecologists (SOGC). (2003). Midwifery. *Journal of Obstetrics and Gynaecology Canada, 25,* 239.

Society of Obstetricians and Gynaecologists (SOGC). (2009). Policy statement on midwifery. Retrieved from http://www.sogc.org/

Society of Obstetricians and Gynaecologists (SOGC). (2008). *Media advisories: Rising c-section. . .* Retrieved from http://www.sogc.org/

Society of Obstetricians and Gynaecologists (SOGC). (2011). Sexuality and U. Ottawa: Author. Retrieved from http://www.sogc.org

Society of Obstetricians and Gynaecologists (SOGC). (2011a). Women's health information: Birth plan. Retrieved from http://www.sogc.org/

Society of Obstetricians and Gynaecologists (SOGC). (2011b). Women's health information: Medications and drugs before and during pregnancy. Retrieved from http://www.sogc.org/

Soderstrom, M. (2007). Beyond babytalk: Re-evaluating the nature and content of speech input to preverbal infants. *Developmental Review, 27,* 501–532.

Soenens, B., Vansteenkiste, M., Lens, W., Luyckx, K., Goossens, L., Beyers, W., et al. (2007). Conceptualizing parental autonomy support: Adolescent perceptions of promotion of independence versus promotion of volitional functioning. *Developmental Psychology, 43,* 633–646.

Soergel, P., Pruggmayer, M., Schwerdtfeger, R., Mulhaus, K., & Scharf, A. (2006). Screening for trisomy 21 with maternal age, fetal nuchal translucency, and maternal serum biochemistry at 11–14 weeks: A regional experience from Germany. *Fetal Diagnosis and Therapy, 21,* 264–268.

Sokol, B. W., Snjezana, H., & Muller, U. (2010). Social understanding and self-regulation: From perspective-taking to theory-of-mind. In B. Sokol, U. Muller, J. Carpendale, A. Young, & G. Iarocci (Eds.), *Self- and social-regulation.* New York: Oxford University Press.

Song, H., Thompson, R., & Ferrer, E. (2009). Attachment and self-evaluation in Chinese adolescents: Age and gender differences. *Journal of Adolescence, 32,* 1267–1286.

Sonnen, J. A., et al. (2009). Free radical damage to cerebral cortex in Alzheimer's disease, microvascular injury, and smoking. *Annals of Neurology, 65,* 226–229.

Sontag, L. M., Graber, J., Brooks-Gunn, J., & Warren, M. P. (2008). Coping with social stress: Implications for psychopathology in young adolescent girls. *Journal of Abnormal Child Psychology.*

Sood, A. B., Razdan, A., Weller, E. B., & Weller, R. A. (2006). Children's reactions to parental and sibling death. *Current Psychiatry Reports, 8,* 115–120.

Sorensen, T. L., & Kemp, H. (2010). Ranibizumab treatment in patients with neovascular age-related macular degeneration and very low vision. *Acta Ophthalmologica, 89*(1), e97.

Sorenson, M. (2011). Vitamin D seminar, Edmonton. Retrieved from http://www.vitamindsociety.org/video.php?id=116

Sottero, B., Gamba, P., Gargiulo, S., Leonarduzzi, G., & Poli, G. (2009). Cholesterol oxidation products and disease: An emerging topic of interest in medicinal chemistry. *Current Medicinal Chemistry, 16,* 685–705.

South, M., Ozonoff, S., & McMahon, W. M. (2005). Repetitive behavior profiles in Asperger syndrome and high-functioning autism. *Journal of Autism and Developmental Disorders, 35,* 145–158.

Sowell, E. R., Thompson, P. M., Leonard, C. M., Welcome, S. E., Kan, E., & Toga, A. W. (2004). Longitudinal mapping of cortical thickness and brain growth in children. *Journal of Neuroscience, 24,* 8223–8231.

SPA. (2010). Alan Ross award. Retrieved from http://www.cps.ca/awards-prix/details/#recipients

Spear, L. P. (2004). Adolescence and the trajectory of alcohol use. *Annals of the New York Academy of Sciences, 1021,* 202–205.

Special Senate Committee on Aging. (2009). *Canada's aging population: Seizing the opportunity final report.* Ottawa: Senate of Canada. Retrieved from http://www.senate-senat.ca/age.asp

Spelke, E. S. (1991). Physical knowledge in infancy: Reflections on Piaget's theory. In S.

Carey & R. Gelman (Eds.), *The epigenesis of mind: Essays on biology and cognition*. Hillsdale, NJ: Erlbaum.

Spelke, E. S., & Kinzler, K. D. (2007a). Core knowledge. *Developmental Science, 10,* 89–96.

Spelke, E. S., & Kinzler, K. D. (2007b). Core systems in human cognition. *Progress in Brain Research, 164,* 257–264.

Spence, A. P. (1989). *Biology of human aging.* Englewood Cliffs, NJ: Prentice Hall.

Spence, J. T., & Helmreich, R. (1978). *Masculinity and feminity: Their psychological dimensions.* Austin: University of Texas Press.

Sperling, H., Debruyne, F., Boermans, A., Beneke, M., Ulbrich, E., & Ewald, S. (2010, in press). The POTENT I randomized trial: Efficacy and safety of an orodispersible vardenafil formulation of the treatment of erectile dysfunction. *Journal of Sexual Medicine, 8,* 261–71.

Spiro, A. (2001). Health in midlife: Toward a lifespan view. In M. E. Lachman (Ed.), *Handbook of midlife development.* New York: John Wiley.

Spironelli, C., & Angrilli, A. (2008). Developmental aspects of automatic word processing: Language lateralization of early ERP components in children, young adults, and middle-aged adults. *Biological Psychology.*

Spruijt, E., & Duindam, V. (2010). Joint physical custody in the Netherlands and the well-being of children. *Journal of Divorce and Remarriage, 51,* 65–82.

Squire W. (2008). Shaken baby syndrome: The quest for evidence. *Developmental Medicine and Child Neurology, 50,* 10–14.

Sroufe, L. A., Egeland, B., Carlson, E., & Collins, W. A. (2005). The place of early attachment in developmental context. In K. E. Grossman, K. Krossman, & E. Waters (Eds.), *The power of longitudinal attachment research: From infancy and childhood to adulthood.* New York: Guilford Press.

St. George-Hyslop, P. (2012). Tanz Centre for Research in Neurodegenerative Diseases, University of Toronto. Retrieved on September 15, 2013 from http://tanz.med.utoronto.ca/profile/peter-st-george-hyslop-director

St. John, P. D., Montgomery, P. R., & Tyas, S. L. (2008, Oct. 6). Alcohol misuse, gender, and depressive symptoms in community dwelling seniors. *International Journal of Geriatric Psychiatry.* Retrieved from http://onlinelibrary.wiley.com/doi/10.1002/gps.2131/abstract;jsessionid=9D5A5577099D70EB1650810FD15822FD.d04t03?denieedAccessCustomisedMessage=&userIsAuthenticated=false

Stajduhar, K. I., Allan, D. E., Cohen, S. R., & Heyland, D. K. (2008). Preferences for location of death of seriously ill hospitalized patients: Perspectives from Canadian patients and their family caregivers. *Palliative Medicine, 22,* 85–88.

Starr, C. (2011). *Biology* (8th ed.). Boston: Cengage.

Starr, C., Evers, C., Starr, L. (2010). *Biology today and tomorrow with physiology* (3rd ed.). Boston: Cengage.

Starr, L. R., & Davila, J. (2008). Clarifying co-rumination: Association with internalizing symptoms and romantic involvement among adolescent girls. *Journal of Adolescence.*

Statistics Canada. (2000). *Research paper: High school dropouts returning to school.* Catalogue no. 81-595-M—No. 055. Retrieved from http://www.statcan.gc.ca/pub/81-595-m/81-595-m2008055-eng.pdf

Statistics Canada. (2001b). Target groups project: Women in Canada: Work chapter updates. Catalogue no. 89F0133XIE. Ottawa: Minister of Industry.

Statistics Canada. (2001c). Trends in the use of private education: 1987/88 to 1998/99. *The Daily.* www.statcan.ca

Statistics Canada. (2003). Among children aged 0 to 14 in Canada 1.4% have a severe or very severe disability. Retrieved from http://www.statcan.gc.ca/pub/89-577-x/4065023-eng.htm#children_0to14_severe_disability

Statistics Canada. (2003a). *Canadian roulette.* Canada Safety Council. Retrieved from https://canadasafetycouncil.org/community-safety/canadian-roulette

Statistics Canada. (2003b). How times have changed! Canadian smoking patterns in the 20th century. Catalogue no. 82-005-XIE.

Statistics Canada. (2003c, May 23). Relationship between working while in high school and dropping out. Retrieved from www.statcan.ca

Statistics Canada. (2004a). *National Longitudinal Survey of Children and Youth.* Statistics Canada.

Statistics Canada. (2004b). Trends in drug offences and the role of alcohol and drugs in crime. *The Daily* (February 23, 2004). Retrieved from www.statcan.ca

Statistics Canada. (2005). Detailed information for 2005. *Canadian Community Health Survey (CCHS).*

Statistics Canada. (2005a). *Report on seniors' falls in Canada, 2005.* Retrieved from publications.gc.ca/collections/Collection/HP25-1-2005E.pdf

Statistics Canada. (2005b, February 2). Secondary school graduates. *The Daily.* Retrieved from http://www.statcan.gc.ca/daily-quotidien/050202/dq050202b-eng.htm

Statistics Canada. (2006a). *Census families in private households by family structure, 1991 and 1996 censuses.* Retrieved from http://www.statcan.ca/

Statistics Canada. (2006b). *Divorces by province and territory.*

Statistics Canada. (2006d). National Longitudinal Survey of Children and Youth (NLSCY). Retrieved from http://www.statcan.ca/

Statistics Canada. (2006e). Social indicators. *Canadian Social Trends* (Catalogue no. 11-008), 35.

Statistics Canada. (2007). Changes in causes of death, by sex, in Canada 1979–2004. Retrieved from http://www.statcan.gc.ca/

Statistics Canada. (2007a). Components of population growth. Retrieved from http://www.statcan.gc.ca/pub/91-003-X/2007001/4129903-eng.htm

Statistics Canada. (2007b). *Family portrait: Continuity and change in Canadian families and households in 2006, 2006 census.* Catalogue no. 97-553-XIE. Retrieved from http://www12.statcan.ca/

Statistics Canada. (2007c). Postsecondary enrolment trends to 2031: Three scenarios (Catalogue no. 81-595-MIE-No. 058). Retrieved from http://www.statcan.gc.ca

Statistics Canada. (2008a). Sexual assault in Canada 2004 and 2007 (Catalogue no. 85F0033M-No.19). Retrieved from http://www.statcan.gc.ca

Statistics Canada. (2009). Canada's population by age and sex. Retrieved from http://www.statcan.gc.ca/daily-quotidien/090115/dq090115c-eng.htm

Statistics Canada. (2009). *Family violence in Canada: A statistical profile.* Ottawa: Author. Catalogue no. 85-224-X.

Statistics Canada. (2010). Arthritis. Retrieved on September 15, 2013 from http://www.statcan.gc.ca/pub/82-229-x/2009001/status/art-eng.htm

Statistics Canada. (2010a). Gap in life expectancy projected to decrease between Aboriginal people and the total Canadian population. Retrieved from http://www.statcan.gc.ca/

Statistics Canada. (2010b). Income of Canadians. Retrieved from http://www.statcan.gc.ca/daily-quotidien/090603/dq090603a-eng.htm

Statistics Canada. (2010c). Leading causes of death (Table 1, 2). http://statcan.gc.ca

Statistics Canada. (2010d). Paid work. Catalogue no. 89-503-X. Retrieved from http://www.statcan.gc.ca/pub/89-503-x/2010001/article/11387-eng.htm

Statistics Canada. (2011a). Canada's population estimates: Age and sex. *The Daily,* Wednesday, September 28, 2011. Retrieved from http://www.statcan.gc.ca/

Statistics Canada. (2011b). Families reference guide (Catalogue no. 98-312-X2011005). Retrieved from http://www.statcan.gc.ca

Statistics Canada. (2011c). Study: Projected trends to 2031 for the Canadian labour force. *The Daily,* Wednesday, August 17, 2011. Retrieved from http://www.statcan.gc.ca/daily-quotidien/110817/dq110817b-eng.htm

Statistics Canada. (2011d). Statistical profile on the health of First Nations in Canada: Leading causes of death (Table 3). Retrieved from http://statcan.gc.ca

Statistics Canada. (2012a). *Body mass index, overweight or obese, self-reported, adult, by age group and sex (2012).* Ottawa: Statistics Canada. Retrieved from http://www.statcan.gc.ca/tables-tableaux/sum-som/l01/cst01/health81b-eng.htm

Statistics Canada. (2012b). Deaths, 2009 (Table 1). Retrieved from http://statcan.gc.ca

Statistic Canada. (2012c). Eating disorders (Section D) (Catalogue no. 82-619-M). Retrieved from http://www.statcan.gc.ca/pub/82-619-m/82-619-m2012004-eng.pdf

Statistics Canada. (2012d). *Health at a glance: Suicide rates: An overview* (Catalogue no. 82-624-X). Retrieved from http://www.statcan.gc.ca

Statistics Canada. (2012e). Highlights (Catalogue no. 84-215-X). Retrieved from http://statcan.gc.ca

Statistics Canada. (2012f). Leading causes of death, infants, by sex, Canada (Table 102–0562). Retrieved from http://statcan.gc.ca

Statistics Canada. (2012g). Life expectancy at birth by sex and by province, May 31, 2012. Retrieved from http://www.statcan.gc.ca/tables-tableaux/sum-som/l01/cst01/health26-eng.htm

Statistics Canada. (2012h). 2011 census: Population and dwelling counts. *The Daily,* Wednesday, February 8, 2012. Retrieved from http://www.statcan.gc.ca/

Statistics Canada. (2012i). *Visible minority of a person.* Retrieved from http://www.statcan.gc.ca

Statistics Canada. (2012j). *Youth court statistics in Canada, 2010/2011.* Retrieved from http://www.statcan.gc.ca

Statistics Canada. (2012k). Overview of family violence. Retrieved from http://www.statcan.gc.ca/pub/85-002-x/2012001/article/11643/hl-fs-eng.htm#a4

Statistics Canada. (2013b, January 8). *Centenarians in Canada.* Retrieved from http://www12.statcan.gc.ca/

Staudinger, U. M. (1996). Psychologische produktivitat und selbstenfaltung im alter. In M. M. Baltes & L. Montada (Eds.), *Produktives leben im alter.* Frankfurt, Germany: Campus.

Staudinger, U. M., & Bluck, S. (2001). A view on midlife development from lifespan theory. In M. E. Lachman (Ed.), *Handbook of midlife development.* New York: John Wiley.

Staudinger, U. M., & Dorner, J. (2007). Wisdom. In J. E. Birren (Ed.), *Encyclopedia of gerontology* (2nd ed.). San Diego Academic Press.

Staudinger, U. M., & Gluck, J. (2011, in press). Psychological wisdom research. *Annual review of psychology* (Vol. 62). Palo Alto, CA: Annual Reviews.

Staudinger, U. M., & Jacobs, C. B. (2011). Life-span perspectives on positive personality development in adulthood and old age. In R. M. Lerner, W. F. Overton, A. M. Freund, & M. E. Lamb (Eds.), *Handbook of life-span development.* New York: Wiley.

Stein, M. T., Kennell, J. H., & Fulcher, A. (2004). Benefits of a doula present at the birth of a child. *Journal of Developmental and Behavioral Pediatrics, 25* (Suppl. 5), S89–S92.

Steinberg, L. (2008). A social neuroscience perspective on adolescent risk-taking. *Developmental Review, 28,* 78–106.

Steinberg, L. (2009). Adolescent development and juvenile justice. *Annual Review of Clinical Psychology* (Vol. 5). Palo Alto, CA: Annual Reviews.

Steinberg, L. Batt-Eisengart, I., & Cauffman, E. (2006). Patterns of competence and adjustment among adolescents from authoritative, authoritarian, indulgent, and neglectful homes: A replication in a sample of serious juvenile offenders. *Journal of Research on Adolescence, 16,* 47–58.

Steinberg, L. D., & Silk, J. S. (2002). Parenting adolescents. In M. H. Bornstein (Ed.), *Handbook of parenting* (2nd ed., Vol. 1). Mahwah, NJ: Erlbaum.

Steinberg, L., & Monahan, K. C. (2007). Age differences in resistance to peer influence. *Developmental Psychology, 43,* 1531–1543.

Steinberg, S. J., & Davila, J. (2008). Romantic functioning and depressive symptoms among early adolescent girls: The moderating role of parental emotional availability. *Journal of Clinical Child and Adolescent Psychology, 37,* 350–362.

Steinhausen, H. C., Blattmann, B., & Pfund, F. (2007). Developmental outcome in children with intrauterine exposure to substances. *European Addiction Research, 13,* 94–100.

Steinstra, D., & Chochinov, M. (2012). Palliative care for vulnerable populations. *Palliative and Supportive Care, 10,* 37–42.

Sternberg, K., & Sternberg, R. (2010). Love. In H. Pashler (Ed.), *Encyclopedia of the mind.* Thousand Oaks, CA: Sage.

Sternberg, R. J. (1986). *Intelligence applied.* San Diego: Harcourt Brace Jovanovich.

Sternberg, R. J. (2000). Wisdom as a form of giftedness. *Gifted Child Quarterly, 44*(4), 252–259.

Sternberg, R. J. (2002). Intelligence: The triarchic theory of intelligence. In J. W. Gutherie (Ed.), *Encyclopedia of education* (2nd ed.). New York: Macmillan.

Sternberg, R. J. (2004). Individual differences in cognitive development. In U. Goswami (Ed.), *Blackwell handbook of childhood cognitive development.* Malden, MA: Blackwell.

Sternberg, R. J. (2007a). g, g's, or jeez: Which is the best model for developing abilities, competencies, and expertise? In P. C. Kyllonen, R. D. Roberts, & L. Stankov (Eds.), *Extending intelligence: Enhancement and New Constructs* (pp. 250–265). Mahwah, NJ: Lawrence Erlbaum Associates.

Sternberg, R. J. (2007b). Finding students who are wise, practical, and creative. *The Chronicle of Higher Education, 53*(44), B11.

Sternberg, R. J. (2008a). Schools should nurture wisdom. In B. Z. Presseisen (Ed.), *Teaching for intelligence* (2nd ed.). Thousand Oaks, CA: Corwin.

Sternberg, R. J. (2008b). Applying psychological theories to educational practice. *American Educational Research Journal, 45*(1), 150–165.

Sternberg, R. J. (2009a). *Cognitive psychology* (5th ed.). Belmont, CA: Wadsworth.

Sternberg, R. J. (2009b). Teaching for creativity. In R. A. Beghetto & J. C. Kaufman (Eds.), *Nurturing creativity in the classroom.* New York: Cambridge University Press.

Sternberg, R. J. (2009c). Wisdom. In S. J. Lopez (Ed.). *Encyclopedia of positive psychology.* Malden, MA: Blackwell.

Sternberg, R. J. (2009d). Wisdom, intelligence, creativity, synthesized: A model of giftedness. In T. Balchin, B. Hymer, & D. Matthews (Eds.), *International companion to gifted education.* London: RoutledgeFalmer.

Sternberg, R. J. (2010a). A triarchic view of intelligence in cross-cultural perspective. In S. H. Irvine & J. H. Berry (Eds.), *Human abilities in cultural contexts.* New York: Cambridge University Press.

Sternberg, R. J. (2010b). Human intelligence. In V. S. Ramachandran (Ed.), *Encyclopedia of human behavior* (2nd ed.). New York: Elsevier.

Sternberg, R. J. (2010c). Intelligence. In B. McGaw, P. Peterson, & E. Baker (Eds.), *International encyclopedia of education* (3rd ed.). New York: Elseiver.

Sternberg, R. J. (2010d). Teaching for creativity. In R. A. Beghetto & J. C. Kaufman (Eds.), *Nurturing creativity in the classroom.* New York: Cambridge University Press.

Sternberg, R. J., Kaufman, J. C., & Grigorenko, E. (2008). *Applied intelligence.* New York: Cambridge University Press.

Stetsone, B. (2002). *Living victims, stolen lives: Parents of murdered children speak to Americans about death value.* New York: Baywood.

Stevenson, H. W., & Newman, R. S. (1986). Longterm prediction of achievements and attitudes in mathematics and reading. *Child Development, 57,* 646–659.

Stewart, A. J., Ostrove, J. M., & Helson, R. (2001). Middle aging in women: Patterns of personality change from the 30's to the 50's. *Journal of Adult Development, 8,* 23–37.

Stice, E., Presnell, K., & Spangler, D. (2002). Risk factors for binge eating onset in adolescent girls: A 2-year prospective investigation. *Health Psychology, 21,* 131–138.

Stice, E., Presnell, K., Gau, J., & Shaw, H. (2007). Testing mediators of intervention effects in randomized controlled trials: An evaluation of two eating disorder programs. *Journal of Consulting and Clinical Psychology, 75,* 20–32.

Stikkelbroek, Y., Prinzie, P., de Graaf, R., ten Have, M., & Cuijpers, P. (2012). Parental death during childhood and psychopathology in adulthood. *Psychiatry Research, 198*(3), 516–520.

Stine-Morrow, E. A. L. (2007). The Dumbledore hypothesis of cognitive aging. *Current Directions in Psychological Science, 16,* 295–299.

Stirling, E. (2011). *Valuing older people.* New York: Wiley.

Stocker, C. M., Richmond, M. K., Rhoades, G. K., & Kiang, L. (2007). Family emotional processes and adolescents' adjustment. *Social Development, 16,* 310–325.

Stone, R. I. (2006). Emerging issues in long-term care. In R. H. Binstock & L. K. George (Eds.), *Handbook of aging and the social sciences* (6th ed.). San Diego: Academic Press.

Stones, M., & Stones, L. (2007). Sexuality, sensuality, and intimacy. In J. E. Birren (Ed.), *Encyclopedia of gerontology* (2nd ed.). San Diego: Academic Press.

Stowe, R., et al. (2008). Dopamine agonist therapy in early Parkinson's disease. *Cochrane Database of Systematic Reviews, 2,* CD006564.

Strandberg, T. E., Strandberg, A. Y., Slaomaa, V. V., Pitkala, K., Tilvis, R. S., & Miettinen, T. A. (2007). Alcoholic beverage preference, 29-year mortality, and quality of life in men in old age. *Journals of Gerontology: Biological Sciences and Medical Sciences, 62A,* M213–M218.

Straus, M. A. (2003). *The primordial violence: Corporal punishment by parents, cognitive development, and crime.* Walnut Creek, CA: Alta Mira Press.

Strauss, R. S. (2001). Environmental tobacco smoke and serum vitamin C levels in children. *Pediatrics, 107,* 540–542.

Strazdins, L., Clements, M. S., Korda, R. J., Broom, D. H., & D'Souza, R. M. (2006). Unsociable work? Nonstandard work schedules, family relationships, and children's well-being. *Journal of Marriage and Family, 68,* 394–410.

Striegel, R., Bedrosian, R., Wang, C., & Schwartz, S. (2012). Why men should be included in research on binge eating. Results from a comparison of psychosocial impairment in men and women. *International Journal of Eating Disorders, 45,* 233–240.

Striegel-Moore, R. H., & Bulik, C. M. (2007). Risk factors for eating disorders. *American Psychologist, 62,* 181–198.

Stroebe, M., Schut, H., & Stroebe, W. (2007). Health outcomes of bereavement. *Lancet, 370,* 1960–1973.

Strohmeier, D., & Schmitt-Rodermund, E. (Eds.). (2008). *Immigrant youth in European countries.* Clifton, NJ: Psychology Press.

Strong, B., Yarber, W., Sayad, B., & De Vault, C. (2008). *Human sexuality* (6th ed.). New York: McGraw-Hill.

Studenski, S., Carlson, M. C., Fillet, H., Greenough, W. T., Kramer, A. F., & Rebok, G. W. (2006). From bedside to bench: Does mental and physical activity promote cognitive vitality in late life? *Science of Aging, Knowledge, and Environment, 10,* e21.

Stutts, J. C. (2007). Driving behavior. In J. E. Birren (Ed.), *Encyclopedia of gerontology* (2nd ed.). San Diego: Academic Press.

Sudheimer, E. (2009). Appreciating both sides of the generation gap: Baby boomers and Generation X nurses working together. *Nursing Forum, 44*(1), 57–63.

Suetta, C., Anderson, J. L., Dalgas, U., Berget, J., Koskinen, S. O., Aagaard, P., Magnusson, S. P., & Kjaer, M. (2008). Resistance training induces qualitative changes in muscle morphology, muscle architecture, and muscle function in postoperative patients. *Journal of Applied Physiology, 105*(1), 180–6.

Sugar, J. A. (2007). Memory, strategies. In J. E. Birren (Ed.), *Encyclopedia of gerontology* (2nd ed.). San Diego: Academic Press.

Sugimoto, M., Kuze, M., & Uji, Y. (2008). Ultrasound biomicroscopy for membranous congenital cataract. *Canadian Journal of Ophthalmology, 43,* 7–8.

Sugita, Y. (2004). Experience in early infancy is indispensable for color perception. *Current Biology, 14,* 1267–1271.

Sui, X., LaMonte, M. J., Laditka, J. N., Hardin, J. W., Chase, N., Hooker, S. P., et al. (2007). Cardiorespiratory fitness and adiposity as mortality predictors in older adults. *Journal of the American Medical Association, 298,* 2507–2516.

Sullivan, H. S. (1953). *The interpersonal theory of psychiatry.* New York: W. W. Norton.

Sunstein, C. R. (2008). Adolescent risk-taking and social meaning: A commentary. *Developmental Review, 28,* 145–152.

Suris, J. C., Jeannin, A., Chossis, I., & Michaud, P. A. (2007). Piercing among adolescents: Body art as a risk marker: A population-based study. *Journal of Family Practice, 56,* 126–130.

Susman, E. J., & Dorn, L. D. (2009). Puberty: Its role in development. In R. M. Lerner & L. Steinberg (Eds.), *Handbook of adolescent psychology* (3rd ed.). New York: Wiley.

Susman, M. R., Amor, D. J., Muggli, E., Jaques, A. M., & Halliday, J. (2010, in press). Using population-based data to predict the impact of introducing noninvasive prenatal diagnosis for Down syndrome. *Genetics in Medicine, 12*(5), 298–303.

Suvas, S. (2008). Advancing age and immune cell dysfunction: Is it reversible or not? *Expert Opinion on Biological Therapy, 8,* 657–658.

Suzuki, A., Sekiguchi, S., Asano, S., & Itoh, M. (2008). Pharmacological topics of bone metabolism: Recent advances in pharmacological management of osteoporosis. *Journal of Pharmacological Science, 106,* 530–535.

Sveen, C. A., & Walby, F. A. (2008). Suicide survivors' mental health and grief reactions: A systematic review of controlled studies. *Suicide and Life Threatening Behavior, 38,* 13–29.

Svihula, J., & Estes, C. L. (2008). Social security politics: Ideology and reform. *Journals of Gerontology B: Psychological Sciences and Social Sciences, 62,* S79–S89.

Swain, S. L., & Nikolich-Zugich, J. (2009). Key research opportunities in immune system aging. *Journals of Gerontology A: Biological Sciences and Medical Sciences, 64,* 183–186.

Swamy, G. K., Ostbye, T., & Skjaerven, R. (2008). Association of preterm birth with long-term survival, reproduction, and next generation preterm birth. *Journal of the American Medical Association, 299,* 1429–1436.

Swanson, C. R., Sesso, S. L., & Emborg, M. E. (2009). Can we prevent Parkinson's disease? *Frontiers in Bioscience, 14,* 1642–1660.

Swanson, D. P. (1997, April). *Identity and coping styles among African-American females.* Paper presented at the meeting of the Society for Research in Child Development, Washington, DC.

Swartz, T. T. (2008, Spring). Family capital and the invisible transfer of privilege: Intergenerational support and social class in early adulthood. *New Directions in Child and Adolescent Development, 119,* 11–24.

Swearer, S. M., Givens, J. E., & Frerichs, L. J. (2010). Cognitive-behavioral interventions for depression and anxiety. In G. G. Peacock, R. A. Ervin, E. J. Daly, & K. W. Merrell (Eds.), *Handbook of school psychology.* New York: Guilford.

Sweeney, M. S. (2009). *Brain: The complete mind, how it develops, how it works, and how to keep it sharp.* Washington, DC: National Geographic.

Sweet, S., Moen, P., & Meiksins, P. (2007). Dual earners in double jeopardy: Preparing for job loss in the new risk economy. In B. A. Rubin (Ed.), *Research in the Sociology of Work.* New York: Elsevier.

Syed, M., & Azmitia, M. (2008). A narrative approach to ethnic identity in emerging adulthood: Bringing life to the identity status model. *Developmental Psychology, 44*(4), 1012.

Szanton, S. L., Seplaki, C. L., Thorpe, R. J., Allen, J. K., & Fried, L. P. (2010). Socioeconomic status is associated with frailty: The women's health and aging studies. *Journal of Epidemiology and Community Health, 64,* 63–67.

Szinovacz, M. E. (2009). Grandparenthood. In D. Carr (Ed.), *Encyclopedia of the life course and human development.* Boston: Gale Cengage.

Szulwach, K. E., et al. (2010). Cross talk between microRNA and epigenetic regulation in adult neurogenesis. *Journal of Cell Biology, 189,* 127–141.

T

Tabira, T. (2009). Decorated plaques in Alzheimer's disease. *Annals of Neurology, 65,* 4–6.

Tacutu, R., Budovsky, A., & Fraifeld, V. E. (2010). The NetAge database: A compendium of networks for longevity, age-related diseases, and associated processes. *Biogerontology, 11*(4), 513–522.

Tafoya, M., & Spitzberg, B. H. (2007). The dark side of infidelity. In B. H. Spitzberg & W. R. Cupach (Eds.), *The dark side of interpersonal communication.* Mahwah, NJ: Erlbaum.

Tager-Flusberg, H., & Zukowski, A. (2009). Putting words together: Morphology and syntax in the preschool years. In J. Berko Gleason & N. Ratner (Eds.), *The development of language* (7th ed.). Boston: Allyn & Bacon.

Taige, N. M., Neal, C., Glover, V., & Early Stress, Translational Research and Prevention Science Network: Fetal and Neonatal Experience on Child and Adolescent Mental Health. (2007). Antenatal maternal stress and long-term effects on neurodevelopment: How and why? *Journal of Child Psychology and Psychiatry, 48,* 245–261.

Taler, S. J. (2009). Hypertension in women. *Current Hypertension Reports, 11*, 23–28.

Talwar, V., & Lee, K. (2002). Development of lying to conceal a transgression: Children's control of expressive behaviour during verbal deception. *International Journal of Behaviour Development, 26*(5), 436–444.

Talwar, V., Lee, K., Bala, N., & Lindsay, R. C. L. (2006). Adults' judgments of children's coached reports. *Law and Human Behavior, 30*(5), 561–570.

Talwar, V., Murphy, S. M., & Lee, K. (2007). White lie-telling in children for politeness purposes. *International Journal of Behavioral Development, 31*, 1–11.

Tam, W. H., & Chung, T. (2007). Psychosomatic disorders in pregnancy. *Current Opinion in Obstetrics and Gynecology, 19*, 126–132.

Tamis-LeMonda, C., & McFadden, K. E. (2010). The United States of America. In M. H. Bornstein (Ed.), *Handbook of cultural developmental science.* New York: Oxford University Press.

Tang, K. L. (2008). Taking older people's rights seriously: The role of international law. *Journal of Aging and Social Policy, 20*, 99–117.

Tang, Y., & Posner, M. I. (2009). Attention training and attention state training. *Trends in Cognitive Science, 13*, 222–227.

Tantillo, M., Keswick, C. M., Hynd, G. W., & Dishman, R. K. (2002). The effects of exercise on children with attention-deficit hyperactivity disorder. *Medical Science and Sports Exercise, 34*, 203–212.

Tappan, M. B. (1998). Sociocultural psychology and caring psychology: Exploring Vygotsky's "hidden curriculum." *Educational Psychologist, 33*, 23–33.

Tarabulsy, G. M., Provost, M. A., Deslandes, J., St-Lautenr, D., Moss, E., Lemelin, J. P., et al. (2003). Individual differences in infant still-face response at 6 months. *Infant Behavior & Development, 26*, 421–438.

Tarabulsy, G. M., et al. (2008). Similarities and differences in mothers' and observers' ratings of infant security on the attachment Q-sort. *Infant Behavior and Development, 31*(1), 10–22.

Tarawneh, R., & Holtzman, D. M. (2010). Biomarkers in translational research of Alzheimer's disease. *Neuropharmacology, 59*(4–5), 310–322.

Tashiro, T., & Frazier, P. (2003). "I'll never be in a relationship like that again": Personal growth following romantic relationship breakups. *Personal Relationships, 10*, 113–128.

Tashiro, T., Frazier, P., & Berman, M. (2006). Stress related growth following divorce and relationship dissolution. In M. A. Fine & J. H. Harvey (Eds.) *Handbook of divorce and relationship dissolution.* Mahwah, NJ: Erlbaum.

Tate, R. B., Lah L., & Cuddy, T. E.. (2003). Definition of successful aging by elderly Canadian males: The Manitoba follow up. *The Gerontologist, 43*(5), 735–744. Retrieved from http://gerontologist.oxfordjournals.org/ content/43/5/735.short on September 6, 2012.

Taveras, E. M., Rifas-Shiman, S. L., Oken, E., Gunderson, E. P., & Gillman, M. W. (2008). Short sleep duration in infancy and risk of childhood overweight. *Archives of Pediatric and Adolescent Medicine, 162*, 305–311.

Taylor, B. (2005, April 22). The little Winnipeg girl who charmed Bay Street. *Toronto Star*, pp. E1, E9.

Taylor, L. S., & Whittaker, C. R. (2009). *Bridging multiple worlds* (2nd ed.). Boston: Allyn & Bacon.

Taylor, L. (2012, April 27). Why Canada is hazardous to their health. *Ottawa Citizen*. Retrieved from http://www.ottawacitizen.com/health/Canada+hazardous+their+health/6206262/story.html

Taylor, P. S. (2007, February 7). The wealth report: Celebrating the RRSP miracle. *Macleans*. Retrieved on September 15, 2013 from http://www.macleans.ca/article.jsp?content=20070226_102281_102281

Taylor, R. D., & Lopez, E. I. (2005). Family management practice, school achievement, and problem behavior in African American adolescents: Mediating processes. *Applied Developmental Psychology, 26*, 39–49.

Taylor, R. L., Smiley, L., & Richards, S. B. (2009). *Exceptional students.* New York: McGraw-Hill.

Teague, M. L., Mackenzie, S. L. C., & Rosenthal, D. M. (2009). *Your health today* (brief ed.). New York: McGraw-Hill.

Temple, B., Janzen, B. L., Chad, K., Bell, G., Reeder, B., & Martin, L. (2008). The health benefits of a physical activity program for older adults living in congregate housing. *Canadian Journal of Public Housing, 99*, 36–40.

Temple, C. A., Makinster, J. G., Buchmann, L. G., Logue, J., Mrvova, G., & Gearan, M. (2005). *Intervening for literacy.* Boston: Allyn & Bacon.

Templeton, J. L., & Eccles, J. S. (2006). The relation between spiritual development and identity processes. In E. Roehlkepartain, P. E. King, L. Wagener, & P. L. Benson (Eds.), *The handbook of spirituality in childhood and adolescence.* Thousand Oaks, CA: Sage.

Terrion, J. L. (2013). The experience of post-secondary education for students in recovery from addiction to drugs or alcohol: Relationships and recovery capital. *Journal of Social and Personal Relationships, 30*(1), 3–23.

Terry, D. F., Sebastian, P., Andersen, P. S., & Perls, T. T. (2008). Disentangling the roles of disability and morbidity in survival to exceptional old age. *Archives of Internal Medicine, 168*, 277–283.

Terry, W., Olson, L. G., Wilss, L., & Boulton-Lewis, G. (2006). Experience of dying: Concerns of dying patients and of carers. *Internal Medicine Journal, 36*, 338–346.

Teti, D. M. (2001). Retrospect and prospect in the study of sibling relationships. In J. P. McHale & W. S. Grolnick (Eds.), *Retrospect and prospect in the psychological study of families.* Mahwah, NJ: Erlbaum.

Teti, D. M., & Towe-Goodman, N. (2008). Postpartum depression, effects on infant. In M. M. Haith & J. B. Benson (Eds.), *Encyclopedia of infancy and early childhood.* Oxford, UK: Elsevier.

Thapar, A., Fowler, T., Rice, F., Scourfield, J., Van Den Bree, M., Thomas, S., Harold, G., & Hay, D. (2003). Maternal smoking during pregnancy and attention deficit hyperactivity disorder symptoms in offspring. *American Journal of Psychiatry, 160*, 1985–1989.

Tharp, R. G. (1994). Intergroup differences among Native Americans in socialization and child cognition: An erthogenetic analysis. In P. M. Greenfield & R. Cocking (Eds.), *Cross-cultural roots of minority child development.* Mahwah, NJ: Erlbaum.

Thavanati, R. K., Kanala, K. R., de Dios, A. E., & Cantu Garza, J. M. (2008). Age-related correlation between antioxidant enzymes and DNA damage with smoking and body mass index. *Journals of Gerontology A: Biological Sciences and Medical Sciences, 63*, 360–364.

Thelen, E., & Smith, L. B. (2006). Dynamic development of action and thought. In W. Damon & R. Lerner (Eds.), *Handbook of child psychology* (6th ed.). New York: Wiley.

Thiele, D. M., & Whelan, T. A. (2008). The relationship between grandparent satisfaction, reaming, and generativity. *International Journal of Aging and Human Development, 66*, 21–48.

Thomann, C. R., & Carter, A. S. (2008). Social and emotional development theories. In M. M. Haith & J. B. Benson (Eds.), *Encyclopedia of infant and early childhood development.* Oxford, UK: Elsevier.

Thomas, A., & Chess, S. (1991). Temperament in adolescence and its functional significance. In R. M. Lerner, A. C. Petersen, & J. Brooks-Gunn (Eds.), *Encyclopedia of adolescence* (Vol. 2). New York: Garland.

Thomas, E. M. (2006). Readiness to learn at school among five-year-old children in Canada. Catalogue no. 89-599-MIE – No. 004. Ottawa: Statistics Canada.

Thomas, M. S. C., & Johnson, M. H. (2008). New advances in understanding sensitive periods in brain development. *Current Directions in Psychological Science, 17*, 1–5.

Thompson, P. M., Giedd, J. N., Woods, R. P., MacDonald, D., Evans, A. C., & Toga, A. W. (2000). Growth patterns in the developing brain detected by using continuum mechanical tensor maps. *Nature, 404*, 190–193.

Thompson, R. A. (2006). The development of the person. In W. Damon & R. Lerner (Eds.), *Handbook of child psychology* (6th ed.). New York: Wiley.

Thompson, R. A. (2007). Unpublished review of J. W. Santrock's *Children* (10th ed.). New York: McGraw-Hill.

Thompson, R. A. (2008). Unpublished review of J. W. Santrock's *Life-span development* (12th ed.) New York: McGraw-Hill.

Thompson, R. A. (2009a). Emotional development. In R. A. Schweder (Ed.), *The Chicago companion to the child*. Chicago: University of Chicago Press.

Thompson, R. A. (2009b). Early attachment and later development: Familiar questions, new answers. In J. Cassidy & P. R. Shaver (Eds.), *Handbook of attachment* (2nd ed.). New York: Guilford.

Thompson, R. A. (2009d). Making the most of small effect. *Social Development, 18,* 247–251.

Thompson, R. A. (2012). Whither the preoperational child? Toward a life-span moral development theory. *Child Development*.

Thompson, R. A., & Goodvin, R. (2005). The individual child: Temperament, emotion, self, and personality. In M. H. Bornstein & M. E. Lamb (Eds.), *Developmental psychology* (5th ed.). Mahwah, NJ: Erlbaum.

Thompson, R. A., & Goodvin, R. (2007). Taming the tempest in the teapot: Emotion regulation in toddlers. In C. A. Brownell & C. B. Kopp (Eds.), *Socioemotional development in toddlers*. New York: Guilford.

Thompson, R. A., & Newton, E. (2009). Infant-caregiver communication. In H. T. Reis & S. Sprecher (Eds.), *Encyclopedia of human relationships*. Thousand Oaks, CA: Sage.

Thompson, R. A., & Virmani, E. A. (2009). Creating persons: Culture, self and personality development. In M. H. Bornstein (Ed.), *Handbook of cross-cultural developmental science*. Clifton, NJ: Psychology Press.

Thompson, R. A., & Virmani, E. A. (2010). Self and personality. In M. H. Bornstein (Eds.), *Handbook of cultural developmental science*. New York: Psychology Press.

Thompson, R. A., Meyer, S., & Jochem, R. (2008). Emotion regulation. In M. M. Haith & J. B. Benson (Eds.), *Encyclopedia of infant and early childhood development*. Oxford, UK: Elsevier.

Thompson, R. A., Meyer, S., & McGinley, M. (2006). Understanding values in relationships: The development of conscience. In M. Killen & J. Smetana (Eds.), *Handbook of moral development*. Mahwah, NJ: Erlbaum.

Thornton, J. G. (2007). Progesterone and preterm labor—Still no definite answers. *New England Journal of Medicine, 357,* 499–501.

Thornton, W. J., & Dumke, H. A. (2005). Age differences in everyday problem-solving and decision-making effectiveness: A meta-analytic review. *Psychology and Aging, 20,* 85–99.

Thygesen, K. L., & Hodgins, D. C. (2003). Quitting again: Motivations and strategies for terminating gambling relapses. *Journal of Gambling Issues, 9.* doi: 10.4309/jgi.2003.9.11

Tiedemann, M. (2008). Health care at the Supreme Court of Canada. *Library of Parliament Research Publications.* Retrieved from www2.parl.gc.ca/Content/LOP/ResearchPublications/prb0519-e.htm

Tierney, M. C., Yao, C., Kiss, A., & McDowell, I. (2005). Neuropsychological tests accurately predict incident Alzheimer disease after 5 and 10 years. *Neurology, 64,* 1853–1859.

Tildo, T., et al. (2005). Exposure to persistent organchlorine pollutants associates with human sperm Y-X chromosome ratio. *Human Reproduction, 20*(7), 1903–1909.

Tjepkema, M., Wilkins, R., Senécal, S., Guimond, É., & Penny, C. (2009). Mortality of Métis and Registered Indian adults in Canada: An 11-year follow-up study. *Health Reports, 20*(4), 1–21.

Toga, A. W., Thompson, P. M., & Sowell, E. R. (2006). Mapping brain maturation, *Trends in Neuroscience, 29,* 148–159.

Toh, S., Hernandez-Diaz, S., Logan, R., Rossuw, J. E., & Hernan, M. A. (2010). Coronary heart disease in postmenopausal recipients of estrogen plus progestin therapy: Does the increased risk ever disappear? A randomized trial. *Annals of Internal Medicine, 152,* 211–217.

Tomasello, M. (2006). Acquiring linguistic constructions. In W. Damon & R. Lerner (Eds.), *Handbook of child psychology* (6th ed.). New York: Wiley.

Tomasello, M., & Carpenter, M. (2007). Shared intentionality. *Developmental Science, 10,* 121–125.

Tomasello, M., Carpenter, M., & Liszkowski, U. (2007). A new look at infant pointing. *Child Development, 78,* 705–722.

Tomiyama, H., et al. (2010). Continuous smoking and progression of arterial stiffening: A prospective study. *Journal of the American College of Cardiology, 55,* 1979–1987.

Tompkins, G. E. (2011). *Literacy in the early grades* (3rd ed.). Boston: Allyn & Bacon.

Tonks, Randal G. (1992). *Identity and generativity in the Canadian context*.

Torges, C. M., Stewart, A. J., & Nolen-Hoeksema, S. (2008). Regret resolution, aging, and adapting to loss. *Psychology and Aging, 23,* 169–180.

Toth, S. L. (2009). Attachment-based interventions: Comments on Dozier, Egeland, and Benoit. In R. E. Tremblay, R. deV Peters, M. Boivin, & R. G. Barr (Eds.), *Encyclopedia on early childhood development*. Montreal: Centre of Excellence for Early Childhood Development.

Totten, M. (2004). Safe school study. Retrieved from http://www.cpha.ca.

Trautner, H. M., Ruble, D. N., Cyphers, L., Kirsten, B., Behrendt, R., & Hartmann, P. (2005). Rigidity and flexibility of gender stereotypes in children: Developmental or differential? *Infant and Child Development, 14,* 365–381.

Travers, C., Martin-Khan, M., & Lie, D. (2010). Performance indicators to measure dementia risk reduction activities in primary care. *Australasian Journal on Aging, 29,* 39–42.

Trefler, D. (2009). Quality is free: A cost-benefit analysis of early child development initiatives. *Journal of Paediatric and Child Health, 14*(10), 681–684.

Trehub, S.E., Plantinga, J., & Brcic, J. (2009). Infants detect cross-modal cues to identity in speech and singing. *Annals of the New York Academy of Science, 1169,* 508–511.

Tremblay, R. E. (2009). Development of aggression from early childhood to adulthood. In R. E. Tremblay, R. deV Peters, M. Boivin, & R. G. Barr (Eds.), *Encyclopedia on early childhood development*. Montreal: Center of Excellence for Early Childhood Development.

Tremblay, R. E., Gervais, J., & Petitclerc, A. (2008). *Early learning prevents youth violence*. Quebec: Canadian Council on Learning.

Tremblay, S., & Pierce, T. (2011). Perceptions of fatherhood: Longitudinal reciprocal associations within the couple. *Canadian Journal of Behavioural Science, 43*(2), 99–110.

Trentacosta, C. J., & Fine, S. E. (2009). Emotion knowledge, social competence, and behavior problems in childhood and adolescence: A meta-analytic review. *Social Development, 19*(1), 1–29.

Trifunov, W. (2009, May 15). *The practice of bed sharing: A systematic literature and policy review.* Prepared for the Public Health Agency of Canada. Retrieved from http://www.phac-aspc.gc.ca/dca-dea/prenatal/pbs-ppl-eng.php

Troll, L. E. (2000). Transmission and transmutation. In J. E. Birren & J. J. F. Schroots (Eds.), *A history of geropsychology in autobiography*. Washington, DC: American Psychological Association.

Trommsdorff, G. (2002). An eco-cultural and interpersonal relations approach to development of the lifespan. In W. J. Lonner, D. L. Dinnel, S. A. Hayes, & D. N. Sattler (Eds.), *Online readings in psychology and culture* (unit 12, chapter 1). Bellingham, WA: Center for Cross-Cultural Research, Western Washington University. Retrieved from http://www.wwu.edu/

Trottier, J. (2010). Atheists and agnostics, stand up and be counted in the 2011 census! Curently, most of us are not. Center for Inquiry. Retrieved from www.centerforinquiry.net/blogs/entry/canadian_atheists_and_agnostics_stand_up_and_be_counted_in_the_2011_census/

True, M., Pisani, L., & Oumar, F. (2001) Infant-mother attachment among the dogon of Mali. *Child Development, 72*(5), 1451–1466.

Truog, R. D. (2007). Brain death—Too flawed to endure, too ingrained to abandon. *Journal of Law, Medicine, and Ethics, 35,* 273–281.

Truog, R. D. (2008). End-of-life decision-making in the United States. *European Journal of Anesthesiology, 42* (Suppl. 1), S43–S50.

Truth and Reconciliation Commission of Canada. (2012). Residential schools. Retrieved from http://www.trc.ca/websites/trcinstitution/index.php?p=4

Trzesniewski, K. H., Donnellan, M. B., & Robins, R. W. (2003). Stability of self-esteem across the life span. *Journal* of *Personality and Social Psychology, 84*, 205–220.

Trzesniewski, K. H., Donnellan, M. B., Caspi, A., Moffitt, T. E., Robins, R. W., & Poultin, R. (2006). Adolescent low self-esteem is a risk factor for adult poor health, criminal behavior, and limited economic prospects. *Developmental Psychology, 42*, 381–390.

Tsai, T., Levenson, R., & McCoy, K. (2006). Cultural and temperamental variations in emotional response. *Emotion, 6*, 484–497.

Tubman, J. G., & Windle, M. (1995). Continuity of difficult temperament in adolescence: Relations with depression, life events, family support, and substance abuse. *Journal of Youth and Adolescence, 24*, 133–152.

Tudge, J. (2004). Practice and discourse as the intersection of individual and social in human development. In A. N. Perret-Clermont, L. Resnick, C. Pontecorvo, & B. Burge (Eds.), *Joining society: Social interactions and learning in adolescence and youth*. New York: Cambridge University Press.

Tulsky, J. (2005). Beyond advanced directives: Importance of communication skills at the end of life. *Journal of the American Medical Association, 294*(3), 359–365.

Tulving, E. (2000). Concepts of memory. In E. Tulving & F. I. M. Craik (Eds.), *The Oxford handbook of memory*. New York: Oxford University Press.

Tulviste, T., & Ahtonen, M. (2007). Child-rearing values of Estonian and Finnish mothers and fathers. *Journal of Cross-Cultural Psychology, 38*, 137.

Turcotte, M., & Schellenberg, G. (2007). *A portrait of seniors in Canada*. Ottawa: Statistics Canada.

Turecki, S., & Tonner, L. (1989). *The difficult child*. New York: Bantam.

Turiel, E. (2006). The development of morality. In W. Damon & R. Lerner (Eds.), *Handbook of child psychology* (6th ed.). New York: Wiley.

Turner, B. F. (1982). Sex-related differences in aging. In B. B. Wolman (Ed.), *Handbook of developmental psychology*. Englewood Cliffs, NJ: Prentice Hall.

Twells, L., & Newhook, L. (2010). Can exclusive breastfeeding reduce the likelihood of childhood obesity in some regions in Canada? *Canadian Journal of Public Health, 101*(1), 36–39.

U

UBC. (2010). http://educ.ubc.ca

Uhlenberg, P., & Dannefer, D. (2007). Age stratification. In J. E. Birren (Ed.), *Encyclopedia of gerontology* (2nd ed.). San Diego: Academic Press.

Umana-Taylor, A. J. (2006, March). *Ethnic identity, acculturation, and enculturation: Considerations in methodology and theory*. Paper presented at the meeting of the Society for Research on Adolescence, San Francisco.

UNAIDS. (2006). *2006 report on the global AIDS epidemic*. Geneva: SWIT: UNICEF.

Underwood, M. (2004). Sticks and stones and social exclusion: Aggression among boys and girls. In P. K. Smith & C. H. Hart (Eds.), *Blackwell handbook of childhood social development*. Malden, MA: Blackwell.

UNESCO. (2008). *Global education digest 2008: Comparing education statistics across the world*. Retrieved from http://www.uis.UNESCO.org/

UNESCO. (2011). *Global education digest 2011: Focus on secondary education*. Retrieved from http://www.uis.UNESCO.org/

UNICEF. (2006). *The state of the world's children 2006*. Geneva: Author.

UNICEF. (2008). *The state of the world's children 2008*. Geneva: Author.

UNICEF. (2010). *The state of the world's children 2010*. Geneva, Switzerland: Author.

UNICEF. (2012). *The state of the world's children 2012*. Geneva: Author.

United Nations. (2004). *Declaration on the elimination of violence against women*. Retrieved from http://www.un.org/documents/ga/res/48/a48r104.htm

United Nations. (2006). *The United Nations Human Development Index report*. New York: United Nations.

United Nations. (2011). *The United Nations Human Development Index report*. New York: United Nations.

University Health Netwook. (2006). Stem Cell Research at UHN. Retrieved from http://www.uhnresearch.ca/news/NR/NRSummer2006.pdf

Upitis, R., Smithrim, K., Patteson, A., MacDonald, J., & Finkle, J. (2003, May). *Improving math scores: Lessons of engagement*. Paper presented at the Canadian Society for the Study of Education Annual Conference, Halifax.

Uppal, S., Kohen, D., & Khan, S. (2006). *Educational services and the disabled child*. Catalogue no. 81-004-XIE. Retrieved from www.statcan.ca/

Urban, J., Lewin-Bizan, S., & Lerner, R. (2010). The role of intentional self-regulation, lower neighbourhood ecological assets, and activity involvement in youth developmental outcomes. *Journal of Youth and Adolescence, 39*, 783–800.

Ursula Franklin Academy. (2008–2013). Ursula Franklin biography. Retrieved from http://www.ufacademy.org/v5/school/bio.php

Usalcas, J. (2011). *The Aboriginal labour force analysis series: Aboriginal People and the labour market—Estimates from labour force survey 2008–2010*. Statistics Canada Catalogue no.71-588-X, no.3. Retrieved from http://www.statcan.gc.ca/pub/71-588-x/71-588-x2011003-eng.pdf

V

Vaillancourt, T. (2008). Bullying: Names will never hurt me ... or will they? Canada Research Chairs. Retrieved from http://www.chairs-chaires.gc.ca/chairholders-titulaires/profile-eng.aspx?profileID=2350

Vaillant, G. E. (1977) *Adaptation to life*. Boston: Little, Brown.

Vaillant, G. E. (2002). *Aging well*. Boston: Little, Brown.

Valiakalayil, A., Paulson, L. A., & Tibbo, P. (2004). Burden in adolescent children of parents with schizophrenia: The Edmonton High Risk Project. *Social Psychiatry and Psychiatric Epidemiology, 39*, 528–535.

Valkenburg, P., & Peter, J. (2007). Who visits online dating sites? Exploring some characteristics of online daters. *CyberPsychology & Behavior, 10*(6), 849–852.

Vallotton, C. D., & Fischer, K. W. (2008). Cognitive development. In M. M. Haith & J. B. Benson (Eds.), *Encyclopedia of infancy and early childhood*. Oxford, UK: Elsevier

Van Buren, E., & Graham, S. (2003). *Redefining ethnic identity: Its relationship to positive and negative school adjustment outcomes for minority youth*. Paper presented at the meeting of the Society for Research in Child Development, Tampa.

van de Weijer-Bergsma, E., Wijnroks, L., & Jongmans, M. J. (2008). Attention development in infants and preschool children born preterm: A review. *Infant Behavior and Development*.

van den Berg, P., Neumark-Sztainer, D., Hannan, P. J., & Haines, J. (2007). Is dieting advice from magazines helpful or harmful? Five-year associations with weight-control behaviors and psychological outcomes in adolescents. *Pediatrics, 119*, e30–e37.

Van Egeren, L. A., & Hawkins, D. P. (2004). Coming to terms with coparenting: Implications of definition and measurement. *Journal of Adult Development, 11*, 165–178.

Van Hof, P., van der Kamp, J., & Savelsbergh, G. J. (2008). The relation between infants' perception of catchableness and the control of catching. *Developmental Psychology, 44*, 182–194.

van Hooren, S. A., Valentijn, S. A., Bosma, H., Ponds, R. W., van Boxtel, M. P., & Jolles, J. (2005). Relation between health status and cognitive functioning: A 6-year follow-up of the Maastricht Aging Study. *Journals of Gerontology B: Psychological Sciences and Social Sciences, 60*, 57–60.

van IJzendoorn, M. H., & Kroonenberg, P. M. (1988). Crosscultural patterns of attachment: A meta-analysis of the Strange Situation. *Child Development, 59*, 147–156.

van IJzendoorn, M. H., & Sagi-Schwartz, A. (2009). Cross-cultural patterns of attachment: Universal and contextual dimensions. In J. Cassidy & P. R. Shaver (Eds.), *Handbook of attachment* (2nd ed.). New York: Guilford.

van Praag, H. (2009). Exercise and the brain: Something to chew on. *Trends in Neuroscience, 32*(5), 990–998.

Van Remmen, H., & Jones, D. P. (2009). Current thoughts on the role of mitochondria and free radicals in the biology of aging. *Journals of Gerontology Series A: Biological Sciences and Medical Services, 64*(2), 171–174.

van Solinge, H., & Henkens, K. (2005). Couples' adjustment to retirement: A multiactor panel study. *Journals of Gerontology B:*

Psychological Sciences and Social Sciences, 60, S11–S20.

van Wormer, K., & McKinney, R. (2003). What schools can do to help gay/lesbian/bisexual youth. A harm reduction approach. *Adolescence, 38,* 409–420.

Vanier Institute. (2010). *Families count: Profiling Canada's families.* Retrieved from http://www.vanierinstitute.ca/include/get.php?nodeid=1907

Vanier Institute. (2012). *Transition: Family roles and responsibilities.* Retrieved from http://www.vanierinstitute.ca/include/get.php?nodeid=2231

Vanpee, D., & Swine, C. (2004). Scale of levels of care versus DNR orders. *Journal of Medical Ethics, 30,* 351–352.

Vasdev, G. (2008). *Obstetric anesthesia.* Oxford, UK: Elsevier.

Vasunilashorn, S., & Crimmins, E. M. (2009). Aging. In D. Carr (Ed.), *Encyclopedia of the life course and human development.* Boston: Gale Cengage.

Vaughn Van Hecke, A., Mundy, P. C., Acra, C. F., Block, J. J., Delgado, E. F., Paralde, M. V., et al. (2007). Infant joint attention, temperament, and social competence in preschool children. *Child Development, 78,* 53–69.

Vazsonyi, A. T., & Huang, L. (2010). Where self-control comes from: On the development of self-control and its relationship to deviance over time. *Developmental Psychology, 46,* 245–257.

Veenhof, B., & Timusk, P. (2009). Online activities of Canadian boomers and seniors. *Canadian Social Trends, 88*(Winter), 26–33.

Veenstra, A., Lindenberg, S., Munniksma, A., & Dijkstra, J. K. (2010). The complex relationship between bullying, victimization, acceptance, and rejection: Giving special attention status, affection, and sex differences. *Social Development, 19,* 480–486.

Vellas, B., & Aisen, P. S. (2010). Editorial: Early Alzheimer's trials: New developments. *Journal of Nutrition, Health, and Aging, 14,* 293.

Vellutino, F. R., Scanlon, D. M., Small, S., & Fanuele, D. P. (2006). Response to intervention as a vehicle for distinguishing between children with and without reading disabilities: Evidence for the role of kindergarten and first-grade interventions. *Journal of Learning Disabilities, 39*(2), 157–169.

Vemuri, P., et al. (2010). Effects of apolipoprotein E on biomarkers of amyloid load and neuronal pathology in Alzheimer disease. *Annals of Neurology* (Vol. 67). Palo Alto, CA: Annual Reviews.

Vendittelli, F., Riviere, O., Crenn-Herbert, C., Rozan, M.A., Maria, B., Jacquetin, B., & the AUDIPOG Sentinel Network. (2008). Is a breech presentation at term more frequent in women with a history of caesarean delivery? *American Journal of Obstetrics and Gynecology, 198,* e1–e6.

Venners, S. A., Wang, X., Chen, C., Wang, L., Chen, D., Guang, W., et al. (2004). Paternal smoking and pregnancy loss: A prospective study using a biomarker of pregnancy. *American Journal of Epidemiology, 159,* 993–1001.

Ventura, A. K., Gromis, J. C., & Lohse, B. (2010) Feeding practice and styles used by a diverse sample of low-income parents of preschool-age children. *Journal of Nutrition Education and Behavior, 42*(4), 242–249.

Venturelli, M., Lanza, M., Muti, E., & Schena, F. (2010). Positive effects of physical training in activity of daily living—dependent older adults. *Experimental Aging Research, 36,* 190–205.

Verhaak, C. M., Linsten, A. M., Evers, A. W., & Braat, D. D. (2010). Who is at risk of emotional problems and how do you know? Screening of women going for IVF treatment. *Human Reproduction, 25*(5), 1234–1240.

Vermeersch, H., T'Sjoen, G., Kaufman, J.M., & Vincke, J. (2008). The role of testosterone in aggressive and non-aggressive risk-taking in boys. *Hormones and Behavior, 53,* 463–471.

Verster, J. C., van Duin, D., Volkerts, E. R., Schreueder, A. H., & Verbaten, M. N. (2003). Alcohol hangover effects on memory functioning and vigilance performance after an evening of binge drinking. *Neuropsychopharmacology, 28,* 740–746.

Vézina, M., & Turcotte, M. (2010). Caring for a parent who lives far away: The consequences. *Canadian Social Trends, 89*(Summer), 3–13.

Vézina, M., & Turcotte, M. (2009, Winter). Forty-year-old mothers of pre-school children: A profile. *Canadian Social Trends, 88,* 34–45.

Victor, E., Kellough, R. D., & Tai, R. H. (2008). *Science education* (11th ed.). Upper Saddle River, NJ: Prentice Hall.

Vidal, F. (2000). Piaget's theory. In A. Kazdin (Ed.), *Encyclopedia of psychology.* Washington, DC: American Psychological Association and Oxford University Press.

Vieno, A., Nation, M., Pastore, M., & Santinello, M. (2009). Parenting and antisocial behaviour: A model of the relationship between adolescents self-disclosure, parental closeness, parental control, and adolescent antisocial behaviour. *Developmental Psychology, 45,* 1509–1519.

Viken, M., Sollid, H., Joner, G., Dahl-Jorgensen, K., Ronningen, K., Undlien, D., et al. (2007). Polymorphisms in the cathepsin L2 (CTSL2) gene show association with type 1 diabetes and early onset myasthenia gravis. *Human Immunology, 68*(9), 748–755.

Villegas, R., Gao, Y. T., Yang, G., Li, H. L., Elasy, T., Zheng, W., & Shu, X. O. (2008). Duration of breast-feeding and the incidence of type 2 diabetes mellitus in the Shanghai Women's Health Study. *Diabetologia, 51*(2), 258–266.

Vitaro, F., Pedersen, S., & Brendgen, M. (2007). Children's disruptiveness, peer rejection, friends' deviancy, and delinquent behaviors: A process-oriented approach. *Development and Psychopathology, 19,* 433–453.

Voelcker-Rehage, C., Godde, B., & Staudinger, E. M. (2010). Physical and motor fitness are both related to cognition in old age. *European Journal of Neuroscience, 31,* 167–176.

Vogel, L. (2011). Advance directives: Obstacles in preparing for the worst. *Canadian Medical Association Journal, 183*(1), E39–E40.

Volberg, R., Gupta, R., Griffiths, M., Olason, D., & Delfabbro, P. (2010). An international perspective on youth gambling prevalence studies. *International Journal of Adolescent Medicine and Health, 22*(1), 3–38.

Von Beveren, T. T. (1999). Prenatal development and the newborn. Unpublished manuscript, University of Texas at Dallas, Richardson.

von Tilburg, T. (2009). Social integration/isolation, later life. In D. Carr (Ed.), *Encyclopedia of the life course and human development.* Boston: Gale Cengage.

Voorpostel, M., & Blieszner, R. (2008). Intergenerational solidarity and support between adult siblings. *Journal of Marriage and the Family, 70,* 157–167.

Votruba-Drzal, E., Coley, R. L., & Chase-Lansdale, P. L. (2004). Child care and low-income children's development: Direct and moderated effects. *Child Development, 75,* 296–312.

Vouloumanos, A., & Werker, J. F. (2004). Tuned to the signal: The privileged status of speech for young infants. *Developmental Science, 7,* 270–276.

Vreeman, R. C., & Carroll, A. E. (2007). A systematic review of school-based interventions to prevent bullying. *Archives of Pediatric and Adolescent Medicine, 161,* 78–88.

Vurpillot, E. (1968). The development of scanning strategies and their relation to visual differentiation. *Journal of Experimental Child Psychology, 6*

Vygotsky, L. S. (1962). *Thought and language.* Cambridge, MA: MIT Press.

W

Wachs, T. D. (1994). Fit, context and the transition between temperament and personality. In C. Halverson, G. Kohnstamm, & R. Martin (Eds.), *The developing structure of personality from infancy to adulthood.* Hillsdale, NJ: Erlbaum.

Wachs, T. D. (2000). *Necessary but not sufficient.* Washington, DC: American Psychological Association.

Wade, C., Tavris, C., Saucier, D. M., & Elias, L. J. (2007). *Psychology* (2nd Canadian ed.). Toronto: Prentice Hall.

Waite, L. (2005, June). *The case for marriage.* Paper presented at the 9th annual Smart Marriages conference, Dallas.

Waite, L. J., Das, A., & Laumann, E. O. (2009). Sexual activity, later life. In D. Carr (Ed.), *Encyclopedia of the life course and human development.* Boston: Gale Cengage.

Waite, L. J., Laumann, E. O., Das, A., & Schumm, L. P. (2009). Sexuality: Measures of partnerships, practices, attitudes, and problems in the National Social Life, Health, and Aging Project. *The Journals of Gerontology: Psychological Sciences and Social Sciences, 64B* (Suppl. 1), S56–S66.

Wakai, K., Marugame, T., Kuriyama, S., Sobue, T., Tamakoshi, A., Satoh, H., et al. (2007). Decrease in risk of lung cancer death in Japanese men after smoking cessation by age at quitting: Pooled analysis of three large-scale cohort studies. *Cancer Science, 98,* 584–589.

Waldron, J., & Dieser, R. (2010). Perspectives of fitness and health in college men and women. *Journal of College Student Development, 51,* 65–78.

Walker, L. J. (2004). Progress and prospects in the psychology of moral development. *Merrill-Palmer Quarterly, 50,* 546–557.

Walker, L. J. (2006). Gender and morality. In M. Killen & J. G. Smetana (Eds.), *Handbook of moral development.* Mahwah, NJ: Erlbaum.

Walker, L. J., & Frimer, J. A. (2009a). "The song remains the same": Rebuttal to Sherblom's re-envisioning of the legacy of the care challenge. *Journal of Moral Education, 38,* 53–68.

Walker, L. J., & Frimer, J. A. (2009b). Moral personality exemplified. In D. Narvaez & D. K. Lapsley (Eds.), *Moral personality, identity and character: An interdisciplinary future.* New York: Cambridge University Press.

Walker, L. J., & Frimer, J. A. (2011). The science of moral development. In M. K. Underwood & L. H. Rosen (Eds.), *Social development.* New York: Guilford.

Walker, L. J., Frimer, J. A., & Dunlop, W. L. (2010). Varieties of moral personality: Beyond the banality of heroism. *Journal of Personality, 78*(3), 907–942.

Wallace-Bell, M. (2003). The effects of passive smoking on adult and child health. *Professional Nurse, 19,* 217–219.

Wallerstein, J. S. (2008). Divorce. In M. M. Haith & J. B. Benson (Eds.), *Encyclopedia of infancy and early childhood.* Oxford, UK: Elsevier.

Walsh, H. C. (2008). Caring for bereaved people 2: Nursing management. *Nursing Times, 104,* 32–33.

Walsh, L. V. (2006). Beliefs and rituals in traditional birth attendant practice in Guatemala. *Journal of Transcultural Nursing, 17,* 148–154.

Walsh, T. J., Pora, R. R., & Turek, P. J. (2009). The genetics of male infertility. *Seminars in Reproductive Medicine, 27,* 124–136.

Walston, J. D., et al. (2009). Inflammation and stress-related candidate genes, plasma interleukin-6 levels, and longevity in older adults. *Experimental Gerontology, 44,* 319–324.

Walter, T. (2005). Three ways to arrange a funeral: Mortuary variation in the modern West. *Mortality, 10*(3), 173–192.

Walters, M. W., Boggs, K. M., Ludington-Hoe, S., & Price, K. M. (2007). Kangaroo care at birth for full term infants: A pilot study. *MCN, The American Journal of Maternal Child Nursing, 32,* 375–381.

Wang, L., Goldstein, F. C., Veledar, E., Levey, A. I., Lah, J. J., Meltzer, C. C., et al. (2009). Alterations in cortical thickness and white matter integrity in mild cognitive impairment measured by whole-brain cortical thickness mapping and diffusion tensor imaging. *American Journal of Neuroradiology, 30,* 893–899.

Wang, S., Baillargeon, R., & Brueckner, L. (2004). Young infants' reasoning about hidden objects: Evidence from violation-of-expectation tasks with test trials only. *Cognition, 93,* 167–198.

Wang, X., Liang, X. B., Li, F. Q., Zhou, H. F., Liu, X. Y., Wang, J. J., et al. (2008). Therapeutic strategies for Parkinson's disease. *Neurochemical Research, 33*(10), 1956-1963.

Ward, L. M., & Friedman, K. (2006). Using TV as a guide: Associations between television viewing and adolescents' sexual attitudes and behavior. *Journal of Research on Adolescence, 16,* 133–156.

Ward, W. F., Qi, W., Van Remmen, H., Zackert, W. E., Roberts, L. J., & Richardson, A. (2005). Effects of age and caloric restriction on lipid peroxidation: Measurement of oxidative stress by F-isoprostane levels. *Journals of Gerontology A: Biological Sciences and Medical Sciences, 60,* 847–851.

Ward-Griffin, C., Oudshoorn, A., Clark, K., & Bol, N. (2007). Mother-adult daughter relationship within dementia care: A critical analysis. *Journal of Family Nursing, 13,* 13–32.

Wardlaw, G. M., & Hampl, J. (2007). *Perspectives in nutrition* (7th ed.). New York: McGraw-Hill.

Wardlaw, G. M., & Smith, A. M. (2009). *Contemporary nutrition* (7th ed.). New York: McGraw-Hill.

Wardlaw, G. M., & Smith, A. M. (2011). *Contemporary nutrition* (8th ed.). New York: McGraw-Hill.

Wark, G. R., & Krebs, D. L. (2000). The construction of moral dilemmas in everyday life. *Journal of Moral Education, 29,* 5–21.

Warr, P. (2004). Work, well-being, and mental health. In J. Baring, E. K. Kelloway, & M. R. Frone (Eds.), *Handbook of work stress.* Thousand Oaks, CA: Sage.

Warren, M. P. (2007). Historical perspectives on postmenopausal hormone therapy: Defining the right dose and duration. *Mayo Clinic Proceedings, 82,* 219–226.

Waters, E., & Beauchaine, T. P. (2003). Are there really patterns of attachment? Comment on Fraley and Spieker (2003). *Developmental Psychology, 39,* 417–422.

Watkins, N., Larson, R., & Sullivan, P. (2008). Learning to bridge difference: Community youth programs as contexts for developing multicultural competencies. *American Behavioral Scientist, 51,* 380–402.

Watson, D. L., & Tharp, R. G. (2007). *Self-directed behavior* (9th ed.). Belmont, CA: Wadsworth.

Watson, J. A., Randolph, S. M., & Lyons, J. L. (2005). African-American grandmothers as health educators in the family. *International Journal of Aging and Human Development, 60,* 343–356.

Watson, J. B. (1928). *Psychological care of infant and child.* New York: W. W. Norton.

Way, N., Santos, C., Niwa, E. Y., & Kim-Gervy, C. (2008). To be or not to be: An exploration of ethnic identity development in context. In M. Asmitia, M. Syed, & K. Radmacher (Eds.), *The intersections of personal and social identities. New Directions for Child and Adolescent Development, 120,* 61–79.

Webb, J. T., Gore, J. L., Mend, E. R., & DeVries, A. R. (2007). *A parent's guide to gifted children.* Scottsdale, AZ: Great Potential Press.

Webber, S. C., Porter, M. M., & Menec, V. H. (2010). Mobility in older adults: A comprehensive framework. *Gerontologist, 50*(4), 443–450.

Weinfield, N. S., Sroufe, L. A., Egeland, B., & Carlson, E. (2009). Individual differences in infant-caregiver attachment: Conceptual and empirical aspects of security. In J. Cassidy & P. R. Shaver (Eds.), *Handbook of attachment* (2nd ed.). New York: Guilford.

Weis, K., & Sternberg, R. J. (2008). The nature of love. In S. F. Davis & W. Buskist (Eds.), *21st century psychology: A reference handbook* (Vol. 2). Thousand Oaks, CA: Sage.

Weiss, R. (1973). *Loneliness: The experience of emotional and social isolation.* Cambridge, MA: MIT Press.

Weissglas-Volkov, D., & Pajukanta, P. (2010). Genetic causes of high and low serum HDL-cholesterol. *Journal of Lipid Research, 51*(8), 2032–2057.

Weisz, A. N., & Black, B. M. (2002). Gender and moral reasoning: African American youth respond to dating dilemmas. *Journal of Human Behavior in the Social Environment, 5,* 35–52.

Wekerle, C., & Tanaka, M. (2010). Adolescent dating violence research and violence prevention: An opportunity to support health outcomes. *Journal of Aggression, Maltreatment & Trauma, 19*(6), 681–698.

Wekerle, C., Leung, E., Wall, A. M., Macmillan, H., Boyle, M., Trocme, N., et al. (2009). The contribution of childhood emotional abuse to teen dating violence among child protective services-involved youth. *Child Abuse and Neglect: The International Journal, 33,* 45–58.

Wellman, H. M., Cross, D., & Watson, J. (2001). Meta-analysis of theory-of-mind development: The truth about false belief. *Child Development, 72,* 655–684.

Wellman, H. M., Lopez-Duran, S., Labounty, J., & Hamilton, B. (2008). Infant attention to intentional action predicts preschool theory of mind. *Developmental Psychology, 44,* 618–623.

Weltzin, T., Cornella-Carlson, T., Fitzpatrick, M., Kennington, B., Bean, P., & Jeffries, C. (2012). Treatment issues and outcomes for males with eating disorders. *Eating Disorders: The Journal of Treatment & Prevention, 20,* 444–459.

Weng, X., Odouli, R., & Li, D. K. (2008). Maternal caffeine consumption during pregnancy and the risk of miscarriage: A prospective cohort study. *American Journal of Obstetrics and Gynecology, 198*(3), 279-e1.

Wengreen, H. J., et al. (2007). Antioxidant intake and cognitive function of elderly men and women: The Cache County Study. *Journal of Nutrition, Health, and Aging, 11,* 230–237.

Wentzel, K. R., & Asher, S. R. (1995). The academic lives of neglected, rejected, popular, and controversial children. *Child Development, 66,* 754–763.

Wermter, A. K., et al. (2010). From nature versus nurture, via nature and nurture, to gene x environment interaction in mental disorders. *European Journal of Child and Adolescent Psychiatry, 19,* 199–210.

Westlake, C., Evangelista, L. S., Stromberg, A., Ter-Galstanyan, A., Vazirani, S., & Dracup, K. (2007). Evaluation of a web-based education and counseling pilot for older heart failure patients. *Progress in Cardiovascular Nursing, 22,* 20–26.

Weston, K. (2007). Exiles from kinship. In S. J. Ferguson (Ed.), *Shifting the center: Understanding contemporary families* (3rd ed.). New York: McGraw-Hill.

Weston, M. J. (2010). Magnetic resonance imaging in fetal medicine: A pictorial review of current and developing indications. *Postgraduate Medicine Journal, 86,* 42–51.

Wethington, E., Kessler, R. C., & Pixley, J. E. (2004). Turning points in adulthood. In O. G. Brim, C. D. Ryff, & R. C. Kessler (Eds.), *How healthy are we?* Chicago: University of Chicago Press.

Wexler, B. E. (2006). *Brain and culture: Neurology, ideology, and social change.* Massachusetts: Bradford Books and M.I.T. Press.

Whaley, S., Sigman, M., Beckwith, L., Cohen, S., & Espinosa, M. (2002). Infant-caregiver interaction in Kenya and the United States: The importance of multiple caregivers and adequate comparison samples. *Journal of Cross-Cultural Psychology, 33*(3), 236–247.

Whayne, T. F. (2009). High-density lipoprotein cholesterol: Current perspectives for clinicians. *Angiology, 60,* 644–649.

Wheeler, M. (2008). Braving the no-go zone: Canada's sub-replacement fertility rate. *Transition 38*(4), 3–8.

Whincup, P. H., Papacosta, O., Lennon, L., & Haines, A. (2006). Carboxyhemoglobin levels and their determinants in older British men. *BMC Public Health, 18,* 189.

Whipple, N., Bernier, A., & Mageau, G. A. (2009). Attending to the exploration side of infant attachment: Contributions from self-determination theory. *Canadian Psychology, 50*(4), 219–229.

Whitbourne, S. K., Sneed, J. R., & Sayer, A. (2009). Psychosocial development from college through midlife: A 34-year sequential study. *Developmental Psychology, 45,* 1328–1340.

White, B., Fredrikson, J., & Collins, A. (2010). The interplay of scientific inquiry and metacognition: More than a marriage of convenience. In D. J. Hacker, J. Dunlosky, & A. C. Graesser (Eds.), *Handbook of metacognition and education.* New York: Psychology Press.

White, C. D., Hardy, J. R., Gilshenan, K. S., Charles, M. A., & Pinkerton, C. R. (2008). Randomized controlled trials of palliative care—A survey of the views of advanced cancer patients and their relatives. *European Journal of Cancer.*

White, J. W. (2001). Aggression and gender. In J. Worell (Ed.), *Encyclopedia of gender and women.* San Diego: Academic Press.

White, R., Wyn, J., & Albanese, P. (2011). *Youth and society: Exploring the social dynamics of youth experience* (Canadian ed). Don Mills: Oxford University Press.

Whitehead, K., Ainsworth, A., Wittig, M., & Gadino, B. (2009). Implications of ethnic identity exploration and ethnic identity affirmation and belonging for intergroup attitudes among adolescents. *Journal of Research on Adolescence, 19,* 123–135.

Whitelaw, N. C., & Whitelaw, E. (2006). How lifetimes shape epigenotype within and across generations. *Human Molecular Genetics, 15,* R131–R137.

Whitley, B. E. (2002). *Principles of research in behavioral science* (2nd ed.). New York: McGraw-Hill.

Whiting, P. (2007). Student mental health at Simon Fraser University. *Visions: BC's Mental Health and Addiction Journal, 4*(3), 10–11.

Wider, C., Foroud, T., & Wszolek, Z. K. (2010). Clinical implications of gene discovery in Parkinson's disease and parkinsonism. *Movement Disorders, 25* (Suppl. 1), S15–S20.

Wiener, J., & Siegel, L. (2010). A Canadian perspective on learning disabilities. *Journal of Learning Disabilities.* Retrieved from http://ldx.sagepub.com/content/25/6/340

Wiersman, W., & Jurs, S. G. (2009). *Research methods in education* (9th ed.). Upper Saddle River, NJ: Prentice Hall.

Wigle, D. T., Arbuckle, T. E., Turner, M. C., Berube, A., Yang, Q., Liu, S. (2008). Epidemiologic evidence of relationships between reproductive and child health outcomes and environmental chemical contaminants. *Journal of Toxicology and Environmental Health, Part B, 11,* 373–517.

Wijngaards-de Meij, L., Stroebe, M., Schut, H., Stroebe, W., van den Bout, J., van der Heijden, P. G., et al. (2008). Parents grieving the loss of their child: Interdependence in coping. *British Journal of Clinical Psychology, 47,* 31–42.

Wilkins, K. (2006). Predictors of death in seniors. *Health Reports, 16*(1), 57–67.

Wilkinson, D., & McCargar, L. (2008, May). Prevention of overweight and obesity in young children, a CCFN watching brief. Canadian Council of Food and Nutrition. Retrieved from http://www.cfdr.ca/

Willcox, B. J., Willcox, M. D., & Suzuki, M. (2002). *The Okinawa Program.* New York: Crown.

Willcox, D. C., Willcox, B. J., He, Q., Wang, N. C., & Suzuki, M. (2008). They really are that old: A validation study of centenarian prevalence in Okinawa. *Journals of Gerontology A: Biological Sciences and Medical Sciences, 63,* 338–349.

Willcox, D. C., Willcox, B. J., Sokolovsky, J., & Sakihara, S. (2007). The cultural context of "successful aging" among older women weavers in a Northern Okinawan village: The role of productive activity. *Journal of Cross Cultural Gerontology, 22,* 137–165.

Willey, J., Sherwood, L., & Woolverton, C. (2011). *Prescott's microbiology* (8th ed.). New York: McGraw-Hill.

Williams, A., Franche, R. L., Ibrahim, S., Mustard, C. A., & Layton, F. R. (2006). Examining the relationhip between work-family spillover and sleep quality. *Journal of Occupational Health Psychology, 1,* 27–37.

Williams, D. R., & Sternthal, M. J. (2007). Spirituality, religion, and health: Evidence and research directions. *Medical Journal of Australia, 186* (Suppl.), S47–S50.

Williams, J. H., & Ross, L. (2007). Consequences of prenatal toxin exposure for mental health in children and adolescents: A systematic review. *European Child and Adolescent Psychiatry, 16,* 243–253.

Williams, L., et al. (2010). Early temperament, propensity for risk-taking and adolescence substance-related problems. *Addictive Behaviors, 35,* 1148–1151.

Williams, M. H. (2005). *Nutrition for health, fitness, and sport* (7th ed.). New York: McGraw-Hill.

Williams, P., & Fletcher, S. (2010). Health effects of prenatal radiation exposure. *American Family Physician, 82*(5), 488–493.

Williamson, J. D., et al. (2009). Changes in cognitive function in a randomized trial of physical activity: Results of the Lifestyle Interventions and Independence for Elders Pilot Study. *Journals of Gerontology A: Biological Sciences and Medical Sciences, 64,* 688–694.

Willis, C. (2002). The grieving process in children: Strategies for understanding, educating, and reconciling children's perceptions of death. *Early Childhood Education Journal, 29,* 221–226.

Willis, S. L. & Martin, M. (2005). Preface. In S. L. Willis & M. Martin (Eds.), *Middle adulthood.* Thousand Oaks, CA: Sage.

Willis, S. L., & Schaie, K. W. (1999). Intellectual functioning in midlife. In S. L. Willis & J. D. Reid (Eds.), *Life in the middle: Psychological and social development in middle age.* San Diego: Academic Press.

Willis, S. L., & Schaie, K. W. (2005). Cognitive trajectories in midlife and cognitive functioning in old age. In S. L. Willis & M. Martin (Eds.), *Middle adulthood.* Thousand Oaks, CA: Sage.

Willis, S. L., & Schaie, K. W. (2006). A co-constructionist view of the third age: The case of cognition. *Annual Review of Gerontology and Geriatrics, 26,* 131–152.

Willis, S. L., Schaie, K. W., & Martin, M. (2009). Cognitive plasticity. In V. L. Bengtson, D. Gans, N. M. Putney, & M. Silverstein (Eds.), *Handbook of theories of aging* (2nd ed.). New York: Springer.

Willis, S. L., Temstedt, S. L., Marsiske, M., Ball, K., Elias, J., Koepke, K. M., et al. for the ACTIVE Study Group. (2006). Long-term effects of cognitive training on everyday functional outcomes in older adults. *Journal of the American Medical Association, 296,* 2805–2814.

Willms, J. D. (2002). Implications of the findings for social policy renewal. In D. Willms (Ed.), *Vulnerable children* (pp. 359–377). Edmonton: The University of Alberta Press.

Wilson, A. E., Shuey, K. M., & Elder, G. H. (2003). Ambivalence in relationships of adult children to aging parents and in-laws. *Journal of Marriage and the Family, 65,* 1055–1072.

Wilson, B., & Smallwood, S. (2008). The proportion of marriages ending in divorce. *Population Trends, 131,* 28–36.

Wilson, B. J. (2008). Media and children's aggression, fear, and altruism. *Future of Children, 18*(1), 87–118.

Wilson, K. G., et al. (2007). Desire for euthanasia or physician-assisted suicide in palliative cancer care. *Health Psychology, 26,* 314–323.

Wilson, R. D. (2007, November). Principles of human teratology: Drug, chemical, and infectious exposure. *Journal of Obstetrics and Gynecology of Canada, 199,* 911–917.

Wilson, R. S., et al. (2009). Educational attainment and cognitive decline in old age. *Neurology, 72,* 460–465.

Wilson, R. S., Mendes de Leon, C. F., Barnes, L. L., Schneider, J. A., Bienias, J., Evans, D. A., & Bennett, D. A. (2002). Participation in cognitively stimulating activities and risk of incident Alzheimer disease. *Journal of the American Medical Association, 287,* 742–748.

Wilson, R. S., Mendes de Leon, C. F., Bienas, J. L., Evans, D. A., & Bennett, D. A. (2004). Personality and mortality in old age. *Journal of Gerontology Psychological Sciences and Social Sciences, 59,* P110–P116.

Wing, R., Tate, D. F., Gorin, A. A., Raynor, H. A., Fava, J. L., & Machan, J. (2007). "STOP Regain": Are there negative effects of daily weighing? *Journal of Consulting and Clinical Psychology, 75,* 652–656.

Winner, E. (1996). *Gifted children: Myths and realities.* New York: Basic Books.

Winner, E. (2006). Development in the arts. In W. Damon & R. Lerner (Eds.), *Handbook of child psychology* (6th ed.). New York: Wiley.

Winner, E. (2009). Toward broadening our understanding of giftedness: The spatial domain. In F. D. Horowitz, R. F. Subotnik, & D. J. Matthews (Eds.), *The development of giftedness and talent across the life span.*

Washington, DC: American Psychological Association.

Winning, J., Claus, R., Huse, K. & Bauer, M. (2006). Molecular biology on the ICU. From understanding to treating sepsis. *Minerva Anestesiologica, 72*(5), 255–267.

Winsler, A., Carlton, M. P., & Barry, M. J. (2000). Age-related changes in preschool children's systematic use of private speech in a natural setting. *Journal of Child Language, 27,* 665–687.

Wiseman, H., Mayseless, O., & Sharabany, R. (2006). Why are they lonely? Perceived quality of early relationships with parents, attachment, personality predispositions and loneliness in first year university students. *Personality and Individual Differences, 40,* 237–248.

Wishart, P. M. (2006). Letting go of preconceptions: A novel approach to creating memorial services. *Health Care for Women International, 27*(5), 513–529.

Witte, A. V., Fobker, M., Gellner, R., Knecht, S., & Fioel, A. (2009). Caloric restriction improves memory in elderly humans. *Proceedings of the National Academy of Sciences U.S.A., 106,* 1255–1260.

Wittmeier, K. D., Mollard, R. C., & Kriellaars, D. J. (2008). Physical activity intensity and risk of overweight and adiposity in children. *Obesity, 16,* 415–420.

Wivliet, M., et al. (2010). Peer group affiliation in children: The role of perceived popularity, likeability, and behavioral similarity in bullying. *Social Development, 19,* 285–303.

Wofford, L. G. (2008). Systematic review of childhood obesity prevention. *Journal of Pediatric Nursing, 23,* 5–19.

Wolfe, D., et al. (2009). A school-based program to prevent adolescent dating violence. *Archives of Pediatrics & Adolescent Medicine, 163,* 692–699.

Wolkowitz, O. M., Epel, E. S., Reus, V. I., & Mellon, S. H. (2010). Depression gets old fast: Do stress and depression accelerate cell aging? *Depression and Anxiety, 27,* 327–338.

Woloski-Wruble, A. C., Oliel, Y., Leefsman, M., & Hochner-Celnikier, C. (2010). Sexual activities, sexual and life satisfaction, and successful aging in women. *Journal of Sexual Medicine, 7*(7), 2401–2410.

Wong, D. L. (2006). *Maternal child nursing and virtual clinical excursions: 3.0 package* (3rd ed.). St. Louis: Mosby.

Wong, D., Hockenberry, M., Wilson, D., Perry, S., & Lowdermilk, D. (2006). *Maternal child nursing care* (3rd ed) St. Louis: Mosby Elsevier.

Wong, S., Ordean, A., & Kahan, M. (2011). Substance use in pregnancy. *Journal of Obstetrics and Gynaecology Canada, 33*(4), 367–384.

Wood, J., Chaparro, A., Carberry, T., & Chu, B. S. (2010). Effect of simulated visual impairment on nighttime driving performance. *Optometry and Vision Science.*

Wood, M. D., Read, J. P., Mitchell, R. E., & Brand, N. H. (2004). Do parents still

matter? Parent and peer influences on alcohol involvement among recent high school graduates. *Psychology of Addictive Behaviors, 18,* 19–30.

Woodgate, R. (2006). Living in the shadow of fear: Adolescents' lived experience of depression. *Journal of Advanced Nursing, 56*(3), 261–269.

Woodgate, R., Edwards, M., & Ripat, J. (2012). How families of children with complex care needs participate in everyday life. *Social Sciences & Medicine, 75,* 1912–1920.

Woodward, A. L., & Markman, E. M. (1998). Early word learning. In D. Kuhn & R. S. Siegler (Eds.), *Handbook of child psychology* (5th ed., Vol. 2). New York: Wiley.

World Health Organization (WHO). (2005). Alcohol use and sexual risk behaviour: A cross-cultural study in eight countries (WHO, Geneva). Retrieved from www.who.int/substance_abuse/publications/alcohol_sexual_risk_crosscultural.pdf

World Health Organization (WHO). 2006. Child maltreatment and alcohol. Retrieved from http://www.who.int/violence_injury_prevention/violence/world_report/factsheets/fs_child.pdf

World Health Organization (WHO). (2008a). What are the key health indicators for children? Retrieved from http://www.who.int/features/qa/13/en/print.html

World Health Organization (WHO). (2008b). Preventable injuries kill 2000 children every day. Retrieved from http://www.who.int/mediacentre/news/release/2008/pr46/en/index.html

World Health Organization (WHO). (2009). *World health statistics, 2009.* Geneva, Switzerland: Author.

World Health Organization (WHO). (2010). *Global strategy to reduce the harmful use of alcohol.* Retrieved from http://www.who.int/substance_abuse

World Health Organization (WHO). (2012b). *Preventing early unwanted pregnancy & pregnancy-related mortality & morbidity in adolescents.* Retrieved from http://www.gfmer.ch/SRH-Course-2012/adolescent-health/Adolescent-pregnancy-WHO-2012

Wortman, C. B., & Boerner, K. (2007). Reactions to death of a loved one: Beyond the myths of coping with loss. In H. S. Friedman & R. C. Silver (Eds.), *Foundations of health psychology.* New York: Oxford University Press.

Wright, J., Briggs, S., & Behringer, J. (2005). Attachment and the body in suicidal adolescents: A pilot study. *Clinical Child Psychology and Psychiatry, 10*(4), 477–491.

Wright, L., & Leahey, M. (2013). *Nurses and families: A guide to family assessment and intervention* (6th ed.). Philadelphia: Davis.

Wright, S. (2013). Start with why: the power of student driven learning. Wright's Room.

Retrieved on October 2, 2013 from http://shelleywright.wordpress.com

Wright S. (n.d.). "The power of student driven learning." TED.com. Retrieved on October 2, 2013 from https://www.youtube.com/watch?v=3fMC-z7K0r4&feature=player_embedded#t=12

Wu, L. T., Pilowsky, D. J., Schlenger, W. E., & Hasin, D. (2007). Alcohol use disorders and the use of treatment services among college-age young adults. *Psychiatric Services, 58,* 192–200.

Wu, Y. H., Cheng, M. L., Ho, H. Y., Chiu, D. T., & Wang, T. C. (2009). Telomerase prevents accelerated senescence in glucose-6-phosphate dehydrogenase (G6PD)-deficient human fibroblasts. *Journal of Biomedical Science, 16,* 18.

Wyn, R., & Peckham, E. (2010). Health and health care access among California women ages 50–64. Policy Brief: UCLA Center for Health Policy Research (PB 2010–1), 1–8.

X

Xie, J., Matthews, F. E., Jagger, C., Bond, J., & Brayne, C. (2008). The oldest old in England and Wales: A descriptive analysis based on the MRC Cognitive Function and Aging Study. *Age and Aging, 37*(4), 396–402.

Xiong, G., & Doraiswamy, P. M. (2005). Combination drug therapy for Alzheimer's disease: What is evidence-based, and what is not? *Geriatrics, 60,* 22–26.

Xu, F., & Baker, A. (2005). Object individuation in 10-month-old infants using a simplified manual search method. *Journal of Cognition and Development, 6*(3), 307–323.

Xu, Q., Parks, C. G., Deroo, L. A., Cawthon, R. M., Sandler, D. P., & Chen, H. (2009). Multivitamin use and telomere length in women. *American Journal of Clinical Nutrition, 89,* 1857–1863.

Xu, X., Hudspeth, C. D., & Bartkowski, J. P. (2006). The role of cohabitation in remarriage. *Journal of Marriage and the Family, 68,* 261–274.

Y

Yamamoto, M., & Schapira, A. H. (2008). Dopamine agonists against Parkinson's disease. *Expert Review of Neurotherapy, 8,* 671–677.

Yang, Q., Wen, S. W., Leader, A., Chen, X. K., Lipson, J. & Walker, M. (2007). Paternal age and birth defects: How strong is the association. *Human Reproduction, 22,* 696–701.

Yang, Y. (2008). Social inequalities in happiness in the United States, 1972–2004: An age-period-cohort analysis. *American Sociological Review, 73,* 204–226.

Yang, Y., & Lee, L. C. (2010). Dynamics and heterogeneity in the process of human frailty and aging: Evidence from the U.S. older

adult population. *Journals of Gerontology B: Psychological Sciences and Social Sciences, 65B,* 246–255.

Yassine, H. N., Marchetti, C. M., Krishna, R. K., Vrobel, T. R., Gonzalez, F., & Kirwin, J. P. (2009). Effects of exercise and caloric restriction on insulin resistance and cardiometabolic risk factors in older obese adults—A randomized trial. *Journals of Gerontology A: Biological Sciences and Medical Sciences, 64,* 90–95.

Yates, L. B., Djuousse, L., Kurth, T., Buring, J. E., & Gaziano, J. M. (2008). Exceptional longevity in men: Modifiable factors associated with survival and function to age 90 years. *Archives of Internal Medicine, 168,* 284–290.

Yen, S., & Martin, S. (2013). Contraception for adolescents. *Pediatric Annals, 42*(2), 21–25.

Yetukuri, L., et al. (2010, in press). Composition and lipid spatial distribution of high density lipoprotein particles in subjects with low and high HDL-cholesterol. *Journal of Lipid Research, 51*(8), 2341–2351.

Yoo, H. J., Choi, K. M., Ryu, O. H., Suh, S. I., Kim, N. H., Baik, S. H., et al. (2006). Delayed puberty due to pituitary stalk dysgenesis and ectopic neurophyophysis. *Korean Journal of Internal Medicine, 21,* 68–72.

Yoo, H., Feng, X., & Day, R. (2013). Adolescents' empathy and prosocial behavior in the family context: A longitudinal study. *Journal of Youth and Adolescence,* doi 10.1007/sd10964-012.9900-6.

Yoon, C., Cole, C. A., & Lee, M. P. (2009). Consumer decision making and aging: Current knowledge and future directions. *Journal of Consumer Psychology, 19,* 2–16.

Yoon, D. P., & Lee, E. K. (2007). The impact of religiousness, spirituality, and social support on psychological well-being among older adults in rural areas. *Journal of Gerontological Social Work, 48,* 281–298.

Young, G. (2011). *Development and causality.* Springer; New York.

Young, K. T. (1990). American conceptions of infant development from 1955 to 1984: What the experts are telling parents. *Child Development, 61,* 17–28.

Youniss, J., McLellan, J. A., & Yates, M. (1999). Religion, community service, and identity in American youth. *Journal of Adolescence, 22,* 243–253.

Ystad, M., Eichele, T., Lundervold, A. J., & Lundervold, A. (2010). Subcortical functional connectivity and verbal episodic memory in health elderly—A resting state fMRI study. *Neuroimage.*

Yuan, T. F. (2008). GABA effects on neurogenesis: An arsenal of regulation. *Science Signaling, 1,* jcl.

Yun, Y.H., et al. (2011). Attitudes of cancer patients, family caregivers, oncologists and members of the general public towards critical interventions at the end of life of terminally ill patients. *Canadian Medical Association Journal, 183*(10), E673–E679.

Z

Zaborowska, E., et al. (2007). Effects of acupuncture, applied relaxation, estrogens, and placebo on hot flushes in postmenopausal women: An analysis of two prospective, parallel, randomized studies. *Climacteric, 10,* 38–45.

Zaghloul, N. A., & Katsanis, N. (2010). Functional modules, mutational load, and human genetic disease. *Trends in Genetics, 26*(4), 168–176.

Zaitoun, I., Downs, K. M., Rosa, G. J., & Khatib, H. (2010). Upregulation of imprinted genes in mice: An insight into the intensity of gene expression and the evolution of genomic imprinting. *Epigenetics, 5,* 149–158.

Zalc, B. (2006). The acquisition of myelin: A success story. *Novartis Foundation Symposium, 276,* 15–21.

Zeifman, D., & Hazan, C. (2009). Pair bonds as attachments: Reevaluating the evidence. In J. Cassidy & P. R. Shaver (Eds.), *Handbook of attachment* (2nd ed.). New York: Guilford.

Zelazo, P. D., & Müller, U. (2004). Executive function in typical and atypical development. In U. Goswami (Ed.), *Blackwell handbook of cognitive development.* Malden, MA: Blackwell.

Zemach, I., Chang, S., & Teller, D. (2007). Infant color vision: Prediction of infants' spontaneous color preferences. *Vision Res, 47*(10), 1368–1381.

Zentall, S. S. (2006). *ADHD and education.* Upper Saddle River, NJ: Prentice Hall.

Zerwekh, J. (2006). *Nursing care at the end of life.* Philadelphia: Davis.

Zeskind, P. S. (2009). Impact of the cry of the infant at risk on psychosocial development. In R. E. Tremblay, R. deV Peters, M. Boivan, & R. G. Barr (Eds.), *Encyclopedia on Early Childhood Development.* Montreal: Center of Excellence for Early Childhood Development.

Zeskind, P. S., Klein, L., & Marshall, T. R. (1992). Adults perceptions of experimental modifications of durations and expiratory sounds in infant crying. *Developmental Psychology, 28,* 1153–1162.

Zettel-Watson, L., & Rook, K. S. (2009). Friendship, later life. In D. Carr (Ed.), *Encyclopedia of the life course and human development.* Boston: Gale Cengage.

Zhang, L-F., & Sternberg, R. J. (2011). Learning in a cross-cultural perspective. In T. Husen & T. N. Postlewaite (Eds.), *International encyclopedia of education* (3rd ed.). New York: Elsevier.

Zhu, D. C., Zacks, R. T., & Slade, J. M. (2010). Brain activation during interference resolution in young and older adults: An fMRI study. *Neuroimage, 50,* 810–817.

Zimmer-Gembeck, M. J., & Helfand, M. (2008). Ten years of longitudinal research on U. S. adolescent sexual behavior: Developmental correlates of sexual intercourse, and the importance of age, gender, and ethnic background. *Developmental Review, 28,* 153–224.

Zins, J. E. (2004). *Building academic success on social and emotional learning: What does* the research say? New York: Teachers College Press.

Ziol-Guest, K. M. (2009). Child custody and support. In D. Carr (Ed.), *Encyclopedia of the life course and human development.* Boston: Gale Cengage.

Zisook, S., & Kendler, K. S. (2007). Is bereavement-related depression different than non-bereavement-related depression? *Psychological Medicine, 19,* 1–31.

Zittleman, K. (2006, April). *Being a girl and being a boy: The voices of middle schoolers.* Paper presented at the meeting of the American Educational Research Association, San Francisco.

Zitvogel, L., Kepp, O., & Kroemer, G. (2010). Decoding cell death signals in inflammation and immunity. *Cell, 140,* 798–804.

Zosuls, K. M., Lurye, L. E., & Ruble, D. N. (2008). Gender: Awareness, identity, and stereotyping. In M. M. Haith & J. B. Benson (Eds.), *Encyclopedia of infancy and early childhood.* Oxford UK: Elsevier.

Zou, Y., Misri, S., Shay, J. W., Pandita, T. K., & Wright, W. E. (2009). Altered states of telomere deprotection and the two-stage mechanism of replicative aging. *Molecular and Cellular Biology, 29,* 2390–2397.

Zucker, A. N., Ostrove, J. M., & Stewart A. J. (2002). College educated women's personality development in adulthood: Perceptions and age differences. *Psychology and Aging, 17,* 236–244.

Zuckoff, A., Shear, K., Frank, E., Daley, D. C., Seligman, K., & Silowash, R. (2006). Treating complicated grief and substance use disorders: A pilot study. *Journal of Substance Abuse and Treatment, 30,* 205–211.

Zuk, C. V., & Zuk, G. H. (2002). Origins of dreaming. *American Journal of Psychiatry, 159,* 495–496.

Zukerman, P. (2005). Top fifty countries with the largest atheist/agnostic populations. Retrieved from http://www.adherents.com/

Zunzunegui, M., Alvarado, B. E., Del Ser, T., & Vtero, A. (2003). Social networks, social integration, and social engagement determine cognitive decline in community-dwelling Spanish older adults. *Journals of Gerontology B: Psychological Sciences and Social Sciences, 58,* S93–S100.

Credits

Chapter 1

p. 1: © Geri Lavrov/Flickr/Getty Images
p. 2 (bottom): Comstock/PictureQuest
p. 3 (top): Prof. Paul Thompson, Ph. D. UCLA
p. 3 (middle): commons.wikimedia.org/ wiki/File: Brain-anatomy.jpg
p. 3 (bottom): © P. Wei/iStockphoto.com
p. 5: PEANUTS@ United Features Syndicate, Inc.
p. 6 (top): Courtesy of Paul Baltes, Margaret Baltes Foundation
p. 6 (bottom): Walter Hodges/Corbis
p. 7: Mark Pearson/ Getstock
p. 8: CIA Factbook - www.cia.gov/library/publications/ the-world-factbook/fields/2102.html
p. 9: Figure 1.2 Source: Adapted from Statistics Canada, Age Groups (13) and Sex (3) for the Population of Canada, Provinces and Territories, 1921 to 2006 Censuses - 100% Data 97-551-XCB 2006005 Census Year 2006 Released July 17, 2007; Population Projections for Canada, Provinces and Territories 2009 to 2036 91-520-XWE 2010001 2009 to 2036, Released May 26, 2010
p. 11 (left to right): ©Brand X Pictures/PunchStock; ©Digital Vision; ©Laurence Mouton/Photoalto/ PictureQuest; ©Stockbyte; ©GettyImages/SW Productions; ©Blue Moon Stock/Alamy Images; ©Doug Menuez/Getty Images; ©Ryan McVay/Getty Images
p. 13: ©Paul Chiasson/The Canadian Press
p. 15 (left): KAREN PULFER FOCHT/The Commercial Appeal/Landov; (right): Getty Images
p. 16 (bottom): ©Rubberball/PictureQuest
p. 17: Courtesy of Douglas Willms
p. 18: © Max Power/Corbis
p. 19: ©Jose Luis Pelaez, Inc. Corbis
p. 25: ©Digital Vision/Punchstock
p. 30 (left): ©AP Wide World Photos; (right): ©Punchstock/Digital Vision

Chapter 2

p. 36: Bettmann/Corbis
p. 37: © Bettmann/CORBIS
p. 40: © Bettmann/CORBIS
p. 42: © Yves de Braine/Black Star/Stock Photo
p. 44: A.R. Lauria/Dr. Michael Cole, Laboratory of Human Cognition, University of California, San Diego
p. 46: Courtesy Albert Bandura, Stanford University
p. 48 (top): Photo by Nina Leen/Life Magazine. © Time, Inc.; (bottom): Toronto Star/GetStock.com
p. 51: Courtesy of Urie Brofenbrenner
p. 54 (from left): Wikimedia; ©Bettmann Archives; ©Yves de Braine/Black Star/Stock Photo; A.R. Lauria/ Dr. Michael Cole, Laboratory of Human Cognition; ©Bettmann/Corbis; Wikimedia; Courtesy Stanford University News Service; Courtesy of Urie Bronfenbrenner

Chapter 3

p. 59: ©2009 Jupiter Images Corporation
p. 60: ©Tom & Dee Ann McCarthy/Corbis
p. 61: ©1996 Photodisc, Inc.
p. 63 (top): Blend Images/Getty Images; Figure 3.2: Baltes, P.B., Staudinger, U.M., & Lindenberger, U., 1999, "Lifespan Psychology," *Annual Review of Psychology*, 50, p. 474, Figure 1. Reprinted with permission, from the *Annual Review of Psychology*, Volume 50. Copyright © 1999 by Annual Reviews, www.annualreview.org.
p. 65: From, *Psychology*, 7th Edition by John Santrock. Copyright © 2003 The McGraw-Hill Companies. Reproduced with permission of The McGraw-Hill Companies.
p. 66 (top): ©Science Source/Photo Researchers; (bottom): Calvin and Hobbes © 1991 Watterson. Reprinted with permission of University Press Syndicate. All rights reserved.
p. 67: © Custom Medical Stock Photo
p. 68: © James Shaffer/PhotoEdit
p. 73 (Figure 3.8): From *Biology*, 6th Edition by S. Mader. Copyright © 1998 by The McGraw-Hill Companies. Reproduced with permission of The McGraw-Hill Companies; (bottom): Source: Larry Berman
p. 77: ©Peter Foley/epa/Corbis

p. 78 (top): Jack Hollingsworth/Getty Images; (bottom): © Brand X Pictures/PunchStock
p. 79 (from left): CP Photo/Tom Hanson; ©Michael Stuparyk/Getstock.com; Tannis Toohey/Getstock.com

Chapter 4

p. 84: Photo Lennart Nilsson/Albert Bonniers Forlag AB, *A Child is Born*, Dell Publishing Company
p. 85: The Canadian Press
p. 89 (all): Photo Lennart Nilsson/Albert Bonniers Forlag AB, *A Child is Born*, Dell Publishing Company
p. 90: Courtesy of Ann Streissguth
p. 93: Courtesy of Ann Streissguth
p. 98: ©Barbara Penoyar/Getty Images
p. 99: Reprinted with permission from Table S-1, *Weight Gain During Pregnancy: Reexamining the Guidelines,* 2009 by the National Academy of Sciences, Courtesy of the National Academies Press, Washington, D.C.
p. 100: Reproduced with permission from the Minister of Health, 2013
p. 102: © Jonathan Nourok/Getty Images
p. 103: © Corbis/RF
p. 106: ©AP Wide World Photos
p. 107: Courtesy of Dr. Tiffany Field
p. 108: From Virginia A. Apgar, 1975, "A Proposal for a New Method of Evaluation of a Newborn Infant," in *Anesthesia and Analgesia*, Vol. 32, pp. 260-267. Reprinted by permission.
p. 109 (top): © Naomi Bassit/iStockphoto; (bottom): © Marc Asnin/CORBIS SABA

Chapter 5

p. 114: ©Marcus Mok/Asia Images/Corbis
p. 115 (left): ©Plush Studios/Blend Images LLC; (right): © Dave Bartruff/CORBIS
p. 117: From Santrock, *Children*, 9th Edition, Figure 6.1. Copyright © 2007 The McGraw-Hill Companies. Reproduced by permission of The McGraw-Hill Companies.
p. 118 (Figure 5.2): Reprinted by permission of the publisher from *The Postnatal Development of the Human Cerebral Cortex*, Vol. I-VIII by Jesse LeRoy Conel, Cambridge, MA: Harvard University Press, Copyright © 1939-1975 by the President and Fellows of Harvard College.
p. 119 (bottom): Courtesy of Dr. Harry T. Chugani, Children's Hospital of Michigan
p. 121: Reprinted with permission from H.P. Roffwarg, J.N. Muzio and W.C. Dement, 1966, "Ontogenetic Development of the Human Dream Sleep Cycle," *Science*, Vol. 152, no. 3722, pp. 604-609. Copyright © 1966, American Association for the Advancement of Science
p. 124: © Bob Dammrich/The Image Works
p. 125: Courtesy of Esther Thelen
p. 127 (Figure 5.8): Reprinted from *Journal of Pediatric*, Vo. 71W.K. Frankenburg and J.B. Dobbs, "The Denver Develoment Screening Test," pp. 181-191. Copyright ©1967 with permission from Elsevier; (photos, left to right): (left to right) © Barbara Penoyar/Getty Images; © Digital Vision/Getty Images; © Image Source/Alamy; Titus/Getty Images; © Digital Vision; Banana Stock/ PictureQuest; Corbis/PictureQuest; © BrandXPictures/ PunchStock
p. 128: ©Aldo Murillo/iStockphoto
p. 130 (Figure 5.10): ©Kevin Peterson/Getty Images/ Simulation by Vischeck; (Figure 2.11): David Linton
p. 131 (top): © Mark Richards/Photo Edit; (bottom): © Jill Braaten
p. 132: From D. Rosenstein and H. Oster, "Differential Facial Responses to Four Basic Tastes in Newborns," *Child Development*, Vol. 59, 1988. © Society for Research in Child Development, Inc.
p. 136 (top): © Doug Goodman/Photo Researchers; (Figure 5.17): From John Santrock, *Children*, 7th Edition. Copyright © 2003 The McGraw-Hill Companies. Reproduced with permission of The McGraw-Hill Companies.
p. 137: Courtesy of Dr. Carolyn Rovee-Collier
p. 141: ©ABPL Image Library/Animals Animals/ Earth Scenes
p. 143: From Santrock, *Child Development*, 10th Edition, Figure 10.2. Copyright © 2004 The McGraw-Hill

Companies. Reproduced by permission of The McGraw-Hill Companies.
p. 144: Blend Images/Getty Images

Chapter 6

p. 148: Meg Takamina/Getty Images
p. 149: Nancy R. Cohen/Getty Images
p. 151 (top, left to right): © Bananastock/PictureQuest; The McGraw-Hill Companies, Inc./Jill Braaten, photographer; © Getty Images; David Sacks/Getty Images; (middle): © Sybil L. Hart, Texas Tech University; (bottom): © Andy Cox/Stone/Getty Images
p. 153: © The New Yorker Collection 1999 Barbara Smaller from cartoonbank.com. All Rights Reserved.
p. 156-157: Tom Merton /Getty Images
p. 157 (bottom): ©MIXA/Getty Images
p. 159 (Figure 6.3): Digital Vision/Getty Images
p. 162: © Martin Rogers/Stock Boston
p. 163 (Figure 6.6): Adapted from M.D.S. Ainsworth & S.M. Bell, 1971, "Attachment, Exploration, and Separation: Illustrated by the Behavior of One-Year-Olds in a Strange Situation," *Child Development*, Vol. 41, (1), pp. 49-67. Reprinted by permission of Society for Research in Child Development.
p. 164: © Martin Rogers/Stock Boston
p. 166 (Figure 6.7): From van Ijzendoorn & Kroonenberg, 1988, "Cross Cultural Patterns of Attachment," *Child Development*, 59, 147-156. Adapted by permission of the Society for Research in Child Development.
p. 167 (Figure 6.8): From Jay Belsky, " Early Human Experiences: A Family Perspective" in *Developmental Psychology*, Vol. 17, pp. 3-23. Copyright © 1981 by the American Psychological Association. Reprinted with permission.
p. 170 (Figure 6.9): Statistics Canada, Canadian Social Trends 11-008-XIE 2003003 Winter 2003, no. 71 Released December 9, 2003
p. 171 (Figure 6.10): From John Santrock, *Children*, 5th Edition. Copyright © 1997 The McGraw-Hill Companies. Reproduced with permission of The McGraw-Hill Companies.

Chapter 7

p. 176: © Ariel Skelley/Blend Images/Getty Images
p. 179 (Figure 7.1): Reprinted from *Human Biology and Ecology*, by Albert Damon, with the permission of W.W. Norton & Company, Inc. Copyright © 1977 by W.W. Norton and Company, Inc.; (top) © DK Stock/ Robert Glenn/Getty Images; (Figure 7.2): From John Santrock, *Children*, 7th Edition. Copyright © 2003 The McGraw-Hill Companies. Reproduced with permission of The McGraw-Hill Companies.
p. 180 (Figure 7.3): From G. J. Schirmer (Ed.), *Performance Objectives for Preschool Children*, Adapt Press, Sioux Falls, SD 1974
p. 181 (Figure 7.4): From G. J. Schirmer (Ed.), *Performance Objectives for Preschool Children*, Adapt Press, Sioux Falls, SD 1974
p. 182 (Figure 7.5): The Chief Public Health Officer's Report on the State of Public Health in Canada Growing Up Well: Priorities for a Healthy Future 2009, 138 pages, http://www.phac-aspc.gc.ca/cphorsphc-respcacsp/2009/fr-rc/pdf/cphorsphc-respcacsp-eng.pdf, Health Canada, 2009 Reproduced with the permission of the Minister of Public Works and Government Services Canada, 2013.
p. 186 (Figure 7.6): From Santrock, *Psychology*, 7th Edition. Copyright © 2003 The McGraw-Hill Companies. Reproduced by permission of The McGraw-Hill Companies.
p. 187 (Figure 7.7): "The Symbolic Drawings of Young Children," reprinted courtesy of D. Wolf and J. Nove.
p. 189 (cartoon): The New Yorker Collection, 1989, Lee Lorenz from the cartoon bank.com. All Rights Reserved.; (photo): Eyewire Collection/Getty Images
p. 190: © Elizabeth Crews/The Image Works
p. 191 (left): A.R. Lauria/Dr. Michael Cole, Laboratory of Human Cognition, University of California, San Diego; (right): © Bettmann/CORBIS
p. 196: Courtesy Carole Peterson
p. 198 (Figure 7.15): From Jean Berko, 1958, "The Child's Learning of English Morphology," in *Word*, Vol. 14, p. 154.

Chapter 8

p. 206: ©Robert Churchill/iStockphoto
p. 207 (song): "I Will Take Care of You" Words and Music by Amy Sky and David Pickell © 1996 Café Music, Fifth Gear Music, and Canadiana Music. All Rights on behalf of Café Music, Administered by WB Music Corp. All Rights on behalf of Fifth Gear Music and Canadiana Music. Administered by Warner-Tamerlane Publishing Corp. All Rights Reserved. Used by Permission of Alfred Publishing Co., Inc.
p. 210: ©LWA-Dann Tardif/zefa/Corbis
p. 216 (left): altrendo images/Getty Images; (right): © Cindy Charles/PhotoEdit Inc.
p. 218: Copyright © 1993 Watterson. Reprinted with permission of Universal Press Syndicate. All rights reserved.
p. 219: © Big Cheese Photo/Punchstock
p. 223: DAJ/Getty Images
p. 224: Digital Vision/PunchStock
p. 226: © Richard Hutchings/Photo Edit

Chapter 9

p. 231: World Literacy Canada
p. 234: © Christopher Futcher/iStockphoto
p. 239: © Archives Jean Piaget, Geneva
p. 240 (Figure 9.4): From Chi, M.T.H. "Knowledge Structures and Memory Development," in R.S. Siegler (Ed.) Children's Thinking: What Develops? Copyright ©1978 Lawrence Erlbaum Associates. Reprinted by permission.
p. 241: The New Yorker Collection 1998 Sam Gross from Cartoonbank.com. All rights reserved.
p. 243 (top): Science Cartoons Plus. Used with permission.; (bottom): With permission of Professor Adele Diamond.
p. 245 (cartoon): © 1992 by Sidney Harris. Reprinted with permission.
p. 246 (top): © Jay Gardner, 1998; (bottom): © New Yorker Collection, 1988, Donald Reilly from cartoonbank.com. All Rights Reserved.
p. 249 (Figure 9.6): Simulated item similar to those found in the Raven's Progressive Matrices. Copyright © 1998 by Harcourt Assessment, Inc. Reproduced with permission. All rights reserved.
p. 250: ©Stockbyte/Veer
p. 253 (top): © Richard Howard; (bottom): No credit.
p. 255: John Woods/The Canadian Press
p. 259: © AP Wide World Photos
p. 262: © Creatas/Punchstock

Chapter 10

p. 267: © Juice Images/Corbis RF
p. 268: "Ladybird Brings Help to the Homeless" Used with permission of The Ladybug Foundation
p. 271: © Pixland/Punchstock
p. 272: © Christopher Thomas/Getty
p. 274: No credit
p. 280 (Figure 10.2): From "Gender Differences in Mathematics Performance" in Psychological Bulletin, 107:139-155, 1990. Copyright 1990 by the American Psychological Association. Reprinted with permission.
p. 282 (Figure 10.3): Reproduced by special permission of the Distributor, Mind Garden, Inc., 1690 Woodside Road #202, Redwood City, CA 94061 USA www.mindgarden.com from the Bem Sex Role Inventory by Sandra Bem. Copyright 1978 by Consulting Psychologists Press, Inc. All rights reserved. Further reproduction is prohibited without the Distributor's written consent.
p. 290: © Stone/Getty Images
p. 293 (Figure 10.4): © Media Awareness Network, Young Canadians in a Wired World-Phase II, Ottawa, Canada, 2008 http://www.media-wareness.ca, quoted with permission.

Chapter 11

p. 297: © David Young-Wolff/Stone/Getty Images
p. 301 (Figure 11.2): From Santrock, Children 7th Edition, Copyright © 2003 by The McGraw-Hill Companies. Reproduced with permission of The McGraw-Hill Companies.
p. 304: No credit
p. 306: Getty/Photodisc RF
p. 307 (Figure 11.4): Rotermann, M. (2008). Trends in teen sexual behaviour and condom use. Health Reports 19(3), 1-5; Rotermann, M. (2012) Sexual behaviours and condom use of 15- to 24-year-olds in 2003 and 2009/2010. Health Reports, 23 (1), 1-5.
p. 309 (Figure 11.5): Preventing early & unwanted pregnancy & pregnancy related mortality and

morbidity in adolescents-Training Course in Sexual and Reproductive Health Research, Geneva 2012. P. 9 World Health Organization
p. 313: © Tony Freeman/PhotoEdit
p. 316 (Figure 11.6): Courtesy of National Institute of Drug Abuse (US)
p. 317 (top): Courtesy of Roger Tonkin; (bottom): © Punchstock/Image Source
p. 320: ©BananaStock/PunchStock
p. 322: © Tony Freeman/Photo Edit
p. 323: Rossetani/QMI Agency
p. 326: Superstock RF

Chapter 12

p. 332: © Ariel Skelly/Blend Images/PhotoLibrary
p. 342 (top): © BananaStock/PunchStock; (bottom): ©BananaStock/PunchStock
p. 346: Kwan Ho
p. 347: © Daniel Laine
p. 352 (Figure 12.4): From "Romantic Development: Does Age at Which Romantic Involvement Starts Matter?" by Duane Buhrmester, April 2001, paper presented at the meeting of the Society for Research in Child Development, Minneapolis, MN. Reprinted with permission from the author.
p. 256: From Santrock, Children 6th Edition. Copyright ©2000 by The McGraw-Hill Companies. Reproduced with permission of the McGraw-Hill Companies.

Chapter 13

p. 362 (photo): © LWA/Taxi/Getty Images; (poem): From Driving in the Blizzard, In Harm's Way by Maureen Hines. Published by Brick Books, 2002. Reprinted with permission.
p. 363: Jonathan Hayward/The Canadian Press
p. 366: Marcos Townsend, The Gazette (Montreal)
p. 368 (Figure 13.1): From National Institutes of Health (US)
p. 370 (Figure 13.3): From Pate, et al., Journal of the American Medical Association, 273, 404. Copyright ©1995 American Medical Association. Reprinted by permission.
p. 375: © 2009 JupiterImages Corporation
p. 382 (from left): Courtesy of Susan Tighe; © Bryce Duffy/Corbis; Toronto Star/GetStock.com
p. 384: Dustin Rabin

Chapter 14

p. 391: Blend Images/JasperCole/Getty Images
p. 394 (Figure 14.1): From Wachs, T.D. "Fit, Context, and the Transition Between Temperament and Personality," in C. Halverson, G. Kohnstamm & R. Martin (Eds.) The Developing Structure of Personality from Infancy to Adulthood. Copyright © 1994 Lawrence Erlbaum Associates, Reprinted by permission.
p. 395 (top): Courtesy of Susan Johnson; (bottom): © RF/CORBIS
p. 398: Lois Tema; http://www.davidroche.com
p. 403 (left): © Fancy Collections/Superstock; (top): © PhotoAlto; (bottom): ©Sigrid Olsson/PhotoAlto
p. 405: Image Source Pink/Alamy
p. 406 (Figure 14.4): Reproduced by special permission of the publisher, Psychological Assessment Resources, Inc. from The Changing Family Life Cycle, 2nd Edition. Copyright © 1989 by Psychological Assessment Resources, Inc. All rights reserved.
p. 410 (Figure 14.5): National Center for Health Statistics, 2000 (US)
p. 413: Digital Vision/Getty Images/Punchstock
p. 414 (Figure 14.5): As outlined by Dr. George Boeree http://webspace.ship.edu/cgboer/genpsymoraldev.html
p. 415 (top): Copyright © 1964 Don Orehek; (bottom): © PhotoAlta/PunchStock

Chapter 15

p. 420: Image Source/Getty Images
p. 424 (top): The Canadian Press/The Globe & Mail; (bottom): sbukley/Dreamstime/Getstock.com
p. 426: Adapted from Newsweek, Health for Life, special section, Fall/Winter 2001. Copyright ©2001 Newsweek, Inc. All rights reserved. Reprinted by permission.
p. 429: Health Canada website and Media Photo Gallery, Health Canada, http://www.hc-xc.gc.ca Reproduced with permission of the Minister of Public Works and Government Services Canada 2008.
p. 430 (Figure 15.3): Adapted from Statistics Canada, Causes of Death 84-208-XIE 20100012 2006 Released May 4, 2010; (photo): © Blue Moon Stock/Punchstock
p. 434: Courtesy of K. Warner Shaie

p. 437: Mackenzie Stroh/Contour by Getty Images
p. 438: Courtesy Mihaly Csikszentmihalyi
p. 439 (Figure 15.7): From Men in Their Forties: The Transition to Middle Age, by Lois M. Tamir, 1982. Used by permission of Springer Publishing Company, New York 10012.
p. 440 (left): Photodisc/Getty Images; (right): Reprinted with special permission of North American Syndicate.
p. 442: © Eric S. Lesser/epa/Corbis

Chapter 16

p. 447 (photo): © Robie Price/Getty Images; (vignette): Dale Auger
p. 450 (left): CP Photo/Kevin Frayer; (right): CP Photo Archive/Jacques Nadeau
p. 451 (from top): Amos Morgan/Getty Images; © RF Corbis; Image100 Ltd.
p. 456 (Figure 16.6): From D.F. Hultsch and J.K. Plemons, "Life Events and Life Span Development," in Life Span Development and Behavior, Vol. 2, by P.B. Baltes and O.G. Brun (Eds.) Copyright © 1979 Academic Press. Reprinted by Permission.; (photo): © RF Corbis
p. 458: © Betty Press/Woodfin Camp & Associates
p. 465: Doonesbury © 1991 G.B. Trudeau. Reprinted with permission of Universal Press Syndicate. All Rights Reserved.
p. 467: CP Photo/Kevin Frayer
p. 468: © Steve Casimiro/The Image Bank/Getty Images

Chapter 17

p. 473: Andersen Ross/Blend Images/Getty Images
p. 474: © Frenc/Dreamstime/Getstock.com
p. 477 (Figure 17.1): From The Psychology of Death, Dying and Bereavement by Richard Schultz. Copyright © 1978 The McGraw-Hill Companies. Reproduced with permission of The McGraw-Hill Companies.
p. 478: © Pascal Parrot/Sygma; © Sarah Maria Vischer/The Image Works
p. 479 (Figure 17.2): Courtesy of Dr. Jerry Shay, PhD., UT Southwestern Medical Center
p. 482 (Figure 17.3): From R. Cabeza, et al., "Age-related differences in neural activity during memory encoding and retrieval: A positron emission tomography study" in Journal of Neuroscience, 17, 391-400, 1997; (photo): © James Balog
p. 488: © Digital Vision/Getty Images
p. 490 (Figure 17.6): Courtesy of Colin M. Bloor
p. 495 (Figure 17.7): © Alfred Pasieka/Science Photo Library/Photo Researchers Inc.
p. 498: © Rick Friedman/Corbis
p. 499: © The Globe and Mail Inc.
p. 510: Richard Lam/The Canadian Press

Chapter 18

p. 515 (photo): © Jonathan Kirn/Riser/Getty Images; (poem): From Users Guide to a Blank Wall, 2006 by Editions du Gref. Reprinted with permission.
p. 516: The Metis Nation of Alberta
p. 518 (Figure 18.1): From "Erikson's View . . . Conflict and Resolution: Culmination in Old Age." Copyright © 1988 by The New York Times. Reprinted by permission.
p. 520 (photo): Ryan McVay/Getty Images; (Figure 18.2): From L. Carstensen, et al., "The Social Context of Emotion" in the Annual Review of Geriatrics and Gerontology by Schaie/Lawton, 1997, Vol.17, p. 331. Used by permission of Springer Publishing Company, New York, 10012.
p. 522 (left to right): Ryan McVay/Getty Images; © Image100/PunchStock; © Image Source/Getty Images; © Corbis. All Rights Reserved.; © Image Source/Getty Images
p. 534: Photodisc/Getty Images
p. 535: John Santrock
p. 537: © Ryan McVay/Getty Images
p. 540: B & C Alexander/First Light

Chapter 19

p. 544 (photo): Lynn Johnson/National Geographic/Getty Images; (vignette): B.A. Cameron (Cam Hubert)
p. 545: Dakota Brant, Youth Delegate, 2005-Aboriginal Spiritual Journey
p. 546: M. Thomsen/zefa/Corbis
p. 548: CP Photo Archive/Chuck Studdy
p. 552: © Patrick Ward/Stock Boston
p. 558: Tim Hall/Getty Images
p. 560 (Figure 19.3): © Stockbroker/PhotoLibrary
p. 564: ©Tao Ming/XinHua/Xinhua Press/Corbis

Name Index

Frick, P.J., 221
Friederici, A.D., 142
Friedlander, L., 353
Friedman, C., 216, 281
Friedman, E.M., 487
Friedman, H.S., 523
Friedman, K., 305
Friedman, K.L., 479
Friedman, R., 320
Friedrichs, A., 243
Friendly, M., 171, 199
Friesen, J., 528, 529
Friesen, W.V., 483
Frimer, J., 276, 277, 278
Fritsch, T., 504
Fritschmann, N.S., 259
Froebel, F., 199
Fromm, E., 30, 41f, 55, 392, 397
Fry, P.S., 564
Frye, D., 194
Fu, G., 269, 277
Fu, V.R., 43
Fuhrman, R., 402
Fulcher, A., 103
Fuligni, A.J., 43, 128, 345
Fuller-Thomson, E., 466, 467, 534
Funai, E.F., 104
Furlong, A., 299
Furlong, M., 339
Furman, E., 464
Furman, W.C., 352, 353
Furth, H.G., 238

G

Gadino, B., 346
Gage, F.H., 481
Gagliese, L., 485
Gajdamaschko, N., 44
Gajdos, Z., 299
Galambos, N.L., 302, 303, 318
Galasko, D., 494
Galavan, A., 303
Galimberti, D., 494
Gallagher, J.J., 243
Gallagher, S., 379
Gallicano, G. I., 93
Galliher, R.V., 346
Gallinger, K., 539
Gallo, L.C., 406
Gallo, W.T., 386
Galotti, K.M., 192
Galton, F., 64, 72
Gamino, L.A., 563
Gan, S., 107
Gandhi, M., 36, 232, 290, 502
Ganguli, M., 506
Ganiban, J., 394
Ganong, L., 283, 411, 532
Gans, D., 468
Gao, L.L., 425
Garasen, H., 527
Garcia, C., 345
Garcia Coll, C., 345
Garcia-Bournissen, F., 91
Gardner, D.S., 182
Gardner, H., 245, 246, 250, 251
Gardner, M., 323
Garner, P.W., 271
Garolla, A., 97
Garrett, D.D., 547
Garrett, E., 555
Garriguet, D., 182, 183, 235
Gartner, L.M., 123
Gartstein, M., 155, 192
Gasser, L., 278
Gates, B., 268
Gathercole, S., 324
Gathercole, V.C.M., 144
Gatz, M., 492, 495, 518
Gauvain, M., 52, 150, 156, 189, 191
Gaziano, J.M., 491
Geary, D.C., 62

Geary-Martin, C., 499
Geda, Y.E., 495
Gee, E.M., 346
Geers, A., 341
Geher, G., 214
Geldart, S., 130
Gelles, R.J., 344
Gelman, R., 188
Gelman, S.A., 186, 195, 198, 322
Genesee, F., 143
Genovese, J.E.C., 322
Gentzler, A.L., 396
Geoffroy, M., 169
George, L.K., 456, 509, 517
Georges, J.J., 548
Gerards, F.A., 72
Gerber, L., 345, 347
German, V.F., 96
Gerrard, M., 323
Gerrotsen, M., 501
Gershoff, E.T., 221
Gerstein, H.C., 94
Gerstel, N., 468
Gervais, J., 226
Gettler, L., 168
Getz, S., 303
Ghanem, K.G., 96
Ghetti, S., 194
Ghisletta, P., 484
Ghosh, S., 484
Giannakopoulos, P., 436
Giannarelli, F., 169
Giarrusso, R., 524
Gibbs, J.C., 276
Gibson, E., 131, 136
Gibson, E.S., 311
Gibson, H.J., 440
Giedd, J.N., 118, 178, 303, 304, 323, 324
Giger, J., 341
Giles, A., 137
Gill, T., 525
Gillanders, D., 453
Gillen, M., 302
Gillespie, C., 369
Gilligan, C., 30, 31, 54, 277, 278, 415, 455
Gilliland, A. L., 103
Gillum, R.F., 443, 509
Gil-Mohapel, J., 481
Gilmore, J., 439
Gilstrap, L.L., 248
Gimenez-Llort, L., 482
Giordano, P.C., 287
Giovannini, M.G., 496
Girling, T., 108
Givens, J.E., 272
Gjerdingen, D., 109
Gladstone, J., 534
Gladwell, M., 281
Glantz, C., 104
Glazer, J., 555, 556
Glick, G.C., 309
Gliksman, L., 371
Gliori, G., 100
Glisky, E.L., 503
Glossop, R., 75
Gluck, J., 502, 505
Glynn, L., 100
Godde, B., 508
Godding, V., 94
Goel, A., 431
Gogtay, N., 179
Goh, Y.I., 100
Golanska, E., 494
Goldberg, W.A., 217
Goldenberg, R.L., 106
Goldman, R., 261
Goldman-Rakic, P.S., 179
Goldschmidt, L., 94, 95
Goldsmith, H.H., 76, 80, 150, 155, 156
Goldstein, A.L., 286
Goldstein, M.H., 144
Goldyn, D.T., 167

Gollnick, D.M., 19
Golombok, S., 214, 224
Gomez Ravetti, M., 494
Gonzalez, R., 257
González-del Angel, A., 68
Goodall, J., 36, 48, 57
Goodman, G.S., 131, 286
Goodman, J., 365
Goodman, J.M., 425
Goodman, S.S., 425
Goodridge, D., 547
Goodvin, R., 150, 153, 156, 165, 272, 393
Goos, L.M., 260
Goossens, L., 339
Gorchoff, J,, 463
Gorchoff, S.M., 464
Gordon, A., 168
Gore, K., 215
Gosden, R.G., 429, 430
Gosselin, J., 284
Gostic, C.L., 370
Goswami, S.K., 493
Gottlieb, D.J., 66
Gottlieb, G., 69, 71, 72, 248
Gottlieb, L.D., 79
Gottman, J.M., 210, 287, 404–405, 406, 463
Gottman, J.S., 404
Gottman, P., 464
Gougeon, P., 220
Gould, M., 320, 351
Goulet, C., 116
Graber, J.A., 301, 302
Grady, C.L., 508
Graham, J., 555
Graham, J.A., 346, 399
Graham, S., 346
Grambs, J.D., 457
Gramling, L.F., 450
Grammatikaki, E., 123
Grammer, J.K., 239, 240
Gray, T.R., 95
Gredler, M.E., 44
Green, R.J., 413
Greenberg, L., 395, 396
Greenberg, N., 441
Greenberg, T., 320
Greene, M.G., 500
Greener, J.M., 91
Greenfield, P.M., 128
Greenough, A., 106
Greenstein, T.N., 387
Greer, F.R., 123
Greydanus, D.E., 260
Griffin, K., 272
Griffin, P.W., 523
Griffiths, M., 317, 555
Griffiths, R., 536
Griffiths, S., 539
Grigorenko, E.L., 248
Grigoriadis, S., 110
Grodin, S., 281
Groen, R.S., 96
Groer, M.W., 110
Grofer Klinger, L., 197
Gromis, J.C., 182
Grossman, I., 505
Grossman, K., 165
Grosz, E., 281
Grotevant, H.D., 285, 339
Grover, S.A., 431
Gruen, J.R., 259
Grünendahl, M., 452
Grusec, J., 18, 212, 217
Gruslin, A., 97
Grych, J., 339
Gu, D., 490
Gualtieri, C.T., 506
Guarnera, M., 501
Gueguen, J., 312
Guelinckx, I., 99
Guerra, N.G., 291
Guerrero, L., 397

Guilford, J.P., 241
Guimond, É, 554
Gulgoz, S., 503
Gump, B., 440
Gunderson, E.P., 109
Gunnar, M., 132, 153, 285, 286
Gupta, A., 283
Gupta, R., 553
Gupta, R.P., 184, 317
Guralnik, J., 430
Gurdon, J., 77
Gurwitch, R.H., 273
Gustafsson, J.E., 248
Gutchess, A.H., 508
Guthrie, W., 474
Gutmann, D.L., 538

H

Ha, J.H., 468
Hackett, J.K., 243
Hagekull, B., 393
Hagg, T., 481
Hagopian, A., 123
Hahn, B., 119
Hahn, D.B., 17, 367
Hains, S.M.J., 161
Hair, E.C., 340
Haith, M.M, 131
Hakvoort, E.M., 347
Halford, G.S., 190
Halford, K.W., 45
Hall, C.B., 507
Hall, D.P., 252
Hall, J.H., 410
Hall, L., 261
Hallahan, D.P., 259
Halldin, M., 425
Hallett, D., 337
Hallinan, E.V., 162
Halliwell, J.O., 206
Halonen, J., 366
Halpern, D., 323
Halpern, D.F., 279
Halpern, I.F., 154
Hamamura, T., 460
Hamilton, M.A., 325
Hamilton, S.F., 325
Hamlin, J.K., 162
Hamm, B., 534
Hammel, R., 426, 536
Hampl, J., 369
Hampton, M., 552
Hamrick, M.H., 370
Han, W.J., 217
Handlin, O., 457
Hanish, L.D., 291
Hankin, B.L., 396
Hannon, E.E., 132
Hans, J., 411
Hansen, M.V., 500
Hansen, R., 157
Hansson, R., 554, 555, 556, 557, 562
Harati, A., 498
Harden, K., 14
Harder, G., 319
Harder, K., 319
Hardman, D., 201
Hardy, M., 529
Hardy, R., 109
Hare, A., 340, 342
Harel, F., 551
Harel, S., 153
Hargreaves, D.A., 312
Harkins, S.W., 485
Harley, T.A., 259
Harlow, H., 162
Harman, S.M., 431
Harms, T., 171
Harootyan, R.A., 537
Harper, S., 10, 257
Harrell, W., 312
Harrelson, A., 486

Torges, C.M., 518
Torode, M., 235
Torrence, C.M., 138
Tosi, G., 96
Totenhagen, C., 427
Toth, S.L., 164, 285, 286
Totten, M., 351
Towe-Goodman, N., 110
Trainor, L.J., 142
Trautner, H.M., 279
Travers, C., 494
Treboux, D., 469
Trefler, D., 171
Trehub, S.E., 132, 133, 144, 168
Tremblay, I., 551
Tremblay, M., 234
Tremblay, R.E., 110, 226, 280
Trentacosta, C.J., 210
Trifunov, W., 120, 121
Trimble, C., 97
Trinh, N., 339
Troll, L.E., 533, 534
Trommsdorff, G., 43, 150
Tronick, E.Z., 107
Trottier, J., 442
Truchon, M., 551
Trudeau, E., 375
Trudeau, G., 465
Trudeau, P.A., 502
True, M., 111
Truog, R.D., 546, 548
Trzesniewski, K.H., 334, 524
Tsai, T., 347
Tseng, V., 43
Tsuyuki, J., 368
Tubman, J.G., 357
Tudge, R.H., 44
Tulsky, J., 559
Tulving, E., 502
Tulviste, T., 111
Tuokko, H., 547
Turcotte, M., 99, 488, 493, 498, 500,
    526, 527, 528, 529, 530, 531,
    532, 534, 536, 537, 538
Turcotte, V., 551
Turecki, G., 80
Turecki, S., 157
Turek, P.J., 74
Turiel, E., 277, 278
Turkeltaub, P.E., 233
Turner, B.F., 538
Turner, F., 67
Turner, J.A., 493
Turner, R.J., 411
Twain, M., 231
Twells, L., 122
Tyas, S.L., 493
Tytus, R., 368

U

Uccelli, P., 141, 198, 252
Udry, J.R., 352
Uhlenberg, P., 422
Uji, Y., 484
Ulbricht, J., 394
Umana-Taylor, A.J., 344, 346
Umberson, D., 537
Underwood, M., 290
Upitis, R., 246
Uppal, S., 262
Urban, J., 339
Urbina, S., 249
Usalcas, J., 439
Utendale, W.T., 213, 280

V

Vahia, I.V., 493
Vaillancourt, T., 291
Vaillant. G., 449, 451, 459, 461
Valente, S., 349

Valiakalayil, A., 284
Valkenburg, P., 288, 398
Vallotton, C.D., 45
Valois, R., 339
van Aken, M., 393
van Balen, F., 413
Van Broeckhoven, C., 494
Van Buren, E., 346
van de Weijer-Bergsma, E., 106
van den Berg, P., 312
van den Boom, D., 413
van den Bout, J., 561
van den Hout, M.A., 561
van der Kamp, J., 128
van Dulmen, M., 287
Van Egeren, L.A., 220
van Gundy, K., 492
van Hof, P., 128
van Hooren, S.A., 506
Van Hulle, C.A., 155
van IJzendoorn, M.H., 165, 166
van Lizendoorn, 396
van Praag, H., 481
Van Remmen, H., 480
Van Schothorst, E.M., 479
van Solinge, H., 530
van Strien, T., 369
van Wormer, K., 349
Vanderhaeghe, G., 391
Vandewater, E.A., 539
Vanpee, D., 547
Vansant, G., 99
Vasdev, N., 104
Vasunilashorn, S., 490
Vaughan, A., 161
Vaughan, K., 236
Vavrinkova, B., 95
Vazsonyi, A.T., 271
Veenhof, B., 530, 531
Veenstra, A., 290
Velasquez, A.M., 343
Vellas, B., 495, 496
Velleman, R., 372
Vellutino, F.R., 201
Velting, D., 320
Vemuri, P., 494
Vendittelli, M., 105
Venners, S.A., 101
Ventura, A.K., 182
Ventura, J.J., 339
Venturelli, M., 483
Verbrugge, L.M., 429
Verhaak, C.M., 74
Verhaeghen, P., 503
Verma, S., 342
Vermeersch, H., 301
Vester, 371
Vézina, M., 99, 527
Vicol, L., 97
Vidal, F., 42, 238
Viechtbauer, W., 459, 462
Vieno, A., 342
Viken, M.K., 91
Vilhena, N., 286
Villegas, R., 123
Vimaleswaran, K.S., 68
Vinnerljung, B., 285
Vinnerljung, B., 285
Virmani, E.A., 150, 208
Vitaro, F., 226, 289, 355
Vodanovich, S.J., 525
Voelcker-Rehage, C., 508
Vogel, L., 334, 546
Vohs, K.D., 270, 442
Volberg, R., 317
Von Beveren, T.T., 102
Von Goethe, J.W., 362
von Hofsten, C., 136
von Tilburg, T., 537
Voorpostel, M., 465
Votruba-Drzal, E., 169
Vouloumanos, A., 141
Vreeman, R.C., 292, 351
Vukelich, C., 200
Vurpillot, E., 192, 193

Vygotsky, L., 28f, 36, 44–45, 53, 55,
    168, 185–189, 189–192, 203,
    226, 239, 244, 338

W

Wachs, H., 238
Wachs, T.D., 393, 394
Wade, C., 15
Wagner, L.S., 6, 31
Wagner, R.M., 30
Wagster, M.V., 506
Wahlin, A., 436
Wahlsten, D., 69, 71, 72
Waite, L., 532, 533
Wakai, K., 372
Walby, F.A., 562
Waldron, J., 367
Walford, R., 475
Walk, R., 131
Walker, L.J., 276, 277, 278
Walker, W.A., 121, 123
Wallace, R.B., 31
Wallace-Bell, M., 371
Wallerstein, J.S., 222
Walsh, L.V., 111
Walsh, R., 441, 443
Walsh, T.J., 74
Walston, J.D., 480
Walter, T., 552, 563
Walters, M.W., 107
Walton, K.E., 459, 462, 523
Wang, C., 312
Wang, L., 226, 496
Wang, Q., 348
Wang, S., 136
Wang, X., 498
Ward, L.M., 305
Ward, W.F., 491
Ward-Griffin, C., 533
Wardlaw, G.M., 122, 181, 368, 369
Wardle, J., 369
Wark, G.R., 277
Warr, P., 385, 529
Warren, M.P., 301, 430
Waters, E., 164
Wathen, C.N., 262
Watkins, N., 348, 349
Watson, D.L., 45
Watson, J.A., 466
Watson, J.B., 45, 69, 152, 195
Wax, J.R., 71
Way, N., 344
Wayman, J., 307
Wearing, H., 324
Weaver, A., 402
Weaver, S.R., 355
Webb, J.T., 251
Webb, R., 525
Webber, S.C., 483
Wechsler, D., 245
Wei, Y., 480
Weiland, P., 341
Weindruch, R., 490
Weinfeld, M., 450, 457
Weinfield, N.S., 394
Weinstein, K.K., 466
Weis, K., 398
Weisner, C., 372
Weiss, C.O., 483
Weiss, L.A., 261
Weiss, R., 402
Weissglas-Volkov, D., 425
Weisz, A.N., 277
Wekerle, C., 286, 307
Weller, A., 152
Wellman, H.M., 195
Wellman, J., 341
Weltzin, T., 312
Wen, W., 101
Wendel, G.D., 96
Weng, X., 92
Wengreen, H.J., 491

Wennergren, G., 123
Wentzel, K.R., 288
Werker, J.F., 131, 132, 141
Wermter, A.K., 80
Werner, L.A., 131, 132
West, M.J., 144
West, S.D., 247
Westlake, C., 531
Weston, K., 413
Weston, M.J., 73
Wetherell, J.L., 492, 518
Wethington, E., 452, 456
Wexler, B., 44
Wexler, N.S., 78, 80
Whaley, S.E., 111, 248
Whayne, T.F., 425
Wheeler, K., 140
Wheeler, M., 62, 74
Whelan, T.A., 466
Whincup, P.H., 486
Whipple, N., 164
Whiren, A.P., 200
Whitbourne, S.K., 450
White, B., 243
White, C.D., 550
White, F., 490
White, J.W., 280
White, R., 299, 319
Whitehead, K., 346
Whitelaw, E., 80
Whitelaw, N.C., 80
Whiteman, S.D., 533
Whitfield, K.E., 506
Whiting, P., 366
Whitley, B.E., 24
Whittaker, C., 18
Wider, C., 69
Wiener, J., 259
Wiersma, W., 22
Wigle, D.T., 96
Wijngaards-de Meij, L., 561
Wijnroks, L., 106
Wiles, J., 481
Wilkins, K., 487
Wilkins, R., 120, 554
Wilkinson, D., 183
Willard, H.F., 91
Willcox, B.J., 476
Willcox, D.C., 476, 540
Willcox, M.D., 476
Willey, J., 70
Willford, J.A., 94
Williams, 393
Williams, D.R., 443
Williams, J.H., 95
Williams, M.H., 368
Williams, M.V., 481
Williams, P.M., 96
Williams, R.W., 371
Williamson, J.B., 532
Williamson, J.D., 490, 506
Williamson, R.A., 138
Williams-Wheeler, M., 318
Willis, C., 554, 555
Willis, S.L., 13, 381, 423, 433, 434,
    435, 507
Willliams, A., 167
Willms, J.D., 17, 28
Wilson, A.E., 533
Wilson, B., 406
Wilson, B.J., 227, 228
Wilson, D., 91, 116, 122, 124, 126,
    132, 236, 308, 319, 320
Wilson, K.G., 549
Wilson, M., 291
Wilson, R.D., 71
Wilson, R.S., 506, 507, 523
Wilson, S., 348, 349
Windle, M., 357
Windley, P.G., 80
Windspoll, R., 527
Wing, R., 369
Wink, P., 460, 461
Winner, E., 251

Subject Index

forebrain, mapping of, 118
four lobes of, 119f
gender and structure of, 78, 279, 294, 431
hemispheres, development of, 118f
infancy, in, 116–119, 120, 139, 145, 150, 156
language and, 142
learning disabilities and brain scans, 259, 259f, 260, 261, 261f
left-brained, 119–120
life span development and, 2–4, 11, 12
lying and brain activity, 45
mapping of, 118–119
middle/late childhood, in, 233, 263
myelination, 117–118, 145
neurogenesis, 481
neurons, development of, 117–118, 118f, 145
neuroplasticity of, 34, 44, 53
prayer and meditation, impact of on, 443, 508, 510, 514
prenatal period and, 2, 4, 89–90, 92f, 100, 112
REM sleep, development and, 120, 121f, 145
right-brained, 119
shaken baby syndrome, 116–117
shrinking and slowing in, 480–481, 511
sixty-five to 120 years, 3
stimulation of during aging, 483
suicide and, 80
ten to twenty-five years, 3
twenty-five to sixty-five years, 3
Wernicke's area, 143f
Brain death, 546, 566
Brain size in primates versus humans, 61f
Brainstorming, 241
Brazelton Neonatal Behavioral Assessment Scale (NBAS), 107, 114
Breaking the Cycle of Violence, 357
Breastfeeding, 18, 122, 123–124, 145
acquired immune deficiency syndrome (AIDS) and, 377
benefits of, 123
bottle feeding versus, 115
contraindications of, 124
human immunodeficiency virus (HIV) and, 115
postpartum depression and, 110
Breast cancer, 123, 302, 327, 392, 429, 439, 477f, 488, 489
Breech position, defined, 105
Broca's area, 142, 143f, 147
Bronfenbrenner's bio-ecological theory, 50–51, 54, 54f, 57, 213, 217, 219, 256, 282–283, 309, 313, 338, 452, 455, 516
chronosystem, 51
exosystem, 51
five environmental systems, 50–51, 51f
five moral orientations of, 413–414, 414f, 418
macrosystem, 51
mesosystem, 50–51
microsystem, 50
Bulimia nervosa, 312, 313, 328
Bullying, 290–293, 295
adolescent, 351
bullied, 290, 295
bully, 290, 295
bystander, 290, 295
cyberbullying, 292, 295, 351
impact of, 291–292
most likely to bully, traits of, 291–292, 295
most likely victims of, traits, of, 291
reduction of, 292–293, 295
relational aggression, 290–291
restitution, resolution, and reconciliation, 292, 351

social contexts and, 290
Steps to Respect program, 292–293
upstander, 290, 295

C

Caesarean section, 105
Caffeine
adolescents, high-caffeine drinks and, 315, 329
prenatal development and, 92, 112
Calorie restriction, life expectancy and, 490–491, 512
Camp Elsewhere, 317
Canada, generations in, 10
Canada Millennium Scholarship Foundation, 385
Canada Standards Association Group (CSA), 429
Canada's Food Guide, 124, 311
Canadian Association for Neuroscience, 53
Canadian Association of Retired Persons (CARP), 526
Canadian Cancer Society (CCS), 429
Canadian Caregiver Coalition, 469
Canadian Child Care Confederation, 170
Canadian Fertility and Andrology Society (CFAS), 74
Canadian Fitness and Lifestyle Research Institute, 310
Canadian Grandparents Rights Association, 534
Canadian Hospice Society Palliative Care Association (CHPCA), 549
Canadian Institute of Health Research (CIHR), 20, 29, 77, 367
Canadian International Development Agency (CIDA), 232
Canadian Labour Code, 529
Canadian Learning Disabilities Association, 258
Canadian Maternity Experiences Survey, 104
Canadian Mental Health Association, 366, 499
Canadian Midwifery Regulators Consortium, 103
Canadian Network for the Prevention of Elder Abuse (CNPEA), 536
Canadian Paediatric Society, 124, 234
Canadian Pension Plan (CPP), 528
Canadian Perinatal Surveillance System (CPSS), 101
Canadian Psychological Association (CPA), 32, 35
Canadian Research Institute for Social Policy (CRISP), 17, 19, 28
Canadian Stem Cell Foundation, 77
Canadian Study of Health and Aging, 547
Canadian Virtual Hospice, 551
Cancer, childhood, 236–237, 263
Cancer, incidence of, 429, 554
Carbon monoxide, pregnancy and, 96
Cardiovascular system
aging and, 486, 511
middle adulthood, changes in, 425, 444
strategies for healthy, 425
stress and, 427
Care, 449, 455
Care perspective, 277
Careers and work, early adulthood, in, 383–387, 389
developmental changes, 383, 389
impact of work, 385–387, 389
occupational outlook, 385, 389
values and careers, 383–384, 389
Careers and work, late adulthood, cognitive function and, 506, 513
Careers and work, middle adulthood, in

barriers to, 440
challenges of, 439, 445
Carriers, 67, 69
Case, Robert, 44, 56
Case study, 24, 28f, 34
Cataracts, 484
children and, 131
Categorization, 139, 146
conceptual categories, 146
Causality, 134–135
Celebrations of life, 565, 566, 568
Cellular clock theory of aging, 479, 511
Centenarians, 475–477
functioning of, 476
gender and, 476
health of, 475
life expectancy and, 9, 9f
predictors of, 477f
Centration, 187, 203
Centre for Addiction and Mental Health (CAMH), 317–318, 427, 428
Cephalocaudal pattern, 116–117, 145, 178
Cerebral cortex, 118–119
lateralization, 145
Cervical cancer, 97, 308, 376
vaccines, 308
Charter of Rights, 525, 529
Chemical pollutants, pregnancy and, 96
Chess and Thomas's temperament classification, 154, 173
difficult child, 154, 173
easy child, 154, 173
slow-to-warm-up child, 154, 173
Child care, 169–171
brain development and, 169
daycare, child development and, 169–170
poverty, impact of on, 169
world policy of, 170
Child maltreatment, 284–286, 295
child neglect, 284, 295
context of maltreatment and abuse, 285–286
developmental consequences of, 286, 295
institutional neglect, 286
prevalence of, 284
prevention of, 286
sexual abuse, 286
Child rearing, culture and, 43
Childbirth settings and attendants, 102–103
doulas, 103
midwifery, 102–103
Child-centred kindergarten, 199–200, 204
developmentally appropriate and inappropriate practices, 200, 204
education for the disadvantaged, 201–202, 205
literacy and numeracy, young child's, 200–201, 205
Montessori approach, 199–200, 204
Child-directed speech, 144, 147
Childhood, early, physical and cognitive development in, 176–205
body growth, 178, 202
brain, 178–179, 202
child-centred kindergarten, 199–200, 204
developmentally appropriate and inappropriate practices, 200, 204
disadvantaged children, education for, 201–202, 205
early childhood education, 199–202, 204–205
health and wellness, 181–185, 203
information processing, 192–197, 203
language development, 197–199, 204
literacy and numeracy, 200–201, 205
motor development, 180–181, 202
nutrition and exercise, 181–183, 203
physical development, 178–181, 202

Piaget's preoperational stage, 185–189, 203
Vygotsky's theory, 189–192, 203
wellness in Canada, 183–184, 203
wellness outside Canada, 184–185, 203
Childhood perspective on death, 554–556, 567
death of a parent, 555–556
terminally ill children, 555–556
Childhood, early, socio-emotional development in, 206–230
divorce, 222–224, 229
emotional development, 209–210, 228
families, 217–225, 229–230
gender, 214–216, 229
moral development, 210–213, 229
parenting, 217–222, 229
peer relations, 226, 230
play, 226–227, 230
self, 208–209, 228
sibling relationships and birth order, 224–25, 230
social media, 227–228, 230
Childhood, middle and late, physical and cognitive development in, 231–266
attention deficit hyperactivity disorder (ADHD), 260–261, 265
autism spectrum disorders (ASD), 261, 265
bilingualism, 253, 264
body growth and change, 233, 263
brain, 233, 263
cognitive development, 237–251, 263–264
disabilities, children with, 258–262, 265–266
disabilities, effect on families, 262, 266
educational approaches and issues, 254–258, 265, 266
educational issues, 255–257, 262
exercise, 234–235, 263
health, illness, and disease, 235–237, 263
information processing, 239–244, 263
intelligence, 244–251, 263
international comparisons, 257, 265
language development, 251–253, 264
learning disabilities, 258–260
motor development, 234, 263
physical changes and health, 233–237, 263
physical disabilities, 261, 265
Piaget's concrete operational stage, 237–239
private schools and home education, 257–258, 265
reading, 252–253, 264
student learning, approaches to, 254–255, 265
vocabulary, grammar, and metalinguistic awareness, 251–252, 264
Childhood, middle/late, socio-emotional development in, 267–296
bullying, 290–293, 295
child maltreatment, 284–286, 295
emotional and personality development, 269–273, 294
families, 282–286, 295
friends, 287–288, 295
gender, 279–282, 294
moral development, 273–278, 294
parent-child relationships, developmental changes in, 282–284, 295
peer statuses, 288–289, 295
peers, technology, and social media, 287–293, 295
self, 269–271, 294
social cognition, 289–290, 295
social media, 293, 295

Visual expectations, 131, 131f, 146
  motor, sensory, and perceptual development, 130–131
Visual perception, 130–131
  acuity and colour, 130, 130–131, 131, 146
  depth perception, 131, 131f, 146
  visual expectations, 131, 131f
Vitamin D deficiency, 122, 145, 491
Vitamins, aging and, 491–492, 512
  antioxidants, 491, 512
Vocabulary, 251–252, 264
Vygotsky's socio-cultural cognitive theory, 44–45, 53, 54f, 56, 168, 189–192, 200, 203, 239, 244, 338
  evaluation of, 191–192
  language and thought, 189–190
  Piaget's cognitive development theory versus, 190–191, 191f
  play and, 226, 230
  private speech, 189, 190
  scaffolding, 189
  social constructivist approach, 191
  teaching strategies, 190–191, 203
  zone of proximal development (ZPD), 189, 190f, 203

W

War Child, 384
Wechsler scales, 245
Weight gain during pregnancy, 99f
Well-being, dimensions of, 452f
Wernicke's area, 142, 143f, 147
Whole-language approach, 252
Wilding, 354
Willis' intellectual abilities and, 433–436, 444
Wilms' tumour, 68
Wisdom, 505, 513
  predictors of, 505
Women's moral development, 414–415, 418
Work, early adulthood, in, 385–387, 389
  dual-career couples, 386, 389
  postsecondary education, work during, 385–386, 389
  unemployment, 386, 389
Work, late adulthood, in, 529, 541
Work, middle adulthood, in, 438–439
  age and job satisfaction, 439f
Working memory, 436, 503, 504, 513
  perceptual speed and, 503
World Elder Abuse Day, 536
World Health Organization (WHO), 32, 115, 258, 284, 286, 305, 309, 313, 318, 443, 446
World Literacy Canada (WLC), 232

X

X-linked inheritance, 67
XYY syndrome, 69f, 82

Y

Young offenders, 354–355, 360
Young old, 478, 510
Youth Criminal Justice Act, 354, 356
Youth in Transition Survey (YITS), 28
Youth Justice Renewal Initiative, 354
Youth violence, 354

Z

Zone of proximal development (ZPD), 189, 190f
Zygote, 65, 66, 81, 86